1 MONTH OF
FREE
READING

at

www.ForgottenBooks.com

By purchasing this book you are
eligible for one month membership to
ForgottenBooks.com, giving you
unlimited access to our entire
collection of over 1,000,000 titles via
our web site and mobile apps.

To claim your free month visit:

www.forgottenbooks.com/free783233

ISBN 978-0-483-02206-5
PIBN 10783233

THE

NINETEENTH

CENTURY

A MONTHLY REVIEW

EDITED BY JAMES KNOWLES

VOL. XL

JULY—DECEMBER 1896

NEW YORK

LEONARD SCOTT PUBLICATION CO., 231 BROADWAY

LONDON: SAMPSON LOW, MARSTON & COMPANY, LIMITED

CONTENTS OF VOL. XL

THE

NINETEENTH CENTURY

No. CCXXXIII—July 1896

RUSSIA, PERSIA, AND ENGLAND

THE month of May has witnessed, in the assassination of the Shah of Persia and the coronation of the Czar of Russia, two events of deep and enduring interest to the world. The two most conspicuous representatives of despotic and autocratic rule in Europe and Asia; the very embodiments of the oldest and newest order of things, the past and the future, so different and yet so near akin, have divided between them the attention of mankind. The one, an astute and strong ruler, sincerely striving to lead his country in the path of reform and regeneration, struck down by an assassin on the steps of a mosque; the other, a young man of unknown capacity, placing on his head an Imperial crown, amidst the congratulations of two continents, and the tumultuous applause of an empire only second to that of the English Queen in extent, population, and power.

What more dramatic than the contrast between the swift and bloody death of the successor of the monarchs whose kingdom had already grown old when Cæsar's galleys first touched the shores of Britain, and the triumphant inauguration of the reign of the ruler of the youngest of European Powers, with princes, ambassadors, and nobles bowing before the throne, an armed host around him, and a dazzled and bewildered nation shouting in their madness : 'It is the voice of a god, and not of a man '? In still more vivid dramatic contrast stands the shining figure of the young Czar in the central pavilion on the Khodinsky plain, surrounded by a gay crowd of laughing women and obsequious courtiers, while the bands play Glinka's 'Life for the

Czar,' and, within sight and hearing, rolls towards Moscow the long line of wagons laden with the corpses of three thousand of his subjects, poor dumb animals, slain by the carelessness, cowardice, and imbecility of his officials. ' Ave! imperator: morituri te salutant.' The catastrophe will, in a country so grossly ignorant and superstitious as Russia, overshadow the whole reign. Why had no care been taken to propitiate a hostile Fortune? Why, as in a Roman triumph, had no slave been placed in the chariot of the victorious general to whisper in his ear that he was mortal?

The duty of moralising may be left to the clergy and special correspondents, and all that is intended here is to suggest considerations which, though familiar to all political thinkers, the majority of Englishmen are too careless or too occupied to work out for themselves. The close of the nineteenth century has seen the interest of the human tragedy transferred from Europe to Africa and Asia. The coming century, which will be full of scientific marvels radically changing the conditions of modern life, will also see the awakening of old world nations whom many have believed to have sunk into hopeless decrepitude; while the savage peoples who have, through long ages, lived in fear and darkness, will, at last, turn to the light and, with glad hearts, prepare to take their rightful places at the feast which civilisation and freedom have provided impartially for all mankind. Everywhere the valley of dry bones begins to stir with new life. The miraculous advance of Japan is no subject for jealousy or fear, but is the happiest omen for all. India, educated and free, will quadruple her wealth; the desert plains of Persia may again blossom as the rose, and the valley of the Nile repeat the glories of the Pharaohs. The crowded ant-hills of Chinese cities will be transformed by the railway and the telegraph; while the spirit of change, like the faint breeze that precedes the dawn, is beginning to wake the dwellers on the slopes of the Atlas, by the far waters of Nyanza, and among the Turkomans' camel-hair tents. The earth is in travail with the new birth that is to be, and the future is of hope and not of despair.

Who, then, and of what spirit are they who shall dominate the twentieth century and lead the expectant nations in the path of progress? For Asia and for Persia, with which this article is specially concerned, there can be no shadow of doubt as to the answer. England and Russia are the two Powers between whom the empire of Asia will be divided, and there is no other to complicate their rivalry. The Monroe doctrine is a chain which binds Americans to their own continent; Germany has no colonising aptitude and all the commercial advantages she may desire are secured to her under the British flag. Austria and Italy are the hereditary friends of England. The day of France is past, with population and power growing each year proportionally less; and, whatever her jealous ill-temper, she may perhaps consider that the shopkeepers and attorneys who rule her to-day are not likely to be more successful than Louis the Fourteenth or Napoleon in a war with England, which would sweep her flag from the seas and leave her with Algeria as her only colony. It is in the conviction that England and Russia stand face to face as the sole pretenders to Asiatic sovereignty ; that the struggle between them for supremacy will be the dominant note of the twentieth century, as the contest between France and England for colonial empire was the dominant note of the eighteenth, that the chief significance of the Moscow celebration is found.

That imposing ceremony signifies the renewed consecration of autocracy ; the fresh dedication of a nation to the service of despotism ; the surrender of independence and free will and intellectual vigour and the joy of life to a fetish as degrading as any that makes the savage tremble in an African jungle. For the young Czar, weighed down with his impossible responsibilities, a god to some of his people, a tyrant to others, we can only feel a profound and respectful pity. For the Russian people our sympathy may be as deep and sincere ; nor is there room for a single shadow of ill-will or hostility to either Czar or people on the part of Englishmen. He and they are alike slaves of a traditional system of government which is an anachronism in this age and a constant danger to the peace and the freedom of the world. What can be more pathetic than the figure of the Czar as he takes his predestined seat on the throne whose pretensions are an insult to heaven and an outrage to man ? He is singularly unfitted for the responsibilities of rule, for, like other princes of semi-civilised states, a jealous tradition has not allowed him any training in public affairs. The dominating influence in his life has been, and doubtless still is, that of the gracious lady so closely allied to our own Royal House, to whose ability, courage, and goodness of heart the peace of Europe owed, during the late reign, far more than is generally imagined. He may possess qualities and virtues which, under a happier system, might bear fruit in the prosperity of his people ; but he, like his subjects, is crushed by the administrative machine, from which, in Russia, there is no escape. A new Czar has as little initiative and is as much at the mercy of permanent officials as is the chief of an English Department reading in the House of Commons the elaborate evasions of his head clerks. If he were really a despot it might be well; for a benevolent despot is an excellent thing ; but he is no more than the irresponsible head of an evil system which is founded on repression, ignorance, darkness and slavery. The chief object of the Russian bureaucracy, whatever official apologists may say, is to exclude the light ; to hold the people in a blind superstitious obedience ; to punish, imprison and banish those who would teach the miserable moujik that he is a man and not a vodka-filled beast, that the peasant has his rights as well as the

Czar and an equal claim to happiness and freedom. This is why political discussion is forbidden in Russia, why every book which opens the windows of the mind, even though of pure science and philosophy, is prohibited by the censorship, and why every unorthodox dissenter who questions the claims of the successor of Ivan and Paul and Catherine to mediate with God for the people is regarded as disloyal and is treated as such. A system like this would never have been tolerated by any race of energy and intelligence, as Englishmen have often taught both Popes and kings. But the Slav people, of an Oriental type, patient, sluggish, mystic and ignorant beyond all imagination, bear and suffer, and allow themselves to be driven, like sheep to the slaughter, into the armies of the Czar. The great majority of Englishmen have no ill-feeling towards Russia, and would rejoice to see her with open ports on the Pacific, stretching her giant limbs in peaceful development. But for the stupid, cruel, and corrupt bureaucracy which dominates Russian policy those who love freedom can have no sympathy, and it is a strange portent that France and the United States, who, in name at least, represent purely democratic institutions, should be the two Powers who express the warmest friendship for the Russian Government. In this ignorant submission of a vast population, directed by a tenacious and unscrupulous bureaucracy, who use the name of the Czar to justify their own selfish ends and his spiritual authority to confuse a simple people, lies the strength of Russia and the danger to Europe and Asia. Freedom and education and constitutional government can alone remove the danger, but these the Czar, however benevolent his personal tendencies may be, has no power to confer.

The strength of the British Empire rests, unless all the results of civilisation be a lie, on surer and deeper foundations, on equal rights, on free speech, on the interdependence of class upon class, and on a reasoned loyalty to the ruling House. Many of those who read this article will have witnessed and will never forget the indescribable scene of tumultuous enthusiasm at the victory of the Prince of Wales in the Derby, and will have understood its significance as a spontaneous expression of the affectionate loyalty of a free people. As significant and instructive to the friends and enemies of England was the interesting spectacle at the Military Tournament, where, in long procession, passed in review the 'Sons of the Empire,' specimens of each division of the multitudinous armies of the Queen, from every quarter of the world. Surely a sight to make each British heart beat fast, to encourage each lover of freedom, and to remind us that Imperial Federation, which some timid statesmen have thought to be an idle dream, is, in some essential particulars, already accomplished. Here, from Canada to the Equator and to the far continent of Australia, are the representatives of a vast host, capable of indefinite increase, who are all free and independent citizens of the great

British commonwealth, whose voluntary service counts high above the unwilling service of compelled soldiers. If the world-empire of England has roused the envy of Powers who would be glad to assist at her dismemberment, she has yet taught the lessons of freedom to her great dependencies so unreservedly that France or Russia, Germany or the United States would not profit by our defeat. Australia, Canada, South Africa, and probably India are strong enough to stand alone against hostile attack. The free trade policy of England which in these days is questioned by impoverished landlords is, in reality, a chief support of our power, as it neutralises the jealousy of other nations, whose vanity may suffer but whose pockets are filled by our success. If, like France or Russia, we closed our foreign possessions to outsiders by hostile tariffs, a league might well be formed against us. But England claims no privileges which she does not share with the rest of the world. It is French stockholders who have most benefited by the pacification of Egypt, and German merchants and financiers amass their fortunes under the British flag preferentially to their own. The so-called selfish policy of England has been, since the triumph of free trade, a cosmopolitan unselfishness unparalleled in history.

Having sketched the positions of the competitors for Asiatic supremacy, we will now consider the country most immediately affected by their rivalry ; which is Persia, geographically the neighbour of both, seeing that Afghanistan, as a subsidised state, may be held to be attached to the British Empire. So much has been written of Persia lately that I will not repeat what may be found in admirable travels and handbooks, but a brief notice of the results of the late reign is needed to make the present position intelligible.

The late Shah Nâsiruddin, signifying Defender of the Faith, was, for his time and country, an enlightened, prudent, and liberal-minded ruler. It is not possible to apply to his conduct and administration a standard of comparison which is only applicable to Western countries and constitutional forms of government where progress is largely due to popular sentiment and initiative, while the slow conservatism of the East opposes its *vis inertiæ* and its traditional and religious opposition to all change, however beneficial. Nevertheless, his reign of nearly fifty years would compare not unfavourably with an equal period of storm and stress and feverish reform and revolution in many Western countries. In every direction substantial progress has been made. The administration of justice has been rendered both more certain and more merciful. Schools and colleges have been founded, for the late Shah was interested in education and was himself acquainted with French, Arabic and Turkish, and in Persian was a poet of some merit, while the diaries which he published after his European tours have had a wide circulation, not only in Western countries but in Persia, where they enjoyed the honour, which English authors may well envy, of compulsory purchase and a special tax. The greatest defect of the Shah was his avarice, which was immense and insatiable; and although this is a fault common among Oriental despots, who feel that their power can only be made secure from attack by the command of a full treasury, yet it injured and often ruined his schemes for the development of his country. If he had been content to spend some portion of his hoards on public improvements, on the repair of ancient reservoirs and watercourses, and the construction of roads and bridges, he would have brought under cultivation tracts of culturable land which are now desert and would have largely benefited both his own revenue and the general trade of the country. But he could not make up his mind to spend money, and required every improvement not only to pay for itself, but to bring a large contribution to his own treasury. The concessions which were given to all comers for manufactures, mines, tramways, roads, banks, monopolies for lotteries, electric lighting, tobacco culture, and other schemes were in no case assisted by State money; but all had to surrender a share of their profits, real or problematical, to the Shah. The consequence was that the greater number of these industrial undertakings, which, in a strange country and among a suspicious population, required constant support and large pecuniary assistance from the Government, soon withered and disappeared, and the Shah not only lost his anticipated profit, but solid and honourable financiers were deterred from adventuring in so unpropitious a country. The ground was left free to less honest speculators, who applied for concessions, not to work them seriously but to pass them on for a consideration to others who might successfully plant them in the often credulous markets of Europe. Disaster followed, the credit of Persia was lowered, and sound enterprises were seriously injured by the collapse of worthless speculations.

There was nothing of the religious bigot about Násiruddin, and there is no probability in the story that his assassin was a Bábi, commissioned to avenge the death of the founder of the sect and the persecution of his followers. The truth is that, with the exception of a few local outbreaks of intolerance on the part of the orthodox priesthood, who find it easy to excite the populace, Bábism, which is to Muhammadanism what the Reformed Faith was to the Church of Rome, or Kukaism to the creed of the Sikhs, has been not only tolerated but protected in Persia by the Shah. At the beginning of his reign, when the extravagant pretensions of the founder had excited both irritation and alarm, the sect was persecuted with some ferocity, but it has been gradually acknowledged that Bábism is a religious and not a political propaganda, many of the Ministers belong to it, secretly or openly, and its adherents are said to include two-fifths of the population. In any case, the Bábis had no grievance against Násiruddin, and their persecution was of small account when compared with the tender mercies of the Inquisition or the cruel treatment of Jews and Dissenters by Russia. Even the Kukas, in the Punjab, some twenty years ago, were ruthlessly suppressed when, like the Bábis in 1850–52, they began to play with rebellion. Reformers must not complain of martyrdom, and the Bábis have only been sufficiently persecuted in Persia to render them interesting. Many of their communistic and socialistic doctrines have of late years been given less offensive prominence, and their general principles, which inculcate freedom of judgment, the abolition of the wearisome ceremonial of Islam, and the emancipation of women, are quite in sympathy with the spirit of the day, and in time may stir the stagnant waters of Muhammadanism throughout the world. The assassination of the Shah is more likely to be due to some private wrong, or to the inflammatory teaching of men like Jamaluddin, an intriguer well known in London society, whose extradition the Persian Government is now endeavouring to obtain from the Porte, and who, in conjunction with others, has been stirring up hatred and ill-will against the Shah and his Government for several years past.

Not only the Bábis were protected by the Shah, but the Jewish, Armenian and Zoroastrian communities, which at the time of his accession were in a very miserable condition, have been well treated, and their position materially improved. Especially has this been the case with the Parsis, mostly resident in Yezd and Kirmán, descendants of the old Zoroastrian rulers and people of Persia. The state of these was so hopeless that large numbers emigrated to India, where they have become loyal and valuable citizens. But they did not forget their poor co-religionists left behind in Persia, and, in 1854, an association was founded for their relief by Mr. Manakjee Nasserwanjee Petit, father of Sir Dinshaw Petit, Bart., who still presides over it. Warmly seconded by the efforts of the Indian Government, Sir Henry Rawlinson and the British ministers at Teheran, the Parsis obtained from the Shah the abolition of all special tribute and taxes which had before been levied upon them, and they are now in no worse position than the Muhammadan community.

The Shah Násiruddin showed much discretion in the conduct of his foreign relations with England and Russia. These are, indeed, the only Powers with which he is vitally concerned, although Turkey, which adjoins the whole western frontier of Persia, is often obstructive and never friendly, for Shah and Sultan are rival potentates in the Muhammadan world, representative respectively of the Shía and Sunn forms of that creed. Especially at the mouth of the united Tigris and Euphrates, with the competing ports of Busrah and Muhamrah, do Persian and Turkish interests come into collision, and the question is still one of difficulty and promises future trouble.   But at Teheran, the English and Russian Legations are the only ones of consequence. Sometimes the exceptional activity or ability of the Minister of France, or Germany, or Belgium, or the United States may give to one or the other an unusual or factitious importance, but these phenomena are transitory, and Persia thoroughly understands that her foreign policy is little more than the conduct of her relations with Russia and England.   This knowledge the Shah utilised both to maintain peace abroad and order at home, and to supply his treasury by playing on the jealousies of each Power by turns, and granting to one concessions which were balanced by subsequent favours to the other.   Nor can Násiruddin be blamed for a line of conduct which was the only one which insured him so long and prosperous a reign. He played the game with skill and success, in strong contrast to Amir Sher Ali Khan of Afghanistan, whose clumsy imitation of the Shah cost him his kingdom and his life.   Only once, in 1857, did Násiruddin come into hostile contact with England, when his armed attempt to recover Herat, the ancient Persian capital of Khorassan, brought Sir James Outram with a British army to Bushire and the Karun, when a swift campaign restored to the Shah the power of seeing clearly the conditions under which a Persian monarch must be content to rule.   It has been plausibly argued that it was unwise for England to have then retired from the Persian Gulf without any territorial indemnity, and that the annexation and permanent occupation of Bushire and Muhamrah would have given us the undisputed command of the Persian Gulf, and the control of the chief commercial routes from the coast to the interior.   But a more far-sighted statesmanship would urge that no policy is so economical as disinterestedness.   Our refusal, at that time, to dismember Persia for our own advantage convinced not only the Shah but the Ministers and the people that we were the sincere friends of Persia, and that our ambitions did not include conquest or annexation of the country. The same lesson taught to Afghanistan when we withdrew from the country and refused to annex Kandahar, for which there was both reason and excuse, has transformed a suspicious neighbour into an ally confident in the honesty of our intentions, and our moderation in Afghanistan confirmed the friendly feeling of Persia to England. Object lessons in disinterestedness convince nations who regard mere protestations as the idle wind.   It may be questioned whether our position in the Gulf would have been favourably affected by the retention of Persian seaports at the cost of the alienation of Persian sympathy.   So long as England holds the command of the sea she will dominate the Gulf and the trade routes from the south.   Should she lose that command, the question of her influence in the Persian Gulf will become of infinitesimal importance.

The policy of Russia towards Persia has been a record of constant aggression, the absorption of province after province, district after district, frontier villages and the head waters of the mountain streams along the whole northern border. The treaty of Gulistan in 1813 merely stereotyped the results of continual aggression by Russia from the year 1800, when Georgia was annexed by the Emperor Paul, Mingrelia, Ganja (now Elizabethpol), Talish, Immeritia, Darband, Báku and Persian Dághistán, Shewán, Sheki, Karábágh and Moghan. Persia surrendered her right to have ships of war on the Caspian sea, and to-day the Shah is not allowed to fly the Persian flag on his own yacht in those waters, a barbarous insult little to the credit of Russian intelligence. In 1825, a three years' war, ending with the treaty of Turkmanchai, gave Russia further concessions ; in 1840, she seized the important island of Ashoráda for a naval station, and although Násiruddin contrived to avoid open war with his powerful neighbour, he had to endure constant encroachment on his northern border, especially on the Atrek river, as a comparison of the map which accompanied Sir Henry Rawlinson's work on England and Russia in the East with the latest published maps of Persia will clearly show. This book may still be recommended to those who desire to study the Persian question, as the best and most authoritative statement of the political situation in Central Asia, and the lapse of time has in no way destroyed its value.

The attitude of England and Russia towards Persia is clear and well defined. England has no desire for territorial aggrandisement at the expense of Persia, and she has proved this by her action in 1857. She is anxious to assist in the regeneration and development of Persia, to encourage its ruler to improve his administration and by his personal example and authority to abolish the system of universal corruption which now prevails, owing to the practice of every office from a governorship to a clerkship being sold to the highest bidder, with the permission to recoup himself from the people, who, though not overtaxed, are tormented by the burden of illegitimate fines, perquisites and requisitions. England would persuade the Shah to start beneficent schemes of irrigation, to restore the reservoirs and water courses which have fallen into decay, to improve the means of communication, especially roads, to develop the industrial resources of the country, which are considerable, both in mineral and vegetable products, to double the revenue from Customs by an honest system of collection, and to reorganise the currency, the disordered condition of which is the cause of constant irritation and discontent, and is the most immediate necessary reform. If England could see Persia strong and prosperous she would be content, and the peace of Asia would secure a new and powerful guarantee. Nor in the industrial schemes which England is ready to assist with her capital does she ask for any exclusive privileges ; and the advantages which may accrue from a more extended commerce and a more secure employment of capital will be open to the whole world in common with herself.

The action of Russia towards Persia has not been less clear than that of England. She has throughout the century missed no opportunity, either in time of peace or war, of increasing her own possessions at the expense of Persia, and the larger part of her Transcaucasian province has been so acquired. She is accustomed, ivy-like, to grow fat on decaying organisms : Persia, Turkey and China furnish but different illustrations of her persistent policy. Her cynical abandonment of the Armenians to destruction because she did not choose to allow other European powers to interfere with her chosen prey is the most shameless scandal of contemporary politics, and Persia will do well to take the lesson to heart. For Persia to become strong and independent would cause Russia infinite annoyance, and her jealousy is directly aroused when she sees any hand approach the fruit which she has determined to gather. All concessions proposed to be granted by the Persian Government to other powers she opposes, and if she cannot cancel them she insists on a still larger concession being given to herself. The development of the industrial resources of Persia she does not desire, further than to divert all foreign commerce to routes where it may pay heavy toll to her own custom houses. Indignation at misgovernment and corruption in Persia she can hardly be expected to feel, for corruption in Russia is probably as high placed and universal ; while, as for moral and intellectual progress, there is to-day in poor, ignorant Persia more real freedom of speech and action, more religious toleration, more practical acknowledgment of the dignity and equality of man than in all the wide dominions of the Czar. There is no doubt that the Persian, who belongs to the purest Aryan type, is far more highly developed than the Russian Slav, who has never shown himself to be possessed of any high intellectual capacity.

There is a very general and excusable ignorance as to the relative influence of England and Russia in Persia. It is assumed that the power of Russia has continually increased at Teheran, while that of England has diminished ; that Russia could, at any moment, overrun and annex Persia without any effective interference from England, and there are writers of repute who argue that it is useless to contend with the inevitable, and that it would be the wisest policy to hasten the disintegration of Persia and come to an arrangement with Russia to divide the kingdom of the Shah. Such a policy would be as foolish as it would be immoral. So far from English influence having decreased at Teheran there was no time in the last fifty years in which England was more powerful in Persia than she is to-day. Sir Henry Drummond Wolff, Sir Frank Lascelles and Sir Mortimer Durand, a succession of ministers of ripe experience, knowledge of the East, energy and enlightened patriotism, have entirely altered the discreditable position to which England had sunk in Persia, when her policy was conducted by apathetic and timid diplomatists. It is obvious that if Russia were to move her armies into Persia she could occupy Teheran and the northern provinces without serious opposition. The Persian army, as we experienced in 1857, is neither numerous, well armed nor disciplined, and England would certainly not send troops so far from their base. But there are many considerations which make it unlikely that Russia will take such a step. In the first place it would probably entail war with England, who could command the Gulf, the more important trade routes and the southern provinces. So far as Russia is concerned, having full command of the Caspian and an excellent road from Resht to the capital, such an occupation would be of little benefit to her trade and would be more costly than it was worth ; while her road to the open sea would be more effectually blocked than ever. In the second place, the industrial development of Persia which, in spite of many difficulties and opposition from corrupt officials and fanatical priests, has made great progress during the last few years, has raised a moral barrier against Russian ambition. Persia, with an elaborate telegraph system, a rudimentary free press and a veneer of Western civilisation in her capital, almost as substantial as that of Belgrade or Bucharest ; with all the nations of Europe represented by their Legations, and enjoying the special regard and friendship of England, cannot be attacked and overrun without outraging the conscience of Europe. Russia has done good service in Central Asia in restoring order and subduing the wild, slave-hunting Turkoman tribes, but she has no superior civilisation to offer to an ancient monarchy like Persia, nor is the fate of the Persian peasant so miserable or degraded as that of the Russian. Nor should it be thought that Persia is a country where life and property are insecure. Crime is of rare occurrence, travelling is safe, and it is from pride and not from necessity that Persians carry arms. The streets of Teheran are certainly safer than those of Paris and London, and a stranger may roam at night in perfect security in the darkest quarters of the capital. Lastly, the Russian Empire, which from various considerations, such as its vast area, the homogeneity of its population and their stolid patriotism, is impregnable as a defensive power, is singularly weak for offence. The very qualities which make the Russian soldiery so formidable at home render them inefficient abroad ; the inferior quality of the officers and generals, the indescribable corruption which makes the transport and commissariat departments invariably break down, the want of communications and the general absence in staff or men of any intelligent spirit—these and other causes render the Russian armies, so overwhelming on paper, altogether unreliable for offensive warfare. Even Turkey, bankrupt and enfeebled, would have beaten Russia in the late war had not the despised Roumanians come to her assistance.

It is most unreasonable to argue, as some English writers are doing, that the present Shah, Muzaffar-ud-Dín, is incompetent and has strong Russian proclivities, when they evidently know little or nothing about him. The very fact that he has succeeded to the throne without any opposition either from the people or rival claimants more favourably placed for a *coup d'état* at Teheran, shows that there is a general belief in his capacity. The statement that he is ignorant of affairs and has no aptitude for government is absurd when it is remembered that he is a man of mature age who has for years administered, through subordinate governors, but still in the independent manner of Persian viceroys, a large and important province where he has been distinctly popular. Rapacity and corruption, which have hitherto been the rule in Persia, have not been absent from his province of Azarbiján, but they have not been so rampant there as in other provinces, notably in those over which the Zill-i-Sultán, the eldest son of the late Shah, holds sway. It is true that the new monarch has, of late years, been careful not to make himself so prominent as to arouse the jealousy of his father, for he knew that this might result in his being deprived of the position of *Walí-'Ahd,* or heir apparent. He had seen his elder brother, the Zill-i-Sultán, who made too conspicuous a parade of his wealth and his troops, suddenly stripped of the greater part of his power and reduced to insignificance, and his readiness to learn the lesson rather proves his intelligence than his incompetence. There is no reason to credit the statement that he has any special Russian tendencies, though his residence at Tabreez, near the Russian border, has naturally inclined him to friendly intercourse with his powerful neighbours. At Teheran he will be able to take a more general view of the political situation. It would be foolish in the extreme for any Shah to set himself in opposition to Russia, or to excite her jealousy by too pronounced a partiality for any other power. A wholesome dread of Russia and a desire to conciliate her by any reasonable concessions was the consistent policy of Násiruddin, and his successor, if he be wise, will continue in the same course. But though a prince and an heir apparent may find it convenient to cultivate Russian friendships which may assist him in maintaining a difficult and critical position, it is not to be believed that an actual ruler of Persia will look on Russia with any more sentimental regard than a rabbit bestows on a boa constrictor. The manners of Russian diplomatists very much savour of their Tartar origin, and persuasion is quickly exchanged for menace with those who are too weak to be audacious. There is reason to believe that if the new Shah, who has safely arrived at his capital and was enthroned on the 8th of June, acts towards Russia with discretion and courtesy, and at the same time relies on the support and assistance of England for the industrial development of his country, he may have a more prosperous reign than that of his father.

As for the suggestion that England should come to terms with Russia for the partition of Persia, it is sufficient to remark that the true policy of England is to work for the regeneration of Persia, which is by no means hopeless, and which both Lord Salisbury and Sir Henry Drummond Wolff believed possible when the charter for the Imperial Bank of Persia was granted by Her Majesty's Government. The proposed arrangement would rival the partition of Poland in infamy, and whatever glamour may attach to success, especially with gallant and adventurous Englishmen, it is not too much to hope that the conscience of England is not debauched by the sordid and stupid muddle connected with the names of Rhodes and Jameson. The morality of writers who cynically advocate the partition of Persia between England and Russia savours of that of the old Cornish parson in Peter Pindar, who was preaching when the cry of 'A wreck! a wreck!' was heard outside the church, and the congregation began, one by one, to steal away. Finding his eloquence unavailing to detain them,

> 'Stop! stop!' cried he, 'at least one prayer:
> Let me get down and all start fair.'

But England, whose name, whatever her enemies may say, stands as a synonym for honour and good faith throughout the East, will refuse to accept the counsels of filibusters, and will honestly endeavour to promote the prosperity of Persia. The continuance of the Prime Minister, or *Sadr Azam*, in office is a signal proof of the good sense of the new monarch. It is exceedingly difficult, as may be imagined, for the Chief Minister of an Oriental state to keep on good terms with the heir apparent, and it is phenomenally rare for the latter to continue him in power when he succeeds to the throne. That it has been possible on this occasion reflects great credit on both the Shah and the Minister. The speech of the Shah on the occasion of his enthronement at Teheran, telegraphed to the *Times* on the 9th of June, contains the following notable passage, which will rejoice all the true friends of Persia:

The Sadr Ázam, who is one of the most enlightened and experienced servants of the late Shah, is confirmed in his eminent post; and, with full powers in civil and military administration, will from this moment execute our decrees, giving us content and satisfaction, and gaining for himself a further increase of royal favour.

The Shah further commences his reign auspiciously by an act of benevolence which will greatly increase his popularity, removing in perpetuity throughout Persia the taxes on meat and bread, which pressed hardly on the poorer classes. In connection with this remission it may be mentioned, as showing the good disposition of the late Shah and the desire of his son to extend his benevolent intentions, that on the day that the telegraphic announcement of this concession reached England, I received the draft of an edict, drawn up by the late Shah, and signed by him a few days before his assassination, showing that this was the very favour which he proposed to grant to the Teheran townsmen on the occasion of his jubilee. As this document has never been published in Europe or Persia, I subjoin a translation, as it is of permanent interest.[1]

The Prime Minister, Mirza Ali Asghar Khan, is well known to European statesmen, as he accompanied the Shah during his tour in 1889. He is now about forty years of age, and is a man of great resource, courage, and ability. He has maintained his position by the force of his high personal qualities, and is favourably regarded by all the foreign Legations at Teheran. He is sincerely anxious for the peaceful development of Persia, and has given constant support to all serious enterprises which he believed would further that object. Especially does he desire the construction of roads and railways, and he was personally interested in the concession granted to the Imperial Bank for a road between Teheran and the southern ports, making over to the Bank his original rights in the section between Teheran and Kum. He has been a warm and constant friend to the Imperial Bank of Persia, and it was largely due to his advice and assistance that it has attained its present position. He is thoroughly liberal in his ideas, and has always been an admirer of England and a friend of Englishmen. So long as he retains the confidence of the Shah there is every hope that a liberal and enlightened policy may prevail in Persia, and in this is the one and only hope of the escape of this ancient empire from the difficulties of the future. The dangers of darkness and barbarism will only be overcome by the weapons which civilisation can furnish. The risk of opposition to the new Shah was never great, and the statement generally made, that Násiruddin had made no declaration as to the

---

[1] 'The aim and object of His Imperial Majesty the Shah-in-Shah being always to provide equally for the welfare and happiness of all classes of his Empire, in order that the rich and great equally with the poor and small may partake of his favour and benevolence, and in return offer their devoted prayers for this ancient and everlasting kingdom, it is decreed that on the occasion of the fifty years' jubilee of His Imperial Majesty's reign, which will be celebrated this month, Zilked 1313, all taxes and imposts which it has been accustomed from time immemorial to levy on meat, as well as all revenues and taxes on bread in Teheran, are, from the date of this announcement, perpetually abolished. No one need pay the smallest coin on these articles of food, and every part of a slaughtered sheep, lamb, or ox, as well as the skin, head, and feet, will belong to the owner. May the wrath of Almighty God visit whosoever should at any time hereafter attempt under any pretext whatever to impose taxes of any kind on bread and meat.

'On the 22nd of this month Zilked [May 5, 1896], which is the day of rejoicing and the jubilee of the august reign, in the walls of all the important mosques of Teheran shall be set slabs of marble, with engraved thereon the purport of this Imperial decree.

'Dated Zilked 6, 1313 [April 19, 1896].'

succession, was absurd, seeing that Muzaffar-ud-Dín has been, for many years past, declared heir apparent, and publicly acknowledged as such by England and Russia. The only possible cause of alarm was in the attitude of the Zill-i-Sultán, the eldest son of the Shah by a plebeian mother, but the day of the Zill has past. Although not more than forty-six years of age, he is broken down in health, and has lost the energy which formerly distinguished him. His cruelty and exactions have made him hated in Isfahán, where he is Viceroy, and the neighbouring districts, and there is little doubt that before many months have elapsed he will be relieved of his charge and permitted to reside in that dignified obscurity which is the usual and convenient fortune of the brothers of despotic rulers. His son Jalál-ud-doulah, who is Governor at Yezd, has inherited some of his father's least amiable characteristics, and will, it may be hoped, follow him into retirement.

All English enterprise in Persia at the present time centres round the Imperial Bank of Persia, established by royal charter in 1889, which was under the special protection of the late Shah and the Prime Minister, and which each year is increasing its popularity and its business. It came forward instantly and energetically as a true State institution on the assassination of Násiruddin, making large advances to his successor to enable him to pay the troops and defray the expenses of his journey from Tabreez to Teheran. This was a service of the highest value and importance, and has at once raised its reputation at the capital. There is no reason to fear that the new Shah will forget this aid, given without hesitation at a critical juncture. The Imperial Bank is an outgrowth of the famous concession of Baron Julius de Reuter in 1872, which was too comprehensive and ambitious for realisation ; but in the Bank concession of 1889 the Shah conferred very large and important privileges, including the monopoly of note issue and the control for a term of years of the more important mining rights in Persia. To this was subsequently added a concession of the right to construct a road from Teheran to Ahwaz, the northern limit of navigation on the Karun river, which had lately been opened to free navigation. Since its foundation the Bank has steadily progressed in public favour, notwithstanding many difficulties, owing to the ignorance of the Persians of the methods of European banking and their disinclination to pay their debts at the appointed date, a trait not altogether unknown to Europe. Its note issue, which was only 13,954 tomans on the 31st of December, 1890, has increased to 387,012 tomans in 1895, and during the present year has increased in still larger proportion. It was stated in an article on the future of Persia, in the *Pall Mall Gazette*, that there was a possibility of the Imperial Bank being allowed to slip into Russian hands, but nothing could be more opposed to the facts of the position. Certain Russian capitalists have been very active in opposition to the Imperial Bank, and started a rival institution named *La Société de Prêts de Perse*, which was little more than a glorified pawn establishment. Unable to do profitable business, the Russian Finance Minister bought up the shares, and the institution is now under restrictions framed by the Petersburg Bank, which cripple it still further, and a large part of its available capital is on deposit with the Imperial Bank of Persia, which has no anti-Russian feeling, and is only too glad to deal with any good customers. The Russians cannot compete with much advantage in banking outside their own country, for the price of money is far higher in Petersburg than in London. The vital question of Persian currency is too intricate to be dealt with here. Suffice it to say that its reform is the necessary preliminary to good government and the future development of Persia. At the present time, the Mint is farmed out for a large annual sum, and as, at the existing price of silver, it is impossible to coin it at a profit, the Mint master endeavours to recoup himself by flooding the country with copper coin in its place. This is at a heavy discount, and the consequent misery and loss to the poorest part of the population, that is ordinarily paid in copper, may be imagined. The only remedy is to abandon the idea of making revenue out of the Mint for the present, and to treat coining not as a commercial transaction, but an Imperial function, carried on for the State by the Imperial Bank or some other independent authority. Thus alone can the currency be regulated according to the requirements of the community, and a uniform standard of weight and fineness enforced.

The concession for mining rights is still alive, though the Corporation which purchased it from the Imperial Bank suspended operations when it found that the apathy and hostility of local officials, and the entire absence of roads, made it impossible at present to carry on its operations profitably. But Persia has great mineral wealth, and under more favourable conditions the concession may yet become a source of profit.

Next to currency reform, the construction of roads is the most urgent need of Persia. The time for railways is not yet, especially as Russia, in 1890, finding herself not prepared for competition in this direction, extorted a promise from the Shah that no railways should be commenced before the year 1900. It is to be hoped that, when that date arrives, England will have prepared herself to take her fair and full share in any railway construction which may be then found feasible and profitable. But roads are more required than railways ; and here England has no jealousy of, or hostility to, German or Russian schemes of road construction which are in progress or about to be started. Everything which tends to the industrial and commercial advantage of Persia should be welcomed by England, whichever nation may inaugurate them, our only care being that no terms are introduced into any road concession which may burden English merchandise with heavier transit duties than those taken from the concessionnaires. The Russian Road Company, with a Government guarantee, is now making a road from the Caspian to Kasvín, where it joins the Teheran road, the whole distance from Teheran to Resht on the Caspian being about 200 miles, and the same contractors propose to continue the line to Hamadán, a great trade centre of the south-west, 150 miles from Kasvín. A German company is proposing to construct a road from Khani Kin, on the Turkish frontier, to Teheran on the one side and Baghdad on the other, and both these roads may be commended and supported if only England does not omit to construct, as speedily as possible, the trunk road from the southern ports to Teheran, the concession for which is still with the Imperial Bank, and the extension of which for a further term of ten years was one of the last official acts of the late Shah. The Bank has already spent a large sum of money on the northern section of this road, but has discontinued active work, although still collecting the tolls, as it did not consider that such an undertaking could be properly or profitably conducted by a banking institution. But British commerce with Persia, which is large and increasing, imperatively demands the road, and seeing that it is from the south that English and Indian goods enter Persia, it was unfortunate that its construction was commenced from the Teheran instead of the Ahwaz terminus, where every mile of road would have been at once remunerative. When the scheme is placed before the public it must propose to commence from the south, working gradually northwards to the rich districts of Hamadán and Isfahán, and the road should at first be of a simple character, without expensive works and bridges, to facilitate and develop the local traffic. As commerce increases, it may be gradually improved into an excellent cart road. Sir Henry Drummond Wolff, when Minister at Teheran, was very anxious to see this work carried out, without which the trade of Persia will inevitably travel by the new German and Russian roads, and the loss to British commerce will be incalculable. The London Chamber of Commerce takes a great interest in the question, and if our Foreign Office gives that hearty assistance which foreign concessionnaires receive from their respective Governments, there should be little difficulty in taking up the work and pressing it to a speedy conclusion. The rapidity with which Russia is developing communications in Central Asia may be estimated by a letter which reached me on the 10th of June from Meshed, whence it was despatched on the 26th of May, probably a record performance. We are fortunate in having at Teheran a Minister, Sir Mortimer Durand, who thoroughly understands Eastern politics, and has both ability and courage; and the interests of England will not suffer in his hands if he receives that consistent support from the Foreign Office without which no Minister can

18 *THE NINETEENTH CENTURY* July

effectively safeguard his country. Some time ago I advocated in this Review [2] the formation of an Asiatic Department at the Foreign Office, with a specially trained diplomatic staff, to thoroughly supervise British interests in the East, and bring to their important duty that local knowledge without which zeal is of no account. The events which have occurred since that time in China and Siam have demonstrated only too clearly the inability of the Foreign Office, as at present constituted, to understand or defend the claims and rights of England in Asia against keen and jealous rivals like France and Russia.

LEPEL GRIFFIN.

[2] 'England and France in Asia,' *Nineteenth Century*, November 1893.

A WARNING TO IMPERIALISTS

AFTER all that has been written about South Africa, one would scarcely venture to approach the subject at this moment, were it not that one side of the question has not received all the consideration it deserves. The passions which the late events have aroused, and the falsehoods which have been disseminated, have tended to obscure the issues; and at the same time the question is such a large one, it is so full of complications and conflicting interests, that it requires a peculiarly calm and dispassionate frame of mind to see all its various sides in their true proportions. While everyone feels bound to condemn the Jameson raid, there are those who still look upon it as a manifestation of the Uitlander grievances. These, they say, are the cause of all the mischief, and until these are redressed there will be no peace in South Africa. Others, on the contrary, think that those grievances have been made use of as a pretext to get the control of a country richer in mineral wealth than any other part of South Africa. Mr. Fort puts forward a third hypothesis. Dr. Jameson's primary object was, not to redress the grievances, but to seize Pretoria and ransack the Government offices for documentary evidence of a secret treaty with Germany. The President and the burghers meanwhile were to stand by passively and be treated 'with the utmost courtesy and consideration.' But this can scarcely be taken seriously. At any rate, the people at Pretoria treat it as a joke, and they seem to have considerably alarmed the gentlemen of the Rand by publishing the imaginary treaty *in extenso*. If, instead of making an outcry about the want of English education, the Uitlanders would condescend to learn the language of the country whose destinies they wish to control, there would be fewer such misunderstandings, and after a few years one would hear much less of grievances.

English people are strangely deficient in the power of putting themselves in the place of others. Whether we are for or against the Chartered Company, we can only look at the South African question from the British point of view. We do not realise, and it cannot be repeated too often, that the Transvaal is a young country. Johannesburg has only existed eight years, and during that time conditions, wants, problems, have developed which tax the highest statesmanship

c 2

to the utmost, and cannot be settled with a stroke of the pen.   Even
Mr. Chamberlain's Home Rule scheme, well intended though it was,
did not commend itself to the Johannesburgers any more than to the
Transvaal Government.   The policy of President Kruger, whatever
his detractors may say, has been simple and straightforward throughout.   The object of his life and of his rule is to maintain the dearly
bought independence of his people.   This is the simple test by which
all legislation in the Transvaal should be measured, and this, it would
seem, is a sufficient contradiction to all the stories about secret
treaties with Germany; but we have besides the President's word :

> I have reason to believe [he says in his official letter of the 25th of February]
> that the British Government has come to the decision to make no alteration in
> this [Art. IV. of the Convention] on account of false representations made to it
> and lying reports spread by the Press and otherwise with a certain object, to the
> effect that the Government of the Republic has called in, or sought, the protection of
> other Powers.   While I thankfully acknowledge, and will ever acknowledge, the
> sympathy of other Powers or their subjects, and the conduct of the last named
> has, in the light of the trials recently passed through, on the whole offered a
> favourable contrast to that of British subjects, there is, nevertheless, nothing
> further from my thoughts than to strive for the protection of a foreign Power,
> which I will never seek.   Neither I nor the people of the Republic will tolerate
> an interference with the internal relations from any Power whatever, and I
> am prepared, if the course proposed by me be adopted, to give the necessary
> assurances for this, in order that her British Majesty's Government need have no
> fear that her interests in South Africa should be injured.

The dignified answer of the President to the German Emperor's
telegram gives the key to the whole position.   It is not to ' friendly
powers' that the Transvaal looks for support.   ' Mit Gottes Hülfe
(with the help of God) hoffen wir weiter alles mögliche zu thun für
die Handhabung der theuer bezahlten Unabhängigkeit und die
Beständigung unsrer geliebten Republik.'

It is always assumed by the advocates of the Uitlanders that they
are a homogeneous party who outnumber the Boers and have therefore an irresistible claim to a voice in the legislation; but what are
the facts ?   As in every mining population, a large proportion are
composed of the worst elements of all nationalities.   Many others do
not care for political rights as long as they can pursue their avocations
undisturbed.   The Hollanders and Germans feel a kinship with the
Boers—they understand them and are in sympathy with them.
French interests are chiefly represented by shareholders.   The
Uitlanders who clamour about grievances are mainly British subjects,
and these do not include the working men.   Their position has been
lately stated in a letter published at Pretoria :

> We have now been in the country four years, have earned on an average 6*l.*
> per week, have saved a few hundreds, and last year had a six months' holiday trip
> to the Old Country.   Would any other country in the world enable us to do this ?
> No.   Then why try to upset the prosperous state of affairs in this country, which

will be sure to continue for many years? If there was any reason for fighting, if England received a blow or an insult, we, as British-born, would be among the first to shoulder our guns in defence of the country we love; but that is a very different matter to fighting against a country which provides, and will continue to provide, bread and enough to spare for thousands who can barely exist in England. We hope this letter will have the intended effect of making the working men think for themselves independently, and not be led by a lot of political agitators whose sole object is to 'compound' Johannesburg, and bring down wages fifty per cent. What do working men care about political rights? Not ten in a hundred would lose an hour to vote if they had the right to do so to-morrow.

Two real grievances from which the working men have suffered are the poisonous state of the water supply, to which a large percentage of the sickness and deaths at Johannesburg can be traced, and the exorbitant house rent, and both water supply and houses are in the hands of the capitalists themselves. The first will, however, be remedied, as there are works in course of construction which will provide Johannesburg with fresh water in a few months; the second is chiefly due to the enormous influx of strangers. It is repeated *ad nauseam* that the Uitlanders have developed the country, that they have enriched it, and yet have no voice in the representation. Now, in the first place, they have developed the country entirely in their own interest—the Boers never asked them to come and, in fact, in the Transvaal as well as in the Cape Colony, there is a strong wish to put limits to immigration. One great complaint of the Uitlanders is that they are highly taxed, but the taxation does not compare unfavourably with that of other mining countries, and it is only reasonable that those who derive their wealth from the Transvaal under the protection of its laws, should bear the expense of the public works which are mainly undertaken for their benefit. Moreover, the President is in the position of the great physician who asks high fees, not because he wishes to be extortionate, but in order to limit his practice. He does not wish to make it too easy for gold diggers and speculators to amass huge fortunes—which they are nevertheless doing. When the President was in England in 1884, he deplored that gold had been found in his country. He knew the difficulties it would bring, and his previsions have been more than justified. 'There is no mistaking,' say the Reform leaders, 'the significance of the action of the President when he opposed the throwing open of the town lands of Pretoria on the ground that " he might have a second Johannesburg there," nor that of his speech upon the motion for the employment of diamond drills to prospect Government lands, which he opposed hotly on the ground that "there is too much gold here already."' It is not difficult to understand the antagonism between those whose actions are governed by the fluctuations on the Stock Exchange and the man who believes in a great cause and devotes his life to it.

Many of the British Uitlanders do not wish to make the Transvaal their permanent home; they do not wish their children to be brought

up with the children of the Boers; they openly state that the Boers
are not their peers; they continually speak of them with contempt
and dislike, and yet they claim equal political rights with them.

Why did not those men have themselves naturalised [asks one of the speakers
in the late debates in the Cape Parliament]? They despised the Government too
much for that, and did not like to do burgher service. If foreigners treated a
Government thus, it could not be expected that the Government would favour
them. Immigrants in Australia and America called themselves Australians and
Americans; but the Transvaal foreigners did not do that: they remained foreigners,
so that they were the cause of their own grievances. A general franchise there
would mean the overthrow of the Government.

The debates in the Cape Parliament are very instructive reading
to those who are constantly being misled by the undue stress that is
laid on the Uitlander grievances in order to condone the conspiracy.
Mr. Innes spoke with great moderation in support of his motion,
expressing the hope that the South African Republic would give
' favourable consideration ' to ' any legitimate grievances,' and though
the House showed no want of friendliness to the Uitlanders, their
grievances found but little recognition, and the motion was thrown
out.

What [said the Attorney-General, Sir Thomas Upington] was supposed to be
the greatest grievance of all? Was it not the franchise? And yet he found, when
he was in the South African Republic at the end of last year, that gross ignorance
prevailed as to what was meant by application for the franchise; that the franchise
could not be given unless they renounced their allegiance which they owed the sovereign under whom they were born. No alien could vote in this country—it would be
well to consider this—no alien could sit as a member of Parliament. No alien on
the same lines should be a voter—should have the franchise—in the South African
Republic unless he did what aliens did in the Cape Colony—renounce his allegiance
to his natural sovereign and take the oath of allegiance to his new ruler. . . .
Who then were going to do it? . . . He thought this cry about the franchise had
been made far too much of.

And even the Premier, Sir Gordon Sprigg, thought

' that the conferring of rights on those people had to be done with very great care
and very great circumspection, considering what was the character of a great part
of the population there—evanescent and unsettled. Moreover, he was not aware
himself whether those people would accept the franchise if it were offered to them
upon the condition which would doubtless be still imposed—that they must renounce their rights as British citizens and become burghers of the Transvaal.

The British Uitlanders look upon the Transvaal as a huge field
for mining operations, and it is reasonable to believe that if they had
a preponderant voice in the legislation, they would use it for their
own temporary interests and not for the permanent welfare of the
country. The Boer attaches far more importance to the vote than
we do in European communities. He looks upon it as the right of
primogeniture of the Voortrekkers and their children, to be jealously
guarded and not lightly shared with the new comer who might use
it against him. Yet he does not shut out from his councils those

whom he can trust. When, after the Jameson raid, the two members of the Free State Volksraad, Fisher and Kleynveld, were sent to Pretoria, these were at once admitted to take a part in the deliberations of the Transvaal Executive. Loyalty is the crucial point on which the whole franchise question turns, and the hostile attitude which the reform leaders adopted prevented President Kruger making concessions.

For months and months [said the President in his proclamation to the Johannesburgers on the 11th of January] I have thought which alterations and emendations would be desirable in the government of this State, but the unwarrantable instigations, especially of the Press, have kept me back. The same men who now appear in public as the leaders have demanded amendments from me in a tone and manner which they would not have dared to use in their own country out of fear of the penal law. Through this it was made impossible to me and my burghers, the founders of this Republic, to take your proposals into consideration.

The President's distrust has been justified by the events. While the Reform leaders were clamouring about grievances and issuing their manifesto, they were secretly plotting in conjunction with the Prime Minister of the Cape to overthrow the Government. It is said in excuse of the Reform leaders that they did not wish to overthrow the republican form of government as such; but what matter the symbol when the reality is gone? Government by the Charter and the ' Gold Wolves ' of the Rand would have been a curse to the burghers under any flag. When Mr. Rhodes was in England in the autumn of 1894, he said to those who were anxious about the future of the Transvaal, that the difficulties would be solved peacefully and naturally in the course of time, and he said the same to his friends in Africa. 'Education and time would remove the race prejudices that existed.' Had the Reform Union confined themselves to constitutional means for redress of any real grievances, his predictions would, no doubt, have been fulfilled. ' More than half the Johannesburg people, English as well as other foreigners, are against the revolutionary movement,' said the British agent in the South African Republic on the 31st of December, ' and will probably side with the Government in every way,' and it is now clear from letters that passed between the conspirators themselves, that the majority of the Johannesburg people did not care for political rights, and that, had they not been instigated to rebellion, they would have abided their time.

In the words of President Kruger :

Under the pretence of striving for political rights, a small number of designing men, within and without the country, have craftily worked upon the feelings of the poor deluded people of Johannesburg, and day by day fanned the flame of rebellion, and then, when in their folly they considered that the time had come, they caused a certain Dr. Jameson to cross the border of the Republic.

Mr. Rhodes had a splendid opportunity. All the Cape Afrikanders looked upon him as their friend, and, with singleness of purpose, his dream of a united South Africa might have been realised, even though the flag of the early pioneers floated by the side of the Union Jack. But such dreams are idle now. What was the cause of Mr. Rhodes's change of policy? *Quem Deus vult perdere, prius dementat.* The late events have changed the whole African situation. One result has been a strong re-awakening of the Dutch Afrikander sentiment. An electric shock of indignation ran through all Afrikanders from the Limpopo to the Cape. All differences between the Cape Colony and the Republic about tariffs, and the like, were forgotten, and it is now quite clear that if ever England wanted to revenge Majuba, there would be an end of her paramount power, although for the moment her arms might conquer. The paramount power cannot live by physical force alone, but by upholding right and justice. It has already received a rude shock. There was at first a strong suspicion that the British Government countenanced the revolution, and it is even now difficult to persuade Afrikanders of the contrary.

Are you now convinced [writes a distinguished Cape Afrikander] of the utter falsehood and cowardice of those who tried to coin out of minor grievances a revolution so as to take the Transvaal from its rightful owners. . . . If all the men and all the money England possesses were given at the present moment, it would not bring back the respect she has lost nor the love of just people here, and if ever England is to be looked upon as great here it will be only after she has had the moral courage to clear herself from complicity, and disavow this scandalous proceeding.

Dutch Afrikanders are too desperately in earnest to be satisfied with what appeared to them half-hearted disavowals, if not of the crime, at least of the criminals. By that light we must read the telegrams of the 19th of June from Pretoria.

Bitterness and distrust have been engendered between the English and Dutch in Africa. In the Free State a President with strong Dutch-Afrikander feelings has been elected as a direct consequence of the conspiracy. Both the Transvaal and Free State are arming in self-defence. Natives are bewildered and rising on all sides, and they scarcely show that predilection for British rule with which they are always credited.

As for the alleged grievances, President Kruger will meet the demand for English education, and there is now a Bill before the Volksraad to give a municipality to Johannesburg; but it is needless to say that the franchise question has not been advanced by the treason of the Reform leaders, and the President will tolerate no dictation in the matter of the internal management of his country. It is too often forgotten here, where public opinion guides the policy of the Government, that President Kruger must take account of the feelings of his own people.

At the same time it is the wish of all who have the welfare of

South Africa at heart, to see peace and good-will restored; but how is this to be brought about? It is clear that no redress of Uitlander grievances will do it. The Republic has done its part; it is now for England to do hers, and, in the first place, the whole attitude of the British people at home, and of British Uitlanders in the Transvaal, must be changed before the Republic can be expected to trust England and her subjects.

The Transvaal Government has behaved with the utmost moderation and magnanimity. While all Continental Europe has acknowledged this, has it wrung anything more than the coldest recognition from England? Even such a conscientious and impartial critic as Mr. Arnold Forster is obliged to confess that he does not love the Boers, and that nine-tenths of the British people do not love them!

Has the British public, indeed, shown by its acts unanimous and unqualified condemnation of the raid and the raiders? Have the Imperialists not tried—and are they not still trying—to shield their idols by obscuring the issues, and accusing the Boers of every kind of treachery which has been, over and over again, disproved by the facts? Has not the charge of corruption been repeated time after time on the authority of the very men who secretly deplored that the law of the Republic prevented them from bribing the electors, in order to ' improve ' the Volksraad!

Hollanders whose ability and integrity are acknowledged in their native country, and who have been entrusted by the President with offices of the highest responsibility, have been systematically abused —whenever they have assisted the Republic in times of trouble—and have had all manner of evil designs attributed to them. What is more natural than that the Boer Government, which requires educated University men that are good linguists, good diplomatists and lawyers, should select them in preference from among those whose language and creed are closely connected with their own, and whose loyalty is above all suspicion? They are men, moreover, whose nationality cannot by any possibility give umbrage to England. They are, in fact, no longer Hollanders, for, like all foreigners who wish to have Burgher rights, they have had to take the oath of allegiance.

The Boers are constantly accused of ingratitude: first because they did not recognise that England by annexing them saved them from the Zulus; but the important fact is always omitted that the reason the Zulus were so dangerous was that the English had provided them with firearms in distinct violation of the Sandriver Convention. British soldiers experienced it to their cost at Isandwana. Then again we are told the Boers did not recognise the generosity of England in giving them back their country after Majuba; but England has never ceased regretting it, as the ominous silence when Mr. Chamberlain made his explanation during the South African debate has once more shown, and it is not easy to be grateful for benefits that are not graciously conferred. Military men say openly that they look forward to the time when they will revenge Majuba. Yet the best people in the Colony declare that nothing has done more to bring together the two races than this act of justice on the part of England.

Let us not forget what our great countryman, Lord Dufferin, said the other day to the British Chamber of Commerce : ' Thanks to the telegraph, the globe itself has become a mere bundle of nerves, and the slightest disturbance at one point of the system sends a portentous tremor through its morbidly sensitive surface.' Every utterance that is published in London is commented upon at Pretoria the next day. Every insult added to the injury inflicted on the Transvaal by British subjects causes profound indignation and may cause permanent alienation.

There are no more loyal subjects of the Queen than the Dutch Afrikanders, but ' blood is thicker than water,' and as long as there is persistent misrepresentation, as long as there are people who try to foment dissension between the two races in order to gain so-called Imperialistic objects, there never will be peace in South Africa. The Transvaal burghers have shown repeatedly what metal they are made of. The spirit of their Huguenot and Dutch ancestors is still alive. The old Calvinistic creed has imparted a strength and an earnestness to their character which has contributed as much to the victories of Majuba and Doornkop as the fact of their being ready fighters and good marksmen. Even though in a minority, they must ever remain the backbone of the country. Their progress is slow, but all the more sure. The President is a man whom Carlyle would have placed among his heroes. Such people—with all their qualities and faults— have a claim not only to our respect but to our friendship.

In the words of Mr. Schreiner in the late debate in the Cape Parliament : ' It is conspicuously the part of any man who loves his country to feel that the methods that must be employed must be those of the most soothing argument and impressed with the one watchword for South Africa, Patience.' England may rely on the assurance of President Kruger : ' Mutual trust must be the basis of our political principles, and that trust the Republic on its side will never put to shame.'

ELISABETH LECKY.

COMMERCIAL UNION OF THE EMPIRE

ONE of the principal and most powerful factors in promoting a mutual good understanding between Great Britain and her Colonies would be the establishment throughout the various parts of the Empire of a scheme, on a sound and satisfactory basis, of commercial federation, which should meet with general approval. Commerce is the life-blood of civilised nations. It is the keystone of the structure which is their mainspring and support. It is the material element which inaugurates their social standing, political progress, and advance in prosperity and wealth. Pastoral and agricultural pursuits comprise the chief industrial occupations of all primitive peoples and savage races for the-supply of their food and for the maintenance of their physical necessities. But, once a nation has emerged from the condition of its first natural environment, and has advanced along the road of an expanding civilisation, new conditions are developed and new wants created, which are supplied by the inventive spirit of man. As these are fulfilled they lead to a desire to circulate the various objects of utility and necessity which human ingenuity has produced, by some system of commercial intercourse between different communities, in the form of barter and exchange.

This is the embryo and germ of what is expressed in the well-known and comprehensive term 'trade.' By instinct, by natural constitution, by the physical and mental energy of the Anglo-Saxon race, by quickness of apprehension for intelligently grasping the elements and cardinal principles of trade, the British nation has been long distinguished for the remarkable aptitude it has shown in successfully pursuing the great object to which for generations it has devoted itself. These principles, there cannot be a doubt, are of vital importance to a people so situated. It has long acquired for them the reputation of being emphatically the one among nations which is in the forefront and van of international commerce and world-wide trade. So decided has been this desire, and so energetically and indomitably has it been pursued by the genius of her people, that England has for centuries shown herself determined to find fresh markets for the development of the manufactures her industry has created by penetrating every clime and endeavouring to exchange her wares for the productions or the gold of other nations which she could induce to trade with her.

All this demonstrated the supreme importance of cultivating as much as possible friendly relations with other States on the part of Great Britain, as well as the vast value of her foreign trade to herself. But if the pursuit of their paramount objects, according to their own ideas and wishes, of cultivating trade, did not appear always attainable with other nations by pacific means, the British people did not hesitate to engage in wars and plunge into the arena of battle and of strife for the purpose of ultimately forcing their rivals, if possible, to acquiesce in their views. Thus they often wrested from others territory which they acquired for their own, and traded on their own terms with the inhabitants of conquered countries that were transferred to them by the fortune of war, as the future subjects of their rule.

This was one of the principal causes of the wars of the eighteenth century, in which Great Britain so greatly triumphed, gaining for her the notable accession of numerous Colonies, which then became the guide of her Colonial policy for the government and control of her already vastly extended Colonial empire.

The loss of the American colonies consequent upon a mistaken policy on the part of the Mother Country on questions of trade left her at the end of the century in the possession of a very limited Colonial empire, consisting of the settlements on the West Coast of Africa, the three islands of Barbados, Jamaica and Newfoundland, and what was termed the insignificant province of Canada. It, however, stimulated the British people to turn their attention to new fields of colonisation; and the discoveries of Captain Cook in the southern hemisphere coinciding with that period, appeared to offer favourable inducements for Colonial expansion in that part of the world. This was the origin of the possession by Great Britain of the island continent of Australia.

Such was the condition of Great Britain and her Colonies at the commencement of the present century.

Since that period it is well known that the great expansion of the British Colonial empire has taken place in all parts of the globe, and new fields for British colonisation and enterprise have been developed by the transplanting of vast numbers of the population to her various Colonies from the British Isles. The British Empire now comprises an area of nearly ten million square miles, combining every variety of soil, climate, and powers of production of everything required for the use and necessities of the human race, so that the demand for every article which is imported from all the various foreign countries into the United Kingdom is capable of being supplied by her own

Colonies. All that is required is the adoption of a course which is really feasible for its accomplishment.

It has unfortunately been too much the policy of our legislators hitherto to regard trade with foreign countries as the most important source of commercial prosperity to Great Britain; hence the foreign trade with the United Kingdom, as compared with Colonial trade, has assumed proportions which it need not have done. The latter would have expanded to a vastly greater extent had it been fostered by more preferential treatment than it has experienced at the hands of successive British Governments. Consequent on this policy treaties have been made from time to time with various foreign countries which have been most serious obstacles to the expansion of our Colonial trade.

It would appear part of a wise Colonial policy, therefore, that these treaties should be terminated with the least possible delay. At the present time our commercial relations within the Empire cannot be regarded as conducive to those principles which ought to tend to promote a perfect federation for trade purposes, and which should eventually culminate in the permanent union of the Empire. It cannot be too emphatically pronounced that all trade is based upon the principle of barter or exchange. This being so, involves a system of mutual estimate of the value of the various articles exchanged. In the case of Great Britain and her Colonies an arrangement would have to be entered into which would apply not only to trade between the Mother Country and the Colonies, but also to the Colonies themselves trading with each other.

Having thus briefly referred to the importance of commerce in its application to British trade, an endeavour will now be made to show that the following scheme will maintain the integrity and strengthen the defence of the Empire, and that it will be permanently advantageous to the various interests whose consent would undoubtedly be requisite for its adoption.

At the outset it is of course understood that it is an essential ingredient of any scheme that it meets with the cordial approval of the Mother Country and the Colonies themselves. The trading relations of the United Kingdom with the Colonies are so vast and important, that their greater development cannot fail to be of incalculable benefit to both. The problem is how to arrange the fiscal conditions between them which would be at the same time advantageous to both parties; and if this can be carried out, no more powerful factor can be found to maintain and strengthen the unity of the Empire. The question is entirely one of give and take. The Colonies, on the one hand, must be prepared to give advantages to imports from the United Kingdom, and the Mother Country must give advantages to the products of the Colonies over those of foreign countries. A way in which this could be done would be by the

Colonies reducing their customs tariff upon the imports from Great Britain as compared with foreign countries, and by this country placing some amount of duty upon those articles of commerce which are imported from foreign countries, and admitting similar Colonial exports free of duty into this country.

In order to provide the necessary means for carrying this into effect, a Fiscal Parliament would have to be formed, consisting of representatives of the Imperial and Colonial Parliaments, who would be entrusted with legislative and necessary administrative powers to fix upon the amount of the tariff, and to amend it from time to time as occasion would appear to demand. Any difficulties which might arise in the first instance would be ultimately overcome by the wisdom and sympathy of such Fiscal Parliament, which could not fail to recognise the immense advantages which must accrue to the Empire as a whole from the carrying out of a commercial federation based on such a scheme.

In order to provide for that part of the scheme which relates to strengthening the defence of the Empire, the following plan is proposed, viz. that a special duty of $2\frac{1}{2}$ per cent. be imposed upon foreign produce imported into the whole Empire. It is estimated that this would amount to nearly 9,000,000*l*., which would constitute a common fund which would be appropriated by the Fiscal Parliament as a contribution to the central Government, which at present bears almost all the entire cost, for the naval defence of the Empire. This would relieve the Colonies from the payment of subsidies, and would be supplied jointly by the Colonies and Great Britain. Besides being relieved from the payment of subsidies the Colonies would enjoy preferential treatment in the markets of the United Kingdom. Compared with the enormous advantages which this plan would bestow upon the general interests of Great Britain, the imposition of so trifling a duty would far outweigh any possible objections to its adoption. It could not fail to be a great attraction to the Colonies, and would establish a connecting link which might eventually develop into a powerful and closer bond of union between them and the Mother Country.

If such an arrangement was carried out, it would involve a change in the clause in the treaties with foreign countries which is technically known as the ' most favoured nation clause.'

It would be necessary, as far as the Colonies are concerned, to provide that when treaties are entered into by Great Britain with foreign countries, that clause should not be applied to the same extent and in the same way as if the Colonies were foreign powers instead of being integral parts of the Empire itself. The policy of every foreign nation having Colonies is to favour its Colonial in preference to its foreign trade. The sole and remarkable exception to this rule has hitherto been the case of Great Britain herself.

In propounding this plan I do not aim at Protection. The idea is rather to promote a cohesive force, which shall at the same time provide a revenue which might be with the least possible difficulty rendered available for a purpose so truly national in its conception as to provide finances necessary for the defence of the whole Empire. It is doubtless in the range of possibility that if some day there should be established one uniform Imperial tariff instead of various local tariffs, it might lead to a system of Free Trade within the various parts of the Empire. Be that, however, as it may, the adoption of this plan for defensive purposes would be no obstacle to the ultimate carrying out of any such policy as is here indicated.

The part of my scheme which relates to defence is based upon one which was suggested at the Colonial Conference held in London in 1887 by Mr. Hofmeyer, one of the delegates from the Cape of Good Hope. It is so simple and comprehensive, and at the same time so practical in its character, that I do not hesitate to embody it in my scheme.

The supreme importance of the British Empire possessing a navy far more powerful than any other nation in the world, in order to maintain her supremacy at sea, cannot be over-estimated. The sea routes must be adequately protected, and the over-sea commerce thoroughly safeguarded and defended, in the interests of both the Mother Country and the Colonies. At present the cost of keeping open the trade routes falls exclusively upon the Mother Country.

The scheme proposed for defence comprehends an equitable and adequate share of contribution to this object in fair and just proportion, without unnecessary friction or insuperable difficulty between the inhabitants of Great Britain at home and her countrymen beyond the seas. Trade follows the flag, and if this plan for extending and protecting it was adopted, the commerce of the Empire would experience a powerful development, and would be enormously increased, creating fresh sources of national wealth and prosperity. I would remark in conclusion that it is not beyond the bounds of reasonable probability that the creation of the Fiscal Parliament here proposed to deal with the question of commercial federation might in the course of time lead to the ultimate attainment of the greater political expansion of the British Constitution which is known by the expressive title of Imperial Federation.

Summary

1. The importance of commerce in its application to British trade.

2. The advantage of promoting the fullest possible intercourse between the various parts of the Empire, compared with the policy of

cultivating foreign trade to the detriment of the expansion of the trade of the Colonies between themselves and the Mother Country.

3. The effect of the loss to Great Britain of the American Colonies in diminishing the extent of the Colonial Empire, and the consequent contraction of Colonial trade.

4. The expansion of the Empire during the present century, and the consequent opportunities afforded for the development of trade within its boundaries.

5. The British Colonies, combining as they do every variety of soil, climate, and powers of production, afford the scope for supplying everything which is imported from various foreign countries into the United Kingdom.

6. Preferential treatment for the trade of the Colonies over that of foreign countries would result in the vast expansion of the trade of the former.

7. That existing treaties with foreign countries should as soon as possible be either abrogated altogether or changed so as to modify the application of what is technically termed the 'most favoured nation clause,' as well as any other clauses which injuriously affect the Colonial trade.

8. The fundamental principle of all trade being the system of barter and exchange, the scheme suggests an arrangement being entered into which should not only apply to trade between the Mother Country and the Colonies, but also to the Colonies themselves trading with each other.

9. The scheme maintains the integrity and strengthens the defence of the Empire.

10. It would be essential that any scheme before being matured must be submitted to and receive the approval of the Mother Country and the Colonies themselves. For this purpose it would be necessary to summon a convention of representatives from the Colonies to approve its adoption. This when ascertained would become the basis of joint legislative action for giving it effect.

11. The trading relations of the United Kingdom with the Colonies are so vast that they cannot be exaggerated.

12. Solution suggested by the scheme for carrying out commercial federation on a satisfactory basis.

13. Formation of a Fiscal Parliament consisting of representatives of the Imperial and Colonial Parliaments, to be entrusted with the necessary legislative and administrative powers.

14. Plan proposed for the defence of the Empire.

15. The policy of every foreign nation, with the exception of Great Britain, is to favour their own Colonial in preference to their foreign trade.

16. Protection not aimed at, but only a system for providing the finances necessary for the defence of the Empire. Suggestion made

that it is within the range of possibility that an Imperial tariff which would have the effect of developing free trade within the Empire might some day be established.

17. Supreme importance of the British Empire possessing a navy far more powerful than any other nation, for the purpose of preserving supremacy on the sea, insisted on.

18. As trade follows the flag, the commerce of the Empire would under this scheme show a powerful development and add greatly to its wealth and prosperity.

19. Commercial federation may be the prelude eventually to Imperial Federation.

FREDERICK YOUNG.

REFORMATION AND REUNION

In the April number of this Review, my friend Mr. Birrell magnified the English Reformation. In the May number, Lord Halifax, certainly not less a friend, pleaded for Reunion with Rome. The two essays afforded an interesting contrast of thought and temper. Each showed intelligence, information, sincerity, and above all a sense of the supreme importance of religion even in the life of this world. But the point of view, the mental environment, the antecedent bias, of the two writers were strikingly dissimilar, and my purpose in this paper is to inquire whether either attains, not to the whole truth of the matter, for that is not given to man, but to so much of the truth as can create a better understanding between members of the Church of England and their fellow-Christians in other communions.

I begin with Mr. Birrell's essay headed 'What, then, did happen at the Reformation?' and here, turning for a moment from substance to method, I hope that Mr. Birrell, who has a scholarlike knowledge of his Dickens, will not be angry if I say that his mode of interrogative argument reminds me of Rosa Dartle. He is so surprisingly ingenuous. He is so conscious of his ignorance. He asserts nothing. He asks much. He insinuates more. 'What, then,' he asks, 'did really happen at the Reformation?' He would not for the world say what; though he has a little notion of his own, and does not mind our seeing what it is. Of Miss Dartle we read that 'she never said anything she wanted to say, outright, but hinted it, and made a great deal more of it by this practice.' Thus:

'Oh, really? You know how ignorant I am, and that I only ask for information, but isn't it always so? . . . . I want to be put right if I am wrong—isn't it really?'

'Really what?' said Mrs. Steerforth.

'Oh! you mean it's *not*!' returned Miss Dartle. 'Well, I'm very glad to hear it! Now, I know what to do! That's the advantage of asking.'

Similarly Mr. Birrell, when asking what really did happen at the Reformation, has a notion that a good deal happened; that, in particular, the Mass ceased to be said in the Church of England;

and that, with its departure, came a severance alike from mediæval·
England and from modern Rome, which it is idle for Anglicans to
ignore and impossible to repair.

This seems to be the idea at the back of Mr. Birrell's mind, but,
Dartle-like, he forbears, out of deference to Anglican feelings, to
formulate it. To him, as a Nonconformist, really things look a·
little as if it were so ; but he very much wishes to be put right if he
is wrong. He 'only asks for information,' and if any one can show.
him good reasons for a different view he will be eager to exclaim,
'Oh! you mean it's *not*! Well, I'm very glad to hear it! Now I
know what to do! That's the advantage of asking.' To lead him
to this happy state of mind, of intellectual satisfaction and moral
peace, is my immediate object.

Now, broadly speaking, I would venture to tell Mr. Birrell that
the following were the most important of the many and far-reaching
events which happened at the period vaguely known as the
Reformation :—

1. The translation of the Bible.
2. The revision of the Liturgy and Offices.
3. The dissolution of the monasteries.
4. The permission of marriage to the clergy.
5. The repudiation of the Pope's authority.

These five great changes will, I think, be found to contain within
themselves the germs of all that distinguishes the modern from the
mediæval Church of England, and together they constitute my
general reply to Mr. Birrell's artless question. For my own part, I
regard the change which I have put last in the list—the repudiation
of the Pope's authority—as infinitely the most important. Mr.
Birrell, on the other hand, seems to think that the most important
is that which I have numbered 2 ; and I will therefore examine it a
little more in detail.

When I speak of the 'Revision' of the Liturgy and Offices, I
include 'translation,' and I use 'Liturgy' in its strict sense, as
meaning the service of the Holy Communion, to which the 'Offices'
of Morning and Evening Prayer are ancillary. The substitution of
a vernacular liturgy for one performed in an unknown tongue was
an immense change, but as Mr. Birrell does not concern himself
with it I may pass it by. Again, he disregards the ancillary Offices,
and so may I. He concentrates his whole attention on the Mass,
and I will do the same. 'It is the Mass,' he says, 'that matters;'
'It is the Mass that makes the difference.' And here it seems to me
that Mr. Birrell attaches to the word 'Mass' some occult or esoteric
meaning, for which, as far as I know, he has no warrant. The
etymology of the word is obscure ; the very language from which it is·
derived has been disputed. Our forefathers did not trouble themselves
with these linguistic problems, but ˎused the word—a short, con-

D 2

venient, practically English, word—to signify the Holy Eucharist.
When Sir Walter Scott describes the Lady Rowena as having got
wet in returning from ' an *Evening* Mass ' he presumably adopts the
less exact use which we find in *Romeo and Juliet*, and which applied
the word to any form of Divine Service. But before the Reformation
all public worship centred in the service of the altar, and the Mass was
the Eucharist. The Reformers regarded the words as synonymous ;
and the Prayer Book of 1549 sets forth ' the Supper of the Lord,
and the Holy Communion, commonly called the Mass.'

The Mass, then, is the service of the Holy Communion—nothing
more, and nothing less ; but Mr. Birrell reads into the phrase some
other meaning of his own. Abandoning for the moment all argument,
historical, theological, or etymological, he makes a sudden incursion
into the region of the emotions, and cries out that he can feel the
presence of the Mass at Havre and can feel the absence of it at
Cromer. Well, it is not for me to disparage the emotions, or the
employment of them in religion. Once Mr. Browning, looking on
with a friend at High Mass in a French cathedral, at the moment of
the elevation, gripped the friend's arm and exclaimed, ' My dear
Arthur, this is too good not to be true.' But an emotion of this kind
affords only a sandy foundation for the faith and practice of a lifetime ; and English Churchmen will look, through the splendid
accessories which so impressed the picturesque sensibility of Mr.
Browning and Mr. Birrell, to the unseen Realities which they enshrine.
We turn from the sound of the Sanct-bell, on which Mr. Birrell is
eloquent, and the divine fragrance of the ' censer's wafted breath,'
to the plain oaken table, the ' fair white linen cloth,' the worn silver
vessels of some English village-church, untouched as yet by liturgical
or æsthetic revival ; and, making our appeal, not to accessories or
trappings however suitable, or beautiful, or instructive, but to the
recorded words and acts of our Lord, to the unbroken usage of His
Church, and to the letter of our English liturgy, we reach a definite
and reasoned conclusion. It may be formulated in the words of a
writer whom I feel instinctively sure that Mr. Birrell dislikes : ' This
day, as I believe, the Blessed Sacrament has been in the church
before our eyes, and what can you or I desire more ? '

So far, I do not understand that Mr. Birrell disagrees with me.
Like a prudent man, he declines to challenge the historic continuity of
English Orders. With a duly commissioned ministry, the words of
institution, and the prescribed elements, we have the essentials of a valid
Eucharist ; but Mr. Birrell seems to say that this is not enough to dis-
prove that organic severance between the mediæval and the modern
Church of England which he would like to establish. A valid Eucharist
we may have, but we have lost the Sacrifice of the Mass, and then he
seeks to prove by (A) the changes in our Eucharistic service ; (B)
the changes in the Ordinal ; (C) the general intention of those who

were parties to these changes; (D) the teaching of the Church of England since the Reformation. Let us examine these proofs one by one.

(A) Mr. Birrell instances, as changes fatal to any sacrificial view of our modern rite, the omission of the Invocation of the Holy Spirit on the elements; and the omission of the Prayer of Oblation.

With regard to the Invocation, it is certainly a liturgical feature of great antiquity and wide prevalence; its insertion in our Office was a gain and its omission a loss. But the Church of Rome has never possessed it; and, if it is essential to the Sacrifice of the Mass, Mr. Birrell, when he fancies that he can perceive the Mass at Havre, is nurturing himself in a delusion, and might as well be worshipping at Cromer.

As to the Prayer of Oblation, it has been, not removed, but displaced, and put as an alternative to the thanksgiving at the end of the service. This, again, was a change for the worse; but surely, if the Sacrifice of the Mass is of our Lord's instituting, it must be found in that part of the service which He explicitly ordained, and not in the devotional additions made by the piety of men. And all that He ordained the Church of England has scrupulously retained.

As to (B), Mr. Birrell merely alleges 'ambiguity' and 'weakening' in the successive changes in the English Ordinal. As he adduces no instance we need not stay to argue, but pass on, merely remarking that here again the Church of England repeats the words of her Divine Founder and the acts of His Apostles; and in so doing she presumably administers a valid ordination, and confers the Christian ministry for all the purposes for which it was instituted.

On (C) Mr. Birrell is even less argumentative, frankly avowing that it is impossible to ascertain the intentions of those who were parties to these changes.

We therefore pass on to (D). And here, without encumbering the pages of this Review with a catena of quotations from Cosin and Sparrow, and Beveridge and Johnson, and fifty more, it may suffice to say that the doctrine of the Eucharistic Sacrifice (or the Sacrifice of the Mass, for it is only a choice of terms) has never ceased out of the Church of England, but has been devoutly held and openly taught in each succeeding age. The chain has never been broken. The Sacrifice in the Eucharist is nowhere set forth with more emphatic clearness than in the hymns, sermons, and devotional manuals of John and Charles Wesley. When John Wesley died, in 1791, Henry Drummond, of Albury, was five years old, and of Drummond Mr. Gladstone wrote: 'No man was in principle more opposed to the Church of Rome; but he expressed in the House of Commons a conception of the Eucharistic Sacrifice so lofty as must have satisfied a divine of the Latin Church.'[1]

Mr. Keble, who was born in 1792 and died in 1866, inherited

[1] 'The Courses of Religious Thought,' *Contemporary Review*, June 1876.

his Eucharistic doctrine from his father and his Nonjuring ancestry, and his teaching about 'our glorious Sacrifice' was widely diffused in the Church of England six years before the Catholic Revival of 1833. Even Bishop Wilberforce (1805–1873), steeped as he was in Evangelical traditions, held, according to Bishop Woodford, 'the doctrine of there being in the Sacrament of the Lord's Supper a Commemorative Sacrifice, wherein the Church on earth pleads before the Father the atoning death of the Son, imitating in a divinely appointed way our Lord's own intercession above.'

And, to add one living link to the chain, Mr. Gladstone himself writes that the 'effacement' of the 'sacrificial idea' from the doctrine of the Eucharist 'could hardly be accomplished without a serious dislocation of the historical relations between that great Sacrament and its historic types; nor again without seriously lowering the general conception of Christian life and worship as a true sacrifice to God, which had the Eucharistic Sacrifice for its central point. St. Paul seems to lift upward the whole fabric of Christian observance when he exhorts the faithful to present their bodies a living sacrifice unto God, which, he says, is "your reasonable service." And if so, whatever tends to impair the efficacy of that idea tends in like degree to lower the Christian obedience from the level of the filial, towards that of the servile standard.' [2]

But perhaps Mr. Birrell will say 'Is this all? There is nothing here that an orthodox Nonconformist need repudiate. The Presbyterian Milligan taught it just as emphatically as you do. This is not the doctrine of the Mass as I understand it.'

Perhaps not; but for all that it is the doctrine of the Mass, as the Catholic Church in East and West understood it; and against this the reformers of the Church of England struck no blow. Certainly they repudiated, and we repudiate, some loose notions, of no theological authority, which had become current in England just before their time. 'The sacrifices of Masses, in the which it was commonly said that the Priest did offer Christ for the quick and the dead, to have remission of pain or guilt, were blasphemous fables and dangerous deceits.' Strong language, though not too strong for the utterly unscriptural and untheological notion which it condemns. But even in this emphatic article there is no word levelled against the true and orthodox doctrine of the Commemorative Sacrifice. Here, as in every other controversy, the Reformers betook themselves to the law and to the testimony—to the recorded words of our Blessed Lord and His express revelation to St. Paul: 'Do this in remembrance of Me.' 'As often as ye eat this Bread, and drink this Cup, ye do shew the Lord's death till He come.' Here is the doctrine of the Eucharistic Sacrifice as stated in Scripture, and to this the

[2] 'The Sixteenth Century arraigned before the Nineteenth,' *Contemporary Review*, October 1878.

Church of England has unfalteringly adhered. 'The Eucharist,' says Bishop Andrewes, 'ever was, and by us is, considered both as a sacrament and as a sacrifice.' I said that I would forbear to quote. Let one famous passage suffice :

> Now what Christ does in Heaven He hath commanded us to do on earth— that is, to represent His death, to commemorate His Sacrifice by humble prayer and thankful record ; and, by faithful manifestation and joyful Eucharist, to lay It before the eyes of our Heavenly Father, so ministering in His Priesthood, and doing according to His Commandment and Example ; the Church being the image of Heaven ; the priest, the minister of Christ ; the Holy Table being a copy of the Celestial Altar, and the Eternal Sacrifice of the Lamb slain from the beginning of the world being always the same.

The doctrine thus stated by Jeremy Taylor has been held by the Church of England since the Reformation as before. But, if Mr. Birrell asks me whether the Reformation made no change in her way of presenting it, I frankly reply that it did. Broadly speaking, the change was this. Whereas in the mediæval Church the idea of Sacrifice in the Eucharist had overshadowed and obscured the primary idea of Communion, the Church of England at the Reformation laboured to restore Communion to its supreme and unshared place in the devotional life of the Christian soul. She reverted once again to the letter of Scripture : to the ordinance of Christ and the usage of His first disciples. She insisted on the presence of communicants at each celebration of the Eucharistic rite ; she repudiated the practice of solitary Masses said on behalf of absentees; and she taught that wherever there is a strict compliance with the conditions of the Eucharist as the Lord ordained It, there is a perfect fulfilment of It in all Its aspects—of communion, sacrifice, and worship.

In the concluding part of his essay, Mr. Birrell, admitting the unquestionable fact that this doctrine of the Eucharist has always been held in the Church of England, refers to the fact, equally unquestionable, that in this as in other matters of less than cardinal importance, there are differences of opinion in the Church ; and calls aloud for an authoritative decision as to which is right. There must, he cries, be in the Catholic Church a defining authority which all her members recognise and obey; and here, having accompanied Mr. Birrell to the end of his journey, I bid him courteously farewell, and transfer my attentions to Lord Halifax; for the question of authority leads naturally to that of Reunion, and Reunion is the subject of Lord Halifax's essay.

> When there was any overture or hope of peace, he would be more erect and vigorous, and exceedingly solicitous to press anything which he thought might promote it ; and, sitting amongst his friends, often, after a deep silence and frequent sighs, would, with a shrill and sad accent, ingeminate the word *Peace, Peace.*

As Lord Falkland, among his friends at Great Tew, ingeminated Peace, so Lord Halifax, surrounded at Hickleton by sympathetic abbés, ingeminates Unity. And in truth it is hardly fanciful to trace some similarity between his character and that of the high-souled Cavalier whom Clarendon depicted, with his 'inimitable sweetness and delight in conversation,' his 'flowing and obliging humanity and goodness to mankind,' and his 'primitive simplicity and integrity of life.'

Now, knowing Lord Halifax's intense convictions on this subject of Reunion, I desire, even when I am constrained to differ from him, to treat his views with the utmost sympathy and consideration. I begin therefore by saying that I entirely concur in his sense of the immense value of Unity among Christian people, and the sacred duty of promoting it. No one who really believes that our Lord uttered the words recorded in St. John xvii. 20, 21, can feel otherwise.

But what is Christian Unity?

It will, I suppose, be admitted on all hands that the first condition of the Unity which our Lord desired for His disciples is that union with Himself by which alone our fallen humanity can be restored and saved. A common Union with the Head is the most potent element of Unity among the members. But is this enough to secure the absolute Unity for which our Lord prayed?

What saith the Scripture?

To the 'one God and Father,' and 'one Lord,' and 'one faith,' the Apostle adds 'one Baptism,' and, in another place, 'one Bread.' In other words, the Creed and the Sacraments are the signs and means of Unity among believers. And it would indeed be an enormous addition to the ideal completeness of the Christian Church as well as to her practical power, if all who hold the same creed could communicate together in the same Eucharist. Intercommunion between different Churches is indeed a consummation devoutly to be wished.

But to some it seems that even this would not be enough; and they say or imply, with greater or less distinctness, that in order to realise Christian Unity after our Lord's own Mind, all Christians must be visibly united in one organisation, governed by one earthly Head, and that Head the Pope. Now, I do not deny the theoretical attractiveness of this ideal of the Christian Church; but has it any warrant in Scripture? And how does it tally with the facts? Do we find after our Lord's Ascension the slightest trace of a visible Head of the infant Church on earth? Do we not find, even in Apostolic days, Christian Churches springing up in different localities, each with its independent life, and governed by no central authority? Do we not see distinct differences of teaching even between one Apostle and another, on matters less than vital? And the Apostles, by mutual consent, taking different departments of the human family under their respective charge? In the Council of Jerusalem we certainly see an instance of appeal, not to an individual, but to a central body; but it is noteworthy that this appeal is made, not on a question of vital doctrine, but on a ceremonial observance of secondary importance. And even if we infer from this instance (what, I think, we have no right to infer) that it is a condition of Christian Unity that all Christians should be ready to refer their disputes to the judgment of one and the same assembly, what becomes of the Papal claim ?

It might be conceivably, though fantastically, argued from the precedent of the Council of Jerusalem, that the visible head of the Church, and the presiding officer at her Councils, must be the successor of St. James in the See of Jerusalem ; but where does the Pope come in ? For my own part, I am unable to recognise that Primacy of Peter which even moderate Anglicans are sometimes ready to concede. St. Peter was indeed a conspicuous figure in the narrative of the New Testament, but conspicuous, alas ! as much by shame as by honour. I believe, with Chrysostom and Augustine and Cyril and Leo, that the Rock on which the Church is built is the fundamental truth of our Lord's Godhead, and that Peter's outspoken testimony to this truth is the great glory of his life, as it is the origin of his name. And, of the two other so-called Petrine texts, I believe that the one merely warned him of his fall, and the other announced his restoration.

I know no proof that Peter had any headship over the other Apostles (certainly he had none over St. Paul, who 'resisted him to the face because he stood condemned') ; or that he ever was Bishop of Rome ; or that he ever was at Rome ; or that, if ever he had been Bishop there and had enjoyed any headship over the rest of the Apostles, he transmitted that headship, or had the power to transmit it, to his successors in the Roman See.

Something may, of course, be said for every one of these notions ; but in the vital matters of Christian faith, and the conditions of our spiritual life, we require something more substantial than an ingeniously constructed system of assumptions and conjectures.

And, turning from history to the actual state of the present world, the Papal theory seems fatally at issue with the facts.

When we look through or over the wall of the Western Church, into the precincts of the Eastern, we seem to find a living confutation of it. For there a vast body, nearly a fourth of Christendom, has subsisted from the great Day of Pentecost to our day, which not only does not enjoy, but which denounces and condemns, the whole doctrine of supremacy ; and which, under the old Patriarchal Constitution of the Church, retains the Christian Faith entire, by the acknowledgment of Rome herself, who invites, and invites in vain, to her councils those unyielding Patriarchs of the East. . . .

· The score of millions of those Christians who inhabit the Turkish Empire have for almost a corresponding tale of generations enjoyed the highest of all honours : they have been sufferers for their faith. They have been its martyrs. They alone have continuously filled that character. . . . Ever since the Turkish hoof began to lay waste the Levant, those twenty millions have had before them, on the one side peace and freedom, on the other side the Gospel. They have chosen the Gospel ; and have paid the forfeit. And, whatever be their faults and errors, it is not for us of the West, amidst our ease and prosperity, our abundant sins and scandals, to stigmatise them as professors of a dead or dying Christianity, and thus to disparage the most splendid and irrefragable perhaps of all the testimonies which man can render to the Religion of the Cross.[3]

No, assuredly the testimony of Eastern Christendom is valid, and it is emphatic against the Papal claims.

But we have among us some who say: 'We do not concern ourselves about the Easterns. We admit that they have strong ground. They stand where they did before the great schism; and we Westerns, who profess the *Filioque*, stand on new ground. But there is no need for further subdivision. Let us leave the East alone; recognise the Pope as Head of the West, and unite ourselves to him.'

But what would be the conditions of such a surrender, and what the resulting gain? First, we should have to admit that the Pope is infallible in matters of faith and morals; and I, for one, no more believe it than I believe that the earth is square. We must abandon our secure foothold on the creeds and the Bible for the varying and perhaps inconsistent decisions of successive Popes. We must exchange the characteristic virtues of the Church of England—an open Bible, a vernacular liturgy, Communion in both kinds, freedom of marriage for the clergy, freedom of Communion for the laity—for the opposite evils of the Roman system. And, in the region of practical effort, we should renounce our passport to the sympathies of the great Anglo-Saxon race, which has, to all appearance, broken finally with Rome and all that savours of her.

We come then to this. The headship of the Pope is unsupported by Scripture or History, is vehemently repudiated by a great part of modern Christendom; and could not be accepted by us without grievous loss to our spiritual privileges and opportunities. Is then the cause of 'Unity,' as between the Church of England and the Church of Rome, hopeless?

If by 'Unity' is meant Reunion, I neither expect nor desire it. But Lord Halifax and his friends seem to see another chance of Unity in a form which would involve no compromising declarations by us. In plain words, they think it conceivable that the Pope may recognise the validity of English Orders, and all that such validity implies. 'Recognition,' then, rather than 'Reunion,' is their immediate object. Now on this I would briefly remark:

1. Lord Halifax, having discussed the matter in confidential conversations with the Pope and other high Roman authorities, is much better able than I am to judge of the likelihood of this recognition; but, for my own part, I do not believe in it. We know that human nature is very strong even in Cardinals; it is part of human nature to dislike being proved to be in the wrong; and this would be most conspicuously the case with the Anglo-Roman body if

[3] 'The Sixteenth Century arraigned before the Nineteenth.'

Anglican orders were pronounced valid. My own belief, therefore, is that, whatever may be the Pope's own sympathies, the Roman authorities in England will fight tooth and nail against Recognition, and will prevail. We have learned from Cardinal Manning's Life that diplomacy and intrigue are not unknown at the Vatican, and that Infallibility is often subjected to a little judicious wire-pulling in order to make its decisions conform with the prepossessions of its environment. We must wait and see.

2. I entirely deny that the Pope and his Commission of Cardinals, whether well or ill affected towards us, have any power to decide for us whether our Orders are valid or not. We are not believers in the Infallibility, and on no other ground could the Pope's decision have binding force. We can judge as well as he of the historical facts of the case, and not less so of the question whether the words and acts of the English Ordinal comply with the requirements of our Lord.

3. Supposing, for argument's sake, that the Pope decides that English Orders are valid, what is the gain? Some weak-kneed Anglicans might be comforted, but people who need the Pope's comfort are better at Rome. Romans could not communicate with us, nor admit us to their altars, for we should still be, *ex hypothesi Romana*, in a state of schism. Rome would regard the Church of England as she now regards the Oriental Churches, and I see no great gain in that. I am told that there is a certain section of Anglicans who long to submit to Rome, but cannot bring themselves to repudiate Anglican Orders and the Sacraments by which they have lived. Well, certainly, if Rome were to recognise our Orders, people of this class would be able to betake themselves to Romanism without disavowing their whole spiritual history. But this, though it might be no great loss, can hardly be reckoned as a gain. Although I do not expect the Pope to pronounce in favour of our Orders, I still sincerely wish that Lord Halifax's aspiration might be fulfilled. It would, at any rate, be an admission by Rome of what we believe to be the truth; it would tend to the increase of Christian charity between two great Communions; and it might, in God's good Providence, do something to accelerate the time when the separated branches of the one great Christian family shall be able, without surrendering their distinctive views of truth, to co-operate for Christian ends.

More than this in the way of Unity I do not expect to see; and even this would be glaringly incomplete if it did not include the great bodies of orthodox Nonconformists. On that word *orthodox* I lay all possible stress, for the great dividing line between religious truth and error is the doctrine of our Lord's Godhead. Between all who accept it there must be a vital union of heart and hope and worship, which those who reject it, alas! cannot share.

Henry Drummond, the Irvingite apostle, used to say that religious people are commonly right in what they affirm and wrong in what they deny. This saying affords a good guide for our dealings with Nonconformist Christians. They affirm the doctrines of the Holy Trinity, the Incarnation, and the Atonement; of sin, redemption, and grace ; and they are right. They affirm that they administer a valid Baptism, and they are right. They do not claim the apostolic succession, with the power to consecrate the Eucharist and to absolve the penitent ; so we have no controversy with them there. If they maintain that in their devout celebration of the Memorial Feast they are spiritually refreshed and strengthened, they speak that which they know, and who is it that dare gainsay them ? If, yearning for the blessings of an authenticated rite, they present themselves for Communion at our altars, ' the English Church offers the Supernatural to all who choose to come. The way is open, it is barred by no confession, no human priest.' If, on the other hand, they choose to abide where they were placed by God's Providence in birth and education, we, while devoutly thankful for our different lot, can surely walk with them in charity and mutual tolerance, and joint efforts for the objects of the Christian Kingdom. After all, we must remember that the Master promised not ' one fold' but ' one flock ' under ' One Shepherd,' even Himself.

GEORGE W. E. RUSSELL.

FROM THE EMPEROR OF CHINA TO KING GEORGE THE THIRD

(TRANSLATED FROM THE TUNG-HWA LUH, *OR PUBLISHED COURT RECORDS OF THE NOW REIGNING MANCHU DYNASTY)*

' *KÊNG-WU* (day).[1]—His Majesty proceeded to the Great Pavilion in the Garden of Myriad Trees, where the English Chief Envoy Macartney and the Assistant Envoy Staunton were admitted to Audience.

' *I-mao* (day).[2]—An imperial order was issued to the King of England in the following terms :

' So then, thou King, far away over many oceans, thou hast inclined thine heart towards civilisation, and hast made a point of despatching envoys to respectfully bear a submissive address. Crossing the seas, they have arrived at Court, and have offered their devout prayers for our imperial welfare, besides submitting articles of local production, by way of evincing thy heartfelt sincerity. We have opened and perused the address, the language of which is sufficiently honest and earnest to bear witness, O King, to the genuineness of thy respectful submission, and is hereby right well commended and approved. As to the chief and assistant envoys, bearers of the address and the tribute, in consideration of the fatigue they have undergone in carrying out the duties of their distant mission, We, in the exercise of our grace and courtesy, have already commanded our ministers to introduce them to the privilege of audience ; have bestowed a banquet upon them ; and have conferred upon them repeated gratifications, in order to make manifest our love and tenderness. As to the six hundred or more of officers and menials in charge of the ship who have returned

[1] Lord Macartney reached Peking on the 21st of August, 1793, and quitted it on the 7th of October. *Kêng-wu* was the 9th day after the kalends of the 8th moon, and as the Chinese moon is usually one moon behind ours, this would be September, or our 9th moon. As a matter of fact, the 14th of September was the date. The scene was one of the old Cathayan capitals now known as Jeho or Zhehol, which the present translator visited in 1870. The Emperor's tent was placed in the middle of the garden. Jeho is 140 miles north-east of Peking. (See Sir George Staunton's *Embassy to China.*)

[2] *I-mao* was the ninth day after *Kêng-wu*—*i.e.* the 23rd of September.

with it to Chusan, though they have not been to the metropolis, We have also bestowed liberal presents upon them, so that they also may have a rich share in our gracious kindness, and one and all be equal recipients of our benevolence.

' As to the earnest prayer in thine address, King, that thou mayest despatch a man of thine own nationality to reside at the Celestial Court [3] and take the management of the commercial interests of thy kingdom, this is quite contrary to the policy of the Celestial Court, and positively can not be allowed.   Hitherto, whenever men belonging to the different states of Europe have shown a desire to come to the Celestial Court and take service there, they have, it is true, been permitted to come to the metropolis.   But, once there, they have submitted to the sumptuary usages of the Celestial Court, and have been quartered in the Hall,[4] never being allowed to return to their own country.   This is the fixed rule of the Celestial Court, with which, it is thought, King, thou must be well familiar.   But now, O King, thou seekest to depute a man of thine own nationality to reside in the metropolitan city.   As such a man would not be bound, like the different Europeans who have accepted service in the metropolis, to refrain from returning to his native land, and as it would be impossible to allow him to move freely to and fro and to communicate information with regularity, it would really be a profitless business. Moreover the area under the administration of the Celestial Court is of exceeding vast extent.   Whenever the envoys of foreign dependencies arrive in the metropolis, the Interpreters' Bureau cares for their entertainment, and all their movements are regulated by strict etiquette : there is no precedent for their ever having been allowed to do as they like.   If thy state were now to leave a man in the metropolis, his language would be as incomprehensible as his attire would appear extraordinary, and there are no quarters suitable for such a case.   If, on the other hand, it were proposed to insist on his changing the style of his attire, after the manner of the Europeans who have come to the metropolis and accepted service there, the Celestial Court again would never be willing to force any man's compliance with the unreasonable.   Just imagine, if the Celestial Court should desire to send a man to reside permanently in thy kingdom, dost thou think that thy kingdom would be able to accept these commands?   Besides,

[3] Some years previously the Emperor had directed that China be invariably described as the ' Celestial Court ' in correspondence with barbarians, in order duly to impress them.   The Emperor here uses it both in the sense of ' China ' and of the ' Court of China.'

[4] The Peking church was destroyed by fire in 1775, but the Emperor contributed towards building a new one.   The King of France and the Pope, after the abolition of the Society of Jesus, arranged to place the Peking mission under the Lazarists; and Father Raux, the first Superior, arrived in 1784.   In Peking the mission is known as ' the Hall of the Lord of Heaven.'   The ' acceptance of service ' refers to the geographical, mathematical, and astronomical aid given, in consideration of which the Jesuits and other priests had been allowed to remain in Peking.

the countries of Europe are very numerous, thy kingdom not being by any means the only one : if all of them were to pray, as thou dost, King, for permission to depute a man to remain in the metropolis, how would it be possible to grant such permission to each one of them in turn ? This matter it is most positively impossible to allow. Is it reasonable to suppose that, in order to comply with the request of thee alone, O King, the century or more old customs of the Celestial Court can be altered ? If it be argued that thy object, O King, is that he should keep an effective supervision over trade, it may be answered that thy countrymen have engaged in commerce at Macao for a considerable time anterior to the present day, and have invariably been treated with every consideration. Take, for instance, the former missions which Portugal and Italy [5] have in turn sent to Court : they also advanced certain applications on the ground of exercising a supervision over trade. The Celestial Court, noticing their heartfelt sincerity, treated them with the greatest commiseration, and whenever any matter occurred in connection with the commerce of the said countries, the most complete satisfaction was always given. On a former occasion, when the Cantonese bong-merchant Howqua [6] was dilatory in paying up the price of a foreign ship, the governor-general under whom the matter arose was ordered to advance the whole of the moneys involved in the first instance from the official chest, and to clear off the debt vicariously, besides severely punishing the defaulting merchant. Probably thy kingdom has heard the facts of this case. Then why should foreign states be so bent on deputing individuals to reside in the metropolis, and make such unprecedented and impossible requests as this ? Again, a man residing in the metropolis would be nearly three thousand miles away from the commercial centre of Macao. How would he be able to exercise an effective supervision ? If it be argued that it is out of veneration for the Celestial Court, and that it is wished that he should acquaint himself ocularly with the arts of civilisation, it may be replied that the Celestial Court possesses a system of rules and etiquette suitable to the Celestial Court, and both of these must be different from those of thy kingdom. Even granting the person of thy nationality so residing were able to acquire the desired knowledge, thy kingdom naturally possesses customs and regulations of its own, and would never be able to follow those of China ; so that, even supposing the person really understood the knowledge thus acquired, he would be unable to make any proper use of it. The Celestial Court conciliates all within the four seas ; its only object is to achieve the solid ends of good government ; it attaches no value to curious and rare objects of price. But as to the things which thou, O King, hast

---

[5] Portugal, 1753; the Pope's Legate, Mezzabarba, 1715-21.

[6] 'Howqua' is a 'pidgin-English' name borne by the head of the *Ng* or *Wu* family at Canton. *Hong* is a Cantonese word equivalent to the American 'store.'

in this instance sent to us, in consideration of thine honest heart and the great distance they have been carried, We have specially commanded the Government Department immediately concerned to take receipt of them.   As a matter of fact, the power and prestige of the Celestial Court is felt far and wide ; innumerable states come to render fealty ; rare and valuable objects of all kinds are ever crossing the seas and accumulating here ; there exists nothing but what We possess it, as your chief envoy and his suite have seen with their own eyes.   Still, We never attach any importance to curious and ingenious objects, nor shall We ever again require articles of thy country's manufacture ; so that thy request, O King, that thou mayest despatch a man to reside in the metropolis, is, on the one hand, contrary to the policy of the Celestial Court, and, on the other, would seem to be totally without advantage to thine own kingdom.

'Thou art thus clearly notified of our pleasure, and thine envoys are hereby dismissed and commanded to betake themselves by comfortable stages back to their country.   And thou, King, thou shouldst do thy best to realise our imperial meaning, make still further efforts to prove thy loyalty, and for ever strive to be respectful and submissive, so as to preserve to thy kingdom its due share of the blessings of peace.

'The chief and assistant envoys, the officials below them, the interpreters, escorts, &c., have been granted both rewards in chief and subsidiary rewards according to the list of objects separately drawn up ; and as thine envoys are now about to return home, these our imperial commands are specially prepared, with presents for thee, O King, of patterned silks and other valuable objects, as by ordinary rule in the first instance ; with, besides, gifts of coloured satins, gauzes, curiosities, and other precious articles, as enumerated in the detailed list.   Accept them all, O King, with deference, as a mark of our imperial love.   These our special commands.'

A further command runs :

'Thou King, having yearned from a distance for the civilising influence, and having most earnestly inclined thyself towards improvement, hast despatched envoys to reverently bear with them an address and tribute, to cross the seas and pray for our happiness. We, observing the honesty of thy respectful obedience, O King, commanded our ministers to conduct the envoys to the honour of an audience : a banquet was bestowed upon them, and rewards conferred in bounteous plenty.   Our commands have already been formally issued to them, and presents to thee, King, have been accorded in the shape of patterned silks, valuable curiosities, &c., by way of manifesting our tender affection.

'But the other day thine envoys raised the question of thy kingdom's commerce, and petitioned our ministers to bring the matter before us.   It all involves tampering with fixed rules, and is

inexpedient to accord.   Hitherto the barbarian ships of the different
European States and of thine own kingdom coming to trade at the
Celestial Court have always conducted their commerce at Macao.
This has continued for some time now, and is by no means a matter
of yesterday.   The stores of goods at the Celestial Court are
plenteously abundant; there is nothing but what is possessed, so
that there is really no need for the produce of outer barbarians in
order to balance supply and demand.   However, as the tea, silk, and
porcelain produced by the Celestial Court are indispensable objects to
the different states of Europe, and to thy kingdom, for this reason
We have in our grace and commiseration established the foreign
hongs at Macao in order that all daily needs may be duly
supplied, and every one share in our superfluous riches.   But now
thine envoys have made considerable demands over and above what
is provided by fixed precedent, in such wise as to run seriously
counter to the principle of recognising the bounty of the Celestial
Court to distant men and its nurturing care of the different barbarians.
Moreover, the Celestial Court exercises a controlling supervision over
all countries, and is benevolent to each in an equal degree.   For
instance, those trading in Canton province do not come from the
kingdom of England alone: if they were all to come clamouring in
the same way, and wantonly to pester us with requests impossible to
concede in this style, is it to be supposed that We could always go
out of our way to grant them?   Remembering, however, that thy
kingdom occupies an obscure corner in the distant wilderness, and is
far removed from us by ocean upon ocean; also that thou art
naturally unversed in the political etiquette of the Celestial Court,
We for this reason commanded our ministers to make all this plain
to thine envoys, instruct their minds, and dismiss them back to their
country.   But, fearing that thine envoys on their return home may
fail to represent matters thoroughly to thee, We again take up their
requests one by one, and prepare these further commands for thy
particular instruction, opining thou wilt be able to grasp our
meaning.

' 1. Thine envoys state that the merchant ships of thy kingdom
would like to come and anchor at Ningpo, Chusan, Tientsin, and
Canton for purposes of trade.   Now, hitherto the traders of the
European States who have set out for places under the Celestial
Court have always found the foreign hongs at Macao available for
them to discharge and ship their goods.   This has continued so for a
long time, and thy kingdom amongst the rest has complied with the
rule for many years without a single contrary word.   At neither
Tientsin in Chih Li province nor at Ningpo in Chêh Kiang province
have any foreign hongs been established, and any ships of thy
kingdom proceeding thither would fail to find the means of disposing
of their produce withal.   Besides there are no interpreters at these

places, and no one would be able to understand the language of thy kingdom. Thus there would be many inconveniences. Apart, then, from the port of Macao in the Kwang Tung province, where trade will continue to be permitted on the old lines, the various prayers of thine envoys that ships may be allowed to anchor for purposes of trade, whether at Ningpo, Chusan, or Tientsin, can in no sense be entertained.

' 2. Thine envoys state that it is desired to establish a separate hong in the metropolitan city of the Celestial Court, for the storing and distribution of produce, after the manner and precedent of Russia, a request which it positively is, even in a greater degree than the first, quite impossible to grant. The metropolitan city is the cynosure of the empyrean for all parts of the world : its etiquette is as severely exact as its laws are of striking majesty; never has there been such a thing there as the establishment of mercantile hongs by foreign dependencies. Thy kingdom has hitherto traded at Macao, partly because Macao is comparatively near to the seaports, and partly because it is the commercial emporium of all nations, access to and departure from which are very commodious. If a hong for the distribution of merchandise were to be established in the metropolitan city, thy kingdom is situated at such a very great distance to the north-west of the metropolitan city that the conveying thither of produce would, besides, be very inconvenient indeed. Formerly the Russians established a trading office in the metropolitan city because this was anterior to the organisation of Kiachta; but they only had houses temporarily given to them to reside in. Afterwards, when Kiachta was established, the Russians did all their trading there, and were no longer allowed to reside in the metropolitan city; and this has been so now for some score or more of years. The Russian trade which now goes on at the Kiachta frontier is, in fact, analogous to the trade of thy kingdom at Macao. As thy kingdom already has foreign hongs for the distribution of produce at Macao, why must thou needs wish to establish another hong in the metropolitan city ? The boundaries of the Celestial Court are defined with absolute clearness, and never have individuals belonging to outer dependencies been allowed to infringe the frontiers or mix with our people in the least degree. Thus the desire of thy kingdom to set up a hong in the metropolitan city positively can not be granted.

' 3. Thine envoys state again that they desire a small island, somewhere about the Chusan group, so that merchants can go thither and make it a resting terminus for the convenience of receiving and warehousing produce. Now, the desire expressed by thy kingdom for permission to reside at Chusan comes from the wish to distribute the merchants' produce. But, as Chusan possesses no foreign hongs, and has no interpreters, no ships of thy kingdom have, so far, gone thither ; and thus the desire of thy kingdom to possess the island in question is a futile one. Every inch of land under the Celestial Court is accounted for in the official survey; the boundary marks are strictly laid down, and even islands and shoals must be considered from this frontier point of view, each belonging to its proper jurisdiction. Moreover, thy kingdom of England is not the only one amongst the outer barbarians which turns towards civilisation and trades with the Celestial Court. Were other states to come clamouring in the same way, and each beg for a gift of land for the occupation of its traders, how would it be possible to grant the petition of each? Besides, the Celestial Court has no precedent for such a course, and therefore it is inexpedient in a yet greater degree to grant this request either.

'4. They say once more that some small place in the neighbourhood of the provincial capital of Canton might be set apart for the barbarian traders of thy country to reside in; or, as an alternative, that those persons residing at Macao might be allowed to travel backwards and forwards at their convenience. Hitherto the barbarian merchants of the different European states, residing for purposes of trade at Macao, have had the boundary line marked out clearly for them, and have not been allowed to transgress it one single foot or inch; nor have the barbarian traders resorting to the foreign hongs to dispose of their goods been permitted to take upon themselves to enter Canton, the object of all this being to check the rise of disputes between the people and the barbarians, and to set a great barrier between China and Abroad. The request now made that a separate place near Canton may be set apart for the residence of the barbarian merchants from thy kingdom is thus, in the first place, contrary to the precedents which have up to this time governed the barbarian merchants of Europe residing at Macao: moreover the different European states have traded in Kwang Tung province for a great many years, and have accumulated great profits: they come in daily increasing numbers: how then would it be possible to set apart a separate piece of land for the residence of each? As to barbarian merchants moving to and fro as they may list, it is for the local officials, assisted by the Chinese bong-men, to institute inquiry as each case may seem to require. If no bounds of any description were set, it is to be feared that the people of the interior might from time to time get into disputes with the barbarian merchants of thy kingdom, which would have results very far from the commiseration intended. Taking into consideration, therefore, the requirements of the case, We must declare for residence at Macao, in accordance with established practice, as being the only satisfactory and desirable course.

'5. Again, they say that the barbarian merchants of the English kingdom might proceed from Canton down to Macao by the inner reaches, and that their goods might either pay no taxes at all, or

reduced taxes.[7] Now, there are fixed tariffs governing all cases connected with the payment of duties by barbarian traders moving to
and fro, and in this regard all the nations of Europe are upon the
same footing. Just as it would not do at the present time to charge
the ships of thy country any excess over the tariff because they
happen to be the most numerous, so is it inexpedient to make an
exception in favour of thy country by reducing the duties payable
by it alone. The only course is to charge a just levy in accordance
with the existing practice, and on the same footing as the other
countries. Henceforth the barbarian merchants of thy state proceeding with their produce to Macao must receive every attention as
before, in order to manifest due commiseration for them.

'6. They next apply that the ships of thy kingdom may pay
duties in accordance with a tariff. Now, the Hoppo of Canton in
levying tonnage dues [8] has hitherto acted under a fixed tariff; and,
as it has now been declared inexpedient to establish trading hongs at
any other seaports, it follows that duties must be paid as before, in
accordance with precedent, to the Hoppo of Canton, and that there is
no necessity for any further notification on the subject. As to the
Teaching of the Lord of Heaven [9] cultivated by thy kingdom, this is
simply the teaching which has up to this time been cultivated by the
different nations of Europe. The Sacred Emperors and Illustrious
Kings of the Celestial Court have, ever since the creation of the
world, handed down the teachings which they have instituted from
time to time; the earth's millions have a standing guide provided for
them to follow herein, and would not venture to befool themselves
with outlandish doctrines. So far as the European men who have
accepted service in the metropolis are concerned, they reside in the
Hall, and are not allowed to form connections with the people of
China, or to wantonly propagate their faith. The distinction between
Chinese and barbarian is strictly maintained. The desire which thine
envoys now express is that barbarian men may be allowed to preach
their faith as they list, which is even more impossible to grant than
anything else.

'The above categorical homily is forthcoming in consequence of
the wanton suggestions made by thine envoys. Thou, King, maybe,
hast not been able to thoroughly comprehend the political principles
of the Celestial Court, and hadst no idea of wanton intrusion thyself.
In all cases where tributary kingdoms with honest heart turn
towards civilisation, We invariably display our commiseration, in order

---

[7] Probably this refers to re-exports or unsold cargoes. The Emperor, like all
Chinese, shows acuteness in evading the main point and betaking himself to generalities.

[8] 'Ships' materials' are the actual words used, but a single extra dot (probably
accidentally omitted) transforms these into 'ships' dues.'

[9] This term is now usually confined to the Roman Catholic faith; 'Jesus teaching' is the common expression for 'Protestants.'

to make manifest our tender affection. ·Should they · crave any matters from us which do not conflict with our political principles, in all cases We go out of our way to grant their requests.   Moreover, in thy case, O King, residing as thou dost in an obscure spot across the oceans, having protested thine earnestness and paid thy tribute, We have conferred upon thee rich favours in double the measure of other countries.   But the requests now submitted by thine envoys not only seriously concern the statutory rules of the Celestial Court, but are all quite futile and impracticable even in thine own interests. We now once more set forth our meaning for thine instruction, O King, who shouldst enter into our views and for ever render obedience, thus enjoying thy due share of the blessings of peace.   If, after this clear declaration, thou, King, shouldst peradventure lend misguided ear to the words of the men under thee, and allow barbarian merchants to go with their trading ships to Chêh Kiang, Tientsin, &c., and seek to land there for purposes of trade, know thou that the statutory rules of the Celestial Court are very strict, and that the civil and military officers in charge of each place will do their duty faithfully, and will not allow any ships of thy kingdom proceeding thither to remain there, but will positively have to drive them away at once to sea, so that the barbarian merchants of thy kingdom will have all their trouble in vain.   Say not thou wast not warned! Tremble and obey, without negligence, this further command!'

'*Jên-yin* (day).[10]—Rescript to the Cabinet Council:

'Chukwei [11] has sent up a memorial reporting that England has submitted an address with tribute.   As certain tribute envoys in previous years had arrived in the metropolis and received handsome rewards from us, the King in question has specially prepared an address, with articles of local origin as tribute, for submission to us. His heartfelt sincerity is sufficiently manifest, and although no special envoy has come to Canton for the above purpose, on what ground should there be any difficulty about vouchsafing acceptance?

'An imperial order [12] is also issued commanding him in the following words:

'"Thy kingdom lying far away as it does across repeated oceans, last year thou sentest envoys to reverentially bear an address with tribute, to cross the seas, and pray for our happiness.   We, observing thy heartfelt earnestness, O King, ordered our ministers to admit them to the privilege of audience, bestowed a banquet upon them, and con-

---

[10] *Jên-yin* is the 24th day after the kalends of the 12th moon in the 60th year of the Emperor K'ien-lung; five days later he abdicated. This would be early in February 1796.

[11] Chukwei must be a Manchu, and viceroy at Canton.

[12] This Emperor often drafted the replies which his officers were to send, and even told them to say 'We dare not trouble the Emperor about this matter.'

ferred rewards in bounteous abundance.   We issued a formal decree of
commands for them to take home with them, and presented thee, O
King, with patterned silks and valuable curiosities, in order to make
manifest our tender affection.   Now, O King, thou hast once more
prepared a submissive address with local articles, which thou hast
sent by barbarian ship to Canton for submission to us.   The honesty
of thy reverent submission is sufficiently obvious.   The Celestial
Court holds in conciliatory possession all the states of the world.
We reck not of the gifts of jewels which come to our Court : what We
value is the senders' honesty of purpose.   We have, however, commanded our viceregal authorities to admit the objects in question, in
order to allow free scope to thy devout respect.

'"As to the punitory expedition which the Celestial Court some
time ago despatched against the Ghoorkas, the generalissimo com-
manding-in-chief penetrated deeply into their country at the time,
capturing successive strong points.   The Ghoorkas, awe-stricken before
our military might, came cringing in to offer submission, and it was
then first that the generalissimo reported the condition of affairs to
us.[13]   The benevolent goodness of the Celestial Court extends far
away over both China and Abroad in equal measure.   Unwilling that
the poor folk of that region should one and all come to annihilation,
We for this reason consented to receive their submission.   At that
time it is true the generalissimo did allude in his report to the fact
that thou, King, hadst sent an envoy to Tibet to proffer a petition,
stating that thou hadst exhorted the Ghoorkas to make their submission.   But the great results of our victory had then already been
achieved, nor was there ever any need to trouble the military power
of thy kingdom.   In thy present address, O King, it is stated that
this affair occurred after the last envoys had started on their journey
hither, and that therefore they had not been able to report it to us ;
but it is evident thou art ill acquainted with the sequence of events.
Still, as thou, O King, appearest able to understand the principles of
right, and art reverently submissive to the Celestial Court, We readily
accord our commendation and approval, and now make thee, O King,
special formal gifts of embroidered satins, &c.   On thy part, O King,
make further efforts in devoted loyalty, and ever merit our imperial
favour, thus giving effect to our high desire that even the most distant may participate in the soothing influence of our benevolence."

'When Chukwei shall have received the above document, he will

---

[13] The *Annals of the Manchu Wars* distinctly states that 'in 1795, when the
English envoy came to Peking [inaccurate, of course] with tribute, he said : "Last
year but one, your general led his troops into the Timi country south-west of Tibet,
and on that occasion we aided you with gunboats.   Should you hereafter desire the
use of European troops, we offer you our services."   It was only then that the
Emperor became aware that, when the Ghoorkas submitted, it was because they were
menaced also on the south.'

at once proceed to deliver it to the *taipan* [14] Brown belonging to the said country for further transmission by him back to his country, so that the King in question may be still further filled with grateful obligation and reverent submission, and our affectionate tenderness be thus made manifest.

'The rule is that officials of the Celestial Court may not have any truck with outer barbarians. Chukwei therefore did right to give him orders to take back the objects presented to the former viceroy and the Hoppo.'

N.B.—In all the above papers there are words which do not admit of exact translation. For instance, the word translated 'barbarian' cannot possibly be accurately rendered: it is rather 'outlandish' or 'strange,' having in it at the same time that suspicion of inferiority which is wrapped up in the vague English word 'natives' as opposed to genuine white men, or in the American expression 'coloured folk.' The use of 'thou' denotes unmistakable inferiority. Such words as 'order,' 'submissive address,' 'policy,' 'etiquette,' 'commiseration,' 'civilisation,' 'devout respect,' 'imperial commands,' and 'tender affection' are susceptible of many turns and shades in translation. However, the rendering is word for word and literal throughout, so far as the Chinese language admits of it.

E. H. PARKER.

[14] *Taipan* is a Cantonese word meaning 'partner' or 'head of a commercial house,' but referring solely to Europeans. The Hoppo—a 'pidgin-English' word—is the Comptroller of Customs.

THE BAB AND BABISM [1]

IN 1845, in the city of Shiraz, the seat of learning, as the Persians say—of rose-gardens and of nightingales, as I would call it—a young Persian began to preach. He had made the pilgrimage to Mecca, and came back full of ideas of his own—mystic and enthusiastic ideas, which evade definition and perplex the downright Anglo-Saxon understanding. However, he made it quite clear that, in his opinion, the people in general, and the priests in particular, had departed widely from the cardinal doctrines of Muhammadanism, and that the priests, in their lives, were far from practising what they did more or less erroneously preach. Now my readers will say that this is very vague ; but I will make bold to say that Bab was at first as vague as myself, but his mystic hints and unintelligible suggestions were taken for the significant, if not for the magnificent. Let anyone who has studied Eastern writings on religion deny, if he can, that to get anything definite out of them is as difficult as the proverbial extraction of a needle from a bundle of hay. However, the young man called himself the Gate of Heaven—the ' Bab ; ' and it is said that he possessed a handsome appearance, engaging manners, and an eloquent tongue—powerful agents at all times for the accomplishment of any ends. A little later, and the Gate of Heaven represented himself as an emanation from the Divinity itself, and then assumed the title of ' Highness,' by which, also, Jesus, the son of Mary, or Miriam, is habitually known amongst Muhammadans. Next he gathered about him eighteen apostles, not that he might have half as many again as had his Highness Jesus, but because a peculiar sanctity, in his opinion, attached to the number nineteen. He, the prophet of God, the latest revelation, was the central point, round which revolved eighteen satellites, and, like the French Revolutionists, he would have renumbered and renamed everything, only with him everything would have had reference to the whole, or to the component parts of the mystic number.

Among his disciples were several persons of courage, eloquence,

[1] This article was written before the assassination of the late Shah of Persia.— ED. *Nineteenth Century*

and resolution, probably superior to his own. Among them was the warrior-priest Hussein, who at once saw that a nation which awaited the coming of the Mahdi—the hidden one, the twelfth Imam— would be more likely to believe in the new religion if its prophet were represented as the Mahdi himself. He thus traded on the ignorance of his public, for this pretension was never asserted by Bab. It is impossible, however, as we have reason to know, to keep the Mahdi out of Muhammadan politics, and this confusion of ideas was almost inevitable.

We have to thank Hussein for giving clear expression to two of the chief aims set before the Babees—viz. the abolition of polygamy, and of the doctrine of pollution. It may here be remarked that, of the many unfair criticisms directed against Islam, there is none it deserves so little as that of encouraging polygamy. When the prophet restricted the number of wives to four, he made an immense advance in morality on the state of things existing in his time amongst the Arabs, where practically every woman in a man's household was in some respects in the position of a wife. If he could have gone further, there is little doubt from his teachings that he would have, and, as a matter of fact, his followers are for the most part husbands of one wife, notwithstanding the indulgence allowed by law. It may safely be affirmed that the English are in one sense, and in a manner that is more demoralising and degrading than the authorised polygamy of Islam, at least as polygamous as the Muhammadans themselves. It has been reserved for a canon of the Church of England to stigmatise a great moral reformer as ' an ignorant and immoral Bedouin,' and ' a lecherous Arab,' to whom Mahomet bore, in fact, no greater resemblance than an agricultural scarecrow does to an impaled Bulgarian.

At the town of Kazveen, on the southern side of the Elburz, and not far from the ruins of the castle of the chief of the Assassins, dwelt, at the time of which I write (1845), the beautiful daughter of a Mussulman doctor of the law. Her name was Zareen Taj, or Golden Crown. Her virtues were equal to her beauty; she was eloquent and well-instructed—an ideal heroine. We have to thank her for the enunciation of another of the tenets of the Babees—the abolition of the veil. She showed her beautiful face without any reserve, perhaps the more readily because it was beautiful, embraced the cause of Bab with heart and soul, and, so say the historians, had no share whatever in the murder of her father-in-law—a priest, who naturally was scandalised beyond all measure by her behaviour, and strove, with her other relations, to reclaim her from perdition.

Now these times were pregnant with other great events; and just as the Babees were beginning to feel their strength, the king died, and his Majesty, Nasir-ed-Din ascended the throne of Persia. This was the opportunity for the warrior Hussein, who gathered about

him the converts he had made in Khorassan, and accompanied by
Golden Crown, the Hypatia of this new religion, entrenched himself
in an inaccessible spot in Mazendaran.   Here Hypatia and Hussein
preached the Church Militant, whose kingdom should be of this world
as well as of the next.   Like the Empress Theodora, when the heart
of her husband sank within him, and his advisers counselled flight,
she was ever present to instil courage into the doubting, and to
promise those who fought, and those who lost their lives in battle, a
golden crown in heaven.   Like Theodora, she would not stop to consider if it became a woman to play the man against men.   She urged
that those were times when women should abjure seclusion, tear off
their veils, not wait for what the men might do, but act themselves.
Her eloquence and beauty kindled incredible enthusiasm amongst the
Babees in Mazendaran, a Caspian province of the Persian realm,
whose thick forests and green foliage form so striking a contrast with
the barren rocks and interminable deserts on the other side of the
Elburz, beyond the talismanic peak of Demavend.   The plan of the
campaign was the conquest of Mazendaran, a march to Ré, the ancient
Rhages of the Apocalypse, around the venerable tower of which ruined
city a great victory was to be gained over the forces of the Shah from
the neighbouring capital.   The new prime minister sent one of the
royal princes with a large army against the Babee chief, who, however, defeated prince and army.   The second attack, though successfully repulsed, proved fatal to the brave Hussein, who died, declaring,
with glorious mendacity, that he would reappear in forty days and
carry his work to its completion.   The prime minister continued for
four months to besiege the mountain stronghold of the Babees, who,
pushed to the last extremities, made flour from the ground bones of
the dead, ate the boiled leather of their sword-belts, dug up and
devoured buried carrion, and suffered all the horrors of a protracted
siege.   At last, the few survivors capitulated, their lives being
guaranteed them, but all were slain in cold blood next day, including
women and children.   All refused to recant.

Contrary to the hopes of the king and his minister, this success
did not stifle the insurrection.   Another of the disciples, the priest
Mahomed, successfully defied the royal troops in Zendjan.   Mortally
wounded in one of the last engagements, he, like Hussein, exhorted
his followers to hold out for forty days, at the expiry of which time
he would return to lead them on to victory ; but soon afterwards they
were overcome by the king's general, who opened the tomb of his
deceased enemy and found him peacefully lying in his coffin with
his sword by his side.   They dishonoured his corpse and cast it to
the dogs.   Three of his chief lieutenants were taken to Teheran and
condemned to death by having their veins opened.   They died pro-
phesying that their persecutor the prime minister would die the same
death, as in fact he did not long after in the peaceful country palace

of Fin by Kashan, where nothing recalls the tragic end of a powerful and erewhile successful minister.

And now the hour of Bab himself was come : summoned to Tabriz by the prince-governor, he was confronted with the doctors of the law, and, according to the side from which one hears the tale, either vanquished them, or was vanquished by them in debate. The prince himself argued a long while with Bab, but finally proved his adversary to be in the wrong by condemning him to death without further ceremony. He probably cared little who won the wordy war. He had conquered the Babees, and might say with Achilles in his grandest speech :

$$\text{Τοῖος ἐὼν οἷος οὔτις 'Αχαιῶν χαλκοχιτώνων}$$
$$\text{'Εν πολέμῳ· ἀγορῇ δέ τ' ἀμείνονές εἰσι καὶ ἄλλοι.}$$

lines I would venture thus to translate :

In council what if others mouth the question and reply?
In battle 'midst the brass-clad Greeks, what other strikes as I?

With Bab was his faithful disciple the priest Mahomed, whose loyalty to his master was cruelly tried in his last extremity. His persecutors called in his wife and children to work upon his weakness, if perchance he had any. They tempted him in vain, and, just before sunset, master and disciple were bound with cords, and suspended from the ramparts within a few feet of the ground in the face of a multitude of spectators. A company of soldiers was told off to shoot them as they hung, and, just before the word was given, the priest Mahomed was heard to say to Bab, 'Master, art thou content with me?' Hardly had he spoken when he received his death wound, but Bab miraculously escaped, and the bullets aimed at him merely cut the cord by which he hung. For a moment all were stupefied, and Bab might have yet escaped had he, in the confusion which ensued, mingled with the crowd, which would have shielded an *enfant du miracle* to save whom God had manifestly intervened. He took refuge, however, in a guard-house close by, where one of the officers of the firing party cut him down with his sword. That there might be no doubt about his death, his corpse was paraded in the streets, and finally cast to the dogs.

So died the Bab at the age of twenty-seven; but his place was at once taken, if not filled, by Baha, a youth of sixteen years, who, for reasons not very clearly established, was considered by the leaders of the faith to be destined to succeed. Pursued by the emissaries of the prime minister, this youth established himself at Baghdad, where, amongst the crowds of Persian pilgrims to the tombs of the holy Imams at Sandy, Kerbela, and gilded Kazimain, he continued to preach the doctrines of his predecessor and to show the way to the gate of heaven. By some in Persia I was told that, following the example of the veiled prophet of Khorassan, he never shows his face, though he interviews all comers.   I must confess that to my annoyance and disappointment I could learn nothing of himself in Baghdad.   Some said the Sultan kept him in prison to please the Shah, but I could discover the existence of no well-known captive, save Suleiman Pasha, who since the Russian war in the city of peace drags out a dishonoured old age.   I learnt even less in the Pashalik than in Persia.

All the above events passed in the decade between 1842 and 1852; and one day in the latter year, when the Shah was out riding, three men approached him with a petition, and when his Majesty drew rein, his attendants being a little before and behind him, one of the supplicants seized his bridle and fired upon him, as also did the two others, whose hands were disengaged.   The king showed great coolness and courage, the escort galloped up, the men were seized, the Shah was taken home, where his wound proved insignificant.   The assassins avowed themselves to be Babees, denied that they had accomplices, and gloried in their act.

When the first alarm had subsided the police set to work to arrest all persons in the capital suspected of being Babees.   Among them was Zareen Taj, or Golden Crown, who had left the camp in Mazendaran before its fall.   The assassins meanwhile continued to protest that they merely obeyed the orders of their chief away in Turkish Arabia, and declared that the king deserved death for having slain their prophet Bab.   No tortures could extract anything else from them.

The king and his minister, perplexed in what way to deal with their captives, offered life and liberty to all who would deny Bab, and began by making the offer to Zareen Taj, who refused unhesitatingly to purchase life by recantation; whereupon she was strangled [and burnt in the citadel, and her ashes scattered to the winds.   Her dreadful fate, contrary to expectation, had no effect whatever on her fellow-captives, who were distributed among different officials for punishment, to accentuate the public indignation which had been excited by the attempt to murder the king.

Most travellers in Persia have seen by the roadside the little pillars in which robbers have been built up and left to starve, and must have heard fairly credible accounts of crucifixions and other cruel [punishments.   Nowadays these things do not happen; but there seems no reason to doubt that extraordinary barbarities attended the execution of the Babees in Teheran.

I have been myself told by a nomad chief, who had been an eyewitness, with whom I camped in Fars, that some were shod like horses, some cut to pieces with knives and whips, and some made to carry torches in apertures made for the purpose in their bodies.   My informant may have exaggerated, but it is certain that extreme cruelty was the rule.   Nothing that is related is beyond belief.   To this day robbers are starved to death in cages in China, and parricides are sliced to death (ling-chih), while the purest and highest morality is the ideal set before the individual Chinaman and the Imperial Government alike.

No tortures that ingenuity could devise sufficed to shake the constancy of these martyred men, women, and children, who died repeating the familiar Arabic text : ' Verily we are God's, and to Him we return.' In the provinces, as well as in the capital, all suspects were hunted down. A relative of my friend the nomad chief was particularly active in this service, and conceived the idea of handing over so many captives to tradesmen of different guilds, whose professional instincts might devise some distinctive and characteristic torture.

These terrible reprisals, which probably far exceeded those ordered by the Government, produced, outwardly at any rate, the desired effect. No man dared name Bab or Babee without a curse as deep as that deserved by Omar. The very subject became a dangerous one to speak of, and it still continues to be so. An official at Teheran, who was I knew conversant with the whole subject, denied all knowledge. Officials all declared not one of the sons of burnt fathers remained. Princes, who are plentiful in Persia, considered a reference to the matter in bad taste and would change the subject. Traders, sitting cross-legged amidst their grain and wares, would suggest that if you wanted to buy nothing you had better move on. The result is that even those Europeans who have been long resident in the country really know extremely little about the tenets of the Babees, or their present position, numbers, and prospects. The writings of Bab and Baha are hard to get, and when got still harder to read with understanding.

In the course of this brief narrative I have already said that Bab abjured polygamy, and removed from woman's face the veil. These were no light innovations. The whole weight of tradition and of the law was bound to uphold polygamy to the extent sanctioned by Mahomet, and every father and every husband in the country looked on the veil as one of the safeguards of women's honour. This appears strange only to those who do not know their Eastern sisters, with their burning love and their simple sins.

The cold in clime are cold in blood.

But the Eastern father must keep his daughter from the sight of man till she is safely married, and her husband thinks the same precaution as necessary in the case of his wife. Both are as jealous of the honour of their women as an English gentleman, and perhaps they know best how to maintain it among their own people. They are aghast at customs which prescribe that women's legs shall be carefully covered, while their faces, by which they are recognised and known, may be exposed to the gaze of any passer-by.

To argue the question is hopeless, and it may be allowed at once
that no bolder or more radical reform could be proposed, or one more
likely to entail hatred and contempt upon its proposer.   The women
themselves are at least as bitterly opposed to such reforms as the men.
Nor indeed do they suffer such restraint as is generally supposed to
result from the custom.   It does not occur to a well-conducted Persian
woman that anyone but her husband should see her face ; and should
she stray from the straight path, what costume so favourable for
assignation and intrigue as the loose trouser, long blue baggy robe
and veil, clothed in which she can pass her husband or anyone else
in the street without fear of discovery, walk to the bath with a female
attendant, or gossip with her friends all day, making known her
identity only when she desires to do so ?

The commission which Bab asserted he had received to expound
the nature of the Godhead included no power of lucid composition,
but thus much is clear : that God is held to be one, unchangeable, and
that the last revelation was more complete than those of previous
prophets which it superseded.   The prophets themselves were emana-
tions from the Deity :

> partem divinæ mentis et haustus
> Ætherios.

The revelation of Bab was not one of the individual, but was made
to the mystic nineteen, of whom one at a time was necessarily the
guiding spirit and spiritual chief, but whose acts and deed were those
of a corporate body.

Though more complete than that of former prophets, the revelation of Bab was not itself complete, and his bible comprises but
eleven chapters of an inevitable total of nineteen.   The next revelation after Bab was, however, like that of Christ at His second coming,
like that of the Imam Mahdi when he reveals himself, to be the last.
An intermediate day of judgment was provided for the termination
of the penultimate prophetic period, but the dead were all to reappear
at the last day, the good to be reunited with God and the wicked to
be annihilated.

So much for the outlines of the doctrines of Bab.   A few details
must be supplied.   Society and government were to be constituted
on a basis something like that existing in Persia, and included a
king, a sacred college, pontiffs, priests, and all the paraphernalia of
patriarchal government.

Unlike Mahomet, Bab preferred silken hangings and decorations
for the house of prayer, and music and singing, and all the pomp
and circumstance of priestly celebration.   He was a great believer
in talismans and the virtues of particular stones.   This fits in well
with the temper of the modern Persians, who to this day will tell
you solemnly that the great volcano Demavend is talismanic, who

believe implicitly in the virtues of a turquoise ring inscribed with the name of Allah. Unbelievers might legally be deprived of all their possessions, which, however, should be returned to them on their professing the true faith. They were on no account to be put to death. Business and other relations with infidels were not forbidden, and, as a matter of fact, the Babees entertain very friendly relations with Jews, fire-worshippers, and Christians, while in their hearts they hate the Mussulman, much as among Mussulmans the Shiahs hate the Sunis, from whom, however, they differ on a merely dynastic and historical question.

The Babees only pray on formal occasions like the Christians. A Babee will not roll out his prayer-carpet and bow his head in prayer on the deck of a steamer, in the public street and on the sands of a desert, as will the devout Mussulman. Nor does the Babee admit the doctrine of legal impurity. Indeed amongst them, ablutions have no religious significance whatever. This doctrine of impurity is said to be a great impediment to free intercourse amongst Asiatics. As understood by the Brahmins and high-caste Hindus it may be ; but as amongst Mahomedans, it merely prescribes ablution before prayer and on certain other occasions. I do not see how this can prove the obstruction it is represented to be. However, it is one of the many refinements of the law which Bab hoped to sweep away. In regard to alms-giving, his doctrines are much those of the Mussulmans. Torture and death are entirely excluded from his penal code. He punished every offence by fines calculated, of course, in nineteens. He held that the rich were only depositories of the bounty of God, and were bound to provide liberally for their less fortunate brethren ; at the same time he altogether forbade mendicancy, which is recognised and encouraged in Islam. Those who have been tormented by sturdy beggars demanding money as a right, and supported by public opinion, will understand what a blessed innovation this was. He exhibited the same favour towards trade as is displayed in the present day everywhere in the East, where there is no suspicion of social inferiority attached to its pursuit, whether in its retail or wholesale aspect. The practical Asiatic mind cannot fathom European ideas on this subject. Everywhere the merchant is held in high esteem and no calling is superior to his. Bab was as sound on this point as are the most despotic Eastern governors, who generally grasp the fact that the oppression of merchants means the ruin of a province. I have dwelt for a moment on the practical nature of the Eastern mind. One may emphasise this, remembering how generally romance is looked upon as the attribute of the East, and how the Asian mystery has become proverbial. It is difficult to imagine whence this belief sprung. I think the *Arabian Nights* may have had something to say to it ; but surely the *Thousand and One Nights* are full of imagination,

but not of romance.   Everything is practical, nothing more so than
love-making, most romantic of occupations.   When the king's son
becomes enamoured of the moon-faced beauty, he goes to bed and
refuses food until she marries him.   He becomes so ill and woe-
begone that all his female relations make a point of bringing his
wishes to accomplishment.   This is very practical, and quite unlike
the knights and troubadours of the West, who went to the crusades
trusting to the constancy of their mistresses, and found them on
their return married, and the mothers of large families.   In the
East men do not greatly strive to arrive at 'self-reverence, self-
knowledge, self-control,' nor will they eat their hearts away from
hopeless love.   They make known their passions and endeavour to
gratify them, be the object who she may and the consequences to
her what they may.   Of imagination there is enough and to spare
in the East, but for romance one must go to the Celts, the Saxons,
and the Scandinavians :

> To the bountiful infinite West, to the happy memorial places
> Full of stately repose, and the lordly delight of the dead,
> Where the fortunate islands are lit with the light of ineffable faces,
> And the sound of a sea without wind is about them, and sunset is red.

Sunset is still redder in the East, but let that pass.   There is sense
in the lines.

To return to our subject.   The new prophet's mild and gentle
disposition prescribed politeness as a counsel of necessity, but exhibited something of the narrowness of mind which induced the Caliph
Omar to destroy the library of Alexandria, for he held that such books
as disagreed with the Word of God were pernicious, and ought to be
destroyed.   He 'commended mirth,' however, and precious stones
were not forbidden to the Babees, who were positively encouraged on
festival days to clothe themselves in purple and fine linen, and to
'rejoice in their youth and walk in the ways of their heart,' remembering only 'that for all these things God would bring them to
judgment.'   In regard to marriage Bab departed in many respects
from the precepts of Islam.   He allowed a second wife.   In this
respect he seems to me to fall short of Mahomet, who in a time of
unbridled licentiousness allowed but four for the frailty of human
nature, and because it was the only means of legalising in Bedouin
life an inevitable *liaison*.   No excuse can be found for Bab, unless he
would urge 'the exigencies of modern society,' any more than for the
Mormons, whose hideous polygamy the United States Government
has happily suppressed with a strong hand.   If it is necessary to
quote others in support of my assertion that polygamy is the exception
among the Musulmans, I will quote M. de Gobineau, who says, '*en
réalité les gens qui ont plusieurs femmes constituent l'exception
même parmi les musulmans.   La majorité se contente d'un unique
mariage.*   The Sheikh-ul-Islam at Constantinople, and Dr. Leitner

have testified to the same effect, but there is in fact a cloud of witnesses. In another respect also Bab improved greatly upon Musulman law in regard to women. Besides the abolition of the veil already spoken of, he abolished the existing law of divorce. The facility with which women are divorced is perhaps the greatest blot in the religion of Mahomet. It will suffice here to say that Bab removed the legal obstacles which exist to prompt reconciliation between husband and wife, when the simple formula of divorce has been hastily and inconsiderately pronounced. For their weakness, Bab prescribed for women short and easy prayers, and he discouraged pilgrimages, saying that wives and mothers were better at home. Other innovations, which, so far as my inquiries went, are at all times honoured in the breach, were his decrees that beards should be shaven, circumcision abandoned, and pipes put out. He was no timeserver and attacked some of the most cherished institutions of the country, amongst which I would certainly include pipes, beards, and circumcision. To the sharers in the property of a deceased believer, Bab added the family tutor—a benevolent addition.

To come to any conclusions as to the extent to which Babees now exist in Persia is most difficult. At Kazneen a Georgian who had been many years in the country, and was at that time in the service of a high official there, told me that he thought that amongst the rich and educated perhaps one-third were followers of Bab. This is probably an over-estimate, but that among the classes named there is a large proportion which is dissatisfied with the Islam of the priests is well known. Among the nomads of the Hills, the Turki tribes and others, there are no Babees, and these tribes form a large proportion of the population of Persia. One ' old White Beard '—to use the phrase of the country—with whom I breakfasted one day, assured me that such a thing as a Babee had never been seen amongst the wandering tribes. He added, however, that he had seven daughters who ate and slept, and that he did not trouble himself much about religion, beyond saying his prayers regularly and observing all due conventionalities. Near Kermanshah one day I met a Seyyad, or a descendant of the Prophet, who was collecting fleeces—suggestive tribute from the faithful—and he said that there was not a Babee left in all Persia. They had been a polyandrous and immoral set of unbelievers, but their fathers were all burnt, that is to say, consumed in hell, and there was an end of them. In Hamadan—one of the largest towns in Persia—I have reason to believe, from inquiries made on the spot, that there are very large numbers who in secret hold to the faith of the young and martyred prophet. At Abadeh there certainly are many such, though gruesome pits full of Babees' skulls exist within the walls of the town.

In Khorassan and the western provinces of Persia I have not travelled, but my inquiries went to show that in the holy city of

Mashad, around the shrine of the Imam Reza itself, Babees abound. It will be obvious from what I have said that I can give no reliable numerical estimate; but this need not be considered a serious omission, as no one knows whether the population of Persia at this day is five or, as I think, nearer eight millions. It will suffice to say that Babees abound, and chiefly among the richer and more educated classes.

J. D. REES.

WALTER VON DER VOGELWEIDE
THE MINNESINGER

THOUGH doubtless unfamiliar to English ears, the name of the greatest of the Minnesingers, Walter von der Vogelweide, should yet not be altogether unknown. Longfellow has retold the charming legend of the poet leaving money for the birds, his masters in song, to be fed daily at his tomb for ever; and lovers of Wagner will remember that among the singers who take part in the poetic contest at the Wartburg, in the second act of *Tannhäuser*, Walter von der Vogelweide plays a prominent part. But, indeed, no excuse should be needed for the endeavour to interest English readers in a name which, after an oblivion of centuries, has once more become almost a household word in Germany, and in the works of a man who has exercised no small influence on the development of modern German poetry. This revived interest in Walter von der Vogelweide and his works was due, not only to the fact that the awakened national consciousness of the German people has been glad to gather up the threads of connection with its brighter past, but also to the new enthusiasm aroused by the great events of 1870, which produced once again a taste for that patriotic poetry of which Walter was so admirable a master. For, of the two greatest names of modern German literature, Goethe had from the first been accused of a lack of national sentiment, while Heine's French sympathies have placed him, so to speak, under the ban of the new empire. Walter's stirring rhymes then, often singularly applicable to the conditions of modern German politics, have served in a measure, whether read in the original Middle High German or in Simrock's excellent translation, to fill a void, and to inspire, in the nineteenth as in the thirteenth century, a certain number of imitators.

It is not, however, as a patriot or a politician that Walter von der Vogelweide would specially appeal to us, but as a character of rare charm and many-sidedness, and a genius which not only reflects and illustrates the movements of an age of deep historical interest, but is also able to express, in a singular degree for so early a period, those human emotions and feelings which are neither mediæval nor modern, German nor English, but transcend the limitations of time or locality.

Born about the year 1170, of poor but not ignoble parentage, Walter von der Vogelweide lived his long and eventful life in an age of great men and great ideas. It was the period of Innocent the Third, in whose person the power and pretensions of the papacy reached their zenith ; of Frederick Barbarossa, whose dream was the restoration of the empire of Charlemagne and of the Roman Cæsars ; of Henry the Sixth and Frederick the Second, under whom the dream was, once and again, all but realised. And in the great world-tragedy of which these were the central figures Walter von der Vogelweide played a distinguished part, exercising, by reason of his clear and patriotic insight into the great issues of the age, as well as by his brilliant poetic genius, no small influence upon the development of the plot.

Of Walter's birthplace and parentage nothing certain is known. His father appears to have belonged to that numerous class of petty nobles (*Dienstadel*) who swelled the train of the great feudal lords ; and it is only with some appearance of probability that the obscure hamlet, or rather homestead, from which he·derived his name, has in recent times been identified, in a remote valley in the Tyrol, with a spot in the forest whence all traces of human occupation have long since vanished. Forced, as it would seem, by the poverty of his parents, Walter had early to leave his home in search of fame and fortune ; and, with the consciousness of his peculiar powers already awake within him, time and opportunity alike pointed the path he should take. For it was now the ' Springtime of the poetry of Love,' and to be a singer or the patron of singers was the part of every gentleman, since, in 1184, Frederick the First had called together the great gathering at Mayence, to witness the knighting of his two sons. There, not from Germany only, but from France, Italy, and the Low Countries, minstrels had assembled to celebrate the occasion in song ; there the future Emperor had himself condescended to enter the lists with the poets, and so brought into fashion that chivalrous poetry which the French had learned from the Troubadours of Provence, and had taught the Germans.

Of all the princes who posed as the patrons of art by far the most splendid and liberal was the Duke Leopold the Sixth of Austria, under whose auspices the Court of Vienna had become a brilliant centre of refinement and culture. Thither accordingly, as at once the nearest and most promising field in which to push his fortunes, Walter turned his steps ; and there, his genius finding speedy recognition, he remained, profiting by the example, if not the actual tuition, of the poet Reinmar, until some eight years later, when his fame had become already established, the death of Duke Leopold's son and successor, Frederick the First (A.D. 1198), broke up the circle of artists and poets who had lived upon his patronage.

To this period, when the poet was still young and full of hope, surrounded by the congenial atmosphere of an art and pleasure-loving Court, and free as yet from those cares and embarrassments which afterwards oppressed him, belong the best of those love lyrics whose charm and spontaneity earned for him the title of the greatest of Minnesingers. And in after years, when age, poverty, and the miseries of the times had all but broken his spirit, he looked back to his early days at Vienna as to a golden age, of which the outward joyousness was but the natural expression of inner excellence.

The earlier poems of Walter von der Vogelweide are almost exclusively devoted to the service of woman and the theme of love; and their character will be best illustrated by quoting a few examples, though no translation, as will be readily understood, can quite reproduce the spirit and form of the original. The following poem displays, perhaps as well as any, the charming spirit and imagination of the poet :—

A DREAM OF LOVE

Lady, accept this wreath
   (Thus spake I to a maiden debonair),
And thy sweet face beneath
   The lovely flowers will make the dance more fair.
If precious stones were mine,
They should adorn thy head ;
This is not idly said—
All that I have, and all I am, is thine.

So fair and sweet art thou,
   My gayest chaplet gladly I bestow
To place upon thy brow.
   Rich store of flowers white and red I know,
In fields afar. In the May weather,
Now that the buds are springing,
And the wild birds singing,
Let us go forth to gather them together.

She took my offering,
   Like a young child to whom a gift is made;
Her fair cheeks colouring
   Like a red rose beside a lily laid ;
Yet though, as if ashamed, her eyelids fell,
She made a courtesy :
That was her gift to me—
If she gave more, be sure I will not tell.

To me it seemed that never
   Could any joy the joy of that surpass;
From the branches ever
   Blossoms fell thick beside us on the grass.

Lo, and I laughed for very gladness' sake.
Such, in my dream, of pleasure
Store had I beyond measure—
Then the day dawned, and I must needs awake.

From her then, in this wise,
  It comes that, when I see a maid this year,
I gaze into her eyes.'
  Can this be she ?   Could 1 but find her here
Among the dancers, all my care were dead !
Lady, be so good
And lift me up your hood—
Could I but see my chaplet on her head !

To the same class belong the two following short poems, both, as
in the case of that last quoted, intended to be sung :—

THE POWER OF LOVE

What gave thee thy strange empire, Love,
  That thou art so exceeding strong ?
Both young and old thy puissance prove,
  And no one may resist thee long.
Praise God then, since I must be bound
With thy firm bonds, that I betimes have found
Where service best may offered be.
That will I ne'er renounce.   Be gracious, Queen !
  Let me henceforward give my life to thee.

LOVE'S PREROGATIVE

Blame me not if, when I meet you,
Lady, I so coldly greet you.
Love with love may angry be,
So it be but lovingly.
Softly chide, and quick forgive ;
Sorrow, and grow glad again :
  That is Love's prerogative.

But of all Walter's poems that which is most justly celebrated,
both for its lyrical charm and the wonderful delicacy with which a
dangerous theme is handled, is the following :—

THE TRYST

Under the tree
Beside the meadow,
Where we two trysted yestere'en,
There may ye see,
Hid in the shadow,
Scattered flowers and fresh green,
By the forest in a vale.
Tandaraday !
Sweetly sang the nightingale.

I came to where
My love should meet me,
And found him waiting there for me.
And oh, when there
He first did greet me !
That will a joy for ever be !
Did he kiss me ? Yes, indeed !
Tandaraday !
Look, my lips are rosy red !

And there meanwhile
He'd fashioned fair
A couch of leaves and blossoms gay :
The folk will smile
To see it there,
If any chance to pass that way.
By the roses they may guess,
Tandaraday !
Whereabouts my head did press.

That he lay beside me,
Should it ever
Be known, for shame of it I'd die !
What did there betide me,
Never, never
Shall any know save he and I,
And a little bird as well—
Tandaraday !
That, I know, will never tell.

The joyous spirit which pervades these earlier poems becomes in time clouded, as the shadow of evil days falls over the poet's spirit :—

What use in tender rhyming ? what in singing ?
What use in wealth ? in woman's loveliness ?
Since all delight the world aside is flinging,
And wrong is wrought, and suffered sans redress ;
Since honour, kindness, faith, and self-respect
Are fallen in neglect,
Hearts, joyous once, are turned to heaviness.

And in the oft-repeated complaints of the corruption and decadence of the times, which are so characteristic of his later poems, Walter, though undoubtedly embittered by a sense of personal wrong, was no mere *laudator temporis acti*; for, in the turmoil of the great civil and religious storm which had meanwhile broken over Germany, manners and morals had alike suffered, and, not least, that artistic refinement of social intercourse, and especially of the relation of the sexes, which it had been the peculiar mission of the chivalrous poets to cultivate.

This chivalrous ideal of the claims and obligations of womanhood, though, with the poetic forms in which it was clothed, it had originated in Provence, had followed in Germany a peculiar development.

In Provence it had always remained a sentiment rather pagan than Christian, and had served more as an excuse for a lax morality than as an instrument for the purification of social intercourse. Transferred to Germany, it had been touched by the more serious spirit of the North; had, through devotion to the blessed Virgin, become influenced by religious sentiment, and perhaps also had been affected by that old Teutonic reverence for women which to the Roman Tacitus had seemed worthy of remark. Not that it always maintained a uniform exaltation of tone in the hands of poets varying greatly in character and genius. Walter is often led to denounce, even in his earlier poems, and before the later decadence of manners had set in, a tendency of certain singers to degrade their art to the service of licentiousness; and even such masters as Wolfram von Eschenbach, and Walter himself, though insisting on the vital difference between true and false love, yet did not in every case exclude illicit relations from the former category. Yet, on the whole, the picture of the ideal woman, painted by the best and most influential of the Minnesingers, is that of a refined lady, modest, reserved, and courteous. Better than all the glories that May brings in its train, sings Walter von der Vogelweide, is it

> When a noble maiden, fair and pure,
>   With raiment rich, and tresses deftly braided,
> Mingles, for pleasure's sake, in company
>   High-bred, with eyes that, laughingly demure,
>   Glance round at times, and make all else seem faded,
> As, when the sun shines, all the stars must die.

Again, he says—

> We men maintain that Constancy
>   Is a good woman's highest pride;
> If she have wit and modesty,
>   'Tis rose and lily side by side.

And if charm, courtesy, and virtue were looked for in woman, a corresponding excellence of character was expected of those who sought to win her love; since, as Walter says—

> Whoso the love of a good woman heeds
> Will be ashamed of evil deeds.

That in this cult of womanhood, and in the poetry that gave it expression, there was much that was artificial and conventional is true enough. Walter, too, is not free from this imputation, which was indeed brought against him by contemporary critics, and which he is at pains to refute:

> Many there are who say it is not truly from the heart I sing.

Not · a little, both in form and matter, he borrowed from older masters, more particularly from Reinmar and Heinrich von Veldegge; and if we seek for genuine depth of feeling we must not look for it in his earlier lyrics, charming as they are in conception and perfect in form, but in those poems of his later years in which he raises his voice for what he believes to be the cause of righteousness, or laments the decadence of the times. A certain artificiality is, indeed, the fault that is most obvious in the work of all the Minnesingers. Till the influence of the French tradition made itself felt, German poetry had erred in the other direction, contenting itself in earlier times with a rude rhythm helped out by alliteration, and, later on, by rough attempts at rhyme. Heinrich von Veldegge had been the first to introduce stricter rules; and, the fashion once set, the artistic canons, which should have been the instruments, soon became the fetters of expression, strictness of form becoming, as it were, a new plaything, which absorbed the attention of the poets of the time, to the exclusion of qualities perhaps more essential. It is one of the most striking features of Walter von der Vogelweide's genius that, under the weight of these formal fetters, he moves in general so easily; and that, with so much that is purely conventional, we have also so much that reveals the striking individuality of the man, and throws such a clear light on the manners and habits of thought of the age in which he lived.

It is probable that, but for the tremendous social and religious cataclysm that convulsed the world at the close of the twelfth century, Walter von der Vogelweide would, like most of his compeers, never have left the traditional paths of chivalrous poetry. But the year 1198, which saw the death of the first and most munificent of his patrons, marked a memorable epoch also in the affairs of Germany and of the world, and, for a time, drew the young poet from lighter themes into the field of political and religious strife.

In September, A.D. 1197, the Emperor Henry the Sixth, after raising the empire to an unprecedented height of glory, and establishing his authority up to the very gates of Rome, had been suddenly cut off, in the mid-career of his success, and at the early age of thirty-two. A few months later, in January 1198, his antagonist, Pope Celestine the Third, also died, and the vacancy of the Holy See was speedily filled up by the election of the Cardinal Lothair, who took the memorable name of Innocent the Third.

Never had the essential weakness of the Germanic empire and the inherent strength of the papacy been contrasted in more vivid relief. The death of the emperor and the uncertainty of the succession undid in a moment the work of years; and, while the empire, deprived of its head, lay distracted and helpless, the new Pope could take up at once the thread of policy where his predecessor had dropped it, and, under the most favourable circumstances, apply his iron will and consummate statesmanship to building up once more the fallen fortunes of the See of Peter.

The death of the emperor was the signal for the emancipation of all those anarchic and disruptive forces which his genius had kept under control; and the succession, which, had he lived a few years longer, would have devolved, in all likelihood, easily and naturally upon his son, afterwards the Emperor Frederick the Second, became the occasion of a long and ruinous civil war. Frederick was at this time a child of but three years of age; and though his father had caused him to be formally recognised as his successor, and though his uncle, Philip of Suabia, at first proclaimed himself the protector of his nephew's interests, the prospect of a long minority was, under the circumstances of the empire, not to be regarded without serious misgivings; and Philip was soon forced, in the interests of the empire, as well as of the House of Hohenstauffen, to put forward his own claims to the crown. For meanwhile Otho of Brunswick, the chief of the House of Guelph, and the hereditary foe of the Hohenstauffen Cæsars, thinking the crisis a favourable opportunity for ousting the enemies of his race, had won a great following among the turbulent nobles of Germany, had, by a concession of all the points at issue with the Church, purchased the support of the Holy See, and finally (in that age a matter of no small importance), having gained possession of the regalia, had been solemnly anointed at Aix-la-Chapelle as King of the Romans.   Into the weary struggle that followed it is unnecessary to enter. For years Germany was devastated by all the horrors of civil war, and for years neither party achieved a decisive advantage; and when at last Otho's power had been completely broken, and he had been forced to acknowledge Philip as emperor, the sword of an assassin did for him, in the pursuit of private revenge, what years of open warfare had been unable to accomplish, and with the death of Philip he found himself undisputed master of the empire (A.D. 1208).

In this struggle the genius and the young and ardent patriotism of Walter von der Vogelweide were from the first enlisted on the side of Philip of Suabia; for the triumph of the Hohenstauffen meant the curbing of those disruptive forces which were destined in time to split up the empire into numberless petty princedoms, and the establishment of a united and powerful German State.

To this earlier period of the civil war, when the rival factions were as yet evenly matched, belong the oldest of Walter's political rhymes.

In the first he pictures the wretched condition to which the country had been reduced by the civil dissensions; in a second, after illustrating from the analogy of nature the necessity for a strong government, he calls upon the Germans to set the crown on Philip's head and curb the ruinous ambitions of the petty princes :—

I heard a fountain brimming,
And saw the fishes swimming,
And marked what in the world did pass:
Forest and field, rush, leaf, and grass;
All things that fly and creep,
And beasts that run and leap;
And saw that of all forms of life
Not one there is lives free from strife:
Wild beasts and creeping things
Have all their quarrellings;
The birds, too, fight right angrily,
Yet in one thing they all agree:
That none would live content
Had they no government.
They choose them kings to make awards,
And some are vassals, some are lords.
Then, wretched Germany!
How ill it fares with thee!
Since ev'ry insect has its king,
While all thine honour's perishing.
Turn e'er it be too late!
The princes grow too great;
These threadbare kinglets press thee sore:
Crown Philip with the Kaiser's crown, and bid them vex thy
      peace no more!

In a third poem, composed in the same form, but probably written somewhat later, in A.D. 1201, when Innocent had pronounced sentence of excommunication on Philip of Suabia, Walter attacks the clergy and the See of Rome with bitter violence, ascribing to their unchristian ambition the evils by which, in Germany, Church and State, 'soul and body,' had been desolated.

For the very arguments which would have commended the cause of the Hohenstauffen to a far-sighted German patriotism had led Innocent, almost instinctively, to espouse the side of Otho; and the casting of the whole weight of the papal influence into the scale on behalf of the weaker and less desirable candidate was but the continuation of the traditional policy of the Lateran, which had been accustomed to look for the strength of the papacy in the weakness of the empire, and to fear, from a strongly established rule beyond the Alps, a renewal of those imperial claims and ambitions in Italy which, under Henry the Sixth, had confined the temporal sway of the popes within the walls of the city.

With the death of Philip and the election and coronation of Otho the policy of Innocent would seem to have been crowned with success. But the jealous suspicion of the papacy was directed, not against a family or an individual, but against an idea; and the very triumph of the Guelph revived once more the old causes of quarrel in the irreconcilable claims of the spiritual and temporal powers, and in due course brought down upon Otho the same thunderbolt that had once been launched against his rival.

The success of the apparently hopeless attempt of the young Frederick the Second to recover from Otho, with the help of the Holy See, the throne of his ancestors, though doubtless accelerated by the emperor's unpopular rule, his incapacity, and his unbridled temper, and consummated by Otho's overthrow, at the hands of Philip Augustus, on the field of Bouvines (A.D. 1212), was none the less a singular proof of the enormous influence which the papal censures then exercised over men's consciences, and makes all the more remarkable the independence of mind of those who, like Walter von der Vogelweide, without losing their reverence for religion or the Catholic faith, ventured, in no mild terms, to criticise the action of the head of Christendom.

For all through the great contest, which was not to end till long after he had passed away, Walter had been consistently on the side of the empire. He had supported Philip until his untimely fate had left Otho the only possible candidate for the crown; he then gave his adherence to Otho, and opposed Frederick the Second, the Priests' King (*Pfaffen-König*), as he was called, until the violence and incapacity of the former made his rejection not only inevitable, but desirable in the interests of the empire; and lastly, when Frederick in his turn had fallen under the displeasure of the Holy See, it was on his behalf that some of the bitterest and most scathing of his attacks on the Pope were composed. Of these anti-papal rhymes the following is one of the most characteristic examples —:

> Aha! how christianly the Pope of us makes mock
> When what he here hath wrought he tells his foreign flock.
> What he proclaims should never even have been thought.
> He says: ' Beneath one crown two Germans have I brought,
> That they the realm may burn, and wreck, and waste ;
> Their wealth the while into my chests I cast.
> I've cudgelled them with my good stick ; their wealth will all be mine !
> Their German silver flows into my Roman shrine.
> Now feast, ye priests, on fowls, and drink your wine ;
> And let the witless German laymen—fast.'

Yet, in spite of all this vigorous denunciation of papal ambition, and the means by which it was furthered, Walter remains to the last a pious Christian and a devout Catholic; and though the number of his religious songs which have survived is small, those that remain breathe a spirit of deep and sincere piety; nor is there in any of them a trace of a premature Protestantism, or of the influence of any of those heresies which had, at that period, gained so wide a hold on the south of Europe.

MORNING PRAYER

Grant me with joy to rise to-day,
Lord God, and go upon my way
Beneath Thy care, what path soe'er I take.
Lord Christ, vouchsafe in me to prove
The mighty power of Thy love,
And guard me well, for Thy sweet Mother's sake.
As angels watched the Mother Maid
And Thee within the manger laid,
Young Child and ancient Deity,
Humble, with ox and ass on either hand,
Though holy Joseph also kept
His happy watch the while ye slept,
And guarded you right faithfully,
So guard Thou me, that Thy divine command
May not be unfulfilled in me.

It was in the Crusades, however, that mediæval piety found its most natural outlet; and though at the end of the twelfth century the crusading spirit was already on the wane, Walter von der Vogelweide's thoughts turned often in the direction of the Holy Land; and in his later poems he laments the infirmity which prevented him from crossing the sea and earning for himself

That eternal crown
Which any churl may gain with sword, and shield, and spear.

Moreover, one of the charges which he frequently reiterates against the Pope is that of diverting the funds, which were ostensibly collected for the defence of the Holy Land, to the prosecution of his own schemes of ambition nearer home:

Little, methinks, of all this wealth will go to aid God's land:
Priests seldom let the money slip that once they have in hand.

Sometimes, even, in his enthusiasm for the cause of the Holy Sepulchre, Walter does not hesitate to criticise even more exalted powers than Pope and clergy, as the following poem will show:—

He who ne'er Himself began,
Yet make begin both will and can,
Can make an end, and one without an end.
Since all creation to His will must bend,
Can there be praise more high than He inspires?
First, then, to Him my song I raise,
Whose praise is higher than all praise;
And holy is the praise that He requires.

Now laud we too the sweetest Maid,
Who to her Son ne'er vainly prayed—
Mother of Him she is who saved us all.
What fairer comfort on our souls could fall

Than that all Heaven her will obeys?
Come, then, the old, and eke the young,
That her high glory may be sung;
Since she is good, she's good to praise.

I ought to praise you angels, too,
But that I'm far too wise to do.
What to the heathen have ye wrought of ill?
Since all unseen ye are and voiceless still,
Tell us, to help the cause, what have ye done?
If God's revenge I too could wreak,
Silent as you, what need to speak?
I'd leave you gentlemen alone.

Sir Michaël, Sir Gabriel,
Sir Foe of Devils, Raphaël:
Wisdom is yours, and strength, and art of healing;
And three angelic hosts, behind you wheeling,
Haste to obey your orders joyfully.
If you want praise, then show some sense!
The heathen mock your impotence:
Praised I you now, they'd mock at me.

In his most bitter denunciations of Rome and of the clergy it is, in fact, the popes and not the papacy, priests and not the priesthood, that Walter von der Vogelweide attacks. He does, indeed, ask indignantly why, if the Pope be St. Peter's successor, he erases the apostle's doctrine from his books; and in one place he speaks of the donation of Constantine as the source of all the woes of the Church. But any attack on the papal idea would, at that period, have been an impossibility. Frederick the Second may, indeed, at one time, envying the subservience of the Oriental bishops to the Emperor of the East, have harboured the thought of establishing independent Churches in Germany and Apulia; but such an idea was too foreign to the whole tendency of Western Christendom to be as yet seriously entertained. The Pope to Walter is still the Lord's shepherd, though he is become ' a wolf among his flock;' he is God's treasurer, though, like a second Judas, he steals from the heavenly store; he is Christ's vicar, though he ' robs and slays with fire and sword!'

No account of Walter von der Vogelweide's religious attitude would be complete without mention of that wide tolerance which he shared with so many of the noblest minds of his age, and of which the Emperor Frederick the Second set so conspicuous an example. For it would seem that the Crusades, begun in a frenzy of fanatical zeal, had ended by inspiring the pilgrims with a certain respect for the character and culture of their unbelieving foes, and some regret that warriors so brave and chivalrous should be condemned to hopeless perdition. Frederick the Second had, indeed, not scrupled to draw down upon himself the censures of the Church by surrounding himself with Jewish and Saracen philosophers and men of letters, whose

services he employed to render into Latin the Arabic version of Aristotle, and other ancient or contemporary scientific works; he had
made, when in Egypt, an advantageous treaty, on equal terms, with
the Sultan of Egypt, and had even admitted him to the Christian
order of chivalry; and if he did not always extend to heretics the
protection which he gave to infidels, it was because to have done so
would have been to endanger his throne, in helping to undermine
those religious principles on which the mediæval polity was based.

If such was the attitude of the emperor, that of the best of the
poets, the true prophets of their age, was no less remarkable. At a
time when the crusading spirit was only beginning to show signs of
decline, when, in Germany, Konrad of Marburg, the cruel and fanatical
tormentor of the saintly Elizabeth of Hungary, was travelling from
town to town, putting hundreds to death on flimsy charges of heresy,
and when the joyous civilisation of Provence was stamped out, in the
name of religion, by the barbarous hordes of Simon de Montfort, it
is strange indeed to come across such a passage as that which, in his
epic of *Willehalm*, Wolfram von Eschenbach puts into the mouth of
a Saracen woman:—

> If for a woman's word ye care,
> God's handiwork ye then would spare !
> For lo, a heathen was the man
> God made when He His work began.
>
> .   .   .   .   .
> As heathens all of us were born.
> Well might the saved in sorrow mourn,
> If He His children should condemn
> To hell, who had begotten them :
> His mercy will on them descend
> Whose store of mercy hath no end.
>
> .   .   .   .   .
> Whate'er the heathen do to you,
> To them ye should no evil do,
> Since God Himself gave pardon free
> To them that nailed Him on the tree.

The moral of mutual respect and toleration which Wolfram wrote
his *Willehalm* to teach is enforced also by Walter von der Vogelweide,
notably in a remarkable little poem in which he shows how, in the
worship of God, ' Christians, Jews, and Heathen all agree.'

There is no doubt that the political and religious rhymes of Walter
von der Vogelweide exercised a deep and wide-spread influence,
serving as models for a host of imitators, who, like himself, wandered
about Germany, and even beyond its borders, singing and reciting,
and everywhere stirring up the national sentiment against the arrogant pretensions of a foreign power. These wandering minstrels
were, in fact, in their various grades, to the middle ages what
journalists and political agitators are to our own times. They not
only represented, but had, in no small measure, a hand in creating

popular opinion ; and of Walter von der Vogelweide in particular his enemies complained that he corrupted thousands by his poems.

Of Walter's private life little is known, save what may be gathered from his own works. After the death of his patron, Frederick the First of Austria (A.D. 1198), which closed the happy and careless period of his life at Vienna, he appears to have wandered from court to court, depending for a living on the precarious patronage of various princes, and that during a period when the civil wars can have left them little time or taste for art and artists. Like Erasmus, he was not ashamed to beg ; and though, unlike Erasmus, he never stooped to solicit help by degrading flattery, the patrons who spared their money at his expense felt the lash of his tongue. Yet, in spite of prayers and scoldings, and of his vast popularity, he lived the greater part of his life a poor man, condemned, as he bitterly complains, to the existence of a mountebank, and depending for house and home on the hospitality of those whom he entertained. At last, however, the Emperor Frederick the Second rewarded his services with the grant of a small fief, and gave him a still more signal proof of his favour in entrusting to him the education of his young son, King Henry the Seventh. This latter charge, indeed, the intractable and perverse character of his pupil soon compelled him to resign, but without thereby forfeiting the goodwill of the emperor, through whose patronage the poet's declining years were preserved from want. He died about the year 1230, at Würzburg, near which his estate lay ; and there his grave remains to the present time.

To the sterling and loveable qualities of Walter's character there are two trustworthy sources of evidence—his own poems and the witness of his contemporaries. In the former we have revealed to us a man who, in an age of storm and stress, kept his own judgment clear and unclouded; a man of deep religious feeling, yet of wide sympathies, scornful of mere superstition, and uncompromising in his opposition to the excessive ambitions of the priesthood ; a poor man, who yet maintained his independence of speech ; and one whose wit, in an age not over-refined, never descended to coarseness. And, amid all his cares and disappointments, one supreme satisfaction, denied to so many, he had—that of being appreciated at his full worth by his contemporaries. To his fellow-singers, indeed, he was the prince of minstrels, the Master ('unsers sanges meister'), as they loved to call him ; and, when he died, many were found to celebrate his memory in song. Of which appreciations the simplest, and, by reason of its very simplicity, the most eloquent, is that of Hugo von Trimberg :—

> Her Walter von der Vogelweide,
> Wer des vergaes' der taet mir leide !

> Sir Walter von der Vogelweide,
> I pity them that him forget !

WALTER ALISON PHILLIPS.

THE MATRIARCHAL FAMILY SYSTEM

THE recollections of the older among us go back to a generation before there was any serious disturbance of the belief that the primitive family life of mankind was of patriarchal type. In its simplest form, the family was held to have consisted of the father with his wife or wives, and their children living under his control and bound together by common descent from him ; this small group expanding in successive generations into larger groups, when the younger families remained under the headship of the eldest ancestor, unless and until they separated from the parent stock and set up independent households. A social framework of this kind was indeed the only one which fitted into general ancient and modern history. Its liveliest pictures were drawn from the traditions of ancient manners in the Bible, whence we have the word patriarch, the Greek designation of the heads of the twelve tribes of Israel in 1 Chronicles xxvii. 22. So far as society in the great ancient nations of the East and West was known, it was laid out more or less rigidly on such lines, and though modern European life did not conform to the stringency of paternal power belonging to old Roman law, it plainly bore the impress of the ancient order in the position of the male line as to authority, descent, succession, and inheritance.

It gave the scholarly world a shock when thirty years ago the Scotch advocate John Ferguson McLennan published in his book on *Primitive Marriage* a theory intended to upset the received patri-archal views, which had just been set forth with especial force and strictness in Maine's *Ancient Law*. McLennan brought forward a collection of evidence as to ancient and modern peoples accustomed to trace their descent not on the father's but the mother's side. This custom he argued to be a relic of the primitive state of the human race, when as yet there was no fixed marriage, so that paternity was not recognised as a social tie, but maternity furnished the only relation on which kinship could be founded and the family held together. This work brought into notice an earlier treatise on Mother-right, the Swiss jurist Bachofen's *Mutterrecht*, in which a similar doctrine had been propounded. The theory of primitive matrimonial anarchy thus set in circulation was in after years

supported with much learning and ability, the evidence adduced in
its proof being on the one hand the accounts of matrimonial lawlessness in the lower and even the higher grades of civilisation, and
on the other hand certain systems of relationships supposed to have
originated in such an unregulated state of society. These doctrines
gained so much acceptance that primæval 'promiscuity,' a stage of
development of human races when there was no such appropriation
of women to particular men as constitutes civilised marriage, came
to be considered almost as a fact established by anthropology. Since
then, however, a reaction has set in before which the theory is likely
to be transformed, or to pass away altogether. The arguments which
have brought about this result are that uncultured man, whose present
organisation of family and tribe scarcely avails under favourable
circumstances to keep up their numbers, was unlikely in past ages
to have existed and increased in a still less organised state; that men
so fierce and jealous as savages could hardly have multiplied in a
social condition which nowadays would break up in flight or murder;
and, finally, that a confused use of terms for relationships is no proof
of the relationships themselves being ignored. I do not propose to
expatiate on this subject, as to which I have little to add to what has
been written by Maine, Darwin, Westermarck, Letourneau, and
Starcke.[1] My concern is with the history and meaning of the great
ancient maternal system, which **McLennan** in his argument on
primitive marriage first brought into prominent notice through its
characteristic practice of reckoning descent rather on the female than
the male side. It is not surprising that he should have looked upon
this rule as the very principle of the maternal system. It was this which
took the mind of Herodotus when he wrote of the Lykians as alone
of all nations taking their names from their mothers, not their fathers,
and tracing their pedigrees through mothers and mothers' mothers.
The Lykians themselves said as much in their myth of Bellerophon,
to whom the Xanthians, when he had slain the wild boar that wasted
their land, gave no thanks; wherefore the hero called on Poseidon
that their soil should bring forth salt; but at the prayer of women
the curse was removed, and thenceforward the Xanthians are named
not on the father's but the mother's side. This myth, told by
Plutarch, is evidence how in his time the real origin of the rule of
female descent had fallen out of memory. There is a pendant myth
showing the antiquity of maternal institutions in the Malay region,
told as follows by the old-fashioned Menangkabau folk. Papeh
Sabatang built a ship and loaded it with gold and jewels, but it
went aground, and the wise men said it could only be launched again
over the body of a princess great with child; the Raja's daughter

---

[1] Maine, *Dissertations on Early Law and Custom*, ch. vii.; Darwin, *Descent of Man*, ch. xx.; Westermarck, *History of Human Marriage*, ch. iv.–v.; Letourneau, *Evolution of Marriage*, ch. iii.; Starcke, *The Primitive Family*, part ii. ch. vii.

refused to sacrifice herself, but his sister threw herself down, and over her body the boat glided out to conquest, and thenceforth in her honour the law of succession to sisters' sons was ordained. The explanation I have to argue for is but commonplace compared with these heroic myths, but the social forces it involves are to be found in action up to our own time, and their effects are conformable to the known social systems of a hundred peoples.

Before entering on the causes which have brought about the rule of female descent, an exacter statement is needed, lest this rule should be supposed to imply that there are any tribes known in the world who take no note of kinship except on the mother's side. As we have just seen, the human race is by some conjectured to have existed at first in this state of pristine ignorance, before they reasoned out the fact that they were related to their fathers as well as to their mothers. To this theory of a legist, a zoologist would probably reply that mutual recognition and kindness between the male and female parents and their offspring appear too far down in the animal world for rudimentary ideas of paternity to be accounted a human discovery. As for peoples within the range of our knowledge, not only are ideas of parentage much the same all the world over, but, so far as can be ascertained, all languages have words denoting kinsfolk both in the male and female lines, which implies that kinship in both lines is taken account of. When necessary, savages define particularly, using such terms as ' he whom I have begotten,' ' he whom I have borne,' according as the father or mother is speaking. But the habit of mankind in ordinary talk is for both parents to use the same word, as with us both say 'my son,' 'my daughter,' or for both sexes ' my child.' The importance of this practice seems to have been overlooked from its obviousness, but it has much significance, showing as it does that father and mother recognise the relation between them and their children as so similar that they habitually use the same word for it. Thus the thought of physical kinship passes into what may be called social kinship, referring not to the physical tie, but to the position in the family. Moreover, even savage tribes have customary rules barring marriage between the nearest kin. Where such restrictions are least regarded is, on the one hand, among degenerate and decaying populations, or wandering outcast groups who can hardly observe them, or, on the other hand, among nations like the old Persians, whom race and religion held together by close intermarriage within the family. The origin of the aversion from such unions, a feeling by which the human species so remarkably parts company with lower species, is an unsettled problem which need not be discussed here, and I will only mention Dr. Westermarck's instructive attempt to interpret it as belonging not to physical kinship for itself, but to the association of the nearest relatives from childhood in the home. What we have to notice is that the lists of prohibited degrees include relatives both in the male and female line. Even the short rule repeatedly given in the Spanish accounts of South America, that a man is excluded from marriage with mother, sister, and daughter, has this effect. So far as appears, the family systems of the world not only recognise both male and female kinship, but with this recognition comes that of family rights and duties. Thus the family system which the late eminent legal anthropologist Dr. A. F. Post of Bremen describes in his text-books as 'parental'—that is, combining the influences of both parents—belongs in its beginnings to early stages of culture, extending onward till it reaches its fullest development in modern civilised nations. All, then, that can be properly meant by saying that a patriarchal tribe follows male and· a matriarchal female kinship, is that their social arrangements, such as membership of the family and clan, succession, and inheritance, are framed on the one line rather than the other.

Which of these two systems may we reasonably consider as the earlier in history? The claim of the patriarchal system to have belonged to primitive human life has not merely long acceptance in its favour, but I venture to think that those who uphold it have the weight of evidence on their side, provided that they do not insist on its fully developed form having at first appeared, but are content to argue that already in the earliest ages the man took his wife to himself, and that the family was under his power and protection, the law of male descent and all that belongs to it gradually growing up afterwards on this basis. The starting point of this doctrine belongs to zoology, in observation of the anthropomorphous species, certainly nearest to man in body and probably in mind. The few and hurried glimpses by hunters and naturalists of the life of the higher man-like apes in the depths of the tropical forests are full of instruction. The full-grown male and female orangs and gorillas have been seen with young ones so far grown up as to indicate that their family life lasts beyond a single pairing season into a more stable union. The male orang-utan passes the night in the fork of a tree hard by the commodious nest lined with dry leaves, occupied by his mate and their young. This agrees with the wonderfully human account from the other side of the world, of the old male gorilla seen sleeping crouched against a great tree-trunk, ready to defend from the leopards his wife and children in the nest. Such observations go far toward justifying an inference that already below the human level the rudiments of the paternal family system had instinctively shaped themselves. The value of such facts may be measured by the impression which they made on Darwin, leading him to declare as most probable that man aboriginally lived in small communities, each with a single wife, or if powerful with several, whom he jealously guarded against all other men. During the human period, so far as we know it, the social order shadowed forth in beast life has been carried on, enforced by reason and language, organised with the inheritance of developed culture, but holding still to the lines first traced by instinct for the rearing of offspring, where the nourishment and care of the young fall especially to the mother, and protection especially to the father.   However the human race may be classified in stages of culture, whether from the lower to the higher Stone age, and thence on to the Bronze and Iron ages, or from savage life supported by wild fruit or game to agricultural and pastoral prosperity, or from the condition of the roaming family to that of the settled nation, the paternal system is to be found in strong if not exclusive prevalence.   Indeed, among the lowest nomad bands of savages of the desert or the forest, no known social bond but that of rough paternal grouping, such as actually appears, would seem even possible.   From these lowest levels and far on in culture, we meet with pictures of the fighting tribes whose habit and glory is to carry off wives in combat with their enemies around, and there are peoples among whom, at peace and at home, it is usual for the strong man to take by main force the wife of his weaker neighbour.   By the civilised mind such practices are held as proof of social rudeness and antiquity.   From the present point of view their interest lies in the obvious fact that they work into the paternal system, and no other.   To the theory of primordial men a little lower than the apes, men among whom the father was of so little consequence that it did not matter who he might be, what sharper contrast could be seen than the actual savage bringing home wives at the risk of his own life, and holding them with spear and club against all rivals?   Among the great ancient and modern nations within the range of history, the paternal system becomes so dominant as to be taken for granted, and the existence of any other rule seems extraordinary.   As Herodotus thought of the female descent among the Lykians, that in this they agreed with none other among mankind, so Montesquieu remarks that it is almost everywhere received that the wife passes into the family of her husband, and mentions as exceptional that in Formosa the husband goes to the wife's.   The system we modern English live under, far as it is from allowing the ancient extreme power of males, yet carries the stamp of male descent and authority.   Thus modern civilisation nowhere disowns the type of paternal society, but brings down to our time the record of continuity, which goes back through law and religion into the region of instinct conducing to the maintenance of the species. I touch these points in order to range our ideas.   So familiar to us are patriarchal family institutions, that they need only be referred to as belonging to common knowledge.   From their well-known features, their principle of formation is seen to be due to the relative positions of the parents.   The father, as defender and leader, has control over the family formed of the wife he has taken and their children, so that descent from him tends to become the main tie of kinship, and inheritance of his property and succession to his authority is guided along the male line.

In examining the rival family system known as the matriarchal or maternal, far more particular description is needed, being as it is neither sufficiently known nor understood.   Let us notice first that if patriarchal society were defined merely as a system of kinship on the father's side, such a definition must be set aside as hopelessly defective and misleading.   Yet through lack of full knowledge, the matriarchal system has been thus treated.   Europeans, who in such countries as West Africa have met with the law of inheritance through the mother, have explained it offhand by remarks on matrimonial laxity and the convenience of following 'the safer side.'   The facts available to McLennan left him little choice but to adopt this current error.   The most essential part of the present argument is to make it clear that the matriarchal system is one framed for order, not disorder.   For this purpose descriptions will now be given of some of its most complete types which have lasted on into modern times.

Malay life, notwithstanding centuries of Hindu and Moslem influence, has kept much of the maternal system once generally prevalent. In an ancient form this has notably lasted on in the Padang Highlands of Sumatra, of which a Dutch Controleur, Verkerk-Pistorius, has published a lively description.   There the traveller, following the narrow muddy paths among dense tropical vegetation, comes on villages of long timber houses almost hidden among the foliage. Built on posts, adorned with carved and coloured woodwork, and heavily thatched, these houses duplicate themselves into barrack-like rows of dwellings occupied, it may be, by over a hundred people, forming a sa-mandei or motherhood, consisting of the old house-mother and her descendants in the female line, sons and daughters, daughters' children, and so on.   If the visitor, mounting the ladder-steps, looks in at one of the doors of the separate dwellings, he may see seated beyond the family hearth the mother and her children eating the midday meal, and very likely the father, who may have been doing a turn of work in his wife's rice-plot.   If he is a kindly husband, he is much there as a friendly visitor, though his real home remains in the house where he was born.   To the European the social situation wears a comic aspect, as when the Dutch Controller describes the '*chassez-croisez*' which takes place at dusk when the husbands walk across the village from their own homes to join their wives and families.   The man's brothers and sisters and sisters' children are the heirs to whom, not to his own children, his property will go when he dies. The mother's elder brother is guardian of her children, and the brother of the eldest grandmother is the mamak, ruler of the whole family settlement. The larger group, consisting of a number of such families, is the *suku* or clan, which is held together likewise by descent on the mother's side, and by the rule of exogamy acting as a bar to marriage between men and women of the same clan.[2]. This Malay account may be supplemented by the Jesuit missionary De Mailla's description of maternal marriage in the island of Formosa. This is the source of Montesquieu's remark in the *Esprit des Lois*, and I may add that, if it had received the notice it deserves, it might long ago have placed the study of maternal institutions on a sounder basis. The Formosan youth desiring to marry makes music day by day at the maid's door, till, if willing, she comes out to him, and when they are agreed, the parents are told, and the marriage feast is prepared in the bride's house, whence the bridegroom returns no more to his father, regarding his father-in-law's house as his own, and himself the support of it, while his own father's house is no more to him than in Europe the bride's home is henceforth to her when she quits it to live with her husband. Thus the Formosans set no store on sons, but aspire to have daughters who procure them sons-in-law to become the support of their old age.[3] The hill-tribes of Formosa are head-hunting Malays, and though their maternal family system is now dying out, the old Malay law forbidding intermarriage within the clan remains in force.

The Kasia of North-east India have a peculiar interest to archæologists as a people who in modern times have continued to set up rude stone monuments, like those we commonly call by their Breton names of menhir or long-stone, and dolmen or table-stone, and which in Europe mark the dim frontier separating historic from prehistoric antiquity. In the Kasia hills, the tall stones are set up to preserve the name of some great man, by relatives unmindful of the fact that the names belonging to such monuments are forgotten in a few generations. The dolmens are tombs in which are placed the ashes of the dead. The hillmen who thus interpret for us our own remote antiquity belong socially to the full maternal period. The young people meet at dances in spring, where the girls find their future husbands. The young bridegroom does not carry his bride to his own home, but takes up his abode in hers, or maybe he only visits there. They call him by the name of his first child, who, of course, is one of the family; thus if he has a son called Bobon, he becomes Pa-bobon. If man and wife separate, which is done by the easy formality of exchanging five cowries, the children belong to the mother. Notwithstanding this legal laxity, Colonel Godwin-Austen, and the Rev. Mr. Murphy, residents who had excellent opportunities of knowing this stalwart and intelligent people, remark on the durable marriage unions among them. Laws of rank and property follow the strictest maternal type: when a couple separate, the children remain with the mother; the son does not succeed his father, but the raja's

---

[2] Verkerk-Pistorius, *Studiën over de inlandsche Huishouding in de Padangsche Bovenlanden.* Zalt-Bommel, 1871.

[3] De Mailla, *Lettres édifiantes et curieuses*, vol. xviii. p. 441; copied in Duhalde, *Description de la Chine*, 1735, vol. i. p. 165.

neglected offspring may be a common peasant or labourer; the sister's son succeeds to rank, and is heir to the property. The Kasia clans of kinsfolk on the mother's side are strictly exogamous: not only is marriage within them forbidden, but in the rough stone dolmens, each holding the ashes belonging to one clan, the remains of man and wife cannot be laid together. This account of the Kasias may be supplemented from the customs of their neighbours the Garos, who have a marriage ceremony illustrating in an extreme form the subordinate position taken by the husband in the matriarchal family. When the Garo youth has been invited by a girl to a preliminary courtship which he cannot easily decline, there follows the wedding day. On that morning the custom is for the bridegroom to hide, and for the bridesmen to seek him. When found they wash him and lead him away, weeping as he goes, to his new home with his mother-in-law.

My own personal knowledge of the maternal community belongs to one of the most picturesque experiences of my life, on a visit made in 1884, under the auspices of the American Bureau of Ethnology, to the Pueblo Indian district on the Californian border. On the high barren plains of soil, below the steep cliffs of the mesas or plateaus, or on this higher ground itself, in places of vantage may be seen in this region the pueblos (*pueblo* is the Spanish word for town; Latin *populus*), where the agricultural tribes fortified themselves against the attacks of the fierce Navajos and Apaches. Built of adobes or mud bricks, reminding the traveller of the villages of the Sahara, a pueblo such as that of Zuñi rises stage above stage, presenting a dreary aspect of mud terraces, and ladders leading up and down to give access to the half-lighted rooms inhabited by families. In the living and cooking room, round the wood fire, the inmates might be seen sitting assembled in the evening, fathers, mothers, and children, so that one might suppose oneself visiting a huge lodging house of the European sort, till one understood the relationships. Enquiry would show that while in a family dwelling the mothers are related together in the female line, and therefore, of course, belong to the same clan, and their children after them, the fathers are not bound together by such ties, and need not be of the same clan, only they must not be of the same clan as the wives. Though the husband takes up his abode in the wife's family dwelling, during her life and his good behaviour, he belongs still to his own family, perhaps three terraces off, up two rude pole ladders and down a trapdoor. How much milder and kindlier the conditions of these people are than what we associate with the name of savages may be well judged from the idyllic record of life among them by Mr. Cushing, in the *Century Magazine* of 1883. He describes how the Zuñi girl, when she takes a fancy for a young man, conveys a present of the thin hewe-bread to him as a token, and becomes his affianced, or, as they say, ' his to be '—how he sews clothes and moccasins for her, and combs her hair out on the terrace in the sun.   When all is settled, with the beginning of his residence with her his married life begins.   ' With the woman rests the security of the marriage ties; and, it must be said, in her high honour, that she rarely abuses the privilege; that is, never sends her husband " to the home of his fathers," unless he richly deserves it.   Much is said of the inferior position of women among Indians.   With all advanced tribes, as with the Zuñis, the woman not only controls the situation, but her serf-dom is customary, self-imposed, and willing absolutely.   To her belong, also, all the children ; and descent, including inheritance, is on her side.'

To these complete maternal systems might be added descriptions of the family life of North American tribes, such as the Iroquois, Crees, Cherokees, of the Arawaks of South America, the Pelew and Mortlock Islanders of the Pacific.   But there is such consistency of principle among them that lengthy accounts may be dispensed with. From Africa may be quoted Livingstone's account of the Banyai, in whose country ' the wives are masters.'   The youth who marries a girl comes to live in her village, serves his mother-in-law in such work as supplying firewood, and treats her with ceremonial respect ; if, tired of such vassalage, he desires to return to his own family, he leaves his children behind.   In equatorial Africa, although patriarchal institutions have come in among the people, there appears among high families a matriarchal counterpart of the Hindu suttee.   In Ashanti the custom was for the king's sisters and daughters to take to themselves plebeian husbands, who, if their royal wives died, must kill themselves on the grave.   Lastly, in Australia, the custom of the husband going to the wife in full maternal fashion is found still, at least in one district.   Some years ago, noticing that among the Kurnai it was the hunter's duty when he had killed a kangaroo to give to his wife's family part of the head, neck, and back, which were his own share,[4] it seemed to me that this was a survival from the time when the husband lived in his wife's family and hunted for them.   Writing to Mr. Howitt to suggest enquiry whether such a mode of life existed in Australia, I received in due course the following remarkable account, obtained by him from Mr. Aldridge, of the tribes near Maryborough, Queensland.

When a man marries a woman from a distant locality, he goes to her tribelet and identifies himself with her people.   This is a rule with very few exceptions. Of course, I speak of them as they were in their wild state.   He becomes part of, and one of, the family.   In the event of a war expedition, the daughter's husband acts as a blood-relation, and will fight and kill his own blood-relations if blows are

---

[4] Fison and Howitt, *Kamilaroi and Kurnai*, p. 207.

struck by his wife's relations. I have seen a father and son fighting under these circumstances, and the son would most certainly have killed his father if others had not interfered.

Although examples of the maternal family of which this is an extreme case are few in number in modern times, perhaps not exceeding twenty peoples, yet the important point has now been made out that they are to be found in all the great regions of the barbaric world. With and around them, moreover, are found twice or thrice as many imperfect systems, which appear from their fragments of maternal rules to belong to the period of transition into the new paternal stage. Meanwhile, the accounts already given of maternal family life are sufficient for beginning the search for its social causes.

It will be already evident that these describe an organised form of society, contrasting in its whole type with the patriarchal. The term 'matriarchal' was an improvement on earlier definitions, but takes it too much for granted that the women govern the family. It is true that in these communities women enjoy greater consideration than in barbaric patriarchal life, but the actual power is rather in the hands of their brothers and uncles on the mother's side. On the whole, the terms 'maternal' and 'paternal' seem preferable. Some eight years ago, in working out a method of investigating customs statistically by ascertaining the frequency of their combination with other customs, so as to arrive at indications of their origin and purpose, I applied this method to the study of laws of marriage and descent. It then appeared that the cause of the maternal system was connected with the custom of the father's residence in the wife's family.[5] I find this inference strengthened by passages showing that the Danish anthropologist,[6] Dr. C. N. Starcke, had come to a similar opinion about the same time, and that Dr. Post admits the principle. While re-stating it as agreeing with the facts, I have now to seek the fundamental motive of the maternal family one stage deeper. The Padang and *K*asia families show that the maternal system may exist without the husband's residence in the wife's house. He may be only a visitor, but the essential point is that the wife remains in her own family, the obvious consequence being that the husband cannot take the position which belongs to him in patriarchal life. If, then, we can ascertain why families keep the married daughters instead of letting the husbands take them away, we shall arrive at an ultimate cause of the maternal system.

For this purpose the Malay islands offer instructive examples. In this region the paternal system is now prevalent, under which the

[5] 'On a Method of Investigating the Development of Institutions applied to Laws of Marriage and Descent.' A Lecture delivered before the University of Oxford, June 1888; Report of the British Association, Section H, Sheffield Meeting, 1888; *Journal of the Anthropological Institute*, vol. xviii. p. 245.

[6] C. N. Starcke, *Die primitive Familie*, 1888, p. 37; English Translation, p. 35. A. H. Post, *Familienrecht*, 1889, p. 87.

wife is purchased from her family and goes to her husband's house, where her children take family descent and property in the male line. But even where this paternal rule is general, the older maternal custom is kept up also, coming into force where circumstances furnish a sufficient cause. Thus the rule is usual that till the whole jujur or purchase-money is paid, the husband is only (so to speak) maternally married, remaining in the house of his wife, to whom the children belong. In some islands the law is that foreigners are admitted only to this maternal marriage. Forbes describes the resulting combination in Sumatra, where the traveller may visit dwellings where one or more sons have brought home purchased wives, and their sisters have taken in husbands to live with them, so that paternal and maternal marriage, with their accompaniments of male and female descent, may be found peaceably together under one thatch. The maternal form of marriage known as ambil-anak, or 'taking a child,' especially comes in where a family ends in a daughter; a young man is taken in as a husband, and the property goes down for a generation in the female line, after which the family returns to the paternal system.

Here the examination of maternal marriage has suddenly brought us into contact with a habit or law which appears again and again across the globe in countries whose social systems are as different as can be from the maternal type. It may be called the custom of the heiress-husband. The Japanese marries ordinarily on a patriarchal footing, but the reverse system is recognised when the iri muko, or incoming husband, marries the daughter of the house to which he succeeds in the wife's name. But his place seems not an honoured one, to judge from a proverb quoted by Mr. Daigoro Goh, in a paper read before the Japan Society, 'If you possess one *go* of rice, do not become an incoming husband.' It is enough to mention three of the well-known European examples. In the South of France, the inferiority of the heiress-husband is pointedly marked by Cordier's comparing him to a Malay maternal husband. In Germany he has a recognised name, Erbtochtermann, from which I take the term heiress-husband. Lastly, let us notice what happens among ourselves when the husband of an heiress goes to live in her house and takes her surname, the children in fact deriving both name and property from the mother. Here, notwithstanding that the husband's position is assured by the law of the land, the maternal family system otherwise holds, though veiled by paternal forms, and its mysterious strangeness as a remote barbaric institution fades away when it is seen to be brought about by practical reasons in modern civilisation.

It thus appears that various social reasons may lead to maternal rather than paternal family life. But such as have been mentioned, though intelligible, are too narrow to account for the presence of the maternal system, complete or partial, among towards half the known peoples of the lower culture. We are led to look for some world-wide influence at work in periods early in time and civilisation, though probably far removed from the primitive state of mankind. Now it has been seen that the maternal Malay, Indian, and American tribes described have the custom of exogamy; by which a people is divided into intermarrying classes or clans, no man or woman being permitted to marry within his or her own. It at once suggests itself that the maternal system and the exogamy thus associated with it are in some way connected by causation, and this expectation is confirmed by the fact that the same combination is certainly or probably general among the other fully maternal systems mentioned. Moreover, it prevails in a majority of the peoples, some sixty in number, among whom the maternal rules partly remain.

. Thus statistical argument tends forcibly to connect the maternal system with exogamy. While maternal peoples are exogamous, exogamous peoples are not necessarily maternal, but may be either maternal or paternal, clanship being reckoned on the mother's or father's side accordingly. In order to ascertain the meaning of these facts, it will be well to enter briefly into the nature and origin of exogamy or marrying-out, which was shown by McLennan, the pioneer of the whole problem of primitive marriage, and to whom, indeed, exogamy owes its name, to be one of the great institutions of the ancient world.

Exogamy may be defined in general terms as a custom of classing a people into two or more divisions, usually by real or supposed kinship, either male or female, marriage within the division being forbidden. The simplest arrangement is that of Melanesia, where there are but two intermarrying divisions, each reckoned to be descended from one mother. More often there are a number of clans, which may be subdivisions of two original clans, and the prohibition of marriage may be within the single clan or the clan-group. To this arrangement are apt to belong the so-called totems, which are names of animals, plants, &c., connected with religion and serving to indicate descent and clanship. Thus among the Wyandots there are recorded two groups of clans whose totems in the female line are (1) Wolf, Bear, Beaver, Turtle; (2) Deer, Snake, Porcupine, Hawk. Without more detailed description, it is clear on the face of the matter that such exogamic rules are not contrived to prevent marriage between kinsfolk, inasmuch as they only take account of one line of descent, prohibiting the remotest unions on the mother's side, while allowing the nearest on the father's, or *vice versa*. Indeed exogamy has to be worked in combination with a law of incest; thus in Melanesia the children of a brother and a sister, being of different classes, might marry so far as the rule of exogamy is concerned, but custom forbids such a marriage. Evidence that the reason of exogamy is not moral but political has been collected by me in the paper already referred to.[7] The explanation there put forward, that the purpose of systematic intermarriage between clans is to bind them together in peace and alliance, is a theory which has the merit of not being ingenious, being simply drawn from what is said by natives who live under exogamic rule, and by foreigners who have observed its results. Thus in the Iroquois league it acted, in the words of L. H. Morgan, 'to break up the spirit of perpetual warfare which had wasted the red race from age to age;' and Munzinger depicts the Bogos of Abyssinia as closely bound together by reciprocal marriages, 'so that internal war is almost impossible.' To this evidence I will only add here that of the Rev. W. Yate, a missionary among the Maoris who was troubled by their incessant destructive wars. Their habit was to marry within the family circle, but he encouraged them to marry their sons and daughters in different and even hostile tribes, with the result that from enemies they became friends. There is something suggestively prehistoric in this story of a Wesleyan missionary teaching exogamy to the New Zealanders. The theory which it illustrates has not received general acceptance among anthropologists, but is advocated by two most thoroughly versed in barbaric law. Professor Kohler, laying stress on the influence of exogamy in promoting brotherly relations, accounts thus for the tendency of peoples at a certain stage of culture to become exogamic, and the late Dr. A. H. Post comments on it to similar effect as a means of protection against blood-feud and war.[8] Modern culture has outgrown and almost forgotten exogamy, but doubtless there was a time in the peopling of the globe when small half-settled hordes, threatened with extinction by intertribal war, found in such compulsory intermarriage their most effective protection, and the means of consolidation into coherent nations. Such social results, even if not representing the complete reason of exogamy, have at any rate contributed to its prevalence, which again must have promoted the maternal system, as may be seen from the following considerations.

While mankind live in small unsettled hordes, keeping to themselves and unfriendly with their neighbours, they tend to marry within their own borders, in a close community which the mutual removal of wives from one household to another hardly disturbs. When, however, population becomes more dense and fixed, and families and clans have more defined property and interests, the manner in which intermarriage takes place, especially that made compulsory by the rule of exogamy, raises most serious questions. There are two alternatives : either for the wife to remain in her own

---

[7] *Journal of the Anthropological Institute*, vol. xviii. p. 265.

[8] Kohler, *Zeitschrift für vergl. Rechtswissenschaft*, 1882, vol. iii. p. 360; A. H. Post, *Afrikanische Jurisprudenz*, 1887, vol. i. p. 72; *Entwicklungsgeschichte des Familienrechts*, 1889, pp. 79, 86.

home, or to be taken by her husband to his home ; according to which of these customs prevails, the family will be prone to become maternal or paternal. Let us now consider the first or maternal case. Here there is no loss to the wife's family, who retain her and her children, gaining at the same time help and defence from the husband. Thus the tendency of exogamous peoples to be framed on maternal lines is practically dictated by self-interest, and works easily from being absolutely just between families, a merit which even savages can well appreciate. There is no proof that at any period the maternal system held exclusive possession of the human race, but the strength with which it kept its ground may be measured by its having encompassed the globe in space, and lasted on from remote antiquity in time.

Against the advantages of the maternal system, however, two evident disadvantages must have told heavily from the first, under the stress of which it has long declined, and soon must disappear. The instinctive attraction which shapes the paternal family among the higher mammalia continually reasserts itself, while the maternal husband emancipates himself from his inferior position whenever the social pressure is removed, and he can become a paternal husband. Among the matriarchal Pueblo Indians, the Hon. J. W. Powell has given me an account how parties leave the villages and go forth to camp on distant spots where some small stream makes the arid alkaline soil cultivable. The consequence is that the wives and children fall under the control of the husbands and fathers, and the first step is taken in the transformation from mother-right to father-right. The complete change is not unknown to modern history. It is probable that, like other Algonquin tribes, the Ojibwas in old times lived under the maternal system, though now, partly at least through white men's influence, they have come over to paternal institutions. I well remember falling in with a party of them on their way to a prayer meeting, and enquiring of a girl what was her totem, to which she answered that she was a Beaver. Then, I said, your mother was a Beaver; but her reply was No, it was my father. They all seemed as much surprised at being thought to count clan-ship on the mother's side as I was to find that the customs of their forefathers had become strange to them.

In the marriage systems of the barbaric world, when classified in a series, the evidence of this change gradually taking place appears in the various modes of overcoming the resistance of the family to being despoiled of their daughters. Elopement belongs to all grades of civilisation. The capture of wives by robbery or in open war is as ancient, though it has not now the glory which belonged to it among the fierce warriors of the Pampas, whose highest virtue lay in slaying their enemies and carrying off their wives ; or among the Homeric captors of Briseis and Chryseis, or the host of Sisera, gone forth to divide to every man a damsel or two. But far more effective than violence in converting family rule to the father's side was the introduction of friendly and equitable means of compensation. The obvious practice of exchange is often remarked on among the natives of Australia, where women of different families are exchanged as wives by their brothers. From Australia to Greenland the custom prevails of betrothing children in infancy, and there are even made, as in the Malay Islands, speculative contracts before the children are born. This widespread practice shows us families already intermarrying voluntarily for the benefit of alliance, as clans do compulsorily on a larger scale in full exogamy. Again, few customs strike the civilised modern reader as more quaint than the pretence of wife-capture in wild countries, as where the Kalmuk bridegroom rides with his armed friends to tear the bride from her people, who meet the sham attack with a sham resistance, till she is carried off with shouts and firing of matchlocks; of course her price had been bargained for beforehand. That this fierce formality is a survival of real warlike capture is no doubt a true explanation so far as it goes, but it has a practical meaning besides. It does justice between weaker and stronger groups; for as soon as the rule is admitted that resistance is to be merely formal, the weaker gains the power of equitable retaliation. Next comes acquisition of the wife by service in her family. When this takes place, after the couple are man and wife it is, in fact, a reduction to moderate limits of the lifelong maternal service, as where in Darfur the husband stays a year or two in the wife's house, and they hardly let him go then. If the service comes before the marriage, as is common, for instance, in the Malay Islands, and familiar to us in the story of the patriarch Jacob, the transaction becomes simply one of payment in labour. If evidence is needed to show that we are here on the track of change from maternal to paternal, and not the contrary, it will be found in the fact that the man's residence in the woman's family may be for the rest of his life, or for any shorter period down to the morrow of the wedding. But he habitually begins in his wife's house and ends in his own, whereas for the couple to set up in the husband's house and remove to the wife's is almost unknown. Last comes actual purchase for goods or money—a custom as much above low savagery as below high civilisation, which improves on rougher methods by estimating the current value of personal attractions, and the pretensions of a rich and powerful family, for their daughter's hand. These different modes of matrimonial agreement, obviously concluded between the families rather than between individuals, do not, however, practically shut out personal inclination or aversion. It is found practically not easy to capture an unwilling damsel, whether it is a Tatar who gallops after her across the steppe, or a Kamchadal who has served his years faithfully, but failed to please after all.

It would be irrelevant to go further into the development of marriage laws, when they pass into new phases in advancing culture, though keeping up lingering survivals, which testify to their descent from the age-long transformation from maternal to paternal. Such are, it may seem, the ideas of close relationship with the mother's brother among the modern Arabs, the horse-race at a Breton wedding where in old times there would have been a sham capture, or the gift of medals as wedding souvenirs in France, which replace the mediæval treizaine or thirteen coins, which again seem to come down from the Frankish marriage by the shilling and the penny (per solidum et denarium).

Further than this I must not go in the history of society. It is enough if I have given some reason to think that the two great regulations of early civilisation, matriarchy and exogamy, have nothing about them fantastic, outrageous, absurd, but are the practical outcome of the practical purposes of people like-minded with ourselves. Moreover, in such enquiries as the present there come before us abundant illustrations of that regularity of human action which makes it possible to deal with it by scientific methods. It may be, for the present at least, too difficult to construct a philosophy of history; but the anthropologist has the easier task of classifying customary thoughts and acts, which recur in distant times and places with high definiteness. Thus the maternal family and the system of exogamy, of which the instances may be scheduled out from Asia, Africa, America, are formations whose regularity reminds us of crystallography and chemistry. In virtue of their compact order they belong to Natural History, and that to Natural Science. They belong, indeed, to a region of Natural Science in which knowledge penetrates more deeply than elsewhere into the meaning of nature. This is due to the happy combination that the anthropologist is himself also a man. All human beings are in body and mind so much of one pattern that each can judge others by reference to his own understanding, intention, and will, and by the consciousness conveyed by language. If a classic dryad could tell his experience, would not a botanist he grateful for knowledge, now out of his reach, of the true inwardness of a tree? Could we hear from the voice of a sun-god about the impulse and purpose of the solar system, we should learn what is dark to the astronomer. But what is mere fancy about botany and astronomy is commonplace everyday fact to the anthropologist, who works a whole stage nearer to ultimate truth than do students who have more doubtfully to translate symptoms into inferences. Directer evidence of personal consciousness stands open to those who have to reason on the thoughts and acts of men like themselves, which might have been their own.

EDWARD B. TYLOR. .

THE WOMAN MOVEMENT IN GERMANY

'ASSOCIATIONS founded for political objects may not have women, scholars, or apprentices as members, nor may women, scholars, or apprentices be present at any meetings of such associations.' So runs the·Prussian Coalition Law, and the laws of Bavaria, Brunswick, and some of the smaller States impose the same limitations on women; while in Saxony, where the law allows women to be *present* at political meetings, they may not be members of political associations. These laws explain in a large measure why there is not in Germany, as in England and America, any strong and well-organised woman movement.

But besides the political there is also a social cause. While the legal restrictions effectually hinder women from carrying on any political agitation, they do not sufficiently explain the lack of a more powerful movement among women of the middle class to obtain equality of opportunity, a movement which has been so very strong in England, and which is only now passing into a new phase more social and less individualistic in its character. This is explained by the very limited income of the ordinary middle-class household, which is also responsible for the German social ideal of woman as *Hausfrau*. Germany is not a rich country, and only a very little observation is needed to see that the incomes of the professional and mercantile classes are much smaller than in England, and that German women are therefore obliged to devote a great part of their time and thought to household work. And just for this very reason, that the women's minds are absorbed in details, German housekeeping is both unscientific and inartistic, and, although it entirely occupies the *Hausfrau*, it seldom attains even its own uncomfortable standard. In this vicious circle, where want of system takes up the time which should be devoted to developing system, it is very hard for a German woman to leave her narrow household interests and to educate and develop her own individuality. All the more honour is due, therefore, to those few thoughtful women who have conceived and led a movement that, though lacking the great and powerful inspiration of a new conception of life, has undoubtedly done a great deal to overcome German prejudices, and to widen German ideas about women. These women have not been aristocrats, for aristocratic women in Germany have never, like the brilliant leaders of French and English society, taken any interest in politics, or influenced leading politicians. The present Empress is entirely absorbed in her children, her dress, the formal etiquette of German Court society, and the work of endowing and building churches. The Empress Frederick undoubtedly takes an interest in the women's movement, but her time of power was too short for her to do much more than help to establish elementary technical schools for girls. The women of the nobility have charitable interests which chiefly take the form of extravagantly arranged bazaars or concerts ; and, though they have some societies for helping the poor and the sick, the hard-working committee of the English aristocratic woman is unknown to them. Their daughters have less freedom than girls of the upper classes in England, and are not expected to take any interest in public affairs ; and it is very difficult for them to get time and opportunity to carry on thorough studies at home. The 'revolted daughter' who leaves home to work is almost unknown, as the Universities are practically closed to women, and nursing is not, as in England, a common occupation for ladies. Sometimes in later life, when a girl has not succeeded in marrying, and if she does not wish to lead the 'drone and dressing-gown life,' as one of them has described it, she becomes a deaconess, but she has even less independence under the strictly organised guardianship of the Church than in her own home.

If unmarried girls of the middle class, on the other hand, have revolted to some extent, the cause has been mainly economic. Just as the married women, absorbed in their assured, though not what we should consider comfortable position, have been economically bound down to their little narrow world, so the unmarried women, whose growing numbers now amount to one-fourth of the German adult female population, have been economically forced to think about an extension of the ways of earning a living. Forced more and more into competition with men, the saying ' Let each one have the work and the calling to which he is suited ' has had for them an economic rather than a social meaning. Self-support rather than self-development was their aim, and though it was a narrow aim, for it applied only to a comparatively small class of women, the intellectual proletariat, it had in it the germ of a larger movement. Their first and most important question was that of higher education, and in this respect Germany was found to offer fewer opportunities to women than any other country in Europe except Turkey. German women could not attend the Universities, though, absurdly enough, foreign women were admitted, and they could not study or practise law or medicine. For years the *Reichstag* and *Landtage* of the different States were besieged with petitions from women's associations, and only now at last are women permitted to practise medicine, though the training and degree for it must still be obtained abroad. There are about ten women doctors practising in different parts of Germany. German women may also now attend lectures in most of the German Universities, but only as ' Hospitirende ' or ' guest students,' without being allowed to matriculate, and generally on the sufferance of the professors.   In Berlin, for instance, where Dr. Adolf Wagner, the present Rector of the University, has this year for the first time made it possible for women to hear lectures, all sorts of difficulties are thrown in their way.   When permission to attend has been obtained from the *Kultusminister*, the individual professor will not always grant it.   One professor is said to have given his servant strict orders to tell all young ladies who might call on him that he was not at home, and that, were he to see them, he never gave permission to ladies to attend his lectures.   According to the papers, the famous historian, Professor von Treitschke, on seeing a lady among his audience, suddenly interrupted his lecture and went up to her and led her out. He is said to have remarked to one of his colleagues afterwards, ' I can't bear women folk at my lectures, and I shall put the Great Beadle at the door to keep them out.'   But even were women allowed to matriculate, it has been impossible hitherto for them to get the necessary preparation, except privately.   The ordinary education of German girls is not very good.   Literature is excellently taught, but in other subjects too many facts are insisted upon, and thinking is not encouraged.   In religion, which forms a large part of the in-struction, the girls are not allowed to express doubts, or to ask ques-tions as to dogmas.   But even this sort of teaching is better than that of governesses, and it is a fortunate thing for girls of the upper classes that, for economy's sake, their parents generally send them to school.   Within the last few years, however, three Gymnasiums or High Schools have been established in Berlin, Leipsic, and Carlsruhe, exactly similar to those which prepare young men for the univer-sities.   Several girls in Berlin will be ready this year to finish the Gymnasium course, and the friends of women's higher education are anxiously watching to see whether the passing of these examina-tions will be allowed to constitute matriculation, as it does with men, and give women the *right*, instead of the mere *privilege*, of attending the universities.

In the course of all this agitation, for even these few concessions have not been won without very great efforts, the women of the middle classes began to realise that their work was not so purely and immediately a personal question as they had imagined.   They found that the existing laws stood opposed to their wishes, and that no real improvement could be effected in their position without some change of the laws.   German law hardly recognises the separate individuality of a woman, especially if she be a wife or mother.   There is nothing corresponding to the Married Women's Property Act, so that a woman is entirely under the guardianship of her husband, and her property and earnings are wholly at his disposal. After her children are four years old, she only has as much control over them as the law allows to those grossly immoral or inebriate fathers whose control has had to be supplemented by legally appointed guardians. And after the death of the father, his will or the law may appoint a third person as guardian, who will have equal control with the mother over the children. The father's will may appoint the mother or any other woman as guardian, but the law courts can never appoint a woman. If the mother marries again, she loses all control over her children.

More and more conscious of the injustice of these laws, the leading women, when they found that their deputations to Government were refused a hearing, and that their petitions were only thrown into waste-paper baskets, tried to organise associations for formal protest, but here again the law was against them, and dissolved their associations as having a 'political aim.' And finally, the younger and more active women, whose centre was in Berlin, were forced to see that the slow, cautious development of the earlier movement was accomplishing practically nothing, that their only weapon lay in the franchise, and that they must concentrate all their power on this one single object, agitating for it in every legal way. At about the same time many Christian women publicly joined the movement, and all the religious bodies, except the Catholic and the Jewish, began to show some interest in the advancement of women. It is a long time since the advanced woman necessarily meant an atheist and a free-thinker to the average Englishman, but public opinion in Germany is only now coming to believe that a woman may take an interest in social and political questions and yet still remain a Christian. Finally, last June, and this was a great triumph, a woman was allowed to read a paper on ' The Position of Women' at the Congress of Evangelical Socialists at Erfurt.

Up to this point, all that has been said might, with some exceptions, be taken as a description of the woman movement in England a quarter of a century ago, and it is only when we come to the working women that we find a striking difference, a phenomenon that is absolutely unique in history, that is to say, a woman movement which has originated with the working women themselves. The middle-class women of Germany, having once seen beyond the interests of their own class, have adopted towards working women an attitude which has hitherto been too much that of the mediæval Church towards the poor, a service of love rendered cheerfully and willingly, but still condescendingly. Instead of going into social questions, they have taken up charity, and their party has justly been characterised as the ' ladies' ' movement.

But that the working women regard them with a settled suspicion and determined distrust is much less the result of this condescending.

attitude than of the point of view of the entire working class in Germany. Since the middle class in Germany did not awake to a full political consciousness until the year 1848, in which year the proletariat also developed a party with strong class interests and class antipathies, they have, at every period of their political activity, dreaded the working class, and withheld from it those political and civil rights from which Democratic Socialism must take its start. Similarly, the women of the middle class did not take up the battle of women's civil rights, and pave the way for the industrial fight of the working women, until the party of the working women themselves had grown conscious of the necessity and possibility of a change, and were ready to agitate for it in their own way.. It is this principle of the *Klassenkampf*, according to which every political party is the party of a class, and every political movement the exclusive movement of a class, which forbids them to co-operate with the bourgeois women. It means nothing to them that the Universities should be open to both sexes, and that numbers of women of the needy middle class should force their way into the ranks of schoolmasters, doctors, or officials. Their goal of admission to the various branches of trade and industry has been practically reached, and, forced by necessity to the severest kinds of labour, they do not demand equality of opportunity, but ask for special legislation and protection. Their lot is thrown in with all other labourers, and they feel that, as the position of woman rises and falls with labour, so the woman question is only one side of the labour question.

The Social Democratic Party, which is the party of labour in Germany, and which includes nearly a quarter of the voters, has not always recognised the equality of women as a necessary part of its programme. At first the working men believed that by restricting the employment of women their own wages could be raised, and their authority in the home as the only wage-earners could be restored. But in spite of all efforts at restriction, and much as it was to be regretted, the employment of women increased rapidly from year to year, and when working men saw that five and a half millions of women were supporting themselves, and out of these over four millions belonging to the proletariat, they realised that women workers were no longer a negligible factor, and that equal duties towards society gave equal rights. At their *Parteitag*, or Annual Congress, held at Halle in 1890, the Social Democrats therefore passed a resolution demanding the full equality of the sexes in state and society; and the next year, at Brussels, the International Socialists' Congress adopted the same resolution unanimously. After 1892 women were permitted to choose delegates to the Annual Congress, and now the members of the working women's associations are an integral factor of the Social Democratic party, and their demands for equal rights with men are the necessary and logical completion of the democratic programme of the working men.

It would perhaps be more correct to say that *theoretically* women are an integral factor of the Social Democratic party, for *practically* their active importance has as yet been very little. This is, of course, largely owing to the restrictions imposed on them by law. If it is hard for middle-class women to find a legal means of carrying on agitation, it is doubly hard for the women of the proletariat. Magistrates and police are always combined to give unjust interpretations of the Coalition Law, where Social Democrats are concerned, and they are especially active in seizing every possible pretext for closing women's associations and meetings. In Berlin, for instance, a number of different associations having been dissolved one after the other, the women formed a small committee of five for purposes of agitation, hoping that a committee could not be interpreted as an association. But the police thought differently, and, after searching the houses of the members of the committee for compromising documents, they had them all brought up and fined in court last May for belonging to a political association. Even a children's Christmas party, only the other day, during the present very severe persecutions of Social Democrats, was forbidden because it was given by Social Democrats and might be considered a meeting of a political association. The agitation is therefore obliged to restrict itself now to the distribution of literature and to the organisation of public meetings. These must always be called by a single person ; and the police, one or two of whom are always present on the platform, may limit the speeches and the discussions which follow according to their discretion. If anything is said which they consider illegal, they can, by standing up and putting on their helmets, dissolve the meeting.

But the law cannot be made altogether responsible for the small number of women who, as yet, take an active interest in the political and labour movements. In Hamburg, for instance, where the law is much less strict, though we do indeed find a certain number of women as members of the political associations, yet the number of those who take a part in public life is very small, and they do not form a centre, as would have been expected, of eager interest and agitation, and especially of Trade Unionism, which is particularly powerful in Hamburg. As a matter of fact, and as the numbers show, it seems almost impossible to rouse the women in Hamburg or in other parts of Germany to take a real interest in Trade Unionism. Only 5,251 women are members of Trade Unions, and these figures are very discouraging to the leaders who have been working since the early eighties to rouse the women of their class from the apathy bred of a feeling of helplessness. The leaders themselves are lamentably few, and most of them, being obliged to work long hours to support themselves, are not able to concentrate all their energies on agitation ; and, though their personal character and hard-working enthusiasm cannot be too highly estimated, their lack of education hinders them from taking the large sympathetic view of the movement on which a leader's inspiration depends.   It is a great pity that the idea of *Klassenkampf*, a principle held rigidly by every Social Democrat rather to the bewilderment of an English person, makes it impossible for them to work with the thoughtful earnest leaders of the middle-class woman's movement, many of whom would be only too glad to co-operate with the working women to bring about certain reforms desired by all women.   For instance, there is at present under discussion before the Reichstag a draft for a new code of Civil Law for the Empire, which has been compiled by legal experts with a view to unifying the laws of the different states.   In adopting that form most widely prevalent and involving the least alteration of existing conditions, they have not realised that reactionary laws are not in accordance with the modern spirit, and they have made the position of women in some points worse than hitherto. The women of the middle classes and the women of the proletariat have organised meetings of protest, and have sent in petition after petition, begging that the new laws might be drafted on new principles, but the lack of unity between them has deprived the movement of that strength which only absolutely solid organisation can give.   Again, in the question of factory laws and factory inspection, the middle-class women, unlike the Liberal women of England, have done all that lay in their power to promote the extension of the factory acts, and to have women factory inspectors appointed.   All Social Democrats are anxious to promote these laws, believing them to be necessary for the health and for the moral improvement of the working people, and their programme demands a maximum eight hours' day, prohibition of night-work, and of the employment of children under fourteen.   And Social Democratic women, preferring the interests of labour to their own narrower interests, are willing therefore, though it may to some extent injure their unrestricted competition with men, that the laws should be made first for themselves, believing that in time they will be extended to men also. Their immediate wish is that the present maximum] work-day of eleven hours for women should be reduced to ten, and that women should not be employed in trades injurious to their health ; already women are not allowed to work for four weeks after confinement, nor for the fifth and sixth weeks unless approved by a doctor.   But even in the matter of these laws they are not willing to work with the middle-class women.   They feel that, though they may both agitate for the same practical reforms in the laws regarding women, yet their own expectations are founded on changes which the middle-class women do not wish for, far more sweeping and fundamental than can be effected by any such surface alterations.   They believe that there is and must be war between the classes of society, that their interests must for ever clash, and that the position of working women, as well as of working men, can only be radically improved when the private ownership of capital is abolished and the means of production are owned collectively.

It is very natural that the middle-class women, while sincerely wishing to improve the economic position of working women, cannot conscientiously agree with this revolutionary doctrine, or that, if able to accept it, they may dread the far-reaching consequences to themselves of joining the Social Democrats. By becoming Social Democrats they would lose their position in society, any situation or paid employment they might have, and, above all, their entire influence with the women of their own class. They would no longer be able to write for the papers of middle-class women, nor speak at their meetings, nor be members of their societies. They would be, in fact, *déclassé*, and obliged to associate only and entirely with Social Democrats. To any English person, accustomed to meeting Socialists and even anarchists in the most commonplace and bourgeois drawing-rooms, such prejudice and persecution hardly seem possible. And yet they do exist, and necessarily exercise an intimidating influence on the bourgeoisie, though at the same time they are the means of drawing the Social Democrats closer together. But that the antiquated intolerance of German public opinion is responsible for such injustice does not make it any easier for the individual middle-class woman to take the only step that will span the bridge between herself and the women of the proletariat, and a belief that she can do more for these women by working and agitating through her own class can hardly be characterised as cowardice.

But the future of the woman movement in Germany undoubtedly lies with the Social Democratic party, the only strong political party in the world that demands the full equality of the sexes. When the middle-class women make demands, they have no political party to represent them; when the working women wish to agitate for anything, they have forty-seven members of the *Reichstag* to push their claims. Led by Wilhelm Liebknecht—the friend and one of the earliest disciples of Karl Marx, who has lately, at the age of seventy, been most unjustly condemned to three months' imprisonment—and by August Bebel, the author of *Woman*, a book which has had enormous influence in Germany, and which has gone through twenty-five editions since its first publication in 1879, the Social Democratic party, though it has not yet attained any of those reforms at which it aims, will undoubtedly control the future developments of German Radicalism, and will never rest until it has secured for German women the most thorough and complete emancipation that they can possibly desire.

ALYS RUSSELL.

ALVAR NUÑEZ

AFTER that God our Lord was pleased to take Alvar Nuñez Cabeça de Vaca out of, captivity and from the hardships which he endured ten years in Florida, he came to these kingdoms (the *Spains*) in the year fifteen hundred and thirty-seven, where he remained till the year forty, in which year there came to this court of your Majesty (*Madrid*) people from the Rio de la Plata, to tell his Majesty of what had happened to the fleet which Don Pedro de Mendoza had sent, and in what straits the survivors were and to ask him to rescue them. This being known to his Majesty, he made an agreement with Alvar Nuñez to go and succour them.

A most gentlemanlike, Christian, and, above all, a most Castilian way to begin a book. Just sufficient references to his perils and sufferings to show that he was no mere courtier. Enough touch of faith to prove that he was grateful for his deliverance. Withal an air of conscious and dignified pride that he was what God had made him. Such a pride Cervantes exhibits in his noble introduction to the second part of *Don Quixote* when he says: 'If my wounds do not shine in the eyes of those who see them, they are valued at least in the estimation of those who know where they were received (Lepanto); for a soldier looks better dead on the field of battle than safe in flight.' Valdivia, Balboa, Ojeda, Pizarro, Cortés, and almost all the 'conquistadores' displayed a similar noble self-consciousness. It seemed to sit upon them as easily and becomingly as their invariable black cloaks and doublets. Indeed, mankind is generally as tolerant of the personal pride of the man of action as it is intolerant of the conceit of intellectual superiority. Pride and conceit [1] are essentially different qualities; one is only a sort of foil to valour, the other a making plain of a weakness in ourselves, which not unnaturally does not appeal to our forgiveness.

Of all the 'conquistadores' of America, Alvar Nuñez and his rival, Domingo de Irala, were the only two who seemed to have realised that the Indians had any rights at all.

Father Charlevoix, in his *History of Paraguay*, says that in his time (1756) three propositions were very generally discussed in

---

[1] Some excellent men of business have never been able to distinguish between 'wit' and 'humour;' and therefore to them it is not unlikely that the difference between 'pride' and 'conceit' is also inexplicable.

reference to the Conquest of America. First, had Europeans any right to conquer America? Secondly, if the conquest had been beneficial to Europe? Lastly, if the conquest (except as regards religion) had been of advantage to the Americans themselves?[2] As regards the first proposition, the general consensus of opinion appears to be that the inhabitants of Europe not only had, but still have, a right to conquer the inhabitants of any country whose arms are inferior to their own.

This I deduce from the fact that at the present moment, and for the last fifty years, a similar 'conquest' is taking place in South Africa to that which took place in America in the sixteenth century. The only difference appears, to be that the modern 'conquest' is infinitely more sordid and even less justifiable than the conquest of America. In the one case a real and even lunatic fervour to extend the Catholic faith was observable in almost all the conquerors. Few will pretend that an earnest and overpowering desire to spread the principles of Wesleyanism, or primitive Methodism, has animated the 'conquerors' of the luckless South Africans. In both cases the desire for personal gain and the thirst for gold has been equal.

It may, however, be put down to the credit of the Spanish 'conquistador' that, in order to enrich himself, he generally had to imperil his private fortune and to run incredible hardships; for, as civilisation was not then so far advanced, it was impossible to be, as at present, a vicarious 'conqueror,' and to spoil the Indians, safely ensconced within the Cadiz Stock Exchange.

Cortés was indeed as avaricious as he was religious and valiant, and though, like a certain 'conqueror' of South Africa, he had some tincture of letters—'speaking in Latin [as Bernal Diaz del Castillo writes], answering those who spoke to him in that language, and even making verses'—yet he endured the defeat and perils of the Noche Triste, and the eventful march to Guatemala. Even the owner of the good horse[3] Motilla, Gonzalo de Sandoval—whose exploits aroused the curiosity of that Prince of Light Horsemen, [the Emperor Charles the Fifth—never exposed his life more readily. ·

Alvar Nnñez was of illustrious birth; his father was 'that Pedro de Vera who won Canaria,' and his mother Doña Teresa Cabeça de Vaca, a noble lady of Jerez de la Frontera. According to the Spanish fashion, he used the name of both his parents.

Only Columbus and Bartolomé de las Casas are to be compared to him in his regard for and treatment of the Indians. Columbus, indeed, seems always to have endeavoured to protect the Indians, and

---

[2] Charlevoix, *Histoire du Paraguay*, vol. i. cap. i.

[3] Bernal Diaz often mentions Motilla, and tells us he was the best horse both in Castille and Mexico. His colour was chestnut—'chestnutted' (*castaño acastañado*) —with a white star on the forehead and one white foot; and he was the best bitted horse who 'passed to the Indies.'

few men had greater influence with them. He, however, was not a
Spaniard, but came of a milder and more civilised race. Las Casas
spent his life in pleading for the miserable Indians, both in his
diocese of Chiapa and throughout the Indies. He, again, was a
Churchman, though on occasions even Churchmen did not disdain to
participate in the benefits of a Mitayo and Yanancona.[4] Neither
Columbus nor Las Casas had ever been prisoners to the Indians,
as Alvar Nuñez had been. Captivity, though it may occasionally
chasten, is seldom known to sweeten the spirit of the captive, at
least towards his captors. However, Alvar Nuñez never avenged
himself upon the Indians for the long years of slavery in Florida,
but, on the contrary, treated them with unvarying kindness.

Who so fit as he to rescue an expedition which had failed and of
which the survivors were in extremity of hunger? Had he not
himself suffered almost everything a man could suffer?

· Having sailed in 1527 with the ill-fated expedition of Panfilo de
Narvaez to Apalache in Florida, he had been shipwrecked, voyaged
in boats, cast without clothes and only four companions, likewise
naked, on an unknown shore. Enslaved by the Indians, risen to be
a peddler, then a doctor, lastly a sacred chief, he had seen the
'rabbits, hares, lions, bears and other savage beasts which roam the
woods of Florida,' observed and written of (for the first time) 'the
opossum, a wondrous animal which carries its young in a pouch after
they are born, had marked the birds, as ducks, and royal ducks, swans,
falcons, herons, kingfishers, pelicans, flamingoes, and others which
are unknown in the Castilles.'

Had he not with the other castaways fashioned a boat with tools
made out of spurs and stirrups, bits and swords, furnished it with ropes
made from the tails and manes of the horses of the expedition, and
sailed for weeks in it, only to fall again into the Indians' power? At
last had he not made his way into New Spain, not as a captive but
leading hundreds of Indians, and, encountering a Spanish horse
soldier, found he had almost forgotten Spanish, and was received as
one long dead and risen by a miracle? Was not his first thought
to entreat the Spaniards not to harm the Indians he had brought
with him, and to beseech the Indians to leave their marching life and
cultivate the soil?

All this he tells us modestly and with excuses (as every now
and then 'me pesa hablar de mis trabajos'), and as befits a gentleman. Lastly, he leaves the reader by informing him, quite quietly
and without comment, that God was pleased to save from all these
perils himself, Alonso del Castillo Maldonado, Andres Dorantes, and
that the fourth was called Estevanico, a Moor, native of Azimur.

---

[4] Yananconas were a sort of grant of Indians who, according to Herrera in his
Historia General de las Indias (decad v. lib. iv. cap. 40), were condemned to perpetual
slavery. Mitayos were a kind of feudal fief, the Indians of which gave a certain
number of days' service a week.

Therefore, being who he was, the king did well to take a certain
'asiento,' and 'capitulacion,'[5] with Alvar Nuñez,[6] and to make him
Governor and Adelantado of the Rio de la Plata and General both of
its fleets and armies.   All on condition that he should furnish 8,000
ducats, with horses, arms, ships, provisions, men and all things
requisite.   So on the 2nd of November (1537) he embarked at Cadiz
with his fleet of two ships and a caravel,

all very well provisioned and equipped. One ship was new, and measured three
hundred and fifty tons, the other one hundred and fifty, and the caravel but fifty.
In these were packed four hundred soldiers and thirty horses. All went well up
to the Cape de Verdes. From thence to the equator, where it occurred to the
'Maestro del agua,' who was in the flagship, to examine his stock of water; and
out of one hundred pipes which had been put aboard he found but three remaining,
and from these the thirty horses and four hundred soldiers had to drink. Seeing
the greatness of the necessity, the Governor—for Alvar Nuñez almost always
speaks of himself in the third person—gave orders that the fleet should make for
land. Three days we sailed in search of it, and on the fourth, an hour before the
sunrise, occurred a very notable affair, and as it is not altogether 'fuera de propo-
sito,' I set it down; and it is this—that, going towards the land, the ships had
almost touched on some sharp rocks we had not seen.

Then as now, I take it, vigilance was not a quality to be found in
Spanish sailors when on watch.   It is probable that, like the sentinels
I remember in my youth who sat on wharves to guard the
ocean, fishing with a pin tied to their bayonets, or slept under a
tent fashioned with a rifle and a greatcoat, the look-out was sleeping
like a dormouse.   However, had he been awake and cried out 'Helms
a' lee,' or 'Hard a' port,' the 'notable occurrence' had not happened.
   Just as the vessels were almost on the rocks,

a cricket commenced to sing, which cricket a sick soldier had put into the ship at
Cadiz, being anxious to hear its music; and for the two months which our navigation had endured no one had heard it, whereat the soldier was much enraged;
and as that morning it felt the land (*sintió la tierra*) it commenced to sing, and
its music wakened all the people of the ship, who saw the cliffs, which were distant
almost a cross-bow shot from where we were, so we cast out anchors and saved the
ships; and it is certain that if the cricket had not sung, all of us four hundred
soldiers and thirty horses had been lost.

Some of the crew and soldiers accepted the occurrence as a
miracle from God, but Nuñez himself is silent on this head, being a
better observer of natural history than a theologian.
   But, 'from then and sailing more than a hundred leagues along
the coast, always every evening the cricket gave us his music, and

[5] 'Asiento' is a contract. The contract which Charles the Fifth, at the well-
meant but unfortunate instigation of Las Casas, made with the Genoese to supply
negroes for America is known as 'El Asiento de los Negros.'
   [6] In the 'capitulacion' occurs the celebrated clause, 'Que no pasasen procuradores
ni abogados á las Indias,' that neither solicitors nor barristers should pass to
the Indies. It is unfortunate it was not persevered in, as in Paraguay at least the
Reptilia were well represented already.

thus with it we arrived at a little port beyond Cape Frio, where the Adelantado landed and unfurled his flag, and took possession for his Majesty.'

If the parallel between the conquest of America and that now going on in Africa exists, the manner of it is somewhat different. In both cases the result is the degradation of the natives and the forcible engrafting of the true faith on the unbelievers; but fewer perils exist to-day by land or even at sea by negligence of the 'Maestro del Agua;' no miracles and certainly no crickets are put aboard the 'ocean tramps' which carry the conquerors, to wile away the hours for ailing soldiers. Better guns no doubt, less superstition— that is, in religion, for the economic superstition is just as crass as ever was the folly of theologians—and a shorter voyage and still the questions, whether or no the thing is right, and if the natives (always excepting the acquisition of the true faith) are going to be the gainers.

After having taken possession for his most Catholic Majesty, the expedition disembarked at Santa Catalina in Brazil. 'There the Governor landed his men and twenty-six of the horses which had escaped the sea, all that remained of forty-six embarked in Spain.' Besides the alarums and excursions incidental to the landing in a new country, the *odium theologicum* gave the Governor some work at once. Two friars, Fray Bernardo de Armenta and Fray Alonso Lebron, Franciscans, had burnt the houses of some Indians, who had retaliated (in the heathen manner) by slaughtering two Christians, and 'the people were scandalised.'

In Africa to-day, when, either to open markets, take away men's wives, or force the people to change their superstitions, they burn a house or two (or even a villlage), the unnatural barbarians retort by murdering a vicarious Christian. The difference is that nowadays whereas the Christian shoots a chief or two and puts the whole affair (distorted) in a newspaper, the Spanish conquerors generally shot and left the bodies for the wolves, and went to Mass. However, Alvar Nuñez sent for the friars, admonished them, and told them that their duty was to try and teach the Indians better ways of life. This was the first false step he made, and set all friars and priests throughout America against him.

Hearing at Santa Catalina that Buenos Ayres was almost abandoned, and that the greater portion of its inhabitants had founded the town of Asunción del Paraguay, Alvar determined to proceed with the soldiers and horses by land and send the vessels into the river Plate and up the Paraguay. This he resolved to do to avoid the stormy voyage down the coast. The two Franciscan friars he told to remain and 'indoctrinate' the Indians; but they refused to do so, giving as their excuse that they wished to reside in Asunción amongst the Spaniards. Had they been Jesuits, it is ten to ·

one they had remained to 'indoctrinate.' The Jesuits alone of the religious orders were ever ready to take all risks.

In the last century, in South America, there was a saying, 'Los Jesuitas van á una, los demas á uña,' meaning that the Jesuits had one aim (*i.e.* to Christianise the Indians), and the others were there to catch at everything.

So on the 2nd of November, 1541, the Governor began his march of something like two thousand miles through an unknown country accompanied by two hundred musqueteers and thirty cross-bowmen, and all the horses 'which had escaped the sea.' In nineteen days he came across the Guaranís, a race of Indians 'who eat human flesh, not alone of Indians [that would be a venal crime], but also of Christians.'

It is curious that both Alvar Nuñez, Hulderico Schmidel, Barco de la Centenera, Padres Montoya and Losano, and almost all the first conquistadores of the Rivers Plate and Paraguay, concur in saying the Guaranis were cannibals. One would have thought it was a thing not easy to make a mistake about. Still Felix de Azara,[7] writing in 1796, and many other moderns maintain it was untrue.

This but confirms a favourite theory I hold to the effect that common-sense with apprehension, power of observation, and even eyesight, were vouchsafed to man no earlier than the middle of the last century.

Leaving these cannibals, or pseudo-cannibals, the Governor advanced to the Rio Iguaçu, where the 'pilots' took an altitude. Pilots always accompanied a Spanish army in America in those days, and seem to have been at least as useful as the modern reporter, who in three lines reports the actions of the army and devotes a column to describe the way he rode to reach the telegraph.

'It was a thing to see, how frightened the Indians were of the horses and how they brought them abundance of provisions, chickens and honey, to keep them quiet and in good humour, and they asked the Governor to tell the horses not to hurt them.'

Perhaps, upon reflection, Don Felix de Azara was in the right, and the Guaranís could never have been cannibals; the description of their terror of the horses and efforts at propitiation savours too much of Arcady. Still, after all, a cannibal who eats an ox is little better than a cannibal who eats a man, the difference seeming to consist in the fact that the four-legged animal cannot (at present) ride a bicycle.

Contrary to all good policy and precedent, the Governor (like Christopher Columbus) ordered that nothing should be taken from the Indians without due payment. To insure this being done, he

[7] Azara, *Descripcion y Historia del Paraguay*, vol. i. Also Dean Funes in his *History of the Independence of Buenos Aires.*

paid for everything himself, and served it out to the soldiery. Fault number two. First having put the friars against him, he now must make his soldiers discontented. In European wars, when, even in the days of Charles the Fifth, Chapin Vitelli, and Pescara, some sort of fitful, undersized gazette appeared at intervals, or when at least there was a chance of history taking notice of the affair, it was advisable to hang a thieving soldier now and then to teach the others not to poach upon the General's perquisites ; but in America, when the enemies were Indians, nothing more absurd than talk of payment. Payment is fitting for men of a (the) superior race. Honour, a fiction to be attended to between the peoples whose governments own navies. But 'niggers,' Indians, or even the Latin races and those who use inferior kinds of rifles, are in another category. For them cases of gin and Bibles. Surely Alvar Nuñez might have known that Pizarro, Cortés, Almagro, and the rest were men who never paid for anything. He, though, persisted in his folly to the end, and so brought ruin on himself. Still the Indians seemed to appreciate his conduct, for he says that 'when the news was spread abroad of the good treatment the Governor gave to all, they came to meet the army covered with flowers and bringing provisions in great abundance.'

After passing the Iguaçu [8] the march continued for several days through a country 'full of game and plentiful in fruits.' Here the two friars went on ahead to collect provisions, and when the Governor arrived the Indians had no more to give. Perhaps the first historical account of the collection of the tithes in South America.

So, passing the Parana and many towns of Guaranis, they came at last to Asuncion on the 2nd of March, 1542, having only lost one man, and accomplished the longest march that any one had hitherto achieved pacifically in North or South America.

Hardly arrived at Asuncion, Alvar Nuñez found himself embroiled on every side. The Indians were in open rebellion, the settlement of Buenos Ayres almost in ruins, and the officers appointed by the king to collect the royal dues badly disposed towards him. After having commanded the clergy to ascertain from them if it was lawful to attack the Guaycurús who had assailed the recently established missions, and received the answer that it was not only lawful but expedient, he despatched a force against them, to which was joined a priest, to require the Guaycurús to become Christians and acknowledge the King of Spain.

Quite naturally the propositions seemed unreasonable to the poor Indians, who probably had never heard before either of Christianity or the King of Spain. The Governor was not satisfied with the

---

[8] Where Alvar Nuñez passed the Iguaçu is not clear, as the 'pilots' have left no recorded altitude, but it was not improbably somewhere in what is now the Brazilian province of Missiones, and possibly at Candelaria, which is the safest place for the passage of an army.

permission given by the clergy, and called another council of priests, who instantly gave him the same advice. This seems to have surprised him, but he probably did not reflect that the clergy would not have to fight themselves, and that the first blood ever spilt on earth was caused by a religious squabble.

Just before the expedition started against the Guaycurús it was found that the two friars who had come from Santa Catalina were missing. It appeared that they had started for the coast, accompanied by a bevy of Indian damsels, thirty-five in number. They were followed and brought back, and explained that they were on their way to Spain to complain against the Governor. The five-and-thirty dusky catechumens remained without an explanation.

The expedition then started commanded by the Governor in person. Only those who know the Chaco or western bank of the River Paraguay can form the least idea of what an expedition in those days had to encounter. Even to-day along the Chaco, the change since the beginning of the world can be but slight. As a steamer slips along the bank, nothing for miles and miles is seen but swamp and trees, swamps intersected with backwaters, called 'aguapeys,' in which lie alligators, electric eels, and stinging rays; swamps and more swamps, a sea of waving Pampa grass. After the swamps thickets of canes (Tacuarás in Guarani), forests of thorny trees, Chañáres, Ñandubay, Jacarandás, Quebracho, Talas, and Urunday, each one hard enough to split an axe, some, like the black Canela, almost like iron. The inhabitants, those who are left, ferocious and intractable as when the 'Governor' himself first saw them, the climate heavy and humid, the air dank with 'vinchucas'[9] and mosquitos, and the little black, infernal midget, called a jején. No roads, no paths, no landmarks, but here and there at intervals of many leagues, a clearing in the rest, where some wretched settlement strives to exist; more rarely a deserted Jesuit mission. Ostriches and deer, tigers, capibaras, and tapirs, and now and then a herd of cattle wilder than buffaloes. Sometimes an Indian on his horse, sitting like a sentinel to watch the vessel pass, with a lance of eighteen feet in length, stuck in the ground beside him, or balanced across his barebacked painted horse, with feathers in its ears.

Even in a steamer one feels outside humanity, the distances are so immense, the men so few; what then it must have been in 1600 we can only guess by reading writers such as Alvar Nuñez.

However, with 400 men he started, accompanied by above a thousand friendly Indians, all well armed and painted, and with plates of metal on their heads to shine in the sun and thus strike terror to the enemy. To save the horses they were put on board

---

[9] Vinchucas are a kind of flying bug with which an all-wise Providence has endowed Paraguay. Their shape is triangular, their colour grey, and their odour noxious.

the ships in which the troops were sent, the Indians marched along the bank.   Horses at that time in Paraguay and in Peru often fetched a thousand crowns of gold, though Azara says that in Buenos Ayres, in the last century, you could often buy a good one for two needles.

At night the vessels anchored close to the bank, the Indians hauled up their canoes, and those who went on foot camped round great fires.

Then, as at present, time was of no account in Paraguay, so almost every day they landed their horses, to keep them in good condition and to chase the deer.   Just the sort of army we would have liked to march with—no reporters, no control by telegraph ; not too much to eat, perhaps, but still a pleasant feeling of independence and a conviction that one marched to spread the true faith and make one's fortune; the only unpleasant feature the foolish system of payment the Governor prescribed.

All was new and strange ; the world was relatively young ; and the Governor seems to have written up his diary every night, now setting down the loss of a horse, the death of an Indian, or commenting upon the fruits, the fish, the animals, the trees, and all the other ' things of God, which differ from those in Old and New Castile ; now and then a fight, as when they met the warlike Guasarapos or the Payaguás, but nothing of much account (*mucha monta*) ; always the tales of gold mines to be met with further on.

Eventually the expedition arrived close to a point not far from where is now the town of Corumbá.   Here, after founding a town called Reyes, long since destroyed, they turned, having first sent on Captain Mendoza to ' discover countries and procure provisions. Captain Mendoza discovered after the manner of captains, but not according to the wishes of Alvar Nuñez, who gave him his orders conceived as follows :   ' What you, Captain Gonzalo de Mendoza, have to do in the towns where you may go to get provisions to support our people, so that they perish not with hunger, is, that you shall buy supplies (and pay for them to the satisfaction of the Indians) ; and tell them from me that I wish to be friends with them ; and be careful that in the places which you pass you do not allow any of your men to do them any wrong, or treat them badly, but, on the contrary, pay for all they give you.   When you come to a village say you want provisions and offer payment, and entreat them with loving words ; and if they will not give you provisions ask them even to three times, offering them the money ; if then they will not give them take them by force, for the necessity of the Armada admits no law ; but in everything behave according to God's laws and those of His Majesty, the which is fitting for you as a servant of the King.'

At the same time another captain, called Ribera, was sent off up the river to try and reach Peru—that is, that portion of Peru now called Bolivia.   Where he *did* get to is a matter of supposition, as the names of the tribes he speaks of cannot be identified. After three months' waiting at Reyes for his two captains, with àll the expedition ill and himself confined to bed with quartan ague, the Governor determined to return. Before returning he gave the death-blow to his waning popularity.

The expedition had failed in finding gold, had suffered much, and was returning poorer than it started. Just as they were about to sail on the return to Asuncion, Alvar Nuñez discovered that some of his followers were taking about a hundred Indian girls. This he forbade, and, sending for their fathers, delivered the girls into their keeping, and, not content with this, published an order that no one on any account should take an Indian female or male aboard the ships.

'With this the natives were much pleased, but the Spaniards rendered angry and desperate, and for this course they hated me.' Nothing more natural. Bishop Colenso was less unpopular in Africa for treating the Pentateuch like a work of sense than for hinting that perhaps a living Kaffir was more useful than a dead one.

On the 8th of April (1543) the Governor and expedition returned to Asuncion, he very ill with fever, and most of the soldiers worn out and dispirited. In Asuncion all was in confusion. Domingo de Irala —a clever, ambitious Biscayan, who had been interim Governor before Alvar Nuñez arrived—had worked upon the people against the Governor, saying that he wished to take away their property—that is, their Indians.

All, of course, was said to be in the sacred cause of liberty, as always is the case when tyranny, murder, or villany of almost any sort is to be done. So, at the hour of the Ave Maria, ten or twelve of the ' factious' entered the Governor's house, where he lay ill in bed, all shouting 'Liberty!' and, to prove they were in earnest and good patriots, one of them, Jaime Resquin, put a bent cross bow to his side, and forced him to get out of bed and took him to a prison, amid a crowd all shouting 'Liberty!' His friends attempted to rescue him ; but the patriots were too strong, and the Governor was thrown, heavily ironed, into a cell, out of which, to make room, they let a murderer under sentence of death. 'He,' Alvar Nuñez grimly remarks, 'made haste to take my cloak, and then set off down the street at once, calling out "Liberty!"' That everything should be in order, they confiscated all the Governor's goods and took his papers, publishing a proclamation that they did it because he was a tyrant. Unluckily, the Indians have not left us any commentaries, or it would have been curious to have learned what their opinion was as to the tyranny of Alvar Nuñez.

Having got him into prison, they had to elect a Governor, and the choice of course ' fell' upon Domingo de Irala. He promptly put his friends in office, like all governors, whether they enter to the cry of Liberty or not. The friends of Alvar Nuñez, in the usual

Spanish fashion, declared themselves in opposition—that is, they fortified their houses, and roamed about the country, proving by theft and murder that their love of liberty was just as strong as that of those in office.

Things came to such a pitch that no one could leave his house in the evening in Asuncion. The Indians burnt the suburbs and threatened the town, and four men, armed with daggers, kept guard on Alvar Nuñez day and night, in case he should escape. As he says himself, his prison was not 'fitting to his health,' for day and night he had to keep a candle burning to see to read, and the grass grew underneath his bed, and 'for the sake of his health' he had a pair of 'first-rate fetters on his feet.'

For his chief jailer they procured one Hernando de Sosa, whom the Governor had put in prison for striking an Indian chief. At the door a strong guard watched day and night. In spite of this he continued to communicate with his friends almost every day.

The method was most ingenious. His food was brought by an Indian woman, whom—so great was the fear his enemies had that he should write to the King or to his friends—they made walk naked into the prison, carrying the dishes, and with her head shaved. Notwithstanding this she used to bring a piece of paper hidden between her toes. The party of Liberty, suspecting that somehow or other Nuñez was communicating with his friends, procured an Indian youth to make love to the girl and to get the secret from her. This he failed to do, owing perhaps to his love-making being wanting in conviction on account of her shaven head. At any rate the correspondence went on for eleven months.

At last Irala and his friends, seeing the tumults did not cease and that things went from bad to worse, determined to send the ex-Governor a prisoner to Spain, taking care, of course, to despatch a messenger beforehand to distort the facts and prejudice the mind of the King against him. His friends contrived to hide a trunk of papers, stating the true facts of the case, on board the ship, unknown to the captain or the sailors.

At dead of night a band of harquebusiers dragged him from his bed, as he says, 'almost with the candle in his hand,' *i.e.* in a dying state. As he left the prison he fell upon his knees and thanked God for having let him once more feel the air of heaven; and then, in a loud voice, exclaimed, 'I name as my successor Captain Juan de Salazar de Espinosa.' At this one Garci Vargas rushed at him with a knife, and told him to recall his words or he would kill him. This, however, he was prevented from doing, and Nuñez was hurried on board the ship and chained to a beam.

On board the ship he says they tried to poison him, but this seems doubtful, as there was nothing on earth to prevent their doing so had they been inclined. Still, like a prudent man, he took the precaution to have a cruise of oil and a piece of unicorn (*pedazo de unicornio*) with which he tried all the food that was set before him. Unicorns he could not have met with in Paraguay, or even in Florida, and he does not explain how he happened to be so fortunately equipped. Nevertheless, of all the discoverers of America he is the man of least imagination—that is, in matters appertaining to natural history—so one must conclude that he brought his piece of unicorn from Spain, where he had it from some dealer in necessaries for travellers to the Indies.

After a stormy voyage he arrived in Spain, to find his accusers arrived just before him. With almost Eastern justice both accusers and accused were cast into prison, a custom well worthy of adoption in other lands. Alvar Nuñez was soon released on bail, and, his accusers having all died, in eight years' time, triumphantly acquitted, but never restored to his government in Paraguay.. Eight years more of trouble must have been little to him after what he had undergone already, and so he never once complains, but, like a gentleman of Old Castile, closes his commentaries merely remarking that his lord the King forgot to repay him what he had expended in his service.

R. B. CUNNINGHAME GRAHAM.

THE STORY OF THE MANITOBA SCHOOLS QUESTION

THE history of the past six years of Protestant domination in Manitoba affords such a display of tyranny and oppression as would seem at the present time to be incredible. The treatment of the Roman Catholics, by which they are wholly deprived of the enjoyment of the rights in the education of their children secured to them by the constitution, comes as near to persecution as can well be conceived in these days of boasted toleration and enlightenment. It is a singular fact that intolerance in matters of religion should be exhibited and carried into practical effect by Protestants in a British colony, while acts of persecution commonly supposed to be peculiar to Roman Catholics are now never heard of. The phenomenon is one well worthy of the consideration of ultra-Protestants in this country.

The controversy arising out of this matter has been fiercely raging throughout the Dominion of Canada during this whole period of six years. No topic has ever secured a wider amount of attention, whether from the public, the press, or in political and religious circles; all available machinery of the courts has been set in motion for the decision of questions of constitutional law, and on two separate occasions the Judicial Committee of the Privy Council has pronounced elaborate judgments on appeal, the only effect of which has been to thrust the matter back once more into the arena of politics; the actual position being that the Roman Catholic minority in Manitoba are fighting for their rights, which the Protestant majority as represented by the Liberal Government of the Province refuse to yield to them, with the result that they have been compelled to look to the Conservative Government of the Dominion for the redress of their grievances. To this end, the Minister of Justice, on the 11th of February last, introduced a 'Remedial Bill' into the Canadian House of Commons, which, however, it was found impossible to pass, on account of the obstruction developed by the opponents of the measure in the short space of time remaining before the end of the term of the recent Parliament, which expired in the latter part of April just past.

Whether to students or to statesmen, the history of this period of incessant strife will be found to involve matters of considerable interest, as, for instance, the modes of life in an isolated colony of pioneers of different races and religions, and their means of education; the erection of the settlements into a province, and its reception into a federation of older colonies, with proper safeguards for the rights of the pioneers; the early provisions for education by law, and their subsequent overthrow; the racial and religious antipathies in consequence evoked throughout the federation, and the amenities displayed by the Protestant majority in the distant province; the conflict between the federal and provincial authorities, and the dependence, for the correct interpretation of the law under which the colonists live, upon the great Imperial Court of the Privy Council.

In the old days of the Red River Settlement in Rupertsland there was no law touching the subject of schools or of education. There were, however, a number of denominational schools established and controlled by the Roman Catholic Church, the Church of England, and the Presbyterian Church respectively. The Archbishop of Rupertsland states that in 1869 he had sixteen schools organised in the different parishes. This settlement is now included in the province of Manitoba, which was received into the Union or Dominion of Canada from the 15th of July 1870 under the provisions of the Manitoba Act of that year (33 Vict., c. 3, Dominion Statutes), afterwards confirmed by Imperial statute. There were then 12,000 Christians in the province, 6,000 of them Roman Catholics, 5,000 of the English Church, and the remainder chiefly Presbyterians.

The Manitoba Act established a legislature for the province, and section 22 of that Act provided that the legislature might exclusively make laws in relation to education, subject to restrictions which will be presently specified, saving certain rights, and reserving power to the Dominion Parliament to legislate in the matter in certain events.

Accordingly, in 1871, the legislature passed a law which established a dual system of denominational schools. A board of education was formed, divided into two sections, Protestant and Roman Catholic, with a superintendent of schools under each section, and the grant for education was divided equally between the two sections. There were twelve districts under each section, according as they comprised mainly a population of the one faith or the other, and the male inhabitants in each district might decide how school funds other than the public grant should be raised. In the course of time the board was enlarged to twelve Protestant and nine Roman Catholic members, and the public grant was rearranged on the basis of the school population. Provision was also made that school districts of the different faiths might overlap each other. Each section had control over the management and discipline of its schools, and prescribed the books to be used therein. In the Roman Catholic section the choice of books referring to religion and morals was subject to the approval of the religious authority. From 1877 to 1890 no ratepayer of one faith was obliged to pay towards a school of the other.

For nineteen years, therefore (1871–1890), a denominational system of education was maintained in full force, being the first system established by law in Manitoba. This, it is to be noted, is the foundation of the whole present difficulty.

Suddenly the whole policy was reversed, the old system swept away, and what is called a non-sectarian system set up in its place. On the 31st of March 1890 two acts were passed by the provincial legislature, which came into operation on the 1st of May. By the 53 Vict., c. 37, a Department of Education and an ' Advisory Board' of seven members were established : four of these members to be appointed by the Department, one by the University Council, and two to be elected by the public and high school teachers, and this board had the power to prescribe the forms of religious exercises. By the Public Schools Act, 53 Vict., c. 38, all Protestant and Roman Catholic school districts came under the Act, and the public schools were to be free. Provisions were made for religious exercises conducted according to the regulations of the board, just before closing time in the afternoon, and for the withdrawal of pupils beforehand if required. They were to be held at the option of the school trustees for the district, who might require the teachers to hold the same, and no others were to be allowed.

Then follow provisions for school districts, the election of school trustees, and the levying of a rate on the taxable property in each district for school purposes. A legislative grant was allotted to public schools, in which no school could participate which did not comply with the Act and the regulations of the department and the advisory board, and no text books were to be used unless authorised by the board.

It must be stated that, owing to the influx of settlers from the eastern provinces and the United Kingdom, the nature of the population had entirely changed in the course of twenty years, so that in 1889 the Protestant school population was nearly 19,000, while the Roman Catholic was less than 4,500.

We will now look at the reasons given for the revolution in the law, and for this purpose it will be satisfactory, so as to avoid the risk of understatement, to take the reasons set out in a paper published under the auspices of the provincial government, which are roughly as follows : The Roman Catholic schools were almost completely under the control of the Church, the teachers being to a great extent priests and sisters, whose qualifications were unknown outside, while the inspectorate consisted of priests alone. The inefficiency of the system is shown by giving instances of the absurdity of papers set in examinations for teachers' certificates, and by the illiteracy of the

French half-breeds.[1]   The whole of the school lessons (except those of arithmetic and geography) were made the means of imparting religious instruction, and the pupils were completely immersed 'in Roman Catholic ideas and influences.'   Instances are given of peculiarly Romanist questions in teachers' examinations, and then the writer says :

'I pass over the following :

' " What are angels ? "

' " What are the occupations of the angels ? "

' " What do you mean by devils ? "

'Any one who could answer the second question at any rate would deserve to be senior wrangler and double first in any hall of learning.'   (*sic*)

The serious charge is made that French ideas and aspirations were fostered to the almost entire exclusion of those that are British.   The study of English was rare in the French schools ; British Canadian history was not taught till the child reached the sixth division, and English history only in the seventh or last division.   Quotations from the text-books and specimens of the teachers' examination papers in this subject are given to substantiate this charge.

This, of course, is all very sad, but there are other ways of improving the growth of a young tree than that of pulling it up by the roots.

Further it is charged that the Roman Catholic Church practically had the disposal of the public grant to its section, and the control of municipal taxation for school purposes in its districts.

In 1889, the last year of the dual system, the number of the Roman Catholic school population was less than a quarter of that of the Protestant, but there were seven times as many Protestant school districts and teachers as there were on the Roman Catholic side.   The average public grant per district was : Protestant, 178 dollars ; Roman Catholic, 304 dollars.   The Protestants taxed themselves on the average per district 538 dollars, the Roman Catholics 242 dollars, which is said to mean that the Roman Catholics avoided taxation and lived on the grant as much as possible.

It is now necessary to examine the powers given to the provincial legislature in the matter of education, and to trace the course of the proceedings taken to obtain decisions on points in dispute in the courts of law.   These powers are contained in section 22 of the Manitoba Act above mentioned, and are as follows :

XXII. In and for the province the said legislature may exclusively make laws in relation to education, subject and according to the following provisions:

---

[1] For the programme of studies in the schools, and specimens of examination papers, reference is made further to the 'Memoir' prepared by the Roman Catholic section of the board for the Colonial Exhibition in London in 1886.   This memoir would probably therefore be accessible in this country.

(1) Nothing in any such law shall prejudicially affect any right or privilege with respect to denominational schools, which any class of persons have by law or practice in the province at the Union.

(2) An appeal shall lie to the Governor-General in Council from any Act or decision of the legislature of the province, or of any provincial authority, affecting any right or privilege of the Protestant or Roman Catholic minority of the Queen's subjects in relation to education.

(3) In case any such provincial law as from time to time seems to the Governor-General in Council requisite for the due execution of the provisions of this section is not made, or in case any decision of the Governor-General in Council on any appeal under this section is not duly executed by the proper provincial authority in that behalf, then and in every such case, and as far only as the circumstances of each case require, the Parliament of Canada may make remedial laws for the due execution of the provisions of this section, and of any decision of the Governor-General in Council under this section.

Upon the passing of the Manitoba Schools Acts of 1890, the Roman Catholic minority protested that they were unconstitutional, and appealed to the federal power for relief.

On the 25th of April 1890 the Hon. E. Blake, leader of the Liberal party in the Dominion House, moved that it was expedient to provide for the reference of questions of law or fact upon educational legislation to a high judicial tribunal. The late Sir John Macdonald agreed for the Government, and the resolution was passed unanimously. In the following session the late Sir John Thompson accordingly brought in a bill to amend the act as to the Supreme and Exchequer Courts of Canada, and the Act c. 135 R. S. C. § 37 was amended, the 30th of September 1891, to provide the means for such reference.

On the 7th of October 1890, one Barrett, a Roman Catholic ratepayer of Winnipeg, obtained a summons for an order to quash certain by-laws of the city, made to authorise an assessment for city and school purposes for the current year, on the ground that the amounts to be levied for Protestant and Roman Catholic schools were united, and one rate levied upon Protestants and Roman Catholics alike for the whole sum. On the 24th of November Mr. Justice Killam dismissed the summons. On appeal the full Court of Queen's Bench for Manitoba dismissed the appeal, Mr. Justice Dubuc dissenting.

On appeal to the Supreme Court of Canada, the 28th of October 1891, the appeal was allowed, the Schools Act declared *ultra vires* of the provincial legislature, and the by-laws in question quashed. The Court held that the words ' or practice ' in the first sub-section of section 22, quoted above, saved to the Roman Catholics the privilege of denominational schools, and that they could not be taxed for Protestant schools.

Next, on the 5th of December 1891, one Logan, a member of the Church of England in Winnipeg, obtained a summons calling upon the city to show cause why a by-law levying the school rate for the current year should not be quashed, on the grounds that the rate was levied upon all denominations alike, and that members of the

Church of England could not be assessed for the support of schools not under its control. Following the Supreme Court the full Court of Queen's Bench granted the application and quashed the by-law.

Both cases were then taken by the city of Winnipeg to the Judicial Committee of the Privy Council, and on the 30th of July 1892 judgment was delivered by Lord Macnaghten allowing the appeals, and reversing the judgments appealed from. Their lordships held that it was intended (sub-section 1, above) to preserve every right or privilege with respect to denominational schools which any class of persons enjoyed at the time of the union; but added that it would be going much too far to hold that the establishment of a national system of education upon an unsectarian basis was so inconsistent with the right to set up and maintain denominational schools that the two things could not exist together, or that the existence of the one implied immunity from taxation for the purpose of the other, and further said that it could hardly be contended that, in order to give substantial effect to a saving clause expressed in general terms, it was incumbent upon the Court to discover privileges which were not apparent of themselves. They held that, notwithstanding the Public Schools Act, 1890, members of every religious body in Manitoba were free to establish schools throughout the province, to maintain them voluntarily, and to conduct them according to their own religious tenets without interference. They could not assent to the view that the new public schools are in reality Protestant schools, for 'the legislature has declared in so many words that the public schools shall be entirely unsectarian.'

I confess, with fear and trembling, that this last conclusion is to me astonishing; but I shall have to refer to the point again, for the dominant party has made the most of it.

By this judgment the rights under sub-section 1 are made clear, and the Church of England now disappears from the fight.

The question of appeal to the Governor-General in Council prescribed by sub-section 2 (above) was the next matter to be disposed of, and in November 1892 a committee of the Canadian Privy Council fixed a date in the following January for hearing the arguments on petitions from the Roman Catholic minority in Manitoba for remedial school legislation. On the 22nd of February 1893 an order in Council was made under which a case was prepared for the Supreme Court, in which certain important questions of law were referred to them for consideration. On the 20th of February 1894 the Court decided by a majority of three to two that the Roman Catholic minority had no right of appeal to the Governor-General in Council.

Thereupon the case (*Brophy and others* v. *the Attorney-General of Manitoba*) was taken to the Judicial Committee, and on the

29th of January 1895 Lord Herschell gave judgment allowing the appeal from the decision of the Supreme Court of Canada. Their lordships held that the questions submitted chiefly depended on the construction of the second and third sub-sections of section 22 (above quoted), and that the second sub-section extends to the rights and privileges of the Roman Catholic minority acquired by legislation in the province after the union. The question was, whether any such right or privilege had been affected by the legislation of 1890. Their lordships were unable to see how this question could receive any but an affirmative answer. They contrasted the position of the Roman Catholics prior and subsequent to the Acts from which they appealed. Prior to 1890 they managed their own schools, selected the books, and determined the character of the religious teaching. They shared the public grant, and the money raised by the local assessment of Roman Catholics was applied only to their own schools. Under the Act of 1890 their own schools will receive no State aid, while they themselves are taxed for the public grant, and assessed for the support of schools which they do not regard as suitable for the education of their children. Their lordships held that the appeal to the Governor-General in Council was admissible, and further that he has the power to make the declarations or remedial orders asked for. It was not essential that the statutes repealed by the Act of 1890 should be re-enacted, or their precise provisions again made law; but all ground for complaint would be removed if the present system were supplemented by provisions removing the grievance on which the appeal is founded, and modified to give effect to those provisions.

The points of law being settled, the Privy Council of Canada met on the 26th of February 1895 to hear the appeal of the Roman Catholics against the school law, with the result that on the 21st of March an order in Council was made in which his Excellency in Council decided that the Manitoba School Acts of 1890 had deprived the minority of the following rights:

'(a) The right to build, maintain, equip, manage, conduct, and support Roman Catholic schools in the manner provided for by the (said) statutes which were repealed by the two Acts of 1890 aforesaid.

'(b) The right to share proportionately in any grant made out of the public funds for the purposes of education.

'(c) The right of exemption of such Roman Catholics as contribute to Roman Catholic schools from all payment or contribution to the support of any other schools.'

And further that ' it seems requisite that the system of education embodied in the two Acts of 1890 aforesaid shall be supplemented by a provincial Act or Acts which will restore to the Roman Catholic minority the said rights and privileges of which such minority has been so deprived as aforesaid, and which will modify the said Acts of 1890 so far, and so far only, as may be necessary to give effect to the provisions restoring the rights and privileges in paragraphs *a*, *b*, and *c*, hereinbefore mentioned.'

This 'Remedial Order' was sent to the Government of Manitoba, and they were requested to take action thereupon. To this the Provincial Legislature, on the 19th of June, made answer alleging the inefficiency of the old Roman Catholic schools, the inadvisability of expending public money on them, the difficulties of maintaining an efficient system of education, which would be aggravated by the establishment of separate schools, and asking for an investigation into the working of the former system.

In July 1895 the Dominion Government asked the Provincial Government whether they would settle the question satisfactorily to the minority, without making it necessary to call in the powers of the Dominion Parliament. To this the Manitoba Government replied on the 20th of December last, stating that action in the schools question was a matter of public policy, flatly refusing to establish separate schools, and again asking for an inquiry.

Here then we have the spectacle of a 'Liberal' Government, supported by a strong Protestant community, refusing the enjoyment of their rights to a Roman Catholic minority, although these rights are specially reserved to them in the constitution of the province, and distinctly defined by the highest court of the Empire. Moreover since the Acts of 1890 that Government has been twice returned to power by the province with a majority of 3 to 1, the second time being as late as the 7th of January 1896, so that their position is impregnable, and they can afford to defy the federal Power. They give us at once an example of Protestant liberality and a practical lesson in 'Home Rule.'

Let us see how far the Roman Catholics are ready to meet the Government, and how much liberty of action it is that they actually require. This was publicly announced by Mr. Ewart, Q.C., of counsel for the minority in all the higher Courts, as long ago as the 29th of April last year, in Winnipeg, subsequently to the issue of the 'Remedial Order.' He says:

> We are willing to work up to the secular standard prescribed by the State; to employ State-certificated teachers; to use State-selected books (if not antagonistic to the Catholic religion); to be subjected to State inspection, and to be free from Church control. That, I think, is all that the State can require of us, and ought to be a sufficient answer to suggestions of inefficiency and illiteracy; and in return we ask that in schools in which there are none but Roman Catholics the religious 'sentiments and sanctions' to be taught shall be such as we choose, and not those selected by others, however free from theological prejudice.

We will now glance at the attitude of the other denominations. The schools do not come up to the requirements of the Church of England, as could be shown by an affidavit of the Archbishop of Rupertsland in *Logan* v. *Winnipeg*.

On the 20th of March 1895 the following resolution of the Methodist Ministerial Association of Winnipeg was sent to the Dominion Premier at Ottawa :

' Fearing lest silence be construed as indifference, we respectfully but firmly protest against interference with the school system of Manitoba as established by law : First, because by this law no injustice is done to any individual ; secondly, because such interference would infringe upon provincial rights, &c.,' and Methodist ministers were requested to preach upon it. This pronouncement is a curiosity in its way.

The following utterances lay stress upon religious requirements, and show how far certain of the Protestant authorities are from desiring religion to be divorced from the school teaching.

On the 21st of November 1895 the Rev. Principal King, in moving resolutions on the schools question before the Presbyterian synod of Manitoba, said that he could not protest too strongly against the view that there should be no connection between religion and the action of the State, including its action in the matter of education— ' a view which, if it obtained, would deprive society as an organisation of all religious sanctions and found it on a purely secular basis.'

On the 18th of April 1895 the pastor of the Central Congregational Church in Winnipeg, during a lecture on the schools question, argued thus : ' It is the business of the State to provide moral training. But moral training will be ineffective unless supported by the sentiments and sanctions of religion. Therefore what ? It is the business of the State to provide religious teaching.' And recapitulating, ' What then is the duty of the State ? First, to teach religion in so far as it can do that without violating the fundamental principles of religion ; and, second, to extend all hospitality and encouragement consistent with justice to the agencies whose business it is to teach religion.'

To come now to the actual facts as to religious teaching and exercises in these ' non-sectarian ' schools. The regulations say : ' To establish the habit of right doing, instruction in moral principles must be accompanied by training in moral practice. The teacher's influence and example, current incidents, stories, memory gems, sentiments in the school-lesson, examination of motives that prompt to action, didactic talks, teaching the Ten Commandments, &c., are means to be employed.'

(*Query*, according to what faith ?)

As to religious exercises, they provide a number of selections from the Bible (either version), which may be read without comment ; a prayer such as would be used by Trinitarian Protestants ; the Lord's Prayer, and the ' Benediction.'

Thus it will be seen that certain ' Protestants ' are allowed to introduce the *quantum* of religion that will satisfy their consciences, while the Roman Catholics are denied the same liberty : such a modicum of religion is to them utterly inadequate for the education of their children ; and they are not allowed a voice in the matter even in the districts where their children form the main school population. And yet it is solemnly affirmed that the schools are not Protestant ! The religious observance prescribed by the advisory board can certainly not be styled Jewish, nor Unitarian, and emphatically not Romanist. What then is the name of it ? Is there any other name for it than ' Protestant ' ? and are not the schools non-sectarian Protestant schools ?

What a farce is the whole proceeding ! Public schools are set up and labelled ' non-sectarian ' in the Act creating them. Then the Protestants are openly permitted to get their foot in as far as suits them, while the Roman Catholics are refused even an inch of standing ground.

Englishmen, I suppose, will scarcely credit the fact that there is no practical difficulty in the way of giving separate schools to the Roman Catholics. The Manitoba Government say that they can scarcely maintain one school in sparsely-settled districts. Quite so : then in such cases it would be clearly impossible and absurd to set up another for two or three Roman Catholic children. The law does not demand impossibilities, and pioneers who go out to reclaim the wilderness do not expect all the advantages of civilisation. In Winnipeg, Brandon, the Portage, and perhaps some other towns, there would probably be enough Roman Catholic children to fill separate schools without trouble. As to the bulk of the Roman Catholic population, they are massed together in their own districts. Their chief settlement is at St. Boniface, a French-Canadian town on the banks of the Red River, opposite to Winnipeg, where is the seat of the Roman Catholic Archbishop. The old Roman Catholic half-breed people are settled in their own parishes on the banks of the Red River, the Assiniboine, and some smaller rivers. Their lands were of the shape of a long piece of tape stretched out. Each strip was a few chains in width, abutting on the river, and going back two miles into the prairie, with two miles further for ' hay-privilege,' known in both common and legal parlance as the ' inner ' and ' outer ' two miles ; while the houses were in a string along the river-banks, for the sake of mutual protection and society for the inmates. Could anything be simpler than such a situation ?

To understand the rancour that has been aroused in this dispute by the stirring up of religious animosities by the Orange Lodges and certain Protestant speakers throughout the Dominion, Englishmen would have to go back to the state of feeling aroused by the Tractarian movement in this country, or the Romanist aggression in the days of Earl Russell. And the irony of the situation lies in the fact that the provision in the Act under which the Roman Catholics are claiming relief was really introduced for the benefit of a future *Protestant minority*, the population having increased in the opposite way to what was at the time expected by many would be the case.

What then is the meaning of the conduct of the Liberal Government of Manitoba ? We can only judge from what appears on the surface, and this subject alone would suffice for a separate article. They have continuously interposed delays and hindrances and opposition to any settlement of the difficulty on the plain lines of justice to the minority, but they have committed the fatal blunder of making too many excuses for their conduct. In their answer to the ' Remedial Order' they alleged the difficulties of maintaining an efficient system of education even under present circumstances, and that the establishment of separate schools for the Roman Catholics would greatly impair that system, while the possible prospect of further separate schools for the Church of England, for the Mennonites, and for the Icelanders would be simply appalling. The position is entirely imaginary, for there is no saving of such rights, except to ' the Protestant or Roman Catholic minority of the Queen's subjects.' It must always be borne in mind that the provincial Government is of one political type, while the federal Government is of the opposite.

Even after the introduction of their own ' Remedial Bill' in February last, the Dominion authorities did not neglect to give the Provincial Government an opportunity of themselves dealing with this matter. After the Bill had been read a second time, they so far endeavoured to meet the wishes of the provincial authorities as to send Sir Donald Smith and two of the Ministers as Special Commissioners to Winnipeg, to see if a satisfactory compromise could not be arrived at, but even these negotiations failed to bring about a settlement. The Government went on with their measure, but were met in Committee by the grossest obstruction, one member reading chapters of the Bible with dissertations thereon, and another spending an hour in giving selections from the *Bab Ballads* with appropriate comments. The committee sat continuously during the whole of Easter week, but the Opposition persistently ' played , to the gallery,' knowing that the whole question would have to be threshed out again at the polls, and thus, as I have said, rendered it impossible to pass the measure in the short time remaining before the dissolution of Parliament.

Such are the main points in the history of the Manitoba schools difficulty, in grappling with which the Dominion Government are to be congratulated on having steadfastly followed the straight line of duty—justice to the minority under the Constitution.

T. C. Down.

THE MUSIC-HALLS

LATE on a Saturday evening, two months ago, I was standing at the portals of Gatti's Music-hall, in the Westminster Bridge Road, reading the programme of the entertainment within. Was it worth while to enter? Every one else had long since made up his mind : the evening was far spent; the sound of the accompanying orchestra —the band in fullest swing supporting some vocalist or dancer on the stage—penetrated to the street ; no one now was expected ; the ticket-giver behind the fortifications of his office was dozing in security ; the functions of the ' chucker-out '—if such there be—were at all events suspended ; and no one stood in the doorway but myself and an undersized, slightly built, ragged-bearded person of uncertain gait, who examined me while I examined the programme. One always knows when one is being looked at, so eventually I turned upon him : was he perhaps labouring under some temporary difficulty of locomotion? He was, in any case, one of whom it was safe to predicate that energetic action was never his characteristic. He was less an active participator in Life than an impartial observer of it. There are those who would have called him a ' loafer ; ' and it may be that a ' loafer ' he was. Anyhow he desired speech with me, and remarked, with an infirmity of deliverance which it would have been charitable to attribute to a quite recent indulgence in whatever may take the place of the wine-cup in the Westminster Bridge Road, that I was looking at the bill of the hall. I admitted that circumstance, and further replied that it appeared to me the bill was not a strong one. He took some umbrage at the statement. He addressed me suddenly with unsuspected eloquence, though in a tone more philosophical than vehement. What, then, was his interest in the hall? It became clear, in a minute or two, that he had no interest in the hall whatever. But he looked at Life largely, and the line of his argument with me—so far as his long-accumulated infirmities and a very recent debauch allowed him to indicate it—was that if a man went into a place of entertainment, he must go to it with the intention of being entertained ; not seeking curiously for any particular artist, nor weighing anxiously the items in the programme, nor wanting any ' specialty,' but minded to ' receive,' and above all to be satisfied with, whatever in the good providence of the management might be proffered for his joy. I had read to me a moral lesson. I wished the ragged-bearded observer of the world Good-night, with the respect due to any fellow creature whose theories are sound—even if his practice be imperfect. I crossed Westminster Bridge again, sadder and wiser. And I trust that the large tolerance so conspicuous in my friend may not be wholly wanting to the tone of this article.

And indeed a large tolerance is very much required from any one who, having seen great Art, the art of Aimée Desclée and Sarah Bernhardt, of Got and Mrs. Kendal and Henry Irving, betakes himself to a little study of the Music-Hall—an institution which, though I would look at it without prejudice, as a thing which meets and satisfies at all events an immense popular demand, I yet cannot take very seriously in regard to the opportunity that it at present affords for the exhibition of the comedian's or the vocalist's art. I am, perhaps, old-fashioned in this matter: I know I lag behind Mr. Walter Sickert, and, I think, behind Mr. Arthur Symons. The music-hall is popular, and will continue to be popular; but it will have to develop itself further, and, in my opinion, to change at least certain of its ways if it is to continue to be fashionable. Indeed, even now it would be very easy to exaggerate its vogue. The fashionable music-halls are chiefly the two or three which have already left behind them many of the music-hall's older characteristics. The Palace·Theatre of Varieties, and yet more the Empire and the Alhambra, rely in great measure upon sources of attraction not known to the earlier successors of the 'free-and-easy'—that is, of the public-house concert, which was the real origin of the halls—and not known much, even to-day, to the average hall, frequented chiefly by the inhabitants of its particular quarter, whether the quarter be Drury Lane and the hall the Middlesex, or whether it be Pimlico and the hall the Standard, or Battersea and the hall the Washington.

At the three great halls that I have mentioned of the newer and more fashionable kind—the Palace, Empire, Alhambra—what has happened is that an immense and novel importance has been assigned to 'spectacle.' Now, the essence of the music-hall proper—taking the word in its older sense—is that the place is a place for the exhibition of what may be supposed to be the talent or the charm of the individual performer; a dozen individual performers—sometimes, with the brevity of the modern 'turn,' two dozen individual performers—succeeding each other rapidly: the chief spectacle, the spectacle of their talent, or of their attire, their art and charm —if you are minded to call it so—exhibited in front of a flat scene which, though frequently changed, as often as not has not, and does not profess to have, any necessary or even discernible connection with the figure strutting its hour in front of it. But at the Palace Theatre of Varieties, which the veteran Mr. Morton manages excellently, you have, along, of course, with other performances, the spectacle of the *tableau vivant*—the one thing which the music-hall has borrowed from the drawing-room ; and it was fair, no doubt, that the music-hall should borrow that one thing, for it has lent the drawing-room the skirt dance, even the ' high kick,' which, for a year at least, was as fashionable as philanthropy, and as much *de rigueur* as ' slumming.'

I said that the *tableau vivant* had been borrowed from the drawing-room ; but, in borrowing it, the display of the nude figure has, of course, been added to—that is to say, the paid model, accustomed to the poses of the studio, has, under artistic direction, exhibited her form to all the world in a degree which the best-endowed of amateurs would doubtless hesitate to follow. And in this has been found cause of offence—cause even of busy complaint on the part of the Puritan, for whom restriction, fussy interference, a narrow and continual forbidding, is as the very breath of life, and who is never altogether comfortable unless he is employed in palliating the mistakes of Providence and energetically bettering the arrangements of God.

That, in a word, expresses, and more effectually perhaps than by elaborate argument, my own view as to the wisdom and reasonableness of the opposition to the *tableau vivant* at the music-halls. I have no great opinion of the refinement of music-hall audiences. It is beyond a doubt that music-hall audiences—like modern theatrical audiences—will stand the very riskiest of jokes. But somehow sight and apprehension are on a different footing ; and just as no audience at an English theatre would endure the action of certain Parisian ' couchers,' or the action in a piece called *Le Dindon* at the Palais Royal this May, so no audience at an English music-hall would tolerate any show of undeniable indecency. Before the intervention of the Puritan became necessary, the public itself would have interfered. But, in the matter of the *tableau vivant*, the public rightly recognised what the Puritan ignored—that the nude in a *tableau vivant*, with all its accessories, with all its associations, is no longer an undressed woman, but the nude in art—the nude to be seen, therefore, with something, at least, of artistic appreciation of refined colour and of ordered and intricate line.

At the Empire and the Alhambra, from which I do not say that *tableaux vivants* are excluded, you have the yet greater spectacle of the Dance ; the dance organised and performed upon a scale that makes the ballet of the opera a comparatively insignificant thing. I am not talking of the art of the single dancer. That may be seen probably almost as well in one place as in another. I am talking of the ballet *en masse* ; the great concerted dance of every kind—*chahut* (which is the pretty word for ' cancan '), minuet, gavotte,

Most dulcet gigs, dreamiest saraband.

These two great variety theatres, the Alhambra and the Empire, have, in the matter of the Dance, conquered new worlds. One or two hundred dancers move or pause on their vast stages with a strange charm of ordered colour, which at first you think you are speaking of with perhaps a little flattery if you compare it with the ·charm of a cowslip meadow, the charm of a tulip garden, the charm of a tract of bluebells among the greenery of a wood in May. But by the comparison, so far as intricate and ordered colour is concerned, you are guilty of an injustice—an injustice not to Nature but to the modern dance. These things are arranged by great artists in scenic effect. And their art is a new thing. Nature, I understand, is stationary; but their art improves with each new effort.

Of course, along with these organised splendours, whether of the *tableau* or the dance, the three great music-halls to which I have thus far confined my comments, have availed themselves, and have profited by availing themselves, of single 'turns' of exceptional—in some cases of temporary—public fascination. At one place you may have some incarnation of animal spirits and of telling eccentricity. At another, the *svelte* grace of a true young actress may be the medium for the mimicry of styles and ways that the young woman has noticed all around her. At a third—this time the Empire—it may be Yvette Guilbert with whom, as in *Les Ingénues*, or in the *Demoiselles de Pensionnat*, you are invited to laugh, and with whom you remain to weep almost, certainly to be most strongly moved by, as, fresh from 'the blithe Ambassadeur's,' she, in a sombre tale of outer Boulevards and nocturnal horrors,

> Sings
> The pity of unpitied human things.

It is a charitable view, at least, that even upon the stage of the music-hall no great reputation is acquired that is not, or that has not been, to some extent, deserved. Yvette Guilbert's reputation is deserved at all events, so magnetic is her personality, so varied her art. In the favour of a large public—not altogether in critical estimation, however, and not at all in the esteem of those whom the occasional violation of good taste distresses—one or two women (children, as I suppose, of Central London) take a place by Yvette Guilbert's side. No London hall is 'too important for them to be welcomed in. They prosper in the heart of things; they prosper in the suburbs. 'By the pricking in my thumbs, something wicked this way comes,' say the Witches in *Macbeth*—anticipating them. I am an old-fashioned person, and, I confess, their songs are not the songs that I would take any woman, of gentle or good mind, to listen to.

Incomparably the most reticent and finished artist among the men of the music-halls, is still Mr. Albert Chevalier. He has gone to

America, to make the polite society of Fifth Avenue and the coster of the Bowery and Fulton Market familiar with the coster of the Old Kent Road and the coster of Hoxton. Very clever as are two or three at least of the men who do low comedy in ways of their own in London halls, from the Eastern Empire at Bow to the Washington at Battersea, no one throws for a minute into the background—no one allows us to forget—the gently incisive art of Mr. Chevalier, more especially as he exercised it before any one of his subjects became lachrymose—as he exercised it in *Mrs. 'Enry 'Awkins*, in the *Little Nipper*, and even if you like (though that was on the confines of exaggerated pathos) in *My Old Dutch*. I always used to think the *Little Nipper* was the greatest triumph of all. The pride of the man in his precocious offspring—the children of the streets are always, like Portia herself, as Shylock said of her, ' so much more elder' than their years—the quick-witted audacity and ' cheek' of the little lad to whom nothing is denied, when he affectionately and confidently asserts equality with his parents—these were in the *Little Nipper* so accurately observed, so very finely rendered.

It is right to say, of course, that the stage of the music-hall may fairly boast two or three other men whose performances are vivid, amusing, not wanting in good taste, and who observe life and render it. But then at the music-hall the list is so short a one of men whom we can praise at all with cordiality. In the regular theatre, when you leave the masters, you find, beneath their rank, dozens and scores of serious, not unworthy students. At the music-hall, below the rank of the big men, you find, I must suppose, here and there a man who has something of his own to give you that you can enjoy and even profit by. But you find him rarely. No. The moment in which I have praised warmly is the very moment for saying that the men, generally, at the music-halls—I mean the singing men and the comedians, not the gymnasts and athletes who give the music-hall a certain *raison d'être*, and bring into the Strand and Leicester Square an ' Olympic game,' as it were, up to date and fitted for the needs of London—that the men, generally, at the music-halls (unless, indeed, they are to be judged from the point of view of the gallery) are incomparably tiresome, incomparably dull—not seldom even revolting.

In discussing women—in estimating something of their charm upon the stage, if not exactly in weighing their pure artistic merit—it may be that the average frequenter of the halls and the occasional visitor, whose interest in an art may be presumed to be more serious, stand more on common ground. The fact may bring a little undue tenderness into the verdict ; but is it, after all, unfair, and is it not, at all events, true that the ladies of the music-hall profession do reach at least a higher average of charm and of attainment than the men ? Here of course the accomplishment of the dance comes in; and must be taken account of, as well as a certain amount of talent, which rarely, I fear, reaches to high 'accomplishment,' in vocalisation or comedy. Very few indeed of the music-hall singers (I am talking now of the ladies) would appear to have ever thought it necessary, in their song, to add Art to Nature—to have studied voice-production. And either the quality of the voice is often pitiably unmusical, or it is strained to hold its own against the too loud accompaniment of the band, or it is practically sacrificed to jerky, loud effects and gestures supposed to be telling. There are, of course, certain exceptions—amongst them, one or two young people whose romping songs, whose graceful dances, have brought them lately from the Music-Hall to the Dramatic Stage.

The halls contain, no doubt, a fair proportion of young women whose intelligence includes humour. Here and there one of them, possessed of the seven devils of her music-hall energy, triumphantly cultivates the eccentric and *bizarre*. But the stage of the halls does not, it seems, present us with many women whose sense of humour is made manifest by any exhibition of their own observation of life; and vivacity, sometimes natural, sometimes forced—animal spirit or the semblance of it—may have to take the place of the real sense of comedy.

Here and there again—it may be in their occasional excursions into pantomime—one sees, in this or that young 'artist,' spontaneous fun and happy humour, more range, more delicate capacity than the music-hall has ever permitted her to show. And then one hopes, of course, that the Stage proper will become that artist's recognised and customary place.

But let me take my reader into my confidence, and tell him, now, that when I venture to express a pious hope of this sort, I never feel quite sure that it will be shared at all, or at all appreciated, by whatever person happens to be the subject of it. For there comes in that which we have always with us—there comes the great question of money; and it needs a pure theatrical success, important, unmistakable, quite out of the common, to permit to gifted youth at the theatre any such receipts as may be gathered by rushing over the town in a professional's brougham, and dancing at three halls every evening. And now that I have raised the question of money, let it be said incidentally that the receipts of the profession vary almost beyond the limits in which they vary in any other calling. There are those who hold themselves, or whose managers hold them, not insufficiently remunerated by the salary of an ordinary ballet-girl— about a guinea and a half a week. Four hundred a week was paid, I think, this season, to Yvette Guilbert at the Empire; and it is said that Chevalier has been able to refuse an engagement which would have brought him in eight thousand a year.

As for the order of dancing seen at the music-halls—except for some survivals at the Empire and Alhambra—most of it is French, or has, at least, affinity with French methods rather than with the Italian operatic dancing for which La Scala yet remains the greatest training-place. The French say it takes ten years to make a fine comedian. We English have it—although Miss Vera Beringer is going to prove the saying untrue—that 'nobody is fit to play Juliet till she is unable any longer to look it.' And in Italy they say—the masters at La Scala say—it takes ten years to learn to do much more upon your toes than other people do upon the soles of their feet. The Italian art, however, such as it is—and I am bound to say that, perhaps because I am ignorant, I am not particularly fond of it—is something more than painfully acquired agility. The merit of such dancing is not obvious. It wants a trained spectator as well as a trained performer. It is a conventional art, in which every movement has a meaning the Italians understand. It is a language of the stage which has been handed down, like Masonic secrets. But, as has been implied already, there is perhaps no reason to be sorry for what must be described as its decline in England. In the English or French skirt or step dance, there is more grace, more joy. At least these give us the quick and lissom and unfettered movement of the whole elegant figure, and swaying lines of supple drapery, and changeful hues.

At music-halls, the songs, or those with the best chances of being popular, are written, chiefly, by only two or three writers ; and to this fact sometimes is attributed what must be called their painful monotony, or, at the least, unhappy paucity, of theme. You have the mother-in-law, and the mother-in-law, of course, is a nuisance and an obstacle. You have the deceiving husband. You have the deceived, or the deceiving, wife. Every one, it seems, is busy in doing that which he pretends not to be doing, yet which all the world assumes that he is certain to do. Along with these out-worn themes, from which one would fain seek relief in some fresh observation of life and of the passing manners of the day, you have, occasionally, if the hall is 'popular' rather than fashionable, some very broad compliment to what are called the ' working classes ' as the base—the inevitable, priceless, base—of society's column ; and you have, in times especially of excitement, appeals to patriotism, some of which are sound, but some of which make one think of M. de la Rochefoucauld's remark that there are ' few of us who have not sufficient strength to bear the misfortunes '—yes; even if those misfortunes be the wounds and death—' of other people.' The effect of familiarity and poverty of theme in the actual songs of the music-halls, is minimised, it is true, to some extent, by the measure of ' gag,' of fresh and personal matter, which the best comedians of the music-hall—and many who are not the best—allow themselves to intro-duce. But, after all, of the songs of the music-hall it has got to be said, in parting from them, that the greater part of their comedy is based on coarseness, and that if you can imagine the relation of the sexes deprived altogether of its carnal side, or, if you will, that carnal side accepted once for all as healthy and above board and so not open to innuendo or comment, the song of the music-hall would at a stroke be deprived of half of its material.

And now, with perfect frankness, though, as I hope, with no great lack of tolerance or charity, I have spoken of some of the characteristics of the entertainment. That entertainment cannot, as a whole, claim to be elevating or refined. There are particulars in which it is worthy of praise; details, too, for which it is to be energetically blamed. I praise it for the occasional daintiness of its appeal to our natural senses of pleasure; and blame it for the little call it makes on our intelligence, and yet more for its too easy acquiescence in the grosser view of Life which is taken, undoubtedly, by no small part of its habitual patrons. Much that it affects to be, it cannot fairly claim to be; but whatever be its qualities or its merits, its variety, its elasticity, no one can contest. And herein lies, one may suppose, its hope for the Future. The managers of music-halls— though, of course, not at bottom more intelligent—are less conservative than average managers of theatres; they vie with each other—many of them—in the presentation of the new thing, whatever the new thing may be.

One of the newest things just now is the popularisation of discoveries. That is better than such feats of the acrobat as involve some danger and little skill—great jumps, for instance, in which, though pluck is there, there is very little besides—feats which are little real test of endurance or of strength, and which, unlike some other acrobatic feats which one witnesses with joy at the same places, permit no exhibition of the disciplined and graceful and finely modelled form. Far better is it too—a thousand times better—than the 'turn' of the extraordinary animal, subdued and trained—taught, as recent accounts tell us, to do wonders on the stage at the cost often of only too much cruelty before the footlights have been faced, or when the curtain has fallen. There are music-halls which put before us—and the audience takes great interest in them—the revelations of the X rays. The Kinetophone is not at the halls yet, perhaps; but it is probably on the way to them. The Kinematograph is already at more than one of them, showing a stormy sea, the Thames at Waterloo Bridge, the race for the Derby. Panorama-like almost in continuity, but, after all, like nothing but life itself, the actual scene, the actual world, there flash before you nine hundred and fifty instantaneous records in a minute, blending in an effect that is that, really, of your very presence on the Downs. The house holds its breath till it is over; cheers lustily the moment it is done. No sagacious person would suggest, of course, that the entertainment of

song and dance and of the observation of Life, more or less comic
generally—in rarest instances a little tender—shall yield place in any
great measure to the popularised science of the Polytechnic. That
suggestion is for the *doctrinaire* who takes no account of what Humanity
is made of—of its need, sometimes, of simple pleasure, simple fun.
But, certainly, these recent discoveries of science—their popularisation
at the music-halls—opens new doors : spreads out a new vista. Anything that brings a better class of people to the performance has an
influence in improving the performance as a whole. It is the business
of the music-hall manager to see to it, that, not only in material
things, but in Art and Tone, his entertainment (which the million
now-a-days flocks to) travels steadily upon the ' up-grade.'

FREDERICK WEDMORE.

ARE MANNERS DISAPPEARING FROM GREAT BRITAIN?

AN American who has seen much of the world and of society once remarked that 'manners had disappeared from America and were rapidly vanishing from Europe.' Is this remark true as regards Great Britain? In answer some cynics might reply, that as Britons never have been known to possess any manners, there can be no question of their disappearance; and in a certain sense the cynics would be right, for, in outward forms of politeness, history and biography unite in telling us that for centuries the art of polite demeanour between man and man, at all events amongst the highest classes, has been more cultivated and practised in the genial climes of France, Spain, and Italy than under the grey and frigid skies of Britain. But although the Englishman has rarely been able to rival the polished manners of his continental neighbours, he has never wholly neglected the art of courtesy, and it is only within quite recent years that it has become reasonable to ask, whether we may not be within measurable distance of the time when all outward forms of polite demeanour between man and man shall have completely disappeared from British soil. This is no extravagant supposition, for, strange as it may seem, a loud, noisy vulgarity has invaded circles which in the olden days were regarded as the strongholds of conventional etiquette, until, amongst a set of persons in London whose social position gives them an influence far in excess of their merits, it is actually considered the 'smart' thing to be brusque, loud, and self-assertive.

It is usually supposed that democracy and democratic institutions are primarily responsible for the decadence of manners, and so, to a large degree, they are; but it bodes ill for the future of the outward signs of personal courtesy if those who desire to be considered in the front ranks of what is called 'Society' join hands with the democracy in sweeping from British soil the last vestiges of outward courtesy of demeanour.

It is quite true that too much importance may easily be attached to the outward forms of politeness, the absence of which from society

137

need not necessarily imply a lack of kindly feeling in its members. Many are truly courteous who are entirely innocent of the conventional forms of politeness. It is, without doubt, possible to keep the human affections warm within one's heart, and yet be ignorant of a courtly code of manners. The French have for long been esteemed a polite nation, and so they are as far as outward forms are considered ; but most travellers will agree that, except within certain circles, there is more genuine courtesy to be found between man and man in Britain than in France. The average Frenchman will be profuse in the bows which he will make on meeting an acquaintance, but he will often not hesitate, should the occasion arise, to sacrifice others to his own personal comfort. I have seen foreigners at a public entertainment make ladies rise by bowing to them, and then deprive them of their seats in the most polite and graceful manner. An Englishman, on the other hand, will often do a really kind-hearted deed in such an abrupt and awkward fashion as almost to give it the appearance of an insult. The Spaniard habitually places his house and everything in it at the disposal of his guest, but he would be greatly astonished if he were taken at his word. A stranger calls upon a Spaniard when he is at dinner. The latter invites the stranger to dine with him, or offers him something which he may have admired, but unless the dinner or article is very much pressed the invitation and the offer must be regarded in the light of mere polite phrases. Under similar circumstances the Briton would either not make the invitation or offer, or, if he did, would do all he could to render the dinner or the gift acceptable to the stranger, and would endeavour to escape being thanked, whereas the Spaniard expects verbal gratitude for the offer he has no intention of fulfilling. So far do we carry this dislike of phrase-making, that some English men and women find it very difficult to give expression to the genuine gratitude they feel for real benefits received ; and there are some men whose modesty is so perverted that they would, apparently, almost rather be accused of doing something positively wrong than be suspected of having yielded to a kindly sentiment. Hence they are sometimes almost brutal in their manner should they feel constrained to make an offer of assistance to a stranger, and will endeavour to prove that any kindness they may have rendered was entirely accidental, or the unforeseen result of selfish action. There can be no doubt that kindness of heart must take precedence of manners; but, granting this to the full, what valid reason can be adduced for the divorce of the one from the other? Love of truth and detestation of all appearance of insincerity are also sometimes responsible for the apparent rudeness of the Briton; and as far as the cold and stiff manner, and the absence from his speech of flattering or complimentary phrases, are really due to these causes he is scarcely open to blame, for truthfulness and sincerity are to be preferred before politeness ; but by keeping a sympathetic and charitable heart he might often honestly, without injury to his conscience, be able to give expression to the polite phrase, and to substitute a warm and cordial for a cold and repellent attitude.   Manners, surely, should be the outward expression of the genuine or presumed inner feelings of man in his intercourse with his fellow-men, and where his heart does him credit the Englishman should not permit it to be discredited by his action.

As civilisation advances, and as man becomes more and more permeated by its softening influences, it would only be natural that manners should improve, but as a matter of fact the exact reverse would appear to be the case.   It seems as if manners were steadily deteriorating.

Each generation as it comes upon the stage of life is a little less polite in its bearing towards its fellows than the generation which preceded it, and unless a reaction should set in, and that soon, it would not be difficult to predict the date when the attitude of men and women towards each other will be softened by none of the restraining influences of a polite and considerate courtesy.   Some will welcome the advent of a time when everything that a man or woman has or enjoys he or she shall possess by right, and not by the favour of any one, and consequently when there shall be no necessity for the giving or receiving of thanks ; when the equality of all shall be so thoroughly recognised that the politenesses and deferences which proceed in a great degree from the recognition in society of differences of station, of age, and of sex, shall have become completely superfluous, and when politeness between equals shall be esteemed a sign of weakness, and an evil survival from feudal and aristocratic ages.   To such it may be answered that, in so far as polite manners are the outward expression of kindly feelings between man and man, they should be welcome to a democratic creed which professes to teach the brotherhood of man.

Britons have lately been made painfully aware of the unpopularity which they enjoy amongst most of the nations of the earth.   It flatters our national pride to think that the almost universal disfavour with which we are regarded is due to jealousy caused by the exceptional prosperity, advantages, and privileges which we enjoy, and in a certain measure this is the real cause of our unpopularity ; but ask the averagely intelligent foreigner why England is disliked in his country, and whether the question be put to the Russian, the German, or the Frenchman, in a large number of cases the answer will show that his dislike of Great Britain is not based on political reasons, nor caused by jealousy, but is the result of personal experience of the rude and overbearing manner of individual Englishmen with whom the foreigner has been painfully brought into contact.

Some of us seem to forget or ignore the fact, that, as oil lubricates machinery, so does politeness facilitate the relationship of men.

Our manners at home are none of the best, but there are some Britons who have no sooner planted their feet on foreign soil than, instead of inquiring what may be the manners and customs of the country in which they find themselves, and then endeavouring to conform to them, they seem to consider that absence from home entitles them to throw off even the light conventional restraints of British manners, and live as though they considered that this planet and the dwellers on it had been specially created by Providence to cater for the enjoyment of the inhabitants of the British Isles, and more especially of certain members of that favoured race in whom they happen to take the deepest personal interest.

How often, with hot indignation, has one seen British men and women behave abroad as he knows they never would dare to do at home—walking in the streets of large towns, or attending places of fashionable resort, the men in knickerbockers and the women in mountaineering attire, ostentatiously and of set purpose attracting public attention by noisy conversation and affected boisterous merriment!

It is not uncommon to see Englishmen in the halls and corridors of foreign hotels wearing their hats, when every foreigner is bareheaded.

Sometimes such conduct is due to ignorance of foreign customs; but very often, when there is no desire on the part of the Englishman to draw attention to himself by outraging foreign opinion, it is due to British pride, which refuses to alter its manners to suit the customs of the foreigner. Both in Norway and in America I have heard of Englishmen accepting invitations to dinner, and appearing at their hosts' houses in shooting-coats. One can hardly believe that such conduct was the result of ignorance.

How many Britons are there who, in order to ensure against unconscious infraction of local rules of etiquette, take the trouble to learn and follow the polite customs of the country in which they happen to be? How many are there, for instance, who, when seating themselves at, or on leaving, a *table d'hôte* abroad, remember that in most foreign countries it is considered exceedingly rude not to bow to the guests on either side; or will bear in mind that the hat should never be worn indoors, and should always be raised when meeting a male as well as a female acquaintance, when addressing any stranger, or when going in or out of a shop or public restaurant; that in Germany, when paying a visit, no well-bred man or woman ever sits on a sofa without being specially invited by the hostess to do so; that in the same country the unmarried girl invariably grants precedence to the married woman; and that in the case of both sexes youth, when walking with age or rank, should place it on the inner side of the pavement? Such forms and ceremonies differ in most places, but there are few, if any, countries in Europe where there does not exist more polite ceremonial than in England. Some may rejoice at this, and denounce such customs as foolish trifling, and reply that true politeness results from kindness of heart, and not from any established code of ceremonies. The truth of the above proposition has already been acknowledged, but there can be no doubt that the existence of such a code exercises a certain restraint on the selfish, vulgar self-assertion of those (the majority of mankind) who only regulate their actions by the consequences which they entail. In a country where rudeness meets with the punishment of social ostracism they will restrain their selfishness within bounds, but where society is indifferent in the matter they will not recognise any necessity for self-restraint.

How much of the unpopularity of the ruling race in India is due to the arrogance of some Englishmen in that country who call the natives 'niggers,' and who, in their dealings with ancient and aristocratic races, possessed of rigid and well-defined codes of manners, care not to make themselves acquainted with them, or to inquire into the social rank and position of those with whom they come into contact, but treat Hindoos and Mahomedans of gentle blood with as little consideration as they do their own servants? Let us reverse the situation, and imagine Britain a dependency of India. What would be the feelings of British noblemen and gentlemen of position if a Hindu official of no birth or manners, sent to govern an English county, were to treat them in the way in which some British officials are in the habit of dealing with natives of distinction? And yet, when one does meet a true British gentleman (and the race is, happily, not yet quite extinct), he is conscious of a feeling that the world cannot show a similar product of finer make.

The word 'gentleman' represents a British ideal, and is untranslatable in foreign languages; but, alas! the fine clay of which he is made is daily becoming so impregnated with coarse admixtures that there is danger lest, by the gradual deterioration of the quality of the clay, society should mistake pottery for porcelain, and should be content to accept the coarser for the finer article. It would be well for British men and women to consider whether politeness is or is not worth preserving. They should make up their minds on this point, and act accordingly. If they should decide that the cultivation of manners is incompatible with nineteenth-century ideas, and should be allowed to die out with other old-world notions, then, though some of us may regret the decision, we must only bow to the will of the majority; but if, on the other hand, thoughtful people perceive that much is lost to mankind, collectively and individually, by neglecting to study and to practise the little courtesies of life, then let them not by negligence, and, as it were, unbeknown to themselves, permit these habits to pass away without a struggle to maintain them.

There are still in our midst many men and women whose thoughtful courtesy and kindly bearing are in marked contrast with the ill-bred manners of the day. Let these bring their influence to bear on society at large, and by example and precept do their utmost to cause the advent of the time when the British nation, both at home and abroad, shall be distinguished for the politeness of its demeanour.

A true gentleman is naturally courteous—he could hardly be the reverse if he tried ; but in these days, when so many lay claim to the title who possess few of the qualifications of gentility, it may be well to point out that a courteous manner is a quality which, especially in the present days of rudeness, possesses a distinctly commercial value. However boorish we may be ourselves, we all appreciate civility and courtesy in others. We would rather have dealings with a man who treats us with civility, not to say with deference, than with one who treads on our corns and generally irritates us.

If British boys and girls were taught to subordinate self, to respect their neighbours, and in non-essentials not to run counter to their prejudices, we should probably in a few years find that, although for political reasons Great Britain might still maintain that ' splendid isolation ' of which we have lately heard so much, her people were no longer disliked, but by their politeness and urbanity had won the respect and friendship of foreigners, and had thereby increased the influence of their country, and taken the most effective steps to diminish the chances of international misunderstandings.

MEATH.

NEW LETTERS OF EDWARD GIBBON

EDWARD GIBBON has hitherto been known to the world by his history, his autobiography, and a selection from his letters. In the stately style of *The Decline and Fall of the Roman Empire* every word has been weighed and measured for its appropriate place in the balanced period. His autobiography is an elaborate composition, written and rewritten to satisfy a fastidious taste, and finally put together by Lord Sheffield and Lady Maria Holroyd from the different drafts which he left behind him. His letters have been carefully selected, edited, and arranged, in order to show him in the light which his friend and executor thought most becoming to the dignity of a great historian. Everywhere it is Gibbon dressed for effect; the natural man behind is practically unknown. It is Gibbon 'the fine gentleman,' as he appeared when equipped for Boodle's Masquerade at the Pantheon, in ' a fine Velvet Coat, with ruffles of My Lady's chusing,' and in a 'sincerely pretty Wastecoat' sent him by his stepmother.

But Gibbon is one of the greatest names in our prose literature, and what the world wants is to see the man in his unguarded moments, when he is most true to himself; to know him as he was known to his valet Caplen, or his housekeeper Mrs. Ford; to catch him in some natural attitude, as when he forgot the presence of the Princesses at Turin, and 'grew so very free and easy, that I drew my snuffbox, rapped it, took snuff twice (a crime never known before in the presence-chamber), and continued my discourse in my usual attitude of my body bent forwards, and my forefinger stretched out.' This autumn the world will have the opportunity of learning something of the real Gibbon. A mass of his letters will be published, most of which have never before been printed, ranging over a variety of subjects, and touching upon the social gossip of the day, his literary pursuits, his friendships, tastes, and domestic affairs, his parliamentary career, and his political opinions. The letters cover the period from 1753 to 1794. They begin with the time when, as a boy of sixteen, he had become a Roman Catholic, had left Oxford, and was sent to Lausanne to be placed under the care of Pastor Pavillard. They end with his death in London in 1794. Almost every detail of his life is laid bare, and the general result of the self-revelation of his character will undoubtedly be to raise the popular estimate of Gibbon as a man.

Suzanne Curchod, afterwards Madame Necker, has left a picture of Gibbon as he was at the age of twenty. ' Il a de beaux cheveux '— it must be remembered that, at the time she wrote, she was engaged to the youth whom she describes—

la main jolie, et l'air d'une personne de condition. Sa physionomie est si spirituelle et singulière que je ne connois personne qui lui ressemble. Elle a tant d'expression qu'on y découvre presque toujours quelque chose de nouveau. Ses gestes sont si à propos, qu'ils ajoutent beaucoup à ce qu'il dit. En un mot, c'est une de ces physionomies si extraordinaires, qu'on ne se lasse presque point de l'examiner, de le peindre et de le contrefaire. Il connoît les égards que l'on doit aux femmes. Sa politesse est aisée sans être trop familière. Il danse mediocrement.

In this picture it would be difficult to recognise the unwieldy figure of the man who fell on his knees to propose to Madame de Montolieu, and could only rise with the assistance of a servant when he had received his refusal. Nor could M. de Bièvre, who was wont to say that he took his daily exercise by walking three times round M. Gibbon, have imagined that the corpulent critic of Christian dogma was ever ' the thin little figure with a large head,' who astonished M. Pavillard by ' disputing and urging with the utmost ability all the best arguments that had ever been used in favour of popery.'

Gibbon did not long remain a Roman Catholic. The second letter in the forthcoming collection describes his re-conversion. It is amusing to find that he was sufficiently a boy to practise the ingenuous stratagems of artless youth, and to base on the good news of his return to Protestantism an appeal to the generosity of his relations. The letter dated February 1755 is addressed to this maternal aunt, Miss Catherine Porten, the ' Aunt Kitty ' who in his childhood supplied the place of his mother. The first part, which has been already printed, states that he is ' now a good Protestant,' and in stilted language remarks on the difficulty of a Church of England man resolving on ' Communion with Presbyterians.' The second part, which is new, confesses in a curious jargon of English and French his loss of 110 guineas at faro. In his despair he bought a horse from the rook who had plucked him, and set out to ride to England to raise the money. He had only reached Geneva when his tutor recaptured him and brought him back to Lausanne. Would Miss Porten lend him the money? His aunt refused to pay his debt of honour, and the letter is indorsed by his stepmother, Mrs. Gibbon, with the note: ' Pray remember this letter was not addressed to his mother-in-law (*sic*), but his aunt, an old cat as she was to refuse his request.'

Aunt *K*itty's refusal did not, however, impair her nephew's affection. In almost the next letter he tells her, with evident delight, that the bird of prey by whom he had been plucked had fallen into the hands of the ' famous Mr. Taff ' at Paris, and had been stripped of 8,200*l.* This is, in all probability, the Mr. Taaffe who, four years before, had made himself notorious at Paris. With his friends Edward Wortley Montagu and Lord Southwell he invited to his rooms one Abraham Payba, a Jew money-lender, made him drunk, and in less than an hour won from him 800 *louis d'or.* Payba paid his debt with bills which he took care should be dishonoured. Finding themselves outwitted, Taaffe and Wortley Montagu broke into his house and helped themselves to a much larger sum in cash and jewellery. For the robbery they were imprisoned for three months in the Grand Châtelet.

For five years (1753–58) Gibbon lived at Lausanne. Here he pursued the literary studies which bore fruit in his *Essai sur l'étude de la Littérature,* published in French in 1761. He joined too in the social amusements of the town, and in philandering with the young girls who called themselves *La Société du Printemps,* or were associated in the *Académie de la Poudrière.* So long as he was in love with the multitude he was safe; but at these social gatherings he met Suzanne Curchod, the only child of the Pastor of Crassy. In his unpublished journal for June 1757 occurs the entry: 'I saw Mademoiselle Curchod; *Omnia vincit amor, et nos cedamus amori.'* The following lines, quoted from some indifferent verses addressed by him to the object of his worship, expand the idea of the Latin line:

> Tôt ou tard il faut aimer,
> C'est en vain qu'on façonne;
> Tout fléchit sous l'amour,
> Il n'exempte personne,
> Car Gib. a succombé en ce jour
>   Aux attraits d'une beauté,
> Qui parmi les douceurs d'un tranquille silence
> Reposait sur un fauteuil, &c.

The affection of Mademoiselle Curchod was deeply engaged, and he was sufficiently in love to implore her to marry him without waiting for his father's sanction. But his passion seems always to have had the exaggeration of unreality, for Julie von Bondeli, the friend of Rousseau and of Wieland, describes him as waylaying the country people on their way to or from Lausanne, and demanding, at the point of a naked dagger, whether there existed a more adorable creature than Suzanne Curchod.

In April 1758 Gibbon, engaged to be married to Mademoiselle Curchod, left Lausanne to return to England. The Seven Years' War, which, as Horace Walpole says, ' reaches from Muscovy to Alsace and from Madras to California,' rendered all roads more or less impracticable, and Gibbon tells his father that he shall travel as 'a Swiss officer,' with ' Dutch regimentals and a passport from the Canton of Berne. I am pretty sure,' he adds, 'that my tongue won't betray me.' He had been in England two months when he wrote to his

aunt, Miss Hester Gibbon, a letter which is interesting from the fore-
taste which it affords of the future historian's style, a style that is
strikingly contrasted with the ease of his ordinary correspondence.
Miss Hester Gibbon, it should be said, had taken William Law, the
author of the *Serious Call,* for her spiritual adviser and almoner, and
supported by her charities various educational and philanthropic
institutions which Law administered at King's Cliff in Northampton-
shire. 'Though the public voice,' writes her nephew and natural
heir in July 1758,

had long since accustomed me to think myself honoured in calling Mrs. Gibbon
my aunt, yet I never enjoyed the happiness of living near her, and of instructing
myself not less by her example than by her precepts. Your piety, Madam, has
engaged you to prefer a retreat to the world. Errors, justifiable only in their
principle, forced my father to give me a foreign education. Fully disabused of the
unhappy ideas I had taken up, and at last restored to myself, I am happy in the
affection of the tenderest of fathers. May I not hope, Madam, to see my felicity
compleat by the acquisition of your esteem and friendship? Duty and Inclination
engage me equally to solicit them, all my endeavours shall tend to deserve them,
and with Mrs. Gibbon I know that to deserve is to obtain.

Gibbon's mode of life would not perhaps have satisfied Miss Hester
Gibbon. He had intended to pass his winters in London, and his
summers with his father and step-mother at Beriton, near Petersfield
in Hampshire. The first winter after his return from Lausanne was
spent, according to this plan, in London, where he was negotiating
the publication of his *Essai sur l'étude de la Littérature.* He was
without acquaintances in the fashionable world, though it was, even
at this time, his ambition to be treated as a man of fashion. His few
friends were chiefly literary men, whom he knew through David
Mallet. The coffee-house which he frequented was the Smyrna in
Pall Mall, the haunt of writers, and still tenanted by the shades of
the *Spectator* and the *Tatler.* He belonged to no club, and lodged
over a 'linnen draper's' in New Bond Street, where he had 'a very
good first floor dining-room, bed-chamber, and light closet, with many
conveniences, for a guinea and a half.' His 'very handsome chair'
cost him twenty-seven shillings. His one fashionable acquaintance
was Lady Hervey, the 'beautiful Molly Lepel' of the Hanoverian
Court in the early quarter of the century, the widow of the 'Sporus'
of Pope and the Boswell of Queen Caroline and George the Second,
and the mother of three successive earls of Bristol.

His plans for the summer were disturbed by the calling out of the
militia as a permanent force. The South Battalion of the Hampshire
Militia, which he joined as captain, and of which he ultimately
became colonel, was kept continuously 'under arms, in constant pay
and duty,' from June 1759 to December 1762. No stranger position
could be imagined for the future historian. Francis Osbaldeston
himself was not more out of his element among his cock-fighting,

fox-hunting, horse-couping cousins than was Gibbon in the society
in which he was compelled to live. In his unpublished Diary he thus
describes his brother officers: 'no manners, no conversation, they
were only a set of fellows all whose behaviour was low, and most of
whose characters were despicable.' The sarcastic lines of Dryden
might have been the motto of the battalion:

> Of seeming arms they make a short essay;
> Then hasten to be drunk—the business of the day.

His Diary is a curious mixture of criticism of Greek and Latin
authors, analyses of the books which he read, reflections on historical
characters, excursuses on Greek particles, and of such entries as the
following:

August 22, 1762.—Last night Captain Perkins led us into an intemperance we
have not known for some time past. I could do nothing this morning but spew.
I scarce wonder at the Confessor who enjoined getting drunk as a penance.

August 28, 1762.—To-day Sir Thomas [Worsley, the Colonel of the Battalion]
came to us to dinner. Pleased to see him, we kept bumperising till after roll-
calling, Sir Thomas assuring us every fresh bottle how infinitely soberer he was
grown.

September 29, 1762.—We drank a vast deal too much wine to-day, and had a
most disagreeable proof of the pernicious consequences of it. I quarrelled when I
was drunk with my good friend Harrison (the Lord knows for what), and had
not some of the company been sober, it might have been a very serious affair.

Yet Gibbon had the good sense to see that his military training
was an advantage to him. If it initiated him into one of the vices
of the age, it also taught the raw youth, 'quiet, retired, somewhat
reserved' as he describes himself, to hold his own in the world. He
agreed with Dr. Johnson in thinking that 'a camp, however
familiarly we may speak of it, is one of the great scenes of human
life,' and, from his own experience, he might have said with Lord
Chesterfield that 'Courts and camps are the only places to learn the
world in.'

In the summer of 1762 the Seven Years' War began to draw to
an end. Peace was in the air. Gibbon was preparing for the Grand
Tour, on which his heart had long been set. His first step was to
break off his engagement with Mademoiselle Curchod, for part of his
plan was a visit to Lausanne. An attempt has been recently made to
show that he behaved badly towards the girl whose affection he had
won. Probably there were faults on both sides. He had heard from
his friend M. d'Eyverdun that Mademoiselle Curchod had been
inconstant, and there is no reason to suppose that he did not believe
the report. When he reached Lausanne he received a letter from
her in which she said that she had never ceased to love him. He
thus comments upon it in his unpublished Diary:

J'ai reçu une lettre des moins attendues. C'étoit de Mademoiselle C. Fille
dangereuse et artificielle! Elle fait une apologie de sa conduite depuis le premier

moment qu'elle m'a connû, sa constance pour moi, son mepris de M. de Montplaisir, et la fidelité delicate et soutenue qu'elle a cru voir dans la lettre où je lui annoncois qu'il n'y avoit plus d'espérance. Les voyages à Lausanne, les adorations qu'elle y a eû, et la complaisance avec laquelle elle les a ecouté formoient l'article le plus difficile à justifier. Ni d'Eyverdun (dit elle), ni personne, n'ont effacé pendant un moment mon image de son cœur. Elle s'amusoit à Lausanne sans y attacher. Je le veux. Mais ces amusements la convainquent toujours de la dissimulation la plus odieuse, et, si l'infidelité est quelquefois une foiblesse, la duplicité est toujours un vice. Cette affaire singulière en toutes ses parties m'a été très utile ; elle m'a ouvert les yeux sur le caractère des femmes et elle me servira longtemps de preservatif contre les seductions de l'amour.

In January 1763 Gibbon left England for the Continent. His letters are not mere topographical descriptions, but are full of interest from their notes on men and things. In the eighteenth century we were almost continuously at war with France ; yet we were then as popular with our avowed enemies as we are now disliked by our so-called friends.

What Cromwell wished [he writes from Paris] is now litterally the case. The name of Englishman inspires as great an idea at Paris as that of Roman could at Carthage after the defeat of Hannibal. Indeed, the French are almost excessive. From being very unjustly esteemed a set of pirates and Barbarians, we are now, by a more agreable injustice, looked upon as a nation of Philosophers and Patriots.

His own position at Paris is interesting. On the score of his *Essai*, which in England was ignored, he was received as a man of letters. The one fly in the amber of his pleasure was that he could not satisfy his ambition to be regarded as a man of fashion. The *salon* at which he was most welcomed was that of Madame Geoffrin, the widow of a wealthy ice-merchant, and nicknamed by Madame du Deffand *la mère des philosophes*. His reception at Paris in 1777 was very different, and marks the advance that he had made in the social position, which he valued more highly than literary fame.

At Lausanne he lingered several months, engaged, as he tells his stepmother, ' in a considerable work, which will be a most usefull preparation to my tour of Italy.' It is the first hint of the design which took shape at Rome in the *Decline and Fall of the Roman Empire*. ' It is,' he continues,—

a description of the ancient Geography of Italy, taken from the Original writers. If I go into Italy with a work of that kind tolerably executed, I shall carry everywhere about with me an accurate and lively idea of the country, and shall have nothing to do but to insert in their proper places my own observations as they tend to confirm, to confute, or to illustrate what I have met with in books. I should not even despair, but that this mixture of study and observation, properly digested upon my return to England, might produce something not entirely unworthy the eye of the publick on a subject upon which we have no regular or compleat treatise.

With this object in view he worked hard at Lausanne and subsequently travelled through Italy. Scarcely a detail of his plan appears in his letters, which are rather written to distract his own mind from such serious subjects than to instruct his father and stepmother. Here, for example, is a picture of Voltaire in his retirement at Ferney, which will serve as a sample of his letters from abroad. It should be mentioned that in 1757–58, when Voltaire was settled at Monrepos, Gibbon had seen him act in his tragedies of *Zaïre Alzire, Zulime*, and his sentimental comedy, *L'Enfant Prodigue*.

After a life passed in courts and Capitals, the Great Voltaire is now become a meer country Gentleman, and even (for the honor of the profession) something of a farmer. He says he never enjoyed so much true happiness. He has got rid of most of his infirmities, and tho' very old and lean, enjoys a much better state of health than he did twenty years ago. His playhouse is very neat and well contrived, situated just by his Chappel, which is far inferior to it, tho', he says himself, 'que son Christ est du meilleur faiseur de tout le pays de Gex.' The play they acted was my favourite *Orphan of China*. Voltaire himself acted Gengis, and Madame Denys Idamé; but I do not know how it happened: either my taste is improved or Voltaire's talents are impaired since I last saw him. He appeared to me now a very ranting unnatural performer. Perhaps, indeed, as I was come from Paris, I rather judged him by an unfair comparaison than by his own independent value. Perhaps too I was too much struck with the ridiculous figure of Voltaire at seventy acting a Tartar Conqueror with a hollow broken voice, and making love to a very ugly niece of fifty. The play began at eight in the evening, and ended (entertainment and all) about half an hour after eleven. The whole Company was asked to stay and set Down about twelve to a very elegant supper of a hundred Covers. The supper ended about two, the company danced till four, when we broke up, got into our Coaches, and came back to Geneva just as the Gates were opened. Show me in history or fable, a famous poet of Seventy who has acted in his own plays, and has closed the scene with a supper and ball for a hundred people. I think the last is the more extraordinary of the two.

After Gibbon's return to England in June 1765, he resumed his old manner of life, spending his summer months at Beriton and the winter in London, occupied either in literary work or in the less congenial task of endeavouring to extricate his father from his pecuniary embarrassments. In 1770 the elder Mr. Gibbon died, and the son succeeded to the wreck of what had once been an ample fortune. 'Economy,' he tells his aunt, Miss Hester Gibbon,

was not amongst my father's Virtues. The expences of the more early part of his life, the miscarriage of several promising schemes, and a general want of order and exactness involved him in such difficulties as constrained him to dispose of Putney, and to contract a mortgage so very considerable that it cannot be paid unless by the sale of our Buckinghamshire Estate. The only share that I have ever taken in these transactions has been by my sensibility to my father's wants and my compliance with his inclinations, a conduct which has cost me very dear, but which I cannot repent. It is a satisfaction to reflect that I have fulfilled, perhaps exceeded, my filial duties; and it is still in my power with the remains of our fortunes to lead an agreable and rational life.

Even this satisfaction he was at first denied. His stepmother had heard a rumour that his own imprudence was the cause of the financial difficulties. He repudiates the suggestion with some warmth and

considerable dignity. 'As a raw lad of one and twenty, unacquainted
with law or business, and desirous of obliging' his father, he had consented to join in cutting off the entail and raising a mortgage of
10,000*l.*   But he had none of the money for himself, neither was it
raised to pay his debts.   His allowance was never more than 300*l.* a
year, and on that he lived.   He had never had any other debts than
common tradesmen's bills, trifling in amount and annually paid.   'I
have never lost at play a hundred pounds at any one time; perhaps
not in the course of my life.   Play I neither love nor understand.'
He had probably, for the moment, forgotten his losses as a boy at
Lausanne.   'I should deserve the imputation,' he continues, 'could
I submit to it with patience.   As long as you credit it, you must
view me in the light of a specious Hypocrite, who meanly cloaked
his own extravagancies under his father's imprudence, and who
ascribed to filial piety what had been the consequence of folly and
necessity.'

Gibbon was now a landed proprietor, and no man could be more
unfitted for the part.   For a few weeks the novelty of the position
amused him, and he asks with some show of interest after the breaking
in of the colt, the progress of the rot among the sheep, or the prospect
of improved prices in wheat.   He even hugs himself with self-
satisfaction at the shrewd bargains which 'Farmer Gibbon' has driven
in letting his farms, or at the judgment with which he has sold his
hops.   But to a man of his tastes and temper the details of estate
management and the strenuous idleness of country life grew intole-
rably irksome.   Dilatory in his habits, his letters are a treasury of
excuses for unpunctuality in correspondence.   He had no country
pursuits.   His sporting friends are savages who hunt foxes.   'Neither
a pack of hounds, nor a stable of running horses, nor a large farm'
had any interest for him.   Magisterial work did not appeal to him.
'I detest,' he says, 'your races, I abhor your assizes.'   The rustic
mind was unintelligible to him, and he to it.   If his tenants wished
to see him, he would make any concession to avoid a deputation of
the 'savages.'   While he is negotiating the sale of one of his estates, he
has an interview with the agent and the proposed purchaser: 'though
we did not speak the same language,' he says, 'yet by the help of
signs, such as that of putting about the bottle, the natives seemed
well satisfied.'   In all matters of business he was careless, forgetful,
impatient of legal forms, helpless as a child.   If his signature is
required to a deed, he is sure to sign his name in the wrong place.
If he is asked to make interest on behalf of a friend, the letter is
probably placed in the wrong enclosure, and 'Lord Milton's heir was
ordered to send me without delay a brown Ratteen Frock, and the
Taylor was desired to use his interest with his cousin the Duke of
Dorset.'   It is not therefore surprising that he soon grew 'tired of

sticking to the earth by so many Roots,' or that before many months
Beriton was let, and Gibbon settled in London.

In 1773 he took from Lady Rous the lease of No. 7 Bentinck
Street. It was now that his real life began. He was like a child
with a new toy, immersed in the mysteries of furnishing, and closeted
for hours with 'Ireland, the Upholder.' His library especially was
to be a triumph of art. Mahogany bookcases were proscribed. 'The
paper of the Room will be a fine, shag, flock paper, light blue with a
gold border, the Book-cases painted white, ornamented with a light
frize: neither Doric nor Dentulated Adamic.' Once settled in his
house, with his books round him, he left his library with reluctance
except for society.

> This abominable fine weather [he says] will not allow me a quiet hour at home
> without being liable to the reproaches of my friends and of my own conscience.
> It is the more provoking as it drives me out of my own new, clean, comfortable,
> dear house, which I like better every week I pass in it. I now live, which I never
> did before, and if it would but rain, should enjoy that unity of study and society
> in which I have always placed my prospect of happiness.

London was to him never dull; there at least he could keep 'the
monster Ennui at a respectfull distance.' For him its heat was
always tempered; even its solitude was 'delicious.' In 'the soft
retirement of my *bocage de* Bentinck Street,' the dog days pass
unheeded.

> Charming hot Weather! I am just going to dine alone. Afterwards I shall
> walk till dark in *my* gardens at Kensington, and shall then return to a frugal
> supper and early bed in Bentinck Street. I lead the life of a true Philosopher,
> without any regard to the world or to fashion.

Master of a good house, possessed of rare conversational powers, as
an Amphitryon *où l'on dine*, the giver of the 'prettiest little dinners
imaginable,' Gibbon soon made his way in London society. He had
come up to the metropolis knowing only a few second-rate men of
letters. His militia training had made him acquainted with the
county members and a few of the county gentlemen of Hampshire
and Berkshire. His grand tour had widened the circle of his friends.
Now he was a welcome guest in London houses. The doors of exclusive clubs, though he was a bad whist-player and never gambled, were
opened to him. He joined the Catch Club; he became a member of
Boodle's, of Almack's, and of Brooks's. At the latter he was a well-
known figure. In some verses written by Richard Tickell in 1780 to
celebrate the election of the Hon. John Townshend for the University
of Cambridge occur the lines:—

> Soon as to Brookes's thence they footsteps bend,
> What gratulations thy approach attend!
> See Gibbon rap his box: auspicious sign
> That wit and classic compliment combine.

As M.P. for Liskeard and subsequently for Lymington (1774–84), his position was still more assured.   The publication of the first volume of the *Decline and Fall of the Roman Empire* in 1776 made him a literary lion.   'I have the satisfaction,' he writes to his stepmother, a month after the appearance of his book, 'of telling you that my book has been very well received' by men of letters, men of the world, and even by fine feathered Ladies, in short by every set of people except perhaps by the Clergy, who seem (I know not why) to show their teeth on the occasion.   A thousand Copies are sold, and we are preparing a second Edition, which in so short a time is, for a book of that price, a very uncommon event.'   Men of letters and men of fashion had been, for at least a hundred years, divided by a gulf which patronage scarcely pretended to span.   Horace W_{alpole}, indeed, dabbled in literature, though scholars unfairly sneered at his literary pretensions.   Gibbon, on the other hand, forced the learned to admit that he was their master with their own weapons, and that his knowledge and industry were equal to his natural genius.   On the whole he bore his honours meekly.   He makes no secret that his vanity was flattered by his success; but he remained the same good-natured, kind-hearted man that he was before he woke to find himself famous throughout Europe.

His correspondence ripens under the pleasant sun of prosperity. For the amusement of his stepmother he becomes the Court newsman, the theatrical critic, the literary adviser, and even the retailer of gossip.   It is for her benefit, for instance, that he tells the story of the duel to which Lord Bellamont challenged Lord Townshend, and its amusing sequel.

> I am so unfashionable as not to have fought a duel yet.   I suppose all the Nation will admire Lord B.'s behaviour.   I will give you one instance of his—call it what you please.   Lord T.'s pistol was raised when he called out, 'One moment, my Lord; Mr. Dillon, I have undertaken a commission from the French Embassador—to get him some Irish poplins.   Should I fall, be so good as to execute it. Your Lordship may now fire.'

Six weeks later, he writes again :

> This morning, the fact is certain, an Address was delivered to Lord B. from the Grand Jury of the County of Dublin, thanking him for his proper and spirited behaviour.   Incomparable Hibernians!   A Judicial Body, appointed to maintain and execute the Laws, publicly applaud a man for having broke them.

For his friend Holroyd, afterwards Lord Sheffield, he collects the latest political intelligence, and flavours his reports with the most recent scandal of the clubs or the green room.   Gibbon sat in Parliament throughout the American War; he was an intimate friend of Lord North, Charles James Fox, and Lord George Germain; he witnessed the overthrow of the favourite minister of George the Third, and the commencement of Pitt's parliamentary career.   The times were full of excitement, and Gibbon, though a silent member, was a shrewd observer. Onlookers often see the most of the game. Some of the interest of the political letters lies in the restoration of passages which Lord Sheffield had suppressed. One example must suffice. In 1788 Fox paid Gibbon a visit at Lausanne, and he describes with enthusiasm the charm of that statesman's conversation. But Lord Sheffield omits the account of Mrs. Armstead, who was travelling with Fox, and of the effect which her presence produced. 'The wit and beauty of his Companion,' writes Gibbon, 'are not sufficient to excuse the scandalous impropriety of shewing her to all Europe, and you will not easily conceive how he has lost himself in the public opinion, which was already more favourable to his Rival. Will Fox never know the importance of character?'

Gibbon carefully studied for himself the questions at issue in the American War. From Israel Mauduit, the agent of Massachusetts Bay, and from Governor Hutchinson, he gathered material for forming an independent judgment. 'I think,' he says, 'I have sucked them very dry; and if my confidence was equal to my eloquence, and my eloquence to my knowledge, perhaps I might make no very intolerable Speaker.' It is curious to note in his letters the apathy of Parliament on the subject. 'In this season and on America,' he writes in May 1775, 'the Archangel Gabriel would not be heard.' His own opinion was, on several points, adverse to the policy of the Government, which, except on one occasion, he steadily supported. He was one of those indolent men who attach themselves to political leaders rather than to political principles. For Lord North he felt a warm affection, and throughout voted with him, sometimes against his better judgment.

His speech would probably have been silver; his silence was certainly golden. In 1778 he was appointed a Commissioner of Trade and Plantations, with a salary of 750*l.* a year. Fox believed that he had been bribed by office, and expressed the belief in the lines :—

> King George, in a fright
> Lest Gibbon should write
> The story of England's disgrace,
> Thought no way so sure
> His pen to secure
> As to give the historian place.

Gibbon held the appointment till the abolition of the office in 1782. The loss of it decided him to leave England, though his friends were influential and active, and he might have secured another post. He was rapidly getting into debt, and he was anxious to finish his History. In 1784 he settled at Lausanne, and there passed the remainder of his life. It was on his second visit to England, in 1793–94, that he died on the 16th of January, 1794, at 76 St. James's Street, the house of Peter Elmsley, the bookseller.

It may be asked, in what way do these letters raise the popular view of Gibbon's character? Indolent and easy-going as he was, he was capable of making moral resolutions and of adhering to them with determination. At one time Gibbon fell into the habit of excessive drinking, which was a vice of social life. But in 1764 at Lausanne, after a drunken orgy, he was made aware that he had forfeited the respect of his better friends, and he cured himself of the vice, without adopting the desperate remedy of total abstinence. It was an age when men staked their fortunes on the fall of cards. Gibbon never gambled. It was an age when the tone of society was grossly immoral. Gibbon could say in 1774 : 'You once mentioned Miss F[uller]. I give you my honour, that I have not either with her, or any other woman, any connection that could alarm a wife.' He went into Parliament with the intention of obtaining a lucrative office. But he valued his own independence so highly that, to secure it, he not only toiled laboriously with his pen, but voluntarily exiled himself from England when, to a man of his age and tastes, such a wrench must have been severe.

For friendship he had a true genius. No trouble was too great to be taken for a friend, and this by a man who loved his ease to excess. To be by the side of Lord Sheffield, who had recently lost his wife, he hurried home to England from Lausanne at a time when the beginning of the Revolutionary War made his journey difficult, if not hazardous. He was a friend of children and a lover of dogs. His letters about little 'Datch' Holroyd, a son of his friend who died in childhood, shows his tender nature. The dogs to which he attached himself were not the breeds that appeal to sportsmen ; but the following passage from a letter, written to thank his stepmother for the gift of a Pomeranian, shows that he loved canine society :—

After drinking coffee in the Library, we went downstairs again, and as we entered the Parlour, our ears were saluted with a very harmonious barking, and our eyes gratified by the sight of one of the prettiest animals I ever saw. Her figure and coat are perfect, her manners genteel and lively, and her teeth (as a pair of ruffles have already experienced) most remarkably sharp. She is not the least fatigued with her voyage, and compleatly at home in Bentinck Street. I call her *Bath*. Gibbon would be ambiguous, and Dorothea [1] disrespectful.

In a note accepting an invitation to Twickenham, he calls the Thames an 'amiable creature.' It is pleasing to relate that on his way he was upset into the water, and received a ducking for the affectation. But an affected manner could not conceal his kindness of heart. For his housekeeper, Mrs. Ford, he was careful to provide a support in her old age ; his butler, Caplen, though he could not speak a word of French, refused a proffered pension and insisted on following him to Lausanne. To young men and boys he took the

---

[1] The Christian name of his stepmother.

pains, even when he was famous, to make himself agreeable. The recollections of the younger Colman may be quoted as a proof. 'The great historian,' says Colman, writing of a time when he was himself a boy, 'was bright and playful, suiting his matter to the capacity of the boy : but it was done *more sua* (*sic*); still his mannerisms prevailed : still he tapped his snuff-box; still he smirked, and smiled, and rounded his periods with the same air of good-breeding, as if he was conversing with men.'

Above all, Gibbon was a straightforward, strictly honourable man. His relations and Lady Sheffield were always seeking him a wife, nor, as his letters show, was Gibbon averse to the idea of matrimony. But he made no secret of his opinions on questions of religion, and was careful that, if inquired into, they should be known. 'The Lady Mother,' he writes,

has given as proper an answer as can be expected. There is only one part of it which distresses me—*Religion*. Your evasion was very able; but will not prudence as well as honour require us being more explicit in the *suite*? Ought I to give them room to think that I should patiently conform to family prayers and Bishop Hooper's Sermons? I would not marry an Empress on those conditions.

After all, what occasion is there to enquire into my profession of faith? It is surely much more to the purpose for them to ask, how I have already acted in life—whether as a good son, a good friend, whether I game, drink, &c. You know I never practised the one, and in spite of my old *Dorsetshire* character, I have left off the other.

Gibbon had his faults; but, judged by the contents of these letters, and by the standard which he himself proposes, there can be but one answer to the questions he suggests, and that answer is emphatically in his favour.

ROWLAND E. PROTHERO.

THE FEDERATION MOVEMENT IN AUSTRALASIA

THROUGHOUT the provinces of Australia, in the Garden Island, Tasmania, and in a lesser degree over the Britain of the South, New Zealand, the idea of a Federated Australasia finds general acceptance. Leaders of men, and they who follow not too blindly, concur in the view that this Federation of the seven constitutionally governed colonies in the Austral seas, together with Fiji, British New Guinea, and any other British territories in the South and West Pacific, must eventually be achieved ; and he who is an enthusiast in the cause, not yet daunted by delays and backslidings on the part of Federationists, asks when, and under what conditions, and by whose agency this splendid dream will be realised. At the National Australasian Convention held in Sydney in 1891, the late Sir Henry Parkes, then Prime Minister of New South Wales, spoke confidently of Federation being accomplished in two years. But those two years came and went, and yet another two years, without any nearer approach to the ' one nation, one destiny ' that had been so confidently predicted by that statesman. And when in January 1895 the six Premiers of Australia and Tasmania met in conference in Hobart, to formulate some plan by which Federation could be urged forward, Sir Henry Parkes, then a private member of the New South Wales Assembly (and soon to become a private citizen, bereft of even his M.P.-ship), spoke in scornful terms of those statesmen who were seeking to achieve that which he had vainly dreamt of as the immediate result of his initiative.

Who will be the instruments that shall lead the peoples to the destined goal ? None of those, I venture to predict, who occupy the recognised position of leaders while the petty, personal jealousies and rivalries of fallen statesmen or discredited politicians intervene to frustrate action—not by these and not at all shall this great end be attained, until the peoples who should be led become the leaders, and the *vox populi* demands that the thing shall be done without further babble. And even if the popular guides could be brought to such a wholesome frame of mind as would induce them to welcome any instrument efficient for their purpose, and hail the accomplishment of Federation while standing humbly aside, self-effaced in their disinterested loyalty—even then Federation, as I see it, must be the act of the people, only to be brought about when the people are educated to this lofty but quite practicable ideal.

And when will the people recognise that herein their prosperity, their strength, and their security lie? When patriotic men shall teach to some purpose instead of leading in purblind fashion only to attain a present object, and when communities shall take a national instead of a parochial view of affairs, and recognise that no nation can be great wherein the individual interest is preferred to the general; that no nation can be wealthy when the common fund is depleted to support exotic industries; that no nation can be powerful where a scattered people, broken up into semi-hostile clans, have no united purpose of defence.

It is sometimes said that the Australasian Colonies will only become one under the shadow of the sword. But what sort of Federation would that be which came of a sudden panic—the haphazard creation of a threatened invasion—even if the invader gave such notice of his coming as would admit of any manner of union? Or what would be the prospect of an effective Federation after a foreign foe had raided and plundered and left an Australasia crippled as to population, wealth, and commerce, and thrown back in the path of progress by half a century? If Federation is to be of practical advantage for the next generation or two, it should be effected now in a time of peace, when statesmen and people can, an they will, give their minds to this great subject.

Australasia (excluding British New Guinea and Fiji) is, except as to population, in advance of the Dominion of Canada; it has greater national resources; it has a larger volume of trade; and (leaving out of consideration the few thousands of aboriginals in Australia, and the Maoris, who number about 40,000) has a population homogeneous as the Canadians are not even now. The Federation of the provinces of the Dominion was effected although Englishmen and Frenchmen had to unite in the common *bund*; although the French language and French laws and customs remained, as indeed, to a great extent, they still endure. Federation is moving on in South Africa, where English and Dutch occupy towards each other much the same position as the English and French in Canada. But in Australasia, where only one tongue is known, whether it be spoken by men of British descent or by nationalised Germans or Swedes or other Europeans, and but one code of laws or manners or customs prevails, Federation is made more difficult by its very simplicity; and men who should be brothers are kept asunder by border Custom-houses that are as inappropriate as would be the raising of an octroi barrier at the entrance to every Australasian city or town.

The idea of a Federated Australasia is no new thing in the Austral Colonies. It may be said to be coeval with the creation of responsible government, for when the colony of New South Wales had her constitution under consideration, one of her statesmen—Mr. E. Deas Thomson—urged the necessity of a central Parliament that should be empowered to deal exclusively with some eight subjects that he specified. Federation was advocated by another and a very distinguished statesman (Wentworth) of New South Wales, while yet that colony was in its infancy. In 1867 it was considered and strongly recommended by a Select Committee of the Victorian Legislative Assembly; and in 1881 a conference was held in Sydney at . which a Federal Council Bill, framed by Sir Henry Parkes, was adopted, but without any practical result, inasmuch as neither the Government of Sir Henry Parkes nor any other Government took any action whatever to give effect to it. The creation of a Federal Council as the first tangible step towards a fuller Federation was the work of the convention that met in Sydney two years later. It should be added, as further proof of the early conception of the Federal idea, that the Constitution Bill passed by the British Parliament in 1849 contained a provision whereby the colonies of Australia might enjoy a uniform tariff regulated by a central body.

It may be of interest if I briefly sketch the history of the Federation movement from the time of the intercolonial convention held in Sydney in November and December 1883 to the present date. It should be interesting also, albeit the tale is one of sadness, if I note the changes that have been wrought by death and other causes in the *personnel* of the *dramatis personæ* engaged in this chapter of Australasian history.

Dealing with the members of the convention of 1883, we find that there were present the following representatives :

For Fiji   .   . H. E. Sir William des Vœux, K.C.M.G.
„ N. S. Wales   The Hon. Alexander Stuart, M.P., Premier.
„   „   •   „   George Richard Dibbs, M.P., Colonial Secretary. .
„   „   •   „   William Bede Dalley, Q.C., M.L.C., Attorney-General.
„ New Zealand   „   Major Harry Albert Atkinson, M.P., Premier and Colonial Treasurer.
„   „   •   „   Fred. Whitaker, M.L.C., late Premier and Attorney-General.
„ Queensland •   „   Samuel Walker Griffith, Q.C., M.P., Premier and Colonial Secretary.
„   „   •   „   James Francis Garrick, Q.C., M.L.C., Postmaster-General.
„ South Australia   „   James Cox Bray, M.P., Premier and Chief Secretary.

For South Australia . The Hon. J. W. Downer, Q.C., M.P., Attorney-
General.
„ Tasmania . . „ William Robert Giblin, M.P., Pre-
mier and Attorney-General.
„ „ . . „ Nicholas J. Brown, M.P., Minister
of Lands and Works.
„ Victoria . . „ James Service, M.P., Premier and
Colonial Treasurer.
„ „ . . „ Graham Berry, M.P., Chief Secre-
tary.
„ „ . . „ George Briscoe Kerferd, M.P., Attor-
ney-General.
„ Western Australia . „ Malcolm Fraser, C.M.G., Colonial
Secretary.

Verily it may be said of these men *tempora mutantur, nos et
mutamur in illis.* Of the fifteen engaged on that occasion, excluding Sir William des Vœux, who appeared in his capacity of Governor,
and not as a colonial politician, six are dead ; two have reached that
haven of rest for weary and strife-worn Attorneys-General, the
Bench ; two have been relegated to the diplomatic circle of Agents-
General in Westminster ; one has been placed in the Speaker's chair,
and one pensioned off in a Government appointment. Of the remaining three not one at the present time occupies a position,
whether as Premier or Minister of the Crown, in the forefront of
Australasian politics.

But it has to be recorded that the work of those men of a bygone political generation was fruitful. That convention laid the
foundation-stone of Federation by the adoption of a draft bill to
constitute a Federal Council of Australasia, out of which it was then
hoped by many (as it still is by a few) that a complete union of the
several colonies might, with the growth of time and the expansion of
the Council, come about.

It would appear, however, that the members of that convention
had not in all instances accurately reckoned with the popular will
of the colonies they represented, or with the jealousies that might
naturally be looked for from some leading politicians who, being out
of office at the time, had no share in the deliberations and decisions
of the convention. Sir Henry Parkes, then still a power in the
land, and shortly to reappear on the scene as Premier of New South
Wales, had no voice in that convention, and from that day to this
New South Wales has stood aloof from the Federal Council. New
Zealand also, where the Federal spirit is languid and for practical
purposes non-existent, has adopted the same attitude ; and South Australia has only been of the Council during one of its six sessions between
1886 and 1895. Delegates of Victoria, Queensland, and Tasmania have

been present at all six sittings, and Western Australia has been represented at five.

It is obvious that no complete or even workable form of Federation is to be expected through the medium of this Council while any of the larger self-governing colonies stand out of it; and more particularly is this the case while New South Wales is the recusant colony, for there can be for Queensland no Federation whatever unless New South Wales is included in it. This is a hard geographical fact of which Queensland statesmen make no secret, true though they be in their allegiance to the Federal Council.

And the last session of the Federal Council, held in January 1895 under its new constitution, duly emphasised the inefficiency and incompleteness that cripple its usefulness and stay its progress. Hitherto the colonies represented in it (except Fiji with its one member) had sent two delegates each. In the last session the enlarged representation gave to each of the self-governing colonies five members; but the twenty councillors who then met (representing Queensland, Victoria, Western Australia, and Tasmania) found themselves powerless to enact any legislation of any kind, and had to be content with passing a resolution to which all the Victorian and some Tasmanian representatives objected, and from which there could by no possibility be any solid result.

This motion was as follows :

1. That in the opinion of this Council the bill intituled 'The Constitution of the Commonwealth of Australia (1891)' should be considered by the various Australasian Parliaments at as early a date as possible.

2. That the Governments of the several colonies of Australia be urged to submit the bill for the consideration of their respective Parliaments, and to take steps for the holding of a second convention to deal with any amendments which may be suggested.

This motion was palpably a mere *brutum fulmen* at which those colonies not of the Federal Council might haply sneer, and by which no colony, whether of the Council or not, need be bound in any way. And even Queensland and Western Australia, whose representatives voted for this resolution, have not given effect to it in their Parliaments.

As a body without an exchequer or any executive functions whatever the Federal Council has only dimly adumbrated the ideal of Federal Government; and although there has come to it expansion as regards the number of delegates, there has been no extension of its legislative powers, which remain to-day what they were at the outset.

The following are the subjects in respect of which the Imperial Parliament has conferred legislative authority upon the Federal Council of Australasia :

(*a*) The relations of Australasia with the islands of the Pacific.

(*b*) Prevention of the influx of criminals.

(*c*) Fisheries in Australasian waters beyond territorial limits.

(*d*) The service of civil process of the courts of any colony within her Majesty's possession in Australasia out of the jurisdiction of the colony in which it is issued.

(*e*) The enforcement of judgments of courts of law of any colony beyonds the limits of the colony.

(*f*) The enforcement of criminal process beyond the limits of the colony in which it is issued, and the extradition of offenders (including deserters of wives and children, and deserters from the Imperial or colonial naval or military forces).

(*g*) The custody of offenders on board ships belonging to her Majesty's Colonial Governments beyond territorial limits.

(*h*) Any matter which at the request of the Legislatures of the colonies her Majesty by Order in Council shall think fit to refer to the Council.

(*i*) Such of the following matters as may be referred to the Council by the Legislatures of any two or more colonies; that is to say, general defences, quarantine, patents of invention and discovery, copyright, bills of exchange and promissory notes, uniformity of weights and measures, recognition in other colonies of any marriage or divorce duly solemnised or decreed in any colony, naturalisation of aliens, status of corporations and joint-stock companies in other colonies than that in which they have been constituted, and any other matter of general Australasian interest with respect to which the Legislatures of the several colonies can legislate within their own limits, and as to which it is deemed desirable that there should be a law of general application.   Provided that in such cases the Act of the Council shall extend only to the colonies by whose Legislatures the matter shall have been referred to it, and such other colonies as may afterwards adopt the same.

In addition to the subjects above mentioned the Council is authorised to legislate on any question relating to the colonies represented in the Council or to their relations with one another which the Governor of any two or more of the colonies shall upon an address of the Legislatures of such colonies refer to the consideration of the Council.

After seven years' experience of the Federal Council, the colonies unanimously, and without regard to the question of their having joined in it or not, resolved that some more complete union was immediately required, and at the Federation conference held in Melbourne in 1890, whereat all seven of the self-governing colonies were represented, the following resolutions were passed:

1. That in the opinion of this conference the best interests and the present and future prosperity of the Australasian colonies will be promoted by an early union under the Crown; and, while fully recognising the valuable services of the members of the convention of 1883 in founding the Federal Council, it declares

its opinion that the seven years which have since elapsed have developed the national life of Australia in population, in wealth, in the discovery of resources, and in self-governing capacity to an extent which justifies the higher act, at all times contemplated, of the union of these colonies under one legislative and executive Government, on principles just to the several colonies.

2. That to the union of the Australian colonies contemplated by the foregoing resolution, the remoter Australasian colonies shall be entitled to admission at such times and on such conditions as may be hereafter agreed upon.

3. That the members of the conference should take such steps as may be necessary to induce the Legislatures of their respective colonies to appoint, during the present year, delegates to a national Australasian convention, empowered to consider and report upon an adequate scheme for a Federal Constitution.

4. That the convention should consist of not more than seven members from each of the self-governing colonies, and not more than four members from each of the Crown colonies.

It will be noted that New Zealand safeguarded herself as a 'remoter Australasian colony under resolution 2, which provided for the union of Australian colonies only, and entitled the remoter Australasian colonies to subsequent admission upon terms to be mutually agreed upon.

The representatives who attended the Federation conference were as follows:

New South Wales .	The Hon.	Sir Henry Parkes, M.L.A., G.C.M.G., Premier.
	,,	William McMillan, M.L.A., Treasurer.
New Zealand .	,,	Captain Wm. Russell Russell, M.H.R., Colonial Secretary.
	,,	Sir John Hall, K.C.M.G., M.H.R.
Queensland . .	,,	Sir Samuel Walker Griffith, K.C.M.G., M.L.A.
	,,	John M. Macrossan, M.L.A., Colonial Secretary.
South Australia .	,,	John Alex. Cockburn, M.D., M.H.A., Premier.
	,,	Thomas Playford, M.L.A.
Tasmania . .	,,	A. I. Clark, M.H.A., Attorney-General.
	,,	B. S. Bird, M.H.A., Treasurer.
Victoria . .	,,	Duncan Gillies, M.L.A., Treasurer.
	,,	Alfred Deakin, M.L.A., Chief Secretary.
Western Australia	,,	Sir James G. Lee Steere, Speaker, L.C.

Of the above-named representatives only one (Sir Samuel Griffith) took part in the convention of 1883, and only five out of the thirteen are at this day in active political life.

The outcome of this conference and its natural sequel was the convention held in Sydney in March 1891, when each of the colonies of Australia and Tasmania were represented by seven delegates each, and New Zealand by three—*i.e.* forty-five in all, of whom some twenty have, in the short space of five years, been removed by death, retirement, or other causes from the political arena. These forty-five were as follows:

New South Wales . .	The Hon. Sir Henry Parkes.
	,, Wm. McMillan.
	,, Joseph P. Abbott.
	,, George R. Dibbs.
	,, Wm. H. Suttor.
	,, Edmund Barton.
	,, Sir Patrick Jennings.
Victoria . . .	,, James Munro.
	,, Duncan Gillies.
	,, Alfred Deakin.
	,, Henry J. Wrixon.
	,, Wm. C. Smith.
	,, Henry Cuthbert.
	,, Nicholas Fitzgerald.
Queensland . . .	,, Sir Samuel Griffith.
	,, Sir Thomas McIlwraith.
	,, John M. Macrossan.
	,, Arthur Rutledge.
	,, Thomas Macdonald-Paterson.
	,, Andrew Jos. Thynne.
	,, John Donaldson.
South Australia . .	,, Thos. Playford.
	,, Sir John Cox Bray.
	,, John A. Cockburn.
	,, Sir John Wm. Downer.
	,, Charles C. Kingston.
	,, John H. Gordon.
	,, Richard C. Baker.
Tasmania . . .	,, P. O. Fysh.
	,, A. I. Clark.
	,, B. S. Bird.
	,, William Moore.
	,, Adye Douglas.
	,, W. H. Burgess.
	,, N. J. Brown.
New Zealand . . .	,, Sir George Grey.
	,, Sir Harry A. Atkinson.
	,, Capt. W. Russell Russell.

Western Australia.   .   The Hon. Sir James G. Lee Steere.

        ,,   Sir John Forrest.

        ,,   Wm. E. Marmion.

        ,,   John A. Wright.

        ,,   J. W. Hackett.

        ,,   Alex. Forrest.

        ,,   W. J. Lotou.

This convention sat from the 9th of March to the 9th of April. The report of the day-to-day proceedings, including the adopted draft bill of the Commonwealth of Australia, fill 188 pages of a very voluminous Blue-book; and the reported debates occupy 455 other pages. The draft bill, even though it may not ultimately be adopted in every detail, will doubtless form more than a mere groundwork of the Constitution Bill that has to be framed by the next and, one may hope, final convention; and it stands as a monument to the drafting skill of Sir Samuel Griffith, C. C. Kingston, and A. I. Clark. The Hansard report of the speeches made should earn for him who wades through its 455 foolscap pages the recognition due to indefatigable patience.

It was, I believe, at this convention that Sir Henry Parkes made his most substantial contribution to the cause of Federation in the effective phrase, ' One nation, one destiny.' The debates teem with effective phrases and fine rhetorical touches that are ornamental if not eminently useful. They are distinguished also, and in a better sense, by much practical knowledge of the matter in hand. And, with one exception, they are characterised throughout by an admirable spirit of loyalty to the British throne and flag. As for the one delegate who thought it seemly to air his republican sentiments on that occasion, it is gratifying to read that he spoke of them at the time as of a bombshell hurled into the assembly of notables present, and that he has since seen fit to sink his republicanism by accepting knighthood (the K.C.M.G.) at the hands of the Sovereign whom in 1891 he would have repudiated.

But the proceedings at this convention lacked in a considerable degree that reality which comes of a determination to master every obstacle, and the confidence that should come to him who, as the chosen of the people, knows that he speaks for the people who have elected him to act in their behalf. They who will deal with the next draft of the Australasian Constitution Bill will be representatives of the people duly elected under the Assembly franchise. They who appeared at the Convention of 1891 were delegates only, and held no mandate from the people.

Thus, in 1891, the delegates, making some show of dealing with the ' lions in the path,' dealt timorously with those animals, and in some instances preferred to walk round them rather than to meet and conquer them. This was especially noticeable in regard to matters of finance, the consolidation of the provincial debts into one Australasian stock, the protection of the smaller States through an equal representation of the States in the Senate, and other points.

As to this, one of the ablest delegates at that convention writes as follows :

The subject which the convention of 1891 failed to grapple with in as satisfactory a manner as could be wished was that of finance, and the cause of that failure was, apparently, a reluctance to make any proposal which would have the appearance of giving any one or more colonies an advantage over the others. The powers of the Senate in regard to money bills were also left in an unsatisfactory state, and a majority of the members of the convention seemed incapable of seeing any difference between the Senate of a Federation and the Second Chamber in a unitary State. But if the experience of other Federations is to be any guide or criterion for the relations of the two Houses of the Legislature in a federated Australia, there is no reasonable ground for anticipating any conflict upon money bills. Both branches of the Federal Legislature will find their ultimate root in popular election, and the Senate will not be the representative of property or wealth, as the Legislative Council is in the majority of the separate colonies.

It cannot be said of both branches of the Legislature in New South Wales, New Zealand, Queensland, and Western Australia that they now have their root in popular election. The Legislative Councils of those colonies are nominee Houses, repugnant to the ideal of the democratic form of government; and it was on this account, and because the Commonwealth Bill of 1891 provided for the election of senators by the Legislative Councils, that some of the delegates hesitated to give to a Senate so appointed the powers that it should have.

For the Commonwealth Bill, as then adopted, while it gave to each State representation in the House of Representatives on a population basis (*i.e.* one member for every 30,000 of population or fraction thereof), made the representation in the Senate equal for all States (*i.e.* eight for each), regardless of the number of population; and it is clearly to the interest of the smaller colonies that at the outset, and until the federated provinces have become welded together as one homogeneous entity—' one nation one destiny '—the Senate should have such co-ordinate power with the House of Representatives, such full power as to amending as well as rejecting money bills, and, it may be, such power of initiating money bills, as will prevent the interests of the smaller colonies being prejudiced by the overwhelming power of the larger colonies in the House of Representatives. Nor can I see why this is not practicable (as it is certainly equitable and expedient) if the members of the Senate are chosen as representatives of their several States by election, as in the case of members of the House of Representatives, so as to realise to the full the idea of two Houses rooted in the popular will.

For myself, I have no fear that, even at the outset of Federal government, there will be occasion for any safeguards against unfair treatment of the smaller provinces by the larger.   There would be, I believe, on the part of the members of the House of Representatives generally a chivalrous feeling that would preclude the employment of a combination of representatives of the stronger States for any purpose calculated to injure States with smaller numerical strength in the House ; there would be in the hearts of the greater number an earnest desire to obliterate the artificial boundaries that on the continent of Australia have divided into separate States a people who are one in race, language, and interests, and one also with the peoples of Tasmania and New Zealand, though these latter are separated from the mainland of Australia by leagues of sea ; and there would be, we may assume, from the beginning, and more particularly then, a feeling animating all that the first duty of the Federal Parliament was to legislate in such wise for Australasia as a whole as would tend most certainly to cement the union of the colonies—large and small alike—that had entered the Federation. But the people have to say 'Aye' or 'No' whether they will enter this union ; and to the people of the colonies with the smaller populations one should be able to point out, as an argument in favour of their voting 'Aye,' that their interests have been fully protected in the Senate.

It will have to be considered at the next convention whether a Senate of smaller proportions and generally a less costly scheme of Federal government may not well be adopted.   In 1891 Australasia had not yet drunk to the dregs, as now she has, the bitter cup of adversity.   In 1891 the foremost plank in the political programme was not, as now it is in most of the Australasian colonies, that of retrenchment ; and in 1891 bloated establishments and high salaries were as generally approved as now they are things to be attacked by the pruning-knife of the unsparing economist.   *Autres temps, autres mœurs.*   In 1897, when the convention may be expected to meet, less grandiose ideas as to expenditure will prevail, and the proposed Federal establishments may be of less magnificent proportions and cost, but not necessarily on that account any less effective in any particular.

Eight members of the Senate were to represent each colony in the Federation according to the proposal of 1891.   Supposing the four eastern colonies of Australia and Tasmania joined the union, there would be, at that rate, a Senate of forty members to a House of Representatives numbering, say, 120 ; Western Australia would be obliged to enter the Federation immediately, and there would then be 48 members of the Senate to 124 of the House of Representatives ; a Senate of about half of that numerical strength, if armed with proper powers, should be sufficient for the work of that branch of the Legislature.

This question of the *personnel* of the Federal Parliament presents itself in another aspect when we ask ourselves where and how the 160 or 172 thoroughly qualified members are to be found. It must be remembered that the Federal Parliament will deal only with certain questions, and the Federal Government administer only in certain matters—either those reserved to it or those not reserved to the provincial or States Parliaments or Governments (questions of defence, Customs, post and telegraphs being among those which have been deemed peculiarly matters of Federal concern), and that the Parliaments and Administrations of the States will absorb some considerable portion of the trained political talent for the conduct of local legislation and affairs. It has to be further borne in mind that the views expressed at the Convention of 1891 were unfavourable to the idea of a State parliamentarian being eligible for election to the Federal Parliament, and that, according to this view (if it should be finally adopted), each colony would have to find an efficient and experienced body for the State Legislature, and another, not less efficient or experienced, for the Federal Legislature; and the question will occur to many, as it has occurred to me, how are these two efficient and experienced bodies to be provided? The difficulty does not arise from the dearth of capable men in the Australasian communities. There are hundreds of men fully qualified to take part in legislation, but those with leisure and inclination are few; and only exceptionally will capable men sacrifice private interest or enjoyment for political work, which enriches none, and exposes all to unsparing and often unmerited criticism.

Let either New South Wales or Victoria be drawn upon for its contingent of forty-eight members of the Federal Parliament, and, if those forty-eight were the picked men of the Parliaments of those colonies, what would be the calibre of those to whom the very important State legislation would be left? But a stronger argument remains in support of the contention that members of the States Legislatures should be eligible for election to the Federal Parliament, and it is this. The best men of the States Legislatures—those enjoying the sweets of office as Ministers of the Crown, and those aspiring to seats on the States Treasury Bench with fair prospect of achieving their aspirations—would probably, in the majority of instances, prefer the greater certainty of the humbler position in the State Executive to the lesser, the very much lesser, certainty of any position at all in the Federal Administration. So it might well fall out that the States would send to the Federal Parliament not their best public men, but a body yet untried and unproved by the test of experience.

I admit that it might in most cases be difficult for any one man to occupy at the same time a seat in both the Federal and State Cabinets, but beyond this I can see no difficulty that should preclude members of the States Legislatures becoming members of the

Federal Parliament or Executive, provided the Federal session were held, as it might very well be, at that season when the States Parliaments would ordinarily be out of session.

But I have allowed myself to be led away from the history of the Federation movement, to which I will now return. And here, if space permitted, I could not do better than give a *précis*, which has been officially prepared, of the proceedings of the several Australasian colonies in this connection from the year 1891 (immediately after the meeting of the convention) to 1894 (just prior to the Premiers' Hobart conference of January 1895). But that *précis* is too lengthy for the purposes of this article, and I must content myself with stating briefly that it shows how the mother colony dallied with the question, albeit Sir Henry Parkes, of 'one nation, one destiny' fame, when Premier in 1891, had made the Federal union of the colonies a question second only to electoral reform in New South Wales, and promptly gave notice of a motion that would have advanced that question if, after being made an order of the day for the 22nd of July, it had not remained intact on the notice paper in all its virgin innocence until the 3rd of November, when the mover was out of office. It also shows how little practical advance was made in the Federation movement elsewhere, and it is principally remarkable because it fore-shadows the course which has now been adopted—viz. the remission of the framing of the Constitution Bill to a convention elected by the people—one man, one vote—and its subsequent submission to the will of the people when finally adopted by the convention. The Common-wealth Bill was not introduced at all in the Legislatures of New South Wales, Queensland, Western Australia, and New Zealand. It was not passed by any colony. In Victoria the bill went through the Assembly, and was returned by the Legislative Council passed with amendments that never came on for consideration. In Tasmania it went through the Assembly, and was dropped at the second reading stage in the Legislative Council. In South Australia it was intro-duced in the Assembly, and dropped there.

Early in 1895 the Premier of New South Wales (the Hon. G. H. Reid) initiated a movement for the restoration of Federation to the list of living questions which may be fairly credited with having fanned the dead ashes of Federation into new life. At Mr. Reid's suggestion, a conference of Premiers was held in Hobart in January of that year, at which all the colonies of Australia, together with Tasmania, were represented as follows:

New South Wales	The Hon. G. H. Reid
Queensland	„ H. M. Nelson
South Australia	„ C. C. Kingston
Tasmania	„ Sir Edward Braddon
Victoria	„ George Turner
Western Australia	„ Sir John Forrest

And it may be remarked that of these six Premiers only two
(Mr. C. C. Kingston and Sir John Forrest) had taken part in any
previous Federation conference.

The six Premiers met on four occasions, between the 29th of
January and the 6th of February 1895. The minutes of their
proceedings occupy less than two and a half pages of foolscap, and
the draft bill 'to enable each colony to take part in the framing,
acceptance, and enactment of a Federal Constitution for Australasia'
(the short title of which is 'The Australasian Federation Enabling
Act') which the conference adopted—comprising forty-four sections
and a schedule—is disposed of in some five pages. Messrs. Kingston
and Turner were the Parliamentary draftsmen to whom the preparation of the draft bill was entrusted, with a confidence in their
skill that was not abused.

Proceedings were by resolution in the first place, and the
resolutions considered were as follows :

1. That this conference regards Federation as the great and pressing question
of Australasian politics.

2. That a convention, consisting of ten representatives of each colony, directly
chosen by the electors, be charged with the duty of framing a Federal Constitution.

3. That the constitution so framed be submitted to the electors for acceptance
or rejection by a direct vote.

4. That such constitution, if accepted by the electors of three or more colonies,
be transmitted to the Queen by an address from the Parliaments of those colonies
praying for the necessary legislative enactment.

5. That a bill be submitted to the Parliament of each colony for the purpose
of giving effect to the foregoing resolutions.

6. That Messrs. Turner and Kingston be requested to prepare a draft bill for
the consideration of the conference.

Upon all these resolutions four of the six Premiers were in
absolute accord; Mr. Nelson dissented as to No. 4. Sir John
Forrest adopted a *non possumus* attitude throughout, giving his
vote only for the abstract resolution No. 1 and the non-committal
resolution No. 6, but dissenting from Nos. 2 to 5. How Sir John
Forrest came to recognise that Federation was the great and pressing
question of Australasian politics, and yet felt himself constrained to
stand aloof from a reasonable plan for dealing with it, is not readily
to be understood.

The members of the conference considered the draft bill on the 4th
and 6th of February, Sir John Forrest being absent on both occasions,
and the draft was, with certain amendments, adopted on the latter date
by all present. On the latter day, at the closing sitting of the conference Mr. Reid intimated that ' as soon as practicable after the reassembling of the New South Wales Parliament his Government would
introduce a measure providing for the chief objects of the bill as defined
in the draft.' Messrs. Turner, Nelson, Kingston, and Sir Edward Brad-

don intimated that, as 'soon as New South Wales had passed the bill, their Governments would introduce measures providing for the same objects, Mr. Nelson reserving the right to dispense with the direct reference to the electors required by the second object of the bill.'

And so, without phrases or speeches levelled at the constituencies. over the heads of the Premiers met in conclave, but in a conversational and practical way, not hampered by Parliamentary procedure and obstructive red-tapeism, the Federation Enabling Bill, which gives to the people the right, and throws upon them the responsibility, of determining their destiny—which makes Federation a living question that shall be settled for weal or woe, one way or the other, within a year or two—was adopted by the five present without even an apology for a Hansard report of their deliberations.

And within the year all the subscribing colonies except Queensland had passed this bill, practically in identical form, through the local Legislatures, by overwhelming majorities or without a division. The Queensland Government hesitated to deal with this measure in the last Parliament; but at a second Conference of Premiers, held in Sydney in March 1896, the Minister who represented the Premier of Queensland gave an assurance that the Federation Enabling Bill would be one of the first measures dealt with by the Government on the assembling of the new Parliament. And there is no doubt that Mr. Chamberlain's very wise decision that the question of dividing Queensland into two or more provinces must follow and not precede Australasian Federation will stimulate the action of Queensland in respect of the Federation Enabling Bill. So it may befall that before the close of this year the colonies that have passed this measure will have commenced proceedings for the election of representatives to the congress.[1]

Briefly stated, the more important provisions of the Federation Enabling Bill are as follows : Each colony shall elect ten representatives, such election to be on the Assembly franchise and for the colony as one constituency. No person to vote more than once at the same election. When such elections shall have been held in three or more colonies, a meeting of the convention shall be convened for a time and place agreed to by the Governors of such colonies. The convention, having framed and approved the constitution, shall adjourn for a period of not less than sixty or more than 120 days. On the reassembling of the convention, the constitution shall be considered with any amendments that may be proposed, and finally adopted. So soon as practicable after the close of the proceedings of the convention, the question of the acceptance or rejection of the constitution shall be submitted to the vote 'Yes' or 'No' of the

---

[1] A press telegram from Queensland, dated the 16th of June, states that the Governor's speech opening Parliament announces a measure to enable Queensland to take part in the convention for framing a Federal Constitution.

Assembly electors in each colony. ' When the electors of three colonies have accepted the Constitution, both Houses of Parliament may adopt addresses to the Queen praying that the same may be passed into law by the Imperial Parliament ; and these addresses being agreed to, the same shall be transmitted to the Queen with a certified copy of the constitution. The Bill gives no power to the Colonial Parliaments to amend the Constitution ; they may suggest amendments for the consideration of the congress when it shall assemble finally ; so may the press direct attention to possible amendments ; but the bill to be submitted to the people shall be one and the same for every colony.

Such is the measure which may be expected to settle for these colonies at an early date whether they shall enjoy a common nationhood or remain isolated provinces. Already public interest has been aroused on this vital question, already candidates for the honourable and responsible position of representatives at the congress are in the field, and before the year 1896 runs out the meeting of the convention may have taken place or be immediately impending.

Meanwhile, those who are earnest in the cause, and who have studied Federation, have imposed upon them the obligation of instructing the people who are to be the ultimate arbiters in this great issue. The men engaged in industries heretofore fostered as exotics by the artificial means of heavy inter-colonial tariffs will need to be taught something of the advantages that come with free trade ; and by this teaching may be surmounted the greatest obstacle that presents itself to such a complete union as will abolish those inter-provincial Custom-houses that now hamper trade and divert industrial effort and capital into unnatural channels. The advantages of that union in improved credit, consolidated strength, and enlargement of Australasia's power in the comity of nations will doubtless be taught. And to a people of such a high average of intelligence as that which distinguishes the inhabitants of these colonies the lesson may come home that the individual interest is subordinate to the general interest, and cannot but be shaped by it for good or evil as it (the general interest) prospers or declines.

To the smaller colonies, such as Tasmania, it should be obvious that they cannot stand out of a Federation into which the larger colonies have entered. Newfoundland is an object-lesson in point. Those smaller colonies are, therefore, well advised that they should take their part in the convention and help to mould the constitution under which, sooner or later, they must come to exist. And it has been already pointed out that this constitution should be considered in a time of peace when hostility, or threatening of hostility, from without interferes in no way with the deliberations of those who frame it. Mr. Deakin, at the Melbourne Conference of 1890, spoke very eloquently upon this head. Others have so spoken from time to time; and always the argument has been with these that it is urgently required of us to settle this great question when it may be viewed and debated in all its aspects calmly, and not delay a settlement until a foreign enemy shall force us to join in an ill-considered union.

But delay may be regarded as dangerous for a reason which has nothing to do with invasion or menace by a foreign foe. It is possible —though I trust not probable—that, with the passing of years, colonies that now experience only insignificant feelings of mutual jealousy may become more and more estranged, may develop racial and hostile instincts fatal to the beautiful idea of 'one nation, one destiny,' with the result that, in addition to Custom-houses along the border of a province, there may be outposts of armed men ready at the word of command to fly at the throats of their brothers on the other side of the boundary. *Absit omen!* May it come about within the next two years, as seems at this moment possible, that Victorians, New South Welshmen, South Australians, and Queenslanders shall be distinguished as such no longer, but be all of them Australasians, under one flag and one central Government!

One lesson there is that happily the people do not need to have imparted to them—that is, loyalty to the mother country. A candidate for the position of representative of Victoria ventured to talk to his audience about a possible separation from England, and at the next meeting of the Australian Natives' Association it was clearly indicated to that candidate that his expressed views about separation met with their cordial disapproval. The Federation Enabling Bill itself discountenances this idea, for it provides for the enactment of the new constitution by the Imperial Parliament with the assent of the Crown.

E. N. C. Braddon.

THE

NINETEENTH

CENTURY

No. CCXXXIV—August 1896

THE DECLINE OF COBDENISM

'Hurrah! Hurrah! the Corn Bill is law, and now my work is done.' So wrote Richard Cobden to his wife just fifty years ago : on the 26th of June, 1846. It is perhaps fortunate for the earnest and sanguine champion of the Manchester School that he did not live. long enough to take part in the chastened festivities with which a few of his followers have endeavoured to celebrate the 'jubilee' of Peel's great measure of fiscal revolution. Assuredly if his work was done in 1846, he would have been forced to acknowledge that a good deal of it has been undone by 1896. Indeed, as the Cobdenite jubilators have sadly to admit, the time is one singularly unpropitious for rejoicing on their part. The half-century, during which the system, described by the somewhat misleading name of Free-trade, has been the prevailing and official economic religion in England, has only served to shake the faith of the orthodox in this country, without in the smallest degree converting the heretics elsewhere. Fate has unkindly arranged a most dramatic array of events to show how limited is the progress which the principles of the Anti-Corn-Law Leaguers have made. We are in the full flood tide of Protectionist reaction, and it is a tide which did not begin to flow yesterday, and shows no sign of ebbing to-morrow. France—the country of Bastiat and Michel Chevalier, the peculiar object of Cobden's interest and patronage—has provided herself with a Premier who is understood to be more resolutely protectionist than any other of her public men. The United States, the constant theme of envious eulogy from the old Manchester

School, is extremely likely to confer the Presidency on the politician whose name stands for the most savagely restrictive tariff of our times.   Germany, which pronounced for Free-trade before England did, now occupies herself in putting on a fresh duty against the foreigner or giving a fresh bounty to her own producers every year. There is hardly one of our colonies which does not live under the shelter of a high tariff; and the solitary fragment of consolation the English Cobdenite can find is that a Conservative and defiantly Protectionist Ministry in Canada has just been beaten at the polls by Liberal opponents, who, however, have shown no disposition whatever to become Free-traders in the English understanding of the term.   So much for that 'civilised world' which Manchester was to have converted long ago.   And in England itself the Protectionists are no longer a party obscure, discredited, half disgraced.   It has ceased to be a mark of mere intellectual obtuseness—as if one should express doubts on the law of gravitation, or the accuracy of the multiplication table—for a man to profess a liking for import duties on other articles besides wine, spirits, tobacco, dried fruits, cocoa, and tea, which things may lawfully be taxed according to the true Cobdenite faith.   On the contrary, Protection raises its head again, open and unabashed; it is vocal on the platform, it is felt at elections, and in Lancashire itself—nay even in Manchester, which was the Mecca of Free-trade, and in Birmingham, which may be called its Medina, since it received the prophet John Bright when the Holy City had cast him out—it is probable that, if a popular vote could be taken, the Free-traders would be left in a minority.[1]   To crown all, one of the most able and popular party leaders of the day, a Minister holding the seals of a Secretary of State, has publicly and emphatically given encouragement to the scheme of a Customs Union for the British Empire.   Mr. Chamberlain's great speech at the Chamber of Commerce dinner on the 9th of June, following on his previous speech to the Canada Club earlier in the year, shows the rate at which we are advancing—or retrograding, as some angry critics may prefer to say.   The Colonial Secretary disclaims any liking for protection; on the contrary, his aim is to break down tariff barriers within the Empire.   But we have certainly moved far from the hide-bound Cobdenite era, when a Minister of the Crown can

---

[1] 'Etrange revirement des esprits! Manchester est précisément la ville aujourd'hui où renaît la réaction économique dans la Grande-Bretagne; on y vante le *fair trade* ou la réciprocité, au lieu du *free trade* ou libre-échange.   Si des élections se faisaient aujourd'hui à Manchester et que les candidats fussent, d'une part, Cobden, l'apôtre du libre-échange, de la paix, de l'autre M. Balfour, le représentant de la politique impériale et ·de l'empirisme économique, la cote des paris serait sensiblement plus favorable au second qu'au premier, et le résultat n'apparaîtrait guère comme douteux. L'âme de Cobden pourrait errer dans la Grande-Bretagne sans être assurée d'y trouver une seule ville restée complètement fidèle à l'ensemble de ses principes.'—M. LEROY-BEAULIEU (in *Cosmopolis* for June 1896). ·

talk, to an applauding audience of merchants and traders, of Great Britain placing moderate duties upon corn, meat, wool, sugar, 'and perhaps other articles of large consumption,' when sent to us by foreigners.

To do them justice, the Cobdenites themselves are well aware that they are in a situation which demands what Bacon calls 'hearse-like songs,' rather than the minstrelsy of triumph. No longer are they the Cocksure School, as they have been harshly called. The big drum and the brass trumpet have given way to rather pathetic fluting in the minor key. The Cobden Jubilee has furnished occasion for a re-issue of Mr. John Morley's excellent Life of the hero of the Anti-Corn-Law League.[2] It is interesting to notice the complacent tone of assured and unshaken success which Mr. Morley, writing fifteen years ago, adopts, and then to contrast it with the depressed apologetics of the latter-day panegyrists. Take, for instance, Mr. Courtney at the Greenwich dinner of the Cobden Club :—

They might confess that a country might be prosperous although it had adopted a protective *régime*. It was prosperous not because of Protection, but in spite of it. They might also confess—though, perhaps, this was a harder statement to accept—that the population and commerce of a country might dwindle though that country had adopted Free-trade. In our own country certain portions had, under our Free-trade *régime*—he did not say in consequence of it—diminished their populations, and had also suffered a diminution in their commercial transactions. And what was possible of a part of this country in respect to the whole might be possible of this country also in respect to the rest of the world. The time might come when, although we had adopted and should continue to maintain the principles of Free-trade, our position might not be unchallenged, our population might have to undergo a decline, and our commercial position in the world might indicate some falling off. But when that happened, if it was to happen, it would not be in consequence of Free-trade.[3]

A 'hearse-like' pæan indeed! Mr. Courtney himself, in his very hour of jubilation, is evidently more in the mood to bury Cæsar than to praise him. No wonder M. Leroy-Beaulieu, one of the few Continental publicists of eminence who is still a professed Free-trader, is even more despondent. All he can say is 'il reste quelques traces des efforts de Michel Chevalier et de Cobden ; ' and he tells us 'il serait excessif d'en désespérer.' We need not quite despair! Chill encouragement this for an army which its chiefs used to tell us was to march from victory to victory, and would presently encompass the world with its irresistible legions.

It is needless to spend words on this point. Most people will be ready to admit that Free-trade is regarded with great and ever-growing disfavour everywhere, and is no longer supreme even in the opinions of Englishmen. It is more profitable, if less easy, to attempt to discover the causes of this strange and striking revulsion.

[2] *The Life of Richard Cobden*, by John Morley. In 2 vols. Jubilee edition. (London: T. Fisher Unwin, 1896.)

[3] See Mr. Courtney's speech as reported in the *Times* of June 27.

The Cobdenite doctors, who recognise the symptoms, give different names to the disorder. Mr. Courtney thinks the set-back is due to the exaggerated expectations of the earlier Free-traders. They had been too sanguine, and hence had naturally suffered disappointment. They thought the repeal of the Corn-laws would abolish pauperism and want, and are discouraged when they find that it has done nothing of the sort. M. Leroy-Beaulieu is inclined to think that the root of the evil is to be found in the depression of agriculture everywhere, owing to increased production and falling prices. Herr Theodore Barth,[4] who is one of the Free-trade deputies in the German Reichstag, puts it all down to the comprehensive wickedness of Prince Bismarck. But these are unwarrantably ' short views,' even if they are true, as far as they go. No doubt there is a good deal in Mr. Courtney's theory. Free-trade has undeniably been a disappointment : nowhere more so than in the only country which adopted it with something like enthusiasm. Every theoretical argument in its favour is as good as it ever was. Rightly considered, the doctrine is no more than an application to the conditions of international barter of Adam Smith's famous demonstration of the advantages of the division of labour. No one who has once mastered that not very complicated proposition in economics can have any doubts as to its general truth. But to reiterate the soundness of general rules of science is not of much use when you come to apply their results in a particular case. An engineer who found that his dams were leaking and his embankments crumbling away would be insufficiently aided by being told to go and study the elementary proposition in hydrostatics which teaches that water tends to find its own level. ' I know that,' he might reply ; ' and I have now to consider whether it is advisable to counteract the tendency in question, and if so by what methods.' The Englishman of the present generation, brought up, as most of us have been, on the ' orthodox ' economics, is rather in that condition. He may be quite ready to admit the validity of many of the generalisations of his teachers, but he turns to experience to inquire whether they have worked out for his benefit. He asks himself, more and more anxiously every year, whether facts do really bear out the contention that Free-trade at home (coupled with Protection everywhere else) has made him more prosperous than he might have been without it. The old-fashioned Cobdenite gives him the easy old-fashioned answer. ' Are not you,' he says, ' a great deal wealthier than you were in the forties ? Don't you own more ships, more railway trains, more steam-engines, more blast-furnaces, more looms and spindles, than you did fifty years ago ? Have you not got more money in the bank, and don't you receive more interest from your investments held abroad ? Then

[4] See his article in *Cosmopolis* for June, ' Ein Jubiläum des Freihandels und der Demokratie.'

what more do you want, and how can you deny that Free-trade has done you all the good in the world?' This is the substance of the vindication which Mr. Villiers—that venerable champion of the Repeal struggle, whose name no Englishman of any party can mention without respect—addressed to the Cobden Club on the morrow of their festival. He summarises rapidly the progress which England has made since 1846—the cheapening of commodities, the rise of wages, the decline of pauperism, the increase of savings, the expansion of exports and imports—and attributes it all to the beneficial operations of Free-trade. His catalogue suggests the inevitable question: Have not other nations, which are not Free-traders, grown in wealth and civilisation and commerce? We know very well that they have. The benefits of mechanical science, of easier communication, of improved means of production, of education, of sanitation, of a progressive civilisation generally, have not been withheld from States which tax their imports. Mr. Villiers credits Free-trade with that cheapening of food which is mainly due to the opening of virgin territory and the lowering of freights, and with that expansion of foreign trade which is the result of a long effort of industrial activity that has not been confined to Britain. He might almost as well say that it is owing to Free-trade that young ladies ride bicycles and old gentlemen no longer get drunk after dinner.

We have shared in the industrial and commercial activity of an era of astonishing material progress. That is true. But the question which Englishmen ask themselves, with an ever-growing anxiety, is whether we have had our fair share, and whether we are now advancing as fast as our rivals. They know that in the protected period—before Cobdenism was by law established—they had a commanding superiority. Mr. Villiers gives figures to show how small, compared with what it is now, was the foreign trade of Britain in the earlier half of this century. Small—yes; but how vast compared to that of our rivals! Not in one great trade, but in many, we had an unchallenged and, as it appeared, unchallengeable lead. In shipping, in cottons, in metals, in cutlery, in hardware, in machinery, England seemed beyond competition. Great is the change to-day. The competitors who have deliberately rejected what Mr. Villiers calls 'the inestimable blessings of freedom of trade' are overtaking us with long strides; nay, in some vital cases have caught and passed us already. In his striking little book, *Made in Germany*, Mr. Ernest Williams, with facts and figures plucked from the Official Returns, shows how far and fast the process is going. Already Germany is abreast of us in the production of iron and steel; America has long since passed us; little Belgium is gaining on us rapidly. The German export of iron and steel rose from 957,000 tons in 1890 to 1,439,000 in 1894; the English export in the same period fell from 2,700,000 to 1,735,000. Even our carrying trade is menaced. We no longer own the first shipping port in Europe.   Liverpool has been passed by Hamburg, and it looks as if it would presently be passed by Antwerp.   Here are the figures of the last few years :—

	1885 Tons	1895 Tons
Hamburg　.　.　.　.　.　.	3,704,312	6,256,000
Antwerp　.　.　.　.　.　.	3,422,172	5,340,247
Rotterdam　.　.　.　.　.　.	2,120,347	4,038,017
Bremen .　..　.　.　.　.　.	1,289,399	2,184,274
Total　.　.	10,536,230	17,818,538
Liverpool　.　.　.　.　.　.	4,278,881	5,965,959

Ten years ago Liverpool was the first port in Europe.   Now she is the second—soon, apparently, to be third.   And here is the general summary of the situation as given by Mr. Williams :

In '72 the total declared value of British and Irish produce exported from the United Kingdom was 256,257,347*l.*; in '95 it had sunk to 226,169,174*l.*; and in the meantime the population of Great Britain and Ireland had grown from 31,835,757 to 39,134,166.   The market is bigger, the ability to supply the market is greater; but, whereas the proportion per head of exported British produce was 8*l.* 1*s.* 0*d.* in '72, it had sunk to 5*l.* 11*s.* 3*d.* in '94·

Such facts as these go a long way to explain the lukewarmness towards Free-trade which Mr. Courtney notices.   Free-trade England stands worse than she did twenty-three years ago.   No wonder Englishmen are puzzled and angry, and look curiously at the protected foreign countries which are reducing the lead we still hold so fast.   If that is what is happening under Protection, says the man of business, may not there after all be 'something in it'?

But if this disappointment and discouragement, this uneasy feeling that all is not well with our industrial condition, goes far to account for the growing impatience with which the 'orthodox' political economy, based on Free-trade and free competition, is regarded by many Englishmen, it is not the sole cause of the revulsion. There are other forces at work, more impalpable, but not less efficient. The antagonism towards Free-trade is, in fact, only part of a much larger movement.   The reaction against Cobdenism is no more than a manifestation of that general revolt against the theories and the ideals of the older Radicalism which is characteristic of our time. For, after all, Free-trade is only the expression, in the economic sphere, of that spirit of *laisser-faire* and exaggerated individualism which dominated English politics during the middle period of the present century.   To see in this revolt nothing but the ignorance of persons too indolent to master the rules of economic science, or the mere selfish greed of a class of producers anxious to grow rich at the expense of the community, is to be blind to the signs of the age. No doubt ignorance and cupidity bear their share in swelling the cry. They have their part in most movements, and were not wanting in the Anti-Corn-Law agitation. But the sceptics of Free-trade include many who have nothing to gain by Protection, and many who do not require to go to school again to learn their political economy. There is nothing cryptic or abstruse about that study, as it was formulated by the 'classical' teachers. Some of the people who talk of it most glibly, with the fluency gained from cheap text-books and popular lectures, are probably not aware that a new political economy working by the historical method, and based on an elaborate collection and analysis of facts, is even now in the making. When it has grown beyond its infancy it will be in the way of giving us a real science of economics, which will be founded on induction and the observation of phenomena, not on *a priori* generalisations, like the political economy which Adam Smith derived from the highly speculative writings of Hume and the French Physiocrats. As for those generalisations, so far as they are axiomatic—based, that is, on such facts of human nature and such circumstances of social life as are matters of common knowledge and common sense—there is no difficulty in accepting them ; nor, I imagine, would any well-informed opponent of Cobdenism deny their validity. The economic justification of Free-trade, as has been said above, is, and always has been, complete. But what is justified economically is not necessarily defensible on ethical, social, or political grounds. The tendency of the old economists, and of the utilitarian liberalism which they inspired, was to lose sight far too often of this all-important distinction. They concentrated too much of their attention on the beauty of buying cheap and selling dear, which no doubt is a very good thing to do when you can ; but they took insufficient account of the numerous cases in which you neither can nor ought to pursue the process. This kind of sentence is perpetually recurring in the works of the 'orthodox' economists :—'In every country it always is and must be the interest of the great body of the people to buy whatever they want of those who sell it cheapest. The proposition is so very manifest that it seems ridiculous to take any pains to prove it.' So says Adam Smith ; but in point of fact the proposition is by no means manifest. Although, no doubt, it is in a general way an advantage to most people to buy what they want as cheaply as possible, it does not in the least follow that it is, always and everywhere, a benefit for a whole nation, or a whole class of producers, or even for a single individual. In private trade it would hardly be considered politic to buy cheap from a rival whose very object in selling to you at a low price was to establish a business which in due time would destroy your own ; to say nothing of the innumerable ethical and social considerations, which may intervene to make cheap buying and dear selling not

merely injudicious but immoral.   Cheapness may be attained by
prison labour, or by sweating, or by oppression and corruption.   Is
it right to take advantage of these wrongs in order to make our
purchases at the best possible rate for ourselves?   Most people nowadays would answer the question in the negative without hesitation.
The older economists were too anxious to put all business on a pure
and unadulterated basis of profit and loss, as if politics and morals
had nothing whatever to do with trade.   They ignored, what Aristotle
had taught long ago, that economics is not the same thing as money-
making.[5]   Adam Smith is quite indignant at the thought that we
could possibly want to give special encouragement to a people like
the Portuguese, who were anxious to favour us.   'As they give us
their custom, it is pretended,' he says loftily, 'that we should give
them ours;' and he goes on to observe with much warmth that
'the sneaking arts of underling tradesmen are those worked into
political maxims for the conduct of a great empire, for it is the most
underling tradesmen only who make it a rule to employ chiefly their
own customers; a great trader purchases his goods always where they
are cheapest and best, without regard to any little interest of this
kind.'   In fact, according to this view, the 'cash nexus' is to be the
only bond between individuals and between nations.   To take into
account considerations of policy, or friendship, or good feeling, is at
best only the sneaking art of the 'underling.'   The really large and
business-like course is to buy cheap and to sell dear and leave everything else to take its chance.   There was to be 'no damned sentiment'
about business; for only when sentiment is eliminated can competition exert to the full its beneficent activities.[6]

It was the curious exaggeration of this same belief in the infallible
virtues of unrestricted competition which made the Cobdenites, at
times, not only anti-national, but anti-social.   When the question of

[5] Οὐχ ἡ αὐτὴ τῇ οἰκονομικῇ ἡ χρηματιστική.   Aristot. *Polit.* i. 3, 2.

[6] Very much the same kind of argument, and the same historical illustrations, are
still considered conclusive by some old-fashioned Cobdenites. Lord Farrer, in a
recently published pamphlet on what he calls the 'New Protection Scheme' of Mr.
Chamberlain, writes these sentences:—

'We have most of us heard of the mischiefs of the Methuen Treaty, which compelled Great Britain to give a preference to the heavy wines of Portugal; but what
shall we say of a treaty which binds England to exclude the low-priced corn, meat,
wool, and sugar of the United States, of Russia, and of Argentina, of France and of
Germany, in order that she may obtain these articles at a higher price from Canada,
India, Australia, and the West Indies? or what shall we say of a treaty which binds
Canada and Australia to buy no articles from the United States or from China which
those colonies can buy, though at a higher price, from Great Britain or from India?'

One might answer Lord Farrer's question by another—'What shall we say of an
agreement between two houses of business, closely connected by family and financial
relationships, to buy goods from one another where possible, even at a slightly higher
cost, rather than to deal with rival firms trying their utmost to drive them from the
markets?' What we should say, we imagine, would be that it was a very sensible
thing to do.

limiting the hours of labour in factories arose, Cobden, as is well
known, was altogether adverse to the reform.   He admitted that the
grievance required a remedy, but he thought the operatives had it in
their own hands.   'I would,' he said, 'advise the working classes to
make themselves free of the labour market of the world, and this
they can all do by accumulating 20*l.* each, which will give them the
command of the only market in which labour is at a higher rate than
in England—I mean that of the United States.   If every working
man would save this sum, he might be independent of his employer.'
On the theory that one country is as good as another, that it matters
nothing to the individual Englishman whether he lives under the
Union Jack or under the Stars and Stripes, and nothing to the State
whether it retains its own children or allows them to become the
subjects of an alien Government, there is little to be said against
Cobden's remedy.   But those who believe that it is advisable to render
the conditions of life favourable to the inhabitants of a country,
instead of inviting them to go and better themselves elsewhere,
would hardly agree with the alternative which the Manchester School
proposed to the Factóry Acts of the late Lord Shaftesbury and his
Conservative supporters.

It was this view of the functions of the State and Society which
turned so many people against the middle-class Liberalism of the
Cobdenite era, even in the day of its predominance.   The enlightened
self-interest theory which Bentham bequeathed to the Manchester
and Yorkshire agitators was repudiated by nearly all the deeper
thinkers and nobler writers of the period—by Carlyle, by Kingsley,
and by Ruskin, by Matthew Arnold and Tennyson, whether they called
themselves Conservatives or Liberals.   They saw (if the present
writer may venture to quote some words he has written elsewhere)
that under the cloak of this plausible theory unnumbered wrongs
were comfortably nestling.   They could not join in that deification
of free contract and free competition, which made it a duty for the
constitutions of a civilised country to hurl themselves upon one
another with tooth and claw,

> Like dragons of the prime,
> That tear each other in their slime,

struggling in the mud for the larger share of those 'utilities fixed
and embodied in material objects' about which the Evangelists of the
Gospel of Pelf and Self wrote so many volumes.   They could not
admit 'that the greatest happiness of the greatest number' was truly
promoted by the unchecked, unregulated, freedom of a blind Industrialism, that brought not peace on earth but a sword, and carried a
mimic civil war into every nation, every city, every household; or that
the first function of the State was to keep the ring while its subjects
pummelled each other inside the ropes.   This was the competitive

ideal, the philosophy of pig-wash, as Carlyle, in some of his most scornful sentences, called it. The author of *Past and Present* was one of those who altogether declined to believe that the competitive theory was in accordance with his favourite Eternal Verities. 'One thing,' he says, 'I do know : never on this earth was the relation of man to man long carried on by cash payment alone. If at any time a philosophy of Laisser-faire, Competition, and Supply-and-demand, start up as the exponent of human relations, expect that it will soon end.' [7]

It was the theory of which it has been said that it ' regarded men and women as if they were algebraical symbols of at best featherless two-legged animals provided only with a stomach and a pocket.' The rise of modern Conservatism is largely the revolt against this soulless and lifeless doctrine. If it can be said it has gone hand in hand with the rise of Socialism, it must also be admitted that Socialism itself is in some sort a similar revolt, and that the mischievous lengths to which it attempts to push the action of the State have been provoked by the individualistic extravagance which almost refused to permit the State to exercise any ethical functions at all.

No doubt the modern Cobdenite, though still all for unlimited Free-trade and unlimited competition, is not, as a rule, anxious to pose as a cosmopolitan and a peace-at-any-price man. He rather prefers to disclaim this doctrine as a mere personal idiosyncrasy on the part of the founder of this faith. But here Cobden was more consistent than some of his 'successors. His refusal to recognise national ideals was in accordance with the general tendency of his teaching and that of his sect. When Tennyson's *Maud* appeared at the outbreak of the Crimean War, he had nothing but condemnation for the poem, and he thought the article in the *Athenæum* praising it merely ' atrocious.' [8]

War was a nuisance because it was bad for trade. The ideal of a nation of shopkeepers could not be realised except in a state of peace :

> Peace sitting under her olive, and slurring the days gone by,
> When the poor are hovelled and hustled together, each sex, like swine ;
> When only the ledger lives, and only not all men lie ;
> Peace in her Vineyard—yes ! but a company forges the wine.

Similarly Cobden had the feeblest belief in the greatness or stability of the British Empire. He was sanguine enough, sometimes, as everybody knows—in fact, absurdly optimistic in his prophecies as

---

[7] Carlyle, *Past and Present*, book iii. ch. x.

[8] It is worth noticing that Mr. Morley at any rate is so far faithful to the teaching of his master that he considers the politics of *Maud* barbarous, though he is too good a critic not to admit that the poetry is beautiful. (See Morley's *Life of Cobden*, Jubilee edition, vol. ii. p. 173.)

regards the industrial future and the speedy triumph of his economic
tenets. To imagine that all the nations of the earth would recognise
the merits of 'enlightened self-interest' and regulate their external
and internal dealings according to the standard of Manchester middle-
class morality caused him no difficulty. But this sanguine temper
disappeared when he came to deal with Imperial politics. Here his
want of faith contrasts curiously with his optimism in economic
matters. When the Indian Mutiny broke out he was at once convinced that the only policy before us was that of Scuttle. 'I am, and
always have been, of opinion that we have attempted an impossibility
in giving ourselves to the task of governing a hundred millions of
Asiatics. God and his visible and natural laws have passed insuperable obstacles to the success of such a scheme;' and in any case, he
asks characteristically, 'what advantage can it confer on ourselves?'
What profit should we make out of it? As for the Colonies, he
regarded them as a mere encumbrance, which we ought to be rid of
as speedily as possible. When the British North America Act was
first mooted, he could see no benefit in it because it held out no hope
of relieving us from the expense and risk of defending the Colony
from the United States—'a task, by the way,' he explains, 'which
everybody admits to be beyond our power.' If he had lived to the
present year he would have discovered that a great many people,
including the entire population of the Dominion of Canada, admit
nothing of the sort. But Cobden adds that he cannot see what substantial interest the British people have in this Canadian connection
to compensate them for guaranteeing three or four millions of North
Americans living in Canada against another community of Americans living in their neighbourhood. Hardly anybody now, except
Mr. Goldwin Smith, who, after all, is chiefly interesting as a belated
survival from the Benthamite era, talks like this. It is worth while
comparing these humiliating words of Cobden with a passage in Carlyle's *Latter-day Pamphlets*, in which he exhorts us by no means to
induce the Colonies to break away from us. Colonies, as he reminds
us, are not to be picked off the street every day. 'Not a colony of
them but has been too dearly purchased by the toil and blood of those
we have the honour to be sons of; and we cannot just afford to put
them away because McCroudy finds the present management of them
costs money. Because the accounts do not stand well in the ledger,
our remedy is not to take shame to ourselves, and repent in sackcloth
and ashes, and amend our beggarly imbecilities and insincerities in
that as in other departments of our business, but to fling the business
overboard and declare the business itself to be bad? We are a hopeful
set of heirs to a big fortune!' [9]

It must be conceded that Cobden had no more confidence in the
future and the magnanimity of other nations than in those of his own.

[9] *Latter-day Pamphlets*, No. IV.

While the United States was engaged in its desperate struggle with sedition and rebellion, Mr. Cobden was one of those Englishmen who believed, with Mr. Gladstone, that the South had made a nation. ' I cannot see my way,' he writes, 'through the American business. I do not believe the North and South can ever lie in the same bed again, nor do I see how the military operations can be carried into the South so as to inflict a crushing defeat.' [10]

The notion that a people would go on fighting for abstract ideas, until a million or so of them had been killed off, and win in the end, failed to fit in with the Cobdenite scheme of human nature. And undoubtedly it is a little difficult for those who believe in Enlightened Selfishness as the mainspring of human action to understand why a man should go and get himself killed in vindication of a thing so intangible as the Constitution, and so unmarketable as the Flag.

One may repudiate Cobdenism without any intention to assail or undervalue the personal character of the leading Cobdenites. Most of them were in many respects highly estimable men; and Cobden himself had a large share of the qualities which Englishmen rightly reverence. He was upright, honourable, and disinterested; kindly and affectionate in his private life; an excellent father, husband, and brother; sedulous in his work, simple in his habits, pleasantly free from ostentation and self-seeking ambition; and no one can question his courage, or the conscientious industry and self-sacrificing energy, with which he served the cause of humanity, according to his lights. Many of his best qualities were shared by the other members of the group with which he was associated, and by his forerunners and successors. Earnestness, sincerity, and an unselfish zeal for the propagation of truth have been characteristic of the leaders of Economic Liberalism—of Adam Smith, Bentham, Ricardo, the Mills, Grote, Molesworth, and John Bright, to come no later. If they preached the Gospel of Self, it was assuredly not because they were personally more selfish than their neighbours; if their economics were 'un-moral,' it was not because they were otherwise than moral themselves. But the fact is their perverted ethics were largely due to the oddly theoretical character of the economical doctrine which inspired them. They prided themselves on being above all things 'practical men;' but the practical man (do we not see it every day?), myopic from much bending over blue-lined ledgers, often discerns the realities of life more dimly than the philosopher who looks at the world through his study windows. Our free-contract Radicals forgot that their political economy was after all the merest *a priori* speculation. It is true their earlier doctors and preachers did not pretend that it was anything else. Adam Smith, for instance, and his masters, Quesnay and Turgot, described what *might* happen under purely

[10] Morley, *Life of Cobden*, vol. ii. p. 389.

hypothetical and, as they thought, quite unrealisable, conditions, not what actually was happening, or would be at all likely to happen, in any society of which they had cognisance. The ' classical ' economics, which professes only to concern itself with tendencies and generalities, could be as unmoral and as *doctrinaire* as it pleased. It dealt with imaginary capitalists paying fictitious wages to unreal workmen ; with shadowy landlords drawing impossible rents from unsubstantial acres tilled by visionary tenants ; with a kingdom of Cockayne, peopled by moral monsters. Eye hath not seen the creatures who inhabit the ' orthodox ' economists' fairy-land—the Consumer who is all stomach, the Labourer who is nothing but a hand and a pair of seven-leagued boots (wherewith he may ' transfer ' himself from China to Peru even as Capital calls him), and the rest. They are phantasms of the speculative brain—mere types and symbols and algebraical x's and y's to do economic sums with, as indeed the more candid of their creators confess. Professor Walker, the great (and far from ' orthodox ') American economist, has pointed out that competition, as the regulator of all production and exchange, will only work effectively if it is ' perfect ; ' and perfect competition means not only that there must be no interference with wages, prices, hours of labour, and the like by Government, but also that in buying and selling no question of sentiment, patriotism, national policy, friendship, custom, vanity, or tradition should arise. But that is only to say that ' perfect competition ' cannot possibly exist anywhere but in the green Utopia of the Economic Cloudland ; it is too perfect for this grey imperfect earth. Now all this dealing in abstractions and hypotheses would not matter if it were confined to the professors, who, of course, know what the limitations of their science are. But a variety of circumstances caused it to be taken up by a large number of Englishmen without any limitations at all. Good men themselves, they pushed the competitive ideal, derived from the works of their theorists, to dangerous and immoral lengths. Fortunately for society, the movement had hardly set fairly in before the reaction came, and the larger part of our recent legislation has been shaped in direct antagonism to the principle of *laisser-faire*. Free-trade is only one application of that principle, and it took the firmest hold because it happened to be particularly well suited to the circumstances of a country, which only wanted to get its raw materials cheap in order that it might sell its manufactured goods where it pleased, and could ask its own price for them. Buying cheap and selling dear is uncommonly good policy if you are lucky enough to have almost a monopoly of a great many articles, which everybody must purchase from you because they cannot get them elsewhere. But Free-trade is no more sacred than any other part of the political creed to which it owes its origin ; and if it is to maintain itself, it must show clearly that it is justified by actual results at the present time. It is not to the purpose to prove that it suited us in the 'fifties and 'forties; still less to quote 'Political Economy' against it, as some speakers and writers do: not very honestly, since, as well-informed persons, they must know that the authorities they refer to, though they may impose on the crowd, are not now accepted unquestioningly in the schools. They are, of course, aware that there is no longer an orthodoxy in political economy; and being, as they must be, familiar with the works of Cairnes, Cliffe Leslie, Cunningham, Walker, Jevons, and Marshall, if not with those of Le Play and Roscher, they should not treat the Smithian political economy as if it were an accepted and unshaken scientific system, instead of a set of rules, generalisations, and personal opinions, some of which are still considered valuable, while others are absolutely discredited. Nothing has done more to accelerate the decline of Cobdenism among the sort of educated people who were once rather pleased to be considered 'Academic Radicals' than the extraordinary refusal of its leaders to recognise the results of modern economic thought. The world has not stood still since John Mill published his *Principles of Political Economy*, or even since the late Lord Sherbrooke 'completed the work of Peel' by his entirely unnecessary and superfluous abolition of the shilling metage duty on corn. It is possible that if Cobden were alive to-day, and face to face with the conditions of latter-day industrialism and international competition, he might be a Cobdenite no longer. It is certain that so acute an explorer of the currents of public opinion would have perceived that such projects as that of an Imperial Customs Union would have to be dealt with on their merits, political and social, as well as financial. And he would have understood that they could not be disposed of by being called 'veiled Protectionism,' or by an appeal to an economic pontificate that has lost its sanctity.

SIDNEY LOW.

THE GOD WHO PROMISED VICTORY TO
THE MATABELE

In the despatches daily reaching us from the scene of the native rebellion in Rhodesia, frequent mention is made of 'Mlimo,' the mysterious and evidently influential being who has ordered the Matabele to rise against the white man, and promised them victory. Any information about this Mlimo and the religious beliefs of the Matabele will probably be acceptable to the British public at the present juncture ; I shall, therefore, in this article attempt to impart some facts upon the subject which I happen to have learned, some-what in the order in which the knowledge came to me, and it will be seen that we have to do with a phase of one of the oldest and most widely spread faiths in the world—something worth our study, both from a political point of view and from that of the history and growth of human religious thought.

On the 27th of March, 1895, I was engaged in surveying that part of Matabeleland where the murdering of white men, women, and children began nearly a year afterwards. I was encamped at the foot of the peaked mountain called 'Ghoko,' between Gwelo and Belingwe. I had a trigonometrical station on the peak, and close by my camp was the kraal of Legulube ('the pig'), who has since joined the rebellion. He was one of the Amalozi tribe, but had become quite Matabele, and had been promoted to be an induna of Lobengula's. I engaged lads from the kraal to carry my instruments up to the top of the peak. In a wood near the summit I happened to catch a glimpse, between the trees, of a structure which, at first, I took to be one of the Zimbabwe-like ruins with which the country abounds. I was reading Bent, and on the look-out for such ruins, but presently I perceived that it was a newly-built hut of a very curious construction. Sitting down to rest near the very top of the peak, I pointed down at the hut and asked one of the lads : 'What is that peculiar-looking house?' He answered gravely, 'It is the House of God' (Mlimo). Now, in order to elicit truth from a native it is always well to avoid putting a leading question, so I went on asking gently, as if ignorant and wishing for information : 'Who is Molimo?' He replied earnestly and ingenuously : 'Don't you know? Molimo made the whole earth—these trees—everything.'

Q. 'But who made the house?'

A. 'We, all of us. He sent his messenger to us all, the people round Ghoko, telling us to build the house there, and we did so, under the direction of the messenger.'

Q. 'Who was the messenger? Is he here?'

A. 'His name is Lusèlé Simpindi; he is down there at that kraal.'

Q. 'And where is God?'

A. 'He is at Matojeni, in a rock. No man has seen him at any time, but he speaks to people in all languages, to each in his own tongue. If you spoke to him, he would answer you too in your own language.'

Q. 'What is the use of making him a house here if he lives at Matojeni?'

A. 'Because he is very kind to people who serve him, so we built his house as he ordered us to do, and the women and girls come up every day to keep it in order, according to his commands.'

Q. 'How does Molimo show his kindness?'

A. 'He makes one happy and fortunate in many ways, and some-times, to one who has served him well, he gives a wife.'

Q. 'Where does he get the wife from to give to the man?'

A. 'Parents take their little girls by the hand and lead them to Molimo, and call out: 'God, here is our child; we come to give her to you,' and God sends his messengers, and they take the little girl and bring her up till she is given in marriage.'

I went down later to look at the hut, and noticed that there was quite a footpath already worn by the steps of the women and girls who came up daily to keep it in order. It was about twelve feet in diameter, and formed by planting tall boughs upright in a circle in the ground and bending them towards and over each other in the centre, so as to form a dome, which was thatched, Zulu-fashion, from the top to rather more than half-way to the ground, with slightly projecting eaves. Below the eaves the walls were converted into a sort of open wicker-work by surrounding them with rings of twisted grass, about two inches thick, tied by means of thin bark to the uprights at intervals of about two inches. In front was an arched doorway some three feet high, and inside, with a similar doorway, was a circular inner chamber formed of perpendicular sticks plastered over with mud. This chamber was perfectly dark inside, while the outer space round it was lighted through the open-work wall. Two calabashes of water stood at each side of the doorway in the outer compartment, and one inside the inner door, and the floor had been freshly 'smeared.' Near the hut stood a tall tree, and against its trunk were placed three sticks four feet high and forked at the top, the branches which forked having been cut off to about four inches in length. Round the fork at the top of the sticks were some narrow strips of bark entwined snake-wise, the effect reminding one forcibly of the 'caduceus' of Mercury in the old representations, with which, indeed, as I shall show, they are apparently absolutely identical.

My servant 'Jim,' a colonial-born Pondo, who had accompanied the pioneers in their first expedition, as well as Jameson's column throughout the war, told me then that he first heard of the Molimo of the country when travelling with Mashona or Makalanga natives near Victoria. A bright meteor had shot from west to east across the sky, and a native at once called out : ' There goes Molimo, home to Matojeni.' On inquiring who 'Molimo' was, Jim learned that he was the god of the natives of those regions, who inhabited them before the invasion and conquests of the Swazi and Matabele. The last ruling sovereign, or 'Mambo,' of these people was of the priestly tribe of the Amalozi, still looked up to by the others with veneration. His seat of government was at the great ruins near the source of the Shangani (where cannon were discovered and a quantity of bullion, &c., dug up by Messrs. Burnham and Ingram). Matojeni, where the oracle of Molimo is heard, is situated about twenty-five miles south-east of Bulawayo, and consists of a cavern in rock, like so many of the ancient oracles. Umsilikaze made use of this oracle and propitiated the god of the country he had conquered by presents. These were always expected to be *black* in colour, whether cattle, sheep, goats, or blankets. Lobengula, the son of Umsilikazi, also made use of Molimo and sent his sister there to learn her fate, which he duly accomplished by strangling her. The worship of Molimo among the Matabele, indeed, appears only in its most evil form, resulting in a political and cruel priestcraft.

The morning after my ascent of the peak of Ghoko, Legulube came to visit me. After chatting with him for some time and expressing the interest I had felt in hearing about the House of Molimo, I said that I should like to see the man who had brought the message from God. He was evidently disturbed by my request, and said there were four messengers, but they had all gone with messages to Chilimanzi and the other chiefs. I could extract nothing further from him about Molimo, and my having learned as much as I had the day before seemed owing to the mere chance of an habitually inquisitive man having fallen in with an uncommonly ingenuous Kaffir lad, and his having caught sight of a queer-looking hut which might just as probably have escaped his notice.

At another time my son saw three such sticks as I have described placed against the trunk of a tree near a Zimbabwe-like ruin, and asked the natives what they were for. He was told that they were used to pray for rain with. One day a very old and jolly Amalozi man showed me another such ruin near my line of route to the west of Ghoko. He called these ruins 'Arupanga.' Walking round the ruin I came to a tall tree, and leaning against its trunk I saw three forked sticks similar to those I had seen before, but in this instance the bark lay folded over the fork and flat against the sides of the sticks. I took the three strange emblems to him and asked him what they were for. He said, pointing to the strips of bark : ' This is *meat*. We pray for meat thus : and turning towards the ruin he cried in a tone of entreaty : ' A-ru-pan-ga !' give us meat, give us meat that we may cut it with a knife !' I said to him, ' You call these ruins Arupanga, do you speak to the *stones* ? ' (I remembered that Bent had stated that the natives did *not* revere the ruins at Zimbabwe.) He only repeated what he had said before. I again asked him : ' Do you address a person or these stones ? ' Then he made a change in his prayer, crying : ' Mambo ! Umlozi ! give us meat that we may cut it with a knife !' ' Mambo ' means Lord, and the title Um*lozi* would naturally be given by one of the Amalozi to the chief of his own tribe. About these ' wishing ' or ' prayer ' sticks, I may mention that Bent speaks of having seen them in another part of the country, but *peeled*, and with the bark twisted round the top, while he heard the natives praying thus : ' Our knives are ready, give us meat !'

The native commissioner of Umtali, Mr. Nesbitt, told me that he came one day upon a hunting party in search of game with several such praying sticks, and that on his telling them that he had shot a buck and that they could have it, they immediately, in token of thanksgiving, cut such a stick, peeled off the bark and wound it round the top.

While surveying in the neighbourhood of Ghoko, I had read Bent's book, but I afterwards re-read it at Zimbabwe, when I became quite convinced that those ruins were once a temple erected to the all-Father and all-Mother, the Creator, as manifested in the generative powers of Nature, by people connected in religion with the ancient Phœnicians and Arabians, a religion many other traces of which still exist in this country. There was probably nothing gross in their reverence for the generative principle, it was the result of their groping after the all-Father who had produced man and all creation. I told a number of people, including officers of the Chartered Company, Mr. J. Dawson (now Captain Dawson), Mr. Selous, and others, of the evidence on which I had stumbled of a living and influencing religion, still utilised on occasion for political purposes, the workings of which were well worth watching. Mr. Dawson told me he had heard much of ' Molimo ' or ' Umlimo,' and that once a rough white trader had gone to Matojeni and entered the sacred cave of the god. Searching it and finding nobody, he shouted mockingly to Molimo, and cursed and swore at him. Afterwards he proceeded to Johannesburg, and was returning with his wagon and a load of goods when he was struck dead by lightning. When the Matabele heard of this, ' You see,' they said, ' not even whites can insult our god with impunity.' Politically considered, I think enough has been told to show that the priests of Umlimo will require to be looked after in future to prevent more mischief being done through their means. Perhaps it would be well to blow up the sacred cave containing the oracle, but it is said that there are several places known where Molimo is to be heard. He must thus be· considered to be present in more places than one, if not everywhere. I once mentioned the above facts to my old friend the Rev. Frédéric Ellenberger of the French Mission in Basutoland, a country which I have long known intimately, and the government of which I administered at one time. I knew that all the Basuto and Bechuana tribes, whose traditions show that they emigrated from the North, were found by the missionaries to be worshippers of 'Molimo' in various ways, and that the missionaries adopted the name of 'Molimo' for God. He told me that the worship of Molimo (Morimo, Modimo, &c.) was found to extend up to Lake Tanganyika at least, though not everywhere throughout the intervening countries. The early Portuguese discoverers mention it under different dialectic changes, as Mozimo, &c. A Jesuit missionary from the Zambesi told me that the people among whom he had been labouring prayed to Mozimo as intercessor with the Supreme Being, whom they called ' Umlungo' or Master, which is the name given to white men by many tribes. The language of Mashonaland will, I am told, take one all over the country, from far north of Nyassa land down to near Delagoa, though a wave of Zulu invasion and language has passed northward through those countries. Mr. Ellenberger, from his critical knowledge of the Basuto language, explained to me what he believes to be the etymology of the word 'Molimo,' pronounced Modimo by the Basutos. He says the root word *dimo* is an almost obsolete word, appearing sometimes as the name of a man, and that it means *hidden, invisible, mysterious.*

It is found in the words :

Modimo, God, the unseen spirit. Plural *Medimo*. The plural *Ba-dimo*, the unseen persons, *i.e.* the spirits of ancestors.

Le-dimo, a hidden person. Plural, *Madimo*, a euphemism (according to the genius of the language, which avoids shocking expressions) meaning man-eaters or cannibals, people who hide to entrap man for food and devour it in secret caves.

Ho-dimo, upwards, towards the invisible world.

Lehodimo, the invisible world, the sky, the heavens.

Dimōla, to reveal the unseen (to *un*-hide, the termination *ola* denoting the reverse action of a verb).

This etymology may not be traceable in the Mashona language, but may, none the less, be the correct one, the Basutos having carried it with them in their migration southward, from the present Mashona or Makalanga country. The Mashonas themselves may not retain it, though it explains the fundamental meaning of the name of the object of their worship. In the same way the Bechuana tribe called

Ba-tsipi, the men of iron (or those who reverence iron tribally), know nothing of the reason of the words they use when praying for success in the chase. ' O Thou of the broken leg,' they cry, ' thou who didst fall from heaven, give us food ! ' This is evidently a hymn descended to them through thousands of years. Hearing such things carries one back into the times of the ancient classics, as I felt once in '74 when hearing a case as British Resident in the Wanskei. It was a charge of murder for alleged witchcraft against Umhlonhlo, the chief of the Pondomisi, and a woman giving evidence told me how, in the subsequently murdered woman's hut, where the lightning spirit had enveloped her, she had, in her sleep, been embraced by the ' thunder bird,' the eagle, the veritable bird of Jupiter Tonans, which produced a sort of possession, by the power of lightning, the worst effect of witchcraft. I may explain that the murdered woman was believed to have dealings with this bird, and her crime was causing the lightning to strike close to the chief's hut.

But these beliefs found in Mashonaland, these temples and praying sticks, carry one further back than any written history goes. Zimbabwe (which in the Mashona language means the ' house of stone ') is clearly a hermaphrodite temple, or temple to the dual generative principle (as Baal and Ashtaroth) as well as to the heavenly bodies and all manifestations of the powers creative of man and Nature. It would be a good thing for some one systematically to visit and to make measurements and plans of the many *other* temples and altars which exist in that country, so that these might be compared with ruins in other parts of the world, especially those of Phœnician origin. There is a peculiar feature in some of these which I shall attempt to describe. An oval stone platform was built, about twelve to fifteen feet high and eighty long, with perpendicular walls, upon a granite rock foundation. Upon this was built another smaller oval platform, and on that two round altars, with steps and a central pillar to each. There was ' Zimbabwe ' ornamentation on the wall over a narrow platform-like projection along one side of the ruin.

. The very peculiar feature of this ruin was that seven well-like circular holes had been made in the platform round about the altars. These holes were about eight inches in diameter at the top but widened as they went down till they reached the solid rock at a depth of from twelve to fifteen feet, where they were twelve or more inches in diameter. They were lined with stone, cut in segments of a circle to fit into their sides. There were no monoliths in this case. In another ruin these holes were larger and proportionately wider at the bottom.

In Bent's book he gives an illustration of an iron smelting furnace, faintly and conventionally showing the female form. All the furnaces found in Rhodesia are of that form, but those which I have seen (and I have come upon five of them in a row) are far more realistic, most minutely and statuesquely so, all in a cross-legged

sitting position and clearly showing that the production or birth
of the metal is considered worthy of a special religious expression.
It recognised the Creator in one form of his human manifestation
in creation. The magistrate of Gwello, when he had his first house
built in 'wattle and daub,' found that the Makalanga women, who
were engaged to plaster it, had produced, according to a general
custom, a clay image of the female form in relief upon the inside
wall. He asked them what they did that for. They answered
benevolently that it was to bring him good luck. This illustrates
the pure form of the cult of these people, who worship the unknown
and unseen God by reverencing his manifestation (in this instance)
in the female side of the creative principle.

I do not pretend to any extensive reading on the subject of the
widespread and ancient prevalence of this cult. I only give
facts as I have picked them up, showing something of a present local
phase of this religion. With regard to the praying sticks I may
mention that I saw a reference in Lemprière and also in an article
in a German 'Konversations-Lexicon' to the caduceus of Mercury, as
having been of Phœnician origin, and originally simply a forked
stick with some band wound about the top of it, just like the praying
or wishing sticks now used by these tribes; also that sometimes a
pair of leaves was represented as growing out of the stick opposite each
other near the fork, and that afterwards these leaves came to be
represented as wings. Mercury Caducifer, the quick messenger
between the gods and men who carried answers to prayer and gave
fertility, carried this symbol and wore similar wings in his ankles
and on the fillet round his head. The writer of the article in the
'Konversations-Lexicon' to which I have referred says that 'the forked
stick appears to be identical with the "wishing stick" of our forefathers
as mentioned in the sagas,' which was evidently a praying stick
used in appeals to the Deity. They remind one also of certain metal
emblems with wings similarly situated which have been found in the
excavations at Pompeii and which illustrate the same principle.
They likewise recall the rods which Jacob peeled and placed before
the flocks of his father-in-law as well as the representation of the
Phœnician god of 'teeming flocks and fruitful fields' which, in after
ages, was used to mark the boundaries of properties, &c., in Roman
times, but the fundamental idea of which was originally identical
with the cult of Hermes and other ancient gods. Thus the use of
these praying sticks and the other customs and modes of thought
which I have mentioned add further links to the chain of evidence
furnished by the ruins in Rhodesia of a near connection between
northern ancient religions and those held by the people who built
the temple of Zimbabwe, and which religious ideas in their present
phase appear to be still spread through a wide extent of country
around the ruins.

Joseph Millerd Orpen.

NATURE VERSUS THE CHARTERED COMPANY

ALTHOUGH from the earliest times, and in almost every country, the efforts of mankind have been constantly directed towards overcoming natural obstacles, and moulding the forces of human nature afresh for human purposes, there has never been, perhaps, in one country, within an equal period, a time when nature has seemed to oppose the progress of human civilisation as in South Africa during the last eight months. The Chartered Company and Mr. Rhodes are to-day fighting two foes, rinderpest and rebellion, each having famine as a possible ally, but of these two evils the much more deadly and powerful is the ' rinderpest,' destroying or paralysing the power of moving necessaries of human life and munitions of war, which are vital to outposts of the Empire, such as Bulawayo or Salisbury. In Rhodesia the real enemy of the Chartered Company not only to-day, but for the next eighteen months, will be, not the Matabele or the Mashonas, but the ' rinderpest.' It would be foolish to state that the native rising was not serious, but the rebellion is nothing like so urgent as the food question. For the past three years a white population, numbering three or four thousand, have received all the luxuries and nearly all the necessities of civilised life from a base at Mafeking, 600 miles away, these food supplies being brought up by ox wagon. The black population is also largely dependent on the ' trek ox ' for its subsistence. The journey, after this manner, generally occupied from forty to forty-five days, each wagon carrying from seven to eight thousand pounds weight of food-stuffs. To-day the position has entirely altered. Fully ninety per cent. of the ' trek ' oxen have died of this plague, and even the small percentage which have recovered are so weak and poor in condition as to make them practically useless for haulage purposes. We thus have, so to speak, a garrison of 4,000 white persons in Bulawayo and Rhodesia, let alone the black allies, to whom food can only now be conveyed by mule or donkey wagon. At first it might seem as if the substitution of the donkey or mule for the ox would make comparatively little difference; but whereas the ox can, by being '' outspanned ' every night, find sufficient nourishment in the grass on the veldt to keep him in excellent condition, the mule quickly dies if mealies, or some other kind of grain foods, are not given· him. Donkeys answer well in places where there is good veldt, but given the hard work of haulage and no grain, they very soon break down. The result is that in the case of mules, and to some degree donkeys also, enough grain food has to be taken on the wagon to supply them for a journey of nearly six hundred miles, and thus proportionately less of human food-stuffs can be taken. In some instances the experiment has been tried of endeavouring to push the mules and donkeys up country as fast as possible, and then shooting them or leaving them to perish on arrival, but this plan seldom succeeds. In the majority of cases the animals fall before they have accomplished two-thirds of the distance.

Nature has placed yet another difficulty in the way of transport, for during the wet season, from November to February, mule sickness is very prevalent, and one of the partners of the firm of Zeederberg and Co., who run the coach service with the greatest pluck and spirit between Mafeking and Bulawayo, and who own over fourteen hundred mules, informed me that they expect every year to lose from fifty to sixty per cent. of their live stock during this period. Then there are diseases affecting oxen, horses, and mules which seem to be peculiar to South Africa, such as 'gall sickness,' 'red water,' and 'lung sickness.' There are also one or two poisonous plants, notably the poisonous lily, which, when eaten, causes almost certain death. This poisonous lily comes up just before the grass, and consequently there is always the risk of its being eaten by hungry animals. It will thus be seen under what difficulties transport work has to be carried on, even in normal times, and when, as now, there are only about five to ten oxen left for every hundred that previously existed the difficulty is enormously and immeasurably increased. The weight usually carried by mule or donkey wagon is also from 25 to 30 per cent. less than that taken by ox wagon. A span of sixteen oxen can reach Bulawayo from Mafeking with from seven to eight thousand pounds weight of food-stuffs, whereas by mule or donkey wagon seldom more than five thousand pounds weight is taken with eighteen donkeys or ten to twelve mules. 'Rinderpest' in this way has been, and will be for some time, a greater enemy to the progress of Rhodesia than the native rebellion. Two years ago the plague was rampant in Uganda and Central Africa, and where this fell disease will stop it is impossible to say, cases having been already reported as far south as Bultfontein, a place near Kimberley. As the infection is largely carried by flies, it is doubtful if even the cattle of Cape Colony, with the most vigorous policy of isolation and destruction, can be saved. In about five per cent. of the cases the animals recover, but amongst all the so-called cures nothing has yet been found really effective, and, as far as can be seen, the only practical means of stopping the plague is to adopt, cost what it may, the most drastic policy of exterminating the cattle, diseased and healthy alike, in all districts in which the disease appears. This policy of course entails compensation in some form or other, but even the most generous, and even lavish, treatment which may be accorded to those who have lost healthy oxen may be cheaper in the long run than a pestilence which in England, twenty or thirty years ago, cost the nation upwards of seven millions before it could be eradicated. But even if this vigorous policy be adopted the difficulty still remains of dealing with the cattle of chiefs who cannot be controlled, such as Sekhome, chief of the N'Gami tribes, the chiefs of the Gazaland district, and along the Portuguese border. If in three years the country is free from this plague, we may rightly consider South Africa lucky. In two years, however, the railway will have relegated the trek ox to the more distant parts of Rhodesia, and the chief mining districts will be in touch with civilisation and independent of the transport rider.

It might be as well to give the reader some idea of the present means of communication between Bulawayo and the south. The first 114 miles of the road—namely, from Mafeking to Gaberones—is, for the most part, fairly good—that is, good for an African road—and the coaches, when the mules are in good condition and not overworked, as at present, owing to the constant strain put upon them by extra coaches and ammunition wagons, perform the journey at the rate of four to five miles an hour, with changes of 'spans' about every ten miles. The next section, from Gaberones to Palla, which is about 120 miles further, is, perhaps, the worst section of the road, the sand in some places being nearly a foot deep, the country monotonous, and there being either bad water or none at all. From Palla to Palapye, another 120 miles, the road is rather better, but the last ten miles into Palapye is heart-breaking work for animals through almost the deepest part of the road, sand in dry weather and mud in wet, finishing up with two or three miles of rock and boulders, which severely try the strength of any team, the nerves of the passengers, and the fabric of all vehicles. Three wagons were hopelessly stuck five miles out of Palapye on this section when I passed on the road returning south. From Palapye to Tati, about 120 miles, is perhaps the best of the road, with the exception of one or two deep 'spruits,' or drifts where there are river beds about as wide as the Thames at Richmond, dry in the autumn, winter, and spring, but roaring torrents in the summer, from November to February, and only crossed then with the utmost difficulty. From Tati to Mangwe, sixty miles, the road is fair, but there is heavy sand in places, and one or two deep drifts. From Mangwe to Figtree, which is at the northern end of the Mangwe Pass, thirty miles in length, the road passes through grand scenery, but the difficulties are consequently greater. Tremendously steep gradients, sand, and almost every species of difficulty to locomotion is met with. The coach-drivers and transport riders are, however, wonderfully skilful in handling their teams, and it is certainly marvellous that so few accidents occur. From Figtree to Bulawayo, thirty miles, the road is comparatively good.

The real question in Rhodesia, as I have pointed out before, for the next year will not be the native question so much as this question of transport and food supply, and this problem remains for the Chartered Company to solve. How can they induce the white population to remain in Bulawayo and Southern Rhodesia, when food-stuffs are at such prohibitive prices, and when there is no work to do, all trades being at a standstill? Naturally no sane individual or wisely managed company is at present building houses, or continuing operations of any sort on a large scale, with prices as they are, knowing that the advent of the railway means cheaper material, cheaper labour, and immunity from native risings. Artisans who were earning 1*l.* a day have now no work, the constructive trades having ceased, and these men are naturally leaving the country. When I was in Bulawayo in May of this year eggs were 40*s.* or 50*s.* a dozen, tins of condensed milk were sold for 7*s.* 6*d.* each—strong buyers, as the Stock Exchange would say—and enough bread for breakfast for one cost a shilling. So long as wages were high and regular high prices were willingly paid, but now, except a man is in the Chartered Company's employ, his chance of work is distinctly poor. For the moment fighting at 10*s.* a day and rations is the best trade, and there are plenty of volunteers at that price. Now that Lord Grey and Mr. Rhodes have settled that 5*s.* a day and rations is ample pay we hear that great dissatisfaction is expressed, and that numbers are leaving the country in consequence. But when the war is over then will come the real pinch, and, unless a system of gratuitous State maintenance is then established at the cost of the Chartered Company, an exodus of the majority of the population must take place. Until, therefore, the railway reaches Bulawayo there can be no real progress in Southern Rhodesia, either in regard to mining, commerce, or agriculture, and no one realises, I feel sure, that a vigorous railway policy is the only solution of the present difficulties more than Mr. Rhodes himself.

Many people will be also tempted to ask, Why is it that Mr. Rhodes, with his wonderful foresight in other directions, has not before now made a point of accelerating the construction of the railway? The Vryburg-Mafeking section was opened in October 1894, and here we are in August 1896, and only another fifty miles is absolutely working—and that only half ballasted—as far as Rabatse. If only a small portion of the money spent in mining, development, and house-building in Rhodesia had been spent upon railway construction Rhodesia to-day would probably not have been suffering from a native rebellion, would have been comparatively well stocked with food for man and beast, and would also have undoubtedly possessed two or three times as many white inhabitants. It is difficult to imagine what can have been the reason of this delay, for the Beira railway was stagnant at the same time, and even if it is true, as is reported, that Mr. Rhodes and the Chartered Company had special reasons for favouring the Beira route, as against the Mafeking route, there is no excuse why, in that case, the Beira line should not have been completed, at any rate as far as Salisbury. Another curious feature is observable. In the United States, and in all other parts of the world where a railway is used as a civilising and developing factor outside any commercial value, the railway precedes the population, and the population afterwards agglomerates round the railway. Where the line crosses streams or fertile valleys, spots particularly attractive to the human eye or convenient for trade, towns spring up. But in Rhodesia the opposite seems to be the case. Take the case of Umtali. Nothing can be stranger than shifting a whole township, and giving the population compensation for disturbances, in order to avoid taking the railway line out of its direct course and over a somewhat severe gradient. Surely in Rhodesia too the railway, even if it does not precede, ought at least to accompany and not follow the incoming population. The delay in pushing on the railway will have proved extremely costly to the Chartered Company and the nation. The Chartered Board must now have realised the supreme importance of the railway, for we learn that it is going to give a bonus to the contractor of 200*l.* for every mile completed in a day.

However, Mr. Rhodes is not the man to be discouraged when the outlook appears bad and possible famine seems to stare the white and black population alike in the face. His personality is worth more, for the moment, in this crisis in Rhodesia, than the agricultural or mineral wealth of the whole country. Rhodesia might to-day be well called ' Rhodes, Unlimited.'

It is true that Mr. Rhodes has no longer any official position with the Chartered Company. But just as a diamond removed from its setting is a diamond still, so Rhodes, whether in the position of Prime Minister of the Cape Colony, or Managing Director of the Chartered Company, or as an individual, is Rhodes still. The same brain, heart, and vigour remain—the rest is as nothing, a mere official halo.

All Nature has striven against him, and large masses of mankind— drought, locusts, pestilences, and famines on the one side, raids, revolutions, and revelations on the other. Should he emerge, as I believe he will, successfully from these troubles, he will have won, and practically won alone, by his own exertions, a country seven times the size of the United Kingdom in the face of Nature and man.

In this case of Nature *v.* the Chartered Company and Rhodes, even though the trial last a year more, and to-day the odds be on the plaintiff, the result will to a certainty be a verdict in favour of the defendants.

JOHN SCOTT MONTAGU.

THE BATTLE OF THE STANDARDS IN AMERICA

I

WAR TO THE KNIFE

THE optimism of the American people blinds them to the approach
of any great political crisis until it is close at hand.   Up to the very
hour when the Secessionists fired on Fort Sumter, the Northern press
ridiculed the possibility of civil war.   It was conceded that there
were a few fanatics in the South who clamoured for secession, and a
few fanatics in the North who would welcome civil war, but that the
South would secede, and the North fight, was thought to be incredible.
But in the flash of the guns of Charleston harbour it was suddenly
seen that the whole South was united in defence of the right of
secession, and that the North was unanimous in the determination
that secession should be crushed on the battlefield.

Two months before the Democratic Convention met last July, the
Eastern States fancied that the movement in behalf of free silver
coinage was of small importance, and that there was not the slightest
danger that the Silverites could triumph in a national election.   To-
day it is apparent that the silver craze has seized upon the entire
West and South, and is spreading with ominous rapidity even in the
East.   As the North was blind to the danger of secession, so the
American people have been blind to the steadily growing danger that
the Federal Government may, at no distant day, fall into the hands
of the Silverites, and that the Eastern States will then be compelled
to choose between utter ruin and withdrawal from the Union.

In the early days of the Southern rebellion, an eminent Democratic leader, one of the few Americans of the period who had a right
to be ranked as a statesman, said, in the course of a confidential
conversation, that the East had signed its death warrant by joining
with the West to crush the South.   'When the war is over,' said he,
'the West will dominate the Union.   It will rapidly grow in population and power, while the East will remain stationary.   In a few
years the East will be powerless, and the crazy financial legislation
which the ignorance and arrogance of the West is certain to bring

about, will make it necessary for the East to accept bankruptcy or civil war.' The speaker was not in the slightest degree in sympathy with the Southern secessionists, and had supported to the best of his ability the Lincoln Government. Nevertheless, he saw that the East had missed its one great opportunity by not following the example of the South, and withdrawing from the shattered Union. A little more than thirty-four years have passed since he made this prediction, and the time of its fulfilment draws near.

The average Western American is a man of unbounded energy, unbounded self-conceit, and unbounded ignorance. The ignorance of the Western man is not the natural ignorance of the Calabrian peasant. The latter can neither read nor write, and he knows nothing except what passes before his eyes in his little mountain village, but with this ignorance there is the humility that accepts the superiority and welcomes the leadership of intelligent men. The ignorance of the Western American is an artificial and acquired ignorance. He absorbs it from the newspapers which form his only reading. These not only teach him the most absurdly false doctrines in matters of political economy and finance, but they also flatter his vanity, and convince him that he is infinitely superior to the men of the effete East. He firmly believes that if the East advocates a revenue tariff and a gold standard, it is because of the influence of British teachings and of British bribery. The West, in its own opinion, has the only true, the only American political gospel, and its mission is to impose it not only on the East but on the world. It is to the ignorant West that the United States owe the Greenback folly, the Protectionist delusion, and the silver craze.

Soon after the civil war was ended, the West made the discovery that an unlimited and irredeemable paper currency was the panacea for all public and private woes. For a time the 'Greenback craze,' as it was called, threatened the American Republic much as the silver craze threatens it to-day. Fortunately, the West had then nothing like the strength that it has to-day, and the efforts of the East to maintain an honest currency were successful. Both the great political parties saw themselves compelled to take firm ground against the Greenback movement, although the Democratic party had at one time showed a disposition to attract Greenback votes by framing platforms that could be interpreted in favour of either honest or dishonest currency. The failure of the Greenback movement was, however, due solely to the fact that the centre of population had not yet shifted so far westward as to make it possible to elect a president without the votes of the two great Eastern States—New York and Pennsylvania. That change has now taken place, and a president can be elected even if he loses both New York and Pennsylvania.

It was natural that a community capable of believing that the *fiat* of the government could make an irredeemable paper dollar worth as much as a gold dollar, should accept the doctrine of the Protectionist, that the American who pays two dollars for a home-made blanket instead of one dollar for an imported blanket is on the high road to wealth. The West is to a large extent an agricultural community, and as such Protection had nothing to offer it except an immense increase of the cost of living. The Western farmer had everything to lose and nothing to gain by Protection, but nevertheless he voted blindly for it, and fastened the McKinley tariff on his back. It is true that there are Protectionists in the Eastern States, but they are certainly in a minority. The strength of Protection lies in the West, and it was by Western votes that it was forced upon the country.

In its beginning, the silver heresy took the shape of a demand for bimetallic currency. It owed its origin to the discovery of large silver mines in certain of the far Western States. Its chief promoters were the mine owners, who sought a market for their silver, but it soon enlisted the support of all who had formerly demanded 'cheap money' in the shape of greenbacks. The silver party was at first confined almost wholly to the West, but it soon enlisted adherents in the South. Its progress was watched with languid interest by the East, where it was believed to be only a weak echo of the greenback movement. It achieved its greatest victory in the passage of the Sherman Law, which provided that the Government should coin every month a certain quantity of silver dollars. In spite of the verbiage with which the Sherman Law was clothed, it meant simply that the Government should be compelled to buy a fixed quantity of silver annually, and pay for it in gold at a price far above its true value. The inevitable result of such a law might easily have been foreseen, but, inasmuch as the purchased silver remained in the vaults of the Federal Treasury, for the very sufficient reason that no creditor would accept it in the place of gold, the people of the East flattered themselves that it would do no harm, and trusted that it would satisfy the Silverites. Of course it brought about the steady depreciation of the price of silver, and the steady flow of gold to other countries, while the Silverites, so far from being satisfied with the Law, were encouraged to demand the free and unlimited coinage of silver. The heresy infects both the great political parties in the West, and there are to-day nearly as many Western Republicans who are in favour of free silver, as there are Western silver Democrats. The recent Republican Convention, knowing that in any event the South was certain to remain Democratic, and that no Republican candidate could possibly be elected without the nearly unanimous support of the East, wisely placed itself fully and fairly on the side of honest money, and for the moment the Eastern people fancied that an overwhelming Republican victory had been thereby made certain. It was not until the Democratic Convention met, and the wild enthusiasm of the advocates of free silver carried all before it, that the East began to think that possibly the strength of the silver craze had been under-estimated.

At the present writing it seems hardly probable that the Democrats will carry the next presidential election, but the supporters of Mr. McKinley no longer feel the absolute confidence which was theirs only a few weeks ago. It is true that in the East all 'gold Democrats' will either vote for McKinley, or will abstain from voting. That this will give every one of the Eastern States to the Republicans is reasonably sure. On the other hand no man can predict to what extent the 'silver Republicans' of the West will abandon McKinley, and vote for the Democratic candidate. If they are sufficient in number to carry Ohio, Indiana, and Illinois, in addition to most of the other Western States, and the solid South, the Republicans may be defeated in spite of their victories in the East. It should not be forgotten that it is not merely the silver question which will influence Western voters. For the first time in the history of the United States the West is arrayed avowedly against the East, and the dislike of the Eastern people, which is universal at the West, will be an important factor in the election.

American optimism shirks the confession that the West dislikes the East. No one, however, who has any thorough knowledge of the American people, can doubt that for some years the East and the West have been steadily growing further and further apart, until they are now fairly in the attitude of hostile communities. The West dislikes the East for two reasons. The Western man is haunted by the fear that his Eastern fellow citizen looks upon him as a social inferior, and in revenge he sneers bitterly at what he calls the 'culchaw' of the East. In point of fact the Eastern American does not care a particle what sort of clothes the Western man wears, or in what fashion he trims his hair and beard. That there is a certain rusticity in Western speech and manners is sufficiently obvious when the West and the East meet socially, but the man from Chicago is mistaken in supposing that by reason of these things he is despised by the man from New York. The Eastern press may occasionally express its amusement at Western ways, but this is rarely done in malice. Nevertheless the Western man, with the painful self-consciousness of the rustic who finds himself in a drawing-room, believes that he is an object of ridicule, and therefore cordially hates the innocent Eastern man. Childish as this feeling may seem, it still exists, and no one can converse half an hour with a Western American without being informed that no Western man cares a straw for the opinion of the East, which is a sure proof that the contrary is the fact.

But the chief cause of the animosity of the West towards the East is the fact that the former is heavily in debt to the latter. The

Western cities have been built with Eastern money, and the Western railways and Western mines owe their existence either to Eastern or English capital. The debtor rarely likes his creditor, especially when it is inconvenient to pay him. Chicago was rebuilt after the great fire by money furnished by the East; but when the lenders ventured to suggest that payment of interest was desirable, Chicago became bitterly indignant at the New York and Boston 'Shylocks,' who were represented as clamouring for their respective pounds of flesh. The Western press uniformly takes a like attitude towards all Eastern creditors, and the mildest epithets given to them are 'Shylocks,' 'sharks,' and 'bloodsuckers.' Gradually the Western man has convinced himself that it is a hard and merciless thing for a creditor to ask for payment, and he is quite ready to take advantage of any method of legally avoiding payment of his debts. The advocates of free silver offer him precisely what he is seeking. If silver becomes the only currency, the Eastern 'Shylock' can be paid in silver dollars that are worth only fifty cents each. The Western debtor can thus rid himself of one-half of his indebtedness, and can at the same time punish the presumptuous East for its insolence in expecting full payment. The West does not favour the free coinage of silver merely because of its ignorant belief that 'cheap money' will make everybody rich. Not the least of the charms of free silver is the expectation that it will serve as an instrument for the chastisement of the East.

The result of the present political campaign will be to intensify the hostility of the West towards the East. For months to come the two great divisions of the country will be in battle array, one against the other. The East will stand for gold and honesty—the West for silver and knavery. The question of the tariff will pass out of sight, and the honest Eastern Democrat will vote for the author of the most preposterous Protectionist measure the world has ever seen, because his only alternative will be to vote for the candidate who represents a policy of highway robbery. Whatever the result of the election may be, the West and the East will have been for months in the attitude of enemies, and the Eastern and Western press will have constantly reviled one another as 'Shylocks' and thieves. If the West dislikes the East to-day, dislike will have grown into the bitterest hatred by next November.

As has been said, the probabilities are at present in favour of the election of McKinley. But a defeat of the Silverites this year simply postpones their victory for four brief years. The Republicans are pledged to re-enact the McKinley tariff, and two, or at most three, years of Protection of the McKinley variety will bring about an inevitable industrial and commercial panic, precisely as the panic of 1895 was brought about. Under the unnatural stimulus of a high Protective tariff manufactories of protected articles will spring up everywhere, and their eagerness to fill the market will ensure the over-production that Protection invariably fosters. Then will follow the closing of manufactories, the idleness and discontent of workmen, and the financial stringency and distress which were, a year ago, the direct results of the McKinley tariff, but which the unthinking voter absurdly charges to the account of the most honest and capable man that has occupied the Presidential chair during the present century. When this panic occurs, the Silverites will insist that it has been the result of the failure to adopt the free coinage of silver. The voters will either be convinced that this is true, or, at all events, they will be ready to give the silver panacea a trial. The defeat of the silver candidate in 1896 will be followed by his triumphant election in 1900, and the East will lie prostrate at the mercy of the West.

That the free and unlimited coinage of silver means the utter ruin of the East, goes without saying. When the Silverites gain possession of the Federal Government, the East must submit, with what grace it can muster, to complete and hopeless bankruptcy, or it must withdraw from the Union, and endeavour to maintain its independence by arms. It may fail as the South failed a generation ago, but it will at least have perished honourably, and its skirts will be free from the stain of fraud and robbery with which the West will have blackened the Federal Union.

W. L. ALDEN.

THE BATTLE OF THE STANDARDS
IN AMERICA

II

SUGGESTIONS FOR A COMPROMISE

THE Republican party has declared explicitly for the maintenance of the existing gold standard, and the Democratic party, at its convention recently held in this city, has declared with equal explicitness for the free coinage of silver by this country alone. The great issue is therefore fairly and squarely joined. And it is the first time in the history of the Republic that a clearly defined issue on this great question has been put before the people. The electoral battle which will be waged between now and November will be beyond all comparison the most important that has been fought in this country since the Civil War.

Which side is going to win? To read the great daily papers in New York, Philadelphia, Chicago, and Boston, one would suppose that there was really no question about it, and that the victory of the Gold men by an overwhelming majority was a foregone conclusion. But these papers can be no more relied on to correctly represent the sentiment of the American people than the daily papers of London can be relied on to correctly represent the sentiment of the English people outside of London. In the prophecies which they make regarding the result, the wish is largely father to the thought.

For my own part, I am convinced that, if every other issue save that of gold against silver were eliminated from the campaign, silver would win. But gold goes into this fight with two great advantages. It is tied to the Republican reaction, and it is tied to the cause of Protection. Roughly speaking, the South and the States and Territories west of the Missouri River are for silver, and the North-Eastern States are decisively for gold. The great agricultural States of the North-West constitute the doubtful territory in which the real battle will be fought. At the State Conventions held in preparation for the National Conventions, the Republicans succeeded in securing gold delegations in these States, but it was evident that there was a strong

minority in favour of silver.   In nearly all of these States, the Democratic party selected delegations instructed for silver.   I am satisfied
that, if the money issue were not in any way complicated by other
issues, the Silver party would carry most of the North-Western States
and that the electoral vote of these States, added to that which they
would receive from the West and South, would suffice to give them a
majority.   But these North-Western States, and in particular the
great States of Illinois and Iowa, have always been Banner Republican
States.   Some of them suffered a temporary aberration during the
landslide to Democracy which took place at the last national election.
But this seems to have only intensified the violence of the reaction in
favour of their old love.   The gold standard now presents itself to
the Republicans in these States as the policy of their party, and they
have to choose between voting for it and leaving the party.   Again,
there is undoubtedly a great reaction in this country in favour of
Protection; and, strange as it may seem to people in England, this
reaction is specially strong in the States of the North-West.   The
Gold cause now comes before the voters of these States linked to the
cause of Protection, and the two must stand or fall together.   Upon
the whole, I hazard the prophecy that gold will win, after a great
struggle, and by a moderate majority.

We are already in the thick of the fray.   At least two-thirds of
the editorial writing done in the daily papers has reference to this
issue.   The Republicans are naturally making a vigorous effort to
keep the Protection issue to the front; but even their papers tacitly
assume that there is no need to argue over this issue, and the Democratic papers avoid it as the burnt child avoids the fire.

Expositions of the familiar rule known as Gresham's law and of
the application of that law to the case of this country if the free
coinage of silver were adopted, the respective merits of the single and
double standards and the possibility of maintaining a stable par of
exchange between the two metals, the sufficiency of the available
supply of gold to meet the needs of the leading nations for money of
ultimate redemption,—these and such as these are the subjects that
are threshed out in the editorials of our leading dailies with a wearisome iteration.   It may not be out of place for me to notice here a
few salient points in regard to the way in which this great controversy
is being conducted.

There are two leading features which seem fated to arise, in a
greater or less degree, in connection with all discussions of monetary
or social topics.   These features are manifesting themselves in a
very marked degree in the newspaper discussion of the money question at present going on in this country.   They are the following:—

1. Each side calls the other side very hard names indeed.

2. While the most absolutely contradictory theories are advocated
on either side, the advocates of each side are supremely certain that

they are entirely right and that their opponents are entirely wrong. Neither side will admit the possibility of a *via media*, and those who talk of compromise are anathematised equally by both sides.

A few words on each of these points :—

1. It would seem to be a peculiarity of the money question that those who argue about it always adopt, more or less, those methods of argument which are said to be popular in the fish market at Billingsgate. The regular thing in this country now is for the Silver men to talk of the advocates of the single gold standard as criminals who have conspired together for the purpose of imposing the yoke of Wall Street upon the necks of the American people ; while the Gold men answer by calling the Silver men knaves, and swindlers, and fools, and idiots, and so forth ; and the amusing part of it is that we frequently find the advocates of one side protesting earnestly against the use of strong language on the other side, and then following up this protest with a perfect volley of abuse against their opponents. When will the disputants, and more especially the newspapers, realise the fact that this controversy has passed out of the stage at which it can be settled, or any good be effected, by calling hard names ? The mere fact that there are numbers of men of the highest intelligence and of undoubted honesty on each side ought to be enough to convince us that the question is one of great complexity on which there is still room for honest and intelligent difference of opinion.

2. Closely connected with, and indeed largely causing, the peculiarity last noticed is the singular confidence of absolute rightness and infallibility which characterises the utterances on either side. As I have said, this is a question of enormous complexity about which men of the highest capacity, who have made a special study of the subject, are still at variance. But to read the Gold papers in this country one would conclude that no man who was not a born idiot could see any merit on the Silver side. And to read the Silver papers one would suppose that no man not a fit subject for the penitentiary could advocate the single gold standard.

In regard to the points which are most commonly argued in this controversy, a man of a judicial turn of mind, who approaches the question without prejudices of any kind, will almost certainly conclude that ' there is a good deal to be said on both sides,' and that the right lies somewhere between the two. To illustrate this by a few examples.

The point about which the controversy rages most fiercely is the question as to what would be the effect on the purchasing power of the silver dollar if this country were to throw open its mints to silver at the ratio of sixteen to one with gold. At present, as your readers know, the silver dollar of the United States has a purchasing power equal to nearly double the bullion value of the silver contained in it. Of course, if silver were admitted to free coinage, the bullion value and the coin value could not keep apart in this way. They would have to come together somewhere. The great question at issue is— where would they come together? The Silver men say that this country alone, by opening its mints to silver at the ratio of sixteen to one with gold, and making the silver dollars unlimited legal tender at that ratio, could fix and maintain that as the ratio of bullion value. In other words, they affirm that the effect of free coinage would be to nearly double the present bullion value of silver relatively to gold. On the other hand, the Gold men say that free coinage means a fifty cent. dollar, which is the same thing as saying that the adoption of free coinage by this country would not raise the bullion value of silver at all, but would leave it just where it is at present. It is obvious that there is plenty of room for a *via media* between these two extremes. There is a good deal of difference between doubling the value of silver and not affecting it at all. For my part, I have not the smallest doubt but that, in regard to this question, as in regard to most of the other questions at issue, the truth lies somewhere between the extremes advocated on either side. I do not believe that this country alone could raise the par of exchange to sixteen to one and keep it at that point, but I am quite convinced that the adoption of free coinage by such a country as this would cause a very substantial rise in the bullion value of silver, and that, therefore, the fifty cent. dollar argument, which is constantly dinned into our ears, is wide of the truth. I am not going to argue the question now, but I will merely say that the experience of the past, and more especially the marked effect on the price of silver recently produced by the shutting of the Indian mints, seems to me to make it as certain as anything of the kind can be that the opening of the mints of this country to free coinage would very materially affect the bullion price of silver.

To take another example. Closely connected with the fifty cent. dollar argument is the question of the honesty of free coinage, about which the controversy also rages with great fierceness. On this question the position of the Silver men is that a great wrong was done to the debtor classes by the demonetisation of silver, and the consequent appreciation of gold, and that the restoring of the right of free coinage to silver is the only way by which that wrong can be undone. They will not admit that there is any dishonesty about it. On the contrary, they say the dishonesty is to leave things as they are. On the other hand, the Gold men use their strongest language on this point. They deny vigorously that any wrong has been done at all, and they say that free coinage would simply mean a wholesale fraud on creditors, and that this is the object which its promoters really have at heart.

Here, again, I think the right lies between the two extremes. If the value of gold relatively to commodities in general has appreciated during the past twenty years, and if that appreciation of gold has been artificially caused by the action of the governments of the commercial nations in demonetising silver, then most certainly a wrong has been done to debtors precisely similar in kind to the wrong which would now be done to creditors by allowing their debtors to pay them in money having a less purchasing power than the money in which the debts were contracted. On the other hand, it is undoubtedly true that by far the greater part of the private debts at present existing in the country have been contracted within the past few years, and that there has been very little, if any, increase in the purchasing power of gold since these debts were contracted. To allow these debts to be paid in depreciated silver dollars would be clearly and unquestionably dishonest. Because a great wrong has been done to the debtor class in the past, it does not follow that it is just to now do a great wrong to the creditor class. The process of falling prices seems to have spent itself, and it is impossible now to remedy the wrong that was done while that process was going on. The friends of the free coinage of silver would very much strengthen their cause with those people who attach any importance to the honest payment of debts if they would consent to have it provided that, if gold did go to a premium, creditors should be entitled to be paid in gold coin or in the silver equivalent of gold coin of the present weight and fineness.

It would be easy to give other cases in which both sides are wrong and the truth lies between them. I may briefly refer, in closing this part of the subject, to the great controversy as to the sufficiency of the gold supply to form a safe basis for the currency systems of the leading commercial nations. According to the Gold men, it is a complete delusion to suppose that there ever has been any mischief-working scramble for gold, or that any of the evils we have been and are suffering from are in any degree due to an insufficiency of the gold supply for the work it is now called on to do. They hold that the general adoption of the gold standard has been a process of natural selection of the fittest, so to speak, and has been entirely beneficial. Of the Silver men it is enough to say that their view is the diametrical opposite of this in every respect. They commonly represent the gold standard in their cheap literature as a hideous octopus fastening the deadly grasp of its many arms upon all the quarters of the earth. Both sides are wrong, and it is by no means easy to say which is the furthest from the truth.

War to the knife and no compromise is now the motto of both of the contending parties. While believing, as hinted above, that the extremists on both sides are wrong, and that the right lies between them, I admit that the ferocious and radical character which the conflict has now assumed has its advantages. Whichever system— the single gold standard or the double standard—may be more in accordance with the principles of sound finance, there can be no doubt as to the fact that uncertainty as to the standard is ruinous. And this stage of uncertainty as to the standard of exchange value is precisely the condition in which this country has been for the past few years. The result has been hard times, far harder, relatively to the average condition, than the nations of Europe have been having. Nothing but the vast natural resources of the country could have enabled us to live through such a condition of things as well as we have done. It is satisfactory to know that the people are now thoroughly aroused to the desperate need of settling this question one way or the other. Macaulay's line, ' One of us two, Herminius, shall never more go home,' expresses very well the spirit by which both sides now seem to be animated; and there is good reason to hope that, when the ballots have been counted in November, the people will feel that one of the most formidable issues which this Republic has ever had to face is in a fair way of being finally settled.

WILLIAM DILLON.

CHICAGO : *July* 1896.

THE TRAINING OF A JESUIT

ONE of the curious phenomena of the modern world is the mystery that hangs around the name of Jesuit. There is a general consent that the Jesuits are a body of men who exert a considerable influence in the world. This at least is conceded to them alike by friends and enemies, by Catholics, and by those outside the Catholic Church. But the secret of their influence, the source whence their power arises, is a matter on which the widest possible opinion prevails. While all, or nearly all, attribute to them an unlimited devotion to the cause of Rome, there is a very considerable diversity of opinion as to the means they employ to carry out the end which they have at heart. A large majority of non-Catholics impute to them an unscrupulous readiness to avail themselves of any means, good or bad, by which they think that their cause can be served. Not a few believe them to be a secret and perfectly organised society, ready to occupy any position, or to fill any office, inside or outside the Catholic Church, in which may be seen an opportunity of carrying on their work of unscrupulous propagandism. They are fully convinced that Jesuits are to be found in her Majesty's Service, in the various learned professions, in the commercial classes, among domestic servants and those who labour with their hands, and even in the ranks of the Anglican clergy. Some among the more zealous Protestants believe in the existence of ' female Jesuits,' who, in the garb of domestic servants, nurses, and governesses, find an opportunity of instilling into the minds of the young children committed to their charge the principles of Popery. Even educated men are not wholly free from the curious superstition that the ' Jesuit in disguise' is to be found everywhere, seeking with unscrupulous perseverance to undermine, by fair means or foul, the foundations of the Protestant Church, and to re-establish the dominion of Rome over the souls of men.

This belief, like all other popular superstitions, has an element of truth in it. In the days of persecution, when Jesuits were hunted up and down the land, and were mercilessly butchered simply because they were members of the proscribed Society, their only chance of escaping the hands of the pursuivant was to be ' Jesuits in disguise.'

Although they were but a handful among the hundreds of devoted priests who laboured and laid down their lives for their religion in the reigns of Elizabeth and the Stuarts, yet they were the objects of the special hatred of the persecutors, and the search for them was carried on with relentless vigour. Even when other priests were tolerated, they were not, and in the present day they still remain an illegal corporation, who are liable at any moment to be expelled from England if the existing laws were put in force. All this engendered a certain policy of caution and concealment, the traces of which linger on even when the necessity of it has happily passed away.

But if this accounts in some measure for their supposed system of secrecy, it does not at all account for the extraordinary influence that they are believed to exert, not in England only, but all the world over. Here the intelligent Protestant is, we think, fairly nonplussed. He cannot but know that the theory that attributes their alleged power in the world to a system of unscrupulous intrigue and deception cannot possibly be maintained. Societies, like individuals, are in due course of time discredited if they violate the fundamental laws of morality. No man of honour and integrity would look with favour on a society which taught that 'The end justifies the means,' (in the sense that means in themselves unlawful are justified by the fact that the end which they are intended to promote is a good one), or which habitually practised deceit and employed underhand means to attain its object. Still less would any man of virtue or high principle dream of belonging to such a body. No parent would think of entrusting his children to be educated by its members. No one who valued his own reputation would have anything to do with such a band of moral lepers. They would be scouted in every civilised community. If Jesuits were what the vulgar Protestant supposes them to be, they would long ago have been crushed out of existence by the just indignation of mankind.

We may therefore dismiss without further comment the absurd supposition that Jesuits owe their influence to deceit and an unscrupulous policy of Machiavellianism, and must look elsewhere for the secret of their power in the world. If they are influential, it must needs be because they employ means that are in themselves calculated to impart influence to those who are willing to adopt them. It will be the object of the following pages to try and explain what these means are.

But first of all I must premise that as I am writing for non-Catholics as well as for Catholics, I shall omit, or pass over very lightly, the supernatural element in their success. Many of my readers will smile if I recall the prayer which their founder, St. Ignatius, used to offer continually for his children. He used to beg of God that they might always be the object of the world's hatred and enmity. He told them that they should wish to suffer contumely, false accusations and insults, so long as they themselves gave no sort of occasion for it, and no offence is thereby committed against the Divine Majesty.[1] He knew from Holy Scripture and from the history of the Church that this has been an essential condition of success in all great works done for God by saints and missionaries, and a mere process of induction taught him to regard persecution and misrepresentation as a necessary accompaniment of every victory won for the sacred cause of Christianity. I should, therefore, be omitting a prominent feature in the history of my Order if I were to pass altogether unnoticed the reproach which always has been attached, and I pray God may always be attached, to the name of the Society of Jesus.

But my object in my present article is rather to dwell on the natural causes that have contributed to gain for us the place of honour which we occupy in the ranks of the Christian Church. And among these marks of honour I include not only our position as theologians, missioners, preachers, confessors, and educators of youth, but still more the invariable selection that is made of the Society as the chief object of the hatred of those who are the foes of the Catholic Church. Whether it be the courtiers of Queen Elizabeth or the sectaries of Germany, the Communists of Paris or the Revolutionary party in Italy, the Bonzes of Japan or the fanatical followers of Mohammed, all who hate the name of Catholic concentrate their deadliest animosity on the unfortunate Jesuit. Even within the pale of the Catholic Church we have sometimes found strenuous opponents. The Jansenists of France were our bitter enemies. Those who rejoice in the name of Liberal Catholics have invariably stood aloof from us. At times even bishops and archbishops have looked coldly on us. Sometimes, indeed, it may be that individual Jesuits have, by their unfaithfulness to the principles of their Order, deserved the ill feeling with which they have been regarded. But in a large majority of cases it is due either to prejudice or defective knowledge on the part of their adversaries, or else to an imperfect grasp of the Catholic system (as was the case with the Jansenists), or to a false impression that the Jesuits exercised an influence which interfered with their own lawful authority, and were a rival power in the government of the Church.

I have still left untouched what I believe to be the real secret of Jesuit influence, regarded, as I desire my readers to regard it, from a purely natural point of view. Not that it can ever be really separated from the supernatural, any more than the ivy can be separated from the oak to which it clings. But as we can consider the growth and means of cultivation of the ivy in itself, so I propose to consider the Society of Jesus in itself, as an organised system of

---

[1] *Summarium Constitutionum Soc. Jesu*, R. 11.

means, adapted, in accordance with the principles that govern human society, to the end that it has in view.   After a quarter of a century spent in its ranks, I can speak with great ·confidence from my own personal experience of the training given to its members.   The study of the training of a Jesuit appears to me to throw a very clear light on the position which the Society occupies in the modern world.

But there is something preliminary to the consideration of its training.   No system of education can produce a well-educated man unless the original material is good.   The first requisite for those who are to do the work of the Society efficiently is that it should select as its members only those who are capable of receiving the Jesuit ' form.' The statue, however deftly carved, will not be a success if the marble have serious defects.   All possible care is taken to admit into the ranks of the Society only those who are naturally qualified to carry out the end that it sets before itself, and who show a capacity for imbibing its spirit and submitting to its discipline.

When any one applies for admission to the Society, he has first of all to satisfy the Head of the Province that he is a likely subject ; and he is then handed over to four of the Fathers to be examined by each of them separately.   This examination is no mere form ; the candidate for admission has to answer the most searching questions, and is submitted to a somewhat rigorous scrutiny.   He is asked about the age, health, and position of his parents in the world ; whether they are Catholics ; whether they are likely to need his help in their old age. He has also to give a full account of himself ; whether he suffers from ill-health or other infirmity, hereditary or acquired ; whether he owes money, or is under any other obligation ; what studies he has made and what are his literary attainments, whether he has lived a virtuous life ; how long he has been entertaining the idea of entering the Society, and what is his motive for wishing to do so ; whether it has been suggested to him by any one else or springs entirely from himself.   The examiner has meanwhile to try and ascertain from personal observation what talent he possesses ; what is his natural disposition ; whether he seems to be a man likely to persevere, and to prove a useful member of the Society.   He is not to be admitted if he has any notable· bodily defect or mental infirmity ; if he is deficient in intelligence ; if he is in debt ; or if he has worn the habit of any other religious body, even for a single day.   Each of the four examiners has to write out at length his report on the above points, and to state in writing his opinion as to whether it is expedient to admit him or not, with any further remarks that he may choose to add.   The four reports are sent in to the Provincial, who after carefully reading them decides whether the candidate is to be accepted or rejected.

In every province of the Society of Jesus there is a day in each year on which candidates are ordinarily received, though exceptions are made in special cases. The new-comers are not at once admitted to the ranks of the noviceship; they spend their first week or ten days separate from the rest, and during that time the rules of the Society are put into their hands, and are explained to them; they are instructed as to the kind of life they will have to live, and the difficulties that they will have to encounter. They have to study the 'Summary of the constitutions,' in which is set forth the end and object of the Society, the spirit that must animate its members, the obedience they must be ready to practise, the sacrifice of their own will and judgment that they must be prepared to make; in fact, they have every possible opportunity given them of ascertaining what it is that they are undertaking when they declare their intention of serving God in the Society according to its laws and constitutions. Of course, there are but few who realise at first all that is involved in the sacrifice they are making; but this must be the case with all who are entering on a new and difficult career. After they have spent a few days in studying the obligation they are going to accept, they are put into retreat for a short time, during which they are kept in perfect silence, and have to spend their time in listening to a series of instructions on the fundamental truths of religion given by the master of novices, each instruction containing a number of suggestive thoughts, on which they have to meditate for an hour after the instruction is finished.

When this time of retirement is over, they are duly received as novices, and are clad in the Jesuit habit. Often one or two fall away during this first probation, discovering that the kind of life is beyond their courage, or requires a higher degree of virtue than they possess. But, generally speaking, those who have made their first probation pass into the ranks of the noviceship as soon as it is over.

From that moment the real process of sifting begins. The new novices enter at once on the routine prescribed by the Society for *all* who desire to fight under her standard. They rise at 5.30, make a short visit to the chapel at 6, in order to make their morning oblation of the day to God, and from 6 to 7 make their meditation. According to Jesuit rule, the points of this meditation have to be studied for a quarter of an hour before retiring to rest on the previous evening. On these points the Jesuit is taught to dwell during the hour devoted to the morning meditation, ending the consideration of them with some good resolution arising out of them, and a short prayer that he may keep it during the ensuing day. As this is a very important element in the training of the Society, I think it may be interesting if I give an example of the points as given to the novices during my own novitiate by the then master of novices, whose holy teaching and loving care will always dwell in the grateful hearts of those who had the privilege of being trained by him.

Subject of the Meditation: ' Let us make haste to enter into our eternal rest ' (Hebrews iv. 11).

Point 1.—How are we to make haste towards eternal rest with God ? It is certain that he who during the hours of the day most frequently does the very thing that his Father in Heaven wishes is he who during that day makes most progress. Penance will not advance us if we do it when our Father in Heaven wishes us not to do penance. Prayer will only retard us if prayer is not our Father's will at the moment. Resting when He wishes us to rest, labouring when He wishes us to labour, speaking and being silent just as He wishes—this is the short and direct road to our eternal repose.

Point 2.—This life is a time of traffic. ' Traffic till I come,' our Lord says. He who traffics most wisely is the one who is making most haste to enter into his eternal repose. St. Paul tells us how to carry on our spiritual business. ' Some,' he says, ' build with gold and precious stones and silver on the foundations of faith. Others with wood, stubble, and hay.' We build with gold and precious stones when our intention is very good ; with hay and stubble when our intention is unworthy. Two men read the same book or work together; how different the value of their work according to their intention !

Point 3.—Of all the ways of making haste to heaven and to God, there is none so rapid as the way of charity and love. ' Many sins are forgiven, because she loved much.' How slow and how weary a task it is to conceal sins by any other process !

Beg very earnestly for an increase of Divine love, in order that you may run in the way of God's commandments.

At 6.55 the bell rings for Holy Mass, and all the novices repair to the chapel. After Mass, which occupies half an hour, another quarter of an hour is assigned to a reconsideration of the meditation and the care with which it was made, and to the writing down of any thoughts that may have suggested themselves in the course of it. Breakfast is at 7.45, and at 8.30 the novices have to be present, each at his little desk, for half an hour's reading of *Rodriguez on Christian Perfection.* At 9 an instruction on the rules is given by the master of novices, after which they have to make their beds and arrange their little cells, and, when this is done, to repair to some appointed place, where one of their number, appointed for the purpose, assigns to each a certain amount of manual labour—dusting, sweeping, washing up dishes and plates, laying the refectory for dinner, sometimes cleaning and scrubbing, and other menial offices of the humblest description. At 10.15 they have to learn by heart, for a quarter of an hour, some portion of the rules of the Society, or such prayers, psalms, or ecclesiastical hymns, the knowledge of which may be useful to the young ecclesiastic. After this they have some free time, during which they can walk in the grounds, pray in the chapel, or read some Life of the saints or other spiritual book. At 11.30 they assemble for ' out-door manual works,' which consist in chopping and sawing wood for fuel, sweeping up leaves, picking up leaves, weeding the flower beds, or some similar occupation allotted to them by one of the older novices, who is termed ' master of out-door works.' At 12.30 they return to the house, and at 12.40 the

bell summons them to the chapel, where they spend fifteen minutes
in prayer, and in examining their consciences as to how they have
performed the various duties of the morning, whether they have kept
silence (for during all this time no talking is allowed), obeyed
promptly and exactly, kept up a remembrance of God in all that they
have done, showed kindness and consideration for others, executed
the work assigned to them in the best manner possible, &c.

The dinner-bell rings at 1, and all repair to the refectory.
During dinner a portion of Holy Scripture is read aloud, and some
useful and edifying book, the life of one of the saints, or the history
of the Society.   After dinner a short visit is made to the chapel, and
an hour's recreation follows.   The occupations of the afternoon are a
repetition of those of the earlier portion of the day, save that on three
days in the week a walk of about two hours has to be taken in companies of two or three.   No one is allowed to choose his companions,
but the master of novices arranges the various companies.   Sometimes a game of cricket or football is substituted for the walk.   At 6
a second hour of meditation of half an hour has to be made in the
chapel, after which the recital of some vocal prayers, and some free
time which they can dispose of for themselves, bring them on to
supper at 7.30.   After this they have an hour's recreation, during
the first half-hour of which Latin has to be spoken.   At 9, night
prayers in the chapel; then fifteen minutes spent in the preparation
of their meditation of the following morning, and after a final
examination of conscience on their performance of the duties of the
day all lights are put out by 10 P.M., and the novices sleep their
well-earned sleep in their dormitories.

I have given in detail the account of a Jesuit novice's day, as
spent in the English province.   In England the Society is deprived
of certain advantages that it enjoys in Catholic countries, where they
undergo two *experimenta*, or trials. which here are impossible.   They
are sent out, wherever the population is Catholic and the Church is
free, to beg alms in the streets, and in the country around, for about
thirty days, and the instructions given by Our Lord to His apostles
are the model which these are taught to imitate.   An amusing story
is told of a young Oxford convert, who, making his noviceship at
Rome in the days when the Pope still ruled in Rome, was sent out
with a companion to beg.   Passing a horseman riding quietly in the
neighbourhood of the city, he asked of him an alms for the love of
God.   The stranger looked for a moment at his shabby Jesuit
soutane and jumped down from his horse.   'My dear X., you don't
mean that you have come to this!'   It was an old Oxford acquaintance, who imagined that his poor friend had been reduced to utter
destitution as the result of his reception into the Catholic Church.
The impossibility of practising this voluntary mendicancy in the
present day is regarded as a misfortune by the Jesuit authorities, as

the humiliations it involved were found to be a most useful element in novice training. Another trial, the month spent in the hospitals, which now can be very rarely carried out, is also much to be regretted. Under normal conditions, the young Jesuits have to repair for a space of thirty days to some hospital, and spend their time in nursing the sick, dressing their wounds, making their beds, and ministering to their various necessities, temporal and spiritual. In England the loss of these two experiments is to some extent compensated by a month spent in the kitchen, during which the novice has to wash up the plates and dishes, to pare potatoes, to grind the coffee, and to perform any other menial tasks assigned to the novice by the cook, whom the novice has to obey implicitly, as for the time being his superior. He has also to take his recreation during this month with the lay brothers, and to make himself one with them in their ordinary life and conversation.

But there is one experiment which is still everywhere retained, and one which is perhaps of all the most important. During one month in his first year every novice has to make what is called ' the long retreat.' It consists of thirty days occupied exclusively in prayer, meditation, and similar employments. Five times a day the master of novices gives points of meditation to the assembled novices, and they have subsequently to spend the following hour in a careful pondering over the points proposed to them, after the manner that I have already described in speaking of the daily morning meditation. A regular system is followed ; during the first few days the subjects proposed are the end for which man is created, the means by which he is to attain that end, the evils of sin and its consequences, and the four last things, death, judgment, heaven, and hell. During the second portion of the retreat the Kingdom of Christ, His Incarnation, Nativity, and His life on earth occupy the thoughts of the novices for a space of ten or twelve days, with separate meditations on the two standards of Christ and Satan, under one of which every one is fighting, on the tactics of the evil one, the choice that has to be bravely made of a life of hardship under the standard of the Cross, and other subjects akin to these. During a third period of four or five days the Passion of Christ is dwelt upon in detail, and finally some two or three days of the joyful subjects of the Resurrection, the appearances of our Lord to His disciples, the Ascension, with one or two concluding meditations on the love of God and the means of attaining it, bring the retreat to an end. Three recreation days are interposed between the various portions of the retreat, which are spent in long walks, and in recovering from the fatigue which is caused by the constant mental strain involved in the long time of meditation and prayer. Except during these three days there is no time of recreation, and silence has to be strictly kept throughout.

This month is certainly a trying one, though a very happy and

fruitful one for those who are in earnest. It generally has the effect
of sending away from the noviceship one or two of those whose aim
in life is not sufficiently high, or whose powers are too feeble to allow
of their undertaking the yoke of Jesuit obedience, and all the sacrifices that it carries with it. It is indeed a searching process, and
generally finds out those who have undertaken a task too difficult for
them to accomplish. This is, in fact, one of its objects, as well as of all
the other trials of the Jesuit novitiate, which are directed not merely
to the formation of the future members of the Society, but also the
elimination of those who have no real vocation to serve in its ranks.

At the end of two years the young Jesuit takes his first vows and
ceases to be a novice. The special object of his life in the noviceship has been to train him up in that spirit of implicit and
unquestioning obedience which is the aim of the Society of Jesus to
cultivate more than any other virtue in her sons, simply because it is
the virtue that underlies all the rest, and without which no other
virtue can attain its full perfection in the soul of man. The routine
of monotonous and often apparently useless employments has for
its object to foster the habit of what is rightly called blind obedience.
The novice is taught to obey his superior without ever questioning
the wisdom of the order given; the perfection of Jesuit obedience
includes not only the obedience of the will, so that he does what is
commanded promptly, bravely, and thoroughly, but also an obedience
of the judgment, so that he regards what is commanded as the best
thing possible for him. Here it is that Jesuit obedience differs from
the obedience practised generally by a good subordinate in the world.
In the army or in a house of business, blind obedience is necessary
to efficient action. No well-ordered system could be carried on
successfully without it; if the subordinate obeyed only where he
approved of the wisdom of the command given the results would be
fatal to any well-organised community. It is the habit, the difficult
habit of abstaining from any mental criticism of the order given that
is the distinctive feature of the obedience of the Society of Jesus.
When still a secular, I once encountered an officer in the army who
had been for some time in the noviceship, and had left because he found
the obedience required too much for him. I took occasion to ask
him how it was that he who had been accustomed to the strict discipline and rigorous obedience demanded of a soldier could not endure the
gentler rule to which he was subject as a religious. 'In the army,'
was his answer, 'you must do what you are told, but you can relieve
your feelings by swearing mentally at your colonel; but you cannot
do that in the Society of Jesus.'

At the same time the obedience of the Society is a perfectly
reasonable obedience. I need scarcely say that in the impossible,
or almost impossible case of a command being given, which could
not be obeyed without sin, the Jesuit would be clearly bound to

disobey.   In the case of the order given being manifestly a foolish
one, obedience does not require that it should be regarded in itself
as wise or prudent.   If the matter is one of any importance, it is his
duty to represent to the superior the undesirable consequences, that
seem to him likely to ensue from the carrying out of the order.
Every superior has certain advisers, to whose opinion he is bound to
give special weight, and the representation can be made either directly
to the superior by the person receiving the order, or through one or
other of these advisers.   Every subordinate has also the right of
appeal to some higher superior, and such appeals always receive full
and careful consideration.   In matters of real moment, he can write
a private letter to the General of the whole Society with a certainty
of redress if the writer has a solid ground for the complaint made.
But in the case of any such appeal he must not act merely on the
impulse of the moment, and must beware of being misled by his own
private judgment.   He must think the matter over with due deliberation, and must recommend it to God in prayer, and must, as far as
possible, make sure that the motive that prompts him is not wounded
self-love, or a pertinacity of judgment, or a dislike of giving up his
own will.   He ought to try and see things from the superior's point
of view rather than from his own.   If, after taking all these precautions, he thinks it right to appeal, he must then be ready to abide by
the decision finally given.   If it is against him, common sense will
tell him that in all probability he is wrong.   The chances are that
his superiors are able to take a wider and more impartial view of the
question than himself.   He will then do his best to conform his
judgment to theirs.   What is then required of him is that he should
consider the command as the best, not perhaps in itself, but the best
for him under the circumstances.   But in all cases where there is any
sort of doubt, he must, if he is true to his rule, and loyal with Jesuit
loyalty, bend his will to a favourable judgment of what has been
ordered by his superior, and abstain, as far as with God's grace he
is able, from all unfavourable criticism, using all the force of a
loyal will, to induce his judgment to approve, and not to condemn,
what his superior has enjoined.   It is this obedience of the judgment
which is one of the chief causes of the power exercised by the
Society.   It ensures a remarkable unity of action, and prevents the
waste of energy, which in other corporate bodies is the result of
disunion, mutual criticism, and internal disaffection and strife.

As soon as the young Jesuit has taken his vows, he enters on
quite a different life.   His religious exercises are now confined to a
comparatively small portion of the day.   The main part of his time
is now devoted to study.   He still makes his morning meditation,
hears Mass, examines his conscience twice a day, and spends a short
time each day in spiritual reading and in prayer before the Blessed
Sacrament ; but the chief portion of the next five years is given up
to intellectual cultivation.   During the first two years he has to

apply himself to classical studies and to a course of rhetoric. This part of his career I can pass over without further notice, because there is in it nothing specially distinctive of the Society. His classical work, which consists in reading the best Latin and Greek authors, and translating from English into Latin and Greek, with a certain amount of English literature, and essay writing, is much the same as that of the higher forms of our public schools, and of those who take a classical degree at the Universities. A certain amount of mathematics has also to be learned, and the practice as well as the theory of rhetoric forms part of the course. All this is carefully regulated by written laws, which lay down in detail the course of study to be pursued.

At the end of these two years the young Jesuit student generally leaves the house of the novitiate, where he has continued to reside even after taking his first vows, and goes to the seminary, where he enters on the new and important study of Catholic philosophy. During the first year he goes through a course of logic, pure and applied, and continues his mathematics. The second and third years are devoted to psychology, ethics, metaphysics, general and special, cosmology and natural theology. He has about two lectures a day in these subjects from Jesuit professors, who are always priests, and are selected on account of their special knowledge, and their gift of a clear power of exposition. Besides the lectures, which are given in Latin, the students are summoned three times a week to take part in an academical exercise which is one of the most valuable elements in the philosophical and theological training of the Society. It lasts an hour, during the first quarter of which one of the students has to give a synopsis of the last two lectures of the professor. After this, two other students, previously appointed for the purpose, have to bring against the doctrine laid down any possible objection that they can find in books or invent for themselves. Modern books are ransacked for these objections, and the 'objicients' do their best to hunt out difficulties which may puzzle the exponent of the truth, who is called the 'defendent.' Locke, Hegel, Descartes, Malebranche, John Stuart Mill, Mansel, Sir William Hamilton, and other modern writers, are valuable contributors for those who have to attack the Catholic doctrine. Everything has to be brought forward in syllogistic form, and to be answered in the same way. The professor, who of course presides at these contests, at once checks any one who departs from this necessary form and wanders off into mere desultory talk. This system of testing the soundness of the doctrine taught, continued as it is throughout the theological studies which come at a later period of the young Jesuit's career, provides those who pass through it with a complete defence against difficulties which otherwise are likely to puzzle the Catholic controversialist. It is a splendid means of sifting out truth from falsehood. Many of those who

take part in it are men of ability and experience, and who have made
a special study of the subjects discussed, and are well versed in the
objections that can be urged against the Catholic teaching.   Such
men conduct their attack not as a mere matter of form, but with the
vigour and ingenuity of practised disputants, and do their best
to puzzle the unfortunate defendent with difficulties, the answer to
which is by no means simple or obvious at first sight.   Sometimes he
is put completely 'in the sack,' and the professor has to intervene to
explain where he has failed, and how the objection has really to be
met.   Sometimes the objicient will urge his difficulties with such a
semblance of conviction as even to mislead some of those present.   I
remember an instance in which an objicient, rather older than the
rest, who had had considerable experience of sceptical difficulties
before becoming a Jesuit, argued with such a show of earnestness
against the existence of God, that the professor, who was a good,
simple man, and new to his work, took fright.   He sent for the
objicient to his room when the 'circle' was over, and, to his no small
amusement, represented to him the misery and hopelessness of
scepticism, begged him to pray God that he might not lose his faith,
and promised to say Mass for him the next morning, that God might
save him from the terrible misfortune that threatened him.   But he
was consoled on discovering that his pupil was as firmly convinced
as himself of the truth of the thesis he had been attacking.

Here I hope my non-Catholic readers will forgive me a remark
which I cannot refrain from making on the present occasion.   I
should like to know what other religion save the Catholic could ever
stand such an ordeal of free discussion as this.   So far from any
check being put on the liberty of the students, they are encouraged
to press home every sort of objection, however searching and fundamental, however blasphemous and profane, that can be raised to the
Catholic doctrine.   In every class are to be found men who are not
to be put off with an evasion, and a professor who was to attempt to
substitute authority for reason would very soon find out his mistake.
This perfect 'liberty of disputation' is one of the many happy results
of the possession of perfect and unfailing truth.

When the two objicients have finished their attack, there still
remains a quarter of an hour before the circle is over.   This time
is devoted to objections and difficulties proposed by the students.
Every one present has full freedom to ask of the professor any question
he pleases on the matter in hand, and may require of him an explanation of any point on which he is not satisfied.   It is needless to say
that full advantage is taken of this privilege, and the poor professor
has often to submit to a very lively and searching interrogatory.   If
any question is proposed that is foolish, or beside the subject, the
questioner is soon silenced by the open marks of disapprobation on
the part of the rest of the class, and a good objection is sometimes

received with quiet applause.   Any fallacy or imperfect knowledge on the part of the professor is very speedily brought to light by the raking fire he has to undergo, and while all respect is shown him in the process, he must be well armed if he is to win the confidence of the class by his answers.

At the end of his first and second years of philosophy, the young Jesuit has to undergo a fairly severe examination in the matter of the year.   If he passes these examinations successfully, he has in all three years of philosophy, at the end of which he has to undergo an examination in the combined matter of the three years, mathematics included.

At the end of this time he begins a new stage in his career. He is sent to one or other of the colleges of the Society to teach or to take part in the discipline.   I will not dwell on this part of his training, as it is not my object to explain the system of Jesuit education in my present paper.   It is enough to say that for some five or six years he is occupied in the ordinary work incident to teaching a class of boys.   Whether he takes a higher or a lower form depends of course on his own classical or other attainments.   Yet there is this difference between the Jesuit system and that of the ordinary public schools, that in all the lower classes the Jesuit teacher generally moves up with his class.   I imagine that the motive of this is to give him a stronger moral influence than can be gained by a master who has the teaching of boys only for a single year.   But the two or three higher forms, corresponding to the sixth and upper and lower fifth, have almost always a permanent master.   This reminds me of another distinction between the Jesuit and other systems, though it is one that does not universally prevail. The time during which the young scholastic is employed in teaching does not, as a rule, extend beyond six or seven years.   Hence permanent masters, in the strict sense of the word, are but rare.   Sometimes, if a man has a special talent for teaching, he will return to the schoolroom after he becomes a priest.   But it is the general experience of the Order that, with the exception of men who have a remarkable power of training boys, those who are in the full vigour of their youth prove more successful masters than those who have passed through the four hard years of theological study, and are already getting on in life.

The time of teaching or disciplinary work generally terminates about the age of thirty, and the scholastic then proceeds to the theological college of his province for three or four years of theology. Here the work is certainly hard, especially during the first two years. On three days in the week, the student who has passed successfully through his philosophical course has to attend two lectures in the morning and three in the afternoon.   The morning lectures are on moral and dogmatic theology ; and those in the afternoon on canon law or history, dogmatic theology, and Hebrew, the last for half an hour only. Besides this, on each of these afternoons there is held a circle or disputation such as I have described above. In theology these disputations are as a rule fiercer and more searching than in the philosophical course. There often arises, not the *odium theologicum*, but the eager advocacy with which even Jesuits defend their own opinions. The men are older, and bolder too, and take a delight in searching out any supposed weakness in the arguments proposed to them, so that there is no danger of any latent fallacy or inadequate proof escaping the observation of the more keen-sighted members of the class. In addition to these constant disputations there is held every three months a more solemn assembly of the same kind, at which the whole house is present and the rector presides, in which two of the students are chosen to defend for an hour continuously a number of theses against the attacks of all comers, the professors themselves included.

During the third and fourth years of the course of theology, lectures in Scripture are substituted for those on moral theology and Hebrew. At the end of the third year the young Jesuit (if a man of thirty-four or thirty-five can be accounted young) is ordained priest, and during his last year his lectures are fewer, and he has privately to prepare himself for a general examination in theology, on which depends in great measure whether he has the grade of a professed father in the Society or the lower degree of what is called a ' spiritual coadjutor.'

Even when his theology is over, and his final examination passed, the training of a Jesuit is not yet completed. He has still another year of probation before he is launched on the world as a fullblown member of the Society. He has to return during that time to the noviceship, and there to repeat all the experimental tests and trials of the first two years of his religious life. He has to sweep and dust the rooms and corridors, to chop wood, to wash plates and dishes, besides going over again the spiritual work of the novice, the long retreat of thirty days included. He has also during this year to study the institute of the Society, and during Lent to take part in some one of the public missions which are given by the various religious orders in the large towns and centres of population. This final year sometimes follows immediately on his theology, sometimes after an interval of a year or two, during which he is employed in one of the colleges or missions of the Society. When it is over he is generally well on in the thirties, and if he has had the full course, he will have spent some seventeen years in the training for his work. Of this period he will have devoted two years to the noviceship, seven years to study, six or seven years to teaching or the work of discipline, and one year to the second noviceship which he has to undergo after his priesthood.

If I were asked to sum up the reasons for the position which the Society of Jesus occupies in the Catholic Church, and the reputation which it enjoys among educated men in every country of the world, I should ascribe it, as far as natural reasons go, mainly to three causes. The first is the extreme care with which its members are in the first instance chosen, and the process of natural selection which eliminates all who are not suited for its work. The second is the length and thoroughness of its training, both moral and intellectual, and the pains that is taken to adapt it to the special talents and capacities of the individual. The third is the spirit of implicit obedience, of blind obedience, in the sense in which I have explained it above, which is absolutely indispensable to every one who is to live and die as one of its members. There are other reasons beside, such as its system of government, the loyalty which animates those who belong to it, and the care with which men are chosen for posts to which they are naturally suited, and removed from positions where they are unable to do their work well. But these are really the result of the three I have mentioned, and would be impossible unless built on them as their basis.

I cannot conclude without mentioning two others, though perhaps they are almost out of place in an article in a Review. The one is the spirit of supernatural charity which is the very foundation on which the Society is built, and without which it would very soon decay and disappear. The other is one I have already alluded to, the almost universal reproach which attaches to the name of Jesuit, in which we gratefully recognise the fulfilment of the words of Him whose name we bear, and who long since forewarned us: 'If the world hate you, know that it hated me before it hated you. If you had been of the world, the world would love its own; but because you are not of the world, but I have chosen you out of the world, therefore the world hateth you' (St. John xv. 18, 19).

R. F. Clarke, S.J.

LI HUNG CHANG

IT would be as easy to under-estimate as to exaggerate the importance of the visit of the great Chinese viceroy to Europe. The Germans, and even the French, may possibly have made too much of him, but that would be an insufficient excuse for our making too little. If his mission is a mystery to us, that may be because our diplomacy has manœuvred itself into a position of isolation in regard to the Far East ; and the continental Powers may have a perfectly clear idea of what they are doing. It is one of our insular ways to consider the rest of the world fools. From the pains which were taken by the Ministers of Russia and France in China to prevent any Englishman, even Li Hung Chang's trusted medical adviser, from being attached to his staff, we may conclude that, in the judgment of those two Powers at least, the mission was not intended to be an empty pageant. And Germany has but followed the precedent she set up in 1884 in the regal reception accorded to the delegates from the Transvaal, who came to England on business, and visited Germany from courtesy.

From every point of view the visit of such a personage as Li Hung Chang to Europe would be an interesting event. He is the first Chinaman of rank who has crossed the sea, except under compulsion, and he is the greatest man China is known to have produced in this century, which out of 300,000,000 is something. He is also the only Chinese statesman who has made any practical attempt to introduce the modern spirit into the polity of his country from a conviction that in that alone is salvation to be found. For thirty years he has been striving against overwhelming difficulties to put his country in a state of defence as the condition precedent to all other reforms, and has thereby entitled himself to our sympathy. Lastly, Englishmen, at least, may remember that it is to Li Hung Chang they owe the discovery of General Gordon. But for the fortuitous contact of these two personalities at a critical period, perhaps neither of them would have gone down to history. The opportunity for Gordon to show his genius might never have occurred elsewhere, for he never would have sought it, and would in all probability have passed his life in the obscurity of service routine, snubbed for his eccentricities by his superiors, and loved by his intimates for the soul that was in him.

On the other hand, but for Gordon and these same eccentricities of military genius China might have been—who knows where?—without government, a scene of rapine on the titanic scale. Judging after the event, it is easy to overlook the special merit of Li Hung Chang, not so much in employing a foreign soldier—-though that made an enormous breach in the wall of Chinese conservatism—but in cordial appreciation of and loyal co-operation with him, which alone rendered his services effective. It was a thoroughly un-Chinese proceeding, which it would have been well for China if it had been more consistently followed out in her recent history. From the principle then introduced Li Hung Chang has never swerved, that the strengthening and regeneration of China necessitated the employment of foreign men and foreign methods; and on this he has staked everything and braved the odium of his peers. He was not, indeed, the father of the idea. That honour belonged to Tsêng Kwo Fan, the father of the late Marquis Tsêng, who was some time Minister to Great Britain. Li was his first lieutenant, and lived to put in practice the policy which his chief had bequeathed to his country. That he has been perfectly successful it would be absurd to contend after the exposure of the military weakness of China in the late war; but if the whole position be fairly considered, the failures of the reformer will excite sympathy rather than contempt. The Chinese statesman set himself to remove a mountain, and only succeeded in carting away a few tons of *débris*. Why was the result so disproportionate to the effort? Primarily, no doubt, it was the inherent difficulty of the task; but the proximate or apparent explanation is that Li Hung Chang stood absolutely alone. The nation was inert, but with a *vis inertiæ* which could be irritated into reactionary activity. The political machinery of the country, massive and complex, was set automatically in motion to thwart and obstruct the reforms which the one man was trying to introduce. His was a task requiring the aid of an enthusiastic propaganda, and the reformer made no proselyte. He did not even make friends, only hosts of enemies. And the few foreigners whose support might have been invaluable have leaned rather towards jealousy of his power than cordial support of his measures.

By sheer force of circumstances Li Hung Chang has been the pivot on which the foreign relations of China have turned for thirty years, the indispensable man, who alone, if we except one member of the Foreign Board who died many years ago, ever dared to deal with foreign questions in a businesslike manner. And so he has come to personate China in the imagination of Europe, and to be the best-known man of that country—so well known, indeed, that his faults and failings have been photographed at close quarters and then enlarged, while his successes have been passed over as flat and uninteresting. But even a glance at the multiplicity of duties that have been imposed on him will impress us rather with the amount

accomplished than with what has remained undone.   For the last
twenty-five years Li Hung Chang has been 'Viceroy' or Governor-
General of the metropolitan province, a territorial office involving
much labour and responsibility.   In addition to that he has been the
Superintendent of Trade for the northern half of the empire, an
office which has brought him into constant relations with consuls,
merchants, and representatives of foreign trade, for he had to deal
with all commercial questions, disputes, interpretation and execution
of treaties, Customs regulations, &c.   In that capacity also he has
had the task of introducing the telegraph and railway systems, with
the responsibility for their operation, and he created and controlled a great steamship enterprise ; also, within the last few
years, cotton mills, in which concerns he took perhaps more than a
platonic interest.

These various duties one would be apt to consider sufficient for one
man, but they represented but a fraction of what was expected from
Li Hung Chang.   Though without portfolio, he was *de facto* Minister
for Foreign Affairs, the general negotiator and the ultimate referee
in the external relations of the empire.   He was Minister of Marine
and Lord High Admiral, Commissioner for National Defence, and
Inspector-General of ' Fortifications.   He was also Minister for
what corresponds in China to the Colonies and India—viz. Tibet,
Mongolia, and Korea.   In a word, this man has been a whole
British Cabinet rolled into one, with perhaps the exception of the
Lord Chancellor and Home Secretary.   If we imagine the strongest
English Minister who ever lived having such multifarious duties
crowded upon him, we shall be better able to perceive how Li
Hung Chang came short of complete success in his labours !   It is
true that some of these high diplomatic and executive functions were
nominally fulfilled by certain Boards in the capital ; but so far from
that easing, it only aggravated the labour of the effective man, who
had not only these Boards to contend with, but had to work without
a staff or an office.   Chinese service is denied both the weekly rest
and the annual vacation, nor have the Ministers of State the relief of
septennial or more frequent refreshing lapses into irresponsible life.
A holiday is almost impossible except on urgent ground of health—
and wonderful details have sometimes to be gone into by the official
applying for sick leave—or on the death of a parent.   Fixed periods
of mourning are of religious obligation, but are occasionally over-
ridden by the exigencies of the public service, as has happened in
the case of Li Hung Chang.   Nor has the plea of sickness always
availed him.   Some five years ago he was prostrated by influenza
and almost given up, but he knew no respite from official duties.   A
local insurrection had broken out in Mongolia, which he was called
upon to put down, and he had actually to conduct a campaign from
what looked very like his death-bed.

' If we but consider that this unrelieved strain has had to be borne for twenty-five years we shall be able to form an idea how the affairs of China are managed, and to understand what a small gift of prophecy was needed to predict the result of the late war. But the case is not yet exhausted. European experience will hardly help us to realise the occult side of this immense problem—how one man is to do the work of a hundred. There was the accumulated inertia of 2,000 years passively opposing its dead-weight to all attempts to move it out of the ruts of ages ; and there were the incessant and insidious plots against the person and policy of the solitary man which have occupied the minds of the official hierarchy of China during the whole period, and are as active to-day as they have ever been. All things considered, therefore, we may well be surprised not that Li Hung Chang has failed to regenerate China, but that he has survived the struggle. A very progressive Chinaman, the late Tong Kin Sing, was, in conversation with Li Hung Chang, recounting the obstruction that met him everywhere, and concluded by deploring his fate in being born a Chinese. ' You might say that,' observed the Viceroy, ' if you had been an official.'

The shortcomings of Li Hung Chang are plain enough, nor have they ever been extenuated. But there is a time for everything, and you need not choose a man's wedding-day to expatiate on the follies of his youth. The occasion of a complimentary visit to our country is scarcely appropriate for setting in array all the demerits of a distinguished man. Artistic justice, to say no more, requires that the lights as well as the shadows of a picture should have their due place. Paragraphs circulate through the Press, not intended to be complimentary, about Li Hung Chang's being the richest man in the world, as if that were the salient feature of his record. But it is ludicrous. Paris, London, New York, and Chicago could each produce its crowd of prominent citizens who could sign a cheque which would buy up the Chinese millionaire, root and branch, while, were the process of acquisition in question, the Occidental would not be able to throw a stone at the Oriental method.

It must, on the whole, be conceded that Li Hung Chang would have well earned his eminent position did his merit extend no further than being the one-eyed man among the blind, a description which has been sometimes applied to him. He must be judged neither by the religious, political, or social laws of foreign countries, but by his own surroundings, traditions, and heredity. See what an enormous change has been wrought by him in the official intercourse between Chinese and foreigners. Think of the impracticable arrogance of viceroys and governors, their studied insolence, their refusal to see foreign officials or to discuss any matter, and their evasions of every practical question ; their listening to no argument short of the *ultima ratio.* It has been the unique merit of Li Hung Chang to take a common-sense view of things, to meet complaints halfway, to receive suggestions with courtesy, and to set an example of concilia-tory demeanour towards foreigners; in a word, to form in his own person a workable joint between the petrified ideas of Chinese polity and the requirements of modern Christendom. He has made himself accessible not only to foreign representatives, but to foreigners of every grade who could show a plausible pretext for occupying his time. His toleration of irrelevant visitors has indeed been remark-able, but it was his only means of studying mankind and of learning something about foreign countries, which fate seemed to veto his ever visiting. Though his conversation was sometimes rough, his etiquette was always respectful; and when there was no serious business on hand, he would ply his visitors with Socratic interroga-tories which afforded him amusement and gave them a high sense of their own importance. A sample of this manner is afforded by the way he is now, as these lines are being written, pulling the legs of French journalists and financiers. Could the Viceroy have read Eng-lish, or French, or German, the solemn reports of correspondents and faddists who attached great value to conversations in which they were made butts of would often have amused him greatly. An ordinary interview with Li Hung Chang in his own Yamên has a curious resemblance to an interview with another astute personage—in Pretoria. They have both a wonderful capacity for sitting, and in their manner there is much in common.

It does not seem a great thing to us, but it was a striking advance for a Chinese official to establish social intercourse with foreigners, to eat and drink with them in public, and even to allow his womankind to emerge from their seclusion, and to share to some extent in the pleasures and pastimes of the Western people. The example in these matters set by Li Hung Chang has not, unfortunately, been followed to any great extent. The initiative was all the more creditable, for it is to be remembered that he braved, it may almost be said out-raged, the whole body of traditional propriety that was extant in the empire. Trivial as these matters appear translated into English, they were really large to a Chinese. We have nothing with which to compare it, having no alien civilisation clamouring for admission at our door; but the moral courage of a bishop carrying a foundling in his arms along the Strand, or of the first Brahmin crossing the ocean, may give some idea of the moral courage required.

Nor, though the effect is not of the ostentatious kind, has this rational bearing of Li Hung Chang been barren of beneficial results in the interests of foreigners, merchants, missionaries, and officials. These results are not the less real for belonging largely to the pre-cautionary order, to the class of unobtrusive things, such as those which preserve our bodies in health. The merit of prevention is only recognisable by contrast with the disaster of its failure. The steamer

Drummond Castle might have made fifty successful voyages to South Africa, and her name remained unknown outside shipping offices. What we know positively of the government of Li Hung Chang is that during his whole incumbency everything has gone smoothly between Chinese and foreigners, and that in spite of the fact that the populace of Tientsin contains a large element of ferocity and lawlessness. Matters were not always so. Under Li's predecessor—himself also a great man—serious disturbances occurred in the province, murders of missionaries unavenged culminating in the historical atrocity known as the 'Tientsin massacre' of 1870. Twenty-one Europeans, most of them Catholic sisters, were savagely done to death on that occasion. The crime excited such a feeling among the foreign representatives, that the Government were constrained to depose the popular and powerful Viceroy, Tsêng Kwo Fan. Li, who was engaged at the time in a campaign against the Mohammedan rebels, was summoned to Tientsin, where he has remained in defiance of the law of the service, which limits the term of office. During these five-and-twenty years peace has reigned in the province, and the unruly character of the town population of Tientsin has been practically forgotten. As for the missionaries of all creeds and classes, they have sat under their own vine and fig-tree throughout the whole province, whose magistrates are held personally responsible by the Viceroy for the protection of foreign missions. To solve the thorny missionary question in China—so far, at least, as mere riot and massacre are concerned—all that is wanted is eighteen men like Li Hung Chang to rule over the provinces. If no one else, therefore, at least those missionaries who do not court martyrdom for its own sake have cause to be grateful to this man.

The selection of Li Hung Chang to succeed Tsêng as guardian of the gate of the capital was the highest compliment that could have been paid to him; and he was there placed in a position where he could give practical effect to the general ideas of national defence originated by his predecessor. The origin of that conception was the invasion of the capital in 1860 by the Anglo-French forces, and the flight and death of the Emperor. 'Such a calamity must not occur again,' was the watchword of the new progress. Everybody admitted the necessity for an effective defence against maritime attack, and Li grasped the plan of achieving it. It was the homœopathic remedy, to take a hair from the dog that had bitten them. Foreign men, foreign weapons, and foreign methods had to be employed. Such was the general idea, which was first reduced to practice in the suppression of the Taiping rebellion in 1862–4, when Ward, Burgevine, and finally Gordon were employed to drill and lead Chinese troops. The dynasty was saved by these measures; from the Chinese point of view by the judicious use of foreign machinery; from the foreign point of view by Gordon, who was the animating spirit of the machine. The efforts of China during the following thirty years to build up a navy, a system of coast fortifications, and even to raise an army, the most difficult of all, originated in the experience gained in the final suppression of the fifteen years' rebellion. A precocious attempt to supply a navy on entirely foreign lines was thwarted by Li Hung Chang, even at the time when the need was pressing, on the ground that the Chinese must use foreigners, but not let foreigners use them.

It is an interesting coincidence that it was at the same time that Japanese regeneration began, an identical incentive having started both. An English squadron had bombarded the capital of the Prince of Satsuma in 1864, and then and there the seed of the new Japanese Empire was sown, for that must also ' not happen again.' Thus two streams sprang simultaneously from the same watershed ; but how divergent their history ! One followed a clear and steady course towards its ocean, gathering force and volume as it proceeded, ferti- lising the country as it flowed, and shedding wealth and blessing. The other meandered through wastes of sand and lost itself in a dismal swamp. Why this difference, the circumstances being appa- rently the same? It is an inquiry which would involve a deep study of national and racial character, for the two peoples who have been coupled together in our thoughts and in popular speech are as wide as the poles apart.

China and Japan entered on their reforms in the same way, and there was as little to distinguish them as there is to distinguish the ' braird ' of two different species of plant on its first springing from the seed. They established schools for Western science, and they sent young men abroad to study. There was no apparent difference, but there was a very real one. The heart of the one nation was in the new enterprise ; of the other not. In Japan it was not one or two particularly far-seeing statesmen who led the reform, but the whole nation, which was sharp-set like a pack of hounds, eager in the pur- suit of knowledge, wealth, and power. The huntsmen had little to do but let them go. In China, on the other hand, the people were densely uninterested, the Government inert, and the governing classes, if they had any passion at all, were passionately opposed to everything foreign and everything new. In Japan the innovators were carried forward on a wave of national enthusiasm. In China the solitary reformer had to drag after him a gigantic mass of dead matter, as well as to contend with both open and covert opposition, from above as well as from below. The different results arrived at in the two countries are precisely what would be expected from the premises. One effect has been that, as Li Hung Chang was the only man who did anything, he is the only man blamed for everything that was not done, just as the one man who was on deck is responsible for the loss of the ship. Such is the world's justice. Yet is there a reasonable side even to that, for a reformer may conceivably block the way of his betters, as 'my lord the elephant' did in Kipling's story.

It is not without interest to note how unequal was even the partial success of Li Hung Chang in the reform of the national defences. The scheme naturally fell into three parts—army, navy, and forts—and the odd thing is that his greatest failure was in the department where success was *prima facie* the easiest. The Chinese knew what an army was, and it might have been thought easier to improve what existed than to make new creations. The contrary was the case. For reasons which are obvious on a little reflection a *tabula rasa* would have formed a more hopeful base for a new army, where no comparisons could be made, nor arguments founded on antiquity drawn from the books of history.

The case of the navy was more hopeful, for though the Chinese had legendary experience of sea-power, by which, in fact, they had been enabled to expel the Japanese from Korea in 1578, yet immense floating batteries propelled by steam, worked by electricity, and carrying terrible explosives, torpedo boats with their lightning speed and deadly weapons, constituted an entirely new thing which had to be created from the egg, so to speak, with nothing to assist comparison or suggest criticism. The navy had the further advantage of moving in an element which was regarded with aversion by the ordinary Chinese official. For that and other reasons the navy could be developed out of sight, without interference from ignorant or preju-diced critics. The whole thing, indeed, was so mysterious that the Supreme Government was but too well pleased to leave its manage-ment in the hands of the only man who was equal to the respon-sibility. The consequence of all this was that Li Hung Chang came very near succeeding with the navy. Where he failed was in relaxing his efforts before adequate progress had been made, probably from sheer weariness, and so letting the fleet fall behind. Moreover, he allowed his foreign officers and advisers to quit the service while their training work was half done. The result was that when the trial came the ships were obsolete, and neither equipped nor disciplined for war. Still, the navy was the sole redeeming feature in the Chinese collapse.

That Li Hung Chang was responsible for the conduct and result of the war with Japan is true, but it is also fair to remember that the war was forced on him. He went as far as he dared in his efforts to avert it, but the power behind the throne was impracticable, and the war was forced on the Emperor, first, by an unprovoked and unanswerable challenge, and next by the opening of hostilities by the Japanese. Some of the Japanese organs have hinted that a little more judgment shown by the representatives of Great Britain would have obviated the war. This is plausible, if not quite true. No doubt had they dealt frankly with Li Hung Chang, and sup-

ported him against the ignorant, insane, and impracticable coterie of
Imperial councillors, a compromise would certainly have been offered
by China, which, if it did not prevent the war, would at least have
cut the moral ground more completely from the feet of the Japanese.
The war would have proceeded *quand même*, but possibly the sympathies of Europe would have gone more with the victim than the
victor—which might have made a difference.

The peculiar position occupied by Li Hung Chang *vis-à-vis* the
foreign representatives deserves a passing remark. He was not
officially Foreign Minister, nor a member of the Board which constitutes the Ministry of Foreign Affairs, neither did he reside in the capital. He was nevertheless the *de facto* arbiter in foreign matters, in
virtue of his being the only man who knew anything or dared to say
what he knew, and the only man whom the Imperial family could
trust with any kind of business. Hence the intercourse between the
Ministry of Foreign Affairs and the foreign representatives has for
a quarter of a century been regulated by Li Hung Chang. The
Yamên dared not take any step without consulting him, because
whenever they attempted to do so they got themselves into a mess
through their ignorance. The situation was of course irregular as
well as inconvenient, and some of the foreign representatives and
others resented the position in which they were placed. They had
installed themselves in formidable array in Peking for the purpose of
being at the very centre of government, though any other residence
would have been more agreeable. Yet they felt there was a man at
a distance virtually controlling the game, as we might conceive a
Bismarck doing under certain circumstances at Friedrichsruhe. It
was found by experience that whoever wanted business put through
did best by dealing direct with Li, who was never reluctant to show
the importance of his position. But this was compounding illegitimacy,
and the British Ministers in particular have always stood out against
it. Did we not, they said, go to war with China mainly to establish
the principle that our dealings should be with the Central Government alone? Have we not in deference to this principle allowed the
interests of British subjects to be sacrificed ever since the war of 1860,
because we would not use the pressure which lay to our hands against
the provincial authorities, who would have given us what we wanted?
And shall we now confess that our theoretical right was a practical
wrong, and go to a provincial magnate, eighty miles away, for that which
the Central Government denies us? Certainly not, your Excellen-
cies, only you will observe that your colleagues, regarding only what
makes for the interest of their respective countries, and being less
tightly laced up in diplomatic purism, enter by the side door, which
is open, while you hammer at the front door, which is closed. Under
these circumstances it was natural that the protesting Ministers should
seek to suppress and even extinguish the disturbing element in their

diplomatic system. To ignore Li Hung Chang and force the Foreign Board to do the same became a kind of policy with them. But a fact remains a fact even though it be ignored. Had Li Hung Chang been really ill-disposed towards the English, which has never been the case, he might have found a reasonable justification in the inveterate hostility to himself evinced by British representatives.

But her Majesty's Government have never really been bound to a fetish of legitimacy. Their attitude was perfectly explicable on the theory that they had alternative channels which offered advantages, and which they also fancied might be a counterpoise to the influence of Li Hung Chang. That was the English head of the Chinese Customs and the English Secretary to the Chinese Legation. Through these channels the British Government imagined it would gain its ends. But if the Li Hung Chang agency was illegitimate, one of these at least was by many degrees more so, and it has produced the miseries which inevitably result from irregularity. A perfectly gratuitous rivalry was set up between the head of the Customs and the Viceroy, whereby their forces, which united would have been nearly omnipotent, have been neutralised, and the Customs service itself brought perilously near dissolution because it was regarded as an English institution. British influence in China has, partly from the same cause, fallen below zero. Instead of maintaining the position of arbiter of the destinies of China which she held in the sixties, she has in these last days become the Ishmael of the Far East.

It is sometimes said that Li Hung Chang is favourable to this or that country, and it has been suggested that he has never been over-friendly to England. This is an error. It would be no credit to any statesman to cherish sentimental fancies, and no man was ever freer from the influence of likes and dislikes than Li Hung Chang. He has always had a leaning towards England on solid grounds, and might still have if she would only be steady and have a policy which would remain in focus for a few seconds. This preference for England is simply dictated by the consideration that on the whole there is less to be apprehended from her than from some other Great Powers. It is true that his continental experiences have shown him clearly how absolutely blind was the statesmanship which has led England to forego her birthright in the Far East, and to lift her rivals into her vacant place; and the moral suggested by analogous exhibitions in common life must be irresistible, that those who fail to guard their own are unfit trustees for other people's interests. So far as Li Hung Chang is anti-English, it is because England herself has been so; untrue to herself, and *therefore* untrue to others.

The only occasion on which the Viceroy came into direct collision with Great Britain was on the occasion of the murder of Mr. Margary on the frontier of Yunnan. The matter was taken up seriously by the British Government, and justice was demanded from the Chinese.

After long and fruitless discussion between the British Minister in Peking and the Tsungli Yamên war seemed near. The British Minister left the capital and proceeded to Shanghai in order to place himself in direct telegraphic communication with his Government. Then the Chinese Government became alarmed, and sent Li Hung Chang post-haste after him to Chefoo, a pleasant summer resort on the Gulf of Pecheli, where negotiations were opened. There was a British Flying Squadron close at hand, and it looked like surrender for the Chinese, which it would actually have been but for an unlooked for turn in their favour. It was in the summer of 1876, when affairs in Europe looked stormy, and news came at the crisis of the negotiations which showed that the British Flying Squadron might bark but would not bite. The representatives of several of the Great Powers were also then assembled at Chefoo. For some reason, personal or official, there was a lack of confidence between the British Minister and his colleagues. They claimed to know what he was doing, as in case of war they must take measures for the protection of their nationals. But the Englishman claimed the right to keep his own counsel. Of course they all knew through the Chinese what turn the negotiations were taking, and that something of the nature of an ultimatum was impending. Having taken the side of the Chinese, these other Ministers were able to communicate to Li Hung Chang most important information, which took the sting completely out of the British Minister's menaces. They knew by their private advices from Europe that the Flying Squadron was muzzled, and they told Li Hung Chang, who was immensely relieved. The Chinese Minister, ably supported by Sir R. Hart, the head of the Customs service, and his very capable lieutenant, Mr. Detring, now became master of the situation, and of course took full advantage of it, as the famous Chefoo Convention testifies. In fact, if the British Minister had not accepted what the Chinese Government was ready to concede, it was arranged that Li Hung Chang should be despatched with full powers to London to treat with the Foreign Office. A steamer was waiting for him in Chefoo Harbour.

The result of the Chefoo negotiations did not perhaps dispose British Ministers to dealings with the astute Li Hung Chang, and may possibly have had somewhat to do with their reserved attitude towards the great satrap ever since. One of the minor effects of the Chefoo campaign was that the experience he had gained of Mr. Detring's capacity induced Li Hung Chang a few years later to get him transferred to his own post, Tientsin, where he has practically remained ever since, as much against the routine of the Customs service as the Viceroy's own extended term of office has been contrary to the official rules of China. It is the same Mr. Detring who has recently been acting as secretary to Li Hung Chang's mission in Germany, and to whose exertions is doubtless largely due the organising of the German reception of the Viceroy ; who also played an effective part in the international combination which saved the Chinese mainland from dismemberment last year.

On some other occasions on which Li Hung Chang encountered British diplomacy he was not the ostensible negotiator, but was behind the scenes pulling the wires. The principal transaction was the Burman treaty of 1885, which was also a surrender to China. Territory which had been undoubtedly Burmese, which made an excellent natural frontier with China,[1] was given up for nothing to China, making such a patchwork frontier that to this day nobody has been able to mark it out. Were it the custom to give black instead of white marks to the signatories of treaties, on the presumption that they were injudicious, there would be fewer instances of giving away the material interests of the empire by officials in a hurry. We should have done better without any such treaty.

Our newspapers have been twitting the Germans about their attentions to Li Hung Chang not being disinterested, while in the next sentence they deprecate English attentions on the ground that he is now powerless and unable to return favours. Between German interestedness and British disinterestedness there would appear to be little to choose. If the Germans really thought that the great Chinaman had brought bags of gold to scatter among them like *confetti* at the carnival, they were naïve. But Germans are not fools, as anyone may satisfy himself who tries a fall with them in business. They know on which side their bread is buttered as well as any race under heaven, with the possible exceptions of the Jews and the Scots, and stand little in need of our condolence. The over-done cordiality of Germany and the insular rigidity which is recommended by some of our leading organs are curiously illustrative of the respective national modes of conducting their commercial competition. The stiff and stand-off attitude suggested to the public for the reception of Li Hung Chang represents too accurately the attitude of British manufacturers in their dealings with customers and potential customers. They refuse to budge or bend an inch from their routine in order to promote trade. This is the universal and continuous report of observers of every class and in every corner of the world. The spirit was typified in a London optician's shop the other day, where a lady had brought a prescription for glasses to be made. Calling attention to the fact that her skin was sensitive, she asked that the bridge should be made so as not to hurt the nose. The optical gentleman, in his downright English manner, on which he no doubt prides himself, merely answered, ' Oh, we can't make

[1] The Burmese have always had a good strategic eye, and their frontiers were ' scientific.' Had we been well advised we should have adhered to them instead of carving out an imaginary frontier on paper, irrespective of terrestrial configuration.

glasses that will not hurt the nose.' Possibly not, but he might have attached a customer for life by merely promising to do his best.

Now the Germans, if they have not booked any contracts with Li Hung Chang, as it would have been childish to expect they would —that is not the way things are done—have at least made themselves favourably known to their guest, and thus prepared the way for future business. It is impossible to deny that a powerful stimulus has been given to German commerce in China, that on the one hand the Germans have been roused in a way they have never been before, and, on the other, the Chinese, as represented by their chief contract-monger, have been deeply impressed with the importance of things German. There was never a better advertisement. Many things which Li has seen in Germany he could have seen as well, perhaps better, elsewhere; but the interesting fact remains that it is there that he has seen them, and the memory will abide. He will not want his face again photographed by the Röntgen rays. That remains a German experience.

The Germans have followed him up scientifically. Krupp's agent appears in the photographs taken as if he were part of the show, which in fact he was. The effect of all this is that when Li returns to China he will always find a German at his elbow ready to render any service— for a consideration. He will not find an Englishman there. And this trait in the English character which is losing us our commercial pre-eminence is surely the last thing the manufacturing and trading communities need to have urged on them by influential journals.

The 'power' of Li Hung Chang will probably remain, as it has been, an unknown and indefinable quantity, and very elastic—the last perhaps the most important element in it. On documentary grounds he has little or no power, any more than Mr. Rhodes has in Charterland. It is force of character and his record, and also the force of circumstances, that give him power. And it is stronger on its negative than on its positive side, so that if he cannot do what he would, he can often prevent others from doing what he would not. No stone has been left unturned by the powerful factions opposed to him to ruin Li Hung Chang; but the foundations of his power have not been materially shaken.

During the war with Japan, though stripped of offices and honours, he remained a power, and, after trying alternatives, the Emperor was constrained to fall back on Li Hung Chang as the only man capable of concluding peace. The Japanese had the same idea, for when envoys were sent to them they said: Not this man, but Li Hung Chang. When he was reported dead on one occasion, the Marquis Ito exclaimed, ' Why, if that man dies, I shall have to bring him out of his grave to negotiate peace.'

The summons to Peking last winter was by no means intended as an honour to Li Hung Chang, nor was it deemed altogether safe for his person, for the Emperor had been got at by Li's enemies, who thought that now peace had been secured, and indemnities provided, there was nothing standing in the way of their conspiring to finally ruin him. But they reckoned without their host, as foreign officials also have done who speculated on his fall. There was a power behind the throne which has always shielded him in extremities, as he has in turn protected it. Between Li Hung Chang and the Empress Dowager the attachment has been lasting and strong. The bond included, during his lifetime, the father of the Emperor, Prince Chun, under whose name and sanction things were done and legitimised. The removal of one leg of the tripod materially weakened the structure, for the Empress Dowager, being a woman, and 'out of office,' was deprived of the usual means of conference with her ally. But force of will overcomes all difficulties, and it is due directly to the energy of the imperial widow that the enemies of Li Hung Chang were baffled, and he has been spared to make a triumphal progress through Europe.

What may be the consequences of Li Hung Chang's tour in the West will obviously depend a great deal on the continuance in health of the august lady we have spoken of, who is sixty-two, and of the Viceroy himself, who is seventy-four. Eliminating these two factors, we should expect little more from it than from the blowing of a soap bubble. Undoubtedly a keen observer, a robust thinker, and a man of affairs like Li Hung Chang will carry back with him deep impressions of what he has seen and experienced. He has had opportunities of learning more about Western countries in general than perhaps any Oriental before him, and though it has been the glittering side of European life that has been shown him, and Sovereigns and statesmen have been his entertainers, yet no door has been closed to him, and he has not been averse in the intervals of regal state to condescend to men of low degree. That is to say, he has kept an eye on commonplace practical things, and while a new heaven and a new earth have been opened to him he will not return to his country without a considerable store of useful information which no diplomat or courtier would have communicated. If only he could have made the experiment twenty or even ten years earlier, as he was often recommended to do, but could not, some important results of the tour would have been soon manifested. Now, the result, though hopeful, is speculative.

A. MICHIE.

RECENT SCIENCE

I

THE beautiful big telescopes which are now at work at several obser-
vatories have rendered a new service to astronomy.   They have given
a fresh impulse to lunar studies, and once again the old questions as
to the existence of air and water and the possibility of organic life
on the surface of our satellite are discussed—this time with some
prospects of a definite solution.

For some time past lunar studies have been decidedly falling into
neglect.   The immense, apparently lifeless plains of the Moon, which
still retain the name of ' seas,' or ' maria,' although no traces of present
or past marine action can be detected on their surfaces ; its immense
circus-shaped craters, which have no rivals in size on our own planet ;
its high chains of mountains and deep rents—all these had been
minutely measured and mapped down to the smallest craterlets, with
the hope of discovering some signs of life, or of change going on on the
Moon's surface ; and yet no such signs were forthcoming, at least in
a definite form.   There was, of course, a small group of devoted
selenographers, Neison in this country, Klein in Germany, Oscar
Schmidt at Athens, who continued to give their lives to a minute
study of the visible surface of the Moon.   With instruments of a
modest power they achieved real wonders in delineating the minor
details of lunar topography, and from time to time they caught
glimpses of such appearances as seemed to indicate the presence of
water in certain cavities, or a periodical growth of some vegetation, or,
at least, a still continuing volcanic activity.   But each time such appearances were studied in detail, it became evident that unless more
powerful instruments were directed towards our satellite, there was
little hope of solving those questions relative to life which, in astronomy as everywhere else, chiefly fascinate man.   Gradually it began
to be said that we already know about the Moon all that can be known,
and interest in lunar studies waned amongst astronomers.

And yet, in reality, our knowledge of the Moon is still very limited.
Our best map of its visible surface, although it is a marvel of accuracy,
represents it only on a scale of 1 to 1,780,000, which is quite insufficient to show even such changes as are still going on on our own

globe.[1]. We know, indeed, that in our lifetime many changes have
taken place in the shapes of our hills, valleys,. river courses, and
ocean shores ; but what could we know of such changes if we only had
small·maps to compare ?   Moreover, only now, with such big instruments as the Lick telescope, which has a glass lens thirty-six inches
in diameter, or the admirable Paris telescope (twenty-four inch lens),
we can distinguish, under the most favourable circumstances, the
valleys and the hillocks, which are from 650 to 1,000 feet in width ;
but until quite lately, all we could see was objects over one or two
miles wide ; so that it has been truly said that if all the knowledge
of the Earth by a man in the Moon were of the same sort, he also
might represent our planet as an arid, dreary body with no traces of
life upon it.[2]

Photography undoubtedly supplied astronomers with a precious
aid.   Already in the admirable photograph of the Moon, which
was made in·1865 by Rutherford, and still more in modern photographs, the circuses, the plains, and the mountains appeared with a
relief and reality of which the best maps gave not the faintest .idea.
But lunar photography is beset with so many difficulties, chiefly on
account of the irregular proper movements of the Moon, that up till
now the largest photographs obtained were less than eight inches in
diameter.   And it was only quite lately that they could be enlarged
ten, twenty, and even thirty three times, without the details being
blurred.   Some of the negatives obtained at the Lick Observatory,
and at Paris by the brothers Henry, in an especially quiet and favourable atmosphere, were even so clear, that it was found advisable to
carefully examine them under the microscope, and to make with the
hand detailed enlarged drawings from the best of them.[3]

---

[1] The Moon has on this map a diameter of 75 inches, while its real diameter is
2,160 miles.

[2] There is no lack of excellent works, most attractively written, in which all
information about the Moon may be obtained.   Suffice it to name the following :—
Gwyn Elger's *The Moon*, London, 1895; Edward Neison's *The Moon and the Condition
and Configurations of its Surface*, London, 1876; the English translation ⸱of
Flammarion's *Astronomie Populaire*; and the excellent work of Miss Agnes Clerke,
A Popular History of Astronomy during the Nineteenth Century, 3rd edition, London,
1893.

[3] Great doubts were expressed at the outset as to the advantages offered by
photography for the study of the Moon.   The advantage of the relief-representation
of the surface is, however, self-evident.   Besides, with the aid of photography, a
continuous record of the Moon's aspect is kept, and every modification of detail
which may occur in it will be settled for subsequent reference by unimpeachable
testimony.   It hardly need be said that in one favourable night many photographs
are taken, and that such a mass of details is thus recorded that it would take one's
lifetime to map them by hand.   As to the enlarged drawings which were made by
Dr. Weineck, who is well known for his skill in that sort of work, they have met with
a good deal of criticism (from Dr. Klein in *Sirius*, 1894 and 1895, and the Belgian
professor W. Prinz in *Ciel et Terre*, ii. 1895, p. 449), but it may now be taken as
certain that they really contain a mass of details which may be seen·directly
even with smaller telescopes, but had been overlooked ; while the appearance of

An examination of such enlarged photographs, which permits us
to embrace with the eye a large surface, filled with a mass of nature-
true details, has led MM. Loewy and Puiseux[4] to some interesting suggestions concerning the origin of the so-called 'rills' or
groups of parallel rents in the Moon's crust.[5]   And on the other side
of the Atlantic, the direct observations lately made by Professor W.
Pickering under the clear sky of Peru, as well as his studies of the
American photographs, have produced such new data concerning the
atmosphere of the Moon, and the possible existence of water on its
surface, as are sure to give a quite fresh interest to lunar studies.[6]

The Moon is so small in comparison with the Earth (its weight is
eighty-one times less), and consequently the force of gravity is so
much smaller on its surface, that, even if it had an atmosphere of the
same composition as ours, its density in its lowest parts would be
from thirty to fifty times less than the density of our atmosphere at
the sea-level.   But it appears from Dr. Johnstone Stoney's[7] investigations, that even if the Moon was surrounded at some time of its existence with a gaseous envelope consisting of oxygen, nitrogen, and
water vapour, it would not have retained much of it.   The gases, as is
known, consist of molecules, rushing in all directions at immense
speeds; and the moment that the speed of a molecule which moves
near the outward boundary of the atmosphere exceeds a certain limit
(which would be about 10,600 feet in a second for the Moon), it
can escape from the sphere of attraction of the planet.   Molecule by
molecule the gas must wander off into the inter-planetary space;
and, the smaller the mass of the molecule of a given gas, the feebler

the same detail on two or three negatives settles all possible doubts as to its
reality. (L. Weineck and E. S. Holden, 'Selenographical Studies' in *Publications of
the Lick Observatory*, 1894, vol. iii.; Loewy and Puiseux, in *Comptes Rendus*, tome
cxix. p. 254, and tome cxxi. pp. 6, 79; Folie, *Bulletin* of the Belgian Academy, 1895,
vol. xxix. No. 1; and Dr. Klein in *Sirius*, 1895, p. 112.)

[4] *Comptes Rendus*, 8 juillet 1895, tome cxxi. p. 79.

[5] To explain the origin of these rents, Loewy and Puiseux look for the time when
the rocks were in an igneous half-liquid state and floating islands of consolidated scoria
were formed on the surface of the molten rocks and drifted like the ice-floes in the
Arctic Ocean.   Remaining in that sphere of ideas, it may, however, be remarked that
the same rents might have originated when the whole crust was already solidified.
When Lake Baikal is covered with a thick sheet of ice, and the level of the water
goes slightly down in the winter, the ice is intersected by long rents, one to ten yards
wide, which usually appear in about the same places and in the same directions.   They
run in straight lines, have vertical sides, and when the water at their bottom is frozen,
they become miniature models of lunar rents.

[6] William H. Pickering, 'Investigations in Astronomical Photography,' in *Annals
of the Astronomical Observatory of Harvard College*, vol. xxxii. part 1 (Cambridge,
Mass., 1895).   See also Dr. Klein's analysis of the same (*Sirius*, 1895, Hefte 7, 8,
und 9).

[7] 'On the Physical Constitution of the Sun and Stars,' in *Proceedings of the
Royal Society* for 1868; and paper 'On the Cause of Absence of Hydrogen from the
Earth's atmosphere, and of Air and Water from the Moon,' read on the 20th of April,
1892, before the Royal Dublin Society.

the planet's attraction, and the higher the temperature at the boundary of its atmosphere, the sooner the escape of the gas must take place. This is why no free hydrogen could be retained in the Earth's atmosphere, and why the Moon could retain no air or water vapour.

However, neither these speculations, which are very likely to be true, nor Bessel's previous calculations, could convince practical astronomers of the absolute absence of any atmosphere round the Moon. A feeble twilight is seen on our satellite, and twilight is due, as is known, to the reflection of light within the gaseous envelope; besides, it had been remarked long since at Greenwich that the stars which are covered by the Moon during its movements in its orbit remain visible for a couple of seconds longer than they ought to be visible if their rays were not slightly broken as they pass near to the Moon's surface. Consequently, it was concluded that the Moon must have some atmosphere, perhaps only 200 times thinner than our own. Of course, a gaseous envelope so thin as that would only be noticeable in the deeper valleys, and it would attain its greatest density within the circus-like cavities whose floor, as a rule, lies deeper than the surrounding country. Towards the tops of the mountains it would be imperceptible. But nevertheless, as was shown by Neison, it would play an important part in the economy of life on the Moon's surface.

The observations made at Lick, at Paris, and at Arequipa, fully confirm this view. A twilight is decidedly visible at the cusps of the crescent-moon, especially near the first and the last quarter. It prolongs the cusps as a faint glow over the dark shadowed part, for a distance of about seventy miles (60''), and this indicates the existence of an atmosphere having on the surface of the Moon the same density as our atmosphere has at a height of about forty miles. A similar result is obtained when the slight flattening of the disc of Jupiter, which takes place when the planet is just going to be covered by the Moon, or emerges from behind it, is measured on the Arequipa photographs. Such an atmosphere is next to nothing, but there is another observation, namely, of a dark band appearing between Jupiter and the Moon's limb when the former begins to be covered by the latter; and Professor Pickering finds no other explanation for it than in some very light haze, partly due to water vapour, which would rise a few miles above the Moon's surface where it is illuminated by the rays of the Sun.

Such a supposition would have been met some time ago with great suspicion. But it must be said that the more the Moon's surface is studied in detail the more astronomers are inclined to think that, in some places at least, a haze, originated from water vapour, is the only possible means to explain certain curious occurrences. Thus, Dr. Sarling has lately reminded us that, in 1774, Eysenhard, a pupil of Lambert, saw the part of the shadow line which crossed one of the plains (the Mare Crisium) brought ·in a wave-like movement which lasted for two hours and was seen by three different persons— only in this part of the lunar disc. Those undulations, which spread at a speed of 1,200 feet per second over a distance of eighty miles, could only be due—as Dr. Sarling truly remarks—to vapours floating over the plain.[8] In several instances, the interiors of deep lunar circuses took a misty appearance at sunrise, and this misty appearance disappeared as the Sun rose higher above the same circus, while in other cases it persisted a considerable time after sunrise, even though all around was sharply marked and distinct.[9] And so on. The temperature of the Moon's surface, when it is heated by the Sun's rays, being very near to the freezing point, as appears from Langley's last measurements, the evaporation of frozen water under the rays of the rising Sun is surely not at all improbable.

It remains, of course, to be seen whether a haze of this sort is not due in some cases to water ejected by volcanoes or geysers; the more so as some volcanic activity, remodelling until now the forms of the' craters, seems to exist. There is, indeed, among astronomers a strong suspicion of a lunar crater, nearly three miles in diameter, being of recent formation. · It was first discovered by Dr. Klein in 1876, in the plain named Mare Vaporum, after he himself and many others had previously so often examined that region without seeing the crater. Besides, the alternate appearance and disappearance of another crater (Linné), nearly four miles in diameter, can hardly be explained unless it is concealed from time to time by the vapours which it itself exhales. As to changes observed in the shapes of small lunar volcanoes, they are too numerous to be due to mere errors of observation.[10]

If free water thus exists occasionally, even now, on the Moon's surface, or has existed at a relatively recent period, it is natural to ask whether it has left no traces of its activity. Are there no river-valleys which would bear testimony to its existence? Till lately, the majority of astronomers answered this question in the negative, even though their earlier predecessors, armed with feebler telescopes, were most affirmative on this point. The maria, or seas, are known to be plains on which no traces of aqueous action have been detected, and the clefts, or large 'rills,' are almost certainly rents produced in a solid surface.

However, beside these clefts, there are much finer formations which only lately have received due attention, and these finer rills have all the aspects of river-beds. They are not straight-lined, but wind exactly as rivers wind on our maps; they fork like rivers; they

[8] *Sirius*, 1895, vi. p. 134.
[9] Edw. Neison, *The Moon and the Condition and Configurations of its Surface,* p. 33 (London, 1876).
[10] *The Observatory*, June 1892; *Nature*, vol. xlvi. p. 134.

are wider at one end than at the other, and one end is nearly always higher than the other. Many such fine rills have been observed and mapped lately, and Professor W. Pickering gives a list of thirty-five presumable river-beds, large, medium-sized, and very fine.[11] However, contrary to most terrestrial rivers, the lunar river-beds—those, at least, which were observed by W. Pickering—have their wider end in their *upper* course, nearly always in a pear-shaped craterlet. This circumstance offers, however, nothing extraordinary, as we know many rivers in Central Asia and South America which originate in a lake and grow thinner and thinner as they enter the arid plains. To take one illustration out of several, one such river, sixty-five miles in length with all its windings, rises in a craterlet, perhaps 2,000 feet wide, but soon its valley narrows to 1,000 feet, or less, and is lost in a plain. Occasionally such ' rivers' occur in groups on the slopes of the mountains. Other river-beds, on the contrary, seem to have the normal characters of our rivers. One of them begins in the mountains as an extremely fine line, gradually increases in width, and, after having received a tributary, becomes a broad but shallow valley. Another bifurcates into two very fine lines in its higher part.[12] In short, it may now be taken as certain that there are river-beds, to all appearance of aqueous origin ; but they are so narrow that we should not be able to discover water-courses if they existed at the bottom of these valleys. We must be content with saying that they have been scooped out by running water.

So much having been won, the next step was naturally to ask if no traces of vegetation can be detected. On Mars, we see how every year a snow cover spreads over the circumpolar region, how later on in the season wide channels appear in it, and how the snow thaws gradually—presumably giving origin to water; even clouds have lately been seen ; and we can notice, moreover, how the coloration of wide surfaces changes, probably because they are covered with vegetation, and how that coloration gradually takes a reddish yellow tint. Of course, if anything of the sort took place on our nearest neighbour, the Moon, it would have been noticed long since. But it would be most unwise to maintain that nothing similar to it happens, on a much smaller scale. On the contrary, Professor Pickering shows that there are some probabilities in favour of plants of some sort or another periodically growing on the Moon as well.

The great lunar circuses or craters attain, as is known, colossal dimensions ; the largest of them have 100 and 130 miles in diameter, and the floor of their inner parts is mostly flat. Now,

[11] *Annals of the Astronomical Observatory of Harvard College*, vol. xxxii. part 1, p. 87.

[12] Dr. Sarling's letter to *Sirius*, March 30, 1895 ; map of the region near Herschel, f, made by J. N. Krieger at the Observatory of Triest, in same periodical, September 1895, p. 195.

Neison had already made the remark that grey, almost black, spots appear on the floor of certain craters at full moon, but disappear later on, and W. Pickering has carefully investigated several such spots during his unfortunately too short stay at Arequipa. Contrary to all expectations, they grow darker just after full moon, that is, when the Sun strikes the visible part of the Moon's surface in full and when it is geometrically impossible for any shadow to be visible, and they become invisible when the Sun is lowest and the shadows are evidently strongest. We know, however, of no stone which would darken under the action of sunlight, and grow lighter when the sunlight fades, and, following two such authorities as Mädler and Neison, Professor Pickering inclines to see the causes of those changes in vegetation. Such spots, whose darkness varies with the Sun's altitude, are not mere accidents. On the contrary, they have been found on all plains, with the exception of one, and in two plains, the Mare Tranquillitatis and Mare Nectaria, they apparently cover the whole floor, their changes being sometimes so conspicuous as to be almost visible to the naked eye. In the craters they always appear in the lower inner edges, but never on the tops of the walls, and rarely, if ever, on the outer walls. As a rule, they are coloured in dark grey, but in one case at least, one of the spots, examined with a great power, was of a 'pronounced yellow colour, with perhaps a suspicion of green.'

These observations,[13] which Professor Pickering unhappily found impossible to continue under the much less propitious sky of Massachusetts, 'on account of the poor quality of the seeing,' are certainly very promising, the more so as they are not isolated. For the last few years, a number of data are accumulating, all tending to prove that it was too rash to describe the Moon's surface as utterly devoid of life. It appears very probable, on the contrary, that volcanic changes continue to go on on the Moon's surface on a larger scale than on the Earth, and that notwithstanding the most unfavourable conditions for organic life which prevail there, such life exists, be it only on a small scale. This is certainly very far from the sanguine affirmations of the last century selenographers, who wanted to see on the Moon 'fortifications,' 'national roads,' and 'traces of industrial activity;' such objects, if they did exist, could *not* be seen with our best instruments. But traces of vegetation which develops at certain periods and fades next, traces of water which runs perhaps even now, as well as indications of volcanic changes of the surface, become more and more probable in proportion as we learn to know our satellite better.

---

[13] In the above-mentioned volume of *Harvard Annals* they are published in full, and are illustrated by a number of excellent photographs.

II

When we examine the animal world in a descending series, from the highest animals to the lowest, we see how their organs of nutrition are gradually simplified, how they become less definite and less specialised in their functions, until we find that functions which are performed in higher animals by special glands are accomplished at the lower stages of the series by mere cells scattered in the tissues, or even by the whole protoplasm of the body. The same gradual simplification is seen in the organs of the senses. They also become less and less definite as we descend the scale; it becomes more and more difficult to separate them from each other, and in the lower invertebrates mere cells, disseminated in the tissues, answer more or less to the irritations from without. At last, at the very bottom of the series, the sense-irritations are received by the whole surface of the animalcule's body.

An immense amount of investigation has been made, especially within the last thirty years, in order to trace the chain of evolution of the sense-organs in the animal world, and to follow the gradual ascent of sense-impressions, from the mere irritability of protoplasm to the highly developed sensations of the higher animals. Anatomists, physiologists, and psycho-physiologists have joined in that colossal work, and by this time it may be said that a result of the highest importance for science altogether, and especially for psychology, has been attained. The series has gradually been reconstituted in full, through the efforts of scores of separate workers. The leading results of these wonderful investigations having lately been summed up by Dr. Wilibald Nagel in a suggestive introductory chapter to a more special work;[14] we may take it, together with a few other works, as a guide for a brief review of the subject.[15]

[14] Dr. Wilibald Nagel, 'Vergleichend-physiologische und anatomische Unter-suchungen über den Geruchs- und Geschmackssinn und ihre Organe; mit einleitenden Betrachtungen aus der allgemeinen vergleichenden Sinnesphysiologie,' in Leuckart and Chun's *Bibliotheca Zoologica*, Heft 18, I. and II. (Stuttgart, 1894 and 1895). A full bibliography will be found at the end of this work.

[15] E. Jourdan's *Les Sens chez les Animaux Inférieurs* (Paris, J. Baillière, 1889) is an excellent little work on the same subject which can be safely recommended to the general reader. Unhappily it has not been translated into English. Haeckel's *Essay on the Origin and Development of Sense-Organs* (English translation) dates from 1879. Romanes's *Mental Evolution in Animals*, Sir John Lubbock's *The Senses and the Mental Life of Animals, especially of Insects*, and C. Lloyd Morgan's *Introduction to Comparative Psychology*, published in 1894, although they do not exactly cover the same ground, are too well known to need recommendation. W. Wundt's *Grund-züge der physiologischen Psychologie* (4th edition, Jena, 1894), and Max Verworn's *Allgemeine Physiologie* are, of course, two classical works, rich in information upon this subject as well, but neither has yet been translated into English. Wundt's *Lectures on Human and Animal Psychology* have at last been translated into English in 1894. Some works on the lower organisms are indicated further on.

What most strikes a beginner in the study of the lowest animals is the variety of those of their acts and motions which apparently imply psychical life and consciousness. Those microscopical animalcules which consist of one single cell, or even of a mere speck of protoplasm, have evidently no traces of a nervous system; and yet their movements and their responsivity to external stimuli are such that one hesitates to interpret them as mere mechanical or chemical processes, such as we see in foams, or even as mere manifestations of 'irritability,' which is a property of all living matter.

In one of the American psychological laboratories, the daily life of a one-celled infusorium—a vorticella—was lately observed under the microscope for days in succession, and all the accidents of its uneventful existence were recorded.[16] A transparent, tulip-like, or bell-like expansion at the end of a thin transparent stalk, which contracts at the slightest jerk; a tiny opening at the top of the bell, representing a sort of mouth, or rather a buccal pore; and a row of extremely fine cilia, which differ from hairs by being mere expansions of the protoplasm of the body—the whole, cilia and all, being covered with an extremely fine cuticle—such is that tiny infusorium which everyone possessed of a small microscope can find in a drop of water taken from a pond. Observed hour after hour under the microscope, while a feeble current of water was flowing over the glass slide, it was seen to swallow still smaller animalcules, after having attracted them into its 'mouth' by the motion of its cilia; it assimilated them, and being well provided with food, it reproduced itself by budding tiny vorticellæ from its sides.

To many stimuli it was insensible. Icy water was made to flow; bright light, immediately following darkness, was flashed upon the little creature; light of various colours was tried, as also musical sounds 'of all qualities and volumes'—the animalcule took no heed of them. But the slightest jerk or jar made it instantly contract its stalk; and it sorted with the greatest apparent precision the floating minute particles, swallowing those of them which suited it. 'The world of relation,' as psychologists say, of a vorticella thus consists of a series of touches, with perhaps some taste and smell impressions, hardly distinguished from each other. With all that, the vorticella displayed memory. When no other food was supplied to it but cells of yeast in sterilised water, it took first to the new food. It filled its body to distension with yeast cells; but in a few minutes the entire meal was suddenly rejected, and for several hours the vorticella could not be induced to repeat the experiment. It must have retained for several hours some unpleasant impression; it manifested powers of 'choice' as it ceased to swallow an unsuitable food; and in some

[16] C. F. Hodge and H. A. Atkins, 'The Daily Life of a Protozoan,' in *American Journal of Psychology*, 1894-95, vol. vi. p. 524.

unknown way it discerned between yeast cells and the animalcules it was used to prey upon.

The vorticella is, however, a considerably developed being in comparison with, say, an amœba, which consists of a mere speck of protoplasm, or with that slimy vegetable organism—a plasmodium—which is made up of thickly interwoven threads of naked protoplasm. And yet, even in these two lowest representatives of the animal and the vegetable world, something in advance of mere irritability appears. The amœba avoids bright light, and if a pencil of light falls upon its path, it retreats; certain chemical substances attract it, while others act repulsively upon it; and when the two poles of a galvanic current are plunged into the drop of water the amœba lives in, it moves towards the negative pole and avoids the positive. As to the plasmodium, it displays a still higher discriminative power. For instance, two beakers, filled with water, are placed close to each other, and in one of them the water is kept at a temperature of 45° Fahrenheit, while in the other it is much warmer (86°). A strip of paper, upon which one of these myxomycetes fungi has spread itself, is then placed in such a way that one end of the paper dips into the cold water, while the other end touches the warm water. Immediately, the slimy fungus begins to slowly stretch out and draw in its threads, and after a time it will have crept over into the warmer beaker. Other plasmodia show their dislike of light by withdrawing from the lighted part of a surface into its shadowy part; while to chemical stimuli they are even still more sensitive. If a plasmodium be placed in a glass tube filled with boiled water, which contains no nutritious substances, and the tube be overturned and plunged by its open end into unboiled water, the fungus will creep out of the tube and spread itself in the water below. It also will invade a paper pellet saturated with the substance it usually feeds upon; but if a crystal of salt is placed on the paper which it is spreading upon, the fungus will at once withdraw its threads and shrink away from the unpleasant matter; and if, while it is spreading itself one way, its front end be cauterised with some acid, the whole plasmodium will at once change the direction of its motion. In short, these lowest organisms have the property of recoiling from harmful substances and of finding the useful ones all through the medium they are placed in. The life-processes which are going on in their protoplasm, as its chemical composition is continually altered and reconstituted, are sufficient to result in a sort of discriminative power between what aids the process of life and what is liable to check it.[17]

[17] The literature of this subject is very large. It is, however, very well summed up in several works quite accessible to the general reader, namely:—Oscar Hertwig's *Die Zelle und die Gewebe*, Jena, 1893 (English translation published at Chicago in 1893); and Max Verworn's *Psycho-physiologische Protistenstudien*, Jena, 1889, which two contain full indexes of the original memoirs; also Binet's *Psychic Life of Micro-organisms*, translated from the French, Chicago, 1890. In Wundt's *Grundzüge*, 4th edition, p. 25 *sq.*, the psychological bearings of these researches are discussed.

With bacteria, the same phenomena become much more complicated. Bacteria, as a rule, are very sensitive to changes in the
intensity of light—some of them preferring light and some others
darkness—as well as to electrical and chemical stimuli. When a
diatom (one of the one-celled plants which swarm in fresh water, and
look so pretty under the microscope, on account of their double
symmetry and the bright green chlorophyll grains they contain) stops
swimming about, bacteria will gather in thousands round it, and
stand motionless, absorbing the oxygen it gives up. Suddenly the
diatom will get out of the crowd of bacteria, but the crowd, after
having remained in the lurch for a second or two, will soon follow it
and reassemble again. And not only oxygen, but various chemical
substances attract them as well. Going higher up the scale, when
we come next to those infusoria which are provided either with
a couple of thin threads (flagellæ), or are adorned with a row of
fine cilia, we find them capable of performing co-ordinate movements
which exclude all possible comparison with the purely mechanical
movements taking place in simple foams. Thus, a flagellate infusorium
will anchor itself by one of its flagellæ to a tiny fibre of weed, and
continually work with the other flagellum in search for food; then it
suddenly will jerk to the opposite side of its anchoring weed and
continue there the same exploration. Or, while hunting, it will
suddenly change the direction of its swim; or it will hunt by jerks.
As to the sensibility of the lowest organisms to chemical stimuli, it
is simply striking. They have their likes and dislikes [18] for different substances, and as they seek for some of them and avoid the
others, they show an admirable discernment. The most wonderful
fact, however, is that these microscopic beings can be attracted not
only by substances which are necessary for their life, but also by some
of those which are no food for them, or even are decidedly harmful
(salicylic natrium, chloride of mercury, or morphine), but seem to
please their tastes. Infusoria will thus abandon a medium containing
nourishing substances, such as extract of meat, which they generally
like, in order to intoxicate themselves with morphine. Drunkenness
thus begins in the animal world at its lowest microscopical stages.

In the presence of a mass of such facts, and of the far more
astounding powers displayed by all the lowest organisms in connection with their reproduction, shall we maintain that all these
manifestations of life are physical processes, which have nothing in
common with what we describe as psychical life at the higher stages?
Or shall we not rather admit that what is described as ' irritability of
living matter ' at the lowest end of the series merges by imperceptible

---

[18] The chemical sense of the lower organisms was admirably explored by Pfeffer,
'Chemotactische Bewegungen von Bacterien, Flagellaten und Volvocineen,' in
Untersuchungen aus dem botanischen Institut zu Tübingen. Bd. iv. 1888; also his
previous work in same periodical, Bd. i. 1884.

degrees into what we are bound to describe as 'sensibility'? . In fact, it·is impossible not to recognise that in the protozoans the first .appearance, the very dawn of sensibility is met with ; but, as shown by Verworn, that sort of·sensibility belongs not only to the animal-cule as a whole, but to each minute part of its body as well. When .one of the cilia of a ciliated infusorium is irritated, the whole row is set into a wave-like motion in the proper direction, and the irritation spreads, not as in a corn-field, by each bent cilium pushing the next ; .it is transmitted through the underlying protoplasm, because the transmission of the irritation may be prevented by making an extremely fine transverse cut between two cilia. But if one cilium .is cut out, together with a tiny portion of the protoplasm behind it— this almost incredible operation has been performed by Verworn—the isolated cilium answers the irritation in the very same·way as if it .continued to make part of the row in the animalcule's body. Each minute particle of the protozoan's body has thus the capacity of responding to the irritation ; and the co-ordinated movements of the animal are a sum total of the movements of the particles. · The protozoan, as Verworn says, can thus be compared to a crowd, in .which there is no conception of the crowd's individuality, because each individual, on receiving a certain impression, acts for himself— the final result being, nevertheless, a movement of the crowd.

It may, of course, be said that as the protozoans have no nervous system, they can have no psychical life. This is, at least, the opinion of Du Bois Reymond. But the nervous system, and even its nerve-cells, must also have had their embryonal stage in the evolution of the animal kingdom, and in the seemingly uniform protoplasm of the infusorium, which performs, together with other functions, some of the functions of the nerve-cells, we must have already the germs of the nerve-cell.[19] In some infusoria there is even a tiny spot which seems to be more sensitive to light than the remainder of the body. However, it is needless to go high up the scale in order to find visible rudiments of a nervous system. They exist in the shape of nerve-cells and nerve-filaments in the next division, in which corals, medusæ, sea-anemones, and so on, are included (the cœlenterata). In this extremely interesting division,[20] sensibility to light and sound, a low sensibility of the skin to pressure, and a high development of the chemical sense are found, together with a first specialisation of the sense-organs, and doubtless signs of voluntary action. · In some subdivisions of this class (the comb-bearers, or ctenophores, and the sea-anemones) Nagel found the sense of taste highly developed ; while the movements which a ctenophore performs to prevent an

---

[19] Max Verworn's *Protistenstudien*, p. 201.

[20] W. Nagel has made it the subject of new detailed studies ('Der Ge-schmackssinn der Actinien,' in *Zoologischer Anzeiger*, 1892, No. 400 ; 'Versuche über die Sinnesphysiologie von Beroë ovata und Carnarina hastata,' in Pflüger's *Archiv*, 1893, Bd. liv. p. 165).

unpleasant stuff, like quinine, from reaching its inner taste-organs, or the movements of the tentacles of a sea-anemone to get rid of a pellet of paper saturated with some unpleasant but not irritating stuff, leave no doubt as to the existence of will and some rudiments of reasoning power. Besides, it is well known from Leudenfeld's investigations that when a sea-anemone or a jelly-fish throws out its stinging threads, this action can by no means be explained in a merely mechanical way.[21] There is no doubt that with this class the first dawn of a dim consciousness makes its appearance, but the general consciousness of the animal is not yet fully attained, because separate radial portions of its body answer to different stimuli as if they were separate individuals. The crowd only begins to be conscious of its individuality as a crowd.

From this point upwards, the gradual and uninterrupted development of the senses is quite easy to follow, up to the highest mammals. One remark is, however, necessary to avoid misunderstanding, and Nagel insists upon it. Even in man it is not always easy to discriminate between what he perceives through his sense of smell and what he is aware of through his sense of taste; in birds, and probably in some mammals too, the auditive sensation may be provoked not exclusively through the organ of hearing; and with the fishes and all the animals living in water, the sense of smell, which has but little opportunity for exercise, is mingled with the sense of taste. Consequently, we must be prepared to find that the usual division of senses into touch, taste, smell, vision, and hearing, will not do for the whole series. The senses must be rather divided into a mechanical, chemical, temperature, and light sense, to which the electrical sense will perhaps have to be added. Such a division, undoubtedly, better answers to the senses which exist in the lower animals, and when the series is considered in an ascending order, the gradual differentiation of the chemical sense into taste and smell, and of the mechanical sense into touch, hearing, and pressure sense, becomes evident. If such a division of the senses be agreed upon, their gradual specialisation can be easily followed, as may be seen even from the following few illustrations.[22]

The star-fishes and the sea-urchins have much more developed senses than might be presumed on first sight. They have organs of vision and a fine chemical sense. They perfectly well discern between a piece of meat and a wet paper pellet of the same consistence, or between a pellet saturated with water and another which is saturated with meat-juice. Nevertheless, it is extremely difficult to separate in them the mechanical sense of touch from the chemical sense;

[21] E. Jourdan, *Les Sens chez les Animaux Inférieurs*, p. 42 *sq*.

[22] Romanes, in his *Mental Evolution of Animals*, pp. 80–125, has briefly sketched that gradual growth. Jourdan's above-mentioned book can be taken as an excellent guide, especially in connection with Nagel's work, in which many doubts, especially with regard to taste and smell, have been cleared away by means of new experiments.

still less taste and smell. With the molluscs, who offer a great variety of sense-development in different species, it is difficult to speak of organs of touch, because the mechanical sense belongs to the whole superficies of the skin, although it is usually more delicate in and around the mouth. On the other hand, they have organs of vision on their tentacles, and the land molluscs are undoubtedly endowed with the sense of smell. A helix will crawl towards a paper sac which contains some food, wet its surface and tear the sac, and thus reach the food; while a snail will crawl towards an apple, and move right and left if the apple be shifted sideways. Most molluscs very well discern their food, while ·some of them have the sense of hearing, and even the direction sense. But in that class of animals the necessity of not too sharp a separation between different senses becomes especially apparent. The same nerve-cells seem to be affected to the transmission of different impressions, which have their own separate organs in man.

That the land-leeches, which come together to assail travellers in Ceylon, possess a finely developed sense of smell, and that the medical leech is not devoid of it, is well known; but it also appears (from Nagel's experiments) that the whole skin of the medical leech is endowed with the sense of taste. As to the presence of visual organs in each of the segments of some worms, it is only what may be expected in animals whose segments have so much maintained of their individuality. It is, moreover, certain that in many cases each segment maintains a good deal of its psychical individuality.

The high development of all the senses in the crustaceans and in insects is quite familiar now through the works of Huxley, Romanes, Lubbock, Forel, Fabre, and so on. The sensibility of crustaceans to sounds and the fine hearing of the spider are of wide repute, although the high qualifications of the latter as an amateur of music have been roughly handled by Forel; the fine discernment of colours by the ants, demonstrated by Lubbock, and the admirable development of smell and taste in various insects—all these are familiar facts. However, even among insects a perfect localisation of the chemical sense does not always exist, and smell attains its full development only with those insects which live in the air; while those which live in water seem, on the contrary, to be almost totally deprived of it. The water-beetle (*Dytiscus*) does not perceive the presence of animals which it preys upon, even within a distance of a few millimetres, so long as they remain motionless. It evidently does not smell them, and it must have but a dim vision. If meat-juice is offered to a water-beetle, it does not notice the juice till it has been approached within half an inch from its mouth. At the same time its sense of taste is very fine. A drop of water carefully brought within its reach at the end of a fine glass tube, so as not to provoke touch sensations, has no effect upon the *Dytiscus*; but a drop of

sugar solution or of meat extract immediately provokes rapid grasping movements. A pellet of paper imbibed with a very weak solution
of quinine, or of vinegar, or of chloral hydrate, is also grasped by the
voracious beetle, but three seconds later it is thrown away, and the
animal clears for a certain time, with its fore-legs, the parts surrounding its mouth, as if to get rid of an unpleasant sensation.[23]

Even in fishes and amphibians the mechanical sense of touch is not
fully differentiated from the chemical sense of taste, while the sense
of smell hardly exists at all. As to the birds and the mammals (with
the exceptions of those which live in water), they not only have as a
rule all senses which man is possessed of, but it is well known that
the sense of vision and partly of hearing in birds and the sense of
smell in certain mammals attain a perfection which is vainly looked
for in man ; while the sense of position and the faculty of almost
instantly adapting the muscles to a variety of requirements during
flight, jumping, running and so on, are always a matter of admiration
to the naturalist.

It will be remarked that in order thus to trace the progressive
specialisation of senses in the animal series no hypotheses of any sort
have to be made. On the contrary, every statement is a direct outcome of most detailed anatomical studies, controlled by physiological
experiments. In order to grasp the whole series of facts we only
need to admit that the appearance of the more specialised senses of
touch, hearing, taste, smell, and vision is preceded by the existence
of the less specialised mechanical, chemical, temperature, and light
senses ; but this is what may have been presumed in advance under
the theory of evolution. Another admission, advocated by Nagel,
namely, the existence of mixed or rather undefined sense-organs—
which appears as a mere development of the same idea—would further
simplify the comprehension of the facts. At the lowest end of the
scale we have what Nagel describes (perhaps not quite exactly) as
'the universal organ of senses,' which means that the whole protoplasm of the animal's body (or, perhaps, some components of it) acts
as an organ for receiving excitations from various stimuli. And
at the other end of the scale there are specialised organs, so specialised
that each of them is capable of transmitting one sort of sensations
only.[24] Between the two Nagel proposes to place intermediate mixed

---

[23] W. Nagel, *Biblioteca Zoologica*, xviii. p. 67 *sq*. Also his earlier more general
work, *Die niederen Sinne der Insekten*, Tübingen, 1892.

[24] A great divergence of opinions still existing as regards the ' specific energy ' of
the sense-organs, Nagel ventures the following hypothesis : Let us take the organ of
taste and suppose that in its simplest form it consists of *three* elements—a sense-cell,
a nerve which surrounds it with its ramifications, and a ganglion-cell in which the
nerve ends. Supposing that the exterior irritation affects chiefly the sense-cell, and
not the ramifications of the nerve, this cell, on being irritated, would secrete on its
superficies some stuff specific to it, and this stuff would irritate the end ramifications
of the nerve. The nerve would accordingly transmit to the ganglion-cell the same
sort of excitations, whatever the outer stimulus may be. Persons acquainted with

organs (*Wechselsinnesorgane,* which, in their normal state, aid the animal in perceiving two or three different sensations, such as taste and smell, or touch, hearing, and taste.　Having no such mixed organs, we evidently have a difficulty in understanding the corresponding sensations, and we may ask ourselves whether the animal possessed of one organ for touch and taste, or for taste and smell, receives from it two different sensations, or has one sensation only, which is neither of the two, but lies between them.　We may not be able to answer this question, but we fully understand that the world of sensations should grow in complexity, precision, and variety, as the sense-organs become more and more definite.[23]

It may thus be said that the joint efforts of anatomists and psycho-physiologists have resulted in reconstituting an uninterrupted series which leads from the vague sensibility of the lowest organisms to the fully developed senses of man.　There is no gap in the series, no boundary to stop at and to say that below it lies something which has not the psychical aspects of senses, and above it begin the senses of the thinking beings.　At the lowest stages there is already some sort of a very vague and extremely simplified psychical life, mechanical and chemical irritations already provoking various co-ordinated movements, which necessarily imply some sort of vague sensations. Then, as we gradually ascend the scale, we notice how rudimentary sense-organs, for receiving and transmitting whole series of irritations, make their appearence, and experiments show that the sensations are broadly differentiated into three or four series, in accordance with their outer stimuli—pressure, heat, light, or chemical processes. And next, by a series of imperceptible gradations we are brought to the stage at which each series of sensations is differentiated in its turn, so that we finally recognise our own organs of the senses, and our own sensations.　This does not mean, of course, that science has mastered the psychology of animals; but it has got an insight into the primary elements of all psychic life—the elementary sensations out of which and upon which that life is constructed.　As to the bearings of these investigations upon psychology altogether, they can only be understood if a glance is cast upon the present standpoint of psychology, which is widely different from what it was very few years ago.

modern theories of vision (they were briefly summed up in this Review, April 1893) probably will feel interested in that hypothesis, which, of course, is only indicated here in its main outline.

[23] The hypothesis of a 'Wechselsinnesorgan' has been met with some criticism in the *Naturwissenschaftliche Rundschau*, by Rawitz, 1893, Bd. viii. p. 91, and R. von Hanstein (same volume, p. 449), which was answered by Nagel in his last work (*Bibliotheca Zoologica*, xviii. pp. 25–42).　It seems, however, from Hanstein's review of this last work that his criticisms are directed less against the theory itself than against the conclusions therefrom as regards the corresponding sensations (*Naturwissenschaftliche Rundschau*, 1895, Bd. x. p. 124).

III

No science has undergone within the last thirty years so deep
a transformation in all its conceptions, its methods, and its very language, as has been the case with psychology.   Thirty years ago the old
conception, mainly worked out in Germany, and according to which
psychology was treated as a mere branch of deductions from speculative principles, was no longer tenable.   Under the influence chiefly
of British psychologists, who had constructed their science upon a
detailed analysis of the experiences of one's own consciousness,
metaphysical psychology was compelled to retire in the background.
But it was a question very much debated at that time whether the
study of the phenomena of consciousness should continue to be carried
on, as most psychologists maintained, by means of self-analysis, taken,
of course, in its widest sense, which does not exclude the study of
psychical acts in other individuals as well, or, as it was advocated by
the younger school of German psychologists, Lotze, Fechner, and
Wundt,[26] the whole matter ought not to be handed over to the
physiologist who would apply the precise methods of his own science
to psychical research.   'Who has to study psychology, and by
which methods?' was the burning question of those days.

By this time, the then much feared transference is an irre-
versibly accomplished fact.   Psychology is studied by the physiologist:
it is a branch of physiology, making its way to become a sister science
to it.   To use the words of an American psychologist, J. Mark
Baldwin,[27] 'we find an actual department of knowledge handed over
to a new class of men,' who treat it by quite new methods, the
methods of accurate measurement and experiment, so familiar to the
physiologist.   They experiment upon sensations, involuntary actions,
acts of memory and thought, and they measure the motions of the
muscles and the chemical changes in the tissues in order to value
in numerical data the intensity of the psychical acts themselves.
And they do not consider their science as philosophy, but know very
well that they only contribute, in common with all other sciences,
the necessary stepping-stones to build up the philosophy of the
universe.

Of course, in all psycho-physiological investigations the analysis
of one's own experiences of his own consciousness remains now, as it
was before, at the basis of psychological conclusions.   When the
experimenter measures the degree of sensibility of one's eye to
luminous irritations, or of one's skin to prickling, or when he records

[26] Lotze's *Medizinische Psychologie* appeared in 1852, Fechner's *Elemente der
Psychophysik* in 1860, and the first edition of Wundt's *Grundzüge der physiologischen
Psychologie* in 1874 (fourth edition in 1894).

[27] 'Psychology, Past and Present,' in *Psychical Review*, 1894, vol. i. part iv. p. 373.
It contains a brief historical sketch

in figures the fatigue of the brain during this or that mental exercise, he may reduce the self-observation of the person whom he experiments upon to its simplest elements; but he also knows that he must appeal in most cases to that person itself; he learns from it what its sensations were during the experiment and by so doing he gets a precious guide in his researches. Self-observation thus continues to occupy a prominent position in all psychological researches; but its very methods have entirely been changed. In the thirty psycho-physiological laboratories which are now in existence,[28] the numerical relations which exist between the energy of the outward stimuli—light, sound, chemicals, and so on—and the energy of the sensations they provoke are measured, and the mathematical law of their relations is sought for. Both the conscious and the unconscious movements which are called forth in man by different sense impressions, under different states of self-consciousness, and under different mental states, are submitted to the same analysis; nay, the mechanism of the growth of ideas, different mental operations, and memory itself are subjects of experimental studies, or of such inquests as the inquest which was carried on by Mr. Galton, and was epoch-making in psychology. And although all these investigations are very young—the first psychological laboratory was opened only eighteen years ago—experimental pyschology has already become a natural science in the true sense of the word, a science of which both the powers and the limits are known, and which has already thrown floods of light upon the mental phenomena which, under the old methods, seemed to lie beyond the limits of understanding.

At the same time another branch of psychology has suddenly taken, within the last ten years or so, a new development. The ambition of psycho-physiology has always been to find for each psychical process its physiological equivalent—in other words, when a sense-impression has awakened in us certain mental images, what electrical or chemical processes, what transformations of energy and, if possible, what molecular movements took place at the same time in our nerve-channels and nerve-centres? That such changes take place every psychologist admits, to whatever school, dualist or monist, he belongs—the difference between the two being that the dualist sees in the psychical and the physiological processes two sets of concomitant but utterly and substantially different phenomena, while the monist considers them as two different aspects of the same process.[29] The study of the physiological processes which go on in man during

---

[28] Fourteen in the United States, four in Germany, two in this country, one in France, and seven in different countries of Europe (Alfred Binet, *Introduction à la Psychologie Expérimentale*, Paris, 1894).

[29] The difference between the two views is very well set out in Dr. Lloyd Morgan's *Introduction to Comparative Psychology* (Walter Scott's 'Science Series, 1894).

each psychical process is, accordingly, one of the main objects of psychology. But until lately such investigations met with an almost insuperable obstacle in our very imperfect knowledge of the intimate structure of the nervous system and the brain. However, within the last few years, a profound modification has taken place in the views upon the minute structure of the nervous system altogether. Through the discovery of the microscopical units of which the nervous system is built up—the so-called ' neurons,' whose protoplasmic ramifications intimately penetrate into the tissues, where they seem to meet with the ramifications of the tissue-cells, and whose axial cylinders ramify themselves to meet the ramifications of other neurons—through this discovery the whole mechanism of the irritations which result in unconscious reflex movements has received a quite new interpretation. Then, the study of the inner structure of the brain, which was chiefly made by Rámon y Cajal,[30] on the basis of the above discovery, has led the Spanish anatomist to attempt a most remarkable explanation of the anatomical mechanism of the formation of ideas and associations and of attention.[31] And finally, the application of the same discoveries to the sympathetic nervous system has lately enabled the German anatomist, A. Kölliker, to make another important step. He has attempted to trace the mechanism by means of which our emotions and the irritations of our spinal cord result in such involuntary movements as affect the activity of the heart and the blood-vessels, and make one turn pale or red, shed tears or be covered with perspiration, have his hair stand on end or shiver, and so on, under the influence of various emotions. Such psychical phenomena and such intimate relations between emotion, thought and will, which it seemed hopeless to explain by means of self-observation on the introspective method, have thus had a flash of light suddenly thrown upon them since the above-mentioned transference of psychology to physiologists took place.

At the same time, a third equally important branch of psychology was lately called into existence. As in all other sciences, the theory of evolution was accepted in psychology ; and by accepting it, psychology was necessarily led to admit that just as we may trace in the animal series the slow progressive development of all organs, including those of the senses and of thought, out of the rudimentary cell-elements, so also we may trace the gradual and uninterrupted evolution of the psychical faculties out of such rudiments of psychical life as are seen in the lowest organisms. Beginning with the irritability of

[30] *Les Nouvelles Idées sur la Structure du Système Nerveux chez l'Homme et chez les Vertébrés*, traduit de l'espagnol, Paris (Reinwald), 1894. His views have been given in this country in a Croonian lecture, in 1894, before the Royal Society. His larger work waits still for an English translator.
[31] *Archiv für Anatomie und Physiologie*, Anatomische Abtheilung, 1895, p. 367.

protoplasm, psychologists now endeavour to trace out the gradual evolution of sensibility and perception, so as finally to reach the highest manifestations of perception, will, and thought, at the highest degrees of the scale. A third large branch of psychology, which may be described as comparative or evolutionary psychology, is thus in elaboration; and in this country we have the good fortune of possessing at least three original works (Romanes's, Sir John Lubbock's and Dr. Lloyd Morgan's) which may be considered as stepping-stones towards the work on the evolution of mind, which is now ripening in science. In the preceding paragraph the progress lately achieved as regards the evolution of senses in the animal world is briefly indicated; but countless researches have been made besides into the progressive evolution of the nervous system and the brain of different classes of animals, and these researches will evidently soon receive a new meaning from the above-mentioned discoveries in the anatomy of the nervous system. Then, and then only, the synthesis of sensation and conception will give us a new insight into the progressive development of the psychical faculties of animals, and throw a new light upon psychology altogether. This is the present standpoint of psychology.

P. Kropotkin.

LIFE IN POETRY: POETICAL CONCEPTION [1]

THERE is a certain irony in the relation between art and criticism. The artist under the impulse of imitation within him follows the lead of Nature, and brings his imaginative idea into being guided only by instinct and judgment. At a later stage in the history of society, perhaps after creative energy has ceased, comes the critic, and traces the idea backward as far as he can through the artist's mind, always stopping short, however, of the real sources of life. Then deeming that he has penetrated the secret of art, the critic begins to lay down the law for the artist, and his law is usually wrong.

Wrong, indeed, he is almost bound to be, because he has followed the order not of Nature but of logic. Yet, so vast is the persuasive power of logic, that deductive criticism, *a priori* criticism, has had an appreciable influence on the course of literature—has, in fact, been the parent of all the Academies. And it is observable that this kind of criticism flourishes most in societies in which the spirit of political liberty has been, or is being, extinguished. Academies began to thrive in the Italian Republics after they had lost their freedom, in France when the nation was tending towards absolute monarchy. As regards the art of poetry, those who helped to found the Academies submitted themselves without reservation to the authority of Aristotle. Misconstruing the text of the *Poetics*, they deduced from their own misunderstanding of the philosopher a code of supposed artistic necessity, which had no basis in the nature of things. They succeeded in getting recognition for a set of rules which Corneille, while submitting to them in theory, was obliged to disregard in practice, and which were of such stringent logic as to convince Voltaire and Frederick the Great that Shakespeare was a barbarian and a bungler.

Criticism, in my opinion, is only of value so long as it follows an inductive method. As I said in my inaugural lecture, the sole authorities in the art of poetry are the great living poets of the world : the business of the critic is to infer from their work the true means of producing lasting pleasure. I propose, therefore, in a series of lectures to discuss the question of life in poetry, regarding it in three aspects : (1) Poetical Conception ; (2) Poetical Expression ; (3) Poetical Decadence. In my present lecture I shall endeavour to

[1] A Lecture delivered in the University of Oxford, June 13, 1896.

trace the course of an imaginative creation from the moment when a design first begins to shape itself in a poet's brain. I shall ask to be allowed to make but one assumption—one, indeed, which has been regarded as self-evidently true by all sound critics from the time of Aristotle—namely, that the end of the fine arts is to produce enduring pleasure for the imagination. With the help of this I shall then attempt to frame a working definition of poetry, and shall inquire from the nature of the art what must necessarily be its fundamental principles. These I shall verify by applying them to poems which are allowed to have attained the position of classics, as well as to others which, after enjoying a temporary popularity, have fallen into neglect. Finally, after establishing my conclusions, I shall consider what practical bearing they have on the production of poetry in our own day.

Now, with respect to life in poetry, as distinguished from life in the other fine arts, it is plain, in the first place, that poetry takes a distinct way of its own to produce pleasure. It proceeds differently from music, because that is an art which appeals to the emotions through the ear, and, except when it is joined to words, cannot raise ideas and images in the mind. It differs again from painting and sculpture, for, though these can suggest ideas and images, they can do so only through the associations of sight. Painting and sculpture can represent movement and action, but their representation is limited to a single moment of time. For instance, in Raphael's great picture of the Fire in the Borgo, there is an extraordinary suggestion of life and passion. You see a mother just handing her child out of a window; a young man in the act of letting himself drop from a roof; other persons energetically striving to save their goods from the flames; and others again, whose property has been consumed, prostrated with despair. But the infant is never actually rescued; the young man remains suspended; we know not how much salvage is effected, or what becomes of the homeless refugees.

Another aspect of this arrested life in painting and sculpture is expressed in Keats's fine Ode on a Grecian Urn:

> Heard melodies are sweet, but those unheard
> Are sweeter: therefore, ye soft pipes, play on;
> Not to the sensual ear, but more endeared
> Pipe to the spirit ditties of no tone.
> > Fair youth, beneath the trees thou canst not leave
> > Thy song, nor ever can these leaves be bare;
> > Bold lover, never, never canst thou kiss,
> Though winning near the goal—yet do not grieve:
> > She cannot fade, though thou hast not thy bliss:
> > For ever wilt thou love, and she be fair.

Poetry, too, can represent ideal life of this kind, but it can do much more. It can call up before the mind, by a kind of inward painting, images of outward forms which the act of sight has stored

in the memory; and though some critics, like Aristotle and Sir
Philip Sidney, have thought that poetry can be dissociated from
metre, still the practice of the greatest poets shows that it is the
nature of the art to produce pleasure by means akin to music.
Beyond this, however, poetry, working through language, can free
itself, as none of the other arts can, from the limitations of time and
space, and can represent in words a series of connected actions.

But this is not all.   Poetry differs from its sister arts not only in
the variety of its means but in the diversity of its effects.   Since it
reaches its ends through instruments so complex as thought and
language, it comprehends many styles; unlike painting, for example,
in which Sir Joshua Reynolds admits only one legitimate method ;
insisting—whether rightly or wrongly I do not presume to question
—that the single aim of every painter must be the Historic or grand
style.   In poetry, on the contrary, the Epic, the Dramatic, the Ethical
Satirical modes of composition are all distinct—each is capable of
producing a different kind of pleasure—and any attempt to introduce
the style proper to one department into another would be a sign of
incapacity in the poet.   Suited to different moods of the mind, these
various kinds of poetry adapt themselves to the wants of opposite
conditions of society.   Satire, that peculiarly Roman form of poetry,
found a congenial soil in the manners of the City under the Empire
when the epic, dramatic and lyric motives of composition all languished.   In England, after the Restoration, the questions which most
strongly stirred men's imaginations were of a religious and political
kind.   To satisfy this taste the representative poet of the day produced works like *Absalom and Achitophel, The Medal,* and *Religio
Laici,* defending his style on the plea of its fitness for his artistic
needs.

> And this unpolished rugged verse I chose,
> As fittest for discourse and nearest prose.

You will observe that Dryden says *nearest* prose; not actually
prose; meaning that his style suited his subject, and that this, though
akin to matter usually treated in prose, had in it an element of
imagination and emotion which adapted it for expression in metre.
When Matthew Arnold, looking solely to the nature of their thought,
says that Dryden and Pope are not classics of our poetry, but classics
of our prose, he is the victim of a verbal fallacy.   For if the end of
poetry be to produce enduring pleasure for the imagination, and if
Dryden and Pope, adopting the usual machinery of poetry, satisfy
this end, these writers cannot be denied a place among our poets
merely because their subjects are less imaginative than is the case
with metrical writers of another kind.   We may, I think, be content
to define poetry as the art which produces pleasure for the imagination by imitating human actions, thoughts, and passions, in metrical

language. The life of poetry is in fact that which is beautifully described by Spenser in his *Ruins of Time:*

> For deeds do die however nobly done,
> And thoughts of men do as themselves decay,
> But wise words, taught in numbers for to run,
> Recorded by the Muses, live for ay,
> Ne may with storming showers be washed away,
> Ne bitter-breathing winds with harmful blast,
> Nor age, nor envy, may them ever waste.

Passing on from our definition to consider the nature of Poetical Conception, we have to remember that Fine Art does not, like photography, imitate real Nature, but the idea of Nature existing in the mind. Ideal Life is subject to laws of its own, and Horace, in his *Ars Poetica*, says very justly: ' Painters and poets have always been allowed a just freedom of conception : this is an admitted fact, and the critic grants the indulgence that the poet asks.' 1. All that the poet is required to do is to create a perfect illusion ; to produce what Aristotle calls τὸ πιθανόν, the effect of poetic probability; or, in other words, that idea of unity which is the essential condition of all organic life.[2] When he is successful in doing this he reaches the standard of the true poet described by Pope in his ' Imitation of Horace : '

> 'Tis he can give my heart a thousand pains,
> Can make me feel each passion that he feigns ;
> Enrage, compose, with more than magic art ;
> With pity and with terror rend my heart ;
> And snatch me through the earth or in the air,
> To Thebes or Athens, when he will and where.

To produce this effect of organic ideal life is difficult, because in the mind Reason acts against Imagination, and because, in critical ages, men apply to Poetic Inventions standards of judgment proper only to scientific analysis. Aristotle, for example, cites some of the criticisms passed in his day even on the *Iliad.* Such and such a thing, said one, was contrary to fact ; something else, said another, was impossible by the laws of Nature ; this and that a third declared to be contrary to experience. But, as the philosopher shows, these objections were all ill-grounded, because—such is his vigorous phrase —' Homer tells lies as he ought.'[3] He is not to be judged by the laws of material Nature ; his conception is poetically true. Our imagination moves easily through his ideal world. We readily grant him his whole stock of marvellous hypothesis—gods, giants, celestial arms, and talking horses—because we feel that it proceeds from a

[2] πρός τε γὰρ τὴν ποίησιν αἱρετώτερον πιθανὸν ἀδύνατον ἢ ἀπίθανον καὶ δυνατόν. Aristotle, *Poetics*, xxv. 17.
[3] *Ibid.* xxv.

living source in his own mind. Yet, if a sophisticated poet were to force himself to invent such things, merely to gratify our taste for the wonderful, it is certain that every intelligent reader would reject his conception with indignation and disgust.

In every genuinely inspired poetical conception there are, as Aristotle and Horace both tell us, two elements of life, one universal, the other individual. The universal element is the idea of the subject, whatever it may be, as it exists in an undeveloped state in the human mind; the individual element is the particular form and character which is impressed upon the subject by the creative genius of the poet. As regards the process of creation by which these two elements are fused into organic life, we cannot do better than attend to what is said by Horace, a poet who attempted various styles of poetry and succeeded in them all. First, says Horace, there must be complete union between the imagination of the poet and the subject he selects. ' All you who write,' such is his advice in his *Ars Poetica*, ' choose your subject in accordance with your powers; turn over in your mind what your shoulders can bear and what they cannot. The poet whose subject is completely assimilated to his genius will not fail in point of eloquence and lucid order.' [4] Every word of this advice is pregnant with thought. There is a modern school of poets which insists that all poetic creation is the work solely of the poet's mind: form, they tell us, is everything, matter nothing. But here you have one of the classic poets of the world declaring that a large portion of the life, and even of the form, of every poem is contained germinally in the subject matter. Artistic creation is not the mere act of the artist's will; the first movement of inspiration comes to him from outside; hence the solemn invocations of the greatest poets for divine aid in their undertakings; as, for example, at the opening of *Paradise Lost*:

> And chiefly thou, O Spirit, who dost prefer,
> Before all temples, the upright heart and pure,
> Instruct me, for thou knowest; thou from the first
> Wast present, and, with mighty wings outspread,
> Dovelike, satst brooding o'er the vast abyss,
> And madst it pregnant; what in me is dark
> Illumine; what is low raise and support,
> That to the height of this great argument
> I may assert Eternal Providence,
> And justify the ways of God to men.

And so too Dante, in the quaint but impressive appeal to Apollo in his *Paradiso*: ' Divine Virtue, if thou wilt but inspire me to make manifest the shadow of the blessed realm which is stamped upon my brain, thou wilt see me come to the tree that thou lovest, and crown myself there with the leaves of which my *matter* and thou will make me worthy.' [4] The reality and power of this inspiration from

[4] Dante, *Paradiso*, i. 22–27.

without are attested by the fact that, in many of the great poems of
the world, the form appropriate to the subject has not been stamped
at once upon the poet's conception. You will remember that
Paradise Lost first suggested itself to Milton in the form of a
miracle play, modelled after the Greek drama, with the accompaniment of a chorus. In the execution of this design he proceeded
some way, and wrote among other passages Satan's speech to the
Sun which is now embodied in the Fourth Book of *Paradise Lost*.[5]
Long meditation and fresh inspirations from without were required
before the poet saw why the dramatic form was unfitted to his
subject, and in what mould poetic necessity demanded that his
conception should come into being.

Not very different was Scott's experience in the conception of the
Lay of the Last Minstrel. A lady asked him to write an imitation
of an ancient ballad. Then, says Lockhart in his very interesting
account, ' Sir John Stoddart's casual recitation of Coleridge's unfinished *Christabel* had fixed the music of that noble fragment in
his memory ; and it occurs to him that by throwing the story of
Gilpin Horner into somewhat similar cadence he might produce such
an echo of the later metrical romance as would seem to connect his
conclusion of the primitive *Sir Tristrem* with the imitation of the
popular ballad in the *Grey Brother* and *Eve of St. John*. A single
scene of feudal festivity in the Hall of Branksome, disturbed by
some pranks of a nondescript goblin, was probably all that he contemplated ; but his accidental confinement in the midst of a volunteer
camp gave him leisure to meditate his theme to the sound of the
bugle; and suddenly there flashes on him the idea of extending his
simple outline so as to embrace a vivid panorama of that old
Border life of war and tumult and all earnest passions with which his
researches on the minstrelsy had by degrees fed his imagination,
until every the minutest feature had been taken home and realised with
unconscious intensity of sympathy, so that he had won for himself
in the past another world hardly less familiar or complete than the
present. Erskine or Cranstoun suggests that he would do well to
divide the poem into cantos, and prefix to each of them a motto
explanatory of the action, after the fashion of Spenser in the *Fairy
Queen*. He pauses for a moment and the happiest conception of the
frame-work of a picturesque narrative that ever occurred to any
poet, one that Homer might have envied, the creation of the ancient
Harper starts to life. By such steps did the *Lay of the Last
Minstrel* grow out of the *Minstrelsy of the Scottish Border*.'[6]

But besides this instinctive, unconscious union between the
imagination of the poet and his external subject, the poet's conception when born into the world must be qualified to live in the

---

[5] Johnson's *Life of Milton*.
[6] Lockhart's *Life of Scott*, vol. ii. p. 24 (1837).

imagination of his audience. On this point too let us hear Horace.
'It is difficult,' says he, 'to clothe universal abstract ideas with
individual life and character, and you would do better to ground a
play on some story as old and familiar as the *Iliad*, than to seek
credit for originality by representing something that nobody has
heard or thought of before.' Yes, and why so? Because as the
subject matter fitted for art exists in embryo in the mind in general,
and not merely in the mind of the poet, the poet must satisfy those
conditions of ideal life which prepare the imagination of the audience
for the reception of his thought. If he attempts to conjure up an
ideal situation entirely out of his own consciousness, it is almost
certain that his creation will have a lifeless or mechanical appearance,
or will provoke a certain instinctive opposition in the reader's sense
of probability. If on the other hand he seeks to vitalise the
inorganic matter already existing in general conception, his audience
will, as it were, conspire with him in the act of creation, and the
general pleasure his work will arouse will insure it immortality. For
this reason the greater Greek dramatists grounded their plays on the
popular mythology, while the Elizabethan poets took their plots, as
a rule, from novels or histories with which their audience were
already familiar.

We conclude, then, with Horace that the secret of life in poetry
lies in the power to give individual form to universal ideas adapted
for expression in any of the recognised classes of metrical composition.
Let us now look at the question from another side, and apply this
law to poems whose position has been finally settled by the judgment
of mankind. . Why, for example, is the *Iliad* so full of life? In the
first place because the subject of the poem was very much alive in
Homer's own imagination : everything in it seems to be of a piece,
and to be said naturally and without conscious effort. It must indeed
be admitted that Homer enjoyed an immense advantage over all his
successors by starting in almost complete unity with his theme.
When he composed the *Iliad* the poetical mode of conceiving things
was the natural mode of conception ; so that we may almost say the
image of the poem pressed itself on his mind from the outside ready
made, and all that he had to do was to find an adequate mould for
the expression. In his verse the commonest objects and actions—
a ship being rowed over the sea; a banquet; a sacrifice—are described in a manner at once grand and simple; not, I imagine, merely
because Homer was a great poet, but because, in his age, almost
everything was conceived as having a divine life of its own. Inability
to conceive of Nature in the same spirit of childlike polytheism
extorted from Wordsworth his passionate cry of regret :

> Great God! I had rather be
> A Pagan suckled in a creed out-worn,

So might I, standing on this pleasant lea,
Have glimpses that would make me less forlorn,
Have sight of Proteus rising from the sea,
Or hear old Triton blow his wreathèd horn.

As regards the individual element in his poem, therefore—the union, that is to say, between the poet's imagination and his subject —Homer had everything in his favour.   What is to be said, however, of the union between his imagination and the imagination of his audience ?   Think how much there is in the *Iliad* to militate against the production of the desired effect !   A scheme of theology which more than two thousand years ago was repudiated by the philosopher ; a view of Nature which is to-day incredible to the school-boy ; a representation of warfare which must seem ridiculous to the soldier ; and a recital of methods of killing and wounding which, since the invention of firearms, has lost its interest even for the surgeon.   What is it, then, in Homer's poetry that produces such unequalled pleasure ? It is the element of the Universal.   Nowhere else, except in Shakespeare, will you find so many characters which are immediately perceived to be living images of mankind ; so many sentiments which at once move the affections ; so many situations of elemental interest and pathos ;—all of them presented in the movement of verse whose majestic roll seems animated by the very life of Nature, and yet is found on examination to be the product of ideal Art.

In the *Æneid* we perceive the case to be quite different.   Here we have evidently a sharp separation between the subject and the mind of the poet, and we understand that Virgil's matter had to be long meditated, assimilated, and transmuted, before the poem was ready to be born into the world.   The hero of the *Æneid* is, comparatively speaking, a poor creature ; the sentiments and manners represented, far from making us breathe naturally heroic atmosphere, provoke question and criticism ; many of the incidents appear improbable, being in fact transferred from Homer, and having lost some of their life in the passage.   We feel through the last six books of the epic that the poet is only carrying on the action because the machinery of his work requires him to do so.   Nevertheless from the very first the *Æneid* has been alive ; it is alive still.   What is the secret of its vitality ?   Partly, no doubt, the fact that Virgil was able to impregnate his subject with certain qualities of his own nature in which no poet has ever equalled him, piety, gravity, sweetness.   But partly also the fact that he has developed out of his subject, with unrivalled art, the elements that it contains of the Universal.   We know how the *Æneid* appeared to Virgil's contemporaries.   They hailed it as something greater than the *Iliad*.   'Nescio quid majus nascitur Iliade,' said Propertius, and though this sounds like patriotic exaggeration, there is a sense in which it is true.   For the *Æneid* is *par excellence* the epic of Civil Life.   It is the poem of a Roman, having for its theme the foundation of the Roman Empire, and reflecting at every point the majesty of the Roman character. That was the special quality in it which so deeply influenced the genius of Dante, and wherever the civilising power of the Roman Empire has been felt, that is, over the whole of modern Europe, there will this element of life in the *Æneid* continue to produce sublime pleasure. But there is a wider, a more human sense, in which the *Æneid* may be said to be greater than the *Iliad*, and that is, the element of the pathetic. Not, of course, that Homer is wanting in pathos; he covers a larger surface of the pathetic than Virgil; but at certain points Virgil goes deeper. His great poetical principle is embodied in the line, 'Sunt lacrimæ rerum et mentem mortalia tangunt,' which a modern poet has beautifully rendered:

> Tears waken tears, and honour honour brings,
> And mortal hearts are moved by mortal things.[7]

Inadequate as the character of Æneas is on the heroic side, it is exceedingly human, and the poet has sounded the deepest feelings of our kind in the description of his hero's adventures and misfortunes. The narrative of the fall of Troy, the death of Dido, the meeting of Æneas and Anchises in the lower world, the deaths of Nisus and Euryalus, these things will move the hearts of men through all time. Virgil in such passages has individualised the Universal; his images live for ever in a stream of verse as deep and full as Homer's is swift and brilliant.

Let me now, by way of contrast, refer to a poem which having once enjoyed great popularity has long passed, not indeed into oblivion, but neglect. When the *Thebais* was first published we know from Juvenal that it was received with general enthusiasm, and even in the Middle Ages the reputation of Statius was so great, mainly no doubt on account of his legendary Christianity, that Dante assigns him a place in his *Purgatory*. To-day he is known only to professed scholars. How is this? If we try to realise the manner in which the *Thebais* came into existence we shall be able to account for its literary fate. Statius so far complied with Horace's advice in the *Ars Poetica* as to choose a subject not less well-known to his audience than 'the tale of Troy divine.' Unfortunately it had no special elements of interest which could touch his heart as a man and a Roman; hence his subject never really passed into his own mind; he hatched it, so to speak, like an artificial incubator. Let us try to watch him composing the Fourth Book, which is much the best in the poem. Here his business was in some way or other to conduct Polynices and the Argive army to Thebes, where Eteocles had usurped the government. Statius sets to work in a style which is eminently logical, and, in a way, scientific. He starts his expedition with stir and bustle, and tells us of all the rumours which the news of the invasion set in circulation at Thebes. Then, said he to himself, 'Now what effect would these rumours have had on the mind of Eteocles?' Eteocles is represented as a gloomy tyrant. Of course then his bad conscience would drive him to consult the prophet Tiresias. Here was a splendid opportunity for what Horace calls 'a purple patch.' Tiresias practised magic in a wood; the wood must therefore be described, and described it is with great effect, and so are the magical incantations. Next it is necessary to learn the future from Laius, the founder of the family, who must be brought from the infernal regions according to the precedent of Æneas, who had gone thither to seek the spirit of Anchises. Statius seems to have thought within himself: 'How can I have a novel and effective other-world scene, something different from Homer's and Virgil's?' and so full is he of this business-like idea, that he puts it into the mouth of his imaginary characters. Tiresias, being blind, has to be helped in his incantations by his daughter Manto, who, after she has performed the necessary rites, informs her father that hell is in view; but, says she, 'what is the use of bringing up the monsters of Erebus, the idly raging Centaurs, the Giants, and all the rest of them?'[8] In other words, Homer and Virgil have done all this kind of thing before. 'Quite true,' observes the practical prophet, 'everybody knows about the rebounding stone of Sisyphus, and the fleeing waters of Tantalus, and the wheel of Ixion: what we want is the spirits of the wicked Argives and Thebans.'[9] And accordingly up they come from the nether world, one after another, 'stern Abas, and guilty Prœtus, and mild Phoroneus, and mutilated Pelops, and Œnomaus all bestained with cruel dust.'[10] Laius appears the last, and delivers himself of an oracle so judiciously obscure that, for all the information it affords his hearers, they and their poet might have spared themselves the trouble they took to procure his advice. Compare this with the Sixth Book of the Æneid, and you will see the difference between Life and Machinery in poetry. Statius is full of cleverness and learning; he is careful to follow poetical precedents; but his creation is not alive; he himself did not care about it; his Roman audience did not care about it, though they applauded it; he can therefore hardly hope to find an audience to care about it in the nineteenth century.

How admirable is the reasoning of Juvenal in the matter! 'These things,' he says in substance, 'have no life. I mean to have life in my poetry: I shall accordingly write Satire, and shall deal with matters that really do interest us, every sort of human action and passion, wishes, fears, anger, pleasure, joy, philosophy, that is my subject.'[11] Hence, though he is only a satirical poet, Juvenal, having this strong individual element in himself, and the element of the

---

[8] *Thebais*, iv. 534-536.
[10] *Ibid.* 589-591.

[9] *Ibid.* 537-544.
[11] Juvenal, *Sat.* i. 85-6.

Universal in his theme, has contrived to produce permanent pleasure for the imagination, while Statius, with his grandiose subject and his sounding verse, has fallen into neglect. Juvenal makes us see, as if they were things of to-day, the perils of the streets in ancient Rome;[12] the bald Nero and his flatterers in council over their turbot;[13] the Trojan-born aristocracy cringing for the rich parvenu's doles;[14] the bronze head of Sejanus's statue turned into pots and pans.[15] When a satirist is so full as this of universal interest, we can listen to him even when he talks mainly of himself. Witness the opening of Pope's *Epistle to Arbuthnot,* where every word seems to throb and tingle with sensitive life:

> Shut, shut the door, good John! fatigued, I said,
> Tie up the knocker, say I'm sick, I'm dead.
> The dog-star rages, nay, 'tis past a doubt,
> All Bedlam and Parnassus is let out.
> Fire in each eye, and papers in each hand,
> They rave, recite, and madden through the land.

And so on, through all the poet's interviews with his literary tormentors, till we reach the climax in the portrait of Atticus, where universal truth lives as lastingly as in the characters of Achilles and Hamlet:

> Peace to all such! But were there one whose fires
> True genius kindles and true fame inspires;
> Blest with each talent and each art to please,
> And born to write, converse, and live with ease;
> Should such a man, too fond to rule alone,
> Bear like the Turk no brother near the throne;
> View him with scornful yet with jealous eyes,
> And hate for arts that caused himself to rise;
> Damn with faint praise, assent with civil leer,
> And, without sneering, teach the rest to sneer;
> Willing to wound, and yet afraid to strike,
> Just hint a fault, and hesitate dislike;
> Alike reserved to blame and to command,
> A timorous foe and a suspicious friend;
> Dreading e'en fools, by flatterers besieged,
> And so obliging that he ne'er obliged;
> Like Cato give his little senate laws,
> And sit attentive to his own applause;
> While wits and Templars every sentence raise,
> And wonder with a foolish face of praise:
> Who but must laugh if such a man there be?
> Who would not weep if Atticus were he?

Even in lyric poetry, which seems above all other forms of the art to contain the expression of individual feeling, if the verse is to have enduring life, the universal must be present either in the simplicity

---

[12] Juvenal, iii.   [13] *Ibid.* iv.
[14] *Ibid.* i. 99-100.   [15] *Ibid.* x. 61-64.

of the emotion or the common interest of the theme. No better illustration of this truth can be found than Gray's *Elegy*, a composition which has perhaps produced more general pleasure than any in our literature. Take the last line of the first stanza: 'And leaves the *world* to *darkness* and to *me*,' where two of the most abstract words in the language are combined with the most personal. Or again, the closing stanza, in which the epitaph on the individual is brought to a climax in the most universal idea that the human mind can conceive:

> No further seek his merits to disclose,
> Or draw his frailties from their dread abode,
> (There they alike in trembling hope repose,)
> The bosom of his Father and his God.

Difficile est proprie communia dicere. Difficult indeed! But to overcome the difficulty is the triumph of art. And here the triumph is complete. How simple and obvious are all the reflections, and yet how individual they seem in the form in which the poet presents them! A single familiar image is selected as the centre of a group of truths which every man acknowledges, and, as a rule, forgets ; each stanza seems to condense in words the experience of human society; and breathes in its solemn harmony the catholic doctrine of the grave.

If then we are justified in believing the law of life in poetry to be what we have described it, we may draw some practical conclusions from it with regard to the poetry of our own day. For is not one of the most striking characteristics in modern poetical conception the exaggeration of the individual element and the neglect of the universal? Many of the spiritual forces in our society, notably reaction from materialism, vulgarity, common-place, impel the imagination towards a state of monasticism, thrust the mind inward upon itself, and urge it to the contemplation of its own ideas without considering their relation to the ideas of others. Poetical conception so formed will by its own innate force command attention and respect from those whose spiritual experience has been in any way similar, and yet, as it has been framed without reference to the wants of human nature at large, must necessarily lack the main element of enduring life. This is the danger that in my opinion threatens the position of one of the most eminent metrical composers of our own generation; I need hardly say that I refer to Robert Browning. No one who is capable of appreciating genius will refuse to admire the powers of this poet, the extent of his sympathy and interest in external things, the boldness of his invention, the energy of his analysis, the audacity of his experiments. But so absolutely did he exclude all consideration for the reader from his choice of subject, so arbitrarily, in his treatment of his themes, does he compel his audience to place themselves at his own point of view, that the life of his art depends entirely on his individuality. Should future generations be less inclined than our own to surrender their imaginations to his guidance, he will not be able to appeal to them through that element of life which lies in the Universal.

If it is an error to look for the life of poetry exclusively in the mind of the poet, it is no less an error to derive its sources from the current tastes of the people. What is universal is always popular in the true sense of the word ; but what is popular is not necessarily universal. Yet the modern poet is under a strong temptation to conceive as if it were so. Invention and Science present the imagination with a dissolving panorama of passing interests, and to embody these in a striking form is the proper end of the art of journalism. The ability and success with which the journalist discharges his functions naturally excite emulation among those who practise the fine arts. They imitate his methods. Hence Realism in the choice of subject, Impressionism, Literary Paradox, and all those other short cuts in art through which seekers after novelty attempt to discover nine-days wonders for the imagination. By the very hypothesis of fine art such methods must necessarily be fallacious ; because when the temporary conditions to which they owe their being pass away the pleasure they excite perishes with them.

The abiding life of poetry must be looked for far beneath the surface of society : the end of poetry, as Hamlet says of the drama, is ' to show the very age and body of the time, his form and pressure.' If there be any of my hearers, and especially of my younger hearers, who say to themselves with the proud consciousness of genius, ' non omnis moriar,' I would urge them to remember that this truth is written on every page of classic English poetry. In the reign of Elizabeth the life of the nation had its centre in the Crown, and monarchical energy found expression in the drama. The eighteenth century was an age of aristocracy and philosophic thought; accordingly the characteristic poetry of that era was ethical or elegiac. With the French Revolution began the great democratic movement which has prevailed for a hundred years, and naturally from that time to this the dominant note in poetry has been lyrical.

I think that one difficulty in the way of forming a poetic conception of Nature and Society in our own day arises from our adhering too tenaciously to a poetical tradition which no longer corresponds with the life and reality of things. Poetry, like politics, is an outward mode of expressing the active principle of social life, and for three generations the master-spirit in Society has been Liberty. In politics we have seen Liberty embodying itself in all that we understand by the word Democracy ; sweeping away privilege, test, restriction ; widening the basis of government ; wakening the energies of free thought ; shaking the foundations of faith and authority. In poetry the same principle finds utterance in the varied emotions we comprehend under the name of Romance. Romance is heard in the voice of Wordsworth sending out his thought into the heart of Nature; in the voice of Byron rebellious against the laws of Society; in the voice of Shelley dreaming of the destinies of humanity; in the voice of Tennyson sounding the depths and intricacies of private sorrow. For universal conceptions such as these Romance has been the fitting vehicle of expression. But alike in politics and in poetry, the productive power of Liberty seems to have reached its natural limits. Can Democracy solve the problems it has itself created? civilise the swarming populations of the city? bind the young and vigorous colony more closely to the venerable Mother Country? charm away the demon of social envy? curb the fury of political faction? Or is it Romance that can most fitly reflect those scientific ideas of Nature and Society which press so powerfully on the modern imagination? It is just because Romance is unable to do this that the school of poetry which has adhered most faithfully to the romantic tradition now sounds in its art the note of lyric pessimism.

There is surely an analogy in the tasks that lie respectively before the modern statesman and the modern poet. It is the part of the one, rising above the indolence of *laisser faire,* to lead, to construct, to consolidate. So too in the world of poetry. The romantic poet regards himself as ' the idle singer of an empty day:' is it, however, just to charge the age with emptiness merely because it affords no materials fitted for expression in a particular poetical mould? The art of poetry has many mansions; and it does not follow that, if one mode of conceiving Nature has become trite and mechanical, the resources of Nature herself are exhausted. Sound reasoning would seem rather to point to the conclusion that since the subjective and lyrical forms of poetry languish, the sources of life are rather to be sought on the objective side and in the dramatic, ethical, and satiric forms of the art.

But perhaps to speculate precisely on this point is to fall into the very error of academic criticism which we started with condemning. It will be best to conclude with reiterating the truth that, while the force of individual liberty and genius is absolutely necessary to inspire poetic conception with the breath of life, obedience to the laws and constitution of the Universal Imagination is no less needful, if the life thus generated is to be enduring.

W. J. COURTHOPE.

THOMAS HENRY HUXLEY

A REMINISCENCE [1]

THE 'personal equation' is often an element very necessary to the true interpretation of a great writer's words. Of the many thousands in England and America who have eagerly read their 'Huxley' few have known the man. They are familiar, perhaps, with his essays on the 'Gadarene pig affair' and the 'Noachian deluge;' and they have in all probability—as the present writer once had—a one-sided impression of the intention and *animus* of such sallies. And a similar difference between the writer and the man extends to many other subjects. If this be so, it may be worth while for those who knew Mr. Huxley in later life to record personal traits which have interpreted for them much of his writing. Doubtless such sketches are necessarily themselves made from a special point of view. But what Huxley was to all his acquaintance can only be learnt by knowing what he was to each. And conscious though I am how imperfectly I shall express recollections which are very vivid, I make the attempt with the less scruple, as it was suggested to me by one whose wishes in the matter should be paramount.

My first direct intercourse with Mr. Huxley was accidentally such as to confirm my original impression of him as a somewhat uncompromising and unapproachable man of war. I was collecting materials about the year 1885 for some account of the old Metaphysical Society, to be published in the biography of my father, W. G. Ward, who was at one time its chairman. I wrote to several prominent members of the society, and received kind answers and contributions from all of them except Mr. Huxley, who did not reply to my letter at all. I remember thinking that I had made a mistake in writing to him, and that probably his antagonism to my father in the debates made him unwilling to say anything on the subject.

I was therefore the more pleasantly surprised when, in the year 1890, a common friend of mine and Mr. Huxley's (Sir M. E. Grant Duff) brought me a friendly message, expressing great contrition in

---

[1] I am indebted to the kindness of Mrs. Huxley and Mr. Leonard Huxley for permission to print the letters from the late Professor Huxley which appear in the present paper.

the matter of the unanswered letter, explaining that it had arrived at a time of total prostration through ill health, and offering to write for my book an account of my father's share in the debates of the society. I gladly accepted the offer ; and the paper came, which, though brief, was very characteristic of Mr. Huxley himself both in its matter and in its manner. As moreover the account it gives will serve to show that side of Huxley which made him and myself afterwards, to use his own words, 'the friendliest of foes,' I here insert it.

It was at one of the early meetings of the Metaphysical Society that I first saw Dr. Ward.[2] I forget whether he or I was the late comer; at any rate we were not introduced. I well recollect wondering what chance had led the unknown member, who looked so like a jovial country squire, to embark in our galley—that singular rudderless ship, the stalwart oarsmen of which were mostly engaged in pulling as hard as they could against one another, and which consequently performed only circular voyages all the years it was in commission.

But when a few remarks on the subject under discussion fell from the lips of that beaming countenance, it dawned upon my mind that a physiognomy quite as gentle of aspect as that of Thomas Aquinas (if the bust on the Pincian Hill is any authority) might possibly be the façade of a head of like quality. As time went on, and Dr. Ward took a leading part in our deliberations, my suspicions were fully confirmed. As a quick-witted dialectician, thoroughly acquainted with all the weak points of his antagonist's case, I have not met with Dr. Ward's match. And it all seemed to come so easily to him ; searching questions, incisive, not to say pungent, replies, and trains of subtle argumentation were poured forth which, while sometimes passing into earnest and serious exposition, would also—when lighter topics came to the front—be accompanied by an air of genial good humour, as if the whole business were rather a good joke. But it was no joke to reply efficiently.

Although my personal intercourse with Dr. Ward was as limited as it might be expected to be between two men who were poles asunder, not only in their occupations and circumstances, but in their ways of regarding life and the proper ends of action, yet I am glad to remember that we soon became the friendliest of foes. It was not long after we had reached this stage that in the course of some truce in our internecine dialectic warfare (I think at the end of one of the meetings of the Metaphysical Society) Dr. Ward took me aside and opened his mind thus : ' You and I are on such friendly terms that I do not think it is right to let you remain ignorant of something I wish to tell you.' Rather alarmed at what this might portend, I begged him to say on. ' Well, we Catholics hold that so and so and so and so [naming certain of our colleagues whose heresies were of a less deep hue than mine] are not guilty of absolutely unpardonable error; but your case is different, and I feel it is unfair not to tell you so.' Greatly relieved, I replied, without a moment's delay, perhaps too impulsively, ' My dear Dr. Ward, if you don't mind I don't ; ' whereupon we parted with a hearty hand-shake, and intermitted neither friendship nor fighting thenceforth.

I have often told the story, and not unfrequently I have regretted to observe that my hearer conceived the point of it to lie in my answer. But to my mind the worth of the anecdote consists in the evidence it affords of the character of Dr. Ward. He was before all things a chivalrous English gentleman—I would say a philosophical and theological Quixote, if it were not that our associations with the name of the knight of La Mancha are mainly derived from his adventures, and not from the noble directness and simplicity of mind which led to those misfortunes.

[2] My father was known in the Society as ' Dr.' Ward, from his Papal degree of Doctor in Philosophy.

Not very long after I received this graphic word-picture, I became a neighbour of Mr. Huxley's at Eastbourne. We exchanged visits, and afterwards had many a talk on nearly every conceivable subject, which were among the most intellectually stimulating that I have ever known.

I shall best describe the impression Huxley made on me by contrasting it with the general idea which I, in common no doubt with many another, had formed of him. He always wrote, as Darwin has said, with his pen dipped in *aqua fortis*, and one naturally conceived of him as a combative and even an aggressive man. Moreover the layman's idea of the professional man of science generally includes something of the pedantic. One anticipates that his conversation, however instructive, will deal largely with very technical subjects in very technical language. Again, the tone of some of the essays to which I have referred was unquestionably Voltairian.

All the greater was my surprise to find the three elements of pugilist, pedant, and scoffer not only not prominent, but conspicuous by their absence. In their place was a personality of singular charm. External gifts of manner and presence, and powers of general conversation which would have ensured popularity to any mere man of the world, were combined with those higher endowments—including great breadth of culture as well as the acquirements of a distinguished specialist—to which no mere man of the world could aspire. I must add that I believe the elements of gentleness and sympathy which gave so much additional charm to his singular brilliancy had become more noticeable in later life; and I have not always found my own impression of a kindliness which suggested great tenderness of feeling shared by those whose acquaintance with him belonged to a much earlier date. But these things were conspicuous at the time I speak of; and while I gradually learnt how to explain their consistency with the polemical style which he preserved to the end in his writing, my first impression was that the man and the writer were very dissimilar people.

His appearance is well known. Above the middle height, the white hair without parting brushed straight back, the lips firm and slightly compressed; a very mobile expression; and I would add (what the current photographs do not represent) eyes full of fire, rather deep-set beneath bushy eyebrows, and a look of keenest interest in all around him, often of great wistfulness. Both in his manner and in his appearance there was marked distinction and dignity. The general impression left by his face was certainly one of intellectual force and activity rather than of scorn.

His conversation was singularly finished and (if I may so express it) clean cut; never long winded or prosy; enlivened by vivid illustrations. He was an excellent *raconteur*, and his stories had a stamp of their own which would have made them always and everywhere acceptable. His sense of humour and economy of words would have made it impossible, had he lived to ninety, that they should ever have been disparaged as symptoms of what has been called 'anecdotage.' I was naturally led to compare his conversation with that of two remarkable men whom I had recently been seeing when first I met Huxley. There was the same contrast between his conversation and that of Tennyson or of Cardinal Newman as there was between their views. Tennyson and Newman alike always suggested more than they said. There was an unspoken residuum behind their speech, which, as Wordsworth once said of the peak of a Swiss mountain hidden behind the low clouds, you felt to be there though you could not see it. Huxley, on the contrary, finished his thoughts completely, and expressed them with the utmost precision. There were not the ruggedness and the gaps which marked Tennyson's speech, nor the pauses, the reserve, the obvious consciousness of suggestion on subjects too wide and intricate for full expression which one felt with Newman. The symmetry and finish of Huxley's utterances were so great that one could not bring oneself to interrupt him, even when this completeness of form seemed to be possible only through ignoring for the moment much that should not be ignored. No doubt the deafness, which increased in later years, made one yet more ready rather to listen than to talk; but the quickness of his perceptions was so great that dialogue was in its place a matter of no great difficulty. If he heard even a word or two he had the clue to the rest, and seldom failed to follow it successfully.

He seemed to me to be almost the ideal of a converser. He was never frivolous and yet never dull. He did not plunge abruptly into deep subjects, but exchanged the ordinary remarks and greetings with naturalness and simplicity, and then talked according to his company. If one cared for the problems of the mind and of human life, one came to them quickly enough. But he was perfectly happy and at home talking about politics or persons, about his garden, or even about the weather, if his hearers preferred it. And there was nothing which he did not contrive to make interesting.

No doubt such exceptional charm followed the law by which natural gifts keep a certain measure of equality in different persons. It was purchased at some cost. Incisiveness and brilliancy went with over-positiveness. Intolerance and one-sidedness appeared at a certain stage. And although to know him was to reject for ever the idea that he was a scoffer, he treated the conclusions of the scientific leaders, even outside the sphere of science, somewhat as the Grand Inquisitor treated the definitions of the Church. Those who called them in question were regarded as being 'outside the pale.' It will seem inevitable that one who differed so widely from him should think him (as I did) more ready to see the weaker side of theological

positions far apart from his own, than to enter into their real
strength. I except, however, from this remark the works of Bishop
Butler and Sir William Hamilton, with whose methods he had much
in common, though he rejected many of their conclusions. The form
of his conversation was dialectical rather than suggestive or meditative. One was often reminded that he was, in some matters, the professed advocate of a cause, and even of a party. It was easy to accept
his own statement in his autobiography that his temper was not
naturally an even one. One could readily conceive, on provocation,
that in word as well as in writing he would be a thoroughly good
fighter ; and one could picture him driven to bay, with his back to
the wall, and dealing out destruction against great odds. I never
felt in his discussions the full measure of philosophic calm.
Opposite considerations to those which determined his own conclusions were indeed often seen and expressed with great lucidity, but
less in the spirit of philosophic inquiry than in that of a just but convinced advocate, whose ultimate positions are absolutely predeter-
mined. Doubtless one felt at the same time that there had been
a more judicial sifting of considerations on all sides before his conclusions had been reached, and that the advocacy was not special
pleading to order, but the outcome of deep conviction. But none
the less his method was distinctly that of the able and lucid exponent
of one side. 'That is my case, my lord,' would have come naturally
at the end. His exposition was not that of the thinker who sees
horizons on every side, too wide-reaching to be fully described, and
yet too unmistakable to be ignored. There were no half-lights or
hesitations. All that was contemplated was very distinct ; the results
arrived at were very definite, and their drift consciously told for the
defence of the clear system he had elaborated.

Yet so far as my own experience went, the intellectual pleasure
he seemed to find in letting each side say its say and do its best, prevented these characteristics of the partisan from marring intercourse ;
although, in weighing the value of his own views of things, they must
be taken into account. In conversation, I nearly always found him,
up to the point beyond which we tacitly agreed not to carry our
debates, tolerant as a listener, though always more brilliant, forcible,
and definite, than convincing, suggestive, or entirely comprehensive
in his replies. His love of the free play of dialectics, irrespective of
the side on which they were exercised, was exemplified in his enjoyment of the *Summa* of St. Thomas Aquinas. I have on several
occasions interrupted him (as he told me at the time) in the act of
perusing its pages. 'Aquinas' bust on the Pincian Hill,' he once
said, ' shows a combination of a singularly simple and devout heart,
with a head of very remarkable capacity. He got his premises from
his heart, and reached his conclusions with the admirable logical
force of his intellect.' ' His marvellous grasp and subtlety of intellect

seem to me to be almost without a parallel,' is the tribute which Mr.
Huxley has paid in print to the ' Angelic Doctor.'[3]

·: The same appreciation of the intellectual drill of the·school-
man is visible in his account (in the Lay Sermons) of a visit he paid
some thirty years ago to a Catholic College—which, after· the lapse
of time, I may mention to have been Maynooth :

> It was my fortune some time ago [he writes] to pay a visit to one of the most
> important institutions in which the clergy of the Roman Catholic Church are
> trained in these islands, and it seemed to me that the difference between these
> men and the comfortable champions of Anglicanism and Dissent was comparable to
> .the difference between our gallant volunteers and the trained veterans of Napoleon's
> Old Guard.
> The Catholic priest is trained to know his business and do it effectually. The
> professors of the college in question—learned, zealous, and determined men—per-
> mitted me to speak frankly with them. We talked like outposts of opposed armies
> during a truce—as friendly enemies.

And after recording the confidence with which the professors prophesied that a Church which had survived so many storms would survive
the existing infidel movement, and describing the systematic training
given to the Divinity students with a view to refuting contemporary
attacks on Christianity, he adds :

> I heartily respect an organisation which meets its enemies in this way, and I
> wish that all ecclesiastical organisations were in as effective a condition. I think
> it would be better not only for them but for us. The army of liberal thought is
> at present in very loose order ; and many a modern freethinker makes use of his
> freedom mainly to vent nonsense. We should be the better for a vigorous and
> watchful enemy to hammer us into cohesion and discipline ; and I for one lament
> that the bench of Bishops cannot show a man of the calibre of Bishop Butler of
> the *Analogy*, who, if he were alive, would make short work of the current *à priori*
> infidelity.

My first talk with Huxley naturally enough turned on the subject
of the old Metaphysical Society at which he had known my father.
The society, which was originated at the suggestion of Mr. James
Knowles, included most of the prominent thinkers on the philosophy
of Religion, amateurs as well as professionals. Mr. Gladstone, Dr.
Martineau, Cardinal Manning, the Duke of Argyll, Tennyson and
Ruskin were among the more distinguished members. Huxley was
very graphic and amusing in his remarks on this subject. ' They were
afraid of asking me to join at first,' he said ; ' they thought I should
be such a firebrand.'

Eventually, however, Huxley did join, and the most friendly relations subsisted between him and (curiously enough) the Catholic
·members of the society, Father Dalgairns, Cardinal Manning, and my
father. But, indeed, members of all schools of thought rapidly became
friendly and sympathetic. . ' This was a great surprise,' said Huxley.
ɩ' We thought at first that it would be a case of Kilkenny cats. Hats

³ See *Science and Morals*, p. 142.

and coats would be left in the hall before the meeting, but there would be no wearers left, after it was over, to put them on again. Instead of this we came to love each other like brothers. We all expended so much charity, that had it been money we should have been bankrupt.' The work of the society was principally one of mutual understanding. Once each member thoroughly understood the position of his opponents, it was seen to involve a divergence in first principles which no argument could affect. Friendliness became the order of the day and debate grew less useful. 'The society died of too much love,' added Mr. Huxley.

I used, rightly or wrongly, to trace to the influence of the Metaphysical Society a very curious mixture of feelings in Mr. Huxley in respect of his theological opponents. No doubt his polemic against the theologians had been, as he said, suggestive of the 'firebrand.' Yet nothing could be more kindly than the two accounts I have cited of the Maynooth priests and of the Catholic theologian. And I believe it was the Metaphysical Society which fashioned this somewhat remarkable blend.

The society was founded in 1869. The years immediately preceding its formation had probably stamped deep on his mind a sense of unjust treatment at the hands of professional ecclesiastics. The advocates of Darwinism and of the 'higher' criticism of the Scriptures—and Huxley was in both ranks—had been for years treated simply as the enemies of religion. The distinctions familiar to all of us now, the admission on all sides of a measure of truth in both these phases of speculation, were little thought of in the sixties. The *Origin of Species* had appeared in 1859, and Colenso had raised the Scripture question at about the same time. 1859 to 1869 had been for Huxley years of war; and with his very direct and practical mind, he saw in the theological protests of the hour nothing but thoroughly unjust persecution of himself and his friends for researches undertaken in the interests of truth. The ecclesiastical 'obstructives' who condemned him without attending to his arguments remained in his mind for a long time as absolute types of bigotry. Their line of action appeared to him to set a *premium* on hypocrisy. The men who had the courage of their convictions were ostracised; and the time-servers among men of science who refused to brave the ignorant clamour of the multitude enjoyed an unenviable popularity. Huxley's moral sense appeared to be simply revolted by this. Some will think that he failed to do justice to the element of instinctive caution which blended with the real bigotry of those critics who took up the narrowest attitude—the element explained by Cardinal Newman in his defence of the condemnation of Galileo. The principle of economy for the protection of weak minds was not at all congenial to Mr. Huxley, although he did in some degree recognise it. His ruling passion was the advance of scientific truth, and this was being impeded, and a noble sincerity to conviction treated as a crime (he thought) by men, some of whom at least did not seem to him even deeply sincere. It was officialism *versus* true genius.

He was not insensible to the element of moral reprobation among the opponents of evolution which made them mark him out as a dangerous man, and which struck, as he has humorously said, at his 'respectability.' And I have always supposed that it was in these earlier years of the struggle that he acquired the deep and genuine sense of injustice on the part of ecclesiastics generally, and of anger at what he considered preposterous superstition, which frequently reappeared, to the very end, in his writing.

On the other hand, in the Metaphysical Society the conditions were so different that he inevitably met theological foes on far pleasanter terms. Intercourse was personal, and candid debate was the order of the day. Notably in the case of the Catholic members of the society he could have no feeling of the substitution of a sanctimonious moral reprobation for frank discussion. The great friendliness which arose between the extreme parties in the society introduced a new element of kindly divergence, and apparently gave birth to a real intellectual respect in Huxley for some of the detested theologians. His two sentiments were perhaps not entirely consistent, for men of intellectual force are not likely to defend absurd superstitions; but both remained. And they occasionally led, in conversation, to a playful combination of language recalling the severest theological condemnation of his views, with the humour and friendly feeling which in almost all cases subsisted in his personal intercourse with opponents. 'We wicked people,' he would often say, in speaking of himself and his allies. A friendly meeting with priest or clergyman was enjoyed, perhaps as a sign that to some extent bygones were bygones; while enough remembrance of opposition remained to give piquancy to the *rencontre*.

I have a good many notes illustrative of some of these phases of his thought. I think it was in 1892 that I saw him just after he had been to a meeting of the Trustees of the British Museum. 'After the meeting,' he told me, 'Archbishop Benson helped me on with my great coat. I was *quite overcome* by this species of spiritual investiture. "Thank you, Archbishop," I said; "I feel as if I were receiving the *pallium*."' A little later he met at Maloja a Catholic professor of some German university, and had many a story to tell of their frequent conversations, and of the pleasure he derived from the priest's company, which he had evidently cultivated.

On another occasion he was at a meeting of the British Association in York, and he and Mrs. Huxley went to visit the Minster. He greatly enjoyed the remark on this occasion of Henry Smith (of Oxford celebrity), who met them there. 'You did not expect to see us here?' asked Huxley. 'Yes, I did,' replied Smith, 'but *on the pinnacle.*'

Something of the same humour, coupled with a remembrance of the days when his championship of evolution was most widely reprobated, appears in a letter which he wrote me from Gloucester in September 1892, in reply to my congratulations on his being made a Privy Councillor:

> Very many thanks [he wrote] for your kind congratulations. Morris has a poem somewhere about the man who was born to be a king, and became one in spite of probability. It is evident to me now that I was born to be respectable. I have done my level best to avoid that honour, but behold me indelibly stamped.
>
> We are staying here with one of our daughters and enjoying the festival. . . . We hope to be back in Eastbourne next week, but we shall have to go to the Grand Hotel, as seven devils in the shape of workmen must be driven out of our house.
>
> See what an opening I have given you for a conclusion to that sentence.

He often resented being identified with simple destruction in matters of religious faith, and disclaimed all sympathy with the scoffing spirit. His opposition to theology had not meant, he said, opposition to religion. I remember his showing me Boehm's bust of himself, and expressing strongly his dislike of its expression. 'It is almost Voltairian,' he said. 'You should not destroy until you are in a position to build up something to replace what you have destroyed,' was another saying of his: 'Descartes saw that, and advocated a *morale par provision,* a system to act upon (pending the conclusion of his philosophical inquiries)—a system which included adhering to the religion in which he had been brought up.' Huxley's application of this principle was very intelligible in his protests against dogmatic infidelity.[4] But it used to seem to me, as I once told him, to be forgotten in his extremely polemical tone, which unquestionably did often lead others to abandon even a provisional adherence to any religious system. But I believe his failure to take this into consideration to have been partly due to the exclusively scientific cast of his mind. The cause of scientific discovery was paramount to all else; and whatever even appeared to impede it he assailed ruthlessly. Moreover he wrote for experts, or at least for careful students. In point of fact, readers include the impressionable and unintellectual as well as the intellectual; and an anti-Christian rhetoric may, for such readers, destroy religious belief wholesale, including positions which the writer himself, to say the least, considered quite tenable to the end. He said to me once, in 1894, 'Faulty and incorrect as is the Christian definition of Theism, it is nearer the truth than the creed of some agnostics who conceive of no unifying principle in the world.' He proceeded to defend eloquently the argument from design, refer-

---

[4] 'Physical science is as little atheistic as it is materialistic' (*Science and Morals,* p. 140. Cf. *Life of Hume.*)

ring me to his volume of *Darwiniana,* to show that he had admitted
in print that it could not be disproved by the evolution theory.[5]
This position, which entirely tallies with his statement that only a
' very great fool' would deny in his heart a God conceived as Spinoza
conceives Him,[6] was distinctly short of the degree of agnosticism
currently attributed to him by those who read him hastily and blended
their own logic with his rhetoric.   Such an attitude towards destructive
thought, coupled with Descartes' maxim, was perhaps the explanation
of his recognising a value and real sacredness in current religious
forms which the aggressive irreligionists of France ostentatiously
despise.

Nevertheless he claimed (half humorously) the sanction of
Descartes, who lived and died a fervent Catholic, for pressing his
speculative doubts to their utmost limit.   He once told me that he
thought his own Lecture on Descartes the best exhibition of his
religious attitude as a whole.   And it was impossible not to recognise
the strenuous honesty which led him to look frankly in the face
problems for which he could find no speculative solution.   Regarded
as a contribution to philosophy, such a method has commended itself
to thinkers whose ultimate positions were various—Catholics like
Descartes and Pascal, Theists like Kant, as well as negative thinkers.
But Descartes did not abandon his religious convictions when he
instituted his 'methodic doubt,' which was to be the instrument of
their theoretic justification.   It is the identification of what is really
only a step towards the analysis of the foundations of belief with
the immediate guide to practical conviction, which marks the difference between Huxley and Descartes.   Apart from this, one felt the
value to the cause of truth of Huxley's lucid and candid exhibition
of the ' case ' of the negative thinker ; and one could not but respect
his enthusiasm for the man who gives forth his deepest convictions
in the face of obloquy, even while one felt that in point of fact
consideration for the effect on society might show what was in intention a protest against insincerity, to have been in effect rash and
misleading.   To Huxley this consideration was not, I think, of weight.
To speak out each fresh fragment of truth which he supposed himself
to have discerned was to him a duty, and not a complex one.   He
who thus spoke was confessor or martyr.   He did not, I think,
realise how often the truest he could see at the moment in science
might mislead from the crudity and inaccuracy of its first statement, and from its apparent conflict with equally true convictions of
society in other departments.   He tended to identify outspoken
candour with love of truth, and prudent reserve or patient suspense
of judgment with insincerity.

This feeling came out in the course of a talk with him in 1894.

[5] See *Darwiniana,* p. 109.

[6] See Essay on *Science and Morals,* p. 140.

He was speaking of Dean Stanley, whose brother Owen he had known in early life, and who had died out at sea in Huxley's arms. 'Arthur Stanley was before all things a sincere man,' he said.

'Men of ability are common enough, but men of character and conviction are very rare. It is the grandest thing conceivable to see a man speaking out and acting out his convictions in the face of unpopularity. What a grand man was your Gregory the Seventh, though I should not have been pleased for his views to have prevailed. But he was a man of strength and conviction.'

He also talked of Kant. 'It is remarkable,' he said, 'that Kant is a very clear writer on Physics, though obscure on Metaphysics.' I said that this seemed a testimony to his depth; it showed the obscurity not to be due to Kant's own want of perspicuity, but to the difficulty of the subject. Huxley, to whom things were always either evident or unknowable, demurred. 'No,' he replied, 'it was because he did not want too many people to understand him. *He would have been persecuted for his scepticism.*'

The Romanes lecture of 1893 has been much commented on as a recantation of his most aggressive theological views, and Huxley resented this account of it. He pointed out most truly that the position taken up in it had been long ago indicated by him. But many will continue to look on it as an example of his insistance in later years on the more religious admissions of his own public teaching. If the logic was that of his other writings, the rhetoric was not; and it was natural that average readers who had ascribed to him an irreligious attitude, much of which was really due to the rhetoric rather than the logic of his earlier works, should now in turn note the change from the hostile tone which they had observed, rather than the identity of his logical position which they had never mastered. I saw him more than once before he went to deliver the lecture, and he was suffering both from weakness and from loss of voice—so much so, that he doubted his being able to deliver it at all.

In the end he went to Oxford and was most cordially received. The lecture was a remarkable one. He shows in it with great force how entirely the struggle for existence and survival of the fittest, as represented in the 'cosmic process' antecedent to human civilisation, fails to account for the ethical element in man. The cosmic process is destructive, and survival in its course is due to the selfish and self-assertive elements in sentient nature. These elements—which in man are the 'original sin' of the theologians—remain in the race, and have to be counteracted, if social life is to be possible, by the more or less artificial cultivation of the sympathetic and conscientious elements. He sent me a copy of the lecture, and I wrote expressing my strong assent to some of its main propositions, although I added that he would no doubt not accept the 'transcendental' conclusion which I should draw from his arguments.

- The Oxford business [he wrote to me in reply], lecture, dinner and all, was too much for me; and even after three or four days' rest in a quiet country house I collapsed on our way to another, and had to come straight home. Since my return I have been almost living in the garden, and otherwise most diligently idle. I read [your] chapter on the Metaphysical,[7] though, and was delighted with the saying that it died of too much love, attributed to me by such a competent witness that I am not going to dispute the fact, though I had utterly forgotten it.

I was quite sure you would agree with my main thesis (in the Romanes Lecture), for it is only the doctrine that Satan is the Prince of this world—from the scientific side.

· Why should not materialists be transcendentalists? What possible difference can it make whether the hypostatised negative ' substance' is the same for mind and matter or different?

I am very sorry my cigar man served you so badly. I cannot make it out, as he invariably sends me the same quality. That confounded ' cosmic process' has got hold of him.

Ever yours very faithfully,
T. H. HUXLEY.

I have said that his conversation had the widest range. Point and humour were always there. If he spoke of persons or scenes, you carried away some definite feature of the personality or events in question.

I well remember his description—given with true Yankee twang —of a lecture he had to deliver at New York, where he was received with great enthusiasm. The reporters of the Baltimore paper called on him, and said they must have the lecture for publication on the day of its delivery. Huxley explained that the lecture existed as yet only in his own head. Still they pressed for it, and he complied with their demand, stipulating that if he rehearsed it for them they must give him a copy, lest they should publish one lecture and he should give another. The rehearsal was made, and the copy sent ; but when he opened it—in the very Lecture Hall itself—it proved to be a wholly illegible transcript on tissue paper. To make the story perfect he ought to have delivered an entirely different lecture from the one reported ; but his excellent memory served him, and the reports of the actual lecture and of the rehearsal, although somewhat different, were not sufficiently so to betray what had occurred.

I felt my impression of Carlyle's dogged Scotch unsympathetic persistency in measuring everything by his own ideas sensibly deepened by a story which Huxley told me of their mutual relations. Carlyle and he were for long good friends, but had a serious difference on the evolution question in the early stages of the controversy. Their personal intercourse ceased in consequence. After an interval of many years Huxley happened to see the Scotchman crossing the street in London, and thinking that bygones might be bygones, went up to him and spoke to him. Carlyle did not at first recognise him, but when he had made out who it was, he at once said,

---

[7] In *W. G. Ward and the Catholic Revival* (Macmillan).

with his Scotch twang, as though he were continuing the last conversation of years ago, ' You're Huxley, are you ?   You're the man that's trying to persuade us all that we're the children of apes ; while *I* am saying that the great thing we've really got to do is to make ourselves as much unlike apes as possible.'   Huxley, who had hoped that the weather or politics might have been admitted for the sake of peace, soon found that the best thing he could do was to retreat, and return to their tacit agreement to differ.

So, too, Stanley's impressionable and imaginative nature was brought out by him in an anecdote.   Stanley, vividly impressed by the newest thought of the hour, liberal, and advanced by family and school tradition, had sympathised with Colenso's treatment of the Bible in some degree ; yet his historical impressionableness told the other way.   Huxley explained his position thus :

' Stanley could believe in anything of which he had seen the supposed site, but was sceptical where he had not seen.   At a breakfast at Monckton Milnes's, just at the time of the Colenso row, Milnes asked me my views on the Pentateuch, and I gave them. Stanley differed from me.   The account of creation in Genesis he dismissed at once as unhistorical ; but the call of Abraham, and the historical narrative of the Pentateuch, he accepted.   This was because he had seen Palestine—but he wasn't present at the Creation.'

Admirably did he once characterise Tennyson's conversation. ' Doric beauty is its characteristic—perfect simplicity, without any ornament or anything artificial.'   Of an eminent person whose great subtlety of mind was being discussed, he said that the constant over-refinement of distinctions in his case destroyed all distinctness.   Anything could be explained away, and so one thing came to mean the same as its opposite.   Some one asked, ' Do you mean that he is untruthful ? '   ' No,' replied Huxley, ' *he is not clear-headed enough to tell a lie.*'

One of the subjects of his enthusiasm was John Bright—his transparent sincerity, his natural distinction, his oratorical power. ' If you saw him and A. B.' (naming a well-known nobleman) ' together,' he said, ' you would have set down Bright as the aristocrat, and the other as the plebeian.   His was the only oratory which ever really held me.   His speeches were masterpieces.   There was the sense of conviction in them, great dignity, and the purest English.'

He once spoke strongly of the insight into scientific method shown in Tennyson's *In Memoriam*, and pronounced it to be ' quite equal to that of the greatest experts.'   Tennyson he considered the greatest English master of melody except Spenser and Keats.   I told him of Tennyson's insensibility to music, and he replied that it was curious that scientific men as a rule had more appreciation of music than poets or men of letters.   He told me of one long talk he had

had with Tennyson, and added that immortality was the one dogma to which Tennyson was passionately devoted.

Of Browning, Huxley said : 'He really has music in him. Read his poem, *The Thrush*, and you will see it. Tennyson said to me,' he added, 'that Browning had plenty of music *in* him, but he could not get it *out.*'

A few more detached remarks illustrate the character and tastes of the man. He expressed once his delight in Switzerland and in the beauty of Monte Generoso. 'There is nothing like Switzerland,' he said. 'But I also delight in the simplest rural English scenery. A country field has before now *entranced* me.' 'One thing,' he added, 'which weighs with me against pessimism, and tells for a benevolent Author of the universe, is my enjoyment of scenery and music. I do not see how they can have helped in the struggle for existence. They are gratuitous gifts.'

He enjoyed greatly the views within his reach at Eastbourne, and his enjoyment was stimulated by the constitutional walk which took him frequently up the downs. 'The incubus of thought is got rid of,' he said, 'if you walk up a hill and walk fast.' He was eloquent on the beauty of Beachy Head. 'Building at Eastbourne is one of the few prudent things I ever did. It contradicts the proverb, "Fools build houses for wise men to live in."'

He spoke of the Royal Commission on Vivisection. 'The general feeling was at first strongly for vivisection,' he said, 'but one German changed the current of opinion by remarking, "I chloroform a cat because it scratches, but not a dog."' This at once suggested possibilities of cruelty, and (as I understood) was the cause of the amount of restriction ultimately placed on the practice. Apropos of vivisection, he spoke strongly of the absurdity of the outcry against it, as long as such things as pigeon-shooting were tolerated for mere amusement.

Speaking of two men of letters, with neither of whom he sympathised, he once said, ' Don't mistake me ; I don't class them together. One is a thinker and man of letters, the other is only a literary man. Erasmus was a man of letters, Gigadibs a literary man. A. B. is the incarnation of Gigadibs. I should call him *Gigadibsius optimus maximus.* When I showed him the various accounts of the Metaphysical Society which had been sent to me, and which revealed certain discrepancies, he said, ' Don't get any more, or the German critics will prove conclusively that it never existed.' Characteristic, too, was his genial pleasure in telling us how his little granddaughter looked at him, and then said emphatically, ' Well, you're the curiousest old man I ever saw.'

My talks with him during the last year of his life were almost entirely connected with the philosophy of religious Faith. In 1894 I introduced to him a young friend of mine, an Oxford man, who lived in Eastbourne. On this occasion he was very eloquent in Bishop Butler's praise, and on the conclusiveness of his argument in the *Analogy* as far as it went. 'But Butler was really one of *us*,' he added. 'That halting style, that hesitancy in expression, show that he was looking for a conclusion—something which he had not yet found.' My friend remarked that Newman thought that that something was Catholicism, and that Newman had developed Butler in a Catholic sense. 'A most ingenious developer,' replied Huxley, with amused emphasis.

He went up to Oxford for the meeting of the British Association, and I saw him shortly after his return. The whole thing had tired him very much, but the enthusiastic reception he had met with evidently gratified him. He criticised Lord Salisbury's address, in which he had spoken of the argument from design, and had attacked Weismann for ruling it out of court.

'After all [Huxley continued] my predominant feeling was one of triumph. I recalled the last meeting of the British Association at Oxford in the sixties, when it was supposed to be downright atheism to accept evolution at all, and when Bishop Wilberforce turned to me in public and said, "Was it your grandfather or your grandmother, Mr. Huxley, who was an ape?" And now Lord Salisbury, though he ventured to attack us, did not venture to question the doctrine of evolution—the thing for which he had really been struggling.'

He was highly pleased with an article on him which appeared in January 1895 in the *Quarterly*. 'It made me feel quite young again,' he said. 'It is a strong attack, of course, but very well written. I know a good bit of work when I see it.' He recurred several times to this article, and the significance of his pleasure struck me when I came to read it. For, like the Romanes Lecture, the article emphasised that side of Huxley's teaching which was consistent with the Theistic view of life—a side so often ignored by his critics. 'I have been attacked all my life,' he added, 'but so are many better men than me. Those whose views ultimately triumph often go through the most obloquy in their own time.'

There is a sad interest in the last scenes of the life of a man of genius which will be sufficient excuse for describing in some detail the last long conversation which I had with Mr. Huxley. Someone had sent me Mr. A. J. Balfour's book on *Foundations of Belief* early in February 1895. We were very full of it, and it was the theme of discussion on the 17th of February, when two friends were lunching with us. Not long after luncheon Huxley came in, and seemed in extraordinary spirits. He began talking of Erasmus and Luther, expressing a great preference for Erasmus, who would, he said, have impregnated the Church with culture and brought it abreast of the thought of the times, while Luther concentrated attention on individual mystical doctrines. 'It was very trying for

Erasmus to be identified with Luther, from whom he differed absolutely. A man ought to be ready to endure persecution for what he does hold; but it is hard to be persecuted for what you don't hold.' I said that I thought his estimate of Erasmus's attitude towards the Papacy coincided with Professor R. C. Jebb's. He asked if I could lend him Jebb's Rede Lecture on the subject. I said that I had not got it at hand, but I added, 'I can lend you another book which I think you ought to read—Balfour's *Foundations of Belief.*'

He at once became extremely animated, and spoke of it as those who have read his criticisms, published in the following month, would expect. 'You need not lend me that. I have exercised my mind with it a good deal already. Mr. Balfour ought to have acquainted himself with the opinions of those he attacks. One has no objection to being abused for what one *does* hold, as I said of Erasmus—at least, one is prepared to put up with it. An attack on us by some one who understood our position would do all of us good—myself included. But Mr. Balfour has acted like the French in 1870—he has gone to war without any ordnance maps, and without having surveyed the scene of the campaign. No human being holds the opinions he speaks of as "naturalism." He is a good debater. He knows the value of a word. The word "naturalism" has a bad sound and unpleasant associations. It would tell against us in the House of Commons, and so it will with his readers. "Naturalism" contrasts with "super-naturalism." He has not only attacked us for what we don't hold, but he has been good enough to draw out a catechism for "us wicked people" to teach us what we *must* hold.'

It was rather difficult to get him to particulars, but we did so by degrees. He said, 'Balfour uses the word *phenomena* as applying simply to the outer world and not to the inner world. The only people whom his attack would hold good of would be the Comtists, who deny that psychology is a science. They may be left out of account. They advocate the crudest eighteenth-century materialism. All the empiricists, from Locke onwards, make the observation of the pheno-mena of the mind itself quite separate from the study of mere sensation. No man in his senses supposes that the sense of beauty, or the religious feelings [this with a courteous bow to a priest who was present], or the sense of moral obligation, are to be accounted for in terms of sensation, or come to us through sensation.' I said that, as I understood it, I did not think Mr. Balfour supposed they would acknowledge the position he ascribed to them, and that one of his complaints was that they did not work out their premises to their logical conclusions. I added that so far as one of Mr. Balfour's chief points was concerned—the existence of the external world—Mill was almost the only man on their side in this century who had faced the problem frankly, and he had been driven to say that all men can know is that there are 'permanent possibilities of sensation.' He did not seem inclined to pursue the question of an 'external world, but said that though Mill's 'logic' was very good, empiricists were not bound by all his theories.

He characterised the book as a very good and even brilliant piece of work from a literary point of view; but as a helpful contribution to the great controversy, the most disappointing he had ever read. I said, 'There has been no adverse criticism of it yet.' He answered. with emphasis, 'No! *but there soon will be.*' 'From you?' I asked. 'I let out no secrets,' was the reply.

He then talked with great admiration and affection of Mr. Balfour's brother, Francis. His early death and W. K. Clifford's (Huxley said) had been the greatest loss to science—not only in England but in the world—in our time. 'Half a dozen of us old fogies could have been better spared.' He remembered Frank Balfour as a boy at Eton, and saw his unusual talent there. 'Then my friend, Michael Forster, took him up at Cambridge and found out that he had real genius for biology. I used to say there was science in the blood, but this new book of his brother's,' he added. smiling, 'shows I was wrong.'

Apropos to his remark about the Comtists, one of the company pointed out that in later life Comte recognised a science of 'the individual,' equivalent to what Huxley meant by pyschology. 'That,' he replied, 'was due to the influence of Clotilde de Vaux. You see,' he added with a kind of Sir Charles Grandison bow to my wife, 'what power your sex may have.' As Huxley was going out of the house I said to him that Father A. B. (the priest who had been present) had not expected to find himself in his company. 'No! I trust he had plenty of holy water with him,' was the reply.

Before he left we had an amusing instance of his positiveness. I reminded him that I had met him a month earlier in embarrassing circumstances. My hat had fallen into a pond, and I had asked him whether to walk home hatless or in the wet hat. 'I took your advice,' I said, 'as the most learned man in England on such subjects. I put on the hat, and I have had a frightful cold in the head ever since.' He replied promptly and quite seriously, 'You would have had pneumonia if you had kept it off.'

After he had gone we were all agreed as to the extraordinary vigour and brilliancy he had shown. Some one said, 'He is like a man who is what the Scotch call "fey."' We laughed at the idea; but we naturally recalled the remark later on.

Shortly afterwards I was anxious to get Huxley's advice as to an illustration I proposed to use in a review of the *Foundations of Belief*, connected with the gradual growth of sensitiveness to light in sentient beings. Being away from Eastbourne I wrote to him. His reply, written on the 27th of February—just before the commencement of his last illness—has a melancholy interest now.

I am not sure [he wrote] that any information of the kind you need is extant. Among the lowest forms of life ' sensitiveness to light ' is measured only by the way in which they group themselves towards or away from light, and it may signify nothing but a physical operation with which sensitiveness in the ordinary sense has nothing to do. The only clue here is in the state of the visual organ, where such exists. It can be traced down from the highest form of eyes step by step to the end of a single nerve filament surrounded by dark pigment and covered by the transparent outer skin. But whether in the last case the nerve ending is as much affected by the light (*i.e.* ether waves) as the nerve endings in the higher eyes are, and whether the affection of the nerve substance gives rise to a state of consciousness like that produced in us by light waves, are quite insoluble questions.

The most comprehensive discussion of the subject I can call to mind is in Tom. XII. of Milne Edwards's *Leçons sur la Physiologie,* and I can lend you the volume, and if you are back here before you want to use your information, I can supply you with oral commentary and diagrams *ad libitum.* There is not much water in the well, but you shall pump it dry with pleasure.

The first instalment of my discussion of the *Foundations of Belief* will be out in a day or two. I am sorry to say that my opinion of the book as anything more than a mere bit of clever polemic sinks steadily.

My wife is much better, and I have contrived to escape the pestilence yet. If I could compound for a day or two's neuralgia, I would not mind, but I abhor that long incapacity and convalescence.

Ever yours very faithfully,

T. H. HUXLEY. .

The very next day he was taken ill, and after four months, in which that vigorous mind and frame struggled with illness and exhaustion, he passed away.

So ended the life of one of whom Englishmen are justly proud for the extraordinary lucidity and brilliancy with which he impressed on his generation the characteristic scientific creed of his time, as well as for much else which specialists will measure with greater accuracy than the general reader.

In the problems of ethics of religion, to which he gave so much attention, I have attempted to convey my own impression, which will not be shared by those who fix their attention wholly on the destructive side of his teaching, that he united two divergent tendencies. Descartes combined the philosophy of ' methodic doubt ' with the faith of a Catholic. The same certainly cannot be said of Huxley. But that an antithesis between his theoretical methods and his practical attitude did impress some of those most interested in his remarkable mind the foregoing pages have shown. I concur with those who believe that his rooted faith in ethical ideals, which he confessed himself unable to account for by the known laws of evolution,[8] implied a latent recognition of the claims of religious mystery as more imperative and important than he could explicitly

---

[8] ' Cosmic evolution may teach us how the good and the evil tendencies of man may have come about ; but, in itself, it is incompetent to furnish any better reason why what we call good is preferable to what we call evil than we had before.'

admit on his own agnostic principles. Careful students of his writings are aware how far more he left standing of Christian faith than was popularly supposed even in his explicit theories ; and this knowledge appeared more and not less significant to many of those who conversed with him.

One thing, at all events, was beyond question—that his occasional flippancy in controversy represented no levity in his way of regarding serious and sacred subjects as a whole. It was in some cases provoked by real narrowness in good people, and sometimes by what I could not but consider his own narrowness, which failed to view minor details of popular Christianity in their true proportion ; and sometimes by the temptation to take controversial advantage of positions current among the orthodox which theologians themselves are likely eventually to abandon. Had he lived in the early seventeenth century he would have represented Christianity as standing or falling with the truth of the Ptolemaic system, and have depicted the theologians, who would not at once break with the Ptolemaic interpretation of Josue, as the most vivid caricatures of unreason.

Such considerations made it seem to many of those who met him more philosophical, as it certainly was more natural, not to attach the weight currently given to his attacks on incidental features of a system whose laws of organic growth he never comprehended.

Apart from these subjects one could not but learn much, even amid great divergence, and feel that divergence itself became less by mutual explanation. Had he found a logical place in his theory of knowledge for the great ethical ideals he so much reverenced in word and in practice, I cannot but think that a far greater change in his philosophy would have taken place than he ever contemplated. At all events, he had the power of intercourse, largely sympathetic, with those who could have had little in common with him, had the man been simply identical with his speculative agnosticism.

WILFRID WARD.

THE QUALITY OF MERCY

WHATEVER we may think of the artistic and critical influence of Mr. Ruskin on his age, we cannot but view with admiration and reverence much of his moral teaching, and there are in his writings innumerable isolated words of wisdom which would be well printed in letters of gold wherever men and women congregate and youth is educated. Amongst these is one which could not be too often reproduced before the eyes of an indifferent, egotistic, and cynical generation. It is this : 'Whosoever is not actively kind is cruel.' It is an absolute truth, but one which is very little heeded.

I will not here speak of the three crystallised and applauded forms of cruelty, war, sport, and scientific experiment. I wish to speak only of what is by the latter termed lay cruelty, but which I would myself call general and scarcely conscious cruelty—the ill-treatment of all sentient creatures not human by human creatures from the apathy, egotism, and unkindness of the latter. It is to this form of cruelty that Mr. Ruskin alludes in the sentence previously quoted.

The cruelty of earlier times had its chief cause in violence ; the cruelty of modern times has its chief cause in cowardice and selfishness. The character of the cruelty has altered, but its prevalence remains equally widespread and its motive is more contemptible. The modern world regards the pillory and the stocks as barbarous ; but it allows the railway signalman to be riveted to his post for eighteen consecutive hours, and sees no harm in it. The human race was then ruder, no doubt but more generous, more violent in some ways, but more magnanimous. Remember the familiar story of the Roman who wrung the neck of the dove which took refuge in his bosom from the pursuing bird of prey, and was stoned by his fellow-citizens. In the modern world there would be no movement of indignation against such an act ; gentlewomen and men see the necks wrung of the wounded birds in the shooting enclosures without the slightest emotion of pity or effort at censure.

Not long ago I spoke of this to a young and beautiful Englishwoman of the great world, and she answered, 'Yes, it is useless to attempt to move them to any feeling for animals. You can get them to do something for people, because they think it does them good with the masses, keeps off revolution, and helps in canvassing. But for cruelty they do not care in the least.' She could not have uttered a greater truth or a more cutting satire.

There are exceptions, doubtless, but they are not numerous enough to leaven the great mass of indifferent and selfish people. Animals find but few friends. Alas! they have no votes!

There is, perhaps, one thing still more nauseating than the world's apathy, and that is its self-praise; its admiration of its own charities, so miserably insignificant besides the extravagance of its own pleasures. When we think how little is done by those who could do so much to influence even their own households to justice and tenderness, one cannot wonder that the populace is unmoved by the occasional invitation to them from a higher world to display those virtues which the rich prefer rather to inculcate than to practise.

Last year in England, in a nobleman's house, a footman beat a small dog which ran into the offices with a red-hot poker, and piled burning coals on it until it died in indescribable agony. I wrote and asked the nobleman in question if he had dismissed this monster from his service, the man having been only punished by the Bench with a slight fine; the nobleman answered me so evasively that it was easy to read between the lines and see that he had retained the footman in his service. This act on the part of the servant was an extreme case of hideous cruelty, but his employer's condonation is by no means an extreme case; it is, indeed, a very common sample of a master's indifference, of that indifference which is practically connivance. People abandon their stables to their coachmen, their dogs to their keepers; even the animals they call pets are frequently allowed to suffer from servants, or children, and are bullied, neglected, and teased with impunity.

The disgusting spectacle of dog-catching by the police is allowed to be presented in the public streets of most capitals of Europe continually, and there is none of that outburst of revolted feeling which such an offence to all humane sentiment and common decency should provoke. If such spectacles excited in the general public one-thousandth part of such disgust as they would excite in any really civilised people, it would be impossible for such scenes to exist in either hemisphere to shock the sight and sense of those of more refined taste and more humane feelings.

There is an excellent association for the protection of birds, but its aims are so little in touch with its generation that it obtains only the most meagre support. Great names and patrician names are very rare upon its lists, and at its public meetings its cause has its neck at once broken by the question of sport being rigorously excluded by its chairman.

There is an institution in London which calls itself a 'home for lost dogs'; under this affecting title it appeals for funds, as though it were inspired solely by love and anxiety for the happiness of dogs, and for the protection and prolongation of their lives. In reality it is an institution for the organised suffocation of fifteen or twenty thousand dogs annually, which have been kidnapped by the police and taken forcibly from their owners; it is a slaughter-house for the abetment and convenience of the police, and as such should be maintained out of the funds of the Government. Nothing but the most criminal apathy in the public could permit a slaughter-house to masquerade as a home and be a petitioner to charity. The word 'home' implies peace and safety, and should not be permitted to cover a place of legalised butchery.

Think how odious to the horse must be the mere forcing of the bit into his mouth and of the headstall over his ears. Without speaking of the torture of the spur, the stinging of the lash, the dreadful weight upon the spine from which the riding-horse suffers, and the dreadful strain upon the lungs and withers to which the draught and driving horse is incessantly condemned, only realise the continued imprisonment and galling servitude in which the equine race are forced to dwell, and ask yourself if, in common pity or justice, that life should not be as much alleviated and lightened as it is possible to make it. Yet is there one owner of horses in a million who takes the trouble to see for himself how his own stables are organised, or maintains out of gratitude in their old age or in their failing speed the horses which have served him in their prime?

Many wild-beast shows of the present hour are as cruel as were the gladiatorial games of Rome, and far less manly. I can imagine no possible argument which can be put forward for the license awarded to the travelling caravans which attend fairs and feasts all the world over, and which are hells of animal torture. What is called the taming of beasts is the most cruel, demoralising, and loathsome of pursuits; the horrible wickedness of its methods is known to all, and the appetite it awakens and stimulates in the public is to the last degree debasing. Yet not the smallest effort is made to end it.

The encouragement of menageries, where wild animals are cowed and maltreated into trembling misery, and forced to imitate the foolish attitudes and comedies of men, lies entirely with the public—with the world at large. If the nations were in any true sense civilised, such forms of diversion would, I repeat, be insupportable to them. Dancing dogs, dancing bears, performing wolves, enslaved elephants, would one and all, from the lion tortured on a bicycle in a circus, to the little guinea-pig playing a drum in the streets—would be one and all so sickeningly painful to a truly civilised public that the stolid human brutes who live by their sufferings would not dare to train and exhibit them.

Not long ago there was a somewhat silly discussion in the English press on the effect of perfumes on desert animals in captivity, of the excitement and pleasure produced on them by such odours. It occurred to no one of the sapient correspondents that such perfumes did no doubt recall to the poor imprisoned animals the intense fragrance of the flowers in their own jungles and tropical forests. All animals are intensely sensitive to odours, because their olfactory nerves telegraph to their brains in a way of which our own dull nostrils are utterly unconscious.

With what pretension can a world call itself humane when in its codes all 'wild' animals are unprotected by laws, and may be treated with whatever brutality is desired? When it is a question for the dweller in a jungle to kill a wild beast or be killed himself, one can understand that he chooses the first of the two alternatives. But this is no excuse for the man in cities to drag a captured lion to make the sport of fools, and to perish wretchedly of diseased joints and thwarted longings.

It is idle to speak of the civilisation of a world in which such things are possible. From a hygienic point of view alone these poor tormented creatures, cooped up in filthy cages, breathing fetid air night and day, hearing each other's piteous cries, having no single want or instinct gratified, ill fed, diseased, miserable, and ravaged by parasites, must be one of the most unwholesome centres of contagion conceivable. A polar bear is at this moment being taken through Europe for exhibition in a caravan; he is kept in a cage in which he cannot turn; he has a pan of water two inches deep; and a few ounces of bread as his only food!

This is permissible by law; and the same generation orders Prince Bismarck and Mr. Gladstone, Count Tolstoi and Sir John Millais, Gabrielle d'Annunzio and Henry Irving, to muzzle their dogs!

There is no animal which is not to be attached by kindness and justice shown to him. The lion of Rosa Bonheur fell into decline from grief at being sent from her keeping to that of the Jardin des Plantes when she was absent on a distant voyage. She returned to find him dying; he recognised her voice and opened his eyes with a feeble roar of pleasure, then laid his great head down upon her knees and died. No one who knows human nature by long experience can assert for a moment that its fidelity can be secured by benefits, or its sincerity insured by affection; but when kindness and regard are shown to 'the beasts which perish,' they never fail to give them back tenfold.

I think that not only is their affection undervalued, but that the intelligence of animals is greatly underrated. Man having but one conception of intelligence, his own, does not endeavour to comprehend another which is different, and differently exhibited and expressed. I have before now said in print that if our mind exceeds the mind of animals and birds in much, theirs exceeds ours at least in some things, as their sight, scent, and hearing surpass ours.

When we remember also that these other races are absolutely alone, are never aided by man, are only, on the contrary, hindered by him, opposed, thwarted, and persecuted by him, their achievements are, relatively to their opportunities, much more wonderful than any of his. The elements which are his great foes are likewise theirs ; they have to encounter and suffer all the woes of tempest, hurricane, flood, the width of barren seas, the hunger on solitary shores ; and they have also in his ruthless and unceasing spite an enemy more cruel than any with which he himself has to contend. If we meditate on this unquestionable fact, we shall be forced to admit that Cristoforo Colombo was not a greater hero than many a little swallow.

But scarcely anyone does meditate on these phenomena ; one in a million, one in a generation, at the most. To nearly the whole of humanity the wonderful and beautiful races with which the world teems, which are for ever living side by side with the human, do not exist except in so far as they contribute to the pleasure of slaughter, or the greed of commerce, or of gambling. For to the majority of men and women all organisms except their own are as though they were not.

There is no sympathy with these interesting and mysterious lives led side by side with man, but ignored by him entirely, except when by him persecuted. The nest of the weaver bird is to the full as ingenious and as marvellous as the dome of St. Peter's or St. Paul's. The beaver state and the bee state are as intricate in organisation as the Constitution of the French Republic and the British Monarchy, and are distinctly superior in many parts of their organisation to either of these. The passage of the white ants through a jungle and across a continent is quite as admirable in unison and skill and order as the human march to Chitral ; and the annual flights of the storks, of the Solan geese, of the wild ducks, exhibit qualities of obedience to a chosen commander, of endurance, of observation, and of wisdom not exceeded by any human Arctic or Australian exploring party.

The vainglorious assumption that we have a monopoly of what is called reason cannot be allowed by those who bring a reason of their own unbiassed to the study of animals, not under the unnatural conditions of the laboratory, but in natural freedom and peace.

No skill of a Stanley or a Nansen ever exceeded that of the hound Maida in tracing Sir Walter Scott, and no journey of a Burton or a Speke was ever so wonderful as the migratory voyage of a martin or a nightingale. I have said this ere now ; and it can never be repeated too often, for nothing is so cruel as the vanity of man, and nothing so opposed to his own true progress as his blind and dogged contempt for all races not shaped exactly like his own.

The recent correspondence general in the English press about the muzzling of dogs has been conspicuous for its silliness, ignorance, and cruelty, but above all by its disgusting selfishness, and an editor of a very popular organ was not ashamed to print that if only one human life could be saved, &c., &c., disregarding the fact that men were at the time being slaughtered by dysentery and fever by the scores for no better object than to go and cut down cotton trees at Coomassie; whilst deaths by starvation, a perfectly preventible cause, are so common in English cities that the reports of them scarcely awaken a passing regret or compassion.[1] The veneration for human life which is developed by journalists when a lion kills his gaoler, or when a dog is supposed to have been the cause of his tormentor's death, is comical in these gentlemen of the press, who to help a speculation, open out a new mart, or influence the share lists, will ravenously demand a military expedition or a naval demonstration, to sabre, shell, burn, and ravage upon distant strands.

The attitude of the Brahmin, to whom all forms of life are sacred, is intelligible, estimable, and consistent; the attitude of the savage conqueror, to whom thousands of dead men and thousands of dead beasts are alike so much carrion, is intelligible and reasonable, whilst brutal. The attitude of the journalist and county councilman is not either; it possesses neither logic or common sense, and is not estimable or reasonable, but only contemptible.

If there be one thing more loathsome than the carnage of war, it is the Red Cross societies following in its train. But the modern world, being conscious that the butchery of war ill accords with its æsthetic and religious pretensions, gives a sop to its conscience by sending the ambulance side by side with the gun carriage. A more robust and more honest temper did not evade the truth that the least brutal war is the one most immediately and conclusively destructive; the slaughter of wounded men was more truly merciful than the modern system of surgery and nursing, which saves shattered constitutions and ruined health to drag out a miserable and artificially prolonged existence.

There is, however, something which the ordinary human mind finds soothing and delightful in this formula of 'the sanctity of human life' when combined with a corresponding disregard for all other life. The good Christian likes to be raised aloft in his own eyes from all those other races which he imagines were given to him by a gracious Deity. He loves to think that both God and the neighbouring policeman are watching over him and taking care alike of his soul and of his great-coat. In the enormous vanity of the Christian who believes all the laws of the universe altered for him, or in the equally enormous

---

[1] In February of this year a working man wrote to Mr. Chamberlain to say that there were over 5,000 working men come up from the country to London in search of work and unemployed, many of them starving; and asked him if he would recommend them to the authorities in the Transvaal. Mr. Chamberlain replied curtly by a secretary that they would not be likely to find work in the Transvaal, and said no more.

vanity of the scientist who arrogates to himself the right to dogmatise
on the mysteries of creation, this attitude is not surprising. But in
either the philosophic mind or the poetic temperament it is so, because to the philosopher the difference between the human and the
other races cannot appear very great, whilst to the poet the solidarity
of all sentient life must always seem unquestionable. That friend and
scholar and poet for whom we mourn as freshly as though he had died
but yesterday did not disdain to greet a brother's spirit in

> That liquid, melancholy eye
> From whose pathetic soul-fed springs
> Seem'd surging the Virgilian cry,
> The sense of tears in mortal things;.

for these lines were written by Matthew Arnold to ' only a dog.'

It is not in foolishly endeavouring to make animals our prisoners
and puppets, in trying to force them to count, to caper, or to play
cards, that we reach insight into their natures and their minds. It
is in loving them and respecting them as he loved and respected
Geist and Kai. I use the latter word advisedly, for whoever does not
in a fair degree, as with a human friend, respect the freedom and the
preference and the idiosyncrasy of an animal will never reach true
comprehension of him.

Let me here tell a little true history, which I should have told to
Matthew Arnold had he been living, with entire certainty of his
sympathy.

A little dog of Maltese breed, who belonged to my mother, was
unconsolable at her death. For three weeks he refused all food, and
was kept alive by nourishment artificially administered. He sat up,
and begged day after day before her bed and before her chair, until
he dropped from sheer exhaustion. He wanted for nothing that I
could give him; and no habit of his daily life was changed; but he
was unhappy. Whenever the door opened he thought she entered.
He ran and looked into every stranger's face. He knew everything
which had belonged to her. His sorrow injured his health; his heart
became weak, and he died of cardiac paralysis at six years old.

What could human affection offer superior in fidelity and feeling ?

> That loving heart, that patient soul,
> Had they indeed no longer span
> To run their course, and reach their goal,
> And read their homily to man ?

A writer wrote the other day, ' People speak of the law of Nature;
but who feels it ? There is no such emotion known in the ordinary
life of the world.' The persons who will let their dinner wait whilst
they watch a sunset fade over sea or moor, or who will leave the share
list unread to see the morning dew make silver globes of the gossamer
in the grass, **are so few** that they may almost be said not to exist, if we

except a poet here, an artist there ; and the sense of kinship with races not human can only come to those whose own kinship with earth and air and sky is strong enough to resist the dulling and debasing influences of artificial life, of life amongst men and their trivialities, frauds, and vanities.

'The sun is God,' said Turner when he lay dying, and, alas ! saw that sun only through the mists of London.   But how many see the sun at all, even when they live where it is most radiant ?   How many think of the sun during the long day it illumines ?   The light is taken as a matter of course, as our breath is drawn through our lungs. There is no gratitude for it.

In similar manner there is no sense of kinship with the winged children of the air, with the fourfooted dwellers beside us on the earth.   Almost the only recognition we give them is maltreatment. At other times the indifference of our unspeakable fatuity rises in a dust cloud between us and them.   Of gratitude for their companionship, their aid, their patience, their many virtues, there is not a trace in those who use them and abuse them, no more than there is gratitude for the beauty of the rose or the fragrance of the violet.

As 'the winds of March take the world with beauty,' and every pasture and coppice is full of blossom, which we too often tread underfoot or pass unnoticed in every daily country walk, so in the same manner do the multitudes trample down and pass by the ineffable charm and fragrance of disregarded affections and unappreciated qualities in the other races of earth.

Hang a poor woodland bird in a cage, if you can bear to look on such a captive, above a blossoming honeysuckle or hawthorn, and note his anguish of remembrance, his ecstasy of hope, his frantic effort to be free.   But the accursed wires are between him and the familiar blossoms, between him and the blue sky ; in a little while he realises that he is a prisoner ; the fluttering joy goes out of his heart and his wings, his feathers grow ruffled and dull, his eyes are veiled, he sits motionless and heartbroken, and the breeze of the springtime blows past him, and never more will bear him on its buoyant way.

Living wild song-birds are sold at a halfpenny each by thousands in the London slums, and as many more die—nay, thrice as many more —before they reach the streets, packed close and jammed together in hampers and crates.

Yet the Home Secretary, on being asked by a deputation to put an end to this abominable traffic, answered that it was desirable to do as little as possible in the way of legislation !

For legislators, always eager to make cruel and coercive laws, prefer to let humane ones be substituted by what they call ' the gradual education of the people.'   But this gradual education is so extremely gradual that its progress is imperceptible, and it may even be justly suspected that it is chiefly a backward movement; and such education, as far as education by example goes, is hindered, not helped, by what are called the cultured classes.

Let us look at the example given by a London leader of fashion and politics as she goes down at election time to shed sweetness and light around her in Poplar or Shoreditch.

In her bonnet is, of course, an osprey aigrette; she knows it was torn from a living heron, but then that was done far away in some North or South American creek or forest, and so really does not matter. Her *Suède* gloves fit like her skin; they were the skin of a kid and were stripped from its living body. The jacket she carries on her arm is lined with Astrakhan fur, which was taken from an unborn lamb; to give to the fur that curl and kink which please her it has been cut from its mother's ripped-up womb. Her horses as they wait for her at the corner of the street have their heads fixed in air and the muscles of their necks cramped by immovable bearing-reins. Her Japanese pug runs after her shaking his muzzle-tortured nose. She has a telegram in her pocket which has momentarily vexed her. She sent her sable collie to the dog exhibition at Brussels, and the excitement, or the crush, or the want of water, or something, has brought on heat apoplexy, and he is dead, poor old nervous Ossian! She really has no luck, for her Java sparrows died too at the bird show in Edinburgh, because the footman sent with them forgot to fill their water glass when it got dry on the journey; a great many people send birds to shows with nobody to take care of them, so she feels that she was not to blame in the very least.

'Why will you show?' says her husband, who is vexed about Ossian; 'you don't want to win and you don't want to sell.'

'Oh, everybody does it,' she answers.

He goes into his study to console himself with a new model of a pole trap; and she, her canvassing done, runs upstairs to see her gown for the May Drawing-Room. The train is of quite a new design, embroidered with orchids in natural colours, and fringed with the feathers of the small green parrakeet, a beautiful little bird which has been poisoned by hundreds in the jungles of New Guiana to make the border to this *manteau de cour*.

If she were told that she is a more barbaric creature than the squaw of the poor Indian trapper who poisoned the parrakeets she would be equally astonished and offended.

Let us now look at her next-door neighbour; he is a very wealthy person and calls himself a Liberal (that is to say, he considers nobody should cry Bo! to a goose without having taken out a licence to do so fully stamped and endorsed); he is a good-natured person, seldom re-fuses a subscription, thinks private charity pernicious and pauperising, attends his church regularly, and votes in the House of Commons in favour of pigeon-shooting and spurious sports. If any one asks him if he 'likes animals' he answers cheerily, ' Oh, dear me, yes. Poor creatures, why not ?' But it does not disturb him that the horse in the hansom cab which he has called to take him to the City has weals all over its loins and a bit that fills its mouth with blood and foam, nor does he notice the overdriven and half-starved condition of a herd of cattle being taken from Cannon Street to Smithfield, but only curses them heartily for blocking the traffic.

He eats a capon, drives behind a gelding, warms himself at a hearth of which the coal has been procured by untold sufferings of man and beast, has his fish crimped and his lobsters scalded to death in his kitchens, relishes the green fat cut from a living turtle, reads with approbation his head keeper's account of the last pair of owls on his estate having been successfully trapped, writes to that worthy to turn down two thousand more young pheasants for the autumn shooting, orders his agent to have his young cattle on his home-farm dishorned, and buys as a present for his daughters a card case made from the shell of a tortoise which was roasted alive, turned on its back on the fire to give the ruddy glow to its shell. Why not? His favourite preacher and his popular scientist alike assure him that all ·the subject races are properly sacrificed to man. It is obviously wholly impossible to convince such a person that he is cruel: he merely studies his own convenience, and he has divine and scientific authority for considering that he is perfectly right in doing so. He is quite comfortable, both for time and for eternity. It were easier to change the burglar of the slums, the brigand of the hills, than to change this self-complacent and pachydermatous householder who represents nine-tenths of the ruling classes.

Let us not mistake ; he is not personally a cruel man ; he would not himself hurt anything, except in sport which he thinks is legitimate, and in science which he is told is praiseworthy ; he is amiable, good-natured, perhaps benevolent, but he is wrapped up in habits, customs, facts, egotisms, tyrannies which all seem to him to be good, indeed to be essential. His horse is a thing to him like his mail. phaeton ; his dog is a dummy, like his umbrella stand ; his cattle are wealth-producing stores, like his timber or wheat ; he uses them all as he requires, as he uses his hats and gloves. He sees no more unkindness in doing away with any of them than in discarding his old boots, and he passes the most atrocious laws and by-laws for animal torment as cheerfully as he signs a cheque payable to self.

His ears are wadded by prejudice, his eyes are blinded by formula, his character is steeped in egotism ; you might as well try, I repeat, to touch the heart of the Sicilian robber or the London crib-cracker as to alter his views and opinions ; you would speak to him in a language which is as unintelligible to his world as Etruscan to the philologist.

The majority of his friends, like himself, lead their short, bustling, bumptious, and frequently wholly useless lives, purblind always and entirely deaf where anything except their own interests is concerned. They think but very rarely of anything except themselves, and the competitions, ambitions, or jealousies which occupy them. But in their pastimes cruelty is to them acceptable; it is an outlet for the barbarian who sleeps in them, heavily drugged but not dead; the sight of blood titillates agreeably their own slow circulation.

Between them and the cad who breaks the back of the bagged rabbit there is no difference except in the degree of power to indulge the slaughter-lust.

Alas! it were easier 'to quarry the granite rock with razors' than to touch the feelings of such as this man or this woman where their vanities, or their more sheep-like love of doing as others do, are in question. Princesses wear osprey tufts and lophophorus wings, and so society wears them too, and cares not a straw by what violence and wickedness they are procured; as the ladies, who attend their State Concerts, sleep none the worse when in their country houses because the rabbit screams in the steel gins and the hawk struggles in the pole trap in the woods about their ancestral houses, and have no less appetite for luncheon amongst the bracken or the heather because shot and bleeding creatures lie half dead in the game bags around, or because the stag often is stretched in his dead majesty before their eyes. Why, then, should they care because in far distant lands little feathered creatures, lovely as flowers, innocent as the dew and the honey they feed on, are killed by the thousand and tens of thousands because a vulgar and depraved taste demands their tender bodies?

What does it matter to them that through their demands the bird of paradise has become so rare that, unless stringent measures be taken at once, it will become totally extinct, and the golden glory of its plumes will gleam no more in tropical sunlight? What does it matter to them that the herons in all their various kinds, the osprey, the egret, the crane, the ibis, are scarcely seen now in the southern and middle States of America, and, when seen, are no longer together in confident colonies, as of yore, but nesting singly and in fear? 'Practically all our heronries are deserted. The birds have been slaughtered for their plumes,' writes a physician [2] dwelling in the Delaware valley. 'What were common birds in their season half a century ago are now rarely seen. The struggle for existence has been a violent one and the herons have been worsted. Scarcely a word of protest has been heard, and none that has been effectual.' Women of the world know this, or at least have been told it fifty times; but it makes no impression on them. They will wear osprey-aigrettes as long as any are left in commerce, and think a humming bird looks so pretty in their hair.

That their example is copied by the women of the middle classes

[2] Charles Conrad Abbott, M.D.

with swallows and warblers, and by the servant girl and factory girl
with dyed sparrows and finches, makes no impression on them ; if the
fact be noticed to them they say that the common people always
will be ridiculous, and stop their carriage in Bond Street to buy
fire screens made of owls or an electric lamp hung in the beak of a
stuffed flamingo.

Why should they care, indeed—they who walk with the guns, even
if they do not do more and secure a warm corner for their own shot ;
they who bring up their young sons to regard the cowardly and
brutal sport of battue shooting as the supreme pleasure and privilege
of youth, and see unmoved their beautiful autumnal woods turned
into slaughter-places ?

One cannot but reflect how different might the world have been
if women had been different, if, instead of their smiling, self-
complacent, tittering approbation of brutality, they had shown scorn
for and abhorrence of brutality. They clamour for electoral rights and
leave all this vast field of influence unoccupied and untilled ! They do
little or nothing to soften the hearts or refine the feelings of the men
who love them, or to bring up their children in any sympathy with
animal life. Sport has become fashionable with them in the last
twenty years, and the crack shot in the coverts of Chantilly this
winter was a woman. Sporting clothes, breeches and gaiters, are
now a recognised part of the fashionable woman's toilet.

I would not affirm (anomaly as it appears) that sport is incompatible with a love of animals, for I have known many sporting men
and hunting men who were in a sense sincerely devoted to animals.
But sport inevitably creates deadness of feeling. No one could take
pleasure in it who was sensitive to suffering ; and therefore its pursuit
by women is much more to be regretted than its pursuit by men,
because women pursue much more violently and recklessly what they
pursue at all, and it is impossible for the sportswoman logically and
effectively to exercise any influence on her young children which
could incline them to mercy, such an influence as Lamartine's mother
had on him to the day of his death.

There are two periods in the lives of a woman when she is almost
omnipotent for good or ill. These are when men are in love with
her, and when her children are young enough to be left entirely to
her and to those whom she selects to control them. How many
women in ten thousand use this unlimited power which they then
possess to breathe the quality of mercy into the souls of those who
for the time are as wax in their hands ? They will crowd into the
Speaker's box to applaud debates which concern them in no way.
They will impertinently force their secondhand opinions on Jack and
Jill in the village or in the City alleys. They will go on to
platforms and sing comic songs, or repeat temperance platitudes, and
think they are a great moral force in the improvement of the masses.

This they will do, because it amuses them and makes them of importance. But alter their own lives, abandon their own favourite cruelties, risk the sneer of society, or lead their little children to the love of nature and the tenderness of pity: these they will never do. Mercy is not in them, nor humility, nor sympathy.

Can written words do much to teach the hearts of those who read? I fear not.

On how many do written words, even dipped in the heart's blood and burning with the soul's fire, produce any lasting effect? Is not the most eloquent voice doomed to cry without echo in the wilderness? And what wilderness is there so barren as the desert of human indifference and of human egotism?

Pity is only awakened in those who are already pitiful. We cannot sow mustard seed on granite. The whole tendency of the age is towards cynicism, indifference, self-engrossment. The small children sneer oftener than they smile.

From Plutarch to Voltaire, from Celsus to Sir Arthur Helps, the finest and most earnest pleading against cruelty has been made by the finest and most logical minds. But the world has not listened; the majority of men and women are neither just nor generous, neither fine nor logical. In a few generations more there will probably be no room for animals on the earth: no need of them, no toleration of them. An immense agony will have then ceased, but with it there will also have passed away the last smile of the world's youth. For in the future the human race will have no tenderness for those of its own kind who are feeble or aged, and will consign to lethal chambers all those who weary it, obstruct it, or importune it, since the quality of mercy will day by day be more derided, and less regarded as one of the moral attributes of mankind.

OUIDA.

A REAL MAHÂTMAN

MANY times the question has been asked of late, What is a *Mahâtman*, and what is a *Sannyâsin*? *Mahâtman* is a very common Sanskrit word, and means literally great-souled, high-minded, noble. It is used as a complimentary term, much as we use noble or reverend; but it has been accepted also as a technical term, applied to what are called *Sannyâsins* in the ancient language of India. *Sannyâsin* means one who has surrendered and laid down everything—that is, who has abandoned all worldly affections. 'He is to be known as a *Sannyâsin*,' we read in the *Bhagavad-gîtâ*, v. 3, 'who does not hate and does not desire.' As the life of a Brâhman was, according to the laws of Manu, divided into four periods, or *âsramas*—that of a pupil, of a householder, of a hermit, and of an independent sage—those who had reached the fourth stage were called *Sannyâsins*, a word difficult to render in English, but perfectly familiar to everybody in India. Another old name for these freedmen of the spirit is *Avadhûta*, literally one who has shaken off all attachment to worldly objects. These Avadhûtas also exist to the present day. They are sometimes called simply *Sâdhus*, good people.

It has been denied that there are any Sannyâsins left in India, and in one sense this is true. If the scheme of life traced out by Manu was ever a reality, it has long since ceased to be so. Boys no longer remain in the house of a teacher till they are grown up. They do not serve their teachers, nor do they, as a rule, receive from them their daily lessons, to be learnt by heart and to be repeated day after day. Nor do they, when they have married and become house-holders, perform the sacrifices prescribed by Manu ; least of all do they think, when their hair turns grey, and when they have seen the children of their children, that the time has come for them to leave their home and retire to the forest, following the life of a hermit, performing penances, and devoting themselves to meditation. But though we hardly ever hear of a man ordering the three stages of his life according to the rules laid down by the ancient legislators, something like the life of a Sannyâsin has been kept up in India to the present day. It is true that, according to orthodox views, no one can be a Sannyâsin who has not spent the required number of years in the three antecedent stages; but on this point the law of Manu had evidently been broken from very early times. The Buddhist revolt was mainly based on this very argument, that if perfect spiritual freedom—considered as the privilege of the fourth stage—was the highest goal, it was a mistake to wait for it till the very end of life. The Buddhist declined to pass through the long discipline of a pupil; he considered the performance of the duties of a householder, more particularly the performance of sacrifices, not only as unprofitable, but as mischievous. The penances performed by the hermit also had been declared by Buddha himself as leading man away from his true calling, and only the state of perfect freedom from the fetters of every passion was recognised by him as the true aim of life. In that sense every Buddhist Bhikshu, or friar, might be called a Sannyâsin, though he had renounced the Veda, the laws of Manu, and all Brâhmanic sacrifices as vanity and vexation of spirit.

This Buddhist spirit seems soon to have extended to the members of the Brâhmanic society also, and we meet at all times, both before and after the Buddhist reform, with men who had shaken off all social fetters; who had retired from their families and from society at large, lived by themselves in forests or in caves, abstained from all enjoyments, restricted their food and drink to the very utmost, and often underwent tortures which make us creep when we read of them or see them represented in pictures and photographs. Such men were naturally surrounded by a halo of holiness, and they received the little they wanted from those who visited them or who profited by their teachings. Some of these saints—but not many—were scholars, and became teachers of their ancient lore. Some, of course, were impostors and hypocrites, and have brought disgrace on the whole profession. But that there were Sannyâsins, and that there are even now, who have really shaken off the fetters of passion, who have disciplined their body and subdued their mind to a perfectly marvellous extent, cannot be doubted. Nor must it be forgotten that from very early times a complete system was elaborated in India, according to which a man by practising different kinds of inhaling and exhaling, by assuming certain postures, by fixing the eyes on certain objects, and by fasting, possibly by drugging himself, could bring himself to such a state of nervous exaltation that in his trance he felt no pain, and was able to do and suffer things which no ordinary mortal could endure. When we read of cases, more or less attested by trustworthy witnesses, of men in such a state seeing what ordinary mortals cannot see, reading the thoughts of others—nay, being lifted into the air without any visible support—we naturally withhold our belief; but that some of these men can go without food for many days; that they can sit unmoved in intense heat and cold; that they can remain in a long death-like trance; nay, that they can be buried and brought back to life after three or four days—these are facts testified to by such unexceptionable witnesses, by English officers and English medical men, that they have to be accepted, even though they cannot be accounted for.

It is generally supposed that these same persons, these so-called Sannyâsins, are also very learned and wise persons. They may have been so in some cases, but, as a rule, I believe they are not. The best Sanskrit scholars of late years have not been among these Sannyâsins, but among the Pandits and professors at the Indian Universities, or in the Maths of Southern India.

Learning is very much specialised in India, and is generally acquired by an immense amount of learning by heart. One Pandit knows Panini's Grammar with commentaries, and commentaries on commentaries, but he remains dumb on logic or rhetoric. Another knows logic in all its branches, but would decline to answer difficult questions in Vedânta philosophy. Many Pandits know poetry and rhetoric to an extraordinary amount, but legal literature seems to have no existence for them. I have myself had to examine young Indian students who knew by heart the whole text in which they had to pass, but who failed altogether when they had to translate unseen passages. The cultivation of memory has been carried to an extraordinary extent in India, so that people who know a whole dictionary like the *Amarakosha* by heart are by no means uncommon. Works like the *Bhagavad-gîtâ*, nay, the *Bhâgavata-purâna*, are committed to memory, and some of the people who have done that travel about the country as professional reciters and support themselves by the alms which they receive. But it is easily understood that all this does not produce anything like independent thought, and in the case of the Sannyâsins of the present generation we look in vain either for great learning, even learning by heart, or for original thought and profound wisdom. Yet these Sannyâsins have often a large following. To visit them is considered meritorious, still more to support them by alms. Some of the descriptions given of these local saints are most repulsive. They are represented as filthy, as impostors, as abettors of crime, even as licentious and dissolute. Indian magistrates do not speak well of them, but with the people at large their prestige is considerable. Nor can it be doubted that, in spite of the black sheep, the true Sannyâsin is really a saint, and that his aloofness from the world is extraordinary. There was, for instance, *Dayânanda Sarasvatî*, who tried to introduce some reforms among the Brâhmans. He was a scholar in a certain sense. He actually published a commentary in Sanskrit on the Rig Veda, and was able to speak Sanskrit with great fluency. It is supposed that he was poisoned because his reforms threatened to become dangerous to the Brâhmans. But in all his writings there is nothing that could be quoted as original beyond his somewhat strange interpretations of words and whole passages of the Veda.

The late *Râmakrishna Paramahansa* was a far more interesting specimen of a Sannyâsin.   He seems to have been, not only a high-souled man, a real *Mahâtman*, but a man of original thought. Indian literature is full of wise saws and sayings, and by merely quoting them a man may easily gain a reputation for profound wisdom. But it was not so with Râmakrishna.   He seems to have deeply meditated on the world from his solitary retreat.   Whether he was a man of extensive reading is difficult to say, but he was certainly thoroughly imbued with the spirit of the Vedânta philosophy.   His utterances which have been published breathe the spirit of that philosophy; in fact are only intelligible as products of a Vedântic soil. And yet it is very curious to see how European thought, nay a certain European style, quite different from that of native thinkers, has found an entrance into the oracular sayings of this Indian saint.   It is difficult to say whether the Vedânta is a philosophy or a religion. It seems to be both, according to the disposition of its followers or believers.   Nor is it possible to speak of the Vedânta without distinguishing between its two schools.   These schools, though they adopt the same name and follow the same authorities, chiefly the *Upanishads* and the *Brahma-Sûtras*, differ on points which form the very essence of any philosophy or religion.

We have first of all the *Advaita School* (non-duality school), which holds that there is only one reality which we should call the Infinite or the Absolute; while whatever is or seems to be finite and conditional is looked upon as unreal, as the result of ignorance which is called *Avidyâ* or *Mâyâ*.   The human soul is considered as identical with the infinite or the Brahman, separated from it in appearance only by *Avidyâ*, or ignorance, though in real reality always Brahman, nay, the whole undivided Brahman, which is supposed to be present or to form the substance of every apparently individual soul.

The second school, called *Visishtâdvaita*, or *Advaita*, non-duality with a difference, was evidently intended for a larger public, for those who could not bring themselves to deny altogether some reality to the phenomenal world, some individuality to their own souls.   Which of the two schools was the more ancient and most in harmony with the teaching of the Veda is difficult to say.   At the present moment, and as far back as about the eighth century of our era, the rigidly monistic school is represented by Sankara, the more practical and accommodating school by Râmânuga (twelfth century).   Sankara makes no concession of any kind.   He begins and never parts with his conviction that whatever is is one and the same in itself, without variableness or shadow of turning.   This Brahman does not possess being and thinking as qualities, but it is both being and thinking.   No qualities whatever can be predicated of Brahman, and to every attempt to define it Sankara has but one answer, No, no!   When, however, the question is asked as to the cause of what cannot be denied, namely, the manifold phenomenal world, the individual subjects, and the individual objects, all that Sankara condescends to say is that their cause is *Avidyâ*, or *nescience*. Here is what strikes a Western mind as the weak point of the Vedânta philosophy. We should say that even this *Avidyâ*, which causes the phenomenal world to appear, must have some real cause; but Sankara does not allow this, and repeats again and again that, as an illusion, nescience is neither real nor unreal, but is like our ignorance when, for instance, we imagine we see a serpent, while what we really see is a rope, and yet we run away from it as if it were a real cobra. This nescience being once granted, everything else proceeds smoothly enough. Brahman as held by *Avidyâ* seems modified into all that is phenomenal. First of all we get names and forms (*nâmarûpa*) coming very near to the Greek λόγοι, or the archetypes of everything. Then follow the material elements, which constitute animal bodies and the whole objective world. But all this is illusive. There are no individual things, there are no individual souls (*gîvas*); they only seem to exist as long as nescience prevails over Brahman. If you ask what is real in all things and in all individual souls, the answer is, Brahman, the One without a Second; but this answer can be understood by those only who know *Avidyâ*, and by knowing it have destroyed it. Others believe that they are this or that, and that the world is this and that. Man thinks he is the ego dwelling in the body, seeing and hearing, comprehending and naming, reasoning and acting, while the true self lies deep below the ego or *aham* which belongs to the world of illusion. As an ego man has become an actor and an enjoyer, instead of a distant witness of the world. He is then carried along in the *sansâra*, the concourse of the world; he becomes the slave of his acts (*karman*), and goes on from change to change, till in the end he discovers the true Brahman which alone exists, and which as being himself is called the *Atman*, or Self, and at the same time the *Paramâtman*, or the Highest Self. Good works are helpful in producing a proper state of mind for receiving knowledge but for nothing else, for it is by knowledge alone that man can be saved or obtain *mukti*, and not by good works. This salvation finds expression in the celebrated words *tat tvam asi*, thou art that, *i.e.* thou art not thou, but that, *i.e.* the only existing Brahman; thy Âtman (self) and Brahman are one and the same.

While Sankara is thus an unyielding Monist, and defies the evidence of the senses with a determined No, no, Râmânuga is less exacting. He is at one with Sankara in admitting that there can be only one thing, Brahman, but he allows what Sankara strenuously denies, that Brahman possesses attributes. His chief attribute, according to Râmânuga, is thought or intelligence, but he likewise possesses omnipotence, omniscience, kindness, and other good qualities. He possesses within itself or himself certain powers (*Saktis*), the seeds of plurality, so that both the material objects of our experience and the individual souls (*gîvas*) are real modifications of Brahman, not merely phenomena or illusions. In this modified capacity Brahman is conceived as *îsvara*, the Lord, and both the thinking (*kit*) and unthinking world (*akit*) are supposed to constitute his body. He is then .called the *antaryâmin*, the ruler within, so that the objects and the souls which he controls are entitled in their individuality to an independent reality which Sankara denied them. Though Râmânuga would hardly accept creation in our sense, he teaches evolution, or a process by which all that existed potentially or in a subtle form in the one Brahman, while in his undeveloped state (pralaya), became individual, gross, material, and perceptible. He distinguishes, in fact, between Brahman as a cause and Brahman as an effect, but he teaches at the same time that cause and effect are always the same, though the cause undergoes *parinâma*, i.e. development in order to become effect. Instead of being merely deceived (by *vivarta*), Brahman, according to Râmânuga, really changes, and thus what was potential at first becomes real at last. Another difference is that while Sankara's highest goal consists in Brahman recovering itself by knowledge, Râmânuga recognises the merit of good works, and allows the pure soul to rise by successive stages to the world of Brahman and to enjoy there perfeet felicity without fear of new births or of transmigration. The soul approaches Brahman, becomes like Brahman, and participates in all his powers except one, that of creating, that is sending forth the phenomenal world, governing it, and absorbing it again. Thus not only does Râmânuga allow reality to individual souls, but likewise to Îsvara, or the Lord, while with Sankara the Lord is as unreal as the individual soul, and both are real in their recovered identity only. What Râmânuga thus represents as the highest truth, and as the highest goal to be reached by a man seeking for salvation, is not altogether rejected by Sankara, but is looked upon by him as the lower knowledge. The Brahman reached on the lower stage is the *aparam*, the lower or the *sagunam*, i.e. the qualified Brahman. He is, in fact, the personal god, and often worshipped by the followers of Râmânuga under such popular names as *Vishnu* or *Nârâyana*. With Sankara this Îsvara would be the *pratika*, the outward appearance only; we might almost say the *persona* or the πρόσωπον of the highest Brahman and his worship (upâsanâ), though ignorant, might be tolerated as practically useful. It leads the virtuous man to eternal happiness after death, while true knowledge produces salvation, that is, recovered Brahmahood, even in this life (gîvanmukti), and freedom from *Karman* (works) and from transmigration hereafter.

This explains why the followers of these two schools have so long lived in peace and harmony together, though differing on what we should consider the most essential point, whether of a philosophy or a religion. The followers of Sankara do not accuse the followers of Râmânuga of error (mithyâdarsana), but only of nescience, or inevitable *Avidyâ*. The phenomenal world and the individual souls, though due to *Avidyâ*, are not entirely empty or false, but have their reality in Brahman, if only a pupil can be brought to see it. What is phenomenal is not nothing, but is the appearance of that which is alone real, the *Brahman*, the *Atman*, or, in Kantian language, *Das Ding an sich*. For all practical purposes (vyavahâra) the phenomenal world is real, for it would not even seem to exist without its foundation in *Brahman*. The only riddle that remains is the *Avidyâ*, or nescience, often called *Mâyâ*, or illusion. Sankara himself will neither say that it is real or that it is unreal. All that he can say is that it is there, and that it must be removed by *Vidyâ*, science, or by *Vedânta*, the philosophy of the Upanishads.

This is a short outline of the background from which such men as *Râmakrishna* and other honest Sannyâsins step out, calling upon the world to have their eyes opened and to discover the way to their true salvation. This is what they preach as Brahma-knowledge, or self-knowledge. The literature in which this Vedântic philosophy has been treated is enormous, and the definitions of every technical term are most accurate and strictly logical. But there is also a poetical spirit pervading this abstruse philosophy, and the metaphors used for the illustration of the most recondite problems are often most striking.

In the extracts from *Râmakrishna's* teachings, some of which have been published by his pupils in their journal, the *Brahmavâdin*, these ancient metaphors have for the first time been blended with European thought; and from all that we learn of his personal influence, this blending had a most powerful effect on the large audiences that came to listen to him. He has left a number of pupils behind who after his recent death are carrying on the work which he began, and who are trying to secure, not only in India, but in Europe also, a sympathetic interest in the ancient philosophy of India, which it deserves as fully as the philosophy of Plato or Kant.

Precepts of Râmakrishna Paramahansa.

(1)
Like unto a miser that longeth after gold, let thy heart pant after Him.

(2)
How to get rid of the lower self. The blossom vanishes of itself as the fruit grows, so will your lower self vanish as the Divine grows in you.

(3)
There is always a shadow under the lamp while its light illumines the surrounding objects. So the men in the immediate proximity of a prophet do not understand him, while those who lie far off are charmed by his spirit and extraordinary power.

(4)
So long as the heavenly expanse of the heart is troubled and disturbed by the gusts of desire, there is little chance of our beholding therein the luminary God. The beatific godly vision occurs only in the heart which is calm and wrapped in Divine communion.

(5)

So long as the bee is outside the petals of the flower, it buzzes and emits sounds. But when it is inside the flower, the sweetness thereof has silenced and overpowered the bee. Forgetful of sounds and of itself, it drinks the nectar in quiet. Men of learning, you too are making a noise in the world, but know the moment you get the slightest enjoyment of the sweetness of *Bhakti* (love of God) you will be like the bee in the flower inebriated with the nectar of Divine love.

(6)

The soiled mirror never reflects the rays of the sun, so the impure and the unclean in heart that are subject to Mâyâ (illusion) never perceive the glory of Bhagavân, the Holy One. But the pure in heart see the Lord as the clear mirror reflects the sun. So be holy.

(7)

As the light of a lamp dispels in a moment the darkness that has reigned for a hundred years in a room, so a single ray of Divine light from the throne of mercy illumines our heart and frees it from the darkness of life-long sins.

(8)

As one and the same material, viz. water, is called by different names by different peoples—one calling it *water*, another *vári*, a third *aqua*, and another *páni*—so the one *sat-chit-ánanda*—the One that is, that perceives, and is full of bliss—is invoked by some as God, by some as Allah, by some as Hari, and by others as Brahman.

(9)

A recently married young woman remains deeply absorbed in the performance of domestic duties, so long as no child is born to her. But no sooner is a son born to her than she begins to neglect household details, and does not find much pleasure in them. Instead thereof she fondles the new-born baby all the live-long day and kisses it with intense joy. Thus man in his state of ignorance is ever busy in the performance of all sorts of works, but as soon as he sees in his heart the Almighty God he finds no pleasure in them. On the contrary his happiness consists now only in serving God and doing His works. He no longer finds happiness in any other occupation, and cannot withdraw himself from the ecstasy of the Holy Communion.

(10)

When the Jews saw the body of Jesus nailed on to the Cross, how was it that Jesus, in spite of so much pain and suffering, prayed that they should be forgiven ? When an ordinary cocoanut is pierced through, the nail enters the kernel of the nut. But in the case of the dry nut the kernel becomes separate from the shell, and when the shell is pierced the kernel is not touched. Jesus was like the dry nut, *i.e.* His inner soul was separate from His physical shell; consequently the sufferings of the body did not affect Him. Though the nails were driven through and through, He could pray with calm tranquillity for the good of His enemies.

(11)

As one can ascend the top of a house by means of a ladder, or a bamboo, or a staircase, or a rope, so divers are the ways and means to approach God, and every religion in the world shows one of these ways.

(12)

Many are the names of God, and infinite the forms that lead us to know Him. In whatsoever name or form you desire to know Him, in that very name and form you will know Him.

(13)

Why can we not see the Divine Mother? She is like a high-born lady, transacting all her business from behind the screen—seeing all, but seen by none. Her devout sons only see Her by going near Her behind the screen of *Máyâ*.

(14)

You see many stars at night in the sky, but find them not when the sun rises. Can you say that there are no stars in the heaven of day? So, O man! because you behold not God in the days of your ignorance say not that there is no God.

(15)

In the play of hide-and-seek, if the player succeeds in touching the grand dame (*Boori*), he is no longer liable to be made a thief of by the seeker. Similarly, by once seeing God, man is no longer bound down by the fetters of the world. Just as the person touching the *Boori* is free to go about wherever he chooses without being pursued and made a thief of, so also in this world's playground there is no fear to him who has once touched the feet of God. He attains freedom from all wordly cares and anxieties, and nothing can ever bind him again.

(16)

If a single dive into the sea does not bring you any pearl, do not conclude that the sea is without pearls. Dive again and again, and you are sure to be rewarded in the end. So if your first attempt to see God proves fruitless, do not lose heart. Persevere in the attempt, and you are sure to obtain Divine grace at last.

(17)

A young plant should always be protected by a fence from the mischief of goats and cows and little urchins. But when once it becomes a big tree a flock of goats or a herd of cows may find shelter under its spreading boughs, and fill their stomachs with its leaves. So when you have but little faith within you, you should protect it from the evil influences of bad company and worldliness. But when once you grow strong in faith no worldliness or evil inclination will dare approach your holy presence, and many who are wicked will become godly through your holy contact.

(18)

Where does the strength of an aspirant lie? It is in his tears. As a mother gives her consent to fulfil the desire of her importunately weeping child, so God vouchsafes to His weeping son whatever he is crying for.

(19)

Meditate on God either in an unknown corner, or in the solitude of forests, or within your own mind.

(20)

If you can detect and find out the universal illusion or *Máyâ*, it will fly away from you just as a thief runs away when found out.

(21)

Should we pray aloud unto God? Pray unto Him in any way you like. He is sure to hear you, for He can hear even the footfall of an ant.

(22)

The pearl-oyster that contains the precious pearl is in itself of very little value, but it is essential for the growth of the pearl. The shell itself may prove to be of no use to the man who has got the pearl. So ceremonies and rites may not be necessary for him who has attained the Highest Truth—God.

(23)

High up in the pure regions under the azure sky the vultures keep soaring on, but have their eyes always directed to the carrion in the field beneath. So worldly men of learning exhibit to all around them their high attainments by clever expositions of sublime spiritual truths and by the utterance of noble sentiments becoming a sage, but their minds are all along secretly and inwardly turned to the attainment of the nearest objects of the earth—to the glamour of shining gold, and the vain applause of worldly men.

(24)

A little boy wearing the mask of the lion's head looks indeed very terrible. He goes where his little sister is at play, and yells out hideously, which at once shocks and terrifies his sister, making her cry out in the highest pitch of her voice in the agony of despair to escape from the clutch of the terrible being. But when her little tormentor puts off the mask the frightened girl at once recognises her loving brother, and flies up to him exclaiming, ' Oh! it is my dear brother after all.' Even such is the case of all the men of the world who are deluded and frightened and led to do all sorts of things by the nameless power of *Máyá*, or Nescience, under the mask of which *Brahman* hides himself. But when the veil of *Máyá* is taken off from *Brahman*, the men then do not see in him a terrible and uncompromising Master, but their own beloved Other Self.

(25)

The vanities of all others may gradually die out, but the vanity of a saint as regards his sainthood is hard indeed to wear away.

(26)

Question: Where is God? How can we get to Him? Answer: There are pearls in the sea : one must dive deep again and again until he gets the pearls. So there is God in the world ; you should persevere to see Him

(27)

How does a true lover see his God? He sees Him as his nearest and dearest relative, just as the shepherd women of Brindâvan saw in Sri Krishna, not the Lord of the Universe (Jagannâtha), but their own beloved one (Gopinâth, the lord of the shepherdesses).

(28)

A boat may stay in the water, but water should not stay in the boat. An aspirant may live in the world, but the world should not live in him.

(29)

What you think you should say. Let there be harmony between your thoughts and words ; otherwise if you merely tell that God is your all in all, while your mind has made the world its all in all, you cannot derive any benefit thereby.

(30)

As when fishes are caught in a net some do not struggle at all but remain calm in the net, some again struggle hard to come out of the net, while a few are very happy in effecting their escape by rending the net, so there are three sorts of men, viz. fettered (*Baddha*), struggling (*Mumukshu*), released (*Mukta*).

(31)

If in all the different religious systems of the world there reigns the same God, then why does the same God appear different when viewed in different lights by different religions? God is one, but many are His aspects. The head of a family, an individual person, is the father of one, the brother of a second, and the husband of a third. The relations or aspects are different, but the man is the same.

POSTSCRIPT.—It was not easy to obtain any trustworthy information about the circumstances of the Mahâtman's life, a life singularly uneventful in his relations with the outer world, though full of stirring events in the inner world of his mind. The following information came to me from India after my article was in type. He was born in 1835 in a village near Jahanabad (Hoogly District) called *K*amarpukur. His chief place of residence is said to have been at the celebrated Rani Rashmoni's temple of Kali on the bank of the Bhagirathî (Ganges) at Dakshineswar, a northern suburb of Calcutta. He died in 1886 in the Kasipur garden, two miles north of Calcutta, and was cremated at the Baranagore Burning Ghat where a Bel tree marks the spot. His ashes have been interred in the garden of the temple of Kacurgachee, about a mile east of the Manicktolla Bridge, Calcutta.

Protap Chunder Mozoomdar, the leader of the Brahma Samâj, and well known to many people in England, tells me of the extraordinary influence which the Mahâtman exercised on Keshub Chunder Sen, on himself, and on a large number of highly educated men in Calcutta. A score of young men who were more closely attached to him have become ascetics after his death. They follow his teaching by giving up the enjoyment of wealth and carnal pleasure, living together in a neighbouring Matha (college), and retiring at times to holy and solitary places all over India even as far as the Himalayan mountains. Besides these holy men, we are told that a great number of men with their families are ardently devoted to his cause. But what is most interesting is the fact that it was the Mahâtman who exercised the greatest influence on Keshub Chunder Sen during the last phase of his career. It was a surprise to many of Keshub Chunder's friends and admirers to observe the sudden change of the sober reformer into the mystic and ecstatic saint, that took place towards the end of his life. But although this later development of the New Dispensation, and more particularly the doctrine of the motherhood of God, may have alienated many of Keshub Chunder Sen's European friends, it seems to have considerably increased his popularity with Hindu society. At all events we are now enabled to understand the hidden influences which caused so sudden a change, and produced so marked a deviation in the career of the famous founder of the Brahma-Samâj, which has sometimes been ascribed to the breakdown of an over-excited brain.

It is different with a man like Râmakrishṇa. He never moved in the world, or was a man of the world, even in the sense in which Keshub Chunder Sen was. He seems from the very first to have practised that very severe kind of asceticism (Yoga) which is intended to produce trances (samâdhi) and ecstatic utterances. We cannot quite understand them, but in the case of our Mahâtman we cannot doubt their reality, and can only stand by and wonder, particularly wheri so; much that seems to us the outcome of a broken frame of body and an overwrought state of mind, contains nevertheless so much that is true and , wise , and beautiful. , Protap Chunder Mozoomdar, who was fully aware that his friend was considered by many, particularly by missionaries, as a self-deluded enthusiast, nay, as an impostor, gives us the following account of him when his influence was at its height. 'The Hindu saint,' he writes, 'is now a man under forty, he is a Brahmin by caste, he is well-formed in body, but the dreadful austerities through which his character has developed appear to have permanently disordered his system, and inflicted a debility, paleness, and shrunkenness upon his form and features that excite compassion. Yet in the midst of this emaciation his face retains a fulness, a childlike tenderness, a profound visible humbleness, an unspeakable sweetness of expression, and a smile that I have seen in no other face. A Hindu saint is always particular about his externals. He wears the *garua* cloth, eats according to strict forms, refuses to have intercourse with men, and is a rigid observer of caste. He is always proud and professes secret wisdom. He is always a *Gurugi*, a universal counsellor, and dispenser of charms. This man, Râmakrishna, is singularly devoid of any such claims. His dress and diet do not differ from those of other men, except in the general negligence he shows towards both ; and as to caste, he openly breaks it every day. He repudiates the title of a teacher or *Guru*, he shows displeasure at any exceptional honour which people try to pay to him, and he emphatically disclaims the knowledge of secrets and mysteries.' This shows that he never was an occultist or esoteric Mahâtman. Mozoomdar declares that his religion was orthodox Hinduism, but, as it would seem, of a very strange type. He worshipped no particular Hindu deity. He was not a worshipper of Siva, of Vish*n*u, or of the *S*aktis. He would not even be considered as a professed Vedântist. And yet, according to Mozoomdar, 'he accepted all the doctrines, the ʿembodiments, the usages and devotional practices of every religious cult. Each in turn was infallible to him. He was an idolater, and yet most faithful and devoted in his meditations on the perfections of the one formless, infinite Deity whom he terms *Akhanda Sach-chid-ânanda, i.e.* the indivisible, real, intelligent, and blissful. His religion, unlike the religion of ordinary Hindu Sâdhus, did not mean much dogma, or controversial proficiency, or outward worship with flowers and sandal, incense and offerings. His religion meant ecstasy, his worship transcendental insight, his whole nature burnt day and night with the permanent fire and fever of a strange faith and feeling. His conversation was a ceaseless breaking forth of his inward fire and lasted for long hours. He was often merged in rapturous ecstasy and outward unconsciousness during the day, particularly when he spoke of his favourite spiritual experiences or heard any striking response to them. Though he did not worship the Hindu deities in the ordinary fashion, each of them was to him a force, an incarnate principle tend.ing to reveal the supreme relation of the soul to that eternal and formless Being who is unchangeable in his blessedness and light of wisdom.'

This last sentence does not convey any very clear meaning. What Râmakrishna seems to have meant when he represented Siva, Krish*na*, and other gods as helping to reveal the eternal and formless Being could only have been the Vedânta doctrine, as explained by Râmânu*g*a, namely, that these gods and even the Lord himself, when conceived as Creator and Ruler of the world (the Îsvara), are only so many forms or persons behind which the true Being (Brahman) must be discovered ; that they are not real in the highest sense of reality, but that nevertheless their phenomenal character derives some reality from their being the transitory manifestations of the only true Being, the Brahman without a second. 'Brahman alone is true, all else is false.' Krish*na*, a god, according to our ideas, of very doubtful antecedents, became to him the incarnation of *bhakti*, or loving devo-tion, and we are told that while meditating on him, his heart full of the burning love of God, the features of the Mahâtman would sud-denly grow stiff and motionless, his eyes lose their sight, and while completely unconscious himself, tears would run down his rigid, pale, yet smiling face. His disciple says : 'Who will fathom the depth of that insensibility which the love of God produces ? But that he sees something, hears and enjoys when he is dead to the outward world, there is no doubt. Or why should he in the midst of that unconsciousness burst into floods of tears, and break out into prayers, song and utterances, the force and pathos of which pierce through the hardest heart, and bring tears to eyes that never wept before through the influence of religion ? '

I have given this description as I find it. I know I can trust the writer, who is a friend of mine and has lived long enough in England and in India to be able to distinguish between the language of honest religious enthusiasm and the empty talk of professional impostors. The state of religious exaltation as here described has been witnessed again and again by serious observers of exceptional psychic states. It is in its essence something like our talking in sleep, only that with a mind saturated with religious thoughts and with the sublimest ideas of goodness and purity the result is what we find in the case of Râmakrishna, no mere senseless hypnotic jabbering, but a spontaneous outburst of profound wisdom clothed in beautiful poetical language. His mind seems like a kaleidoscope of pearls, diamonds, and sapphires, shaken together at random, but always producing precious thoughts in regular, beautiful outlines. To our ears, no doubt, much of his teaching and preaching sounds strange, but not to Oriental ears, or to ears accustomed to the perfervid poetry of the East. Everything seems to become purified in his mind. Nothing, I believe, is so hideous as the popular worship of Kali in India. To Râmakrishna all that is repulsive in her character is, as it were, non-existent, and there remains but the motherhood of the goddess. Her adoration with him is a childlike, whole-souled, rapturous self-consecration to the motherhood of God, as represented by the power and influence of woman. Woman in her natural material character had long been renounced by the saint. He had a wife, but never associated with her. 'Woman,' he said, 'fascinates and keeps the world from the love of God.' For long years he made the utmost efforts to be delivered from the influence of woman. His heartrending supplications and prayers for such deliverance, sometimes uttered aloud in his retreat on the riverside, brought crowds of people, who bitterly cried when he cried, and could not help blessing him and wishing him success with their whole hearts. And he succeeded, so that his mother to whom he prayed, that is the goddess Kali, made him recognise every woman as her incarnation, and honour each member of the other sex, whether young or old, as his mother. In one of his prayers he exclaims : ' O Mother Divine, I want no honour from man, I want no pleasure of the flesh ; only let my soul flow into Thee as the permanent confluence of the Gangâ and Jamunâ. Mother, I am without *bhakti* (devotion), without *yoga* (concentration); I am poor and friendless. I want no one's praise, only let my mind always dwell in the lotus of thy feet.' But what is the most extraordinary of all, his religion was not confined to the worship of Hindu deities and the purification of Hindu customs. For long days he subjected himself to various kinds of discipline to realise the Mohammedan idea of an all-powerful Allah. He let his beard grow, he fed himself on Moslem diet, he continually repeated sentences from the Koran. For Christ his reverence was deep and genuine. He bowed his head at the name of Jesus, honoured the doctrine of his sonship, and once or twice attended Christian places of worship. He declared that each form of worship was to him a living and most enthusiastic principle of personal religion ; he showed, in fact, how it was possible to unify all the religions of the world by seeing only what is good in every one of them, and showing sincere reverence to every one who has suffered for the truth, for their faith in God, and for their love of men. He seems to have left nothing in writing, but his sayings live in the memory of his friends. He would not be a master or the founder of a new sect. ' I float a frail half-sunk log of wood through the stream of the troublous world. If men come to hold by me to save their lives, the result will be that they will drown me without being able to save themselves. Beware of Gurus ! '

F. MAX MÜLLER.

ARBITRATION WITH AMERICA

THERE may possibly be two opinions as to the course that Lord
Salisbury has taken in making public the correspondence with the
Government of the United States, in an intermediate stage, while
negotiations are still pending. It may be said by some that both
the petty question (and it will be ridiculous or criminal if it ever
becomes more than a petty question) of Venezuela, and the great
question of a general treaty of obligatory arbitration in all or some
classes of dispute between ourselves and the United States, are
matters which the executive power should deal with on its own
responsibility, and should make up its own mind without seeking
outside counsel in the middle of the voyage as to the tack on which
they would do best to sail. 'We have need to know,' Lord Salisbury
explained to the House of Lords (July 17), 'what is the trend of
public opinion on these matters. We desire, in a question which is
certainly not one of party, that the best intellects that we have on
both sides should apply themselves to a matter that affects the welfare of the human race in a singular degree, and especially the
good relations of a State with which we so desire to be on good
terms as the United States of America. Therefore we have laid the
papers on the table, and we hope to derive from such attention as
noble lords on both sides of the House may devote to them, *much
guidance with respect to the subsequent conduct* of the negotiations
that we have to pursue.' All this would have made Lord Palmerston
and the Foreign Office of his day gasp with horror, and I do not
know that one could pay Lord Salisbury a higher compliment.

The Prime Minister would hardly have taken this unusual though
perfectly defensible step, or have invited public discussion of negotiations still pending, unless he believed that the two governments were
approaching pretty closely within sight of one another, and that
public discussion would supply whatever momentum may be required
for overcoming the obstacles that still remain. The papers themselves confirm this impression. They deal with two matters—first,
the dispute with Venezuela, and second, proposals for a general
scheme of arbitration, which the question of the Venezuelan

boundary brought once more into prominence. On the first of these issues, as can easily be shown, the difference between the British and American Governments has become so narrow, that a rupture would be preposterous and intolerable. On the second, though the principles at stake go deeper, and demand a wider survey, yet things have advanced far enough to justify Mr. Olney's hope in the closing despatch of the series (June 22) that 'persistent effort in the line of the pending negotiations will have results which, if not all that the enthusiastic advocates of international arbitration anticipate, will be a decided advance upon anything heretofore achieved in that direction.'

In spite of the promising aspect of either of the two questions, Lord Salisbury's speech, his publication of the papers, and the papers themselves, all indicate that, both in the narrower and the broader issue, a miscarriage of the event is still possible. This would not be the first time in history that a favourable moment had been allowed to pass; that an indolent assumption that things were sure to turn out well, was the very circumstance that ensured their turning out ill; that an excessive fear of a too rapid or summary decision ended in smothering the whole faculty of decision; and that an easy-going trust in Providence and a fatalistic confidence in the wisdom of Downing Street lulled the nation into a slumber from which they awoke to find a very disagreeable storm whistling about their ears. What is important for us at the present hour is that as many people as possible in this country should know both plainly and precisely how matters stand between ourselves and the American Government, what position is taken by Lord Salisbury and what by Mr. Olney, and what are the definite points on which the Prime Minister desires to ascertain 'the trend of public opinion.'

Whatever may be said for it or against it, we must bear in mind that the American position on the question of Venezuela is not affected by proposals for a general scheme of arbitration. The American Government stands in that matter just where it stood before. Writing so late as the 12th of June, Mr. Olney says with some emphasis : [1]

I deem it advisable to recall attention to the fact that, so far as the Venezuela boundary dispute is concerned, the position of this Government has been plainly defined, not only by the Executive but by the unanimous concurring action of both branches of Congress. A genuine arbitration issuing in an Award, and finally disposing of the controversy, whether under a special or a general Treaty of Arbitration, would be entirely consistent with that position, and will be cordially welcomed by this Government. On the other hand, while a Treaty of General Arbitration providing for a tentative decision merely upon territorial claims, though not all that this Government deems desirable or feasible, might nevertheless be accepted by it as a step in the right direction, it would not, under the circumstances, feel at liberty to include the Venezuelan boundary dispute within the scope of

_____

[1] Enclosure 3 in No. 24.

such a Treaty. It is deemed advisable to be thus explicit in the interest of both Governments, that the pending negotiations for a general Treaty of Arbitration may proceed without any misapprehension.

We shall see more particularly what Mr. Olney means by the distinction between a genuine arbitration issuing in an award, and a merely tentative decision on territorial claims. Meanwhile, whatever form the general treaty may· ultimately take, it is well to remember that the secondary but more dangerous question still confronts us, as it confronted us six months ago. The telegram of the correspondent of the *Times* (July 19) contains a comment on the above passage which ought not to be overlooked, to whatever determination we may incline ultimately to come :

> That is equivalent to saying that, in the event of a report from the present Commission adverse to the British claims and a refusal of Great Britain to accept that report and retire from the territory declared to be Venezuelan, the menace of the President's Message would become operative.
>
> There is reason to believe that this contingency is kept steadily in view in Washington, and that the President, with the memories of last December fresh in his mind, still thinks that, should the need arise, a reassertion of his former warning would be supported by the multitudes who supported him before. He is still President, and will remain President till next March. His personal influence has waned, but the authority of his great office is what it was. If he tried to use it to revive the animosities of last winter, he would probably fail. Still, few Americans wish to see such an experiment tried or would be perfectly confident of the result.

A series of despatches is seldom very easy reading, and in the present instance the arrangement tends to confuse two questions which, though not wholly unconnected, are practically distinct, and ought to be considered separately. It may be useful, therefore, to set out pretty briefly the contents of these most interesting and important papers. Three or four pages will suffice to present the Venezuelan question, and the question of a permanent tribunal of arbitration, as each of them now stands. The former is, for various reasons, much the more pressing, contains more elements of real and actual peril, and ought less than any other to be allowed to drift.

So far as the Venezuelan question goes, it is hardly possible that Lord Salisbury can have a shadow of doubt as to ' the trend of public opinion.' A quarrel with America on the question of arbitrating a boundary line that has been in active and lively dispute at intermittent periods for more than half a century, has been viewed from the first with the deepest incredulity and abhorrence. It is safe to say that this feeling will grow a thousand times stronger when the public have mastered, as half a dozen pages of these papers enable them to do, the point to which the controversy has now been contracted.

This is not the place for any inquiry into the merits of the respective claims of the British and Venezuelan Governments to the territory in dispute between them. Whether the Aberdeen line, the

Schomburgk line, the Granville line, the Rojas line, be the boundary best justified by the history of the matter; whether grants from Popes or ancient treaties with aboriginal tribes are of any valid force; to what extent the exploration of streams and tributaries, and the constitution of post-holders by the Dutch, or the recognition by the Spanish of this river or that as the frontier of Spanish possessions —all these and the thousand obscure and intricate questions of fact through which the industrious reader may, if he pleases, thread his way in the heavy jungles of the two bluebooks, are happily not to the purpose now. The more diligently one endeavours to master this entangled mass, the clearer does it become that the whole field of the controversy, settled lands and all, presents matters with two sides to them, and claims for all of which something is to be said, and that if ever there was in the world a set of circumstances proper for arbitration, and if ever arbitration is to be good for any case, this is such a case. The question discussed here is whether there should be an unrestricted arbitration, with a final settlement for its result; or a limited arbitration, with only an optional acceptance of any award that should go beyond these limits.

In his speech in the House of Lords, the Prime Minister seems to have used some language that rather understates the extent to which the correspondence shows him to have been willing to go in meeting the American Government.

The difficulty lies in the fact that the claim of Venezuela embraces a very large proportion—I think two-thirds—of the colony of British Guiana, including a considerable quantity of territory *that is settled and that has been settled for a great number of years.* We have never thought, and *we do not now think,* that the ownership of that territory is a matter which ought to be submitted to arbitration. At the same time, with respect to the unsettled territory, we have always been willing that that should be submitted to arbitration, but it is necessary, of course, to distinguish between the two. Our view has been that at this stage arbitration is not a suitable remedy; that the first thing which has to be ascertained is the real state of the facts in respect to the past history of Venezuela and of Spain and of Holland in those countries; and, when the facts are fully ascertained by a Commission in which both countries have confidence, I do not myself believe that the diplomatic question that will follow will be one that will be very difficult of adjustment. When once we know what the facts are, I do not think there will be much difficulty in coming to an agreement as to their result. But even if there is, that would then be the time for applying the principle of arbitration. In order that arbitration may be satisfactory, the issue presented to it should be clean, clear, and simple; and when we know enough of the facts to be able to say what are the precise points on which the two Governments differ on the question of boundaries, I think then the question of arbitration will probably be dealt with without difficulty and without involving—what we deprecate—*exposing to the hazard of a tribunal which is comparatively untried the long-inherited and long-possessed rights of British colonies.*

From the first, says Lord Salisbury, 'our objection has been to subject to the decision of an arbiter, who, in the last resort, must of necessity be a foreigner, the rights of British colonists who have settled in territory which they had every ground for believing to be British, and whose careers would be broken, and their fortunes possibly ruined, by a decision that the territory on which they have settled was subject to the Venezuelan Republic.'

It is worth while to note in passing that the papers shed no light on the number, quality, situation, or other particulars of these colonists. Mr. Olney asks for information as to the precise meaning attached by the Government to the expression of ' settled districts,' and Lord Salisbury promises to communicate this desire to the Secretary of State for the Colonies. So far, the result has not been made public. Yet the point is of much practical importance. The exact magnitude of these colonising operations does not affect the right and wrong of the matters in issue; it does not touch the general duty and obligation of protecting British colonists in their lawful rights. But the magnitude of the colonising operations has much to do with the expediencies of the particular problem. As we shall see in a moment or two, Lord Salisbury does not shut out these colonists from possibility of treatment. And in any event, if public opinion is to be consulted, it is indispensable that we should know, in an exact and concrete way, what is the size of the obstacle to such an arbitration as would finally dispose of the possibilities of a dangerous quarrel. There is no objection to a little rhetoric. But besides rhetoric, we must have arithmetic and mensuration.

Lord Salisbury's proposed basis of settlement is as follows:—[2]

1. A commission of four, two British and two American, to investigate and report upon the facts of the Dutch and Spanish rights respectively at the date of the acquisition of the Dutch territory by Great Britain.

2. Upon the finding of this commission as to the historic facts, the two governments to try to agree to a boundary line.

3. If they cannot agree, a tribunal of three to be appointed—one nominated by England, another by the United States, and a third nominated by these two, and the three to fix the boundary line upon the basis of the report of the commission of four, and this line so fixed to be binding upon England and Venezuela. Here, however, we come on the fatal proviso: ' Provided always that, in fixing such line, the Tribunal shall not have power to include as the territory of Venezuela, any territory which was *bona fide* occupied by subjects of Great Britain on the 1st of January 1887.' This is the sharp stumbling-block which at the present moment threatens to break off negotiations.

Lord Salisbury, however, speedily takes a long stride towards its removal by adding a remarkable rider to his proviso. ' In respect ' he says, ' to any territory with which, by this provision, the Tribunal is precluded from dealing, the Tribunal may submit to the two Powers

[2] No. 17, May 22, 1896.

any recommendations which seem to it calculated to satisfy the equitable rights of the parties, and the two Powers will take such recommendations into their consideration.' That is to say, it may inquire into the case of the settled lands, may arrive at a decision about them, and may make recommendations about them, but neither decision nor recommendations will be absolutely binding. This opens a very wide door.

The position of the British Government is concisely summed up by Lord Salisbury in the closing sentences of the despatch :—

It will be evident from this proposal that we are prepared to accept the finding of a Commission voting as three to one upon all the facts which are involved in the question of Dutch and Spanish rights at the time of the cession of Guiana to Great Britain. We are also prepared to accept the decision of an arbitral Tribunal with regard to the ownership of all portions of the disputed territory which are not under settlement by British subjects or Venezuelan citizens. *If the decision of the Commission shall affect any territory which is so settled, it will be in the power of either Government to decline to accept the decision so arrived at so far as it affects the territory alleged to be settled. But I need not point out to you that even upon that question, although the decision of the arbitral Tribunal will not have a final effect, it will, unless it be manifestly unfair, offer a presumption, against which the protesting Government will practically find it difficult to contend.*

Obviously, if this is a very weak position in one respect, it is just, on that account, very encouraging in another. Surely the last sentence comes very near to that exposure to the hazards of an untried tribunal of the long-inherited and long-possessed rights of British colonies, against which Lord Salisbury in his speech protested. ' I will not accept an unrestricted arbitration about the settled districts,' says Lord Salisbury, ' but I shall not complain if the Tribunal should choose to make an unrestricted award even about the settled districts ; and, between ourselves, I may tell you in confidence that unless the award about the settled districts were manifestly unfair, I should find it impossible to resist.' In other words, broken careers and ruined fortunes or not, Lord Salisbury admits that the decision of the Tribunal against the title of the British occupiers would raise so strong a presumption that it would not be much less difficult to resist than if it were a definite award. That is where Lord Salisbury stands. Now for the American Secretary of State.

Mr. Olney, in reply, says that his Government with regret find themselves unable to regard the English proposals as likely to bring the boundary dispute to a speedy conclusion, or as duly recognising the just rights of the parties concerned. Your Commission of Facts, Mr. Olney argues in effect,[3] will probably stand two and two, and so no decision will be reached. The chances of a peaceful settlement will even be made worse rather than better, because each party will be hardened in the conviction of the soundness of its own contention.

---

[3] Enclosure in No. 25, June 12, 1896.

Therefore the Commission of Facts should be so formed, by adding one or more members, that it must reach a conclusion.

In the next place, Mr. Olney proceeds, this Commission of Facts is confined to the facts of the year 1796. But how are you going to ascertain the facts about the occupied lands which you withdraw from arbitration? Who is to find out for us what and where these settlements exactly are? You talk of *bona fide* occupation. How are we to get at the circumstances showing the *bona fides* of the occupation? Yet the Tribunal of Three are to make recommendations about the settled lands, if they should be so minded. How can they do that, unless they have supplied themselves with a report of all the facts and circumstances of the settlements? In any case the Tribunal of Three will be bound to receive, and will undoubtedly have laid before them, all matters pertaining to *bona fide* occupation by settlers. This you cannot prevent. Surely the sensible course would be to invest the Commission of Facts with the power of reporting upon all the facts necessary to the decision of the boundary question, including the facts of the occupation of the disputed territory by British subjects?

So much for two comparatively minor matters. There is no room for quarrel about either of them, and Lord Salisbury will undoubtedly make no difficulty either about adding a new member to the Commission of Facts, or about including all the facts within the scope of the inquiry.

Mr. Olney then proceeds to press more closely to the heart of the thing. You tell us, he says, that if the Tribunal of Three should fix as the true boundary a line cutting off from your territory lands *bona fide* occupied by a British subject, that line must be so deflected in every case of that sort as to make such lands British.[4] By what conceivable course of argument can this exclusion of the occupied lands from arbitration be justified? Is the rule you lay down just in itself, so as to give England a right to impose her will upon Venezuela in the matter?

Suppose it to be true that there are British subjects who, to quote the despatch, 'have settled in territory which they had every ground for believing to be British,' the grounds for such belief were not derived from Venezuela. They emanated solely from the British Government, and 'if British subjects have been deceived by the assurances of their Government, it is matter wholly between them and their own Government, and in no way concerns Venezuela. Venezuela is not to be stripped of her rightful possessions because the British Government has erroneously encouraged its subjects to

---

[4] Of course, Lord Salisbury proposed that the same rule should apply to a case of territory *bona fide* occupied by a Venezuelan. But, as matter of pretty obvious fact, the rule would undoubtedly serve the interest of England, and prejudice the interest of Venezuela.

believe that such possessions were British. Such a claim might be plausible if Venezuela had ever in any way, tacitly or in words, directly or indirectly, assented to it, or allowed the right of occupation morally to consolidate itself by any default of hers. Everybody knows that, on the contrary, Venezuela's claims and protests have been constant and emphatic. So, in short, the proviso about the occupied lands ought to disappear altogether. At any rate, you should agree to substitute for your proviso this proviso of ours, namely, that in fixing the true boundary line, 'if territory of one party be found in the occupation of the subjects or citizens of the other party, such weight and effect shall be given to such occupation as reason, justice, the rules of international law, and the equities of the particular case may appear to require.'

This last is the crucial and cardinal proposal in the controversy, and deserves the reader's closest [attention. Lord Salisbury says: 'I will not promise to accept the line which the arbitrators may find to be the true boundary, if it should prove to hand over to Venezuela lands in the occupation of British subjects. But I shall feel myself bound not to disregard any recommendations which the arbitrators may make as to these occupied lands, and which seem to be' "calculated to satisfy the equitable rights of the parties."' Mr. Olney says: 'Let the arbitrators draw the true boundary on the historic and legal merits of the case; if the arbitrators find British subjects in occupation of what, on the merits of the case, is established as Venezuelan territory, such weight and effect shall still be given to this occupation as international law and the equities of the particular matter may seem to require.' What Lord Salisbury desires, and rightly desires, is, as he says, to protect certain British colonists from having their careers broken and their fortunes possibly ruined. Mr. Olney is willing to direct the arbitrators to give such weight and effect to the position of these colonists as reason, justice, law, and the equities of the particular case may seem to require. But reason, justice, and the equities of the case would manifestly forbid the breaking of the careers and the ruin of the fortunes of men who had settled in the territory which they had every ground for believing to be British. Nobody who will take the trouble to scrutinise the difference between these two positions, and to realise how narrow it is—narrower, I think, than Lord Salisbury's speech would lead us to suppose—will doubt that an accommodation is inevitable, unless the same spirit of loitering which has for so many years haunted the Foreign Office in Venezuelan matters, should still preside over these negotiations.

A precedent has been mentioned which is worth recalling. Five years ago the French and the Dutch could not agree about a boundary in Guiana. They both held that a certain river was the boundary, but they disputed the identity of the river. One said that the river in question, as marked on the map, was a certain stream; the other said it was quite another stream. The question was referred to the Czar. The Czar declined to accept the task unless he was allowed to go into the whole question of the frontier. This was conceded. He decided that the Dutch were in the right, and that their river was the true boundary. But he added to his award the proviso—which is apt to the business that we now have in hand—that his award was to be without prejudice to the rights acquired *bona fide* by French settlers in the limits of the territory in dispute. This comes to pretty much the same thing as Mr. Olney's proviso; and who would say that the French would not have been wrong to refuse arbitration, lest they should be breaking the careers and possibly ruining the fortunes of the settlers whose rights the Czar thus safeguarded? Be the aptness of the particular precedent what it may, no reasonable man will deny that it is absolutely impossible for us to continue to hold ground which is capable of being fairly described, as it is fairly described, in such a way as this, that 'though the Arbitral Tribunal may find certain territory to belong to Venezuela, and may even find that there are no equities which should prevent her having it, whether she gets it or not is to depend upon the good pleasure of Great Britain—upon her generosity, her sense of justice, her caprice, or her views of expediency generally.' This is not a position in which, I venture to hope and believe, the trend of public opinion in this country is at all likely to leave the question.

Let us now turn to the larger sphere of discussion—to the scheme for a treaty of obligatory arbitration between ourselves and the United States, and a permanent tribunal for conducting such proceedings, as they may arise. No fault can be found with Lord Salisbury for proceeding, as he says, with 'very considerable caution and circumspection.' The more thoroughly he now explores doubts and difficulties, the more likely he is at the end of his journey to achieve a solid and stable result. The attempt to reduce a deep and general sentiment to practical working shape is novel. An untried field may conceal many possibilities of hazard and surprise. The Minister of a great State cannot afford to expose any vital part of its interests or its strength to any avoidable risk. The British Empire is unlike any other that the world now sees or has ever seen, in the multiplicity, the diversity, the complication, the interdependence of all its relations and concerns by land and by sea, and its rulers are under an unsleeping obligation not to be tempted, for the sake of healing a mischief in a part, to overlook the possibility of mischief to the vast whole. The spirit of international peace has dreams as the spirit of conquest has them, and it is possible that a policy of adventure in pursuit of the blessings of peace might bring with it as many dangers as a policy of adventure in the less blessed sphere of aggrandisement and war.

On the other hand, Lord Salisbury, though he shows abundance of incidental acuteness and sagacity, hardly conducts the controversy with the vigorous grasp of a man who has energetically thought the thing out as a whole, or with the resolute faith of a man who means to drive lions from the path, and to bring the business strenuously through. The Minister, sometimes, almost carries circumspection to the point of timidity. This timidity seems mainly to arise from his failure, in the language of science, to isolate his phenomenon—from his failure, in other words, to keep steadily in view that he is dis- cussing not a great system of universal peace all over the civilised world, but only a particular scheme for promoting peace between England and the United States. Even here there is no small need for caution, for a treaty between two such Powers as these, with their many points of daily contact and the many underlying and subtle elements of antagonism, is by no means so simple a thing as, for instance, the project of a permanent treaty of arbitration between Switzerland and the United States, which was adopted by the Swiss Federal Council in 1883. Still Lord Salisbury sometimes argues as if he were debating with Kant, or Saint-Pierre, or any of those other grand utopians whose noble and benignant speculations have been the light of a world ' swept with confused alarms of struggle and flight, Where ignorant armies clash by night.' Mr. Olney is no Kant, but an acute lawyer. He is as far removed as possible from being a disputant of the utopian stamp. The Olney despatches are not altogether in the key of the Olney Hymns. He has made up his mind that the end desired by English and American alike is attain- able, and he makes for it with a directness of vision and will that always marks the way in which great things are done.

When all has been said that can be said on the possible excess of critical spirit, it is satisfactory to know that everybody will re- cognise, as the President of the United States recognises, 'the enlightened and progressive spirit' which animates Lord Salisbury's despatches upon a general system of arbitration between the two governments, and 'the earnest and serious attention' which the subject is evidently receiving in his mind. There is everything to hope from a statesman who had the courage and good sense to act as the Prime Minister acted in Heligoland.

Of the strength and depth of American sentiment, and of its thoroughly rational and practical aims, there can be no doubt. Few more interesting or significant conferences have ever assembled than that which met at Washington last April. Three hundred members .from six-and-thirty states, speaking what Lincoln called the 'sober second thought of the people,' containing many of the most serious leaders of opinion, men recognised as among the best and most responsible citizens in that vast community, assembled to focus or concentrate the manifold movements all over the Union in favour of such a treaty between America and England as would secure the settlement of international difficulties by the establishment of a standing international tribunal. The discussion was more specific and definite than such discussions usually are; the moving common-places of peace and goodwill did not obscure the perception of practical difficulties; and the proceedings ended in the establishment of a permanent organisation, containing many men of important station and influence, whose business it will be to keep vigorously alive the feeling in favour of erecting a great standing barrier against war between England and America.

No misty love of mankind in general was allowed to dim the spirit of a firm patriotism. Disagreeable facts were not blinked. One speaker actually founded his argument on the inevitable elements of conflict between the two countries. 'We wish to carry our com-merce and manufactures all over the world in competition with England. Furthermore, we cannot fulfil this mission of ours, a mission of commerce, of civilisation, and of the extension of the principles of the right of man to self-government—we cannot fulfil our mission without becoming a sea power. It is a dream of the future to think that nations are going to lay down their arms and dwell to-gether as sisters. As long as other nations strengthen their influence all over the globe, we are bound to build ourselves up, in fair degree, as a sea power. Now, for the precise reason that we are two great, ambitious, commercial powers, we want, and we greatly want, such a system of arbitration as will act as a check upon popular clamour and prejudice.'

The whiff of jingoism evoked some protest. The general feeling seemed to be that the flag of the United States ought to fly in every quarter of the globe, but only as the flag of the commercial navy of the United States, carrying products, ideas, civilisation—things all declared to be more important than guns. But there was no evasion of unpleasant contingencies: they were turned, as they ought to be, into arguments for making civilised provision against them.

'We are told even now, in this country,' said Mr. Carl Schurz,

that Great Britain is not the power with whom to have a permanent peace arrangement, because she is so high-handed in her dealings with other nations. I should not wonder if the same thing were said in England about the United States. This, of course, is not an argument against an arbitration agreement, but rather for it. Such an arrangement between nations of such temper is especially called for, to prevent that temper from running away with calm reason. Between perfect angels from heaven an arbitration treaty would be superfluous.

The institution of a regulated and permanent system of arbitration between the United States and Great Britain would not be a mere sentimental cooing between loving cousins, nor a mere stage-show gotten up for the amusement of the public, but a very serious contrivance intended for very serious business. It will set to mankind the example of two very great nations, the greatest rivals in the world, neither of them a mere theorist or sentimental dreamer, both intensely practical, self-willed, and hard-headed, deliberately agreeing to abstain from the barbarous ways of bygone times in adjusting the questions of conflicting interest or ambition that may arise between them.

This is exactly the temper in which the question should be approached, and it is the temper in which both Lord Salisbury and Mr. Olney conduct the discussion.

The questions on which differences arise are really three. What shall be the machinery? What are the subjects which the parties to the Treaty are to bind themselves to submit to the award of the standing tribunal? Is there any advantage in inquiry before the tribunal, if its award is not to be finally and unconditionally accepted? The main stress of the controversy is on the second and third questions.

Both sides agree that not all matters in dispute should be subjects of arbitration. Some exceptions must be made. 'Neither Government,' says Lord Salisbury, 'is willing to accept arbitration upon issues in which the national honour or integrity is involved. But in the wide region that lies within this boundary, the United States desire to go further than Great Britain.' [5] How are you to define issues in which national honour and integrity are involved? How is the presence of elements of honour and integrity to be discovered and decided? This is the central pivot of the discussion.

The matter is one of infinite delicacy and difficulty. In the Swiss-American draft treaty the parties agree to submit to arbitration all difficulties that may arise between the two States, 'whatever may be the cause, the nature, or the object of such difficulties.' This is obviously impracticably wide for our case. In the plan adopted at the Pan-American Conference of 1890, the only excepted questions were to be such as, 'in the judgment of any one of the nations involved in the controversy, may imperil its independence. This is a qualification which, in controversies between us and the United States, would be merely futile. In some proposals made at the Peace Congress at Chicago three years ago, obligatory arbitration was not to extend to any question respecting the independence or sovereignty of a nation, or its form of government, or its internal affairs. In the treaty of 1848 between the United States and Mexico, arbitration may be excluded, if ' deemed altogether incompatible with the nature of the difference or the circumstances of the case.' A formula so vague as this leaves everything open and offers no help.

Subjects proper for arbitration may be divided into two classes, says Lord Salisbury: (1) private disputes in respect to which the

State is representing its own subjects as individuals, such for instance as a claim for indemnity or damages. Here international arbitration may be admitted without reserve. (2) Issues that concern the State itself considered as a whole, that concern it in its collective capacity, such for example as a claim to territory or sovereign rights. Here more than one formidable difficulty stands in the way of unrestricted arbitration.

In a later despatch Lord Salisbury somewhat simplifies this twofold division. He draws a distinction only between territorial claims on the one hand, and non-territorial on the other.

The latter class he treats as arbitrable as of course. The territorial claim he regards as not arbitrable of course, and for three reasons.

First, the difficulty of securing an impartial arbitrator. ' It would be too invidious to specify the various forms of bias by which, in any important controversy between two great Powers, the other members of the commonwealth of nations are visibly affected. In the existing condition of international sentiment, each great Power could point to nations whose admission to any jury by whom its interests were to be tried it would be bound to challenge; and in a litigation between two great Powers the rival challenges would pretty well exhaust the catalogue of the nations from whom competent and suitable arbiters could be drawn. It would be easy, but scarcely decorous, to illustrate this statement by examples. They will occur to any one's mind who attempts to construct a panel of nations, capable of providing competent arbitrators, and will consider how many of them would command equal confidence from any two litigating Powers.' [6]

Second, the probable multiplication of territorial claims of a speculative character preferred by enterprising governments willing to hazard experiments before a tribunal where they might win, and if they lost would be little the worse. Facility of procedure would be sure to augment litigants, and all sorts of surprises would arise.

Third, international law in respect of territorial rights is in a most rudimentary condition, and this would aggravate the danger arising from the doubts as to the competence and impartiality of the arbitrator. The law of territorial rights has yet to be constructed. The laws of individual rights to land are well known, but who will undertake to say in respect of national rights to land what length of time constitutes international prescription, what is effective control, and the exercise of what clearly defined acts builds up a valid title? ' The great nations in both hemispheres claim, and are prepared to defend, their right to vast tracts of territory which they have in no sense occupied, and often have not fully explored. The modern doctrine of Hinterland, with its inevitable contradictions, indicates the unformed and unstable condition of international law as applied to territorial claims resting on constructive occupation or control.' [7]

These three general grounds of objection lead Lord Salisbury to the position that obligatory and unconditional arbitration on territorial claims, and the compulsory acceptance of a final award, involve a complete surrender of freedom of action in the event of an unjust award, which might prove to be highly dangerous. A nation must retain some control over the ultimate result of any claim that may be advanced against its territorial rights. So, while willing to bind himself to submit territorial claims to arbitration, he suggests arrangements for the protection of national interests by conferring on the defeated litigant an appeal to a court in which the award would need confirmation by a majority of the judges belonging to its own nationality. On this particular form of protection, however, he does not positively insist. 'It would be equally satisfactory and more simple to provide that no award on a question of territorial right should stand if, within three months of its delivery, either party should formally protest against its validity. The moral presumption against any nation delivering such a protest would, in the opinion of the world, be so strong that no government would resort to such a defence unless under a cogent apprehension that a miscarriage of justice was likely to take place.' These are remarkable words.

An arbitration without a final award, says Mr. Olney in reply, is no arbitration at all : it is no more than an uncommonly ceremonious and elaborate investigation, which is to end in smoke if the defeated litigant does not like the result. Not only is this not arbitration in any true sense, but 'it may be better to leave controversies to the usual modes of settlement than to enter upon proceedings which are arbitral only in name, and which are likely to have no other result than to excite and exasperate public feeling in both countries.' At the same time Mr. Olney admits the need of some security, and what he proposes is that the freedom of action which Lord Salisbury desires after the arbitration is over should operate before the arbitration is entered upon. What he proposes is that in the case of a territorial claim, either Congress or Parliament, at any time before the Arbitral Tribunal shall have met for the consideration of any particular subject-matter, may, by Act or Resolution declaring such particular subject-matter to involve the national honour or integrity, withdraw the same from the operation of the Treaty; and if a controversy shall arise when either Congress or Parliament shall not be in session, and such controversy shall be deemed by either Government to be of such nature that the international honour or integrity may be involved, the controversy shall not be submitted to Arbitration under the Treaty, until Congress and the Parliament shall have had the opportunity to take action upon it. In other words, every claim

[7] No. 15, May 18.

shall be *prima facie* arbitrable, and shall be arbitrated, unless Parliament or Congress declare that it is a claim involving national honour and integrity. Both sides agree that claims of that character should be withdrawn from the compulsion of the arbitration treaty. The difference is that Mr. Olney wishes people to make up their minds on this point before they go to arbitration, and Lord Salisbury not until they have found out which way the arbitrators have gone. As Mr. Olney trenchantly puts it, ' under the British proposal, the parties enter into an arbitration and determine afterwards, when they know the result, whether they will be bound or not. Under the proposals of the United States, the parties enter into an arbitration having determined beforehand that they will be bound. The latter is a genuine arbitration—the former is a mere imitation which may have its uses, but, like all other imitations, cannot compare in value with the real article.' [8]

We may agree with Mr. Olney here—that to leave to either Government the bare power of putting aside an award at its discretion is to nullify the arbitration. It would be far better than this to accept the proposal for an appellate tribunal, composed of three jurists from each Power, and three from outside (perhaps the three outside jurists might go) ; though it is hard to see, if this tribunal is to be more efficiently constituted than the tribunal of first instance, why it should not become itself the first and the last court, instead of setting up an intervening tribunal of inferior weight and secondary moral authority.

Mr. Olney's own proposal of a preliminary reference to Parliament or Congress seems not a little cumbrous, though he makes an ingenious defence for it. [9] The whole policy of arbitration rests on the expediency of removing international disputes from the atmosphere of passion, and to ask a great national and popular assembly to decide beforehand whether a given dispute involves national honour or not will perhaps strike many persons as a questionable experiment for suppressing passion.

The truth is that the word ' honour ' is a word of such breadth, subtlety, vagueness, and emotional intensity ; so little definite, positive, and objective, that it is a very hard word to introduce into the articles of a treaty. Do we want, for the purpose of Lord Salisbury's draft proposals, more than integrity of territory ? Certainly, as between ourselves and the United States (or those smaller American governments of whom the United States now constitute themselves the champions and representatives), that description is open to no misunderstanding. A boundary, for instance, that has been disputed for fifty years or more, and as to which our own Government has taken three or four perfectly different positions, can hardly be decisively

[8] Enclosure in No. 26, June 22.
[9] Enclosure in No. 12, p. 8.

labelled as an integral part of our territory, and no sensible man would pretend that it is so. If the tribunal were rightly constituted, and the specified majority fairly settled—and the two negotiators are really not far apart on these two points—there should be little difficulty in finding words for the territorial cases to be excepted from obligatory arbitration, and demanding special agreement. A tribunal would be very worthless if, 'with proper conditions as to its machinery and working such as are indicated in these papers, it could not be trusted —we are talking of the American continent, not the African —to settle such territorial cases as Lord Salisbury has in his mind.

Lord Salisbury suggests the conclusion of a Convention for referring to arbitration secondary or non-territorial claims, such as claims by individuals for damages or indemnity, questions affecting diplomatic or consular privileges, alleged rights of fishery, and the like. Here both governments agree that an arbitrator's award might be final ; and Lord Salisbury says that it would be matter for regret if so much as that view at any rate should not be embodied in a treaty.[10] To this the pertinent objection is made that the point of national honour might just as well arise, as indeed it has often in the past arisen, in connection with an individual or pecuniary as with a national or a territorial claim. The same difficulty faces us, therefore, in framing a limited, as in a general, convention.

As for the two main grounds on which Lord Salisbury finds himself at a deadlock, I confess that his apprehensions seem exaggerated. In his speech in the House of Lords he recurs to the fear of speculative territorial claims starting up, if arbitration were made obligatory. This might be a well-founded objection, if we were discussing a great scheme of General Treaties. But Mr. Olney is surely right in his remark that a treaty of that sort between Great Britain and the United States being the only thing now contemplated, it is not easy to imagine how its consummation can bring about the perils referred to. 'From what quarter,' he asks, 'may these numerous and speculative claims to territory be expected to come? Is the British Government likely to be preferring them against the United States, or the United States' Government likely to be preferring them against Great Britain? Certainly this objection to including territorial controversies within the scope of a General Arbitration Treaty between the United States and Great Britain may justly be regarded, if not as wholly groundless, as at least of a highly fanciful character.'

It has been suggested that a clause might be added to the treaty of arbitration upon the basis of existing possessions, definitely prohibiting the raising of any question relating to territory now in undisputed occupation. There is something like this, though not quite the same, in the sixth article of the Pan-American project. At any

[10] No. 15, May 18.

rate this ground of anxiety might be removed by the acceptance in the treaty of an authentic map of existing territories. So far as I am aware, the not very momentous dispute about the Alaskan boundary is the only ragged edge in territorial matters between Great Britain and the United States.

Then as to the difficulties of the law which the standing tribunal would be called upon to administer. The rules of international law applicable to territorial controversies, says Lord Salisbury, are uncertain. Without doubt there is the utmost uncertainty about the rules that may rise out of the new doctrines about Hinterland and spheres of influence. But these doctrines, at any rate, have no application to any boundary disputes that now exist or are likely to arise on the two continents of America. Nor, says Mr. Olney, is it to be admitted that, so far as territorial disputes are likely to arise between Great Britain and the United States, the accepted principles of international law are not adequate to their intelligent and just solution.

On the critical point of settlements, ' each case should be left to depend upon its own facts. A State which in good faith colonises as well as occupies, brings about large investments of capital and founds populous settlements, would justly be credited with a sufficient title in a much shorter space than a State whose possession was not marked by any such changes of status.'

The truth is that the creation of a permanent tribunal would be the best way of improving the rules of what is called international law. Sir Henry Maine has some weighty remarks on the advantages of a permanent court or board of arbitrators over occasional adjudicators appointed *ad hoc*. He is arguing from the memorable Geneva arbitration upon what are known as the *Alabama* claims. He does not deny that this famous proceeding conferred great benefit for the moment both on Great Britain and the United States, but he insists that the tribunal did not look at the subject in all its bearings, and forgot the future effect of their award in the particular case upon the rights of neutrals—the neglect of which does more than anything else to enlarge the area of maritime wars. A permanent board, well constituted, ' could be better trusted to adjust its awards to the entire body of international principles, distinctions, and rules, ... and it might be .employed more freely as a body of referees on critical questions which are now left to themselves for want of any authority to which their consideration might be committed.' [11] In short, a permanent board is the only hope of building up coherently that fabric of international rules about territorial claims, the non-existence of which is one of Lord Salisbury's main arguments against the proposals before him.

To insist upon a plan which shall make a miscarriage of justice

---

[11] *Lectures on International Law* (1888), p. 220. The whole chapter deserves to be read in connection with the present discussion.

impossible is of course equivalent to throwing up the task. Miscarriages of justice happen in law courts, but law courts, with all their imperfections, are better than duels and free fights. What we have to ask ourselves, among other things, is whether in any arbitration that could be held under treaty between ourselves and the United States, we can possibly suffer any detriment of honour, of material interest, or in respect of any principle of national strength, integrity and power, that would be at all or in any degree comparable to that which would be inflicted on both nations by war. This thought is the strongest stimulus to further the continued effort in the task that Lord Salisbury has undertaken. Defects in the tribunal, such as experience might reveal, could be remedied. It is not necessary that the Treaty should be perpetual: Mr. Olney himself suggests that it should be terminable after a short term of years on notice by either party. If the principle of arbitration and a permanent tribunal were once established, and with reasonable securities and safeguards embodied in practical shape, that in itself would be an immense step towards lessening the chances of war, even in cases which lay outside the specific operations of the tribunal.

The things to be done are to frame the exception clause, which, though difficult, is not beyond the expert skill of Lord Salisbury and Mr. Olney; and to shape the constitution and functions of the tribunal, as to which the two ministers could evidently come to an understanding in twenty-four hours. If these two things are done, the award should be final, or else we might almost as well or better leave the project alone.

To leave it alone would, in the opinion of the present writer, be nothing short of a disaster to one of the greatest causes now moving the Western world. If Lord Salisbury fails, the question, we may be sure, will be set fatally back for many a year to come. Congress and Parliament may go on passing benevolent resolutions in favour of arbitration in the future, as they have in the past; but everybody will feel that no such favourable moment is likely soon to recur. Even the indirect consequences of failure will be highly mischievous to the general interests of peace. It is to be fervently hoped, therefore, that the Prime Minister will strenuously persist in the most important enterprise that he has ever had in his hands.

JOHN MORLEY.

WHY SOUTH AFRICA CAN WAIT

TO THE EDITOR OF ' THE NINETEENTH CENTURY'

SIR,—Mr Edward Dicey contributed an article to the May number of your Review, in which he advocates a policy of force against the South African Republic; a policy the only possible result of which would be to envelope South Africa in the flames of war. It is difficult to suppose that he will find many sensible men to agree with him; or that moderate-minded men will not recognise the fact that hitherto Transvaal affairs have been presented to the British public almost exclusively from an anti-Transvaal point of view, and that a great deal remains to be said on the other side. It is my intention at an early date to publish a short review of British policy towards the two South African Republics, as viewed from the Boers' standpoint, in the pages of your Review, should you be willing to afford me the space required for the purpose; meanwhile it may be allowed to me to make a few remarks on the article in question. Having only just read it, and having to forward this communication at once, I am unable at present to attempt fully to reply to Mr. Dicey's arguments and allegations.

As regards the footing upon which the two languages, Dutch and English, are placed in the Cape Colony, the facts are these. About twenty years after the acquisition of that colony by Great Britain, and whilst the overwhelming majority (at least seven-eighths) of the population understood only Dutch, an order was issued by the Imperial Government that from a certain date all official documents, and from a certain other date, three years thereafter, all proceedings in courts of law, should be exclusively in English. This was done in spite of the remonstrances of the Dutch-speaking population. A couple of years afterwards a notice was issued that all documents addressed to the Government must be written in English, or have a translation attached, otherwise they would be returned to those who sent them. Great inconvenience, of course, resulted to the Dutch-speaking inhabitants of the country; in one instance all criminal cases were removed from a country town by one of the judges, because though the prisoners and witnesses spoke Dutch only, a sufficient number of English-speaking men could not be found to form a jury. Some years afterwards, however, the difficulty thus experienced in respect to jurymen was removed by an ordinance. In 1853 a constitution was granted to the Cape Colony, one of the provisions of which was that no other language than English should be used in either of the Houses of Parliament, and that their proceedings should be recorded in that language. In 1872 responsible government was introduced into that colony; and it was not till 1882 that the Dutch-speaking population, being in a position to command a majority in Parliament, first secured the same rights for their language as the English enjoyed. This was effected in the face of strong opposition; the present Premier of the Cape Colony, I believe I am not wrong in saying, being one of those most bitter in their hostility to the placing of the two languages upon a footing of equality. Even as it now is, the two languages do not stand side by side upon anything like equal terms; for instance, all University, Civil Service, and school examinations are conducted in English, so that the children of Dutch-speaking parents have to prosecute their studies in an acquired language. The Dutch language shows, indeed, a marvellous vitality considering that under such circumstances of discouragement and repression it has not utterly perished. Now, if this was the policy adopted in the Cape Colony for so many years towards the old inhabitants of the country forming the industrial backbone of that colony, how absurd it is to wish to deal out death and destruction to the South African Republic, because, amongst other reasons, it does not at once grant equal rights in respect of language to British subjects, who came into that country well knowing that Dutch was there the official language ! Should there hereafter be a sufficiently large influx of Germans or of Chinese into that country, it might possibly be found difficult to withstand a similar demand made on their behalf; and it is questionable whether in such a case those who now claim equal rights in respect of language would so readily grant the same privilege to others.

Now, I do not wish for one moment to suggest that concessions on the score of language should not be made to the English-speaking population, or that the Dutch-speaking community should do to others what has been done to itself, but at all events I make free to think that any person, before making comparisons between the Cape Colony and the South African Republic unfavourable to the latter, ought at least to have a clear grasp of the actual state of affairs. If it is just that concessions should be made, the Afrikander sense of justice will, if allowed fairplay, see to it that those concessions are effected; and the less talk there is of force and of violence, the sooner they will be made.

As regards the franchise (supposing this not to be an entirely fictitious grievance and that Mr. Lionel Philips was wrong in assuring his correspondent, Mr. Beit, that he did not 'think many people care a fig about it '), it is surely absurd also to compare the case of the Cape Colony, where an old-established and perfectly loyal Dutch-speaking population enjoy the franchise, and the case of the Transvaal, with a new population, the vast majority of whom knew, or ought to have known, at the time they came thither, exactly what their political status there would be, and who men like Mr. Dicey, I have very little doubt, in their heart of hearts desire should not be loyal to the Government of the country. Mr. Chamberlain is reported to have said, 'Time is on our side'—that is to say, on the side of the British Government; he is also stated to have advised ' a modified oath of allegiance' (!); and, most curious of all, is very anxious that British subjects should enjoy the privilege of casting off their allegiance to the British Crown. I think better perhaps of Englishmen than Mr. Dicey does, and believe that the great majority of British subjects who shall in course of time have become Transvaal citizens will be perfectly loyal to their new allegiance; but taking all these matters into consideration, as also the manner in which the annexation of the country was at one time effected, surely any impartially minded man must see that the question is for the Transvaal one of very great difficulty. That if patience is exercised the difficulty will be overcome there can be no reasonable doubt; but badgering and bullying the Government of the Transvaal will not bring about that consummation. It is perhaps an exercise of charity to believe that Mr. Dicey really desires that it should be brought about; for his mind seems bent upon a war the progress of which he can calmly watch from afar, at a distance of 6,000 miles away.

I cannot animadvert in detail upon or controvert any of Mr. Dicey's further allegations in support of his plea for war; if he be not the devil's advocate, he has certainly been doing devil's work. He disagrees, as a political economist, with the Transvaal Government as to the value of concessions, and would apparently, if he had the power, break faith with concessionaires. To attain that end and other ends he would make war upon the Transvaal. South Africa, he maintains, cannot wait. South Africa knows better what it wants than Mr. Dicey does, and it certainly does not want war. Time is on the side of the Transvaal; for time will explode the mass of fiction and misrepresentation of which that country is now the victim.

MELIUS DE VILLIERS.

BLOEMFONTEIN :
   June 15, 1896

The Editor of THE NINETEENTH CENTURY *cannot undertake
to return unaccepted MSS.*

THE

NINETEENTH CENTURY

No. CCXXXV—September 1896

THE HIGH OAKS.

BARKING HALL, JULY 19th, 1896 [1]

FOURSCORE years and seven
Light and dew from heaven
Have fallen with dawn on these glad woods each day
Since here was born, even here,
A birth more bright and dear
Than ever a younger year
Hath seen or shall till all these pass away,
Even all the imperious pride of these,
The woodland ways majestic now with towers of trees.

Love itself hath nought
Touched of tenderest thought
With holiest hallowing of memorial grace
For memory, blind with bliss,
To love, to clasp, to kiss,
So sweetly strange as this,
The sense that here the sun first hailed her face,
A babe at Her glad mother's breast,
And here again beholds it more beloved and blest.

---

[1] *Verses written for the birthday of the Author's mother.*—ED. *Nineteenth Century.*

Love's own heart, a living
Spring of strong thanksgiving,
Can bid no strength of welling song find way
When all the soul would seek
One word for joy to speak,
And even its strength makes weak
The too strong yearning of the soul to say
What may not be conceived or said
While darkness makes division of the quick and dead.

Haply, where the sun
Wanes, and death is none,
The word known here of silence only, held
Too dear for speech to wrong,
May leap in living song
Forth, and the speech be strong
As here the silence whence it yearned and welled
From hearts whose utterance love sealed fast
Till death perchance might give it grace to live at last.

Here we have our earth
Yet, with all the mirth
Of all the summers since the world began,
All strengths of rest and strife
And love-lit love of life
Where death has birth to wife,
And where the sun speaks, and is heard of man ·
Yea, half the sun's bright speech is heard,
And like the sea the soul of man gives back his word.

Earth's enkindled heart
Bears benignant part
In the ardent heaven's auroral pride of prime:
If ever home on earth
Were found of heaven's grace worth
So God-beloved a birth

Here, for mine and me,
All that eyes may see
Hath more than all the wide world else of good,
All nature else of fair:
Here as none otherwhere
Heaven is the circling air,
Heaven is the homestead, heaven the wold, the wood:
The fragrance with the shadow spread
From broadening wings of cedars breathes of dawn's bright
bed.

Once a dawn rose here
More divine and dear,
Rose on a birth-bed brighter far than dawn's,
Whence all the summer grew
Sweet as when earth was new
And pure as Eden's dew:
And yet its light lives on these lustrous lawns,
Clings round these wildwood ways, and cleaves
To the aisles of shadow and sun that wind unweaves and
weaves.

Thoughts that smile and weep,
Dreams that hallow sleep,
Brood in the branching shadows of the trees,
Tall trees at agelong rest
Wherein the centuries nest,
Whence, blest as these are blest,
We part, and part not from delight in these; .
Whose comfort, sleeping as awake,
We bear about within us as when first it spake.

Comfort as of song
Grown with time more strong,
Made perfect and prophetic as the sea,
Whose message, when it lies
Far off our hungering eyes,
Within us prophesies
Of life not ours, yet ours as theirs may be
Whose souls far off us shine and sing
As ere they sprang back sunward, swift as fire might spring.

All this oldworld pleasance
Hails a hallowing presence,
And thrills with sense of more than summer near,
And lifts toward heaven more high
The song-surpassing cry
Of rapture that July
Lives, for her love who makes it loveliest here;
For joy that she who here first drew
The breath of life she gave me breathes it here anew.

Never birthday born
Highest in height of morn
Whereout the star looks forth that leads the sun
Shone higher in love's account,
Still seeing the mid noon mount
From the eager dayspring's fount
Each year more lustrous, each like all in one;
Whose light around us and above
We could not see so lovely save by grace of love.

ALGERNON CHARLES SWINBURNE.

SISYPHUS IN IRELAND

25 *LAND ACTS IN* 26 *YEARS*

On the 15th of February, 1870, Mr. Gladstone, then Prime Minister, favoured the House of Commons with one of the many perorations in which he has guaranteed the finality of each of his successive legislative efforts with respect to Ireland. He spoke of the Land Bill which he was introducing, and he said :—

> What we desire is that the work of this Bill should be like the work of Nature herself, when on the face of a desolated land she restores what has been laid waste by the wild and savage hand of man. Its operations, we believe, will be quiet and gradual. We wish to alarm none ; we wish to injure no one. What we wish is that where there has been despondency there shall be hope ; where there has been mistrust there shall be confidence ; where there has been alienation and hate there shall, however gradually, be woven the ties of a strong attachment between man and man. In order that there may be a hope of its entire success it must be passed, not as a triumph of party over party, or class over class ; not as the lifting up of an ensign to record the downfall of that which has once been great and powerful, but as a common work of common love and goodwill to the common good of our common country.

It is interesting, in view of these magnificent aspirations, to test their value by the criterion of facts. Let us see what are the benefits which this saving measure has really produced. Since 1870 no fewer than twenty-four Acts dealing with Irish land have been passed by the Imperial Parliament, and the present year has produced a twenty-fifth. In 1881 came the second great Land Act, by which the confusion created by the Act of 1870 was enormously increased. The introduction of that Act was of course accompanied by the usual peroration.

> Justice, sir, is to be our guide ; we proceed upon a reckoning which cannot fail. It has been said that love is stronger than death ; even so justice is stronger than popular excitement—stronger than the passions of the moment, stronger even than the grudges, the resentments, the sad traditions of the past. Walking in that path we cannot err. Guided by that light—that divine light—we are safe. Every step that we take upon our road is a step that brings us nearer to the goal.

And so on, and so on, in the usual common form.

Now let us see how much nearer the goal we have really got, whither ' the path in which we cannot err' is leading us, and what is

the spectacle which the 'divine light,' as manipulated by Mr. Gladstone's magic lantern, has revealed to us. It is perhaps scarcely yet
realised by the public generally that in the present year of grace we
have come back to precisely the point from which we started in 1881,
and that the term of fifteen years, described as the 'judicial term' in
that Act, having expired, we are now deliberately starting once more
upon the same vicious round, and commencing once more the same
impossible task which we first set ourselves to perform fifteen years
ago. But it must not be supposed for a moment that the mere fact
of our having returned to our former starting point after fifteen years'
progress down the road in which we can 'never err' is the sole or the
principal mischief which has been inflicted upon the nation by the
reckless legislation of 1881.

'As in 1881, but worse'

Attempts have been made from time to time to encourage the
belief that each successive Act brings us nearer to a conclusion ; that
what one measure leaves undone, the next in part at any rate accom-
plishes. There could not be a greater delusion. Sisyphus was a
practical business man, the Danaides were wise virgins improving
the hours and engaged in a hopeful and useful occupation, in comparison with the perpetrators of a modern Irish Land Act. Not only
is the goal never approached, but at every succeeding step we see it
recede further and further into the distance. Not only do the original
difficulties remain practically untouched, but each addition to the
Statute-book produces new difficulties from which we have hitherto
been free. Like some of the lowest forms of the animal kingdom,
the creature which has been let loose in Ireland breeds and spreads
from every knot and joint of its shapeless form, till it threatens to
fill the land.

Twenty-five statutes, 261 pages of laws, judges and commissioners
by the score, lawyers like locusts, and what is the result? In 1896
we are precisely at the point which we left in 1881. All over Ireland
applications for fair rents are once more raining in ; once more we
are told the courts are to be choked with suitors, the old judicial
terms are coming to an end, and the new ones are to begin.

That the Irish Land Acts should have failed is not a matter of
surprise; the amazing thing is that any one in the world could ever
have expected them to succeed. To carry out an elaborate mathematical calculation under the impression that two and two make five,
and that the less contains the greater, would lead to remarkable
results. But the authors of the successive Land Acts have been far
more ingenious in their methods of ensuring triumphant error than
our hypothetical mathematician. Knowing well what was the result
at which they aimed, they have shown a perfectly amazing skill in

providing against its attainment. They have laughed at political economy; they have ignored experience; they have departed as far from common fairness as they have from common law; they have made no allowance for human nature; they have not even imparted the merit of consistency into their aberrations. And entering on these terms into a struggle with the eternal verities, they appear to be surprised that they have come second best out of the encounter.

These are strong expressions, but they are justified by the facts. That the conditions of Irish land tenure in 1870 were unsatisfactory, and were in need of reform, no man can deny. Civil war, race differences, and the frequent 'settlements' which transferred landed property by force from one section of the population to the other, had brought about a condition of things which was unsound and unsatisfactory both from the political and from the economical point of view.

The disease existed, and a remedy was required, but never was a stranger treatment adopted.

THE RELATIONS BETWEEN LANDLORD AND TENANT

The people of Ireland were divided by a sharp class division which was absolutely conterminous with a division arising out of the agrarian difficulty.

On the one side were the landlords and on the other the tenants. The problem was to destroy the line of division and to produce harmony and good feeling between the parties. By what method have the authors of the Land Acts sought to accomplish this desirable end?

Have they removed the dividing line between tenant and landlord? Not at all; it exists more sharply defined than ever. Have they produced a better feeling? If they have it is a miracle, for they have so contrived that of all the relations in which landlord and tenant ever met, one alone shall survive. They have ordained that the only place in which the landlord shall meet the tenant shall be the County Court or the Land Court; the only terms on which either party shall have dealings with the other shall be as a litigant in a bitterly contested lawsuit.

It is deeply to be desired, and it is indeed essential to the agricultural welfare of Ireland, that the owners of the soil should be encouraged by every means to invest their capital in the improvement of the soil, and to give the benefit of their personal interest and attention to the development of their estates. It has been the deliberate aim and intention of each successive Land Bill to prohibit the owner of the soil from exercising any rights whatever with respect to it, and to make it absolutely absurd for him to entertain the idea, even if he possessed the power, of investing a brass farthing in its improvement. Not content with making the landlord a mere rent charger on his own estate, the framers of the Acts have shown the most extraordinary ingenuity in removing every sort of inducement which might retain him upon his estate after he has been deprived of his principal rights over the soil. The exhibition of a desire to serve his neighbours and to oblige his tenants has now been made statutory evidence against him, and every concession which kindly feeling, gratitude for long service, or other good motive may have prompted him to make, is to be construed by the Courts as proof of the deliberate conveyance of a right which may be sold by the new owner to the highest bidder.[1]

The literature of the century is largely occupied with the description of the social and economical disadvantages which have resulted from the absenteeism of Irish landlords. Nearly all that has been said is true; absenteeism is from every point of view a misfortune to the country. How have our legislators sought to remedy the evil? By depriving the Irish landlord, who, whatever may be his faults, is the true leader of Irish society, of every amenity and occupation which residence on his property could furnish, they have provided a motive for absenteeism more potent than any which all the outrages which have darkened the annals of Ireland could supply.

Impoverished, impotent for good, unoccupied, the landlord has every motive to leave the country of his birth and of his affection. It is conceivable that, the separation once made, the landlord might in other lands and among happier surroundings find a useful outlet for his energies. But even this chance of escape has been denied him. Whatever happens, he must remain a useless incumbrance upon what was once his estate; for the law in its wisdom has still left him two duties to perform. In the first place he must still, in person or by deputy, struggle for the recovery of such part of his former income as the sub-commissioners may have left him. Recourse to the ordinary methods of recovering a debt which prevail in every civilised country will expose him to universal odium, and he may consider himself fortunate if some member of the Executive Government, in the hope of gaining a transient popularity, does not openly, or by innuendo, join in the chorus of condemnation.

One other duty remains to be performed. It is still the privilege of the landlord to disburse his scanty means in feeing attorneys to appear on his behalf in the Land Court, in order to ascertain, with what precision they can, under which particular provision of the thousands which compose the Irish Land Code their client is to be mulcted of the remaining portion of his property. These are the two

---

[1] Thanks not to any sense of justice or equity on the part of the Government which fought for this scandalous clause in the House of Commons, but thanks solely to the House of Lords, the most unjust features of this particular provision are not embodied in the new Land Act.

duties—among the most odious, the most ungrateful that can be imposed upon man—which our laws have reserved to the landowners of Ireland. Rendered powerless for good, they are still chained to the land for the express purpose, as it would seem, of aggravating and prolonging those very evils which their ruin was to have removed.

THE REVIVAL OF THE 'LAW OF THE MAXIMUM'

The Price of Commodities cannot be fixed by the State

It is not necessary to quote authorities for this plain statement of a plain fact. It is one of the earliest axioms of political economy, taught by the aid of a score of examples to every boy who begins the study of his Fawcett or his Mill. The plan has been tried. It was probably tried in Egypt in the time of the early Pharaohs, and failed. It was tried in Rome under the emperors, and failed. It was the practice of the Middle Ages, and the victims of the experiment suffered smartly enough in consequence. It was tried during the French Revolution and the Commune, and though many persons were murdered under circumstances of peculiar brutality in order to secure its easy working, it failed again. It has usually been resorted to during a state of siege, and the principle is sometimes accepted in times of famine in the East. As a recognised basis for the laws of a sane community, it has long ago been abandoned by the Government of every civilised State, save that of the United Kingdom, which has revived it in favour of Ireland alone. The plan that failed in the time of Pharaoh Necho has unluckily retained its evil reputation in the days of Queen Victoria. With an odd inconsistency we still teach our youth that the State cannot with advantage fix the price of commodities, we laugh at the law of the 'maximum,' and speak with scornful pity of the economical blunders of our ancestors, and yet at the very same time we pass volumes of statutes for the express purpose of fixing by the authority of the State the price of the commodity which is most universally in demand and most frequently dealt with in the whole of Ireland. And now we are apparently astonished because we are still a little short of perfect peace and contentment in that unhappy island.

No serious attempt has ever been made to justify this midsummer madness, though occasionally efforts are made by false analogies and misleading comparisons to distract attention from the true nature of the scandal.

The Indian Land Settlement is quoted, a precedent which is as irrelevant to the Irish system as are Kepler's laws or the custom of gavelkind.

The rents of the Indian holdings are fixed for the purposes of taxation only, and are based upon the necessities of the State, not upon the commercial and exchangeable value of the land affected.

The fixing of prices as between buyer and seller is peculiar to the Irish system.

FIXED RENTS AND FREE TENANT-RIGHTS

But granting for a moment that the crazy plan of fixing prices by Act of Parliament be justified by the urgent necessities of the case, and by the peculiar conditions of Ireland, what is to be said of the system as we have elected to inflict it upon that unhappy country? Conceive the commandant of a besieged town ordaining that a 4 lb. loaf of bread should be sold by the bakers to the apothecaries at 4*d.*, and thereupon not only permitting but encouraging every apothecary to put his purchase up to auction and to sell at famine prices to the highest bidder.

Such a proceeding would be considered illogical by an impartial judge, but it would be heaven-inspired wisdom compared with that of the authors of our Irish Land Acts. The rent of every holding is fixed by a so-called judicial tribunal, and is made subject to what is commonly known as a 'fair rent.' The object, we are told, is to relieve the tenant from the intolerable evil of rack-renting, and to save him from himself by relieving him from the competition of the open market. But no sooner has the right to purchase the use of the land under these fortunate conditions been conceded, than to it is added the right of selling the use to a third party. And this second sale, be it noted, is trammelled by no such conditions as those which limited the first. No judge decides, no court records. The owner goes into the open market with his tenant-right, and sells it in open competition to the highest bidder. The consequence is obvious, foreseen, unavoidable. Every penny that comes off the rent is automatically added to the tenant-right. The new tenant borrows the money to pay for the enhanced tenant-right, and the interest on the money represents the increase in the rent which all the Queen's lawyers and all the Queen's men have by the exercise of their joint wits and authority been conspiring to keep down.

CONFIDENCE AND CAPITAL

Whatever may be the rights and wrongs of the various questions, political, social, and economical, which have disturbed Ireland during the last half-century, there can be no doubt at all that they have resulted in a lamentable unsettlement of the country, and in a partial paralysis of industry which only tranquillity, confidence, and the expenditure of large amounts of capital can remove.

Confidence and *capital*, these are the great requisites of Ireland. Let us see what our precious land legislation has done to promote the one and to attract the other. Confidence is a plant of slow growth, there are some soils in which it will never grow. It will never grow

in ground which is constantly disturbed. We· have deliberately
ignored this obvious truth, and like the ostrich have imagined that
what we refused to see had no existence. Twenty-five Acts in twenty-
six years represent our efforts to reassure the doubting and to encon-
rage the cautious. It may be truly said that the only thing of which
the owner of the most important class of property in Ireland is absolutely certain is, that the law under which he lives at the beginning
of the year will not be the law under which he may attempt to live
at the end of it.

The Law of the Land

Year after year the Land Law of Ireland has been ripped up,
patched, tinkered, amended, repealed, till no man knows, or has the
means of knowing, what are his own rights or those of his neighbours.
This is hardly the way to encourage the growth of confidence.

No one is likely to deny that among the most crying needs of
Ireland is a greater respect for the law and for those who administer
the law than is at present observable. To inculcate such a feeling
and to furnish an adequate reason for its existence should be the first
care of the statesman who has to deal with Irish problems. If the
first care of our statesmen had been to destroy all confidence in the
law, all respect for its authority, and to inspire a hearty contempt for
those who administer it, they would probably have acted in precisely
the manner in which they have acted during the last twenty years.

With regard to the law itself, no man in Ireland knows what it is.
In the 261 pages of statute law and the countless thousands of pages
which contain the judicial decisions or the *obiter dicta* of the judges,
there is no real body of law at all. There are, it is true, an infinite
number of casual and often contradictory provisions, thousands of
categorical propositions, every one of which is modified, or nullified,
by some cross reference, by some decided case, or by some expression
of opinion in Parliament or in Court.

But this is not all. The ponderous and unintelligible statutes
which are turned out with infinite effort by the Imperial Parliament
are not and never have been the expressions of any single thought or
consistent plan. They have been a patchwork of compromises adopted
under pressure, of amendments hastily considered and rashly adopted.
Striving to embrace all things great and small connected with Irish
land, they have failed to anticipate a hundred petty difficulties, a
hundred incoherences or inconsistencies which practical working was
certain to reveal. Each original error has in a vicious geometrical
progression been productive of a host of subsidiary errors and absurdities. A is included in the benefits of the Act; it is absurd that A
should be included, but if A, why not B ? A whole class of contracts
is set aside by Parliament; another set of contracts is allowed to

remain unimpaired. What can be more monstrous? The logic of the situation demands that the surviving contracts should be broken in order to restore the harmony of error. And thus it has come about that each Act has been merely the seed of a new series of Acts, each error and discrepancy as it has been discovered has been made the subject of legislation, and each new law has in turn been made the excuse, and the logical excuse, for another and yet another.

So much for the methods by which the laws are made which Irishmen are supposed to respect. It is no exaggeration to say that no man in Ireland knows or can pretend to know at the beginning of the year what is likely to be the law under which he lives at the end of it. He is, however, entitled to form a very strong presumption that it will not be the same, and that, whatever may be its form from day to day, he may be certain that its provisions will be so complicated, so involved, so uncertain of interpretation that they will be intelligible to no man, a curse to the community, a danger to the individual and a priceless treasure to the attorneys. It is one of the axioms of statesmanship that laws to be respected must be clear, certain, and unchanging. And yet we expect Irishmen to believe in the law as we have made it.

So much for laws and the making of laws with regard to Irish land. We now pass to the instruments by which the sanctions of law are invoked and secured in Ireland. It is said that in the early days of man, before the dawn of civilisation, the law of contract was unknown. In Paris during the days of the Commune, when the assassin and the petroleuse were the rulers of the city, the law of contract and the obligations attaching to it were deliberately abandoned. At the present moment it has no existence in some of the more remote islands of the Pacific and in Ireland. The precedents hardly seem sufficiently favourable to induce us to believe that the destruction of the law of contract will prove of great benefit to the people of Ireland; but our politicians have thought otherwise, and have produced the state of things which Englishmen hardly yet realise. It is absolutely impossible for the most ingenious, the most learned lawyer to draw any agreement between man and man in Ireland, the subject of which is land, or any right or obligation connected with land, which shall be worth the paper on which it is written. The parties may sign, may seal, may deliver, may register, may go through every conceivable formality which the ingenuity of jurists or the custom of mankind has consecrated as an outward sign of the efficacy and binding force of an agreement. Parliament itself may in the name of the nation give the solemn pledge of an Act of Parliament as a guarantee for the fulfilment of a promise deliberately made to an individual or a class; and yet, with contract and bond, with seal and deed, with Act of Parliament and the solemn obligation of the nation's promise, the end is the same in every case. Not one of them is of more value than a Confederate greenback ; nor is the promise made by the contracting party of greater significance or more to be relied upon than the oath of a Kerry juror. Agreements for one year have been made ; they have been set aside. Leases for twenty-one years made for good and valuable consideration, signed and sealed with due formality, have been torn up like waste paper. Leases for perpetuity have fared no better. Judicial rents fixed by the ridiculous tribunal called a Land Court, acting under statutory authority, have been deliberately altered during their currency by that most dishonest of all the Land Acts, the Act of 1887. It is no exaggeration to say that, as far as land is concerned, there is no such thing as a legal contract in Ireland, and now the only engagement which can be entered into by two willing parties is a bargain that they will mutually keep their agreement until one party being tired of it chooses to get out of it, or until Parliament in its wisdom declares the bargain to be of no effect, an event which will probably take place within the next ensuing twelve months.

The Land Commission

And now a word with regard to the individuals who are employed to administer this kaleidoscopic law. If owners of property in Great Britain could once truly realise what is the nature of the tribunal which, under the name of the 'Land Commission,' has been set up in Ireland, the mere instinct of self-preservation would lead them to destroy it at the earliest possible opportunity. And here be it said that, in speaking of the owner of property, it is not only the owner of land who is referred to. Every man and woman who owns a sixpence honestly acquired is equally threatened by the policy which is embodied in this predatory institution.

For if the methods adopted for making the law respected or its guarantees of value be inadequate, what are we to say of the administrators of the law themselves and of the prestige attaching to them ? The absolute integrity and independence of the judge are the foundation stones of British justice. By every means that reason and experience can suggest we seek to enhance the dignity of the office and to ensure the independence of the office holder. Selected after years of service, tried by the fierce competition of the Bar, learned in the law, acquainted with human nature, trained to understand and to appreciate the judicial habit of mind, such is the judge as we have hitherto known him, a fit minister of the national justice. The salary of the judge assures his position ; he is appointed during pleasure, which means for life. He has nothing more to seek, no higher ambition to pursue. He deserves, and he obtains, the respect and confidence of suitors.

Now let us turn to the so-called judicial authority which we have created in Ireland.   Let us consider the men who, under the title of 'Assistant Land Commissioners,' have been let loose on the country.   They are all 'honourable men,' no doubt, all provided with good intentions sufficient to pave a most extensive 'Inferno;' they all desire to do their duty.   So much may, at a pinch, be admitted. But that is the extreme to which courtesy and a regard for the facts compel us to go.   Selected not because they are at the head of the profession or trade in which they have respectively failed or won some small measure of success, but because the bewildered Chief Secretary, overwhelmed with conflicting recommendations of men whom he has never seen and does not know, thinks that the least mischief will be done by making this or that particular appointment.   Such are the men to whom we have entrusted, practically without appeal, the right to ruin large sections of her Majesty's subjects in Ireland. To-day a man is living a decent honourable life in peace with his neighbours ; to-morrow there come down from Dublin a pair of unknown gentlemen.   Within half an hour these two gentlemen have decreed, and without appeal, that their victim shall be then and there ruined, that 25 per cent. of his property shall be handed over to somebody else, who shall be at liberty instantly to go into the market and sell the property which he has got for nothing, at the highest price which a willing bidder will pay for it.

But the regular Assistant Commissioner—the gentleman who is a civil servant of the Crown and whom the British taxpayer is compelled to keep for the rest of his days—is a dignified and respectable person compared with the *temporary Assistant Commissioner*.   At the present moment the temporary Commissioner is in abeyance ; the individuals who formerly held the post have been relegated to those spheres of private influence and utility which they adorned before they were commissioned.   But the breed is shortly to be revived ; and one of the crowning blessings of our healing legislation is the certainty that within a few months we shall see scores of these temporary three-guinea-a-day gentlemen hired by the job to administer justice and equity as between man and man in Ireland. It would be nothing short of impertinence to expect any reasonable man to have confidence in judges appointed under these conditions.   They come for the most part from a class which has a direct interest in lowering the rents of the land.   To that class they will go back as soon as there is no man to hire them.   From the fact that the applications to the posts are to be numbered in hundreds, it is to be presumed that those who obtain the posts value their position.   It does not, therefore, require much foresight to prophesy that rent reductions will be the invariable rule.

Lastly, there remains one other blessing which our Irish Land Acts have conferred upon us. It has been said over and over again that the Irish landlords are the English garrison. The fact is to a certain extent true, but the conclusion which has been deduced from it is a strange one. The principle that the sole use of a British garrison is to abandon and betray it has not yet been universally accepted, though from the days of Khartoum downwards it has found, no doubt, an increasing number of adherents. To many it would seem that if the necessities of the State compel Parliament to inflict upon Irish landlords a treatment which is meted out to no other class in the community, it is the peculiar and obvious duty of the State to give the fullest and most liberal measure of compensation to those whom it is compelled to interfere with. Among all the dangers that threaten us in Ireland, perhaps none is greater than that which we have made for ourselves. We have many enemies in Ireland; we have had them long, and we have not been much the worse. But if the day ever come when we add to the list of our enemies the gentry of Ireland, who, despite all contradiction, are the true leaders of Irish society, and if they become our enemies because we have treated them meanly and unjustly, we shall be face to face with a danger greater than any which has yet confronted us.

It is idle to contend, as some persons do, that the fact that there have been large voluntary reductions of rent in England furnishes an absolute justification for all the reductions made by the Land Commissioners in Ireland. In the first place, the circumstances of Ireland in this, as in so many other particulars, are different from those of England, and the value of agricultural property in one country is by no means a certain criterion of its value in the other. But quite apart from these considerations there is the fact that the reductions in one case are compulsory and permanent, and that as long as human nature remains what it is there can be no analogy whatever between a voluntary gift and a surrender under compulsion. This distinction, which indeed seems elementary, would be appreciated by Englishmen with extraordinary rapidity the moment an attempt was made to try upon them the experiment they have so lightly inflicted upon Irishmen.

And while on the special subject of the landlords and the treatment they have received, a word may be said with regard to the extraordinary inconsistency of our dealings with the owners of land on the one hand, and their tenants on the other. At this moment there are many landlords whose estates are subject to incumbrances. It is fashionable to sneer at the folly and improvidence of men who have incumbered their estates. The taunt is a peculiarly foolish one, for it is probable that there are not five men in a hundred in any rank of

life in the United Kingdom who have not at one time or another
borrowed money on the security of their property in land or goods,
their personal reputation, their labour, or their skill. The man who
does not occasionally use his capital as the security for an advance,
is not a very wise one. The improvident man is he who pledges
his security for more than it is worth. The Irish landlords and
their predecessors raised charges on their land, many of them
for most excellent purposes, and the value of the land at the time
was fully sufficient to cover the charges and to leave a surplus. The
British Government has now stepped in, and by a series of operations
unknown in any civilised country, and therefore not to be anticipated,
has for the benefit of the State made enormous and permanent reductions in the value of the landlord's property. It has done more—it
has strictly forbidden him to test the value of his property by the
ordinary method of offering it for sale to those who wish to purchase
it. To the tenant, on the other hand, the Government has given the
enormous advantage of the Imperial credit, which enables him to buy
the property which the landlord is compelled to sell, with money at
3 per cent. Meanwhile the landlord, who is met at every turn by
exceptional laws directed against his interest, finds that the laws which
regulate his own outgoings are enforced with the most punctual
regularity, and that if he desire to pay off the incumbrances upon
his estate, he must borrow the money, if he can borrow it at all, at
4, 5, or 6 per cent. interest, and is forbidden to look to the State for
the loan of a farthing. At this moment there are hundreds of landlords who have hitherto managed to live upon the margin of rent
which they still receive. The reductions which have now become the
fashion will sweep away the whole of these margins, and will leave
the landlords with a debit balance, and utterly unable to meet the
interest on their incumbrances. In other words they will be absolutely ruined. The equity of enabling the landlords to borrow money
on Government security for the discharge of the whole or a part of
their incumbrances is so obvious that it may safely be assumed it will
not commend itself to a British Cabinet.

THE WAY OUT, 'BACK AGAIN'

We have now enumerated some of the consequences of the amazing remedy for Irish disorders which Parliament in its wisdom has
adopted. It would be hard to conceive a more unsatisfactory and
unpromising result. And depressing as is the result itself, the
attitude which many Englishmen have thought fit to adopt in regard
to it is more depressing still. Those who are most ready to admit
and deplore the evil are often the most ready to submit without
protest to its indefinite prolongation. ' We are in presence,' they say,
' of a *fait accompli*; what is done cannot be undone. The Act of

1870 was bad, the Act of 1881 is worse, but we cannot go back upon
them.' This is a counsel of despair, and the sooner it is abandoned
the better. We *must* go back on this legislation. We *must*
repudiate it; we must admit that it was legislation for the hour and
the emergency only, not for the daily life and the ordinary needs of
a civilised people. If we do not, the penalty is certain. In Ireland
the reign of the attorney will be for ever prolonged; litigation is
already becoming the only profitable industry; it bids fair to survive
all others. The ill feeling between classes, which it is our professed
object to remove, will and must continue, if it does not become
aggravated. The weary task of fixing sham values by the aid of
sham courts, which we are beginning over again, will have to be
renewed, at ever-shortening intervals, *in sœcula sœculorum.* The
infinite series of additional land bills with which we are threatened
will engage and waste the time of the Imperial Parliament. But the
mischief which will be done in Ireland will be insignificant in comparison to that which will assuredly be inflicted upon Great Britain.
Once admit that the principles and the practice of the Irish land laws
are anything but rules for a state of siege, hasty expedients to meet
an emergency, and we thereupon accept them as reasonable bases for
the laws of a civilised community. Every departure from common
honesty and from true economy which the Irish Land Code contains
will be cited here, and justly cited, as the foundation for new claims
and new methods, not in regard to land only, but in regard to every
other form of property. The English members, who with such a light
heart have given *carte blanche* to successive governments to play
the mischief in Ireland and in Ireland only, will find to their cost
that the principles to which they have so wantonly given their
adherence will come back and will grow with a vigour which will
astonish them in English soil. It is, therefore, not only desirable, it
is essential, that the whole system of Irish land tenure as it now
exists should be destroyed. Dual ownership must cease to exist.
The land courts must be abolished and men once more allowed to
earn their living with some confidence in the future. Purchase—
the one and only method by which we can escape from our present
difficulty—must be made easy, universal, and just. Sir William
Harcourt pretends to be shocked at the idea of purchase being proposed by those who are supporters of the Union and the cause of law.
To buy out the landlords is to buy out the English garrison. But to
keep a garrison in an enemy's town after you have deprived that
garrison of its leaders, of its arms, and its organisation, is a folly which
should be apparent even to an enemy like Sir William Harcourt.

PURCHASE

Moreover, there is no reason whatever why an honest scheme of
purchase should not give the same facilities to the landlord to become

the purchaser of the tenant's interest as are now accorded to the tenant
who wishes to purchase the interest of his landlord. Lastly, there
must be no more Land Acts of the pattern of 1887 and 1896, Acts
which in themselves are makeshifts of the poorest kind, which solve
no problem, which bring us to no goal, and which, above all, are calculated not to facilitate but to postpone that extension of purchase to
which, and to which alone, we can look for a real remedy for some of
the troubles of Ireland. As to how purchase shall be effected, that
is another matter. There are various ways in which the object can
be accomplished ; but, whatever method be selected, success can only
be hoped for if certain essential features of the situation are recognised
at the outset. It must be recognised that the only justification for
such a step is a national emergency. If the measure be attempted in
a petty spirit of animosity against any particular class, and be made
the opportunity for giving effect to the prejudices and the hatreds
of one section of the community, it will fail, and it will deserve to
fail. Sir George Trevelyan, Mr. Byles, late of the Shipley Division,
and others of their way of thinking, have announced that though
the skies may fall they will never 'give a penny to the Irish
landlords.' That is the language of spite, not of statesmanship.
To begin with, whatever the Irish landlord has done or left undone,
he has acted in strict accordance with the laws which the Imperial
Parliament, it may almost be said the Parliament of England, has
enacted. Every law up to a comparatively recent date has been made
in the supposed interests of England, and the landlords have done
precisely what every other British subject would do under similar
circumstances, lived and acted under the law as he found it ; some
wisely and well, some ill and unwisely. The basis of purchase
must be a generous recognition of the landlords' rights, and an
admission of the iniquity of atoning for the errors of a nation by
the sacrifice of individuals.

There is good reason to believe that not even the most extreme
members of the Separatist party in Ireland are anxious to ruin the
landlords, provided that purchase can be effected ; the opposition to
a reasonable scheme will not come from them.

ULSTER AND THE NEW LAND ACT

There is, moreover, a special reason why the terms of purchase
should be generous. It is one of the many blessings of our Irish land
legislation that it has invariably rewarded bad men, and inflicted
special disabilities on good men. The murderer, the perjurer, the
boycotter have found their respective professions pay. The rogue can
point with satisfaction to the indisputable truth that roguery has
proved to be the best policy. And now in Ulster, and to a limited
extent in other parts of Ireland, we are face to face with the fact that

tenants are being denied the benefits of the purchase clauses simply because they have been honest, industrious men, who have earned and paid their rents. Landlords who by their forbearance, their good sense, and their enterprise have made their properties valuable, are threatened with confiscation because other men, less provident and less well behaved, have brought down prices in the South and West. Indeed, the condition of affairs in Ulster is the only real excuse for the Bill of the present Session. The Bill itself is full of the most patent absurdities. It is part of a system which is replete with injustice and pregnant with failure. But certain rough considerations of equity seemed to require its passage. If after the storming of Badajoz the Duke of Wellington had given permission to the Portuguese troops and to the King's German Legion to sack the city, but had forbidden the British troops to take part in the operation, there would have been a certain amount of injustice in the prohibition. There would have been something to be said for allowing the British soldier to 'go in' with his comrades. But even that would not have furnished a good argument for sacking towns as a general principle; still less for plundering a city which happened to be occupied by your friends.

It is permissible to claim that the provisions of the Land Acts should be extended to Ulster without admitting that the Land Acts are either wise, just, or expedient.

But to return to the question of purchase. The terms on which compulsory purchase is based must be sufficiently generous to prevent gross injustice. If necessary, the State, which hopes to reap the benefit, must bear at least a portion of the cost. To the tenant should be given the first option, or rather to him should be transferred the fee of his holding subject to the rent-charge. But facilities should also be given to the landlord, and he should be encouraged and enabled to purchase their tenant-rights from his tenants by agreement. To achieve this object money should be advanced to the landlord on the same terms as to the tenant; the security will be as great, probably greater, and the Exchequer cannot suffer. If it does suffer, the loss will not be comparable to the expenditure past and future upon the paraphernalia of land courts, land commissions, and all the complications and miseries which have followed in their train.

Purchase once made universal, what will follow? Not necessarily peace, not necessarily prosperity; but, at any rate, the chance, the possibility of peace and prosperity. We cannot produce either of those blessings by Act of Parliament, but we can refrain from making their attainment impossible. Is it not at least worth while to try the experiment?

H. O. ARNOLD-FORSTER.

THE INFLUENCE OF BAYREUTH

SOME years ago, in the earlier days of Bayreuth as a centre of Wagnerian music, an appalling amount of literature used to be published
in which various German philosophers or quasi-philosophers were
wont to discuss the tendency and true inwardness of Wagner's art,
and of the institution founded by the munificence of the King of
Bavaria.   One of these pamphlets, which were formerly hawked about
Bayreuth at the time of the summer festivals there, bore for its
partial title the words, 'Was soll Bayreuth?' which might be interpreted, 'What is the intended function of the undertaking, or of the
Wagner Theatre, or Wagner's works as a whole?' (for all these meanings
have been for a good many years implied in the utterance of the
sacred word 'Bayreuth' by the initiated).   Now that the twentieth
anniversary of the first performance in the Wagner Theatre at Bayreuth has been celebrated (the 13th of August is the exact day) by
a revival of the Nibelungen cycle in the theatre specially built for it,
it may not be out of place to review the progress of all that is meant
by the mystic word.   Has the influence of Wagner himself, of the
ideal theatre which he made an accomplished fact, and of the festival
performances that are visited by pilgrims from all parts of the world,
been a good influence for his own art, for the art of dramatic music in
general? or is the astounding statement true, which appeared at the
beginning of an article in this Review some years ago, 'The Wagner
bubble has burst'?

    That statement seems to have been a little premature, and for a
bubble, the creations of Wagner have shown a remarkable unwilling-
ness to vanish.   The world in general has accepted Wagner, and the
case of the professed anti-Wagnerians is more hopeless than ever.
In respect of the permanence of Wagner there seems no room for
question; things which, at first received with doubt, if not actual obloquy,
live down the prejudices of the world, and increase in general appreciation for many decades, as Wagner's works have done, do not belong
to the class of productions which are merely transitory, and have been
buoyed up by fashion or the interested admiration of partisans.   But
it is not simply the popularity of Wagner's music as a whole that
need be discussed, but the working of that great plan of his which

included something like the artistic regeneration of German operatic tradition. The central fact of the scheme is, of course, the building itself, that wonderful theatre which proves Wagner to have been as great an architect as he was a poet, a composer, or a designer of pictorial effect. This was not all, however. The master's own home, Wahnfried, was to become the social centre of all that was worthiest in that artistic world which should visit the Bavarian town, and in some sort a school of instruction in the traditions he wished to establish. In addition to this, an actual school was instituted, the first products of which were this year allowed to try their skill in important parts. Bayreuth, in fact, was to be the ' hub of the universe' as far as the new dramatic music was concerned, and the choice of this dull town, with the departed fragrance of its little Court, and its fast-fading souvenirs of Jean Paul Richter, was eminently a wise one. The difficulty of getting there by train was not the only advantage it presented from Wagner's point of view: it is true that he wished to make it more or less hard of access, in order to keep away the average holiday-seeker, and in some measure to make sure that those who came thither should be distracted from the main object of their journey by no rival excitements or dissipations, such as in a large capital must always divert the mind from serious study of an artistic creation, more especially when that artistic creation requires for its embodiment a theatre, with its associations of frivolous pleasure.

These objects have been fulfilled to a degree that Wagner himself can never have anticipated ; and the vogue of Bayreuth has increased with every succeeding festival year. At the same time it has not lost its pleasantly primitive character, nor has the tide of fashion converted the town into a mere pleasure-resort of the usual kind. There are, as there must always be, a certain amount of people who go to Bayreuth mainly out of curiosity, but these form but a very small part of the crowd, and among them there are many who come to gape and remain to admire. The revolution worked in stage illusion by the various ingenious devices that the Bayreuth theatre has been the first to exhibit has had an influence that may be described as world-wide, and although no great theatre has yet been built on the exact model of the Wagner Theatre, yet scarcely a theatre in the world has failed to feel its influence in some degree. In lighting generally, and more particularly in effects of cloud and storm, this stage can still produce pictures altogether beyond the attainment of its rivals ; this is in great part owing to the arrangement of the auditorium, which of itself removes many difficulties of ordinary stage perspective. In theatres of the usual shape the scene can only be perfectly illusory to those who sit at a certain distance and look at the stage from a certain angle ; generally the front of the dress-circle, or the dividing-line between the pit and the stalls, is the point at which everything falls into its proper place. As a certain amount of

illusion must be secured for the stalls and the boxes, the difficulties
of the scene-painter are much increased, some compromise has to be
arranged, and some of the illusion is necessarily lost, even by those
who sit nearest the points already mentioned.   At Bayreuth, for
all practical purposes, every spectator occupies a position of equal
advantage in relation to the stage.   This result is accomplished, of
course at considerable sacrifice of space, by setting the whole stage
much farther back in the building than is usual, and by placing all
the seats on a gradual slope, the number of seats in each row increasing towards the back.   The angle at which the seats are raised brings
about the delightful result that everyone gets a complete view of the
stage, the heads of those in front of him appearing to be in one plane,
conveniently below the level of that hood which at once conceals the
orchestra from sight, and causes its sounds to blend with the voices
on the stage in a way that cannot be described.

As for the influence of Wahnfried, it may be briefly described as
resembling more or less closely the influence that is exerted by one
of the smaller German Courts, such as Bayreuth itself formerly possessed.   That Frau Cosima Wagner should receive from the most ardent
Wagnerians the kind of homage that is usually reserved for crowned
heads need not be a matter of much surprise, for this lady's work in
connection with all the festivals that have taken place since her
illustrious husband's death has been far-reaching and all-important.
Her quasi-royal position is due not only to the memory of Wagner,
but is mainly the result of her own labours in engaging artists, in
teaching them every gesture and pose on the stage, and in superin-
tending every detail of the production.   The preservation of the
Wagnerian tradition, if it is preserved, will be mainly her work, and
for this self-appointed mission who shall censure her ?   We may
smile at the ceremony that is observed at the Wahnfried receptions,
but it is impossible to ignore the fact that the reins of government
are held in a strong hand, and that the policy adopted has
been in general a wise one.   As a matter of subordinate importance,
it may be observed that the work of the Bayreuth school, as exhibited
in two of its pupils, Herr Burgstaller (Siegfried) and Herr Breuer
(Mime), has been proved this year most satisfactorily.   If the standard
of vocal art is in neither case very high (as it can never be where
German methods of instruction prevail), the technique of stage
business has been thoroughly acquired, and both the young singers
move with ease and appropriateness of gesture.

Frau Wagner's independent work began with the production of
Tristan und Isolde for the first time at Bayreuth in 1886 ; though
she had, of course, superintended the *Parsifal* performances of 1883
and 1884, yet there was nothing to do but see that the composer's
intentions were strictly adhered to.   With the new production there
was also little difficulty, for the German stage could offer superlatively

.fine individual impersonations, and the best scene-painters were only too glad to get a chance of their work being seen with all the advantages conferred by the Bayreuth theatre. In 1888, *Die Meistersinger* was added to the repertory, and the three works were given again in the following year. With this programme, so worthily representing the master's ripest works in three different spheres of dramatic art, the work of Bayreuth may be said to have reached its culminating point. In *Parsifal* the highest development of the sacred drama or 'mystery-play' is attained; in *Tristan* we have the supreme achievement in musical tragedy; and in *Die Meistersinger* the ideal comedy in music. In 1891 and 1892, *Tannhäuser* formed part of the scheme, and the revival was not uninstructive, for the opera had become sadly conventionalised in the course of years, and it was most desirable to bring it out with all the reverence for the text and the gorgeous mounting that Bayreuth can command. In 1894, *Lohengrin* was taken up in the same spirit; so that with this the cycle was completed of those works which Wagner would have acknowledged as representing the maturity of his creative faculty.

With these later performances a new question presented itself for consideration by the Bayreuth authorities. That old one, 'Shall Wagner be allowed to exist?' had long ago been answered; now there arose the discussion as to whether his music was to be the exclusive possession of the German race, or to become the heritage of all the nations in equal measure. At first the singers engaged were all German by birth and education; but the fact that German vocalisation is often far from satisfactory—a fact which, from Wagner's writings, it is clear that he grasped many years before it was generally admitted—was gradually assimilated by his successors, and in some of the later reproductions of *Parsifal* foreign artists of exceptional ability, such as Van Dyk and Blauwaert, were occasionally seen on the Bayreuth stage. As a natural consequence, their finer methods of singing threw the German singers into the shade, and these were very soon made to feel that with the cosmopolitan Bayreuth audience their popularity was not as great as that of their rivals.

When the later operas were mounted it became ever more and more evident that the many passages requiring beautiful singing could not be safely entrusted to German artists, and thus engagements were given to a wider circle of musicians, including, for the *Lohengrin* performances, Madame Nordica, Miss Marie Brema, and others, all of whom made acknowledged successes. These successes very naturally stirred up a good deal of artistic jealousy, and gradually a new party has been formed within the Wagnerian camp. This party of 'protectionists,' as they may be called, has taken for its watchword a certain speech of Wagner's on the memorable occasion when the foundation-stone of the new theatre was laid. 'You have now a German Art' is the equivalent of the famous sentence, and it is contended that the master intended his music to remain an exclusively German possession. The words spoken in 1872 undoubtedly carried with them an implied reference to the then newly re-created German Empire, whose first, and in some ways greatest, product was, without question, the creation of all that is implied in the word 'Bayreuth'; but it is clear from many passages in Wagner's writings that he was fully aware of the shortcomings of German singers, and that he was no enemy to his music being sung by vocalists who should also prove themselves persons of ordinary artistic intelligence. · In going far afield for her singers Frau Wagner was most amply justified; and, after all, German singers were not forgotten, but whenever a German artist was found to be competent preference was given, as it naturally would be, to the performer who, though possessing no other crowning merit, would yet be able to pronounce the German words as his or her native language.

When the arrangements for this year were being made, it was rumoured that engagements had been offered to, and in some cases contracts actually signed with, a number of distinguished non-German singers. That the De Reszkes were approached on the subject is an open secret, and both Miss Macintyre and Miss Susan Strong were talked of for the part of Sieglinde. Madame Nordica and several other foreigners were contemplated; but when the final cast of the dramas appeared, it was found that all the principal parts had been filled either with old stagers of German origin, or with young aspirants for fame in Germany. Miss Brema was, indeed, engaged as Fricka, and, if the truth must be told, made the part of supreme importance by her fine singing, noble presence, and artistic conception of the character; Miss Marion Weed, an American lady, appeared without much success as Freia, in a particularly hideous costume, but there was hardly another foreign name in the cast. As Frau Sucher was a Sieglinde of absolutely unsurpassable merit, the preference given to her over the foreign singers is amply explained; but the numerous cases in which these rumours of foreign appearances proved false give rise to a strong suspicion that the changes were made in partial deference to the protectionist party. Frl. Gulbrandson, of whose Brünnhilde high opinions have been expressed, is indeed a Swedish lady, but apparently she is an artist of German training, so that she is no representative of the 'bel canto,' as it is called. The other Brünnhilde, Frau Lilli Lehmann-Kalisch, is one of the three artists who took part in the original performance of the *Ring* in 1876; she then sang one of the Rhine-maidens, but since that time her fine singing has been displayed in more dramatic parts, and though she is now a very mediocre actress, the splendid voice told with all possible effect in the last two acts of *Götterdämmerung*. In the former dramas she was evidently not completely at ease, and her want of conviction was a great surprise to those who remember her ideally beautiful performances of Isolde and Leonora more than ten years ago in London. The Wotan of Herr C. Perron was another impersonation that improved, in the first cycle, from day to day; at first the excellent singer was sadly perfunctory, but in *Siegfried* the fine passages allotted to the Wanderer were given with much dignity. Those who attended the first cycle had the great advantage of hearing two Siegfrieds, for Herr Grüning, after a moderately successful appearance in that part of the drama named from the hero, was succeeded by Herr Burgstaller on the final day. This artist should make a great career: his voice is of fine quality, and he acts with delightful conviction and point; he has also the nameless quality by which a personality of distinct charm conveys itself to the audience. In the first rank of the female impersonations stands the Waltraute of Frau Schumann-Heink, who also sang the music of Erda and the First Norn with great vocal beauty and distinction. Frau Reuss-Belce was a good Gutrune, and the representatives of Rhine-maidens, Norns, and Valkyries were quite efficient. The Siegmund of Herr Gerhäuser was a sad failure, but Herr Breuer did well as Mime, Herr Grengg was a first-rate Hagen, and Herr Gross a manly Gunther. The ponderous voice of Herr Elmblad was exactly suited to the music of Fafner, whose bodily representative in *Siegfried* was a triumph of mechanical skill. No more fearful dragon than this has been seen upon the stage; and another very meritorious monster was the serpent into which Alberich transforms himself in the *Rheingold*. The acting of Herr Friedrichs in the latter character was admirable, though his singing was scarcely above the average attained by non-musical actors. The return of Herr Richter to Bayreuth as principal conductor is a matter on which the management is to be heartily congratulated.

The mounting of the whole cycle was extremely fine, at least in respect of the scenery; while the most famous scenes of 1876 were repeated almost exactly, down to the smallest details, certain scenes that were not so remarkable then are now transformed into stage-pictures of the utmost beauty. The opening scene with the Rhine-daughters is entirely successful, and the new machinery by which their motions are controlled is a complete success. The second act of *Die Walküre* and certain passages in *Siegfried* and *Götterdämmerung* were also most commendable. It is hard to bestow unqualified praise upon the costumes, the majority of which were exceedingly disappointing; German taste in such particulars is notoriously bad, and here is a point in which a little cosmopolitanism would come in most usefully. And it is hard to see how Bayreuth is to keep up its position if it does not move with the times to some extent. The absence of innovations in the text hardly calls for praise, since any such piece of vandalism would be wholly foreign to the spirit in which the institution is managed; but against one piece of inter-

polated stage business an emphatic protest must be made.   There is
a celebrated point near the end of *Das Rheingold* where Wotan,
shortly before leading the procession of the gods across the rainbow
bridge, conceives the idea of redeeming the treasure, with the power
of the magic ring, by means of a hero whose parentage and education
are dealt with in the two successive dramas; the use of the
'leitmotiv' afterwards connected with the sword here enabled the
composer to tell the audience what Wotan is thinking of, without
any help from words or action.   It has struck someone at Bayreuth
that the musical theme alone might possibly not be recognised by
many of the audience; and in deference to their stupidity an actual
sword is introduced at this point which appears to have formed part
of the Nibelungen treasure, a theory that is entirely unsupported by
the words of the later dramas, where the sword Nothung is stated
to have belonged in the first instance to Wälse, *i.e.* Wotan, in the
disguise adopted by him for the sake of generating the family of the
Wälsungs or Volsungs.   To attribute the sword to the treasure, and
to produce it in tangible form, is to vulgarise one of the most
refined touches in the whole trilogy, and one which more than
perhaps any other single passage justifies the principles upon which
Wagner worked.   The power of suggestion by means of a musical
theme previously identified, or afterwards to be identified, with some
definite dramatic factor is the great advantage of the system carried to
such a point of development by Wagner, and anything which material-
ises his ideas, as is done here, is sincerely to be regretted.[1]

Bayreuth must hold the highest standard in every department
of the dramatic and musical arts; if it ceases to give the pattern, as
it were, on which other performances are to be modelled, its *raison
d'être* will cease also, and the moment it lowers its ideals its vogue
must pass away, and the noble building fall into disuse.   For,
considering the absence of any other attraction to the Bavarian town,
which is on the way to no special pleasure-resort, it cannot hold its
own unless the attractions of its performances are infinitely greater
than those of any other theatre on the Continent, at least in the
way of artistic presentment of the works given; and although that
part of Wagner's original scheme which was concerned with the
production of important operas by other men may well be allowed to
be ignored, yet the Wagner performances must maintain their importance if the place is to continue its work in the world.   It would
be disaster if it all came to naught, and those most deeply interested
must see to it that this veritable 'Götterdämmerung' shall not
arrive for many years to come.

J. A. FULLER MAITLAND.

[1] It has been asserted that this 'business' was permitted by Wagner himself in
1876, as a concession to the less acute among the audience; but if this is so, it is
strange that Herr Richter, who conducted the festival of twenty years ago, should
know nothing about it.

THE BAPTISM OF CLOVIS

THERE is nothing which indicates more strikingly the growth of the historic sentiment among all classes during the last twenty or thirty years than the fashion which has sprung up of celebrating the anniversary of some great event in the remote past, or the birth or death of some distinguished or heroic personage. These celebrations have been rapidly increasing upon us of late, not without causing some little bewilderment to worthy people whose knowledge of history is not their strong point. They are surprised to hear that Hungary, for instance, can lay claim to a millennium of anything; or that there could be any reason why excited experts should go into hysterics because eight centuries had actually been completed since the Domesday Book was drawn up; or that there was so much that was worth remembering at Durham or Ely or Norwich all those hundreds and hundreds of years ago. Cynical Philistines, on the other hand, have been prone to ask whether it might not be just as well to let bygones be bygones—whether we are any the better for loading our memories with facts which have travelled down to us from so very long ago that a critical age may be prepared to question whether they are likely to be true ; or whether, if true in the main, much of the glamour which surrounds them may not be due to the mists through which we look back at them—inasmuch as ' the past will win a glory from its being far,' and also inasmuch as we are agreed that ' distance lends enchantment to the view.'

It is always better to let the cynics have their say and to forbear from arguing with them. We and they do not stand upon the same platform, nor start from the same premises. In this particular instance they are in an evil case as being a small sect of unfortunates who count themselves wiser than the rest of us, and yet who are bound to find themselves more and more in a hopeless and soured minority. The spirit of the age is against them, and, however little they may be able to understand it, the truth is that the cynics are always behind, never before, their time.

Our near neighbours across the Channel have of late been throwing themselves with a great deal of excitement into one anniversary which in its multifarious pomps and ceremonies has been, and is, making its appeal on the one side to the patriotism of Frenchmen, and on the other side to the religious beliefs and aspirations and hopes of the devout and fervent millions of the Catholic population of the great Republic. The Government has betrayed no little anxiety as to what may come of it all, and have actually put forth stringent orders to restrain the French bishops from meeting in too large numbers simultaneously, lest a religious demonstration on too large a scale should result in some frenzied outbreak which might be dangerous to the public welfare. *Surtout pas trop de religion!* seems to be the ruling principle of philosophers who profess unbounded liberty of thought.

And yet this great French anniversary will celebrate nothing worse than the baptism of Clovis, King of the Franks, in the Cathedral of Reims, on Christmas Day, 496—the baptism, that is, of the man whom Frenchmen regard as the founder of their national institutions, the beginner of their national life, the establisher of their national faith, the saviour of European society in an age when things were tending towards chaos. Whether this view of the case be anything but a hugely exaggerated view is one question—that it is the view of the average Frenchman whom one meets by the way-side, and who has anything to say of Clovis, is hardly a question at all. Much less is it a question that the event commemorated by this year's anniversary in France has been one of almost incalculable importance in its influence upon the social, religious, and political sentiments and beliefs of European peoples, nations and languages down to the present hour, and that it marked an epoch in the history of the world.

Who were these Franks? When Julius Cæsar, after eight years of ceaseless warfare, effected the complete subjugation of Gaul, fifty-one years before our era, Rome found herself not only with a new dependency to govern, but she found herself with a new race to take account of—a race which for centuries afterwards became an enormous source of wealth and power to the Empire. Gaul in its widest extent comprehended all that is now included in France, Belgium, the Netherlands, and Alsace-Lorraine.

The inhabitants of this wide territory were of the same blood, with a religion and with a polity of their own. They had something like national assemblies; they had a powerful priesthood, which exercised great influence over the people; they were brave, intelligent, rich, and civilised up to that point at which a nation is prepared to assimilate and absorb whatever better things its neighbours or its masters may have to offer. What the Celts are to-day, that they were on the Loire and Seine in Cæsar's days; and what that means I must refer to the great historian of Rome to tell those who would fain

know.[1] The point is, those Gauls were Celts; while on the other
side of the Rhine there were the teeming and restless Teutonic
peoples, who for some time past had been finding their own land too
strait for them. Not only that, but the climate and the soil of
the South were a clime and a soil of a land of promise; for generations they had longed to possess that good land so much better than
their own. It was in consequence of a great emigration from the
upper Rhine by some of these German tribes resolved on finding a new
home for themselves across the river that Cæsar was sent to drive
them back. The end was that the Rhine became the boundary
between Rome and Germany. When Gaul became a Roman
province it was supremely necessary to defend it against the barbarians who should try to cross over. All along its left bank, from
Mayence to Cologne, there was a wide belt which was in fact a
gigantic military district occupied by an army of no less than eight
legions, or an aggregate of 100,000 men, cantoned in fifty for-
tresses or fortified camps. Up and down the stream two fleets were
always moving, watching the navigation and the movements of the
dwellers on the opposite bank, who were continually threatening
to force a passage across the barrier and pour in upon the plains of
Gaul.

It was not long before it was found politic to cut off the northern
portion of the new territory, and make of it a new prefecture, under
the name of Gallia Belgica. Draw a line on the map from Dieppe
to Strasburg, and you may take it that the triangle of which this
line is the base, and the Rhine with the coast along the North Sea
and the Channel the other two sides, roughly indicates the boundaries
of this province, of which in the fourth century the father of St.
Ambrose was the governor. Under the wise administration of the
Romans this country became one of the most thriving and prosperous dependencies of the Empire. When the poet Ausonius
made a voyage hither in the middle of the fourth century, he was
enraptured with what he saw as he sailed down the Moselle, more
beautiful and more populous than it is to-day. Trèves was accounted the fourth city of the Empire. It possessed what may be
called a university, in which, under the supervision of Lactantius,
Constantine's son Crispus probably pursued his studies. Here
St. Ambrose was born, and here St. Jerome seems to have spent
some years; and here we are told he went through one of those
religious crises in his life which determined his after career. By
this time, and perhaps a century at least before this time, the
Belgic Gaul was emphatically a Christian land. Soissons, Strasburg,
and Reims had each its bishop, and at Trèves there was an archbishop or metropolitan. Trade, commerce, manufactures, and litera-

---

[1] Mommsen, *History of Rome*, Book V. chap. vii. vol. i. pt. i. p. 286, English
translation.

ture too, flourished to a far greater extent than, till comparatively lately, has been thought. Paris, or Lutetia, in the fourth century could not compare with the splendour of the Belgic cities. Between Reims or Trèves and Bordeaux there was no city of any great extent and importance, except perhaps Tours, which was the centre of South Gallic as Reims was of the Belgic Christianity.

It was within the borders of this much-favoured land that the Franks had succeeded in establishing themselves at least as early as the beginning of the fifth century, when Rome had been compelled to withdraw the legions from the defence of the Rhine, and had left the Belgian Celts to protect themselves. We first meet with the name of Franks in the year 242, when they were so inconsiderable a company that a tribune of a legion could disperse and crush them ; and during the third and fourth centuries we come upon them as mere bands of marauders, always beaten and put to flight, but collecting again in formidable associations, as gatherings of outlaws on a small scale have been wont to do in unsettled times, and are likely to do again. In the latter half of the fourth century the pressure upon the Goths and German tribes by the movements of the Huns was continually increasing, and forcing the former across the Danube and the latter across the Rhine. Gradually and somewhat rapidly these Franks appear to have become constituted into something like a nation, and under the name of Ripuarian and Salian Franks—the one hovering upon the right bank of the Rhine, the others roaming among the fastnesses of the lowlands at the mouth of the Schelde or the great forests of the Silva Carbonaria and the Ardennes—had developed into a disciplined force which even Attila and Aëtius had to reckon with, and whose tactics in warfare were peculiarly their own. When Attila crossed the Rhine somewhere near its mouth, he appears to have driven the Franks before him, only to make them join the legions of Aëtius ; and under this commander they contributed materially to the reverse which the Huns suffered at Châlons. Attila led his hosts back across the Rhine at Cologne, and as he retreated we may reasonably infer that the Franks followed in his wake and returned to their settlements in the Belgian province.

At this point in Frankish history we find ourselves very much in the dark. We are confronted by legend and fable ; mythical personages appear out of the mists, and names of kings who are like the knights of King Arthur, and of whose actual existence grave doubts have been expressed by scholars with a right to the opinions they hold. Meanwhile we have not yet found a distinct answer to the question who these Franks were, and whether they were in any true sense a nation when we hear of them first, or whether they only grew into an organic polity out of a mere aggregate of hungry and desperate vagabonds, pretty much in the same way that Saxons and Frisians and Angles, and other marauders who poured into Britain when the island was deserted by the Roman legions, became consolidated into a nation among ourselves.

The tendency of German scholars is to maintain the view that the Franks were the lineal descendants of one or other of those Teutonic peoples whose valour and whose virtues Tacitus has immortalised ; and one of the last supporters of this theory has gone so far as to suggest that they were the descendants of that great group of tribes whom Tacitus calls the Istævones, and who claimed to be descended from the gods of the land. How these people lost the old name and got to adopt the more modern one we are not informed. Gibbon, with that unique sagacity of his, forbears from anything which could pledge himself to more than a single phrase might express, and speaks as if there could be no doubt that the Franks were a *confederacy* ; implying that their early organisation was the result of a settled compact among the members of which it was composed. On the other hand, the French school of historians, under the inspiration of a thinker of brilliant genius, the late M. Fustel de Coulanges, rejects even the theory of a confederacy of Germanic tribes, and, dismissing it as a pure hypothesis lacking any evidence for its support, denounces with vehement emphasis the notion that the Franks, when we come upon them first in the third century, were a *nation* at all. M. Fustel, with his usual exhaustive elaboration and argumentative force, insists thát, long before the third century, those German tribes of whom Tacitus wrote—perhaps more as a philosopher than as an historian—had, by their continual internecine wars and by the frightful and pitiless slaughter inflicted upon them by Rome, ceased to exist as organised clans or tribes ; and that the Franks were the mere scattered survivors—the wrecks—of the Chauci, Catti, Cherusci, and Sigambri, who were simply swept away like the doomed aborigines of America and Africa ; that their very names would have been blotted out of human memory if it had not been that the bards and popular singers of a later time kept up the old traditions of their fabled prowess. This view, in the main, seems to the present writer the only view that serves to explain the facts that have come down to us, and the only view that helps us to account for the origin and significance of the name Franks which these people earned or adopted, and in which they gloried. For the word seems to mean *Roamers* or *Wanderers*, and may well have been applied to restless companies of soldiers of fortune who, as we know they did, were ready to take service in the Roman armies (in which some of them rose to be commanders of eminence) or, failing to find what they sought in the way of pay, engage in expeditions on their own account—like the White Companies of the Middle Ages —wandering as far as Spain, or preying upon the outskirts of the Rhenish border when the chance of making a raid occurred, as it must have done from time to time.

The passage of the Danube by the Visigoths in 376 was the beginning of the end for Rome's imperial prestige. The passage of the Rhine thirty years later was, as Gibbon pronounced, the invasion that sealed the fate of Roman civilisation. Burgundians and Suevi and Vandals came pouring in upon the broad lands and cities made ready for the spoil. The stream went rushing over Western Europe; it did not stop till it had overflowed Gaul and Spain and North Africa. Everywhere there was pillage, devastation, obliteration. Four times during that dreadful fifth century was Rome herself stormed and sacked. Practically, however much theorists of the *doctrinaire* class may protest against the admission, the Roman Empire in the West came to an end in the year 476; it was Charlemagne who restored it and once again made the name of Roman Emperor a reality. But while the Teuton hordes were spreading themselves over the more southerly regions, plundering, burning, and slaying, the Franks in the old Belgic province were, as far as appears, content to remain at home. They were not all men of war, there were those who were tillers of the soil; the land could not be left desert. Moreover, though the fighting class might be pagans, if anything, all below the heroes were Christians, with a strong attachment for and confidence in their clergy, and an almost unbounded reverence for their bishops, in whose hands the civil administration was left: they were the arbiters of all disputes which did not require to be settled by the sword—their word was law. The true Franks, as by this time they had got to call themselves—the Franks who were the warrior class and looked down with immeasurable contempt upon priests and people, in whose veins no royal blood was coursing—they let their hair grow to its full length and fall over their shoulders—in battle they managed to pack it under their helmets; ferocious and careless of life, they knew no fear, and loved fighting for fighting's sake, as men love hunting for hunting's sake while recking nothing of the quarry. But these haughty swashbucklers all boasted of their divine origin—whatever that might mean—and every one of them, in his own opinion, was worthy to be a king. Such 'kings' were for ever starting up among them, enjoying here and there a brief reign. The time was sure to come when some strong man higher by a head and shoulders than all the rest, like Saul, the son of Kish—a man of force of will and force of brain, masterful, irresistible—a king by the grace of God indeed—should win the ascendency which none could gainsay, and who at some great crisis should be recognised as the peerless leader and commander of the people. When such a man was firmly seated on his throne he would be likely to think of founding a dynasty. And thus it came to pass.

When, in the spring of that dreadful year 451, Attila led his enormous hosts across the Rhine, he seems to have passed that river at several points, extending his front all along the bank from Stras-

burg as far as Cologne. He himself with the central force appears
to have got possession of Coblentz and laid waste the valley of the
Moselle. The right wing of the invading army, crossing at Cologne,
made straight for the valley of the Meuse, and, finding themselves in
face of the Carbonarian forest, revenged themselves for their disappointment at discovering less booty than they looked for by perpetrating
every kind of hideous cruelty upon the miserable inhabitants whereon
they came. This seems to have been the army that at one time
threatened Paris and spread agonies of terror among the panic-stricken
inhabitants. What Joan of Arc did for Orleans a thousand years
later, that Genoveva, the sainted heroine of the fifth century, is said
to have done for Paris. But the truth seems to be that Attila, though
giving a certain measure of licence to his auxiliaries, had no design
of letting them go their own way. He had a definite plan of campaign : his objective was Orleans, and the scattered hosts, though
allowed to ravage and slay, were to be concentrated at Châlons-sur-
Marne for a forward movement against the Visigoths. At the right
moment the pack of bloodhounds that were plundering here and
there were called back to heel when they had advanced no further to
the west than Reims, from which place the legends seem to indicate
that they were summoned to headquarters before they had had time
to complete the looting of the defenceless city. All that portion of
Belgic Gaul to the west of a line from the right bank of the Marne
below Châlons, and taking in the whole basin of the Schelde, suffered
comparatively little from the Huns ; and when Attila, foiled at
Orleans and compelled to retreat from Châlons, made his way back
again to the right bank of the Rhine, Belgic Gaul found itself
nominally indeed still a Roman province—but in point of fact it
was a territory that was derelict. If the people could find themselves
a king, there was little or nothing to prevent them from making
their choice.

Some ten years after the death of Attila, two strong men were
rivals for the supremacy over this no man's land : Egidius, a representative of a powerful family among the Gallo-Romans of the south,
and therefore probably of Celtic blood, represented the old Roman
domination ; and Childeric, son of Meroveus the Frank, and therefore
presumably sprung from a Teutonic stock. Egidius perhaps bore
the title of 'King of the Romans,' Childeric that of King of the
Franks; the first held his court at Soissons, the second at Tournay.[2]

In the autumn of 464 Egidius died of the plague ; he left a son
behind him, Syagrius by name, who succeeded to his father's possessions and was 'king' at Soissons. Two years later to Childeric a
son was born, Clovis, the real founder of the empire of the Franks.
Of his boyhood and early youth we know hardly anything; indeed

[2] *Soissons*, on the left bank of the Aisne, midway between Reims and Compiègne.
Tournay, on the Upper Schelde.

only this, that his father died in 481 and that the lad of fifteen succeeded to the crown. From the time of the young hero's birth till the year 486, *i.e.* till he was twenty years old, there is a provoking blank in Frankish history. We are left to conjecture what course events were taking by reasoning back from the crisis that came at last. It looks as if Clovis, during the first five years of his reign, was making his preparations for what was inevitable, and was extending his influence in the basin of the Schelde and along the left bank of the Meuse. Probably, too, he pushed southward and westward as far as the Somme, making himself master of Cambray, Arras, and Thérouanne—possibly too of Boulogne.

To the south of the Somme were the rich valleys of the Aisne and of Marne, and further still there were the boundless possibilities which invited with irresistible allurement the ambition of a young warrior whose heart was all aflame with thoughts of conquest.

Observe that Soissons was at this time almost the richest and the most beautiful city of Belgic Gaul. When the mixed multitude of barbarians rushed across the Rhine in 406, Soissons had escaped the havoc. When Attila, again, and his motley host spread themselves over the Belgic plains, Soissons once more was spared. It had its aqueducts, its churches—six or eight of them, it seems—its splendid palace for the governors of the city in the old Roman times ; great roads ran from it to Amiens on the west, to Reims on the south-east, to Vermand on the north. There had been great factories here of military engines, and farms ; outside the city walls there were splendid monuments to the nobles whom Soissons delighted to honour. And but a day's journey off there were Rouen and Beauvais, and Senlis and Meaux and, noblest and grandest of all, Reims, where the great bishop, the sainted Remigius (about whom there is so much to tell, if this were the time and place to tell it), was exercising a mighty moral and intellectual influence which to the fierce men of battle was inexplicable, awful, and at times inspired in them a mysterious overmastering dread. All this goodly region seems to have been in some sort Syagrius's patrimony ; it counted as his kingdom. And he called himself a king by right of imperial appointment ; he and none other was *Rex Romanorum*.

A Roman forsooth ! A Roman ! When there was no longer any emperor nearer than Constantinople, and when ten years before this the giant Odoacer had scornfully flouted the puppets that were playing at sovereignty on the Tiber and had gone very far indeed to make the world recognise that Rome's empire, in the West at any rate, was a sham. Let the new nationalities rouse themselves and awake from their dreams ; there had been enough of dreaming ! The time had come when such a born king of men as Clovis—he was twenty years old now—could no longer tolerate the empty fiction of a Rex Romanorum on his borders.

. ·'Let us bring this matter to an issue, thou and I. Let us look one another in the face and play the game of battle for high stakes and *not* for love. Let us see which is the stronger, thou of the Celtic blood or I the Teuton—thou the Roman, I the barbarian. Let us see whether thy land shall be mine or mine thine !'

So they joined battle a league or two to the north of Soissons. Syagrius, with the remnants, or it may be the shadows, of the Roman legions in Gaul and such other men-at-war as he could muster, was smitten hip and thigh and his army was scattered, and he himself fled away to the court of the Visigoths at Toulouse. Thence they sent him back in chains to Soissons ; and there Clovis smote off his head. For the duties of hospitality—or any other duties for that matter—and the softer emotions of pity or generosity—or any other soft emotions—existed only in embryo in those terrible days ; such virtues were for women and priests to talk about, not for men of the flowing locks and the sword that wins plunder and carves out empires for such as can greatly dare.

There was no stopping now. To the long-haired Franks victory meant pillage unsparing. Soissons was sacked, the churches looted, the sacred vessels piled up in giant mounds of plunder for division among the spoilers. Hence that famous incident of the chalice or vase that St. Remigius—if it were he—begged might be reserved. Clovis would fain have kept it back; an unnamed fierce soldier shivered it with his battle-axe. But take note that already we find the grim king in some intimate relations with the Gallic episcopate. The bishops were clearly a power to reckon with ; if the Franks were to go on conquering and to conquer, the Church, through her clergy, must be left to govern the lands that were won. In that fifth century there was no country—not even Italy—that was from end to end so completely christianised as Gaul. The Church was the only organised force that men looked to for protection, for justice, for hope of salvation in this world and the next. 'The Church,' as one has well put it,[3] 'had grown in esteem and wealth . . . the bishops became both spiritual and temporal lords. The Bishop, invested by the simple barbarians with a strange sanctity, was listened to with awe. His confidence in his mission, his high training, his dress, his education, the spiritual power he asserted—all deeply touched his conqueror. It is said that even Attila carried Lupus, Bishop of Troyes, with him to the Rhine that he might get the benefit of his sanctity as a kind of charm. Remigius certainly acquired a mighty influence over Clovis.'

The king had by this time deserted Tournay ; he made Soissons his residence now. But Soissons might be a fortress or might be a palace ; forty miles off to the eastward lay Reims, the city which was regarded in the fifth century as the religious metropolis of all Gaul to the north of the Loire, as Tours was, and perhaps more truly was, the sacred

---

[3] Dean Kitchin, *History of France*, vol. i. Book I. c. vii.

city of the south. Reims had not only its amphitheatre, its baths, 'which Constantine the Great had built there,' its triumphal arches, 'one of which remains,' its circuit of walls, and, outside these, splendid villas which represented the wealth and grandeur of the neighbour-hood, in that happy fourth century of our era when there were no dangers from barbarian invasions; but the city was rich in churches and oratories, tombs of saints and martyrs with a local reputation, and, above all, the cathedral, then of small proportions as compared with the superb and magnificent edifice which now stands up proudly as the matchless triumph of mediæval architecture and the despair of our modern artists, who have lost touch with the enthusiasm and the aspirations of the past. Obviously Reims in that year 486 swarmed with clergy, all held well in hand under the authority and discipline of a prelate whose courage, sanctity, elevation of character, quickness of wit, and lofty wisdom contributed to secure to him as boundless an ascendency over those who had everything to gain by peace as Clovis himself, colossal as his image appears to us as we look back upon him, could exercise by the tremendous force of his irresistible will upon the grizzly warriors who had everything to gain by war. A sort of tacit understanding seems to have been come to which was but the continuation of the understanding between the Romans and the Celtic nobility and landed gentry in the earlier times. The Franks were to be men of the sword. The bishops were to be the civil rulers—of the subdued.

The men who make empires for themselves are and must always be men of policy as well as men of war. Clovis was both to a pre-eminent degree. He saw that with the effective support of the bishops, in whose hands the administration of the country lay, there would be no fear of any revolt of the people. He was a pagan, as were the majority of his Frankish captains, but this paganism of theirs was rather a confused superstition than a religion; a matter of omens and magic and sorcery, of witches and prophetesses and unmeaning observances and irrational terrors. We hardly hear anything of gods or demons, and, I think, nothing of temples or idols or sacrifices— the Franks knew not what they believed. As for these Christian folk, somehow they were the better for their creed; let them keep to it, why meddle with them? Yes! and there was something more. Those other barbarian invaders had got themselves wrong with the bishops and clergy in the lands where they had settled. Vandals and Visigoths and Burgundians were not pagans; they were professing Christians, and had brought a form of Christianity with them which was hateful to the people whom they had subdued. These latter called it a degradation of Christianity; they branded it with the name of Heresy; they spat at the heretics whom they stigmatised as the worst of all heretics, Arians to wit, and shut them out of their churches where they dared till they should renounce and abjure their

errors. Then was war in the gates! Visigoths and Burgundians
and Vandals turned persecutors of the orthodox creed, and there was
variance and hatred between the new comers and the old dwellers
in the conquered lands. Dissension everywhere, harmony nowhere.
Only Theodoric the Great, Arian though he were, let his people
believe and worship pretty much as they pleased; even the very
Jews he would protect and defend. Clovis saw that the man who
had the bishops of Gaul on his side would become master of Gaul
from end to end. From the first he pursued the policy of conciliating them; and in all the wars and annexations of territory that were
crowded into the next few years, and which ended in making him
master of all Gaul north of the Loire, the clergy were his staunch
supporters. In humbling the Arians he was strengthening his
bishops and himself.

Then came a proud moment for the king. In 492 Theodoric the
Great asked for the hand of Adolfleda, one of the sisters of Clovis,
in marriage. It was an alliance which brought together in friendly
relations the two greatest potentates in Europe, though the empire
of Theodoric did not last. Clovis was in his twenty-sixth year, and
was still unmarried; he too determined to take a wife, but she
should be a princess. Along the eastern borders of his dominions
there lay the Burgundian kingdom. This people were settled in the
valley of the Rhone; they too were Arians. Be it remembered, as I
hinted just now, that this Arianism—this *exotic* as I may say—this
outlandish religion imported from foreign parts, necessarily brought
it about that between the dominant new rulers of the land and the
older tillers of the soil, with their bishops and clergy at their head,
there were 'strained relations;' much in the same way as it is over
more than half of Ireland now, when the landlords profess one faith
and the masses another.

In these days there were two brothers who were 'kings' of the
Burgundians; the one, Gondebald, reigned at Vienne on the Rhone,
the other, Godegisil, at Geneva. There had been a third brother,
Chilperic, who had reigned at Lyon, but he had lately died, leaving
a widow—she was *not* an Arian, but one of the orthodox Catholics—
and a daughter Clotilda, who was being brought up under her
mother's care. When Chilperic died, mother and daughter put
themselves under the protection of Godegisil at Geneva, and there,
says the chronicler, they busied themselves in works of charity and
devotion. Of course we are told that Clotilda was beautiful as well
as good, and certainly she was zealous for her religion and true to
her mother's creed. There are some reasons for believing that Godegisil himself had less sympathy with the Arian heresy than his
brother Gondebald. Clovis asked for the hand of Clotilda, apparently
at the same time that Theodoric had made his advances to Clovis for
his sister's hand; and in the year 492 [or 493 ?] the nuptials of the

pagan king of the Franks with the Christian maiden were celebrated
with great pomp at Soissons. The event produced a profound
impression; it clearly was sanctioned by the Church, it opened out
a great future for the faith once delivered to the saints—for is it not
written that 'the unbelieving husband is sanctified by the wife'?—it
seemed to foreshadow that the Gospel might have great triumphs to
exult in even in the near future. In very truth the marriage of Clovis
was one of those events the consequences of which it is difficult to
exaggerate.

Clovis, looked at from our modern standpoint, was a monster of
wickedness—cruel, false, relentless, implacable, fiercely vindictive,
sparing none in his wrath, and, if we may believe all that is told of
his atrocities, with a certain wild beast's joy in bloodshed. But this
savage with the tiger's temper was not profligate. He was the only
one of his race who, as far as we know, was true to the woman who
was his wife, and the only one whose relations with the other sex
exhibit anything approaching to tenderness and romance. The
wandering loves of the Merovingians are continually befouling the
pages of Gregory of Tours. They are scarcely less shocking and
detestable than the wanton carnage. But on Clovis his wife Clotilda
never ceased to exercise an influence for good.

In her presence there appears to have flashed upon him now and
then gleams of the inner light that comes from God. She spoke to
him out of her own experience of the beauty of holiness. She had
a mysterious language which prattled of 'the soul' and 'the spirit,'
words that, coming from her, might for all he knew have some
occult meaning. So much of the thing men call their hearts this
woman had made him suspect there might be under that shaggy
bosom of his, something that thrilled with a tremor that was not all
animal passion as he gazed into her unfathomable eyes. She spoke
to him of the Crucified—the highest, holiest manhood, the human
and divine—that came to suffer and save; the strong Son of God,
'stronger even than thou, my Clovis! Yea, very much stronger
than thou!'

Then a child was born to the pair. There was an heir to the
throne. 'Christ claims him,' said Clotilda, and Clovis acknowledged the claim. So the babe was brought to the font in the
cathedral of Soissons, decked out for the ceremony with all imaginable splendour, and there they gave him the name of Ingomir—hope
of the dynasty that was to be. Alas! the child had scarcely been
stripped of his baptismal robe than the light went out from the palace.
The little heart stopped beating, and he was gone.

'It's his baptism that was the death of him,' cried the king in
his wrath. 'Had I but given him to those old gods of mine he
would have been alive now!' Clotilda knew when to speak and
when to be silent. She bowed her head and made no murmuring.
The Christ had found a better home for the child.

Next year another son was born. Unshaken in her faith, Clotilda claimed that he too should be baptised. Again after the child had been admitted into the Christian Church he began to sicken. 'He too will die as his brother did,' growled Clovis brutally. 'What else could happen to him? Of course he'll die!' But he did not die; he recovered and grew strong. The leaven was working, we cannot doubt, silently, peradventure sullenly. It is surely, surely, a very superficial view of such cases as this of the conversion of Clovis to account for them on the simple hypothesis that they were brought about by the huckster's way of settling everything— to wit, by striking a balance between profit and loss.

When we look at it, how small a part does what we call *motive* play in the heroism, the romance, or the self-surrender which glorify with a celestial radiance some few pages of human history! 'Who can understand his errors?' says the Psalmist; those tortuous mazes in whose labyrinthine entanglements moves that undistinguishable throng of hopes and fears which kindle hope, the whispers from worlds not realised, the regrets, the yearnings, the aspirations, the unaccountable whims that play upon the surface, or the outbursts of heat and flame that seem to come from the central fires. Who can tell how these mysterious factors contribute, each in some inexplicable way, in determining what decision we shall come to, or what course we shall take, at this or that turning-point of our careers? One thing is quite certain—namely, that we are not all brain, neither does logic rule the children of men.

Just at this time two sisters of Clovis gave up their Arianism or their paganism—it is not clear which—and were admitted to baptism. There are other hints, or at least indications, that there was a propaganda going on. Remigius was all this while the Primate, exercising his mighty influence at Reims, and Principius, the Primate's brother, was Bishop of Soissons. The fame of the elder brother and the splendour of his genius—his moral and his intellectual genius—have tended, perhaps unfairly, to rob the younger of his due. It can hardly have been but that the continued presence of one or other of the brothers—their example, their conversation, and the high estimation in which they were held—must have made itself felt, and that the 'continual dropping' was doing its work.

In the year 496 the crisis came. The Franks by this time had become what the Roman legions were in the first half of the fourth century, the warders of the left bank of the Rhine. On the right bank there had grown up a strong people whom Julian had tried conclusions with—whom Probus, a hundred years before Julian, had attempted to keep back by constructing that tremendous rampart known as the 'Devil's Dyke,' and which proved such a vain defence against these same Alamanni only a few years later. Gradually the

Alamanni had become a great host, fierce and aggressive, bent on conquest. They seem to have crossed the Rhine at Coblentz, and were threatening to wrest the valley of the Moselle from the Franks now settled there. What followed we are not told, for at this point we are once more tantalised by the silence of historians; and where the final conflict took place we cannot tell. As the battle raged, the issue seemed to be dreadfully doubtful, for the Alamanni were gaining ground, the Franks were giving way. In the heart of their great leader there came a horror, a weird shiver of dread. Were the gods, from whom he was sprung, forsaking him at this supreme moment? Was there to be no more help from them? He lifted up his hands to heaven and a cry came from his lips: 'O Thou, Jesus Christ, whom my Clotilda proclaims to be the Son of the living God. Thou who art said to give help to those in trouble and victory to those that hope in Thee. Give me but a token of that power of Thine which the people called by Thy name affirm that they have found in Thee, and I too will believe in Thee and be baptised in Thy name! For, lo! my gods have gone away from me, and I find they have no might. Thee now I call to mine aid! In Thee will I trust to grant me deliverance from the foe!' The answer came with no lightnings from heaven nor any thunders from the clouds; but in the king's heart there blazed forth the flame of a new enthusiasm. The wavering and half-beaten Franks rallied, charged, and drove the barbarian host before them as chaff before the wind. Their leader was slain on the field. Of the Alamanni we hear no more. ' On that day,' says one, ' the centre of gravity of history was changed.' By which I suppose he means that stable equilibrium for European society in the future was to depend not upon the support which mere brute force could supply, but upon that which it could receive from the spiritual and moral forces which are the real arbiters of human destiny. On that day, whatever there was that was good in the old civilisation was saved from shipwreck. The cause of progress for our race became identified with the cause of the Christian Church. A new era had begun.

Clovis kept his promise. It was a hard promise to keep, and nothing can show how immense was the influence which the barbarian conqueror exercised over those wild warriors than that they joined him by the thousand in renouncing the old gods of war and in bowing their knees to the Prince of Peace. History has many instances of the same acceptance of the gospel by a rude people where their king has had the courage to show them the way. But the significance of this great event lay here, in that Clovis dared to take the first great step. Others might follow, he led.

Between the great victory over the Alamanni and Christmas Day 496 some months elapsed. Of course there are the usual traditions, legends, peradventure, too, devout inventions, some of them one would wish to be able to believe; but for the most part they come to us from sources that are not above suspicion. As for the magnificence of the ceremonial when the king was admitted to the font, it may be read in the pages of Gregory of Tours, and in this instance we can hardly be wrong in thinking that the good man's pen, so far from exaggerating, was not by any means equal to the occasion. Reims was all astir with the men of war and the men of peace. No such magnificent ceremonial had ever been seen, at any rate north of the Alps. Through the streets of Reims, lined by his Franks on this side and on that, Clovis walked, the Bishop Remigius holding him by the hand, conducting him on his way to the cathedral church. Banners and tapestry were, we are told, hung out from the windows as the procession moved on—bishops of the province and ecclesiastics of this grade and of that, in copes and chasuble and dalmatic, gorgeons in colour and dazzling with gems and gold, singing the praises of the Lamb of God in barbaric tones that a hundred years later were brought into new measures and lifted to the glorious level of the Gregorian chants. As they entered the great western doors, where the blaze of a myriad tapers was wellnigh lost in the clouds of incense that filled the church with an overpowering fragrance, Clovis for one moment paused. 'Is this the heaven that ye bring me to?' he asked of the Bishop, who still held his hand. 'Nay! my king; this is not heaven, but it is the way to heaven for thee!'

The great moment came at last. The saintly Bishop, standing by the font, was really the commanding figure at that solemn moment. 'Bend low thy head, Sigambrian,' cried he. 'Adore thou that which aforetime thou gavest to the flames! Let the flames have now what aforetime thou didst adore!'

.   .   .   .

There is no need to carry on the story of Clovis and his conquests to the end. It is a story which is not edifying—at any rate not edifying to those who, as they read the great dramas of the ages behind us, have no eyes but for the acting of the puppets on the stage. It is for the philosophic historian to justify the ways of God to men. I do but aim at pointing out briefly the meaning of a single anniversary and the transcendent importance of the event which Frenchmen are celebrating now. Few great conquerors have achieved so much as Clovis with resources, at first sight, so inadequate to the success achieved. When he died he was but forty-five years old. At fifteen he began his career as little more than a leader of outlaws; he ended by being king of almost the whole land from the Pyrenees to the Rhine. He founded a dynasty, but he did very much more: he founded an empire. The dynasty came to an end, the empire lasted. For wellnigh four hundred years after that Christmas baptism at Reims, there was no people in Europe, except the Franks, which developed into an organised national community or could boast of an uninterrupted national history. If the title of the First Christian King which has been bestowed upon him be something more than he deserved, it still remains true that he was the first barbarian chieftain whose profession of Christianity was the beginning of that recognition of the Gospel as the religion of his people which since his days no European sovereign has ventured to regard as the ground of his claim to rule. If in any real sense he was a Christian at all, if his daily life was in hideous contrast to the creed he professed, and his career was a hideous reproach upon the religion which he called his own—so much the worse for him, we may perhaps be inclined to say. But he was not the first, nor by any means the last, whom God has used to work out His divine purposes and, in spite of themselves, their errors, or their crimes, to assist in the evolution of the Kingdom of Heaven.

[In writing about Frankish history I adhere to the French way of spelling proper names. I do so for more reasons than one, but especially for this reason—that it is the simplest way of escaping from the chaotic *orthography* (?) which modern writers with Germanic tendencies seem to flounder about in. M. Fustel gives a dozen forms of the name 'Clovis,' and Guizot almost as many of the name 'Clotilda,' for which authorities may be adduced. Romans and Teutons were sorely puzzled to spell the Celtic names phonetically.]

AUGUSTUS JESSOPP.

No. I

In a German garrison town—let us call it Philistia—lived and practised one Dr. Franzel, and his friend and colleague, Dr. Claus. The
two men had been fellow students at the University of —— and
boon companions—good comrades, it might be said, from their earliest
infancy. Born of pious parents, worthy burghers, swaddled, drilled,
ruled, and cut out strictly according to the pattern of young men prevailing in Philistia, they had eventually escaped from the parental
clutch and the pedagogic strait-waistcoat to the real dignity of half
shares in a furnished room in Z——, in which town the two young
men had cultivated their moustaches together, attended their first
lecture together, revelled in their first *Kneipabend* together, eaten
their first meal at a public restaurant together, and together, on the
same memorable day, attained to the coveted distinction of a hideous
slash across the right cheek-bone of Dr. Claus, and a manly gash across
the inquiring nose of Dr. Franzel. Thenceforward they were true and
worthy citizens of the Fatherland, baptised with the holy water of
German sentiment, German beer, and German blood. Life was certainly worth the living under these highly gratifying and peculiarly
God-ordained circumstances. And Dr. Franzel and his friend Dr.
Claus were both eager and ready, as the entire Fatherland long had
been eager and ready, and on the tiptoe of brutal expectation, to
pick a quarrel on the first occasion that offered with any stranger, or
with any barbarous nation, that should have the colossal impudence
to question the rights of *Deutschland, Deutschland über Alles*, even to
the three quarters of the globe if the German Emperor so willed and
telegraphed it. Full-fledged doctors, the two friends returned to
Philistia, and settled down—the one, Dr. Claus, in a practice which
had been purchased for him by his father ; the other, Dr. Franzel, in a
less aristocratic quarter, where grand opportunities offered for a pushing, energetic man to work up a practice for himself. The next step
was to marry and so set the social stamp of medical respectability on
their private lives. This Dr. Franzel lost no time in doing, for his
banking account was slowly dwindling down to a humiliating sum.

He married an orphan with a considerable fortune of her own and a thriving manufactory in the country, whose yearly output helped to flood the world's market-places with cheap underclothing, bearing the magic words 'Made in Germany' stamped upon each article. Dr. Claus obstinately refused to marry, or rather his mother refused to allow him to do so; and in the course of a year, his father dying, his father's wife was installed the proud and boasting mistress of her son's establishment.

To this little town flocked many English and American visitors, who, staying a few weeks or months, were, of course, highly delighted with its very foreign air and quaint Continental ways. They perfectly revelled in the funny idea of asking permission of the police to stay up a few hours later on a birthday night, with extra permission to play the piano and dance and drink unlimited lemonade, on the understanding that there should be no disturbance of the Public Rest; and they hung out of the windows in delight upon discovering an emissary from the police station before the house to see that no treason was plotted behind the window-curtains.

Dr. Franzel was a short, stout, florid, fussy, self-assertive little man, and wore gold spectacles, which gave him a very wide-awake look, and made him appear ten years older, and twenty years wiser, and thirty years more experienced than he was. Without his spectacles he was a very commonplace individual with nothing noticeable beyond a short-sighted look in the eyes. But with his spectacles, astride his somewhat aspiring nose, he was a typical German, brimful of encyclopædic information, from A B C to X Y Z, in all living languages, with the Alpha and Omega of the dead tongues to give classic basis to the whole conglomerate mass—a little man with information on the brain and active intelligence running out at his finger-tips, a man with a brain large enough for anything, which might, indeed, one day spell discovery to startle the passive intellects of Europe withal. With such a man all things were possible—with one humiliating exception, namely the attainment of a dignified use of the English language, together with something approximating to finality in English orthography and English orthoepy.

Now it came to pass one day during a period of grass-widowhood that Dr. Franzel numbered among his new patients several English ladies who could speak German without being able to make him understand what was the matter with them; and in his distress at not having comported himself in the consulting-room with his usual dignity, he hastily asked the advice of his friend Dr. Claus, who promptly recommended instruction and a teacher.

'A man looks such a fool mumbling over lesson-books at the age of five-and-thirty,' Dr. Franzel demurred.

'He looks a bigger fool when he loses a rich patient because he cannot make some idiot understand the meaning of " Put out your tongue." '

' I do not see why we doctors should give ourselves the trouble to learn their idiotic language in our own country. This is Germany. Let them learn to speak German. In Rome one——'

' This is not Rome,' Dr. Claus interrupted ; ' this is Germany. And in Germany the Germans must learn to speak English, because the English swarm all over the country and cannot learn German. I must rub up my bit of English too. We are both in the same boat ! '

The result of this conversation was that the two friends made up their minds to take English lessons, and an agent was set to work to find an English lady teacher, who, to the advantage of being a married woman, should be able to advance the warm recommendations of being middle-aged and cheap, since giving English lessons to German professors carried social advancement in its train, and was in itself as good as a fee.

' The English are bad teachers,' Dr. Claus explained by way of a solatium for professional dignity, seriously compromised by the national commercial spirit. ' They have no method. They do everything, even teaching their own grammar, on the John Bull hectoring system. It is so and so, because it is English, and if you don't like it you can leave it and be d——d to you, and there's an end to the matter. What can you do with such a people and such a language ? ' Dr. Claus laughed contemptuously in the bored, fatigued way he did everything which had to do with lay matters.

Dr. Franzel was silent—he was day-dreaming again, arranging an English grammar and an English orthography on the rational German method. And after the lapse of a few days an English lady-teacher was found, who was discovered to be neutral in two of the three necessary qualifications for the post : that is to say, she was married, yet neither middle-aged nor young ; and further, she was decidedly cheap.

The two doctors consulted together.

' We must be careful,' Dr. Franzel remarked. ' My wife tells me—she speaks English—that in England it is not safe for a man to enter a railway compartment if a woman is there alone.'

' This is not England. And we are Germans,' returned Dr. Claus a little drily. ' You forget we shall be two. There will be no opportunity for her to fascinate us.'

Dr. Franzel flashed his friend a grateful look. ' Good. Otherwise I should decline. I see enough of women in the consulting-room, and the hospitals. There is nothing new in the sex. Much study of them is only madness—and expense,' which diatribe was tantamount to a confession that he, Dr. Franzel, was a grass-widower again.

The matter was nearly settled by old Frau Pastor Claus, whose husband had been a pastor of the good old Martin Luther school, and might have been twin-brother to him, in the muscularity of his. practical faith and in his sturdy love for wife and children. She argued with many secret rejoicings that the lessons should be given in her son's apartment, where the presence of a lady of the social standing of a Frau Pastor would lend decorum to the somewhat irreverent proceeding. But a polite letter from the lady teacher in question, to the effect that she was unable to give the lessons away from home, put a new complexion on the matter—and the Frau Pastor pursed her lips—and again the doctors consulted.

'I will tell her that I am a married man,' Dr. Franzel at length remarked, seeing a way out of the dilemma. He glanced at his friend seriously. Dr. Claus was a man who looked as if he had been born sneering.

'No necessity at all,' Dr. Claus returned. 'Never embark upon personalities with a stranger—and this is an Englishwoman. They call themselves free.' Dr. Claus made a gesture expressing his scorn and medical contempt. 'Too free for me. She will have nothing to do with our private lives. And we are not bound to say we are married or single.'

'I wonder if she is a widow,' Dr. Franzel remarked with gathering anxiety.

An exclamation of impatience escaped his friend. 'To us it is a matter of supreme indifference. We shall have no time in the lesson to consider whether she is a woman or a man, married or single. She will give us instruction in English—we pay her one mark fifty pfennigs each the lesson—and there the matter ends.'

'I think,' said Dr. Franzel with a degree of nervousness, 'I think I had rather say I am a married man, you see.'

Dr. Claus lifted his brows. 'As you will, my dear fellow. It can do no harm.' And thus the subject closed. And a letter penned by the exact Dr. Franzel—of which he took a copy in all seriousness— was despatched by post the same evening, fixing the hour and the day of the first lesson, also mentioning the exact fee by way of German precaution.

It was a winter's evening in this same little garrison town, about the hour of Divine Service, when the Hoftheater was opening its doors to a pagan congregation of devout enthusiasts of the Wagnerian cult, while the bells of the English and the American churches were ringing to church the scattered members of their flocks.

The doctors took an English lesson every evening in the week, Sunday not excepted. This was no matter for scruple, on the part of Mrs. Marion Carr, their English teacher, who rarely went to church, which was one of the reason why she did not 'get on,' she was told by kind inquiring friends, who probably did succeed in their under- takings, if only to put an emphatic seal on their own assertion, that going to church was good for business, and that in taking thought for the soul one could expediently kill two birds with one stone.

The pupils were late, and Marion Carr awaited their coming, seated in her quiet little study, at the head of a small oval table, with her back to the dormer-window, and her restless eyes continually interrogating the blank stupidity of the closed door. She wore the usual mask upon her face, with the feeling of irritation which all restraint necessarily brings with it. And there was a good deal of mental disturbance going on which was in the course of the lesson to settle down into more positive emotion. There was a pile of ill-used books at her right hand, and before a fair white square of blotting-paper, somewhat ostentatiously placed, an inkstand, a pen and a pencil, and a priggish-looking pen-wiper.

These are mere details. But it is the common details of every-day life which too often decide whether that life shall set to tragedy or comedy, pure romance or commonplace story, to the happiness or the misery, the salvation or complete demoralisation of that infinite thing, the soul. Details may be vulgar and uninteresting, and there may be little in a name, and a rose, no doubt, by any other name would smell as sweet. Yet there is sufficient stubborn force in unsympathetic surroundings, in a bigoted sanctimonious arrangement of household effects to afflict the artistic temperament with violent spasms of revolt, and more provocation in the Puritanic disposal of German tables and chairs, and what not, than is afforded in a thrice-heated Chauvinistic article in the *Vossische Zeitung*.

Mrs. Carr suffered more or less from such surroundings; in other words, from details—which was absurd. It would seem she had been glued to that identical chair at the head of that small oval table, with a pupil on her left-hand, and a pupil on her right, with her back to the window in which bloomed everlasting India-rubber plants with sickly leaves, and that short, squat, stout vulgar little door regarding her abject misery with a complacent grin, ever since the beginning of things. More than ever that evening she longed to revolt from the oppressive tyranny of German domesticity, longed to upset the sanctimonious order of things, to set the *causeuse* at a rakish angle suggestive of Louis le Grand and scarlet high-heeled shoes, and charming Dresden china shepherds and shepherdesses—to shake the stupid stolidity of the little oval table, and to introduce pandemonium into the serried ranks of her dull chairs. She had a feverish desire to jump up and pin Japanese fans on the walls where pictures should be hanging; to swathe her flower-pots in Liberty silk bows; to hang a Toby frill round the white throat of the stuffy stove; to introduce milking stools into the corners of the room, Japanese umbrellas over the lamp, to turn her writing table into a mad asylum for *bric-à-brac* gone demented: in a word, to play at keeping shop in her own religious little study.

The harsh jangling of a bell in the corridor set Marion Carr's teeth and nerves on edge, and roused her from a brown study. For there was just the difference between the quality of the expected pupils' ring and that of an unexpected visitor which lies in the *morale* of a lesson given and a lesson received—the whole difference of a fee. Indeed, the announcement was that of one who in each and every action of his public and private life invariably demanded his full pound of flesh. That the law allowed, that the law prescribed no more than the pound of flesh, with no jot, no drop of human blood, was matter for devout thanksgiving on the part of all English teachers and Christian Antonios. The jangle of the bell died away, and Marion Carr with an effort assumed a pedagogic attitude and carefully arranged her expression.

There was a knock at the door and the two doctors entered. The short, stout, florid little man, blinking through his spectacles with a busy expression, is Dr. Franzel. Towering a head and shoulders above him follows Dr. Claus, a tall, dark, noticeable man with heavy, tired, rather melancholy-looking hazel eyes, and a slow, languid, sinuous mode of progression, and a figure whose muscular proportions would have been set off to more advantage in the costume of a barbaric chief than they were in nineteenth-century dress, showing a slovenly inattention to the details of toilet, such as betrayed itself in the soiled edges of crumpled cuffs, in a limp collar, and in a suit of clothes that had seen hard work in the operating-room that day; indeed, the whole man appeared rather uneasy in his clothes. Both men bowed with stiff formality. 'Guten Abend' was their laconic greeting, given with the almost ungracious concession of two German professors who were come strictly on business (when the amenities of social intercourse were not to be thought of), and who privately deplored the fact that German society prescribed no more business-like formula of greeting between masculine German pupils and English female teachers. So wary, indeed, was their every look and movement that had a caricaturist been present he might have seized the impression of the moment to dot them both down in his album in the shape of two German blue-bottles, one wearing spectacles, caught in a web of fine English manufacture, but with every intention of extracting themselves without losing so much as a leg or a wing, while the spider looks out of a corner in the shape of a midge.

'Good evening, Dr. Claus. Good evening, Dr. Franzel.' The midge—that is, Marion Carr—responded, equally cold but a little more courteous. She spoke in English and mouthed her words, so that Dr. Franzel, who was listening, and who appeared to absorb information through the pores of his skin, could catch every syllable, carefully articulated as it was. For though he had been six weeks studying hard the vagaries of English pronunciation, having a book always open, even in his dressing-room, he was not yet quite satisfied that

he had thoroughly mastered the true pronunciation of the word
' evening.'

The two friends seated themselves, each in his own characteristic
way. Dr. Franzel plunged into his chair and drew it close up to
the table, and without wasting a moment, opened his note-book and
seized a pencil and squared his elbows and blinked across the table
at his friend by way of exciting stimulus to lethargic effort. Dr.
Claus was of another temper of mind and mood. There was marked
reluctance, indeed something aggressive and provocative, in the slow
way in which he dragged his chair to the table; and more than a
hint of roughness and rudeness in the oblique turn of his shoulder
upon Marion Carr, so that she was compelled to address a side view
of his head, or his large ear, or an angle of his nose, whereas she
would have preferred to address him with her gaze turned full upon his
face, as she was in the habit of addressing everybody. This reluctance to be looked in the eyes, which is not to be confounded with
an inability to look another person in the eyes, by a woman who was
a lady and an English teacher—therefore, a note of interrogation—
was one of the doctor's most marked, most disagreeable singulari-
ties. Marion Carr laughed at it in her quiet contemptuous way;
but her gaze never faltered. The mistake which Marion Carr
made was that of standing by her rights, one of which was to consider
herself, as in truth she had a perfect right to do, one on a social
equality with her pupils. This to all appearance Dr. Claus stiffly,
proudly, coldly, bitterly resented, with true petty German professional
pride and bourgeois hauteur. His answers, when answer he gave,
dragged forth from the profound depths of his self-centred *ego* by
his teacher's laborious, nay, desperate efforts to get at the man, and
make him both understand and speak the language which it was to
his advantage to learn, were given with positive reluctance, and
Marion Carr's observant eye detected, with growing embarrassment,
how painful a matter it was to the doctor to be subjected to this
riddling process, to the humiliating position of pupil to a woman,
when, with very little bodily trouble or brain condescension on his
own part, the position of pupil or teacher might with profit to either
be creditably exchanged. When Marion Carr became eager, persistent,
anxious, enthusiastic, Dr. Claus became disagreeably satirical, quiz-
zing her almost girlish ardour with a smile which well-nigh drove her
out of the room; it was so set and cold, so priggish, so intensely
artificial, so barren of everything that was manly, courteous, well bred,
chivalrous in the sex.

This uncomfortable state of things had lasted for about six weeks,
during which Marion Carr had preserved her composure, taken—and
earned—her fees, and swallowed her pride, with sundry mental reser-
vations, and a certain slow wonder at herself, pointed with the query,
How long shall I be able to endure this man's insufferable egoism?

Dr. Franzel was of another type, eminently practical, commercial, and thorough, that is to say, German.   He was a little man who knew not only exactly what he wanted, but exactly where to get it, and precisely how to get it, and to a farthing what he meant to pay for it, to the uttermost farthing exactly what it was worth, which was quite another matter, and not always the price Dr. Franzel gave for it.   He was come that evening to have an English lesson, and to obtain something in exchange for the fee he paid, and there was not a moment to lose, and without the slightest *mauvaise honte*, he plunged into the middle of things.

'It is a very cold evening,' he began.

Now this was not a brilliant opening for a medical intellect ; indeed, it smacked of the *Backfisch*.   But it was eminently useful, and committed him to no unnecessary waste of sentiment, and brilliant conversation, it must be remembered, was not required ; indeed, would have been seriously reprimanded by both doctors as unprofessional and dangerous, both in the consulting-room and in Mrs. Carr's little study.   It was, in fact, one of the few stock phrases of correct and decorous expression which German medical gentlemen might in their intercourse with English patients of the opposite sex use safely, use with the utmost propriety, without in any way damaging their reputation as German doctors.

Marion Carr found herself on the brink of a smile.   Recovering herself she responded as coldly, but with alacrity, since she must not keep Dr. Franzel waiting : 'Bitterly cold.'   Dr. Franzel took up the words and tried their sound several times, laying the proper accent on each syllable, while Marion Carr added, with an expression that might be called 'harnessed,' 'These east winds are terrible.'

'Ach,' ejaculated Dr. Claus, speaking for the first time.   'There gives not such east winds in England.'   He looked of course intensely bored and miserable, for the atmospheric affairs of a country of so purely local a fame as England were necessarily mundane matters entirely out of the sphere of his, the doctor's, interest.

'Oh yes, indeed we have,' Mrs. Carr corrected with *élan*.   She was always intensely thankful for any weather to talk about, it was so safe a topic—one of the recognised formalities of social discourse, licensed by the proprieties and warranted not to corrupt the morals of an infant.   She had even slyly 'got up' the technicalities of weather physics ; gravely tried to reduce degrees Fahrenheit to degrees Centigrade by the simple process of subtracting 32 degrees and multiplying by five-ninths.   But arriving at no sane results therefrom she had in her despair attempted a compromise by reducing Centigrade degrees to degrees Fahrenheit, which was another simple process of multiplying nine-fifths and adding 32 degrees.   Thus her zeal as a teacher, her conscientiousness in her labours, could not be questioned, and she continued with enthusiasm, 'East winds in

England are not iced, if I remember rightly, as they are here—they are generally raw.' She groaned internally and made a grimace, for this again was neither original nor brilliant, nor did it appear to offer much consolation to Dr. Franzel, who was always keen on the scent of new words. Still, it was weather, and although they had been discussing the weather, every rise and fall of the barometer, every change of wind and fall of snow, for the last six weeks, Marion Carr could not remember to have used the word 'raw' before.

Now, the two doctors had each his own peculiar views upon mastering a language. Dr. Claus required rules, a Justinian code of laws and a constitution for everything, from *a b—ab*—to a golden key of all the symbols of pronunciation; which it was quite safe to assume he would master in the course of a hundred years or so—a line-upon-line, and precept-upon-precept system, written down and engraven upon two tables of stone—with a duplicate copy of the same for the waistcoat pocket. He found too much doctrine, too many principles of faith, and not enough precept in English grammar, where there seemed to be more exceptions than rules, and a truly deplorable lack of finality in matters concerning English orthography and English orthoepy. The words rough, plough, lough, tough, puff, through, thought, roused his derision and stirred his contemptuous anger. And why and wherefore one, two, and sometimes three modes of expressing one and the selfsame idea? 'Taller than he is'—'Taller than him'—'Taller than himself,' he scoffed, picking out these examples with a scornful finger.

'True,' gravely replied Marion Carr.

'And all three are correct?'

'You will find all three forms used by our classical writers.'

'And not one rule to prove which is the most correct form of the three?'

'I fear not,' Marion Carr answered, looking guilty. '"Taller than him" is good English. One of our masters of style, Thackeray, uses it. In this case there is a preposition and the object following in the objective case, according to rule.'

'And taller than he is?' Dr. Franzel eagerly looked up and pushed his spectacles back with thumb and forefinger.

'Here there is a conjunction, and the object following in the nominative case.'

'And one may use both forms?' said Dr. Claus fretfully.

'Both forms may be used with equal and perfect propriety, Dr. Claus. Though "taller than him" is now becoming obsolete. Why it should be going out of fashion I know not. It is good English.'

Dr. Claus glanced at his friend across the table with a shrug and a I-told-you-so air.

Now, Dr. Franzel could not be bothered with rules; he was in too much of a hurry. What he wanted was a plentiful supply of words—

a vocabulary, in fact ; a careful collection of idioms—a few polite
social phrases and absolute literal translation—not the idiom of the
German language rendered by the idiom of the English language, or
the equivalent of that idiom ; but downright autocratic translation,
syllable for syllable, word for word, phrase for phrase, not bating to
useless, partial, or a single redundancy. This literal translation out of
florid German into close, terse, compact, nervous English, could have
but one disastrous result (as any one will acknowledge who has
practised it)—could but result in English nonsense. And of this the
greedy little doctor was as fully cognisant as was his teacher. As
we have intimated, he was by no means a fool. But he *was* greedy.
He wanted, he exacted, the full value of his money. And, once having
mastered the *sense* of a phrase, he hung it up on its own particular
peg in readiness for future use, and then lovingly returned to the
beaten track to pick up all the little untranslatable particles, gather
together all the mangled remains of the phrase as it were, which he
would obstinately insist upon translating into a sort of glossary of his
own, since banishing them out of the English rendering was so much
waste of precious German material, and argued reckless English
extravagance on the part of Marion Carr. This was the whole gist
of the matter.

After a fortnight's persistent struggle—Dr. Claus looking on with
melancholy eyes and a contemptuous, disdainful air of strong disapproval, since it was perfectly futile to argue or to wrestle with so
truly feminine and capricious a thing as the English tongue—Marion
Carr herself succumbed, and allowed the little man to revel in literal
translation at his own sweet will, listening to the mangling of her
mother tongue with philosophic phlegm. There was no other way
to deal with Dr. Franzel, and, strange to say, he made rapid progress.
Rules or no rules, the man and his system triumphed.

Dr. Claus's particular fad and peculiar crotchet was not so much to
learn as to improve the style and correct the composition of the different English authors he read. He had a mania for triumphantly
selecting a passage upon which to operate with his scalpel. It was
in vain that the indignant and patriotic Marion Carr would assure
him that such an author in writing English dialogue produced the
English language as it is spoken in English drawing-rooms by well-
bred Englishmen and Englishwomen, and not by Board school
masters—sometimes carelessly; occasionally, alas! ungrammatically;
never, or rarely, pedantically. Dr. Claus would shake his large head
with solemn disapproval. But the climax of endurance was reached
in a muttered aside to his friend, in which he remarked that though
the English had their Shakespeare, the German race had by no
means decided whether he was Shakespeare or Bacon.

The lesson languished. The two doctors were each in his
own peculiar and most difficult mood. Nothing went right. Dr.

Claus's cool and arrogant disdain of guidance in the tongue he was professedly learning bordered on downright impudence, and every attempt to set him right was contemptuously waived. Dr. Franzel was distressed and indignant because his brain refused to hold any more new words and flatly refused idioms, and to progress without new words was impossible. He blinked through his spectacles at Marion Carr with a look that plainly charged her with the offence.

'Dr. Claus,' she at last insisted, with a heightened colour and a throbbing brow, 'I must really protest against the pronunciation of that word. I have corrected you six times in the course of the lesson. It is believe, not be-live.'

'Why believe?' Dr. Claus inquired, smiling across the table at his colleague. Both men retained something of the arrogance of their blood-and-beer student days.

'Why believe?' Marion Carr quickly retorted. 'Really, Dr. Claus,' and she managed to command a momentary view of his eye, 'that is a frivolous and mischievous question, and the answer lies entirely outside my province. I am here to teach my mother tongue; not to reconstruct its rules, or introduce new methods of pronunciation, or reduce the number of its anomalies. I am neither a verbal critic nor a specialist. If you wish to go into verbal criticism or literary research, you must go elsewhere. I have neither the time, nor the inclination, nor the scholarship, nor yet the cranial development necessary for literary pugilism. You should consult authorities on those subjects. I cannot give, I would not, if I could, give you the legal why and wherefore of some seventy or eighty thousand words. I am not a philologist, nor have I ever advertised myself as one. You have wholly mistaken my calling, as I your purpose in seeking my services. Your demands are much too exorbitant and quite beyond me. With reading, translation, conversation, English dialogue, dictation, and grammar, and literature if you will, you must rest satisfied in the short time we have to study. When you have a larger grasp of the language——'

'B-e-l-i-e-v-e, believe; r-e-c-e-i-v-e, receive;' repeated Dr. Claus derisively, and with a gesture and an expression of abominable rudeness he closed his book with a bang and pitched it across the table, so that it fell into the lap of his friend. Dr. Franzel burst out laughing.

Marion Carr's eyes flashed. 'You are forgetting yourself, Dr. Claus,' she said, a little sternly, and she likewise closed her book with every evidence of finality in the action.

Dr. Claus stared across the table; then, with a clumsy attempt at a laugh, he requested his friend to return his book.

'Excuse me, Dr. Claus,'—Marion Carr rose from her chair and stood with her hands on the back of it. 'I regret that I am compelled to bring the lesson to a conclusion.'

' A conclusion,' repeated the doctor ; but at a sign from Dr. Franzel he continued more suavely, ' Ach, Mrs. Carr, you must not be offended because I do not love your funny tongue—I am a German.'

' Exactly,' Marion Carr returned drily. ' You have just demonstrated the fact, Dr. Claus. But I am an Englishwoman, and therefore I say I regret that I am compelled to bring the lesson to a conclusion.'

' And wherefore ? ' rather haughtily inquired Dr. Claus.

' Wherefore ! ' Marion Carr exclaimed, with equal hauteur. ' Really, Dr. Claus, your question is but an aggravation of your offensive attitude. I am not accustomed to have books pitched across my table by my pupils, nor to listen to maledictions against my mother tongue. That I am only a teacher is no palliation of the offence.'

' Ach, Mrs. Carr,' remarked Dr. Franzel suavely, ' you are too— too passionate, too impulsive.'

' And I do not think,' continued Dr. Claus, ' I do not think you will make much progress in Germany if you treat your other pupils as you are treating us.'

' Possibly—probably not,' was the calm reply. ' And you, Dr. Claus, as you come more in contact with my country-people, you will doubtless make the discovery that we are as a nation less known for our commercial than our national spirit. We never sell our pride. And I for one refuse to barter my love of independence for a mess of German pottage.'

' Perhaps,' remarked Dr. Franzel, who seemed disinclined to budge from the table, ' perhaps you are dissatisfied with your fee, *Gnädige Frau.*'

Marion Carr enveloped the little man in a look of withering contempt.

' My actions are not always bounded by—fees, Dr. Franzel,' she made answer. ' Though a teacher—and teaching is not a lucrative profession in any country—though a teacher, I am never so poor that I cannot indulge myself with a little honest indignation.'

' It is true,' Dr. Claus remarked with a degree of awkwardness, that I am a German. I did not——'

' Equally true that I am an Englishwoman,' Marion Carr quickly returned.

' Are we to understand then—— ' Dr. Claus began.

' I shall be glad, Dr. Claus, if you will seek another teacher.'

The two doctors rose to their feet, and stood with their books under their arms. Marion Carr calmly packed her books together and left them in a pile on the table, then, with a courteous inclination of the head to both gentlemen, quietly turned and left the room.

KATHARINE BLYTH.

SOME RECOLLECTIONS OF

CARDINAL NEWMAN

WHEN first I made acquaintance with Newman I was young and impressionable, and for that reason all the more able to appreciate at least a portion of what was most remarkable about him. It was late in 1838, and Oxford, apart from its illustrious inmate, would have well repaid me for my journey from Ireland, not then a short one. The sun was setting as I approached it, and its last light shone brightly from the towers, spires, and domes of England's holy city. Such a city I had never seen before, and the more I saw of it the more deeply was I touched. Its monastic stillness is not confined to its colleges; much of the city besides, in spite of modern innovations, wore then an aspect of antiquity; and the staid courtesy of those whom I met in the streets contrasted delightfully with the bustle, the roughness, and the surly self-assertion encountered in the thorough-fares of our industrial centres. I had often to ask my way, and the reply was generally an offer to accompany me. It reminded me of what I had heard respecting Spain, viz. that every peasant there is a gentleman. As I walked I recited to myself Wordsworth's sonnet on Bruges, and wondered why the most patriotic of poets had not rather addressed it to Oxford. There seemed a rest about that city, bequeathed to it by the strength of old traditions, which I have nowhere else enjoyed so much except at Rome.

'While these courts remain,' I said to myself, 'and nothing wors e is heard than the chiming of these clocks and bells, the best of all that England boasts will remain also.' 'Nothing come to thee new or strange' is written upon every stone in those old towers, whic h seem to have drunk up the sunsets of so many centuries and to be quietly breathing them back into modern England's more trou bled air. How well those caps and gowns harmonise with them! Certainly Oxford and Cambridge, with all their clustered colleges, are England's two anchors let down with the past. May they keep her long from drifting from the regions dedicated to piety and learning into those devoted but to business or pleasure.

The ancient spirit is not dead :
Old times, I said, are breathing here.

In Oxford there then abode a man, himself a lover of old times,. and yet one who in fighting his way back to them had in the first place to create an order of things relatively new—John Henry Newman. I had left for him a letter of introduction from an eminent Fellow of Trinity College, Dublin, the Rev. J. H. Todd, to whose learning, liberality, and patriotism Ireland has owed much. Early in the evening a singularly graceful figure in cap and gown glided into the room. The slight form and gracious address might have belonged either to a youthful ascetic of the Middle Ages or a graceful and high-bred lady of our own days. He was pale and thin almost to emaciation, swift of pace, but, when not walking, intensely still, with a voice sweet and pathetic both, but so distinct that you could count each vowel and consonant in every word. I observed later that when touching upon subjects which interested him much he used gestures rapid and decisive, though not vehement, and that while in the expression of thoughts on important subjects there was often a restrained ardour about him, yet if individuals were in question he spoke severely of none, however widely their opinions and his might differ. As we parted I asked him why the cathedral bells rang at so late an hour. ‘ Only some young men keeping themselves warm,’ he answered. ‘ Here,’ I thought, ‘ even amusements. have an ecclesiastical character.’ He had asked me to breakfast with him the next morning and meet his young friend Frederic Rogers, afterwards Lord Blachford, a man later as remarkable for high ability as high principle, and especially for what Sir Henry Taylor called his marvellous gift of ‘ sure-footed rapidity ’ in the despatch of business. After breakfast he placed me in the hands of Mr. Mozley, who became my guide among the objects of especial interest at Oxford, an office not less kindly discharged the next day by Mr. Palmer, well known from his theological works. I shall never forget the kindness which I received at that time, and later, from distinguished men, several of whom reminded me that my family name had old associations with Oxford, while others gave me letters to eminent persons in Rome.

I did not see Newman again till after the lapse of three or four years. Many things had occurred in the interval. He had read much, he had thought much, and he had written much. His fame had grown ; so had the devotion of his friends, the animosity of his enemies, and the alarms of many admirers. Those alarms had been much increased by one of the recent *Tracts for the Times*, the celebrated Tract No. 90. The wits were contented with averring that No. 90 only meant ‘ No Go.’ Several of the University authorities, however, thought that the tract was no laughing matter, and in—

stituted proceedings against its author, Newman, probably with
regret, but in the conviction that it was injurious to the 'Thirty-
nine Articles,' which Mr. O'Connell had called the 'forty stripes save
one' inflicted by Queen Elizabeth on the Church of England;' but
the High Church reply was that if the 'Thirty-nine Articles' felt
aggrieved so much the worse for them, since in that case they must
be opposed to 'patristic antiquity,' by which the Church of England
professed to stand.   Many pamphlets were written on the subject,
one of them by a layman, my old friend R. M. Milnes, afterwards
Lord Houghton.   I remember Wordsworth's reading it and giving it
high praise ; and I remember also Dr. Whewell's reply to some one
who expressed surprise at Milnes's holding any opinions upon such a
subject.   'Oh, he holds none; but he took a fancy to write a philosophic essay on the subject of the day ; so he wrote what he thought
a philosophic mind like Thirlwall's might think.'   It was a very
brilliant essay.   The stir made by 'Tract 90' gave it an immense
circulation, with the proceeds of which Newman bought a library,
now included in that at the Edgbaston Oratory; but though he
bore with a dignified self-control what his friends regarded as a
persecution, yet a tract generally regarded as one that explained
the Thirty-nine Articles by explaining them away could not but
increase the distrust with which he had long been regarded both by
the Evangelical and the Establishmentarian party in the Church of
England.   Several recent occurrences, on the other hand, had impaired Newman's confidence in her position, especially the 'Jerusalem
Bishopric,' which he regarded as a fraternisation of that Church
with a German non-episcopal community, and also as a hostile
intrusion into the diocese of an Eastern bishop possessing the
'apostolical succession and primitive doctrine.'   Against that measure
he and Dr. Pusey had solemnly protested, but in vain.   Their interference had given great offence in high ecclesiastical quarters ; and not
a few made themselves merry at the war between the bishops and
their chief supporters, while a story went round that the wife of some
dignitary had openly stated that she could not approve of the
indiscriminate study of 'the Fathers' among the clergy, because it
tended to 'put thoughts into the heads of young curates.'   Newman
was then 'quadraginta annos natus,' yet even he apparently had not
escaped this danger; for, though his mastery of 'the Fathers' was
almost as much an acknowledged fact as his mastery of Holy Scripture,
their teaching no longer, as once, seemed to him much to resemble
that of the Established Church.   He wished to be at liberty, and he
resigned his Oxford preferment and retired to Littlemore.   That
voice the 'solemn sweetness' of which, as Mr. Gladstone described it,
had pierced all hearts at St. Mary's, was heard there no more except
in sad memory and sadder anticipation.   Men remembered that
pathos so much more powerful than any vehemence could have been,

that insight which made his gentleness so formidable a thing, those dagger-points of light flashed in upon the stricken conscience, and, most of all, that intense reality which sent a spiritual vibration over the land, with the warning, 'Words have a meaning whether we mean that meaning or not.' These things men remembered, perhaps the more because they saw the man no more.

Littlemore was but three miles from Oxford. He had retired there to a hermitage stiller even than Oxford—that Oxford described by 'Wulfstan the Wise' as serener than the summit of Olympus, the Olympus which he thus describes :—

> So tranquil were the elements there, 'tis said
> That letters by the finger of the priest
> Writ in the ashes of the sacrifice
> Remained throughout the seasons uneffaced.[1]

To Littlemore I walked alone through the fields from Oxford. The little hermitage had been changed to a little monastery by the addition of some small rooms which sheltered a few young men who, like those that accompanied Plato in the gardens of Academe, walked with him that they might learn from him. One of these youths was afterwards well known as Father Ambrose St. John, who, but for his premature death, would have been Newman's biographer. Another was Father Dalgairns. I asked one of them whether they recited the 'Canonical Hours' of the Breviary, and understood that they did so. I was deeply interested that day by my interview with Newman, though he seemed to me more reserved than when I had first made his acquaintance, and very grave, if not actually depressed. The final casting up of an account is a more difficult process than the preliminary ranging of the figures one beneath another. Newman's long and arduous studies had collected a vast mass of philosophical and theological materials ; and the details were doubtless arranging themselves in his mind and pointing towards the sum total. That sum, total, perhaps, looked daily less like what he had contemplated in his youthful anticipations—a Church of England triumphant here below, pure as the earliest day-dawn of the Faith, venerable as the sagest antiquity, cleansed from mediæval accretions, enriched by modern science, daily rising up out of the confusions of the sixteenth century, and delivering itself from secular bonds at no loss but that of diminished revenues ; one with a gradually increased colonial extension, making her the inheritor of a second 'orbis terrarum ;' and ultimately a reunion with the earlier one. Such ever since my boyhood had been my aspiration : how much more must it have been his! Yet that day as we walked together—for he was good enough to accompany me most of the way to Oxford—those aspirations did not seem to smile upon him amid the summer field flowers as they had smiled four years previously that night when the cold Christmas

[1] *Edwin the Fair*, by Sir Henry Taylor

winds blew the cathedral chimes over us. Newman's mind, however, was not like Mr. Ward's, which always saw with a diamond clearness what it saw at all; it included a large crepuscular region through which his intelligence had to pass before its dawn broadened into day. No one could appreciate better than he the subtlety of illusions, or their dangerous consequences; no one could feel more profoundly the pain of severing old ties; but he has told us that he could never see why any number of difficulties need produce a single doubt as regards matters of faith; and perhaps he might have added that he could never see why any amount of suffering need paralyse action in matters of duty, when at last certainty had emerged from the region of doubt. Daily I heard reports which he met neither with encouragement nor denial, but with reserve. Some of his followers began to whisper, ' Our great admiral will transfer his flag to another ship.' Others said, ' The Church of England will be the better for losing a formidable guest. The acorn blown by a chance gust into a china vase, if it continued to grow there would break it up.'

In 1845 Newman's secession was not attended by that of as many others as had been expected, though it included one, a great power in himself, the poet Faber, who renounced poetry for a higher work; but it left profound misgivings in the breasts of others, who continued their researches, carried their principles out in their parochial labours, and watched the signs of the times. They had not to wait long. The ' Gorham judgment' was pronounced, and within a few ·years about 300, some say 400, of the Anglican clergy, as I am informed, had followed his example, many of them to their worldly ruin and that of their families, together with a far larger number of highly educated laymen. Newman's ' Lectures' were believed to have assisted many persons in doubt at that crisis. Mr. R. H. Hutton, whose work on Newman appears to me far the best thing on the subject which I have seen, wrote in it as follows :—

When Newman at last made up his mind to join the Church of Rome his genius bloomed out with a force and freedom such as he never displayed in the Anglican Communion;

and elsewhere he thus illustrates that remark —:

The *Lectures on Anglican Difficulties* was the first book generally read, amongst Protestants, in which the measure of his literary power could be adequately taken. . . . Here was a great subject with which Newman was perfectly intimate, giving the fullest scope to his powers of orderly and beautiful exposition, and opening a far greater range to his singular genius for gentle and delicate irony than anything which he had hitherto written. . . . Never did a voice seem better adapted to persuade without irritating.

I was among the many present at those Lectures in 1850, and to me nothing, with the exception of the *Divina Commedia* and Kenelm Digby's wholly uncontroversial *Mores Catholici*, had been so impressive, suggestive, and spiritually helpful. I was also struck

by their impassioned eloquence, which brought to me the belief that
'if this man had chosen for himself a parliamentary career he must
have carried all before him.'   The extreme subtlety which belonged
to his intelligence was then shown to be but one of many faculties,
and opposed no hindrance to his equal power of exciting vehement
emotion, though he did so apparently unconsciously, on this occasion,
perhaps, restrained by the solemnity of the subject discussed and the
circumstance that the Lectures were delivered in a church.   Many
passages might be cited in illustration of this remark, such as the last
half-dozen pages of Lecture 10, contrasting the calamitous condition
of the Church in the days of Jansenism, the French Revolution, and
Napoleon, when the Pope was his prisoner, and when many among
the Church's enemies boasted that the Papacy was at an end, with
the sudden change when her chief enemies had vanished, and there
had returned to her an energy and health not hers for a very long
preceding time.   Nothing about those Lectures was more remarkable
than the celerity with which they were composed. They were written
as they were read—once or twice a week, I think—a rapidity as great
as that with which the successive chapters of his *Apologia* followed
each other many years later.   His genius was always stimulated by a
sudden pressure.

I had become a Catholic more than five years later than Newman.
The time when I saw most of him was in 1856.   Soon after the
Catholic University had been opened by him in Dublin at the
command of Pope Pius the Ninth he requested me to deliver at it a
series of lectures on literature.   I thought myself incompetent for
such a task ; but I could not refuse compliance with a wish of his,
and, although not a professor, I delivered about a dozen, the substance
of two among which was long afterwards (A.D. 1889) published in a
volume of essays.   When the day for the delivery of the first lecture
arrived Newman invited me to take up my abode in the larger of
the two University houses, over which he presided personally, surrounded by a considerable number of Irish students, together with a
few foreign youths of distinguished families attracted by his name.

The arduous character of Newman's enterprise in Dublin became
the more striking from the contrast afforded by the humble houses
which bore the name of the ' Catholic University ' to the monumental
buildings of Trinity College, Dublin, not to speak of the magnificent
homes provided for learning and religion at Oxford and Cambridge
by the piety of Catholic ages.   The difficulties connected with the
creation of a new University are great under the most favourable
circumstances; here they were immeasurably increased by the
determined opposition of successive Governments and Parliaments,
which steadily refused to concede to the Catholic University a
charter, a public endowment, or University buildings.   The opposition was stimulated by a vehement doctrinaire enthusiasm in favour

of the ' Queen's Colleges,'. long since admitted to be (excepting that at Belfast) a failure.   The purely secular character of those colleges was solemnly protested against by the larger part of Ireland, both Catholic and Protestant, on the double ground that they violated the ' rights of parents,' nearly all of whom preferred ' religious education,' and also because in them, though not in popular education, religion was banished from those higher studies with which it is so vitally connected, and banished at a time when youths are deprived of the safeguards of home.   The error was a grievous one, and both England and Ireland feel its consequences to this day.   It added a new secular ascendency to the sectarian one.   The poverty to which religious education was thus condemned, besides its more serious consequences, had others with a touch of the ludicrous about them ; but, as some one remarked, ' no one who laughs with consideration would laugh at such a jest.'   I confess I was pained by the very humble labours to which Newman seemed so willingly to subject himself.   It appeared strange that he should carve for thirty hungry youths, or sit listening for hours in succession to the eloquent visitors who came to recommend a new organist and would accept no refusal from him.   Such work should have fallen on subordinates ; but the salaries of such it was impossible to provide.   The patience with which he bore such trials was marvellous, but he encountered others severer still.   I cannot think that he received from Ireland aids proportioned to what ought to have been his.   The poor, who had no direct interest in the University, paid for it in large annual contributions several hundreds of thousands of pounds ; the middle and higher classes were proportionately less liberal ; and there were, perhaps, jealousies besides to which it is now needless to advert.   In Ireland, however, Newman found many private friends who honoured him aright and were greatly valued by him.   Among these were Dr. Moriarty, long the head of ' All Hallows College,' and later Bishop of Kerry ; Dr. Russell, Principal of Maynooth, the learned, the accomplished, and the kind ; Dr. O'Reilly, S.J. ; the late Judge O'Hagan, and others.   He worked on, cheered by the grateful sympathy of men like these, including that great Irish scholar Eugene O'Curry, to whom he had given the Irish professorship, and whose lectures, the most valuable store-house of Irish archæology, he attended.   He was cheered by the great interests of religion which he believed to be at stake, and by the aid which Irish genius and Irish aspirations, if true to their noblest mission, must largely, as he also believed, have ministered.   In that hope he gave Ireland three of his noblest volumes and seven of the best years of his life. Newman was one of those who could work and wait.   I remember his saying to me once, when things were looking dark—

We must not be impatient.   Time is necessary for all things.   If we fail at present to create a Catholic University there remains another great benefit which

we may confer on Ireland. We can in that case fall back upon a second college'
in the Dublin University, one on as dignified a scale as Trinity College, and in all
respects its equal; one doing for Catholics what Trinity College does for Protestants. Such a college would tide over the bad time, and eventually develop into
a Catholic University.

Many years have passed since he spoke, but neither a Catholic
University nor a Catholic college, founded at once on the two
principles of 'religious education' and of educational equality, has
yet been provided. A Newman was given to Ireland, one longing to
make of her what she was named in early Christian times, viz.
'the School of the West,' and apparently she knew as little what to
do with the gift as England had known. The opportunity was lost.
A foundation-stone was laid. On that occasion I wrote an ode, not
worthy of its theme, but one aspiration of which may yet be fulfilled.
It was that the statue of Newman might one day stand in the chief
court of an Irish Catholic University.

When I had been but a few days in Newman's house I fell ill of
scarlatina, and the first of my lectures had to be read aloud by another
person. I wished to be taken out of that house, lest the infection
should spread ; but for some time that course was interdicted ; and
every day, in spite of countless other engagements, Newman found
time to sit by my bedside occasionally and delight me by his conversation. When advancing towards convalescence I went to Bray
for sea air, and he drove out to see me. I remember urging him to
make an expedition with me, when I was well enough, amid the
beautiful scenery of Wicklow, and his answering with a smile that
life was full of work more important than the enjoyment of mountains
and lakes—a remark which Wordsworth would have thought highly
irreverent. I remember also saying to myself, ' The ecclesiastical
imagination and the mountain-worshipping imagination are two very
different things : Wordsworth's famous *Tintern Abbey* describes
the river Wye, its woods and waters, its fields and farms, as they
could only have been described by one whose eye saw things visible
and things invisible both. The one thing which it did not see was
the great monastic ruin, for of it that poem says not one word ; and
now here is this great theologian who, when within a few miles of
Glendalough Lake, will not visit it, though St. Kevin consecrated it
by flinging the beautiful Cathleen from the cliff into its wave
beneath.' I had to pass many a day at Bray, for my scarlatina was
followed by other maladies, and so exhausted my strength that my
poor attempts at exercise often ended by my having to lie down at
full length on the road. A little later I went to Wicklow, and thence
to Killarney, in hopes that the mountain air might restore me. That
hope was long unfulfilled. I used to look at Mangerton and say, ' Is
it possible that I ever climbed a mountain ? ' But I am degenerating
into ' inferior matter.' At Killarney I met my honoured friend Dr.

Moriarty, with whom I had first made acquaintance when he was the head of that admirable missionary college All Hallows, which the Irish Church owes to a priest of lowly degree and of no high ability, but rich in charity and faith—a man to whom far lands have owed many of their best pastors. The Bishop was making a visitation of his diocese, and offered me a place in his carriage. I gladly accepted it ; and rejoiced the more when I found that our road passed through some of the most beautiful scenery in Europe—that combination of mountain and sea coast which has ever to me appeared to surpass in spirit-stirring beauty every other kind of scenery. As we drove along by cliff and bay our discourse was chiefly of Newman. One night we slept at Derrynane, O'Connell's home. He would have liked Newman better than Newman would have liked him.

It was one of Fortune's strangest freaks that brought two of Oxford's most eminent sons to Dublin, Dr. Whately, Protestant archbishop there, and Newman. For seven years they dwelt nearly opposite to each other, at the northern and southern sides of St. Stephen's Green ; but, I believe, never met once. Newman considered that it was not for him to pay the first visit, and the archbishop perhaps thought that a renewed intimacy with his old friend might excite polemical jealousies in Dublin. I was present, however, at a meeting, the first since their Oxford days, between Newman and Gladstone. It was at the hospitable board of my dear friend Sir John Simon. They sat next each other after the ladies had left the dining-room, but their conversation was confined to the topics of the day. Newman, however, at a later time, when in London, was the guest occasionally of Dean Church and of Lord Blachford.

Newman and Sir Henry Taylor had also a singular sympathy for each other, though they had never met, and though there was so much antagonistic in their opinions and dissimilar in their characters and pursuits. If they had met early they would probably have been friends. They had in common a fearless sincerity and a serene strength; but one of them had found his training in the schools and the other in the world and in official duties. Another man of letters for whom Newman had a great love was Walter Scott. He delighted not only in the *Waverley Novels*, but, like Mr. Ruskin, in Scott's chivalrous poetry. His own great poem, *The Dream of Gerontius*, Sir Henry Taylor used to say resembles Dante more than any poetry written since the great Tuscan's time. Sir Henry could not have failed to admire also some of his short poems, such as his beautiful *Lead Thou me on*, so strangely called a hymn; and another poem not less admirable, though little known, respecting that painless knowledge of earthly things possessed by the happy Departed. The last stanza of it expresses the theological teaching that it is neither with merely human feelings nor with eyes turned towards the earth that the souls of the blest regard the shapes of this lower earth. On

the contrary, their eyes are fastened on the Beatific Vision ; and it
is in the ' mirror of the Divine Knowledge ' that they contemplate so
much of earthly things as is needed, in that region where charity
is perfected, for the exercise of intercessory prayer. The mode in
which they possess a serene knowledge of earthly things is thus illustrated in connexion with a well-known passage in the Apocalypse :—

> A sea before
> The Throne is spread.   Its still, pure glass
> Pictures all earth-scenes as they pass ;
>   We, on its shore,
> Share, in the bosom of our rest,
> God's knowledge, and are blest.

The *Dream of Gerontius*, as Newman informed me, owed its
preservation to an accident.   He had written it on a sudden impulse,
put it aside, and forgotten it.   The editor of a magazine wrote to
him asking for a contribution.   He looked into all his ' pigeon holes,'
and found nothing theological ; but in answering his correspondent
he added that he had come upon some verses which, if, as editor, he
cared to have, were at his command.   The wise editor did care,
and they were published at once.   I well remember the delight with
which many of them were read by the Bishop of Gibraltar, Dr. Charles
Harris, who was then on a visit with us, and the ardour with which
we all shared his enjoyment.

Newman's tale of *Callista* is a book singularly different from his
Loss and Gain, one being a vivid picture of a certain section of
modern English life and the other a not less vivid picture of life in
the days of the old Roman Empire.   The last was written, as he
informed me, chiefly with a pencil in railway carriages, during a
Continental tour.   No one who has read that work can doubt that it
was no less within the power of its author to have become a master
of prose fiction than to have become a great poet or a first-rate
parliamentary orator.   Such versatility would to most men have
proved a serious peril, and we have probably lost much of the best
poetry we might otherwise have inherited from Scott, Coleridge,
Southey, and Landor, owing to the circumstance that they had equal
gifts for other things as for poetic tasks ; but Newman was saved
from such snares by his fidelity to a single and supreme vocation.
He was eminently fitted, as I believe, to be a great historian, and a
history of the early Church by him, as his *Historical Essays* prove,
even if it had descended only to the time of Charlemagne, must have
been among the most valuable of historical works, from the absorbing
interest of the theme and the many years which Newman had given
to the study of early Christian times.   Newman's other avocations
prevented us from having such a book from his hand.   In the meantime we possess in the work of a great friend as well as ardent
admirer of Newman (I allude to Mr. Allies's work, *The Formation of*

Christendom) a treatise on the Philosophy of early Ecclesiastical History, at once so profound and so eloquent that it may largely console us for the loss of one more work by Newman.

At one time the Pope had given Newman a commission to make a new English translation of the Holy Scriptures from the Vulgate. He told me that he had heartily desired to undertake the task, but that unexpected difficulties, connected in part with vested interests, had presented themselves, in addition to those inherent in such a work; and thus another 'frustration' was added to the many which beset his life, frustrations of which I never heard him complain; and certainly self-pity was no weakness of his.

If he had translated the New Testament and the Psalms alone into English worthy of them, it would have imparted to countless readers 'the freedom of no mean city,' opening out to them those treasure houses of manly and spiritual devotion the Breviary and other office books of the Church.

After Newman had ceased to be connected with the Catholic University of Ireland, which I trust may yet reward his labours, even if it does not wholly fulfil his ideal, I saw him chiefly through my annual visits on my way to the Cumberland mountains and to Wordsworth's grave. I never stood beside that grave without a renewed wish that those two great men, surely England's greatest men of thought in her latter day, had known each other. In many of their opinions they would have differed; but the intensely English character of both and the profound affection cherished for his country by each would have been a bond between them.

There often exists between very different men a latent resemblance, sometimes even a physical resemblance, which long escapes observation. I was interested by hearing that after Wordsworth's death, several friends permitted to take a last look at one whom they had long loved and honoured, as he lay on his bed of death, were deeply impressed by the resemblance which his face then bore to that of Dante, as preserved in the best portraits, a resemblance which they had never noted before.

One of my most interesting visits to Newman was paid when I was on my way to Rome, early in 1870, the year of the General Council. Of course we spoke of the definition of the 'Papal Infallibility' then regarded as probable. I well remember the vehemence with which he exclaimed, 'People are talking about the definition of the Papal Infallibility, as if there were and could be but one such definition. Twenty definitions of the doctrine might be made, and of these several might be perfectly correct, and several others might be exaggerated and incorrect.' Every one acquainted with Newman's teaching was aware that he fully believed the doctrine—nay, that he had expressed that conviction in nearly every volume published by him subsequently to his conversion. Consequently, when a letter of his written to a private friend in Rome, and published without his knowledge, had been misunderstood, and had consequently produced a considerable though transient excitement, all such persons knew at once that what that letter contested was not the doctrine of the Papal Infallibility, but the expediency of defining it at that particular moment. When, some months later, the definition was made, it proved to be a most moderate one, and therefore much disappointed some so-called ' Ultramontanes.'   Several years later Newman, in his *Letter to the Duke of Norfolk*, replying to Mr. Gladstone's *Vatican Pamphlets*, distinctly stated that the definition made by the Council, so far from being an extreme one, was a strictly moderate one.   It therefore belonged to that class of definitions which, six months before it was put forth, Newman had spoken of to me as being perfectly correct.   As he has been much misrepresented in this subject I deem it a duty to him to record that conversation.

To men who were acquainted with Newman only through his books it was rather as a mind than as a man that he presented himself; but the converse was the case with those who enjoyed his intimacy. To them his great attraction lay in what belonged to his personal being, the strange force of which often made itself felt almost at once, so entirely free was he from conventionality. Amid the society of those with whom he was not in sympathy it is true that the shyness of his nature bred a marked reticence, but, notwithstanding, with that reserve there was mixed a frankness. You might be left with a restricted knowledge, but not with an erroneous impression.

W. S. Landor makes some one say that the thoughts of a true man should stand as naked as the statues of the God of Light ; but he might have added a converse assertion, viz. that a man's most sacred feelings should be shrouded in a dimness like that of the same God's Delphic laurel grove.   There was much in Newman which could only be made known to those deeply in sympathy with him, and the disclosure of which to others could only have led them into error.

What men felt most in him was his extreme, though not self-engrossed, *personality*. It was a very human personality, one that imposed upon him a large share of human sensibilities, and, perhaps by necessary consequence, of sorrows, cares, and anxieties. He had also, it is true, a strong sense of humour ; but in all serious matters his seriousness was exigent, and nothing came to him lightly, although he had, notwithstanding, a strength that raised him up under the weight of sadness.   Silence and stillness but kindled more the interior fires ; and a narrow limit increased their force. His nature, one

> Built on a surging, subterranean fire,
> That stirred and lifted him to high attempts,[2]

---

[2] *Philip van Artevelde.*

was far more likely to be stimulated than kept down by the pressure of adversities.   He had vehement impulses and moods which in his *Apologia* he calls 'fierce;' and these were stung into activity in him, as in Edmund Burke, by the sight of oppression or injustice.   But his temper was also one that abounded in sympathy. He was full of veneration.   It was thus that, as he tells us, the lightest word of his bishop in his Anglican days was a conclusive challenge to his obedience.   When some one pointed out Mr. Keble to him for the first time, he looked upon him with awe, and 'when Mr. Keble took his hand he seemed sinking into the ground.' He tells us also that the *Christian Year* had largely helped to teach him two great truths to which he had always clung closely, and that he had ever considered and kept the day on which Mr. Keble preached the assize sermon in the University pulpit as the start of the religious movement of 1833.

In others also he greatly valued veneration, and thought that even when a snare it was still a thing entitled to sympathy.   He told me that Mr. Keble possessed that quality in an extreme and even unfortunate degree; that it had always been directed especially to his father; and that the thought that in becoming a Roman Catholic he would place a gulf of separation between him and his father must have rendered it difficult for him seriously even to ask himself the question whether such a step had become a duty. With Dr. Pusey—'dear Pusey' he almost always called him—the obstacle to conversion was of another sort.   He remarked to me that with many great gifts, intellectual as well as spiritual, Dr. Pusey had this peculiarity, that 'he never knew when he burned,' the allusion being to a sport among children, when they have hidden something away and encourage the searcher by exclaiming as he gropes his way nearer and nearer to it, 'Warm,' 'Hot,' 'You burn.'   Dr. Pusey, he said, might see a doctrine with clear insight, yet take no cognisance of another proximate to it—indeed, presupposed by it.   'For years,' he said, 'many thought Pusey on the brink of Rome.   He was never near it.'   Thus, strange as it seems, the two old friends co-operated even in separation; they stood at two ends of the same bridge, and the one at the Anglican end of it passed the wayfarer on towards the Roman end, though he always strove to hold him back.

The intellectual ardour of Newman is curiously illustrated by a remark made by Mr. Woolner, the sculptor, when he contemplated the plaster cast which he had made of Newman's bust as placed at last in his studio when finished.   He turned to a friend and said, ' Those marble busts around us represent some of the most eminent men of our time, and I used to look on them with pride.   Something seems the matter with them now.   When I turn from Newman's·

head to theirs they look *like vegetables*.' What he was struck by was the intense personality of Newman's face—a still intensity.

Newman's humility was not more marked by his relations with Mr. Keble than by his relations with Dr. Pusey. In the early years of the 'High Church' movement, to which he contributed more than all its other supporters put together, he had no desire to be its head, and was ever pushing Dr. Pusey into that position. And yet with that humility he united a strong belief in his own powers and a conviction that God had imparted to him a high and special mission. That conviction must have been a great support to him during all the numerous trials of his long life. One of the severest of those trials came upon him towards the close of that life. During its last two years the state of his eyes rendered it impossible for him to say Mass. Few of his many afflictions pained him so deeply.

Nothing more characterised Newman than his unconscious refinement. It would have been impossible for him to tolerate coarse society, or coarse books, or manners seriously deficient in self-respect and respect for others. There was also in him a tenderness marked by a smile of magical sweetness, but a sweetness that had in it nothing of softness. On the contrary, there was a decided severity in his face, that severity which enables a man alike to exact from others, and himself to render, whatever painful service or sacrifice justice may claim. With his early conviction that he had a mission there had come to him the 'thought that deliverance is wrought not by the many, but by the few.' In his *Apologia* he says, 'I repeated to myself the words which have ever been dear to me from my schooldays: *Exoriare aliquis*. Now too Southey's beautiful poem of *Thalaba*, for which I had *an immense liking*, came forcibly to my mind.' The saying 'Out of the strong came forth sweetness' was realised in Newman more than in any one else whom I have known. In other matters also apparent opposites were in him blended. Thus while his intellect was pre-eminently a logical one, and while it seemed to him impossible or immoral to disown the authority of logic, when plainly exercised within her legitimate domain, yet no one felt more deeply that both the heart and the moral sense possess their own sacred tribunals in matters of reasoning as well as of sentiment. It was this consciousness which protected him from the narrowing tendencies to which the logical passion, or habit, when acting by itself, so often leads. Many a vigorous mind includes but a single section of a mind like his. The logical faculty was in his case most fortunately supplemented by an expansive imagination, which grasped thoughts immeasurably beyond the range of the mere logician. The largeness of his intellect thus, as well as his reverence and humility, protected him from the scepticism imputed to him by men who, in his place, would have become not sceptics only, but unbelievers. It was that wide imagination which made him grasp the hidden but substantial analogies between the chief schools of religious thought in the nineteenth century and the corresponding schools in the fifth, analogies which had never revealed themselves to minds perhaps as logical as his own, but which he could never repel, however much they distressed him. In Newman, again, above both the logical and the imaginative faculty there ever hung the spiritual mind, a firmament full of light, though clouds at times overswept it. These were the characteristics of Newman which made him write the memorable sentence, 'No number of difficulties *need* produce a single doubt'—he meant doubt in a mind capable of real convictions. His mind swung through a wide arc and thoughts apparently antagonistic often seemed to him supplemental each to the other. Thus he tells us in his *Apologia* that the existence in the world even of such sin and suffering as sometimes seem to make it incapable of reflecting its Maker's countenance implies, *for the true Theist*, nothing disparaging to true Theism. What it teaches *him* is that the world cannot have remained what the Creator made it; that some dreadful catastrophe must have overtaken it, and wrecked its chief of creatures, Man—viz. the Fall— that, to keep due proportion, a second mystery, not less wonderful than that of a Creation, must be true no less, viz. an Incarnation, a Redemption, a Deliverance—in other words, that not only Theism is true, but that Christianity, the practical Theism, is its supplemental Truth.

Another most remarkable union in Newman of qualities commonly opposed to each other was that of a dauntless courage with profound thoughtfulness. The men of thought and study are often timid men, and, when not timid, are indolent and averse to action, a thing which takes them out of that region in which they can trust themselves and into a region in which their battle is a left-handed one. Men of this order may not on that account be consciously false to their convictions; but they wish to serve Truth, a jealous divinity, in their own way, not in hers; and they swerve aside from it on specious pretexts, when approaching near to that point from which the conclusion must be rudely plain, and where there can remain no other alternative except that of avowed faithlessness, or—serious inconvenience. In Newman there existed the rare union of the contemplative mind and the heroic soul. Otherwise he might have pointed out its way to another generation; but he would not have 'led forth the pilgrimage.'

It would be a mistake to suppose that Newman's imagination, religious as it was, could spare no space for earthly interests. Had its energies been thus restricted it would have dealt less vigorously with heavenly subjects. Many of his writings show how keenly he had studied human character, and the degree in which it affects that great drama of providence called by us 'History,' in which whole nations have their entrances and their exits, like actors on the stage of life.   Nothing except his zeal for the highest spiritual truths could exceed the sympathy felt by him with all that concerns the 'Humanities;' and I well remember the look of stern disapproval with which he spoke to me of the Abbé Gaume's theory of education, one that must have excluded the Greek and Latin classics from the schools of Christian youth, or left them but a small place therein.   Another able and excellent man, Dr. Ward, would, I think, in that matter have sympathised with the Abbé's opinions more than with Newman's.   I recollect once, when I had remarked in a letter to him on the lamentable loss which the world must have sustained if all the works of Æschylus and the other Greek dramatists had perished, as most of them have, Dr. Ward's replying that in the surviving works of those men he could really find almost nothing of a character to be called 'ascetic,' and that therefore he could not see what loss would have followed if the whole of them had disappeared.   Newman could heartily admire also, in spite of its limitations, the heroism of the early world.   His admiration for the greatest of early heroes, Alexander the Great, was ardently expressed in a letter to me on my sending him my drama bearing that name.   It demanded, 'Who was there but he whose object it was to carry on civilisation and the arts of peace, while he was a conqueror?   Compare him to Attila or Tamerlane.   Julius Cæsar compared with him was but a party man and a great general.'

I have thus recorded some of those traits that struck me as most remarkable in Newman's character.   His career bore a singular resemblance to that character.   Till his forty-fifth year it was a disturbed one.   If, as he informs us in his *Apologia*, his submission to the Roman Catholic Church imparted to his soul a profound and lasting peace, while (a fact admitted alike by friend and foe), far from chilling or contracting, it greatly stimulated his genius and energies, it is not less true that the antecedent process of conversion was to him an unusually painful one.   That conversion meant a separation from all whom he most loved and honoured, and also, but only apparently, a desertion of what was then regarded by many as the battle-field of great principles, and as, in its place, at least an external fellowship with many to whom he had long felt a strong antipathy on the ground of their philosophic 'liberalism,' or of the part they took in political 'agitation.'   Newman was an intense loyalist, and he had once deemed it a duty of loyalty for him, as a Churchman, to see matters theological, as long as that was possible, from an Anglican point of view.   Eventually he had to choose between thinking independently and discarding those great main principles which for so many years had been consolidating themselves both within his intellect and his heart, but which, as he had reluctantly discovered, could not be realised in England's Established Church, and were realised, as they had ever been, in the Roman Catholic Church.

Some persons have expressed surprise that a mind like Newman's should have been so slow in making that discovery. They forget the difference ' 'twixt now and then.' They should remember that the wild cry of ' The Mass is idolatry ! ' had rung for several centuries over the land, and that its echoes, though dying away in the distance, had sounded in the ears of Newman's generation. When passionate polemical errors have lived their time, and died, so far as the intellect is concerned, their angry ghosts continue yet for a season to haunt the imagination. We should also remember that when, in the sixteenth century, the very idea of the Church seemed to have been suddenly sponged out of the Northern mind (otherwise the practical reforms then doubtless much needed must have been sought in a General Council, not imposed by local authorities), and when, in the nineteenth century, that idea had been partially restored, the last part of it to reappear was that of the Church's visible unity. The new reformers thought it sufficient to resist Erastian tyranny and to revive the general teaching of Christian antiquity.

It is easier to measure the swiftness or slowness of purely intellectual movements than of mixed movements, intellectual and spiritual both, because in the latter case we have to deal with Grace and with Reason both ; in the former with Reason alone. Even in scientific enquiries, the philosopher's pace has not the regularity which belongs to that of the man of business or the man of fashion. The philosopher does not grudge the time he spends on reiterated experiments, though he often asserts that, in the end, the great discovery is reached by a bound, no one can say how. In Science that bound is commonly a flash of that genius which is an inspiration in itself. In the case of Religion it is often an act of the highest Faith, when to the humility and insight of Faith it has added her courage.

AUBREY DE VERE.

AT SEA

I

DR. JOHNSON is reported to have said that being in a ship was like being in a gaol, with the chance of being drowned; and without doubt one's 'cabined, cribbed, confined' position, even on the largest modern steamers, is a prison; but with regard to 'the chance of being drowned,' I was assured that on board one of the great transatlantic liners was about the safest place in the world. In spite of all assurances, however, I am inclined to think that it is generally, if not in reality, at least in feeling and conjecture, rather a pitch-and-toss affair! In mid-ocean, on a precipitous and moving island, in a state of constant warfare with the most powerful elements of nature; now rocked from side to side by the enormous heaves of the ocean swell, and now breathlessly buffeting the thunderous beats of wave and wind, we must feel, even under the most favourable circumstances, that we are tiding over a time of considerable danger and risk. And accordingly, with or without good cause, I certainly found that an atmosphere of very great timidity and precaution permeated the whole ship.

We see, also, that we are weathering the rough assaults of forces which, though equally inimical to all, are yet not such as are best confronted, in case of a mishap, by a united struggle, but that, on the contrary, so strong and merciless are they, that the only way of escaping from their sweeping and wholesale devastation is by single, selfish efforts—*sauve qui peut.* For we know that collective salvation will not then be the belief or order of the day, but that the survivors will be few and far between. It is true that in the meantime we are all in the same boat; but similarity of situation does not in these particular surroundings encourage much sympathy or friendliness, but tends rather to rouse special feelings of rivalry and hostility. We are therefore strangely on the defensive in our conduct and relations to one another. In fact, it is really quite ludicrous to see how careful and suspicious we become. We are on our guard from every quarter, north, south, east, and west; for, like weathercocks, we know not whence an ill wind may come blowing nobody any good. Every person and thing seems labelled 'Dangerous,' for does not each represent a possible collision and upset, or at least unpleasant disturbance? A touch, a word, a look may do it. One fears lest any injudicious remark or rash act should disarrange our machinery or that of the vessel, and perhaps spring a leak somewhere. Like the notable pots that were fellow-travellers down a stream, it is all right so long only as we take care not to crack one another. So we move gingerly; we look askance; we speak disjointedly. Our sounds are signals; our movements balances; our seats anchorages. Nobody is at their ease. Everything is angular and awkward, and liable to fall or slide at any moment. It is a shaky experience, where there is truly many a slip 'twixt the cup and the lip. It is a world out of plumb, where levels are constantly varying and lines crossing. We are, in fact, the whole time perilously bordering on an upside-down state of affairs.

Every one therefore takes up a position of stern personal vigilance and reserve, and each passenger is as isolated on board the ship as the ship herself is on the ocean. They look like mere colourless bundles of human ballast. Their expressions are as blank as mummies, and their manners as frigid and congealed as the frozen mutton below. Not a pore is open that can be shut. Weatherproof and water-tight, all their desires and interests are self-centred. Egoism reigns supreme. Dante's Inferno is not more individual. Thus the boat is peopled with little human skiffs, separated and estranged from one another through this strong sense of the general risk and jeopardy of the situation and of the imminent possibility of rivalry and antagonism; and thus, in coats of mail, as it were, we breast the dangers of the voyage, and such are the prevailing influences that regulate our conduct and sentiments: and of some such sort, also, is man, I fear, when placed between the devil and the deep sea. The truth is, we are only too thankful to be thus left high and dry both by the receding waves and our retiring companions, and would in neither case invite more intimate relations.

This nervous spirit dominating everything, and our defensive, unfriendly appearance and bearing to one another, are not attractive. In fact, on board a ship is not for many reasons a sociable place, and most travellers are very near land again before they consent to become even nodding acquaintances. Such close quarters—on deck and at table, sharing state-rooms and sitting-rooms—seem to enforce a companionship that most people dislike and resent; and so, if only for this reason, we are as cool and distant in manner as is possible under the pressing circumstances, until we have had time to recover from the shock of this inevitable and ubiquitous proximity. Nor is this climatic pillory a becoming place to the physical or even sartorial sides of our being. Saturated on deck with the salt sweat of the brine and unstinted fresh air, or pent up in air-tight holes for hours, or perhaps days, our physical appearance is in neither case shown off to advantage, while the costumes worn, especially the ladies' marine garments, look extremely ugly.   So we are not, or rather we are, taken altogether, a pretty kettle of fish.   Indeed, a collection of passengers at sea is uncommonly like a great cargo of human rubbish gathered from all parts of the globe, and heaped together in one discordant pile for the purpose of being carted out into mid-ocean and there ignominiously consigned to the waves and deeps of oblivion.   If, however, it should luckily escape this appropriate and timely end, and, thus as it were reprieved, should reach in safety a landing-stage, there is some justification for this merciful prolongation of life in the remarkable transformation scene that takes place when the happy hour of release approaches.   Grace and chivalry once more relate the sexes; there is an extraordinary change for the better in their physical appearance; colour and expression again declare themselves, and hair falls into place and shape, while their figures and limbs seem actually to take a new shape as they stand once more on steady ground, and, with autochthonic pride, tread in the well-worn footsteps; and clothes become again decorative.

Verily, to disembark is to escape as from a gaol, and the minute the 'unplumbed, salt, estranging' gulf that separates us from home and hearth is bridged by the gangway, pushing forward, bag and baggage, we hasten across to coveted freedom and exercise of mind and body, to roam and to stretch to our heart's content after our long, cramped confinement.   Without delay we settle down in the soft lap of luxurious earth, and, shaking the spray off the hem of our garments, we would, in our great joy and delight, like dogs, like donkeys, like anything, roll and roll in the dust and the grass.   For physical and moral, as well as æsthetic reasons, a landscape is a necessary background to human figure.

II

Any one who has ever been on a long sea voyage knows its little excitements and diversifications—the reading of the log-book, which is the daily newspaper, the standard concert, the drawing of sweepstakes, &c.   It is not lively.   There is nothing entertaining or dramatic in a sponge-bag, and suchlike is our *milieu* for the time being.   But any life and fun there was seemed to me to be among the steerage passengers.   There humour and pathos, love and laughter, accidents and tragedies might be seen.   But, curiously enough, a great part of their time was passed in religious exercises, singing and preaching and praying.   Some were apprehensive and earnest, some were content to do at Rome as Rome does, and some evidently found it an amusing pastime.   One young man, with a damsel on each arm, and followed by a procession, paraded about singing snatches of hymns in a very convivialist, if not revivalist, fashion.   But beyond such mild efforts the voyage was quite uneventful.   We saw no sea-serpents.   Nobody fell overboard.   There were no deaths, nor were there any births, as there often are, and, though there may have been some betrothals unknown to me, there were no marriages.

I am not an ancient mariner. This was, in fact, my first really outlandish expedition, and I must say I found it gratified, with one exception, none of the ordinary pleasures and tastes of life. For even the best ship can hardly be said to be a cosy or comfortable place. Like some huge lavatory, there is everywhere a cold, petrified aspect, and I thought one's narrow berth preferable only to the rather too wide bed of the ocean outside. Then the food tastes insipid and artificial. Meat kept in ice seems as though it had been washed and rinsed till all the essence was gone, while, strange to relate, fish at sea are not as good as coals at Newcastle. There is no delicious flavour of clay in the vegetables, and the water one drinks has come from no fresh mountain spring. But it is the paradise of the idle and lazy. On the sea one has no use for feet at all, since the ship does all the motion, although she even, as in the Irish song, 'walks through the water without any feet.' One cannot stand, or walk, or run except on a few short planks. The unwebbed toes and unfledged arms of the human kind are useless and out of place. Man is an exotic on the water. He is most distinctly out of his element. He is, in fact, every bit as bad as a fish out of water. Only a Dagon, with fishy tail, could possibly enjoy himself. There is, therefore, nowhere to go, nor is there anything to do. One does not read or write much, and people are not even conversational at sea, and any talk there may be is but far-fetched reminiscences of the distant land and its faded interests. Nor can one even think. This vast void of wind and water takes one's very breath away, suffocating both mind and body. Man's physical properties and cares, at all times a danger to his soul, are ruinous to it at sea. In fact, it is quite awful to contemplate how sterile and dull we should become if long at sea. The infinite volume of the ocean would, I fear, mentally drown us. Such interminableness and monotony do not conduce to intellectual fruition. Eternity is, I suspect, thoughtless. Philosophy in the clouds is only true very metaphorically, for I believe no system of thought will ever be worked out in a ship or a balloon. After all, it is in the study, or at least in the fields, that the brain of man is at home. But voyaging in this boundless space, where clouds only are formed and rain made, there is nothing to catch the wandering eye or fix and occupy the vacant mind. There are no objects, no distinctions, no limits, no standards, no contrasts. To select or discriminate is impossible. Who knows one wave from another? We are swimming in a basin of liquid, and the solids of life, so to speak, have been left behind. It is a soupy, sloppy fare, tasteless and unpalatable to the mental appetite.

Thus, sundered from the body of life, we reel and we roll and we gasp, and flounder hopelessly in our efforts to find bottom. Like Archimedes, one is sadly in want of room to stand on in order to set

to work. For at sea there is no *locus standi*. Man is in every way
out of his depths. His calculations are unsound; his views undefined; his reflections unfathomable. The products of the mind are as
unstable and fruitless as the bubbles rising and bursting in the surf.
Neither can escape into separate existence. A mental vacancy seems,
indeed, to pervade the whole of this watery realm of fish, of whom
the complaint has been made that it is impossible to obtain from
them a single instructive look or sound. A spiritual chill possesses
us in their domain as though we also were cold-blooded animals.
We, too, become deaf and dumb in this voiceless world; for, as you
know, 'the things that live in the sea are all mute.' Our thoughts
and feelings lie dormant. It is a hibernating season, as it were. A
low-lying stagnancy oppresses us, and we succumb to the degraded
level of jelly-fish. And how abhorrent is this negative existence to
the soul and consciousness of man, who, in order to thrive, must,
like a flower of the field, be planted and rooted ! For he cannot live and
bear fruit while drifting, like some plants of seaweed whose roots even
float upon the surface of the sea. He cannot, like the halcyon, build
his nest on the water. He is rather a bird of passage, who finds here
no home or resting-place.

It is a precarious existence too—just keeping our heads above
water. For we are but puppets, bobbing for very life in the storm
and stress of the ocean, on the secret brow of which, even when at
rest, dreaded doom treacherously broods. Even the smooth desert of
the ocean is too ominous of the calm that precedes a storm to be
called a peace. The sleep of the sea is that of a sleeping dog.
Tragic uncertainty, in its most unrelenting form, reigns throughout
these unfamiliar regions. So we are all fatalists on the ocean, just
as those who live on its shore always are, and mere human character
and will are completely submerged in the mysterious depths of
destiny and chance. Man is, in fact, no longer a free agent in mind
or body, but the victim of strange, unearthly powers.

And how impersonal we must and do become ! Dipped, as it
were, in the waters of Lethe, we have shaken off all manners, morals,
and customs, as antediluvian remnants of some now remote order of
things. All old associations, local, national, legal, of birth, name,
home, class, country, of kinship and friendship, evaporate in this
realm of nothingness. Variations of age, sex, character, of religion,
habits, pursuits, have no room or opportunity for display. Passion
and purpose have no vent and become obsolete.

Wiped off the face of the earth, we are lost in the splash and the
mist.

How wanting, too, in local colour it all is ! For on the ocean there
is none of the music and beauty of the sea. It is on the shore that
the sea breaks into resounding speech and song. There, among the
shells and pebbles on the beach, she finds her human voice. But in
mid-ocean there is no tide or current of any sort. No ebb and flow

is perceptible there. It is an unvaried scene without feature or expression. It has everywhere a tiresome, obvious aspect.

O this great, unimpressionable power! What can I hope to do or see here, when even the hand of the Creator is not visible or present? For is not this the material, ' without form and void,' which the Divine Sculptor left untouched on the day in that memorable week when He made 'the dry land appear'? It may be difficult to see the trees for the wood, but who can see anything for the overwhelming ocean? or can we even see it? We have heard that Cortez stared at the Pacific, but we have wondered how he managed to do it, and agree rather with Charles Lamb who complained that he had never seen the ocean, but only an insignificant bit of it. The very progress of the ship through its multitudinous waves is impossible to detect and is hard to believe in, and at the journey's end the land comes as a surprise, and I, for my part, should not have been much astonished if we had never reached our destination. For, in this world of motion without change, there are no landmarks or signposts, to say nothing of milestones, and so I never felt that we were getting over any ground or approaching anything; but for all I could see we were moving round and round in a circle, which but for the compass—the sailor's cross of salvation —we might, I suppose, still be doing.

Thoreau found it employment enough to watch the progress of the seasons at Walden, but he would have been idle at sea; for, unlike nature elsewhere, the ocean has no seasons, no spring, no summer, autumn, or winter; no fresh life and growth, no new scents, no birth or death. It has been well called evergreen. Snow even does not cover or affect it; while after rain the ship seemed the only wet place. Nor can time imprint any tale or tidings on its fluctuating surface. The past leaves no traces. History can find no records. Unlike crumbling ruins, wrecks are quickly swallowed up, and all vestiges obliterated. The ocean has no memory. The fields of Marathon and Waterloo outlive Salamis and Trafalgar. All experiences are buried too deep for even the most adventurous and searching diver or wet-as-weed antiquarian. For who has seen the ' untrampled floor' of the sea? Who can sound the bottom of the ocean, *au fond*? Unless, perhaps, the poet, thus :—

> Methought I saw a thousand fearful wrecks;
> A thousand men that fishes gnaw'd upon;
> Wedges of gold, great anchors, heaps of pearl,
> Inestimable stones, unvalued jewels,
> All scatter'd in the bottom of the sea.
> Some lay in dead men's skulls; and in those holes
> Where eyes did once inhabit, there were crept,
> As 'twere in scorn of eyes, reflecting gems,
> That woo'd the slimy bottom of the deep,
> And mock'd the dead bones that lay scatter'd by.

Or, more naturally, thus :—

The world below the brine,
Forests at the bottom of the sea, the branches and leaves,
Sea-lettuce, vast lichens, strange flowers and seeds, the thick tangle, openings,
    and pink turf,
Different colours, pale grey and green, purple, white, and gold, the play of light
    through the water;
Dumb swimmers there among the rocks, coral, gluten, grass, rushes, and the
    aliment of the swimmers;
Sluggish existences grazing there suspended, or slowly crawling close to the
    bottom;
The sperm-whale at the surface blowing air and spray, or disporting with his
    flukes;
The leaden-eyed shark, the walrus, the turtle, the hairy sea-leopard, and the
    sting-ray;
Passions there, wars, pursuits, tribes, sight in those ocean-depths, breathing that
    thick-breathing air, as so many do.
The change thence to the sight here, and to the subtle air breathed by beings
    like us who walk this sphere;
The change onward from ours to that of beings who walk other spheres.

But to return to us poor mortals on its surface. Sea and sky everywhere. Billows and breezes above and below. One wash of blue and grey. It is truly a vain and vague existence, floating in this nebulous world of froth and vapour. Within such fluid and aërial envelopments we can well realise how all nature is indeed one and the same, how ether is perhaps a more rarefied form of matter, permeating even the solid structure of crystals, and matter a more compressed form of ether, or both but forms of energy, since all things then seem very cognate and interchangeable. In a long-continued storm, are not the limit and distinction between sea and air said to become completely annihilated, 'the heaven all spray and the ocean all cloud'? But although there may be this natural kinship, there are no feelings of human familiarity or homeliness in the scene, for the sea and sky are most distant and foreign to our physical organism. Man may have been a mere animal at one time of his development, but, as far as I can, by hints and possible inclinations in myself, revive his earliest aboriginal habits and instincts, he was never either fish or fowl, although, of course, scientists tell us there was at one time nothing but water-life in the world, and that land animals are late inventions, and point to the snail wandering over the earth with his sea-shell still on his back, and will also explain to us how the worm crept up a tree and had to grow wings in order to get down again. But all this, if ever, was a long time ago, and I, for my part, found this atmosphere of wind and wave so strange and uncongenial that I doubt very much if my ancestors were at any stage of their gradual evolution able to swim or to fly, though I believe they may once have been able to crawl and climb. It seems, indeed, clear to me that we human beings are essentially land-lubbers, and that we must, like leeches, stick to earth for our very

life-blood. Is it not actually true that when life begins to fail our
senses swim and our wits vanish into the air? Is not death an inundation, as it were, a sort of unpleasant drunkenness, by which the
equipoise that sustains life is upset?

And, in this vapid sphere of water and air, how ardently one longs
for a good handful of dry brown clay! How one's feet itch for the sure
touch of soil! How divine earth now seems! On the dead, barren
boards of the deck one thinks of her as teeming and sprouting with
luxuriant life. A particle of dust even is now a sacred and treasured
relic of past terrestrial bliss, and as for a blade of grass or a sprig of
green foliage, they would be as manna from heaven to one's famished
senses and orphaned soul. Verily, earth is our mother. Amid these
aquatic surroundings, hemmed in by the ocean on both sides, I confess I found myself to be a gross, unabashed materialist, and ardently
wished to be, as they say, 'immersed in matter.'

And how deeply pathetic it was to watch the antics of her exiled
children as, by diligent pacing up and down the deck and stamping
on the boards, they vainly endeavoured to recall the solid joys of
terra firma and the voluptuous delights of a long, unbroken walk!
For no amount of tramping will draw from the hard, cold, close-
shaven, and well-scrubbed boards of a ship's deck a vestige of earth's
soft touch and fond, caressing warmth—what the poet means when
he says :

The press of my foot to the earth springs a hundred affections,

and the futile attempt to do so only reminded me of a tame sparrow
I once saw that used to flap its wings and try douse itself in the
polished, glossy surface of a mahogany table.

Thus cooped up like hens in the middle of a great pool, the time
passes away in slumberous vacuity, much feeding and roosting, and
a certain amount of discontented croaking and picking.

III

But there were times in this rather squalid life when the soul
could emerge and rise to the purest exaltation; rare moments when
the true purposes of life become evident and conscious realities, and
the soul, touched with emotion, breathes eternal loyalty to its high
possibilities; hours, by day, spent in sea-dreaming, and by night in
star-gazing; calm days, when all above is a dome of light and the
waters around one smooth, resplendent flood; clear nights, when the
sea 'bares her bosom to the moon,' whose bright shadow, soft and
evanescent like a golden rainbow, lights and adorns her deep, dark
rest; stirring, dashing times, when the width and freedom and wild-
ness of the scene are most exhilarating to the rebellious spirit in one;
fickle moods, when the perpetual motion of this fleeting world
delight one; lovely, chaste mornings, when the electric purity and
freshness of the sea and air enchant one; gorgeous, fiery evenings,

when the blaze of the setting sun and the glow of the spreading ocean vie with each other in surpassing magnificence and glory. And how often—drifting between two oceans, one infinite arching overhead, and one fathomless sweeping underneath, the vast space of the sky with its countless stars above, and the unknown depths of the sea with its myriad waves below, alone, in the solemn stillness of 'the huge and thoughtful night' and bathed in the eternal mystery of life and death—would I wistfully look up at the deep vault of the veiled heavens and then searchingly peer down into the dark hollow of the hidden waters !

> Stars silent rest o'er us,
> Graves under us silent.

It was strange and startling indeed to think of ' this fragment of a world hastening to rejoin the great mass of existence,' of this little oasis of life and humanity in the wide wilderness of the desert-ocean. For I found the Atlantic very uninhabited, except by fish, and they were mostly beneath one's notice. We seldom sighted a passing ship and only occasionally saw ' the backs of plunging dolphins ' or the ' foam-fountains ' of the ' sea-shouldering ' whale. Birds only were our almost constant attendants. But I must not forget to mention how one beautiful, clear afternoon four magnificent icebergs 'mast-high, came floating by.' We were very fortunate in meeting them, as some passengers on board had crossed thirty times without ever having seen one. Their dazzling lustre in the bright sunshine, glowingly reflected in the watery mirror around, was superb. As the ship passed close by them one after the other in procession, they seemed to me like great ocean swans that had strayed from their northern nests and were now aimlessly swimming about this shoreless pond in search of rest, some with their stately necks reared high above the luminous water in crystal glory, some with their heads gracefully buried, in Arctic repose, in the fluffy, snow-white plumage of their softly folded wings. And as the sun's rays fell on them and the sea breezes blew around them, they sparkled all over in shimmering sprays of silvery radiance, their feathers of frost and foam were gently ruffled, and the sheen of the encircling blue broke against their emerald-hued sides into rippling waves of motion and light—one star-quivering, sun-flashing, sea-glittering scene of glacial splendour. Or, again, as we got farther from them, I fancied them to be the loveliest of sea-lilies, cruelly torn from their white bed in the north and wafted down the world's great Gulf Stream, and, as they listlessly floated towards warmer climes, little by little fading and melting away into its absorbing depths, pure water-blossoms, dissolving pearls of snow.

These ocean phantoms looked so peaceful and innocent that it was difficult to regard them as one of the greatest dangers of the voyage, which in foggy weather they are, though there is, I believe some slight chance of seeing them in time owing to their brilliant whiteness and towering size. Apart, however, from the mere danger, I am glad that we met them in full daylight and escaped a collision, since in such a catastrophe, though doubtless the unholy part of my nature would have been inclined to curse this 'harmless albatross,' all my poetic and spiritual sympathies would have been on the side of so fair and fascinating an opponent. For, in spite of the ship's orthodox gender, I imagined her to be a mighty, screw-driving, smoke-belching, blacksmithy Vulcan—I had but lately been over her hot interior, inspecting the furnaces and many gigantic instruments of force that propel her—with club-footed blades forging his iron way and will in a brutal attempt to assault the cool, fresh, morning purity of a spotless goddess, born of the sea. Certainly, as these icebergs, aurora-like, tremulous, and delicate, calmly glided along, our noise and motion, as, leviathan-like, with smoking nostrils and burning eyeballs, we ploughed and splashed by, seemed rude, indecent, and unpardonable.

We did not catch sight of another danger, 'derelicts.' I regret this, as I should have much liked to have seen a great naked-ribbed vessel, adrift and unmanned and deserted by every living creature— its skeleton hulk still lying unburied on this fluid field of seafaring and storm-fighting.

But we did have a view of, in my opinion, the greatest 'derelict' of all between this and America. For I shall not soon forget how, as the first morning broke after leaving Liverpool, we found ourselves anchored in the beautiful harbour of Queenstown, with its picturesquely situated cathedral on the brow of the sloping declivity on which the little town is built. This lovely glimpse of my native land was especially dear and touching to me, since, meeting her thus out at sea, it seemed as though she had come out a part of the way on purpose to see me off and bid me a 'God-speed' on my journey; and well might we have said when, with the hearty good wishes of the natives, we started on our voyage across the ocean,

> The ship was cheered, the harbour cleared,
> Merrily did we drop
> Below the kirk, below the hill,
> Below the lighthouse top.

And long shall I remember also, as with lingering regret we slowly receded, gazing back through the whole of that afternoon at the dim, distant tinge of the land's edge, and how, as I thought of the Old World we were leaving behind and of the New World we were hurrying to, it seemed to me like the faint thin outline of an old moon, pale and indistinct, yet clearly visible; and so it remained in my eyes, even after, continuing our globular course, we had come round on the first crescent of the rich new moon.

MARTIN MORRIS.

THE JEW-BAITING ON THE CONTINENT

JEW-BAITING is no novel phenomenon in history. Ever since the dispersion of the Jews amongst the nations, rulers or classes of men, both heathen and Christian, have practised that sport extensively. In former times, it is true, they did it in very rough fashion, and untold numbers of Jews were massacred all over Europe by crowds hounded on by that peculiar hatred which all nations have felt for the chosen people of God. Nowadays the persecution of Jews is more in conformity with our polished manners. Now, instead of the club and the hatchet, is used the poison of calumny, and the scandal of accusations, denunciations, and aspersions of crimes opprobrious and ignoble. Formerly there were persecutions *pur et simple*. No one cared to find another name for it. Now there is *Antisemitism*. A new word was needed, and it were folly to regard that new word as a mere catchword of ephemeral value, and as hiding under its novel garb only an old and stale fact. Words, like men, have their successes, and in success there always is a certain measure of truth. The word Antisemitism does mean something novel. It is not altogether the old persecution of the Jews, or rather it is not the persecution of that kind of Jews which was set upon by people in previous centuries. It is, I take it, the persecution of the reformed Jew, of the emancipated Jew, of the Jew who is a doctor, a professor, a banker, a playwright, a journalist, a lawyer—in one word, of the gentleman Jew. The Stoeckers, and Ahlwardts, and Luegers, and Drumonts, and likewise all other leaders of the antisemitic movement on the continent, do not really hate the small Jew, the orthodox Jew, the petty trader in foreign garb and of strange manners. With regard to him, the meanest of Antisemites has the great satisfaction of despising him. Nobody really wants to destroy the subjects of his disdain. To look down upon a whole class of people, to feel oneself superior to them—is not this a satisfaction far too exquisite to be lost to the disdainer by the extermination of the disdainee? How true; if brutally so, was that Hungarian countess who used to hear the reports of her young Jewish steward in her bedroom early in the morning, lying on her bed in a state of nature! When being asked how she could so forget herself, she replied, with an astonished mien, ' To be ashamed of Moses ? ' (meaning the steward)—' why, Moses is no man ! He is only a Jew.' No, it is not the Jew proper, the old-style and forbidding Jew whom the Antisemites are after. What they aim at is the Jew who has practically abandoned the law and ritual of Judaism ; and the appearance of that sort of Jews in large numbers being a novel phenomenon, their persecutors necessarily adopted a new party-name.

The new name is thus fully justified ; it actually means a novel thing. This has been largely lost sight of by the writers on Antisemitism. Both Jews and Christians have, as a rule, insisted on the obsolete traits of Antisemitism. They have in tones of indignation or broad learning essayed to show that modern Jew-baiters are using old and worn-out armoury ; that their accusations of Jewish rites have long been refuted ; that the whole movement is a preposterous relapse into mediæval obscurantism. It is well known that the late Emperor Frederick the Third, as well as Professor Theodor Mommsen, have publicly declared German Antisemitism to be a stain on the honour of Germany. The sovereign as well as the scholar regarded any persecution of the Jews as attempts at reviving the worst and long outgrown diseases of a low and despicable stage of civilisation. Yet, with utmost deference to the noble Emperor and to the great historian, I beg to differ. Modern Antisemitism is not a mere revival of mediæval obscurantism. It has a *raison d'être* of its own ; and it is inconceivable how a scholar endowed with the fine historic instincts of Mommsen could be misled by some of the manœuvres of Antisemitism into misconstruing the real purport of that movement. For the Antisemites have indeed had recourse to measures used by the lowest sort of Jew-baiters in long bygone times. They have revived the old calumny that Jews need the blood of Christians for the preparation of their Passover bread. Of the numerous trials to that effect in recent times, the most gigantic was that of the alleged murder of Esther Solymossy by the Jews of Tisza-Eszlár, a village in Central Hungary, in 1881. In that ghastly case the young son of the Jewish butcher of the village declared before the judge, and in presence of his father, that he had seen through the keyhole of the synagogue how his father, together with a number of other Jews, were slaughtering Esther, and letting her blood run into a receptacle used for religious rites. The trial lasted for nearly two years, and kept all Hungary, nay Europe, in a state of ever-growing intense excitement. The Jews were acquitted in all the three instances permitted by Hungarian law ; but I must add, and from personal knowledge too, that the number of persons other than Jews believing in the innocence of the Tisza-Eszlár Jews was, and probably still is, exceedingly small, although the innocence of the Jews was established beyond the shadow of a doubt. Nor need that astonish any one. Popular rage wants its victim. The Hungarians, for reasons to be mentioned hereafter, were enraged against the gentlemen Jews. They wanted their victim; and what could satisfy them more than to cast the unspeakable ignominy of ritual child-murder on the subjects of their hatred? A few years later, in 1891, at Xanten, a small place in Westphalia, a child five years old was found dead in a barn with its throat cut. The barn being near the shop of a Jewish butcher, Buschhoff, he was accused of murdering the child in order to provide blood for Jewish rites. No clue to the actual murderer was found, and Buschhoff was put on trial. After two weeks' hearing of the case, during which time the whole of learned Germany was completely absorbed in and frantically excited over the guilt of the Jew, the public prosecutor himself asked for the prisoner's acquittal, claiming that the accused had proved an *alibi* for every minute of the day of the murder. Buschhoff was of course acquitted by the jury. I do not entertain the slightest doubt that the majority of Germans did not acquit Buschhoff at all. In vain did learned Christian Hebraists, such as Francis Delitzsch, publish ponderous treatises on the absolute lack of foundation in all these stories of ritual murder by Jews : the trials for such murders were steadily increasing. After Tisza-Eszlár in 1881 came the trials at Dohilew and at Grodno, in Poland, in 1886 ; the trials at Constantinople, Caiffa, Budapest, Pressburg, in 1887 ; at Saloniki, Samacoff, Kaschau, Pressburg, in 1888 ; at Varna, Kustendji, Aleppo, Pressburg, in 1889 ; at Damascus, Beyrout, in 1890 ; at Xanten, Philippopoli, Smyrna, Budapest, Corfu, in 1891 ; at Malta, Rahova, Posen, Kolin, in 1893, &c. &c.

This apparent resuscitation of past methods of persecuting Jews has given much colour to the view that modern Antisemitism is but an incomprehensible revival of mediæval fanaticism in the midst of our enlightened century, or one more type of 'degeneration,' atavism, social psychopathy, &c. However, none of these explanations will hold water. In Antisemitism we are bound to recognise a social and political phenomenon growing out of the present constitution of the continent with inevitable necessity; and since this constitution is certainly not identical with the frame and tenor of society in the Middle Ages, or any other previous period, Antisemitism too is largely an historic phenomenon of its own. To scoff at it, to indulge in bleak indignation over it, to minimise its various aspects by regarding it as a passing fad of the masses—any such attitude will at once preclude us from rightly comprehending it. It is passing strange to note how utterly incapable contemporary historians and philosophers have been to assign Antisemitism its adequate significance in modern history. In England, it is true, there has appeared no elaborate essay or work on that question. To my knowledge, Mr. Lecky alone, in a review of M. Anatole Leroy-Beaulieu's book, *Israel amongst the Nations* (in the *Forum*, Dec. 1893), has offered a few remarks on the subject. Mr. Whitman's article on ' Antisemitism ' in the *Contemporary Review* (May 1893) is interesting and full; it does not, however, study the subject as a problem of history in the first place.   On the continent, on the other hand, the number of treatises, essays, pamphlets, and articles in journals published on Antisemitism is legion.[1]   Some of the greatest of continental sociologists, economists, historians, and philosophers have pronounced upon that movement, and vainly tried to account for it.   In the seventies, when Antisemitism was in its first stages, they did not, with one single exception (the late Professor Treitschke), even surmise the coming growth of the movement.   In the eighties, when all Germany and Austria-Hungary were drenched by Antisemitism, they offered a most amusing variety and divergence of opinions as to its causes and cure.   A philosopher of the description of Edward Hartmann may perhaps be pardoned for having, in his book on the Jewish question, avoided touching upon the real issues of the problem at all.   Herr Hartmann's very system consists of the art of writing round his subjects and never by any means on them, whereby he amply merited the name of the Philosopher of the Unconscious.   But ought not historians and historic economists proper to have given us a satisfactory explanation of this remarkable contemporary phenomenon?   If history is not meant to help us, by the comprehension of the past, to a fair understanding of the present, if not also of the future, what then *is* History meaning?   Do we not quote Gibbon's absurd misconstruction of the French Revolution, or Niebuhr's utter failure in judging contemporary politics, as examples of the then backward state of historic methods and historic science?   Yet our modern continental historians have so far not proved much more able in unlocking the present with the keys of the past.   I am not overstating the case by attributing this peculiar inefficiency of history to the neglect of that powerful method of comparison which in other fields of inquiries has yielded such surprising results.   What we want is comparative history.   Organic beings cannot be understood by any other process of thought.   Comte has said so long ago, science has verified it.   Let us try that method in the study of Antisemitism.

II

I premise a few words about the contentions and allegations of continental Antisemites.   These are simple enough.   In their opinion all the evils in society, commerce, and more or less in any other sphere of life come from the Jews.   The Jews oppress the labourer, corrupt the capitalist, bribe officials, contaminate the press, mislead justice, and, by marrying Christians, deteriorate the blood of the

---

[1] See the *Bibliographical Hand-list* to the 'Jewish Question, comprising the literature from 1875 to 1884, by Mr. Joseph Jacobs (London, 1885, 8vo).   For later bibliographies see the *Revue des Études Juives* (Paris, 1885, &c.)

Aryans. The Jews as Semites—that is, as a race totally distinct from that of the Aryans—cannot but be antagonistic to the latter. The Aryan, and chiefly the Teutonic branch thereof, is an idealist born; the Semite is an unmitigated materialist. The Aryan, and more especially the German, is frank, slow, and unselfish; the Semite is cunning, shrewd, and selfish to the core. In short, the Aryan is all white by nature; the Semite is all black, also by nature. There is no compatibility between these two races, and to insist on the removal of the Jews from the communities of Aryans is only to obey nature's own imperative demand. The Jew has no fatherland, or rather, as Schopenhauer has put it, the fatherland of the Jew is the other Jews. They are a state within a state, as another great German philosopher, Fichte, has said long ago; and, adds that same thinker, the Jewish question could be radically solved only by cutting off each Jew's head, and putting in its stead another head in which not a single Jewish idea is to be found. The Jews cause financial paralysis by congesting all funds at the exchanges where they dominate. They likewise cause mental consumption by sullying the intellectual atmosphere, through the press, with its perfidious and mendacious misrepresentations of things political and social. They are moreover the chief promoters of that Bright's disease of modern nations, of Socialism, the two founders of which, Karl Marx and Ferdinand Lassalle, were Jews, as are its chief leaders at present. Nor must it be forgotten that the Jews, by supplanting the small trader and the small landowner, have, like locusts, devastated and depopulated the 'flat land,' or the country proper, and thereby only increased those plague-boils called large cities, which, according to Prince Bismarck, ought to be razed to the ground one and all, and at an early convenience too. The Jew is, in the beautifully inane words of Richard Wagner, 'the plastic demon of man's decadence.' He is purely negative, uncreative, imitative, and destructive. In music Jews have done nothing but bastard matters, and Aryan taste naturally revolts from such tone-hebraisms as Mendelssohn's violin-concerto, or his music to *Midsummer Night's Dream*; let alone Meyerbeer or Goldmarck, whose music is sheer talmudistic *yodlers*. In literature Jews are only successful in a kind of verbal bartering, and dexterous dazing of the reader. Heine, it is true, was a Jew; but it is equally certain that he ought not to have been one; and then he is far too witty to be a true German writer. And as to Spinoza, he proves nothing. Having been declared a nuisance by nearly all professors of philosophy, how can we expect him to be more accommodating for the professors of Antisemitism? The fame of so many Jewish writers is owing only to a concerted mutual admiration society of theirs, rendered very efficient by their preponderance in the international press. Last, and yet first, the Jews have all the gold and other money in their hands. They are rich, all of them.

There is really no poor Jew ; and the Russian Jews were a mere farce palmed off on innocent Europe by the late Baron Hirsch, who, after fleecing the Turks—since which time they are so barefaced—posed as a founder of hospitals and other diseased objects. The Jews have the Mammon ; and more particularly the Rothschilds have it. They own all governments. All ministers are in the pay of the Vienna or Frankfort house of the famous bankers. All posts are in their gift and patronage. They really run Europe. And if the Christian people of Europe will not pull themselves together ere long, then history will be reversed, and the Ghetto, wherein in former times Jews were locked up, will come to be the panel for Christians, kept under lock by their superiors, the Semites.

This is the sum total of the countless antisemitic writings published on the continent during the last eighteen or twenty years. To these theories practical responses were not missing either. Jewish merchants were boycotted, and annoyed in all imaginable manners. In the parliaments, in the press, from the pulpits of Catholic and Protestant preachers alike, Jews were and are being exposed to all the opprobrium and scandal that their opponents can muster. In vain did some Christian and a host of Jewish writers and journalists exhort the Antisemites. The current of hatred went on increasing in bulk and rapidity, and finally reached a definite political organisation. Both at Berlin and at Vienna the Antisemites, not content with the social taboo they had succeeded in spreading against the Jew, formed into parliamentary parties, with a programme and working staff. Their number steadily increased ; their example was imitated in the various diets and councils of the provinces and towns of Germany and Austria proper ; and quite recently, as is well known, the Antisemites gained such an overwhelming majority in the municipal council of Vienna as to enforce in the face of opposition on the part of the Austrian Government the appointment of Lueger, their leader, as temporary vice-mayor, and in due time as Mayor of Vienna. In consolidating themselves into numerous and thus influential parliamentary parties, the Antisemites have become a real power in the state-life of Germany and Austria. In France they have not yet reached that stage ; but it is nowise impossible there too. In Italy there is little Antisemitism. Not on account of the small number of Jews though ; for numbers do not have much influence in that matter. In France there are scarcely over 70,000 Jews ; yet Antisemitism rages there just as wildly as in Germany, where there are 600,000, and in Austria with its 1,500,000 Jews. In fact no one can at present conceal from himself that Antisemitism is, in one way or another, a fixture of the political and social life of the continent. The Jews will no doubt survive it. Have they not survived all the attacks and onslaughts levelled at them by all the nations of Europe, and for nearly a score of centuries ? Nor is it, to my mind, difficult to see why they survive all attacks. They never seriously resist. Since the reign of the Emperor Hadrian, when the Jews, broadly speaking, for the last time offered real and obstinate resistance to their assailants, they have, as a body, never seriously essayed to combat those that attacked them. They suffer and endure; they moan and wail; they bandy wit or sarcasms at their oppressors; but they never show real fight. The Protestants, whether in France or Germany, in Austria or Hungary, have, at the risk of millions of lives, fought their oppressors on hundreds of battle-fields or in innumerable party strifes. Having shown tangible resistance, they were in some countries crushed out altogether, in others reduced to an insignificant minority. So fared the Albigenses, the Hussites, and the Waldenses. So have fared, in antiquity, the Semitic Carthaginians and the Iberians in Spain. Not so the Jews, and least of all the modern Jews. They go complaining to everybody, and write in the *Revue des Études juives*, or in similar learned periodicals, long-winded articles where, paragraph by paragraph, and especially by means of foot-notes, it is proved that the Jews are really not *méchants*; that they are good, law-abiding, and quiet citizens; that one Jew, in 1801, provided food for French prisoners at his own expense, and that another in 1806 actually died in the interest of a French patriotic cause; and that in law, medicine, mathematics and other sciences, Jews like Stahl, Lassalle, Jacobi, Lombroso, &c. &c. have contributed to the stock of knowledge no inconsiderable share. That is to say, to the men who brandish real swords over their heads, they answer by showing them drawn revolvers indeed, but drawn on paper. The Jews harp on their undying tenacity and indestructibility. So may the gipsies do. Neither Jew nor gipsy ever resists; hence both indefinitely survive. Do not the German Jews, especially the better class among them, more than merit their treatment at the hands of the Antisemites for enduring without any serious revolt the shame of being refused the rank of officers in the German army, although by law they are fully entitled to it? People who can stand that will stand anything. Where is the body of Jews in Germany that has publicly declared, and then manfully acted up to its determination to get access to the ranks of officers by means of agitation unrelenting and uncompromising? Had Catholics in Prussia been excluded from what by the constitution of Germany is their right, they would certainly not have rested until they could have forced the Protestant majority to admit them to the honour of officers in the army. The Jews in Germany have never made the faintest attempt, beyond incidental woeful reproaches in Parliament, and very funny remarks on the Prussian lieutenant in feuilletons. It has been said, every country has the Jews it merits. Truly, every aggregate of Jews has the Antisemites it deserves. That a certain class of people is hated by other classes : nothing occurs more frequently in history. All real history is full of violent party struggles, and all parties cordially hated and fiercely fought one another. But here is a novelty. Here is a well-hated class, so gorgeously hated that many an ignored class might well envy them such solid hatred. They are fought in public and private, by means fair and foul, systematically and at random, from above and from below. What splendid occasion for people ambitious for greatness ! But here is the worm. The Jews never coalesced into parties openly fighting their opponents. The individual Jew is virile enough. In no one case has the individual gentleman Jew refused or shirked a duel; and even in cases of so-called American duels, or forced suicides, no Jew has been known to go back on his word. All the more strange is their absolute passive resistance as a body. The modern Jews are, in history, the only class of people that, being openly attacked, recoil from openly fighting their assailants. And this is the historic novelty.

Or, rather, not quite novel. For there has been indeed, and there still is, another class of people equally hated as the Jews by immense numbers of civilised men, and who have likewise never resisted attacks in an open and recklessly bold manner. Hence, having been not only persecuted and chased, but positively exterminated and declared to be non-existent, they yet exist, and will continue to exist for many more centuries. It is by comparing the case of the Jews to the case of their historic parallel that we will get at the right point of view wherefrom to judge and analyse the antisemitic movement on the continent. This other class of people are the Jesuits. They, like the Jews, are openly hated, and have been exposed to attacks and aggressions of a formidable character, and for the last hundred and fifty years. Their order was solemnly abolished by Pope Clement the Fourteenth in 1773. But their lease on life has been renewed and again renewed, and they still continue to wield very considerable power. And all this they achieved *because* they never offered open resistance. The famous phrase of their General Ricci, ' Sint ut sunt, aut non sint,' indicates an iron firmness and obstinacy which the Jesuits really never possessed. Had they acted according to their general's dictum, they would have long ceased to exist. They acted, however, otherwise.

III

Of the numerous orders of monks founded by the Catholic Church some have, at times and by certain people, been ridiculed or hated. The Franciscan friars of the thirteenth and the Capuchins of the sixteenth century were objects of strong antipathies in many a country. However, the Jesuits, and they alone, have been and largely still are the best-hated organ of the Roman Church. Their name alone of all names of monastic orders has given rise to a new adjec-

tive, 'Jesuitic;' and this testimony of language is sufficient to prove
the intense animosity arrayed against them. It is in adjectives where
nations store up their likes and dislikes. This general and lasting
hatred—can it be explained by racial antipathies? The members of
the order of Jesus are of all races and nationalities. Can it be accounted for by a peculiar mental or emotional temper innate in such
people as become Jesuits? They are of all possible tempers and
emotional calibre. It remains only to ascribe that general hatred of
Jesuits to the fact, instinctively or consciously present to all their
enemies, that they are essentially strangers—strangers in every country, in any kind of commonwealth, under all circumstances. They
have neither nationality nor race, neither family nor other social ties.
They are outside all communities, and thus absolute strangers. By
their system of education as founded by Loyola, and developed by
Lainez, their disciple necessarily becomes a being attached to no
single person or groups of persons, to no particular or collective
interest other than that of his order. He is the ideal stranger.
Callous to the world of emotions engendered by the ordinary affilia-
tions of human life, he becomes as it were extra-human, and so, in
a sense, superhuman. But while this estrangement makes him unsympathetic, it also renders him more powerful. No wiser word ever
fell from the lips of John Selden than the remark that they who
want to rule people make themselves as different from them as possible. The stranger, by the very isolation in which he stands to the
people around him, acquires a superiority over them. Their foibles
are not his; and therefore where they are weak, he is strong. Their
virtues are not his; and therefore where they recoil, he will boldly
push onward. Their perils are not his; and therefore where they
succumb, he will survive. But chief of all, where they are agitated
by passion and blinded by violent desires, he is cool and collected.
In all history strangers have exercised an enormous influence. As
so many other chapters of history, this too has not yet been written.
There is no history of strangers. Historians, from patriotic motives
and from ignorance, have never dwelt upon that point. Yet pause a
moment to weigh the influence of strangers in England, from King
William the First, the Norman, to King William the Third, the
Dutchman; or from Anselm, of Aosta in Piedmont, Archbishop of
Canterbury, to Panizzi, the Italian, the creator librarian of the British
Museum; in France, from Alcuin of York to Cardinal Mazarin the
Italian, and Napoleon the Corsican; in Austria, from Rudolf of
Habsburg in Switzerland, to Eugen, Prince of Savoy, Van Swieten
the Dutchman, Count Beust the Saxon, and Count Andrassy the
Hungarian; in Russia, from the first Ruriks from Sweden to
Catharine the Great, the German Princess, &c. It need not astound
us that in countries where over fifty per cent. of the population are
strangers, or the first generation of strangers, as for instance in the

United States, the most marvellous progress has been made in all matters requiring push, enterprise, and feverish activity. The backwardness of Latin America has been ascribed to their Latin race, which is alleged to be a race unfit for the struggle of life, as witness the ancient Romans. It has also been ascribed to the Catholic religion, which is alleged to be an inferior equipment to Protestantism, as witness Catholic France. The simple truth is, Latin America has a very much smaller influx of strangers. Where the United States receive hundreds of thousands, Latin America receives a few thousands. This characteristic energy of the stranger is so true that it also applies to what we might call relative strangers— that is, the constantly increasing rural element in our large towns. Within less than three generations the population of London, Manchester, or Paris, Bordeaux, is entirely changed. The Londoner proper is supplanted by the man coming from the country with the keener energies of a stranger. Nearly all leading men of the French Revolution were provincials that had come to Paris hungry for money, glory, or blood. They were to the *Parisien* proper, strangers. In fact, although Paris is the centre of France, nay all France, it is so mostly owing not to the *Parisien*, but to the *provincial* coming to Paris. So it was in ancient Babylon; so in Athens; so in Rome. Not a single great writer of Latin literature was a Roman born, except Cæsar.

The Jesuits, then, and the Jews are the great types of the stranger. Being clearly distinguishable—one by their costume and organisation, the other by certain physical features and social habits— they cannot submerge in the mass of the strangers generally. When, therefore, circumstances prepare an attack on either of them, they are a clear aim, and the simplest know where to hit. Having arrived at this, the only correct standpoint, we need not trouble ourselves with ethnologic or historic researches in order to reconstrue the Jew and his mental or moral features. If we steadily keep in mind that he is, generally speaking, not only a stranger, but also that he has been so these fifteen or sixteen hundred years and in all countries, his innermost *esse* will become quite clear to us. He has the energy, aggressiveness, shrewdness, and frequently the recklessness of the stranger, but with threefold intensity. Being constantly on the alert either against danger or for rapid advance in fortune, he must needs be sober and temperate, and particularly keen in judging men and events. Being severed from broader interests of large aggregates of men, such as town, county, or nation, his emotions feed chiefly on family sentiments, and he becomes the most feeling of fathers as he is the most devoted of sons. Up to recent times he had only to gain by a change of *régime*; hence he readily enlisted with revolutionists. And finally, whenever he is received into society, he is practically an upstart, a *parvenu*; and hence he manifests all the objectionable qualities of that class of strangers. Upstarts, whether individuals or nations (witness the Prussians), are ostentatious, self-centred, vain, and boastful. These qualities are inevitable in upstarts. It is equally inevitable that good society resents these qualities very keenly. Good society—*le monde*, as the French rightly say—is in reality a state of its own ; the laws, officers, and procedure of which are even more finely developed than in states proper. In classical antiquity society proper did not exist. Laws were given by the public assemblies both on matters treated in modern parliaments, and on matters now left to the sway of fashion and other social powers. Hence the Jews in their antique *diaspora* could not commit the specific crime that they are perpetrating at present. For there is little doubt that the main and most general cause of the dislike for Jews at present is their lack of social tact. The laws of society are unwritten, because everybody knows them. They form an organised whole covering the smallest detail, the minutest eventuality. No man can conform to them unless he has been in the habit of so doing from childhood onward. In consequence of the more or less complete emancipation of the Jews on the continent in the course of the last hundred years, a very large number of Jews have, by entering liberal professions, received access into society. In the years 1876–81 the Jewish students at the Berlin *Gymnasien* (colleges) formed no less than 17 per cent. of the total. In 1887 the Jews furnished 10 per cent. of the students at Prussian universities, although they formed only $1\frac{1}{3}$ per cent. of the population of Prussia. Nearly 10 per cent. of the judges in Prussia are Jews ; and at the highest law court of the German Empire, at Leipsic, there are ten Jewish judges among a total of seventy-nine. In single towns the proportion is still higher. Thus, of the fifty-seven barristers at Breslau, thirty-one are Jews ; and of the three hundred and sixty lawyers of the law court called *Landgericht* in Berlin in 1889, no less than two hundred and sixty were Jews. In the twenty-one universities of Germany there were, in 1888, one hundred and four Jews as regular professors, that is, 8 per cent. of the total ; and of the *Privatdocenten*, or tutors and prospective professors, the Jews formed 18 per cent. In the University of Vienna there were in 1885–86 two thousand and odd Jewish to three thousand and odd Christian students. In Hungary and Italy, and also in France, the statistics show similar results.

From the above facts it will be seen that the Jews of the continent have been given access to professions and social preferments which had been closed to them for centuries. The stranger was given a chance of blending with a native. How did the stranger use his privilege : Did he really assimilate himself with the world into which he was admitted ? Did he do what Grillparzer, the Austrian sage and dramatist, once required of any one who entered on a profession or trade ? Did he appropriate both the faults and virtues of his new profession ? The most favourable critic of the Jews cannot

assert that. And how could the Jews have done so? Old Cato used
to say : ' Quod initio vitiosum est, tractu temporis convalescere nequit.'
I have already hinted at the fact that the Jews in modern times
never fought for their emancipation as did the Protestants or other
sects. They got it indeed, but without fighting for it. They reaped
the harvest that they had not sown; and here, here is the vice ' quod
tractu temporis convalescere nequit.' The ideas of the French Revolution had such a profound influence on the peoples of Europe that
governments were fairly ashamed of the bondage in which Jews were
held by them. So these governments hastened to liberate the Jew.
Had the Jews been going through all the anguish and terrors of
religious wars, had they acquired their citizenship by efforts as immense as were those of other oppressed religious sects, they would
have come out of the struggle diminished in numbers indeed, but
worthier of their privilege. As it was, the Jews were not only upstarts, but upstarts by dint of sheer good luck; that is, the worst of
upstarts. In countries like Hungary for instance, where the liberal
professions were, up to 1867, exclusively in the hands of the nobility,
the sudden influx of Jewish lawyers, teachers, judges, and writers
could not but be most injurious to the interests of the hitherto
privileged class. For a nobleman to be obliged to treat as his peer
the son of the Jew whom his father had kept as ' village-Jew ' was a
most tantalising position. What made it absolutely unbearable was
the lack of all social tact on the part of the *novi homines*. In the
ball-room, in the ' casino,' or club of the town, in the street, the
newly-emancipated Jew displayed a familiarity and forwardness with
the men and women of the old Hungarian society, that, as it was in
the worst taste, so it was most bitterly resented. Duels among
Jews and Christians began to increase at a terrible rate. To no avail.
That initial vice mentioned above went on cankering the whole
relation. I am fully aware of the fact that the Jews constantly harp
on the principles of ' humanity,' ' civilisation,' ' enlightenment,' throwing them wholesale into the face of whosoever wants to exclude them
from social or legal equality. This modern humanity, this modern
civilisation, this modern enlightenment, however, was it won by the
Jews? Was it not won by Christian peoples labouring and fighting
for it in the blood of their bodies and in the distress of their souls?
This world of Europe is a sword and rifle begotten world. He who
has kept outside that secular fight has no claim to the benefits
thereof. If the fighters generously admit him within their ranks,
let him practise many virtues, but foremost of all let him practise the
virtue of modesty. And here is the heavy and unanswerable indictment against the emancipated and reformed Jew : he is profoundly
immodest. The old orthodox Jew is perverse and uncouth if you
please, but he is a character. There is system and logic, and even
poetry, in his weird consistency of forbidding exclusiveness. If pro-

perly roused he, and he alone, may still show fight—real, honest, fatal fight. He is absurd perhaps, but true. There is a grandeur in his stintedness, and fascination in his self-inflicted isolation. The greatest of Jewish luminaries in science or philosophy have nearly always come from among the orthodox Jews. He is not immodest or forward, for he does not crave for Christian society. He is an erratic block on the surface of Europe. But the reformed Jew, he who abandons the ritual of his fathers without adopting the creed of the Christians, he who is ashamed of meeting his lowly and still orthodox relative, and arrogantly struts on the boulevards and other public places of great capitals, he is downright absurd and worthy of the lash of society. And thus far modern Antisemitism is quite right. It was and is a just and legitimate reaction against the preposterous arrogance of the New Jew. Nor has this reaction been without its beneficial effect on many of these New Jews. No inconsiderable number of the fiercest Antisemites have arisen from among Jews. Thus to the funds for the 'mission' of Stoecker, the arch-Jewbaiter of Berlin, Jewish bankers of that town contributed very largely. A still larger number of New Israelites have taken the lesson of Antisemitism to heart, and have seriously tried to blend with the nation whose members they are. But much, very much, remains to be done, and unless Christianity will be embraced by the reformed Jew, he will, it is to be feared, never quite assimilate himself with the Christian. This change of religion, however, is almost impossible. The central fact and belief of Christianity, that is the coming of salvation through and in Jesus Christ the Son of God, will scarcely ever be accepted by the orthodox Jews ; and for the simple reason that they already possess and fully believe in a medium, in another Son of God, through and in whom salvation is coming to them, namely, through and in the community of Jews, the 'chosen people' whom the prophet Daniel called 'the Son of God.' In this regard too the orthodox Jew is infinitely superior to the *Neologue*. It being certain that every system of Monotheism necessarily leads to a mediator between the Godhead and man, the orthodox Jew, in accepting his own chosen tribe as the mediator, remains within the due demesne of that exalted religious concept. The reformed Jew, on the other hand, throws over the mediatorship both of the 'chosen people' and of Jesus of Nazareth, and yet boldly declares himself to believe in one God. He is therefore, in point of religion, no less absurd than in point of social conduct. The Antisemites, if frequently in a clumsy and boorish manner, distinctly felt and pointed out this grave and dangerous failing of the modern or New Jew, and in doing so they have again done great service to the cause of civilisation, this cause being largely the cause of Christianity. In studying these causes and these effects of what might be called social Antisemitism, many differ with its promoters as to some of the means they have employed in pro-

pagating it.   But there is another and more serious species or aspect
of Antisemitism—the political—and as the former is vested in a
socially intolerable failing of the New Jew, so this is arising from a
politically poor constitution of the nations of the continent.

IV

The study of movements in the past, similar to that of political
Antisemitism in our time, reveals the fact that nations either unripe
for, or decadent from, parliamentary government show their inferiority
especially in the incapacity of producing real political issues of parliamentary struggle.   Their parties take up 'platforms' which in times
of high parliamentary development would have been left to the regulation of the home or the drawing-room.   Instead of rallying round men
and principles of truly political drift and weight, they try to hush up
their inaptitude by falling foul of relatively harmless classes or
institutions.   This generally happens when, after long wars, a period
of peace is setting in.   The excitement of the war having subsided,
people long for new modes of excitement.   The evils of war have
been shown up by many a well-intentioned writer.   The evils of
peace have scarcely been pointed out.   Yet they are almost as glaring
as the former.   No sooner had the Romans, by the middle of the
second century B.C., conquered the Mediterranean world than they
began to interslaughter themselves; and agrarians, socialists, and
religious reformers were calling upon the citizens to remedy the
' terrible diseases' of the commonwealth.   It was exactly the same
after 1763.   Europe, sick of three immense and useless wars—that of
the Spanish succession (1701–13), the Austrian succession (1740–
1748), and the Seven Years' War (1756–63)—Europe wanted peace but
could not stand it.   Political life was just beginning to grow, first
in the heads of thinkers and writers, then in the bosoms of the
bourgeois classes, and this new life wanted issues, aims, centres of
struggle.   Having absolutely no parliamentary issue proper in that
they had no parliaments, the *Zeitgeist* forthwith created a surrogate
which was sufficient to animate the masses and the governments.

This surrogate was the fight against the Jesuits.   In all Catholic
countries of Europe a deluge of pamphlets and skits, popular books,
and elaborate treatises was poured forth . containing all imaginable
accusations and denunciations of the Order of Jesus.   The Jesuits
were the root of all evil.   They had clandestinely caused by their
intrigues all the late wars.   They were the perdition of the youth
whom they taught, of the nobility whom they confessed, and of the
kings and princes generally whom they ruled.   The accusations
levelled against them by Pascal and the Jansenists in the seventeenth
century were mere sops and child's play beside the fearful insinua-
tions now raised against them.   They were murderers; for had they
not attempted to assassinate the King of Portugal?   They were

harpies and usurers of the worst description ; for had not Father **La** Valette implicated by his treacherous commercial enterprises nearly all the south of France ?   They were slave-dealers; for had they not in Paraguay enslaved and vilified a whole nation of innocent Indians ? They were the bane of the world, the curse of the Church, the out- laws of humanity.

By this time we are pretty fairly informed about the truth of all these fearful incriminations.   In common fairness we cannot any longer write history and hold the Jesuits guilty of one hundredth of the crimes imputed to them at about the middle of the last century. We do know that they then abused their power indeed, but far less— nay, infinitely less—than from 1550 to 1650, and that on the whole they were not much more harmful than any other of the then ruling classes.   That they were and are hateful on account of their very constitution as absolute strangers, this much we may and do grant. That they were or are the root of all evil is untrue, and preposterous to hold.   No parliamentary fight will kill *and* exterminate them. They must be met by means over which parliaments are powerless : by a change in the minds of the people.

The parliamentary fight against the Jews at present is precisely on the lines and has the same origin as had the fight against the Jesuits in the last century.   After the gigantic wars of the French Republic and Napoleon the First, Europe was held in a state of siege from 1815 to 1848—in some countries as late as 1860 and 1867. During that long torpor the various nations were constantly clamour- ing, if in subdued tones, for parliamentary government.   In reality, however, they were not ripe for it at all.   It was only a timid imita- tion of the theories of the French Revolution.   They cried for modes of government which they had long unlearned to practise, and of which they had no clear idea.   The revolutions of 1848 affrighted the rulers ; and fearing lest all Europe should break out in a second and still more formidable French Revolution, they slowly consented to grant parliamentary governments, and at the end of the sixties nearly all continental countries had been granted parliaments of their own.   After the wars of 1864, 1866, and 1870–71, peace settled down on Europe.   The various parliaments were opened, and the necessity was felt to create parties.   This is easily and naturally done in countries of long parliamentary habits and wants.   In the New Parliaments, however, this was the chief stumbling-block.   Parties arose indeed, but they were so unnatural, so far-fetched, that they had scarcely any vitality in them at all.   The ' fractions ' of the German Reichstag rose and fell and changed like fractions of coloured glass in a kaleidoscope.   Their number sometimes reached twenty. Likewise in the Reichstag at Vienna.   And now it was that men endowed with considerable insight into the needs of the time began to work at the formation of a new nucleus of party-crystallisation.   As had been done a century ago by the Jesuit baiters, so now those clever agitators, feeling that the politically untrained masses in Germany and Austria would never get enthusiastic over purely political issues, substituted for it one of the ready-made social antipathies. Society indeed was, all over the continent, in a stage of maturity infinitely superior to that of the parliamentary state. Society had material enough for party organisation, and among these none was surer of general acceptance than the hatred of the New Jews arising from circumstances related above. Here then was a nucleus of a party endowed with enduring vitality.

And now followed with necessity, as in the case of the Jesuits, the string of accusations, all the more exaggerated the less they were founded on truth. The Jews are the root of all evil; they corrupt the administration; they are murderers of children; they enslave the labourer and bribe all governments, &c. All this as in the case of the Jesuits. In reality the Jews have, either in commerce or in other walks of life, not done more harm than many another class that had, and abused the chance of power. In reality Jews are, *as a rule*, very far from rich, and any one of the rich monastic orders is far richer than they, as, for instance, the Præmonstratenses in Hungary, the Benedictines in France, or the Jesuits in Belgium. In reality Jews have a particular and almost craven horror of blood, and have never murdered children for ritual needs; several Popes have declared this blood accusation to be the most absurd of allegations, and in no single modern case have Jews been convicted for such a crime by a court of law or a jury. Yet, and again as in the case of the Jesuits, nothing will convince or can convince the Antisemites, and for the simple reason that their existence as a strong political party depends on the belief in those alleged atrocities. And if all the Jews of Germany and Austria suddenly left Europe altogether, the Antisemites, far from ceasing their agitations, would continue to exist as heretofore. They would fight the 'semitic' element in Christians generally or in Turks, Russians, or—Englishmen. This is no mere assumption. For so far have things Antisemitic come to develop that the word 'Semite,' again, and precisely as the word 'Jesuit,' is used in a general sense, and quite irrespective of Jews. The large portion of Frenchmen who cordially hate the English have, in an elaborate book written by one Louis Martin, given utterance to their firm belief that the English are Jews. The Antisemites of Vienna carry on a crusade against the Jews and the Hungarians at the same time. Lueger, their leader, is a Magyar-eater of the darkest dye, and his Antisemitic agitations against Hungary will before long cause serious trouble in the dual empire.

The political aspect of Antisemitism on the continent is thus an unmistakable symptom of the poorly developed political instincts of most of the continental nations. Should they ever reach political manhood, they will drop Antisemitism as too barren a means of great political work. The Hungarians, for instance, whose political life dates back to centuries before the French Revolution, have soon dropped Antisemitism altogether. They do have real political issues to work on. They do not need surrogates. Most of the other nations on the continent, however, still need it as a first schooling in public business. And this is the redeeming feature even in political Antisemitism. It indicates that Germans and Austrians are beginning to wake up from their inertia in matters public and political. It is a prelude to something better. The New Jews will not benefit by that. They will continue to practise their policy of abstention. They will not crystallise into parliamentary parties, and their most likely fate is to get swamped by the orthodox Jews. The sooner this will happen the better. In this well-knit and plastic Europe of ours we do not need hybrid, colourless cosmopolites like the New Jews. And if Antisemitism had done nothing but bring the great question of nationality into still stronger relief, it has well deserved of Europe.

EMIL REICH.

ON INDUCTIVE MORALITY

I

ENGLAND is the birthplace of experimental philosophy, to which she has remained faithful from the time of Bacon up to our own day, nor has she since had any reason to repent of this fidelity. While other nations subjected their vitality to a dogmatic yoke, or spent it fruitlessly in the abstractions of transcendental philosophy, England has made rapid progress in every branch of her national life, built up a free and solid political constitution, and attained her present prosperity and greatness.

The rest of the world, more or less rapidly according to the diverse moral and intellectual conditions of each nation, did not long hesitate to follow the same road, soon to be illumined by such marvellous conquests of science as the discovery of the system of the universe, in which discovery the chief figure is another great Englishman, Newton, who gave definite order to conflicting theories by establishing the law of universal gravitation.

But, while proceeding in this way, hardly had experimental philosophy begun to deal boldly and fully with the problems of the physical than it was confronted with those of the moral world: owing to long-established prejudices, and, above all, to their peculiar nature, these last did not seem to lend themselves readily to this treatment.

Under the impression of that first contact of experimental philosophy with the moral world a third great Englishman, after the frank and decided manner of his race, made up his mind as to the impotence of philosophy on the subject. Thus, as Bacon was the founder of experimental so it may be said that Hume was the founder of positive philosophy.

This designation contains in itself the idea of limitation, permitting experimental philosophy to deal only with such applications as can be made with profit, to the exclusion of subjects which are, or„ rather, seem, to be incapable of scientific demonstration, or of being submitted to examination and led to scientific conclusions.

Hence a widespread difference between the two schools. Experimental philosophy—by subverting the Aristotelian system, on which were founded not only the physical sciences, but the moral ordering of the world—logically and inevitably tended to destroy the one as it had refuted the others. But while, in regard to the physical world, the scientific observation of facts enabled it to substitute a new system for the one it had refuted, not less complete, and having in itself a far greater presumption of truth; as for the moral world, it was marvellously ready to destroy, but utterly incapable of reconstructing. By the simple application of its fundamental principle, that nothing should be accounted true which had not been scientifically demonstrated, it confined itself to considering any hypothesis, nay every belief, belonging to that order as incredible and absurd.

The instinctive sense of the great void made in the world by the destruction of an order of ideas on which had reposed, and still repose, the social and moral relations of countless generations soon brought about a reconsideration and a certain hesitation in the more thoughtful and intelligent in presence of the mystery of the unknown. From this sprang positive philosophy.

This school modestly confined itself to recognising its own utter incompetence in these matters without accepting or rejecting whatsoever concerns them; while the logical and natural procedure of experimental philosophy induced the latter to abound in negation and rejection.

It was, in fact, this last conception which had evidently inspired the entire intellectual and moral movement initiated by the great Continental revolution of the end of the last century. The practical results which concerned the moral world, having gradually given greater relief to that void to which we have alluded above, confirmed primitive apprehensions, and lent credit, especially on the Continent, to positive philosophy as a kind of compromise, or truce, by which, without renouncing any of the benefits of experimental philosophy, the .question remained unprejudiced in regard to the fields upon which it had been unable up to the present to enter.

This was a great step in advance from the exclusiveness of science as a means of conciliating the two worlds, past and present. It was even opportune, as it practically induced a *modus vivendi*, since very varied beliefs and opinions may live together under the shadow of liberty. But this also entails as a logical consequence a complete abstention on the part of science, and a real scepticism corresponding in the human conscience to an unlimited freedom of thought upon subjects the most essentially important to the moral world.

In presence of this logical and unavoidable process, and with regard to the results which must proceed from it, it seems but right to ask whether it be true that, in the moral world, with which is connected the most important part of human life, there be nothing stable or scientifically true ?   And whether, according to apathetic contemporary philosophy, the most shallow and fantastic ideas have equal rights not only to a political tolerance which, in a certain measure, may be opportune and even necessary, but also to the respect and consideration of men's consciences?   Can it be true that religion, country, family, property, everything which has been until now the basis on which is constituted moral order, are nothing more than mere opinions which may or may not be professed ?   Is it true that a man may act in conformity to his personal opinion, as far as the material coercion of the law will allow ?   Is he bound to any truth or abstract principle, or is he simply inspired by momentary social opportunism?   Is there nothing true nor universal outside this empiric practical and temporary utilitarianism ?   In a word, can it be really true that good and evil are merely abstract ideas, their application left to the will of all, or any, making plausible the recognition of opinions and practices which corrupt the family, demand the dispersion of property, and even the destruction of society?   Indeed, taking into account all that occurs before our eyes in contemporary literature and jurisprudence, everything seems to be inspired in this spirit, which, given the premises to which we have alluded, is logical and natural.

As a matter of fact, in the shadow of this philosophical tolerance there exists no ordinary crime which does not assume a sort of special qualification which, in many cases, is convertible into a philosophical classification.   Attacks on property, if only sufficiently considerable, find their justification in a business code so involved and indulgent that a French comedian of our day simply defines business as *l'argent d'autrui*.   The lesser attacks are in their turn indulgently considered as justified by social injustice.   The poor devil caught red-handed in the wrongful possession of five francs need hardly fear to be looked upon as a real thief.   Infractions of the respect due to the family have a complete literature of their own.   Writers of this kidney discourse indifferently on every subject, from the worship of Vesta to that of Astarte, from the Palatine to the Suburra, and even beyond these natural limits.   They treat with *esprit*, often with genuine seduction, and always on the same footing, vice and virtue, as they occur in all the varied inventions which the human mind is capable of producing in that fertile field.   The public is amused, academies confer prizes, women study the various types of their sex, and men learn a lesson.   Small wonder if their practice be in conformity, and that an occasional shock to the most elementary natural instinct can alone avail to induce a court of law to condemn a culprit, who is, then, rather an object of curiosity than of reprobation to the general public.

The forms of rebellion against society are classified in a number of officially recognised classes ; it is sufficient to be a republican under a monarchy for a man to consider himself justified in doing almost anything against the established order of things. Under a republic it is only necessary to declare oneself a socialist. Nay, to take the worst instance, it suffices to profess anarchism to be no longer considered as a vulgar rebel or disturber of public peace, but as the follower of a recognised school, and a sort of philosopher, who may become a martyr just as he may become a minister, but who will no longer be a vulgar delinquent.

In default of these categories, already sufficiently numerous, whoever does not fall under them has recourse to an equally minute pathological classification. Psychological and physiological studies have created so many and such varied qualifications that there hardly exists a delinquent who is not far more interesting from a scientific standpoint than from that of the public security. Even criminality has a literature of its own, which reacts upon contemporary jurisprudence so much that some recent legislation, thanks to the unduly scientific mind of its makers, has found no other definition for certain degrees of crime than the material punishment connected with them.

All this is not in the natural order of things, nor is it likely that the world will quietly acquiesce in it; indeed, it is strange that this abnormal condition should escape serious attention. Man has never paid so little attention to his *raison d'être* and to his finality as in our time. He is contented with the contemplation and observation of himself and of his work. He has perhaps never been so attentive to it, but does not attempt to draw any consequence or rule which would help to the reconstruction of the moral edifice, so deeply shaken on its very basis. Can societies and man grow accustomed to this void and be satisfied with this state of things? Every society that has existed and prospered has been founded on certain fixed principles; and with the decay of these, societies have generally 'decayed and disappeared.' The example of an eclectic society without principles and fixed notions of right and wrong as a condition of normal and lasting existence would be without parallel.

In order that, in opposition to the testimony of history, this should be believed to be possible, and that this condition should be considered, according to the views of its defenders, rather a result of the progress of the human intellect than a sign of decadence, it would be necessary to believe that both experimental and positive philosophy had said their last word. If it were true that the experimental method were not applicable to the moral world—and it is not thought that any other method can give any evidence of truth—one would be obliged to conclude that whatever concerns this question was utterly beyond scientific investigation, that moral order was beyond hope of reconstruction, and was therefore necessarily to be abandoned to the personal judgment of each, and consequently to human folly and wickedness, which is simply absurd.

But is it really true that the moral world is outside the sphere of the experimental method?

There are facts of an enduring nature in the moral as well as in the physical world. Now, in the latter, methodical study has enabled us to discover the laws which govern it. And no one would to-day hold a personal opinion different from the one commonly existing as regards cause and effect in relation to the natural laws, strictly so called. It is no longer possible to entertain two opinions on the greater number of these subjects.

If, on the contrary, it be possible that there should exist as many opinions as there are men on the laws and rules which ought to govern, and in fact do govern, the moral world, we must conclude that the facts which belong to that world have not been so studied, observed, and classified as to lead to the same results. Hence it is not the matter which is wanting to the experimental method, but the application of the method to the matter.

The principal reason why this application has not been made is that, while it is impossible to deny the constancy and recurrence of moral facts, a variable element manifests itself in them, which, without altering the qualities common to both, essentially differentiate their nature from that of physical phenomena. The presence of such an element, which is nothing else than the human intellect and will, and of which it may be said that it is ' *degno d'immensa invidia e di pietà profonda*,' has so reacted on the moral world as to disturb thought, and to prevent the application of methodical observation and the deduction of rational and impartial conclusions. It is because man did not know how to look into himself with his own intellect that, though he has succeeded in knowing what is outside, he is unable to know himself, whom, however, he ought, for his sake, to know better than anything else.

Nosce te ipsum was said by the oracle. Had this precept been understood in all the fulness of its meaning, humanity would have been spared many evils.

II

We do not mean that human actions have not been described and even studied and discussed; on the contrary, they have been not only observed, but brought under rule in every age and from every point of view, though generally, and for a long period, they were considered *a priori* and in accordance with pre-established principles. Moreover, as to the application of these principles to practical life, they have been treated so empirically that entire generations have died for what they considered to be right according to one order of ideas; and successive generations, with equal faith and perseverance, have rejected, condemned, and abandoned that very order of things which previous generations had accepted, respected, and venerated.

It is true that all this occurred for the most part in an age and at a time when it was believed that the earth was the centre of the universe, that Nature abhorred a vacuum, and so forth; in a word, when the knowledge of the physical world was not more advanced than that of the moral world.

But when the secrets of the physical world had been revealed, this parallel ceased to exist, and things proceeded differently as regards the moral world. Not a single attempt was made to study the past in order to draw instruction for the future. And the same contradictions continued to occur as before in various states of civilisation and even among various populations. What seemed good and honest to one seemed bad and reprehensible to the other. Different peoples and fractions of the same people came into collision, testifying with their blood, which is the supreme testimony of sincerity and devotion to a cause, to opposite beliefs. Both were equally convinced that they lived in the truth, and were ready to give their life for the truth. Scarcely a century has passed since blood flowed in rivers in order to suffocate whatever belonged to a faith and to an order of ideas which in its time had been built up with blood and martyrdom; since then, more than once the past has tried to avenge itself, and the present, believing itself to be the future, has renewed its aggressiveness.

Only lately, in one of the most cultivated and civilised countries of Europe, one party declared science and reason bankrupt, while the other party has reasserted its doubts and renewed its protests against religion and faith. On the one side is a vast number of persons, worthy of respect from every point of view, while the other counts a large proportion of cultivated and scientific men.

Generally speaking, in both cases, all these people, alike in the past and in the present, have believed and believe firmly, act conscientiously and honestly, and cling to their own ideas with absolute faith. Who is right or who wrong? or are both parties to be regarded as unhappy maniacs? Are they equally victims of hallucination? Neither science nor philosophy, not even the most accommodating and tolerant, can furnish us with an answer, because they do not know.

Our concern is more particularly with the struggle between reason and faith, since it interests us more directly as being that which has been fought with the greatest vigour in our very midst. Fortunately the tendencies of the present time seem to point out a compromise of a practical kind; and therefore its latest effects are no longer as disastrous as they were in the past. But it is just its present state of transition, or rather of indifference, which constitutes the gravest peril for society, because absence of principle is more dangerous than a conflict between divergent principles.

Now, it must be remembered that this indifference and neglect are principally the result of the state of knowledge on the subject, which in its turn is produced by the defective method with which this most important part of human life has been hitherto treated.

This is so true that the consciousness of this defect, in spite of all manner of prejudices, has begun to make itself felt among contemporary thinkers, and some of them have arisen from various quarters, and under the inspiration of various theories, with tendencies towards a scientific treatment of that important part of universal life, although up to the present they have not attained their object.

The attempts at a scientific treatment proceeding from the known to the unknown in studying the moral life of humanity have been of two kinds. One has been called the philosophy of history. It had for its parent Gianbattisto Vico, who called it a new science (*scienza nuova*). Since his day, and especially of late years, this science has been largely cultivated; still, it has not gone beyond the limits of history properly so called. According to its principles human facts have been observed and studied, but chiefly from the standpoint of the political life of nations. And in this respect it is as old as Macchiavelli, who, from the observation of certain facts, passed to the enunciation of more or less acceptable rules concerning the government of society.

But the philosophy of history as it has been understood, and as its name indicates, has rather concerned itself with the verification of certain facts and their recurrence in relation to the public and political life of society, than with drawing conclusions therefrom and applying those conclusions impartially to all public and private, general or individual facts in regard to the moral life of humanity.

Other methods of endeavouring to study moral facts have been supplied by both the psychological and physiological sciences, and also by the exuberant literature of realistic fiction which discovers and elucidates all the secret moral recesses of the human heart, from the most exalted virtues to the most abject vices, setting in relief, not its ordinary feelings, as a reasonable method would dictate, but, in preference, the most extravagant ones, as presenting the greater interest to the reader.

In the first place, these inquiries have been, one and all, rather subjective than objective.

Putting aside the fact that psychology is necessarily led to deal with the unknowable, and that the use of hypotheses is unavoidable, it concerns itself with the human soul rather as a very source of action than as taken in reference to the entire life of humanity.

Indeed this last field of investigation has been divided into other sciences, as the Philosophy of Law and Sociology, and also in part Political Economy; but in their turn these sciences treat the subject one-sidedly, and from different standpoints.

Physiology, with all its various developments and schools, counts among its disciples many sagacious and gifted observers, but, being unable to detach itself from sensible nature when studying and judging human actions, it has not been allowed to consider all those parts of the moral life which are beyond physical and chemical analysis. For this reason not only has its work remained incomplete, but in many cases it has rather served to lead astray and to minimise than to rectify and generalise thought.

Of so-called realistic literature it is useless to say much, because its analysis of the human heart is not always faithful, but often exaggerated, and has not shown any tendency to co-ordinate or to draw general conclusions. On the contrary, it prefers to particularise and to satisfy curiosity rather than to prepare matter for study, and, instead of developing laws, it is specially attracted in a particular way by exceptions. After reading works of this school one is often inclined to believe the world worse than it is, and rarely to know it as it is. In any case, there is nothing in this species of literature which tends to bring about a complete co-ordination of ideas upon moral life.

Therefore there exists no science which, while observing and classifying human actions as they are, or at least as they appear, without seeking their origin and essence, sets in relief the circumstances in which they are produced, their recurrence, and establishes the relation between cause and effect the better to infer the rules that govern them.

This science might be called inductive morality, that is to say, the science of the great moral laws as they are discovered by proceeding from the known to the unknown, by the accurate study of facts; in a word, by the experimental method.

It may seem an exaggeration to assert the need of a new science in an age when sciences are even too numerous, but we should say that it is the one thing which is wanting. We need a co-ordinated and logical judgment upon moral facts, carried out methodically in such a way as to be the basis of the knowledge of the laws which govern them. Even if, from time to time, these views have been ventilated, they have never been summarised nor presented in so clear and synthetic a form as to enable them to penetrate the popular conscience and to serve to restore it to a sound and distinct idea of the moral order.

The times are favourable to the formation of such criteria. Never before as now have the various religions, civilisations, arts, beliefs and customs of all ages and types been placed before the eyes of the philosopher so readily and completely. Nèver have men enjoyed greater liberty in the development of their own powers. And this development has never been more evident nor has it ever proceeded in so full a light as in our days. History and contemporary literature take note of everything, both from the past and in the present, from great political and national events down to the most private actions of the lives of individuals. Never has the philosopher had a wider prospect before him nor a larger number of elements upon which to found his judgments.

But the most important point lies in the fact that, if on the one hand the times are propitious to the renewal of these studies, they also proclaim the need of them in a way hitherto unknown. In the general shock given to the principles on which society was based it is necessary for us to know upon which of them we may rely as having their foundation in the very nature of things, so that on them we may be able to maintain the civil and moral order of society, and save it from the alternating chances of polemics and the changeable will of majorities.

III

The first impression arising from this study, if carefully and widely made, is that, despite the unlimited variety of opinions that have been expressed and of the systems which have been tried; despite varying and contradictory legislative enactments and the powers of every kind used in their realisation; in the midst of the agitation and incessant contradictions which are found in the history of humanity, there may be distinctly recognised a series of facts which, while differing in form and manner, have always and everywhere recurred on account of their identical substance.

These facts occur in every phase and in the most vital manifestations of the life of humanity, such as the constant and intense strain for the preservation of the species, its reproduction, its constitution into societies, the foundation and growth of religions, the evolution of science and the cultivation of art; in a word, they comprehend all its developments.

If men, even though possessed of different sorts and degrees of intellect and will, all do the same things equally and in all ages, this can only be because they are constrained thereto by constant forces and by influences in a certain measure independent of, and superior to, themselves. Hence the fixed and determined character of these forces and influences of man, which, under the form of feelings and affections, order the existence of men and societies.

And, as a matter of fact, who has ever been able to give any other explanation why he adheres to his religion, why he loves his country, why he chooses one partner for life rather than another, why he loves his children more than any other human beings, if not because they please him, or, better, because a sentiment, neither submitted to, nor capable of being submitted to, explanation or discussion, draws and impels him in an almost irresistible way towards these objects of his affection ?

And how few men could state that they have never made profession of, or at least in any way considered themselves as belonging to, any religion.   How few could aver that they have never belonged to nor loved a country, that they have never loved a woman, their own family.   Who could pretend not to love himself?   There may be some exceptions here and there, and especially in times of disturbances and social or moral crises ; but these exceptions to the general rules represent a *quantité négligeable* in comparison with the great and enduring movement of humanity.

As we have said, the universality, the constancy, the fixedness of these feelings and affections, their origin, independently of the intellect and will of man, give to them the character of real laws, which, like those regulating the physical world, have their cause in nature itself.   Nay, more, as all these laws, apparently different from each other, have but one sole object, namely, to preserve humanity and keep it connected with, and in relation to, the general order of things, so they may be easily reduced to one single energy, the sentiment which, like the universal attraction which governs the order of the physical world, as an even more mysterious part of it, in its manifold but equally universal action, presides over the moral order of the world.

From this same force proceed the noblest actions, the great sacrifices, the acts of heroism and certain sublime follies, called so precisely because, though inspired by a strong sentiment, they cannot find justification in reason.   We have spoken of science and art, and, as far as concerns art, the creation of great ideals and the inspiration of masterpieces have no other cause.   But even as regards science, how great a part of its success is due to the inextinguishable thirst for truth which lies in the heart of every man, and which, when further developed in certain more elevated natures, impels them to concentrate all their faculties and even their life to it alone.   The man of science who is not animated by this sacred fire is little more than a mechanical cipherer, or apparatus for arguments.   Indeed, those who study the most intricate scientific problems or produce the masterpieces of art, the geniuses and the heroes, are like all the general run of mortals, subject and obedient to this great law, which, like all great natural laws, is to be recognised by its effects and not by its cause.

In the sphere and on the plan traced by this universal and in a certain sense irresistible force—so irresistible that the practical daily evidence of its effects has originated in some schools the idea.

of determinism or fatalism to the exclusion of individual freedom—moves and acts the *Angelica farfalla,* the spontaneous and original power of man consisting of his intellect and will.

From the objective point of view, and in regard to the life of the universe, the action of the human intellect and will is hardly sensible. Although individually and collectively endowed with power and energy, these faculties are unable to sensibly change the fated course of humanity. Each time they have endeavoured to attempt it they have been severely punished, and the greatest disillusions and the most deplorable catastrophes signalise in history all the attempts at rebellion and violence which have ever been made against nature by violating any of the laws which form a substantial part of the moral order of the world.

But from the subjective point of view, namely, with regard to the government of men and even of things within the limits traced by natural law, the human intellect and will exercise a determinate and efficacious action, and reveal themselves as a real force capable of controlling the strongest feelings and affections in order to make them tend whither they are naturally disposed.

Moreover, the beneficent action of this force is so necessary and needful in human things that without its control sentiment deviates and produces the most formidable illusions and catastrophes. Hence the principle professed by the great religious and philosophical schools of every age, that the dominion of the feelings and affections by means of intellect and will constitutes one of the essential conditions of the moral order in the world.

The importance of this force has in its turn appeared so great (in opposition to determinism and fatalism) as to have induced some spiritualistic schools to disregard the value and constancy of the natural forces which preside over the development of human life ; hence the doubt of the possibility of founding any scientific system upon them to which we have alluded. The most acceptable doctrine between these two opposite schools appears to be that intellect and will, however gifted with initiative and in a certain measure free and independent, not only cannot substantially change their fatal work, but are themselves by their very nature submitted to the general law which connects cause with effects and scope with means. From this intimate connection between cause and effect, scope and means, man is led to the knowledge of right and wrong, and to the feeling of duty, which together are the directing principles of human action and the very basis of morality.

There is nothing vague and indeterminate in these processes.

The mysterious origin of these forces and the prejudice that their action is not in subjection to scientific research have allowed men to exceed alternately in two opposite directions, and for a long time they almost unconsciously devoted themselves either to cultivating sentiment and faith, or to worshipping intellect and reason with equal exclusiveness. The partisans of religion and faith have maintained that there was no salvation outside their peculiar fold, while the partisans of intellect and reason have maintained that beyond their field there existed nothing but falsehood and folly. And now that, by dint of lack of observation and knowledge, indifference seems to have succeeded to arduous struggle, the matter remains abandoned to the variability of opinions with an accentuated tendency towards complete scepticism.

But what is more conform to the truth is that moral order is the result of the combination of these two forces. Indeed, the results of their action are all the great institutions which provide for the wants of humanity. Such are religion, family, fatherland considered as a constituted society, and property. Such is morality considered as a complexus of rules extending to the whole of humanity. Such are science and art. All these institutions and rules represent the concrete form and the application, by the intellect and will of man, of the great natural laws to real life. And as both these forces have been proved to be far from being irreconcileable with the method which proceeds from the known to the unknown, namely, with the experimental method, but capable of being submitted to it; if all this is true, as it appears to be, there is no more reason why, even from the standpoint of positive philosophy, the foundations on which moral order reposes should be abandoned *disputationibus eorum*, nor why they should not be scientifically formulated and rationally fixed in certain canons just as are those revealed by the same process applied to the natural sciences.

And indeed it would be strange if, while we know with certainty all about the customs, wants, and rules which govern other animals, we should be still in the greatest confusion and contradiction of opinions as to the laws which govern mankind.

Hence, by way of example, if self-preservation and everything which pertains thereto require the observance of certain rules and the practice of certain virtues, these are not matter of probable opinion, but are as certain as any other physical or chemical law. If the reproduction of the human species is necessarily bounded by the existence of the family, its constitution and sanctity acquire equal certainty. If the necessity of self-preservation, combined with family feeling, produce property, this social institution is beyond discussion as depending upon a natural law, with the same relation as in any other case exists between cause and effect. If men are compelled to live in society, and if the fact of living in society brings a certain limitation of individual action, certain obligations and duties, and if for their fulfilment it be necessary to determine them in certain concrete forms, these forms may vary according to time and circumstances; but the principle of order and government which they represent cannot be indefinitely discussed, because it would prevent any one of them from being stable and efficacious, which would be in opposition with one of the most evident natural laws.

If men have never succeeded in summarising all the rules and duties hitherto prescribed, universalising them, and in giving them efficacy without referring them to an absolute principle; if the worship of this absolute principle has always and in every age been constant in human societies, taking the concrete form of what we call a religion, which tends to satisfy certain wants of consolation and justice, and of noble and ideal aspirations irresistible to humanity, it is evident that, though religions may in a certain measure vary and be discussed in their forms and developments, they cannot be substantially and absolutely rejected without undermining the foundations of moral order and contradicting the natural laws which preside over it.

The same may be said of science and art. For the former, an accurate and constant observation would demonstrate not only its beneficence and necessity in order to satisfy certain wants of humanity, but also the limits assigned to it in proportion to the strength of human faculties,'which are not always sufficiently recognised by its devotees.

For the latter, the same observation would help us to realise its high scope, as consisting in revealing certain ideals to which we aspire, but which are different from, and superior to, reality; another truth often misunderstood by its cultivators, who make of it a reproduction or copy of reality, with all its lights and shades, very often perverting by vulgarity and bad taste one of the noblest and most delicate manifestations of the human soul.

It has been said that, from the constant observation of facts, moral order appears to be the result of two forces—namely, sentiment combined with intellect and will. By the same method it may be recognised that the regular succession with which these factors operate is manifested in the history of humanity. Feelings and affections greatly prevail in the youth of humanity and in the beginning of societies, because in conformity with natural law its own genuine energy presides over their foundations and formations. The intellect and will predominate in a more advanced age of men and societies, because they preside over their development and progress. And still no age can do without them both.

We have in the past lamented the effects of the excessive predominance of faith; to-day we see the perils of the exclusive dominion of reason.

And still all the great things in the world—religions, reforms, the constitution of societies, charity in all its forms—owe their creation to sentiment, just as they owe their development and progress to the intellect and will. Nothing is done in this world without a strong and intense affection, and nothing is preserved, developed, nor progresses without a healthy intellect and a strong will.

Intellect gifted with will, in the maturity of our civilisation, has reached the higher grade of power, has discovered the laws which govern the physical world, and has equal power to recognise those which uphold the moral world. But in both fields man may only know the *why*, but he cannot comprehend the *wherefore*; in this last inquiry, despite the marvellous progress of science, he has not advanced a step. In a word, by his intellect and reason man can ascertain the laws which govern both of them, but he cannot come to a knowledge of their primary causes and ultimate objects. This is the field reserved to sentiment, because in deficiency of intellect and reason in the human mind, faith replaces the knowledge of the first causes and hope that of the last ends. Reassuming all we have said, it evidently appears that as reason is possessed of the knowable, the unknowable is in the dominion of faith, and by the clear apprehension of this distinction in moral life is filled up a great part of that void which we have alluded to as having been left by positive philosophy.

We do not mean by that distinction that they never act simultaneously in both fields; on the contrary, we have seen what a great part sentiment has as an impulse and stimulus in the first field, just as reason has an important function as a limit and a restraint in the second. Because both are equally integral factors of the moral life of humanity and both are equally indispensable to mankind.

If the one party of the disputants to whom we alluded had considered this, they would not have declared the bankruptcy of science, nor would the other party have urged the inefficacy of faith, both forgetting that the different faculties had in different times, circumstances, and ways equally contributed to the greatness of the civilisation and societies to which they belong. Nor would there be any further continuance of a strife which has proved so fatal to humanity, and is one, perhaps, of the last obstacles remaining to its pacific and undisturbed progress.

Many other conclusions and more numerous corollaries might be drawn from a rational and methodical observation of human facts besides those to which we are led by a superficial glance; and their results would be neither few nor unimportant.

What is still more important is the fact that by this study certain fixed and controlling laws would become evident to men and societies, and the many who are not disposed to acquiesce in authority would understand that certain fundamental principles on which their very happiness and existence repose are outside of discussion because founded upon nature itself; that public and private virtues and vices are not, as they appear from a certain kind of literature, indifferent

manifestations of life and merely an object of curiosity, but real
virtues and vices in opposition to each other as they appear when
there is a clear discernment of right and wrong.

Consequently there would be no further necessity either for
violent revolutions or for not less violent reactions; no more need of
the *Conciergerie* to correct the *Bastille*; no more would adventurers,
communists, or anarchists, covered with the blood of their fellow-
countrymen, stand as acceptable rivals in the struggle for life, on
.the same footing with the slaves of honour and victims of duty.

The world of to-day yearns for guidance to a secure path in the
labyrinth created by the neglect of contemporary philosophy of the
moral order of things. And everywhere is felt a tendency to again
take into consideration all that has been hitherto respected, so as to
reconstruct with its ruins a place of safety in the solitude which has
been made around the human soul. So far we have had isolated
attempts, and they need co-ordination to produce efficacious conclusions.

This subject not being one which can be adequately treated
within the margin of a Review, the writer has endeavoured to
develop it more fully and completely elsewhere.[1]

But big volumes do not find their way to the crowd, and in so
vast and complex a matter a simple enunciation such as this cannot
be otherwise considered than as a germ and seed which, if it have
any value, should find a kindly soil in the mother country of both
Experimental and Positive Philosophy.

F. Nobili-Vitelleschi.

[1] *Morale Induttiva*, Tip. Forzani, Roma, 4 vols. 8vo.

BOILING MILK.

'THERE can be no shadow of doubt,' said the *Lancet* now many years ago, 'that the contagia of typhoid and scarlet fever are disseminated by milk, and that boiled milk enjoys a much greater immunity from the chance of conveying disease.'

This decided expression of opinion was given when the study of bacteria was yet in its infancy, and before any direct experimental evidence had been obtained on the behaviour of microbes in milk or concerning the part played by them in the dissemination of disease. Our information now is, however, of a very different order; innumerable investigations of a most laborious character have been made on this subject, and there is now no longer any question as to the great and continual risk of spreading disease which is run by the consumption of unboiled milk.

Amongst our articles of diet there are very few which we tolerate in their raw condition, and the number has recently been still more curtailed by the not perhaps altogether unwarranted scare about oysters transmitting typhoid fever; milk, however, whilst one of the most attractive of foods to the microbe which is contained in our bacteriological *menu* is, at the same time, the material which in this country is most largely consumed in its natural raw, uncooked condition. Knowing as we do that bacteria flourish and multiply abundantly in this rich fluid, it ought not to surprise us to learn that milk as we receive it contains enormous numbers of microbes, that one investigator, for example, found as many as 960,000 to 1,600,000 per cubic inch, or, in other words, from *thirty-three to fifty-six millions per pint*.

There is not much difficulty in surmising from what sources this vast microbial population is obtained if we recall the conditions under which the process of milking is carried on. The stifling atmosphere of the milking-shed rich in germ life, the carelessness which prevails as regards cleanliness not only in the condition of the animals themselves, but only too frequently in those entrusted with the milking of them, the impure water used in the washing of the vessels, &c., &c. If we consider again the number of hands through which milk passes before it is finally placed on our tables, it is surely not astonishing to find it so abundantly supplied with germ life.

We have pointed out that once provided with such a rich diet as milk, the fortunate microbe will thrive abundantly; the following instance will, however, give some approximate idea of what this thriving really means. A sample of milk was collected and found to contain 153,000 bacteria in a cubic inch; it was put on one side and kept at a constant temperature of 59° Fahr.; one hour later it was examined and found to contain 539,750 bacteria; at the end of seven hours the process was repeated, and 1,020,000 were discovered; whilst after the lapse of twenty-five hours as many as 85,000,000 were present per cubic inch.

The multiplication of bacteria in milk goes on even more rapidly if the temperature of the surrounding air is somewhat raised; thus another sample of milk was collected and found to contain 391,000 bacteria per cubic inch; twenty-four hours later, during which time it had been kept at a temperature of 77° Fahr., there were 13,702,000,000 bacteria present per cubic inch! But it may be urged that these germs are not necessarily capable of producing disease or dangerous to health. Quite so, but on the other hand what guarantee have we that amongst all this multitude of germs those associated with disease will not also obtain access to milk? That they do find their way into milk has been, moreover, proved over and over again, and the responsibility of communicating scarlet fever, typhoid fever, diphtheria and tuberculosis are only some of the heavy charges which have justifiably been brought up in connection with our milk supplies. Moreover, there is the strongest reason to believe that the gastric and intestinal disturbances, so common in young infants during the summer months, are due to the presence of certain fermenting organisms in milk which, favoured by the higher temperature, multiply most abundantly, elaborating products of a highly toxic character.

One frequent source to which the presence of these obnoxious organisms in milk has been directly traced is the outbreak of disease amongst the *employés* or amongst those connected with the *employés* of dairies from which milk has been distributed; there are, however, many other means by which milk may become contaminated.

As regards tuberculosis and milk, our information is perhaps more precise, for a large number of investigations have been successfully carried out on this subject, and it is now known that bacteria may not only obtain access to milk through the employment of persons suffering from tuberculosis in the dairy, but that the source of infection may be, and often is, the cow itself.

Recent research has shown that cows may be affected with tubercular disease in cases where the udder appears to be perfectly healthy, and that animals thus affected are capable of infecting the milk derived from them with the germs of tubercular disease.

The unsuspected existence of tubercular disease in cows, and its transmission to other animals fed with their milk, has been shown in a striking manner in the investigations carried out and just published by the Massachusetts Society for the Promotion of Agriculture.

In one case as many as over 33 per cent. of the calves fed with milk from tuberculous cows succumbed to the same disease. According to Hirschberger, 10 per cent. of the cows living in the neighbourhood of towns where the conditions of their environment are not generally the most satisfactory or conducive to health suffer from tuberculosis, and 50 per cent. of these animals yield milk containing tubercle bacilli.

Accepting these facts, 5 per cent. then of the samples of town milk contain these microbes. Freudenreich states that in Copenhagen four out of twenty-eight samples of mixed milk, derived, therefore, from a number of cows which he collected at random and carefully examined, proved virulent or induced tuberculous disease in other animals when injected under the skin.

Although the chances of infection are diminished by the fact that the milk derived from a number of cows is generally mixed together before being sent into the market, so that any infected sample will be largely diluted, yet in the above instance two out of the four samples came from dairies where from twenty to thirty cows were kept, and in each case suspicion only fell upon one cow.

It is sufficiently obvious what a source of danger such milk is, more especially as it has been proved that tubercle bacilli can live for upwards of 120 days in butter and over thirty-five days in cheese ! In 1890 a Royal Commission was appointed to inquire and report upon ' What is the effect, if any, of food derived from tuberculous animals on human health ? ' The results of the inquiries instituted by the commissioners were presented to Parliament a few months ago. In the summary appended to the report we read : ' Tuberculous matter in milk is exceptionally active in its operation upon animals fed either with the milk or with dairy produce derived from it. No doubt the largest part of the tuberculosis which man obtains through his food is by means of milk containing tuberculous matter.'

That the commissioners are alive to the great importance of this means of spreading disease is further shown by the following significant paragraph : ' In regard to milk, we are aware of the preference by English people for drinking cow's milk raw, a practice attended by danger on account of possible contamination by pathogenic organisms. The boiling of milk, even for a moment, would probably be sufficient to remove the very dangerous quality of tuberculous milk.'

As regards the last statement we cannot help feeling that it may lead to some misapprehension of the immense powers of endurance so characteristic of the tubercle bacillus, for Currier has shown that to effectually destroy this micro-organism in water a temperature raised to the boiling point maintained during ten minutes is necessary. The power to withstand exposure to high temperatures is possessed in very different degrees by different microbes; thus the cholera bacillus cannot survive even a momentary exposure to a temperature many degrees *below* boiling, whilst typhoid and diphtheria bacilli are destroyed when the water reaches the boiling point.

There are, of course, various methods of obtaining germ-free milk; some are, however, attended with too great labour and inconvenience to admit of their practical application. Thus some time ago, wishing to prepare some sterile milk for bacterial cultivation purposes without altering its chemical composition, I had to patiently heat it for from one to two hours on five successive days, watching the while that the temperature remained between 58 and 65° Centigrade! The milk was sterile and I kept it for months, but such a process of course is impossible for domestic purposes.

The addition of chemicals to milk is both undesirable and ineffectual; amongst such substances boracic acid, borax, and salicylic acid are employed; but whilst the two former have been found to produce but little effect upon disease germs present in milk, salicylic acid hinders curdling more than other substances, but even if added in the small proportion of twelve grains per quart gives a taste to the milk and is not capable of destroying typhoid bacilli.

Authorities are, moreover, not agreed as to the harmlessness of this ingredient, and in France the employment of salicylic acid in the preservation of food is strenuously opposed by doctors who consider its habitual use injurious to health. The application of heat to milk is the only advisable and reliable method for rendering it free from germs, but a great deal depends upon the manner in which the heat is applied.

It is unnecessary here to detail the numerous efforts which have resulted in the elaboration of various descriptions of so-called 'milk-sterilisers,' the efficiency of which have all undergone searching investigations at the hands of bacteriologists as regards their destruction of disease germs.

The difficulties which have to be mastered consist, firstly, in the remarkable power of resisting heat which characterises not only some disease germs, but also some of the microbes which are most partial to milk; secondly, in the sensitiveness of milk to heat as exhibited by its alteration in taste and other respects through exposure to high temperatures.

To overcome these obstacles many ingenious pieces of apparatus have been devised, based upon a process originally introduced by Pasteur for preventing certain defects in wine and beer, and which consists in the application of a temperature of about 140° Fahr.

The process is usually described as the 'pasteurisation' of milk, and very perfect apparatus has now been provided in which milk is maintained at a temperature of from 154–156° Fahr., generally through the agency of steam. A special contrivance is also provided by means of which during the process the milk is kept in continual movement, so that it does not acquire a burnt flavour; the temperature is also prevented from rising to 158° Fahr., at which point the change in taste, which it is desirable to avoid, commences. By observing these precautions much of the popular objection raised to boiled milk is removed. It is extremely satisfactory to learn, on the authority of so careful an experimenter as Dr. Bitter, that pasteurisation in the most approved apparatus for from twenty to thirty minutes kills with certainty all the disease germs such as those of tuberculosis, cholera, diphtheria, and typhoid which are likely to be found in milk.

It must not be supposed that the pasteurisation of milk necessarily relieves the dairyman of all responsibility as regards the conditions of his dairy, that he may with impunity neglect precautions of cleanliness, &c.; on the contrary, more and more attention is being directed to the importance of cleanly milking and the observance of other hygienic considerations in dairy work, for experience has shown that it is far easier to sterilise clean milk than milk contaminated with thousands of bacteria obtained through neglect of, and inattention to, simple sanitary requirements. Some idea of how imperative such precautions are may be gathered from investigations recently made on the milk supply of Berlin, for Dr. Backhaus has estimated that this city alone consumes daily with its milk 300 cwt. of cow-dung!

Pasteurised milk may be prepared in bottles, and special devices have been introduced so that the latter are closed whilst still heated and under pressure, thus avoiding any chance of bacterial infection taking place at the moment of closing the bottles.

There is no reason why cream should not also be pasteurised before being sent out from the dairy, not only for direct consumption but for the production of butter. Pasteurised cream lends itself very readily for this purpose, for although the actual yield of butter is said to be rather less, it is stated to be of a superior quality.

Another application of pasteurised milk is in the manufacture of cheese. Such milk curdles very readily with rennet, and investigations are now in progress for the production of particular varieties of cheese from pasteurised milk by means of particular microbes; for although many varieties of bacteria are not only not wanted in, but are detrimental to the quality of, as well as safety of, dairy produce, there are many germs which play a most useful and indeed absolutely indispensable part in the dairy. Our exact information on this branch of the subject is at present very limited, but researches are being vigorously pursued, and some already of the useful and friendly dairy bacteria have been distinguished; for example, a bacillus has been found which is responsible for the production of that variety of Swiss cheese known as 'thousand-holed' on account of its porous or cavernous structure. This appearance is due to the production of bubbles of gas by a bacillus which causes the curd to 'heave,' thus leading to the formation of large holes.

There is a wide field for research open for workers in this direction, and it is one which will doubtless occupy the attention of the authorities in some of our recently created agricultural colleges. There can be no doubt that, before long, a well-appointed dairy will have its supply of particular bacteria much as a chemical laboratory is furnished with suitable reagents, and instead of depending upon chance for the production of particular cheeses, any desired variety of the latter will be produced at will by means of special microbes with almost the same certainty as a chemist can obtain a particular chemical reaction.

It is earnestly to be hoped that before long the public will themselves insist upon the distribution of untainted milk; at present, the request for sterilised milk at any of our dairies would be met with blank ignorance on the part of the *employé* as to what was meant by the inquiry. On the Continent a very different state of things exists, and so strong is the prejudice against drinking unboiled milk, that in Leipzig and other cities in Germany serious endeavours have been made by charitable and other societies to encourage the use of sterile milk amongst the poorer classes. It has also been recently claimed that the introduction of pasteurised milk among the poor people of New York city, through the philanthropic efforts of Mr. Nathan Straus, has done much to reduce the infant mortality during the hot summer months.

The Swiss, alive to the pecuniary importance to be derived from the supply of such milk, have established milk sterilising associations, and in Paris important companies exist for the production and regular delivery of 'lait pur stérilisé.' There is surely room in this country, were but the facts sufficiently well known and the dangers realised of using raw milk, for the successful establishment of such associations, not alone on hygienic grounds, but from a purely commercial point of view.

Who would not thankfully exchange, for example, the tumbler of dust-laden, germ-swarming milk which is handed round at our railway stations, or provided in our crowded non-alcoholic luncheon saloons, for a flask of milk guaranteed to be sweet and free from all contamination?

If only in the extension of its keeping power, surely pasteurised milk has a future which must commend itself sooner or later to agricultural authorities here as it has already done on the Continent.

It is satisfactory to learn that some of the objections which have

been raised to the use of boiled milk, on the grounds of its unwhole-
someness are not regarded, by those best qualified to form an opinion,
as proven. Some years ago, after the National Health Society had
circulated a leaflet which I wrote for them on the advisability of boiling all milk before use, I was invariably confronted with arguments
as to its unfitness for children on account of its indigestible character.
My personal experience is, however, quite contrary, and although the
use of raw milk has been for years most rigorously prohibited, none
of the evil results foretold have resulted.

This question has, however, been thoroughly investigated by the
present Director of the Institut Pasteur, Dr. Duclaux, who published a
short time ago an exhaustive article on 'La digestibilité du lait
stérilisé,' in which he carefully examines and weighs all the facts
which have arisen, and reviews the numerous special researches which
have been made in connection with this subject.

I cannot do better than quote some of the words with which he
concludes his article : ' Ceci nous amène,' he writes, 'à une conclusion qu'il faut bien avoir le courage de tirer, c'est que ces études
chimiques sur la digestibilité du lait ne sont pas adéquates à la
question à résoudre. . . . En attendant, tenons-nous-en à cette conclusion générale, que le lait pasteurisé, chauffé ou stérilisé, est encore
du lait, devant la science comme devant la pratique, et que si son
emploi présente parfois des inconvénients, ceux-ci sont légers et
amplement compensés par les avantages.'

G. C. FRANKLAND.

A NORTHERN PILGRIMAGE

LONDON was hot—very hot. The season was growing stale. 'No more dining out,' said the wise physician; 'try a few days in a bracing atmosphere.' A bracing atmosphere! I drew in a long breath of the tepid air. I might have been inside an oven. Where, at such a time as this, was there anything that could truly be called bracing to be found short of the Arctic Circle? And then in a blessed moment of inspiration there suddenly flashed upon me the vision of my native county—practically unseen for two-and-thirty years. As in a dream I saw the league-long roller breaking in silver on the iron coast, and heard the plovers calling on the rolling moorlands that look down on Coquet and Aln, and felt the city of my youth quivering beneath the blows of her 'clamorous iron flail.' Unseen for two-and-thirty years, and the generation I had known gone from it for ever, all the dear remembered faces of my childhood vanished with it! It was the memory of that generation that stood between me and the place I longed to see again. How could a man go back to the old home that was home no longer? But out of the far-off past came a sudden call before which my hesitation vanished—a call that found an echo in my heart; and thus it came about that, four-and-twenty hours later, I found myself seeking repose in the Station Hotel at Newcastle-on-Tyne.

One station hotel resembles another as closely as twin peas in the pod. When I breakfasted next morning in the coffee-room there was nothing in my surroundings to remind me of the town once so familiar. That which struck me was the distinctly cosmopolitan air of the company at breakfast. At one table they were talking Russian, at another Spanish, whilst at a third, a demure Japanese with almond-shaped eyes was studying the *menu*. It was not thus in the early sixties; but since then the world has discovered Newcastle, and has learned what the men of the Tyneside can do for it. By-and-by some neighbouring chairs were filled by a party of honest country-folk, and then there fell upon my ears the long-lost music of the Northumbrian tongue—the rolling gutturals, the sing-song cadence, that can be heard nowhere else in this world. I knew that I was at home at last.

The Central Station at Newcastle, familiar to all who take the East Coast route to Scotland, is a vast bewildering place. The great bridge by which it is approached, spanning the Tyne at a height of more than a hundred feet above high water mark, the blackened Norman keep that guards its portals, give it an air of distinction that no London railway station can command. It is the same station that I saw opened to the world more than six-and-forty years ago, when the opening ceremony consisted of a dinner to Robert Stephenson, the famous son of a still more famous father. But it has been more than doubled in size since then, and where once there was comparative spaciousness and leisure, there is now crowding and bustling, such as even Charing Cross cannot show. One was bewildered by the labyrinth of sidings and main lines that covered the vast roofed-in area. This after all was not the station I had once known. Out in the streets the landmarks of my youth were still to be seen. The noble lantern tower of St. Nicholas—the most graceful edifice of the kind in England—remained unchanged, though in my absence the building it adorns had been transformed from a mere parish church into a cathedral. Grey Street, the thoroughfare which Newcastle owes to the genius and courage of Richard Grainger, and which is a glorified Regent Street in stone instead of stucco, was as stately as of yore ; and the other well-planned harmonious thoroughfares that once made the town an example to the cities of the earth, were what they used to be. But now hurrying crowds filled the pavements, whilst beyond this central portion of the city spread a vast town of which I knew nothing. It had more than doubled in population since I last dwelt within its walls, and the area it covered had increased in a still larger proportion. As I wandered through the once-familiar streets that morning, or traversed new thoroughfares where houses had taken the place of hedge-rows, effacing the meadows where I had played as a child, two lines of Tennyson's were constantly running in my brain :

> There rolls the deep where grew the tree.
> O Earth, what changes hast thou seen !

The deep seemed to have rolled above my own head. Like Esmond at his mother's grave, I felt as one who walked beneath the sea. It was sad enough to have to go to the quiet cemetery beside the moor, in order to find one's friends. It touched one's heart to the quick to stand again before the house that had once been a home, and to find that, instead of the far-reaching prospect over hill and moor and sea, all that the dwellers in it could now command was 'the other side of the way.' But these are the necessary incidents of a return after so long an absence, and being in the nature of private griefs they can hardly be obtruded here.

There was much, however, in this new view of a place which still dwelt freshly in my memory, as I had known it in 1860, that had a more public interest. It was impossible not to be struck by the immense advance in material wealth and luxury of life that had taken place in the interval. There were fewer ragged children in the streets. The houses were bigger and better decorated. The shops were infinitely better supplied than of yore. There were many handsome carriages. There was a general air of prosperity about the place that was not to be mistaken, and that I had not known in the past. For that prosperity Newcastle is largely indebted to the genius of one man. As a youth I remember a plain house in Westgate Street, upon the door of which was a worn brass plate bearing the words, ' Mr. Armstrong, solicitor.' The Mr. Armstrong of forty years ago was an eminently respectable member of his profession. Some good people, it is true, shook their heads when they heard that instead of attending to conveyances and writs and mortgages, he had taken to dabbling in mechanics. Not that way does fortune lie in the profession of the law. But one day I was taken as a boy to see a remarkable new toy— it seemed nothing more—that had been placed upon the Quayside at Newcastle, where a few small steamers and Dutch merchantmen were in the habit of coming with cargo. It looked like a metal box, with some curious handles not unlike water-taps, upon the lid. A good-natured workman turned one of these handles, and lo! as he did so, a great crane hard by rattled its chain, and slowly but surely swung a heavy load into the air. It was like magic. ' Now try it yourself,' said the man, as he stopped the movement of the crane. Timidly I moved the handle, and straightway the miracle was repeated. At the touch of a child the heavy load was at once borne upwards. ' It's arl dune by watter,' said the man, ' and it's Armstrong the solicitor in Westgate Street that's invented it.' That was the first hydraulic crane.

' Mr. Armstrong, solicitor,' had found his true calling in life. He still kept up the practice of his profession. But he bought a small bit of ground by the side of the Tyne, away from the town on the Scotswood Road, and there he raised a modest building within which the manufacture of his new hydraulic machinery was undertaken. I remember the place well. Many a time I accompanied my father on a round of pastoral calls among the plain people who lived at Elswick, in small cottages with little gardens attached, in which marigolds and carnations bloomed, and the fragrant lad's love was invariably to be found. There are no gardens there now. From that humble beginning of more than forty years ago has sprung the vast Elswick establishment, which knows only one rival in Europe. Fifteen thousand workmen are busy from day to day at furnace, forge, and lathe. Where once the flowers bloomed and the cattle fed on the riverside meadows there is now a range of industrial buildings a mile in length ; and a whole town has grown up in that which I can still remember as rustic Elswick— the place where as a boy I roamed in the fields, or rowed in one of Harry Clasper's boats upon the river. Of course the place had begun to make great strides forward before I left Newcastle in 1862. The famous rifled gun had been invented, and was becoming almost as important an article of manufacture as the hydraulic cranes and rams. But since then the development of the establishment has been almost appalling, and I could not recognise the scenes once so familiar. It is ' Mr. Armstrong, solicitor,' now Lord Armstrong, who has given the impetus to the industrial progress of the Tyne. He is the magnet who draws to the old town that cosmopolitan company I noted at the breakfast table.

But it is not my business to describe the vast Elswick works, the greatest of their kind in the United Kingdom, if not in the world. I have but to note them among the many changed features in the life of Newcastle. Incidentally they have brought about another change, not less remarkable than the creation of the great industrial suburb of Elswick. I have said that as a boy I have spent many an hour rowing on the Tyne opposite the place where the Elswick works now present their mile-long frontage to the stream. At that time it was almost possible to cross the river dry-shod at low water. The King's Meadows, where the buttercups bloomed in profusion among the grass, formed a group of islets in mid-stream, and no vessel of heavier burden than the characteristic keel of the Tyne—the subject of the familiar song ' Weel may the keel row '—was ever to be seen above the old bridge. Now the King's Meadows have disappeared ; the river has been deepened from its mouth to far above Elswick ; the old Tyne bridge has been removed, a huge swing bridge moved by hydraulic power taking its place, and great battleships—ships as big as the ill-fated *Victoria*—are not only built at Elswick, but are able to traverse the river safely from that spot to the sea. The story of what has been done for the Clyde by local spirit and engineering genius is matter of history. It is not so generally known that a work at least as great has been done for the Tyne. The river I could have waded across as a boy now bears ships of thousands of tons burden at any state of the tide. I watched with amazed eyes the opening of the huge swing bridge to allow a great ocean steamer to pass down stream. It was swung by a single man just as easily as the hydraulic crane which once stood hard by was moved by my fingers as a boy, and, like the crane, it was the offspring of the brain of the Newcastle solicitor.

Politics ! One cannot keep away from them even on a holiday. Of late years Newcastle has been chiefly known in the political world in connection with the name of John Morley, its representative in four successive parliaments. But my Newcastle dates from a time when Mr. Morley was still unknown, and it is with other names that I connect it. Between the fifties and sixties Newcastle had a distinguished son, of whom it was half proud, and perhaps a trifle

afraid. He went about its streets a plain man among plain men.
He spoke with a strong Northumbrian burr; he dressed not unlike
a pitman in his Sunday best, wearing always that soft black felt hat
which in those days was regarded by timid persons as being in itself
the badge of the incendiary and the revolutionist. He was dreaded
by the timid Whigs, who were then in the ascendant in the political
world, and detested with a whole-hearted intensity by every true Conservative. A great many good citizens sincerely pitied the respectable
Mr. Joseph Cowen, senior, because fate had afflicted him with a son so
erratic as his namesake, Joseph Cowen, junior. But the more he
was dreaded by Whig and hated by Tory, the more ardently was
young Joseph Cowen adored by the workpeople and Radicals of
Tyneside. His gift of speech—that burning eloquence which in after
days was to thrill the House of Commons, and stir the admiration of
the coldest and most critical audience in the world—was the pride
and the delight of those of us who flocked in those far-off days to
the dingy lecture-room in Nelson Street to attend a meeting of the
Northern Reform League, or to pass some red-hot resolution against
the tyrannical Powers of the continent. For the distinguishing
mark of Newcastle Radicalism in those times was its cosmopolitanism.
We were all strong for the granting of the suffrage to the working
man, and unanimous in our groans when the name of Lord Palmerston
fell from the lips of one of our favourite orators. But under
'Joe Cowen's' inspiration we were even more enthusiastic in our
interest in the fate of the Pole, Hungarian, and Italian, and our
loudest cries of scorn and indignation were reserved for 'the man of
the Second of December,' and the King of the Two Sicilies. How we
crowded into the old lecture-room in those days of youthful illusion
to join in cheering 'Joe,' as he poured forth the burning flood of his
tempestuous eloquence against kings and emperors and grand dukes!
And with what shouts of heartfelt joy and reverence we received
from time to time some scarred victim of the oppressor, or some
hero of the war of liberation, who, having reached the hospitable shores
of England, found his way as a matter of course to Newcastle, and to
the warm shelter of Joseph Cowen's modest house at Blaydon Burn.
Garibaldi was one of these, though that was nearly fifty years ago,
when, even as a spectator, my part in the reception was but a passive
one. But later came Kossuth—grave, pallid, earnest-faced; and Felice
Orsini, fresh from his Mantuan dungeon, and with the shadow of the
guillotine even then descending upon his head; and Louis Blanc,
bristling with witty epigrams against Napoleon the Little; and Dr.
Bernard, saved from a French scaffold by the turgid rhetoric of Edwin
James; and many another, whose name must live in history. It was
good to be alive in those days of generous illusions. Newcastle
Radicalism believed in itself then at any rate, and believed also in a
cause which was not its own alone. Alas! there are few signs now
of the survival of that old spirit of generous sympathy with the

oppressed of every land that led the working men, at the close of
a day of toil, to give their evenings to the hot and crowded meeting,
where they denounced the tyrant with a vociferous heartiness that
ought to have made him tremble on his throne.   As I walk through
the streets of Newcastle to-day I see many announcements of sports
of every kind, cricket, golf, bicycling, bowls, but not so much as a
handbill summoning my fellow-townsmen, as in the days of old, to a
meeting in the lecture-room on behalf of the alien victims of oppression.   *Tempora mutantur et nos* . . . !   Here, as elsewhere, a change
has come over the spirit of the people.   Newcastle has more theatres
and music halls than in those days ; more recreation grounds and
public sports.   It travels more on pleasure.   Its grand old moor and
leazes have fallen into the hands of the improvers.   They are more
ornamental; they are more in harmony with modern taste.   But
are they better ?   And in any case, despite the political clubs which
I see in every district, is there more of the real political spirit than
there was in the days when Joseph Cowen, with half-a-dozen foreign
spies dogging his footsteps even in the streets of his native town,
was summoning us to take our part in the battle of freedom ?

Mr. Cowen represented, as I have said, the extreme Radical
element in Newcastle in those days.   But we were not without
politicians of eminence of a different school.   There still survived
amongst us Charles Larkin, the Chartist orator, who won a passing
notoriety by his declaration (in the Reform agitations of 1830), that
' a fairer head than that of Adelaide, Queen of England, had already
rolled upon the scaffold.'   That was an outburst marking the epoch
when the favourite cry of the disappointed was that ' the Queen has
done it all.'   In my time Mr. Larkin had ceased to be an active
politician ; I believe had even ceased to be a Radical.   He was an
extinct volcano ; but one that spoke eloquently to us of a great
eruption.   With him one must place dapper Sir John Fife, the
eminent surgeon, who had won his knighthood by boldly charging
the assembled Chartists, when as Mayor of Newcastle he led the
forces of the Crown against the unlucky people who had the misfortune to be born before their time.   Sir John Fife was a plucky
fellow, and a good horseman, and his horsemanship most appropriately
gained for him his knighthood.   Of men of letters in those days we
could boast few.   Prominent amongst those few was Dr. Collingwood
Bruce, the historian of the Roman wall, dear to the elder men of the
North to-day because his was the one great public school of Northumberland, at a time when Eton and Harrow were still the preserves of
the great and their parasites.   But there was one distinguished writer
of whom some at least of the people of Newcastle were proud thirty or
forty years ago, and concerning whom I venture to tell a simple but
veracious tale.   Somewhere in the fifties a certain boy in the old
town showed a strong desire to embark upon the perilous career of
journalism.   To him entered one day an old friend of the family,

anxious if possible to snatch the lad from the doom to which he was rushing unheeding. 'Thomas,' he said, in tones of solemn warning (and nobody but the boy in question knew how much he hated to be addressed as Thomas), 'ah'm sorry to hear that ye want to go to London, and to take to this writing in the papers. It'll bring ye to no good, my boy. I mind there was a very decent friend of mine, auld Mr. Forster, the butcher in the Side. He had a laddie just like you; and nothing would sarve him but he must go away to London to get eddicated, as he called it; and when he had got eddicated, he wouldn't come back to his father's shop, though it was a first-class business. He would do nothing but write, and write, and write; and at last he went back again to London, and left his poor old father all alone; and *a've never heard tell of that laddie since!*' It was thus that the fame of John Forster, the author of the *Life of Goldsmith* and the destined biographer of Charles Dickens, was cherished in his native town by his father's ancient friends!

One name was still held in special honour in Newcastle forty years ago. That was the name of Thomas Bewicke, the ornithologist and wood engraver. His fame was dear to the people of Tyneside, and the fact that members of his family were still living in the place was regarded as a matter of local pride. I have talked with some of Bewicke's old cronies, and heard more than one story of his life. He was a jovial person, and like most jovial persons of that generation had a weakness for late sittings at the public-house, which represented the club of modern times. His wife did not appreciate this side of the character of her distinguished husband; and her tongue was sharp and bitter. One evening, according to a legend I heard from one of Bewicke's friends, the great man came home late—very late. But when he entered the nuptial chamber, to his relief he saw that his wife was, to all appearances, wrapped in profound repose. Quickly and silently he undressed and slipped into bed. Scarcely was his head upon the pillow, however, before the good lady had laid aside the mask she had chosen to don, and had begun to pour forth all her grievances in a flood of angry words. For half-an-hour by the clock she continued to berate her erring spouse after the manner of Mrs. Caudle, and then paused for want of breath. 'Thomas Bewicke,' she said, as her last words, 'hast thou nothing to say for thyself?' Now Bewicke was a shrewd man. He had seen the ruse practised upon him by his wife, and was quick to copy it. Turning slowly in his bed as his exhausted spouse paused in her speech, he yawned ostentatiously, and then, as though suddenly awaking to consciousness, murmured in his softest tones, 'Hinny, wast thou talking?'

There was a worthy, long since forgotten, in my time who was a kind of prototype of Rogue Riderhood in *Our Mutual Friend.* He was known as Cuckoo Jack, and he lived upon the Tyne in a well-patched old boat, picking up any trifle that came in his way, from a derelict log to a corpse. One day an elderly and most estimable Quaker of Newcastle, in stepping from a river steamboat to the quay, slipped and fell into the stream. Cuckoo Jack was at hand with his boat, and quickly rescued the luckless 'Friend,' and landed him dripping on the quay. The good man drew half-a-crown from his pocket and solemnly handed it to his preserver. Jack eyed the coin a moment with lack-lustre gaze, spat upon it solemnly 'for luck,' and having placed it safely in his pocket, said in a matter-of-fact tone to the soaked Quaker, 'Man, ah'd hev gotten five shillin' for taking ye to the dead-hoose !'

Newcastle has always been too busy, too much engrossed in the practical, to care much for literary fame, and, so far as I know, its only literary poet is that respectable mediocrity, Mr. Mark Akenside. Its real poets have been its Stephensons and Armstrongs, and other masters of the forces of nature, who have known how to make the poetry of life out of more stubborn things than words. Yet in the history of the town, even within living memory, there have been incidents that might have moved the poet's heart. Among these the outbreak of cholera in 1853 may well be counted. No similar visitation of that dread scourge has occurred in this country within the half century. It was the story of the Great Plague of London on a smaller scale. The epidemic descended upon us like an armed invader.

But he did not come unheralded. One day I went out to school, and found that a mysterious gloom brooded in the sunny September sky. It was not an ordinary cloud that made all things dark. It was a plague of minute flies. They filled the air; one could not breathe without swallowing them. They were everywhere—a host as terrible and as loathsome as that which subdued Gulliver in Lilliput. Even a schoolboy could not face such a plague. I covered my face with my handkerchief, and only in that fashion was it possible to pursue one's way to school. Everybody else I found had adopted the same expedient, and on that dreadful day none but veiled faces were to be seen in the streets of Newcastle. We had heard that the 'cholera flies' invariably preceded the cholera itself. Such was the legend. Whether true or false, our experience served to verify it. Within a couple of days the cholera was upon us, and then for six terrible weeks we were at its mercy. I remember the dead being wheeled in common barrows to the churchyard, for the undertakers were done to death. I remember the men who went about the streets at night, carrying burning vessels of disinfectants, whose acrid odour is not yet forgotten. On one dreadful day more than a hundred persons died, and at that time the population of the town was only some 80,000. A death-rate of 450 in the 1,000 *per annum* was something to startle even the most callous. But the plague passed, and we had almost ceased to compare it with that of which Pepys has left an undying record, when the parallel between the fate of London and Newcastle was made strangely complete by the great fire of 1854. The scars of that fire, which was attended by a great loss of life and the destruction of nearly a million pounds' worth of property, are still visible in the old town. But the worst of the narrow alleys abutting upon the river were destroyed, and the Quayside of to-day, with its handsome buildings, dates from that calamity.

It is not generally known that Northumberland has a picturesqueness which can vie with that of any county of England. From the city of many memories I made my way to Rothbury, a village on the banks of the delightful Coquet, one of the best trout streams of England. It was forty-one years since I had last stayed in the hamlet. Here time had dealt gently with the scene. The lovely valley was the valley I remembered. Old Simonside had not changed a jot or a tittle. His contour was precisely that which I remembered as a boy, and the most beautiful of all Northumbrian valleys was as beautiful as ever. An excellent hotel—the County—furnishes admirable accommodation for the visitor. From the window of my sitting-room I could see the very spot where I caught my first trout, and experienced one of the keenest pleasures of life. In few districts of England is there to be seen such a combination of the grand and the gentle in nature as here. The noble Cheviots rise in the distance ; heather-clad moors with precipitous walls of rock crown the sides of the valley ; whilst below are the greenest of meadows, through which the Coquet pursues its way, musical at every step. The keen air that sweeps down from the north is as exhilarating as iced champagne. London was grilling in a temperature of 80° in the shade. Here I found a fire a pleasant incident in the evening. In one thing only had there been any great change in Rothbury during my forty years of absence. Lord Armstrong has made his home here, at one end of the oval cup which forms the vale of Rothbury. At Cragside the master of the Elswick works has built himself the lordliest of pleasure-houses. About that pleasure-house I have little to say. The great genius who has made it his home has a right to its beauty and its seclusion. But one who remembers Rothbury in the old days, and who roamed freely over the rocks and crags of the moors before any millionaire had thought of fixing his abode here, may be pardoned if he does not enjoy the transformation of the wild moorland into a sumptuous pleasure garden, in which artificial waterfalls and rockeries and ferneries have taken the place of the bare hillside of his youth. Perhaps it was the intimation on the ticket by which I obtained admission to this rather cockneyfied paradise that smoking was strictly prohibited that hardened my heart. Whatever may have been the cause, I preferred Cragside in its original form to that which it has now assumed.

One purpose with which I came to Rothbury was to ascend the valley of the Coquet as far as Alwinton. Forty years ago I had

walked from the one place to the other. It was a long walk for a
boy of fourteen, and the recollection of it had never been lost. My
companions in that memorable walk had long since passed away.
But they lived again as I set out in the dogcart provided by my host
of the County Hotel, to retrace the steps of my lost youth. A fairer
day's drive no man need wish. Ascending from the delightful
summer meadows of Rothbury, I followed the Coquet in its upward
course by Thropton, Sharperton, and Harbottle, until I reached the
remote hamlet of Alwinton at the foot of the Cheviots. All along the
valley the scenery was typically English of the best kind. At
Harbottle the remains of the old castle where one queen was imprisoned and another born, were still to be seen. This mouldering
keep was in the old days the stronghold of the Warden of the Middle
Marches, the warrior whose business it was to keep Central Northumberland free from the encroachments of the reiving Scot. At Alwinton,
as at Harbottle, an eminence near the village bore the name of
Gallows Law. It was the old place of execution, in the days when
the chief of each small border hamlet held power of life and death in
his hands—and used it freely. From the Gallows Law at Alwinton
there is a wonderful view into the very heart of the Cheviots. These
billow-like hills, covered with grass and heather, have a charm peculiar
to themselves. The pity is that so few persons visit them, and that
one of the healthiest and most picturesque districts of England is
practically unknown to the tourist. Here at least the tired Londoner
can revel in absolute solitude. As I stood on the Gallows Law, where
many a moss-trooper had met his death of old, I could not see a
single human being, I could hardly see a human habitation. The
distant barking of a dog was the only sound that broke the stillness
of the summer air. The voices of the dead who had been my companions all along the valley were the only voices that I heard.

There was one other spot familiar in times past to which my
pilgrimage led me. This was Tynemouth, the picturesque old
watering-place which faces the German Ocean at the mouth of the
Tyne. It was changed, as were all the spots I visited, but changed
wholly for the better. Its gardens and the sea-banks were better
kept than of yore. Unlike most of our watering-places nowadays, it
had not been over-built; and the splendid sea, with its silvery waves
breaking on the Long Sands or the rocks at the Ox Ford, was the
same rushing, resistless ocean as of old. The finest feature of
Tynemouth is the Castle Rock, a bold promontory of sand-stone
jutting out into the sea, crowned by the grand ruins of Tynemouth
Priory, and by the white lighthouse, which from time immemorial
has guided the mariner seeking to enter the river below. The place
has now a new attraction in the shape of the majestic crescent-shaped
piers which stretch forth into the sea from either side of the river.
The North Pier is more than half a mile in length, whilst its sister
pier jutting from South Shields is longer still. These massive

structures have been for more than forty years in course of construction, and their like is hardly to be found elsewhere upon the surface of the globe. They have converted the once dangerous entrance to the Tyne into a vast harbour of refuge, where a fleet of ironclads might lie in safety. How many times during the past forty years the whole work of a summer—for it is only in summer that real work is possible—has been undone in a single night of tempest, I dare not say. But at last the piers are practically finished and their formal opening is at hand. One cannot conceive a more picturesque spectacle than that which is presented as one stands at the end of the North Pier. Between it and the South Pier there is an opening a third of a mile in width, and through that opening the commerce of one of the greatest English ports passes daily. 'There go the ships,' from the humble ocean tramp to the mighty ironclad fresh from its cradle at Elswick. One of these same ironclads passed out upon its steam trial trip as I watched the scene, and for six hours it cruised up and down in front of Tynemouth at a speed of nineteen knots. Why a watering-place which possesses such special attractions of its own is so little known beyond the limits of Northumberland is a point that baffles understanding.

I renewed my acquaintance with picturesque Cullercoats, beloved of artists, and Whitley, where for many a summer I had enjoyed myself as a child among the sands and rocks, in the course of a long drive. Unlike Tynemouth, these once beautiful spots had been altered for the worse. The plague of cheap building had afflicted them, and the fields I knew of old were now a wilderness of bricks. But my drive carried me beyond the building limit. I went as far as Seaton Delavel Hall, once one of the stateliest of English mansions, the work of Sir John Vanbrugh, and generally recognised as superior in beauty and majesty to Blenheim itself. The greater part of the mansion has stood for more than a century in ruins. The 'wicked Delavels' have disappeared, and the strange rites and unholy sports which were once carried on within the grey walls are now only matter of tradition. One of the three huge pavilions which constitute the hall has been restored by the present owner, Lord Hastings, and he lives there on the scene of the former grandeur of an ancient family.

It was at Delavel Hall that I had an unusual experience. As we drove near the front of the house, my companion bade the coachman stop, and pointed out the different features of the building to me. 'Do you see the housemaid standing at that window?' said my host's wife, indicating an upper window in the central pavilion. I saw some one at the spot indicated, but my defective vision did not allow me to recognise the sex or condition of the stranger until I had donned my spectacles. Then I saw plainly and unmistakably a woman clad in the dress of a housemaid apparently watching us as we sat in the carriage. 'Well,' I said by-and-by; 'what about the housemaid?' 'Oh, don't you know? That is the ghost!' I laughed at the notion, for there was certainly nothing ghost-like about the figure I was watching. At a sign from my host, the carriage advanced a few paces, and instantly the woman at the window vanished. I saw at the same moment that the window at which I had seen the figure belonged to the ruined portion of the hall. The apparition was of course nothing more than a curious optical illusion, the effect of the lights and shadows from the carved stone-work adjoining the window; but so real was the spectral appearance, that I was not surprised that local tradition claimed it unhesitatingly as the ghost of a building which, if tradition speaks truly of its former owners, might certainly well be haunted.

But it is not Seaton Delavel Hall, it is the engine-house of a colliery that stands within a stone's throw of the gates at the foot of the long avenue, that furnishes the haunted ground of this part of Northumberland. As I drove up to the well-remembered pit-buildings, I was surprised to see that smoke was issuing from the tall chimney, and that there were signs of cheerful life about the place. When last I had seen it the shadow of doom hung over it, and the rusting iron-work, the mouldering pit-heap, the disused tramways all told their own tale of ruin and death. Four-and-thirty years ago, in the month of January 1862, all England was awaiting in breathless suspense the issue of a struggle which was being carried on at this spot. More than 200 men and boys had been made prisoners in the pit, by the blocking of the single shaft which gave admission to it. The accident was due to the breaking of the great beam of a pumping-engine, which worked directly above the opening of the shaft. When the beam broke one-half fell into the pit, and choked it. For a whole week, a bitter week in mid-winter, I was one of those who stood on this pit-heap and watched the ceaseless and heroic efforts of brave men to rescue the imprisoned miners. To the last we hoped against hope, telling ourselves tales of the signalling we had heard from the prisoners beneath our feet, and fondly deluding ourselves with the idea that, as they had a sufficiency of food and water, they must be safe. Only a few men could work at once in the confined space of the shaft, and their task was one of excessive peril. They hung suspended by ropes in the depths of the pit, with water pouring incessantly upon them, with the crumbling sides of the shaft continually giving way, threatened at every moment by a terrible death, but not for a single instant by day or night desisting from their efforts. In the meantime, all England was thrilled with the story of the imprisoned miners, and shared in the suspense which chained the wives and mothers of the captives to the pit-heap, day after day throughout that week of anguish. It was in the dead of the winter night that those of us who stood upon the platform at the mouth of the pit learned the dreadful truth. A sharp signal had been given from below, and at once the sinkers working in the shaft had been drawn up. For a moment we hoped that the signal meant that the lost had been recovered, and our hearts beat quickly with joyous anticipation. But too soon the bitter truth was made clear. As the sinkers were brought to the surface, it was found that all were unconscious, and we knew that they had succumbed to the deadly gases of the mine. Restoratives were at hand, but before they could be applied to the victims, the master-sinker, Coulson by name, whose own son was among the men lying on the pit-heap unconscious, stooped and kissed his boy, and then calmly took his place in the dangling noose, and bade them lower him into the shaft. There was not one of us who would have given sixpence for his life at that moment. That has always seemed to me to have been the bravest deed I ever witnessed.

When Coulson disappointed our fears by coming back to the surface alive he told the awful tale. The obstruction had been at last removed, but 'the pit was foul,' and we knew that it held none but the dead. As I look at the place on this bright July day of 1896, I find it difficult to realise all the horrors of which I was a witness here thirty-four years ago. Yet I can still see the uncoffined dead being brought to bank—twenty hours being occupied in that task alone. I can recall the smile of peace which rested upon every grimy face ; ay, and I recollect the tears with which the brave men who had gone down into the depths of the pit told me of how they had found the victims sitting in long rows side by side, waiting for the help which was to come too late, and of how the fathers had their boys folded in their arms, whilst brothers and friends sat with clasped hands, in patient silence. One slight record of the captivity was left in the shape of a cheap memorandum book, in which one of the prisoners had pencilled a few words telling of the prayer meeting that had been held and the 'exhortation' that had been given in the early hours of their imprisonment. But the record broke off little more than four-and-twenty hours after the closing of the shaft, and we comforted ourselves with the thought that their agony had been brief, as their end was undoubtedly painless. Away yonder stands the grey tower of Earsdon Church, steeped in the summer sunlight. At its foot, in one vast common grave, lie the two hundred men and boys who died thus in the New Hartley Pit in January 1862. I can still see the long procession of coffins being carried between the leafless hedges. I seem to hear again the wail of the old hymn, 'O God, our help in ages past,' which filled the air as the whole manhood of the village of Hartley was borne to the tomb. It is haunted ground, truly, on which I stand ; and I realise afresh not only the perils and heroism of the miner's daily life, but the fact that the man who, after the lapse of a generation, revisits the home of his youth, must of necessity sojourn among ghosts.

WEMYSS REID.

AN ATTEMPT AT OPTIMISM

IT seems at the present moment probable that pessimism and consequent dejection will share the fate of all the pegs on which men have hung their theories since they have begun to think consecutively. They are momentarily in possession of the field; therefore pessimism and its result dejection are made to appear the sufficient cause of masses of phenomena for which they do not really account.

An important consideration seems to be ignored, not only in the easy and cheap form of pessimism to be found as the keynote of books of inferior value, but in some works of real merit. It deals with the necessity of realising, however positive our knowledge, that the margin which extends beyond it is limitless. There is more comfort to be derived from the ' Je ne sais pas ' of Pascal than from the ' Que sais-je ? ' of Montaigne; for in that unknown tract which lies beyond our powers of conception, our imagination can conjure up the possibility of the sudden appearance of a factor, at present undiscovered, which may alter the aspect of the problem so completely as sometimes to appear almost to reverse it.

Instances of this may be shown in the study of, let us say, the science of chemistry, where the qualities of a chemical substance may be altered by combination with a new element. And what of the inexact sciences, medicine for instance, all the greater for being inexact—for where would the sudden inspiration of the great physician come in if he could fall back on exact knowledge? This difficulty is still greater in the scientific study of heredity; with the countless possibilities of unknown and undiscoverable elements making anything like a rigid deduction from the known to the unknown a sheer impossibility. We are confronted here by a double puzzle; since, if deluded for an instant by the belief that we are in possession of undoubted facts unrolling themselves in orderly sequence from generation to generation, we are immediately repulsed by the perception that the effect of peculiar and special surroundings on each agent must modify the problem as a whole and make it more complex than ever. And there are greater mysteries than either of these behind the science of the Psychology or the Pathology of mind. The human brain—its marvellous powers, its dismal failures, its latent and unexplored potentialities—who can fathom it? It is of the utmost importance that men of science should wholly refuse to admit the authority of any hypothesis which cannot be proved; but they are the first to own that they deal only with relative truths subject to the conditions of time, space, and the construction of our own brain.

Mr. Pearson (the author of *National Life*, &c.) says with some justice that science being thus positive in the assertion of the omnipotence and the irrevocableness of law, fatalism and consequent dejection must needs follow—a dejection and horror greater than any produced by the gloom and spiritual fear consequent on a belief in predestination. True, it may be that a knowledge of the laws of heredity and of the subjugating effect of surroundings is sufficient to drive a weak spirit, nay, even a strong one, into an abyss of horror and despair, and to take from it all power of volition. But let us admit for an instant that we have only got hold of a fragment of the whole truth, would it not be wiser, instead of bewailing this, to summon up all the courage we can muster and try fully to grasp that it is not and never can be any more than a fragment; that there is an immense margin of the unknown round the very small nucleus of positive (though relative) knowledge which we have within our reach, for we must accept and be content with incompleteness, as we have no choice in the matter.

All honour, we repeat, to the men of science who guard this relative knowledge and protect it from the inroads of fanciful and unstable reasoning. The wretched attempt to disparage philosophic thought on the laws of evolution, and the desire to ridicule the logical deduction of the inevitableness of the succession of phenomena by demonstrating, as M. Bourget seeks to do in *Le Disciple*, that if a man be an evolutionist he must needs be a villain, a liar, and a profligate, is really an attempt below the line of talent of that very clever author. The consequences of an opinion, philosophic or scientific, are not to be considered for a moment in a serious discussion. It is of no avail to point out that the holder of such an opinion, and they whom he may persuade to hold it, will, by their beliefs or unbeliefs, hasten the decay of all aspirations, all strivings after the ideal. That is not the question, and to bring such considerations into court at all only complicates an already too perplexing and difficult problem. Yet, after doing homage to the relatively true, it is refreshing to return for a moment to the mysterious unknown. It is obvious that to multiply the terms of an equation is not to solve it. If it be true that by means of the telescope and the microscope we have now to apprehend that billions instead of thousands of worlds exist within and yet beyond our ken, infinity and immensity may seem to overwhelm us, but the mystery underlying all remains the same.

The following propositions are indisputable. With our greatest efforts of thought we find that we can get comparatively no distance whatever from the 'here' of space and the 'now' of time, and that the 'present' as a mathematical point appears to be hurrying and bearing us with it along the line stretching from the past to future eternity; but in reality we are no further from the one or nearer to the other. If it is also indisputable that nothing exists as we suppose it to be, that nothing we do or say or think is apparently of any importance—in short, that nothing matters—it is impossible that the human brain should not reel before this sea of uncertainty. The pressure, the sensation of being hemmed in on all sides, by infinities and immensities, until we fail to grasp the position in which we stand in this endless spiral, beginning nowhere, ending nowhere, seems too much for endurance, and our poor powers of thought, if we pursue the investigation, will finally fail us. Has the moment then arrived when pessimism must of necessity be the outcome of such speculations? No; it only means that our ignorance is more profound than we imagined. Do we say nothing matters? It is more true to say that everything matters.

How valueless every thought, word, and deed? Perhaps each is full of infinite meaning and importance. Light and sound never cease vibrating in space, so that these poor thoughts, words, and acts of ours have gone forth never to be lost or recalled. Each day—what a limited thought is conveyed by this form of speech and this division of time—may be filled by an awful sense of mystery and of the poetry of the unknown, and this sense will pursue us in the form most congenial to each personality.

In everyday life we must needs adopt the ways of science and stand courageously by our relative knowledge, and, in homely language, 'do our best' according to the light that is in us; but when weighed down and crushed by the sense of evil apparently incurable and by the incomprehensibility of the most elementary data, it would be well bravely to turn to the other side. Surely the balance is more evenly hung than pessimists would have us think. A single detail in the discussion will show that we cannot go by any foregone conclusion. It seems strange that, as more of life lies behind us and less prospect of joy and happiness before us, while fewer possibilities of enjoyment and appreciation remain to us, so does the force of the optimistic view increase, and it happens that with decreasing powers and diminished energy life becomes brighter. It is a paradox, but, like many other paradoxes, undeniably true. Why is it true? Because things of beauty become more and more precious to those who are no longer young; they gladden the old with a sense of surprise at their own power of appreciation, a power which in youth is often neglected in the hot pursuit of the unattainable and the mad desire for untested experience. The old turn more willingly away than the young from that scale of the balance in which are cruelty, injustice, cowardice, sickness, misery—the whole brood of horrors, in short, that flesh is heir to; they turn more hopefully to that scale in which things of joy and beauty are striving to make their weight be felt, while they yet puzzle the beholder in the attempt to appreciate and to measure them. We look and ponder, and cannot tell how the matter stands, for it is of the very essence of the difficulty that in either scale the controlling power lies in the least distinguishable and most impenetrable elements. In the scale of misery who can calculate the power of the bitter word, of the sweep of disillusion, of the untrustworthiness of affection, of the distrust of self, and, worse than all, of the loss of love? Who, again, can put a just value on the beauty of a rose-leaf, on the smile of a child, on the joy of the poet, of the artist, of the lover, on the passionate tears of admiration wrung from the most hardened by nobleness of conduct, by the small unconscious acts of self-devotion, by the unworldliness of the worldly, by the unselfishness of the selfish, by the tolerance of the intolerant? It is in the appreciation of these almost intangible instances of beauty and ugliness, of good and evil, on either side that we are met by almost insuperable difficulties in making a true estimate. Each scale rises or falls according to the vision of the beholder. All is ephemeral, all is relative—who can tell?

So let us leave the religious man to his mystic dreams, built it may be on the sternest dogmatism, and on a rigidly enforced rule of conduct, yet penetrating far beyond these into the sublime height and depth of the love which passeth all understanding. In considering the unknown and the inexplicable, the cup of cold water, the silent look which lived in St. Peter, will assume proportions they never had before when works were weighed and accounted great or small. Let us likewise leave the man of science to soar into the great ' beyond,' leaving for a time his accurate but relative knowledge, and by means of his 'scientific imagination' to construct theories, build up distinctions which he may never turn to account or ever translate into positive knowledge; for is he not now dealing with poetry and mystery, not with the known but with the unknowable?

Above all, let the puzzled, the ignorant, those who fail in conduct and those who cannot follow or grasp the apparent conviction of the great ones in the intellectual world, deal tenderly with themselves. Let these limited ones, owning humbly their limitations, have their moments of joy in dreams. When they have done their small day's work, let them look into the far blue and rejoice that all is not known even to ' the wise and prudent.'

A poor conclusion some will say; but ' Le Rêve est bon et utile pourvu qu'on le tienne pour ce qu'il est. Souvenez-vous du grand principe de Hegel, " Il faut comprendre l'inintelligible comme tel." '

MARY E. PONSONBY.

SAILING FOR LADIES IN
HIGHLAND LOCHS

SAILING in a fresh or salt water loch which is surrounded on all sides by mountains is a somewhat risky amusement. Yet there is many a summer's day in which the most inexperienced person might learn to sail without any danger by attending to a few simple hints. Unfortunately, when women take up outdoor amusements they seldom pursue them in moderation. If they hunt, they must be in the saddle eight hours a day for six days a week; if they row, they row till they faint; and if they bicycle, they ride till they go off in hysterics. It is not surprising, therefore, that sailing in Highland lochs should be discouraged by fathers and husbands; for the careless management of a sailing-boat, or the attempt to sail at all in squally weather, may mean, not loss of health, but loss of life itself. Still, when the sportsmen are away on the hills, taking with them all the available men to carry their lunch or bring back the game, it seems rather hard that the ladies of the party should have to pass their days in knitting stockings, or walking up and down the one and only road, when they might be spending a most enjoyable afternoon in sailing about the loch.

There is just as great a difference in the pleasure of sailing a boat oneself and being in a boat sailed by some one else as there is between driving a pair of spirited thoroughbreds and sitting in the carriage while the coachman holds the ribands. The one is tame and dull, while the other is exciting and pleasantly dangerous. But I should advise no woman to learn to sail without a practised boatman at her side, unless she has had previously some considerable experience in boating. I do not mean the experience she would acquire by punting or sculling on the Thames in smart clothes, but the rough work she would have to do when boating alone in the Highlands. For instance, she should be nimble and active—able to push a boat off the shore and scramble after it, on to the bows, on one knee; or, when a boat has struck the shallows some feet from dry land, she must slip round the mast without losing her balance, and jump on shore from the bows, rope in hand, so as to pull the boat up after her.

No woman who is naturally awkward ought to be allowed to sail a boat herself, neither should one who has not a strong sense of danger; but she must be strong of arm and cool of head, and she must not mind a knock on the temples from the yard or an occasional blow on the shins from the boom. In short, she must be *hardy* without being *foolhardy*, and brave without being daring.

It is of the utmost importance to have a boat which will not sink under any circumstances, and this is a matter which should not be left to chance; therefore it is better to test it yourself. First put whatever ballast you are going to carry for sailing purposes into your boat, then fill it with water, then stand on the seat. Naturally, you cannot expect a boat full of water to *remain* right way uppermost, because the very first wave would turn it over; but it is something to feel that it will not sink, though the chances of being able to cling to the bottom of a boat in ice-cold water until assistance should arrive are in the highest degree remote.

The boat in which I learnt to sail was built for me in London. It is about ten feet long; light enough for one person to row when sailing is impossible; shallow enough to take within a jump of the shore, and small enough for me to manage entirely alone. So far it has proved perfectly seaworthy, as I have been caught in some terrible storms without being capsized; but I do not consider that it sails as well as it might if it had been made on different lines; however, a first experiment is never quite successful, and I hope that my next boat will be as perfect for sailing as my present one is in all other respects. This boat has a centreboard, copper air-tight compartments round the inside to keep it from sinking, and it is partially decked over. The space between the air-tight compartments and the deck forms a shelf on which cloaks, lunch, and life-jackets can be stowed away, and anything else which is to be kept dry. In ordinary little boats there is no such place, and everything has to be thrown to the bottom, where, besides being in the way, things generally get very wet. The stern seat is double the usual width, and has a raised back, so that with two cushions you can recline luxuriously while sailing. Instead of the ordinary tiller, I had a piece of a young tree bent into a half circle and fixed with wire to the back of the rudder, so as to be able to steer with either hand, or, in a steady high wind, with one elbow leaning on the deck, thus leaving both hands free for managing the sail. The rowlocks have to be extra high in order ·to free the oars from touching the coamings. In some respects my boat is like a rather tubby dinghy, but it is infinitely less rickety, as you can step on one side of it without fear of its slipping away from under you and leaving you in the sea.

In hoisting a simple lugsail no knots are required and none should be used. The gear consists of a fixed mast, and the sail, the top of which is laced to a yard, and the bottom corner tied to a boom (these fastenings are permanent and need never be altered).

Only four ropes are necessary: (1) called a *painter*, to tie the boat to her moorings; (2) called a *halyard*, to haul up the sail; (3) called a *sheet*,[1] which is fixed near the end of the boom. *This rope must never under any circumstances be tied to the boat*; it is either held in the hand or allowed to fall loose. The danger of making fast this rope cannot be too strongly enforced, as half of the accidents to small sailing boats are caused by carelessness on this point. The fourth rope, called the *tack*, fastens the sail to the bottom of the mast. With sculls, rowlocks, baler, rudder, and the centreboard (the latter a fixture), you have everything complete for sailing, with the exception of ballast, and the amount of ballast required to sail a boat to the best advantage, as well as the position in which it should be placed, can only be learnt after long and careful study of the matter.

The ballast used for my boat consists of three or four sacks of small shingle, which I can scarcely lift, and three smaller bags, which can easily be moved from side to side of the boat to keep her from heeling over too much when tacking. Some people might prefer to use heavy stones for ballast instead of sacks of shingle, as these can be pitched overboard to lighten the boat when the wind drops and you have to row.

It is best to learn to sail in a light breeze; and, before attempting to put up your sail, let the boat be well away from the shore, either tied to a buoy, or rope, or floating about loose. If the boat be near the shore, the rudder and centreboard, which should both be in their places ready for a start, may be scraping along the bottom, and possibly damaged, before your sail is set.

The hauling up of the sail is a difficult matter and requires great strength of arm; for, unless it is pulled right up to its proper place, it cannot set without creasing. On a calm day, when you can stand on the seat in the bows and lift up the sail by the yard, it is easy enough; but when a high wind is blowing this is impossible, as the sail envelops you entirely, and the yard bangs you on the head and face till you are stunned and stupefied. I have sometimes felt quite sick after tussling with the sail in a high wind, only to find that, after all, my exertions were in vain, as there was a large crease right across its middle. Before hauling up the sail, it must be hooked on to the halyard (there being a thimble, or eye, on the yard for that purpose), and the short end of the yard should be on the left of the

---

[1] It is a common mistake among those who have had no practical knowledge of sailing to suppose that a *sheet* is another name for a sail, and that the mainsheet is the same as the mainsail. I fancy that Allan Cunningham must have been under the same misapprehension when he wrote the well-known line,

'A wet sheet and a flowing sail,'

as, in former days, buckets of water used to be thrown over certain parts of the sail to make it stand better; but there could be no particular reason for laying stress on a wet rope.

mast. When the sail is up, give the halyard one twist round a cleat you will find at the bottom of the mast on the right side, and then, instead of tying it, pass a loop of the rope between the mast and the halyard just above the cleat, and bring the long end over the seats to the stern. By pulling at this end from your place in the stern, the loop will come out and the sail be let down without your being obliged to leave go of the tiller in the event of a sudden squall coming on.

Having hauled up the sail as far as it will go, you must next hook the end of the boom into a metal loop fixed for that purpose in the centre of the bottom of the mast, and finally lace the *tack*, which is hanging from an eye or loop in the corner of the sail, into the loop on the left side of the bottom of the mast, passing it four or five times backwards and forwards through each loop and pulling it as tight as it will go. Every time you haul up your sail (after letting it down), you will have to loosen this cord several inches, or you will find that you have not the strength to pull the sail up to the proper place again. *The set of the sail depends entirely on the tightness of the halyard and the tightness of the tack.*

The boat is now ready to start ; you loose her from her moorings, and seat yourself rather to the windward side of the stern, then take hold of the sheet and draw in the sail towards you, and thus your first lesson in the art of sailing will commence.

As you draw the sail towards you the boat will begin to move. If she sails along at an even pace, when you have pulled in the sheet till the sail and centre of the boom are above the edge of the lee side of the boat, you may be sure that your ballast is in the right place for sailing up to the wind. If, on the contrary, the head of the boat turns right up to the wind and the sail begins to flap, you must use the rudder to put it off again ; but remember, the more you use the rudder the more drag there will be on the boat to keep her back ; you must therefore try, by altering the position of the ballast—putting it more to the stern, for instance—to get the boat to sail with the smallest possible strain on the rudder.

Now watch the way the wind strikes the sail. The wind should strike the centre of the sail, and if there is the slightest possible shiver or bulge *behind the sail near the mast*, you must use the rudder to put the boat off the wind; that is, if the wind is blowing from the east, you must turn the boat away until the wind strikes the east side of the sail again. If you have a flag at your masthead, it should always blow *behind* the sail. If the flag is blown between you and the sail, there must be wind at the back of the sail, and if the wind blows from the back of the sail, the boat will fail to get the full advantage out of it ; you must therefore draw in the sail nearer to the boat, or else turn the boat away from the wind by the rudder—the pace at which the boat sails will tell you which it is best to do.

Having thoroughly mastered the above instructions by keeping the boat sailing in the same direction till you understand them perfectly, you must now *tack*, or put the bows up to the wind till it strikes the other side of the sail. To do this you must pull in the sheet till the sail is above your head, lifting it over with one hand, at the same time turning the boat with the rudder, and shifting your seat to the other corner of the stern. If the boat fails to come round, or *misses stays* from lack of wind, you must turn her head up to the wind with an oar; but if she fails from bad management, you must let her go back to the old tack and put her a little more off, or away from the wind, with the rudder; she will then have more way on (or sail faster), and that will give her the impetus to send her round up to the wind. In a very light breeze it is sometimes necessary to hold up the boom to make a bag of the sail at the moment of turning, so that the wind may catch it sideways; but under no circumstances is it allowable to turn a boat round *away* from the wind—that is, with her stern to the wind; in calm weather it is unseamanlike and in a storm most dangerous.

You have now been learning how to sail a boat *up to the wind* in a light breeze, and most likely your course has been away from home; to return home it will not be necessary to tack at all, as you will be *running before the wind,* and to do this you sit nearly in the centre of the stern, put your ballast aft—*i.e.* to the stern—and gradually let out the sheet till the boom is almost at right angles with the boat. Though it does not need as much skill to run before the wind as it does to sail up to the wind, it requires even more caution; for, if a puff of wind suddenly catches the sail from behind—a most common occurrence in Highland lochs—the sail will *gybe* without any warning, and, even if the boat is not capsized, you may easily be thrown out by the unexpected jerk, from one side to the other, of the sail. The only way to avoid this is by carefully watching the sail, and if the boom begins to fly upwards you must be ready to catch it in your hand as it passes over your head, or else you must catch the sheet close to the boom and let the sail out gradually. In a light wind this is not a difficult matter, but when the wind is high and gusty you have not a moment's security when running before it, though the sensation of rushing through the water with the waves curling after you is most delightful, and the distance it has taken you a long time to traverse when tacking is all too short when flying before the wind.

A boat should not sail on an even keel, but should have a slight list to leeward—the side on which the sail is. Some sailing boats are intended to *lie over* more than others, but it is always safer for a beginner to keep the boat pretty upright; nothing, however, looks worse than to see a boat with a list to *windward*.

If you wish to land on a shore towards which the wind is blowing, you must take down your sail in deep water, and get to the bows with an oar in your hand ready to keep the boat from striking on the rocks before you jump out and pull it up. Remember to push a boat off or on shore with the butt end of the scull, or you will soon split and spoil the blade against sharp stones.

If you wish to land at a pier, you must sail some yards to the right or left of it, and then turn the boat round till the bows are towards the wind, when the sail will flap, and the boat gradually stop. If she overshoots the mark, let her sail round again till you are near enough to hold on to the pier. Nothing but experience can teach you how much to allow for the ' way ' a boat will have on her when turned up to the wind, as it varies with the strength of the wind. In stormy weather it is better to take down the sail and use the oars rather than to run the risk of knocking the varnish off your boat against the pier.

I have now given a few hints about sailing and landing in fair weather; the next thing to be considered is what to do in a small boat in stormy weather. In the first place, see that she has no water in her when you start, for water rushing from side to side at the bottom of a boat will help to turn her over. Then, every time a squall comes up let out the sheet so that the wind does not strike the sail so hard; and, at the same time, let the head of the boat go up to the wind. It is difficult to do this in a small, short boat without losing way, but it *has to be done*. Sometimes you can see a squall coming towards you and beating down the waves on its course; to be prepared for it you must turn the boat *away* from it, to get more way on her, for the wind always slacks suddenly before a squall, and then, as the wind strikes it, let her head come up and loose the sheet out. If you were not to turn a short boat away from the wind before a squall, she would be standing still when the wind struck her, and, most likely, capsize.

From my own experience I should say it is never safe for a lady to go out sailing by herself after the 1st of October, nor do I consider it safe to sail in a *cross* wind or a *north* wind. If the wind blows up or down the loch, you can judge more or less of its strength, and go out or stay at home accordingly; but a cross wind will blow down from the tops of the mountains, and it will strike the sail before it strikes the boat, and probably turn it over before it has way on. If there is a dead calm underneath the shore and a line of blue waves with ominous white edges across the loch, you had better stay at home, especially if the tide be against the wind, which makes the sea choppy.

That October is a treacherous month for sailing I have good reason to remember, as will be seen from the following experiences. On the 1st of October last year I was anxious to try some experiments with the ballast in my boat. It was like a summer's morning, with a hot air just ruffling the surface of the loch. It sufficed, however, for my purpose. In the afternoon I intended sailing over the loch to meet a friend. The wind had risen, and I had a long tussle with the sail, and was quite exhausted by the time I had hauled it up and tied it down. As I let go the moorings the wind dropped, and I found myself almost aground with the rudder scraping the shingle. However, I just managed to keep off the shore without using the oars till the next gust, when I got away clear of the pier. A fresh breeze soon sprang up, and I had a nice sail across the loch. Finding that the train by which I expected my friend was an hour late, I decided to sail across again, and, by the merest chance, I picked up the keeper and took him with me. Before we got to the middle of the loch a squall struck the boat and deluged us with spray, while the waves rushed down and off the deck. The boat was completely on one side in spite of the extra weight, and I was glad indeed to have some one with me to look after the sail whilst I steered. *I did not return to fetch my friend.*

One instance will be sufficient to exemplify the uncertainty of October weather. Last season my little boat was towed some seven or eight miles out to the open sea by a steam yacht. It was a glorious day, and the sun shone brilliantly. There was only the faintest ripple on the surface of the water, but before leaving the yacht to set sail in my boat I took the precaution to ask the skipper what I was to do in case the wind should get up. He pointed to some rocky islands to the north—my destination being west—and told me to steer in their direction.

Long before the yacht was out of sight the breeze had died away, and I had to take to the oars. I did not particularly enjoy the idea of having to row several miles in a boat which had been heavily weighted for sailing, but, as it is always pleasant to be on the water in the midst of beautiful scenery, I paddled contentedly along, and amused myself by watching the little black and white razor-bills as they appeared and disappeared round me—popping now a head and now a tail out of the sea—and wondering at the marvellous size of the seagulls, which looked like fleets of white-sailed yachts on the opal surface of the water.

Presently a little breeze sprang up, and I took hold of the sheet, leaving the sculls in the rowlocks. In another minute it was blowing half a gale. I had no time to put the oars away, change the ballast, or make any other preparations; the storm was upon me, and for miles and miles I fought against wind and waves, not knowing from one instant to another whether the boat could live in such a sea or not. I kept her head towards the islands, but it was like a pivot—never still a second. Every time a squall struck the boat the bows turned up to the wind; then, as it heeled too far over, I had to loose the sheet; next I had to leave go of the tiller and use both hands to haul in the sheet; besides this the bows had to be turned up to meet every big wave, and a little away, when there was something of a lull, to keep in the right course—for the gale was from the north-east, and the islands were to the north; then the tiller had again to be left so that I might make a grab at the oars to get them inside the boat, where they were continually rolling into my way; and all this time the gale kept on increasing in violence, while the waves got bigger and bigger and rushed along the deck, but fortunately were kept out of the boat by the coamings. At length, after a severe struggle, I found myself to leeward of the islands, and here my instructions ended; so, not knowing in the least whether it was wrong or right, or would be safer or more dangerous, I let out the sail, turned the head of the boat further away from the wind, and steered for a rocky shore about a mile off. The boat now simply flew along, accompanied on its course by big waves which rushed beside it and behind it. The strain both on the boat and on my own mind and body was less than when sailing up to the wind, but I doubt if the danger was any the less. However, I arrived in due course under a precipitous coast where there was no possibility of landing, and no wind, but plenty of swell, which tried to heave the boat against the cliff. I stayed here for some little time—not from choice, but because I could not get away; and I was obliged in the end to row out into the wind again, and sail before it for another mile or so, under a lee shore; till at length, battered and broken in spirit, I was picked up by the yacht, which had steamed back to look for me.

It was the worst storm we had ever been out in. The water dashed over the deck of the steam yacht and poured down into the cabin; and, long before we reached home, my poor little boat, which was being towed behind, had filled, and when the yacht was stopping rather suddenly in a sheltered place, the water rushed from the stern to the bows, and it turned bottom upwards!

I have said enough to show that sailing in the late autumn is not a very safe amusement for ladies, but not too much, I hope, to deter them from enjoying many a pleasant day on the water earlier in the season. Even then I should advise them to run no needless risks, for I do not much believe in the chances of escape from drowning when riding on the bottom of a capsized boat. An ordinary pocket handkerchief will sink when dropped into the sea, and heavy woollen clothes would drag one under like so much lead. Besides this, the water is ice-cold, and every wave would wash over one; how, then, could anybody expect to cling for hours to a slippery boat while waiting for the chance of being seen and rescued?

A word now about dress. Sailing is cold work. Have woollen gloves with leather inside the palms and fingers, or the ropes will soon cut them to pieces, and be sure to put them on *before you start*, or you may find you are unable to do so until you land again, both hands being always occupied with managing the sail and helm. It is useful to have a macintosh within reach in case of a sudden shower, or to put over your knees when the tidal waves are against the wind and the spray dashes over you. I have a loose jacket of the water-proof material used in the navy, and a skirt of the same stuff, made to fasten with three or four large buttons up one side. I often use the skirt as a cloak, either for warmth or when rain comes down unexpectedly, as it can be thrown on in an instant.

One word more. In sailing, as in other outdoor pursuits, you must take the rough with the smooth. Unfortunately, when the rough comes one cannot really be prepared for it, as nothing but experience will show how much of wind and waves a little boat can stand without capsizing. Nor does the presence of a professional sailor teach one much, as a boat behaves differently with an extra top-weight to what it does when one person is alone in it with all the ballast at the bottom. There is, I think, only one way to learn to sail in a high wind with any safety, and that is by having a steam yacht in close attendance. I tried this once with a little 9-ft. canvas boat, in which another lady and myself sailed for about four miles before the wind, at the commencement of a gale, in order to see how it would behave. And it behaved wonderfully well, bobbing over the tops of the waves like a cork, and never shipping a drop of water; but I believe that its appearance to our escort on board the steam launch was ridiculous in the extreme.

When steam is not within hail in the event of an accident, I cannot too strongly impress upon my readers the danger of sailing in stormy weather. Let them be satisfied with a gentle, steady breeze, and if it is inclined to be squally, let them stay at home, for it is far better to be over-cautious than it is to be too venturesome.

CAROLINE CREYKE.

JOHN STUART MILL

ALMOST a generation has passed since a most strenuous and magnanimous spirit was laid to rest in the cemetery of Avignon along
the Rhone. In that majestic and melancholy spot, beneath dark
pines and beside his beloved wife, lies John Stuart Mill, one of the
most intense workers, one of the most upright spirits of our age.
The age itself, we must admit, has been flowing on, like the Rhone
to the sea, and has left the philosopher at peace in his distant grave.
His work was completed, he himself said with his dying breath; and
his most devoted friends will not dare to claim for him the influence
and the reputation he undoubtedly possessed some thirty years ago.
They are few to-day who will re-echo quite literally all that John
Morley said in the two fine pieces written on the death of Mill in
1873, now to be read in the third volume of his *Miscellanies*. His
tribute, if deepened into rare passion and pathos by the unexpected
loss of a friend and master, was substantially just and true. He did
not say too much when he wrote: 'A strong and pure light is gone
out, the radiance of a clear vision and a beneficent purpose;' 'We
have lost a great teacher and example of knowledge and virtue.'

It is, however, obvious that the influence of John Stuart Mill has
been waning in the present generation. They who would use the
language just cited are not so many as they were, nor are they themselves in so strong a force. It was said at the time of his death that
with the reputation of Mill would stand or fall the reputation of
a whole generation of Englishmen. Something of that kind has
already happened. The young lions of to-day, whether in politics,
literature, or philosophy, are very far from caring much for what was
said 'by them of old time,' *i.e.* in the early manhood of their own
fathers. Their motto is, ἡμεῖς μὲν πατέρων μέγ᾽ ἀμύμονες εὐχόμεθ᾽
εἶναι. They are not familiar with the reputations of the last generation, and are apt to wonder how these were made. If the reputation
of Mill has waned, the reputation of a whole school of leading minds
of his generation has waned also. It was the dominant school of the
'sixties': it is dominant no more.

For this reason it is much to be wished that John Morley would
now give us that estimate of Mill which in 1873 he said would one

day have to be made, and that *Life* which we have so long awaited. But since he is otherwise employed (alas! for letters, alas! for philosophy), a few words may be permitted to tell the younger generation wherein lay the influence over us elders of Mill's character and mind some thirty years ago. For my own part, I can pretend to none of the qualifications which so eminently meet in Mr. Morley. Though I knew Mill in the later years of his life, I could not in any sense lay claim to his intimacy. With very deep respect for him, I was in no way his disciple. My own education, habits, tastes, and temperament were so utterly different from his as to awaken in me the interest of contrast and surprise. I felt, and I still feel, vehement aversion to some of Mill's cherished ideals and doctrines. And so far from his being my master, he has attacked my own master with unsparing, and I hold unjust, criticism in an important volume. I can, therefore, pretend to no claim to speak of him except it may be some knowledge of his life, nature, and writings; a deep reverence for his noble qualities; and, I think, a sympathetic, but real, impartiality of mind.

These few pages will, of course, not admit of any proper criticism of Mill's philosophy, social and moral teaching, or his political theories, much less any estimate of his character, example, and life. To attempt such a task would be to compile a treatise on Logic, another on Political Economy, a third on Ethic, a fourth on Politics, to say nothing of Metaphysics, Natural Theology, and Positivism. No such high aim is mine. We shall have this in good time, we all trust, when Unionists and Nationalists, Imperialists and Englishmen shall have lain down together at last. In the meantime, I wish to say a few words (*caret quia vate sacro*) as to the influence of John Stuart Mill upon his own generation—what of it is left and is destined to remain—what of it lies silent beneath the pine trees and cypresses at Avignon—into what form some of the best of it has matured.

Those who are familiar with the sermon on the death of Mill I have cited, will remember how deeply it is charged with enthusiasm for the character of the man, more than with praise of the work of the teacher. It is, perhaps, not easy for those who did not personally know him to do justice to all that was great and good in Mill's nature. By education and by temperament alike he was one of the most reserved and self-contained of men, formally and externally not very sympathetic, a Stoic by birth and training, cramped from childhood by an unnatural and almost inhuman type of discipline, a man to whom the ordinary amusements, humours, and passions of life were as utterly unknown as were its follies and its vices. His punctilious courtesy was such as to seem somewhat pedagogic to the ordinary man of the world; as his generosity was so methodically rational as to seem almost ungracious to the idle good fellow. Infinitely patient, just, tolerant as he was, he was always dominated by the desire to strike the balance of right and wrong, of the weight of evidence, the force of argument, *pro* and *contra* every act under observation and every proposition that he heard. This produced on the ordinary and casual observer an impression of pedantic formalism most undeserved by a nature that was the very soul of compassion, benevolence, and honour. As his books are curiously devoid of anything like literary grace or mastery of the 'pathetic fallacy,' the ordinary reader does not easily perceive how much enthusiasm, what magnanimity, what tenderness underlies the precise statements even of such pieces as the *Autobiography*, the *Subjection of Women*, and *Liberty* : pieces which are red-hot within with affection, pity, and passion. Some of us were always more attracted by Mill's character than by his intellect : we rated his heart above his brain : and his failures seemed to us mental, not moral perversities. But of his fine and exemplary nature it is indeed needless for me to speak. It has had full justice done to it by John Morley, who has so well placed Mill's distinction in the 'union of stern science with infinite aspiration, of rigorous sense of what is real and practicable with bright and luminous hope.' We listened to him just because we found in him a most systematic intellect in a truly great heart.

It must always be borne in mind that Mill essentially belonged to a school, that he was peculiarly the product of a very marked order of English thinkers, and gave their ideas a new development. Coleridge, Carlyle, Ruskin, can hardly be said to have been either the sons or the founders of any school of thought. John Mill was a singularly systematic product of a singularly systematic school of philosophers. And he was himself at one time the recognised head of a group of men of a more or less kindred type, with more or less similar aims in mental and social science. Locke, Hume, Adam Smith, Bentham, Malthus, James Mill, Austin, Grote, Bowring, Roebuck, the philosophic Radicals of the first Reform era, maintained a real filiation of central ideas which reached their complete general systematisation in the earlier writings of John Stuart Mill. He in turn worked on general lines with Professor Bain, T. Hare, G. H. Lewes, Professor Cairnes, W. E. Forster, and Henry Fawcett. John Morley and Leonard Courtney still maintain erect the standard of their former chief. And Herbert Spencer, building on an analogous general ground-plan, has raised a yet more encyclopædic system of his own.

John Morley hardly over-stated the intellectual authority of Mill when he wrote, in 1873, that the leading men of that day bore traces of his influence, whether as disciples or as opponents. The universities (he said), journalism, popular reading, and foreign opinion concurred in the same testimony. Mill held, moreover, a very unusual position —at once head of a school of philosophy, and also a most active social reformer, a politician of mark, and the inspirer of many practical movements, moral, economic, or religious. Hume, Adam Smith,

Carlyle, Spencer, have each poured forth very pregnant ideas upon
social problems : but they did not discuss Bills in Parliament or found
Leagues. It was the essence of John Stuart Mill, which he inherited
with his Benthamite blood and his Utilitarian nurture, to unite ' stern
science with infinite aspiration,' to regard social philosophy as the
instrument of social regeneration. If he was far more the philosopher
than Bentham, he was quite as much as Bentham the social reformer
—far more than was any other follower of Bentham and his school.
Mill indeed was a compound of Bentham corrected by the ideals and
thinkers of modern France, especially by Auguste Comte.

Those who admit that the influence of Mill has been waning in
the last generation have also to admit that the whole school of thought
which came to its flower in Mill has been waning also in the same
time and for the same cause. John Mill is not to-day what he was
a generation ago, because Utilitarianism, Benthamism, Political
Economy, Radicalism, the Philosophy of experience, moral and social
Utopias have somewhat gone out of fashion. It is rather the school
than the man which has lost vogue. It is not so much Mill as
social science, which ceases to absorb the best of the rising generation. We live in an age of reversion to more early types—theologico-
metaphysico-dilemmas—and aristocratic incarnations of the beautiful, the wise, and the good. To-day our aspirations are imperial,
our *summum bonum* is national glory. War, armaments, athletic
triumphs fill the souls of our patriotic and heroic youth. Philosophy
retires into a higher region of mist and invisibility. Philosophy
must wait and possess its soul in peace.

If the larger doctrinal treatises of Mill have a wider teaching
power, his distinctive ideas and the keynote of his mind and nature
are to be found rather in the three short popular essays to which he
gave his whole soul in later life, and whereon he placed his chief
claim to leadership. These are *Liberty* (1859), *Utilitarianism*
(1863), and *The Subjection of Women* (1869). They are all sum-
maries of his beliefs, manifestoes, appeals, almost sermons in their
inward fervour, addressed to the people, condensed and published in
sternly popular form. To reach the essence of Mills's nature and
influence we must always go straight to these short but typical
works of his mellow and widowed age.

The literary history of the *Liberty* has no small interest. It was
planned and written as an essay in 1855 ; in the following year, he
tells us, whilst mounting the steps of the Capitol at Rome, he
conceived (like Gibbon) the idea of making it a book. For two
years his wife and he worked at it, writing it twice over, and then
revising every sentence separately and criticising it with their joint
labour. After years of thought it is published with a magnificent
dedication to his dead wife as part author of the work, inspired ' by
her all but unrivalled wisdom.' And it may be bought, in sixty-

eight pages, for sixteen-pence, in which form it has found an immense circulation. None of his writings, he says, have been so carefully composed or so sedulously corrected; and he believes it destined to survive longer than anything else that he has written, with the possible exception of the *Logic.* It is designed to be, in his own words, ' a philosophic text-book of a single truth': 'the importance, to man and society, of a large variety in types of character, and of giving full freedom to human nature to expand itself in innumerable and conflicting directions.' But this ' single truth' covers the whole field of the relation of the individual to society, *i.e.* Ethic, Sociology, Education, Politics, Law, Manners, and Religion. It was, therefore, not strange that a code of maxims thereon should absorb the thoughts of two thinkers for many years, and, when formulated with a sort of stern passion, should strike fire¬ in some millions of brains.

The ' simple principle' on which the *Liberty* expends so deep a passion and so much logic is this: that self-protection is the sole end for which society is warranted in interfering with the liberty of action of the individual. This principle is *absolute*, and includes all intervention, physical force, or moral coercion. The independence of the individual is absolute, of right, implies the sovereignty of the individual over his own mind and body. The only part of his conduct for which he is amenable to society is that which concerns others. And this liberty includes liberty of conscience, liberty of tastes and pursuits, liberty of combination. No society can be called free in which freedom in all these forms does not exist, absolute and unqualified. On this great theme John Mill has composed a truly monumental manual of acute and impressive thoughts.

It would be futile to attempt in these few pages either a defence or a criticism of these far-reaching dogmas. The only purpose of this slight essay is to consider how far the book of Mill impressed his own age, and how far it can be said to have a growing or permanent influence. It is certain that the little book produced a profound impression on contemporary thought, and had an extraordinary success with the public. It has been read by hundreds of thousands, and, to some of the most vigorous and most conscientious spirits amongst us, it became a sort of gospel—much as for a time did Rousseau's *Social Contract* or Bentham's *Principles of Legislation.* It was the code of many thoughtful writers and several influential politicians. It undoubtedly contributed to the practical programmes of Liberals and Radicals for the generation that saw its birth; and the statute book bears many traces of its influence over the sphere and duties of government. But in the present generation, or broadly speaking, since the great Franco-German war, that influence has been waning, and is now at its lowest point. The book is still read, it is still admired, it has not been refuted or superseded. But much of it is accepted to-day as truth needing no argument; much of it is regarded as quite outside of modern conditions; and a good deal of it is condemned as contrary to all the movements and aspirations of the newer schools of social reform. Why is this: and what are the parts of the book to which these remarks may apply?

The second chapter, on 'Liberty of Thought and Discussion,' is a masterpiece of wise and generous pleading for toleration in opinion, freedom of speech, and liberty of conscience. On such a topic it is impossible to be original; but it condenses, with a mastery of touch and a measured passion, all the best that has ever been said in defence of freedom of opinion, and will stand beside the *Areopagitica* as one of the classics thereon. Few of us are still so much in love with Debate as to share in Mill's exaggeration of the moral and mental value of discussion itself, so that he seems to think that Truth must languish if it were not constantly opposed to the counter-stimulation of some *advocatus Falsi*. But Mill would not be himself if he did not exaggerate the value of discussion. Yet the argument is lighted up with so much moral enthusiasm, and (what is so rare in Mill) with so much eloquence, that we easily pass over its defects. This chapter also has that typical example of free speech in the concrete—the daring and somewhat unjust arraignment of Christian morality. But even those who are forced to dissent from many of its arguments and conclusions will agree with Professor Bain that 'it stands as the chief text-book on Freedom of Discussion.'

The third chapter is an ardent plea for *individuality* as an element of well-being, and it is that part of the book which makes it a sort of Gospel to many a brave and honest soul. No one can gainsay the manly enthusiasm and convincing logic which rings in every passage. No one outside a Jesuit seminary is ever heard to maintain the contrary: but the eloquent and reasoned justification of individuality as the essential basis of civilisation does certainly give a moral stamina to life, and many a man will echo Charles Kingsley's words, that it made him 'a clearer-headed, braver-minded man on the spot.' The question still remains, whether there has been visible of late any waning of individuality in our country or in Europe: is there any real danger of its being undervalued? Is it true that 'the danger which threatens human nature is *the deficiency of personal impulses and preferences*'? There are undoubtedly many molluscous and sheepish natures which show such deficiency. There always have been, and there always will be; and if anything can make men of them, such a warning as that of Mill on *Liberty* ought to rouse them. But a cool review of the facts, after the thirty-eight years that have passed since this appalling prophecy was made, compels us to doubt if any such danger now 'threatens human nature'—to doubt if the last generation showed any want of 'individuality'—if 'individuality' has been growing weaker amongst us in the present generation. A very strong and growing opinion to-day is that we are still rather overstocked with 'the sovereignty of the individual.'

It is when we come to the fourth chapter—'The limits of the authority of society over the individual'—that the breach grows widest between Mill's absolute individualism and the current of contemporary thought. The steady tendency of opinion and of policy in the last generation has been to strengthen the authority of society over individuals. Though it is only a jest to say that 'we are all Socialists now,' it is quite true that recent opinion and legislation have shown evidence of a socialist bias. Mill laid it down as an axiom 'that society has now got the better of the individual.' But the dominant, and I will add the best, ideals of our time tend still further to assist society in getting the better of the individual. Indeed, the book on *Liberty*, so far from helping to curb the authority of society and limit its range, coincided with a very strong lift throughout the whole of society, from top to bottom, to make the authority of society more stringent and more ample. The old legal saw ran : ' It is the part of a good judge to enlarge his jurisdiction.' The political maxim to day more nearly runs thus : ' It is the part of the wise legislator to enlarge the authority of law.' And whatever be the errors of detail, most thoughtful and patriotic citizens are not dissatisfied with the general spirit of the rule.

It does not at all follow that Mill's protests in the central chapter of his book are unnecessary or mischievous. His general propositions are far too absolute and doctrinaire ; but his practical warnings are invaluable, and his concrete examples of State meddling and muddling are full of sense and point. Thousands of social reformers and scores of politicians are every day clamouring amongst us for repressive legislation, of which Mill expounds all the folly and mischief. Nearly all the examples he gives in the chapter on the *Limits of Authority* and in the chapter on *Applications* may be gratefully accepted as contributions to political philosophy, by those who very much object to Mill's general doctrines of non-intervention by society as absolute and rigid axioms. Even they must see how many things are wise, how many are noble, how many are inspiring in this memorable and sagacious book.

The real weakness of the book, the cause of the aversion it inspires in so many minds, lies in its ultra-absolute dogmatism and its violent exaggeration of individualism. Mill's canons as to State intervention are stated with the rigid generality of mathematical axioms. His propositions bristle with such words as 'absolute,' 'unqualified,' ' of right,' ' sovereignty,' ' independence.' Now, the science of politics abhors any 'absolute,' ' unqualified ' rule : it uses 'right,' 'sovereignty,' ' independence ' only in a legal or else in a metaphorical way, never as constituting a rigid social law. Mill is far too deeply versed in the history of sociology and jurisprudence to appeal to ' rights ' with the reckless sophistry of so many metaphysicians. But when he speaks of a thing as 'not warranted,' as being 'of right,' or 'not rightfully,' he is appealing to a theory of right. But we know now that sound principles of social organisation cannot be founded upon 'rights' exclusively. 'Rights' are primarily what the law will secure for each, and secondarily, what each may think himself worthy to receive—an idea on which no doctrine can be framed. At bottom, the book on *Liberty* is an attempt to ascertain what are the 'rights' of the individual against the State. We know that this is like asking what are the 'rights' of the stomach against the body?

An even more fundamental fallacy is the way in which 'Society' and 'the State' are used almost as if they were interchangeable terms; and there is a want of steady distinguishing between these two throughout the argument. The true problem is, not 'what are the limits of the authority of Society over the Individual?' but 'what are the respective limits of State Legislation and Social Opinion?' The essence of Social Science is to determine the respective provinces of Law, Force, Government on the one side, and of Public Opinion, Social Morality, Religious Discipline on the other side. The progress of civilisation means the restriction of the former power, and the correlative enlargement of the latter power: the transfer of control over individuals from Law to Opinion. As the poet says:

Molto è licito là che qui non lece.

Most thoughtful men agree with the practical examples that Mill gives us of the evils of legislative meddling. But they are not at all willing to bind the legislative power within absolute and cast-iron bonds. There are no absolute and immutable limits: it is a practical problem, to be determined for different societies and various occasions in tentative ways, by skilled statesmen, as Aristotle says, ὡς ὁ φρόνιμος ὁρίζει—*i.e.* as practical sagacity may suggest.

Most of us to-day deeply revolt against the arbitrary dogma—that the only part of conduct for which one is amenable to society is that which concerns others; that, as to what concerns oneself, the individual is sovereign. That may be the practical limit of legislation, but it is no absolute bar to moral and social influence. If a man chooses to be a sot, a hog, a savage, it is the bounden duty of his fellow men to bring the whole pressure of society to bear on him; of '*society*,' we say, not necessarily of *law*: that is a question for experts, or statesmen. What 'part of conduct' concerns the individual merely and does not concern others? No part whatever. 'Conduct' is *ex hypothesi* a social act. No man's life is, or can be, solitary. The whole of 'conduct' concerns society, concerns others; for human life simply means a continual action upon, and reaction from our fellow beings. 'We are all members one of another,' said the greatest of religious teachers. And the strength of all religions has lain in their bringing home to the believer the continuous and inevitable relation of every act and thought of the individual soul to the great Power which he believes to represent the sum of things and men around him. Nor can any Gospel look to supersede the old Gospels of theology, unless it will base itself on the organic unity of the Individual and of Humanity, and discard vain dreams about the isolated autonomy of the *auto-man*.

What does 'the individual' mean? It is no doubt a physical, mechanical, and biological fact. It is a convenient term of logic, and is useful as an abstract idea for purposes of analysis or classification. But in sociology there never was, is not, nor can be, any absolute 'individual' in real life, as a normal human being living a complete and continuous human life. In social science, an 'individual' is a term of art, not a substantive organism, just as we may speak of the 'nervous system,' or 'the digestive apparatus' in anatomy, or the 'vertebrate series' in physiology. We cannot find, or even imagine, any 'nervous system,' or 'digestive apparatus,' living and continuously in function in a normal way, whilst being absolutely isolated from the rest of the organism, 'sovereign over itself,' and rigidly absorbed in what 'merely concerns itself.' So, in social science, we cannot find, we cannot imagine, an 'individual,' living a complete and continuous human life, as an individual. Living men and women are, and always must be, organic members of a social system. Any social philosophy founded upon 'individuals' as such, is founded not on real facts and living beings, as we find them and know them, but upon mental abstractions, that is, upon postulates, not on realities. Of course we can temporarily get individuals isolated, just as we can dissect out a nerve, or even a cell, but these isolated individuals can no more function normally as men and women than can the dissected nerve or cell.

To talk, in social science, about the 'rights of individuals,' or the separate life of individuals, or the independence of individuals, or the conduct that solely concerns the individual, unless we are using these terms as convenient hypotheses of abstract analysis, not as real, permanent, substantive facts of nature, is as incoherent as to talk of 'the rights' of the nervous system, or the separate life of a detached nerve or organ in the dissected body. In social science, the smallest substantive organism of which society is composed is the Family, not the Individual. A Family, as such, has a rudimentary organic life of its own, but an Individual has not. A Family on an isolated island can conceivably continue a normal, but very low, type of human life, physical, moral, intellectual, and progressive, and can transmit somewhat that can be called the germs of human civilisation from generation to generation. An Individual cannot do this, and therefore is not, normally speaking, *man* at all. The unit of society is the Family, not the Individual, which is an abstract artifice of analytic classification. And the social science which starts with Individuals, not with Families, is based on a radical sophism. It is this fundamental error which vitiates Mill's book on *Liberty*, and vitiates indeed the whole scheme of Mill's Social Philosophy.

In the 'Introduction' to the *Liberty* Mill does make some reference to the difficulty that whatever affects the individual may *indirectly* affect society, and he promises to meet this objection in the sequel. But he entirely fails to meet it, and he states the difficulty itself far too slightly. The attempt to distinguish between conduct which concerns oneself, and conduct that may remotely concern others, is quite fallacious. No distinction can be drawn, for human acts are organically inseparable. Not only *may* the conduct of the individual, as concerns himself, affect others, but it *must* affect them—the individual never can know when, or how, or whom it will affect. The belly might as well say to the brain, 'What can it matter to you what I take?' as the individual can say to his family, or even to his countrymen, 'What can it matter to you what I eat or drink?' Society does not indeed possess the all-seeing Eye which the Christian believes to penetrate the most secret thoughts or acts; but it has quite as real an interest in those thoughts and acts, and they far more intimately concern its own well-being.

The book on *Liberty*, from beginning to end, is an invaluable text-book for the legislator, for the politician, for the social reformer; and its powerful protest against all forms of over-legislation, intolerance, and the tyranny of majorities, is rich with perennial wisdom and noble manliness. But as a piece of social philosophy it is based upon a sophism as radical as that of Rousseau himself, with his assumption of a primordial Contract. And, if these absolute dogmas as to 'the sovereignty of the individual' against even the moral coercion of his fellow-citizens were literally enforced, there would be a bar put to the moral and religious development of civilised communities. Mill has left it exceedingly vague what is the line that he draws between the 'persuasion,' exhortation, instruction, and apparently even the boycotting, which he admits, and the 'moral coercion of public opinion,' which he regards as iniquitous. As in the famous trades-union cases, it seems to be left to the temper of the judge to decide where 'persuasion' ends and 'moral coercion' begins. The real *crux*, in the problem of individual liberty, as in that of 'picketing,' is to decide where lawful 'persuasion' becomes wrongful 'coercion.' And this part of the problem Mill has left uncertain and vague. To many of us, 'moral coercion,' of a wise and guarded sort, may become a great engine of progressive civilisation.

Not only is the language of the *Liberty* somewhat vague in defining the respective limits of 'persuasion' and 'coercion,' but the practical illustrations of lawful restrictions by the State seem at times hardly consistent with so absolute a doctrine. It is somewhat startling, after such trenchant assertion of the absolute freedom of the individual, to find a defence of the Malthusian laws of some continental States, which forbid the marriage of needy adults. The vehement language against the 'mischievous act' of poor persons in breeding sounds strangely in the mouth of an apostle of freedom. And it is even more startling to find it preceded by an elaborate plea for '*the duty of enforcing universal education*,' the instrument being public examinations, extending to all children, and beginning at an early age, the parent being punished if the child fails to pass. Here is indeed a Chinese tyranny of an ominous kind, which is hard to reconcile with the absolute freedom of the citizen. Many of us from the first protested against State compulsion even in the sacred cause of education, and we see the results of it to-day. *Hinc illæ lacrymæ—illæ iræ—illæ rixæ*—which resound in our midst. The result of forcing children into school, cramming them for mechanical examination, and fining the parent, has proved to be a source of religious bitterness, and the disorganisation of our public education.

The root error of ancient States, according to Mill, was in their belief ' that the State had a deep interest in the whole bodily and mental discipline of every one of its citizens.' It is quite true that the codes of the ancient commonwealths erred in a monstrous amount of over-legislation—(*Mulieres genas ne radunto*, XII Tab.)—which culminated in Plato's Utopian Republic. This primitive error Mill would meet by the dogma that the Individual, and not the State, is sovereign over all that concerns himself alone. The correction is as sophistical and as mischievous as the original dogma. The error of the ancient legislators lay in their extravagant idea of the State. Put the term Society for State, and the doctrine is right. Society has a deep interest in the whole bodily and mental discipline of every one of its citizens : though it is but a small part of that discipline which the magistrate can enforce or laws prescribe, and but a part of it which even Society can control. How to distinguish the one from the other is the great problem of Polity, of Ethic, of Religion. And that problem Mill has not solved, in spite of all the wise warnings he impresses on the legislator, and all the courageous and inspiring virtue that breathes throughout his essay.

The little treatise on *Utilitarianism* was also a compact manual of Mill's ethical system, elaborated for years and diligently revised. It was begun in 1854, recast and finally published in 1861–63. It contains a wonderful amount of thought ; it has had a great influence ; and has met with incessant criticism and comment. It remains, after all deductions and corrections made, far the most ample and rational text-book of the principle of Greatest Happiness as the foundation of Ethic. It is better reasoned, more fully developed, more enlightening and ennobling than anything produced by Bentham and his school. If it had been wholly detached from the formulas and associations of

Bentham, if its type of social morality had been worked out in ampler forms and made its central doctrine, if it had been more purely Mill's own work, and if he had gone on to define and expound his own doctrine of Happiness—perhaps, if it had borne another title—it would have been the most important and effective piece that Mill ever produced.

The worst thing about it is its name—the term which Mill himself adopted in order to describe the Benthamite principle of the greatest Happiness of the greatest number. In spite of all that Bentham, Mill, and their followers have said, the ordinary man will continue perversely to associate *Utility* with *Expediency*, with self-interest, with material value, with practical commodities. It is ignorant, unfair, uncandid to do so—but it is human nature. It must be admitted that *Utilitarianism* is a very awkward term to describe the pursuit of the highest welfare of mankind ; to mean indeed what has been happily called—The Service of Man ; and to include all the devotion of self to others that we may find in the lives of Alfred, or Washington—nay, we must add of Socrates, St. Paul, or Christ. Can these be the types of utilitarian morality ?

In substance, Mill's book is a plea for Ethic as being a demonstrable science founded on analysis and experience of man as a social being eminently adapted to social development. When he says that actions are right in proportion as they tend to promote Happiness, and that by Happiness he means Pleasure, he makes it clear in the sequel that he really intends to say, that Happiness, in the best sense, is the general and purest welfare of Mankind, and that Pleasure, in the true and highest degree, is the satisfaction of man's best instincts of Benevolence and Devotion. So understood, the book is a solid and convincing addition to moral philosophy, in spite of its title and its associations.

The weakness of the argument admittedly lies in the want of a more scientific definition of Happiness, and an ample exposition of the elements, constitution, and production of Happiness. And an even more serious *hiatus* lies in the absence of all these explanations as to Pleasure. What constitutes Happiness: how is it created, maintained, and lost ? What Pleasures are high, what low : what are the qualities of Pleasure, and how should we distinguish between them ? It is quite clear that Mill's own conception of Happiness is both practical and elevated, reasonably adjusted between *each* and *all* ; and that his conception of Pleasure is a wise and noble harmony between the personal and the altruistic pleasures. But he does not systematically work out this. He leaves all this in sketch. And he does not, therefore, give us a substantive scheme of ethical science.

That Mill's conception of Happiness and of Pleasure is of this rational and elevated order appears in his whole argument, but especially in that truly grand passage in the third chapter, where he claims as the natural basis of morality the social feelings of mankind, the desire to be in unity with our fellow creatures; and where he goes on to show that the social state is the normal destiny, and, under civilisation, becomes the instinctive habit of mankind. The true basis of Ethic is that which, with Aristotle, starts with the conception of Happiness as normally to be attained by the free development of man's natural function, and man's natural function to be fulfilling his part as a social being. And Comte has completed that view by proving man's natural function to be the systematic control of the personal desires by the benevolent instincts, with regard to and by the aid of the entire Human Organism. Mill coincides with that theory, and is entirely saturated with it; he certainly urges nothing to the contrary. But he has not worked out any theory of Ethic so definitely as Comte has done, and indeed as Herbert Spencer has done.

How Mill himself reconciled the tone of militant Individualism in the *Liberty* with the tone of enthusiastic Altruism in the *Utilitarianism* he entirely fails to explain in his *Autobiography*, or elsewhere. The two pieces were both composed about the same period—that of his short married life—and both were published at nearly the same date. He was evidently not conscious of any divergence of view. Without saying that they are in verbal or direct contradiction, or that they do not coincide in many things, the paramount importance given to the social feelings as the firm foundation of morality does not seem compatible with the *spirit* of the *Liberty*, which is to assert the sovereignty of the individual and the absolute independence of each man and woman. Take this noble passage in the third chapter of the *Utilitarianism*:

The social state is at once so natural, so necessary, and so habitual to man, that, except in some unusual circumstances or by *an effort of voluntary abstraction*, he never conceives himself otherwise than as a member of a body; and this association is rivetted more and more, as mankind are farther removed from the state of savage independence. Any condition, therefore, which is essential to a state of society, becomes more and more an inseparable part of every person's conception of the state of things which he is born into, and which is the destiny of a human being. . . .

In an improving state of the human mind, the influences are constantly on the increase, which tend to generate in each individual a feeling of unity with all the rest; *which feeling, if perfect, would make him never think of, or desire, any beneficial condition for himself, in the benefits of which they are not included.*

This fine burst of altruistic sentiment is as true as it is eloquent. It is entirely consistent with Mill's own nature and with the facts of his life, and it inspires the whole spirit of his *Utilitarianism*, of which it is the best and central idea. A follower of Comte would even say that the altruism is exaggerated in the last cited phrase, and that the legitimate claims of Self are ignored. Mill, we know, called Comte ' a morality-intoxicated man : every question with him

is one of morality, and no motive but that of morality is permitted.'
Potest retorqueri; for here Mill appears as intoxicated—not so
much with morality as with altruism.   But if this fusion of the
personal with the altruistic feelings is so natural, so complete in a
high civilisation, so essential to the stability of morality, what
becomes of the defiant sovereignty of the individual—'whose independence in all that part of conduct which merely concerns himself
is, of right, absolute'?   In the *Utilitarianism* we are told that a
man of high moral culture in a society of high civilisation will come
to feel about himself, to think of himself, not as an isolated individual
but habitually and naturally as an organ in a social organism.   How
are we to reconcile the *Liberty* of Mill with his *Utilitarianism*?

I turn now to the last of his completed books, *The Subjection
of Women*, 1869—in many ways the most eloquent of his works, the
most characteristic, and perhaps that which has had the most direct
and immediate effect.   Like the *Liberty*, it was written many years
before it was published, and was to a great degree a joint production.
His biographer, Professor Bain, very justly calls it 'the most sustained exposition of Mill's life-long theme—the abuses of power.'
And Mr. John Morley calls it 'the best illustration of all the best and
richest qualities of its author's mind.'   'It is fortunate,' he adds,
'that a subject of such incomparable importance should have been
first effectively presented for discussion in so worthy and pregnant a
form.'

The form is indeed pregnant, and in every sense worthy of a
scheme which touches us all home, and reaches so far and wide.   It
is one of those very rare examples of a short treatise on a weighty
topic, packed with accumulated thought, and fused with ardent conviction.   In four short chapters it condenses a scheme of social
Ethics.   It is in its passionate logic the most 'notable result of this
ripest, loftiest, most inspiring part of his life.'   And its practical effect
on legislation, manners, and opinion has no doubt been greater than
anything else which Mill gave to his generation.   The law has
already been amended on many points which drew down his indignation
and satire.   A great number of the disabilities of women arising
from prejudice, habit, or torpor have been practically removed.   At
least, there remains no legal or moral bar to the aspiring woman,
except in one or two exceptional cases.   Literature, art, medicine,
science, law, the universities, athletics, sport, political agitation, the
public service, are now practically open to women.   Their admission
to Parliament, to the franchise, to the Bar, to Degrees, is still an open
question, which would be decided in their favour at once if the
majority of women seriously resolved to claim it.   There is nothing
now to prevent any woman who wishes it from competing with men
in composing an epic, playing in a polo match, orating on platforms,
in building a cathedral, in presiding over a hospital, in inspecting a

factory, or sitting on a parish council and a school board. One or two disabilities remain, really because many of the best and greatest women we have earnestly oppose their removal. The change which 'the present generation has witnessed in law, practice, and in opinion is mainly due to the passionate school of Reform which Mill inspired, and very largely to the little book in which his aspirations were concentrated.

This is no place to discuss how far these changes are salutary, for the aim of this brief essay is to call attention to the effect of Mill's influence on his age. It is impossible to dispute what Mr. Morley justly calls 'the sagacity of his maxims on individual conduct and character,' and 'the beauty of the aspirations for collective social life' in this eloquent treatise. There are whole pages which would furnish forth a dozen sermons on the coarseness, the cruelty, the arrogance which men so often show towards women who fall into their power, towards the women of their own family, to their sisters, to their daughters, constantly to their wives, and occasionally even to their mothers. It is a scathing indictment : and few men will dare to say that they have not known some loathsome examples of the brutalities it depicts. And all honest men will agree that there are few homes into which this insolence of sex does not from time to time intrude ; that the rebuking of this temper is indeed a primal duty of morality and religion ; that no more powerful sermon on this duty has ever been preached by man.

The Subjection of Women, however, is not a simple sermon against male arrogance. It is a systematic effort to recast the whole form of our domestic, social, and political life, and, as such, it must be judged. The real question is, not whether the book contains many salutary warnings and some noble aspirations, but whether it shows adequate ground for a vast revolution in law, opinion, habits, and ideals, both of private and of public life. Has civilised life between the sexes been based on a selfish tyranny : must it be reformed root and branch ? Here some of those who honour most the memory of Mill entirely decline to assent. That he has denounced with a noble freedom gross tendencies in our social and domestic life is most true. That these tendencies are so enormous, so universal, so poisonous as he asserts is a monstrous exaggeration. That they can only be overcome by the tremendous revolution which he preaches is an even more dangerous delusion. The subjection of women is a mere hysterical sophism in itself. The remedy proposed to cure it is rank moral and social anarchy.

The whole argument is an example of what we know so well—the fiery denunciation of some too common failing or vice, to be stamped out by some revolutionary process. Nearly all that teetotallers say about drunkenness is true ; but it does not follow that we need penal laws to prevent all mankind from obtaining alcohol. Marriage is not seldom a cruel purgatory for one or both of the married pair; but it does not follow that all marriages should be terminable at will or on trivial grounds.   There is practised a great deal of cruelty to brutes and much wanton slaughter; but it does not follow that we ought to make it a misdemeanour to hurt or kill a vertebrate animal, even in order to save human life or provide human food.   Calmly judged, and regarded as a serious contribution to sociology, the *Subjection of Women* partakes of the fanatical extravagance found in Abolitionists, Vegetarians, and Free Lovers.   The assertions of fact on which it professes to rest its plea are caricatures of practical life of truly grotesque extravagance.   And the results at which it aims would logically involve the dissolution of civil and domestic existence as civilisation has slowly evolved it.

It is said to be ' a joint production'; but in truth the *Subjection of Women* is much more the production of a woman than of a man. Mill himself was a man with a heart of truly feminine sensibility. His heart was even richer than his brain.   Under the stimulus of indignation for the outrages and obstacles of which he saw women to be frequent victims, his acute reasoning powers caught fire.   Indeed, there are purple patches in the book where we seem to hear that spiteful wrongheadedness of some woman who has grown old in nursing her wrongs, out of touch with actual life and with her own sex.   These Hecubas, whose married life was a failure or who have never known it at all, are suffered to rail at male wickedness with a burlesque exaggeration which disturbs no one, and which none disregard so completely as the sensible, amiable, average woman.   We had hardly got over the conventional satire upon Woman which disgraced the age of Swift, Pope, and Congreve, when there was founded the feminine caricature of Man.   And for this new terror to quiet life, Mr. Mill, with his female inspirers and imitators, have to answer at the bar of Good Sense and Good Feeling.

A revolution so vast as that involving the mutual relations of the sexes is not to be decided by reference to one country or one generation.   The supposed uprising of women against the tyranny of man is still a mere fad in the other advanced nations of Europe.   And to pretend that women are slaves in the United States is too ludicrous to be attempted.   In what is far the largest part of the English-speaking race we are assured that Woman is absolute mistress of the situation, and Man with shame begins to take a lower place.   The American girls who so freely accept English husbands are not thought by their sisters to descend into the ranks of degraded slaves.   The anomalies of the feudal law which long lingered on our statute book, for the most part survivals of antique manners, were in practice corrected by appropriate modifications.   It is an instance of this feminine want of balance, of knowledge, and of impartiality, when Mr. Mill calls these modifications of the old law ' special contracts setting aside the law.' The rules of Equity and the system of settlement are, of course, quite as truly law as the old Norman common law; and, instead of 'setting aside the law,' they are improvements in law made by lawyers and enforced by judges. It is childish to ask for a change which will shake to its foundations every household in civilisation, on the ground of an obsolete doctrine which survives in the text-books of our old ·English law, but which no longer seriously affects any number of families. English law bristles with anomalies under the heads of property, family, Church, and State, and we have a dozen different types of agitation which propose radical changes on the strength of these obsolete and paradoxical anomalies. It is melancholy to find a great sociologist such as Mill heading one more of these rhetorical revolutions.

Let us guard against misconception, if that be possible, on this thorny topic. We admit that many changes are needed in law, in opinion, in our habits, before all the powers of women can be fully developed. There is permanent value in Mill's invectives against male tyranny in the past and male arrogance in the present. And his impassioned rebukes have much nobility and no little truth. But they do not justify the radical sexual revolution that he heralds. It would be quite as easy to frame a wholesale indictment against the cruelty, selfishness, and meanness of women—not in the brutal ways common to bad men, but in the feline ways common to bad women. There are bad wives, mothers, sisters, daughters, alas! in all ranks, although the bad are not so savage as bad men, and the good are often nobler than the best men. Men of the world know as many homes made wretched by the defects of the women as by the arrogance of the men. Selfishness, alas! is common to both sexes, and is too often latent, if it be not blatant, in the average home. It takes different forms with men and with women, but there is not so much to choose between the secretive selfishness of women and the domineering selfishness of men. The vices of both are to be met by purer morals, manners, religion—not by social revolutions and anarchic experiments in the New Life. To argue that the arrogance of many men requires us to turn our social institutions inside out is quite as foolish as it would be to argue that the meanness of many women justifies the subjection of women as really practised by ancient Romans and modern Mussulmans.

I have no intention whatever of discussing the specific changes recommended by Mill; and it would be idle in this place to touch upon problems so vast and so universal. The institutions of Family and the relations of the sexes concern the whole human race and the general course of human civilisation. It is pedantry to debate them from the point of view of Britain to-day. A favourite argument with some academic debaters founds this vast social revolution on the slightly greater proportion of women to men—a phenomenon in itself trifling, which is due to the accidents of emigration in the British Empire for the time, but which is reversed by similar reasons in the United States and some other countries. The famous argument that it is impossible to say what women may one day become, since for generations they have never had a chance, is too much like the pretext of the spiritualists that the presence of an incredulous person makes every test unfair. A whole generation has now been bred up in the light of the new movement that Mill led and inspired; and few of the disabilities he denounced have now any practical effect. It is difficult to believe that, in these twenty-seven years, women have proved themselves so greatly superior to their mothers and their grandmothers, that the passage from slavery to freedom has wrought any change so vast—or indeed any change at all except a certain perceptible loss in tenderness, modesty, and charm, and a very marked increase of restlessness, self-assertion, and conceit.

The specific proposals of the book need not be considered whilst it confronts us with the root misconception on which it is founded. Women are not a subject race in civilised Europe and America, not slaves, not victims: and men are not tyrants, jealous task-masters, and inhuman brutes. And the plea for the vast social changes involved is founded on the same theory of the Individual that is the root error of *Liberty*. Nothing can be made right in sociology whilst society is regarded as made up of Individuals instead of Families. If this individualist doctrine is logically carried out, and husband and wife are to be but temporary 'partners' with identical rights and separate lives, monogamic marriage as now understood must disappear. Mill for once failed in his accustomed courage when he shrank from frankly dealing with the problem of Marriage. It is certain that he was really prepared for a very large relaxation of its actual conditions and laws. But Marriage is only one of the institutions over which these absolute dogmas of individualism would cast a blight. The Family as an institution would be dissolved; the fine flower of Womanhood would become cankered; the brutality of Man would become a grim reality; and the Subjection of Women would be a fact—and not an epigram.

With all its defects, the book has great beauties, lasting merits. All that could be done by a most generous, pure, and noble spirit starting with a vicious theory, Mill has done. To me it reads like a sermon of St. Bernard on the miraculous gifts of the saints, or some other transcendental figment. Beautiful and impressive as an occasional homily, as philosophy it is vitiated, not only by its metaphysical apotheosis of the Individual, but also by unsound physiological, cerebral, and ethical data. The truth lies not in the *equality* but in the *interdependence* of the sexes: not in their *identities* or *similarities* but in their *heterogeneities* and *correlations*. This truth Mill's own beauty of soul is continually leading him to affirm, even whilst the romance of his personal life is seducing him to adopt most extravagant delusions. The co-operation of man with woman has never been more finely described than in Mill's own statement of the ideal marriage—'in the case of two persons of cultivated faculties, identical in opinions and purposes, between whom there exists that best kind of equality, similarity of powers and capacities with reciprocal superiority in them—so that each can enjoy the luxury of looking up to the other, and can have alternately the pleasure of leading and of being led in the path of development.' Be it noted that this picture is in the very spirit, nay, in the actual words, with which Comte has drawn the ideal marriage. This ideal is at once the gem of Mill's book on Women—and its refutation. It is not, as he fancies, 'the dream of an enthusiast.' It is an ideal which is often, even in our own day, attained in perfection; and which they who have been blessed in such attainment well know to be the normal and natural type to which the relations of the two sexes steadily tend to conform, even, to a certain extent, in the relations of family, friendship, and association, beyond and outside of the marriage union. The true function of men and of women is to be the complement each of the other. The effort to assimilate them is a step towards barbarism.

This is no place to deal with the great works of Mill's earlier life —the *Logic* and the *Political Economy*. They are still standard works which every student of these sciences is bound to master; they have exercised a really dominant influence over the thoughts of the thinking world; and they are doubtless destined to colour the minds of many students for some time to come. It is true that their authority has been rapidly waning since Mill's death; and they are, perhaps, as much undervalued now as they once were unduly extolled as manuals of final and absolute truth. Forty years ago these works were the text-books of a large and influential school of students, especially at Oxford: and, as is the unhappy fate of text-books, they were regarded by the youthful philosopher as infallible revelation. This, of course, they are not; nor is any one of them the summary of a coherent and complete system of thought. In the *Political Economy* especially we find two incompatible schemes of thought; and the first and the second volumes of the *Logic* are not wholly consistent throughout. The truth is that Mill, for all his apparent proof armour of dry logic, was continually moved by what has been called 'the logic of feeling.' He was excessively sensitive and indeed impressionable; and was often carried away by new ideas and intense feelings. In the course of his career he passed through the tremendous grinding of Bentham and James Mill's cast-iron machine, and ultimately ended in social utopias and sentimental ideals. It was said of the great Condorcet that he was a volcano covered with snow. And Mill had something of that temperament—without, a method of severe logic, within, intense sympathy and aspirations after new ideals. Both of these may be traced in most of his writings, in antinomies that he failed to harmonise, of which he is obviously unconscious himself.

This is especially marked in the *Political Economy*, which went through three modifications, as has been explained by Professor Ingram, who has admirably described both its weakness and its strength. It has been, as he says, the source from which most of our contemporaries have derived their knowledge of the science. And it still remains the most important English text-book of the older school. It marks an epoch. For, if it cannot be said to be the introduction to the new methods with which our generation approaches economic problems, it undoubtedly closes the canon of the older methods. For in its final form, and still more in connection with Mill's later economic doctrines, it makes admissions and encourages ideals of a social future which knock the ground from under the feet of the old orthodox school of abstract dogmas and unlimited Competition. Of this tendency Mill himself was quite aware, and he admitted that he had imbibed it in the school of St. Simon and Comte. But, if the absence of any perfectly coherent scheme is a defect in the *Political Economy*, the fact that it combines so much of sound reasoning on economics with a serious attempt to expand plutonomy into sociology, makes it the most valuable general treatise which our language in this century has produced.

The *Examination of Sir W. Hamilton's Philosophy* is so full of acuteness, of interest, and of pregnant argument as to make one regret that Mill's chief metaphysical work should have been cast in a controversial form. It would have been far better had he stated his own metaphysical position in a systematic body of doctrine. He has not altogether satisfied such thinkers of his own school as Professor Bain, G. H. Lewes, and Herbert Spencer. Few metaphysicians, alas! ever satisfy any of their fellow philosophers altogether. But although there is much in this most interesting criticism of Hamilton that has not won general assent or even a very important following, the volume as a whole contains so many characteristic and memorable lines of thought, and has so much that is at once subtle, and rich with sterling good sense, that it is especially valuable in this age of Intuitional Reaction and in the welter of half-hearted hypotheses in which we are told to-day that true philosophy consists.

With the work on *Auguste Comte and Positivism* I shall not deal, for it has been treated so exhaustively by Dr. Bridges in his admirable reply, and I have in other places dealt with it at such length that I have nothing further to add. I associate myself entirely with the whole of Dr. Bridges's essay. He has amply shown how very large and fundamental are the points of agreement between the two, and how deeply Mill had assimilated the philosophical, ethical, social, and religious ideas of Comte. Mr. Leslie Stephen states it truly when he says, 'Comte's influence upon Mill was clearly very great, especially in his general view of social development.' It has been remarked by Professor Bain and by Professor Ingram that Mill had been influenced by Comte far more than he was himself disposed to believe. Readers of Bain's *Life of Mill* and of Mill's own *Autobiography* will observe how early, how intimate, how profound was the effect of Comte's work upon the mind of Mill. The grand difference—whereon they eventually parted company—was that Mill was (in theory) an Individualist, whilst Comte was (philosophically speaking) a Socialist. To Comte Synthesis was the great aim: to Mill it was Independence. Both aimed at combining Liberty and Duty. But Mill would put Liberty first: Comte gave the prerogative place to Duty.

In the supreme point of religious aspiration there is essential agreement. It is clear from a concurrence of testimony that Mill looked forward to what in his last considerable piece he describes as 'that real, though purely human religion, which sometimes calls itself the Religion of Humanity and sometimes that of Duty.' In his last interview with John Morley he expressed the same thought. The three posthumous *Essays on Religion* develop and expound it. Written at intervals of some twenty years, they are not quite consistent, and to Bain and Morley they present certain difficulties hard to reconcile with each other and with their knowledge of the writer. The last essay on *Theism* admits, in a loose and sentimental way, a certain *concurrent* and purely hypothetical Theism as likely to aid and colour the Religion of Duty. This Comte himself certainly did not contemplate, and all Christians and most Theists would reject it with scorn. But Mill's religion was not after Comte's model, though it virtually amounted to the same result. Fairly considered, the three posthumous *Essays on Religion* do not vary more than the development of a single mind over twenty years may explain. They combine to surrender all forms of belief in the Supernatural, in Revelation, or Christianity, and they practically close with a definite acceptance of the Religion of Humanity, as in some form or other the permanent religion of the Future.

With Mill's political activity and his writings on politics we are not now concerned. They belong to his own generation, not to ours. And, however rich with light and leading to the movements which they founded or inspired, their effect was in no sense either so great or so permanent as that of his books. His whole conduct in public was that of a courageous, conscientious, and noble-minded citizen, who gave his countrymen a rare example of how to play that most perilous of all parts—the philosopher as ruler. Whether we agree or not with all his aims, his bearing was always a combination of patience, justice, a lofty morality, and unflinching courage.

In summing-up the peculiar powers of Mill and his special services to English thought, it would seem that his work marks a certain transition or combination between two very different movements, and also the return to the fusion between French and English ideas. Hume, Gibbon, Priestley, Godwin, and Bentham, with the societies around them, had saturated Englishmen with the philosophical and political ideas of France. Scott, Coleridge, and Carlyle saturated them with German romanticism and philosophy. The influence of Mill again was almost wholly French, and to a very small degree German. In spite of the formal reasoning of his method, and the laborious precision of his form, he can hardly claim the highest rank as an original, or systematic, thinker. He is neither so original nor so systematic as Bentham or Spencer. And nearly all his work shows evidence of competing currents which are far from completely harmonised. His social philosophy is made up of Bentham and Comte, his Economics of Plutonomy tempered by Socialism, his Metaphysics are based, either by agreement or antagonism, on Sir W. Hamilton. His *Liberty* is deeply coloured by the memory of his father, and the *Subjection of Women* is an echo of his romantic devotion to his wife.

Yet as one turns over the roll of Mill's labours in philosophy, in metaphysics, in ethic, in economics, in sociology, in politics, in religion, it is difficult to believe but that such solid achievement will have a permanent place in English thought, although it may never regain its original vogue. In any case the name of Mill must stand as the most important name in English philosophy between Bentham and Spencer. But, to the diminishing band of those who knew him, it will be his nobility of nature which dwells deepest in their memory, rather than his sagacity of mind. And those who did not know him should read in his *Autobiography* the modest yet resolute presentment of a life of indefatigable industry, conscientious effort, and beautiful ideals. The sensitiveness to social improvement and the passionate nature of his own affections, which led him so to exaggerate the gifts of his own dear ones, and to plunge into such social revolutions, not seldom overpowered his science and involved him in inconsistencies, little to be expected from the external form of logical and patient induction. The inconsistencies and sophisms will be forgotten, as his great services to thought and his sympathetic trust in humanity are more and more remembered and prized.

FREDERIC HARRISON.

The Editor of THE NINETEENTH CENTURY *cannot undertake to return unaccepted MSS.*

THE

NINETEENTH
CENTURY

No. CCXXXVI—October 1896

WHY RUSSIA DISTRUSTS ENGLAND

THE visit of the Emperor of Russia to the Queen coincides with a momentous crisis in the affairs of Europe, and above all in the relations of the countries over which the two monarchs reign. England and Russia seem to be standing at the parting of the ways, and to have before them the choice either of a permanent friendship, with all its attendant blessings, or of a lasting estrangement and hostility, accompanied by perils the unspeakable gravity of which cannot be exaggerated. It is natural in these circumstances that all who wish well to their own country, and who are not inspired by any feeling of deadly hostility to Russia, should be asking themselves whether something cannot be done to bring about a change for the better in the relations of the two States. Their anxiety to see such a change effected is increased by their knowledge of the fact that a good understanding between Great Britain and Russia would mean the termination of the orgies of devilish cruelty in the dominions of the Sultan. There is apparently no other way in which the occupant of the Yildiz Kiosk can be reached and curbed. We have therefore a double motive for wishing to come to terms with Russia, the motive of an enlightened self-interest and the motive of common humanity.

The Czar visits the Queen as a friend and ally, closely connected by marriage with the royal family of this country. In this character he has received a welcome of the genuine warmth of which he can make no complaint. Yet it is impossible to forget that every effort has been made, not only by the Russian press but by the journals of France and Germany, to convince us that the nation over which the Czar rules is our enemy, and that under no circumstances will she abandon her attitude of confirmed suspicion and hostility with regard to this country. It is difficult to withstand the evidence which is brought forward to support this contention. It is almost impossible, in face of the daily insults and malignant innuendoes showered upon us by the journalists of the four chief capitals of Europe, to feel that there is any hope of a change for the better in the situation. When we are told that such a movement as that we are now witnessing for expressing horror at the massacres of the Armenians is a crafty device on the part of English statesmen to enable them to carry out unobserved some secret plot of their own against the peace of Europe and the interests of Russia, it is almost impossible not to give way to a feeling of despair. How can we ever hope to be on good terms with those who misunderstand us so completely and so maliciously?

Yet it is well to bear in mind two facts that forbid this feeling of despair. The first is that not so many years ago it was this country which cherished an inveterate suspicion of Russia, and refused to believe in the goodness of her motives, no matter what might be the apparent worthiness of her actions. The other is that when we survey the history of Europe during the last forty years, we are driven, in common fairness, to admit that the Russians have some excuse for their present sentiments towards us.

During the greater part of the lifetime of most of us Russia has been the acknowledged bogey of the Englishman. Our older men remember the Crimean War, when we fought her openly, inflicting upon her enormous material injury and gaining for ourselves victory that few of us now regard as having been worth the price paid for it. Since then we have been afflicted by recurrent panics, of all of which Russia has been the cause. On the Bosphorus, in Asia Minor, in Afghanistan, in Central Asia, she has been the nightmare of our dreams, for ever disturbing our rest and filling us with apprehension. How many names of remote Asiatic cities and passes have we not had upon our lips during the last thirty years, each one of which has seemed for the moment to be the final, long-sought *casus belli*, and not one of which the average Englishman, on searching his memory, could now recall? More than once during that period we have come dangerously near to war; and on one memorable occasion we seemed, as the late Earl of Derby declared, not to be drifting, as in the Crimean days, but to be positively rushing into such a conflict. When we look back we can all see for ourselves that not one of the matters which seemed at the moment to have so much importance—neither Merv, nor Kandahar, nor Herat, nor Penjdeh —was really worth the sacrifice of a single army corps. And yet for all these years we have honestly believed that each new crisis as it arose was to lead to the downfall of the British Empire unless we resisted Russia to the death.

. And during all that period we have scoffed at the explanations offered by St. Petersburg, have persistently refused to believe in Muscovite good faith, and even when men like the late Emperor have taken steps to make that good faith indisputable, have hinted pleasantly that, after all, behind the Emperor there were other men not quite so scrupulous whom, autocrat though he might be, he was powerless to control. When we remember what our own attitude towards Russia was during this period in our history—a period which has only just been closed—we may possibly view with greater tolerance the present attitude of Russia towards ourselves.

But we are deeply and rightly hurt at the insulting imputations which it pleases the St. Petersburg and Moscow Press to cast upon the genuineness of our pity for the perishing Armenians. It adds to our chagrin to discover that in Paris and in Germany the official view of the popular uprising in this country is practically the same as that taken in Russia. But can we find no cause or excuse for suspicions which every Englishman knows to be absolutely unfounded? For such an excuse we have only to go back for twenty years. September 1876 saw the United Kingdom convulsed by an agitation far more remarkable than that which we are now witnessing. Men of all classes and of both political parties joined in what seemed to be a holy war against the Sultan—the same Sultan who still sits in the Yildiz Kiosk, watching with cynical eyes that outer world in which he has never mixed. If one thing seemed certain after the memorable St. James's Hall Conference—greatest and most striking of all the public meetings this generation has witnessed—it was that Great Britain would never again stand between Abdul Hamid and his just doom, that Turkey would never again find protection under the shadow of the English flag, and that we would welcome gladly any hand that was stretched forth to save the Christians of the Ottoman Empire from their oppressors. In 1877 Alexander the Second took upon himself the task of rescuing Bulgaria from the assassins and ravishers of Asia Minor. He accomplished that task successfully at an enormous cost to himself. Russia was crippled for years by her campaign in the Balkans. What was her reward? She saw the Treaty of San Stefano torn up at Berlin, chiefly through the influence of England ; she had to surrender almost everything she had gained; and she found that whilst she was thus despoiled of the fruits of her victory, Great Britain, under the Anglo-Turkish Convention, not only gave her guarantee for the safety of the Sultan's dominions in Asia Minor —that is to say, the territory most directly threatened by Russia— but carried off for her own benefit a substantial piece of loot in the shape of the island of Cyprus. I do not recall this old story for the purpose of raising a party controversy. Lord Beaconsfield's policy in those days may be left to the judgment of history. But is there any fair-minded man, whether he be a Liberal or a Conservative, who, trying to put himself in the place of a Russian, and remembering the events of 1876–78, can feel surprised that Russia is distrustful of our present policy, and is even cynically unmindful of the protestations of absolute disinterestedness with which we accompany our expressions of sympathy with the Armenians? The misfortune is that, whether well or illfounded, so long as this is the temper of the Russian people—so long as they believe in their hearts that Great Britain, whatever policy she may appear to be pursuing, is thinking only of herself and is chiefly desirous of procuring her own aggrandisement at the expense of her great rival in the East—there can be no real security for the peace of Europe, and the nightmare of constant anxiety must continue to weigh upon the statesmen of Great Britain.

Is it not time for us to do something to convince Russia that we have changed our views with regard to her position in Europe? That we *have* changed them is now recognised by everybody in this country. Whether the change is due to Mr. Gladstone's unceasing attempts, whilst he remained in public life, to convince his fellowcountrymen of Russian good faith, or to the logic of facts, or, as is more probably the case, to one of those psychological waves which from time to time affect the opinions of nations as well as of individual men, I do not pretend to say. But the change is real and unmistakable, and proofs of its reality may be gathered not only in Parliament, where the raiser of the Muscovite bogey is now a discredited personage, but in our newspapers and political clubs. The policy of the Crimean War—the war which ought never to have been waged—is dead. The policy of the Berlin Treaty is evidently moribund. It is hardly necessary to say in an English review that this country has never wanted Constantinople for itself. But every year that has passed since 1878 has witnessed an increased indifference in England with regard to the ownership of that great city. The common sentiment for some years past has been summed up in the words 'anybody must be better than the Turk.' The 'anybody' may not have consciously included Russia; nay, it may even consciously have excluded that particular settlement of the ownership. But the mere fact that the Turk should have been deposed from his old place in our favour as the necessary ally of this country on the Bosphorus, and 'the bulwark'—heaven save the mark!—'against the barbarism of the North,' speaks volumes to those of us who can remember the old days. He is no longer 'such a gentleman' and 'such a good fellow.' We have ceased to be anxious to furnish him with money, or to slobber over him at banquets and in newspaper articles. Our former idol has, in fact, been cast beneath our feet. This is undoubtedly a great change in public opinion, and it alone would make an arrangement with Russia not quite impossible—if only we could convince the Russians that the change is a fact.

The absolute ownership of Constantinople is a question far too vast and complicated to be discussed offhand in these pages, but it is something to feel justified in saying that Great Britain would be able to approach the discussion of that question with a comparatively open mind, and that she would certainly not seek to resist any con-clusion regarding it which the other Powers of Europe might arrive at. It has, in fact, ceased to be a question of paramount interest to this country, and we are in consequence able to consider it dispas-sionately, if not absolutely without prejudice. We know that at this moment Russian influence is paramount at Constantinople. Of that fact we have had during the past twelve months conclusive evidence. But where are there any signs of a revival of the old feeling of panic because this is the case? Twenty years ago the country would have been convulsed with anger and filled with apprehension if it had learned that the English ambassador had ceased to be a power at the court of the Sultan, and that the representative of Russia was supreme. This is what has happened now, and yet nobody troubles, nor does anyone raise a cry of alarm. The sole regret of the people of Great Britain appears to be that, having secured this overwhelming influence in the counsels of the Sultan, Russia should be using it to such little purpose so far as the interests of outraged humanity are concerned.

As for the question of the opening of the Dardanelles, opinion in Great Britain, so far as it is possible to gather it, is still more *com-plaisant* towards Russia than upon the question of Constantinople. Experts, both political and military, have published opinions with regard to the effect of that measure which are decidedly reassuring. Our chief national interest in the Eastern Mediterranean is the Suez Canal. But apparently the judges on such questions agree in the conclusion that in time of war the Canal can be used by none of the Powers. That would have been a very serious matter for England five-and-twenty years ago; but now, with our triple- and quadruple-expansion engines, we can in case of need do without the Canal and keep up communications with India as regular and as swift as those we had by way of the Canal only a few years back. No doubt the alliance between France and Russia is a very serious factor, affecting materially the question of the admission of Russia to the Mediterranean by way of the Dardanelles. But it is more serious for Austria and Italy than for England, and it is, at all events, one about which the British public do not seem particularly to concern themselves. Against any arguments founded on the Franco-Russian *entente* the average Englishman is disposed to set the enormous advantages that would be derived from a friendly understanding between the two greatest empires of the world—an understanding which would not of course be procured without some sacrifice on both sides, but which, if it were to be attained, would compensate both parties to it a hundred-fold for all the sacrifices they might have made in arriving at it.

My purpose is not, however, to discuss questions, either of detail or of high policy, that can only be properly treated by those who have access to the most authoritative sources of information. It is rather to state what I conceive to be the present attitude of the people of this country towards Russia, and to show how real and how remarkable is the transformation that has taken place in public opinion since the days of the Berlin Treaty. Russia is at present bitterly hostile to us, though, as I have tried to show, she is not without some excuses for her hostility. So long as this feeling exists on her side, the peace of Europe must be in danger, while the Turkish assassin will continue to enjoy full liberty to carry on his devilish work against the Christians who he at his mercy. But is it not possible that we may bring about a change in Russian feeling towards Great Britain analogous to that which has unquestionably taken place in British feeling towards Russia ? Can we not convince the Czar and his people that there is on our side no desire to keep up the old antagonism at Constantinople ? Taught by the bitter lesson of 1878, they suspect our intentions now, and foolishly delude themselves with the idea that our deep sympathy with the Sultan's victims —a sympathy which exists in every household in the land—is an artful piece of hypocrisy covering some scheme of selfish wickedness. If we can remove that delusion from their minds, if we can satisfy, not only the Emperor of Russia, but his ministers and his people, that they have nothing to fear from us so far as any designs antagonistic to Russian interests in Turkey are concerned, we shall have rendered the best possible service to ourselves and to the whole world. That we desire to draw nothing for ourselves out of the seething cauldron of intrigue and passion at Constantinople, that our interest in the Armenian question is absolutely generous and unselfish, and that we would infinitely rather see Russia undertaking the chastisement of the Sultan single-handed than see that task unattempted, are, I believe, sentiments common to the overwhelming majority of the people of this country. But are they sentiments which are shared by Lord Salisbury and his colleagues ? That, after all, is the crucial question so far as the establishment of better relations between the two governments is concerned.

At present the Russian people stand upon the unpleasant memory of the Berlin Treaty, and with that memory enshrined in their hearts they listen with sullen indifference to the cries of distress which reach them from Turkey. If we could pluck that memory from their breasts, if we could give them reason to feel confident that if they undertook, either single-handed or along with others, the work of liberation and chastisement in the dominions now given over to the Sultan, they would not find that when the work was done England would snatch the fruits of victory from them, they might assume a different and nobler attitude, and the world might be relieved from the shame under which it now lies. So far as one can understand it, the opinion of this country would be warmly in favour of such a pledge being given by our statesmen. Are our statesmen themselves of the same way of thinking? One hopes that they are; but in any case it may, I think, be said with some show of confidence that, whatever happens, the British people will never again allow a Prime Minister to use the might of this country for the purpose of defending the Ottoman Empire, and will never sanction any fresh engagement which makes them responsible for 'keeping a ring' for the Sultan and his fiends while they indulge in such a saturnalia as that of Sassun. Whether they care to believe it or not, the Russians are secure henceforth from such a policy on the part of England as that which twenty years ago they felt so keenly and which they still resent so bitterly.

The late Mr. Froude, in his *Life of Lord Beaconsfield*, used certain pertinent words which, coming from a man who was certainly not 'a Little Englander' or a friend of latter-day Radicalism, ought to have some weight with those who may regard the opinions of living Radicals with suspicion. Speaking of the Jingo agitation of 1878 he says:

> Of the tens of thousands who gathered in Hyde Park to shout for war, how many had considered what a war with Russia might involve? Bismarck could not understand Disraeli's attitude. 'Why cannot you be friends with Russia and settle your differences peacefully?' he said to him at the beginning of the dispute. 'Why not put an end once for all to this miserable Turkish business, which threatens Europe every year or two with war?' Why not, indeed? . . . In such a war we stand to lose all and gain nothing, while in itself it would be nothing less than a crime against mankind. We are told that a cordial co-operation with Russia is impossible. It will not be made more possible by a quarrel over Turkey. Yet to a peaceful arrangement we must come at last if the quarrel is not to be pursued till one or other of us is destroyed.

There is happily no war feeling on our side at this moment. It is peace with Russia, not war, that we want. Will our statesmen be wise enough and strong enough to take advantage of this feeling on the part of the nation to put an end to the old jealousies and hatreds, and to establish that cordial understanding with Russia which alone can make impossible a struggle such as that which Froude justly described as 'a crime against mankind'?

Wemyss Reid.

THE CRY FOR FRAUDULENT MONEY
IN AMERICA

WHEN a man with good reputation suddenly goes wrong, it is natural
to seek some explanation for his conduct. Sometimes his fall is
attributed to heredity, or laid to the art of successful concealment.
Again, it may be claimed that misfortune has merely developed traits
long dormant, or that, in the latest cant, he is the victim of 'degeneration.' So when a great national political party in the United
States, from being conservative, careful, even to cautiousness, of
rights and interests, proud of its traditions and its history, and
anxious for the respect of its adherents and the country, as well as
for votes and power, makes itself deliberately the ally of the worst
elements in the eclectic population of a great country ; when it places
over the doors of its Convention Hall the sign 'Danger: Beware,'
shamelessly proclaiming that it is devoted to the policy of repudiation,
that plunder and anarchy are among the most innocent of its purposes,
and that it welcomes the adventurers it has always opposed, it is
certainly time to ask some questions. It is a phenomenon, and, as
such, it must be interesting to attempt to trace, even in the most unsatisfactory way, some of the processes which accompany the appearance of signs and wonders. This becomes the more imperative when
one has long been attached to such an organisation, has given to it
such support as he could, and has found in it congenial associations,
both as to doctrine and individuals.

When the Civil War closed in 1865, the Democratic party, torn
asunder by division five years before, was able at once to resume its
work more or less systematically in every State in the Union, and
thus to show that it was a truly national organisation. Its partisans
had fought, in perhaps equal numbers, on either side during a great
contest, and so were better able than others to understand what civil
war meant. During the struggle its leaders were in a hopeless
minority in both Houses of Congress, and were only able in the most
fitful way to gain control of a few State Legislatures. Among them
were many men of character, ability, and patriotism who, firmly
attached to the Union at all times, were peculiarly fitted to bind up

the wounds it had made. They did so with a devotion and a heroism truly great, and so became the brake upon the wheel of fanaticism at a time when it was difficult, almost to impossibility, to find such a thing as conservatism.

Scarcely was the conflict over, when great financial problems pressed for solution. From a simple country, without taxes, without even the annual expenditure now made in a fourth-class European State, with no necessity or desire to study or master questions of finance, there had sprung into being, almost without thought, a great nation, with new impulses and ambitions, and with a debt unexampled in human history when the brief period in which it was incurred is taken into account. Few men had thought of finance, fewer had had an opportunity to deal with it, and none of them was in the Democratic Opposition. Much uncertain, tentative work followed. Gold payment had been suspended, vast amounts of irredeemable paper were in circulation among a people never over-familiar with the value and appearance of gold, and for whom during all their history a currency in the form of paper has had a strange and unaccountable fascination.

The debt had been created largely on a paper basis, and when the first hints of liquidation came, the issue was raised that the bonds representing this indebtedness ought to be paid in 'greenbacks'—the name given to the legal tender currency created by the Act of February, 1862. Many of the leading men of the dominant party assumed this position, among them some who for many years have shown forth fruits meet for repentance by strenuous and successful efforts to assist and maintain the national honour. After full discussion, this issue was settled by a declaration that the bonds should be paid in coin—a decision from which the people of the United States have never wavered. But the Democrats were in opposition. Although they were gradually regaining power in some of the States of the North, their friends in the South were struggling with reconstruction schemes and with those financial questions of purely personal interest which marked the border line between starvation and plenty. Naturally, they had no time, and less inclination or power, to make any contributions to the elucidation of great fiscal difficulties.

Within a few years it became apparent that the prosperity which had been supposed to accompany inflation was not, after all, the highest and most enduring kind; so when the Government ceased to print new issues of currency and began to pay some of its bonded debt, times were said to have become hard, and there was a sigh in many quarters for the return of the days of a dollar worth only forty cents, instead of one which had gradually appreciated until it was worth more than twice this sum. This sentiment was particularly strong in what was then known as the West—the country beyond the Alleghany Mountains. In Ohio, Indiana, and Illinois there was a fairly continuous demand for the payment of the bonds in green-backs, for a cessation of the process of retiring this irredeemable currency, which had come to be spoken of as 'money,' and for its taxation.

In 1868 the first Presidential canvass after the close of the war was entered upon. The Republicans nominated General Grant as their candidate—although it is not known that he had ever voted a Republican ticket—and declared the following to be their creed on finance :

We denounce all forms of repudiation as a national crime, and the national honour requires the payment of the public debt in the utmost good faith to all creditors at home and abroad, not only according to the letter, but the spirit of the law under which it was contracted.

A few weeks later the Democrats held their convention, and put forth the following as their confession of faith :

Where the obligations of the Government do not expressly state upon their face, or the law under which they were issued does not provide, that they shall be paid in coin, they ought, in right and justice, to be paid in the lawful money of the United States.

A demand was made for the equal taxation of every species of property, 'including Government bonds and other public securities,' and was followed up by this glittering generality: 'One currency for the Government and the people, the labourer and the office-holder, the pensioner and the soldier, the producer and the bondholder.' This was vague, but it was understood to mean, and did mean, attachment to the greenback. The platform was made to fit an Ohio candidate; but the convention defeated him, and nominated Horatio Seymour, then recently Governor of New York, one of the noblest and highest-minded men developed in our politics, and he was com-pelled to go to defeat repudiating the platform upon which he stood.

As a result of this, the Democrats veered round rapidly toward sound finance, and in 1870 their convention in New York enume-rated, among other Republican shortcomings, 'inability to devise an intelligent financial policy and the restoration of a sound currency.' In the same year the Supreme Court of the United States declared that the law which gave the greenbacks legal power was unconstitu-tional, Chief Justice Chase, who, as Secretary of the Treasury, had issued them, delivering the majority opinion. This was reversed by the full bench the next year, but its effect was that no national con-vention of either of the great parties endorsed such a currency until this year. Another result was that the labour organisations, then much more potent in the making of political opinions than now, began to condemn the national bank system—also devised during the war period—and to demand the substitution of 'legal tender notes as the exclusive currency of the nation.' Within a few years this doctrine had no party authority behind it, other than that represented by a faction whose members called themselves 'Greenbackers.'

We are concerned just now with the attitude on questions of finance of the Democratic party only, except in so far as the position of other organisations may have a bearing upon this history. In 1872 an independent element inside the Republican party held a national convention in Cincinnati, and nominated Horace Greeley for President. The Democrats endorsed this ticket, both standing on the same platform. It would be difficult to find a financial sentiment more diverse from that just quoted out of the platform of 1868. They declared that 'the public credit must be sacredly maintained, and we denounce repudiation in every form and guise. A speedy return to specie payments is demanded alike by the highest considerations of commercial morality and honest government.' The candidate was defeated, but as a result of the movement—and especially because of its changed attitude on finance—thousands of men who had left the party in the days of the war came back to its ranks, while other thousands of active and intelligent young men in every part of the country were drawn into it. From that time it can date its revival. It began at once to gain victories in every part of the Union, and was able in 1874 to regain control of the House of Representatives and to increase its membership in the Senate. Most important of all was its ability to promote the return of good feeling between the long-sundered sections of the country; to reward the devotion of its followers, not only with official recognition, but with something more valuable in the way of influence; to regain its power as representing once more, in an organised way, the conservative ideas and instincts of its earlier history. It had men like Bayard and Thurman in the Senate, and in the House of Representatives some leaders worthy of the new position and power it had conquered for itself.

No man ever did more conspicuous or timely service in any country within the same time than did Thomas F. Bayard during this period as a senator from the State of Delaware. His ability and lofty character, his relations with his associates on the personal side, his knowledge of every part of his country, but, above all, his never-failing courage and honesty in opposing every financial scheme of doubtful soundness, gave him a unique position. Had his advice been followed, either by his opponents when in power, or by his friends when they succeeded to it, the United States would long ago have been placed in the most advantageous position so far as their finances were concerned, and the party to which he was attached would not have been subjected to attack and capture by a gang of political pirates. His public service was of an all-round character, but he always gave an emphasis to sound finance which led him to place it above and before all others. It would not be possible to pay too high a tribute to the unselfishness and patriotism of one whose fortune it was to render to his country the most conspicuous service; the value of which, not yet fully recognised, is certain to command for him a high place in our history.

In 1876 the Democratic party came under the domination of the late Samuel J. Tilden, whose wonderful organising mind, severe training in the political principles which underlie our government, and knowledge of practical affairs, tended to fix anew the policy of the party on a sound basis. No man could know better how to resist the advance of movements dangerous at once to the country and his party. He knew how to manage men, making appeal at once to reason and interest. His canvass for the Presidency was one of the marvels of modern politics, and its success was conspicuous in fixing for a long time the policy of his party. Among a long list of reforms declared to be necessary by the convention which nominated Mr. Tilden, was one ' to establish a sound currency, restore the public credit, and maintain the national honour.' This buried ' greenbackism,' that dangerous doctrine never making another serious appearance in a national convention of any recognised party.

But the unsettled condition of public sentiment on financial questions soon led to an assault of a different kind. In 1873, after an extended debate, Congress, in making a revision of the coinage laws, dropped the silver dollar from the list of coins. This was done, after careful investigation, without opposition from any serious element, and the bill was signed by the President without protest from any class or interest. It was found that only about 8,000,000 of these dollars had been coined since the establishment of the mint in 1792, and as the ruling price of silver made them worth more than the gold dollar, it was deemed useless to continue the coinage only to have them seek some other market. Besides, since the suspension of specie payment almost none had remained in the country. There was nothing in the Act which, under existing conditions, discriminated against silver. But with the discovery of masses of this metal in the Rocky Mountain region, the advance in scientific methods, which cheapened production, together with the approaching resumption of specie payments, fixed in 1875 for the 1st of January, 1879, there arose a great outcry about ' the conspiracy of 1873 against silver ' and ' the poor man's dollar.' Those elements which had been attracted to the greenback because it was cheap, turned their attention to silver, which, as it was steadily declining in price, promised in due time to meet their demands in the matter of cheapness.

The final settlement, during the administration of President Hayes, of the sectional issue left the South free to take part in political questions of a general character. Although no people could have had less practical experience in financial management, there was soon manifest a strong sentiment in favour of the various forms of cheap money, demand for which had previously been confined to a small part of the West. Many of the leading men in the South steadily resisted this sentiment, even against their own personal and ambitious interests ; but the people were poor and were paying their full share of the taxes made necessary by the war ; their products were already sharing in the decline which has been going on steadily for many years, and demagogues were ready at hand to inflame passion by attributing this to the demonetisation of silver, and to the consequent disappearance of a coin of which probably not one person in fifty then living in the South had so much as seen a specimen. Then began the first talk of an alliance between the West and the South, than which nothing could be more unnatural, because these widely sundered parts did not then, and do not now, come into anything like such intimate relations, personal, business, or political, as both had and continue to have with the East. They really differ widely in origin, sentiment, and productions.

The first form taken by the silver agitation was the passage in the House of a bill providing for the free coinage of silver. This was changed in the Senate into a bill, which was made into law over the President's veto, providing for the purchase by the Government of silver bullion of the value of not more than 4,000,000 dollars or less than 2,000,000 each month, and for its coinage into dollars of standard weight and fineness, at the rate of sixteen to one with gold. No Secretary of the Treasury under any President belonging to either party ever exceeded by any considerable sum the minimum amount, as it soon became evident that the silver dollar could not be forced into circulation. Every device was tried. When the coin itself was rejected, certificates were issued ; but, in spite of all, no large proportion of the new coinage or its representative was in the hands of the people. The Government vaults were soon filled, and resort was had to such rooms in public buildings in various cities as could be spared from other uses ; and still the cry arose from each succeeding President and Secretary of the Treasury for more storage facilities. Each vied, too, with his predecessor in demanding the repeal of the law, and yet none was able to command in Congress the support necessary to bring this about, and it continued in force until 1890, when the Republicans, in order to avert the danger of a threatened Free Coinage Act and to avoid the party risk involved in a Presidential veto—with the prospect that it would be ineffectual—secured the repeal of the Act of 1878, and the enactment in its stead of a law which directed the purchase each month of 4,500,000 ounces of silver —practically the entire silver product of the country at the time— and the issue upon it of a new form of certificates, to be known as

'Treasury notes.' Strangely enough, this came to be known as the 'Sherman Act,' in spite of the denial by the veteran Ohio senator of responsibility for it.

The Democratic position on the silver question, as defined by the platform of its national conventions or by its candidates for President and Vice-President, has never been equivocal. In 1880 it declared sententiously for 'honest money, consisting of gold and silver and paper convertible into coin on demand; the strict maintenance of the public faith, State and national;' and in the resulting canvass no leader of influence in its ranks joined in the cry for free silver. This sentiment found expression through a third party, an order of organisation which has been the safety-valve of American politics. In 1884 the National Democratic Convention, held in Chicago, went still further, adopting the following as its creed on finance: 'We believe in honest money, the gold and silver coinage of the Constitution, and a circulating medium convertible into such money without loss,' and nominated Grover Cleveland for President. In 1888 it reaffirmed the same doctrine, renominated Mr. Cleveland, and he went to defeat. In 1892 the propagandists of silver had become more active, and sought from the National Convention a declaration in sympathy with their objects. After a protracted contest in the committee, their demands were rejected by a decisive vote, and the party adopted the following declaration:

We denounce the Republican legislation known as the Sherman Act of 1890 as a cowardly makeshift, fraught with possibilities of danger in the future which should make all of its supporters, as well as its author, anxious for its speedy repeal. We hold to the use of both gold and silver as the standard money of the country, and to the coinage of both gold and silver, without discriminating against either metal or charge for mintage; but the dollar unit of coinage of both metals must be of equal intrinsic and exchangeable value, or be adjusted through international agreement, or by such safeguards of legislation as shall ensure the maintenance of the parity of the two metals and the equal power of every dollar at all times in the markets and in the payment of debt; and we demand that all paper currency shall be kept at par with and redeemable in such coin. We insist upon this policy as especially necessary for the protection of the farmers and labouring classes, the first and most defenceless victims of unstable money and a fluctuating currency.

The attitude of the Democratic party in six quadrennial national conventions and the resulting canvasses, with no variableness or shadow of turning, and the agreement—except for certain minatory accusations common to partisan tactics everywhere—of the two great parties, shows that no sentiment was more firmly fixed in the public mind than devotion to a sound financial system. It is emphasised by the fact that during the period under examination no man, however strongly intrenched he might be in the affections of any State or section, was ever seriously considered for nomination as a candidate for President or Vice-President unless he was in thorough accord with this sentiment. It is interesting, too, to note that no man who has become President, either by election or succession, to whichever party he may have been attached, has failed in what he deemed his duty, or because of any unpopularity, real or threatened, to use the great powers of his office, the right of veto and all his personal influence to assert and maintain the honour and the good faith of the Government of the United States and its citizens. Every attempt to pass a bill for the free coinage of silver has come to naught because of this determined attitude of one President after another, and all have so administered the laws, dangerous though they were, as to maintain credit at home and abroad.

This review of party position would be incomplete if it failed to recognise the work of Grover Cleveland, now President, who, as the only Democrat to hold the office since 1861, has, so far as finance is concerned, had upon his shoulders a burden which few men would willingly assume. He has so effectually resisted the demands of demagogues and destructives, that he has been able within a few years to render to honest government a service quite unparalleled. In July 1884, when Mr. Cleveland, then Governor of New York, was nominated for the Presidency, he had never been called upon to give any practical attention to large financial problems, nor was he widely known to his countrymen. But his character for courage and honesty was so well recognised that he was elected over one of the best known and most brilliant statesmen. Even before his inauguration in March 1885 he was called upon to repulse the adherents of a debased coinage. For many years, in spite of the general soundness of the national platforms, and of the majority of the adherents of his party, a larger proportion of the advocates of the free coinage of silver had been found in its ranks than in any one organisation. Naturally, they expected more from one of their own partisans than from their opponents. Great, therefore, was their surprise when, under date of the 24th of February, 1885, he addressed a letter to the leading free silver advocate, refusing to consent to the enactment of further schemes in favour of silver coinage, and insisting instead upon the repeal of the compulsory coinage law. Then, as always, he avowed himself a convinced bimetallist, and every act of his in opposition to independent coinage has been taken in spite of his opinion that, with an international agreement, a greatly enlarged use of silver would be both possible and right. In his first annual Message he insisted upon the suspension of coinage, and repeated this demand in each regular or special Message bearing upon the financial question. After his defeat in 1888, and during the canvass carried on by his friends for his nomination in 1892, he pursued the same policy, and his selection again by a national convention of his party as its candidate was made in the face of unyielding but impotent opposition from the advocates of free coinage. His election, by an overwhelming majority on both the electoral and the popular vote, was the result of his courage on this and other questions.

In August, after his inauguration on the 4th of March, 1893, President Cleveland called Congress in special session to discuss the Silver Purchase Act of 1890· Three months later the last law on the Statute-books of the United States requiring the coinage or purchase of silver was repealed. After fifteen years of unremitting effort by the friends of sound money and national honour, this concession had finally been wrung from a reluctant Congress by the official representative of the Democratic party. During this period the cost, in addition to mintage expenses, of the silver dollars coined under the law of 1878, and of the bullion purchased under the Act of 1890, had been 464,210,293 dollars (more than 95,000,000*l.*), and the loss, at the going market rate, when all laws were finally repealed, was 170,170,967 dollars (or more than 35,000,000*l.*)

This harmony of sentiment among a people, secluded upon a great continent, is interesting as showing the unity of mankind. It arises from a desire to take part in the movements of the time, and from the aspirations inherent in the Teutonic peoples from which the United States has, in the main, drawn its population. It has been inspired by loyalty to honesty, good faith, and the best traditions, by confidence in what the experience of mankind has found good, and by the belief that all these elements contribute to their prosperity as individuals and as a nation.. The teaching in school and college, the experience of men who have risen from humble surroundings, the traditions of accumulated wealth, have all contributed to this acceptance of the financial system common to the whole Western world. In getting away from primitive ways, the slow, tedious development everywhere incident to colonial life, the necessity for credit, and its agency in promoting industry and enabling the country to make more rapid strides towards wealth, became apparent.

Above all considerations of interest or belief in destiny has been the moral side. It was felt that, although plenty might be produced or bought, national greatness could only come when honour had been recognised to be both expedient and right. This sentiment, having its beginning and making its growth among the people, found expression—always in words with the same meaning, however different they might be in the phrasing—in the utterances of the two great political organisations. If any party had failed to see this moral significance, it would have been swept out of existence with a swiftness and a certainty which nothing could have resisted.

Coming so suddenly out of small conditions into the presence of great ones, emerging within four years from a peace expenditure in 1861 of 62,616,055 dollars to a war expenditure in 1865 of 1,296,517,159 dollars, and from a debt of just over 90,000,000 dollars to one of 2,700,000,000 dollars, it is not surprising that there was hesitation over these staggering totals, that wild theories found advocates, or even that men of character and patriotism made mistakes. None of those destined for recognition and influence failed when the time for action came, or when great responsibility was thrown upon him.

, The three men to whom at different times it was given to lead in this work in the Democratic party have already been indicated. Meeting different and, in some respects, harder conditions, many men did well, but credit of the highest order must be given to two men in the Republican party. President Grant, by the effective veto in 1874 of the bill increasing the legal tender currency, was able to do as much as any other man in our history to recall a great nation to itself, and to promote the national honour and good faith. If this position had not been taken then, we might have drifted long since into the repudiation and ruin which belong to anarchy. It was General Grant's fortune to do his country and the world a great service in war, but this single act in time of peace required as much courage, and probably had results reaching farther than all his military operations together.

John Sherman entered the Senate of the United States from Ohio in the early days of the Civil War. His training for work in the field of finance came to him through mistakes and misconceptions from which no ordinary man could have emerged. But if he took an untenable position, he abandoned it when he discovered that he had been mistaken. If one financial experiment failed, he gave it up to try something better. He has been the financial rock of refuge of his party, and to him, more than to any man in it, is to be attributed the attitude which it now occupies on the silver question. As he is never likely to be President, honest finance would be safe if when his party is in power he could be perpetual Secretary of the Treasury.

These are some of the elements, and such are the men, who have contributed to a great result. It now becomes necessary to account, if possible, for the deliberate abandonment by one of the political parties of the conservative doctrine which it has held with so much constancy, and under which only has it been able, with varying fortune, to attain to a large measure of power, and to command since 1876 the support of more than half of the American people.

Reference has been made to the presence at all times since 1868 of a considerable element—always noisy, confined at first to the West, and then to the West and South—which has opposed these accepted theories of finance. It began by favouring the payment of bonds in greenbacks—a position it never abandoned so long as any of the original bonds remained unpaid   It took up the demand for the free coinage of silver, and while never able to carry out its programme, it saddled upon the country two laws, which would have bankrupted any nation in the world other than the United States and England.

The leaders of this agitation have gone from one dangerous position to another. Considerations of national honour or good faith have been alien to them. If they could not get a paper basis, they sought such a silver currency as might come nearest in lack of value. Failing in this, they demanded at one time that the Government should issue currency for loan directly upon landed property at 2 per cent. interest, and at another that it should establish warehouses at convenient points for the storage of farm products, upon which it should make an advance. If shown in a worthy cause, the untiring persistence in these schemes would commend itself to the world as admirable. Alliance with any party willing to treat, even in the smallest political division, has always been sought, and partisans of these demands have been ready, however insignificant in number, to stand up and be counted, and have been able at different times to modify the policy of the two great parties in every State from Pennsylvania to California. If some advocates have lost heart and returned to reason and party allegiance, others have appeared in due time to take their places and to carry on the propaganda. In one place they have inclined to protection, in another to revenue reform; here they have gone cheerfully into prohibition or woman's suffrage conventions, while there they have welcomed as associates the advocates of disruption and disorder. With all their activity, they have never been national. They have never had a serious following in any of the New England or Middle States, except for a time in Pennsylvania. In one Presidential canvass after another, never twice under the same name, they have had candidates for President and Vice-President, but until 1892 they never carried an electoral vote in any State. In that year, under the name of the People's Party, and with the wildest demands imaginable, they were able to command twenty-two electoral votes in Colorado, Idaho, Nevada, Kansas, and Oregon. The two last named returned, however, at the next election to their old allegiance. Soon after, the Republicans of North Carolina, Louisiana, Mississippi, and Arkansas, discouraged by long-continued defeat, united with the People's Party advocates, utterly defeating the Democrats in the first, while the Democrats of South Carolina, accepting all the distinctive doctrines of the Farmers' Alliance, without severing their nominal party association, ceased to be in harmony with their national organisation.

This year the Republicans as a party have maintained their old position, although not without a struggle. Foreseeing this, the Populists, free silver Republicans, and Anarchists joined their efforts with the free silver Democrats of the West and South. They have been able to capture the organisation, to overwhelm the advocates of sound money, to adopt a platform which fits the new elements, and to nominate a candidate who, committed fully to the worst and most extravagant of their purposes, is neither better nor worse than the most dangerous of his competitors. He is known to the country only for those achievements and doctrines necessary to command for him his present position. If he has opinions upon any other question than the one he has been chosen to represent, nobody knows them. His canvass thus far, carried on in every part of the country by a series of the most extraordinary speeches ever made by a candidate for any office, has been thoroughly in keeping with the character of his supporters and with the doctrines he avows. He has shown himself to be without dignity, ready to appeal to the lowest elements in human nature, profligate in speech, but parsimonious in idea, and full of a vanity which, though it may draw hearers, drives away votes. In all the political history of the country no man has been put forward by a great party who to all outward seeming had in a smaller degree the qualities which people expect to find in their candidate, or insist upon having in their President.

It would take too much space even to enumerate, much less to discuss, the elements which enter into this decay, for the time at least, of a party, and the new danger with which it threatens a great country. The change in the methods of production which has been going on all over the world during the past quarter of a century, with the continued decline in prices; the gradual, but no less apparent enhancement of wages, and the wider and more equitable distribution of the rewards of human labour which has resulted; the competition arising from the development of machinery; the necessity for closer management in every branch of industry, and for an increased investment in order to ensure the profitable development of land and the natural use of credit to supply the capital; an improved standard of living, producing greater comfort; the change from the old economies, which often concealed unfavourable surroundings and conditions—all these have done their part, not only by introducing changes to which mankind only slowly adapts itself, but by producing dissatisfaction with the slow gains with which all were once content. The great mass, still progressive, satisfied, and prosperous, are adapting themselves to new relations as their predecessors have done for generations. Intellectual conditions have changed with the material. Every man lives in the midst of a publicity once impossible, has an education once thought hurtful, and indulges in aspirations once deemed the exclusive possession of the few.

In America, accumulated money is just beginning to show its effects. In the main these are wholesome. They are promoting leisure, which is bringing education, refinement, and consideration for others, and reducing the fierceness of competition. But even these are hateful to the Jacobin character everywhere, and the fact that they are seen in every community on the American continent

gives the man always ready to appeal to the discontented an object
lesson under his eye, and promotes the perfect working of human
envy.

On the other hand, some ill-effects of accumulated wealth are no
less apparent. It is often flaunted in the face of a society little
patient with such exhibitions, generally with most offence in times
of distress. Together with the idleness which has never known discipline, the ill-got gain which puts itself forward with dauntless persistence, and the bribery which sometimes, though much less often
than is supposed, attempts to attain its end in politics or business—
they are magnified as causes by the demagogue, the ignoramus, or the
man who has failed, when they are only the effects of bad conditions.
Then there is the tendency of some creditors to be hard and heartless,
and of some debtors to think themselves downtrodden, even though
they are merely unfortunate, or suffer from their own fault. All have
combined to produce a kind of literature, intrinsically worth neither
attention nor study, yet widely read and mischievously believed, an
example of the flippant opinion of the man in the street! One such
publication, known as *Coin's Financial School*, has had a phenomenal
circulation. It was beneath contempt as writing or notice as argument
—merely the sign of an epidemic which must run its course—
but it has no doubt done something to reveal the storm centre of
politics.

One development which has seriously affected industry in the
United States is often overlooked. Nothing in history is more remarkable than the influx between 1870 and 1895 of more than
11,000,000 immigrants from every quarter of the world. The
country has welcomed and attempted to assimilate this vast multitude,
who have come with little knowledge of its language, society, business,
or system of government, and little capital other than strong and
willing hands ; but the strain upon industrial, social, and political life
has been terrible. It means that a single country has been compelled
to expand its power of production and all the multifarious agencies of
life in order to accommodate, within a quarter of a century, an abnormal population, which with its descendants outnumbers the inhabitants of any country in South America ; is one and a half times
that of all the English-speaking people in the British Colonies
scattered round the globe ; is nearly equal to all the people of Spain,
to half those in Italy, a third of those in France or the United Kingdom, and a fifth of its own population. The wonder is that, out of
the presence of so large an extraneous element, no serious problem has
arisen to tax the resources of both government and philanthropy, and
that our troubles are not ten times as many as they are. The Republic
has always had a capacity for assimilating vast multitudes from the
ends of the earth ; but as there must be a limit to the digestive power
even of that capacious maw, it would be impossible to exaggerate

the seriousness of the difficulties raised by such a vast addition to population in so short a period.

The existence of all these problems is an additional reason why the country should not be confronted at the same time with one more serious and hurtful than all of them together. So long as national honour and private credit—inseparable elements in the life of a people—can be maintained, there is solid ground upon which to stand.

Some attention must be given to a consideration of the probable success or failure of such a movement. Are the American people, without notice, ready to abandon all that they have heretofore believed, and to turn against themselves as fiercely as Jacobins or Communards have done in France? Or is this to be the final struggle against the forces of disorder, so that they may go on confidently to fulfil their destiny, and to solve those problems distinctly their own? No man cares to assume the possession of the ' gift of prophecy,' but I do not believe there is the least danger that Bryan and his hosts will be commissioned to carry on the affairs of the United States during the four years from the 4th of March, 1897.

The capture of the Democratic organisation does not ensure success at the election in one of the close States usually carried by the party in Presidential elections. For the purposes of the present canvass the Democratic party is a divided army, fighting against itself, the division claiming regulants having new commanders. But change of leadership to be wholesome must be gradual. Mutineers may capture a ship, or deserters attempt to reorganise a regiment after they have deposed its officers, but neither is likely to be of much use against what has been a common enemy. Bryan, Bland, Blackburn, Jones, Harris, Daniel, Vest, Tillman, even the unspeakable Altgeld, may have the qualities of leaders; but as the party has not been looking for them, and as they have usurped authority out of due time, they cannot command enough confidence and support to make themselves effective. Before they can do this, their Falstaffian army will have gone to battle and defeat.

Already the dissentients, organised in more than forty States, have held a national convention at which they have nominated candidates for President and Vice-President, and perfected arrangements for putting electoral tickets into the field in every important State. In doing this thing they have nominated men of the most lofty type known to American statesmanship, whose names are synonymous with character, ability, and devotion to principle under many discouragements; one a soldier of the North, the other of the South, who, in an important command, met each other face to face in battle. This has been done with the avowed purpose of making more certain the success of the sound money movement and the election of the Republican candidate. It is also intended as a nucleus for a reorganised party when the pre-

sent crisis of Democratic fate has once been passed.   Enrolled among
the supporters of these men are every Democrat in the country who
would be deemed of Cabinet rank, and the men who, for many years,
in one canvass after another, have managed the affairs of the party.

On the other hand, the Republican party was never better organised, better led, or more thoroughly disciplined than it is now, in the
States where these elements are a necessity.   It stands for sound
money and financial stability, the only real issues before the people.
It has for candidate a man of high character, honest in belief and in
life, with the courage of his opinions, whatever they may be, without
personal enmities, and with many attractive qualities.   He has risen
to the situation, showing himself manly, dignified, and patriotic.   He
has remained in the quiet of his home, instead of running about the
country to speak wherever two or three could be gathered together to
listen.

The Independent voter, who has elected every President since
1876, must be reckoned with.   This is the man, always of property, education, and position in his community, who, disliking the
policy of his party or distrusting its candidate, votes for the man
more nearly in accord with his opinions or his interests, not only
proclaiming his intentions boldly, but seeking to influence his
neighbour, and to mould public sentiment by means of organisation.
Allied in purpose, but different in method, are a great number of
voters of all professions and employments, who, refusing to proclaim
their intentions from the housetops or in the newspapers, go to the
polls, and, with a secret ballot, do their work so effectively that the
demagogue or the objectionable machine is unable to deal with
them.   These classes are widely distributed, uniformly attached to
good government, or to things which have commended themselves
by experience at home or observation abroad, opposed to agitators,
demagogues, disorganisers, and disagreeable people generally, and
opposed to free silver almost to a man.

In all the agitations through which the United States have passed,
no foreign-born element, as such, has given encouragement to
questionable financial schemes.   The Germans, or the Irish, or the
Swedes and Norwegians, have at various times had a controlling vote,
and in every case it has been cast for sound money.   The Germans
especially have arrayed themselves in opposition to such doctrines
everywhere, and have turned the scale against inflation or free silver
in Ohio, Indiana, Illinois, Iowa, Missouri, Michigan, and Wisconsin.

In no society, however new or old, is there so much machinery,
so many wheels within wheels, so many checks and balances, to preserve popular institutions from harm by the people themselves.
One House of Congress is dependent upon another, equal in power as
well as in name, and both together are co-ordinate with the President,
who, in the veto, holds a power which can rarely be overcome.

Co-ordinate, in theory, with the legislative and the executive, the judicial power passes both in a review that is absolutely final. The same checks exist in every State, in addition to those exercised by the Federal Constitution and the powers at work under it. At every turn local government in county, township, and municipality is subject to limitations from the Federal Government, in some of its many ramifications, as well as to the intervention and authority of the executive, legislative, and judicial powers of the State. When to all of these is added that curious system of choosing a President by electors and not by popular vote—under which it becomes difficult to carry on agitations against a settled system which commends itself in general—the rooted conservatism of the American people is emphasised.

In movements which affect business interests, all these constitutional and legal bars are as nothing compared with the universal distribution of property, the fruit of industry, thrift, and law. Of the 14,000,000 heads of families, half are landowners—three-fourths of them free from debt. The investments in banking, manufactures, and commerce are widely distributed, in small amounts, and every owner is interested in preserving the value of his holding. The 5,000,000 depositors in savings banks—not institutions for investors, but really used for the purpose implied in the name—with an average saving of 400 dollars each and a total of 2,000,000,000 dollars, are not likely to encourage any scheme which threatens values. The result of this universal distribution of property and material comfort —in spite of the talk about the rich growing richer, and the poor becoming poorer—is that only 5 per cent. of all the wealth of the United States is held by persons worth more than 1,000,000 dollars each, and only 25 per cent. of it by persons with fortunes between 100,000 dollars and 1,000,000 dollars. On the other hand, 27 per cent. is owned by those worth from 10,000 dollars to 100,000 dollars, 37 per cent. by those worth from 1,000 dollars to 10,000 dollars, and only 6 per cent. by those worth less than 1,000 dollars.

In this crusade, of which free silver coinage is only an incident, it is continually represented that it is for the relief of a class—the farmers. Yet of the 5,000,000 farm families, two-thirds own their own holdings, worth on the average 3,400 dollars, half of them free from encumbrance. From these farms come probably one-half of the students in all the colleges, three-fourths of the men in the professions, and a large proportion of those who own and manage the railroads, banks, mines, and manufactories. From them are drawn the majority of the men who hold offices, Federal, State, or local. Nowhere does the soil and its owners bear so close a relation to all the influences which combine to make a wholesome society. Agriculture has its own difficulties and drawbacks everywhere; but in the United

States the men who follow it are dominant in all that makes for independence and greatness. They are partakers in the enterprise which impels them to adopt improvements, in the energy with which a people must surmount difficulties, and in all the movements of a varied national life. Every attempt to push to success the demand for a depreciated currency has been made in States distinctly agricultural. Each one has failed most disastrously, and must fail again.

In spite of all appeals, the man with the town lot, who lives in his own home ; the man with the unencumbered farm, honest in his own business, and anxious to live under an honest government ; the man with the pass-book, which records his savings ; the pensioner, who, as a faithful soldier, has become the recipient of a popular bounty freely and liberally bestowed ; the holder of a life insurance policy, who, whatever he may do, is still unlikely to vote to cheat his heirs ; and the man whose name is borne upon a wages roll, may be relied upon together and of themselves to settle the fate of a set of men who have robbed a party and have avowed it to be their purpose to pass 'laws impairing the obligations of contracts.'

The pending canvass is a bitter one. Nothing since the war period has aroused so many passions. It is viewed not simply as an effort to change a fiscal system and so to unsettle values, but as an attack upon property, a threat to industry. Old party distinctions will disappear for the time, and every effort will be made to assert the national honour and to preserve public and private credit.

The American people have a way of carrying on a Presidential contest with as much energy when they feel sure of the result as when they must win every point. From this time forward they will take no chances ; the new forces of disorder will have no rest. Anarchy, it may be assumed, is not to get its full meal among the intelligent, self-governing people of the United States.

GEORGE F. PARKER.

ON THE ETHICS OF SUPPRESSION
IN BIOGRAPHY

In his *Historical Sketches*, Cardinal Newman wrote as follows in reference to omissions in great histories:

> Here another great subject opens upon us, when I ought to be bringing these remarks to an end; I mean the endemic perennial fidget which possesses us about giving scandal; facts are omitted in great histories, or glosses are put on memorable acts, because they are thought not edifying, whereas of all scandals such omissions, such glosses are the greatest.
>
> But I am getting far more argumentative than I thought to be when I began, so I lay my pen down and retire into myself. (Vol. ii. p. 231.)

Cardinal Newman in his own person had a painful experience of the effects produced by the 'endemic perennial fidget' which he so aptly describes. They, who in his day managed Catholic affairs in England and at Rome for a long period of years, were possessed by this endemic fidget in regard to John Henry Newman himself. It broke out by fits and starts. Now, it was feared lest the illustrious Oratorian, by making admissions imposed upon him by a sense of justice and love of truth, or by accepting documents which, though impugned, he knew to be authentic, or by refusing to put the required glosses on historical facts, might give scandal to Protestants. Now, lest scandal to Protestants might be given by independence of judgment in criticising, on occasions, the policy pursued by ecclesiastical authorities; or in objecting to the unreasoning prohibitions imposed, at times, on legitimate freedom of action on the part of the laity. The mere mention of the name of Newman, or of his writings, or of advice given to his friends and disciples sent a shiver, as it were, through the letters which, for ten years or more, passed between Archbishop Manning and Monsignor Talbot of the Vatican. This endemic fidget in regard to Cardinal Newman endured to the end.

On the first appearance of the *Life of Cardinal Manning* the endemic perennial fidget of giving scandal to Protestants fell on the sudden, like a shiver penetrating marrow and bones, upon some effeminate or mistrustful Catholics among us. Many for a time lost their heads or their tempers, or both.

Fear of giving scandal to Protestants in matters which seem, however remotely or relatively, to touch the Catholic Faith, amounts in men of over-sensitive temperament or of limited capacity almost, in its acutest form at any rate, to mania.   In their fear and fidget such men are incapable of discerning the distinction between the human agencies, which play their subordinate part and which in their nature are fallible and open to criticism, and the divine elements which sustain the Church in its infallible teaching-authority, and in its spiritual life.

Fear of giving scandal to Protestants was the cardinal element in the outcry which was raised against the publication of Cardinal Manning's letters, diaries, and journals.   To take one instance only as an illustration : Fear accounted for the almost insane desire for the suppression of the now famous correspondence between Arch-bishop Manning and Monsignor Talbot.   What wringing of hands, what gnashing of teeth, what lamentations were not uttered by good but timid Catholics lest scandal should be given !   These pious people, happily but few in number, are mistrustful of their Protestant fellow-countrymen ; mistrustful of the effect of simple historic truth ; know not, or have forgotten, that in all ages the Church at times has had to bewail or reprove or condemn the human agents to whose hands the divine work had to be entrusted.   The pure springs were, alas ! but too often defiled.   In the divine constitution of the Church such risk of evil was not excluded.

Even if in the diplomatic correspondence between Archbishop Manning and Monsignor Talbot at the Vatican, human motives may have obtruded themselves, or human weaknesses be at times detected, the guiding motive of Archbishop Manning's action was not, accord-ing to the evidence recorded, personal antipathies or a desire for self-advancement, but a deep-rooted determination to safeguard in a critical transition period, and at all costs, no matter who suffered in the conflict, the interests of the Catholic Church in England.   Even if Manning's action had been a corrupt intrigue ;   even if the Pope, by Monsignor Talbot's secret and underhand influence, in ' making,' as he himself declared, ' every other candidate impossible,' had been cajoled into an unrighteous nomination—what then ?   Are corrupt intrigues at the Vatican to be suppressed lest scandal be given to Protestants, or is the truth to be told ?

That is the vital question raised in the controversy of the last few months.   It concerns not Catholics only, but non-Catholics. It concerns the British reading public, which loves truth and hates suppression of facts and documents, no matter what the motive, as almost a lie.   The question touches nearly the honour and honesty of the literary world, and not of England only.   The question has been taken up on both sides of the Atlantic : Is it a virtue to suppress historic truth or no ?   The broad issues once raised cannot now be evaded.   The advocates of the art of suppression, in great histories or biographies, of historical facts, or of documents on which such facts are based, are now trembling in their shoes. They cannot lay the Frankenstein's monster they have raised.

By force of circumstances, by its candour and outspokenness, and, perhaps, still more by the blunderings of its Catholic critics, the *Life of Cardinal Manning* is become a test-book, as it were: a criterion of the rival methods in the art of writing history or biography. In all the lands where the English tongue is spoken, the question of the hour is asked: Is the publication of historical facts based on authentic documents 'almost a crime' or a virtue?

By a careful estimate it is computed that the Life has already been read in England and the United States, in the Colonies and India, by well-nigh 200,000 persons. As a consequential result of the unprecedented circulation of such a book, or rather as the result produced by action and reaction, it has been criticised over and over again by more than 200 writers in the daily and weekly press, in monthly reviews and magazines on two continents. And yet the authenticity of no single document has been impeached or imperilled.

In regard to this test-question the all but unanimous verdict is in favour of candour and truthfulness in biography as well as in history. They who run may read; unless it be those who elect to walk through life blindfold.

What readers at home and abroad are, perhaps, most concerned to learn from me is the opinion of Catholics, first in regard to the Life, and, secondly, as to whether truthfulness and candour in biography is a virtue or no. In the nature of things I am in a position to learn many opinions on the subject from various quarters which find no public expression. Numerous letters from Catholics come to my hands; many more from Anglicans and others. Many of the former indignantly complain of the suppression of their letters. Catholics of position and experience maintain that Catholic opinion on the *Life of Cardinal Manning* is not fairly represented in *The Tablet* or the *Weekly Register*. They draw a broad distinction between those Catholics who have read the Life and those who have only read criticisms in the Catholic papers. They who have read the Life as a rule, in the teeth of its many faults, approve of it; those who have only read Catholic reviews of it denounce it. I will give two typical instances: a priest only the other day denounced it as 'an abominable book,' but admitted he had not read it. This was in England. A nun in Australia refused to read the Life, which was within her reach, because she had heard it was a 'bad book.' Both priest and nun were honest. They took the opinion of their pet newspaper as gospel truth. They are types of fortunately not a numerous class. On the other hand, fervent and loyal Catholics of independent judgment, who far exceed both in numbers and capacity these good people who believe implicitly what is told to them, have read the book and find it neither bad nor abominable. Quite the contrary. I might justify 'this assertion by many quotations from letters sent to me by personal strangers, if space and modesty permitted.

Still more convincing, perhaps, than the opinion expressed in private letters is the judgment given in conversation by literary people, and at clubs, and in general society. One personage, a Catholic of high ecclesiastical position, of wide experience and knowledge of men, recently expressed the following opinion: 'The *Life of Cardinal Manning* justifies itself by results. By common consent it is acknowledged that a higher estimate has been formed alike by Catholics and Protestants of Cardinal Manning's character and career than was held before the publication of his Life.'

From the other side of the wall of separation which unhappily divides the Church of Rome and the Church of England—a wall, it is devoutly to be hoped, destined sooner or later, in the inscrutable designs of Providence, to be removed—I am enabled by the kindness of Lord Halifax to recite the following testimony given by his Grace the Archbishop of York: 'I always had a high opinion of Manning's powers, but since reading his Life I look upon him as a saint. The chapter on " Hindrances " is the most attractive and edifying record in the book.'

Such testimonies, however valuable as coming from representative men on either side, are in the nature of things dwarfed by the following words spoken a short time ago by his Holiness Pope Leo the Thirteenth. Though, of course, unofficial, these weighty words will be received with all the more reverence and gratitude inasmuch as they touch upon the test-question raised to-day in all the lands where the English tongue is spoken—namely, whether in great histories or biographies truth is a virtue or a crime?

Someone in the presence of the Pope was regretting that Manning's character should have been so hurt by what had appeared in his biography, and Pope Leo the Thirteenth spoke as follows: ' Truth is the only thing that matters. What would the Bible have been if the writers had considered the effect of what they wrote? What would have become of Mary Magdalene and her sin; what of Peter and his fall?'[1]

Such a verdict is in keeping with all the known acts and utterances of his Holiness. It is not so long since that the well-known author of *The History of the Popes*, before recording the life of Alexander the Sixth, consulted Pope Leo. His Holiness's advice to the eminent German priest was in substance: ' Tell the truth and the whole truth, no matter though the reputation of a Pope should suffer thereby.'

---

[1] The correspondent—a personage of honour and truthfulness—who conveyed to me the above words of the Pope writes as follows: ' This is, as far as I can remember, what I heard, but of course it was spoken in Italian, and I cannot vouch for the accuracy of every word.' The accuracy of this statement is confirmed by another witness of equal authority.

In the face of the verdict of ͏public opinion in England and America, all but unanimous, as already recorded, in favour of candour and truthfulness in biography, his Eminence Cardinal Vaughan ought to look to it lest he come to be regarded as a sort of *introverted* 'Athanasius,' standing alone, *contra mundum*, in defence of an almost condemned proposition.

At the beginning of this brief article I quoted an effective passage from Cardinal Newman's *Historical Sketches* on the endemic perennial fidget among Catholics of giving scandal. I cannot do better in bringing my remarks to a close than to recite Cardinal Newman's judgment on the true method of writing a biography. The authority of the illustrious Oratorian on ethical and literary questions is recognised to-day by the world at large. Even they who in their haste suggested the suppression of contemporary letters will, I am persuaded, in deference to such a judgment, be only too eager to abandon, or at least qualify, an ill-considered opinion.

In a letter addressed to his sister, Mrs. Mozley, John Henry Newman wrote as follows :—

> It has been a hobby of mine, though perhaps it is a truism and not a hobby, that the true life of a man is in his letters. . . . Not only for the interests of a biography, but for arriving at the inside of things, the publication of letters is the true method.
>
> Biographers varnish, they assign motives, they conjecture feelings, they interpret Lord Burleigh's nods ; but contemporary letters are facts.

In these pregnant sentences Cardinal Newman touched by anticipation the heart of the· controversy which was raised by the publication of the *Life of Cardinal Manning*. Even before publication I· was urged, with singular vehemence and pertinacity, to adopt the policy of suppression. What would have been the result of such a disastrous policy ? Contemporary letters, which Newman says are facts, would have disappeared from an emasculated Life. The relations between Manning and Newman would never have been known in their truth and fulness had I consented to the suppression of their letters. The disclosure of those relations was absolutely essential, not only for the sake of historic truth, but for the real manifestation of Manning's character in one of its most salient aspects. In like manner, the suppression of the Manning and. Talbot correspondence, out of fear of giving scandal to Protestants, would have been in itself the greatest of all scandals.

In a word, had I in writing *Cardinal Manning's Life* not followed Newman's leading, but had regarded, according to the suggestion of men of faint heart, the suppression of letters, not their publication, as the true method of biography, the world would never have arrived ' at the inside of things ' in regard to the character and career of Cardinal Manning. Happily, I was inspired to follow Cardinal Newman's precept and example. Unfairness in controversy or in writing history is a detestable practice. I can conceive little or nothing more prejudicial to Catholic interests, especially to-day in England, than the policy of suppressing historical facts and documents. In his *Essay on the Development of Christian Doctrine*, page 185, John Henry Newman uttered the following warning, which Catholics of the timid and mistrustful sort might well take to heart to-day :—' If the Catholic hypothesis is true, it neither needs nor is benefited by unfairness. Adverse facts should be acknowledged, explained if but apparent, accounted for if real; or let alone and borne patiently as being fewer and lighter than the difficulties of other hypotheses.' In like manner, in his preface to the *Life of St. Chrysostom*, Newman points out the virtue of letters as forming the best sources or materials of biography. The personality of the saints is known to us, he says, not by their learned treatises, but by their letters. Nothing is known of the personality of St. Thomas Aquinas, called by his contemporaries the ' Dumb Ox,' though his learned works extort the admiration of all men ; whereas, on the other hand, the letters of St. Augustine bring his personality home to our hearts. Speaking of Cicero, John Henry Newman said, ' Cicero is personally known to us, not by his Orations, but by his letters.'

What should we have really known of the personality of Cardinal Manning from his sermons and lectures had his letters, journals, and diaries been suppressed, or such portions of them as revealed his real character or mind in its most salient features ?

Let the robuster faith and trust of Cardinal Newman prevail over the wave of mistrust and timidity, over ' the endemic perennial fidget of giving scandal' which for the moment possesses the heart of a small minority, at all events, of the educated Catholics of England. The old English proverb, ' Honesty is the best policy,' has come true in regard to *Cardinal Manning's Life*. His character, public and private, as Archdeacon of Chichester, as Archbishop of Westminster, as Father of the Vatican Council, as Cardinal and champion of the Holy See, has been brought in its true light and colour to the knowledge of all men. The crowning labours of his later life as Father of the Poor, as social reformer, as champion of the oppressed ; his incessant work, his mental vigour displayed to the end without the remotest trace of ' senile decay '—a cruel slur cast on his closing years which Mr. Sydney Buxton, his fellow-labourer to the last, indignantly repudiates—endeared Cardinal Manning, as no man of his generation was endeared, to the hearts of the toiling masses of London. The upshot is that without an attempt to conceal his faults and weaknesses, the character of Cardinal Manning is held to-day in higher esteem than ever ; his personality—the real Manning as he lived and breathed—is known far and wide ; honoured and appreciated by all men, Catholic and Protestant alike ; honoured all the more because his whole nature stands revealed, and because no gloss is put on human frailties, which were indeed overshadowed by the virtues of his higher spiritual nature. After the experiences of the last few months, it would be politic, to say the least, on the part of the advocates of suppression to forego their fears and their folly, and take to heart the words of Pope Leo—' Truth is the only thing that matters.'

To the biographer of Cardinal Manning, truth was indeed the only thing that mattered. To me it is a supreme and singular satisfaction that it fell to my lot to be called upon to stand up before the world against the faint-hearted or craven advocates of suppression in defence of the cause of historic truth : to write, if I may say so, my name on the annals of the day as a champion of candour and outspokenness, at all events in biography.

Before concluding this brief survey there are two special points to be noted.

It is curious as a psychological study to examine for a moment the mental attitude of Catholic critics in regard to the *Life of Cardinal Manning.* Not one of them has ventured to utter a word on Cardinal Manning's change of front in regard to the Temporal Power of the Pope. This conspicuous and startling change has been absolutely suppressed in the Catholic newpapers ; not one of those pious Catholics, whose knowledge of the Life is derived solely from what is told to them in their newspaper, is aware to this hour that Cardinal Manning, not long after the death of .Pope Pius the Ninth, declared that the policy of upholding the Temporal Power was bringing spiritual ruin and disaster on the Catholics of Italy. The motives of this suppression on the part of Catholic newspapers was not fear of giving scandal to Protestants, for, as a fact, Protestants were not scandalised by such a change of principle. The habit of suppressing what they regard as awkward facts seems to come naturally to these light-hearted papers. Cardinal Manning's inconsistency about the Temporal Power, it was considered, would give scandal to pious but weak-kneed Catholics. What easier, then, than to suppress the fact ?

On the other hand, Cardinal Manning (which is the second special point I wish to note) was consistent from beginning to end in his opposition to the Jesuits. But consistency on this point was also regarded as an ugly fact, and therefore to be kept out of sight.

Cardinal Manning's opposition to the Jesuits came too near home to the hearts of Catholics, was too prolonged and obstinate, to be altogether concealed even by the adroit handling of the astute suppressors of things that be. From Protestants, Cardinal Manning's relations with the Jesuits were, even during his lifetime, carefully concealed. It was feared that if Manning's disputes with the Jesuits got abroad, Catholics would be taunted with suffering just as much as Protestants from the plague of internal dissensions. Catholic quarrels, however, are not on theological questions, but on matters of policy or

Church government; but if otherwise, in either case suppression of facts is almost a fraud. Protestants have no doubt often looked with interest on Jesuit colleges and schools in the neighbourhood of London. But it never occurred to their minds that the Jesuits, with all their teaching apparatus, were exiles from London, that their colleges at Beaumont, near Old Windsor, and at Wimbledon were, as far as his own diocese was concerned, under Cardinal Manning's ban; that the Diocese of Westminster was guarded, like the Garden of Eden, by two flaming swords against the intruding Jesuits.

Cardinal Manning has put on record his rooted antipathy to the Jesuits. In one of his latest autobiographical notes, written in the year 1890, he said:

> There is only a plank between the Jesuits and Presbyterianism. . . . They are Papal by their vow, but in their spirit they are less Papal than anti-episcopal. The claim of special dependence on the Pope breeds everywhere a spirit of independence of local authority. This is a grave danger to them, and few of them escape it. Their anti-episcopal spirit shows itself in their treatment of their own men when they become bishops. . . . They are like the Low Church Evangelicals in the Anglican Church, who look upon their bishops as 'enemies of vital godliness.'

Cardinal Manning could not endure—it was not in his nature— to be looked upon by the Jesuits as an 'enemy of vital godliness.' They fell under his ban. Metaphorically he 'cursed them with bell, book, and candle.' In a laughing fashion, their retort came quick:

> Cardinals may come, Cardinals may go;
> But we go on for ever.

Cardinal Manning, as is known of all men, regarded the suppression of the Society of Jesus in 1773 as the work of God's hand; he likewise looked upon its restoration in 1827 as God's work. But his abiding hostility to the Jesuits, based, as he declared, on their corporate action in England and Rome, was testified by the prediction which he uttered on various occasions: 'I foresee another 1773.'

EDMUND S. PURCELL,
Author of the 'Life of Cardinal Manning.'

· PostscrIptum. ·

Some months ago, in reply to Mr. Gladstone's refutation in a letter to me of the charges brought against him in the *Month*, Father Smith addressed a letter to the editor of this Review. Instead of frankly withdrawing his misrepresentations, whether with or without an apology matters but little, Father Smith, in spite of Mr. Gladstone's absolute contradictions, reiterated his charges under cover of putting a gloss on Mr. Gladstone's words. For instance, in regard to Mr. Gladstone's conversation with Manning in the summer of 1848 in St. James's Park, Father Smith suggested that Manning had likewise spoken of his difficulties and perplexities. Mr. Gladstone's denial was plain and positive : 'According to my recollection, not a word.'

Again, in regard to Mr. Gladstone's statement that, speaking of Newman and his fellow-converts of 1845, Manning had said, ' Their common bond of union is their want of truth,' Father Smith suggested that, ' owing to a failure of memory, Mr. Gladstone had inverted the respective parts taken by himself and Manning, and put his own words into Manning's mouth.'

When compelled by Mr. Gladstone's unanswerable evidence to back out of this charge, Father Smith excused himself for his misstatement by saying that his ' suggestion was pleasantly rather than seriously meant.' After such treatment, no one would have been in the least surprised had Mr. Gladstone not condescended to expend another word on such a special pleader. But in his kindness Mr. Gladstone placed ' at my free disposal ' the following letter, with the liberty of making use of it when a fit opportunity occurred :

Hawarden : April 1896.

Dear Mr. Purcell, —I do not know how far you may desire to follow up the question which Mr. Smith, S.J., discusses in the new *Nineteenth Century*. I am, however, glad to say that I have found here the collection of my letters to Anglican Manning, which he gave me (a reluctant party to the exchange) in return for his letters to me, of which the destruction has created an irreparable loss. In this collection I find two important letters. In the first, of November 6, 1850, I recite to him the conversation (which, indeed, in substance was all on his side) of 1848. The second is of December 20, 1850, I having heard from him in the interval. In this letter I say ' we are sadly, strangely at issue on the facts of the conversation,' and then go on to specify in what way he contested my narrative :

' If I have any one clear recollection in my mind, it is that your assurances then did not relate at all to God's mercy to those who faithfully follow their light, be it what it may, but to your perfect sense of security in the Church of England from its objective character.'

It is, therefore, plain to me that the way in which he contested my narrative was not by any direct denial of the propositions I had put into his mouth, but by contending that I misconstrued him, and that he meant to refer to Divine mercy for the invincibly ignorant.

In other words, all the evidence we possess exactly agrees with my recollections, though Manning's unfortunate destruction of his own letters has cancelled the best evidence of all.

I also find that the cessation of intercourse was not so entire as we had all supposed. He wrote a letter to me in the latter part of 1852, and I replied to him referring to the great gap between us, but entirely in terms corresponding with our old relations.

[After thus dismissing Father Smith, Mr. Gladstone, referring to the *Life of Cardinal Manning*, said :] The importance of your work rather grows upon us than loses in weight with the passage of time. I do not think any of us exaggerated the importance of the Life as an *event*.

I remain, sincerely yours,
W. E. Gladstone.

In corroboration of the statement in the above letter regarding the now famous conversation in St. James's Park, 'which, indeed, in substance was all on his (Manning's) side,' I may fitly recite a passage from an earlier letter, dated Biarritz, the 2nd of February, 1896, written before Mr. Gladstone knew even of the existence of Father Smith, far less that he had been betrayed into the folly of misrepresenting Mr. Gladstone's letters and conversations given in the *Life of Cardinal Manning*. The passage is as follows:

'I have just been looking into a point which you might have emphasised more strongly: the utter contradiction between the spontaneous declaration to me in St. James's Park, in June, I think, or July, 1848, and the letter he had written in March to Robert Wilberforce'

E. S. P.

BHOWÁNI, THE CHOLERA-GODDESS

SOME EXPERIENCES IN HINDOO SANITATION

THAT an Englishman on visiting an Indian village in which cholera was raging should be able to offer the inhabitants no advice which he was certain was good and at the same time practicable, except that they should pray to Bhowáni, the Cholera-Goddess, may appear a matter for surprise to people in England. When it is further explained that the Englishman had come to the village furnished with such resources of modern science as a portable bacteriological laboratory, which included an autoclave and an immersion lens, and that he had had some experience of cholera epidemics under different conditions in India, the surprise will not be lessened; neither will it be diminished when it is learnt that Bhowáni is another form of Kali, the terrible goddess of the Thugs, those road murderers who used to appease her by offering human sacrifices. Nevertheless, this was my experience on the occasion of a visit which I made to the Balrampur district in the autumn of the year 1894, and I venture to think that an account of my experience may prove of some interest.

Balrampur is a small native state, about half as large as England, situated to the north of the River Gogra, and lying within sight of the snow-clad ranges of the Himalaya Mountains. Much of it is frequently flooded. Fever is constantly present, and cholera breaks out almost every year. No railway exists nearer than Gonda, which is twenty-six miles distant from Balrampur, the chief town of the state. One or two roads run through the district, away from which travelling is difficult, especially during the rains, when, as was my own experience, the tracts are impassable for horses and heavy going even for elephants.

My object in spending a few days' leave in this place was to see if it might not be possible to check the march of cholera by disinfecting wells. Thanks to the kindness of Colonel Anson, the Political Agent, I found myself installed in a comfortable bungalow, with the town in which cholera was present on one side, and the village of Dhusaha, in which the disease was also raging, on the other. A soldier belonging to the state had died in the compound, and one of the only two Europeans in the place had died of the same disease, in each case a few days before I arrived. I afterwards found that two out of the three wells in use in the compound contained the microbe of cholera, and were probably responsible for these deaths.

The villagers at first objected to my putting any medicine in their wells. I regret to say that, so far as my experience goes, the first symptom of civilisation among the lower classes in India is that they develop a sort of inverted conscience, which pricks them whenever they tell the truth. In Dhusaha this influence had not yet arrived, and consequently my suggestion to put a medicine in their wells was met with a plain-spoken and unambiguous refusal. I therefore spent my first few days in the place in making bacteriological observations and in studying the beliefs and customs of the inhabitants.

The village Dhusaha consists of a collection of mud huts. There had been about 320 inhabitants, but seventy-eight had died of cholera in the epidemic that was then existing. The water supply is obtained from four shallow wells. The mud huts are constantly falling down in the rains, and mud to repair them being taken from a piece of waste land, the hollow thus formed has gradually formed a tank. Refuse is usually thrown down on the margins of the tank; hence, its water is so putrid that the inhabitants not only do not drink it, but I believe do not use it even for washing clothes. The inhabitants pointed out to me that the reason why the water in one of the wells was bad was that it was situated near the tank, and that the bad water from the tank travelled along under the ground to the well and gave a disagreeable taste to the water. I afterwards found that the water of this particular well contained no less than 7,000 microbes per cubic centimetre, and thus thoroughly deserved the character the villagers gave it.

The inhabitants are all high-caste Hindoos, mostly Brahmins. Not a single sweeper or other low-caste man was in the place. Being of high caste they only eat food which has been cooked by themselves, and this only when it is perfectly fresh. They eat no sweetmeats or other food brought from the bazaar in the neighbouring town. Their food consists almost entirely of rice and pulse, with occasionally a little unrefined sugar or dried mangoes.

But what chiefly aroused my interest was their views of cholera, and their religious observances in the presence of this scourge. If cholera breaks out in a village, the inhabitants say that it is due to Bhowáni their goddess, or to the army of Bhowáni being present in the place. They regard it as a judgment for their sins and shortcomings, and, as in other religions, they consider this evil to be a blessing in disguise. They immediately commence to propitiate the goddess by sacrificing flowers and rice. When travelling through the district the first sign of the presence of cholera which struck the eye was a small booth of grass mats surmounted by flags borne on long bamboos. In Dhusaha such a booth had been erected on the margin of a well which contained the cholera microbe, and in this booth the chief 'jogi,' or priest, of the village prayed with about a dozen of the older villagers. I myself heard him praying on three successive days in a loud voice, and I believe he prayed the whole day long with scarcely an interval for refreshment. I shall mention him again later on.

The villagers in this district, however, not only attempt to propitiate Bhowáni by prayers and sacrifices, but also by certain rules of conduct, which appear to me to be of interest and importance. Firstly, they say that Bhowáni will be angry if any of the inhabitants leave the village. Secondly, they say that she will be angry if any outsiders are allowed to come into the village at a time when cholera is present. A curious incident illustrating the good effect of this belief happened at about this time in a couple of villages some distance from the town of Balrampur. There was only one well between the two villages. Cholera one day broke out in the village which possessed the well. On the next morning women came as usual from the other village to fetch water. But the inhabitants of the first village turned out and refused to allow them to approach, on the grounds that Bhowáni was among them and would be angry at being disturbed. The inhabitants of this second village had to get their water from elsewhere, and consequently came into the town to make a complaint. It may be noted that the official to whom they chose to bring their complaint was not the native prime minister or the native secretary for home affairs, or any other native official, who might be supposed to be better able to sympathise with their wrongs, but the head stableman, who was the only English official in the district at the time. I have no doubt that he pointed out to them that if they could not get their water, they were equally unable to get the cholera through this source.

Granting that the spread of cholera is chiefly furthered by human intercourse (and this at the present time few people seem inclined to doubt), it appears to me difficult to see how cholera could spread if these simple rules were rigidly enforced.

But there are other ways of avoiding the wrath of Bhowáni which appear to me to be only slightly less admirable than those above mentioned.

Firstly, they say that Bhowáni will be angry if any one takes medicine when cholera is about. Perhaps I owe some apology to medical men in suggesting that this rule is good. But when it is considered that if the natives were willing to take medicine, they would often have to walk twenty miles to the dispensary to get it, thus increasing the risk of spreading the disease through the four thousand villages that are in the district in question, it will be seen that there are advantages in the plan. Further, it would often

happen that the medicine would arrive too late to have any effect on
the patient, and probably it would have a bad effect on the relatives
in making them doubt the efficacy of English drugs. Cholera in this
district often kills in a few hours, and when a fairly unanimous
choice has been made as to which of the thousand and one now
existing remedies is most likely to be able to cope with it, it will be
time to object to the custom in question. The wish to do something
when one sees a fellow creature in pain is very natural. I saw an
old woman dying of cholera in Dhusaha. The sole treatment to
which she had been subjected was that a mud plaster had been
spread over the stomach, and small doses of holy water from the
Ganges were being poured into her mouth. The latter treatment
was intended as a medicine for her soul rather than for her body, as
every Hindoo should, according to the prevalent belief, drink this
water before his death. Her relatives were too troubled by the
occurrence to object to my putting some salol which I happened to
have with me into this water, but it certainly did no good to the
patient, and had I at the time known more about their religion, I
should have avoided the risk of hurting their feelings.

When Bhowáni is in the village, it is also necessary to avoid
feasting and other forms of indulgence. The excellence of these
rules is sufficiently obvious.

What is the origin of this worship of Bhowáni, every detail of
which, excepting the sacrifices, appears to be a sanitary precaution?
Is Bhowáni the name of some primeval bacteriologist, who has since
been deified? Or of some early sanitary commissioner, whose studies
on the nature of cholera have since earned him a place in the
Hindoo pantheon? Or, on the other hand, has the form of worship
arisen by some process of evolution from a simpler and perhaps less
admirable model? *A priori* the latter alternative would appear to be
the most probable, and it agrees the better with some inquiries I have
instituted since my return to Agra. Bhowáni is another name or
incarnation of the goddess Kali.[1] There are not many worshippers
of this goddess in the parts of the North-West Provinces with which
I am acquainted. They occur more frequently, however, in the
neighbourhood of Calcutta; and here I made inquiries. I found,
however, no trace in her worship of the above-described sanitary
precautions. After some search, I met in Agra with a most devout
worshipper of Kali, who had given up his business in order to be able
to devote his time to religion. He showed great willingness to tell
me everything connected with the ritual, and further gave me
free permission to chop off his head if he could not stop a cholera
epidemic by offering sacrifices and prayers. He was, however, more.

[1] Kali is the Destroyer. Diseases and pestilences are caused by her emissaries.
The views of the Thugs were that they could please her by acting as her emissaries.
Consequently they regarded the murder of their fellow creatures as a religious act.

shocked than interested in the ideas of his fellow religionists in Balrampur, and I found in his worship of Kali no trace of any · hygienic precaution.   He told me that if cholera is present in a village, it is necessary to sacrifice to Kali every day, and that while the public worship, which may last about two hours, is going on, it is necessary that no one of the inhabitants of the village should stay away. Further, while the worship is proceeding, the inhabitants do not like strangers to come into the village and interrupt them, either by drawing water or in any other way.   It would seem that, in Balrampur, it is these details of the ritual that have been more developed than they are elsewhere.   In other places the worshippers of Bhowáni or Kali seem content with enjoining that the inhabitants should remain in the village during the two hours during which the religious ceremony is going on.   In Balrampur, on the other hand, it is considered necessary that every one of the inhabitants should remain in the village during the whole of the twenty-four hours.   Elsewhere the worshippers merely object to their service being interrupted. In Balrampur they object to strangers coming into the villages at any time when cholera is present, as if the worship were proceeding continuously.

I have left to the last a curious custom, rather than a religious observance, which is met with in the Balrampur district.   It relates to the disposal of the dead.   The body of a person dead of cholera, instead of being burnt, is buried.   This may appear at first sight to be an insanitary proceeding.   But in reality it is the reverse. Usually the bodies of Hindoos are burned.   It is a necessary part of the ritual that on the fifth, tenth, eleventh, or thirteenth day after the burning, according to the caste, all the relatives of the deceased should meet in his house with as many Brahmins as can be obtained, and that they should have a feast.   Supposing this to be done at a time when cholera was present in the village, there can be no doubt that it would lead to the diffusion of cholera over the surrounding district.   A case in which this appears to have happened is mentioned in a recent report by Surgeon-Captain Pratt on cholera in the Gonda district.   The worshippers of Bhowáni, on the other hand, prefer to bury the bodies until cholera has vanished.   The burying of the body is not followed by the assemblage of the relatives for the funeral feast, but after the cholera is over they dig up the body, burn it, and then carry out the religious ceremonies. I cannot find that this apparently insanitary proceeding has ever re-started the cholera.   Nor is it likely that it should, for it has recently been shown that the cholera microbe rapidly perishes in buried corpses.   How far this disagreeable custom may be objectionable in respect of other diseases I am not prepared to discuss, but I have little doubt that it tends to prevent the spread of cholera.[2]

[2] In many parts of Oudh it is a custom to throw the bodies of persons dead of

As already stated, my object in coming to Balrampur was to dis-
infect wells, and my proposal to do so had been met by a direct
negative on the part of the Dhusaha villagers. After learning their
belief as to the nature of cholera, and the nature of their objections
to the presence of a disinfectant in their wells, I was in a position to
attack them again on the subject. Knowing that it is more easy to
convince people by education than by argument, I collected about a
dozen jogis and other kinds of fakirs and some Brahmins, and gave
them a lecture which, with the accompanying experiments, lasted
about two hours, and was completely successful in its object. Those
who know fakirs chiefly, as I have seen them, hanging for hours
head downwards, over a hot fire in the burning Indian sun, or
attempting to earn their salvation by other eccentric methods, such
as sitting on a bed of upturned nails, may think that I was too
sanguine in hoping to succeed, and a short account of this lecture
may therefore be of interest.

I commenced my lecture by showing them a human hair under
the microscope, first slightly magnified, and then under increasing
degrees of magnification, until, as they affirmed, it looked as large as
a tree. Then I showed them some mildew growing in a test tube ;
this they recognised. Then, under a low power of the microscope,
they saw that the mildew consisted of a mass of threads. Under a
higher power (a magnification of 750 diameters) they recognised with
evident interest that it was a plant, and they themselves pointed out
the branches, the roots, the flowers, and the seeds. I then showed
them a large collection of microbes which I had at that time collected
from different wells in the neighbourhood. In each case I gave the
name of the well in the hope of increasing their interest in the subject,
and with the *arrière-pensée* of suggesting that their water was in need
of improvement. The first microbe which I showed them was a large
bacillus, that had grown out into long rods similar in thickness to the
threads of which the mildew consists, and containing rows of spores
which they recognised as seeds. I then showed them the same
bacillus at an earlier stage of its growth, when the individual rods
were shorter and slowly moving through the culture liquid. The
next microbe I exhibited was still smaller and rapidly motile. The
last was the smallest, and moved so quickly across the field of view
that they could only see it with difficulty. This was the cholera
microbe. I told them that it was the army of Bhowáni, but afterwards referred to it as the ' cholera mildew.' I pointed out how in
some respects these creatures resembled plants, in others animals.

cholera into rivers. In other parts of the country this fate happens to the bodies of
persons dead of snake-bite. Still more widespread is the custom of disposing of the
bodies of lepers in this way. For this I believe there are religious reasons. The
bodies of young children are not cremated. In the case of poor people the cremation
is often very partial, and the greater part of the disintegration is left to the sacred
turtles which are always waiting at the burning ghats.

Since they had seen them moving, it was no use asserting that they were merely plants, so I contented myself with asking the question, 'Who can tell which they are, animals or plants ?' I then told them that the food of these creatures is dirt. I showed them some peptone under the name of the 'essence of dirt taken from the inside of a pig.' The nomenclature may appear strange, but if I am right in believing that peptone is usually made by allowing a pig's stomach to digest itself at a warm temperature, it at least cannot be described as highly inaccurate. I then showed them some water to which some of this 'essence of dirt' had been added. I told them the name of the well from which the water had been taken, and explained that on the previous night the cholera mildew had been present in such small quantities, that I was unable to see it by means of the microscope, but that owing to the 'essence of dirt' having acted as food, the water now looked as if milk had been added to it, and the reason of this was that many thousands of the cholera mildews were now present in every drop. It may be explained that the addition of peptone to water in this way is the ordinary method of testing for the cholera microbe.

I then somewhat changed the subject by asking why it was that no one ever got cholera by drinking holy water, whereas many persons died of cholera every year by drinking water out of ordinary wells. Holy water, it may be explained, is water taken from the Ganges or Jumna.[3] Many bodies of persons dead of cholera are thrown into these rivers. Natives constantly drink the water of the river while cholera corpses are floating past, yet none of them contract the disease from so doing. Yet it is certain that the cholera mildew gets into the water. Further, this must also happen when cholera breaks out at religious festivals at Hurdwar and Allahabad ; yet there is no evidence that cholera spreads to villages downstream more quickly than it does to other villages, to which it is carried by the returning pilgrims. I suggested that the reason of this is that the water of these rivers contains no dirt suitable for the cholera mildew. Consequently, when it gets into these rivers it quickly perishes owing to lack of nourishment. The water of these rivers appears to be muddy. If some of the mud floating in their water is examined under the microscope, it is seen to consist of nothing but little pieces of stone. If the mud from a well, on the other hand, is examined, pieces of leaves, of clothes, of human skin, and of other particles of animal origin may be discerned. Such things furnish food for the cholera mildew. Consequently, if a trace of the cholera mildew gets into one of their wells, finding there a suitable food, it rapidly reproduces until the cause of cholera is present in quantities in every drop. Here in Balrampur the wells were dirty, and hence cholera came and

[3] Evidence of the extraordinary purity of the Ganges and Jumna may be found in a paper which I read at the Indian Medical Congress in Calcutta (December 1894), entitled 'On the Microbes of Indian Rivers.'

was bad every year. In Agra, on the other hand, where I came from, the wells were cleaner and cholera was far less frequent.[4]

I then went on to ask how cholera could be stopped. This · could be done by adding to the .wells a medicine which I possessed, which had the wonderful power of destroying·dirt. The medicine, it may be explained, was potassium permanganate. To exhibit its action, I placed before them two glasses of water. To one I added a small quantity of the ' essence of dirt.' The other was pure water, or, rather, the best that I could obtain. I showed them some potassium permanganate, dissolved it in water, and added a few drops of the solution to each of the glasses. The purple colour produced by the addition remained permanent in the glass containing clean water; but in the other, owing to the presence of the peptone, the colour was destroyed in a few seconds, giving risé to a yellow colour; and presently a brown precipitate was deposited. I pointed out to my audience that where dirt was present the medicine had combined with it. The medicine was destroyed, and also the dirt, both falling to the bottom as a precipitate. I pointed out that this might be done in a well just as easily as in a glass, and that by so doing they inevitably render the water less fitted to support the life of the cholera mildew, and make the water like that of the Ganges.[5] I did not ask them to take away the life of any living creature, for this I knew was contrary to their religion ; but I did ask them to remove its food and thus prevent this living creature from reproducing itself, and so giving them the cholera. Further, I said that I knew that drinking an English medicine was also contrary to their religion, and I did not ask them to drink it. There was plenty of dirt in their wells with which it would combine, and if they added it at night, it would, before the morning, have fallen to the bottom. Further, as they could see for themselves, if a trace of the medicine was present in the ·water, it produced a purple colour, and therefore if they waited till the purple colour had disappeared, they would be safe to avoid the chance of swallowing the medicine.

. Whether they were most impressed with the cogency of my arguments, or the exceeding badness of the Hindustani in which I

---

[4] I have stated some of the grounds on which this and other opinions expressed here are based in *The Annual Report of the Chemical Examiner and Bacteriologist to the Government of the North-West Provinces and Oudh* for 1894, published at the Government Press, Allahabad. But since writing the above, I have been led to the view that there is something in the water of the Ganges and Jumna which kills the microbe.

[5] Some evidence that permanganate really acts in the way here described—namely, by removing the food of the microbe and thus 'starving it out—was subsequently obtained in an epidemic of cholera in Shahgunj. Here the cholera microbe vanished from the well water a few hours after the addition of the permanganate, but reappeared on the following morning. But within three days it had wholly disappeared from the wells which had been treated, though it continued to exist for weeks in other wells that had not been medicated. Less than two ounces of the permanganate had been added to each well.

expressed them, or by the price of my microscope, I do not know ; but they appeared to be satisfied that it was a good thing to add the medicine to the wells ; some of them even appeared to be eager to do so, since cholera was in their villages.

After giving this lecture I went to Dhusaha, and at last persuaded the chief jogi, Mahadeo Purhit by name, to allow me to put medicine into his well. The natives crowded round, showing much surprise at the quantity of colour produced by so little of the substance. The addition was made at evening, and on the next day both the colour of the permanganate and the cholera microbe which had previously been in the well had completely vanished.

Later in the day news was brought to me that Mahadeo Purhit was dangerously ill. I hurried over to see him, and to my dismay found that he was dying of cholera. In the afternoon he died. I went again immediately to the village, not feeling very sure of the reception I should get, since it was inevitable that, sooner or later, the inhabitants would come to the conclusion that his death was a judgment from Bhowáni for his allowing a Sahib to come into the village and to put medicine in his well. However, I thought that it might be possible to prevent their arriving at this conclusion by first getting another idea into their heads. I spoke to the villagers, and pointed out that his death proved the truth of what I had been saying, for I had said that the cause of cholera was in his well at a time when no one who drank its water was suffering from the disease. Now he had died from drinking this water. If I had put the medicine into the well a week earlier, he would now have been all right. I then seized the opportunity of making some prophesies about other wells which were in the village, and in which I had found the cholera microbe ; and without more ado the villagers allowed me to put permanganate into all these wells.

It may be noted that it was most important that the villagers should have no objection to this medication of their wells. For if they did not approve of it, they might obtain their water from a tank or some other source which might be worse than the well itself. Although I succeeded in showing the natives that the addition of this medicine implied nothing dangerous to their caste, I could not help their being at first a little frightened of it. So I drank some water (and this was the second of the two occasions only on which I have drunk water since I have been in India) from one of the wells in the village, to which permanganate had been added ; this I had to do in order to convince the natives that it was not poisonous.

The cholera stopped within three days of the treatment of the wells, that is to say within a time covered by the probable incubation period of the disease. It is not the object of this paper to prove that the disinfection of wells during cholera epidemics is useful, so I will confine myself to saying that the results obtained in other epidemics, as in this have been encouraging, but not conclusive, as to the value of the method.

I wish rather to suggest that a help to progress in sanitation in India may possibly be secured by studying the customs of the people in the light of recent knowledge, and by encouraging those which appear to be of use. The customs above described exist, so far as I am aware, over a limited area only, and from the standpoint of others than the inhabitants themselves, this religion which makes quarantine in the presence of cholera one of the cardinal virtues, is little more than an ethnological curiosity. In other parts of India the religious beliefs of ,the people impel them to the most insanitary actions, especially at their religious festivals, which are known to be so potent in spreading diseases.

But I have come across customs which exist over a far wider area, and which I believe to have a beneficent influence in limiting the spread of epidemic disease. Take for instance the customs connected with giving water to strangers. I have been told that in some districts Brahmins keep a bucket and rope at each well for the special use of travellers, these not being allowed to lower their own buckets into the well. In other places a man also is provided to draw water for strangers. Sometimes, in the case of villages situated near to the high road, a man brings water from the village to sell to the passers by. But I believe a more frequent plan is for the villagers to subscribe, and to keep going a house in which passers-by can obtain water free of cost. A man of high caste sits inside the house at a little window. A traveller comes up and asks for water. In England he would receive it in a glass which he would put to his lips, and after having deposited on the edge of the glass any objectionable microbe which he might happen to have about him, whether influenza, diphtheria, or whooping cough, would return the glass in a condition in which it might possibly be ready to infect the next comer. In India the simple process of giving a cup of cold water to a traveller is carried out with more regard to sanitary laws. Firstly the traveller states his caste. If he is of high caste, immediately he holds out his hands, and washes them with water poured into them. Then more water is poured into his hands and thus conveyed to his mouth. If by any chance he should happen to touch the drinking vessel, it would be necessary to heat it in a fire to sterilise it, or, as the natives say, to remove the defilement, before it could be used again for the next comer. Supposing the traveller is of low caste, that is to say one engaged in some filthy occupation, then the water cannot be poured direct from the vessel into his hands, because, as was explained to me by a Brahmin, it is possible that some defiled water might plash back from the man's hands on to the vessel. Hence the low-caste man has to drink from a little spout called a 'tonti,' usually made of bamboo, projecting from below the window. The

water-provider pours water from his vessel into a sort of funnel.
Thence it issues by the spout, and if any water does splash back
from the man of dirty occupations, it merely falls on to the spout,
and there is no risk of its infecting the water supply for the
next comer. If one realises the complete absence of the dirt-
fearing instinct, among, for instance, the sweepers, and the fact that
it is their business to remove the most filthy offal, which they
generally do with their hands, and that consequently their hands are
liable to be polluted with the most objectionable microbes, it will be
understood that the above precautions are by no means a useless
refinement. When I was examining one of these places the water-
provider offered me a drink, adding that he had a glass. When I
reflected that I had only just recovered from a mild attack of cholera,
owing to an infection contracted in my laboratory from a moment's
carelessness, I felt more inclined to drink from the spout than
to run the risk of infecting his water by drinking in the English
fashion.

It is now abundantly proved that the cholera infection is often
carried into villages by returning travellers. There can be no doubt
that it then infects others by the intermediary of the village well.
In reading certain reports which contained much evidence in favour
of this statement, I was struck by the fact that the traveller in each
case appears only to have brought the disease to the village to which
he returned, but does not seem to have deposited the infection in the
villages through which he passed. There is the possibility that this,
if true, is due to the above described arrangements for giving water
to strangers. This inference, however, cannot be made with certainty
until investigations have been made, both as to the customs in the
villages in question, and as to the amount of cholera in villages
situated on the high roads. Against this idea may be stated the fact
that cholera is known to be frequent along great pilgrim routes. But
it is possible that this is an exception which helps to prove the rule.
Owing to the vast numbers of pilgrims passing along the roads, it
would, I suspect, be impossible for the villagers to provide water for
them all to drink, and it thus becomes necessary for them to draw it
for themselves.

I have had opportunities of watching the customs of these pilgrims at the large religious festivals held annually near Allahabad,
at the point of junction of the Ganges and Jumna. For miles along
the roads leading to the fair, and all over the plain near the site of
the fair, families of Hindoos (chiefly Brahmins) can be seen encamped,
and cooking their simple food. Before eating they take off all their
clothes, except a loin cloth, and wash themselves all over, for fear
some defilement may be present on their clothes or bodies. As is
well known, they object to a person of another caste coming near to
them while they are eating. It is not so well known that they have

no such objection if their food has been heated to a temperature sufficient to kill microbes, that is to say, if it has been fried in oil, except so far as persons are concerned who belong to the five lowest castes. The occupations of members of these castes are regarded as unclean, and they are not allowed to come near high-caste Hindoos while they are eating under any conditions, neither are such persons allowed to bring the uncooked food of Brahmins from the bazaar. It is obvious that each one of these rules has a tendency, though it may be slight, to prevent men of higher caste from swallowing the microbes which can cause diseases. Unfortunately, when at pilgrimages, they do not appear to pay much attention to the precautions which at that time are most required. I questioned several of them on that point, and they told me that they took no care as to what water they drank. I may parenthetically remark that I was walking alone among these natives without any imposing array of police or other officials. The only sign that I was an official was the doubtful one that I was carrying a notebook. Yet frequently as I passed the natives would turn round and call out after me, ' God bless the power and property of the English Government.' I was particularly struck by their using the term English, and I commend the fact to the attention of the members of the National Congress.

Sometimes the customs attending pilgrimages are fearfully insanitary. For instance, at the site of a pilgrimage in the Madras Presidency is a hill which is supposed to be a god. It is surrounded by twenty-four small tanks. On the great day of the festival nearly a hundred thousand persons bathe in, and drink, the water of each of these tanks. Each tank is thus defiled by every body, since, for religious purposes, everyone must go round the hill and bathe in each of the tanks. Little wonder that these pilgrimages are potent means for the spread of cholera.

The idea that natives in certain parts of India, when in their villages, habitually take precautions to insure the purity of their water supply, may seem strange not only to English readers, but also to Anglo-Indian officials stationed in certain other parts of India where no such care is taken, as, for instance, is, I suppose, the case in localities where the supply of drinking water is derived from tanks. Here, I am informed, the natives are in the habit of washing themselves, their cows, and the Sahib's shirts, in the tank that also acts as the village cesspool and the village water supply. Personally, I know nothing of these parts of India. The following account is based on experience obtained near Agra, and in other parts of the North-West Provinces.

In every village at least one well is reserved for the supply of drinking water. Only vessels especially reserved for the purpose are allowed to be lowered into such wells. Great care is taken to preserve the drinking-water vessels from pollution. Musalman water-carriers or bhistis [6] do not allow any one but themselves to touch their water buckets, or the skins in which they carry their water. Hindoos generally draw water in an iron vessel known as a ' dol.' This is only used for drawing the water. When required the water is poured into another vessel, and only from this other vessel is the water poured into the hands of any one requiring a drink. No one is allowed to go on to the platform of a well without removing his shoes.

Other wells in the village are reserved for household purposes. The vessels used to draw drinking water are never allowed to be lowered into these wells by Hindoos. I suspect that Musalman bhistis are not so particular ; at any rate, this is the case with bhistis employed by English people. The poorest Hindoos have two separate sets of vessels, one to hold drinking water, the other for water used in household purposes, such as washing the cooking vessels.

Houses, being generally made of mud, are constantly in need of repair. The workmen (or coolies) who need water for carrying out this work necessarily employ very dirty earthenware vessels. I am certain that these are not allowed to be lowered into drinking-water wells, and I believe they are not allowed to be lowered into wells used for household purposes. A small tank containing dirty water is generally attached to each well, and from this the workmen take the water which they need in repairing houses. When first I saw these tanks I thought it was rather unsanitary to have such dirty water so close to the well. But the above statements, I venture to think, make it obvious that it is better to have such tanks than that coolies should lower their dirty vessels into a well used for drinking purposes.

I once asked a completely uneducated native why it was necessary to have dirty wells in the place, why the dirty wells could not be closed, and all the water, whether for drinking or household purposes, be obtained from clean wells. His answer was that if this were done diseases would become prevalent. Whatever truth there may be in this answer appears to me to depend on the practical necessity that in some cases dirty vessels have to be lowered into wells ; and hence it seems to be a good plan, as things go, to reserve some wells into which alone such vessels may be lowered.

I recently had to do with a cholera epidemic in which certainly most of, possibly all of, the infection was derived from wells used for household purposes, and it is probable that the disease would have been far more widespread if the water of such wells had been actually drunk by the mass of the population. The epidemic [7] in

---

[6] Bhistis are always Mahommedan, and only draw water for Mahommedans or for English people. Hindoos usually draw water for themselves, but sometimes water-drawers are employed. These are always of Brahmin or Cahar castes.

[7] Some details concerning this epidemic will be found in my Annual Report already quoted.

question occurred in Shahgunj, and at the time it was stated to be inexplicable on the grounds that only women had been attacked. I found that the latter statement was true so far as the first part of the epidemic was concerned. The women who were affected had no supply of drinking water in common. Some of them obtained their drinking water from a well situated a couple of miles away from their houses. But out of seven cases I found evidence that six had been in the habit of going to one well which was used, not for drinking, but only for household purposes, and consequently was chiefly frequented by women. A few poor Musalmans, however, were in the habit of using the water for drinking purposes. Hindoos used a better well situated about sixty yards away. The epidemic affected twenty-six Mahommedans and only one Hindoo. I have little doubt that the first part of the epidemic was due to accidental infection from the water brought by the women for household purposes. In the latter part of the epidemic the cholera microbe appears to have spread to other wells in the place; but in these cleaner wells the microbe seems to have assumed a less virulent form, for the cases which now affected both men and women in nearly every instance ended in recovery, and on my putting disinfectants into the wells the epidemic ceased.

It is commonly supposed that the natives are in the habit of washing their clothes and themselves at the wells, and that the water frequently runs back into the well. This is not quite accurate. Women generally wash themselves either in their houses or in the river, if one is near. Men wash themselves and also their dhoti or loincloth at the wells, and owing to the platform of the well sloping away from its mouth, very little water, if any, gets back into the well, provided it is in good repair. Clothes, both of men and women, are washed by dhobies, who are never allowed to carry on their business near a well. They are obliged to use either the river or a tank. It is considered that the occupation of dhobies is unclean, and consequently they belong to one of the five lower castes who are not allowed to come near a well used by higher castes.

Perhaps the most interesting precaution taken by Hindoos about their drinking water is that those who are supposed to be engaged in dirty occupations, or vessels belonging to such persons, are not allowed to come near a well. In towns and larger villages it sometimes happens that a well is especially reserved for the use of Chamars and sweepers. More generally, if a sweeper wants water, he has to sit down at a distance from the well and wait till some one of higher caste comes and draws water for him.

This does not exhaust the list of precautions taken by natives in this district to insure the purity of their water supply. I was astonished to discover that they take pains to prevent the contamination of the River Jumna. While staying the other day in a bungalow in the

Ram Bagh Garden, which is situated above Agra on the banks of the river, a fisherman came to me and complained that my servants had dug a drain from the cook house and that from it dirty water was running into the river. The servants had made this drain by my orders, as I had a prejudice against the accumulation of stagnant water near to where my food was being prepared. On the fisherman making the complaint I hazarded the statement that it did not matter, since all up the banks of the river everywhere the natives were in the habit of depositing on its banks, as they often did at the margin of a tank, refuse which frequently fell into the water. The fisherman somewhat indignantly denied that this was the case, saying that men who would do such a thing must be of very low caste, and that higher caste people certainly always took pains to prevent the pollution of the river. To this I objected that the natives did not care whether the water was dirty or not, because a mile or two lower down the stream they were bathing at the ghats just where a large drain ran into the river. The fisherman admitted that they did this, because their ancestors had always bathed there, but at the same time he said they do not like the drain being run into the river, because the river is holy and they make many prayers to it. It appears to me that this incident well illustrates to what extent with these people cleanliness is godliness, and tends to make one regret that cleanliness has not been left a matter of common-sense instead of having become incorporated with their religion.

I have only attempted to describe some of the customs of the Hindoos in respect of their supply of drinking water. A further study of their customs would show that, with the higher castes of Hindoos, cleanliness and the avoidance of defilement are virtues to be cultivated in one's self and admired in others. Among the poorer classes and among men of lower castes these hygienic virtues are apt to be tempered with much original sin of the insanitary kind. But it cannot, I think, be denied, that even when only a few members of higher castes are present in a village they exert a beneficial influence in preserving the supply of drinking water from contamination. Unfortunately, their influence does not go far enough, but it appears to me that this is only a reason for trying to extend it in those directions in which it appears likely to be of use.[8]

The above remarks may seem like a eulogy of the caste system. This is far from my wishes. A system which enjoins that persons

[8] For instance, I am engaged in writing a tract in Hindustani on the prevention of cholera in India. By way of advocating the imposition of a quarantine on persons returning from a pilgrimage who may possibly bring back the cholera virus with them, I suggested in my rough draft of the pamphlet that such persons should be regarded as unclean for a week after their return. But on translating it into Hindustani, I was unable on the one hand to find any word for unclean that did not mean unholy; and on the other hand I found that the custom already existed in the case of certain distant pilgrimages. My informant, whom I have every reason to rely on, tells me that

who are careful in avoiding defilement should be admired and respected, but not imitated, at any rate by part of the population, is
far from satisfactory even from the hygienic standpoint.   From the
ethical standpoint, a system which tends to keep certain classes in a
low position and to prevent them from rising to anything higher, no
doubt leaves much to be desired.   Further, it seems to make no distinction in importance between matters which might be of great use, such
as those relating to the water supply, and those of trivial import, such
as the position of the cooking vessels while food is being prepared.

E. H. HANKIN.

pilgrims returning from Goya and Budrinath are not allowed to eat with other members of their families or, I believe, to come near their wells, until they have bathed in
the Ganges.   I believe this custom to be the reverse of widespread, but in my tract I
have explained its advantages, and suggested that it should be applied to every
returning traveller, that his clothes should not be washed until they have been exposed in the sun to dry, that he should be allowed to bring none but dry food back
with him into the village, &c.

OF WOMEN IN ASSEMBLIES

I PROPOSE in the present paper to treat of the question of woman's co-operation with man in public work from a single point of view. I wish to support the general proposition that a real discussion of important matters, on which practical action is to follow, is impossible by men in any assembly in which women sit with them as fellow-debaters and fellow-voters. By real discussion I mean a discussion which shall be at once fair, exhaustive, and penetrating to all the vital issues of the matter. I make the proposition general because I believe the impossibility to be founded on a necessary relation between men and women, a relation as old as the Garden of Eden, or as any historic or semi-historic record. If this aspect of the matter has struck others, it has not, so far as I know, been publicly noticed, and it is possible that, unless noticed in the abstract, it would not force itself upon the general attention till public mischief had resulted in various directions from the neglect of it.

It will be granted that, with exceptions, woman is physically weaker than man. It will be granted also that, with few or no exceptions, she has enormous influence over him. If I could find a stronger word than enormous I would use it without fear. How did she obtain it? By fascination. Fascination is a word of wide and vague meaning, and therefore is a suitable one. One does not want to tie down fascination to one or two special methods, we are concerned chiefly with its results. Ugly women have fascinated men, and pretty ones, and old ones and young ones, and robust ones and very weak ones, and talkative ones and silent ones where found. I am not sure that a woman both ugly and silent has often reigned supreme, but I may be wrong. If so, she probably spoke to some purpose once. If they have all prevailed, it must have been from something which they had in common. The quality in common may be expressed by the word fascination. May fascination be described (not defined) as an effect not wholly dependent on the facts of the case? Woman's strength lies in having something to grant which can only be granted to the favoured;[1] also in establishing such a relation with the other sex that any attempt to snatch the

[1] It is a proverb that 'kissing goes by favour.'

favour roughly will be resented by other possible aspirants to it.
From this has resulted a different way of speaking to the man from
the man's way of speaking to her; an unfair way, let us say at once,
if we assume the point of view and the object aimed at by both sexes
to be the same. And there has resulted, too, that woman has prevailed to have it assumed as a social axiom that the way shall be
different, and to have the sense of its unfairness lost in the sense of
the objects of intercourse being different, as between man and man
and between woman and man. And at this early period of my
remarks I can conceive a champion of woman's public appearances
saying, 'Oh, but this is all so antediluvian. It is assuming the
perpetuity of an old-fashioned relation. This old-fashioned relation
is one of the very things we are incidentally going to destroy.' It is
of no use to reply, 'Are you?' The other side will not regard the
question as conclusive. And it is enough to call the attention of
the impartial to the fact that the very women who wish to establish
the right to every responsible public appearance are, rather more
than the old-fashioned woman, precise upon the point of etiquette,
rather more ready than the old-fashioned woman to say, 'Oh, of
course, he could not contradict a woman,' 'Of course he could not
say that to me, because I am a woman.' Roughly speaking, men
are polite to one another because they fear something; they fear
retaliation. And this retaliation is a defence of exactly the same
kind as their attack. And, roughly speaking, they know that words
may be backed up by deeds, which, as between themselves, are
exactly of the same kind. Ignoring all the finer issues of feeling
which have grown up upon these original fears, such are the foundations of manly courtesy, with the result that manly courtesy is
unexaggerated, tempered, and moderately truth-telling. That is, it
fears no plain speaking but such as a man must give an account for
to his equal. There is no shrinking whatever in an assembly of men
from expressing the sense that folly is folly, and had better be cut
short as soon as possible. And on this expression, and the fear of it,
is all sensible and fruitful debate founded. No man yet has gained
influence in a useful public assembly of men who had not been made
to feel that he had conquered a hostile atmosphere and could live in
it. He has been made to feel that he is acceptable to a body of men
who, while friendly to all comers, would have shown their sense of a
fool or a bore. It is not said from love of paradox, but from conviction which could be justified in detail, that the possibility of rudeness
is the indispensable condition of fruitful debate. So is the rod an
indispensable condition of a good school, though rarely used.

And there is no doubt that, neglecting the finer issues which are
results and after-growths, the courtesy of man to woman is founded
on the fear of retaliation, but what a different retaliation it is! The
retaliation is the loss of favour, and the whole attitude of man to

woman is a request for favour. 'Here is this antediluvianism again,'
says the New Woman. But the New Woman, like the Old, can dispense favour, except perhaps that she wishes to be asked for it rather
more, and that she dispenses less. · It results from this that in dis-
cussion· woman, within her womanly limits, speaks to man pretty
much as she likes, and will continue to do so. She will continue to
·do so whether emperors or presidents govern and whatever be the
limits of suffrage. She will do so not as voter or non-voter but as
woman. There is no form of government which has not been already
tried, and under all of them the relation of man to woman has been
the same—that of a despicable and cowardly tyrant whose every toil
has been undertaken for her sake, who has been rewarded by her
smile and abashed by her frown, and two-thirds of whose spoil, holy
or unholy, she has less appropriated than had thrown upon her.

I shall by this time be gleefully reminded that the principle of
the admission of women into assemblies which propose to take practical and legislative action founded on discussion has already been
established in more than one sphere, and that I cannot hope to push
back the hands of the clock. It is so. And the whole question of
the public development of women has been attended with assertions
of limitation of their ultimate intentions which it is difficult to think
can have been believed by any one at the time they were made, and
which certainly were not believed by the opponents of the general
principle. This system, however, of laying down a new limitation to
demands at every step, and then crying out for logic, is not confined
to the woman's movement, though it has been more systematically
used there than in any political departure.

It will be well first for any reader who has attended a discussion
club where the sexes are mixed to try and remember what has
generally happened at these comparatively harmless institutions.
No make-believe is absolutely harmless, but here, since practical
action does not result, there has already been opportunity to study
facts, which have developed themselves freely because no exaspera-
tion of a cause won or lost has followed. In mixed discussion clubs
I think it will be allowed by the impartial that the arguments of the
women are not really met and answered. I mean that the men
consciously do not dissect and answer them as thoroughly as they
can. The women think they do. This is all part of the usual social
game, with its usual limitations. It is much like mixed lawn-tennis.
The real deadly unapproachable serve does not get delivered by the
man to the woman, not even to the professed lawn-tennis-playing
woman. If the man has had a nice father and mother I defy him to
deliver it. · In this matter of the body the women are more ready to
acknowledge this, though they often ·dispute it; but in the matter
of the discussion club the same thing happens, though it is not so
readily acknowledged by the sex. And why are the arguments not

really dissected ?   The man fears loss of favour.   The retaliation of
fair argument he does not fear, but something else ; something disturbing of social pleasantnesses to come.   And the consequence is
that the women are apt to go prosing on, with infinite self-belief,
innocent of the sturdy interruption which would be administered to
males.   There is mischief even here, for it leaves in females the
sense that that which is not is ; and it is a sense to which as a sex
they are already too prone.   And it leaves especially a sense of
having vanquished males and left them behind ; from which comfortable platform they step forth to other and more practical conquests.

I would appeal also to those who have taken part in serious
meetings upon subjects in which both sexes are interested, and at which
both are speakers, to consider whether latitude of subject, and
exceeding of time-limits, and silence of men in the face of direct
observations, is not conceded to women in such assemblies.   And I
should like to ask the question whether it is not felt that among
gentlefolk it must always be so, and to ask all to consider the import
of such facts, if there be fact in what I say, upon the admission of
women to yet more practical public discussions.

It will be well to give a more detailed illustration of what is likely
to happen by the free blending of women with men in discussions
from which the most important action is to follow, by considering
the case of parish councils.   Here, of course, the system is already
in full swing.   Women are already important factors in them.   Let
us take a purely imaginary case of a small country parish.   It is in
these small country parishes that more important results might
follow from the Act under which they are created than in any other.
In such places it has always been taken for granted that two or three
houses round the village green will manage everything.   The parson's
is one, the squire's, or the so-called squire's, is another ; and there
are two or three more who are permitted to dine with these.   There
is a great deal of management of small local rights going on in a
small parish.   In these rights a great deal of law is really involved,
and in the course of years a great deal of law and right is given up ;
and this through the presumption that everything will be managed
by these two or three families.   The peasant has lost all initiative,
and in scorn of this loss Lord Salisbury offered him a circus instead
of a council.   It is difficult enough in any case to bring him back
to a true and wise initiative.   Yet it can be done.   There are
parishes where peasants and small tradesmen can be brought to vote
one of their own number into the chair in the presence of the parson
and the squire.   At first, where it comes, it will be done with strain
and rudeness, but later, when the institution works as a thing of
course, it will be done naturally and without strain or rudeness.   I
am not meaning that a peasant or a small tradesman should always

be in the chair, and a landowner or titled person never, but that the right of the small person to be there when his interests are real, or his personality influential, needs establishing, and among males meeting for business can be established. But put a woman or two among them and the whole mutual relation is altered. The peasant and the small tradesman will stand or sit tongue-tied in their presence. She herself will rise with easy nerve, and will perhaps speak on and on ; and if, as will more often happen, her remarks are towards the Tory side, the case of the uninfluential will never be presented. And I wish the reader to remark that this silence and deference will be conceded to her, not as property-owner, if she be one, but as woman. To the property-owner as such a certain plainness of speech and standing up for themselves will come to the uninfluential, at first with rudeness and, as a habit of firm discussion sets in, without it. But the presence of a woman or two may make parish councils inoperative on the side of the peasant for ever. A perception of this probably increases the willingness of Tories to see them there, and not only there, but in other public places. And if in this small place the lady happens to be a titled one, and it happens very frequently, then her influence in silencing discussion, in quietly managing that things shall be decided her way, will be out of all proportion to the position which she would have held there as a man of whatever station. And here one may fitly recall how Dr. Johnson with wise sarcasm observed that the influence of woman over man was so supereminent that the law had wisely deprived her of all legal rights which were possible.

The real public mischief is that things will not get themselves thrashed out in her presence, but this can better be considered where we speak of her presence on some wider field. And of this mischief the root mischief is that to very many the things will appear to have been thrashed out when they are not, and especially to herself and to her sex. This is not a mere negative evil, it is a positive one, introducing the poison of a false consciousness as to facts into the body politic.

If the mischief of their presence can be seen more acutely on the small important stage of a parish council, it can be seen working evil over a wider area and as affecting more general interests on a municipal council. And here comes in the all-important question of humour. Women are not without humour, and in the few instances in which it has been controlled and chiselled enough to give a finish to literary power it has been of a rare and delicate kind. But in the general intercourse of life, humour, or humour so-called, between man and woman has been exercised under unfair conditions (if we are to look at the humour alone), and the unfairness of the conditions will be recognised by women who have added any large qualities of mind to their womanly ones. The matter is a part of

what I said at first about the retaliation feared being different in
kind. In general society a woman may practically say what she
likes to a man, and from time to time rudeness from her passes for
wit by a tacit consent. And the man takes it, or answers in other
tones, for the reasons that I originally gave, that he fears a different
retaliation, and that his objects in society are other than verbal
success. Habits introduced with the blood are not thrown off by
entering a council hall, and there they will be mischievous. The
women who wish to enter council halls are the last to wish to throw
them off. Nor is there any serious wish on the part of males that
women of any type should do so.

But such considerations have a very serious bearing upon the
possible entering of Parliament by women. It is not to be denied
that there is some serious danger of their ultimately doing so. This
would be the natural result of their voting at all, and of concessions
already made, whatever protestations may be expedient from time to
time. It has come within the region of possible danger through the
tendency of either side to coquet with the female vote when the
polling of the constituencies threatens to be well balanced. This
coquetry is, perhaps, a little more pronounced among Tory members
through a not ill-founded belief in the Toryism of the bulk of women.
And it leaves more to be explained from them, because such an
admission of women is contrary to the general set of their principles.
Whereas the employment of women (and so naturally the voting of
women) has always been akin to the general re-examination of the
framework of society which seems essential to Radicalism. And
before glancing at the probable results, as affecting honest discussion,
of admitting women to Parliament let us look at what is taking place
around us, their joining men in public dinners where speeches are
delivered, and where they themselves deliver them. If there be an
enjoyable element in the dining parties of clubs and societies in what
does it consist? In easy freedom, in the possibility of natural badinage,
in the cutting short of a bore even, if need be. That a certain sequence
of speeches will be delivered more or less in decorous silence where
the sexes are mixed is not to be denied. They will probably be
listened to, whether liked or not. But will the easy freedom of
enjoyment remain? These remarks, and many more besides them,
are certainly not specially made by those who are averse to female
society as such, they are even made by those specially alive to the
charm of mixed social intercourse, as opposed to meetings where the
real ventilation of public topics is the reason of the gathering, though
its form be convivial. The introduction of the matter would be
impertinent but for the light it may throw on some part, at least, of
the results following from a Parliament which shall be open to both
sexes, and into which even a few women shall have entered.

The time when veterans like Mr. Gladstone were entering it is with reason believed to have been a great time of Parliament. The reminiscences of the very old may still be gathered by those who are admitted to them, and they may be found abundantly in memoirs. And the general impression left of this time is, that it was a time of great freedom of expression. Humour, often boisterous humour, was allowed to play freely over the solemn subjects of debate, and in this way reality of treatment was attained. The matters really were discussed, and the vital points were not shirked ; and those who were not pertinent or interesting were left under no self-delusions. When it is sometimes pretended that women would raise the tone of debates by preventing freedom, there is an utter confusion of thought. There is no reason to suppose that there would arise a less venomous way of looking at things by women taking places in Parliament. The restraining men from saying what they have to say, in the way in which they would naturally say it amongst themselves, would be not a good but a real evil, tending to prevent the fatuity of solemn pretences from being exposed, and turning debate from an engine for getting at the realities of the case, into a sequence of decorous declamations, not really contradicted on the points in which contradiction and exposure are necessary. In this matter the mere fluency of woman is not so much a qualification as a drawback. That she is capable of making speeches of a certain length no one doubts, nor speeches of a set coherent cogency. The vital point is that the mere presence of her sex must necessarily disturb the freedom of style and the possibility of rudeness where necessary, which is indispensable to the real treatment of public questions.

It is much to the point to remark that on many less observed platforms there is little doubt that she is hindering that reality of treatment now. Even in a matter which seems to give more than any other a promise of her beneficial agency, her appointment as Guardian of the Poor, I believe that her presence in debate among other male guardians, considered as a hampering presence, stopping the free play of natural remark and contradiction, and securing to her own share of assertion and discussion a far larger immunity from reflection by reason of her sex than her influence and position could give if she were male, is more calculated to do harm by the hampering of truth than her special aptitudes for finding out certain facts of public import could do good. Unreality, and the thin dropping of uncontradicted assertion, a lack of contradiction which to a large extent must always come to her by reason of her sex, must, I think, outbalance the advantage of her sitting at the board. Yet these are but illustrative matters, and it is in view of a danger of wider and more vital operation on broader fields that the remarks are offered. At the risk of repetition I say in fewer words, that the vital object of debate is that the realities which underlie a matter, and which often come out best by collision, by contradiction, and by irritating interruption, should be revealed there and then in the council chamber. That whatever claims may be made by New Women, the radical relations of man to woman have been settled by nature long ago; that these are incompatible with an uncompromising sifting of truth in common public debate; and that this public debate, whether in the large field of Parliament, or in the lesser fields of parish councils, hospital boards, or boards of guardians, and especially in boards which relate to public education, is of more importance to a nation than any other thing. If there be any truth in this point of view, it would seem to follow from it that the public functions of women would be limited to the collecting of evidence, which men must afterwards debate. This seems at first sight arrogant on the part of males. And there is no doubt that it will be received with indignation by those who are most serious in the claims which they make for public position. But it has a really humble side. The sarcasm of Johnson is worth attending to. So supereminent is the influence of woman over man that we must protect ourselves. By rightly constituted men, women will never be subjected to the immediate sifting or heckling in public debates which we must needs give to one another; and those who respect woman much and love their country more, must in self-protection do their best to keep her out of them.

CHARLES SELBY OAKLEY.

LORD RANDOLPH CHURCHILL
AS AN OFFICIAL

HAMLET, in his most cynical humour, hopes that a great man's memory may outlive his life half a year. It almost seems as if Shakespeare, in the person of his hero, foresaw the fickleness of those who live at the close of the present century, when popularity is attained and lost, when fortunes and reputations are made and marred, when men and questions alike fill the public imagination for an hour, it may be a day, and are then hurried off the scene to make way for new men and new ideas. Those who have held a great position, or who have been brilliantly successful in their lifetime, or even who have achieved some important work, are often soon forgotten; but not so the possessor of an individuality that is unique of its kind. Him the world does not willingly let die. So it seems to me unlikely that Lord Randolph Churchill will ever disappear from the memory of his countrymen; for rarely has English political biography furnished one gifted with a personality of such dazzling brilliancy. For a time—alas, too short—he held a position in the world of politics second only to that of Mr. Gladstone or Mr. Disraeli. He could draw together the largest audiences in London and the provinces, and he always inspired them with his own enthusiasm. Not a newspaper but was full of his speeches as he traversed the country from Woodstock to Belfast, or from London to Edinburgh; not a caricaturist but exercised his talents on his features, his mustachios, and his collars.

Is it possible that

> . . . now the painful warrior famoused for fight,
> After a thousand victories once foiled,
> Is from the boke of honour razed quite,
> And all the rest forgot for which he toiled?

To some other writer and to a remoter time it must be left to deal with that part of Lord Randolph Churchill's life when, in the face of the overwhelming majority opposed to him in 1881, in spite of the ill-concealed disapproval, and to the dismay of what he somewhat disrespectfully termed the old gang, he charged over the heads of a dejected and dispirited party into the serried and then unbroken

ranks of the Liberal phalanx.   Like the youth in the old classical
story, he hurled his lance, before the awe-struck worshippers, into
the side of the idol they knelt to and adored.   My object in this
short sketch is to show the impression Lord Randolph Churchill produced on the minds of old and staid officials who had been educated in
the school of Lord Palmerston, Lord John Russell, Mr. Gladstone, and
Sir Stafford Northcote.   At first they regarded him as an impossible
man 'whose breath was agitation and his life a storm on which he
rode.'   He was to their eyes a visible genius, an intense and un-
quenchable personality, an embodied *tour de force*; but as a serious
Minister of the Crown he was to them an impossibility.   In his fierce
assaults on Mr. Gladstone he had attacked the best friend the Civil
Service ever had; and it was a moot point which was in greater
dread—they of his entrance within the portals of a Government
department, or he of having to associate in daily business with men
whom he curtly described to a friend as 'a knot of d——d Glad-
stonians.'   He was a man to whom the words of Hookham Frere in
Monks and Giants might as suitably be applied as they were to that
kindred spirit, the brave and fiery Peterborough.

> His birth, it seems, by Merlin's calculation
> Was under Venus, Mercury, and Mars;
> His mind with all their attitudes was mixed,
> And like those planets wandering and unfixed.
> His schemes of war were sudden, unforeseen,
> Inexplicable both to friend and foe.
> He seemed as if some momentary spleen
> Inspired the project and impelled the blow.

Such was the impression we had of him, not unnatural and
certainly not wholly wrong.   But there were other aspects to his
many-sided nature—the reckless knight-errant of debate proved
at the same time a patient, strenuous, thorough, and far-sighted
administrator.

The following is the character he won at the India Office from
Sir A. Godley, the Under Secretary of State for India:—

He was, as every one knows, exceedingly able, quick, and clear-sighted.
Besides this, he was very industrious, very energetic and decided when once his
mind was made up, and remarkably skilful in the art of ' devolution,' by which I
mean the art of getting the full amount of help out of his subordinates.   He knew
at once whether to take up a question or to leave it to others.   If he took it up,
he made himself completely master of it; if he left it alone, he put entire confidence
in those to whom he left it, and endorsed their opinion without hesitation.   I need
not tell you how invaluable this quality was both to himself and to those who
worked with him.   It should be added that his perfect candour and straight-
forwardness were not only admirable in themselves, but were a great assistance to
business.   What he said he meant; and if he did not know a subject, he did not
pretend to know it.   The duties of the Secretary of State for India are, as you
know, somewhat complicated by his relations with the Council, over whose deliberations he has to preside.   In this part of his business he showed great skill.

For some time, and until he had learnt the methods of procedure, he took no part whatever in our debates. But as soon as he began to feel at home, his method was to decide beforehand which were the subjects as to which he wished to use his influence, and having done this, to send for the papers and master them thoroughly before the meeting of Council. Then, having his brief, and with the advantage of his parliamentary training and natural readiness, he interfered with decisive effect, and I believe I may say, invariably carried his point. Few high officials can have been his superiors, or indeed his equals, in the art of *getting things done*. Those who worked under him felt that, if they had once convinced him that a certain step ought to be taken, it infallibly would be taken and 'put through.' . . . He was, as he freely said, extremely sorry to leave this office, and I believe that all who had worked with him, without exception, were sorry to lose him.

Lord Randolph's brief tenure of the India Office was marked by some achievements of first-class importance. The annexation of Burma, a country with an area of 83,473 square miles and a population of 3,000,000, was his policy for which he was responsible. The conquest of the country was effected with remarkable rapidity. In November 1885 Lord Randolph gave the order to advance; on the 1st of December Lord Dufferin announced that the conquest was completed; and on the 31st of the same month Lord Randolph sent out his despatch detailing what had happened and authorising the annexation. Another important piece of work, the formation of the Indian Midland Railway, which has now a length of line of 700 miles and a capital of 7,000,000*l*., was carried out by Lord Randolph against considerable opposition. It was he also who finally sanctioned the increase of the British (European) army in India by 10,000 men; and several other important measures were passed during his administration of the India Office.

Lord Randolph, between the fall of the Tory Government and his return to office as Chancellor of the Exchequer, made himself the mouthpiece of an attack with a venom not his own on the Chairman and Deputy-Chairman of the Board of Inland Revenue. 'Those were,' as he said, 'my ignorant days.' When he returned to office as Chancellor of the Exchequer in 1866, notwithstanding the reputation he had made for himself at the India Office, he still appeared to the minds of Treasury officials as a Minister who would in all probability ride roughshod over cherished traditions and habits which were very dear to them. That such a man, with all his faults and glaring indiscretions, whose inclinations became passions, should have attached to himself a body of men like the Civil Service of this country, was little short of a miracle. A Frenchman, in a conversation with Pitt at the end of the last century, expressed his surprise at the influence which Charles Fox, a man of pleasure ruined by the dice-box and the turf, had exercised over the English nation. 'You have not,' was the reply, 'been under the wand of the magician.' It was not long before those who were brought into close communication with Lord Randolph fell under his magic spell. I confess that I, at that time Chairman of the Board of Inland Revenue, was as much dismayed as any man at the prospect of his becoming Chancellor of the Exchequer. I was soon reconciled, and I well remember our first interview in the old historical Board Room at the Treasury, the stiff and formal cut of his frock coat—the same that he always wore when he was leader of the House—and the somewhat old-world courtesy of manner with which he received me at the door. But it was not long before he produced the new-world cigarette-case and the long mouth-piece, which so soon became familiar. A very few meetings were enough to show me how sincerely anxious he was to learn all the little I had to teach; and from that first hour our acquaintance gradually ripened into a friendship which not all the vicissitudes of his stormy life, nor even his agonising illness, ever interrupted. The last letter he wrote before he left England on his sad journey was to me. In it he spoke of our long years of friend_ship, of his return, and of years to come; but the handwriting told how impossible that return and those future years were to be.

Our early official meetings at the Treasury were soon superseded by more intimate conversations at Connaught Place. On my first visit there I found him in a room bright with electric light, and the eternal cigarette in his mouth. He was seated in a large armchair having a roomy sofa on one side, which I afterwards learnt was known in the family as the 'Fourth Party sofa,' and on the other, much to my surprise, a large photograph of Mr. Gladstone. Whether the photograph and the sofa were thus placed opposite each other for the convenience of the party in rehearsing their attacks I do not take it upon me to say. Although Lord Randolph certainly had never made a study of finance, he was not, when he became Chancellor of the Exchequer, so ignorant of it as Charles Fox, if the story be true which reports him to have said that he never could understand what Consols were—he knew they were things that went up and down in the City; and he was always pleased when they went down, because it so annoyed Pitt. A story is also told of Lord Randolph, that a Treasury clerk put some figures before him. 'I wish you would put these figures plainly so that I can understand them,' he said. The clerk said he had done his best, and he had, pointing them out, reduced them to decimals. 'Oh!' said Lord Randolph, 'I never could understand what those d——d dots meant.' But it soon became clear that besides a wonderful intuition, Lord Randolph possessed many of the qualities which had always won for Mr. Gladstone so high a reputation as a departmental chief—indefatigable assiduity, that energy which Dr. Arnold said is of more value than even cleverness, a vehement determination to learn his subject *ab ovo usque ad mala,* a strong intellectual force which, while it in no way interfered with his attention to the opinions of his subordinates, absolutely preserved his own independence of judgment and decision. He possessed the very rare gift of keeping his mind exclusively devoted to the subject in hand, and impressed on all those with whom he worked the idea that the business on which they were employed was the only one of interest to him. For a man of his rapid thought and excitable temperament he was scrupulously patient and quiet in discussion; and from frequent conversations with him on financial subjects I can safely affirm that no one ever ended an official interview with him without at any rate having arrived at a clear knowledge of his views and intentions. No time spent with him was ever wasted, nor would he suffer any interruption from whatever source it came.

In the autumn preceding the session of 1887 he knew that the duties of leadership would absorb all his time and strength, and, like a wise and prudent statesman, he prepared himself for his financial statement by a performance such as was never equalled, in getting ready and passing through the Cabinet the Budget for the forthcoming year. On the evening of the day on which he carried his Budget through the Cabinet, after describing to me how he had done so, he said, 'There in that box are all the materials of our Budget. They are unpolished gems; put the facets on them as well as you can, but do not speak to me on the subject again till the end of the financial year.' What that Budget was cannot yet be told; but it may be fairly said that it far exceeded in importance any Budget since Mr. Gladstone's great performance in 1860. It was often said that Lord Randolph won his popularity among the permanent officials by his subservience to their views. Nothing could be farther from the truth; and when some day his Budget comes to light, as I trust it will, it will be seen how original were some of its provisions, and how unlike to any plans that would probably have emanated from the ordinary official brain.

He did not bear fools gladly, and was hardly capable of being even civil to people who bored him. On one occasion he went in to a formal luncheon, where the places were arranged. He looked to the right of him and he looked to the left of him—he gathered up his plate and napkin and knife and fork and sat himself down at the other end of the table, which reminds me of a story of a very distinguished statesman, Lord John Russell, who took the Duchess of Inverness in to dinner. When he got to his place he looked behind him and walked round to the other side of the table, and sat down next to the Duchess of St. Albans. Lady John said to him afterwards, 'What on earth made you leave the Duchess of Inverness and go across to the Duchess of St. Albans?' 'Well,' he replied, 'I should nave been sick if I had sat where I was put, with my back to the fire.' 'But I hope,' said his wife, 'you explained it to the Duchess of Inverness.' 'No, I didn't,' he said, 'but I did to the Duchess of St. Albans'!

His cynicism was delightful. When the dreadful subject of

bimetallism cropped up, he turned to Sir A. Godley and said, 'I
forget, was I bimetallist when I was at the India Office ?'

Lord Welby, who was Secretary to the Treasury, writing to me
his impressions of Lord Randolph, says :

One could not be otherwise than anxious as to our relations with our new
chief. But that anxiety was soon dispelled. He met us from the outset with
perfect frankness, which soon became cordiality, and I cannot recall a word or a
line of his during his autumn office which I should have wished unspoken or unwritten. Not that he was an easy or an unexacting chief. He expected subjects
to be laid before him fully, clearly, and intelligently, and he was keen to mark
default. This, however, was only as it should be. He was, in short, a Minister
of the type that Civil Servants appreciate. He ruled as well as reigned. He had
a mind and made it up, a policy and enforced it. He was quick in acquiring
information, quick in seizing the real point, and quick in understanding what one
wished to convey to him; impatient in small matters and details, and contemptuous
if one troubled him with them. Above all he was accessible, ready and willing
to hear what one had to say, whether it accorded with his own views or not.
Doing business with him was most interesting; not being a respecter of persons
he criticised freely and pointedly men and matters, and the consciousness that we
were working under so keen a judgment did not lessen the interest of our intercourse. You and I know well that in 'chaff' he was unsurpassed, and that it
was difficult to find his equal. From my recollection, I should say that when he
was at his best, in quickness, readiness, and versatility of reply he stood first ; and
this struck one the more since he had not the resource of a well-stored memory on
which to rely. He was singularly free from affectation of knowledge he did not
possess. Once, criticising a statesman, he said: ' So-and-so makes the mistake of
conveying or implying to the House that his decisions are based on his own knowledge of the subject; whereas the House knows perfectly well that his own
knowledge of technical subjects is not greater than that of the majority of members
around him. He should say that his skilled advisers have put the pros and cons
before him, and that, applying his common-sense to the information then before
him, he has arrived at the conclusion which he recommends to the House. If you
are frank with the House in this fashion you get their confidence.' Could one fail
to take interest in a chief ' who always showed us sport '? Alas, that this should
all be a tale of the past.

From the very commencement of his career as Chancellor of the
Exchequer, Lord Randolph began his struggles for economy, his love
for which was sincere and earnest. He determined that as long as he .
was responsible for the finances of the country he would enforce it.
It has often been the subject of discussion whether a man who is
careful in his domestic affairs would naturally be an economist in
public affairs, and *vice versâ.* No one would ever have accused Lord'
Randolph of being a careful or even a prudent man in the manage--
ment of his private concerns, but his ruling idea as Chancellor of the
Exchequer was for economy. Lord Welby, in his letter to me, gives
two good instances.

Of old times sums were issued out of the Civil List to the Secretary of the
Treasury for secret service. No public account, of course, was rendered of the
money thus expended, and there was opportunity for abuse or worse. An important
step was taken in the right direction when Parliament in 1783, following the lead

of Burke, limited the grant to 10,000l. a year, and that amount was yearly issued to the Secretary of the Treasury from 1783 to 1886. It must be borne in mind that this branch of secret service was quite distinct from that which is ordinarily known as foreign secret service. This sum was used, according to general belief, for party purposes. There was no reason, indeed, to think that of late times it had been applied to other services than those of legitimate party organisation; but the principle of a grant of public money for party purposes was an anachronism under popular government. Yet such is the innate conservatism of English parties and English statesmen that the grant was never seriously questioned for over a century. A remark by the Comptroller and Auditor-General in one of his reports to Parliament drew attention to it, and Lord Randolph began his Chancellorship by abolishing it. By this act he showed how closely he watched the progress of public opinion, how much in this respect he was ahead of his contemporaries, and how instinctively he knew when a position or a policy was no longer tenable. In the other instance of administrative action to which I have referred he refused to ask Parliament to renew the octroi duty on coal coming into the Metropolis, the proceeds of which were divided between the City and the Metropolitan Board of Works. One would not have been surprised if he had answered the application of the Metropolitan Board of Works in the ambiguous terms which are dear to party leaders. He had not been a student of economical subjects. The principle of the duty was not unpleasing to his party. The Metropolitan authorities were anxious to obtain money in a manner which would enable them to incur expenditure without being hauled over the coals. Powerful interests objected to a rise in the rates, while the abolition of a duty which affected the poor consumer did not elicit much enthusiastic support. Lord Randolph, to his credit, did not play with the question. He looked into the subject for himself, saw that an octroi duty was out of date, that it was a survival of a financial policy which had been emphatically condemned, and he returned a decided refusal to the application. His speech to the deputation was admirable, and it may be read with interest and advantage by any who care to see the arguments against such an octroi put tersely, forcibly, and without reserve.

Lord Welby adds:

On other points he was not so orthodox. He had doubts about the Sinking Fund, and a doubt as to the Sinking Fund will shock a man trained under Mr. Gladstone in the Treasury as much as a doubt about the Creed will shock an orthodox Churchman. I always had hopes, however, that on further reflection he would finally recognise the worth of a weapon so useful in peace, and of such priceless value in emergency of war.

I well recollect also his indignation on learning that specie had to be conveyed in merchant ships because the cost for freight charged by naval officers was so great that H.M.'s gold could not be conveyed in H.M.'s vessels—a discreditable state of things, which he took immediate steps to remedy.

In a letter he wrote to me shortly after his resignation, Lord Randolph said : 'The Budget scheme we had in contemplation will now be relegated to the catalogue of useless labour. The essential principle of any financial policy which I cared to be identified with was zeal for thrift and economic reform. This was wanting, and the scaffolding was bound to come down.' It was the extravagance of the spending departments that induced him to write that fatal letter which could only bring about his absolute supremacy or his resigna-

tion. No new fancy it was that dictated it. In October 1886 he had
said that 'unless there was an effort to reduce the expenditure it was
impossible that he could remain at the Exchequer.' Again he said:
' If the decision of the Cabinet as to the amount of the Estimates was
against him, he should not remain in office.' I recollect after his fall
his appealing to me and saying that I knew that his resignation was
not the consequence of a moment's irritation, but was from his
deliberate determination that in matters financial he would be supreme.
This I was able fully to endorse.

On the 20th of December, ever anxious to learn all he could
by personal study, he spent nearly three hours with me at Somerset
House, seeing for himself all the working of that huge department.
The following day he went to the Custom House, and that same
afternoon to Windsor, where he wrote the letter to Lord Salisbury
which has since become historical, threatening his resignation. On
the evening of the 22nd he walked down to Printing House Square
and communicated what he had done to the Editor of the *Times*.
Then, on the 23rd, I got the sad and startling news of his resignation.
In a note which followed close upon it, his secretary, Mr. A. Moore,
who by his ability and devotion had contributed so much to Lord
Randolph's fame, said: ' I have really not the heart to write anything. Moreover, there is nothing to add to what was said in that
terribly irregular and premature *communiqué* to the *Times*. I look
upon the whole thing, from every point of view—patriotic, party, and
personal—as simply an irreparable calamity.'

It is strange that a man endowed by nature with quick perception,
should not have seen how gladly Lord Salisbury would dispense with
his services, or should have forgotten Sir Stafford Northcote's prophecy
and hope in 1880, that a Conservative cave would be formed on the
Liberal side with Goschen in its centre.

So Lord Randolph became officially dead, and a cruel fate has
made him one of the great might-have-beens in the financial history
of his country.

After leaving office, Lord Randolph went to work laboriously to
master and unravel the complicated question of publican's licenses.
He prepared a wise measure founded on a compromise between Tories
and Radicals, publicans and the advocates ·of temperance. The
Temperance party had recently suffered a great defeat, and he
thought they would be amenable to reason. The Tories were in
power, and could induce the publicans to accept reasonable terms.
The Opposition would be glad to get this thorny subject out of the
way; and the Government would have the credit of settling this
difficult question. There were all the elements of compromise.
County Councils in counties, and Town Councils in boroughs were
to have power, without interfering with magisterial prerogative, to
oppose the renewal of licenses and then to purchase the houses, the

value of which was to be settled by the Commissioners of Inland Revenue on the basis of the annual value of the house with or without a license, and the difference of value between the premises as licensed and as unlicensed was to be taken as the annual value. The purchase money was to have been, in the year 1891, ten times the value of such difference, and the purchase value was thereafter to diminish annually by one tenth, so that a license extinguished after ten years would not represent any value for which any purchase money would be payable.

The Bill also provided for an increase of duty to be paid by the publicans in a county or a borough in proportion to the number of houses purchased; and it proposed to give to ratepayers a large control of the number of public houses, hours of opening, &c. It also dealt fully with clubs, a part of this complicated question which has long cried for solution. The Bill, however, did not find favour with the Government, and the Liberals objected on the score of compensation, that rock of offence on which all liquor measures have been, and I fear will be, wrecked. For I am perfectly convinced that no satisfactory drink bill will ever be passed without compensation in some shape or another.

A brilliant, but anonymous, writer in the *Saturday Review* of the 26th of January, 1895, says that Lord Randolph was the greatest elemental force in English politics since Cromwell, and compares his tragic life to that of Byron. He tells of his epigrams that stuck like burrs, and of his confession that he ornamented his discourse with every variety of vituperation. He tells, too, how the Duke of Devonshire spoke of Lord Randolph as a man he had learned to respect as an opponent and to trust as an ally, and who led the House of Commons with genius, and was the greatest leader he had ever known.

Lord Randolph has been compared to Madame Sarah Bernhardt. A less sensational, but, I think, more appropriate comparison may be made between him and Charles James Fox in his early days. Lecky, speaking of Charles Fox and his loves, his play, his racing, his politics, says:

> That a man of whom this can be said should have won for himself the perennial love of some of the best Englishmen of his time is not a little surprising; for a life such as he had led would have with most men destroyed every fibre of intellectual energy and moral worth. But in truth there are some characters which nature has so happily compounded that even vice is unable wholly to degrade them; and there is a charm of manner and temper which sometimes accompanies the excesses of a strong animal nature that wins more popularity in the world than the purest and the most self-denying virtue.

Fox certainly was not goaded by the curse of an irritable brain; yet while making due allowance for this, I think it is possible to show some interesting points of resemblance between the two states-

men. The merit of Fox's speeches, like Lord Randolph's, lay not in
rhetorical adornments, but in the vigour and quickness of the
thought. In his invective, Fox could be as severe as the leader of
the Fourth Party. Lord G. Germaine he once described as 'that
inauspicious and ill-omened character, whose arrogance and presumption, whose ignorance and inability, had destroyed the country.'
As Ministers, they both gave up the turf and play for real hard
work; yet on neither did office exercise any restraint. Both were
economical reformers. Both advocated a generously popular system
of local government for Ireland. Both were opposed to coercion.
Lord Randolph, indeed, was ready in his negotiations with Parnell to
pledge himself to a no-coercion policy ; and Charles Fox would rather
have seen Ireland totally separated from England than allow her to
be kept in obedience by mere force. Fox even approved of the Irish
associations and their appeal to arms as a *dernier ressort* : and it was
in the same spirit that Lord Randolph told the Belfast men, in words
not yet forgotten, that in the event of Mr. Gladstone's Bill passing,
' Ulster would fight, and Ulster would be right.' Not that he objected
so much to the principle of the Bill, but he was of opinion that it
could never be passed into law. As he said : ' If the wisest, cleverest,
and most experienced parliamentarian that ever lived could not pass
it, nobody could, not even if there were a Cabinet composed wholly
of angels from heaven.' Fox possessed a courage that knew no fear ;
but Lord Randolph once confessed to me that there was a limit to
his courage, for he did fear two men—Bismarck, and Gladstone.

It has been said of Fox by Sir George Trevelyan that there was
nothing that he did not feel himself equal to accomplish. He succeeded because when once in the front all the world in arms could not
have put him in the background, and because when once in the front
he played his part with a prompt intrepidity and a commanding ease
that were but the outward signs of the immense reserve of energy on
which it was in his power to draw. He went into the House of Commons
as into the hunting field, glowing with anticipations of enjoyment,
assured that nothing would stop him, and that however often he
tumbled he would always be among the first—and first or among the
first he always was. He was not a political adventurer, but a knight-
errant roaming about in search of a tilt, or still better, a *mêlée*, and
not much caring whether his foes were robbers or true men, if only
there were enough of them. This description of Fox in the days of
Wilkes might, *mutato nomine*, have been written of Lord Randolph
in the days of Bradlaugh.

Equally applicable to Lord Randolph is what Horace Walpole said
of Fox, that

Fox displayed such facility in comprehending and executing all business as charmed
all who approached him. No formal affectation delayed any service or screened
ignorance. He seized at once the important events of any affair, and every affair

was then reduced within a small compass—not to save himself trouble, for he at once gave himself up to the duties of his office. His good humour, frankness, and sincerity pleased, and yet inspired a respect which he took no other pains to attract.

The great and indelible blot on the fame of Fox was his coalition with Lord North. No such blot besmirched the escutcheon of Lord Randolph. ' Once or twice,' he said, ' as in the case of Pigott, I broke out against folly and ineptitude ; but I never opposed my party as a policy.' Abandoned by his colleagues on his resignation ; thwarted by them at the time of the Birmingham election, a treatment he felt keenly ; his advice as to the Parnell Commission wholly disregarded ; snubbed on the occasion of his Licensing Bill—to the last he was loyal to the party whom he educated far more successfully than ever Disraeli did in the arts and moods of the Tory democracy, and thereby contributed largely to their triumph in 1895. Disraeli had idealised it long ago in *Sybil*, but Lord Randolph hardened the idealised material into good practical concrete. At Dartford, Birmingham, and elsewhere he laid great stress on the power of the democracy, and at the Carlton Club at Cambridge he told his audience that we had an hereditary monarchy, an hereditary Chamber and a representative Chamber ; but what, he asked, is the foundation of this very ancient and curious structure ?

The foundation is totally new, purely modern, absolutely untried ; you have changed the old and gone to a new foundation. Your new foundation is a great seething, swaying mass of some five million of electors, who have it in their power, if they should so please, by the mere heave of the shoulder, if they only act with moderate unanimity, to sweep away entirely the three ancient institutions which I have described, and put anything they like in their place ; and my state of mind when these problems come across me, which is very rarely, is one of wonder—or I should say, of admiration and hope, because the alternative state of mind would be one of terror and despair. . . . My especial safeguard against such a state of mental annihilation and mental despair is my firm belief in the ascertained and much tried common-sense of the English people. That is the faith of the Tory democracy, in which I shall now abide. It is not many years since the most prominent man in the present Cabinet said he did not believe in a Tory working-man. He had challenged a meeting at Birmingham if they could produce such a thing. ' I am one,' said a man, and a shout went up—'Ah, he's the Parish Beadle ! '

But that triumph and the harvest of the seed he had sown he did not live to see. From his fall to his tragic end he bore with him to the grave much affection, much admiration, and many regrets of true friends and political opponents. He might have used the words put into the mouth of the unfortunate Queen Mary by Schiller : ' I have been much hated, but I have been much beloved.'

Nothing, I am sure, is more curious in political biography than the fascination Lord Randolph Churchill possessed over his political opponents. Notwithstanding his exaggerated invective, Mr. Gladstone could not altogether resist the charm and sympathetic genius of his

younger opponent.   He frankly and fully admired Lord Randolph's
short leadership of the House of Commons, his insight, and his dash
and courage, and he sympathized with his not unsuccessful struggles
over his loved economy.   Modesty is not, perhaps, among the virtues
attributed to Lord Randolph; but there was some far off touch of it
in a letter he wrote to me, in which he says : ' I am not so conceited
as to suppose that Mr. Gladstone could care for or even notice any
speech of mine.'   But Mr. Gladstone did notice the rising man, and,
turning to a colleague on the occasion of one of Lord Randolph's early
speeches, he said prophetically : ' That is a young man you will have
to reckon with one of these days.'   They met several times, and Mr.
Gladstone often spoke in warm terms about the power Lord Randolph
possessed of making himself loved and respected by the various heads
of departments in which he worked, of his aptitude for learning, of
his admirable and courageous work towards economy, of his personal
courtesy and his pre-eminent qualities as a host, which could not be
exaggerated.   And Lord Randolph's admiration for Mr. Gladstone
was unbounded and sincere.   I recollect on one occasion when Mr.
Gladstone had been talking after dinner, as the men were leaving the
room, Lord Randolph said to a Unionist friend : ' And that is the
man you have left.   How could you have done it?'

Dr. Johnson said: ' When I was beginning the world and was
nobody and nothing, the joy of my life was to fire at all the established
wits, and then everybody loved to halloo me on.'   Disraeli followed
the great Doctor's example in his attacks on Peel; and Lord Randolph,
probably with similar motives, attacked Mr. Gladstone with an **exaggeration we now all deplore**.   But if Lord Randolph was violent and
even unscrupulous at times in his attacks, when a conviction came to
him that he had been mistaken he was generous in acknowledging it.
In language of real eloquence he had denounced the policy of Mr.
Gladstone's Government in the Transvaal.   But when years afterwards
he was face to face with the facts on the spot, he wrote a letter to a
London newspaper which attracted great attention at the time, and
which contained a retractation of the rash judgment he had pronounced, so complete and at the same time so judicious that it is
well worthy of being remembered at the present critical juncture in
our relations with that Republic.

> The surrender of the Transvaal [he wrote] and the peace concluded by Mr.
> Gladstone with the victors of Majuba Hill, were at the time, and still are, the
> object of sharp criticism and bitter denunciation from many politicians at home,
> *quorum pars parva fui*.   Better and more precise information, combined with cool
> reflection, leads me to the conclusion that had the British Government of that day
> taken advantage of its strong military position and annihilated, as it could easily
> have done, the Boer forces, it would indeed have regained the Transvaal, but it
> would have lost Cape Colony. . . . The actual magnanimity of the peace with the
> Boers concluded by Mr. Gladstone's Ministry after two humiliating military
> reverses suffered by the arms under their control, became plainly apparent to

the just and sensible mind of the Dutch Cape Colonist, atoned for much of past grievance, and demonstrated the total absence in the English mind of any hostility or unfriendliness to the Dutch race. Concord between Dutch and English in the Colony from that moment became possible.

A retractation so generous and hearty as this covers a multitude of rash vituperations.

In his strongest political animosities Lord Randolph ever retained his sense of humour. Shortly after he had written a letter to the *Times* containing a violent attack on Lord Granville, he was crossing the Channel and was dreadfully sea-sick. 'How Granville would like to see me now,' he said. Indeed I should have thought that no one could ever have doubted his sense of humour; yet in the obituary notice in one of the leading papers it was said he was totally devoid of it. Not only had he a sense of humour, but he is one of the few parliamentarians who have left sayings that have become proverbial. The elder of his colleagues were known as 'the old gang.' The Unionists as the 'crutch of the Tory Party.' His was the mint from which came 'the mediocrities with double names,' 'the old man in a hurry,' 'the duty of an Opposition is to oppose,' and many more.

It seems a paradox in God's providence that a man of genius, great talent, and splendid promise should in the prime of his life have been stricken down by a disease which appears cruel to us who see only through a glass darkly. 'But as in a piece of tapestry, where on one side all is a confused and tangled mass of knots and on the other a beautiful picture, so from the everlasting hills will this earthly life appear not the vain and chanceful thing men deem it here, but a perfect plan guided by a divine hand unto a perfect end.'

When present at his funeral service in the Abbey, I could not but think sadly of what he many a time said humorously: 'Mr. Gladstone will long outlive me; and I often tell my wife what a beautiful letter he will write on my death, proposing my burial in Westminster Abbey.' I cannot better conclude this inadequate sketch than by quoting the words used by Mr. Gladstone in writing to his poor mother:

You followed your son at every step with, if possible, more than a mother's love; and on the other hand, in addition to his conspicuous talents, he had gifts which greatly tended to attach to him those with whom he was brought into contact. For my own share, I received many marks of his courtesy and kindness, and I have only agreeable recollections of him to cherish.

ALGERNON WEST.

ON THE DERVISH FRONTIER

PARTS of Africa have to be discovered and other parts rediscovered, and each little war and each little journey contributes to the accomplishment of both these ends with alarming rapidity, and the geographical millennium is looming in the distance when the traveller will no longer require his sextant and his theodolite, but will take his spade and his pruning-hook to cultivate the land this generation is so busy in mapping out.

This last winter we have added a few square miles to a blank corner of the map where rediscovery was necessary, and where rediscovery will go on apace and produce most interesting results when we have conquered the barbarous followers of the Khalifa, and restored law and order to that wide portion of Africa known as the. Eastern Soudan ; for the Soudan, meaning in Arabic 'the country of the blacks,' really extends from the Atlantic to the Red Sea. Little did we think when we started to explore the western shores of the Red Sea that the explosion with the Dervishes was so near, otherwise I think we should have turned our steps in another direction.

To effect our ends we hired an 80-ton Arab dhow at Suez, and after placing it in the hands of a carpenter, who boarded off two cabins for us four whites in the big open stern cabin of the antiquated craft, leaving a sort of verandah in front of them where we lived by day, we embarked with a consumed plum pudding inside us and another in our hands for future consumption, last Christmas Day.

Our captain, Rais Himaya, turned out an excellent fellow, as also did the seventeen sailors he had under him, and though at times they would quarrel loudly enough amongst themselves, the only points of discord which arose between us always had reference to the length of time they wished to stop in harbour and the length of distance they wished to go in a day. Ill-fed, dirty, unkempt men as our sailors were, we got to like them all, from the elderly, dignified Mohammed, who thought he knew more about navigation than the captain, to the buffoon who played the tomtom and made everybody laugh ; this worthy individual was the recognised leader of all the festivities with which they regaled us from time to time, consisting of very ugly songs and a yet uglier dance, the chief art in which consisted in wagging their elastic tails with an energy which mortals further removed from monkey origin could never hope to approach.

Four days' sailing with an excellent north wind behind us brought us to Kosseir, our last comparatively civilised point, where we stayed for two nights to do our final victualling arrangements. Kosseir is a wretched place now, though twice in its existence it has been of importance, owing to its road connection with Keneh on the Nile. The ruins of the old Ptolemaic town Myos Hormos are five miles to the north of the present one, where the Red Sea fleets in ancient days assembled to start for India, and twenty years ago it was a favourite point for the departure of pilgrims for Mecca, and the P. & O. had offices there, which are now turned into camel stables. Kosseir is waiting for a railway before it can again recoup its fortunes.

Along the whole coast-line from Kosseir to Sawakin we may say that there are no permanent places of residence, if we except the tiny Egyptian military stations with their fort and huts for the soldiers at Halaib, Mohammed Gol, and Darour; it is practically desert all the way, and is only visited by the nomad Ababdeh and Bisharin tribes, when after the rains they can obtain there a scanty pasturage for their flocks. During the Ptolemaic and early Arab periods the condition of affairs was very different; several considerable towns stood on this coast, now marked only by heaps of sand and a few fallen walls. In spite of its aridity this coast-line has a wonderful charm of its own, its lofty, deeply serrated mountains are a perpetual joy to look upon, and the sunset effects were unspeakably glorious, rich in every conceivable colour and throwing out the sharp outline of the pointed peaks against the crimson sky.

The nature of this coast-line, too, is singularly uniform, and offers tremendous obstacles to navigation, owing to the great belt of coral reefs along it, through which the passage was often barely wide enough for our dhow to pass, and against which on more than one occasion we came in unpleasant contact. The bay of Berenice, for example, was for this reason known in ancient times as ἀκάθαρτος κόλπος, and is now known as 'Foul Bay;' it can only be navigated with the greatest care by native pilots accustomed to the various aspects of the water, which in many places only just covers the treacherous reefs. All boats are obliged to anchor during the night either just inside the reefs, or in the numerous coves along the coast, which are caused by the percolations of fresh water through the sand-beds of rivers into the sea, and these preventing the coral insect from erecting its continuous wall.

Sometimes when the coral reef rises above the surface low islets have been formed with sandy surface and a scant marine vegetation. By one of these named Siyal we were anchored for a night, and on landing we found it about three miles in length, some fifty feet in width, and never more than four feet above the surface of the sea. On its eastern side the shore was strewn with cinders from the numerous steamers which ply the Red Sea, and quantities of straw cases for bottles, out of which the ospreys which live here in large numbers have built their nests. Turtles revel in the sand, and corals of lovely colours line the beach, and at one extremity of the islet we found the remains of a holy sheikh's hut and his grave hard by. Many such holy men dwell on promontories and on remote island rocks along this coast in sanctified seclusion, and they are regularly supported by the Bedouins and pearl fishers, who bring them food and water, neither of which commodities are to be found in such localities. Our sailors on New Year's Eve took a handsome present of bread and candles to a holy man who dwelt on the extreme point of Ras Bernas, and had a long gossip with him concerning what boats had passed that way and the prospects of trade—*i.e.* the slave trade—in these desert regions. They burnt incense before his shrine and the captain devoutly said his evening prayer, whilst he of the tom-tom stood behind and mimicked him to the great amusement of his fellows, a piece of irreverence I have never seen before in any Mohammedan country. Still, I think our sailors were as a whole religious ; they observed their fasts and prayers most regularly during Ramadan, and their only idea of time was regulated by the five prayers, ' We shall start to-morrow at " God is greatest," and anchor at the evening prayer,' and so forth.

The rapidly succeeding little harbours formed in the coral reef are called ' Mersa ' or anchorages by the Arabs. Khor Shinab is a typical specimen of one of these ; it is entered by a narrow passage between the reefs about 20 feet across and runs sinuously inland for about two miles, and is never more than a quarter of a mile wide. The flat ground for miles inland is nothing but madrepore, and is covered with semi-fossilised sea-shells, which have probably not been inhabited for thousands of years. We walked over this for three miles before reaching the first spurs of the mountains, and it is impossible to conceive a more barren or arid spot. Khor Shinab is a well-known resort for slave-trading craft—small boats can easily hide in its narrow creeks and escape observation. We had to stay there for two nights in order to have three of our sails mended, which had been torn into shreds by a strong north wind as we entered the harbour, and our sailors spread them on the beach and spent the whole day patching their wretched canvases, which were little better than rags.

The navigation of an Arab dhow is no easy task, with its clumsy arrangements for sails, when there is a strong north wind behind it and reefs in every direction. Three men are perpetually in the bows on the look out for rocks, and indicate the presence of danger to the steersman by raising their hands. The gear of these boats is exceedingly primitive. They do not understand reefing a sail ; hence they are obliged to have no less than five different sizes, which they are constantly changing as occasion requires. They use a clumsy cogwheel for raising and lowering the sails, and do it all by main force, singing silly little distichs and screaming at the top of their voices as they haul the ropes. The arrangement for baling out the bilge water is extremely laborious : a large trough with channels on either side is erected in the centre of the boat, into which the water is baled by skins from below, and the stenches during the process are truly awful.

It is difficult to estimate how far these coral reefs have changed since ancient days ; there is a lagoon at Berenice which looks as if it had been the ancient harbour with a fort at its extremity. Now there is scarcely two feet of water over the bar across its mouth ; but all ancient accounts bear testimony to a similar difficulty of navigation down this coast. At the same time, it is manifest that this coast-line is just the one to have tempted on the early mariners from point to point with its rapid succession of tiny harbours and it reefs protecting it from heavy seas. More especially must this have been the case when the boats were propelled by oars, and in one's mind's eye one can picture the fleets of the Egyptian Queen Hatasou and of King Solomon from Eziongeber creeping cautiously along this coast and returning after three years' absence in far-distant regions laden with precious freights of gold, frankincense, and spices. In later days Strabo and Pliny tell us how flotillas of 120 ships proceeded from Myos Hormos to Ocelis in thirty days on their way to India, going together for fear of the pirates who marauded this coast, and in those days the settlements on the Red Sea must have presented a far livelier aspect than they do now.

On both shores of the Red Sea we find a curious instance of the migration and adaptation of an entirely foreign kind of boat. Some Arabs who have lived in Singapore—and Singapore is as favourite a point for Arab emigration as America is for the Irish—introduced ' dug outs' in their native harbours, and these have been found so useful in sailing over the shallow coral reefs in search of pearls, that they now swarm in every Red Sea port, and steamer loads of ' dug outs' are brought from the Malay peninsula. The Arabs call them ' houris'—why, I cannot think—for a more uncomfortable thing to sit in, when half full of water in a rolling serf, I never found elsewhere.

At the present moment the coast below Ras Bernas and above Sawakin, is the hot-bed of the slave trade, carried on between the Dervishes of the Nile valley and Arabia. Regular Egyptian coast-guard boats keep matters pretty clear north of Ras Bernas, and we can testify to their activity, for we ourselves were boarded and searched by one; but south of this, before the influence of Sawakin is reached, there is a long stretch of country where the traffic in human flesh can be carried on undisturbed. Troops of slaves are sent down from the Nile valley to the Dervish country at certain seasons of the year, and the petty sheikhs along the coast, owing a doubtful allegiance to the

Egyptian Government, connive at this transport; and the pearl fishing
craft which ply their trade amongst the coral reefs are always ready
to carry the slaves across to the opposite coast, where the markets of
Yembo, Yeddah, and Hodeida are open to them.   This will of course
be the case until the Dervish power is crushed, and the Soudan
opened out for more legitimate trade.   As we sailed along we passed
hundreds of these pearl-fishing boats engaged in this dual trade, and
nothing could be more propitious for their pursuits than the absolutely
lawless condition of the tribes by the coast.   At Berenice, for instance,
there is absolutely no life or government of any sort.   Nominally, one
of our Nile frontier subsidised sheikhs, Beshir Bey Gabran, of Assouan,
has authority over all the country between the Nile and the Red Sea,
but the coast-line has been visited more frequently by Dervish Emirs
than by Beshir Bey.   One Nasrai, a Dervish Emir, is said to have
resided in the mountains behind Berenice for some time, and with a
small following collects tithes of cattle from the nomads, and sees to
the safe conduct of slave caravans.

We spent several days amongst the ruins of this old Ptolemaic
town, and made sundry excavations there.   In its centre is an old
temple of the date of Tiberius Cæsar, the hieroglyphs in which are
rapidly becoming obliterated.   All around is a sea of mounds covered
with sand, where the houses stood, mostly built of madrepore and laid
out in streets.   On the surface are to be found numerous glass beads,
Roman coins, bracelets, &c., and a great number of fragments of rough
emeralds from the celebrated emerald mines in the mountain behind;
we picked up fully fifty of these, besides a large quantity of olivines
or peridots, carnelians and crystals, testifying to the wealth of these
parts in precious stones in ancient days.

A few startled Ababdeh nomads came to visit us; at first they
only inspected us at a distance, but gradually gained courage, and
came to our camp, and we were able to purchase from them two lambs
to replenish our larder.

With its emerald mines, its harbour, and its great road centre, in
ancient times Berenice must have been one of the greatest trade
centres of the Red Sea, but under the present state of affairs its condition is impossible.   The wretched Ababdeh tribes are constantly at
war with one another, and the Dervish Khalifa can make his authority
felt about here with a small handful of resolute men judiciously
placed, and I believe Nasrai has done this for some time past with only
thirty men.

It is hard to imagine anything more squalid than the Egyptian
fortress of Halaib on the shores of the Red Sea, which was our next
halting-place, and from which we succeeded in getting a little way
inland.   The governor, Ismael, has been there seven years, and he
and his family inhabit some wicker cages near the small white fort,
and gathered round them are the huts of his soldiers and the cabins

of a few Bisharin, who live under the immediate protection of the fort.   Ismael is possessed of the only patch of cultivated land that we saw during the whole of our expedition, where he grows gourds, peas, and aubergines.   The man of most authority in the place is Mohammed Ali Tiout, head of the Bisharin tribe of Achmed Orab, and he is called the *Batran* in the local dialect.   He appointed his son, a fine intelligent young fellow of five-and-twenty, to act as our guide and protector during our exploration of the Shellal range, which rises some miles inland at the back of Halaib.

After our somewhat long experience of life on a dhow, we were delighted to become Bedouins once more, and wander amongst the fine rocky range of mountains, but we were disappointed that our guide would not take us far behind this range for fear of the Dervishes, and as shortly after the outbreak of the war a party of Dervishes came right down to Halaib, there is every reason to believe that had we gone far inland at this point we might have been compelled to pay the Khalifa a not over pleasant visit at Omdurman.

The people of this portion of the Soudan between the coast and the Nile Valley, who do not own allegiance to the Khalifa, belong to the Morghani confraternity of Mohammedans ; their young religious sheikh, a self-possessed, clever lad of about seventeen, lives at Sawakin, and his influence amongst the tribes not affecting Mahdism is supreme.   He is devoted to British interests, and no doubt in the present condition of affairs his co-operation will be of great value. The Egyptian Government instructed him to write to the sheikhs around Halaib and Mohammed Gol to insure our safety, and to this fact I am convinced we owe the safety we enjoyed and the assistance given to us in penetrating inland from Mohammed Gol.   The Morghani have the three cicatrices on either cheek, and as a confraternity they are not the least fanatical and well disposed to Christians ; very different from the Arabs we met in the Hadramaut, and very different from the Dervishes with whom they are on such hostile terms.

As a race the Bedouins by the Red Sea mostly trace their origin to the Nile Valley.   It would seem that the original inhabitants, the Bejas, of whom we read so much in early Arab geographers as living on this coast and owning all the land from Abyssinia to the borders of Nubia, must have become extinct : to them are probably due the large circular tombs which are dotted about in all directions, and which are admitted by the present race to belong to a period anterior to themselves.   The prince of the Bejas lived at Sawakin, and they owned another considerable town called Aydab, of which we were fortunate enough to identify the ruins about twelve miles north of Halaib, which was a great point of commerce between the Nile Valley and the opposite coast of Arabia.   We find the Bejas occurring on the old monuments at Aksum in Abyssinia, and from the Arab geographers we learn that they were the recognised guardians of the old gold mines which existed in this district, and concerning which I have more to say presently; and though vassals of the Egyptian kaliphs, nevertheless they seem to have had considerable local authority, and to have carried on wars on their own account.

In course of time the Bejas seem to have disappeared from the face of the earth and left nothing but their tombs and a few ruined towns behind them; and for some centuries it would appear that the coast of the Red Sea, north of Sawakin was uninhabited until in later years came fresh Bedouin colonists from the Nile Valley, whose descendants occupy it now.

The tribal traditions of the district are all that we have now to rely upon, and they state that two brothers with their families, one named Amer and the other Amar, came from the Nile Valley near Wadi Halfa, and settled along the coast of the Red Sea; from them are descended the Beni Amer and Amarar tribes of Bedouins. These brothers were followed in due course by four other brothers, Ali, Kourb, Nour, and Gueil, from whom the tribes and sub-tribes of the Aliab, Kourbab, Nourab, and Gueilior are respectively descended. These tribes have never been anything but pastoral nomads, living in miserable mat huts and spreading themselves over the district at wide intervals in search of pasture for their flocks. They entirely disown having anything to do with the remains of buildings and tombs found in their midst, and it seems to me only reasonable to suppose that these were erected by their predecessors, about whom Aboulfeda and Edrisi have so much to tell us, ruled over by the princes of Kush and Beja, the hereditary guardians of the gold district.

Everything connected with the various tribes of Bedouins amongst whom we travelled savours of the Nile Valley—their wild, shaggy locks with curls stiffened with lard, their round skin shields with eye holes, their long, straight swords bulging at the end, are objects familiar to all travellers on the Nile in Nubia. Moreover, their quaint adornments, too, are apparently all of the same origin—the tall headdress, two feet high, thickly covered with cowries and with long danglements decorated with shells, in which their figures at weddings and dances have been brought thence. Their elaborate camel trappings for females when they travel, their silver and gold nose rings, bracelets, meat-safes, and the few other ornaments one finds in their tents, are all relics of a higher state of civilisation, when they lived in greater affluence on the banks of the Nile.

As we found them last winter, the nomad tribes around the great mountain centres in this district, known respectively as Mounts Elba and Erba, appear to be in the last stage of decadence and miserably poor. We travelled for a week without seeing any trace whatsoever of human habitation, and we travelled for three months without seeing a single inch of cultivated land belonging to them. We never saw more than half a dozen tents together, wretched tenements made of matting spread on sticks, and the sole sustenance of the inhabitants is derived from their flocks, which they with difficulty keep alive during the dry season by driving them up to the loftier slopes of the mountains.

For many years past the Egyptian authority in these parts has been nil, and confined only to a few wretched forts on the coast. Dervish raids from the interior and the stoppage of whatever caravan trade there ever was has contributed to the miserable condition of affairs now existing. The Batran of the Achmed Orab tribe told us that all the way from Ras Bernas to just below Halaib, a distance of more than a hundred miles, over which his tribe has nominal territorial rights, he can only count upon a force of 300 fighting men, and that scattered over a too hopelessly extended area for any practical resistance to their more powerful enemies inland ; and it would seem that if this condition of affairs were to continue much longer the country would soon be again uninhabited. One can well understand why these miserable hounded tribes are wavering in their allegiance between the Egyptian Government and the Khalifa whom they dread, and that they countenance the slave traders from the reason that they have no power to resist them.

For all practical purposes it is a wretched country, waterless during a great part of the year, except where some deep ancient wells, scattered at wide intervals over the country, form centres where camels and flocks can be watered ; and as we travelled along we were struck by the numbers of these wells which had been quite recently abandoned. But the mountains are magnificently grand, sharp in outline and with deep and lovely gorges. Formerly they abounded in mines, and were celebrated for their mineral wealth, and if there is ever to be a revival in this country it will be from this source that hope will come.

At Mohammed Gol, to which port our dhow next conducted us, our prospects of getting well into the interior were much brighter, and our ultimate results beyond comparison more satisfactory than they had been at Halaib. Mohammed Gol is distinctly a more lively place than Halaib, possessing more huts, more soldiers, and actually a miniature bazaar where, strange to relate, we were able to buy something we wanted.

The governor or mamour of the little Egyptian garrison there summoned three sheikhs from the neighbouring mountains, into whose hands he confided us, and though several travellers had visited the Red Sea side of the massive group of Mount Erba on holidays from Sawakin in search of sport, no one as yet had been behind it ; and thither, with the assistance of our three sheikhs, we were determined to go.

Little did we dream when we left Mohammed Gol with our rather extensive caravan that behind that gigantic mountain, which, though it only reaches an elevation of 7,500 feet, looks considerably higher from the sea as it rises almost directly out of the level plain, we were to find an ancient Egyptian gold mine, the ruins in connection with which would offer us the first tangible comparison to the ruins which had exercised our minds so much in the gold-fields of South Africa.

In the summer season, when the waters of the Red Sea are low, traders come to Mohammed Gol for salt. The salterns are situated on the narrow spit of land called Ras Rowaya; consequently, the people about here are more accustomed to the sight of Europeans, and the governor, who is young and energetic, seems far more in touch with the world than Ismael of Halaib. He complains much of the dulness of his post, and passes his weary hours in making walking-sticks out of ibex horns, a craft he has learnt from the Bedouins of Mount Erba, who soften the horns in hot water, grease them, pull them out and flatten them with weights and polish them, using them as camel sticks. The governor gave us several of these sticks, and also presented an ibex horn head scratcher to Mrs. Bent, remarking, as he did so, with a polite gesture, that it was a nice thing to have by her when her head itched.

Two Kourbab sheikhs, the rulers over Mount Erba and its adjacent spurs, and one Keilab sheikh, whose dominion extends over a vast area in the adjacent valleys, after much haggling and many palavers in the reed council chamber by the shore, consented to take us where we wished; 'right round Mount Erba, and as far inland as possible,' being the crucial sentence in our agreement with them.

He of the Keilab tribe, Debalop by name, was the most important of them, and he took one of his wives with him; all had their servants and shield bearers, and most of them were wild, unprepossessing-looking men, with shaggy locks and lard-daubed curls, and all of them were, I believe, thorough ruffians, who, as we were told afterwards, would willingly have sold us to the Dervishes had they thought they would have gained by the transaction. These things officials told us when we reached Sawakin; but to do our guides justice I must say they treated us very well, and inasmuch as we never believed a word they said, the fact that they were liars made but little difference to us.

Some miles inland on the plain behind Mohammed Gol are certain mysterious towers some twenty feet high, of unknown origin. They have every appearance of belonging to the Kufic period, being domed and covered with a strong white cement; they have no doors, but windows high up; some are hexagonal, some square, and they are apparently dotted all along the coast. Whether they were tombs, or whether they were landmarks to guide mariners to certain valleys leading into the mountains, will probably not be definitely proved until some one is energetic enough to excavate in one. They are found as far south as Massowa, but as far as I could ascertain those we saw were the most northern ones. In one we found two skeletons of modern date, with the scanty clothing still clinging to the bones, as they had laid in the agonies of death, poor sick creatures, who had climbed in to die.

At the tower which marks the entrance to the Hadi valley we halted, and bade adieu to the governor and officials of Mohammed Gol, who had accompanied us thus far. Our parting was almost dramatic, and the injunctions to the sheikhs to see to our safety were reiterated with additional vehemence.

The dismal journeys of the next few days are by no means pleasant to look back upon. Our road led us in and out of desert and uninhabited valleys, with no object of interest to look upon save the numerous circular buildings crowning heights, and clustered on elevated ground, which I put down as the tombs of the departed Bejas ; tombs of a somewhat similar nature are found all down this coast—down to the confines of the Ethiopian Empire ; they originally built circular walls about three feet high and ten feet in diameter, and filled up the centre with stones, with a slight depression in the middle.

As we wandered up the valleys to the north of Mount Erba, occasional glimpses of the fine peaks of the range would relieve the monotony of the landscape, but the barren hills around us, with a few mimosa trees dotted here and there, long stretches of sand, and scarcely any animal or vegetable life, made the daily hours on our camels extremely wearisome.

We were in Debalop's country now, the chief of the large and powerful Keilab tribe, half of which owns avowed allegiance to the Khalifa, and the other half with their chief is put down as wavering by the Government at Sawakin. Luckily we did not know this at the time, or otherwise I question if we should have ventured to put ourselves so entirely in his hands, with the horrors of a visit to Khartoum, as experienced by Slatin Pasha, so fresh in our memories.

A halt of three days was called for, after we had marched steadily for six, at a spot called Hadai, close to which Debalop's own huts were placed, and where he took the opportunity of changing his wife, having presumably had enough of the other's company on the road. The Debalop family mausoleum is also here, the tombs of which consisted of piles of white stones, with little paths around them made of the same material, and headstones towards Mecca, neat but not gaudy.

At Hadai for the first time during the whole of our journey our interests were keenly aroused in certain antiquities we found here— antiquities about which Debalop had said a good deal, but about which we had never ventured to raise any hopes.

Hard by the Debalop mausoleum was another Kufic tower, though much smaller than those we had seen on the coast, and not covered with white cement, and in the same locality were several foundations of circular buildings very neatly executed in dry masonry, which appeared to have at either end the bases of two circular towers and curious bulges, which at once reminded us of our South African ruins. On climbing an adjacent hill we found a circular fort, evidently constructed for strategical purposes, with a door with rounded ends leading into it, quite a counterpart of the smaller ruin on the Lundi river in Mashonaland. The analogy was indeed curious, and we talked about it hesitatingly to ourselves, as yet unable to give any satisfactory reason for its existence. On various heights around were cairns erected as if for landmarks, and we felt that here at last we were in the presence of one of those ancient mysteries which it is so delightful to solve.

We rested our camels and our men at Hadai, and drank of some fresh water, the first we had seen in this barren country, which was supplied by a tiny stream which made its appearance for a few yards in a sheltered corner of the valley, a stream of priceless value in this thirsty land. Debalop suggested that he knew of some ruins in a neighbouring valley to which he could take me, but it was not without considerable hesitation that I decided to go. A long day's ride in this hot country, supposed to be almost, if not quite, within the Dervish sphere of influence, was not lightly to be undertaken, more especially as I had been on so many fruitless errands in search of ruins at the Bedouin's suggestion, and returned disgusted; and when I mounted my camel next morning, without any hope of finding anything, and sure of a fatiguing day, if a reasonable excuse had offered itself I should probably have not gone. But the unexpected in these cases is always happening. The long ride turned out only to be one of three hours. Wadi Gabeit was infinitely more fertile and picturesque than any we had as yet seen, and as a climax to it all came the discovery of an ancient gold mine, worked in ages long gone by doubtless by that mysterious race whose tombs and buildings we had been speculating upon.

Diodorus, in his account of an old Egyptian gold mine, describes most accurately what I found in the Wadi Gabeit. For miles along it at the narrower end were the ruins of miners' huts; both up the main valley and up all the collateral ones there must have been seven or eight hundred of them at the lowest computation. Then there were hundreds of massive crushing stones, neatly constructed out of blocks of basalt, which had been used for breaking the quartz, lying in wild confusion amongst the ruined huts, and by the side of what once was a stream, but now only a sandy, choked-up river-bed. On a high rock in the centre of the valley I found a trifle of a Greek inscription scratched by a miner, who had evidently been working the rich quartz vein just below it.

On an eminence behind the valley was another of the circular forts in ruins, similar to the one on the hill above Wadi Hadai, intended evidently for a look-out post to protect the miners at work below. Burnt quartz and refuse of quartz lay around in all directions, and on either side of the valley stretched for a mile or more seams of the auriferous quartz just as it had been laid bare by the ancient workers. There was no question for a doubt that I had come across the centre of a great mining industry of ages long gone by, lost in these desert valleys behind the mighty wall by which Mount Erba and its spurs shut off this district from the Red Sea littoral.

Naturally one's ideas were a trifle confused at being confronted with this unexpected discovery, and in the short space of time then available it was impossible to grasp it all. So I rode back joyfully to tell the news to my party at Hadai. I told Debalop that we would move our camp thither, and stay as long as it was possible.

Difficulties again confronted us. Our two Kourbab sheikhs did not want to go at all, and Debalop himself had to be firmly spoken to on the subject, but at length we all made a start to visit my new Eldorado. A short time before reaching the spot we were met by a small band of natives, who tried to stop our advance with menaces, which we were determined neither to understand nor recognise. Possibly they were some of the Keilab tribe, who owned allegiance to the Dervishes, possibly they were actuated by the inherent dread the Moslem has of Christian enterprise reaching their secluded vales. However, our show of fire-arms and determination to go on had the effect of intimidating them, and after a somewhat feeble hostile demonstration and many palavers, we found ourselves comfortably established in our tents in the heart of the ancient industry, and peacefully distributing medicines from our chest to our whilom foes.

Thus we had ample time to look around us and gauge the extent of the former industry. We marvelled at the multiplicity of the crushing pans scattered in every direction, and the number of huts there must have been; and we also found several miners' scratchings, representing gazelles, birds, &c. on the rocks, and we visited a spot higher up the mountain sides, where we saw large blocks of quartz that had been cut out of the vein ready to be removed to the valley below for crushing purposes.

Since returning home I have consulted various ancient authorities on the subject of these mines, and have come to the conclusion that they form a portion, at least, of those referred to by Edrisi and Aboulfeda as the gold mines of Allaka, in one allusion to which they are placed in the vicinity of the Red Sea, four days from Aydab. There is an interesting old map, said to be the oldest in the world, given by M. Chabas in his *Inscriptions des Mines d'Or*, now in the Turin Museum, and dating from the time of Seti the First, and it is highly probable that this is a rough sketch of these very mines;

but they were abandoned by the Khalifas, one gathers from the Arab geographers, for want of water, when our era was still young.

Will this mine ever be available again for those in search of the precious mineral? is the first question that suggests itself. Unfortunately I am no gold expert, and am therefore absolutely unable to give an opinion as to the possibilities of the still existing quartz seams being payable or not, but there is abundance of it both in the Wadi Gabeit and in the collateral valleys, and it is improbable that the ancients, with their limited knowledge of mining, could have exhausted the place. Specimens of quartz that I picked up at haphazard have been assayed and found to be auriferous, with the gold very finely disseminated : an expert would undoubtedly have selected even more brilliant specimens than these. Against this the absence of water and labour seemed to me at the time to negative any possible favourable results ; but, on the other hand, the mine is so conveniently near the sea, with comparatively easy road access, that labour might be imported, and such wonderful things are done nowadays with artesian wells, that if the experts report favourably upon it, there would be every chance of good work being done, and these desert mountains of the Soudan might again ring with the din of industry.

The morning after we reached Wadi Gabeit an express messenger reached us from Sawakin, bidding us return to the coast at once, as we were supposed to be in considerable danger. Dervish raids were expected in this direction, and the authorities were evidently afraid of complications. A solemn palaver forthwith took place, at which our three sheikhs showed that they thought little of the supposed danger, and said that though we were nominally in Dervish country at the time, there was no armed force near of sufficient strength to attack us. So we decided, and backed up our decision with a promised bribe, to stay another night in Wadi Gabeit, and to continue our course round Mount Erba as we had originally intended, and with us we kept the messenger of woe with his gun and spear as an additional protection.

We left Wadi Gabeit next morning, and on the following day another messenger from Sawakin met us with a similar mandate ; but as we were now journeying in a presumably safe direction we annexed him too, and went on our way rejoicing. Personally we felt that we knew the condition of the country better than the authorities of Sawakin, who had never been there. If our sheikhs had meant treachery they would long ago have put it into practice; our two Kourbab sheikhs, whose property is in and around Mohammed Gol, were ample guarantee for our safety; and, moreover, the country was so absolutely destitute of everything, that we gave the Dervishes credit for better sense than to raid it.

It was at this juncture that we lost our little dog, a pet that had journeyed everywhere with us ; when search failed, we gave it up for lost, and drew mournful pictures of the dear creature's dying agonies in the desert, foodless and waterless. The clever animal nevertheless retraced its steps, how we know not, to Mohammed Gol in five days, without food and very little water, over the desert paths we had come— a distance of about 120 miles, and terrified the governor out of his wits, who naturally thought it was the sole survivor of our expedition. It made its way straight to the jetty and swam to our dhow, and was picked up by our Arab sailors more dead than alive. After resting and feeding on the dhow for two days the dog jumped overboard once more, and went off by itself to the mountains for three days in search of us; when this failed it returned again, and reached our dhow the night before we did, and was ready to welcome us on our return with a wildly demonstrative greeting. We eventually gave it to a sergeant at Sawakin, and have reason to believe that it is at present taking part with its regiment in the Soudan campaign.

The day's journeyings after leaving Wadi Gabeit were very similar to those before reaching it: now a valley of black shale void of verdure, now a sand-choked valley with herbage as black as if it had been burnt, now a valley with a few arrack trees, the mustard tree of the Bible, on which young camels and their mothers were feeding; and as we reached Mount Erba we descended the stupendously lovely Wadi Kour, where many donkeys are bred, and from which, they told us donkeys often escape and form the bread of wild asses, one or two of which we saw among the mountains.

From the heights above us, as we wound our way down Wadi Kour, stones were rolled down on us by natives of hostile intent, and our sheikhs would not let us encamp under the shadow of the rocks, but right in the middle of the valley, for fear of our being treated to a volley of stones during the night. Far richer vegetation here existed at the foot of Mount Erba; deep pools of water were to be found in the crevasses, trees, plants, and rushes grew here, in the sight of which we revelled after our desert wanderings.

At the instigation of one of our sheikhs we made a long detour from here to visit his father's encampment at a spot called Sellala, concerning which he drew such lively pictures of rich vegetation and plenty that we hoped we were going to a real oasis in the desert, but instead we found a wretched sand-choked spot, and pitched our tents in a raging sandstorm, by no means pleased at the deception that had been played upon us.

At Sellala is a deep and probably ancient well, which is the point of assemblage for many Bedouins with their camels and their flocks. Ali Hamed, the aged sheikh of this branch of the Kourbab tribe, here has his settlement, the largest we had seen anywhere in this district, and actually consisting of ten huts. He is a wicked old man to look upon, with a hooked nose and cunning eye, with a wide-spread reputation, doubtless well deserved, of being a hardened old

slave-trader; he was very civil to us nevertheless, and in his village
we sat for some time and purchased various native commodities—a
gold nose ring and earrings, and elegant camel trappings, for the
evidence of wealth here was in excess of any we had yet seen. But
the greatest good that accrued to us from our visit to Sellala was a
long ride. Ali Hamed's son Mohammed took us to see some rock
scribblings, and I am confident they were the best 'antikas' he had
to show us, for he was very jealous of the interest we had taken in
those in Debalop's country. On a knoll covered with basaltic rocks
we found the smooth surfaces completely covered with representations
of various animals, similar to those we had seen in the Wadi Gabeit,
only a larger assortment. Here we recognised the elephant, the
mongoose, the gazelle, and the camel, and interspersed amongst them
were two letters of the Sabæan alphabet, suggestive of the theory
that visitors from South Arabia had done them. The spot was only
a few miles from the sea, and the tiny harbour of Salaka, the port of
Ali Hamed's country, and we naturally connected these scribblings
with the gold industry inland, and came to the conclusion that this
harbour was one frequented by the ancient miners. Near the mound
was another of the curious towers in ruins, but otherwise the country
around was void of all interest—an absolutely barren expanse of desert
sand.

Before finally returning to Mohammed Gol and our dhow, we
decided to pass a few pleasant days in exploring the fastnesses of
Mount Erba and its spurs. One of our party was exceedingly anxious
to go in pursuit of the ibex, which occur in great numbers on this
rocky mountain. So accordingly we clambered up the Wadi Ambaya,
which penetrates far into the heart of the mountain, and pitched our
tents in the dry bed of the mountain stream amid gigantic boulders.
It was a perfectly delightful change to be amongst these mountain
gorges with streams of water and rich vegetation, and no fear of
Dervishes to prevent us wandering hither and thither, where we
wished.

Nabidua, Sherbuk, and Emeri are the three highest peaks of
Erba, the former reaching an elevation of 7,500 feet, and running
like needles into the sky. The scenery is exceedingly wild and rocky,
and in whichever direction we turned the rise was very precipitous.
Scattered up the valleys are several native settlements, the huts being
hardly distinguishable from the boulders around them; the pasturage
seemed exceedingly good, and we regaled ourselves with the luxury
of an unlimited supply of milk. These mountain Bedouins have dogs
of a breed peculiarly their own, which they keep for the chase of the
ibex; and these people here are exceedingly lithe and active, leaping
from rock to rock, with their shields and spears, with the nimbleness
of-goats.

In the lower valleys gazelle and antelope are very numerous, and these the natives trap with a peculiar snare manufactured by themselves, consisting of a ring in which many thin strips of wood are fastened, meeting in the centre. This ring is just covered with sand and tied to a tree, so that when the animal steps upon it its leg is caught and it is easily captured; there are great numbers of these ingenious traps to be found in every hut.

We spent one pleasant day on an expedition to a mountain hamlet high up in the recesses of Kokout—a spur of Erba, and approached by a curious gorge, so narrow in places that we thought it must end soon, and requiring considerable agility to get up. The women were all busy making butter by shaking the milk in skins tied to a tree, which product is the principal one on which they subsist for a livelihood; their children were learning the art of war with toy shields and toy swords, and the men played us tunes on long reed pipes, most suitable to their pastoral pursuits and wild surroundings, and on our return home we had ibex for dinner, which we did not like much, being in flavour too closely related to old goat.

Then we bid adieu to our wild roving life, and returned to our dhow, which took us in two days to Sawakin, where war and rumours of war were the order of the day.

J. Theodore Bent.

COUNTY COUNCILS & RURAL EDUCATION

The following pages upon the recent educational proposals of the Government are in no sense prompted by political considerations. They are simply intended to embody certain conclusions suggested by a long and fairly wide interest and experience in connection with rural elementary schools, and by the experience gained and the interest awakened in secondary education in the conduct of the business (as chairman) of the Technical Education Committee of the Devon County Council, which was appointed immediately upon the passing of the Act in 1890. That committee has worked zealously and steadily, and with a measure of success such as only the boldest and most sanguine would have ventured to predict from the reception which was usually accorded to their proposals during the first four or five years. It is some satisfaction to be able to remark that the lines upon which they have principally run have been in most matters closely paralleled by the lines followed in other counties of a comparable size and of circumstances at all similar; and this fact to some extent justifies the inference that the conclusions to be drawn from our experience in Devonshire and the western counties are far from being inapplicable to other rural districts.

I have therefore ventured to put forward these suggestions solely from a sincere anxiety to promote, as far as in me lies, sound permanent progress in education, both elementary and secondary, in rural districts. In urban districts the solution of the problem is as child's play compared with the overcoming of the difficulties that attend its solution in 'the country;' and it is mainly with 'country matters' that county councils have to do. It is of rural and not urban districts that I write. And it may be well to remind the reader that while it is with regard to rural districts that those interested in education find the most numerous and the most serious obstacles in their path, it is also in rural districts that the need for energetic action is greatest and the reward of success would be the most encouraging.

It would be difficult to say which were the greater, the hopes or the fears excited by the educational project so unexpectedly sprung upon the country by the Government during the session of 1896, and not less suddenly withdrawn.

On the one hand were those who for the moment congratulated themselves on seeing the problem solved of how to combine financial aid to voluntary schools with 'Local Control,' in such a manner as to steer clear of the parochial ratepayer; while, on the other hand, at least an equally appreciable number of persons looked with dread upon what they regarded as a proposal to introduce sectarianism into the minds of children at the very outset of their education, and viewed with intense anxiety the proposal to entrust to county councils the administration of so vital a subject as elementary education.

But probably when the bill was withdrawn, and time was thus given for the mature consideration of an experiment so revolutionary (as regards education), the sense of relief was both more general, and stronger than any feeling of disappointment at the postponement of what may have at first sight appeared to some to be an ingenious practical solution of a difficult problem.

The tendency to decentralisation in administration, which is regarded by some as one of the phases of democracy in this country, presents a curious variety of aspects. Any one who has taken part in local affairs during the last quarter of a century must have been struck by the antipathy felt by the local authorities to interference and control, and the healthy hatred of red tape and of the official uniformity which is the necessary result of excessive centralisation such as is often attributed to 'my Lords' and the 'Board above.'

At the same time it is by no means an uncommon experience among local authorities to find a collision between them and the 'Board above' in such matters as the appointment and efficient remuneration of competent officers, or as to the outlay necessary for efficient sanitary precautions, and so forth. And cases are frequent enough in which the 'guardian' watches far more carefully over the rates than over any of the other subjects entrusted to his charge.

On the other hand, there can be no question that some devolution of responsibility for the conduct of ordinary local public business is essential to a combination of efficiency and economy. Nor can there be any reasonable doubt of the general soundness of the maxim that taxation and representation ought to go together, although as regards parochial affairs there may have been amply sufficient reasons for its having been disregarded in the establishment of parish councils and meetings.

In this connection there is probably no greater difficulty in legislation (and perhaps it may be said in administration also) than the due appreciation of the differences between the aspects presented by problems affecting similar subjects in urban and rural districts respectively.

In the one case it is easy to collect at any time an assembly of intelligent men bound together by membership of the same community, with many interests in common, and with minds kept alive and in constant activity by daily contact with their equals in intellectual power and in social station, sharpened by business, and impatient of waste of time. In the other case, long distances have to be travelled; the men available are fewer, their minds are of a different order, their occasions of intercourse with their fellow-men are also different; time is not so precious to them, the very nature of their employment accustoms them to wait long for results; and their shrewdness is more often shown in the personal conduct of their own separate business than in the active participation in the local affairs of their immediate neighbourhood, and the community of which they are fellow-members has a much less definite and corporate existence.

The result is shown in a far less rapid formation of public opinion in rural than in urban districts, and consequently a much slower rate of progress, much less elasticity or fertility of resource, and much less evidence of public spirit or devotion to public duty.

In no department of public business has this difference already produced more evident effect than in matters connected with elementary education.

In the working of the School Board system two very opposite effects have been produced, which tend to illustrate the complexity and difficulty of the questions connected with this subject.

While in some cases in urban districts the effect of entrusting education to bodies locally elected *ad hoc* has been a steady growth of expenditure reaching almost to extravagance, the other extreme —namely, economy amounting to foolish parsimony—has been not less frequently the fault of such bodies in rural districts.

It is hardly going too far to say that, so far as elementary education is concerned, that system which has been a success in urban districts has been comparatively, in rural districts, rather less than more successful for the most part than the voluntary system. And unquestionably the 'intolerable strain' spoken of by Mr. Balfour as inflicted upon voluntary schools can only fairly be considered to exist in those urban districts where the supporters of voluntary schools have been compelled to support by rate the Board schools from which it was their main object to save their children.

In country districts, on the other hand, the voluntary school has ordinarily been regarded by its supporters as a more economical, and at the same time equally efficient means of discharging the public duty of providing elementary education of which in nearly all cases by far the greater part has been paid for from Imperial funds, so that while, in urban districts, the supporters of voluntary schools have been fair objects for sympathy, in rural districts they may rather be congratulated, as far as expenditure has been concerned, though the burden on subscribers is often heavier than the rate would be if borne by the whole community.

It is difficult to believe that the authors of the Education Bill had really thought out the results which must follow the proposals embodied -in it. One can hardly wonder at their feeling a very strong tempta- tion to seize the opportunity of sailing round the parochial ratepayer, and obtaining 'Local Control' without his interference, which appeared to be afforded by the existence of the county councils. But can they have carefully considered all that would be involved in so far-reaching a proposal?

Did they examine the composition of the county councils?

Did they endeavour to ascertain the amount of unpaid work which falls necessarily upon county councillors, even exclusive of what they already have in connection with education, which will certainly become the heaviest work of all when the whole area of local secondary edu- cation is brought under their superintendence? The presence of experts on the Education Committee may no doubt be desirable, but it would in no way lighten the pressure of the increased burden upon the shoulders of county councillors.

Did they realise all that is involved in exposing county councils to the inevitable attacks from all sides in connection with the financial and religious difficulties about which those who have the management of elementary—especially voluntary—schools have made so loud an outcry?

It must be remembered that upon the shoulders of county councils as 'paramount' authorities it was proposed at once to place the whole burden not only of elementary, but also of secondary education, excepting only the non-local schools.

The financial part of the elementary school business alone brings with it such a train of other details as to render that part taken by itself more formidable than any other division of the present duties of managers. But what evidence of the willingness (not to say desire), and what evidence of the fitness of county councils for the duty of keeping up the standard, by efficient inspection and even- handed strictness of administration, has been forthcoming? Did the Government seriously entertain the belief that the utmost efficiency of administration of which county councils might be capable could be comparable to that of the existing Department?

And were the evils of divided government, dual control, present to their minds?

There is one consideration which has not as yet been much brought to the front, but which might have been expected to have had some influence where evidently it has had none—namely, a fundamental and essential distinction between the nature and aim of *elementary* as distinguished from *secondary* education.

The field and scope of 'public elementary education' are clear, distinct, and homogeneous throughout the country. They are the in- struction and religious and moral training of the children of that section

of the nation of which the following, as regards education, are important characteristics : (1) The proportion of children whose parents are
uneducated is the largest.   (2) The time which can be devoted to instruction is the shortest.   (3) The prospect of the children being able
to follow up and maintain that which they have gained at school is the
most precarious.   (4) All other circumstances affecting their education
are less favourable than those of the other sections.   (5) The proportion of those to whom in future years education may appear (falsely,
of course) of· small importance is the largest.   (6) The cost of any
sacrifice on the part of the parents for the sake of education is the most
serious in proportion.   (7) The whole cost of the teaching in most cases
is supplied by other than the parents—either wholly or partly from
State funds, rates, or voluntary subscriptions.

Whether in town or country, North or South, Board or voluntary
school, the above characteristics are in the main true, distinctive, and
fundamental.   No doubt there are other considerations, but the above
seem to me to point to the following inference : namely, that the provision of the education required under conditions so uniform, and on a
scale of magnitude sufficient to meet the requirements of the working
millions, is eminently and properly the function of the nation at large,
acting through its central administration.   The plea that officialism
and rigid uniformity are the vice of that administration, if it were
true, would be no answer—it would only tend to enforce the necessity
of parliamentary vigilance with regard to that Department.

It cannot be seriously pleaded that the requirements of the
children from five to twelve years old of uneducated parents, and of
a nearly uniform social grade, present a variety too great to be
amply met by reasonable elasticity in the administration of a
central Department which has already a well-trained and able staff,
and an accumulation of half a century of experience.

It is no doubt true that the long neglect to provide an efficient
system of secondary education, linked by evening continuation schools
to the public elementary system, has led to the addition to the code
by which that system has been worked of subjects which were not
originally contemplated as part of that curriculum, and which it is
often, and not without some grounds, contended do not properly
belong to it.

Now, not one of the seven characteristics specified above is true
of the field and scope of secondary education.

On the contrary: (I) It is not limited to any one section of
the community.   All sections ought to have access to its benefits.
(2) The time which it ought to occupy is longer and more fruitful—
say, from ten to eighteen, instead of from five to twelve.   (3) It should
expressly lead up to some further commercial or professional training.
(4) The greater part of the children for whom provision has to be
made in it are in more or less educated families, and they spend their

leisure hours among companions and in circumstances more favourable to education than are, for the most part, the homes of the poor. (5) This last fact tends to impress upon them the necessity for attaining at least a similar standard of education with those around them. (6) The parents have not the same amount of difficulty in providing some part, at any rate, of the cost. (7) By far a larger number of endowments available for education are being used for the provision of this grade of education.

And when to the above comparison of essential characteristics is added the more important consideration that at the very age when the elementary education terminates the divergence of requirements with a view to after-life commences, it would seem that no further argument can be needed to prove that the provision of secondary education is eminently and specially an unfit function for a central Department, very slightly fitted for parliamentary interference, and distinctly to be met by a local, rather than by a national system.

To this argument, *a priori*, in favour of entrusting secondary education to county councils, while elementary education is still regarded as a national rather than a local matter, and remains therefore centrally and not locally administered, further confirmation is afforded by the experience with regard to technical education gained during the last seven years.

It has become clear that even in villages it is quite feasible for successful evening continuation classes (the first, largest, and in some ways the most important part of secondary education) to be maintained, both by the county council and by the Department, either jointly or separately (Sir John Gorst cannot have realised this when he spoke upon the Education Estimates on the 10th of July last).[1] It is no doubt open to question whether it would not be far better, on grounds of simplicity of administration, adaptation to local requirements, and stimulation of local interest, that the maintenance of evening continuation schools should be regarded as a function not of the Department, but of the county council—as these schools are secondary and not elementary, and therefore should be local and not national in character.

The difficulties hitherto attending these schools in connection with the restrictions attached to the supplying or aiding the supply of technical education to children still learning the three R's are transitory, and will soon entirely cease, as the number of children

[1] 'A great deal had been said with which he entirely concurred upon the desirability of promoting continuation schools, particularly in country districts. How could they promote continuation schools in country districts unless they had some county authority charged with the duty? That, again, was a reform which must await the passing, the expected passing, of the Education Bill next year.'—*Times* report, 11th of July, 1896.

N.B.—There were more than 175 continuation schools in Devon last winter and the winter before.

gradually diminishes who discontinue their schooling altogether when‛ they pass the standard of exemption.

In all probability, as time goes on, and the supply of adequately trained teachers of a grade higher than elementary grows more equal to the demand, it may become possible to organise a thorough system of peripatetic teachers whose special function it shall be to keep the teaching of these evening schools up to the highest level that the elementary teacher can reach, and in the course of time gradually to raise it higher. But if this be done, it would be in connection, not with the public elementary day schools under the Department, but with the system of secondary schools which it would be the duty of county councils to create. The teachers in such secondary schools would have been trained to teach secondary subjects to students of secondary age, and should be available for such evening work in their neighbouring villages, it being easier to send the teacher to the taught than the taught to the teacher in *rural districts*, while in towns it is exactly the reverse.

At this point it may not be amiss to draw attention to the impor-. tance of remembering the necessarily elementary character of the education in village day schools, whether voluntary or under School Boards.

Those who are most conversant with the routine of these village schools, and the results produced by even the best work done in them, will be most fully aware of the wisdom of completing in the elementary school, as thoroughly as possible, the real elementary work up to the highest standards, and of special emphasis being laid upon the thoroughness of the mastery gained over the three R's. The children whose mastery over these subjects is the most complete are those who will form the most certain, the most regular, and the most profitable pupils for the evening continuation classes.

Any sacrifice of such thoroughness in the elementary school, for the sake of a little science or a little cookery, means a corresponding future sacrifice both of the time in the evening continuation school and (which is more important) of the inducement to attend it.

But none of these considerations point in the direction of the necessity for submitting elementary as well as secondary education to county councils.

The case for devolution of the administration of elementary education cannot be said to have been made clear, and before it commands general assent it will require a far more detailed defence. In the opinion of a very large proportion of the community there would be a serious disadvantage in the interposition of a local authority between the central Department dealing with the subject as a matter of national and therefore parliamentary interest, and the fathers and mothers of the children whose tender years keep them still under the parental roof. No need is felt for any authority more remote than the managers of the village school, *in whose election the parents unquestionably have a claim to share.* It must be remembered that whatever matters are too local for departmental management in the affairs of village schools are also too local for anything except village management, and that nothing will be gained by devolution if intimate knowledge of local circumstances is not secured ; on the contrary, increase of correspondence, conflict of interests, more opportunities of friction will be the result.

Much of the difficulty already felt with regard to the village school has its origin in the confusion between the *parent* and the *ratepayer.* It may almost be said that wherever in rural districts this distinction has been borne in mind, and fair representation on the body of managers has been provided for voluntary subscribers and for parent, it has practically been found that the interests of all concerned have been amicably adjusted, and the burden has not been intolerable. It is indeed difficult to see what advantage there is to be gained at present in the interests either of the parents or of the subscribers by the interposition of any local authority with regard to public elementary schools. The county council would not possess the intimate knowledge of local circumstances. No district committee appointed by the county council would have the requisite immediate touch with the parents. Our experience in country districts so far is not encouraging as to direct election for educational purposes even for elementary schools alone, and it hardly requires argument that for successful development or organisation of secondary education the area of district councils would not suffice either for administration or for finance.

And we are thus driven back to the conclusion towards which the considerations urged in the earlier part of this paper also seemed to point—namely, that the distinction between elementary and secondary education should be clearly admitted and practically recognised, that the administration of the one should be regarded as the function of the national Government, and should be direct and complete ; while with regard to the other, the extremely complicated nature of the problem of secondary education, and the very great variety of considerations affecting it, point to a local treatment which should cover as large an area and as wide a limit of age as may be found feasible.

The more clear the distinction and the more complete the administrative separation between elementary and secondary education, the lower down can be placed the first rung of the ladder which it is the object of all persons interested in education to construct.

The first step in the ascent of that ladder must be the step out of the elementary school. The way should then be clear to the top. And for the construction of that ladder a county educational authority is an eminently fit body.

With regard to the construction, functions, and powers of that body there is a good deal of difference of opinion. It is a point of considerable practical difficulty. The question really is, on what lines can most steady progress be made with the least resistance ? The resistance will come from the ratepayer. The motive power must come from the parent. The authority has to accumulate the power, and steer through, or past, the resistance.

The ratepayer's power is wielded by the councillors—the parent's interest is entrusted to the committee. In what way, then, can the committee get most support from the parent ? And by what means can the ratepayer secure economy ?

While it is eminently undesirable that county councils should be elected with special reference to education, it is, on the other hand, in so far as the limitation of expenditure of local rates is concerned, inevitable that the voice of the council should be final. Hitherto the difficulty has arisen usually in the submission of educational projects for consideration by a rather heterogeneous body, with an agenda paper already formidable in its length and in the variety of subjects contained in it.

Some county councils have shown considerable reluctance to give a free hand to their Education Committees, and the committees in consequence have felt to some extent hampered in the formation and organisation of their schemes, as well as in the appointment of their staff. But, if secondary education is to prosper in the hands of county councils, it is essential that (except as regards the total amount of rates expended) the hands of the committee on education shall be absolutely free to form and to put into execution its own schemes, and to appoint its own officers.

If they are given a free hand in details, and a power to spend within certain limits, with the consent of the council, there is no reason why the organisation of an adequate supply of secondary education in its various forms should not at once be placed in the hands of properly strengthened committees of county councils. They would probably welcome the provision—as a kind of Court of Appeal—of some such central authority as was suggested in the Report of the Royal Commission on Secondary Education (pp. 256–259), but the fewer the trammels and officials they are hampered with the better will be their work.

The most important practical point to be considered is the constitution of the County Committee. The suggestion of the Commissioners (Report, p. 268) seems to be one upon which it will be difficult to improve—namely, a majority appointed by the county council freely, from within or without its own number; one-third of the remainder nominated by the Education Minister (or central authority); the remaining members being co-opted by the members already chosen. Such co-optation should be absolutely free.

There is hardly room for doubt that in this manner, whatever resources a county contains for the formation of an earnest and efficient educational authority would be called forth.

But it is worth while to consider for a moment what would be the consequences (or some of them) of imposing on such a body the duties of a 'paramount' authority on elementary education. We know already, with regard to secondary education, something about the amount and the nature of the work likely to be imposed upon them, from our experience with regard to the technical side of it, including such technical instruction as can be given in evening schools.

We know that such work has not brought upon them any serious difficulties in the way of discipline among teachers, inspection or examination of schools or of scholars, statistics of attendance, or in the way of apportionment of grants.

It is possible that the necessities of a certain class of secondary schools may entail some further apportionment of public money. But, at the worst, if this should turn out to be the case, such duties would grow gradually out of the work of the committee itself, and would easily be met by provision made as the necessity should arise. But the assumption (or, rather, as it would be, the most unwilling acceptance) of the duties of a 'paramount authority' on elementary education would immediately bring down upon the committee, all unprepared and inexperienced in such matters as they would be, a hailstorm of difficult problems, and a heavy mass of duties in connection with them; for the whole system of elementary schools in the county would at once turn to the unfortunate committee, in hopes of getting better terms from them than they ever could expect from the Department. All the financial business of the multitude of schools, with the attendant examination of details and checking of registers, and the thousand and one other minute points affecting grants, &c., would be referred to them.

Is it possible to contemplate this (leaving altogether on one side the worst of all, the religious difficulty) without seeing that one of two results must follow? Either (1) a body which might perform thoroughly well such educational functions as in connection with secondary education have been above referred to, must be paralysed and overwhelmed under a mass of clerical and other work already efficiently performed in the central offices of a national department, or (2) a new office must be got together, as best it can be, in each county, which would be very far from representing, or in any way being part of, the county council, and its work would have to be superintended, not by county officials (even if there were any fit for the task), but by such amateurs as may be zealous enough to devote their leisure hours steadily to this purpose, and who reside near enough to the county town to be in constant daily attendance without inordinate waste of time and money in travelling.

For this kind of work cannot be done by occasional periodical committee meetings, with a staff of less than half a dozen clerks. It will require steady attendance of persons in authority, made competent by experience to give rapid decisions on a variety of points, and responsible for expenditure—and such persons it is not easy to gather daily from a county area. If this be not so, it is difficult to see in what sense the contemplated authority would be ' paramount,' or what was meant by the phrase ' decentralisation.'

Further, no allusion has so far been made to one of the most formidable objections to the proposal—namely, the impossibility of maintaining satisfactorily a national standard of attainments. The appointment and employment of inspectors is one (probably the most important) of the chief duties of a paramount authority. Therefore, under the proposed arrangement, either (1) the inspector must be appointed by one body and report to another; or (2) there must be double inspection, divergent reports, and varying apportionment of grants ; or (3) the county paramount authorities must take entire charge of the inspection (*i.e.* appointment and employment of inspectors), and the resulting apportionment of grants.

It is difficult to say which of these three systems would be most disastrous in its effects.

Again, it has been somewhat thoughtlessly assumed that after this function has been put upon county councils, or upon committees acting with their authority, the composition of these bodies would remain the same as it is now. Reasons have already been given for doubting whether it be desirable that this assumption should be realised—such as the unfitness of county councils for such functions. But it is certain that they would not remain the same, and equally certain that they would not be improved from an educational point of view.

The introduction of a really important educational question among the subjects upon which a county council election has to take place would immediately alter the whole complexion of the contest. And· as surely as it is true that individual experts in educational matters· can hardly be chosen in a worse way than by direct popular election, so surely is it also true that a body chosen upon issues such as those attending School Board elections is not likely to show a degree of practical efficiency for other and more mundane subjects (such as roads, county buildings, asylums, pollution of rivers, and so forth)· equal to that which has hitherto characterised our rural municipal authorities.

It has been argued in some quarters that some such proposal regarding elementary education as that contained in the Bill is necessary to create and maintain an ' intelligent interest in education.' In reply, it may fairly be maintained that when the county· authority becomes responsible for the organisation of a supply of education adapted to the wants of all classes, except that provided for with a parliamentary grant by the nation, there will be an ample field, and an adequate stimulus, for the exercise of such 'intelligent interest.' Attention may also be directed to the very great interest already shown in the various forms of technical education during the last five or six years. And it will hardly be suggested that for the chance of adding a little to that which has been already manifested it would be worth while to incur the risk, which amounts indeed to a certainty, of kindling, with reference to secondary education, the blaze which has burnt so fiercely and so detrimentally with regard to elementary education around the question of religious teaching.

There are, it must be remarked with regret, already some clouds lowering upon the horizon which threaten a storm when the wind really gets up and fills the sails of secondary education. One sees in the newspapers from time to time signs that the religious question is not to be allowed to be quietly settled, nor will even the present peace be permitted to continue undisturbed.

But it is tolerably certain that if the functions of county educational authorities with regard to secondary education could e allowed to be developed as occasion requires, without legislative restriction in religious matters, and if provision of secondary schools by rate becomes a necessity, the religious denominations will see efficiently to the provision of such teaching as they desire, and there will be no more sectarianism in county councils about secondary schools than there has been about roads and asylums.

The difficulties natural to the position of village public elementary day schools will not arise. Various denominations have already shown their capacity for establishing successful and efficient secondary schools. And the wise course in this respect is to let well alone, and leave it to each denomination to provide religious teaching for its own children.

What is really wanted is a free hand, coupled with adequate realisation of responsibility and adequate powers. If these are conferred upon the education committees of county councils, strengthened in the manner suggested (as mentioned above) by the recent Royal Commission; and if these committees are not overwhelmed by work, and smothered with details which do not properly appertain to them, and for which they are in no way fitted and are not at present capable of adapting themselves, there is no reason to anticipate failure.

If the Government are in earnest about education, let them pass quickly an efficient measure for the registration of teachers; let them provide for the constitution of a central authority which, through the system of registration, and as a centre of advice, and possibly of sanction, may render valuable assistance to local authorities; let them strengthen and set free the hands of county council committees,

and give them adequate powers with regard to rating and endowments.   But no further burden need be placed on the Department.
Evening continuation schools may be taken off its hands.   No
Imperial grant need be given for secondary education, and therefore no
departmental interference will be necessary.   With such encouragement as would thus be given to the practical manifestation of 'intelligent interest in education,' and with the prospect which would
be afforded of some speedy, practical result, there can be no question
that local energy would be quickly and effectually stimulated.

Evening continuation schools, exhibitions, scholarships, various
grades of secondary schools, public and proprietary, will be provided to
meet local requirements.   The supply of qualified teachers, registered
by a central authority, will be developed by the demand, and it may
be hoped, if not confidently anticipated, that the universities will
rise to the occasion, and seize the opportunity thus opened to them
of guiding, stimulating, and to a large extent providing, the instruction for which an appetite is among all classes manifesting itself in
the reception of the efforts already made to perform a task for which
county councils have, as far as in them lies, proved their fitness by
their success.

CHARLES THOMAS DYKE ACLAND.

HORSE AMBULANCES

AMONG the many remarkable movements of the present generation for the relief of suffering humanity, none are more worthy of support and encouragement than those having for their object the wider dissemination of the means whereby temporary help may be given in the case of illness or accident, and the better and quicker transportation of the patient.

There can be no doubt that the lessons in giving first aid imparted by skilled instructors to the police, the army, and to numerous other classes and individuals throughout the country, have resulted in numberless instances in the prevention of a vast amount of needless suffering, that would otherwise have ensued as the result of unskilful handling of the patient in the first instance.

But it may be doubted whether that part of the ambulance system that deals with the actual transportation of the sufferer from the scene of accident to the hospital or home has advanced as rapidly towards perfection.

The ambulance in England is still, as a rule, in the nature of a hand stretcher.

The more rapid system of an ambulance wagon drawn by either one or two horses is seldom, if ever, employed, as it is in New York, where the system originated, in other cities of the United States, in Vienna, and to a limited extent in Paris, where it was started at the time of the war between France and Germany.

The idea of instituting horse ambulances, that should be summoned and sent out in cases of illness or accident with the same speed and regularity with which fire engines are called and despatched in the case of fire, originated in the year 1868 with Dr.. E. B. Dalton, at that time the superintendent of the New York Hospital. Owing to a change in the disposition of that institution's property the suggestion was not acted upon at the time, but in the following year the Department of Public Charities and Correction approved of Dr. Dalton's proposals and the code of rules he had drawn up, and in consequence an ambulance service was adopted at Bellevue, the Municipal or Free Hospital of New York.

From that time forward the system has proved so useful and beneficial that it has gradually extended to all or nearly all the other hospitals in New York, as well as to many other cities in the United States, and has become an integral part of the hospital work, and numberless lives are saved by its agency, and by the speed with which help is brought to the sick and injured.

The ambulance service of New York is conducted by means of vehicles kept continually ready at the different hospitals, the stables being either in the grounds of the institution or at a very short distance.

The system employed varies in slight details in the different hospitals in New York, but, speaking generally, on a telephonic or telegraphic call for an ambulance being received at one of the hospitals, it is automatically and simultaneously transmitted to the room of the surgeon on duty, and to the driver and the gatekeeper.

The horses are immediately attached to the ambulance, improved methods of swing or suspended harness being employed—as in the case of the fire departments—all the parts adjusting themselves properly when pulled down on the horse, and being fastened by a few snaps, so as to reduce the time occupied to a minimum. The driver springs to his seat, the gates are thrown open, and the ambulance starts out, picking up on the way the surgeon, who has received a slip of paper on which is written the source of the call, and the time and the place where the accident has occurred, which last information he calls out to the driver.

The whole process from reception of the call to the start requires on an average about one minute.

The instructions to the driver are that ' in responding to a call the ambulance should always be driven at a rapid, but never at a dangerous rate. In returning, the rate should always be moderate, except when with cases which must be brought to the hospital without delay.'

By Act of Legislature ambulances have the right of way over all vehicles excepting those of the Post Office and the Fire Departments, and each ambulance is provided with a gong, which the driver sounds when necessary, to warn other vehicles to keep out of the way, and not to obstruct its transit.

On arrival at the scene of the accident the surgeon applies such treatment as is immediately advisable, and with the help of the driver lifts the patient into the ambulance bed, which by an ingenious arrangement is run out from, but remains attached to, the wagon, and the bed is then carefully run back into its place. Should the patient express a desire to be taken to his own home, instead of to the hospital, his wish is complied with, provided he lives within the city limits, unless the surgeon, with whom the decision rests, sees any reason to the contrary.

Should the patient be conveyed to the hospital, he is on arrival handed over to the care of the house physician, the ambulance surgeon making his report at the same time on the case. The ambulances, it should be added, are kept ready to start out at any hour of the day or night.

Such is the general system observed by the hospitals in sending out their ambulances, and it is to be specially noted that from first to last the whole service is entirely gratuitous, though naturally many of the patients, on leaving the hospital, present a donation towards its funds.

In reviewing next the means whereby the ambulances are maintained, distributed, and regulated, it may be best to give a brief description of the American hospital system generally, differing as it does in many respects from our own.

In the United States the chief cities provide, through their Department of Charities or other similar body, a free hospital, supported by yearly taxation, at which all citizens can obtain indoor or outdoor treatment. These hospitals, however, do not answer to the Poor-law infirmaries of Great Britain, but correspond more to such hospitals as Guy's, St. Thomas's, St. George's, the London, and other general hospitals in the English metropolis.

There are also in New York private or partially self-supporting hospitals, maintained by private charity or by endowments, at which the rule is to charge a weekly or daily rate graduated according to the room that is occupied, or, in the case of a bed in the general ward, by the circumstances of the patient. Many of these hospitals, however, admit a great number of free patients, but this does not alter their private character.

It may be mentioned in passing that the use of this free or municipal hospital is not looked upon in the United States as having the pauperising effect that admission to the English workhouse infirmary has; in a similar manner, in that country education is free—even to the higher grades—and the parents of children of all classes avail themselves of the advantage in their children's early education, a procedure that would probably provoke unfavourable criticism in England.

The hospital system in New York may be divided into three classes :

Municipal or free hospitals, supported and carried on by the city from money raised by yearly taxation ; and private and public hospitals, supported by individual contributions or by income from endowments. The public hospitals are such private ones as have established public ambulances, and they are public only in so far as regards their ambulance service.

As has been mentioned before, the municipal or free hospital of New York is Bellevue, where the first ambulance service was adopted in December 1869. In that month there were seventy-four calls; in the next year the number was 1,466.

The following table will show the increase from this time forward, not only in Bellevue, but in the other hospitals which have adopted the system, and the year of their so doing :—

Name of Hospital	Year when System adopted					
	1870	1877	1878	1879	1881	1892
	Number of Cases in each Year					
Bellevue	1,466	1,217	1,606	1,888	2,282	4,858
House of Relief	—	1,155	1,253	1,321	2,293	3,216
New York	—	—	651	585	1,154	1,520
Roosevelt	—	—	273	291	352	1,675
St. Vincent	—	—	—	823	1,387	2,066
Presbyterian	—	—	—	—	387	1,730

In 1893 the total number of cases was upwards of 20,000.

The ambulance service of New York City consists of the following number of vehicles :—

Bellevue (the Municipal Hospital) 10
Government ⎫	2
Harlem ⎬ Dependencies of Bellevue Hospital [1] . . . 1
Fordham ⎭	2
New York 2
House of Relief (a branch of the New York Hospital) . . . 2
Roosevelt 3
The Presbyterian 3
St. Vincent 2
Manhattan 2
Flower 2
Total number of Ambulances 31

With the exception of those of the municipal hospitals, these vehicles are under the management of, and maintained by, the respective hospitals, without any assistance from the municipal authorities.

The service is controlled by three separate departments :—the police, the health, and the commissioners of public charities and corrections.

The police commissioners only exercise control in so far as the allotment of an area is concerned, from which individual hospitals receive casualty cases.

The commissioners of public charities and corrections maintain and have special charge of and control over the municipal and public hospitals, but the private institutions are independent of their orders.

---

[1] These dependencies of Bellevue Hospital are emergency hospitals, situated in the remote parts of the city, and are only intended to accommodate accident and other cases until they can be transferred to Bellevue itself.

⸫ But by arrangement between the hospitals, both public and private, and the commissioners and the police, all sick and injured persons may be taken to whichever hospital may be the nearest, the object being to insure the quickest possible medical or surgical treatment.

The private hospitals enter into such an agreement because of the experience and practice it affords to the physicians and surgeons connected with them; indeed, so much has the ambulance service become a part of the New York hospital system that there is a great desire to secure an allotment of an area, so as to ensure a share of the accident and emergency cases that occur.

No hospital, in fact, in New York could now be carried on without ambulances; a hospital without an ambulance would be without patients. The ambulance surgeons are not students merely, but are sub-juniors of the hospital house-staff, holding the degree of M.D., and they give their services gratuitously on account of the experience they gain.

As regards cases of contagious disease, the Health Department takes exclusive charge of them, and arrangements are made that prevent any danger of infection being communicated to others.

To ensure no time being lost in summoning an ambulance when required, the city of New York is divided into police precincts, each having its station house or headquarters, while there is one general headquarters for the entire Police Department. These several headquarters are in communication with the general headquarters by telephone or telegraph, and it again is in communication with the several hospitals maintaining an ambulance service. In the case of a street accident, therefore, the policeman on duty where it occurs communicates by telegraph, telephone, or other expeditious way, with his headquarters, they pass the message on to the central headquarters, and the message is transmitted from there to the nearest hospital provided with ambulances.

Though this is the regulation way, other methods of summoning an ambulance are naturally made use of—when, for instance, the accident occurs near a hospital, and it is summoned direct by a spectator or by a policeman by word of mouth, or a call is sent over the general public telephone or telegraph.

The Fire Department of New York has also introduced ambulance calls into its code of signals, and these may be sent out from all the signal-boxes throughout the city.

The ambulance used in New York is of the Abbot-Downing type, and has a covered arched roof, room for the bed before mentioned, on which the patient can lie at full length, and for the surgeon and the various instruments and appliances he carries with him.

The cost in New York is $550, or, allowing for the difference in the purchasing power of money in England and in America, about 85*l.* to 90*l.* in English money.

The cost of maintaining an ambulance in New York is about $920 to $1,000 (190*l.* to 208*l.*), which may be considered equal to about 150*l.* in England, this estimate including the wages and board of the driver, forage for the horse, and keeping the ambulance in repair.

The excellent example set by New York in regard to its ambulance service has been copied in its general principles by most of the other big towns in the United States, though the systems pursued differ in various details. For instance, in Philadelphia, Norwich (Connecticut), and Chicago, the police have the chief charge of the service, though in Philadelphia other ambulances are maintained by private hospitals and institutions.

In St. Louis one ambulance is kept by the police and one at the Railway Hospital, while others are maintained by their Department of Health.

At Pittsburgh twelve patrol wagons are used by the police for ambulance purposes, while at the same time all the hospitals in that city have ambulances ready.

In Boston five of the general hospitals have six ambulances in use altogether, the municipal hospitals have three, while the Police Department has seven.

In New Orleans the service is under the direction of the administrators of their Charity Hospital, which is supported in a manner that in one of its details would scarcely be recognised in this country.

It is maintained by ' license fees paid by auctioneers, and on account of public entertainments, such as theatres, balls, shows, &c., an annual contribution of $40,000 from the Louisiana State Lottery Company, and voluntary contributions.'

The custom there is for two surgeons, instead of one, to go out with the ambulance, and the hospital authorities exercise their discretion as to whether to answer calls or not—a practice that would scarcely seem advisable, as liable in a great measure to destroy the main object of the whole ambulance system, which is to reach the sick or injured in the shortest possible space of time. False calls will occur, as the Fire Brigade in London and elsewhere know only too well; but if time were to be lost while an investigation is made into the genuineness of the call, what terrible disasters would result!

In other respects the service in New Orleans seems to have been brought to a great state of perfection.

A report says : ' By one electric action a gong is sounded in the ambulance station, and in the bedroom of the students on duty above ; the chains of the horse stalls drop, a trap in the ceiling opens, and the officers on duty slide down a polished steel shaft just behind the wagon, which, by the time they can do so, is harnessed and ready to start. The average time between the striking of the gong and the departure of all concerned upon their mission is fifteen seconds. They have gone forth in ten.'

This time is certainly remarkable, and would seem to deserve to rank as a record; but those who have seen the Fire Patrol turn out in Chicago will remember that with them still more extraordinary celerity is attained. The horses having been trained to spring to their places of their own accord on the striking of the alarm gong by electric mechanism, their harness, suspended above them, drops down on their backs, and is attached with one or two snaps; the gates fly open, and, should the call be at night, the clothes are pulled off the beds on which the firemen sleep on the floor above; the beds themselves are at the same time tilted over to one side, and the firemen, who sleep ready dressed, with the exception of their boots, which are ready on the patrol wagon, find themselves deposited on the floor at the entrance to a sloping wooden chute so arranged that, gliding down it, they alight on the wagon, which immediately starts out.

The average time taken from the striking of the gong to the start is five seconds.

The operation of gliding down the chute, simple as it would seem, requires some confidence, as an English visitor to Chicago found to his cost when he attempted to perform the feat. Losing confidence when halfway down, he endeavoured to stop his wild career, alighting instead with a severe fall and a badly damaged leg.

In New Orleans, those who can afford to do so are expected to pay for treatment in the Charity Hospital or for being transported to their homes by its ambulance.

Turning now to the Continent, Vienna is the city which appears to have advanced most in the matter of ambulance service. But, owing probably to the military character of the nation, the terrible floods to which the city is exposed, and to the great disasters that have from time to time occurred there, the object would appear to be to combine a system of providing relief against famine and exposure, together with the ordinary ambulance in case of sickness or accident.

The Volunteer Humane Society of Vienna was established after the burning of the Ring Theatre in 1881. It is supported entirely by voluntary contributions, receiving no assistance from the State or the municipality, and its services to the public are given gratuitously It has at its disposal the services of a volunteer fire brigade, in case of fire, numbering nearly 400 men, with all necessary apparatus; of 200 trained watermen, with boats and the newest appliances for saving life; and of 221 doctors and 100 volunteer assistants (all medically educated).

The society owns 20 ambulance wagons for the transport of the sick and wounded, besides other vehicles; 25 doctors, whose residences are distinguished by coloured lamps, give their services gratuitously to the society for night work.

Two ambulances by day and one by night, with the horses ready harnessed, are kept in readiness at the central station.

In addition to the ordinary ambulances, the society owns vehicles called 'kitchen ambulances,' fitted with all the necessary apparatus for forming soup kitchens, which they send out, with cooks in attendance, in time of floods and other disasters.

In Paris, the 'Ambulances Urbaines,' a private philanthropic enterprise, was started in the year 1888. The society sends out a special ambulance carriage on being communicated with at the Hospital St. Louis, their headquarters.

One of their ambulances is always kept ready harnessed, provided, as in the case of the New York service, with a stretcher, and containing the medical appliances necessary for first treatment, a doctor accompanying the vehicle, who conveys the injured person to the hospital or to his home.

Numberless lives have been saved, not only in New York, but in the many other cities that have followed the admirable example it first set, by the speed with which the ambulances reach the sick and injured, bringing help that literally wrests back the sufferer from the jaws of death, as the last flickering spark of life is leaving the body.

As, in the case of fire, the first few seconds or minutes are proverbially the most critical, so is it often in the case of accident or illness, and many lives are lost by injuries received in the streets of London and the other great cities of England, owing to the delay in reaching the scene of accident with a hand stretcher, that might be saved were the New York system in universal use.

And if a conveyance is employed in any English town in the case of accident, what is it? Generally a four-wheeled cab or suchlike unsuitable vehicle—perhaps to convey the patient for a distance of several miles to the nearest hospital, when suffering from broken limbs, the cramped position necessary in such a conveyance causing the sufferer excruciating agony.

The official annual reports issued by the Commissioner of Police of London dispel an illusion sometimes entertained that practically no accidents occur there.

The excellent manner in which the traffic is regulated in London, to the admiration and envy of foreign visitors to the city, cannot prevent an appalling number of accidents occurring in the course of the year, even allowing for the fact that the return has reference to an area of nearly 700 square miles.

The last report issued, that for the year 1894, shows that over 5,600 accidents that were known to the police occurred in the streets of London, and 156 persons were killed, in the course of the year.

Probably this return would compare very favourably with that from any other city where the traffic is not so well regulated, but still it shows that there is an ample field for such an ambulance service as has been described.

Finally, in considering the methods whereby such a system of ambulance service could be introduced into London, a consummation devoutly to be hoped for, two points of essential difference between the hospital systems in London and New York present themselves —the absence in London of municipal hospitals, and the exemption of the New York hospitals from taxation, rendered possible by the centralisation there of the taxing power, there being but one body to levy rates for the entire city; whereas the division of London into separate parishes renders taxation necessary, in order that certain districts may not be unduly burdened in comparison with others.

These two points of difference constitute a severe handicap in the case of the London hospitals.

In addition to which, the impecunious state in which far too many of them find themselves renders it extremely doubtful whether they would care to launch forth into any fresh undertaking that would entail further expenditure.

But still there are other methods to be considered whereby the end indicated might perhaps be attained.

One is by private philanthropy; another by the Metropolitan Asylums Board undertaking the matter; a third by the Metropolitan Police Department joining such ambulance wagons to their present hand-ambulance system; or, lastly, by the London County Council adding such a scheme to the improvements they are proposing, either in conjunction with the hospitals or otherwise.

As to private philanthropy, it would be doubtful wisdom waiting for it to tend in that direction—an event that might never happen.

The Metropolitan Asylums Board is a Government Department dealing with infectious cases, and is akin to the Department of Health of New York, that has been mentioned before.

It might be possible to have horse ambulances for cases of accident and non-contagious sickness added to their present system. But some difficulty might arise in keeping the two departments separate, and in giving confidence to the public that no danger would exist of an ambulance that had carried a patient suffering from an infectious disease being used in other cases.

Still, if the matter were taken in hand by the Board it might be able to cope with this difficulty.

The Police Department, if it were so decided, might introduce and take charge of the ambulances, as the police do in Chicago and other cities of the United States.

But probably the most satisfactory way of all would be for the London County Council to take up the matter, either by subsidising the hospitals according to the number of ambulances employed by each, as in Brooklyn, U.S.A., or by working them by means of their own employés, in conjunction with the hospitals.

The first plan of the two would probably prove the more satis-factory; but as to the details, it would be for the future to decide them.

It has only been attempted in this slight sketch to draw some attention to what is being done by other countries in the alleviation of human suffering, and it seems impossible not to believe but that in the greater London of the future the same kind of system will ultimately prevail, by whatever means it is set in motion.

And certainly, when ambulance wagons take the place of the present old-world stretcher, or the worn-out cab so often made use of in this great city, it will be a matter of wonder that, with all our many philanthropic schemes, and all our efforts to minimise the terrible suffering that flesh is heir to, we have so long neglected an example set us by far younger cities than our own.

DUDLEY LEIGH.

HOARDED among the archives of the kingdom of Würtemberg, and unknown, it would seem, to our historians, there exists to this day the confidential report of an envoy despatched to England on a difficult and delicate mission. In the year 1563 the future of England and of the English people hung, men said, upon a woman's life; and that woman was Queen Elizabeth. It was not only that her death, issueless, would leave the succession doubtful: the nation had too good cause to fear that to the miseries of civil war would be added the horrors of invasion and the fury of religious strife. From the prospect of these dangers there was but one escape—Queen Elizabeth must marry. This, indeed, was no new discovery; but the recent and dangerous illness of the Queen, together with the threatening outlook abroad, had brought out vividly the danger. A fresh and urgent remonstrance from Parliament impressed, it was thought (or at least hoped), upon Elizabeth the absolute necessity of sacrificing her anti-matrimonial feelings to the welfare of her people.

Now among the Queen's many suitors the Archduke Charles had met with a considerable degree of favour. Some years younger than the Queen—an important consideration with Elizabeth—he was barely twenty when his father, the Emperor Ferdinand, sent an ambassador, Count George of Helfenstyn, to negotiate for his marriage with the Queen. His Catholic faith had created difficulties; and, as usual, it was gravely doubted whether Elizabeth was in earnest. Possibly she could not make up her mind; in any case the matter dropped. Since 1560 the project had not been revived. But Cecil, three years later, had more reason than his standing anxiety to see the Queen married for urging that, after all, she should marry the Archduke Charles. There was a rival in the field. The Cardinal of Lorraine was known to be scheming to bring about a marriage between the Archduke and his own great-niece, the dreaded Queen of Scots. To Cecil this match presented an alarming prospect; and yet so probable did it seem that in the autumn of this year it was thought to be a settled thing. Whether or not he hoped to play upon the Queen's jealousy, he set himself to do what he could, knowing that almost any marriage would be rapturously acclaimed by the people, while a marriage with the

Archduke would at least be as popular as any other. As for the
Queen herself, she was beyond all calculation; but Charles was by no
means devoid of attraction. His inventory, as it were, was taken by
Lord Sussex, acting on Elizabeth's behalf, a few years later; and the
Queen learnt, among its contents, that ' his hands (are) very good
and fair; his legs clean, well-proportioned, and of sufficient bigness
for his stature; his foot as good as may be.'

 · We had at the time in Germany a confidential agent, Christopher
Mundt by name. To him Cecil addressed himself; and the correspondence which ensued is still in Lord Salisbury's possession.
Writing from Windsor, he asked Mundt whether negotiations could
be resumed. ·But diplomacy had to reckon, in those days, with unforeseen delays, and it was not till the 9th of October (1563) that
Mundt received Cecil's letter of the 25th of August. He promptly
replied that the best plan would be to approach the Duke of Wurtemburg, who had favoured the match when originally proposed, and he
promised to leave Strasburg in search of the Duke the following day.
He was as good as his word. Pointing out that Parliament was eager
for the Queen's marriage, and that the Archduke would prove an
acceptable consort, he lightly alluded to the Queen's relations with
the Lord Robert Dudley—over which there had been, in Germany,
much shaking of heads—and assured the Duke that, while rightly
gracious to so loyal and noble a subject, she had not the least idea of
marrying him, and had given no ground for supposing it. He implored him to consider favourably the suggestion as to the Archduke,
which (he was, of course, careful to add) was entirely his own. The
Duke allowed himself to be persuaded to act as intermediary, and
wrote on the 17th of October to sound the Emperor on the subject.
Ferdinand's reply was not encouraging. He reminded the Duke,
with much dignity, of the unsatisfactory treatment his mission had
encountered on the previous occasion, and observed that to court a
renewal of it would expose his son and himself to ridicule. They
had, therefore, abandoned all thought of the marriage, while entertaining towards the Queen perfect goodwill and friendship. The
Duke sent for Mundt and read him the letter. Undeterred, the
sturdy agent insisted that the Queen could not be expected to make
the first advance; her modesty as a woman, her dignity as a sovereign,
alike forbade her even to appear to be in search of a husband. But
to no prince in the world could it be unbecoming to risk all for such
a bride and such a dowry.[1] Then he implored the Duke to put an
end to the *impasse* by sending an envoy himself to England to sound
the Queen on the subject.

To this the Duke at length agreed, and set himself to find a

[1] His letter to the Duke (December 1) is in the archives of Stuttgart. He
repeated his arguments in the personal interview, when the Duke showed him the
Emperor's letter.

plausible excuse for approaching his cousin of England. He found it in the close of the Council of Trent, and in the condemnation of their common cause by its decrees. Authorship, theological authorship above all, had for the Duke, as for Henry the Eighth, an irresistible fascination. Mundt, it may be, worked upon this weakness; but in any case the Duke had endeavoured, some months before, to convert from the error of their ways two of the leading cardinals by sending them certain books 'refuting' the abuses of the Mass and the decrees of the Council of Trent, and by personally exhorting them 'in a friendly manner' to devote themselves to piety and to propagating the true faith. While ingenuously confessing that to these letters he had as yet received no reply, he now wrote to Elizabeth informing her that the old friendship between their fathers, and their own, which he eagerly desired to maintain, compelled him to send her by his envoy certain little books, which he hoped she would find time to read carefully, and would find acceptable. Then, reminding her of the dangers and uncertainties of human affairs, he begged her to listen graciously to his envoy, who had certain secret communications to make to her, and ended by expressing the pious hope that all might tend to the glory of God and the propagation of His eternal word as well as to the weal of her royal person and of her realm. To Cecil he wrote more plainly, commending his piety, wisdom, and loyalty, and expressing his earnest hope that the Queen might be induced by his envoy's arguments to turn her mind to matrimony as ordained by God Himself, and to choose a worthy and suitable husband. To bring this about would be a good work, and one pleasing to God.[2] At the same time he drew up a paper of secret instructions for his envoy, explaining in minute detail what arguments he was to employ. The Duke was careful to mention that the Queen should be shown, if she expressed a wish for it, copies of his letters to the cardinals, but soon came to the point, and urged that Elizabeth should be warned of the dangers awaiting her realm if she should die childless. The envoy was specially to impress upon the Queen the eager efforts to bring about a marriage between the Archduke and the Queen of Scots, and was to leave her in no doubt that the Duke was acting on his own initiative, without the knowledge of the Emperor or his son, and that Ferdinand was resolved to send no embassy to England till it was absolutely certain that the marriage would take place.[3]

Allinga, the envoy selected, reached Antwerp on the 4th of January, and started at length, on the 8th, on the perilous passage to England. He had found the men of Antwerp furious at the seizure of their merchantmen by English pirates. French pirates also scoured the narrow seas, and if, as happened to him on his return, the hapless traveller was driven too near to the French coast, *magnæ bombardæ*

---

[2] Letters of the Duke, December 28, 1563 (Archives of Stuttgart).   [3] *Ibid.*

lay in wait for him, and the Calais gunners made excellent practice. His ship, as it was, ran upon a rock, and the seamen promptly betook themselves to their prayers. He reached Windsor, however, safely on the 15th, and was kindly received by Herle, who found him quarters, and proved himself equally at home in Latin, French, and German. The following day he was sent for by Cecil, who, after a mutual exchange of compliments, assured him that his mission was most welcome, and that all the leading men in England were anxious for an heir to the crown. But his own efforts to prevail upon the Queen had hitherto been unsuccessful, and he hinted, as to the Archduke Charles, that unless he came to England the Queen would be hard to persuade. It was not till the day after that 'Augusta' was free at length to receive the envoy, who received a final warning from Cecil that she was stubbornly attached to the single state.

Passing through the palace, Allinga was conducted, by a secret staircase, to a remote bedchamber. There he waited till the Queen entered, accompanied by the faithful Cecil and two maids of honour. He kissed, 'after the manner of the country,' the hand she held out to him, and presented the Duke's letter. Elizabeth asked for the books it spoke of, and he handed them to her, kissing them as he did so, one by one. As she opened the one entitled *De Missa*, 'Ah,' she exclaimed, 'the mighty name of the Mass!' Then, reclining on a coffer by the door, she waited for the envoy to begin.

Now Allinga had not received a University education for nothing. In fluent Latin he set forth first the argument his master had prescribed, the danger impending over England and its Queen, from the Popish sovereigns north and south of it; and then, painting in vivid colours the horrors awaiting her 'orphan realm' if Elizabeth died childless, he boldly urged that she could only avert them by marrying, as her nobles wished. Elizabeth sighed appropriately at the allusion to her realm and its dangers, but when matrimony was mentioned she begged him, seeing that her ladies were listening, not to pronounce the name she thought he was going to mention, lest it should give them a clue to his business. The envoy promised that he would not do so; but the constant repetition, as he warmed to his subject, of the word 'matrimonium' roused anew the fears of the Queen; she bade Cecil talk to her maids, lest they should understand, while she alone listened to Allinga. Then he exhorted her in his master's name to enter 'the holy estate,' the oldest, the noblest, the most excellent, and, above all, the most necessary. He carried her back to the garden of Eden, 'the most sacred spot on earth;' he appealed even to the gods of the heathen, who made marriage their chiefest care, so that 'Gamelius' was among the most glorious titles of Jove and 'Jugalis' of his consort Juno.

It was too much for Elizabeth's gravity; a smile crept across the Queen's face. Delighted at the favourable impression he had produced, the envoy continued with renewed ardour. Vain and laughable though such fables might be, they proved that marriage sprang, as it were, from natural religion. How much greater was their own call, proceeding not from nature only, but from the approval of the Christian and true Catholic Church! He passed from Genesis to the New Testament, in which Christ Himself described the Church as His spouse; he exalted marriage as the bond of society, as the greatest of human joys; and then he resorted to the arsenal of the classics. He quoted Homer, he appealed to Euripides, and with these he mingled the Divine commands and the teaching of recent history. What had not kingdoms and nations suffered from the deaths of their rulers childless? The sorrows of Hungary, alas! were notorious; Poland, invaded and divided, was doomed to destruction. Surely her Majesty should not expose her glorious realm to such ills as these, but should listen to the voice of her sorrowing subjects, and endeavour, God's grace helping her, to leave a son who should worthily represent the best of mothers in the zeal of his piety and the perfection of his ways.

The Queen inclined her head.

History proved, resumed the envoy, that as the prince was, so were his people. Cicero had observed that the tastes of the Romans changed with each of their emperors. Aristotle held that the best of laws were an actual evil to the state unless observed by those who made them. Unless there were an heir to whom she could hand on her own lamp, and who would rival her in piety and the pursuit of virtue, what could happen to that flourishing realm but the destruction of a polity so wisely ordered, and the terrible uprooting of the pure doctrine concerning God and His holy word? Somewhere, the envoy cautiously added, Pliny had said that a good successor was the surest mark of divinity; was there anything wanting to her Majesty's attainment of divinity (so far as possible for men) save only the desire for children? If only the weal of her people and of posterity could overcome her Majesty's inclination, the name of Elizabeth, Queen of England, would ring most glorious for all time, crowned with every virtue.

Again the Queen bowed.

In the fifth book of his *Politics*, pursued the ruthless envoy, Aristotle asserted it was the duty of parents to provide for their children's welfare. And was not her Majesty the mother of her realm? Princes, said Plutarch, were the ministers of God; it was theirs to care for the happiness of men. He quoted Socrates, he appealed to John; he even insisted with doubtful wisdom—for the Queen was now thirty years old—that every day, every moment, was bringing her nearer to death, and that, as Cicero had reminded Sulpitius, she would die, if not that day, at least before long. Pliny the younger was here brought in to enforce the desired conclusion; Xenophon and Cicero were advanced in support.   Her Majesty was known to think of her kingdom alone in the present.   But would she not turn her thoughts to the future ; would she not remember how the Emperor Constantine had thought less, in his dying moments, of his own sufferings than of the welfare of the Church—nay, how her own brother Edward had cared for it even with his latest breath ?

At her brother's name the Queen sighed.

Let her Majesty, Allinga implored, offer herself in this, a sacrifice to the commonweal and to God.   Cicero, Euripides, Menander had urged marriage as a duty ; it was the only way by which she could save her people from the woes awaiting them.   Then would her Majesty be depicted to posterity as ' some celestial animal,' more like to Deity than to man, sent by God Himself to relieve the woes of mortals.   Could this amazing envoy soar higher still ?   Yes ; he proceeded to detect in the Queen the living likeness of God (*vivum Dei simulacrum*).

And again the jewels quivered and flashed ; and that gorgeously enshrined head was bowing in acknowledgment of his words.

Once more he pictured in harrowing terms the coming of a prince ' more demon than man,' the agonies of her faithful subjects, due to her single life.   Once more he summoned the classics to his aid : Isocrates, Seneca, Cicero were hurled at the virgin Queen ; then in a lowlier strain, on behalf of his lord and prince, he begged her to take his 'exhortation' kindly, for the Duke had only wished to prove his devotion to the Queen and the English realm, and to offer his services in the matter to the utmost of his power.

Elizabeth rose.   A chair was brought her ; and the eager envoy bent over her, to catch her almost whispered words.   She began by thanking him for the Duke's exhortation, which she knew was prompted by his care for the realm, for the Church, and for posterity. She confessed that she herself had seen the dangers imminent, and the need that she should marry ; and yet, from her youth up, while in a lowlier station, neither the prospect of advantages or honours, nor even the fear of danger, could move her to marry.   It was known what she had suffered for her religion, and how the French King, for his son, and afterwards the King of Sweden also, had fitted out fleets to rescue her from captivity with a view to marriage ; yet not even her peril could induce her to marry.   Nor had her brother's dying words, with all their weight, prevailed on her.

Here the Queen broke off abruptly, and bade her maids chatter less loudly ; then she apologised for expressing herself so ill, said that rumour had much to answer for, that it gave her credit for more than she deserved, and that she was not so learned as was reported.   She rarely (she explained) spoke Latin, usually French or Italian : hence she was troubled when they told her that Allinga would address her in Latin.   The courtly envoy hastened to praise the elegance of her

Latin and the charm of its delivery. Elizabeth, mollified, returned to the point, and insisted that, incredible though it seemed to many, she distinctly shrank from matrimony (*a matrimonio abhorerre*). When she ascended the throne in the twenty-third year of her age,[4] there was nothing to prevent her marrying whom she would ; nor had any one imagined that she would put off marrying so long. Nevertheless she had resolved to do so, and, so far as she knew her own mind, nothing could prevail on her to marry. Her realm was more dear to her than anything on earth ; she would die, if she could, ten deaths for it ; her love for it had, she confessed, made her hesitate. Yet she could not think that its salvation depended on her alone. She admitted, however, that the estate of matrimony was good and pleasing to God : it was not from principle that she lived single, but from her own inclination.

The poor envoy expressed his grief, in the interest of the public, at her words ; he reminded her what her realm had suffered from the change of religion at her brother's death.

But the Queen stood firm. She met, she parried, the envoy's arguments ; she assured him that, though her Parliament had taken her last answer to their prayers to imply that she intended to marry, she had not the least idea of doing so. She marvelled why such a supposition should be entertained in Germany, and even more did she marvel at the rumour being spread there that she was betrothed to one of her nobles.

Allinga protested that no such rumour had come to his ears. To the Queen's inquiry whether he had really heard nothing of the kind, he lightly replied that there had been a rumour that she was going to marry the King of Sweden ; but that it was only gossip, to which no one of consequence gave credit. The Queen significantly expressed her wonder why his master should have sent him on this mission at such a cruel season. The envoy fell back on the Council of Trent and the anxiety with which it had inspired the Duke for the future of religion in England, unless the Queen married. Hence his earnest desire that the Queen should hear his views. Elizabeth professed herself grateful ; she would not refuse absolutely, but it would not, she added, laughing, be an easy matter to persuade her. 'And now,' she exclaimed, ' have I detained you, for to-day, far too long with my chattering.' The interview had lasted some two hours, and the baffled envoy, like others before him, left the palace no wiser than he came.

When Cecil received him the following day, and heard what the Queen had said, he blandly observed that she had often given his friends and himself a similar answer, but that he had hoped the remonstrance of Parliament had produced some effect on her. Perhaps, he added, she did not care to reveal her intentions at a first interview.

[4] It was, as a matter of fact, in her twenty-sixth year.

This was but cold comfort for Allinga, who protested that Mundt had led him to expect a very different result. The cautious Cecil replied that he had not authorised him to do so. Allinga thereupon querulously retorted that he did not see how any good could be done : if the Queen objected to marriage in general, still less was he likely to convert her to marriage with the Archduke Charles, or any one else in particular. The wily secretary hastened to appease him. The Queen, he assured him, had spoken most highly of all his proceedings the previous day ; what he had to do was to persevere, for the glory of God and the good of the kingdom. His logic might be sound, yet one often had to proceed in the reverse order, especially with women, who, even though they had determined not to marry, could often be persuaded if they were wooed for some individual man. Even so, sick folk might say they could touch no food, and yet be tempted by the mention of some special dish. To Allinga's legal mind this seemed a lame argument. Besides, he urged, he would hardly be justified in making overtures as from the Archduke, when neither Charles nor his father even knew of his mission. Cecil replied that it was useless to expect the Queen to confess that she wanted to marry the Archduke ; still less could she suggest the terms. It would be a subject of reproach to her if the wooing came from her. Allinga persisted that the Emperor would send no fresh embassy unless he had good ground for believing that the matter would be settled. 'Then,' was Cecil's rejoinder, 'we can only leave it to God.' Neither he nor any mortal man could make the Queen declare herself till she was formally approached. Allinga reminded him that he was not authorised to propose for the Queen's hand. Cecil expressed his regret that it was so, and solemnly asserted that Mary would never have married King Philip unless he had come to England to show himself. When evening drew in, the two men were no nearer an agreement. It was settled that Allinga should on the morrow do his best on his own lines to persuade the Queen.

It was a bitter winter ; the Thames was frozen over by the middle of December, a thing which had not been known for nearly half a century. On the following day the envoy was conducted to the same chamber as before. The Queen had drawn close to the hearth. Although the eloquent Allinga confessed his surprise and his distress at the failure of his previous arguments, he craved leave to renew his persuasions. Again he produced, as it were, a prize essay on marriage, which, more fortunate than the Queen, we may be permitted to skip. Once only did she interrupt the flow of his pedantic periods. Matrimony, he explained, was a desirable evil. 'Think you it desirable ?' she laughingly inquired. But Allinga was in no laughing mood.

When he had finished, Elizabeth told him that she had taken note of his arguments, but that she was not learned enough to reply

to them.   She was grateful to his Prince for the trouble he had taken ;
but there was no need for all these arguments, since arguments would
never move her.   Necessity alone could induce her to marry, not as
Elizabeth, but as Queen.   She reminded him how she had been wooed
for years by the Princes of Spain, of France, of Denmark, of Sweden,
by the Emperor, and by many others.   The lot of her suitors had
varied in all but refusal.   As to the Emperor, she knew not who had
broken off the negotiations.   The envoy, clutching at this straw, expressed the grief with which their termination had filled the Christian
world.   Elizabeth retorted that the fault had not in any way been
hers.   'The Emperor,' she loftily protested, 'did me therein some
wrong ; I think that he deemed me unworthy of his son.   And I, as
Queen of England,' she exclaimed, 'trow that I am at least worthy
of the Emperor's son.'   Allinga protested that all the godly, especially
those of the Augsburg Confession, had set their hearts upon the match ;
the difficulty, he reminded her, of bringing it about lay in the Emperor's wounded pride and in her own modesty.   'And the Emperor,'
bitterly protested the Queen, 'behaves like an old shrew, who begins
the quarrel, when the fault is her own, in order to throw it on some
one else.   Never yet have I told any one how the Emperor treated
me ; and yet will I briefly tell you.'   With real or simulated indignation, Elizabeth related her version of the facts.   She had told the
Emperor's envoy of her vow that she would never marry a man she
had not seen.   There was nothing in that vow displeasing to God ;
and she meant to keep it.   It had been promised her that Charles
should come ; she had guaranteed his safety while here ; but, she
added, laughing, she would not summon him ; to do so would have
been immodest.   Some one, she believed, had slandered her to the
Emperor ; he had broken off the negotiation.   These were the facts,
and she could prove them.

·Real or calculated, Elizabeth's emotion had proved too much for
her Latinity.   She had not, she protested, spoken Latin since she
addressed Count Helfenstein.   'He has spread abroad,' she insisted,
'a false report of my learning.   Had I him here, I would charge him
with falsehood.'

'Your Majesty's speech is perfect,' replied the scholarly courtier ;
'no man could praise it too highly, because no man could praise it
enough.'

Sharply reverting to the subject in hand, Elizabeth again protested
that the Emperor was behaving like a shrew.   At the envoy's suggestion that the time had come to begin the negotiation anew, 'What !'
she exclaimed.   'Would you, then, have me run with open arms to
meet him, and beg him to give me his son ?   Fitting, indeed, would
that be for me—I, who have had the noblest suitors in Christendom.'

The envoy hastened to admit it was impossible ; but another way
could be found, would she only agree to the marriage.   He praised

the Archduke as young; he termed him the Rising Sun; he dwelt on his gifts, on his piety, on his knowledge of tongues; he was of polished manners, gracious, charming, devoted to all the virtues and brought up in obedience to his father. ' Yea,' broke in the Queen, ' he clings to his father's side; his father keeps him to his bed-chamber and fondles him, as it were, in his sleeve, because he would not have him marry.'

The envoy, however, dwelt on the advantages England would derive from such a match—on the danger if the Archduke should marry the Queen of Scots. He assured her that his master would arrange it all, if only he could count on her favouring the scheme.

' Favour Charles! ' she exclaimed; ' what is that but to court him ? Why not first make sure of him ? '

Again Allinga pleaded the natural anxiety of the Emperor not to be made a laughing-stock if she had already resolved not to marry his son.

' Let him try,' she retorted; ' I shall not ask him to come here.'

In vain was the advantage of such a match pressed on her; woman-like, she soon flew off at a tangent. ' The nobles of my realm would have had me, at one time, marry an English peer. But it moved me to wrath; I will never bring myself,' she exclaimed, ' to marry a subject.'

Then she reverted to the Archduke Charles. To give hope that she would marry him would be to bind herself to part with her freedom; she feared it could not be. As she rose to go, she observed that her nobles were about to meet for six days; she would send Allinga to some bishop that he might seem to have come on a matter of religion, and their business remain more secret. When her nobles had dispersed, she would recall him. Allinga urged that time was pressing, for the Cardinal of Lorraine was driving on the match with the Scottish Queen.

' I know that,' Elizabeth replied; ' and as I write to her,' she laughingly added, ' every week, I congratulated her, last time, on her marriage with the Emperor's son, and told her I was going to marry the father.'

To Allinga her humour was by no means welcome; he implored her to give the matter her more anxious thought, as all depended on her alone.

' I know not,' she laughed, ' what will come of it;' and so left him.

On the following day, the 20th of January, the envoy visited Cecil to implore him to use his influence with Parliament on behalf of the match. The secretary assured him that in that quarter there were no obstacles to fear. No one would object if the Queen were willing and ' Cæsar ' made the request. But neither the Queen nor her Estates would ever consent unless ' Cæsar ' made the advance. Otherwise, he warned Allinga, all his efforts would be vain; he would only have given the Queen offence. Then he pleaded press of business, and hurried off.

The Bishop of London was the prelate selected by Cecil and his mistress as the means of concealing the real purport of Allinga's mission from the public. This we know from his own letter, preserved among the Lansdowne MSS., in which, writing to Cecil on the 24th of January, he tells him that 'the Duke of Wurtemburg's gentleman' was about to leave him, much to his regret; for they had been at Strasburg University together, and it was only on 'Brentius' doctrine of ubiquity' (that which was held at the Court of Wurtemburg) that they now found themselves unable to agree.

On the 26th, Allinga, now back at Windsor, urged Cecil to hasten the matter. 'At noon,' the secretary replied, 'you will hear from her Majesty's lips, it may be, what you desire.' 'God grant it!' the envoy exclaimed.

. Admitted to the presence that afternoon, Allinga answered the Queen's inquiries as to what he thought of England, and of his visit to the bishop, but reverted, as soon as possible, to his master's anxiety for her marriage. 'I thank your master,' the Queen replied, 'for his care of my realm's welfare; but, plainly, I will not fall into a snare by declaring that I wish to marry the Emperor's son. Let him,' she added, 'come here and try. For I, if not an Emperor, am at least a Queen: there is something due to me also.' To the envoy's entreaty that she would allow the advantages of the match to influence her, '.Let them influence,' she retorted, 'the Emperor.' The poor envoy protested that he knew not what to report to his master. 'I have told you more,' the Queen replied, 'than I have ever told an envoy yet, and more than I have told the Estates of this realm. For they have had no other answer than that, burdened with my cares, I could not give my mind to marriage. Love was mostly bred, I told them, of idleness; and the pressure of business had not yet allowed me time to think of it. Therefore, as I had not thought of marriage, I could not discuss with them this man or that.' She had, she continued, revealed to him that, although by inclination she would rather be a beggar and single than a Queen and married, yet she had resolved to marry if compelled; but compulsion only could prevail upon her. This must suffice him: she could not enter into the merits of this man or that. As to what she had told him of a foreign prince, it had been wrung from her rather than said by her.

Allinga felt that the end was near. Speaking in the tongue of modern diplomacy, he expressed the grief that her firm determination would cause to his master and to all well-wishers. Would she listen to a last appeal? The Queen, now also speaking in French, again threw the blame upon the Emperor. He had heard evil of her, so he broke off the match. 'And how,' she exclaimed with delightful irrelevancy, 'could I talk to Charles when he tells me, in German

(for I understand it, though I speak it not), of Constantinople ? ' The
envoy suggested that he spoke Latin well, and French also. ' Not
so,' Elizabeth imperiously rejoined : ' he speaks but little French, and
less Latin ; the Kings of Denmark and of Sweden, and the King of
Portugal's son were willing enough to come here and show themselves,
even though I asked not for them ; and that barbaric King of Sweden
has been at great cost for the marriage. But how,' she persisted,
' could we have agreed, our manners so greatly differing ? For, do
the best I would, they would give up none of their customs.' There
would, the envoy suggested, be no such difficulty with the Archduke ;
no nations in the world had manners and customs so similar as the
Germans and the English. Bred at the Court of a great prince, and
in the most ceremonious country in the world, the Archduke could
not be other than the pink of courtesy. For in those parts they
modelled themselves somewhat on Italy. ' That,' said the Queen, ' is
charming : I love the manners and the ways of Italy ; methinks I am
half an Italian myself ("me semble que je suis demie Italienne ").'

The moment favoured a final effort. ' Madam,' cried the envoy,
' will not your Majesty give me a word of comfort for my master ? ' ' I
can say,' she replied, ' nothing else : I must needs remain *in majore* ;
si minorem addam, you will draw a conclusion.' From this position
she would not stir. An embassy would be welcome ; the more so if
it came with his master at its head ; but it was not for her to solicit
any one ; the Emperor might do as he would. Should not, Allinga
urged, the consent of the Estates of the realm be sought in a matter
touching the kingdom ? ' Not for the marriage,' was the prompt reply ;
' I am not their subject : they are mine.' So they fenced, the sovereign and the envoy. Elizabeth ever returned to the point. The
Emperor might begin again, if he liked, but she was as deserving of
consideration as he was. ' I shall stand now on tiptoe, as he does. If
he send his son here of his own accord, I shall be all the better
pleased ; but it will be for the [Queen of Scots, who is young and
pretty.' That, the envoy hastened to assure her, would not be. ' Nay,'
urged Elizabeth, ' she counts on his coming. And why should it not
be ? ' The Archduke, protested the envoy, would never marry a
widow. ' Yes, he will,' persisted the Queen ; ' I thank heartily your
Prince, and would show myself grateful to him. My secretary shall
hand you my letters to-morrow.' She placed her hands on Allinga's
shoulders, and then withdrew.

' What ! Girded for your journey ? ' was Cecil's greeting, when
the envoy, his cap on his head, entered his chamber on the morrow.
' Yea,' he replied, ' it were vain that I should stay here longer.' To
all Cecil's remonstrances Allinga remained deaf. It was clear to him
that nothing could be done, if neither party were willing to take the
first step. The Englishman pressed for an embassy from the Emperor ;
and indeed, whatever Elizabeth intended, it is evident, on comparing

Allinga's report with a letter from Roger Strange, written a few days later,[5] that Cecil was wholly in earnest. He gave Allinga a letter for the Duke, thanking him for his intervention and assuring him that his envoy had been enabled to speak more freely to the Queen than he, as her Minister, could have done.

Elizabeth's own reply to her 'friend and dearest cousin,' that illustrious and most excellent prince, the Duke of Würtemberg and Teck, is preserved, with Allinga's report, in the Stuttgardt archives. A touch of simple pathos, a certain ring of truth, makes us loth to dismiss it as a mere diplomatic subterfuge. She thanks the Duke for his friendship, for his books, for his kind advice, and admits that his care for the reformed faith is shown even in his anxiety for her marriage. She had never regretted her single life, and had no more heartfelt desire than to die unmarried. But she foresees and fears that her fate will be far different. As the last child of Henry the Eighth, the most famous king of his time, her subjects pray and implore her, her friends abroad exhort her, the weal of her realm and the dangers of the future, reproaching her conscience, are driving her to abandon her happy celibacy for that estate which she has always disliked. She sees but too clearly that dire necessity will force her to accept the yoke, and that she must decide on a husband (hateful word). She must not disappoint her people, who have set their hearts upon her marriage, and who have left her a freer choice than ever sovereign had. And in that choice she will be guided wholly by the safety and the honour of her realm.

One seems to hear her people shout, ' God save Queen Elizabeth !

J. H. ROUND.

[5] *Calendar of Hatfield MSS.*, i. 291.

THE UNAVOIDABLE USELESSNESS OF
PRISON LABOUR

I HAVE observed that whenever discussion arises as to the mode in which prisoners should be occupied, the question is considered almost entirely from the moral point of view only—that is, whether it is or is not desirable or essential to promote the industrial employment of prisoners with a view to their moral well-being or reformation, or in order to provide them with means of earning an honest livelihood on discharge. The pecuniary view sometimes comes in, that is, the advantage of turning the labour to profitable account, so as to di- minish in some degree the cost of maintaining the prisoners ; and it appears as if it was supposed that the only difficulty the question presents is how far it is right that prison labour should compete with free labour, or under what safeguards to prevent unfair competition. It is assumed as a matter that requires no demonstration that it is always possible to employ all prisoners profitably, and that if this is not done it is from want of goodwill in some quarter or that somebody does not see the advantage or will not take the necessary steps.

I think my experience may be useful in the discussion, and as I shall have to show that these assumptions are very far from being warranted, it may be well that I should commence by some autobio- graphical recollections, which will make it clear that my prejudices have been in favour of the advantage of industrial employment of prisoners from all points of view, and also of the capabilities of prison labour.

My connection with prisons, which terminated only last year, commenced in 1851, when I was sent as a subaltern attached to a company of Royal Engineers (Sappers and Miners they were then called) to Western Australia, to help in directing the labour of the convicts who had lately been sent to that colony. I was put in charge of a large district in which the convicts were to be employed in making roads and bridges. These convicts had all arrived at that stage of their sentences in which they might be released on ticket of leave if they could find an employer, and until this happened they lived in ' depots,' which they had to build themselves.

I had a detachment of sappers under me, some of whom were employed to instruct the prisoners, and to act as foremen and in charge of detached parties. There was no great number of artisans among the prisoners—free artisans were expensive to hire, and the company of sappers could not spare nearly so many to act simply as artisans as were required. In course of time, nevertheless, we got the prisoners to do nearly everything that was required for our works. We made our own bricks, sent parties into the bush to cut and saw timber, others to split shingles for the roofs, others to burn charcoal for the blacksmiths and lime for the building, and in fact provided almost everything for ourselves; and of course I acquired a high opinion of the capabilities of convict labour.

After returning home from this service and working for some years in the War Office in designing fortifications, I was again brought into connection with the prison service by being appointed a Director of Convict Prisons, especially in connection with those prisons in which large public works were being carried on by the convicts. These works offered great opportunities for teaching convicts trades, and the convict prisons were in fact, and still are, schools of technical instruction in various trades. After some years I became head of the department, and as it happened at a moment when the number of convicts was rapidly increasing on our hands on account of the cessation of transportation, the question how these increasing numbers were to be employed loomed in the not distant future. With a view to inviting suggestions on the subject, I read a paper at the Society of Arts, supposing that among the members would be found many who could tell of manufacturing processes in which the prisoners could profitably be employed. The fruit of that paper was lamentably disappointing; the only proposal came from a patentee of some sort of compressed peat, that we should embark on the manufacture of this fuel. The discussion on the paper was all directed to the moral question; many who took part in it described the advantages to the prisoners of industrial work, but nobody gave any help in solving the practical question which it was my object to raise—what employment could they in large numbers be put to?

Sir Henry Cole afterwards suggested the manufacture of a certain kind of marble mosaic in slabs for floors, and this was adopted as an employment for women, whom it suited admirably. A good deal of this work was done for the South Kensington Museum, where it may now be seen. By personal efforts I got orders for a certain quantity at St. Paul's and elsewhere, but the demand was limited. The product was at a disadvantage in comparison with that which could be executed *in situ* by free labour with the ordinary tesseræ, because of the cost of packing and transport and laying the slabs, which had to be done by free labour. This experience gave a practical demonstration of the necessity, and also of the difficulty, of insuring a market for the produce of prison labour, a difficulty which all persons who set up a factory have to overcome or else to fail, and which some fail in while others succeed by methods which are not all open to a Government Department.

A great deal of very valuable employment was found in erecting all the buildings required in the prisons. These had been executed by free labour until my predecessor commenced employing prisoners on them.

A very large amount of this work has been done, and it is of the most valuable kind, because it gives the opportunity for learners to acquire practical knowledge of various trades. One or two instances of these works may be given, because of the peculiar circumstances under which they were undertaken. The large prison at Wormwood Scrubs, containing some 1,400 cells, was commenced by surrounding the site by a timber hoarding, and placing inside it a temporary building of wood lined with iron to accommodate 100 prisoners. From this beginning the whole building has been erected by convict labour, the bricks made on the spot, the stone supplied from Portland, castings and forgings from various prisons, and the mechanic's work done in the prison itself, of which the population was increased as the accommodation grew. The circumstances of the construction of Borstal Prison near Rochester are still more remarkable. The site was surrounded by a hoarding, and convicts were brought out daily in omnibuses three miles or so, under suitable guard of course, to erect the buildings inside it. When the buildings were finished the convicts proceeded to construct certain adjoining forts and defensive works, and to cultivate the ground, all in the open country ; and when in course of time it was desired that certain more distant forts should be undertaken, a steam tramway was laid, and the novelty might be witnessed of convicts being taken daily in trams backwards and forwards some two miles from their prison to the site of the fort, where they worked surrounded by a palisade.

About the same time printing was introduced as an employment for convicts, but it was limited to supplying our own requirements, for we never could get any other Government printing. Continual attempts were made to induce the Admiralty and War Departments to give employment in manufactures to our prisoners ; but these departments naturally, perhaps, looked on the question of supplies from their own point of view only, and considered the prison department like any other manufacturers and not at all as being broadly a Government interest which should be encouraged. When supplies of certain articles were wanted we got them to send us notices that we might tender in competition against ordinary manufacturers, and this sounds fair enough, but it did not enable us to undertake much, for we could not set up a factory merely to execute one order, or unless we were certain of continuous employment, nor could we with our fluctuating population and our large proportion of learners or half-skilled workers be sufficiently certain of making the large quantities of articles usually contracted for in the short period given for their supply. There was another serious difficulty : the articles when made had to be examined and passed by the official inspectors to see that they corresponded with the sample. Even articles which were practically quite good might be rejected because they might in appearance be inferior to articles made by machinery and by skilled workers. If rejected we had not the same facility for disposing of them as a large manufacturer with extensive connections selling to other buyers goods of the same nature, and they might therefore be a dead loss to Government.

The Post Office gave us a good deal of work making mail bags, baskets, &c. The Office of Works gave little or none beyond getting mats from us. It always seemed to me that Portland stone might very well have been supplied to that department from our quarries at Portland as it was for Admiralty and War Office and prison buildings, and in the same way as we supplied Dartmoor granite for the new Scotland Yard.

A good deal of work was done for the police in making boots and clothing, and this went on until the number of convicts decreased so much that we could not keep up the necessary supply. I may here refer to one of the limitations which must of necessity exist in the supply of articles by prison labour. Shoemakers, tailors, and indeed artisans generally, do not come in any numbers ready trained into prison. They have to be taught ; until they have gained a considerable degree of skill they cannot turn out work which will pass scrutiny as up to the sample which supplies, whether from contractors or from prisons, must conform to. Whilst they are learning, they are more or less spoiling material, and necessarily produce inferior articles. What is to be done with these? The only answer to this is that the prison department must consume them itself. The number of skilled hands that can be created, therefore, depends on the number for whom this inferior work can be found, and in the aptitude of those who go through the training. This applies to all trades : unskilled men cannot be made into carpenters, bricklayers, smiths, masons, stone dressers, &c., except by employing them on some work which is going on, in which a small proportion may learn their trade in doing under instruction first the rougher kinds of work, and gradually acquiring skill to do the more finished work. For this reason, and because of the scope afforded to unskilled labour by large public works of construction, this mode of employing convict labour has always been preferred, a preference which has been affirmed by more than one Royal Commission, and particularly by the committee appointed specially to consider the best application of convict labour, which reported in 1882 in favour of the construction of Dover Harbour.

What I have said so far relates to the employment of convicts whose sentences keep them several years in prison. In 1877 I was brought into relations with the question from another point of view, viz. the employment of prisoners who are under short sentences, the great majority for only a few days, and only a small proportion for more than a few weeks.

The law of prisons, *i.e.* the Prisons Act 1865, gives little or no encouragement to industrial employment. The report of the committee on which it was founded laid it down very distinctly that the employment of prisoners for profit, or with a view to recouping some of the cost of their maintenance, should be considered quite subordinate to the other object the punishment is intended to serve, *i.e.* briefly the prevention of crime. Accordingly the Act ordained that all adult male prisoners should during the first three months be employed on 'hard labour of the first class,' and also for the remainder of any longer sentence, unless specially ordered otherwise. Great efforts were made, when the bill was being drafted, to devise a general definition which should indicate what was intended by the above phrase, and a proposal which was made, though not adopted, that it should be defined as ' work which visibly quickens the breath and opens the pores,' sufficiently indicates the idea intended. The purpose of a definition was ultimately effected by giving an example. It was to be 'tread-wheel, crank, capstan, stonebreaking, or other like kind of hard bodily labour.'

Shortly before the Prisons Bill 1876 and 1877 was introduced, the Secretary of State did me the honour to consult me as to whether the period of three months for compulsory 'first-class' hard labour should be shortened. I proposed that it should be shortened to one month, so that all the rest of the sentence might be employed on industrial labour. This amendment was introduced into the bills of 1876 and 1877, and is now the rule of all prisons.

There are many persons, and I am one, who in the abstract dislike and object to this purely penal labour, but I know that it has its uses, and in this as in many other matters there is only a choice of difficulties. Prisoners who are in for only a few days, and who know of no sedentary or indoor trade which can be carried on in the prison—for instance, agricultural labourers, porters, dealers, &c.—have no time to learn or to carry on industrial work, and must therefore either be idle or doing some pretence of work, or else be employed on that which is merely mechanical, and if this sort of labour is enforced only for a short period the disadvantage to the prisoner is practically reduced to nothing. It is also in actual practice turned to account as a spur to good conduct for those who are in prison long enough, by holding out the prospect of relief from it as a reward for conformity to the rules and orders.

An alternative is suggested by some who feel the disadvantage to the prisoner of unprofitable labour, or labour without industrial result. They think the moral disadvantage of mechanical labour, such as the tread-wheel, &c., may be surmounted by connecting it with machinery which does useful work, such as grinding corn for the prisoners' own consumption.

It seems to me that this view is founded on an amiable delusion as to the imagination prisoners are likely to indulge in on these subjects, and further in an absolute failure to perceive the mode in which, or the reason why, industrial employment may have a good effect on a prisoner's mind. According to my belief, such good effect results from the stimulus which industrial labour may give to a prisoner's mind by his efforts to do good work, or to his moral qualities, such as industry, by his desire to turn out a full amount of work, these results being before his very eyes. But such stimulus is obviously quite absent in the case of a prisoner working a tread-wheel, whose share in the result is just the same as is due to the weight of a clock or the action of a mill-horse or the steam of a steam engine. Those who hold that the mind of a prisoner on the wheel is occupied in thinking of and rejoicing over the work which is being done by the millstones, and that in some mysterious way a good moral influence is conveyed from them to the prisoners who are turning the wheel, but that this moral influence is not so conveyed if the wheel is only working against a brake, must be prepared to hold that when the mill has ground as much flour as is required, and the machinery is therefore thrown out of gear, there is a sudden cessation of moral effect on the prisoners at that moment on the wheel! If there were no reason against the provision of the grinding machinery except that the moral advantage is only fanciful, there would be no harm in gratifying such a harmless delusion. But unfortunately it is a costly fancy to gratify. A millhouse with the apparatus for grinding, sifting &c. costs a good deal of money, and the services of a skilled miller are needed to carry on the work properly; and this is by no means always compensated by any saving in the cost of the product, for all these expenses, together with others, such as of carriage, very often indeed make the prison-ground flour dearer than flour can be bought by contract and ground by steam mills with the newest apparatus according to the modern method. The tread-wheel itself is an expensive mode of providing even the mechanical labour. A tread-wheel with its house giving employment to fifty men would cost about 1,600*l.* the flour-mill it would work would cost about 820*l.* more. Cell cranks of the best kind for an equal number would cost only 500*l.*, and the difference amounts to a large sum in providing for a large number of prisoners. There are cell cranks which grind corn, but these are objected to on medical

grounds on account of the dust they create and the difficulty of
regulating the pressure according to the strength of the prisoner—a
most important necessity—so they do not afford a way out of this
difficulty.

I have pointed out above that the necessities of the case arising
from the shortness of the sentences as well as the law of prisons
compel the employment of prisoners on mechanical or penal
labour as distinguished from skilled or industrial labour. It will
be well to show to what an enormous proportion of the prisoners
sentenced the shortness of the sentence almost forbids any other
sort of labour. In 1894–5 about 113,000 male prisoners received
sentences of imprisonment in local prisons. Of these upwards of
42,000 received sentences of a week or less, upwards of 70,000
received sentences of a fortnight or less, upwards of 94,000 received
sentences of five weeks or less, probably really of not more than a
calendar month. This very large proportion of the prisoners must,
therefore, by law be employed on labour of the tread-wheel type, with
the exception, of course, of a portion excused for medical or other
like reasons. And if the law did not enforce this, it would still be
necessary to use it or something equally unprofitable in a very large
number of cases unless somebody can suggest or devise a trade which
prisoners can learn and profitably carry on with little or no instruction.
Oakum picking may be said to fulfil this condition, but I do not think
that those who advocate the industrial employment of prisoners would
consider that this type of work satisfied their requirements. Indeed,
we now and then hear of indignant complaints because an anti-vaccina-
tionist or an unruly member of the Salvation Army who is committed
to prison is employed on this work for want of anything better.
But, however this may be, the oakum-picking business affords a
very narrow field. The demand is gradually being diminished as
wooden ships are replaced by iron, and at the same time the supply
is being increased indefinitely by the adoption of this employment
in tramp wards and similar institutions, and the result of this, as I
have been told, has reached the point that some workhouses actually
pay for the privilege of picking junk into oakum, a condition of things
which shows that nobody has yet been able to discover a new mode
of employment which the unskilled can be put to in a prison or workhouse, and exemplifies what we must be prepared for if, in order to
carry out the doctrine of industrial work for all prisoners, those who
are in prison for periods too short to acquire skill are set to execute
work which for want of that skill is unsaleable.

But the figures I have given above have still to be supplemented
in order to show what a small part of the prisoners sentenced can,
from the nature of things, be put to industrial work with any practical
result. Of the 19,000 male prisoners these figures left to be accounted
for as having longer sentences than one month, all have to be accord-

ing to law employed for at least one month on labour of the tread-wheel type, so that it is only at the end of that period that they can begin learning a trade if they do not already know one which can be carried on in a prison. Supposing that it takes a man a month to learn a trade well enough to do good work, then he must be in prison for at least two months before he can begin to do work of much profit. If he is in prison for another month or more, he may turn out a certain amount of useful work, or, in other words, the useful work must be done by those who are sentenced to three months or more, *i.e.* by about one in eleven of the whole number sentenced.

These facts have evidently never been considered by those who assume that industrial work can be introduced as the general practice in prisons, on the supposition apparently that the moral effect is the only point to be considered. It is only a small residue who can be profitably employed.

To find employment even for this limited number is not without difficulties, the principal of which is to find customers for the work they can do. Evidently the prison department itself has wants which prison labour can supply, and accordingly since the prisons have been united into one department a great development of this work has taken place, such as was not possible when each prison was an isolated unit. Tailoring, shoemaking, tinworking, weaving, knitting, and many other like trades are now carried on in certain local prisons for the supply of the whole number; a very large amount of building work involving carpentering, bricklaying, and iron work has been carried on in local prisons, and this, with the baking, cooking, washing &c. absorbs a large number of the available prisoners. But there is still a large residue for whose work outside consumers must be found, and this residue will be larger if the gross number of prisoners should again increase.

In the days when prisons were under the local authorities, mat-making and its allied trades for sale to the public formed the staple of the industrial employment of prisoners. This of course gave rise to pressure from rival manufacturers or workmen, who complained of prison competition as unfair, but the Visiting Justices of Quarter Sessions, not being elected by household suffrage, could deal with this matter on its merits, and so had an advantage over a department which acts under political heads who never can be indifferent to even ill-founded grievances pressed on them by supporters whose seats might be affected by the question.

The late Prison Committee, indeed, very truly state that the amount of the competition from prison-made mats was so small compared with the total volume of the trade that it practically could make no difference to the free employers or workmen, and the committee on foreign prison-made goods express the like opinion. But this abstract truth is of no avail against a number of agitators and voters, whose 'invincible ignorance' leads them to maintain that it does, and I am quite sure that no Government, especially a weak one, would care to alienate support by insisting on an abstract truth as to the profits of mat-making. This trade therefore gradually and largely diminished as a prison employment; and there was another reason which illustrates one of the difficulties of prison trading. Those who discuss these matters with only theoretical knowledge to guide them think to avoid the charge of unfair competition by laying it down as a condition that prison-made articles must not be sold under the market price. But what is the 'market price' of anything? It is not a divine decree sent down from heaven, but is the result of what has been called the 'higgling of the market,' in which sellers get as high a price as they can and buyers pay as little as they can— in which they are helped by the sellers being ready to undersell each other. The practical effect of the condition so laid down is that outsiders may undersell the prison, but the prison may not undersell the outsiders. Of course a prison-made article might *prima facie* be sold for less than an article made by paid labour, and there are other items of expense which a trader must cover by his profits, but which a Government department can neglect, so that the outside trader could easily be undersold by the prison. To avoid, therefore, unfair competition of this kind, it was the practice in Government prisons to fix a reasonable price for the prison produce, but the traders at once took advantage of this, their commercial travellers were authorised to undersell us, and we found our stocks accumulating on our hands. Of course we could have played the same game, but a Government department has its hands tied in carrying through that sort of business.

In foreign countries there is a very common practice which seems at first sight to have much to recommend it. A contractor buys, so to speak, all the labour of the prison, and sets the inmates to work on anything he can turn their hands to. In places where the prisoners are all day in workshops and not in cells, this becomes more feasible, but it does not really provide employment for prisoners with very short sentences who know no trade, and who therefore practically do nothing useful.

We tried a version of this with our mat-making. We invited makers and dealers to compete under an arrangement by which they were to supply all raw material, plant, and necessary instruction, and to take away the produce at the price they tendered. This arrangement, however, which seems fair enough, aroused most strenuous opposition from rival manufacturers and workmen, who alleged they were undersold, and yet would not themselves give any higher price or compete for what they professed to consider such an advantageous contract. We also tried selling our mats by auction, with the result that the dealers combined to keep down the price realised at the sale. These experiences show how difficult it is for Government to carry on trade and to turn prisons into factories of articles for sale to the public.

There is one other point on which I must make an observation as to the general advantage of industrial labour in prisons—a point which I find is generally overlooked. It is assumed as a general rule that by teaching a prisoner a trade he will be less likely to fall again into crime, and this is apparently founded on the idea that people fall into crime from want of employment or ignorance of any mode of earning their own livelihood. I believe that it is an entire delusion to suppose that this is true of any considerable number of criminals, and, moreover, I believe that it would be rather a misfortune than otherwise if any large number of men who are in the habit of earning their bread by outdoor or unsedentary labour should be tempted to adopt indoor work instead, especially any such as they could be taught in prison.

Even of those who might profitably carry on an indoor and sedentary employment, a little consideration will show that manufactures in a prison must in many cases at all events be carried on under conditions so different from what prevails in factories outside that the skill acquired in a prison can be of comparatively little use in obtaining employment after discharge. It has been stated quite erroneously that this sort of inefficiency is due to prisoners not being properly instructed, but it is not so at all. The evidence given before the Prison Committee was to the effect that in these modern days most articles are made partly or wholly by machinery, and with a great division of labour, and it is skill in working under these conditions which is required, but which cannot be obtained under prison conditions.

To justify the setting up of machinery it would be necessary to be sure of a constant and large demand and a considerable infusion of highly skilled workmen, which could not be depended on when, as in a prison, they are constantly changing at short intervals. Moreover, all idea of separation and of good discipline among a naturally disorderly body of men would have to be entirely abandoned.

The only solution of all the difficulties, as I believe, is that prisons should be looked on as workshops for articles required for the Government service, considered as a whole: that is, they should be made sources of supply of articles required by other Government departments; and that it should be clearly established as a general principle that it is the duty of the officers of those departments to find employment for prisoners in making some of the numerous articles they require in such large quantities. Prisoners are in fact workmen maintained at Government cost, and as Government requires plenty of work to be done it is perfectly natural that the workmen it maintains should be employed for its benefit. I am well aware of

the difficulties that may be urged against this. It is no doubt
much simpler to call upon contractors to tender to supply articles
just when they are wanted than to go into the details necessary to
have them made in workshops in which the number of workers
fluctuates. Then there is the question of patterns of articles to be made,
and if these are decided on without any reference to the capabilities
of prison labour it is likely enough that the precise article required
could not be produced in a prison; but a little good will would get
over this difficulty if it were once accepted and recognised as an
obligation to find work for prisoners. Difficulties of much the same
kind have presented themselves as regards the construction of public
works by convict labour; but this I know, that when once prejudices of
this sort have been surmounted the officers of the Government
departments which are carrying on the public works find that there
are many countervailing advantages in having at their disposal a
large amount of unpaid labour, and those who were opponents have
often become the strongest supporters of this mode of employing
convicts.

The upshot of the considerations I have brought forward is, I
believe, incontrovertibly this : that however desirable industrial
labour for prisoners may be from a moral point of view, it is impossible
to apply it to more than a small proportion of those sentenced to
imprisonment, both on account of the law applicable to prisons and
on account of the shortness of the sentences of the large majority; that
it is a delusion and a costly one to imagine that mechanical labour
such as the tread-wheel can be made to produce the moral advantages
of industrial labour by connecting it with milling machinery or other
like method ; that the advantage of industrial labour in local prisons,
considered as enabling them to find employment in discharge, is
considerably overrated, and that it is only in a very limited degree
that crime arises from want of employment ; that prisoners under
the longer sentences may with facility and advantage be employed
on industrial work so far as the law allows, providing consumers can
be found for the work they produce ; that the Government itself,
considered as a whole, is the most appropriate consumer of such
articles, and that prisons should therefore be looked at as Government workshops, for the inmates of which other Government departments should as a matter of duty and obligation be required to find
employment.

E. F. Du Cane.

FRA FILIPPO LIPPI.

.I ᴀᴍ not ashamed to confess that, in my earlier days, I refused to
believe that a Carmelite friar could have been the father even of a
very celebrated son by a Carmelite nun. I thought it unlikely that
a Carmelite friar who had transgressed the rules of his order should
have remained a dignitary of the Church. But I have since learned
that the lax morality conspicuous in the age of the Borgias was not
less apparent a century earlier; and, painful as the fact may be, I
cannot but admit that, amongst the religious artists of the Florentine
revival, there were as many disreputable men as there were men of
respectable lives.

What pains me most is to think that the art of Fra Filippo, the
loose fish and seducer of holy women, looks almost as pure, and is
often quite as lovely, as that of Fra Giovanni Angelico of Fiesole.
We must therefore learn to count the moral qualities as part
and parcel of the charm which is so inexpressibly attractive in
Angelico at the same time that we endeavour to forget that the
candour of Fra Filippo's angels is not the reflex of any similar
quality in that painter.

No contrast is more striking than that which is afforded by the
lives of the two Florentine friars who equally acquired fame and large
practice in art in the fifteenth century without having any one
feeling in common.

Belonging to different monastic communities, they both laboured
inside and outside the edifices in which their vocation took them to
live; each of them was a popular and finished craftsman. In one
respect they differed greatly : one was a pattern of good conduct; the
other a notorious example of corruption and foulness.

Fra Angelico, who was born in 1387, was a Dominican; Fra
Filippo, born about 1405, was a Carmelite. Their pictures were of
the same class : altar pieces or frescoes, Madonnas or illustrations of
saintly legends. Their patrons were amongst the highest ranks of
the aristocracy of Florence. Both reaped wealth and renown, and it
was no doubt because they were so equal in their success that I felt
so much inclined to doubt whether it could be true that the
Dominican was a saint and the Carmelite a demon; though, when I

went so far as to try to clear Fra Filippo of a crime which seemed to contrast too strongly with the duties usually inculcated by the Church to be founded on reliable evidence, I was soon constrained to admit that I was mistaken in believing that a friar could not commit a most serious offence against morality without meeting with instant condemnation.

It now appears that Fra Filippo's career was marked, not only by offences against morality, but by breaches of the criminal law as administered in his time at Florence; yet that, in spite of the stain on his character, which was quite public, he kept his station as a painter, earned a competence, and was hardly less successful professionally than Angelico, who was acknowledged to have led the most blameless of lives.

Vasari seems to have felt that there was something unfair in the distribution of rewards to Angelico and Lippi. He contrasts their lives in a few sentences, observing that never was a churchman more devoted than the Dominican to the service of God, the benefit of the world or duty towards his neighbour, or one of such great and varied gifts, whose habits were so simple, whose thoughts were so pure, and whose piety was so conspicuous. He might have had wealth and enjoyed dignities; but he scorned them all, dying, as he had lived, a poor friar.

Fra Filippo enjoyed both honours and riches. He, too, was by nature gifted. But he was neither simple nor virtuous nor pious, and he was mostly prosperous without deserving to be so.

The fact is, adds the historian, men do not acquire fame because they are honest, or fail because they are dishonest. It is important only that they should excel in the profession they have selected. Honest men who excel do not fail to enjoy honours and wealth; but their reward is as nothing in comparison with that which may accrue to one who has no moral quality of any kind to boast of. An honest man of ordinary parts, who falls into dishonest ways and has the ill fortune to be detected, generally receives condign punishment. A talented man of lax morality guilty of a similar offence, will be considered, in virtue of his gifts, as not having sinned. Not only is he not punished, but compassion is felt for him and justice itself deals mildly with his offence, even though he has but a shadow of honesty to recommend him.

Shall I confess that I was at first greatly distressed to learn that Fra Filippo, a Carmelite friar and an ordained priest, had a son who afterwards became a painter almost as celebrated as his father? I did all I could to rehabilitate his memory; but as evidence came piecemeal out of the dusty repositories of the Florentine archives, and I had to acknowledge that Fra Filippo was not only a man of dissolute life, but an offender against the ordinary laws which regulate the conduct of individuals, I was soon forced to look a-field and inquire how it was that a man who had gone through his experiences should not only have remained unpunished, but found unusual indulgence, and had the fortune at last to captivate a patron of high station who caused his memory to be preserved in the splendid polish of a marble monument.

Fra Giovanni Angelico lived to be prior of the Dominican monastery of Fiesole; Fra Filippo died in harness whilst painting the frescoes of the choir vaulting in the cathedral of Spoleto. Some difference in their education may explain why one should have been good and the other bad.

There was no doubt a better chance for a friar who settled down to his profession after taking vows at twenty-one than for one who was thrown as an orphan into a religious order at a tender age. Angelico, who learnt painting as a boy amongst laymen, went through his novitiate and took the cowl in the full responsibility of his manhood. Lippi, the child of penniless parents, was thrust into the convent of the Carmine when hardly more than eight years old. It may be that the Dominicans were more strict as an order than the Carmelites of that time. The Dominicans were on their good behaviour at the opening of the fifteenth century. They were involved in quarrels with the Archbishop of Florence, which ended in their withdrawal to Foligno. The Carmelites were not in similar straits, but the strictness of their discipline may have been impaired during the rebuilding of their monastery in the first twenty years of the century, and there may have been some laxity in the rules, which allowed children to be taken in, either because they were waifs and strays, or because parents found it cheaper to pay the convent fees than to rear their progeny themselves. The Carmelites of Florence took in boys; the Carmelites of Prato girls. It was a Carmelite confessor from Florence who had charge of the souls of the nuns at Prato. It was as chaplain to the convent of Prato that Fra Filippo ran away with the Carmelite nun who became the mother of Filippino Lippi. At Florence, as he grew up in the cloisters of the Carmine, Fra Filippo was thrown into the company of the painters who were engaged to decorate the interior of the new edifice, and, instead of learning his grammar and preparing for his examinations, the boy probably adopted the manners of free and easy artists, who initiated him into the life of a layman. At all events, whilst Angelico was going through the severe discipline of a strict monastery at Fiesole, Filippo breathed quite another atmosphere, and when at last he left the Carmine and faced the world as a professional painter, he fell easily a prey to disorder, whilst accidents soon occurred which made him thoroughly acquainted with the seamy side of human nature.

It is not unnatural to assume that, even amongst friars, a bad one may here and there have leavened the main body which included a majority of honest and reputable persons. Yet when I look into the

˙story of Fra Filippo and weigh all the circumstances which left their
impress on' his career, I find reason to be surprised that there were
any good friars to counterbalance by their virtues the vices of the
bad ones.   I discover that morality was not prized as it should have
been even in that age ; that immorality was not very thoroughly
reproved ;˙ and that offences of that kind were very frequently
condoned.˙ It may be said, indeed, that the ways of the fifteenth
century were not unlike those of the nineteenth.   But that is another
matter altogether.

In the literature of the sixteenth century there are passages which
illustrate the status of˙painters of the monastic orders as well as that
of artist laymen.   Churchmen and painters were always intimately
connected, because art was traditionally at the service of ecclesiastical corporations, and the best customers of painters were pious
people.   But the religious orders were not without perception of the
advantages which might accrue from the education and enrolment of
artists amongst their members ; and hence, no doubt, the career of
Fra Angelico, Fra Filippo, Lorenzo Monaco, and Fra Bartolommeo.
But clever as the orders were in recruiting painters, they never
succeeded in keeping up an absolute exclusiveness.   Either the monk
took a layman for his apprentice, as Angelico took Benozzo Gozzoli, or
he entered into partnership with a guildsman, as Fra Bartolommeo
did with Mariotto Albertinelli ; or the chiefs of orders allowed the
friars to leave their monasteries and practise beyond the discipline of
the cloister.   Under these circumstances it might well happen—and
it certainly happened in the case of Fra Filippo—that churchmen
mixed in the world with laymen, whose liberty they shared,
whether more to the detriment of the Church or to that of the public
it is difficult to say.   In most cases, as Leonardo da Vinci is reported
to˙ have observed, the profession of art was enabled to prosper and
thrive ; and honour was done to painting independently of the
painter's worth.

˙ It has not been usually credited that Fra Filippo was captured
by a Moorish pirate, as Vasari relates.   But I have discovered that
there is more foundation for the story than has been hitherto assigned
to it ,since Vasari's time.   I find that the history of Fra Filippo's
career was a common subject of conversation in the painting rooms
of the great masters of the sixteenth century ; and Bandello the
novelist actually tells it in one of the tales in which his hero˙ is
Leonardo da Vinci.   According to this version, Fra Filippo was the
son of Tommaso Lippi, who lived at Florence in the fourteenth
century and died leaving him in charge of his mother.   The boy at
that time was but eight years old, and the widow was so poor that,
instead of rearing her child, she gave him in charge to the brethren
of the Carmine, who took the necessary steps to educate him.   The
fraticello, instead of learning to read, began to practise sketching ; a

chapel had been recently painted in the convent church by an excellent master, and it was there that Filippo and other boys, his comrades, came to draw. His progress was rapid, and when he was ordained a deacon he threw off the friar's frock and painted a series of beautiful pictures for the magnificent Cosimo de' Medici. Unfortunately, the painter was inordinately fond of the company of women, and when in that humour he scarcely touched a brush. One day, at a time when Cosimo de' Medici was pressing for the completion of an altarpiece intended as a present to Pope Eugenius the Fourth, Filippo neglected his work so thoroughly that Cosimo caused him to be locked up in order that he might not play truant; but this was not an effectual bar to the painter's inclination. He knotted the sheets of his bed and dropped out of the window into the street, where he enjoyed the liberty which his patron had been desirous to curtail. Leaving Florence and wandering into the March of Ancona, the friar led a free and easy life, and, amongst other pastimes, indulged in a boating trip in company of some friends. He had soon reason to repent of his imprudence. He was captured at sea by the great corsair Abdul Maamen, who enrolled him as a galley slave and made him wield the oar instead of the brush. After some cruising, the season came to an end, the corsair lay up for the winter, and employed Fra Filippo in gardening. But Lippi disliked digging as much as rowing. He exercised his leisure by drawing with charcoal on a garden wall a likeness of Abdul, and this so pleased the corsair, that he bid the galley slave to paint some pictures for him. Ultimately he gave him his liberty, and finally landed him on the Neapolitan coast. Later on Fra Filippo found means to obtain possession of a beautiful Florentine girl, daughter of Francesco Buti, by whom he had a son, also a celebrated painter, and Pope Eugenius would have given Fra Filippo a dispensation to marry, though he was in deacon's orders, but that the friar preferred his liberty and remained single. It is a remarkable fact that this story of Lippi which Bandello put into Leonardo's mouth and Vasari only in part transcribed, has since been confirmed in many ways. Records, it is true, give no information as to the friar's captivity. But they show that Fra Filippo did not refuse the Pope's dispensation to marry; and they confirm his relations with the chief of the Medici family, his connection with the Carmelites, his adventure with Lucretia Buti, and the Pope's offer to make that lady his lawful wife. In addition to these passages, other incidents in the friar's life have been discovered, which denote that he was a scoundrel of the worst class, and that if he was by chance reduced to the position of a galley slave as a Moorish captive, he deserved later on to row in the galleys of the Florentine State as a swindler guilty of perjury and forgery. Thus the boy who had distinguished himself as an associate of artists at the Carmine, fell into bad courses when he left the monastery, became entirely corrupted under the discipline of the corsair's galley, and returned to the practice of the arts to show that, though he was still a master of extraordinary skill, he really deserved to be treated as a reprobate. Yet Leonardo himself is made to tell the friar's story as if he felt indulgence rather than regret for the culprit's conduct. The cool way in which he relates that Lippi refused to accept the Pope's dispensation for his marriage shows that da Vinci thought as little of the sanctity of religious vows as the friar himself. He thought more of art as conferring honour on bad men than of the actions which displayed the friar's moral turpitude. Meanwhile the fact that Fra Filippo sinned, whilst Fra Angelico's fame remained unsullied, may be attributed to the misfortune that Filippo passed from childhood to adolescence, and thence into manhood, without the care of parents or the guidance of strict monastic discipline. Separated at an early age from his mother, he found no substitute for her amongst his companion friars. He was then led into temptation by the facilities which the constitution of the Church in the fifteenth century gave to ecclesiastics in holy orders to associate with women, chiefly when serving the office of chaplains to nunneries; and the small command which he had over himself, as well as the bad experiences which he had made, completed his moral ruin.

The date hitherto assigned to the birth of Fra Filippo is 1412. But the books of the Carmine reveal that he took the vows on the 8th of June, 1421, after a year's novitiate; and the regulations which forbade any youth to become a novice before the age of fifteen must lead us to conclude that Lippi was born, at the latest, in 1405 or 1406. If he entered the Carmine at eight years of age, as historians relate, he had the run of the cloisters as early as 1414. He learnt as much reading and writing as the Carmelites were able to cram into him, at the same time that he associated with the workmen and painters who at that time were rebuilding the church, founding new chapels, and adorning them with frescoes. The convent accounts tell us how he professed in 1421, and what was paid to his debit for the frock and cowl in which he afterwards wandered through the cloisters and aisles of the Carmine. It was at this very time that momentous events occurred in the monastery. The Brancacci chapel was finished and consecrated, and Fra Filippo, who had hitherto only been a subordinate, covering his grammars and the grammars of his playmates with sketches, became an assistant to the painters, who were his daily companions, saw Masolino da Panicale and Masaccio begin the frescoes which gave the Carmine an undying repute, and became himself a master. There are clear traces of his residence at the Carmine from 1422 to 1430, and Vasari mentions his frescoes of a Pope confirming the rules of the Carmelites, St. John the Baptist, and St. Martial, and scenes from the life of the Baptist in various parts of the church. His labours met with approval. In 1431 he doffed the cowl, after having been ordained a priest, and, entering the world under good patronage, he bid fair to become an artist of high, rank as well as a respected member of society.

The first evidence of Fra Filippo's activity after he left the Carmine is the picture of the Nativity which he painted for the ornament, of a cell or chapel in the convent of the Camaldoles of Florence, to which the wife of Cosimo de' Medici habitually resorted. At the, Academy of Arts in Florence, where this masterpiece is now preserved, it was long considered to have been the work of Masolino da Panicale, but it is now acknowledged to be by Lippi, and it is generally assumed that the predella which Cosimo de' Medici sent to Pope Eugenius the Fourth at Rome was that which Fra Filippo was painting when locked in by his jealous patron. There is no improbability in the assumption that it was about this time (that is, in 1431–1432) that the truant friar left Florence for the northern provinces of Italy. Records show that he was painting in the Santo of Padua in 1434, and it may be that this is the period when Lippi's adventure with the corsair happened. Not till 1436 did he venture back into Tuscany. But then he remained, as it seemed, permanently at Florence, where he produced the Virgin and Child with saints, which long adorned the Sacristy of Santo Spirito and was carried away at the close of the last century to Paris, where it now remains and is exhibited at the Louvre. For many years Fra Filippo was industrious, and his capacity for work was proved in numerous portable pictures. But the struggle for life proved severe, because the friar, according to his own account, had six marriageable nieces to support, and according to contemporary scandal-mongers, his expenditure on pleasure was quite beyond his means. He wrote in 1438–39 to Piero de' Medici that he was the poorest friar in all Florence, and it is, perhaps, in consequence of this complaint that, on the 23rd of February, 1452, a bull was issued by Pope Eugenius the Fourth giving him the office of rector and abbot *in commendam* of the church of San Quirico in Legnaia, near Florence.

During these and subsequent years the friar's practice continued large; he employed assistants, and in other ways he indulged in luxury and extravagance. About 1459 he took into his painting room Giovanni di Francesco della Cervelliera, who had been apprenticed to Andrea del Castagno, and engaged him for an annual salary of forty gold florins. At the end of the term, he not only refused to pay Giovanni his wages, but swore that the claim for salary was not justified, as he had already paid it in instalments. Giovanni summoned Fra Filippo before the archiepiscopal court, and the judge, in order to decide whether the receipt which the master tendered was genuine or not, put the accused as well as the accuser to the torture. Giovanni, on the rack, repeated his charge against Filippo. The friar, unable to bear the pains to which he was subjected, confessed, that he had forged Giovanni's signature. .

There was little room now for Fra Filippo in Florence. He was not tried for perjury or forgery. But he withdrew to Prato, where Inghirami, superintendent of the cathedral, gave him commissions to. paint several panels illustrating the legend of St. Bernard. He then obtained permanent employment, and Prato became to the friar a mine with very productive seams. Fra Filippo worked more or less. regularly for years at a large and important series of frescoes, which. still adorn the cathedral; and, thanks to his interest with the Medici, who were amongst the patrons of that foundation, he obtained a new piece of preferment and was made in 1452 chaplain to the nuns of San Niccolò de' Fieri at Florence. It was a timely appointment. Complaints of Fra Filippo's neglect of his duty at San Quirico, had been sent in to the Archbishop of Florence, who after many warnings and admonitions had suspended and then deprived the chaplain of his benefice. Yet Lippi's interest, even then, was so great that on appeal to Rome he obtained a revision of the sentence, and the papal authorities appointed Ugolino Giugni, Bishop of Fiesole, to reopen the case. The Florentine *curia*, however, disregarded the papal injunctions. The Bishop of Fiesole received an intimation that he had not to intervene, the Archbishop of Florence reported to the Vatican that Fra Filippo, in his appeal, had distorted the facts, and Pope Calixtus the Third, in a brief of the 15th of June, 1455, confirmed the original sentence, ordered Lippi to be deprived ' because he had been guilty of many infamous crimes,' and the benefice was transferred in due course. It is characteristic of the times and of the man that, in spite of these adverse proceedings, Fra Filippo managed to keep the temporalities of the office of which he had been deprived, and in a public document of 1457 he is still called rector *in com-mendam* of San Quirico of Legnaia.

Meanwhile, and as early in the century as the year 1452, Fra Filippo had bought the freehold of a house at Prato on the hire and purchase system of annual payments to the Hospital of Santa Maria Nuova of Florence. On the square opposite this house lay the convent of the Carmelite nuns of Santa Margarita, to which Fra Filippo, early in 1456, became attached in the capacity of a chaplain. An order to paint a Madonna for the high altar of the church was obtained by the friar, and permission was given him at the same time to take sittings for the Virgin's head from Lucretia, daughter of a Florentine, Lorenzo Buti, who had placed her in charge of the abbess, either for purposes of education or that she might become a nun. Fra Filippo took advantage of the occasion to declare his passion for Lucretia; she confessed her desire to leave the convent, where she was really confined for the purpose of being immured, and the lovers seized an early opportunity for a flight, which they successfully accomplished in the early days of May.

ͺ. Prato, it is well to remember, is celebrated as a place of pilgrimage to a chapel in which the Virgin's girdle is preserved as a relic. During the annual Festival of the Girdle in May, at which it was the custom of the nuns of St. Margaret to attend in a body, Lippi carried off Lucretia, who meanwhile had become a nun, and the pair, accompanied by Spinetta, Lucretia's sister, took refuge in Lippi's house, where they lived from 1456 till 1458. But the scandal had been so great and so public that steps were taken to put an end to it. When Lorenzo de' Medici heard of the new adventures of the friar to whom he extended his protection, he laughed and made light of it. But the people of Prato did their best, and although Lucretia had already borne a son to the chaplain (who called him by his own name and afterwards taught him his own art of painting), the authorities forced Lucretia and her sister to renew their vows and return to Santa Margarita two days before Christmas 1459. Little more than a year elapsed, and the two Butis had again left the nunnery and were traced without any difficulty to the house of Fra Filippo, and then it became clear to the painter's patrons that nothing would retrieve his character but the intervention of the highest ecclesiastical power, and they obtained a dispensation for Lucretia Buti, who became Fra Filippo's wife and bore him a daughter in 1465. But the action which rehabilitated the friar, did not improve the painter's worldly position. He was deprived of the chaplaincy of Santa Margarita of Prato, as well as of his rectorship at Legnaia, and his creditors at Florence distrained upon the properties of his painting room at Florence. From that time till 1469, when Fra Filippo died at Spoleto, where he spent three years in decorating the choir of the cathedral, he had to work for his daily bread, and did an enormous amount of pictorial work ; now and then he showed signs of neglect and produced altarpieces of unequal merit. But throughout his chequered career Lippi kept his character as an artist of great ability, and though he lost the noble simplicity and sweetness of conventual art which Angelico preserved to the last, it is not to be doubted that he is a representative example of the highest form of painting in the fifteenth century at Florence.

We saw that he had the good fortune to witness the first appearance at the Carmine of Masolino and Masaccio. Vasari tells us that his frame was entirely filled with the spirit of Masaccio. But Masaccio in Vasari's view is always a master who painted in two styles : the style illustrated by Masaccio at San Clemente of Rome, in which the influence of Masolino appears, and that which displays its varieties in the later frescoes of the Brancacci Chapel at Florence. The beautiful Nativity and Adoration of the Infant Christ in the Academy of Arts at Florence, which was so long attributed to Masolino

as it came from the cell at the Camaldoles in which the wife of
Cosimo de' Medici said her prayers, that delightful picture which
embodies the traditions of holy simplicity and taste peculiar to
Masolino, and in a still higher degree to Angelico, reveals that Fra
Filippo was the disciple of Masolino rather than a pupil of Masaccio,
and that before he became completely tainted by vice he had the
stuff in him to emulate all the qualities of his immediate precursors.
The charming angels, whose presence enlivens the space, the pretty
figure of the boy Baptist, and the fine presentment of a bearded friar
of the Camaldoles, who was probably confessor to the wife of Cosimo
de' Medici, form a thorough combination of grace with brightness of
scale in tints and balance of harmonies in tone which show Fra
Filippo's preference of the Allegro to the Penseroso. The colours
are of great transparence in a very light key; the outlines are clean
and minutely finished, revealing the individuality of a young artist
who intently watched the expansion of Masolino's art, in contrast
with the more powerful and manly style which Masaccio finally acquired. The sweet expression of the figures and the delicacy with
which they are presented are as attractive as the tender blending of
rosy flesh, the pleasing selection of gay dress and the elegant fall of
draperies. In all this we discern the teaching of the monastery.
But the spirit which gave simplicity and candour to Angelico's
creations is alloyed even thus early in Lippi by a sensuous feeling
which contrasts with the meditative calm and purity that dwell in all
the creations of Angelico. As he proceeded, Lippi became more and
more mundane. But he never attained the masculine power which
might justify Vasari in saying that he was filled with Masaccio's
spirit. What he wanted in order to bring him up to that level was
grandeur of conception, majesty of line, skill in grouping, and a
monumental style of drapery. He had none of these qualities in their
greatest development. Form, as he conceived it, was cast in the Giot-
tesque mould rather than the realistic shape of Uccello and Castagno.
There was no searching after new mediums or scientific principles of
perspective. Drawing was defective, especially in articulations and
extremities. Minute and dry detail of rocks and shrubbery, architecture of poor style, and ornament of doubtful taste, were constantly
obtruding, and were only redeemed by high finish, delicacy of touch,
and perfection of blending in bright colours. A new influence only
became visible when Lippi studied and adapted principles derived
from the practice of sculptors. As Ghiberti, in the gates of the
Baptistery of Florence, had carried into the execution of bas-relief
the system of line perspective which scientist painters had perfected,
Donatello had realised form in very shallow working of marble
surfaces. Lippi adopted Donatello's system in his painting, in which
he imitated the flatness of the works of Desiderio da Settignano,
whilst he acquired some of the breadth of Donatello in the shaping and

Morally he deserved the pillory, yet Lorenzo de' Medici caused a monument to be erected to his memory on a model furnished by Filippino, and we still enjoy the lovely productions of the artist, whilst we are taught to abhor the actions which debased the character of the individual man.

J. A. CROWE.

THE MASSACRES IN TURKEY

I

BY THE REV. DR. J. GUINNESS ROGERS

WHATEVER doubt may have existed in any mind as to the feeling of the nation in regard to the successive outbursts of insane fury at Constantinople has been set at rest by the extraordinary demonstrations of the opening weeks of September. On the 5th of that month the *Speaker* expressed the keen disappointment which was being felt by numbers who were concerned alike for the safety of the persecuted Armenians, and the good faith of the British people, which was virtually pledged on their behalf, at the seeming apathy with which the Constantinople Terror was viewed. The challenge was distinct, the reply was immediate, and in its volume and intensity leaves nothing to be desired. The passionate feeling of the hour is sweeping every-thing before it, and the fire blazes all the more fiercely because of the persistent efforts which have been made to keep it under. My own conviction is that it would have been possible at any time within the last few months to kindle a feeling in the country as strong and resolute as that which put an end to the Bulgarian atrocities of twenty years ago. But so far from any movement in that direction, the contrary course has been adopted. Popular agitation has been discouraged, and then it was confidently said that the country had reached a state of callous indifference, like that of Prince Bismarck when he said the Eastern question was not worth the sacrifice of a single Pomeranian soldier.

For days after the present movement began it was the fashion of the London correspondent of country journals to assure his readers that any appearance of excitement was delusive, and as I happened to be the first who took up the *Speaker's* challenge, I was treated as the victim of a midsummer madness. These correspondents were quite right as to their own field of observation. But that field was not the world, was not even the country. These gentlemen may be very useful, if their readers remember that they are only repeating the gossip picked up in lobbies and smoking rooms, and that outside these there

is a wide circle of opinion—opinion which is intelligent and influential
—of which they know nothing. It has proved so in the present instance.
Clubland was all but unanimous, and they reflected its views. It was
extremely inconvenient for various reasons that the country should be
stirred, and it was therefore dogmatically asserted that it cared
nothing for the whole matter. Was not Lord Salisbury, strongest
and bravest of Foreign Ministers, at the helm ? Was not the European
concert in active operation ? What more could be done, or indeed
desired, in this best of all possible worlds ? Meanwhile if the people
did not speak they observed and they reflected ; while they were musing
the fire burned (and now, to use the old Psalmist's words) they speak
with their tongue.

Whether, even now, there is a clear perception of the extent to
which the character and influence of Great Britain are involved in
the matter, is open to very serious doubt. Passion is at white heat,
but mere sentiment, whether of indignation at the tyrant or of
sympathy with his victims, however natural and laudable, is not
statesmanship. It is affected, rightly affected, by the outrage done
to our common humanity, but it does not take the trouble to appraise
the exact measure of our national responsibility, nor does it care to
inquire how far our national status is likely to be affected by the
decision that is reached. Sober-minded politicians will be more
affected by considerations of this nature, and they are certainly those
which must be pressed home upon every statesman. This is not
one of those occasions on which a nation can stand by with the
cynical and scoffing question, 'Am I my brother's keeper ? ' Our
own honour is at stake, and what some seem to value more than
our honour, our influence and position in the world.

It is not necessary here to repeat the long and melancholy story
of that Berlin treaty which at the time was said to have brought us
peace with honour, but which it is now seen scattered seeds of disaster
and trouble, whose harvest we are reaping. The connection between it
and the present Armenian persecution is too direct and obvious to
admit of doubt or require demonstration. Had the treaty of San
Stefano been confirmed, the crimes which have shocked all Europe
could never have been perpetrated ; and as on Great Britain rests the
responsibility for tearing up that treaty, on her must come also a
large measure of responsibility for the crimes resulting from this
fatal indulgence to the Turkish tyrant. Alas! the memory of that
ill-advised act has haunted our diplomacy ever since, and it paralyses
its efforts still. This is one of the facts that must be borne in mind
in shaping the policy which is to deal with this emergency. In
some way or other its evil effect has to be counteracted. But however this is done, it is, at all events, clear that the whole transaction
has fixed on us obligations which we cannot evade.

But if there are any who are inaccessible to an appeal of this kind, there is another of an entirely different character which it is impossible to ignore. The Sultan hardly conceals the fact that his action is a distinct defiance of Great Britain. It is Great Britain which has sought to check him in the exercise of his murderous proclivities, and it is her policy which he has been endeavouring to circumvent, unfortunately with only too much success. He will humiliate himself before Russia, he will intrigue with Germany, he will send his ribbons to French statesmen, he will even try to conciliate Austria in order that he may be able successfully to defy Great Britain. Unfortunately these Continental Powers have shown themselves only too ready to fall into line and to support him in his resistance. We have been assured over and over again that Great Britain is without a friend on the Continent, and, it must sorrowfully be said, if she has any they are very slow to act in her support. It is in vain that the sympathy and aid of the Great Powers have been sought; in vain that we have waited upon their convenience, until that waiting has come very near to a humiliation to ourselves; in vain that such excessive stress has been laid upon the European concert that it might almost seem as though we were afraid to call murder murder until the European concert had first given us permission to speak the truth; in vain that this European concert has, in fact, been exalted into a very demigod, on whose fiats the statesmen and people of this free nation must wait in humble submission. The more our statesmen have sought thus to clear themselves of any suspicion of selfish aim or sinister purpose by consultation at every point, the more cold and chilling has been the response which they have received. If this were to be the end, and the Sultan, resting upon the indirect help which he receives from other Powers, were able to laugh to scorn the remonstrances of Great Britain, it is hardly possible to exaggerate the blow which would be given to our national influence. The present insulting attitude of the Sultan may seem ridiculous enough looked at from one side. But there is another side of a very different character. Here is a monarch who sits on his throne solely in virtue of the tolerance of other Powers, assuming the airs of a mighty prince who can afford to meet sober and rational remonstrance with lies and insults, can pose as the victim of misrepresentation and calumny at the very time when his deeds are crying to heaven for vengeance, and secure in the immunity which he enjoys through the mutual jealousies of those who ought to suppress him and his crimes, can still persevere in his career of cruelty and blood. The spectacle is too ludicrous, but, alas! this miserable caricature of a monarch is able to work his own will. Our Government may enter its protests, and this may be soothing to our consciences, but it is humiliating to the last degree. What it really means is that England has parted with the power which she wielded when Milton sang, and Cromwell, 'before whose genius' (to use Macaulay's words) 'the young pride of Louis and the veteran craft of Mazarin stood rebuked,' and ' whose imperial voice arrested the sails of the Libyan pirates and the persecuting fires of Rome,' interposed on behalf of the persecuted Piedmontese, and that on the suggestion of our modern Imperialists. For her own sake as well as for the sake of those who are looking up to her for protection, England is bound to see that her remonstrances have another and a different issue.

The first and most essential condition of this is, that we get rid both of the party and international intrigues which in reality make the capital on which the Sultan trades. So far as our internal affairs are concerned, our first business is to lift the whole question out of the region of party strife. Our one concern should be to put an end once and for ever to the possibilities of Turkish despotism. How that may best be secured is a problem which statesmen have to solve. It is ours to make it clear to them that it must be done, and that no apology will be accepted for failure, or at all events until every possible method has been exhausted. It is simply pitiable to find men trying to turn the incidents of a crisis like this to the advantage or disadvantage of any particular statesman. Policies must be judged, but it should be on their own merits, and not on their bearing on the interests of a particular leader or party. It is for this reason that I personally welcome the letter which Lord Rosebery addressed to myself. That does not mean that I agree in every word or in every opinion, but simply that I approve of his attitude as worthy of a statesman occupying his distinctive position as leader of the Opposition. When Mr. Gladstone raised his trumpet voice in 1876 he was not hampered by his relation to a party, and yet his work had hardly commenced before the Prime Minister of that day took fright and treated the whole as an attack upon the Government. Much more certainly would this have occurred had Lord Rosebery put himself forward as the leader of any opposing policy.

Never indeed was there a subject in relation to which a party strife would be more utterly discreditable. Unfortunately there are those who seem unable to contemplate any subject except through party spectacles. They are so intent upon the battles of factions, and even of individuals, that they seem to forget that there are numbers of earnest politicians in the country, who care little or nothing about the personnel of a ministry, but who are intensely anxious as to the success of principles. They have no axe of their own to grind, are far removed from the temptations of place, have not even the faintest desire for a title. Naturally they are disgusted by the intrigues of the lobbies and the log-rolling of journalists. It is these unselfish politicians who are the strength of the present movement, and they are determined that it shall not have a party character. It is bad enough that the Armenians should suffer from the jealousies of contending potentates. It would be worse still if they were sacrificed to the ambitions of English parties. But it would be worst of all if their cause were to be prejudiced by intestine dissensions in the English party which specially prides itself upon undertaking the defence of its interests. In saying this, I do not for a moment mean to suggest that any Foreign Secretary ought to be sustained in power regardless altogether of the character and success of his policy. Speaking as a Liberal I must express my strong opinion that any attempt to promote the interests of Liberalism by an Armenian agitation would be impolitic in the highest degree. If we are to help these unfortunate people, we must have a singleness of eye. The law holds good here : we cannot serve God and Mammon.

But the second point which I wish to emphasise is not less important than the first. Personally, I do not share the anxiety which so many express as to the possible results of our taking an independent position in defence of Armenia. Every one outside diplomatic circles ought to speak with extreme reserve on such a point, since his knowledge of the situation must necessarily be very restricted. But it would require a good deal to convince me that the European Powers could ever be brought to unite to save the Sultan from the righteous penalty of his own misdeeds. Their bond of union is distrust of England rather than sympathy with Turkey, and it is hard to understand how, with views so divergent that they must necessarily become antagonistic as soon as any positive action was attempted, they could agree on measures of hostility to this country. It is, to say the least, extremely doubtful whether any resistance would have been offered if Great Britain, having invited the other Powers to unite in repressive measures and been refused, had taken independent action.

Be this as it may, it is eminently desirable that a work of humanity in which all the Powers are interested, should be undertaken by them conjointly. It is idle to deny that the chief difficulty in our way is the distrust and jealousy of Great Britain which evidently prevails on the Continent and perhaps especially in Russia. Russia has certainly been the most powerful obstacle to the success of our policy. Her representatives have hitherto thwarted us at every point, and there is no reason to hope for anything different until some better understanding is established between us. I venture to think that it should be the aim of our statesmen to secure this. Diplomacy has not yet exhausted all its resources. But if it is to succeed it must be prepared to exercise trust in order that it may inspire it in return. Russia is in no sense our natural enemy. It is not even an ancient foe. The policy which began with the Crimean War set aside the best traditions of our Foreign Office, and our action at the Berlin Conference fostered the antagonism which had thus been engendered between two hitherto friendly peoples. That alienation and rivalry must cease, or there is little hope for the Armenians. The Berlin Convention blocks the way. The obstacle ought to be removed. If our are told that everything possible has been done, and now that we have simply to wait until the European Powers come to a different mind. Advice more cowardly and pusillanimous could hardly be tendered, and it is safe to say that the English people are not in the mood to brook such a confession of impotence. We can at least withdraw our Ambassador, and so cease to play our part in consultations which have too much the character of a farce, and at the same time save ourselves from giving any sanction to so detestable a rule. What further action we take must be determined by events. No sane man counsels war, but to say that we will do nothing that would lead up to it is to make war a certainty. Even were we compelled to act alone, Great Britain is not so impotent as some would fain represent her. But for myself I have no love even for splendid isolation; I long to see the end of the insane jealousies which have separated Russia and this country, and I believe that the establishment of better relations between these two great peoples would inaugurate a new era in the history of the world.

J. Guinness Rogers.

II

By the Right Hon. the Earl of Meath

'CONSTANTINOPLE Riots. Further details of massacres. Six thousand defenceless people murdered.' So run the headlines of a sober, unsensational, leading newspaper, appearing this 9th day of September, in the year of our Lord 1896.

Six thousand defenceless people murdered! One's breath is taken away if one thinks of the meaning of these words. If 6,000 people had passed away within a few days by the visitation of God; if they had died of, say, the cholera, or of any similar deadly disease; if they had suddenly been swallowed up by an earthquake, or had been overwhelmed, as sometimes has occurred in China, by a gigantic flood, we should all have been horrified; but to be murdered, and murdered in cold blood by their fellow-subjects and fellow-citizens, suddenly and without warning, not in China or in some far-off, semi-civilised or uncivilised land in Asia or Africa, but in Europe, and in a capital largely inhabited by Europeans, under the very walls of the palace of their sovereign, to whose ears their dying shrieks may quite possibly have reached, within sight of the Embassies representing the most powerful and most civilised countries of the world, and under the very eyes of the police and soldiery paid by them for their protection and defence, but who, under the spell of some mysterious influence, stood passive spectators of these horrible scenes of carnage! What more sickening and ghastly story of wholesale murder is it in the power of the imagination of man to conceive?

One has to return in thought to the awful massacres of St. Bartholomew, when a sovereign hounded on his soldiery to the destruction of his own people, for a parallel to the fearful situation which now reigns in Constantinople. But this dreadful crime occurred more than three centuries ago, and it might have been hoped that the world had made some progress since those days.

Let it not be said that the 6,000 men suffered for the crime committed by some twenty-five of their co-religionists in seizing by violence the Ottoman Bank and in hurling bombs at the Turkish soldiers.

These few misguided men were responsible for their own crimes and assuredly deserved punishment, but what had the innocent 6,000 done that they should be massacred in cold blood? As well say that because some Protestant Englishmen have been wounded by the bombs of Roman Catholic Irish dynamiters, that therefore it would be legitimate for the British to massacre 6,000 Irish Roman Catholics in the streets of London.

The Sultan is directly responsible for these murders, and should not be allowed to escape from the just punishment of such an awful crime. When massacres occurred in Armenia it was possible for him to plead inability to restrain the passions of his Mohammedan subjects in distant portions of the Empire. He could urge that inefficient police and undisciplined soldiery far from the restraining hand of his centralised power had broken loose from his control, and, excited by their Mussulman fanaticism, had committed crimes in the heart of Asia which he greatly regretted and which should never be repeated. He might, I say, plead this in extenuation of the horrible massacres in Asia Minor which have justly excited the wrath and indignation of Europe, though every indication has gone to show that, far from restraining his soldiery and officials in these distant regions, he directly encouraged them in their bloody work of massacre; but no such excuse can be made in the present case.

The Sultan of Turkey, whatever may be his power in the distant portions of his Empire, is certainly supreme and all-powerful in his own capital. He surrounds himself with the most trustworthy and best disciplined men both in the army and in the police. It is notorious that nothing can take place in his capital without his being instantly acquainted with it. His spies are in all parts of the city, and report direct to him the conversation and movements of all suspected persons. A revolutionary movement in which so many persons were engaged as in the attack on the Ottoman Bank could hardly have been organised without some intimation of the intention of the conspirators having reached the ears of the Sultan through his numerous detectives, and in the excited state of the populace it would only have been natural to anticipate that some reprisals would be made by the Mussulmans on the Christians, if precautions were not taken to prevent them.

Had the Sultan desired the massacre of the Armenian Christians in his capital he could not have planned a better course of action than to allow these twenty-five mad revolutionaries to carry out their foolish and wicked designs, knowing that the Mussulmans would certainly revenge the outrage, and that if the police and soldiers were held aloof from the disturbances for forty-eight hours, the discontented and, from his point of view, dangerous Christian Armenians, the source of so much trouble and annoyance, would be wiped out of existence, and that he and his advisers would be freed for ever from their hateful presence in the capital of his Empire.   It is impossible to say what actually occurred in the palace, but knowing the power of the Sultan, and the means at his disposal for becoming acquainted with all that was going on in his capital, and for suppressing at once any riot or disturbance, and considering that murder was permitted to go on practically unchecked for some forty-eight hours, and that 6,000 men lost their lives during that time, almost within sight of the palace of the all-powerful autocrat, the man who can acquit him of some share in these atrocious crimes must indeed be gifted with a charitable spirit.

'The Assassin who sits on the throne of Turkey. . . . Him whom I wish always to call the Great Assassin.'

Such are the terms applied in recently published letters by Mr. Gladstone to the Sultan.   To most men the name will not appear exaggerated or undeserved.

Righteous as is the indignation which we may feel towards the Assassin on the throne, we cannot, in justice, forget that there are exalted and distinguished personages in other countries who cannot be exonerated from all blame in regard to these massacres.   We know from the despatches published in the official Blue-books that the Prime Minister of England was prepared after the first massacres of Armenians in Asia Minor to have put a stop, if necessary by force, to any recurrence of these horrors, had he received the smallest encouragement from the great European Powers, and that he reluctantly desisted from interference on hearing that Russia would not only not assist England in her efforts to stop further massacres, but would resent any independent action on her part.   It has been stated, with what truth I know not, that private approaches were made by the Government of Great Britain to that of the United States (whose people had shown marked sympathy with the victims of persecution, and whose missionaries had been eye-witnesses of many atrocities, and had personally suffered from the disturbed state of the country), and that Lord Salisbury declared his readiness to risk the dangers of foreign hostility could he be assured of the support of the Republic of the West, but that such an assurance could not be given, as American traditional policy did not permit the Republic to entangle herself in European alliances, or to take any part in the political affairs of the Old World.

Whatever others may have done, the Prime Minister of Great Britain has, at all events, performed his duty.   Short of plunging his country and Europe into a general war for the sake of the Armenians —an act of quixotic madness, which even such a righteous cause has failed to bring about a concert of Europe for the purpose of compelling the Turk to cease his murders and brutalities and to conduct himself like a civilised being, the fault lies not with Great Britain, but with those Powers whose selfish jealousy forbids them to combine with their neighbours in enforcing peace and respect for law and order on the bloodthirsty tyrant of the Bosphorus.

As I write, a telegram from Paris states that while at breakfast together on the journey from Breslau to Goerlitz, the German Emperor spoke with the Czar upon his approaching visit to France. His Majesty is said to have alluded to his projected stay in the French capital as a fresh pledge of peace, and then, referring to his late visit to Vienna, he announced that a complete understanding had been arrived at between Russia and Austria, with the object of effecting a pacific solution of the Eastern Question. In any case, the telegram continues, the Czar stated that Russia and Austria would only actively intervene in the event of any third Power endeavouring to act alone.

Of course, this statement may be perfectly untrue, and may have its sole foundation in the brain of a Parisian reporter; but if it be true, it means that whilst Russia and Austria decline to interfere in the internal affairs of Turkey, they will not permit any other Power to do so.

In the meantime the blood of 6,000 men, murdered in Europe, in addition to that of the thousands who have already met their deaths during the last six months in the Sultan's dominions on the other side of the Bosphorus, cries aloud to Heaven for vengeance.

How long will the populations of Christian Europe permit these atrocities to be committed with impunity by the crowned assassin of the Yildiz Kiosk?

His object is evidently to sweep from his dominions the hated Giaour—either by death or banishment. Having murdered 6,000 Armenians, he is now deporting the rest to the inhospitable shores of Anatolia and to other distant portions of his Empire, where death awaits them either by starvation or at the hands of mobs of fanatical Mussulmans, who assuredly await their arrival.

Encouraged by the jealousies between the Powers, which in the past have ensured him impunity, the Sultan seems to have become reckless. If he be permitted to destroy the Armenians, who can guarantee that in his madness he will not attempt similar violence against Christian foreigners residing within his dominions? Are we to wait for justice to be executed until he commits such a final act of murderous folly? In such a case, the one remaining satisfaction would be that this scene would be the last in the horrible drama, as the Assassin, his throne, and his dynasty would once for all be swept from the soil of Europe amidst the universal execrations of an outraged world.

Let us hope that the Powers of Europe will awake to their responsibilities and anticipate such a fell catastrophe by deposing the reckless Imperial madman before he can shed further blood, or finally exterminate the last remnants of an ancient Christian race.

MEATH.

III

By John Burns, M.P.

There is a time in the history of a nation like Great Britain, whose general interests are best served by permanent peace, when it should face dauntlessly, and with a heart of steel accept, the alternative even of war for a just, inevitable, and humanitarian act towards a suffering people.

Such a time and crisis have arrived for our common country over the Armenian atrocities.

By doing the right thing boldly, through the inspiring influence and contagious example of a speedy intervention, England can palliate the awful reproach that Europe has incurred, stop the flagrant injustice to Armenia, and avert the continued stain on our common humanity. Unless some step is taken by England somehow, a further policy of drift will be disastrous, and our masterly inactivity in the East will cause us to regret, perhaps in India, the day when our statesmen construed indifference as neutrality and desertion as diplomacy. Further delay on the Armenian Question will be dangerous for England's prestige. The waiting upon others is inimical to her power and that strength amongst nations which have almost solely been sustained by the spontaneity and independence of her ' splendid isolation.'

The gravity of the last phase of the Eastern Question, serious though it be, is fortunately not accentuated by political partisanship. Our Ministry, without fear of men or favour for any particular method of intercession, can, if they have a prompt remedy, have a unanimous country at their back. Certain it is that other Powers are expectant of England's lead. In them that attitude is instinctive; because, as has been often proved, England is alone ' the one free voice in Europe.' The civilised world hopes and believes England will lead the way in telling the Sultan, and if necessary compel him, to cease the ruthless slaughter of an unarmed people. For less provocation England has often risked life and treasure. In her highest moral interests which have been assailed she should exercise her traditional responsibility and carry out the international obligation due to a weaker people from such a first-class Power. That the time for active intervention by some Power has arrived is beyond question.

Whether through joint or by isolated action England does her bounden duty is immaterial. As the country to which oppressed people have always turned, and, I hope, will ever appeal, England is by virtue of her geographical situation and her political isolation the only Power that can take the initiative. I want that dutiful honour to be England's, and in so being and doing save the Armenians from that effacement evidently now intended. Any objection that may have been urged for delay has been removed. Every corroboration of past massacre has been produced, and the horrors of the recent holocaust established. The universal denunciation of the character and extent of Constantinople murders compels England, failing co-operation from others, which is improbable, to chivalrously suppress, single-handed if necessary, the satanic lust for blood that the Sultan has displayed.

A year ago, perhaps, active isolated intervention by England would have been premature and inexpedient, and might have led to international complications. But since then in other crises activity in well doing led to arbitration over Venezuela. A flying squadron to deliver a firm message taught an Emperor the art of polite letter-writing whilst England was daring to curb her own rebellious Præ-torians in South Africa. These and other acts show that 'grasping the nettle' within and without our Empire pays. But is this alarm as to the possibility of war through our intervention justified? I think not. The undue apprehension of war over the right issue has often, by the excessive fear of it, made war inevitable, and enabled the daring despotisms to exploit the nervous scruples of their more civilised neighbours and opponents. Less consideration for the material and commercial interests at stake, and a greater regard for the moral obligation, has by its transcendent influence averted what, under less noble impulses and ideals, would have been forcible action.

But why speculate upon results of intervention and hypothetical combinations of Powers and other complications when all the signs of the times point to practical unanimity? The co-operation of the Powers through their ambassadors by the collective notes to the Porte on the 27th and 31st of August would of itself justify any action England may take, and cause the chief Powers, if diplomacy is not duplicity, to support her demands upon the Porte. The refusal of France to hand over the bank raiders, our past waste of blood and treasure for Turkey, her indebtedness to England, all prove our *bona fides.* Whether or no, England, not for the first time, must do her duty, even though it be alone, in demanding reforms. What those reforms may be can best be determined as recent past action and present negotiation determine.

If England for the moment specifically confines her action to the prevention of further outrages, and the concession of such reforms or autonomy to Armenia as will secure its people there, and through the Turkish dominion, life and liberty, that temporarily will suffice.

And it is only because British aggrandisement is feared that some Powers do not join England. That fear dispelled by pledges, they will allow England to be the Garrison Police of Europe to keep the Turks in order.

If doing this, however, should open up, as it may, the deposition of the Sultan, the repartition of Turkey, and the allocation of its dominions to other states in Europe, that must be faced.

But I believe the cost of Europe's armed peace, in the main due to the untenable position of Turkey, will very soon lead all the Powers to settle without war, perhaps by arbitration, as soon they must, the distribution of the Turkish Empire to better hands than those who now palter with its possibilities, plunder its people, and prey upon its resources. Pending that decision, which is inevitable, England would be supported in her attempt to secure an armistice from assassination for the Armenians.

It does not need enthusiasm for the social and political aims of the Armenians as a people to justify their prompt rescue from their present condition on the part of England.

I cannot enthuse over the Armenian. He is not an ideal subject for help or sympathy, but he is, with all his faults, human, and should not be hunted like a beast. That the Armenians are the least favoured of the polyglot peoples that submit to, but do not accept, Turkish rule is true.

I have no love for the Armenian, his Christianity is in many instances a cloak for crafty commercialism, his huckstering and usurious pursuits are incapable of defence. That he is the Jew of the East we know, and, like the Jew of the other hemisphere, he may look upon the Mussulman as his commercial Mecca and to prey upon him his religion. A dash of the vigour the Cretans recently displayed would have been to his credit. The undue cultivation of the worst form of commercial spirit has evolved in the Armenian faculties that do not endear him to the Turk. We have the same thing under another name nearer home. The Jewification of the Armenian is in no small degree the cause of the recent troubles; but that is no excuse for persecution as a preliminary to extinction. All this given and admitted, the senseless slaughter of otherwise innocent, if undesirable, people must be stopped.

On the other hand, I do not share even now the wholesale denunciation of the Turks as a people. Not even the number of Armenians killed by them decides my opinion for intervention. I venture to believe that the ordinary Turks, if left to themselves, are incapable of the organised brutality that, under the inspiration from their rulers, the dregs of its population have assisted in.

The broad fact that tells with me is that, without sufficient cause or provocation, an Eastern oligarchy is plundering and murdering a section of its people under the corrupt domination of its pashas. Worse than this, they were secretly, then openly, now defiantly stirring up the fanaticism of its otherwise decent people, and for their own ends importing the most savage of their auxiliaries to carry out what the real Turkish people at Constantinople do not approve.

The fact is, and the past and present history of the Ottoman Empire proves, that there are two Turks to be reckoned with : the governing element, which is nearly always criminal and corrupt, and the governed, who, considering their race, religion, and Oriental customs, are not the immoral replicas of their infamous rulers. In a word, the autocracy of degeneracy which stands for government in Turkey has to be destroyed, and in its destruction the overtaxed, blackmailed, Turkish people would rejoice, and good administration for Armenia would begin.

Turkey has for generations been in the hands of a brutal bureaucracy. This official despotism that combines Oriental craft with Western hypocrisy, and both with Eastern vice, must go. Its puppet and embodiment, the Sultan, must be deposed. In the permanent interests of Turkey itself the Sultan and all his *entourage* must be sacrificed, or, for lack of this, the Turks will provoke universal hostility and, as a nation, must disappear.

As a Turkish proverb pertinently says, ' Their fish now stinks at the head.' That ghoulish head must be severed to save the whole Eastern peoples from moral putrefaction, administrative decay, and social dissolution.

How best and quickest can relief to the Armenians be given and the better Turkey saved from its wicked parts ? For any one, not of the Government, it is difficult to say, and through the curse of our secret diplomacy it is difficult to suggest what to do. That is the business of our governors and parliamentary pashas, the Cabinet. The details of it is their work, its necessity is their mandate, and their political responsibility as an administration makes it their duty.

When they will apply the vital spark of kindling action I cannot say. Europe is indignant, England is agreed, and it commands the only voice that can order the Porte to desist. Such an order given by our fleet in forcing the Dardanelles would suffice. This decisive act, once before taken for less justification than has recently occurred, would have created a situation the outcome of which would not be war, but the agreed dismemberment of Turkey.

Risks must always be run. England was made and lives by them at home and abroad.

A bold venture would have exposed the bluff of the reptile Press of Europe, and disclosed not a unity of Powers against England, but a rupture amongst them over the division of an empire that England alone can and must tumble to its doom.

But what has come over our statesmen that they should hesitate even at strenuous mediation, when a real *casus belli*, as the condition of Armenia is, exists? Is their hesitancy and apprehension due to a knowledge of factors in the Eastern Question that the public do not possess? If so, it is time the English people were informed, so that if the dread arbitrament of war alone will suffice, they should know it, and on that knowledge decide, or if a bargain with Russia is needed, discuss the terms, accepting or rejecting as humanity, not territory, decides. There have been few European troubles that possessed the justification for English initiative and collective action of the Powers which these massacres have furnished. Had some crisis been wanted for reasons of *la haute politique*, it would have arisen and been created over the matrimonial alliance of some petty prince with another member of a royal house, and war would have been declared ere this. Had some irritable ambassador had a violent dislike to another, means would have been found for the ' suspension of friendly relations.'

Had the Sultan been at Coomassie instead of Constantinople, at Zanzibar or Khartoum, or anywhere else than in his lair at Yildiz Kiosk, the long fingers of our commercial interests would have found some sordid trade reason for pulling him up, as our sailors say, with a round turn. If the sanctified political exigencies of palm oil, cotton, and trade gin have driven us to the splendid and heroic audacity that has marked some of our expeditions, and often illumined the pages of our history, we have yet, I am certain, conscience and courage enough for the rescue of millions of human beings from a cruel and obsolete despotism.

Surely in the heyday of our naval supremacy and military preparedness, our statesmen have the firmness to indicate what our sailors and soldiers would cheerfully do and dare?

Over the Armenian atrocities there has been greater incentive for interference than evoked the courage of the Crusaders. In some form, in varying degrees, the subject peoples of Turkey have been oppressed by a continuity of crime in their rulers. What in more barbarous times we could have tolerated, we now must take active steps to suppress.

I decline to accept the view which recent events have seemed to justify, namely, that women and children, the aged, and the deliberately unarmed, must continue to be killed in Turkey because the armed giants of Europe are jealous as to who shall be the first or last to stay the murderer's hand.

Have the ' Big Battalions' taken the other side and now become the bodyguard of his Satanic Majesty the Sultan? Is it safer for the Great Assassin to ply his murderous mission with an armed host surrounding him, while he, in proportion to their strength, craftily exploits their rival plans, their hidden antagonisms, and their secret policies ? If this be so, England, exempt from territorial aggrandisement in that part of Europe, is driven to plainly telling the other Powers that, in their desire to divide the Turkish dominions in the future, they must help to stay the annihilation of its people in the present.

If war is out of the question singlehanded and collective deposition impossible, these do not exhaust the versatility and resources of the potential Pitts and embryonic Cromwells who aspire to direct our policies and govern our Empire. I at least await their action with some degree of doubt. But if they can prove that their hand is stayed because intervention will mean the intensification of Armenian massacres and universal persecution, we perhaps will have to wait. But how long? Judging by recent references to the impotency of England, Armenia is always to be the theatre of atrocity because some statesmen and journalists regard England as weak and as nervous as themselves.

But at least the convening of a conference of the Powers is possible. Let the world know which nation shields the Sultan, and what for. Let England at that conference or now boldly exploit for humanity the real divisions amongst the Powers, with a full knowledge that some of them dare not attempt war abroad for fear of revolution at home, whilst at the same time subordinating those ' British interests ' that a false pride and a mistaken policy have maintained too long in Turkey, and caused the present difficulty.

The pity of it all is, that the impression created on Europe and the Porte by the spirited action of our Consul at Constantinople was allowed to pass away. It was the plucky preliminary of further action by his superiors at home ; at least it foreshadowed what their policy should have been.

The withdrawal then or even now of our Ambassador, and the substitution of an admiral with an hour's notice for all four-footed beasts to vacate Yildiz Kiosk and a bombardment if reforms were not granted within an hour. Audacious well-doing would have solved the situation.

The Concert of Europe, however, is to be waited upon, and the chief element in it, as I regard England to be, must await, I suppose, another tragedy to invoke its aid. If that should come—and vacillation is its chief stimulus—then even with the Powers against us, but America and our colonies helping England, the Sultan must be thrown from that pivotal position he now occupies, and from which he has dexterously lured, or drawn to his side, or kept neutral, the very forces and powers that, in preserving their diplomatic balance, sent the Armenians to their fate and made a murderer master of the Eastern Question.

JOHN BURNS.

IV

By Professor H. Anthony Salmoné

THE darkest record in the pages of modern history is unquestionably that of the reign of Abdul Hamid. What is still more lamentable is the fact that an indelible stain blemishes the fair repute of European chivalry and honour. With all the boasted claim of Western nations to civilisation, culture, love of justice and humanity, and the protection of the oppressed, they have of late remained inert witnesses of the most barbaric treatment that a subjugated people ever received from its rulers. All this notwithstanding that the six Great Powers stand pledged by treaties to afford protection to the persecuted subjects of the Sultan. But they have continued passive, lest by active intervention some spoke may thereby be put in the wheel of their political machinery.

It is true that the Powers, following the lead of Great Britain and Russia (I do not mention France, for her latter-day statesmen have made her the puppet of the Tzar), made strong representation last year to the Sultan. This was followed by several others. Every one is now acquainted with the result. His Sultanic Majesty, after months of tedious exchange of polite remonstrances, granted some modified reforms—on paper. This, be it understood, he took the precaution to make publicly known to the world, and especially for the edification of his wretched subjects, as voluntarily 'emanating from the fountain of his limitless mercy and boundless love for his people!' Despite the apparent absurdity of the whole affair, the representatives of the Powers were constrained to make a virtue of necessity and accept this magnanimous concession. Months elapsed and not a sign was made as to putting this into force. On the contrary, the officers and officials at whose instigation and by whose aid the atrocities in Armenia took place were decorated and promoted.

The tone of the press on the Continent has been, throughout the period of the sad occurrences, modified and extremely cautious. But, on the other hand, I venture to ask what real good has accrued from the voluminous writings in this country and the tirades made against the Sultan and his Government. Worse than nothing. Abdul Hamid retaliated by a repetition of his former dark deeds of blood! Numerous indignation meetings were held, eloquent platform speeches

were delivered, and every feasible step was taken to prove that
the feelings of Christian England were outraged at the merciless
slaughter of so many thousand Armenians. Surely, no greater or
more influential and representative meeting was ever held than that
which took place at the St. James's Hall last year in May! Yet,
after the lapse of fifteen months, over five thousand Christians are
butchered by orders of the Sultan within a stone's-throw of his fast-
ness, Yildiz, and actually within sight of some representatives of the
European Powers. Can history furnish a greater outrage upon the
honour of the civilised human community?

With regard to the St. James's Hall meeting, I venture here to
state briefly that it is my firm conviction that (1) had the speakers
refrained from attacking the Muhammadan faith; (2) had they
expressed the desire for the introduction of general reform in Turkey
(both to Christians and non-Christians alike); (3) had a formal
resolution been passed appealing to the other Powers to support
Great Britain in taking immediate measures to compel the Sultan
to carry out those reforms—long ere now the desired end would
have been attained. This would have contributed, in a great
measure, to lubricate much of that friction which has since existed
between Great Britain and the Powers over the Turkish Question. It
would have helped to allay the discontent of the Muhammadans and
brought about peace and contentment throughout Turkish dominion.
That meeting, with all its subsequent appendages, had a baneful
effect! It increased the madness and fury of the bloodthirsty
Sultan, roused the suspicion of foreign politicians, and augmented
the hostility of Russian statesmen to this country.

The question of imminent importance at present is to consider the
manner in which this complex problem can be solved. Affairs have
now reached so acute a stage that unless some speedy solution be
found a disastrous European war is inevitable. It must be evident
to all that the persecuted suffering subjects of the Sultan are determined to maintain their present attitude, and will not rest until they
get the much-needed reforms. The voice of the leaders of the reform
movement has had a telling effect. Committees have sprung up in
every part of the Turkish Empire. Some of these are absolutely revolutionary, as has been proved; but their action was independent
of the leaders of the Central Committee at Paris. The power of the
latter has grown to enormous dimensions, and I have the best
authority for stating that these have the support of the bulk of the
Turkish Army officers. Indeed, with the exception of a small minority
(who surround the Sultan), every inhabitant of the Empire secretly
supports the league of reform.

The only solution of the difficulty—the only means of checking
the flow of bloodshed in perturbed Turkey—*is the immediate deposition of Abdul Hamid!* In this idea the Press and public of this

country are unanimous. On the other hand, no practical suggestion has been offered as to the manner of procedure. It is true some have advocated that England should, single-handed if needs be, effect the dethronement. Such a step without some understanding with Russia would be fraught with danger. I do not mean that this country in reality need fear any active opposition on the part of Russia or of the other European Powers. The Government of the Tzar knows right well that, by supporting Abdul Hamid actively against the will of the whole nation, Russia would defeat her own ends and jeopardise her policy in appearing as the champion of Turkey. The danger would really emanate from the people of the country themselves—I refer to the Muhammadan population. These— although they have been equally the victims of misrule, and are in reality anxious to terminate the existing *régime*—would resent the active intervention of England, which they would regard as made on behalf of the Armenians and Christians alone. Unless these doubts be dissipated they would resort to arms, and—though powerless to withstand the power of Great Britain—they would avenge themselves upon the hapless Christians. I repeat what I have often said before, that it is much to be regretted that this country should have so strenuously striven to obtain redress for the Armenian sufferers, with such total disregard of the condition of the non-Christians of Turkey. But this may yet be amended. I rejoice at the fact that Mr. Gladstone has latterly in one of his letters stated that it is not the Muhammadans who are to blame, but the Sultan. It would be beneficial if his lead were to be followed by others who have waged an incessant war against the creed of Islam.

The time has arrived when the Young Turkey party should be fully recognised by the European Powers. Without their support, direct or indirect, nothing can be effectually or peaceably done. They, on the other hand, should have some countenance from one or more of the European Powers, so that when the hour arrives for them (especially those at Constantinople) to openly proclaim themselves opponents of the present *régime*, they may do so securely and effectively. They would, moreover, take the necessary means to ensure the fulfilment of reforms by Abdul Hamid's successor.

The deposition of Abdul Hamid could be effected in a single night without the shedding of one drop of blood ; for should it be felt that Europe would even only stand neutral the whole nation would openly rise, and the *Sheikh-ul-Islam*, the chief Turkish Muhammadan dignitary, himself would be at their head and readily grant the necessary *fetwah* for his deposition. In this connection I may add that, according to Muhammadan law, the edict of a few priests of Islam is all that is needed to dethrone the Kaliph and appoint a successor. Such was the case with the four former Sovereigns of Turkey who have been deposed during this century.

It is somewhat strange that in all that has been said regarding the deposition of the Sultan no mention has been made of his possible successor, and no reference made to the possible condition of the country after the event. Does this not show a heedless disregard of the future—with all its possible complications? Does it not show the irresponsible ignorance of those who would at any cost have their country plunged in a hazardous situation?

It is both amusing and painful to reflect upon the conduct of a person who, while labouring under mortal fear and in imminent danger, seeks to dispel from his mind the inevitable evil by thinking of some fantastic good. Such has been the case with some of the leading men in this country over 'the Eastern Question.' At the time of the appearance in this Review of my article in May 1895, the editors of two leading London morning papers expostulated with me for having so strongly shown the real condition of Turkey, intimating 'that such exposures may lead to the re-opening of the Eastern Question, which is most undesirable at present.' This wilful blindness is almost incomprehensible, and I even venture to say that its consequences are as disastrous as those of the conduct of people who imagine they see what does not exist. The conduct alike of those who ignore a fact and of those who exaggerate it is reprehensible.

I trust that I may be pardoned for referring to my past writings in this Review, but it may somewhat serve to emphasise what I feel it my duty now to say. As far back as May 1895 I declared that the persecuted suffering subjects of Turkey have at last realised that they must no longer hope for succour from Europe, and that they are determined to endure their sufferings no longer; that they were resolved by themselves, unaided, to fight for liberty or die in the struggle. And this statement has since been fully realised. Macedonia, Crete, Mount Lebanon, and again the Armenians, have risen in arms, and many thousands in truth have died in the struggle.

The British nation and its Government have repeatedly been accused of seeking self-benefit at whatever sacrifice it may entail to others, and that self-considerations alone for the purposes of national aggrandisement sway the mind of public men in this country. There may be some amount of truth in the indictment. On the other hand, can the other Christian nations of Europe plead guiltless of the crime of aiding and abetting the shedding of the blood of thousands upon thousands of innocent lives in Turkey at the close of the nineteenth century? Should not France, once the mighty champion of Christendom, with all its historic chivalry, bow its head in shame for helping to support a cold-blooded tyrant upon his throne? And how can Russia—the avowed enemy, until within a year or so ago, of Turkey and of all oppressors of Christians—reconcile her former attitude with her present conduct in giving encouragement to that worthless jects than all his predecessors put together.

In conclusion I will briefly summarise the opinions of one of the most influential leaders of the Young Turkey Party and the chief editor of *La Jeune Turquie*, of Paris, as expressed to me in a conversation a few days ago. He said:

Present affairs in Turkey are replete with danger—not only as regards that Empire, but as threatening the peace of the world. The danger does not arise so much from the disturbances in the country as from the attitude of the Powers in connection therewith. Their apathy and contentment with diplomatic remonstrances (instead of taking decisive steps) have made affairs much worse than they would have been. It was thought that the matter would blow over. Mere protests and threats had no effect upon the Sultan, who has become well acquainted with 'European representations.' But things now have gone beyond all the arts of diplomacy. Further disturbance and massacres are inevitable! These sparks in Turkey will cause a European conflagration, the result of which God alone knows. The Muhammadans are wrongly accused of fanaticism. The idea is erroneous. They likewise cry out for reforms and are sick of the present Sultan. Moreover Muhammadans are always ready to submit to superior power, as is the case in India, Algeria, Egypt, and other places.

As to the Sultan, he is possessed of intelligence, but he is in reality insane—and who would not be so after twenty years' imprisonment at his palace, surrounded by adventurers and liars, knowing only what he is told? There is only one way to save Turkey, and save Europe thereby from a fruitless war; and that is by the deposition of Abdul Hamid. Why should not Queen Victoria, for instance, ask the Tzar, as a humane act, to agree to the deposition, for the sake of saving the heartless massacre of thousands of innocent helpless people? Such a step would be hailed with acclamation throughout the civilised world, no less than by the people throughout Turkey.

The above is, with some reserve, what was said. I can only add, from my intimate knowledge of the forces at the disposal of and employed by 'awakened Turkey,' that nothing but the speedy deposition of Abdul Hamid can possibly remove the danger which now threatens all the subjects of Turkey with destruction and Europe with a disastrous war.

H. Anthony Salmoné.

V

By the Right Hon. W. E. Gladstone.

THE foregoing articles, with which I have become acquainted through the kindness of the Editor, appear to me likely to attract the public attention, not only by ability and integrity, but by the remarkable diversity in the points of view from which the several authors approach the discussion, and the not less remarkable decision with which they arrive at a common conclusion : that conclusion being, that the 'situation' in the East is intolerable, and that action with a view to a remedy has become indispensable, and ought not to be delayed.

It may be worth while to remark that that situation, besides being intolerable, is unexampled. It is not without example that the Great Assassin, now Sultan of Turkey, should have defied all Europe.: but on two occasions when he made the attempt, in 1876–7, and in 1880, it cost him the severance of fourteen millions of people from his Empire, whereas his daring has now effected this defiance, up to the present point, with absolute impunity, and with triumphant success. In a witty and pungent sarcasm, Dean Swift set forth that, when ten men well armed enter into conflict with one man in his shirt, the man in the shirt is nearly sure to be beaten. In the present case, not indeed ten but six men well armed have fought with one man in his shirt, and that a very ragged one, but the man in the shirt has thus far been victorious, and has exhibited his consciousness of victory by the periodical repetition of his crimes now blazoned throughout the world.

Nor (to do the six men justice) has this been because they were insensible to the enormity of the offences. On the contrary, though we do not know all, yet it has become known even to us on the outside of all charmed circles, through channels which if accidental are authentic, that a remedy the strongest and most direct of all has been deliberately proposed and variously advanced in their deliberations, and has only failed to take effect through certain reciprocal jealousies, independent of the merits of this particular controversy before us. Now it may be laid down as a general rule that the failure of strong remedial propositions is not a mere return to the *status ante*, but worsens the general position. They are sure to have become known to the criminal who is unhappily also a sovereign : their collapse is like an assurance of impunity : and that assurance of impunity becomes for the time absolute, when the Six Powers cast aside their weapons of offence, and descend to the prosecution of an illimitable diplomatic war, which has been based upon the method of still-born remonstrance, and which, not from fault of execution, but from the law of its nature, was doomed from the first to be, and to become with the lapse of time more and more, a thing pitiable and contemptible.

The last feature of strangeness, in this successful contumacy by the single hand, remains to be stated. When a particular sovereign defies the world, it is sometimes with the love and veneration, always at least with the assent and support, of his subjects. There is no evidence that the Sultan has any one of these props to sustain him. His people are not indeed permitted to express their sentiments ; but all the evidence before us is to the effect that as a body they, the Mahommedans as well as the Christians, are thoroughly disaffected. The motive power, which has directed these atrocities, and is only watching the movement of the hand on the clock to direct more, consists in the Sultan himself, sitting in the Yildiz Kiosk, with his dishes tasted lest his cook should poison him, and surrounded by ten or, as some believe, twenty thousand troops in his capital, whom, contrary to his general practice, he regularly pays, feeds, and clothes, and on whom, rightly or wrongly, he thinks he can rely.

Such is the unexampled character of the Eastern controversy in its present phase. The interrogation, however, of the hour, to which the British nation is from day to day heaping mountain high the materials of an affirmative reply, is whether, besides being unexampled, it is also intolerable. I venture to add that we have already passed the point at which a doubt could be raised whether the Eastern Question had been really opened or not. Quite apart from the present national movement, or its immediate consequences, opened that question is by the weight of facts, and so effectually opened that unless by the application of effective remedies it never can again be closed.

Upon the humiliation, which Europe has been suffering for the last eighteen months through its diplomacy, the people of this country appear to be well agreed. They seem also to be of one mind in the belief that action is absolutely demanded by the intolerable character of the situation. Further they have no doubt as to the title of the Powers collectively, or it may be individually, to undertake such action ; the ground or reason of it being found in the hideous character, and the vast extent, of the Armenian massacres, together with the certainty that nothing but fear on the part of the Assassin will prevent their indefinite repetition. For, though the wonder be scarcely less than the crime, it really seems as if he had marked out for himself as an infernal mission, even the extirpation of the race whose blood, as we understand, he shares ; and as if he would not consider his business was at an end until the last Armenian was at his last gasp.

Now, the action which is contemplated is humane ; and it is also of the class which is called humanitarian. But, as between nations, the fact that a given course is agreeable to humanity does not of itself amount to a sufficient justification for entering upon it. Neither is it enough to say that we have made a careful examination of means and ends, and are well convinced that the undertaking is within our power. But there is still something more that we lack : for we have not had the sword of the Almighty entrusted to our keeping, and while we are bound to follow and require humanity in our own house, we may not have a title to enforce it in the house of our neighbour. We ought therefore to examine whether our case is complete, and whether we have the specific rights and obligations, which suffice, in the case that may be before us, to invest us with a jurisdiction that, apart from these specific rights, would not properly belong to us.

The specific right, then, which the Powers of Europe possess, and which entails a corresponding obligation, to prevent the recurrence of atrocious and wholesale crime in the Turkish Empire, is the right conferred, and the obligation imposed, by Treaty ; let us say *nominatim* by the Treaty of Berlin. This right, and this obligation, attach to all the Powers. It is the shameless violation of it by Turkey which entails her liability as towards them all. There are two of them, however, from whom sound moral judgment would entitle us to expect a special forwardness. One of them is Russia, who by the Treaty of San Stefano had promised so much to the Christians. And the other is England, to whom unhappily were owing in a principal degree such shortcomings as attach to the Treaty of Berlin in comparison with the Treaty of San Stefano.

But while the argument for action as opposed to mere expostulation is under the Treaty of Berlin complete and even imperative for all the Powers, it cannot be too pointedly borne in mind that over and above everything which belongs to the five sister States, England is invested with an altogether separate right, and bound by an equally separate obligation, in which they have no share whatever. Were the Treaty of Berlin swept to the bottom of the sea, the Five Powers would have no rights in the matter save those of generalised humanity. But, in that same contingency, the rights and obligations of England would remain absolutely unaffected, as she draws them, distinctly but cumulatively, from another source.

It pleased us, in the year 1878, to conclude, without the intervention of the Powers, a separate Treaty with Turkey, which however became known to them before the transactions at Berlin were completed. It was thus tacitly accepted or allowed by them; but, whatever their attitudes in regard to it may now have been, it is absolutely binding as between the contracting parties. This Treaty differs from most others in two important particulars, of which the joint effect is, if I mistake not, to give a great amount of additional point and force to the obligations we have spontaneously incurred.

The name of honour is one, which has often been abused in political discussion. It has been made a cover for miscarriage, for mistake, for crime. It has been profaned for evil purposes quite as much as the name of Liberty, even (perhaps) almost as much as the name of Order. But it is a great and a sacred name: and, where it can be invoked under a valid plea, the man who hesitates to make whatever sacrifices it may require, degrades both himself and the nature which he bears.

Under the Treaty or Convention of 1878, a great advantage was obtained by Turkey; for England became engaged to defend not Armenia only, but the whole Turkish Empire in Asia against Russian attack. On the other hand, the Sultan undertook to reform his government in concert with England. So that we actually made ourselves in honour partakers of the government of those widely extended countries, and such we should have been in act, had the Sultan fulfilled his promise. He not only did not fulfil it. In Armenia, he read Reform to mean ' Massacre.' The peculiarity of the Treaty was that his promise of reform was stipulated as being ' in return' for the truly valuable engagement he had already obtained. Not only was the pledge broken, but it was broken after he had received actual and weighty value in return.

The Armenians were no parties to the Convention. They have no treaty rights, no international existence. They are only men: for, though they happen to be also Christians, this does not affect the substance of the case. But who can deny with ' honour ' that, when we made this Treaty over their heads, we undertook not only heavy juridical obligations as towards Turkey, but also real and profound moral obligations as towards them ?

But there is another enhancing consideration, which has not I think as yet been sufficiently borne in mind. We too in this Treaty took ' value received ;' and we have it, so to speak, at this moment in our pockets. The Sultan made over to us, without limit of time, the occupation and administration, that is the virtual dominion, of the Island of Cyprus.

Perhaps it may be said, and I might concur in the opinion, that Cyprus is of no value to us. But that reply is wholly foreign to the purpose. If it did not add to our strength or resources, it added, as we were told, to our *prestige.* It was boasted of in Parliament at the time as a territorial acquisition, and was highly popular. We cannot now turn round upon it and declare it valueless. We took it as value, and as value we have now to abide by it in the present argument.

The case then stands briefly thus.

We are entitled to demand of the Sultan the immediate fulfilment, under his treaty with us, of his engagements, and to treat his non-compliance as, under the law of nations, other breaches of treaty are, or may be, dealt with.

We have in the face of the world bound ourselves to secure good government for Armenia and for Asiatic Turkey.

And for thus binding ourselves we have received what we have declared to be valuable consideration in a virtual addition to the territory of the Empire.

And all this we have done, not in concert with Europe, but by our own sole action, on our own sole responsibility.

However we may desire and strive to obtain the co-operation of others, is it possible for us to lay down this doctrine: *England may give for herself the most solemn pledges in the most binding shape, but she now claims the right of referring it to some other person or persons, State or States, not consulted or concerned in her act, to determine whether she shall endeavour to the utmost of her ability to fulfil them?*

If this doctrine is really to be adopted, I would respectfully propose that the old word 'honour' should be effaced from our dictionaries, and dropped from our language.

W. E. GLADSTONE.

The Editor of THE NINETEENTH CENTURY *cannot undertake to return unaccepted MSS.*

THE

NINETEENTH CENTURY

No. CCXXXVII—November 1896

ENGLAND AND
THE CONTINENTAL ALLIANCES

I DO not intend to write here about the well-thrashed and hackneyed theme of the visit of the Tsar to France. This last stage of an historical tour has been studied under all its aspects and discussed per-haps even *usque ad nauseam* in its most immediate features. What I want is to take it, with its universally admitted consequences, as the departure for a short inquiry into the relations of the great Powers between themselves, with a special view to the case of England.

The public opinion of the outer world, as mirrored in its press, has gone through three different stages concerning the mutual under-standing of which this visit is both the solemn affirmation and the tightening. There was first the phasis of unbelief pure and simple, though more or less affected. It was—not yet so very long ago—the fashion to jeer and scoff unmercifully at those poor credulous French-men about their pretended friendship with the Russian autocrat. No article about the international condition of Europe was judged good without a jesting parallel between the solid, strong, silent mass of the Triple Alliance and the fanciful, noisy, blustering phantasm of the dual understanding.

When facts became decidedly too unmanageable for this comfort-able scepticism, public men and public writers betook themselves to the second point of view. We entered upon the stage of compassion for poor gulled-France. It was ironically asked what advantage the Government of the Republic flattered itself with the hope of gaining from a friendship where all the profits were for Russia. It was currently said that France had given to the Tsar the key both of her heart and of her money-chest, and had to be satisfied with a return in *monkey's currency.* It was pointed out that everywhere, in the far East, in the Levant, in the Balkans, Russia had received an accession of strength and prestige, while nowhere, neither in Egypt nor on her eastern frontier, had France yet got back the smallest assistance.

Well, this shower of sympathy not unmixed with some cynical *Schadenfreude* is for the present come to an end. We hear now quite another song. People are not content to acknowledge the reality, the strength, the mutual cordiality, and the reciprocal beneficence of the Franco-Russian understanding: they must fain exaggerate the power, and by the same token the perilousness, of this new international constellation. Assuredly, it is a good and a reasonable thing to silence once for all these cavillers, who foolishly make it their wisdom to look for spots in the sun or blemishes in a gift horse, and who have sadly and sapiently shaken their heads because a certain word was not pronounced where a certain thing was established and put beyond all doubt before the whole world. However, the proceeding is a little too gross when, for instance, the *Cologne Gazette* expatiates at length on the dangerous omnipotence of the new *Duplice* as contrasted with the old innocuous and safe *Triplice*, and insinuates, in glaring contradiction to its own avowals during the meeting itself, that thoughts of the *Revanche* received a deplorable impulse and found a frequent expression during the imperial visit.

These tactics of the German officious press, though singularly unscrupulous, are not, after all, particularly dangerous. It is enough, in order to confute them, either to appeal to their own acknowledgments in their unguarded and therefore more truthful moments, or to call to witness any unprejudiced spectator of these memorable days. For is it not beyond doubt that during this short but epoch-making stay there occurred not only a political pact of the first rank, but at the same time a great soul-stirring moral event? We must dare to say it: the people of France, in their unreasoning impulse, have known how to solve with the utmost simplicity the difficulties and to avoid the perils of this reception. Republicans they were and they are, and they have perfectly understood how to make themselves hoarse by clamouring 'Vive l'Empereur!' without shaking the foundations of the Republic. They knew how to distinguish between home and foreign policy. This ignorant and fickle democracy knew how to follow the example of a Richelieu allying himself in Germany with those Protestants he was crushing in France, or of a Cromwell meeting halfway the friendship of the French King, that is to say of the first cousin of the proscribed Pretender. These masses—the men in the streets—knew how to redeem the innumerable mistakes of the Protocol, and how to make good by the innate dignity of nobodies the errors of the vulgar some-bodies or busybodies of the official world. While they enjoyed to the full the feeling of reconquered security, of France's place in the world recovered, they have not compromised by a gesture or by a clamour the peaceful character of this visit, and they have held in the leash the unfeigned feelings or the factitious passions of so-called patriotism.

In short (I beg pardon of the *arbitri elegantiarum* and universal doctors of the German press), it has been a great and beautiful spectacle —and, what is more, without the blemish of imprudent and foolish mishaps. Both parties—Tsar and people—have brought to bear the same goodwill, the same unshaken love of peace, the same unassailable consciousness of right and of strength upon this solemn promulgation and outburst of the Franco-Russian understanding. Even bad faith, which alone has dared to misrepresent these unmistakable displays and to slander their meaning, has borne an unwilling witness to their real value. If there is henceforth a fact solidly settled among the data of European politics, it is that France and Russia have tied a love-knot between themselves, and formed for the nonce an indissoluble league. Henceforth politicians have to take into account this dualism. If not precisely a brand-new contrivance, at any rate it is sufficiently new in its official acknowledgment, and chiefly in the tightening of its bonds, to introduce a novel element into international politics.

It has even appeared as if this coming up of the *Duplice* had already occasioned some searchings of heart among the members of the *Triplice*. Not only is poor, nearly bankrupt Italy unmercifully held up to her heavy undertakings, and casting longing eyes towards a more natural and less expensive relation with her nearest neighbour, no longer delivered up beforehand to the first assaulting whim of Germany. Other more or less premonitory crackings have been heard. In a portion, at any rate, of the German press, chiefly that which takes its cue from the unforgetting and unforgiving hermit of Friedrichsruh, advances—not even very self-respectful ones—have been made to the Tsar. The friendship of Russia has been depicted as immeasurably more valuable to Germany than the unattainable goodwill of England, or even than the easily gained intimacy of Austria —in fact, as the corner-stone of the true policy of the young Empire.

However, significant and worthy of all attention as are these symptoms, it would be wrong to put upon them too large or too immediate a meaning. The triple alliance is yet, for good or for evil, a great, stubborn, immutable fact, and with it we must deal as with one of the primary data of the international situation. Just now two great systems of states are facing each other in the political heavens: The era when numerous erratic bodies wandered isolated through space, crossing and recrossing their ways, is definitively gone. England alone remains, between two constellations following each its own path, a solitary comet. Naturally the drawing near and moving together of all these stars of the first rank have created both new attractions and new repulsions—in a word, have totally altered the state, not only of the bodies subject to these new relations, but of the others too.

England, then, finds herself under the necessity of a political self-examination. It will be well for her, first of all, to clear her vision and to see things as they are. High-sounding formulas, burdens of songs for the use of the music hall, all the self-deceiving paraphernalia of a pinchbeck jingoism, are to be shunned more than in the past. For instance, ' splendid isolation ' is neither more nor less than one of those hollow, resounding, dangerous phrases such as: ' L'Empire c'est la paix,' or ' masterly inactivity,' or ' Peace with honour,' with which people let themselves be deluded.

If it were even ' proud aloofness,' that is to say, if it connotated a real attitude of abstaining, non-intervention, and solitary security, it might pass muster. But the truth is that this so-called ' splendid isolation ' means, not the refusal of all compromising, troublesome engagements, not the holding aloof from all entangling meddlesomeness, but purely and simply successive and contradictory flirtings. Its true name ought to be the ' semi-detached policy.' Now, this plan does not seem to bring better results in diplomacy than it does when a builder scatters on a whole estate the sorry suburban monster of semi-detached villas. It is a policy of make-believe, of self-deceit, and it ends by discontenting everybody.

The history of the present year of grace bears sufficient witness to this melancholy truth. From the Transvaal to Zanzibar it has been a sequence of cross purposes, of self-contradicting undertakings, of half-matured designs. Begun by a violent explosion of anger against the German Emperor, of which the coarse polemics of the German press did not fail to fan the flames, it seemed to set towards an understanding with France, the first-fruits of which were the regulation of the Mekong and Siamese difficulty. Suddenly the policy of Lord Salisbury veered from point to point: French friendship was thrown overboard, German favour was ardently sought for; Italy was taken in tow, a little against the grain on account of her African disaster; and Egypt, the touchstone of Anglo-French relations and of the value put by the Cabinet of St. James on its word, was once more an object of quarrel between the two great liberal countries of the West.

However, it was not yet the end. Once more the pendulum swung back. The Zanzibar succession has been much less the cause than the pretext of a new war-whoop of the German press. Little by little the paper-war has widened its ground, the heavy ordnance has begun fire. The *Times* and the *Cologne Gazette*, not to name the smaller fry, are just now engaged in an exchange of rather uncomplimentary truths, among which it is difficult to see where comes in the boasted reconciliation of last spring.

Such, then, are the fruits of the system of 'splendid isolation,' so dear to the heart of Mr. Under-Secretary Curzon. It does not belong at all to my province to come and tell Englishmen: 'Take this or take that side in exchange for your so-called freedom.' What I mean to try and set before my readers is only the fact that England *must* choose, that she cannot remain in a *status quo*, which would not be a true one, since the change of everything outside could not but react on the position of the isolated kingdom itself.

My next aim is simply to examine shortly under what conditions England, if she makes her choice, would be able to join the diplomatic combination in which France has got part and parcel. It is the business of Englishmen and of them alone to see if the periodical outburst of hate against their country in the German press is merely a childish symptom to be overlooked, or if it is a rather unamiable way of fishing for the friendship of England —in contempt of that popular saying according to which flies are not taken by vinegar—or if finally it is the weighty sign of a deep-seated antagonism of temper and of interests, making, even against the will of the majority of the citizens of both lands, for a fatal struggle sooner or later; in which last case, the incidents of the present year would take, to the eyes of clear-headed, sagacious observers, something of the character of that Luxemburg scrape which in 1867 nearly precipitated, three years before its time, the Franco-German War.

Let us then suppose that England, after full and mature consideration, advisedly and with open eyes, resolves to feel her way to an understanding with the Franco-Russian combination. Even by this simple statement I have already pointed out one, and perhaps the most important, of the conditions antecedent to this happy consummation. It is not, it cannot be, a question of substituting one country for another in the intimacy of Russia, of wriggling or worming in another partner into the Tsar's friendship instead of France. No divorce is to precede this match. International marriages admit perfectly well of a third party. Notwithstanding the old saying that 'two are company and three are none,' there can be for England no association with Russia, if France has no part and lot in it.

And, what is more, it is not to be fancied that France's friendship may be thrown into the bargain or got for the asking. The two partners are both equally to be met halfway, both equally to be wooed, in order to be both equally won. Such advice is not at all superfluous, to judge by the tone of too many of the papers which have advocated, after the visit of Nicholas the Second at Balmoral, an agreement with Russia. Those among them which did not own a little cynically as their purpose the substitution of England for France in the Russian friendship, have all along built on the supposed willingness of France to follow blindly her great ally, and to accept dutifully any new bedfellow. As a matter of fact, the negotiators of this beneficent understanding will have to deal with two partners at once.

However, I must hasten to add that, in the majority of cases at any rate, what would satisfy the one would also satisfy the other. The crux of the whole matter is, before all, a matter of trust. The past is heavily handicapping the present. Everybody is beginning to see it in relation to the Armenian agitation. Thus Cyprus and Egypt stand in the way of the acknowledgment by Europe of the good intentions and disinterestedness of the forward policy. It is no less true that they bar the road to a fruitful understanding with France and Russia.

This Armenian business is in some sense a symbolic exponent of the whole state of things. Here is a hideous nightmare of cruelty, vileness, and madness oppressing the whole of Europe, or rather of Christendom. Here is the old spectre of the Eastern question reappearing within a dark and bloody cloud before the conscience of the people and of the governments of the civilised world. The mere continuance of the *status quo* is a scandal, and holds up over the peace of our continent the gravest dangers. In the meanwhile the whole of the great Powers remain stricken as with palsy. Diplomacy is just strong enough to paralyse philanthropy; philanthropy is just strong enough to paralyse diplomacy.

England has just seen such an outburst of right-minded indignation as in 1876, during the never to be forgotten campaign against the Bulgarian atrocities. Twenty years more on the hoary head of Mr. Gladstone have not prevented the old man eloquent from sounding from Land's End to John o' Groats the trumpet calls of his magnanimous anger. If the right honourable gentleman is no longer the member for Midlothian, he considers himself as the member for oppressed and martyred mankind, and he has nobly fulfilled his mandate. English opinion, without distinction of parties, has rallied around the grand leader of old days. A series of meetings, crowned by that in St. James's Hall, where bishops, peers of the realm, mayors of great cities, Anglican divines, Nonconformist ministers, professors, politicians have met on the same platform, have given loud expression to the mind of the country.

I am not here just now discussing the policy so passionately proclaimed at these meetings. Much as I admire the moral inspiration of the movement, much as I am disposed to subscribe with my whole heart to the ends it has in view, I should have to enter my strongest protest against the childish and hot-headed scheme of a separate action of England and of the recall of Her Majesty's ambassador at Constantinople, as well as against the exaggerated unjust, unfounded, and unchristian charges promiscuously hurled against the unfortunate heir of a deplorable system. For the nonce what I look for is the cause why this great agitation, instead of finding sympathy, not unmixed with criticism, among the nations of the continent, has loosened a perfect tornado of ill-will and bad words.

Undoubtedly there is among too many of the inhabitants of other countries an unshakeable conviction that English feeling is hypocrisy. Nothing is more absurd than this impression. It is not necessary to be a very far-looking student of human psychology to know that the English temper is at once uncommonly practical with a kind of matter-of-fact hardness, and strangely emotional. There is in the English soul, under a superficial coat of proud reserve, of affected coldness, of pragmatical *no-nonsense-ness*, a rich vein of true sensibility, of humanitarian eagerness, of an even aggressive philanthropy. Only we must not forget that the human mind is not without its contradictions or its phases; that Englishmen, if they have their vigils of holy and crusading zeal, have their morrows of practical reaction; and that history—I mean the most contemporary history—teaches us to fear a little the swingings of the humanitarian pendulum.

How could we forget the tears we or our fathers mingled twenty years ago with those of the generous champions of Bulgaria, but how could we, too, obliterate the memory of that painful awaking from the noble dreams of 1876, when a Semitic statesman knew how to confiscate for the purposes of his egoistical policy the powerful movement initiated by Mr. Gladstone, and how to intoxicate with jingoism, imperialism, and hate of Russia, the selfsame masses which had cheered to the echo, on Blackheath Common, the burning words of the great Liberal leader? We had witnessed an indisputable philanthropic crusade; but an Eastern magician had brandished his wand, and, hey presto! the whole scène had changed, the holy war had degenerated into a political rivalry, and Cyprus was the only monument which remained of this great upheaval of conscience!

Since that time we have seen Egypt occupied under a wholly disinterested pretext; we have heard the solemn promises of a short stay and a prompt evacuation given by Mr. Gladstone, ratified and reiterated by every successive Government; and we see now the Nile Valley incorporated in fact with the British Empire, the reconquest of the Soudan undertaken against the advice of Lord Cromer, in order to put back to the Greek calends the execution of engagements which the principal organs of the press and a whole school of politicians begin to treat as null and void. Verily an instructive lesson about the value of self-denying ordinances!

Such then is the past which weighs so heavily upon the present. It is a very encouraging sign of the times to find a growing number of public men openly advocating the only means of retrieving these mistakes. A letter like that of the Right Hon. Leonard Courtney to the *Times* is not only a new proof of the unequalled and incomparable independence of this hero *sans peur et sans reproche* of true freedom of thought: it is an evidence, among many others, of the progress of sounder views on the questions jingoism has so long succeeded in confusing and entangling.

This way lies the hope of a renewal of the *entente cordiale* of former times. This way, too, lies the chance of an agreement with Russia. If England begins to tread the road of conciliation in Africa, the chances are for her following the same impulse in Asia. Thus would be made easy the new triple alliance which alone, as we are told by those who know best, is able to resolve by pacific means this Eastern question so dreadfully weighing on the conscience of mankind.

After all, there is no mischief in trying to fancy what would be the results of the conclusion of an understanding, without which it seems there is no motive power sufficient to put into activity the European concert and to set it towards the right ends. As for the general prospects opened by such a consummation, imagination reels before their vastness. Once more I do not presume to answer for England the questions I have brought before my readers. My aim has been all along simply to expound not what England ought to do, but what she ought to do *if* she wanted one of the two solutions I indicated at the beginning of this article. It is for the English people, and only for them, to make their choice. It is for them to say once for all if they share yet the feeling so eloquently expressed by Shakespeare in his *Henry the Sixth*:

> *Hastings.* Why, knows not Montague that of itself
> England is safe, if true within itself?
> *Montague.* But the safer when 'tis backed with France.
> *Hastings.* 'Tis better using France than trusting France.
> Let us be backed with God and with the seas,
> Which He has given for fence impregnable,
> And with their help only defend ourselves;
> In them and in ourselves our safety lies.

They may equally try the Triple Alliance and give as epilogue to the Homeric exchange of amiabilities with the German press the acceptance of German hegemony. One thing only is out of their power, and that is to remain as they are, without either an accession or a loss of strength, in a world which has completed the work of consolidation and where two great systems are henceforth to attract in their orbit or to repulse out of their sphere of influence the few remaining isolated bodies.

FRANCIS DE PRESSENSÉ.

LA TURQUIE ET SON SOUVERAIN

LA CRISE ACTUELLE, SES ORIGINES, SA SOLUTION

QUELQUES semaines après l'avénement au trône du Sultan Abd-ul-Hamid, lorsqu'on se préparait à célébrer la cérémonie de Kilidj-Ala-yi (prise de possession par le nouveau souverain de l'épée du fondateur de la dynastie, qui équivaut en Turquie au couronnement des souverains d'Europe), le grand-vizir Mehmed Ruchdi pacha, écœuré des intrigues qui commençaient à se fomenter, avait offert sa démission. Le Sultan, mal assis sur le trône qu'un double changement venait de mettre à sa disposition, désirait s'entourer de ceux qui avaient été les auteurs de ces changements et dont l'énergie et la popularité seules pouvaient lui assurer le règne. Mehmed Ruchdi pacha était une force sur laquelle on pouvait s'appuyer et le Sultan désirait particulièrement le garder au pouvoir pour montrer à ses sujets, imbus d'idées de liberté en ce temps, qu'il marchait d'accord avec le parti de réformes ; aussi envoyait-il émissaire sur émissaire auprès du grand-vizir pour le persuader à retirer sa démission ; mais le vieux *Sadrazam* restait inébranlable ; las enfin de l'insistance qu'on mettait à l'inviter à rester au pouvoir, Ruchdi pacha a fait à un ami, homme d'honneur et de confiance, les déclarations suivantes :

> Il m'avait fallu dix ans pour connaître à fond le caractère d'Abd-ul-Aziz ; dix jours m'ont suffi pour pénétrer celui d'Abd-ul-Hamid ; depuis la fondation de l'Empire, un homme si atrocement dangereux n'était jamais monté sur le trône ; les calamités qui vont fondre sur la Turquie durant ce règne, dépasseront de beaucoup tout ce que l'histoire de ce pays a enregistré ; n'insistez pas sur le retrait de ma démission ; je ne veux pas mêler mon nom à l'histoire du démolissement de ce grand empire.

Il avait bien prévu, le malheureux grand-vizir, l'avenir que la nature perverse d'Abd-ul-Hamid préparait au pays ; et il a bien eu sa part dans le malheur, puisqu'il est allé finir sa vie, faite de travail et d'honnêteté, dans l'exil !

Jamais l'Empire ottoman ne s'est senti si près de l'abime et tout le monde est d'accord pour rejeter la responsabilité de cette catastrophe personnellement sur le souverain. Comment cet état de choses a-t-il été créé ? quel état d'âme a conduit le Sultan à saper de ses mains, dans ses plus profonds fondements, le patrimoine que ses aïeux lui avait laissé ? c'est ce que nous nous proposons d'étudier en évitant de répéter tout ce qui avait été dit jusqu'à présent sur ce sujet.

I

C'est une révolution qui a fait monter Abd-ul-Hamid sur le trône ; la déposition de son oncle et la maladie de son frère ont formé devant ses yeux un tableau qui ne s'est jamais effacé depuis. ·En même temps, il a vu dans ce qui s'était passé un enseignement dont il devait faire son profit.

Le courant libéral et constitutionnel ne convenait pas à la nature et aux idées du monarque ; pourtant ce courant présentait dans le pays une force respectable ; il fallait une autre force pour remplacer celle-ci ; quelle pouvait être cette force ?   Abd-ul-Hamid y a pensé sérieusement et après mûre réflexion a trouvé la *force musulmane,* le *fanatisme* pour faire contre-poids ; et tandis que d'un côté il promulguait la Constitution et ordonnait l'ouverture de ce malheureux· parlement ottoman qui ne devait avoir que deux sessions, de l'autre il invitait à Constantinople les plus influents Cheikhs et Mollahs des· diverses provinces de la Turquie et quelques notabilités religieuses d'autres pays islamiques pour s'entourer d'eux et en faire ses organes.

Grandi entre les mains de quelques ulémas et eunuques fanatiques, ayant reçu une éducation exclusivement religieuse, dans laquelle la superstition tient la place la plus importante, Abd-ul-Hamid était porté par sa nature soupçonneuse et par son éducation intolérante à subir les influences de ces serviteurs du Coran, qui ont presque tous exploité les faiblesses du souverain dans un but de profit personnel.

Le Sultan et ses créatures ont travaillé la population musulmane pendant plus de quinze ans en excitant ses passions fanatiques contre la chrétienté ; après avoir créé, sous l'impulsion de l'eunuque Hafiz Behram (mort depuis), l'affaire d'Arabi pacha en Egypte, après avoir caressé pendant quelque temps, sous l'influence du Cheikh Eb-ul-Huda (celui qu'on appelle communément à Constantinople le jésuite musulman) le rêve de jeter avec les pays islamiques les bases d'une grande union musulmane dont le Sultan serait le chef en sa qualité' de Calife (qualité contestée en Perse, au Maroc et dans une partie du Hédjaz même), la camarilla du Palais a changé de tactique et toute l'action a été centralisée dans le pays même.

Les libéraux ottomans, les auteurs de la Constitution, avaient dit· aux populations de l'Empire ⁚

Ce sont l'égalité et la justice qui régneront désormais dans le pays ; le musulman y gagnera autant que le chrétien ; ce qui lui est soustrait comme prépondérance politique, sera sans doute gagné par les progrès matériels et moraux qui résulteront d'un régime tolérant et juste ; régime qui consolidera en même temps l'existence chancelante de l'Empire.

Le Sultan et la camarilla du Palais, pour donner le change à l'opinion publique musulmane et la détourner de sa direction, ont dit à l'adepte du Coran : 'Constitution ! . . . Parlement ! . . . Égalité ! . . . mais ne vois-tu pas que c'est là ta perte à toi ? Tes pères ont conquis ce pays avec leur sang, ils ont réduit les *guiavours* (infidèles) à l'état d'esclaves et tu veux en faire tes égaux ! ne sens-tu pas qu'en agissant ainsi non seulement tu méconnais la loi du Prophète, mais encore tu lèse tes propres intérêts ? Ce pays est à toi et ta religion te défend de traiter d'égal celui qui est destiné à n'être que ton esclave ; au lieu de lui faire de nouvelles concessions, tu dois au contraire lui retirer les avantages qu'il a su conquérir dans le courant des temps ; c'est là ton vrai rôle ! '

Et tandis que le Gouvernement essayait avec une mauvaise foi manifeste d'annuler les privilèges des communautés chrétiennes, ne craignant pas même de provoquer la fermeture des églises grecques, comme cela s'est produit en 1890, tandis que les chrétiens se voyaient écartés des fonctions publiques et on leur rendait difficile l'accès de plusieurs écoles supérieures pour qu'ils ne pussent se créer des titres aux fonctions publiques, une pression économique était simultanément opérée sur eux, afin de les réduire à la misère et faire ressortir par là leur situation de nations conquises ; on espérait en même temps prouver aux yeux des populations musulmanes la supériorité de ce nouveau courant, qui leur procurerait des avantages matériels.

Comme tous les hommes d'une éducation bornée, Abd-ul-Hamid a toujours cru à la toute-puissance de l'or ; l'expérience qu'il a faite de certains hommes publics d'Europe et d'une partie de la presse européenne n'a pas été pour peu dans cette conviction ; aussi en créant une question économique dans son pays au détriment des chrétiens, il espérait leur enlever tout moyen d'action, tandis qu'il croyait s'attacher davantage les musulmans qui, suivant son opinion, devaient gagner le terrain perdu par les chrétiens.

Il ne prévoyait pas, le malheureux souverain, que rendre la vie impossible aux chrétiens, c'était provoquer chez eux des velléités de révolte et que cette politique aurait en même temps pour contre-coup de tourner contre lui l'élément musulman, dont la situation économique est intimement liée à celle des chrétiens, le commerce du pays se trouvant entre les mains de ceux-ci.

Il ne prévoyait pas surtout qu'en mettant le hola contre l'élément chrétien ce qu'il encourageait ce n'était pas l'esprit de progrès chez le musulman, mais bien le fanatisme, cette soif de massacre et de pillage dont l'Europe avait vu de si tristes exemples en Bulgarie et qui devaient se renouveler d'une manière plus cruelle encore en Arménie et à Constantinople même.

II

C'est dans.lès premières .années du règne d'Abd-ul-Hamid qu'un diplomate ottoman, élève du grand-vizir Réchid Pacha, et incarnant en sa personne les idées du parti rétrograde vieux-ture, qui avait été écarté des affaires publiques durant tout le règne d'Abd-ul-Aziz, a eu l'occasion de s'approcher du souverain et de lui présenter un manuscrit qui n'était autre que la traduction en turc du *Prince* de Machiavel. Ce diplomate-traducteur qui devait avoir une si malheureuse influence sur les destinées de la Turquie et qui, lors de l'ouverture de la question bulgare, a mis dans le palais de Yildiz les fondements de cet effacement à outrance devant la Russie, s'appelait Youssouf Riza bey (depuis Youssouf Riza pacha, mort en 1893), président de la Commission des Réfugiés après la guerre turco-russe et conseiller, intime de Sa Majesté.

Après les détrônements successifs de son oncle et de son frère, la hardie tentative d'Ali-Suavi qui, peu de temps après l'avénement d'Abd-ul-Hamid, a attaqué avec trois cents réfugiés musulmans de Roumélie le palais de Dolma-Baghtché et a réussi à pénétrer jusque dans les appartements mêmes du souverain, avait eu sur le caractère soupçonneux de celui-ci une influence désastreuse. On a souvent dit que le souverain actuel de la Turquie était hanté par la folie de persécution ; le Sultan n'est sans doute pas un irresponsable ; mais il est évident que son caractère le pousse à voir noir partout et à douter de tout.

Déjà immédiatement après le coup de main d'Ali-Suavi, un certain Youssouf bey, mort plus tard en exil, le tcherkess Ahmed Djelaleddine, de l'entourage du souverain, et le général de division Hadji Hassan pacha, gouverneur de Béchiktach, avaient organisé, par ordre d'Abd-ul-Hamid, une espèce de police politique autour du Palais et dans la ville. Cela avait été le premier pas dans le système de 'rapports secrets.'

La lecture de la traduction du *Prince* et les conseils intéressés du rusé Youssouf Riza ont raffermi Abd-ul-Hamid dans cette voie ; il est arrivé graduellement à faire de toute l'organisation administrative, judiciaire et militaire de la Turquie une vaste filière de police secrète dont le centre se trouve au palais de Yildiz dans son cabinet de travail même. Pensant avec raison que tout espionnage sans contrôle ne peut être qu'une duperie, le Sultan a voulu contrôler les faits et gestes de ses 'serviteurs' les plus 'fidèles,' et jusque de ceux que sa confiance chargeait d'espionner les autres ; on a établi au Palais un 'cabinet politique' dont le premier titulaire fut Ahmed Djelaleddine (actuellement général de division, quoiqu'il n'ait conquis ses grades que dans le noble métier d'espionnage), et dont le titulaire actuel est Cadri bey, ancien secrétaire d'Ahmed Djelaleddine, devenu plus tard son ennemi et son dénonciateur. Mais à côté de ce cabinet officiel, d'autres cabinets politiques pullulent dans le palais, dans les bureaux des ministères, dans toutes les classes de la société, dans les résidences des personnalités en vue, dans les *harems*, et jusque dans certaines maisons malfamées de Péra.

Depuis les grands dignitaires de l'Empire jusqu'au dernier greffier de tribunal tout le monde se moucharde réciproquement ; et comme les hommes de réelle capacité et d'honneur ne pouvaient pas être utiles au Sultan dans cette nouvelle voie, ils ont dû céder leurs places à des sycophantes sans conscience qui se signalaient par leurs intrigues et dont le favoritisme insensé du souverain faisait des personnalités importantes.

La conséquence de ce système a été que pendant les vingt dernières années toutes les grandes charges de l'Empire, toutes les fonctions importantes ont passé entre les mains des mouchards.

Lord Salisbury, parlant il y a un an sur la situation actuelle de la Turquie, déplorait cette pénurie d'hommes d'état capables qui est vraiment la plus grande pauvreté pour un empire ; cette pénurie, c'est le système d'espionnage d'Abd-ul-Hamid qui l'a créée et rien ne peut actuellement y remédier, car pour rendre à l'administration sa marche normale il faudrait renvoyer ou pensionner plus de cinquante mille fonctionnaires !

Les suites de cette politique du Sultan ont été incalculables ; les conditions les plus élémentaires d'une administration régulière ont été négligées. Les confusions créées par des rapports secrets contradictoires ont paralysé la marche régulière des affaires ; les créatures du Palais et les mouchards de l'administration ont profité des circonstances pour contenter des animosités personnelles et pour rançonner de paisibles citoyens. Et comme avec un rouage pareil il est naturel que tout le monde ait des griefs—le voleur autant que le volé, l'un pour ne pas pouvoir voler davantage, l'autre pour être privé de son bien—il en est résulté un mécontentement général qui, par une fatalité compréhensible, s'est tourné contre le souverain. De sorte qu'aujourd'hui à Constantinople ceux qui parlent avec plus d'aigreur contre le Sultan sont souvent ses grands espions mêmes.

Quelques chiffres d'ailleurs suffisent pour prouver à quelle extrémité sont arrivées les choses. Le nombre des ' rapports secrets ' adressés journellement de Constantinople et des provinces à des personnes ayant des *relations directes* avec le souverain est évalué à six mille et le nombre de ceux soumis au Sultan lui-même à plus de trois cents ; quatre chambellans sont chargés de dépouiller cette volumineuse correspondance et d'en donner connaissance au souverain ; il y a dans le palais plusieurs commissions qui s'occupent d'enquêtes sur les faits rapportés et des tribunaux exceptionnels sont formés pour questionner les personnes dénoncées. Les grands-vizirs mêmes, tout en gardant leurs charges, passent quelquefois devant ces tribunaux pour répondre d'un fait dénoncé.

· La méfiance du Sultan a augmenté d'une manière exagérée le personnel du Palais, qui monte actuellement à douze mille personnes, tandis que l'infanterie et la cavalerie chargées de la garde de la résidence impériale présentent un nombre de vingt-cinq mille soldats campés dans diverses casernes aux environs du Yildiz et formant un triple cordon.

Beaucoup de nouvelles fonctions ont été créées pour caser les soi-disant ' dévoués ' de sa Majesté et on a prodigué outre mesure titres, dignités et décorations. Le nombre des maréchaux et des vizirs dépasse actuellement les cent-cinquante et il existe un nombre incalculable de généraux de division, de généraux de brigade et de colonels qui n'ont jamais vu le feu autrement que dans des tableaux.

Et tandis que les dépenses augmentaient sans cesse, la pression exercée sur les chrétiens venant s'ajouter aux effets de la mauvaise administration, diminuait les revenus. C'est ainsi qu'a été créée, aussi au point de vue financier, une situation presque inextricable.

Et il ne faut pas croire que toutes ces combinaisons ont eu au moins pour résultat d'assurer au Sultan un service de renseignements exacts ; s'il y a quelqu'un mal renseigné en Turquie, c'est assurément le Sultan ; tout le monde est intéressé à le tromper, car c'est à force d'alimenter ses craintes que les grands et les petits espions réussissent à garder leurs places ! [1]

III

Ainsi d'un côté on excitait le musulman contre le chrétien, tandis que de l'autre le système d'espionnage inaugurait un nouveau régime dans lequel toutes les injustices étaient possibles.

Après les massacres bulgares, après la guerre turco-russe, la question arménienne a eu le malheur d'éclore juste au moment où ce double courant cherchait un nouvel aliment.

L'Anatolie, dont l'Arménie forme une partie importante, a toujours été considérée par les ' diplomates ' du régime actuel comme le dernier refuge des Turcs ; ces ' diplomates ' se sont habitués depuis longtemps à l'idée d'être les *mussafirs* (les hôtes) de l'Europe, et ils connaissent très bien les visées de l'Autriche sur la Macédoine, de la France sur la Syrie et de l'Italie sur la Tripolitaine ; d'autre part ils ne sont jamais sûrs du Hédjaz, où l'élément turc est exécré

---

[1] Au sujet de l'extension qu'a prise l'espionnage, voilà une parabole qu'on raconte souvent à Constantinople et qui ne manque pas de saveur :

'Le bon Dieu va un jour à Constantinople pour s'enquérir *de visu* de la situation ; accompagné de l'ange Gabriel il s'approche du toit de la première maison qu'il voit et regardant d'une fenêtre il aperçoit une foule de gens qui écrivent des lettres, en évitant chacun que leurs voisins lisent la lettre écrite.

— Que font ces gens ? demande le bon Dieu à l'ange.

— Ils font des rapports secrets au Sultan.

Et l'ange Gabriel d'ajouter malicieusement :

·—Ne vous penchez pas tant, Seigneur ; s'ils vous apercevaient ils seraient capables de faire un rapport secret même contre vous ! '

et qui se trouve d'ailleurs en état de perpétuelle révolte. A la première guerre européenne il faudrait sans doute aux Turcs de reculer vers l'Asie, si même Constantinople restait entre leurs mains ; or, en cédant quelques provinces de la frontière à la Russie, il restait encore assez de place pour faire bonne figure comme puissance asiatique de second ordre, et voilà que les compétitions arméniennes venaient créer des difficultés de ce côté.

On a persuadé le Sultan qu'il hâterait la perte de son empire en acquiesçant à la moindre concession en faveur des Arméniens ; incapable de comprendre qu'en défaut de tout avantage politique il devait au moins à ses sujets arméniens une administration impartiale et juste, le Sultan a, au contraire, voulu étouffer la question en opprimant le malheureux peuple auquel cette question appartenait.

La seule consolation de l'Arménien avait été jusque là la liberté relative avec laquelle il pouvait exercer sa foi, parler sa langue, vénérer les grandes figures de son histoire. Quand l'Arménien de Constantinople, à la fête du héros national Vartan, chantait à l'école de son quartier la cantate de vengeance et allait voir le soir au théâtre l'épopée de la guerre religieuse de 451 (p. J.-C.), il était content. Il y avait là une vie idéale, faite de souvenirs, qui suffisait à satisfaire ses aspirations.

Le Sultan, aveuglé par son fanatisme, a attaqué la nation arménienne de son côté le plus sensible ; il n'existait encore aucun comité révolutionnaire quand le Sultan a défendu l'impression dans son empire et l'étude dans les écoles arméniennes de l'histoire d'Arménie, ainsi que les représentations théâtrales tirées de cette histoire. Peu à peu l'oppression s'est accentuée ; il a été défendu aux journaux d'employer le mot 'Arménie,' de faire allusion au passé de la nation, de traiter même les affaires nationales. On a commencé à arrêter les Arméniens sous de futiles prétextes ; porter la coiffure nationale dite Arakhdji même était considéré un crime et les délinquants jetés dans les cachots.

Les espions enchérissant sur les tendances du Palais, se sont mis de suite à signaler des complots et révolutions alors qu'il n'en existait aucun. Tout le monde s'attaquait à l'Arménien et une animosité de race et de religion, alimentée aussi en partie par la presse turque de Constantinople, s'est ainsi enracinée peu à peu dans le cœur du Turc.

Il n'en fallait pas davantage pour donner l'éveil à l'Arménien ; privé de son histoire passée, il était naturel qu'il désirât s'en faire une nouvelle ; l'oppression morale et économique l'y poussait déjà ; c'est presque sous le coup d'une nécessité que les comités se sont formés et les Turcs s'en sont effrayés avec d'autant plus de raison que l'existence des comités se révélait à Constantinople et dans les provinces par une activité calculée et méthodique.

Un gouvernement sage aurait vu dans la formation même de ces comités et surtout dans la facilité avec laquelle ils réussissaient à enrôler des adeptes la condamnation de sa politique, puisque cette politique donnait naissance à une organisation dangereuse pour l'Empire. Le Sultan y a vu, au contraire, la confirmation de la justesse de la direction qu'il avait donnée à la cupidité de ses fonctionnaires et au fanatisme de ses sujets musulmans.

Alors, les régiments kurdes de Hamidieh ont été formés, tandis que le régime des suspects devenait de jour en jour plus sévère; des arrestations en masse ont eu lieu et les tortures les plus barbares ont été données aux Arméniens dans les prisons.

Les ulémas et les cheikhs excitant continuellement leurs coreligionnaires, les fonctionnaires et les espions opprimant sans cesse les Arméniens qu'ils signalaient au fanatisme musulman comme ' les ennemis de la foi et de l'empire!' (*duchmeni dine ou devlett*), il en est résulté une tension de rapports qui devait naturellement avoir pour conséquence l'effusion de sang à la première occasion.

L'écho que les massacres de Sassoun ont trouvé en Europe y a servi de prétexte; le courage avec lequel les Arméniens ont mis sous les yeux du monde civilisé les circonstances dans lesquelles leurs malheureux compatriotes avaient été passés au fil de l'épée a encore aiguisé la haine du Sultan, qui se voyait cette fois personnellement en cause.

Ayant ordonné lui-même le massacre, c'était sa responsabilité personnelle qui se trouvait engagée; le Sultan a vu qu'il y allait peut-être de son trône et n'a pas hésité à jouer son atout.

Aussi son premier soin a-t-il été de mettre le hola sur l'Arménien qu'il a dénoncé cette fois comme en état de rébellion ouverte; il s'est ensuite servi du fanatisme musulman comme d'une arme à opposer à toute intervention étrangère en faveur des Arméniens et même à toute tentative de protection morale.

En effet, avant que les massacres eussent commencé, il signalait déjà l'éventualité de l'explosion du fanatisme musulman aux diplomates étrangers toutes les fois que ceux-ci le mettaient au pied de mur pour obtenir quelques concessions!

Et il faut noter que le courant libéral chez les Turcs reprenait de force juste au même moment; on avait découvert des sociétés secrètes a l'école militaire, à l'école de médecine et à l'école préparatoire de Kouléli; et au journal *Hurriett* (La Liberté) publié depuis plus d'un an à Londres par un éminent publiciste arabe qui signe Djivanpire, étaient venus s'ajouter le *Mechverett* (Le Parlementarisme) et le *Mizan* (La Balance). Le danger grondait aussi de ce côté, il fallait une nouvelle diversion.[2]

---

[2] Au lendemain de la manifestation arménienne du 30 septembre 1895 le parti jeune-turc a publié un manifeste à Constantinople approuvant les revendications des Arméniens et invitant les musulmans à s'unir à eux; l'avocat Adjem Izzet effendi, chef du Comité Hurriett, a été arrêté et on ne sait pas ce qu'il est devenu depuis.

Porte (30 septembre 1895) qui avait provoqué les massacres ; c'est une grande erreur : la manifestation armée, si regrettable qu'elle soit, n'a servi que de prétexte ; elle n'a nullement été une cause ; c'est la politique du Sultan, des ordres émanant directement du Palais qui ont été cause des massacres ; les consuls étrangers en Arménie pourront déclarer que les préparatifs en étaient faits depuis trois mois et que la menace en était proférée partout publiquement.

D'ailleurs les derniers événements de Constantinople n'ont laissé aucun doute quant à la culpabilité et la complicité des autorités dans l'effusion de sang.

IV

Et   présent quelle solution pourrait dénouer la situation ? voilà la question, très grave, qui occupe en ce moment le monde politique.

Avant de dire quelques mots sur ce sujet, nous voulons détruire certaines illusions qu'on se fait encore en Europe.

On croit que tout en laissant au Sultan continuer sa manière de gouverner, on peut améliorer la situation des Arméniens et par conséquent la situation générale de la Turquie. C'est une erreur.

Le Sultan doit régner mais non pas gouverner. Rien à espérer tant qu'il aura la faculté de se mêler des affaires d'état ; cela doit être le premier point du *credo* dans la solution à adopter.

Il faudrait donc établir à Constantinople un contrôle européen ou une représentation nationale, qui aurait alors pour base une constitution élaborée conformément au principe de décentralisation, seul principe qui puisse donner satisfaction aux différents éléments formant la population de l'Empire ottoman. Cela serait le système autrichien de *nationalités*, atténué et approprié aux circonstances locales.

Pourtant, même en cette seconde éventualité la surveillance européenne serait nécessaire pour plusieurs années, afin de contrecarrer les velléités du souverain qui voudrait sans doute attenter de nouveau aux droits de ses sujets, comme il l'a fait une première fois.

Et l'agrément du Sultan à la solution, comment l'obtenir ?

Voici notre idée là-dessus : Si les ambassadeurs des six grandes puissances, agissant loyalement (mais avec une loyauté sincère), se rendaient ensemble au Palais de Yildiz et présentaient au Sultan, *comme à un condamné*, les *décisions* de l'Europe, avec la menace réelle d'une rupture collective immédiate, tout serait accepté en dix minutes.

Mais tant qu'il se trouvera une puissance quelconque, qui intriguera, ouvertement ou dans les coulisses peu importe, ou qui gardera simplement une attitude réservée, le Sultan n'acceptera rien.

Il y a encore l'emploi de la force ; là il s'agirait de la manière dont la force serait employée.   Si l'on agit énergiquement, le Sultan, poltron de nature, cédera ; mais si l'on emploie la force graduelle- ment, d'une manière soi-disant méthodique, une opposition plus ou moins sérieuse est possible ; le Sultan brûlerait alors ses vaisseaux en tâchant de provoquer une guerre européenne ; mais l'Europe se rendrait ridicule si Abd-ul-Hamid pouvait faire la pluie et le beau temps suivant ses convenances.

DIRAN KÉLÉKIAN.

When the first Board schools were established the Voluntary schools, then without rivals in the field, were educating about two-fifths of the children who ought to have been in elementary schools. At the present date, after a quarter of a century of severe competition, they are educating four-sevenths. The number of children in Voluntary schools was in 1870 little more than a million; in 1895, nearly two millions and a half.[1] It is instructive to inquire why the promoters of a system which has shown such a marvellous power of growth should be now crying out for their schools to be saved from extinction. A review of the facts will prove that the difficulties which are now occupying the public mind have been before statesmen for half a century, and that, although they have been much discussed, and to some extent successfully evaded, they have never been solved. It will also show how ignorant of the history of the past those party politicians were who brought against the proposals of the Government in the Bill of 1896 the accusation of novelty.

The education of the people had been taken in hand by the Church of England, and other religious societies, long before the nation awoke to its obligations in that regard. The first Treasury grant, amounting to 20,000*l.*, and appropriated to the erection of 'schoolhouses,' was made in 1833. From that date to 1870 the action of the State in promoting national education was confined to the grant of continually increasing subsidies to Voluntary schools established and managed by religious bodies, and to such control as conditions attached to the reception of the grant conferred. For a long time the idea of establishing schools which should be independent of all religious bodies was not within the sphere of practical politics; separation between secular and religious instruction was generally scouted. In 1840 the Government were 'strongly of opinion that no plan of education ought to be encouraged in which intellectual instruction is not subordinate to the regulation of the thoughts and habits of the children by the doctrines of revealed religion.' As late as 1853 a grant was refused to a secular school on the ground that 'education grants had not hitherto been applicable

[1] The actual numbers were—in 1870, 1,152,389; in 1895, 2,445,812.

to schools exclusively secular, and that they' (the Committee of
Council) 'believed that such a decision was in accordance with the
views of the great majority of the promoters of education.' On the
other hand, many Voluntary school managers resented the mild State
interference which was the accompaniment of State aid; some would
accept neither the one nor the other. State control was as much a
bugbear fifty years ago as control of ratepayers is to-day. The
'management clauses' which it was proposed, in 1847, should be
inserted in the trust-deeds of all Church of England schools as a
condition of a building grant provoked an angry controversy extending over many years. The right of the State to interfere at all was
denied. It was maintained that the education of the people was the
exclusive prerogative of the religious denominations. Freedom from
State control was demanded by Nonconformists and Roman Catholics
as earnestly as by Churchmen.

In 1853 Lord John Russell introduced the first Education Bill.
It was a permissive Bill, and applied to boroughs only; the absence
at that time of any suitable local authority in rural districts was an
insuperable bar to its extension to them. It made the town council,
acting through a committee, to which persons not members of the
council might be appointed, the education authority. Schools which
were eligible for grants from, and were regularly inspected by, the
Committee of Council might, on their own application, be aided out
of the borough rate. The rate aid was to be in the form of a grant
on average attendance, and was to be supplementary to a prescribed
amount derived from subscriptions, endowments, or school fees. The
charge on the borough was limited to the produce of a 6*d.* rate.
Aggrieved managers had an appeal to the Committee of Council.
Lord John Russell disclaimed, on the part of the Government, any
attempt to disturb the then existing system, based on voluntary effort;
the object of the Bill was to strengthen and improve it. The Government were against secular education, and thought there should be
religious training in the schools; but there was a provision in the
Bill giving parents a right to withdraw their children from religious
instruction. Objection was made then, as it is made now, that
individuals might refuse to pay rates that were to be applied to purposes of which they disapproved. But the rate was not to be ear-
marked, but paid out of the general borough fund. A conscientious
and recalcitrant ratepayer would have to refuse to contribute at all
towards the revenues of the borough, on the ground that some part
of its expenditure was such as he could not conscientiously approve.
Scruples of this sort, if general, would put a stop to all social combination, either for local or national purposes. The establishment
by a municipality of schools of its own, supported out of the borough
rate, side by side with the schools under voluntary management,
does not seem to have been contemplated in the Bill. It was thought

that with rate aid Voluntary schools would in boroughs have covered the ground. The country schools, excluded by the Bill of 1853 from the possibility of rate aid, were to be consoled by an increase of the capitation grant. It was a scheme of State aid to country schools and rate aid to town schools. The Bill was coldly received. It was accused of novelty. The town councils were reluctant. The Bill was dropped. The Government declared they would pass it 'in another session, but they never did. On the collapse of the rate-aid scheme of the Government the increased capitation grant, originally intended for the counties only, was extended to the boroughs, and for seventeen years longer the financial assistance given out of public funds to elementary education was exclusively State aid.

Simultaneously with the Government two other parties in Parliament were promoting education Bills. The one party aimed at the establishment in every place of a system of free schools, supported by local rates, and managed by local committees specially elected for that purpose by the ratepayers; these schools were to impart secular instruction, only leaving to parents, guardians, and religious teachers the inculcation of doctrinal religion. But opportunity was to be given for denominational schools to come under these local committees, and obtain support from the rates, upon condition that they restricted the inculcation of doctrinal religion to fixed times, and allowed scholars to be withdrawn by their parents from such lessons, and that they provided free secular instruction. The other party relied for the advancement of national education upon voluntary effort, stimulated and supported by State subsidies, although they admitted the necessity of some provision for establishing schools in places where voluntary effort failed, and proposed that it should be a condition in such schools that the Bible should be read.

In 1855 there were three education Bills before the House of Commons, all of which embraced provisions for aiding the existing Voluntary schools out of local rates. First, there was a Bill introduced by Lord John Russell, which permitted both towns and country parishes to submit schemes to the Committee of Council for both aiding and establishing elementary schools. The second Bill was brought in by Sir John Pakington, and may be considered to embody the views of the progressive Conservatives of that day. The educational areas were to be boroughs and Poor-law unions. The education authority was to be a school committee specially elected by the ratepayers for the purposes of the Act. The committee might levy an education rate not exceeding 6d. in the pound, to be paid out of the borough fund in towns, and the Poor-rate in the country. All the existing schools which were recognised by the Committee of Council were to share in the rate, and in the case of new schools established by the local committees the religious teaching was to be in accordance with the religion of the majority. of the persons in the district for which the schools were to be established. No child was to be excluded from any rate-aided school in consequence of its religion. The third Bill, promoted by the partisans of secular education, proposed the establishment of a Board of Public Instruction, which was to divide England and Wales into convenient education areas, in each of which there was to be a committee, specially elected by the ratepayers, with power to establish and maintain out of rates free secular schools. But, in order to afford the scholars the opportunity of receiving definite religious instruction, the committee of each district was to set apart certain hours in every week, not exceeding one-fourth of the time devoted to general instruction, during which the schools should be closed. The treatment which this extreme party was at that time willing to extend to denominational schools is significant. The managers might sell the school to the committee, retaining the right to give such religious instruction as they thought fit in it on Sundays, and during those hours in the week on which the schools of the committee were closed for the purpose of allowing the scholars to attend religious instruction; or they might retain the management, and receive rate aid from the school committee, on condition that the inculcation of distinctive doctrinal religion did not take place on any week-day between 9 and 11 A.M., or between 2 and 4 P.M. All these three Bills were discussed, and finally dropped without any definite decision having been arrived at.

After abortive attempts at legislation in succeeding sessions, it appeared to the Government of the day that the education question was ripe for being hung up for some years by a Royal Commission; and a Commission was accordingly appointed in 1858, presided over by the Duke of Newcastle, which finally reported in 1861.

A minority of the Commission, which represented a considerable body of opinion out of doors, still clung to the doctrine that voluntary effort was sufficient to provide education for the people, and that all State interference should be resisted. If the religious bodies accepted State subsidies for the erection of schools, it should be on the distinct condition that the State should take no part in their maintenance or management; and, in accordance with this view, they desired that the annual grants then made for maintenance should be gradually withdrawn. But this party, finding itself in a minority on the Commission, deferred to the opinion of the majority, and, 'on the rejection of their own view, cordially adopted in the second resort the scheme of assistance approved by the majority of their colleagues, which they regarded as better in every respect, and, above all, a far nearer approach to justice than the extremely partial system' then in operation. It is remarkable that in the whirligig of time those who are in many respects the successors of this party should now.

occupy the position of contending that, while the religious bodies may properly be called upon to furnish the whole cost of erecting and keeping in repair school buildings, the entire cost of school maintenance, teachers' salaries, apparatus, books and so forth, ought to be paid out of public funds.

The report of the Duke of Newcastle's Commission became, by this yielding of the minority to the views of the majority, a unanimous one in favour of rate as well as State aid to all elementary schools, and of their supervision by municipal and county authorities. The Commission thought that all assistance given to the annual maintenance of schools should be reduced to grants of two kinds—the first paid out of the general taxation of the country, and the second paid out of the county rate ; that every county should appoint a county board of education, six to be elected by the court of quarter sessions (at that time the only governing body in the county), and six others co-opted by the members so elected. In municipal boroughs containing a population of more than 40,000 inhabitants the town council was to act as its own county authority, and was to appoint a borough board of education. They recommended that the State grant should be paid direct to the managers of the schools, in consideration of the fulfilment of certain general conditions as to the sanitary condition of the buildings and the discipline, efficiency, and general character of the school, and that the amount should be based on average attendance. The payment out of the county rate was to depend upon results ascertained by the county, and was to be a specific payment for each child which passed a satisfactory examination before a county examiner in reading, writing, and arithmetic, and, if a girl, also in plain work. They wished to preserve the leading features of the existing system, and they especially adhered to the principles to which it was, in their opinion, indebted for no small part of its success, viz. :

(a) Non-interference in the religious training which is given by different denominations of Christians ;

(b) Absence of all central control over the direct management of schools ; adding, that it might become the duty of the council to make provision for insuring to the children of the poor the benefit of education 'without exposing their parents to a violation of their religious convictions.'

These recommendations shared the common fate of the recommendations of royal commissions : no attempt was ever made by the Government to carry them into effect. They suggested, however, to the Government a most pernicious change in the mode of dispensing the State grant. No rate aid was to be given to elementary schools, but by the Revised Code of 1862 the State aid was to be henceforward given, not on the general conditions recommended by the Commission, but upon the system of payment for results on which the Commission had recommended that the local authorities should dispense their subsidy. Elementary education has scarcely yet recovered from the disastrous effects of this change.

In 1867 and 1868 Bills were brought in by Messrs. Bruce, Forster, and Egerton, supported by moderate members of both parties, to give rate aid to the existing schools, and to establish those local education authorities whose existence is a condition-precedent to the distribution of such aid. The authority was to be a committee appointed in boroughs by the town council, and in other places by the ratepayers. The committees might, in case of local deficiency, build and maintain schools of their own; but all existing schools might place themselves in union with the committees, and were entitled on the fulfilment of certain specific conditions to payments out of rates on a scale fixed by the Bill. The conditions were that the school should be open to inspection, conform to the Code, and have an effective conscience clause. But the school committee was 'not to interfere with the constitution, management, arrangements, discipline, or instruction.' These well-meant efforts to provide rate aid on fair terms to existing Voluntary schools, without impairing their distinctive religious teaching, were coldly received, and the Bills had ultimately to be withdrawn.

Finally, in 1870 the strong Liberal Government of Mr. Gladstone, in its second session of Parliament, brought in an Education Bill. The fundamental principles of the Bill introduced by Mr. Forster differed very widely from those of the Elementary Education Act, 1870. The fatal error of making every rural parish, however small, into an independent school district is common to both. But in the Bill the School Board which was to be the education authority was to be appointed in boroughs by the town council, and in rural parishes by the vestry. Mr. Forster, like all other promoters of education Bills, was greatly hampered by the non-existence in country districts of any efficient organisation for local self-government. The education of the people was beginning to be regarded as one of the more important functions of Government, and one that could be most effectively discharged by means of local administration. But while in the boroughs the town councils furnished a fairly effective machinery, in the country districts the promoters of national education were confronted with the almost impossible task of having to establish a system of local administration without any local body being available to which it could be properly entrusted. The county area furnished nothing but the court of quarter sessions; the union, nothing but the board of guardians; the parish, nothing but the vestry. If county and district councils had been in existence in 1870, it is impossible to believe that parishes and vestries would have been selected as the areas and authorities for education purposes. In the Bill the function of the local education authority was not confined to the provision and maintenance of schools of its own to supplement deficiencies, as is that of the School Board under the Act. It could grant pecuniary assistance, of such amount and for such purposes as it thought fit, to all Voluntary schools in its district willing to receive it, provided that such assistance was to be granted on equal terms to all Voluntary schools, upon conditions to be approved by the Education Department. This general and elastic power of giving rate aid to Voluntary schools was in accordance with Mr. Forster's own Bills of 1867 and 1868, and with the various legislative proposals made to Parliament from 1853 downwards. Its adoption would have prevented the rivalry which afterwards sprung up between Board and Voluntary schools. In towns, where this rivalry is most prevalent, the school board of the Bill would have been practically a mere committee of the town council, bound to have regard in the exercise of its powers to the general interests of the town. It would have clearly been the interest of the town at large to keep the already existing schools on foot, to make them perfectly efficient, and to build new schools only so far as it might become necessary to supplement existing accommodation. The interest of the managers of Voluntary schools would have been identical with that of the town; and when interests are identical, parties easily come to terms. In large and populous parishes of an urban character the same considerations would have prevailed. In rural parishes the contest, such as it is, has been between the two systems, not between the two kinds of schools. In the country, Board and Voluntary schools scarcely even co-exist in the same district, and their rivalry is almost unknown.

The two fundamental changes which the Bill of 1870 underwent in passing through Parliament, both of which were brought about by the friends of Voluntary schools, were :

(1) That the local education authorities were to be independently elected, and that education was to be thus separated from the other functions of local self-government.

(2) That the new authorities were to be deprived of the power of using the machinery of the existing schools for the establishment of a comprehensive scheme of national education. They were to set up a rival system.

Those who uphold the separate election of school authorities with independent rating powers have a very narrow view of the principles of local administration. Education, though an important, is not the only function of Government. A system by which a separate body is to be separately elected for the performance of each separate function of government, and is to levy such rates as it deems necessary for the performance of its particular duty, without any regard to the other wants, the rate-paying capacity, and the general finance of the district for which it acts, will soon bring local self-government into

disrepute.   There must be one body, by however many committees
it may act, to exercise paramount control.

The result has proved that the friends of Voluntary schools were
not wise in rejecting the provisions of the Bill which rendered possible a concord between the representatives of the ratepayers and
the managers of Voluntary schools.   The School Boards in the towns
and populous places have well performed the duties put upon them
by the Act of 1870.   They have constructed a system of elementary
education which is inferior to that of other nations only because of the
early age at which children are withdrawn from instruction.   They
have, not unnaturally, pushed and extended their system in every·
direction; they have regarded efficiency before economy, and have
never spared the rates out of regard to the necessities of their districts
other than educational.   Unless some radical change can be speedily
made in the position of Voluntary schools in School Board districts,
all of them, except such as the strong religious feeling of their supporters can succeed in keeping on foot, must shortly disappear.

After a quarter of a century of the present dual system of
national education, the position and prospects of Voluntary schools
are found to differ diametrically in the country and in the towns.   In
rural districts the Board-school system is not spreading, and many
parishes which have come under it would rejoice in being emancipated,
if any practical means of getting rid of their School Boards were provided.   The Voluntary schools are in no danger of extinction.   The
dread of the cost of a School Board is so great that in a great number
of parishes the ratepayers are paying a voluntary rate to the Voluntary
school managers to escape the higher one which the establishment of
a School Board would impose upon them.   Nor are those who desire
educational progress at all anxious to see voluntary management
replaced in rural districts by that of School Boards.   Unsatisfactory
as the former may be to educational experts, the latter is generally
worse.   Rates are high because of the costs of elections, offices, and
management, not because in Board-school districts better salaries are
paid or a larger proportion of teachers supplied.   The class of people
who form a rural School Board are often quite unfit to have the control of a school.   The country parson, with all his alleged shortcomings,
is generally by character, by education, and by experience a better
manager, even from a secular point of view.

Urgently as country education demands reform, the universal
substitution of Board for Voluntary schools would be a step in the
wrong direction.   To improve country schools, Board and Voluntary,
two things are requisite—more money and better organisation.
Country School Boards have not unlimited resources : there are
many parishes in which any increase of the already monstrous
school rate is practically an impossibility.   Many Voluntary schools
have no endowments, and their subscriptions in times of agricultural

distress are difficult to keep up. Small schools are much more costly per head than large ones. Efficiency suffers from lack of means. In any grant made by the Exchequer to country schools, it would be difficult to defend upon any principle of justice its restriction to those under voluntary management. Two parishes may exist side by side in which there is equal need of additional funds to make the village school efficient. The parish which is under School Board management is probably the poorer of the two, lacking the wealthier residents whose subscriptions help to keep up the Voluntary school. It has greater burdens, for it has to pay for elections and management as well as for schools. It would be impossible to give a grant from the Exchequer to the richer parish and leave the poorer out in the cold. But in either case, unless effective precautions were taken, a grant would do little to relieve the financial difficulties of the managers. It would be swallowed up in relieving ratepayers or subscribers, and there would be nothing left for managers to spend upon the schools. It is indispensable that the additional grant should be under the supervision of some county authority if it is intended that it should reach the schools. But country schools want something much more than money. They want some system of organisation which will enable them to co-operate for common objects. The parish is too small an area to establish alone efficient education. The great success of Board Schools in towns is largely due to the fact that the School Board furnishes a centre of federation for the individual schools. The teachers have the prospect of promotion from school to school. Apparatus, pictures, and books can be transferred. Organising teachers and special lecturers can be employed. Centres for cookery classes, laundry-work, and manual instruction can be formed. Pupil-teachers can be taught more cheaply and more effectively in a common school. There is nothing of this kind in the country. I have heard of places in which confederations for such purposes of rural School Boards exist, but these are exceptions. Church schools dare not federate, for fear of losing their subscriptions. People will subscribe to their own village school who would, it is believed, cease to do so if the school became merged in a diocesan federation. Only a county education authority could form an effective nucleus for common action amongst the individual schools of the county.

But whilst in the country Voluntary schools are every bit as good as, if not better than, Board schools, and, although a little straitened at times for lack of money, are in no danger whatever of extinction, the result of the dual system in the towns has been disastrous to Voluntary schools, and the continued existence of a great many of them is in jeopardy. The Board-school system has spread over most of the towns, and flourishes in them. The Boards have in the rates a source of income which is practically unlimited, and their manage-

ment is never stinted for want of funds.   Moreover, the rate contribution to the Board school is drawn from the subscribers to Voluntary
schools equally with the rest.   Thus the supporters of Voluntary
schools have to pay twice over.   Many of them regard this as unjust ;
they cannot escape the rate, so they withdraw their subscription. The
rate of voluntary subscription per child is far lower in districts which
have School Boards than in those which have none.   The managers
of Voluntary schools in towns want the same things as those in the
country—money and organisation—whilst their rivals are amply provided with both.   The natural consequence is that, with some conspicuous exceptions, Voluntary schools in towns are generally inferior.
to Board schools.   They have worse buildings, worse apparatus, worse
paid head-teachers, assistants with inferior qualifications, and larger
classes for these teachers to manage and instruct.

How much more money do the Voluntary schools want, and
where is it to come from ?   The difference between the expenditure
of Board and Voluntary managers on school maintenance is in London
25s. per child, and in the large towns is, on the average, 12s. per child.
The first question that arises is, whether this difference can be
diminished by curtailing the expenditure of the School Boards.   It
is said that they are extravagant.   They are probably not so economical as they would be if they were responsible for the general finance
of their district as well as for its education ; but there is little doubt
that, on the whole, the ratepayers get excellent value for their money.
Increased economy will not do much to bridge over the difference
between Board and Voluntary school expenditure.   Neither is it possible that the cost of education can be arbitrarily fixed in advance, as
some persons have suggested.   It depends on the cost of buildings,
the price of apparatus, and the salaries of teachers.   These are regulated by the law of supply and demand.   Salaries, in particular, which
are frequently denounced as extravagant, are undoubtedly higher in
England than in France or Germany ; but as the general level of
elementary education amongst the mass of the population of this
country is lower than abroad, those who are to be teachers have to be
raised to a much greater height above their fellows.   They form a
class with special qualifications which cannot quickly be augmented,
and they command, in consequence, high salaries, without which their
services cannot be obtained.   It is thus impossible to place a limit
on the cost of education.   The State may fix its contribution, the
power of the School Board to rate may be restricted, but there must
be some authority behind whose liability is unlimited if the efficiency
of the Board schools is to be maintained.   It is contended by some
persons that the cost of School-board education might be lessened
by restricting it to the teaching of certain subjects, to be called
‘ elementary,’ and forbidding the Boards to give instruction in any
subject not included in the definition.   In many places the Boards

have responded to a popular demand for higher education, and have established excellent secondary schools. Until some better public provision is made for secondary education it would be the height of folly to stop these laudable efforts, highly popular among the rate-payers concerned. But whatever reasons may arise hereafter for placing secondary education in other hands, economy is not one of them. The Boards, as purveyors of higher education, allege that they make a profit which enures to the benefit of the ratepayers, and that the general cost of education to them is diminished, and not in-creased, by their operations. But so long as our industrial population is so inferior in elementary and technical knowledge to their rivals in other countries, any attempt to lower the quality of education is dangerous to our national interests, unless we could persuade other nations to step down to the same low level. There is a competition in these days among civilised nations in education as well as in arma-ments, and our national prosperity depends upon our keeping abreast of our rivals at whatever cost.

If Voluntary schools are to continue to exist in towns in a state of efficiency at all comparable to that of Board schools, the managers must be provided with means something like equal to those which their rivals enjoy. Whether aid can be accepted without destruction to the religious character of the school from the rates is a question upon which for fifty years the friends of Voluntary schools have been unable to make up their minds. It is impossible to settle such a question in the concluding lines of an article. But it may be useful to state some conclusions which seem to spring from the history of the past, and which must be borne in mind in any solution proposed:

1. An additional State subvention, given in towns to Board and Voluntary schools alike, will not redress the existing inequality in their resources. Whatever is given to the Voluntary schools must either be withheld from the Board schools or be such as the latter already possess. Whether it is possible to persuade Parliament to give to schools, because they are Voluntary, exceptional grants, which are neither now nor in the near future to be extended to Board schools, or whether, after so many schemes of rate aid have been proposed and none accepted, it is now possible to devise something which Parliament will adopt, are questions for the party politician.

2. The aid must be adequate. It must be sufficient to enable the managers of Voluntary schools to give an education as efficient as that of the Board schools. Any part of the excess of School-board expenditure which is due to extravagance, any saving which can be made in Voluntary schools by reason of unpaid services, may be deducted from the existing difference of resources; but the rest must be made up in full. Some plan will also have to be devised to secure that the aid will go to the school, and not to the subscribers,

otherwise it will be swallowed up by the latter, and the former will be no better off than before.

3. The aid must be elastic. It is impossible to regard the existing cost of education as a maximum which will never be exceeded. If the cost in Board schools increases, the Boards have the rates to fall back upon. The managers of Voluntary schools must have a source of income capable of simultaneous augmentation.

4. The aid must be permanent. Any relief given now to Voluntary schools which might be withdrawn a few years hence will only ensure their destruction. Differential treatment by the Exchequer, unless it is generally accepted, is a perilous expedient. There are so many ways in which a policy of this kind can be reversed—either by cutting off the supplies, or by extending the grants to the Board schools, and thus reviving the present inequality—that its permanence can only be relied on if it is the result of a common understanding.

5. Lastly, the managers of Voluntary schools must make up their minds to accept, along with increased grants of public money, increased public control. If aid come from the State, Parliament is sure to impose conditions with the view of securing the application of the special grant to increasing the efficiency of the schools. If from the rates, the representatives of the ratepayers must have some sort of voice in the management of the schools. The ingenious expedient of the Duke of Newcastle's Commission, to make rate aid a payment for results, is not likely to be accepted now. Payment for results is discredited as mischievous to education. Managers must submit to such conditions as ratepayers may properly require for securing the efficiency of the secular education in their schools; they may have to surrender some part of that independence of management which the Duke of Newcastle's Commission thought so valuable; the only thing which they cannot surrender, and for which they must stand out to the last, is full liberty to teach their distinctive religious doctrines to the children of their own communion. There is no reason from past history to suppose that Parliament will seek to take that liberty away.

JOHN E. GORST.

THE WESTRALIAN MINING 'BOOM'

BETWEEN the first day of March 1894 and the last day of September 1896 not less than 731 Western Australian gold-mining companies, with an aggregate nominal capital of 75,871,372*l*., have offered their shares for subscription to British investors. The greater part of these companies—to be exact, 423—made their first bow to our public during the last twelve months. One hundred and eighty were floated when the late lamented 'boom' in South African mining shares, which I discussed in this Review for October 1895, was in its zenith; and about the same number were children of the spring of the present year.

To the 80,000,000 Westralian mining shares now in existence the Stock Exchange has long since conceded a special 'market;' and it has even conferred upon these stocks a nickname—the surest indication of importance and popularity. And that 'Kangaroos,' as they were fondly called, could boast of importance and popularity nobody would dare to gainsay. During many months they were the only class of stocks which furnished stockbrokers and company promoters with a living, financial newspapers with advertisements, and dabblers in shares with an opportunity to dabble. When the South African market was in a chronic state of collapse; when Home Railways had been carried to such high prices that nobody could muster pluck enough to touch them; when Argentine stocks had been 'worked for all they were worth;' and American railways were going to the dogs, along with the Democratic party—when, in short, every department of the Stock Exchange was inactive—Westralians came to the rescue, and the creation and distribution of these shares kept the financial community profitably employed.

I propose to enter presently into a brief examination of the methods pursued in creating these 80,000,000 shares, and particularly of the means adopted to distribute them among the public. I also intend to show how little reason the public have to congratulate themselves upon their new acquisitions. But before I do that I must show what foundation there is for these shares and their market—in other words, what are the position and the prospects of the gold industry of Western Australia, which provides the basis of this gambling mania.

The Western Australia Goldfields, first somewhat vaguely known as 'Coolgardie,' really consist of a large number of districts spread over an area considerably more than 100,000 square miles in extent, and almost exclusively consisting of arid lands situate between the thirtieth and thirty-fifth degrees south.   Until quite recently the whole colony of Western Australia had neither future nor history; and, as far as the latter is concerned, it has only just begun to manufacture the article.   Although the honour is claimed by two men named Ryan and Sweetman, the first important discovery of gold is generally placed to the credit of two prospectors named Bayley and Ford, who in 1892 discovered some rich gold-bearing quartz from which they extracted 700 ounces of gold.   They took this gold to Southern Cross, then a small mining camp.   Within one day every able-bodied person in the town was prospecting, and needless to say a rush also ensued from the coast.   It is a curious fact that the principal drawback with which these pioneers had to contend whilst they were making many important discoveries was excessive rain.   Horses and carts had to be left in the mud, we are told, and 'dry-blowing' was impossible.   That was in the summer of 1892. By Christmas water sold, in some places, at five shillings a bottle, and it has been at a premium ever since.

By degrees many fresh discoveries were made, and 'Coolgardie' was divided into sections, whilst new fields—Pilbarra, Murchison, Yalgoo, Kurnalpi, Kalgoorlie, and others—were added.   Many of the 'finds' created a sensation, and numerous 'pockets' were found that eclipsed the most famous 'bonanzas' of the halcyon days of California. Gradually, also, mining operations were extended.   Foreign capital and foreign experts were attracted, and the goldfields soon became by far the most valuable asset of one of the least prosperous of British colonies.   Many mines were started, although most of them remain in an embryonic state until the present day.[1]   And there has been this peculiarity about these enterprises, that people often embarked upon them without ascertaining the extent of the mines, their probable permanence, or their presumable prospects as commercial ventures.   'Westralian' mining companies, as I have already shown, were promoted by the hundred rather than by the score; but hardly anybody seems to have taken the trouble to ask for, or to provide, proof that these mines, into which scores of millions have been sunk, would ever repay the original outlay, let alone yield profits.   This omission appears the more remarkable, since it has always been known that these rich fields had serious drawbacks.   There were no means of communication except camels; there was no adequate supply of labour; there was little timber; there was hardly any surface water; and, worst of all, the auriferous deposits—one can hardly call them

---

[1] It is but right to add that this seems in part due to the cost of transportation, and its prospective reduction owing to the construction of a line of railway.

who bought shares. For a time, indeed, the Londonderry *fiasco* damped the ardour of the promoter to bring out more companies, and suppressed the eagerness of the 'investor' to purchase more shares. But the patience of the company promoter is long, and the memories of shareholders are short, and after a time promotion was resumed afresh and soon reached truly unprecedented dimensions. As many as eighty-one companies have been brought out in a single month—April 1896. And yet there never were any sufficient hard, solid facts, reliable data, or results worth speaking of, to explain this renewed favour. Herr Bergrath Dr. Schmeisser, a German geologist whose name is well remembered in this country in connection with a very sanguine report written by him a couple of years ago on the Witwatersrand mines, had been sent to Western Australia by one of the leading 'finance companies' interested in these fields. His report, translated by his employers, was by no means wholly favourable, and received but scant publicity. It emphasised the unreliable nature of the strata, already known to everybody not wholly devoid of the faculty to observe; and it went so far as to say plainly that 'the richness of the outcrops, either in the " pockets " or for continuous stretches . . . has repeatedly led to erroneous valuations of the deposit.'

The richness of these 'outcrops' is explained by the gradual decomposition of rock near the surface. The decomposed layer, the layer where Nature has been doing imperfectly during many centuries what mercury and cyanide of potassium accomplish in a few days, varies in depth from about 60 feet in the Cue district to 140 or 150 feet in Mensies or Kurnalpi. Beyond that depth the ore is, as a rule, poor.[2] It is true that no great depth has yet been reached. On the Rand—where people have, at any rate, always had confidence in the continuity of the strata—very deep bore-holes have been sunk, and the diamond drill has established the existence of the well-known series of reefs at a vertical depth of over 3,000 feet. In Western Australia nobody has ventured to sink deep test holes or shafts; there are not ten mines which have followed their reefs down to a vertical depth of more than 200 feet. That is to say, most companies have kept within the semi-decayed zone, within the rich upper layer. It is undoubtedly true that this upper layer has in many cases proved very rich. Some bodies of ore—for instance, on the Hill End mine—have

[2] See note on next page.

yielded as much as fifteen ounces per ton, whilst most mines on the
Rand do not yield as many pennyweights.   Three or four ounces of
gold per ton is a common figure, and four ounces means 15*l.* worth of
gold.   But there is no doubt whatsoever that these ores are selected ;
even the boldest of ' experts ' does not assert that they are not.   And
it is necessary to select, because the cost of treatment is so high that
it would be rank folly to work low-grade ores.   All the necessaries of
life and all materials are dear.   There are no transportation facilities.
Water is unobtainable in most places ; where it can be had, it costs
money.

This question of water supply, indeed, is one of the most important
with which the fields are confronted.   The Government is, no doubt,
anxious to assist in providing the life-blood of the mines ; in fact,
Sir John Forrest, the Premier of the colony, who has learnt that these
mines must create a strong political force, has virtually undertaken
to supply water.[3]   But Western Australia is a sparsely peopled colony,
which has less than 100,000 inhabitants ; and the fields are very extensive.   Even if water can be procured—which is not by any means
certain in any bar a few cases, and very doubtful in many—it will be
at a heavy cost.   Ten million gallons a day, which would not go very
far, would, according to a Mr. O'Connor, require an initial outlay of
5,323,000*l.*, and would cost 3*s.* 10*d.* per 1,000 gallons.   But it remains
yet to be seen whether water can be had in such large quantities.
Then there are difficulties of transport.   Even an imperfect railway
system would require an outlay of at least 3,000,000*l.* in addition to
the sum already spent upon the trunk line to Coolgardie, and it would
leave the vast majority of mines dependent upon supplementary means,
chiefly camels.   Also, there is a great scarcity of labour.   But coolies
and Chinamen can probably be had for the asking, and the question is
less how to provide muscle and sinew than how to maintain them at
reasonable cost.

I have in the foregoing endeavoured to point out the four salient
characteristics of this young mining region.   First, the gold strata
are unreliable and erratic ; they decrease in value at small depth,[4]

---

[3] A special correspondent of the *Economist*, whose letter from Perth, Western
Australia, can be found in that journal of the 10th of October, says concerning this
matter : ' The goldfields are absolutely without fresh water, and the most feasible
method of supplying Coolgardie and the surrounding district with fresh water is
considered to be by means of a line of pipes 300 miles long and involving pumping
the water not only along that distance, but raising it in the process some 1,500 feet.
For this project a loan of 2,500,000*l.* will shortly be asked for in the London market.'

[4] Dr. Schmeisser says in his report : ' This irregularity in the distribution of the
pay ore makes it necessary to determine by careful sampling and examination during
the progress of the development work which portions will pay to work.   Another
fact which I have frequently observed is the richness of the outcrops, either in pockets
or for continuous stretches.   This circumstance has repeatedly led to erroneous
valuations of the deposit.   *For as soon as mining operations are extended in depth, a
considerable decrease in the value of the bulk of the ore takes place,* and corresponding

and they have not been shown in one single case to afford a safe basis for a large permanent outlay. Second, there is lack of water ; it has not yet been demonstrated that it can be supplied, and if it can be had it will be at considerable cost. Third, there is the problem of providing transportation at a reasonable price ; and fourth, labour will have to be made more abundant and cheaper. Ere these conditions are fulfilled it will be impossible for the industry to develop at all ; whether they can be fulfilled, and whether, if they can be fulfilled, the industry will prove to possess vitality, is, to say the least, open to grave doubts in the majority of cases.

Yet our public has been persuaded to sink scores of millions in these enterprises. Have, then, the drawbacks and disadvantages just enumerated—the uncertainty of the formations, the inaccessibility of the mines, the difficulty of obtaining water, and the scarcity of labour —been offset by other, more tempting conditions? Not that I am aware of. The yield of the mines is poor ; if allowance be made for the 'expansion of the industry,' it is poorer even to-day than it was two years ago. In the year ending the 30th of September, 1894, 185,000 ounces were produced ; in the year ending with September last only 254,529 ounces were mined, although the capital engaged in mining is at least six times larger now than it was two years ago. Moreover, there has been a constant string of disappointments owing to the foolish faith of the public in the rash and optimistic predictions of the 'boomer' and the promoter. Those interested in these mines have always held out bright prospects with which actual performance had better not be compared. Sir John Forrest, the Premier, himself predicted at the beginning of the year that the output of the current year would reach one million ounces of gold ; during the first three quarters of the year only 193,406 ounces have been produced, and the output for the whole of 1896 is certain to be less than 30 per cent. of the total foretold by the sanguine Sir John. The case is but typical of the disagreement between actuality and prediction, as I shall show more conclusively anon. But let us for the moment assume that Sir John's one million ounces will be reached in 1897, which I hold to be impossible. A million ounces of gold would be worth about 3,500,000*l.* Let us assume that one half of this sum will represent profits, which will certainly not be the case. Then the shareholders can divide on their 75,000,000*l.* of share capital 1,750,000*l.*, being an average return of 2⅓ per cent. For the present year the profit can at best represent but a miserable fraction of 1 per cent. The dividends paid so far by *mining* companies aggregate

disappointment. In the more favourable of such cases the ore at a depth, even if considerably poorer, will still be payable. In other cases, however, it becomes poor even to barrenness.' The italics are the writer's.

only 221,825*l.* A list of these distributions is soon given. Here it is:[5]

Name of Company	Amount paid per share in dividends	Percentage of dividends	Amount disbursed in dividends
	s.	per cent.	£
Golden Link	5	25	22,500
Great Boulder . . .	19	95	152,000
Great Fingall Reef . . .	1	5	8,750
Menzies Gold Reefs . . .	2	10	16,500
Murchison New Chum . . .	1	5	16,000
Pilbarra Goldfields . . .	2	10	6,075
Total	...	...	221,825

So much for the mines. Let us now look at the market.

The 1*l.* share, one of the most pernicious of financial innovations, is the standard share. There are occasional departures from this rule in the shape of shares with a face value of 10*s.*, 5*s.*, and even less; but the 1*l.* share is the rule, and the others are exceptions.

Some figures given above have already shown that the vast majority of companies have been floated during the last eighteen months. They have been brought out ' by a large number of promoters, professional and amateur. Almost every self-respecting city man who has no business in particular takes a hand at promoting ' Westralians ' nowadays, and, in spite of the huge crop of companies that has already been gathered, there are hundreds that have not yet made their appearance and are waiting for a revival of the markets. On the whole, the professional promoter is far better versed in his *métier* than the occasional godfather of companies; but space does not permit me to draw fine distinctions between the two, and I must content myself with a general description of how the work is done.

First of all it is necessary to procure a mine; but this is easy enough. Plenty of ' finds ' are made, and miners are, as a rule, ready to sell, and rarely take the trouble to extract the gold themselves. Such unselfishness seems too good to be human; but to avoid the appearance of bias I will not enter into any conjectures of my own as to the explanation. I will content myself with a quotation from Dr. Schmeisser's report, written, be it understood, for one of the great Westralian 'interests.' ' The Australian prospector,' says the Bergrath, ' is well acquainted with the fact that the surprisingly rich pockets frequently found at or near the outcrops of the reefs quickly disappear as depth is attained. He therefore tries to sell his find with as little loss of time as possible.' I have been told that the price of these ' finds ' ranges between 500*l.* and 3,000*l.*, and the claims are usually purchased by local speculators.

[5] Compiled from ' *Mathieson's Mining Handbook* ' and '*Mining Dividends and Rights.*'

The first thing these speculators do is to procure experts' reports. But it is not difficult to obtain these. Westralia teems with experts. But they are often not of the right kind. Says Dr. Schmeisser:

Experts of very doubtful capacity and character undoubtedly exist in these goldfields. Members of all trades—formerly sailors, officers, physicians, chemists, merchants, bookkeepers—become mining experts with a surprising rapidity, from the moment they breathe the air of the goldfields and get a sight of the shining yellow metal in its natural state. The most extraordinary things take place. One of these experts reported on a deposit solely on the basis of samples found and submitted to him. It will not be difficult to mention similar occurrences as illustrative of the knowledge and conscientiousness of some mining engineers. In consequence of judging the whole deposit to be equal to the rich outcrops, many totally exaggerated opinions about the value of many mines got into existence.

Dr. Schmeisser represents the case far too mildly. Many of these experts write, for a consideration, reports of the most brilliant kind without having the slightest ground for their roseate opinions. Either they do not inquire at all, or their examination is wofully superficial, or they must lack the knowledge without which their opinion is altogether worthless. And yet these reports are embodied in prospectuses to guide the investor!

The local speculators sell their claims at a good profit to the London promoters who have created a large demand for them; and in their turn these promoters endeavour to sell their 'valuable properties' to an eager public. Needless to say, the capital of the companies is in almost every case highly inflated. The nominal capital of the various companies is, on the average, just in excess of 100,000*l.* Of this sum, as a rule, only from 15,000*l.* to 25,000*l.* are working capital—are put into the mine.[6] Of the 75,000,000*l.* which constitutes the nominal capital of the Westralian gold mines some 60,000,000*l.* have probably gone to the promoters, partly in shares and partly in cash. There is no doubt whatsoever that the vast majority of mines will sooner or later find their working capital too small; indeed, there are already at this early time of day several cases where it can be demonstrated that this is the case. Dr. Schmeisser has called attention to the same evil.[7] But to return to the promoter. That gentleman does not always at once realise the huge profits at which he aims. The public does not without fail

[6] The writer may speak with some authority on this matter, as he has during the past year critically examined over two hundred Westralian prospectuses.

[7] I quote once more from Dr. Schmeisser: 'The European company promoters thought they could not float rich deposits at prices high enough. In some of the larger mining fields ground was hastily taken up which had not even been seriously prospected, with a view of forming subsidiary companies with as high a capital as possible. In this way mining properties have been floated with considerable capital which could only produce dividends by being worked on a small scale and in the most economical manner. The unheard-of high capitalisation excludes, of course, in most cases, the payment of dividends.'

respond to his appeals for capital, the biggest advertisements, the most promising of prospectuses, and the most skilful of puffs notwithstanding. Cash subscriptions rarely reach an aggregate total of one-fifth of a company's capital; but I have heard of several cases where the amount subscribed for fell short of 200*l.* Yet 'letters of allotment and regret' are posted, and notices to that effect appear in the newspapers. But nevertheless the promoters and their friends the underwriters still have to complete their task. Huge blocks of shares which they have kept on hand are still to be sold to the public.

Before entering upon some details pertaining to the means by which this often difficult task is accomplished I must pause for a moment at the prospectuses. These documents constitute in themselves a fit subject for a critical essay; but I will satisfy myself here with bringing not more than three of their peculiarities to the reader's notice. The first is that the subscription lists are in many cases open for such a brief period that criticism is ineffective. The second is that the finance companies are in the habit of publishing the prospectus of their bantlings ' for public information only;' but information regarding the shares which anon will be worked off on the public is as a rule deplorably meagre. The third point is that *nowadays no reliance whatsoever can be placed upon the statements made in most prospectuses. They abound in mendacious statements clearly made with the object to deceive.* This abuse is so frequent and so general that one frequently wonders what object there is in having Companies Acts or a Public Prosecutor.

But to return to the sale of shares in new companies by the promoter. This work is, as a rule, accomplished by means of various subtle devices. The great point is to create a market as soon as the prospectus appears, and this is often done by so called ' wash sales' on the Stock Exchange. Wash sales are ' formal' transactions, to which the most reputable brokers do not lend themselves. But many small members of the Stock Exchange are willing to act as brokers to doubtful companies and to push them, and in this way the fictitious quotation of a practically unknown mine gets on the 'tape,' and from there into the newspapers.

The next thing to be done is to obtain favourable reports relating to the mine in the press. I am sorry to say that this is easy work. I have already shown with how little difficulty favourable expert reports can be obtained. Managers seem quite anxious to cable good news relating to marvellous strikes or wonderful crushings; and there are several obscure ' news agencies ' which undertake, for a small consideration, to arrange for the insertion of these reports—and, indeed, of almost any paragraph—in a large number of newspapers. Local country papers are freely used for this purpose, but so-called leading journals also lend themselves to the practice. I have a list containing the names of nineteen provincial dailies and of two London weeklies, all of ' good standing,' in which I have found such paid puffs. But the financial press is especially guilty of inserting such notices. With three or four honourable exceptions most financial journals are ready to insert and to recommend anything as long as they are paid for it. And apart from the 'tape' and the press, the ' bucket shop ' is also pressed into the service of the promoter of bad companies. Some of these run their own paper; all have tens of thousands of addresses on their lists, and freely circularise investors all over the country.

By such means as these, all devious and dark, are the shares sold by degrees—if possible at a premium, but where it is necessary at a discount. It often happens that large blocks of unabsorbed shares are bought from promoters at a heavy discount by finance companies, who hold them until a market for them has been created. These concerns are to a certain extent characteristic of the 'Westralian' market. They are, as a rule, worked by powerful financial groups, and are little else than huge promoting concerns; and if we are to draw inferences from the dividends of some of these companies, promoting must be a very paying trade indeed. Several of these institutions have paid from 100 to 200 per cent. on their share capital in dividends, and in consequence the shares of most of them quote at a high premium. But these profits are not derived from the working of the mines, as everyone who looks at the foregoing list of dividends will readily understand. They come entirely from successful promotions and profitable transactions in claims.

These finance companies are in the Westralian market what the controlling firms are in the South African; and this leads to the inference that the Westralian market, too, is largely cornered, artificial, and unhealthy. Indeed, those at all conversant with money matters and in touch with the stock markets will find hundreds of small indications that point with irresistible force to this deduction. There is no doubt whatsoever that a large part of the eighty million Westralian gold mining shares created during the last three years are still in the hands of the finance companies, which practically dominate this market. These companies are at once the creating, the moving, and the ruling spirits. But whilst their ultimate object is as clear as the object of gain can be, their means are dark in more senses than one. We outsiders only know that they deal and barter with each other—that they are sometimes at battle and sometimes at peace—that they silently resist each other here and support each other there—that they are now destroying each other's work and then shoring up each other's shams. But their true mutual relations are complex and mysterious like those of the components of a 'nest' of eels, or of one of those curious litters of rats which are for ever tied together by their entangled tails.

Let us now briefly summarise the facts cited above, and see to what deductions they lead. We have in the first place seen that some inordinately rich gold deposits have been discovered in Western Australia. But the auriferous formations are unreliable for the purposes of ordinary mining, owing to the irregular course and uncertain quality of the auriferous deposits. The depth and course of formation have nowhere been tested to any extent, but numerous disappointments have already been caused by the pinching out of reefs, and there will no doubt be more of them. Crushings are very irregular, and development has not advanced beyond initial stages. In consequence it is foolish to profess unbounded faith in the future of these mines, and still more foolish to 'back' such faith. The most favourable attitude which cautious persons can assume is, as Dr. Schmeisser hints, to 'wait for a year or two until more extensive developments have taken place;' but the balance of evidence provided by the experience that has hitherto been gained forces us to conclude that scepticism is wiser than even an open mind. There are already thirty mines that have absolutely failed; there are few indeed that may be regarded as permanent successes, as fit media for the safe investment of capital.

There never was inflated, unreasoning speculation yet which did not come to grief, from the tulip mania of 1634 down to the Kaffir boom of 1895; and the Westralian craze of 1896 is not likely to be the first exception to the rule.

S. F. Van Oss.

WITHIN the last few weeks there has been a renewal of interest in the discussion on commercial morality which, recurring at intervals throughout the last few years, has directed attention to the ethics of commerce. The facts upon which the present discussion is based are by no means new. Mr. Herbert Spencer, writing thirty-five years ago, gave a number of similar instances of corruption in his essay on 'The Morals of Trade,' where, summing up the general opinion expressed by his mercantile informants, he says: 'On all sides we have found the result of long personal experience to be the conviction that trade is essentially corrupt.' Nevertheless, he demurs to the suggestion that the commercial morality of the time was inferior to that of a hundred or a hundred and fifty years earlier, when, as Defoe showed in his 'Complete English Tradesman,' a state of things existed which was not only no better than that prevailing to-day, but was in many respects decidedly worse. 'There was scarce a shopkeeper,' says Defoe, 'who had not a bag of spurious or debased coin, from which he gave change whenever he could.' After dealing with this and other facts which he adduces, Mr. Spencer comes to the conclusion that while the great and direct frauds have been diminishing, the small and indirect frauds have been increasing, alike in variety and number; and against this state of things he suggests that there is no remedy save a 'purified public opinion.' 'When,' he says, 'that abhorrence which society now shows to direct theft is shown to theft of all degrees of indirectness, then will these mercantile vices disappear. When not only the trader who adulterates or gives short measure, but also the merchant who overtrades, the bank director who countenances an exaggerated report, and the railway director who repudiates his guarantee, come to be regarded as of the same genus as the pickpocket, and are treated with like disdain, then will the morals of trade become what they should be.'

Such a higher tone of public opinion Mr. Spencer did not regard as likely to be reached in the near future. 'Throughout the civilised world, especially in England, and above all in America, social activity is almost wholly expended in material development. . . . And as, in times when national defence and conquest were the

chief desiderata, military achievement was honoured above all other
things, so now, when the chief desideratum is industrial growth,
honour is most conspicuously given to that which generally indicates
the aiding of national growth.' These sentences are eminently
fitted to preface a consideration of commercial morality in a country
which at the present time is exciting much interest by reason of its
phenomenal progress. In Japan the military period was supplanted
by the industrial period, not, as in other countries, by a process of
natural evolution, but as the result of a sudden convulsion, which
in less than ten years converted the State from feudalism and
autocracy to industrialism and constitutional government. The
results have been curious and striking, as well as instructive to the
sociologist. The territorial noble or clan leader, of ancient lineage,
holding his own court, and possessing with his army almost complete
administrative autonomy, suddenly found himself a cipher, unless he
chose to embrace politics and maintain a constant struggle for personal
supremacy with his fellows. The *samurai*, accustomed to estimation
by the common people as a hero, but with little education save
in the art of war, found himself at the same time in a position
where the military tactics he had learned were of no value to him,
and where he must labour with hands or brain to save himself
from starvation. On the other hand, the merchants, hitherto
occupying the lowest rung on the social ladder—lower than the
labourers who tilled the soil, and but little above the *Eta*, or pariah
class—discovered that trade, erstwhile despised, was now a passport
to position, industrial exploitation ranked as a virtue, and wealth
conferred honour and power.

But though trade now became an honourable and recognised profession, in which even the ancient territorial aristocracy could engage
without losing caste, but little change occurred in the methods
which characterised it in the centuries of military supremacy, when
trader was but another name for trickster, and the pursuit of commerce practically argued lack of integrity. To recognise a low ideal
in one class, and to speak and act as if in the circumstances there
could be no higher ideal, is to originate and encourage a defective
standard which no sudden change of environment can immediately
alter. And thus we find it the unanimous opinion of those in a
position to judge, that Japanese commercial morality is of a defective
type when compared even with the standard prevailing in China,
where trade has never been stamped as degrading, or with the
standard of those nations which, amid all the trickery immemorially
associated with trade, have yet kept before them a certain standard
of integrity in business as in other walks of life. It is, indeed, a
common belief among those who have investigated the conditions of
trade in Japan, that commercial morality there stands almost on the
lowest plane possible to a civilised people, and that, with few excep-

tions, even Japanese who prove estimable and high-minded in every other matter are not to be trusted when business transactions are in question. As a direct outcome of the contempt and degradation visited upon trade in feudal days, all classes now appear to regard commerce simply as a game of 'besting,' and the man who fails to take advantage of his neighbour when opportunity serves is looked upon rather as a fool than as one whose example should be praised and imitated.

It is well, therefore, at a time when Japanese merchants are endeavouring to enter into direct relations with firms abroad, that the position should be clearly understood; and as a page of illustration is worth more than a volume of comment, I propose to relate some facts of recent occurrence, from which the reader will be able to draw his own conclusions. A case decided by the Japanese courts last year affords a good insight into Japanese methods of carrying on business. It has attracted much attention locally, in view of the fact that by the Revised Treaty with Japan which has now been signed the foreign merchant will come under Japanese law and Japanese administration, and mercantile transactions will consequently be decided by Japanese custom. A firm of British merchants last year imported a hundred bales of yarn to the order of a well-known and wealthy Japanese trader, who at the time was president of the Yokohama Yarn Guild. By the time the goods arrived, however, the market had declined, and the transaction promised to result in a loss to the Japanese importer. He therefore adopted a course which foreign merchants bitterly complain is a common practice with the Japanese trader in similar cases, and refused to take delivery of his goods, his pretext for not fulfilling his engagement being that he had ordered goods with a purple and not a red 'chop' or mark. Finding that their customer obstinately refused to take delivery of the goods he had ordered, the British firm brought an action against him in the Japanese court, and eventually judgment was given in their favour, the Japanese yarn importer being ordered to pay the full claim of 29,528 dollars, together with insurance, interest, and warehouse rent. This was so far satisfactory, but the sequel was far otherwise. Some days before the judgment was delivered a deputation from the Yarn Guild waited upon the representative of the British firm in Yokohama, and proposed a compromise very favourable to the defendant, and proportionately against the interests of the plaintiffs. The foreign merchants refused to entertain it; whereupon they were told that unless they agreed to the proposal and stopped proceedings, they would be placed under a boycott, and none of the Japanese yarn merchants would have any dealings with them in future. Refusing to be intimidated, the firm allowed the case to proceed to judgment, and instructed their counsel—a Japanese who is a barrister of the Inner Temple—to inform the

court of this attempt to interfere by threats with the administration
of justice. He did so, but without effect, for the judges, while giving
a decision for the plaintiffs, refused to take any notice of the gross
contempt of court which had been committed by the defendant.

Naturally, the fact of the judges declining to pass any comment
on their conduct, or to take any action against them, emboldened
the Japanese merchant and his business friends, and the threat of
boycotting was renewed in more precise terms than before. The
British firm found themselves in a position where there appeared
no hope of any protection from the law, while they were aware,
from previous cases of this nature, that the boycott would be
strictly carried out, and might mean ruin to their business. After
anxious consideration, it was at last decided to give way to the
pressure of the Guild and accept the so-called compromise, by the
terms of which they were losers to the extent of 2,150 dollars. Thus
the Japanese business men of Yokohama were able to thrust an
unfair and wholly inequitable arrangement upon the firm of foreign
merchants, in sheer defiance of the law, and without the shadow of
excuse or justification in any code of commercial morality.

The case is only one of many, differing in details, but alike in
illustrating the standing complaint among foreign merchants in
Japan, that the native trader will not honourably fulfil his engagements if by so doing he is likely to suffer loss. On the one hand,
orders given and contracts signed are regarded by Japanese as so
much waste paper when the market declines ; while, on the other, the
foreign merchant is held strictly to his agreement should the prospective loss be his. The serious point is, that we have here an
example of a Japanese court giving an equitable decision, but remaining absolutely passive in the face of information as to deliberate
measures taken to nullify its judgment. Another very significant
feature is that in the discussion which ensued not a single Japanese
journal expressed any condemnation of the methods pursued by the
defendant and his Yarn Guild ; several, indeed, went so far as to
justify them, and a correspondent, who appeared to voice the general
feeling of the native traders, wrote to a Japanese journal a quaint
sentence in English that will be found very instructive. It ran
as follows :—' The *saibansho* (court) had its say from a legal point of
view of the question, but the trade practices long established at
Yokohama [*i.e.* of holding native traders to their contracts], so
often objected to by Japanese merchants, but maintained with dogged
obstinacy by some of the foreign merchants, are not such as would
justify, in the name of equity, an appeal to court in every case of
differences between the parties.' The meaning of which is, that the
decisions of the courts are to be ignored and rendered of no effect
because they are not approved by the persons supposed to be subject
to them !

Thus has evil been worked by the practice of placing commerce outside the sphere of morality, and making the position of the trader one of degradation. The merchant class is now constantly being recruited from among those who, fifty years ago, would have considered themselves disgraced by any connection with trade; but, unfortunately for the hope that a better state of things will be brought about in the near future, even the higher walks of what may be called commercialism are not free from the questionable methods developed by a long period of commercial debasement. For example, it might have been supposed that the promoters of last year's industrial exhibition at Kioto, held under the sanction and patronage of the Government, and associated with the name of the Emperor, would have aimed at setting a good example to merchants in general. It was not so, however, as the following incident shows. A visitor who saw some articles at the exhibition which took his fancy, and found they were marked 'sold,' went to the shop of the exhibitors in Kioto, and attempted to purchase similar goods direct. To his surprise, he was asked a price just fifty per cent. above the figure marked on the goods in the exhibition. On asking for an explanation, he was told that had the firm's goods in the exhibition been marked at their actual retail price they would have been refused by the committee, which insisted on the manufactured articles being all marked at low figures; consequently, it was necessary for exhibitors to place a fictitious price on their goods, and then to send agents on the first day the exhibition opened and purchase them back, so as to avoid loss. If the statement is correct—and it came to me on the very best authority—it is possible we have here some explanation of the remarkably low price marked on Japanese manufactured goods exhibited at Kioto: a fact to which attention was called by articles in the commercial journals of every manufacturing country in the world, and which was especially commented upon in England, as exemplifying the competition with which British manufacturers would have shortly to contend. Yet it seems much of the argument was founded on false information, suggested and encouraged by the exhibition committee, and Japanese goods have thus secured an advertisement for cheapness which they do not deserve, and which can be of no practical benefit to Japanese trade in the long run.

Even if we go higher in the social scale than exhibition commissioners, we are still confronted with conduct in commercial matters seriously lacking in integrity. Quite accidentally it was discovered some time ago by foreign merchants that, notwithstanding definite provisions in the Treaties placing them on an equality with Japanese in the matter of Customs duties, the Government was secretly discriminating against the foreigner. The Customs tariff provides that specific duties upon certain articles of import and export shall be paid in *boo*, an ancient Japanese silver coin defined as weighing 134 grains and containing not less than nine parts of pure silver. Article VI. of the

Convention made with Japan by Great Britain (1866) and other Powers, provided that, in conformity with those articles of the Treaties which stipulated for the circulation of foreign coin at its corresponding weight in native coin, dollars were to be received in payment of duties at the rate of 311 boos per hundred dollars, and this method of calculating the amount of duties still remains in force. About ten years ago there was issued an Imperial Rescript, countersigned by the Minister for Finance, which stated that hereafter the exchange would be calculated at the rate of 31½ *sen* per boo, or boos 317·44 per hundred dollars; but, strange to say, no copy of this Imperial Rescript found its way into any foreign Legation or Consulate, and foreigners continued to be charged duties at the old and higher rate of exchange, while Japanese were permitted to pass their goods through the Customs at the new and lower rate. The Chairman of the Hiogo and Osaka Foreign Chamber of Commerce has compiled the following table, showing amounts that were actually paid by Japanese importers, and contrasting them with what foreigners would have been charged :

Imports	Paid by Japanese Importers	If Foreigners had passed Goods	Difference
	$	$	$
206 bales Yarn	973.35	993.57	20.22
33 bales Yarn	155.92	159.17	3.24
2,277 bags Sugar. . . .	537.94	549.11	11.17
600 bags Sugar	141.75	144.69	2.94
1,000 bales Cotton	1,166.15	1,190.37	24.22

Showing an advantage in favour of the Japanese of more than 2 per cent. upon the total duty paid—an advantage which is not to be despised in these days of close competition. Now this discrimination against foreigners and in favour of Japanese had been going on for some nine or ten years, and it is difficult to believe that it was unknown to the high authorities, or was the result of any misunderstanding. The secrecy shown by the issue of the Rescript to Customhouse officials only, the fact that not a single Legation or Consulate managed to get hold of a copy, and that the only foreign employé at the time in the Customs was kept in ignorance of its provisions, all go to show that the Japanese Government was knowingly concerned in a trick to 'best' the foreigner by placing the native 'direct' importer at an advantage, not only over his foreign rival, but over the Japanese merchant who imported his goods through a foreign firm.

As the result of a memorial addressed to the foreign Consuls, upon which action was taken by the various Legations in Tokio, the Japanese Government has abandoned this method of discriminating between foreign and native importers, and the former as well as the latter now pay duties at the uniform rate of 31½ sen per boo. But the Government has not attempted to clear itself of the charges brought against it. The foreign Chamber of Commerce in Kobe commented in its next report on the significant fact that, though the disability had been removed, and the Government practically admitted that there had been a distinct breach of the treaties going on for nine years, no explanation had been vouchsafed, nor was there any suggestion of restitution. The matter is not so trifling as may appear at first sight. It has been estimated by an authority upon trade in Japan, that the loss to foreign merchants by the discrimination in Customs duties amounted to as much as 100,000 dollars annually, some firms, dealing mainly in goods subject to these specific duties, being losers to the extent of from four to five thousand dollars per year.

The actual loss suffered is serious enough, but the chief interest of the facts here set forth comes from the light thrown upon the standard of commercial morality prevailing throughout all classes in Japan, from the Government bureau to the stall of the huckster. A Japanese merchant, discussing the yarn case with a foreigner, remarked, in defence of the Yarn Guild's president, ' But if he had taken delivery he would have lost money ! ' That is the attitude which, with some few honourable exceptions, is almost invariably taken up by the Japanese merchant. The profit on a transaction *must* be on his side. If he perceives that he is likely to lose money, he will repudiate his bargains and his contracts, and will permit all manner of evil things to be said of him rather than fulfil his obligations. Unfortunately, those who rank above the merchant in social status, and who might be expected to take a higher view of the country's commercial reputation, do not, as we have seen, set him a much better example. It is ' business ' to secure the greatest advantage for one's self at all costs to reputation, and this seems the only touchstone which, in Japan, is applied to commercial matters. We see in this the direct outcome of the contempt for trade and for all who concerned themselves in barter, which was one of the features of feudal days in Japan. Ethical considerations were held to be out of place in the field of commerce, and as a result we find that men who would not dream of doing their neighbours injustice or injury in the ordinary affairs of life have no hesitation in overreaching them in a commercial bargain. Trade is thus placed by immemorial custom outside the sphere of morality—it is something to which ethics do not apply, any more than they apply to the differential calculus—and the result is what might be expected.

Thirty years of a non-feudal state of society in Japan have not availed to establish commerce in a much higher position than it occupied a hundred years ago. The period is much too brief. The leopard does not change his spots in a day, but by a long process of evolution in a different environment ; and we may hope that the same forces which for centuries have been at work in the West, and which, with all the commercial dishonesty prevailing in certain quarters, have done much to make probity in business as much a virtue as in other relations of life, will gradually bring about improvement in Japanese commercial methods.   The only remedy, as Mr. Spencer says, is a ' purified public opinion,' and if there are, unfortunately, no signs at present in Japan of any such pressure being exercised in the near future, it may be because there has been no Defoe or Spencer to expose the evil and its tendencies, or even one Japanese newspaper to lift up its voice in remonstrance.   It is difficult to believe, however, that things can go on very long as they are without Japanese traders and all interested in commerce being forced to look at business methods from a somewhat higher point of view than at present.   Already Japanese Consuls have reported that the country's foreign trade is being seriously injured by merchants who send abroad matches that will not strike, rice that is not up to sample, and stuffs whose only merit is cheapness.   Within the last few years guilds have been formed to introduce better methods into certain branches of trade ; and though it may be admitted this is a welcome sign, they have not yet worked much improvement, for it is clear there can be no radical change so long as there is no public opinion to support the application of morality to commercial transactions.   Japanese publicists and statesmen have to consider that until such improvement is evident Japan will certainly not take the leading place among the commercial nations of the world which—mistakenly, as I venture to think—has been predicted for her.   Her exports and imports will go on increasing in volume, but the trade will remain in the hands of foreign merchants, as at present, and the direct trading with foreign countries, in which her merchants desire to engage, will remain a dream of the dim and distant future.   The life of trade is confidence, and confidence is the very last thing to be generated by the standard of commercial morality at present prevailing in Japan.

ROBERT YOUNG,

Editor, *Kobe Chronicle*, Japan.

II

FRAU JORGON was giving a 'coffee' to four of her most intellectual friends, who made a weekly rendezvous of her private sitting room, meeting every Wednesday afternoon for a little serious reading aloud in French, English, and German, with dilettante criticism on the same, and the Frau Doctor, of course, in the armchair. It pleased Frau Erna Jorgon immensely—who was nothing if not to her taper finger-tips a trifling, coquettish, calculating, rather hard and superficial woman of the world—to affect the pose of a spoiled woman of society, secretly enamoured of intellectual pursuits, while reluctantly engaged in the more distracting duties of wifehood and maternity. And it filled up a void, this weekly re-union, in the calm, methodical, domestic life of the Frau Doctor, who had nothing in the world to do but indulge her taste for reading and live up to the European reputation of her distinguished husband. Frau Jorgon was a young and handsome woman of five and twenty, dark as a gipsy, and the spoilt and wilful wife of an opulent merchant in this same German garrison town. Frau Doctor Lehmann was the wife of the great *savant* of that name, a childless, gruff-voiced, manly-looking woman of fifty, with short iron-grey hair and a tendency to *embonpoint*. The other members of the friendly quintet were Frau Flink, a little widow of thirty; Fräulein Hedwig Schneider, a nervous, deprecating woman, who wrote 'Rentier' and 'lediglich' on the census papers, and learned articles in a Berlin monthly journal; and last, though by no means least, Anna Löser, a peculiar and distinctive character, a difficult personality of twenty, gifted, artistic, vain of her personal appearance, musical to a supercilious degree, rather overweighted with self-consciousness, and inordinately ambitions.

It was a cold January afternoon, about four o'clock. The grand porcelain stove in Frau Jorgon's charming boudoir, a Hirschvogel, was throwing out too much heat, and the folding doors of the adjoining apartment were thrown wide open, revealing deep, cool vistas of a shrouded salon, darkened, into which the Frau Doctor, who loved fresh air and free space, was casting longing glances. Coffee was just over, and Frau Jorgon's picturesque maid was carrying away the coffee cups. There now remained nothing in the way of the serious purport of the meeting, which, this week was English reading; hence Frau Erna Jorgon's inconsequent mood and discursive remarks, laughingly adjusted to disturb the mental serenity of the other ladies, who had taken up their needlework and were waiting for Fräulein Anna Löser to read. A woman's needlework is always suggestive and characteristic. The Frau Doctor knitted—she knitted yards, miles, leagues in the course of a year. Little Frau Flink, everlastingly occupied from January to December in the plaintive renovation of a somewhat *bric-à-brac* wardrobe, was for the nonce immersed to her pink ears in second-hand millinery, listening to the reading with a deeply critical expression and a mouth full of pins.

'Ach, please Anna, you read too quickly, I cannot understand.'

Fräulein Hedwig Schneider was sadly sorting crewels under the askant glance of the practical and industrious Frau Doctor, and, being a nervous creature, she made very little visible progress. When she would finally start, her 'Tischläufer' was matter for the curious speculation of the Frau Doctor, who had a truly marvellous knack of evolving little garments out of a single ball of wool, and in the course of a short winter's afternoon—to the secret envy and chagrin of poor Hedwig Schneider. And Frau Jorgon was crocheting nursery lace, with considerable condescension for a ' *Gnädige Frau* ' who kept a maid, and with some play of expressive feature, as though she were all the time marvelling at her own inconsistency or complacently admiring her bejewelled hands. She crocheted with her small dark glossy head a little inclined and her dark mischievous eyes now and again mockingly directed to little Frau Flink's new hat.

'Mietzel, what a hat!'

'Do not be stupid, Erna, I cannot buy me a new one, can I?'

'English, English,' called Frau Doctor Lehmann from the chair.

'Ach Gott!' Frau Jorgon sighed, with a glance at a clock supported by a shepherd and shepherdess engaged in an immortality of frail Dresden-china courtship.

Anna Löser read on as fast as she could. She invariably managed to do her own and somebody else's share of reading, for she was having lessons in elocution and gave the true dramatic touch to everything she read. Moreover, she was always carried away to unconscious excess of emphasis by the pleasing sound of her own voice. As she paused to turn over a leaf and to take breath, the Frau Doctor again looked up from her knitting and dryly said:

'If you are tired, Anna, perhaps Frau Jorgon will read a little.'

'I thank you,' said that lady, who, was getting tired of crochet work, but even that was better than English reading. How fearfully dull it was, and what was it all about, and had she understood a word ?

Anna Löser was beginning again when little Frau Flink and the indignant Frau Doctor exchanged glances.

'I will read a little, if you please, Anna,' said Frau Flink, who was a decisive little person in her way, and she lovingly laid down her hat and took the book, and commenced reading rather badly, so that poor Fräulein Hedwig Schneider looked up from her tangled crewels, and blinked with a distracted expression through her ugly blue goggles, and passed her hand over her narrow wrinkled brow.

'Oh, please, Frau Flink, I have not understand.'

'Understood,' prompted the Frau Doctor.

'It is quite the same,' laughed Frau Jorgon, admiring the work of her hands at arm's length. Then she laid it down and slily took up Frau Flink's wonderful hat and tried it on, glancing at her own ridiculous reflection in a Venetian mirror opposite her; even the Frau Doctor was constrained to smile much, against her will.

'Ach, mein Gott, what a hat!'

But little Frau Flink was by this time fairly wound up and set going for a good five minutes, and Frau Jorgon's frivolity was entirely lost upon her; so, with another sigh, Frau Jorgon resumed her crochet work, devoutly wishing it were supper time.

Meanwhile Frau Flink read on proudly but execrably, and it was as much as the learned Hedwig Schneider could do to disentangle the sense of what she read. The Frau Doctor had philosophically given up even listening, and was calmly counting stitches for a new little garment. Anna Löser never listened to anybody's reading but her own.

'"The progress of the mind of Frances Burney ——"'

'Fran—ces Bur—nie!' Frau Jorgon exclaimed in some astonishment. 'I thought we were reading about that delightful Lord Byron.'

'Erna! You said last week that Lord Byron was too difficult, and so we began Madam D'Arblay.'

'Ach so,' said Frau Jorgon carelessly. 'But I do not know Madam D'Arblay.'

'She wrote books.'

'All Englishwomen write books. And what books?'

'She wrote a famous diary,' Frau Doctor rather impatiently explained.

'What is—diary?'

'Diarium. Do let me read, Erna.'

'But I will know what you read. When did she live, this Madam D'Arblay? And why not Mée-sis D'Arblay?'

'Du lieber Gott, Erna, she married a Frenchman.'

'Then why did she live in England ?   Surely it would have been much nicer to live in La belle France.   If I married a Frenchman I would live in Paris.'

'I believe she did live in France for several years,' remarked Hedwig Schneider.

'Was she not the friend of the great Dr. Johnson ? '

'I believe she was,' said the Frau Doctor shortly.   'Give *me* the book, Metzil ; I will read a little.'

And the Frau Doctor began.

' "The progress of the mind of Frances Burney, from her ninth to her twenty-fifth year, well deserves to be recorded." '

'Wie . . . How ?   I do not understand a word, dear Frau Doctor,' said Fräulein Hedwig.   Frau Jorgon laughed.

With a look of irritation, Frau Doctor Lehmann, who read well and translated better, laid down the handsome volume of Macaulay's *Essays* and took refuge in knitting once more.

'It is perfectly useless reading with these constant interruptions,' she said.   'Since December we have begun no less than four different essays, not one of which have we finished.   And I must read very ill, Hedwig, if you do not understand me ! '

Frau Jorgon looked up roguishly, and drew her crochet needle slowly through the wool, and attempted broken English.

'Not ill—not at all, dear Frau Doctor.   You read very good —very good, but I too, myself, have not understand—understood.'

'Ich auch nicht,' mumbled little Frau Flink distressfully.   And she took another pin from between her lips.

'Mietzel, how can you eat pins ?   You will choke yourself one of these days and then there will be an inquest, and my husband will say it is my fault.'

Anna Löser stirred.   'We ought to have some one to overhear our reading and correct our mistakes and pronunciation.   The Myers have a Fräulein.'

'An English Miss—you mean.'

The Frau Doctor shook her head and closed her lips firmly, and then spoke.

'I for one decline to waste another pfennig on lessons.   I never learnt anything in a lesson which was ever of the slightest practical use to me in my life.   All the English I know I have taught myself, in my husband's study, with my husband for a dictionary and a grammar.'

'But dear Frau Doctor,' remarked her hostess rather slyly, 'your pronunciation——'

'Is bad.   I know it.   I desire to master the English language for the pleasure of reading English literature.   I shall never need to talk English.   No more lessons for me.'

one did teach me anything; they did not amuse me.'

'I find English *so* easy,' said Anna Löser, without further committing herself.

Frau Doctor Lehmann gave the young lady a peculiar look, but said nothing.

'I know an English lady,' began Fräulein Hedwig Schneider, and then stopped abruptly, abashed by a look in Frau Jorgon's brilliant eyes, who held up her hand in mock despair.

'Ach, dear Hedwig, I have tried all the English teachers in the town. They bored me to death. They could not laugh. I could not be serious. They could not talk about the opera and never went to balls. I could not talk about lawn tennis and never went to church. Mee-sis Porter—Ach, mein Gott!—was like a Puritan, tall and straight, and severe and black, and solemn and miserable. Poor thing, she had much trouble. Her husband had deserted her. If I had been her husband, I too would have deserted her. She was horrid.'

'This lady is quite a stranger, dear Frau Jorgon. You have not seen her.'

'Poor thing! No pupils I suppose.'

'Oh yes. But not many. She might have many, but——'

Frau Jorgon tossed her head. 'Ach, do I not know. She is difficult, you would say. All Englishwomen are difficult, too difficult for me.' And Frau Jorgon shivered. 'The wife of the English pastor invited me to five o'clock tea last week, and my husband made me promise that I would go—*nimmer, nimmer mehr.* It was dread—ful.' With a smile Frau Jorgon went on, in charming broken English: 'I would laugh for I was merry. Why not? But no man did laugh. All sat up upright and crossed their feet. So I too sat bolt upright, but I did not cross my feet. It was funny. And then I must drink English tea and eat English—*wie sagt man heimgebackenen Kuchen auf englisch, Hedwig?*—I must drink English tea and eat English home-made cake. And I did not like it. I could not speak one word, for I was shy. And no man did spoke German with me but Mee-sis Perry, and she was too busy. And then I come away and my husband laugh. *Voilà!* that is English five o'clock tea.'

Once again did Frau Hedwig Schneider attempt an oar.

'I know a lady, she is a good teacher. One can understand all what she says—*Alles was sie sagt.* But she speaks not a good German.'

'A point strongly in her favour,' said the Frau Doctor approvingly: she spoke excellent English with very little foreign accent. 'Speaking little German herself, there will be more opportunity for her pupils to speak English.'

. 'Exactly,' chimed in little Frau Flink. 'Ach! I like to speak English. But always must I know how the difficult words are spelled.' *Sonst*——'

'And this lady, Hedwig?' the Frau Doctor inquired, suspending her knitting.

'Is a friend of me. At least I have made her acquaintance; for I will improve in English.'

'Ach, my dear Hedwig, you have every week a new friend,' said Frau Jorgon, rather contemptuously.

Fräulein Hedwig Schneider coloured and continued: 'She has taught me much. She has given lessons to Herr Doctor Claus.'

'How! Dr. Claus! Then my husband was right. He is going to marry a rich and charming *Amerikanerin*. Well, I wish her joy,' and Frau Jorgon laughed a little maliciously and with a conscious air. 'She will not be happy.'

'I do not believe it,' said Frau Flink. 'How cruel you are, Erna!'

'Ach! he is not in love with me any more,' said Frau Jorgon coolly. 'But I would like to hear him speak English. I will tease him when we meet at the ball next week—I will talk only English with him. And this lady, how did she teach him? I would not like to teach him anything. Perhaps——' Frau Jorgon reflected a moment or two with her chin in the palm of her hand and a mocking smile on her lips, and presently astonished her friends by clapping her hands. 'I have it,' she said. 'How would it be, Hedwig, if you brought this lady with you next week and introduced her to us—of course as a friend, not as a teacher? I will have no more teachers. Teachers have not a large acquaintance, I believe. It would be very nice for her. She need not speak German, if she is shy. She could speak English' (roguishly). 'I would not object. She could come to coffee, and stay to supper. I will order cutlets. She will not eat cutlets every day. Do you think she would come, Hedwig?'

'I can ask her.'

'Of course she will come,' said Anna Löser, who was getting tired, and was dying to be asked to play, for she knew all Frau Jorgon's love affairs by heart and did not approve of coquettish matrons.

'Why should she refuse?' said Frau Flink, who seldom ate a meal at her own expense.

'Indeed, why?'

'She will want a fee,' gruffly remarked the Frau Doctor, putting a damper on everybody.

'Not if she is invited to coffee and supper. And Erna gives such nice suppers.'

'I tell you she will want a fee.'

'Ach was!' said Frau Jorgon pettishly. 'I ask her out of kindness. She will give no lesson. Is it any trouble to sit in my boudoir and drink coffee and eat cake and talk a little English? Teachers are not rich. Meesis Porter was dreadfully poor. And Miss West, poor thing, wore cotton gloves summer and winter, and was always hungry. Ach, thank God I am no teacher. I will give her a nice supper—perhaps cutlets, green peas, a little cake, a little fruit, and perhaps wine. What more can she desire? And my husband can talk as much English as he will, *meinetwegen*; but I shall talk German. How is she called, Hedwig, and what is she like, your friend?'

'Ach, dear Frau Jorgon, she is not my friend. But I have met her in several families. She is very thoughtful and helpful, and takes great trouble to make one understand her mother tongue.'

'Ganz recht,' put in the Frau Doctor with an expression of strong approval. 'But I doubt we shall have to pay her something—some little trifle.'

'I will pay nothing,' said Frau Jorgon, rather haughtily. 'But I will give a good supper.' .   .   .   .   .

'O, it can be arranged,' Anna Löser remarked rather eagerly. 'My cousin's Fräulein receives one mark fifty pfennige the hour.'

'But Fräulein is a young and inexperienced girl, and this is a married lady.'

'Ach, it is quite the same.'

'And from coffee to supper is not one hour, but three.'

'But what can she do with her time in the evening? Surely it is much more agreeable to sit and talk in my boudoir and have a nice supper than go to sleep and be miserable in a furnished apartment. It is no trouble to come to coffee and eat " a nice supper —cutlets, peas, *compot*." Only I shall not talk English. She can talk to me. And perhaps, after all, I will not give wine, only beer.'

'Wine is not at all necessary,' said the Frau Doctor.

'Then it is quite settled, and how very good you are, Erna! I do so long to improve in English.' Anna Löser spoke enthusiastically.

'But, Anna, you must talk. Why will you never talk unless gentlemen are present. It is not nice in a young girl.'

'I have a headache.'

'Ach, you always have a headache when only ladies are present.'

'Is this lady's English quite—quite the English of good society, Hedwig?' It was Frau Flink who spoke.

Fräulein Hedwig looked up and blinked through her goggles in mild surprise. 'My dear Frau Flink, she comes from London.'

'Ach, then, I must tell my husband. He *schwärms* for London. He would like to live in London. I tell him I have no objection. But I shall stay in Germany with my children.'

'I must go,' said the Frau Doctor, looking at her watch. 'It is getting late and my husband lectures to-night.'

'We have not read much to-day. It will be better next week.

Bring this Englishwoman with you, Hedwig. And Anna, my dear, do not be late.'

'Thank heaven, I have finished my hat,' Frau Flink murmured to herself. 'I can wear it home, and next week I will come in my brown silk. Are you coming, Hedwig?'

The friends, accompanied by their hostess, went out into the corridor, where a maid attended to help the ladies on with their outdoor things. Here they gossiped and trifled away another ten minutes, when, seized with compunction, the worthy Frau Doctor made good her escape.

Fräulein Hedwig Schneider was the last to go, and Frau Jorgon watched her from the corridor door, as she slowly descended the great stone staircase.

'Good-bye till Wednesday, and mind you bring the Englishwoman with you.'

.   .   .   .   .   .

It was Wednesday again and Frau Jorgon with her friends was awaiting with some impatience and much lively curiosity the advent of Fräulein Schneider with the Englishwoman. Frau Jorgon—who, it must be said, had an excellent taste in dress—was looking charmingly fresh and girlish, and radiantly handsome. Her eyes shone almost as brilliantly as the diamonds on her fingers. She held an illustrated paper, at which she was languidly looking, making impatient little ejaculations and continually glancing at the clock. Anna Löser, too, had found it expedient to come in a new and extravagant gown, since teachers were proverbially poor and ill dressed, and the thought of shining resplendent in the eyes of one of the grand army of martyrs was inexpressibly soothing and comforting to the girl's ignoble mind. On the other hand, Frau Doctor Lehmann was in her homely blue serge, and of course she was knitting at a furious rate.

Presently voices were heard in the corridor. Frau Jorgon jumped up with a sigh of relief, and made a rush to the door, where she paused and listened and whispered:

'I will meet her in the corridor. It will not be so stiff and ceremonious. If she is solemn I shall be taken ill and go to bed, and Marie can bring me my supper, and you can entertain her; also—' and Frau Jorgon disappeared with a frou-frou of silken petticoats.

Frau Doctor Lehmann knitted on as a matter of course, studying in odd disapproving glances Anna Löser's extravagant gown, while that young lady, not quite at ease in her dress, sat somewhat stiffly on a high-backed chair and turned over an album. An earthquake alone would have roused Frau Flink from the blue silk corsage, which she was decorating with pink rosebuds. Certainly there was no love lost between little Frau Flink and Frau Jorgon's maid.

Five minutes elapsed. Above the murmur of voices in the corridor was heard Frau Jorgon's clear voice cajoling somebody in coaxing tones, and certainly she was not contemplating retiring to bed. This augured favourably for the Englishwoman.

'I am curious,' said Frau Flink, breaking silence and snapping the stalk of an impossible rosebud.

'She cannot be solemn,' remarked the Frau Doctor, with a faint smile.

There was a burst of laughter. Anna Löser reared her head and tried to appear at her ease. For some unaccountable reason she was regretting that she had come in her new gown, which really fitted her admirably, and how was any one to know that it pinched her horribly across the chest?

Presently the door was flung joyously open and enter Frau Jorgon in one of her most fascinating, irresistible moods, with her right arm completely encircling the waist of the Englishwoman, who appeared to be struggling between the embarrassment of the situation and a strong desire to wear an expression suitable to the occasion.

'Ach, dear Frau Doctor,' said Frau Jorgon, as she sailed across the room, skilfully piloting the embarrassed Marion Carr between cabinets of costly china and innumerable low chairs, one of which she overturned.

'Let me introduce Mee-sis Carr—Frau Doctor Lehmann—the great Dr. Lehmann. (In a whisper) Anna, Anna, how shy you are! This is Mee-sis Carr—My friend, Fräulein Anna Löser—Frau Flink. Now you shall sit in this chair and have a cushion to your back, so. Mietzel, put away that horrid corsage, and ring the bell. Coffee, Marie. You drink coffee, Mee-sis Carr? Yes? It is much nicer than English tea. Pardon—you will not be offended with me, but I do not like English tea. In the Russian fashion, in glasses, and with lemon, O yes. It is another thing. But English tea with milk—and Heimgeback.'

'Home-made,' suggested the Englishwoman, with a smile.

'Ach, but you understand German very well. I must talk English? Ach, it is too ugly a language. French, I speak French like a native, but English——You must eat my cake. My cook has made it especially for you. It is much nicer than English cake—what you call home made.' Frau Jorgon paused to take breath.

'How do you like Germany, may I ask, Mrs. Carr?' demanded the Frau Doctor in magisterial tones, and, laying down her knitting, she sipped her coffee and looked at the Englishwoman.

Marion Carr was about to make a reply when she caught a quizzical look in Frau Jorgon's sparkling eyes. She passed the question by. 'It is a wonderful country,' she said, which was a perfectly safe answer and might mean anything.

Frau Jorgon wagged her head. 'Ach, Mee-sis, you will not say. But you will not offend me. I do not say that I admire the English

language, or that I like English five o'clock tea and cake and English
ladies.   On the contrary, I think they are detestable.'

Frau Flink looked horrified, Anna Löser rather amused than otherwise, while the Frau Doctor exclaimed chidingly :

'Erna ! '

'Ach, I am only teasing Mee-sis Carr.   But I cannot make her
angry ; ' and Frau Jorgon bent forward, rested one arm on her knee,
and looked up into the Englishwoman's face.   'Of course I do not
mean that English ladies are detestable, only so *schrecklich* cold and
stiff and proud.   And are they never merry ?   I grant that they are
handsome, for I have seen them in the English Church, and at the
Opera, and they have fine figures, and beautiful complexions, and
long hair.   But oh! they are so cold and stiff.   Ach, I see you are
very sensible.   You do not look offended.   One lady who gave me
lessons was always offended because I would not say that I liked the
English language.   She was too stupid.'

'I understood that—we were to speak English, Frau Jorgon,' said
Marion Carr seriously, and for the third time she was compelled to
decline cake, much to her hostess's astonishment.

'But first we must make each other's acquaintance, and I cannot
say all this in English.   I will not talk English to-day.'

'But, Erna, I should like to talk English,' said Frau Flink, with
pleading eyes.

'Have you many pupils ? ' demanded the Frau Doctor, for she
could manage a straightforward question with remarkable fluency.

'Very few,' was the cheerful answer.

Frau Jorgon lifted her handsome black brows, 'Very few ?   And
you are not sad—sorry ? '

The Englishwoman smiled.   'I do not wish for many, Frau
Jorgon.   I live a very busy life, and every hour of the day is
occupied.'

'So ?   But how ? '   demanded the hostess with blunt but lively
curiosity.   'If you do not teach many pupils, what do you do ? '

'Teaching, Frau Jorgon, is but one of my irons in the fire—a
means to an end.'

'Irons in the fire !   Oh, please how does man spell "irons."   I must
know how the difficult words are spelt.'

'Ach, I do not understand ; and, Mietzel, do me the favour not
to spell to-day.   I wish to talk to Mee-sis Carr.   Please tell me, you
say you do not speak German, yet you understand quite well.   And
it is remarkable I understand you perfectly.'

'But, Erna, I want to know how the words are spelt.'

'Get a dictionary, then,' suggested the Frau Doctor, rather impatiently.

'I will tell you, Mietzel,' whispered the good-natured Hedwig.

Again Frau Jorgon turned to the Englishwoman, but noticing

'Are we not going to read to-day?'

'No, no, no. No reading. I will not read. Give me the book. I will hide it.' Frau Jorgon stooped and threw the book under the *causeuse*. 'It is better there. Marie will find it in the morning. It is getting late; my husband will be home early to-night, you will see, because he knows that he can talk English with Mee-sis Carr.'

'I fear I shall not have that honour,' said Marion Carr, a little ironically. 'It is already half-past six. And——'

'Oh, but you must not go yet. You must stay to supper, and then I will introduce you to my husband. You will love—like my husband. All women love—like my husband.'

'Erna!'

'He is a great favourite. He is very kind. He looks like an Englishman, but that is because he is a Pole and has lived in England and wears English clothes—*meinetwegen*. I do not object. I have all my gowns from Paris.'

'But really, Frau Jorgon——'

Frau Jorgon laid forcible hands on the unfortunate Englishwoman. 'Ach, I will not hear a word. I have already ordered supper—a very nice supper. I have an excellent cook. I pay her very high wages. My husband is very satisfied. It is good policy. A wife should always have a good cook—and charming gowns. They cost money, it is true, but my husband is indulgent. He spoils me. Do you dine at home, Mee-sis Carr, or do you go to a restaurant, as so many of the English people do here?'

'I seldom dine, Frau Jorgon,' was the demure answer, and instantly five pairs of eyes were focussed upon her.

'Wie?'

'How?'

'Not dine?'

'Seldom dine! You say so. But how then do you live? One must dine. What do you eat?'

'My meals are very simple, Frau Jorgon. I live mostly on bread and butter and milk.'

'But you cannot be strong without meat. I am not very strong, and my doctor tells me that I must eat much meat three times a day. He is very angry with me when I do not eat meat.'

At this juncture Frau Jorgon caught the pleading eye of the little Frau Flink, and changed the order of her cross-examination. She rose from her chair and sat down next to Marion Carr and began examining the texture of her gown, giving her an approving pat.

'It is a very nice gown, Mee-sis Carr. It is an English gown— yes? Look, Mietzel, look, Anna, how perfectly it fits. Now why

cannot Madame ' —— fit like that ? Her charges are enormous.
What do they charge in England for making a dress like this ? '

'I paid ten guineas for it,' said the Englishwoman coolly. 'About
two hundred marks.'

'Herr Je, two hundred marks ! How ? You pay two hundred
marks for a gown ! But you are a teacher. How can a teacher pay
two hundred marks for one gown ? '

The Frau Doctor looked up. 'It is a charming gown, Mrs.
Carr. I have heard before that English tailor-made gowns are very
expensive.'

'It is a ridiculous price to pay, two hundred marks !' said Anna
Löser rather acrimoniously.

'Not for a well-made gown,' returned the Englishwoman. 'I
cannot afford to be shabbily dressed.'

'What is shabby ? ' Ah, *schäbig*, so. But why not ? You must
have many pupils to pay two hundred marks for a single gown.'

'Oh no. I am very careful with my dresses. With care this
one will last quite two years.'

'But you cannot wear a tailor-made gown in the evening. What
do you wear——'

'My dear Erna,' Frau Doctor protested. 'Do let us talk a little
English. The afternoon is gone, and I cannot stay this evening.'

Marion Carr remarked with alacrity, 'I am quite at your service,
Frau Doctor. Shall we read ? '

'No, no, no. I will not read. Mrs. Carr shall talk to us. Tell
me about your travels, please ? You can speak in English, for I
understand very well. Only I will not talk.'

'My travels, Frau Jorgon ? '

'I have heard that you have travelled much.' Frau Jorgon
bent forward and touched the Englishwoman's hair approvingly. 'It
is nice hair. I like it. Then you have had many adventures,
Mee-sis Carr ? '

'Adventures ? '

'Ach, you know quite well what I mean. And Anna, you need
not listen. You are a girl. You can play to us. Mee-sis Carr is
fond of music. Play—play—'

Not waiting for a second invitation, Anna Löser gladly escaped to
the salon and began playing Liszt, without a light. This was an
excellent opportunity for Frau Flink, who, with loving fingers and
an ecstatic sigh, took up her blue silk bodice.

'Now tell me '—Frau Jorgon settled herself comfortably in a
corner of the *causeuse*, and folded her arms, and riddled the Englishwoman with looks—'now tell me, what have you seen and where
have you travelled ? You are quite young and quite, quite nice, I
find.'

'You are very kind,' was the ironical reply. 'If you will put the questions, Frau Jorgon, I will endeavour to answer them to the best of my ability. It will be easier for both of us.'

Frau Jorgon bent forward and whispered, 'Tell us first, why have you not married again? You are a widow, I believe—very sad.'

Marion Carr's face and figure took the coldness and immobility of stone. Frau Jorgon laughed: 'Now,' she said triumphantly, ' you are a real Englishwoman, cold and proud and shy. Why are you offended with me? Your eyes are angry, nice eyes. I will tell you all about *my* husband. *I* am not stiff and cold and reserved. You may ask me any questions you like.'

The Englishwoman maintained a dead silence.

'Ach! now I see why you will not tell me. You have secrets. Ah! yes, yes, yes. You blush. I am curious. Why do you blush? But it is very becoming. Ach well, you shall tell me all your secrets another day when the Frau Doctor is not here. *She* has no secrets. Neither has Hedwig secrets. Hedwig, Hedwig, put down those stupid crewels and say, have you any secrets? Only one, Mee-sis Carr, and I will tell you it. She is (in a loud whisper) an authoress. But she will not acknowledge it. Ach, here comes my husband.'

Marion Carr took a deep breath, and the Frau Doctor rolled up her stocking and consulted her watch. Frau Jorgon's brilliant eyes were laughingly fixed on the door, when it presently opened and a tall, foreign-looking man, with broad shoulders and a clean-shaven face, entered. His wife jumped up and introduced the two who were strangers to each other in her own off-hand way.

'Conrad, Mee-sis Carr—my husband, and now'—waving her hands—' you can talk as much English as you please.'

'Madam,' said Herr Jorgon—he came forward and shook hands heartily with the Englishwoman, his wife watching him—'Madam, I am pleased to welcome an Englishwoman to my house. I have lived in England, and received much hospitality at the hands of your compatriots; therefore I bid you welcome.'

There was a mocking laugh, and Frau Jorgon laid her two jewelled hands heavily on Marion Carr's shoulders.

'There, is not that a fine speech? Did not I say that my husband was very clever, and could talk English like a book?'

'Erna,' said her husband quietly, but with a heavy look of entreaty in his kind eyes. Then he turned to Marion Carr, who was looking and feeling excessively uncomfortable. 'On the contrary, Mrs. Carr, I have much forgotten. But I am very pleased to talk English again.'

'You will have plenty of opportunity now. And, Conrad, what do you think? You say I am an extravagant wife. But Mrs. Carr is extravagant. She pays two hundred marks for a gown, and she is not rich.'

Conrad Jorgon looked distressed, and excessively ashamed of his wife. But here a diversion was created by the opening of the folding doors which faced the salon where Anna Löser was still playing in the dark, and a well-spread supper table was displayed with two maids in attendance.

'Ach, I am hungry.' Frau Jorgon darted a keen glance at the supper table. 'Come, Mee-sis Carr, you shall sit by me,' and she linked her arm within that of the Englishwoman, calling to the others but not waiting for them. 'Anna, come! Marie, lower the lamps.'

One by one the ladies passed on into the supper-room, followed more slowly by Conrad Jorgon, who left the door ajar, for the maid was extinguishing the lamps in his wife's boudoir.

And the meal began with much energetic play of knives and forks and everybody talking at once—as a matter of course. The inquisitorial conversation was necessarily of a hybrid nature, shrewdly directed by practical housekeeping minds, each intent on its own particular bargain. It is needless to state that throughout the meal, and although she was looking fagged and wan, and her voice was growing hoarse and her throat ached, Marion Carr was furiously assailed with appeals and questions on a hundred and one different topics, to all of which she made answer with slow, clear, careful enunciation of every syllable. Herr Jorgon alone it was who at last put in a plea in behalf of the unfortunate Englishwoman.

'You are looking extremely tired, Mrs. Carr. Do rest a little. My wife is a perfect magpie.'

At this juncture Marion Carr was compelled to consult her watch. It was ten o'clock. She had been hard at work since four o'clock. How she managed to make her escape that night was never afterwards quite clear to her. But escape at last she did, descending the great stone staircase which led from Frau Jorgon's apartment on the first *étage* to the courtyard below, preceded by a sleepy maid carrying a lamp which she held high above her head. The great house door opened, then closed and locked behind her. With a stolid *Gute Nacht* from the maid, Marion Carr passed out into the deserted street. She breathed quickly and walked passionately, with her grave eyes fixed on the eternal stars.

'Another day's work done,' she murmured. 'But am I any nearer to my goal?'

KATHARINE BLYTH.

ARBITRATION IN LABOUR DISPUTES

·AMONG the 'hardy annuals' of the House of Commons, one of the most regular is the Bill for promoting arbitration in labour disputes. Every important strike, moreover, brings a whole crop of leading articles in which the journalists, of one party or another, either blame the Opposition for obstructing, or praise the Government for introducing, so beneficent a measure. Let us examine this panacea for industrial disturbances.

The essential feature of arbitration as a means of settling the condition of employment is that the decision is not the will of either party, or the outcome of negotiation between them, but the fiat of an umpire or arbitrator. It is distinguished from that organised negotiation between trade unions and employers' associations which is now termed collective bargaining, in that the result is not arrived at by bargaining at all, the higgling between the parties being, in fact, expressly superseded. On the other hand it is not legal regulation, though it bears some resemblance to this form, because the award is not obligatory on either of the parties, and their refusal to accept it, or their ceasing to obey it even if they have promised to do so, carries with it no coercive sanction.

These characteristics of arbitration, as a method of settling the conditions of employment, come to the front on every typical occasion. We see the employers and workmen at variance with each other. Negotiations, more or less formally ·carried on, proceed up to a point at which a deadlock seems inevitable. To avert a stoppage of the industry, both parties agree to 'go to arbitration.' They adopt an impartial umpire, either to act alone or with assessors representing each side. Each party then· prepares· an elaborate 'case,' which is ·laid before the new tribunal. Witnesses are called, examined and cross-examined. The umpire asks for such additional information as he thinks fit. Throughout the proceedings the utmost latitude is allowed. The 'reference' is· seldom limited to particular alternatives, or expressed with any precision. The umpire, in order to clear up points, is always enter-· ing into conversation with 'the parties. Practically no argument, however seemingly irrelevant, is excluded; and evidence may be given in support of claims founded on the most diverse economic theories. Finally, the umpire gives his award in precise terms, but usually without stating either the facts which have influenced him or the assumptions upon which he has made up his mind. The award—and this is an essential feature—carries with it no legal sanction, and may at any moment be repudiated or quietly ignored by any capitalist or workman.

Yet arbitration has one characteristic feature in common with the higgling of employers and workmen, which it supersedes. The arbitrator's award is a general ordinance, which, in so far as it is accepted, puts an end to individual bargaining between man and man, and thus excludes, from influence on the terms of employment, the exigencies of particular workmen, and usually also those of particular firms. It establishes, in short, like collective bargaining, a common rule for the industry concerned. We can therefore understand why the trade unionists from 1850 to 1876 so persistently strove for arbitration, and so eagerly welcomed the gradual conversion of the governing classes to a belief in its benefits. At a time when the majority of employers asserted their right to deal individually with each one of their 'hands,' habitually refused even to meet the men's representatives in discussion, and sought to suppress collective bargaining altogether by the use of ambiguous statutes and obsolete law, it was an immense gain for the trade unions to get their fundamental principle of a common rule adopted. During the last twenty years arbitration has greatly increased in popularity among the public, and each ministry in succession prides itself on having attempted to facilitate its application. Whenever an industrial war breaks out, we have, in these days, a widespread feeling among the public that both parties should voluntarily submit to the decision of an impartial arbitrator. But however convenient this solution may be to a public of consumers, the two combatants seldom show any alacrity in seeking it, and can rarely be persuaded to agree to refer their quarrel to any outside authority. Although arbitration has been preached as a panacea for the last forty years, the great majority of 'captains of industry' still resent it as an infringement of their right to manage their own business, whilst the leaders of the organised workmen, once enthusiastic in its favour, now usually regard it with suspicion. The four years 1891–95 saw, in Great Britain, four great industrial disputes in as many leading industries. But neither in cotton manufacture nor in coal-mining, neither in the great machine industry of boot-making nor in engineering, could the capitalists and workmen agree to let their quarrels be settled by an impartial umpire. What happened in each of these instances—and they were typical of many others—was the breaking off of collective bargaining, a prolonged stoppage and trial of endurance, ending, not in arbitration but in a resumption of collective bargaining, and the conclusion of a fresh agreement under new and more favourable auspices.

At first sight this disinclination of workmen or employers to submit their claims to an impartial tribunal appears perverse and unreasonable. Business men, it is said, almost invariably refer disputes between themselves to more or less formal arbitration, and would never dream of stopping their own industry, or drying up the source of their own profits, merely because they could not agree upon an impartial umpire. And if this be true in commercial transactions, where the alternative is nothing worse than an action at law, how much stronger the need must seem when the alternative may easily involve the bankruptcy of capitalists, the semi-starvation of thousands of operatives, and the temporary paralysis, if not the permanent injury, of an important national industry? Unfortunately this taking analogy, drawn from the arbitration between business firms, rests on the old confusion between interpreting an existing agreement and concluding a new one. Commercial arbitrations are invariably concerned with relations already entered into, either by existing contracts or under the law of the land. No business man ever dreams of submitting to arbitration the terms upon which he shall make new purchases or future sales.[1] Arbitration in commercial matters is therefore strictly confined to questions of interpretation, both parties resting their claims on a common basis, the existence of which is not in dispute between them. Now, issues of interpretation of this kind are incessantly occurring between employers and employed, even in the best-regulated industries. In these cases, as we shall hereafter point out, whilst there is no insuperable objection to arbitration, there is no real necessity to resort to it. Nor is it for this class of disputes that arbitration is usually proposed. The great strikes and lock-outs which paralyse a whole industry almost invariably arise not on issues of interpretation, but on the proposal of either workmen or employers to alter the terms upon which, for the future, labour shall be engaged.

The position of the employers who object to the fixing of the terms of the wage contract by the fiat of an arbitrator has, from the first, been logical and consistent. In a weighty article which appeared, twenty years ago, in the official organ of the National Association of Employers of Labour, we find the case stated with perfect lucidity.

[1] The frequently cited 'Conseils de Prud'hommes' of France are strictly confined to the settlement of disputes arising out of existing contracts, or (as regards minor matters) the application of the law. In no case do they presume to fix the rate of wages for future engagements. They are indeed merely cheap and convenient legal tribunals, which make efforts to compose a dispute before proceeding to pronounce judgment upon it. We understand that this is the character also of the similar tribunals which exist in various German States and elsewhere.

The sphere of arbitration in trade disputes is strictly and absolutely limited to cases of specific contract, where the parties differ as to the terms of the contract, and are willing, for the sake of agreement and an honourable fulfilment of their engagements, to submit the points in dispute to competent men mutually chosen. Where there is a basis and instrument of agreement by the parties to which they wish to adhere, and on which arbiters have something tangible to decide upon, it is seldom difficult for impartial men to elicit an adjustment fair and equitable to both sides. Arbitration is thus constantly of use in business matters on which differences of view have arisen, and is as applicable to questions between workmen and employers where there is a specific contract to be interpreted as in any other branch of affairs. It is better than going to law, much better than running away from the contract, striking, coercing, and falling into civil damages or criminal penalties, and raising on the back of such unfortunate consequences a blatant and endless protest against 'the labour laws.' But cases in which there are specific contracts absolutely define the sphere of arbitration. To apply the term ' arbitration' to the rate of wages for the future, in regard to which there is no explicit contract or engagement, and all the conditions of which are unknown to employers and employed, is the grossest misnomer that can be conceived. It is certain that neither workmen nor employers could be bound, nor would consent to be bound, even were it possible to bind them, by such arbitrary decrees; and that the law, therefore, can never give such decrees even any temporary force, unless we are to fall back into the long obsolete tyranny of fixing the rate of wages by Act of Parliament, or by ' King in Council,' or by ' Communal Bureau of Public Safety,' or whatever the supreme power may be.[2]

Thus, from the employers' point of view, the supersession of the higgling of the market by the fiat of an arbitrator is, on its economic side, as indefensible an interference with industrial freedom as a legal fixing of the rate of wages. But an arbitrator's award has additional disadvantages. A law would at any rate be an authoritative settlement, which disposed of the question beyond dispute or cavil. An arbitrator's award, on the other hand, even if it is accepted by the trade union, may not commend itself to all the workmen. The employers who accept it may not unnaturally feel that they have surrendered their own freedom, without securing any guarantee that the workmen, or some indispensable sections of them, will not promptly commence a new attack on which to provoke a stoppage of the industry. A law, moreover, is a common rule, enforced with uniformity on all alike. The arbitrator's award, on the other hand, binds only those firms and those workmen who were parties to it. In almost all industries there are some establishments, and often whole districts, which remain outside the employers' association, and in which masters and men persist in conducting their businesses in their own way. And there is no guarantee that some firms will not break away from the association, and join the ranks of these unfettered outsiders. If the arbitrator's award has secured better terms to the operatives than the masters are unanimously willing to concede, the good and honourable employers are

2 *Capital and Labour*, June 16, 1875.

penalised by their virtue. The proceedings of the 'Boards of Conciliation and Arbitration' of the boot-making industry contain many complaints by employers that the awards are not enforced on rival firms, who are consequently undercutting them in the market. If our factory or mines legislation had been enforced only on specified good employers, and had left untouched any firm who objected to the regulations, so intolerable an injustice would quickly have led to a repudiation of the whole system.

If we turn from the employers to the trade unionists, we find a steadily increasing disinclination among workmen to agree to the intervention of an arbitrator to settle the terms of a new wage contract. This growing antipathy[3] to arbitration is, we think, mainly due to their feeling of uncertainty as to the fundamental assumptions upon which the arbitrator will base his award. When the issue is whether the 'standard earnings' of the Lancashire cottonspinners should or should not be decreased by ten per cent., there is no basis accepted by both parties except the vague admission that the award should not be contrary to the welfare of the community. But this offers no guidance to the arbitrator. Judge Ellison, for instance, acting in 1879 in a Yorkshire coalmining case, frankly expressed the perplexity of an absolutely open-minded umpire.

It is [he said] for (*the employers' advocate*) to put the men's wages as high as he can. It is for (*the men's advocate*) to put them as low as he can. And when you have done that it is for me to deal with the question as well as I can; but on what principle I have to deal with it I have not the slightest idea. There is no principle of law involved in it. There is no principle of political economy in it. Both masters and men are arguing and standing upon what is completely within their rights. The master is not bound to employ labour except at a price which he thinks will pay him. The man is not bound to work for wages that won't

---

[3] We may cite as evidence of this antipathy some recent declarations made in the names of the three most powerful organisations in the United Kingdom. It is expressly stated (for instance, in the Derbyshire Miners' Executive Council Minutes of the 2nd of June, 1891) that it was the idea that the Royal Commission on Labour was intended to introduce a 'huge arbitration system;' that determined the whole Miners' Federation steadfastly to refuse to have anything to do with that inquiry. 'We are opposed to the system altogether,' declared Mr. Mawdsley before that Commission (Group A, Answer 776), on behalf of the Lancashire cotton operatives. And Mr. Robert Knight, giving evidence on behalf of the United Society of Boilermakers (Group C, Answer 20, 833), definitely negatived the idea of arbitration, explaining as follows: 'I speak from long experience of the working of this large organisation that I represent here to-day, and I say that we can settle all our differences without any interference on the part of Parliament or anybody else.' The same feeling is shared by smaller societies. 'Our experience of arbitration,' states the Secretary of the North Yorkshire and Cleveland (Ironstone) Miners' Association, 'was that we always got the worst of it, and so since 1877 it has been firmly refused.'—Joseph Toyn, in *Newcastle Leader* '*Extra*' *on Conciliation in Trade Disputes* (Newcastle, 1894), p. 9.

assist (subsist) him and his family sufficiently, and so forth. So that you are both within your rights ; and that's the difficulty I see n dealing with the question.[4]

But this cold-blooded elimination of everything beyond the legal rights of the parties is neither usual in a wages arbitration, nor acceptable to either side. Each of the parties implicitly rests its case on a distinct economic assumption, or even series of assumptions, not accepted by the other side, and not often expressly stated. The employers will often hold that, in order to secure the utmost national prosperity, wages should rise and fall with the price which they can obtain for their product. Or it may be urged that the wage bill must under no circumstances encroach upon the particular percentage of profit assumed to be necessary to prevent capital from leaving the trade.[5] These assumptions would, at one time, have been acquiesced in by many leading workmen, although, perhaps, not by the rank and file. But during the last twenty years, the leaders of the most powerful organisations have definitely taken up the view that considerations of market price or business profit ought, in the interests of the community, to be strictly subordinated to the fundamental question of ' Can a man live by the trade ? ' It is urged that the payment of ' a living wage ' ought, under all circumstances, to be a ' first charge' upon industry, taking precedence even of rents or royalties, and of the hypothetical percentage allowed as a minimum to capital in the worst times. The skilled mechanic moreover will claim that the length of his apprenticeship warrants him in insisting, like the physician or the barrister, on a minimum fee for his services below which he cannot be asked to descend. The arbitrator's award, if it is not a mere 'splitting the difference,' must be influenced by one or the other of these assumptions, either as a result of the argument before him, or as the outcome of his education or sympathies. However judicial he may be in ascertaining the facts of the case, the relative importance which he will give to the rival assumptions of the parties can scarcely fail to be affected by the subtle influences of his class and training. The persons chosen as arbitrators have almost invariably been representative of the brain-working class—great employers, statesmen or lawyers—men bringing to the task the highest qualities of training, impartiality, and judgment, but unconsciously

[4] *Report of South Yorkshire Collieries Arbitration* (Sheffield, 1879), p. 49. The umpire was the Judge of the Sheffield County Court.

[5] Mr. Mawdsley (Amalgamated Association of Cottonspinners) is very emphatic on this point. ' If we had arbitration we should have much less wages than we are getting now. Arbitrators generally go in for a certain standard of profit for capital —generally speaking, it has been 10 per cent. Mr. Chamberlain has always said that capital ought to have 10 per cent. If the arbitrator went in for 10 per cent. in the cotton trade, we should have a very big reduction of wages ; and we are not going to have it.'—Evidence before Royal Commission on Labour, Group C, Answer 774. We believe the case to which Mr. Mawdsley referred is Mr. Chamberlain's award in the South Staffordshire Iron Trade in 1878.

imbued rather with the assumptions of the class in which they live than with those of the workmen. The workmen's growing objection to arbitration is, we believe, mainly due to their deeply rooted suspicion that any arbitrator likely to be accepted by the employers will, however personally impartial he may be, unconsciously discount assumptions inconsistent with the current economics of his class.

There is however one industry in which, for five and twenty years, arbitration has been habitually resorted to, for the settlement of the terms of new wage contracts. This one exception to the usual dislike of arbitration will, we think, prove the correctness of the foregoing analysis. 'The Board of Conciliation and Arbitration for the Manufactured Iron Trade of the North of England,' which has existed since 1869, has long been the classical example of the success of arbitration. Besides providing by the machinery of a standing committee for the settlement of interpretation differences, and by half-yearly board meetings for discussing general questions, the rules direct the reference of intractable disputes to an outside umpire. On twenty separate occasions during the last twenty-five years this provision has come into operation with regard to the settlement of the conditions of future wage contracts; and on every occasion the arbitrator's award has been accepted by both employers and employed.

It is an interesting confirmation of the view we have taken that, in this one industry in which arbitration has achieved a continued success, we find the workmen and the employers agreeing in the economic assumptions upon which wages should be fixed, and upon which therefore the arbitrator is asked to proceed. It has for more than a generation been traditional among ironmasters that the wages of the operatives ought to vary with the market price of the product. Since the formation of the board, in 1869, this assumption has been accepted by both parties as the main, and often as the exclusive, rule for the settlement of wages. In the reports of the arbitration proceedings we find both parties constantly reaffirming this principle, each in turn resorting to other considerations only for the sake of argument when the main assumption is for the moment calculated to tell against them. 'We entirely agree,' declare the operatives in 1877, 'that our wages should be regulated by the selling price of iron.'[6] Next time it is the employers who assert the same rule. 'The eight years sliding-scale arrangement,' states their spokesman in 1882, 'we believe was the principle of determining wages by the selling price of iron, and it would be extremely difficult, if not dangerous, permanently to depart from that.'[7] There is, in fact, as a careful student observes, 'a general understanding running through the cases and pleadings, both of masters and men, that

[6] Report of Arbitration before Mr. (now Sir D.) Dale, July 1877.
[7] Report of Arbitration before Mr. (now Sir J. W.) Pease, April 1882.

wages should follow the selling prices of iron.'[8]   This was expressly
stated by Dr. R. Spence Watson in the letter which accompanied
his fifth award as arbitrator for this board.   Whilst observing
that

the wages paid in the Staffordshire district, which competes with the North of
England in the employment of ironworkers, as well as to some extent in the trade
itself, is a factor which cannot be disregarded, [he declares that] in the course of
the arguments it was admitted on both sides that . . . the realised price of iron,
as shown by the figures taken out by the accountant to the board, may be considered the principal factor in the regulation of wages. . . . It is upon this statement [he continues] and these admissions that I am called upon to give my
award.[9]

It will be apparent that arbitration on issues of this kind comes
really within the category of the interpretation or application of
what is, in effect, an agreement already arrived at between the
parties.   The question comes very near to being one of fact, answered
as soon as the necessary figures are ascertained beyond dispute.   It
is therefore not surprising to learn that, during eight of the twenty-
five years of the board's existence, variations of wages were automatically determined by a formal sliding scale, and that even during
the intervals in which no definite scale was adopted the board itself
was able, on eight separate occasions, to agree to advances or
réductions without troubling the arbitrator at all.   We need not
discuss whether the acceptance by employers and operatives alike
of the assumption that wages must follow prices is, or is not,
advantageous to the workmen, or to the industry as a whole.   But
it is evident that the continued success of arbitration in the North of
England Iron Board, dealing, as it does, mainly with the interpretation or application of an existing common basis of agreement, affords
no guide to other trades in which no such common basis is accepted,
and in which the claims of the respective parties rest on opposite
assumptions.

But the success of the North of England Manufactured Iron
Board, whilst it gives no real support to arbitration as a panacea for
strikes, seems at first to open up a new field of usefulness for the
arbitrator in the settlement of issues of application or interpretation.
These questions of interpretation or application to particular cases
are always arising, even in the best-regulated trade, and to provide
machinery for their peaceful and indisputable decision is of great
importance.   Here we have not merely identical assumptions by the
two parties, but a precise bargain by which both agree to be bound.
Unfortunately it is just in these issues, for which arbitration seems a
natural expedient, that its adoption has been found, in practice, most
difficult.   The application of a general agreement to the earnings of

---

[8] *Industrial Peace*, by L. L. F. R. Price (London, 1887), p. 90.

[9] Letter and award of the 28th of November, 1888; *Report of Wages Arbitration
before R. S. Watson, Esq., LL.D.* (Darlington, 1888).

particular individuals, or to the technical details of particular samples or processes, is at once too complicated, and of too little pecuniary importance, to make it possible to call in an outside arbitrator.[10] The intractable questions, to take one trade as an example, which perplex the local boards in the boot and shoe industry relate only to a few shillings, and frequently concern only one or two workmen. For such issues it is obviously impossible to obtain, either for love or money, the services of any personality eminent enough to command the respect of the whole body of employers and workmen. Where the standard of earnings of large bodies of men, or the prevention of a serious industrial war, are concerned, public spirit will induce men of the calibre of Lord James or Dr. Spence Watson to spend whole days, without fee or reward, in bringing about an adjustment. In commercial arbitrations which involve considerable sums, recourse is had to eminent lawyers, who are paid large fees for mastering the intricate details of each case. This sort of arbitrator is far too expensive a person to be available for the application of general wage contracts to particular cases, and the statesman or philanthropist cannot spare the time. On the other hand, if, as in the boot and shoe trade, recourse is had to some one engaged in the industry, it is difficult to avoid the suspicion of class bias. The big employer from another district, whose services are usually called in, can hardly be expected to content the workmen. The employers, on the other hand, will not consent to be bound by the decision of an operative.

It is fortunately unnecessary for the employers and workmen to get into this dilemma. The correct analogy from the commercial world for all these issues of interpretation is not the elaborate and costly reference to arbitration, but the simple arrangements for taking an inventory, in connection with a contract of purchase or hire. Instead of calling in an outside authority, eminent enough to be known and trusted by both sides, each party is represented by an inexpensive expert habitually engaged on the particular calculations involved. The two professional men seldom find any difficulty in agreeing upon an identical award. This corresponds exactly to the

[10] Thus, when in 1891, in an arbitration between the West Cumberland Iron and Steel Company and their workmen, the arbitrator (Dr. Spence Watson) was asked to fix the actual rates at which particular men were to be paid, he declined the task as one outside the possible capacity of any arbitrator. 'What has always happened,' said Dr. Spence Watson, 'in every arbitration I have had hitherto? There has been a general question of percentage. . . . The principle of the thing is the thing to leave to arbitration. The detail of the thing, as to how it is to affect this or that or the other, never can be left to arbitration. . . . Already over this matter I have given up several nights to go through these papers and work them in this way and that way, but I have not the knowledge, and you cannot give me the knowledge. . . . Surely the question of individual payment is a question for the manager of the works and the men of the works, and not for a third party.'—MS. proceedings. We are indebted to Dr. Spence Watson for permission to examine these and other papers, and for many valuable suggestions and criticisms.

machinery which is employed with such success in the Lancashire cotton trade. The two secretaries who visit the mill in which any question of interpretation has arisen correspond in all essentials to the two house agents employed respectively by the owner and the incoming tenant of a furnished house. In the interpretation of wage contracts there is even more justification for this method than in taking an inventory. The object of the house agent on either side is to get the best terms for his client. But the professional experts who visit a cotton mill, in response to a complaint from operative or employer, are not employed by or responsible to either of the parties directly concerned. And though one represents the associated employers, and the other the combined workmen, both are retained and paid to secure an identical object, namely, absolute uniformity between mill and mill. So far as regards the application to the particular cases of existing general contracts between employers and workmen, arbitration, though possible, is therefore but a clumsy device. The only way of getting an efficient umpire for such technical work would be permanently to employ a professional expert of high standing to give his whole time to the business. But directly an industry is sufficiently well organised to afford the expense of an efficient paid umpire, it can find in the joint meeting of the salaried experts of both sides a far more speedy, economical, and uniform method of settling questions of interpretation than any arbitration could provide.

The reader is now in a position to estimate how far arbitration is likely to serve as a panacea against strikes or lock-outs, or even to become a permanent feature of the most highly organised machinery for collective bargaining. In the really crucial instances —the issues relating to the conclusion of a new agreement—habitual and voluntary recourse to an umpire may be expected, we think, only in the unlikely event of capitalists and workmen adopting identical assumptions as to the proper basis of wages. We have seen how unreservedly the best-educated workmen of the North of England accepted, between 1870 and 1885, the capitalists' assumption that it was only fair that wages should vary with the selling price of the product. For twenty years the miners of South Wales have acquiesced in the same doctrine. If this view were to become accepted in other trades, it is conceivable that arbitration would become more popular among them. On the other hand there is growing up among workmen a strong feeling in favour of a fixed minimum standard of life, to be regarded as the first charge upon the industry of the country, and to be determined by the requirements of healthy family life and citizenship. If the capitalists should accept this view, arbitrations might become common, the explicit reference in every case being what conditions were required in the industry to enable the various grades of producers to lead a civilised life. But no such agreement on fundamental assumptions is at present within view. We are therefore constrained not to place any high expectations upon the fiat of an umpire as a method of preventing disputes as to future conditions of labour. Nor can we estimate very highly the practical value of arbitration in the application to particular cases of existing general agreements. In promptitude, technical efficiency, and inexpensiveness the ' impartial outsider ' is inferior to the joint meeting of the salaried secretaries of either side.

But although arbitration is not likely to supersede collective bargaining, or to prevent the occasional breaking off of negotiations, it has great advantages, in all but the best-organised trades, as a means of helping forward the negotiations themselves. The first requisite for efficient collective bargaining is for the parties to meet face to face, and in an amicable manner to discuss each other's claim. But this initial step is often one of difficulty. We are apt to forget, in view of the regular negotiations in such highly organised trades as the cotton operatives, the boiler-makers, and the Northumberland and Durham coalminers, how new and unusual it still is for capitalists and workmen to meet on an equal footing, to recognise each other's representative capacity, and to debate, with equal good temper, technical knowledge, and argumentative skill, upon what conditions the employer shall engage ' his own hands.' Even to-day, in the great majority of trades, the masters would think it beneath their dignity voluntarily to confer with the trade union leaders on equal terms ; and they would resent as preposterous the idea of disclosing to them their profit and loss accounts, or even the prices they are obtaining for their product. Yet it is upon these facts that they base their demand for a reduction of wages, or their refusal of an advance. The workmen, on the other hand, especially in such half-organised trades, are full of prejudices, misconceptions of the acts, and utopian aspirations. Under these circumstances, even if the employers consent to meet the men at all, there can be no frank interchange of views, no real understanding of each other's position—in short, no effective negotiation. Recourse to an impartial umpire is one way out of these difficulties. The employer's dignity is not offended by appearing before an eminent jurist or statesman, sitting virtually in a judicial capacity. It is regarded as only natural that the arbitrator should ask for the statistical facts upon which each party bases its case. The mere fact of each having to set forth its claims in precise terms, in a way that can be maintained under cross-examination, is already a great gain. But if the arbitrator is tactful and experienced, he can do a great deal more to bring the parties to agreement. He discovers, by kindly examination, what precisely it is that each party regards as essential, and persuasively puts on one side any irritating reminiscences of past disputes, or theoretic arguments going beyond the narrow limits of the case. In friendly conversation with each side in turn, he draws out the really strong arguments of both, restates them in their most effective form, and in due course impresses them, in the most conciliatory terms, on the notice of the opponent. Those who have read the proceedings before such an experienced arbitrator as Dr. Spence Watson will, we are sure, agree with us in feeling that his wonderful success as an umpire is far more due to these arts of conciliation than to any infallibility in his awards. In case after case we have been struck by the fact that, long before the end of the discussion, many of the issues had already been disposed of, the points remaining in dispute being so narrowed down by a mutual recognition of each other's case that when the award is at last given each party is predisposed to accept it as inevitable.

In this patient work of conciliation lies the real value of arbitration proceedings. There is no magic in the fiat of an arbitrator as a remedy for strikes or lock-outs. If either party really prefers fighting to conceding the smallest point to its adversary—that is, in those cases in which either employers or the workmen have an overwhelming superiority in strength—there will be no submission to arbitration. If both parties are willing to bargain, and are sufficiently well organised and well educated to be capable of it, no outside intervention will be needed. In those industries, however, where organisation has begun, but has not yet reached the highest form; where the employers are forced to recognise the power of the men's union, but have not yet brought themselves to meet its officials on terms of real equality; where the workmen are strong enough to strike, but do not yet command the services of experienced negotiators, the intervention of an eminent outsider may be of the utmost value. It is of small importance whether his intervention takes the form of 'arbitration' or 'conciliation'—that is to say, whether he is empowered to close the discussion by himself delivering an 'award' as umpire, or whether he must wait until he can bring the parties to sign an 'agreement' drawn up by himself as chairman. In either case his real business is not to supersede the process of collective bargaining, but to forward it. And in view of the usual impossibility of agreeing upon any common assumption as to the proper basis of wages; in face of the workman's suspicion of the brain-worker's training, and the employer's fear of electioneering considerations; and remembering the importance of securing universal concurrence in the result, we are, indeed, inclined to believe that the intervention of the 'eminent outsider' will, as a rule, be at once more acceptable and more likely to be successful if he avowedly acts only as a 'conciliator.'

This inference is supported by the events of the last few years. On four notable occasions outside intervention has been evoked to settle a serious industrial conflict. In 1893 Lord Rosebery, at the express desire of the Cabinet, settled a dispute which had for sixteen weeks stopped the coal trade of the Midlands of England. The next year saw the intervention of Mr. Asquith, as Home Secretary, in the quarrel between the London cabowners and their drivers. In 1895 Sir Courtenay Boyle, Permanent Secretary of the Board of Trade, drew up the agreement which terminated the great strike in the boot trade. And Lord James, a distinguished member of the Conservative Ministry of the day, in January 1896 brought about, after protracted negotiations, a settlement of the dispute between the Clyde and Belfast shipbuilders and their engineers. But notwithstanding the official position of these magnates, it is significant that in no case were they asked, and in no case did they attempt, to cut the Gordian knot by the judicial decree of an umpire or arbitrator. It was not their business to inquire into the merits of the case. They were not called upon to make up their minds whether the employers or the workmen were in the right. They had not even to choose between the rival economic assumptions on which the parties rested their respective claims. Their function was to persuade the representatives of both sides to go on negotiating until a basis was discovered on which it was possible for them to agree.

This work of conciliation is, we believe, destined to play a great and for many years an increasing part in the labour struggles of this country. In the present state of public opinion the intervention of an outside 'conciliator' is, as regards the imperfectly organised trades, a precursor of regular collective bargaining. In many trades the employers themselves are not united in any association : in many others they still haughtily refuse to discuss matters with their workmen. In any prolonged dispute public opinion now almost forces the parties to resume negotiations, and the intervention of an eminent outsider is found the best lever for collective bargaining. His social position or official status secures for the proceedings, even among angry men, a certain amount of dignity, order, and consideration for each other's feelings, whilst it prevents any hasty rupture or withdrawal. So long as Lord Rosebery was willing to go on sitting, it was practically impossible for either the coalowners or the coalminers to stop discussing. But prolonged discussion does not lead to agreement unless the parties get on good terms with each other, and are brought into a friendly mood. It is the conciliator's business to see that this atmosphere of good humour is produced and maintained. The excellent luncheon which Lord Rosebery provided for owners and workmen alike was probably more effective in creating harmony than the most convincing arguments about 'the living wage.' All this, however, is but preliminary to the real business. We have already described the important part played by a tactful and experienced arbitrator in drawing out the best points in each party's case, restating them in the most persuasive form, and eliminating from the controversy all unnecessary sources of irritation

or non-essential differences. The ideal conciliator adds to this a
happy suggestiveness and fertility in devising possible alternatives.
Throughout the discussion he watches for the particular points to
which each party really attaches importance. He has a quick
eye for acceptable lines of compromise. At the right psychological moment, when discussion is beginning to be tedious to both
sides, he is ready with a form of words. This is the crisis of the
proceedings. If the parties are physically and mentally tired, and
yet pleased with themselves and no longer angry with their opponents ;
if the conciliator is adroit in his drafting, and finds a formula which,
whilst making mutual concessions on minor points, includes, or seems
to each party to include, a great deal of what each has been contending for, the resolution will be agreed to, if not by acclamation, at any
rate after a few minor amendments to save the dignity of one side
or the other ; and almost before some of the slower-minded representatives have had time to think out all the bearings of the compromise the agreement is signed, and peace is secured.

We see, therefore, that outside intervention in wages disputes
may be of the highest value, and we anticipate that it will, for many
years to come, in all but the best-organised trades, play a great, and
even an increasing, part. But its function will not be that of 'arbitration,' properly so called, but rather that of 'conciliation,' though this
will continue to be sometimes carried on under the guise of arbitration. Instead of aiming at superseding collective bargaining, the
arbitrator will more and more consciously seek to promote it. In
fact, so far from being the crown of industrial organisation, the reference of disputes to an impartial outsider is a mark of its imperfection.
Arbitration is the temporary expedient of incompletely organised
industries, destined to be cast aside by each of them in turn when a
higher stage, like that of the cotton operatives or the boiler-makers, is
attained. The present Government has therefore done well to cut
down its arbitration bill to a modest 'Conciliation Act.' The preten-
tious legislation of 1867 and 1872, from which so much was expected,
is now simply repealed. The Board of Trade is empowered, in case
of an industrial dispute, 'to inquire into the causes and circumstances
of the difference.' It may intervene as the friend of peace, to persuade the parties to come to an agreement. If a conciliator is
desired, it may appoint one. Finally, if both parties join in asking
that the settlement shall proceed in the guise of arbitration, and wish
the Board of Trade to select the arbitrator for them, the Board of
Trade may accede to their request, as it might have done without any
Act at all !

This conclusion will disappoint those who see in arbitration not a
subordinate and temporary adjunct to collective bargaining, but a
panacea for stoppages of industry. The popularity of arbitration has
deep roots. At the back of the peremptory public demand for the

interests of the whole community neither employers nor workmen ought to be allowed to paralyse their own industry. If one side or the other persists in standing out, we have a clamour for 'compulsory arbitration:' that is, the intervention of the power of the State. We need not enter into the numerous suggestions that have been made for 'State Boards of Arbitration,' authoritative intervention by the Board of Trade, or the deposit, by both parties, of sums of money to be legally forfeited upon breach of the award. The authors of such suggestions always find themselves in a dilemma. If resort to this kind of arbitration is still to be voluntary, the liability to penalties or legal proceedings is not calculated to persuade either employers or workmen to come within its toils.[11] If, on the other hand, it is to be compulsory, it will amount to legal regulation, of a novel kind. It may well be argued that the community, for the protection of the public welfare, is entitled to step in and decide the terms upon which mechanics shall labour, and upon which capitalists shall engage them. In such a case the public decision could perhaps best be embodied in the award of an impartial arbitration tribunal, invested with all the solemnity of the State. But here we pass outside the domain of 'arbitration' properly so called. The question is then no longer the patching up of a quarrel between capitalists and workmen, but the deliberate determination by the community of the conditions under which certain industrial operations shall be allowed to be carried on. Such an award would have to be enforced on the parties whose recalcitrance had rendered it necessary. This does not imply, as is sometimes suggested, that workmen would be marched into the works by a regiment of soldiers, or that the police would open the gates (and the cash box) of stubborn employers. All that the award need decree is, that if capitalists desire to engage in the particular industry they shall do so only on the specified conditions. The enforcement of these conditions would become a matter for official inspection, followed by prosecutions for breaches of what would in effect be the law of the land. Here, it is true, we do find an effective panacea for strikes and lock-outs. Although industrial history records plenty of agitations and counter-agitations for and

[11] The following extract from a recent report of so experienced and well-informed a society as the United Textile Factory Workers' Association is significant: 'Boards of Conciliation.—Any number of Bills are constantly being introduced on this question, but your Council do not see that any useful purpose can be served by their becoming law. The assumption on which all these proposals are based is that . . . when the return goes down the wages of labour and the profits of capital should go down together. . . . The umpire is never a workman, but always a member of the upper class, whose sympathies and interest lie in the direction of keeping wages down. . . . They believe that the Bills now being brought forward are meant as so many traps with which to catch a portion of the workers' wages, and they have consequently opposed them.'—*Report of the Legislative Council of the United Textile Factory Workers' Association* for 1893-4, p. 17.

against the fixing by law of various conditions of employment, there has never been either a lock-out or a strike against a new Factory or Truck Act. But by adopting this method of avoiding the occasional breaking off of negotiations which accompanies collective bargaining, we should supersede collective bargaining altogether. The conditions of employment would no longer be left to the higgling of masters and men, but would be authoritatively decided without their consent in the manner which the community, acting through an arbitrator, thought most expedient. 'Compulsory arbitration' means, in fact, the fixing of wages by law.

SIDNEY AND BEATRICE WEBB

1

THE WELL AT THE WORLD'S END [1]

THE creative gift of Mr. Morris, his distinctive power of imagination, cannot be defined or appreciated by any such test of critical comparison as is applicable to the work of any other man. He is himself alone, and so absolutely that his work can no more be likened to any mediæval than to any contemporary kinsman's. In his love of a story for a story's sake he is akin to Chaucer and the French precursors of Chaucer: but if he has not much of Chaucer's realistic humour and artistic power of condensation and composition, he has a gift of invention as far beyond Chaucer's as the scope of a story like *The Well at the World's End* is beyond the range of such brief romances as *Amis and Amile* or *Aucassin and Nicolette*. Readers and lovers (the terms should here be synonymous) of his former tales or poems in prose will expect to find in this masterpiece—for a perfect and unique masterpiece it is—something that will remind them less of *Child Christopher* than of *The Wood beyond the World*: the mere likeness in the titles would suggest so much: and this I think they will not fail to find: but I am yet more certain that the quality of this work is even finer and stronger than that of either. The interest, for those who bring with them to the reading of a work of imagination any auxiliary or sympathetic imagination of their own, is deeper and more vivid as well as more various: but the crowning test and triumph of the author's genius will be recognised in the all but unique power of touching with natural pathos the alien element of magical or supernatural fiction. Coleridge could do this: who else till now has done it? And when we venture to bring in the unapproachable name of Coleridge, we are venturing to cite the example of the most imaginative, the most essentially poetic, among all poets of all nations and all time.

It should be remembered that when an allegorical intention was

[1] *The Well at the World's End.* 2 vols. By William Morris. London: Longmans & Co., 1896.

detected in the beautiful story of adventure and suffering and love which enchanted all readers in *The Wood beyond the World*, Mr. Morris for once condescended to disclaim the misinterpretation of his meaning, and to point out the difference between allegorical and simple narrative in words of perfect and conclusive accuracy. No commentator, I should hope, will ever waste his time on the childish task of inventing an occult significance for the incidents and adventures, the lurid and the lovely landscapes, set before him and impressed upon his memory in this later and yet more magically beautiful tale. The perfect simplicity and the supreme nobility of the spirit which informs and pervades and quickens and exalts it must needs make any but an inept and incapable reader feel yet once more a sense of wonder at the stupidity of the generations which could imagine a difference and a contrast between simple and noble. The simplest English writer of our time is also the noblest: and the noblest by reason and by virtue of his sublime simplicity of spirit and of speech. If the English of the future are not utterly unworthy and irredeemably unmindful of the past, they will need no memorial to remind them that his name was William Morris.

ALGERNON CHARLES SWINBURNE.

2

WINDFALL AND WATERDRIFT [1]

THIS little square book, the colour of meadow forget-me-nots, is so modest and simple that it may very easily be passed over in a period which has little sympathy with tenderness of feeling and simplicity of expression. The verses, of which this small volume is full, resemble the *stornelli* and *rispetti* of Italian songs rather than any kind of verse which has preceded them in English literature, unless it be the earliest and briefest songs of Robert Lytton, with which they have a certain kindred, both in their measure and in their themes. Auberon Herbert is known to the world as a daring and original thinker, a sociologist who lives three centuries before his time, a fearless preacher of new liberties and ideal creeds; in this tiny azure booklet he is also a poet, or, as he would rather himself say, a singer. The verse springs from the depths of his heart, and calls to those who, like himself, have loved and suffered and found nothing endure except the consolations of natural beauty.

[1] *Windfall and Waterdrift.* By Auberon Herbert. London: Williams & Norgate.

As the great king goes to his rest;
In the East the purple staineth
The hills from foot to crest.

And I stand and look in wonder
Till my heart is cleft in twain,
Half for the vision of glory,
And half for the dying pain.

Like the Italian *canzone*, these little lyrics, brief as a summer breeze, which momentarily sways the stalks of grass, must be heard with the ear of the heart. Coldly criticised by the mind alone, they will lie like the gathered field-poppy, inert and colourless. They are the cries of the heart, like those *stornelli* which the Tuscan lover sings to the sobbing lute beneath the moon. He who has killed his heart in the pressure of the world will find nothing in them. They who are steeped in the chill indifference of mundane interests will no more heed them than such heed the skylark's or the linnet's song which they resemble. They were not written in the study, or fashioned with the pruning-knife; they were born by the edge of the sea, in the woodland shade, by the clover path of the country hedge, in the falling rain of the peach and pear-blossoms, in the starlight above the olives. They are the elder children of the lonely shores and flowering pastures; they have never known the gaslight of the streets or the electric light of the drawing-room. They are as sweet and pure as violets.

To those who know, and respect as they should be respected, the virile and original philosophies of the writer, there is an added charm in these tender blossoms in the fact that they spring from the same intelligence as that which proclaims individualism in its boldest forms and attacks the tyrannies of social and political superstitions.

They are but little songs, short as a ripple of music from a wood-lark's throat, of no more account, if you will, than the blue stars of mouse-ear by the brook's side, than the dog-rose on the bank; too simple it may be said, speaking of emotions too trite, of sorrow too common, of sights too familiar, in language that the dullest can scarce fail to understand. Yes; no doubt, they are like field-flowers, like hedge-birds; they claim to be no more than these; they were not wrestled for as Wordsworth wrestled for an ode beneath the shadow of Rydal, or as Coleridge strove with the rebellious forces of a halting sonnet when lying down face foremost amongst ' the common grass.' They are spontaneous utterances, as natural as the ripple of the water over the cresses in a brook's bed beneath willow and alder. It may be easy to dismiss them with indifference, to underrate them with hypercritic sneer, and assuredly those who take pleasure in the strained archaic obscurities of much modern verse will find no more

charm in them than the languid æsthete, musing over the pages of
Verlaine and Mallarme, would find in a sea-wet breeze blowing across
a hayfield at early morning.　There is no studied mannerism,
no sought-for darkness of expression, no exaggerated ecstasy or
pessimism; there is such a natural feeling of joy as of sorrow,
which come to the soul at once robust and sensitive; and these
are expressed with frank, unstudied *naïveté,* with the candour as of a
child, and the self-control of a man blent in their simplicity.　' Look
in your own heart and write,' has been the only precept which their
creator has obeyed.　The most intense attachment in them is for the
sea.　The sea, whether those grey sad tides which sway from the
sands of Christchurch to the rocks of Freshwater, or that azure
radiance which rolls from the headland of Antibes to the gardens of
Porto Fino, has the same magic for Auberon Herbert that it has for
Algernon Swinburne; a charm much calmer and more peaceful, but
not less strong.　Many of these little poems speak of the sea only;
are full of that happy sense of return and recognition which so many
amongst us feel when, after absence from the sea, we tread again its
wet salt sands, and feel its white spray dance against our cheek.
Swinburne is the great laureate of ocean, the charms of whose mighty
lyre reverberate with the ocean storm and echo the thunder of
breakers breaking upon iron shores, and of billows sweeping from
pole to pole.　The song of Auberon Herbert is the homing cry of the
sea-swallows swaying on the crest of the waves.

' Back to the Sea Mother ' he calls those yearning lines :—

> Kindest of mothers, from whom I have strayed,
> 　Back again, tired, I come to thee,
> Chaunting and crooning the old wave-song;
> 　Sing it, oh! sing it again to me!
>
> Weary and spent as the hour draws near,
> 　Hush me to sleep with the soft wave-song,
> Wash all the cares away, wash all the strifes away,
> 　All the old pains that to living belong.
>
> Down at thy side I place me to rest;
> 　Slowly my senses are stealing from me;
> Passions and pleadings have ceased in my breast,
> 　Gently my spirit floats away free.

And yet again :—

> Thou great strong sea, fast lock'd in dreams,
> 　Clouds journeying to and fro,
> Whose tender blue the stars come through,
> 　I can but love ye so!
>
> Ye take possession of my heart,
> 　And all my life renew ;
> Like grain of dust I grow a part,
> 　A small stray part of you.

As thou stridest over the sea ;
And we need thy breath from many a taint
To set us clean and free.

But when thou comest on mighty wings,
Deal gently with forest and tree,
For my heart is woe for the goodly things·
That to-morrow will cease to be.

Yes! I shall go and you will dream,
And drink the pale blue sky,
Beneath the hill that hugs you round
As silver days go by.

When others come your love to claim
You still, you pale, blue sea,
Oh, shall you mean for them the same,
That once you meant for me ?

And shall they look on you with eyes
As tender true as mine,
And love each changing gleam that flies
Across that face of thine ?

I dislike the translation of expression from one art to another, otherwise I would call these verses impressionist. They have the quickly captured forms, the frail fugitive colour, the infinite suggestiveness, which are the notes of the highest impressionism in painting.

See these eight lines :—

The sun is at rest—for the storms are o'er ;
Just touch'd with the hand of night,
And a line of shadow creeps to the shore,
Then flashes in silver light—

Like a note that stoops in its flight and droops,
And clings for a while to the ground ;
Then trembles and wakes from its trance and breaks
Into passion and glory of sound.

How entirely true are these to the breaking of a smooth, pale expanse of water into motion and light ; the sudden flashing as of a million spears with which the sea, when smitten by the sword of the Sun, rises to the challenge of Morning. And yet by what simple and common words this strong effect is produced !

Or this :—

Only a bit of land-locked bay,
With a haunting face on the further side ;
Yet the ocean as well might bar·the way,
So far from each other our lives divide.

> For you jest at times, and at times you pray,
>   And you tread a path that cannot be mine;
> And the world is with you from day to day,
>   And all that you are I dare not divine.

Or this :—

> In the glory of youth the young man went;
>   His heart with pride was stirred;
> 'They should yield,' he cried, ' to the message sent,
>   And force of the burning word.'

> The long years passed and a wearied man
>   Crept back to the old home door:
> ' I have spoken my word and none has heard,
>   And the great world rolls as before.'

Or this :—

> Forward we look and we gild it all,
>   Rich is the picture and tender and fair,
> Backward we look and the blue mists fall,
>   Veiling the troubles that once were there.

> Ah! well, and ah! well, and lighter the load,
>   If heart the enchanter weave his web;
> If he tells love-stories to cheat the road,
>   And binds in our dreams the purple thread.

It will be seen that the store of words at the singer's command is limited; his palette is set with few colours; his lute has but few strings; and it is in this that he resembles the singers of the Italian folk-songs and couplets which have only the limited vocabulary of the peasant to express so many of the deepest chords of human feeling. These English verses, like those Italian *canzone*, might be created by one to whom all the stores of knowledge and of culture were sealed books. They are cast in the simplest of all possible forms of expression, and there is not one which would not suit the plaintive measure of a crooning ballad sung in twilight by the embers of a cottage hearth. They suggest their own music, and it would be difficult to read them aloud without falling into some rhythmical balance of their lines.

Auberon Herbert is, we know by his prose works, master of rich stores of language and of scholarship; therefore, this simplicity of style in his verses springs, not from poverty of resources, but from correctness of instinct. These songs are *naïf* as a child's prayer at its mother's knee at eventide; were they ornate or elaborate they would cease to be, as they are now, the frank and spontaneous utterances of the soul, natural, I have said, as song of linnet or of lark.

Let those who love pure, simple, unstudied, and unborrowed things send for the little azure book and read it for themselves; not in noisy railway train, or metropolitan library, or fashion-filled country-houses; but in the solitude of some quiet rural place, beside some nameless streamlet where the willow-leaves touch the blue brook-lime and the bees hum amidst the flowering thyme.

When we take it home, as the day dies, let us place it on a shelf between the hymns of George Herbert and those earliest love-songs which were signed Owen Meredith. There it will find its fit companionship.

OUIDA.

3

PRIMOGENITURE [1]

I REMEMBER my old friend and master, Sir Henry Maine, once expressing his hope that some competent scholar would write a book on primogeniture. I am not sure that he did not from time to time contemplate addressing himself to that task. Certainly the subject, cutting, as it did, so to speak, into his special line of studies, was very much in his thoughts from the year 1861, when he published his book on *Ancient Law*, shortly after resigning his Regius Professorship at Cambridge, to the year 1883, when he embodied in his *Early Law and Custom* the most important of the lectures delivered by him as Corpus Professor at Oxford. Both these works contain some admirable pages upon it. So does his work on *Early Institutions*, published in 1874, in which he enlarges on the reasons that had led him thirteen years before to call primogeniture one of the most difficult problems of historical jurisprudence. I incline to think that his strong sense of its difficulty disinclined him for grappling with it. He was, as one of his most intimate friends described him, ' physically incapable of severe continuous drudgery.' And for fully exploring this matter a good deal of such drudgery would have been necessary. Mr. Evelyn Cecil has not shrunk from it, as the pages of his book sufficiently show. And in the work with which he has begun his literary career, Maine's aspiration is at last fulfilled. In his preface he modestly endeavours to extenuate his ' audacity' in undertaking the task. It is related of George the Third that when presented with Bishop Watson's *Apology for Christianity* he observed, ' Christianity needs no apology.' We may say the same of Mr. Cecil's book. It is a valuable contribution to an important topic of jurisprudence. And he has laid all students of law and sociology under a very considerable obligation by publishing it. He has collected, from numerous sources, a great number of facts helpful for the

[1] *Primogeniture : a Short History of its Development in various. Countries, and its Practical Effects*, by Evelyn Cecil, M.A., of the Inner Temple, Barrister-at-Law, and a member of the London School Board (London : John Murray, 1895).

elucidation of his subject. He has stated them perspicuously ; he
has marshalled them skilfully ; and he has indicated his conclusions
in a spirit of moderation and candour by no means general even in
purely scientific treatises. He follows in the footsteps of Maine, who,
as Sir Frederick Pollock has happily remarked, ' forged a new and
lasting bond between history and anthropology,' and treated jurisprudence as ' a study of the living growth of society through all its
stages.' And in executing his task he has carefully observed what
I may call the rules of literary perspective. He has brought his
chief facts into bold relief, and has kept his less important ones in
their proper place of subordination. Throughout his pages there
reigns that unity of composition which enables him to present his
materials in the light of a dominant idea. Such are some of the
merits of Mr. Evelyn Cecil's book. A distinctly noticeable book, I
account it, as being the first serious attempt made by an English
scholar to deal adequately with a subject no less complicated and
obscure than it is interesting. The faults of the book are chiefly
three, which, happily, may all be easily removed in a future edition.
In the first place certain important lines of inquiry are too hastily
dismissed. For example, the subject of primogeniture in India is
dealt with in six pages. Sixty would not have been too many for
treating it even in the barest outline. Secondly, authorities are not
always very discriminatingly cited. Thus at pp. 83–4 a quite worthless extract from an obsolete book—Craig's *Right of Succession*—fills
a long note, and at p. 116 Dr. W. Roberston is referred to as though
his opinions were conclusive regarding a difficult point as to fiefs for
life. Thirdly, here and there are statements lacking in precision.
Thus at p. 30 we read ' William the Conqueror took care that the
rule of primogeniture should develop [in England] under his pilot-
age.' But as Messrs. Pollock and Maitland have pointed out in their
History of English Law—published subsequently to Mr. Cecil's book
—' what William and his sons insisted on was rather " impartible
succession " than a strict application of the primogenitary rule.'

It would be manifestly out of place here to follow Mr. Evelyn
Cecil through details interesting chiefly to the student of jurisprudence ; but there are two questions of general interest dealt with in
his last chapter as to which I should like to say a few words. Primogeniture properly means the right of the eldest among males to
succeed to real property. That right is of much less consequence
now than it was in ancient times, before alienation of such property
by will was permitted. But it is a right which our law still recognises
and enforces in cases where a landowner dies intestate. In such
cases, ' provided,' as Mr. Cecil observes, ' that he has not overwhelmed
his land by an avalanche of creditors,' the law appoints his nearest male
relative to succeed him. That is the *right* of primogeniture. The
custom of primogeniture is a distinct thing, although no doubt it

arose from the ancient right. The modern custom of primogeniture is a device for keeping a landed property together, or, as the phrase is, tying it up, by means of settlements, the operation of which is by law restricted to the lives of existing persons and a period of twenty-one years after their decease. Now there are two practical questions which arise. Should there be legislative interference either with the custom or with the right of primogeniture? Let us consider them a little.

First, then, as to the custom. Should a man be allowed to tie up his land, as at present, in order to keep the property together? Let us look at the matter from the point of view of ethics, to which law ought to conform. There are those who tell us that a man has a moral right to do what he will with his land; that he should be free to dispose of it as he likes. I take leave to call this absurd on the face of it. A man has no moral right to do what he will with what he terms his own, which, after all, is his own in a very limited sense. A right is a moral power residing in a person—that is, in an ethical being—a truth expressed with equal brevity and force in Trendelenburg's dictum, 'Alles Recht, so fern es Recht und nicht Unrecht ist, fliesst aus dem Trieb ein sittliches Dasein zu erhalten.' Now the right of private property, like all rights, rests upon personality. Its true *rationale* is that it is necessary for the development and explication of personality in this workaday world. It implies and demands the performance of correlative and commensurate duties. And it is subject to the just claims of the community in which it is exercised, and from whose sanction and recognition it obtains validity and coercive power. It is not absolute. Only from creation can spring absolute ownership. It is relative, as all human rights are, to moral ends. True is this of all property. It is especially true of land. For land differs from other property in that its quantity cannot be multiplied. The deep distinction between realty and personalty, so emphatically recognised by the law of England, is founded in the nature of things. The underlying idea of the feudal system is that the land of the country is the common heritage of the country—that a man can have only an estate in it. The feudal system has passed away; but its fundamental principle that the ownership of land—this is true, in a measure, of all property—is fiduciary, that it is weighted with duties to the social organism, that it must be made a common good, is not of an age, but for all time. And this is the doctrine of Aquinas. Private ownership in land he regards as just, according to the *jus naturale*, not *in se* and absolutely considered, but relatively to the results which flow from it.

The question, then, whether any particular form of ownership in land is justifiable, must be determined in the long run by the common good. In Mr. Cecil's last chapter the reader will find what seems to me a very fair and candid discussion as to the respective advantages of the system of large landed properties existing in these islands and the system of small landed properties prevailing in certain parts of the continent of Europe. Mr. Cecil's conclusion is that in the present state of civilisation in this country the system of large landed properties is more for the common good ; and in the fact that such properties cannot be kept together without the *custom* of primogeniture he finds a sufficient defence of the custom. I must leave my readers to consult his arguments in his own pages. It must suffice here to say that, so far as I am concerned, I entirely agree in his conclusion. I do not, however, agree with him in his view as to the *right* of primogeniture. which comes into force when a landowner dies intestate. Mr. Cecil does not appear to deny—I do not see how any reasonable man can deny—that this right, which arises, generally, in the case of very small properties, for the large ones are almost always settled, is usually, in practice, a wrong, resulting in great hardship and injustice. He would, apparently, substitute for it the German system of *Anerbenrecht*, whereby all the children are allowed adequate shares of the inheritance, while one son, usually the eldest, receives the landed property undivided, in a share amounting to a somewhat larger aggregate than the others. My own view is that the argument for abolishing the right of primogeniture generally is overwhelming. I think that when a landowner dies intestate his land should devolve as personal property devolves, except in the case of estates belonging to lunatics or to minors, where the custom of primogeniture has been followed for at least three generations immediately preceding. In these special cases alone the right of primogeniture should subsist. In all other cases it should be abolished. That this reform would be for the common good, that it would render the defence of the custom of primogeniture easier, that it would be in the truest sense Conservative, seems to me as clear as daylight. And it fills me with unspeakable reflections to see so-called Conservatives resisting it. But *mit der Dummheit!*

W. S. LILLY.

4

ILLUMINATION [1]

THE moral deterioration of the Reverend Theron Ware, a young American Methodist minister in charge of a number of unpleasant souls who wanted ' straight-out, flat-footed hell ' in their sermons, at

----

[1] *Illumination*, by Harold Frederic (London : Heinemann).

Octavius, U.S.A., is a singularly powerful study. It is interesting even in its weaker places, and notable for many of those pages of brilliant description which Mr. Frederic sometimes flashes before his readers just when they are beginning to discover they are bored. But in 'Illumination' there are few opportunities for boredom, even though the local politics of a narrow and ignorant Methodist community, somewhere in the heart of New England, are not in themselves alluring, while the terrible Yankee jargon does, for all that may be said about its raciness, too often grate on English nerves. Theron Ware's history contains little enough of plot or action. He is treated badly by many people, and entirely demoralised by a pretentiously intelligent and unscrupulous woman, but his sufferings and wrongdoings are all of a subjective order. The interest of the book lies in the masterly drawing of this man's character, in the experiences which develop its latent mean qualities to the gradual subversion of his better nature, and of his happiness with his wife while dominated by an influence which he took to be a superior one.

It is the tale of the bull-frog over again, a poor little bull-frog who might have been good and happy if only a female vivisectionist had not encouraged him to attempt impossible feats of expansion and then abandoned him when the results were troublesome and uninteresting.

Celia Madden, the papist, began by playing Theron's soul away with her music and by the use of grosser arts in strange assortment with an assumption of personal distinction and refinement. She subsequently brought him 'illumination' in various disastrous forms, but on the whole she is a less convincing, more indefinite piece of character drawing than are the other women, the poor simple wife, who rings so true, and Sister Soulsby, that delightful mountebank who proves the Wares' good angel. It is not easy to realise her creator's intentions with regard to Celia, but most readers will accept her old friend Dr. Ledsmar's description of her in a moment of petulance, as more seriously accurate than he intended—'A mere bundle of egotism, ignorance, and red-headed immodesty . . . with a small brain addled by notions that she is like Hypatia, and a large impudence rendered intolerable by the fact that she has money.'

The interest of the reader is carried on from one striking scene or brilliant piece of description to another, with but little drooping over intermediate passages of lesser merit and more uncertain delineation. Amongst the most powerful must be named (with regret that space forbids quotation) the death of the workman, where Theron first meets Celia and sees the impressive last rites of the Roman Church ; the revivalist meeting where, already half disillusioned, he watches with consternation his wife going through the process of conversion supported by Lawyer Gorringe, and last but not least the weird and semi-grotesque effects of the camp meeting in the forest. Whether the end be altogether unhappy the reader must decide for himself. Things might certainly have been many degrees worse both for Theron and his wife.

THE SCRIPTURE READER OF ST. MARK'S [1]

OF slum 'novels' the ordinary reader who does not love to take his pleasure too sadly has had almost enough.   Vivid pictures of sordid want and sheer brutality unredeemed by the compensating human emotions only serve to remind him of unpleasant things which he cannot help and to make him sick and sorry.   It is probably this absence of all ordinary feeling, rather than its setting, which makes the modern realistic slum study so painful a diversion ; for here is a tragic romance, the scene of which is laid in the darkest desert of the East End, with a poverty-stricken Scripture reader for its hero, and a cockney working girl for its heroine, and yet it is delightful reading. 'The Scripture Reader of St. Mark's' is not a story of adventure or of stirring incident, neither is it a mere study of sordid life. It is the drama of a strong and austere man's sudden passion for a beautiful and fascinating woman belonging to the devastating tribe of human cats who have done so much mischief since the world began.   It sets forth his struggle to overcome the temptation which chance and duty so abruptly flung in his way, his yielding to Alexandra's determination not to go through the form of marriage at the outset of their life together, and the consequent mental agonies suffered by this innocent St. Anthony.   After the struggle comes a period of domestic peace and exquisite happiness in fatherhood, described in scenes full of humour and tenderness.   But even here a warning note is sounded more than once.   Alexandra combined 'the fresh beauty of a girl with the intuition and knowledge of a woman, a child's unrestricted zest in life and the serpent's art in making black look white.   But she was, in fact, more a kaleidoscopic train of awfully unexpected phases than she was girl, woman, child, or serpent.'   She revealed a portion of her past to Lee when he saved her from suicide, but, as usual, she reserved something—in this case it was her actual marriage to the other man, and another detail equally important. Alexandra's past of course assumed the present tense again in time and became the almost unwilling instrument of avenging fate, which the reader feels to be as resistless and inexorable here as in a Greek tragedy.   The climax is finely wrought out, and the honest workman's horror at having to inflict the blow on the man he has learnt to respect is an effective feature of it.

---

[1] *The Scripture Reader of St. Mark's*, by K. Douglas King (London : Hutchinson & Co.)

Alexandra's moral deficiency almost paralyses him at the last; after their flight with the child is arranged, he cannot understand how she can spend another twenty-four hours under Lee's roof on the old terms, without revealing her purpose. 'Well, God Almighty!' he cried with almost vindictive blasphemy, when he was once more in the street, 'You made this woman—this wife of mine, and I guess You aren't astonished at anything she does! But she's knocked me off my feet this time.'

In a story so powerfully written, slight defects call for small notice. A certain want of proportion and balance between the first half and the last, a tendency to isolate scenes from one another, alone betray the inexperienced novelist. The writer's style is admirable; she has drawn a strong man with an emotional nature as few people can do nowadays. It is to be hoped the Scripture reader may soon have a successor worthy of him.

A LADY OF QUALITY [1]

'Not I,' said she. 'There thou mayst trust me. I would not be found out.' Such are the characteristic words of Clorinda Wildairs, the 'strong woman' of this year's novel show, and certainly the most remarkable of her creator's heroines. As an embodiment of sheer robustness in female shape, indeed, this young 'lady of quality' stands alone in recent romance. She is a *tour de force* or an extravaganza, according to the view of the individual reader, but she is as impressive a piece of work as any the year 1896 has brought forth.

Mistress Clorinda was wise enough to be born as long ago as 1690. The rich decoration of the time suited her, and the stout nerves of a generation which was not reared on tea, philanthropy, and small scruples gave her a clear field for performances before which the aspirations of the most hysterical New Woman seem pale and attenuated. The daughter of a coarse, hard-drinking country squire, she was brought up chiefly in the stables, rode to hounds like 'an infant jockey,' rapped out round oaths, and was 'the scandal of the county by the day she was fifteen.' Suddenly this state of affairs changed. Clorinda discovered that she had a woman's heart and more than an ordinary woman's beauty. She changed her garments and her manners with the deliberate purpose of becoming a great lady, and of course succeeded, but not before she had shown that she was, after all, vulnerable. The remembrance of Sir John Oxon, an unscrupulous rake whom she met as a young girl in the old rose garden, would have burdened any ordinary woman with 'a past' sufficient to weigh down her future. Not so Clorinda; she tossed

[1] *A Lady of Quality*, by Frances Hodgson Burnett (London: F. Warne & Co.)

aside troublesome memories along with the frightened remonstrances of her saintly sister Anne, also an excellent character sketch. She made the old Earl of Dunstanwolde entirely happy till his death, and kept her word. She did 'not cheat him, as weaker women do their husbands.' When free to bestow her hand on the noble gentleman who had won her heart Clorinda suddenly found her way to happiness barred by the resurrection of the ugly old secret. How she strode over all the laws which govern sophisticated humanity, onwards to virtue and honour, must be sought in the brilliant pages of this astounding story. Its power and its weakness are alike patent, there is the old tendency to a certain riotous exuberance, both in words and sentiment, the need for a male restraint matching the strong and male conception, and there are certain faults of taste and exaggerations which are not new in Mrs. Burnett's work. But *A Lady of Quality* is a strong book and a bold adventure in days where strength and originality are less common than excellence of literary style.

MABEL C. BIRCHENOUGH.

5

CHARLOTTE BRONTE AND HER CIRCLE[1]

WITH a modesty that deserves recognition, Mr. Shorter tells us in *Charlotte Brontë and her Circle* that his book is not a biography, but a collection of letters. The remark is to a certain extent true, and yet it is an act of bare justice to Mr. Shorter to say that in those parts of his work which are distinctly biographical he displays so keen an instinct and so deep a sympathy that one is compelled to regret that he has not attempted upon a large scale, and in the light of the new material he has at his command, a full biography of the great woman of whom he has written. As it is, we owe him a debt of gratitude that cannot easily be repaid. With extraordinary success— a success which can only have been achieved by an untiring industry and an unfaltering devotion to his subject—he has brought to light and placed in the hands of his readers all those records of Charlotte Brontë's noble life that were left untouched and almost unsuspected by previous writers. If his book contains no great and novel revelations, it is simply because his heroine lived her life from first to last with a simple consistency that made her at all times as nearly as

[1] *Charlotte Brontë and her Circle*, by Clement K. Shorter (London: Hodder & Stoughton, 1896).

possible true to her own ideal of duty. What he has done has been to supplement the materials employed by his predecessors with a lavishness that will astonish no one so much as those who laboured before him in the same field. He has added a great many letters of Charlotte Brontë's to those which the public already treasured. He has brought to light one or two that are of peculiar interest and significance, as casting light upon the innermost mind of the writer; and he has given us that fresh chapter in her life which of necessity had to remain unwritten, not only when Mrs. Gaskell produced her great- biography, but twenty years later, when I had the honour of following her afar-off in the same task. The chapter of which I speak is that which touches upon Charlotte Brontë's life as the wife of Mr. Nicholls.

It is superfluous now to speak of the extraordinary fascination which the story of Haworth Parsonage and its illustrious inmates possesses for most cultured men and women. Charlotte and Emily Brontë have taken their place with the immortals, and their lives as well as their works have become part of the national heritage. Mr. Shorter enables us to study the simple and pathetic story from a new point of view, and there is no possible point of view from which it is not worth studying. If there are any still ignorant of it, this book may be safely commended to them; for, though it cannot supersede the brilliant work that we owe to the genius of Mrs. Gaskell, it will still convey to them, in the words of Charlotte Brontë herself, a true conception of two careers, each of which may fairly be described as being in its own way unique in the history of English letters. To those who know the story already Mr. Shorter's volume will be doubly welcome because of the fresh light it throws upon its subject, and the new material which it places in the hands of its readers.

But in the brief space at my command I am compelled to touch upon one or two points on which I find myself at issue with the author of *Charlotte Brontë and her Circle*. The little book which I published twenty years ago on the same subject has long been out of print; but Mr. Shorter has paid me the high compliment of dealing with some of the theories I advanced in that volume, and, whilst treating me with a courtesy which it is my duty to acknowledge, has not concealed the fact that he differs from me. In the first of these questions of controversy he differs also from an infinitely greater authority, Mrs. Gaskell herself. This is as to the character of Mr. Brontë, the father of Charlotte and Emily. 'It would seem quite clear,' he says, 'to any careful investigator that the Reverend Patrick Brontë . . . was a much-maligned man;' and, continuing, he distinctly challenges Mrs. Gaskell's portrait of the old gentleman. That there was exaggeration in that portrait I ventured to point out twenty years ago. But that Mr. Brontë was 'maligned,' or that he was anything, in his youth and manhood, but an extremely difficult person to live with, I cannot admit. Mr. Shorter has had to gather the materials for his work more than thirty years after Mr. Brontë's death. It is not surprising that the stories which made so deep an impression on Mrs. Gaskell, and which still retained their original shape when, nearly thirty years ago, I began my own inquiries into this fascinating subject, had been softened and toned down by time long before they reached Mr. Shorter's ears. Mr. Brontë himself was softened and subdued after the death of his children. I remember a letter written to me by Mrs. Gaskell in 1859, or thereabouts, in which she described at length a visit she had paid to Haworth, and spoke of the extraordinary and touching change that had taken place in Mr. Brontë's manner and character. It is not surprising that those survivors who still remember the old gentleman should instinctively recur to those six years of chastened tenderness and penitence rather than to the many preceding years when he lived his life almost alone in the midst of his family, and when his eccentricities and foibles, to use no harsher word, made him an object of wonder and apprehension to his neighbours. This phenomenon, the effacement by time of the harsher features of the dead in the memory of the living, is too common to call for explanation. But if any evidence is needed of the fact that Mr. Brontë was the reverse of an amiable or reasonable man in his relations with those around him, one has only to turn to the remarkable chapter in which Mr. Shorter has told us, through the medium of Charlotte Brontë's own letters, the story of her engagement to Mr. Nicholls. Her sense of justice, outraged by her father's furious and flagrant injustice, was beyond all question the force which drove her into that engagement. That it was in all respects a happy one for her, and that Mr. Nicholls proved himself not only a devoted but a worthy husband, does not affect this indisputable fact.

The only other point of difference between myself and Mr. Shorter on which it is necessary to touch in these pages has reference to Charlotte Brontë's visit to Brussels, and to its effect upon her life and character.

The second visit of Charlotte Brontë to Brussels (says Mr. Shorter, p. 207) has given rise to much speculation, some of it of not the pleasantest kind. It is well to face the point bluntly, for it has been more than once implied that Charlotte Brontë was in love with M. Héger, as her prototype Lucy Snowe was in love with Paul Emanuel. The assumption, which is absolutely groundless, has had certain plausible points in its favour, not the least obvious, of course, being the inclination to read autobiography into every line of Charlotte Brontë's writings. Then there is a passage in a printed letter to Miss Nussey which has been quoted as if to bear out this suggestion: 'I returned to Brussels after aunt's death,' she writes, 'against my conscience, prompted by what then seemed an irresistible impulse. I was punished for my selfish folly by a total withdrawal for more than two years of happiness and peace of mind.'

This remarkable passage in Charlotte Brontë's letter Mr. Shorter father practically unprotected from the enticing company of a too festive curate.'

I shall not dispute the existence of the festive curate, and alas! I cannot ignore the evidence that, not only at the period to which Mr. Shorter refers, but at other times in Mr. Brontë's life, that unfortunate man fell into temptation. But as I was the first to draw attention to the special significance of Charlotte Brontë's experiences in Brussels, and to the undoubted effect they had upon her life and character, I am bound to re-state my position. I never applied the term 'falling in love' to her feeling towards M. Héger. What I did say [2] was that 'her spirit, if not her heart, had been captured and held captive in the Belgian city;' and I cannot, even in the light of Mr. Shorter's new evidence, alter my opinion. Surely the 'irresistible impulse' which drew her back to Brussels when she felt that she ought to have remained at home, and the yielding to which was punished by 'a total withdrawal for more than two years of happiness and peace of mind,' was something real. There never was a saner woman than Charlotte Brontë, and she could never have written in this fashion to her friend if she had merely imagined this thing. Nor is it possible to ignore the evidence which supports the theory that Charlotte Brontë, pure and noble woman as she was from first to last, had been fascinated by her brilliant and eccentric master in Brussels. Not even her genius would have enabled her to draw the portrait of Paul Emanuel if she had not herself experienced something of that overmastering intellectual influence which in her novel he exercises over Lucy Snowe. I have no desire to press the unconcealed dislike and jealousy which was felt towards her by Madame Héger too far; but the evidence of her great book, and of her own letters after her return from Brussels, points unmistakably to the one logical conclusion that is to be drawn from the words she wrote to Miss Nussey regarding the 'irresistible impulse' which drew her back to Brussels when she knew in her heart that she ought to have stayed at home. She had found a mind there which fairly dominated her own, and held it captive for the time; and all the deeper experiences of her soul, all the higher flights of her intellect, may be said to date from that period in her life. Who is there who will honour her the less because she was thus susceptible to the influence of a mind which she believed to be stronger than her own? Nobody has said, and nobody believes, that M. Héger was Charlotte Brontë's lover, even in the most platonic sense of the word. But that for a time he was her master, the controlling influence in her intellectual life, cannot, I think, be seriously disputed.

There are many other portions of Mr. Shorter's fascinating volume

[2] *Charlotte Brontë: a Monograph*, p. 60.

which, if space permitted, it would be a delight to dwell upon. It would have been interesting, for example, to discuss the claim set forth on behalf of Branwell Brontë to a share in the authorship of *Wuthering Heights.* The claim was absolutely unfounded, but the evidence by which it was supported is stronger than Mr. Shorter is disposed to admit. The fact that I differ from him on some points only makes me feel, however, the more strongly the debt which, in common with all who love and honour the memory of Charlotte Brontë, I owe him for the labour which has enriched our knowledge of his heroine so greatly. His book will always hold a prominent place by the side of Mrs. Gaskell's noble *Life,* and will remain a permanent magazine to which those who desire in future to understand or criticise the character of one of the greatest of Englishwomen will resort for the materials on which to found their judgment.

WEMYSS REID.

'OF WOMEN IN ASSEMBLIES'

A REPLY

THE value of one ounce of practice being by general consent accredited as worth pounds of theory is the only excuse I offer for this article. It has lately been advanced in this Review as a truism that the self-consciousness of sex prevents men from being outspoken and businesslike on such public boards as have women members. I prefer to contend that the meeting together of men and women for public work lessens exaggerated sex-consciousness by bringing men and women together on a sound and easy union of common duty.

Thirteen years' experience as poor-law guardian, member of a rural sanitary authority, and frequenter of parish vestries, with just one opportunity (by invitation) of arguing an important subject before quarter sessions, on a matter in which that body and several of the boards of guardians throughout the county were at variance, followed by further experience under the Local Government Act 1894, both as rural district councillor and first chairman of a parish council, ought to entitle me to speak on the utility of the joint work of the sexes in local government; even though my statement be regarded—as of necessity it must be—as an *ex parte* one.

The theory which has been ventilated in this Review is so charged with life-destroying character that we women, most of us being proud to be united to men by near and dear ties, may well be excused if we fail to accept anything so derogatory to the character of men in general. We are told that the inherent differences of sex so dominate the nature of men as to preclude full and free discussion on their part of any subject when women are present. ' That things will appear to be threshed out, but will not be threshed, and yet they will appear so to the woman,' and that she, the woman, will delude herself with having been victorious when in reality she has not been clearsighted enough to correctly apprehend the situation. This reticence on the part of men will be owing to some ' fascination ' which women always possess, and which men must always feel, because this ' fascination ' has existed since the days of the Garden of Eden. And yet, propounding this theory as to the inability of men to be businesslike and candid, the writer goes on to say, ' And yet men would not like women to lose this "fascination" even in the council hall!' And further, alas! 'This great sensitiveness is so extensive that even if women be old and ugly—unless possibly they keep silence—there is no guarantee that this dominating "fascination" of the sex will not tongue-tie male auditors.' Now, I think we should ask, where are we? Surely at a point where pathos is dissolved in bathos!

It would seem that women are akin to serpents, which, whether beautiful, old, or ugly, alike exercise in a greater or lesser degree so dangerous a fascination that men must be protected from having to face them. They are advised to double round and scotch them if they can, the result of which advice, if taken, will be that the snakes—*i.e.* the women—will thrive and multiply in the land of public debate. There is another suggestion to protect men, and that is that women might ' be allowed to collect evidence for men to use in debate.' We therefore presume that there should be an end to women giving evidence before committees of the Houses of Parliament or Royal Commissions. In the future we ought to lose such valuable testimony as was given years ago by Miss Louisa Twining on workhouse management, or that of Dr. Annie M'Call and other ladies before the recent Commission on Midwifery. We should dispense with that verbal testimony which from time to time able and philanthropic women can give to the nation.

We are asked to believe ' that the possibility of rudeness is the indispensable condition of public debate;' that women will never—by rightly constituted men—be subjected to that heckling and sifting which those 'who love their country' give to men. Therefore women should be kept not only out of Parliament, where they would intensify the already too venomous style of debate, but also off local councils.

Those who are conversant with the modern work of women in local government know that even if women have not been exactly heckled on boards of guardians, they have certainly not been received with uniform courtesy. The success of lady guardians has not been due to any fascination which has struck dumb their male co-workers, but to the signal ability and ease with which they have grasped the possibilities of the poor law. This has doubtless been in part owing to their superior knowledge to men of the needs and characters of the poor.

The women who have taken part in such forms of local government as have been open to them do not believe—nor do the public who have watched the joint work of men and women on boards of guardians believe—that the presence of women has stultified freedom of speech or discussion for men. The Local Government Board and both Houses of Parliament have in every way encouraged the election of women, both as poor-law guardians and as members of the Metropolitan Asylums Board. Those governing powers have realised that poor law work cannot be thoroughly done without the co-operation of women. Both sexes can bring to the application of the poor law the full complement of facts, and in this way both the poor and the public have been the gainers. I will give as an example of the need of the womanly mind the consideration of three of those Acts of Parliament which for brevity I will call Permissive Acts—they may be applied or not applied—viz. the Notification of Diseases, the Vaccination, and the Cow Sheds and Dairies Acts. Who would say but that women ought to have a voice and vote in the working of those Acts, or that the interest of women in those Acts should be confined ' to collecting evidence for men to debate' thereon? There have been most full and free discussions of the working of those Acts on councils composed of men and women, and surely it is *reductio ad absurdum* to suppose that the most susceptible of men to female influence felt unequal to say all he required to.

If it be granted, as indeed it must be, that questions will some-times arise touching the most miserable side of the relations of the sexes, I can say that from my fifteen years' experience there need be no reticence in discussion, except that which is of pre-eminent impor-tance in all public work, viz. the choice of fitting and appropriate language.

Long before the modern movement had arisen among women for taking their share in local government, they and men had worked together on joint boards for the management of refuges for fallen women and kindred institutions. 'To the pure all things are pure.' A loathsome subject carries with itself an antidote for all except those who, if they have attained office, are really not fit to act as public representatives.

Parish councils have been in existence so brief a time that it is not possible to report much experience, but so far as that experience has gone it has tended to show that the presence of women, far from being considered a hindrance by men, has been valued and appreciated by them. Two at least of the lady chairmen who were elected at the first election were unanimously chosen by councils composed entirely of small village traders and labourers, in one case dashed with the Nonconforming element. One at least of those lady chairmen (Mrs. Barker of Sherfield) dealt with the powers under the Act in so systematic and exhaustive a manner as to serve, in my humble opinion, as a pattern for many a parish council under male control. Both Mrs. Barker and myself (though unknown to each other) resigned at the end of our first year of office, strangely enough for the same reasons. Both were anxious that the educational power of the chair of parish councils should not crystallise, and both were desirous of proving beyond a doubt that a woman could act as chairman and re-turning officer at the annual parish elections. This would have been impossible had we been candidates for office. By singular good luck,

one, if not both, the elections were decided by the casting vote of the
lady chairman.   Before the publication of this Review Mrs. Barker
will have given her most interesting experience at the conference of
the Women's Emancipation Union held in London.

If we could gather together the opinions of those women pioneers
who have borne the brunt and burden of the day as co-workers
with men in public assemblies, there is little doubt but that their
testimony would tend to show that sex distinction has been much
less oppressive than even they hoped it could be.   It is not far-fetched
to suggest that the novel position assumed by them minimised sex
fascination.   Men possibly regarded them as hybrid creatures, par-
taking of the characteristics of two species, curiosities of nature ;
but, like all hybrids, limited in sexual power, therefore (though, like
the mule, good for hard work and surefootedness) of depreciated value
in the scheme of Nature.

I think we touch the crux of the matter when we say that a great
vantage-ground has been taken from men who have to sit with women
on local boards.   It is less easy to air a sex biassed opinion, or give a
sex biassed ruling, than of yore.   In the past but few men cared to
earn the gratitude of women by being enthusiastic on the woman's
side of a question.   It was much more comfortable when only one
side need be debated, and that the male side.   Though, according to
Mr. Oakley, two thirds of the spoil (I question the proportion), ' holy
or unholy,' gained by men may be appropriated by the women they
favour, there will always be some women who will appreciate simple
justice above all the good things of this life.

This terrible theory of the impossibility of men doing justice to
business in the presence of women has been backed up by a quotation
from Dr. Johnson.   It is now more than a century since the grand
old lexicographer was placed in his grave, and men and women and
theories have moved on since then.   Yet I cannot say an unkind
word of Dr. Johnson.   His practice in regard to women so often
excelled his precepts ; the good husband of an old wife, the kind
protector of destitute women, even to the sheltering of some of them
for years in his own home, has gained my love.   Even to the wealthy
and fascinating Mrs. Piozzi he could blurt out his opinions.   He
never became weak-kneed in the presence of women.

Experience has taught some of us that many men are more fearful
of ventilating their opinions before members of great ability among
their own sex than they are of enforcing opinions opposed to those
of women.   The fear of woman is as nothing compared to the fear of
a clever scathing male tongue.

Women have desired that their public work should be on the broad
line of *homo* man—' male and female created He them '—not on the
narrow one of sex affinity, much less of sex antagonism.   George
Meredith, by deep and generous intuition, has sounded in his latest

enlightened husband is made to say : ' I do not believe that anything higher than respect can be given to a woman ; ' and again ' When . . . woman breathes respect into us she wings a beast.' How different are these sentiments from those of Mr. Oakley, who would base all human relationships between men and women on sex fascination alone !

If the disorder be but half as bad as it is represented, there can be only one certain cure. We must have an increase in the representation of women. Women cannot go back, it is undesirable from the enemy's point of view that they should remain where they are, consequently they must go forward. This will reduce the number of men likely to be affected, and secure for women the exercise of those higher qualities of mind, heart, and brain which belong alike to spiritually-minded men and women. Every age has produced women for whom the serious concerns of life have had a greater attraction than its pleasures. The Vestal Virgin exists no longer but as a pure symbol. The Sister of Charity has been for ages among us. The spear of progress presses us on. This generation of women is awake not only to the need of religious but also of civic devotion on the part of women to do battle with ' dirt, discomfort, and disease.'

HARRIETT McILQUHAM.

THE MODERN BABEL

THE author of the 11th chapter of the Book of Genesis felt profoundly how great a lever of civilisation a common language among men must be. He represents Jehovah as foreseeing that with this bond of union ' nothing will be withholden from them which they purpose to do.' Hence human speech, he tells us, was confounded; the too rapid growth of human power was indefinitely stayed by the separation of language into divers tongues. Those who still believe in a Special Providence regulating the temporal affairs of men may fairly point to the same interference operating at the present day. Whenever a number of neighbouring nations or races, separated by their speech, have been brought into that large and constant contact which is implied by a common civilisation, they have endeavoured to over-come this great obstacle; they have striven towards a common language, or a common graphic system; and yet when the goal of unity, at least so far as common intercourse, had been wellnigh attained, hostile causes interfere. With the confounding of speech all the labour of approximation by mutual understanding of a common language is undone, and we begin again from the Tower of Babel.

There is no clearer proof than this to an historian that human pro-gress is not a continuous advance, but something spasmodic, which often recedes from unclaimed ground, which often resigns conquered terri-tory. There was a time, not many centuries ago, when any man who chose to learn Latin in addition to his mother tongue could con-verse easily with any other educated man in Europe. There never was a better practical solution of a great difficulty. By keeping up as the medium of communication a dead language, if we may so term a language freely spoken, but no longer the mother tongue of any European people, all difficulties of international jealousy, which are now the greatest obstacle to a solution, were evaded. Latin was by com-mon consent regarded as the purest, the most grammatical, the most logical idiom which a man could learn; there were to be found in it not only all the learned works of the day, but also great ancient masterpieces, not since equalled as standards of literary taste. This language had its alphabet perpetuated in its daughters; it was de-void of that exuberance of flexions and of particles which makes other great languages so difficult to learn. It was the language which had been spoken by the world's conquerors, and was therefore the language of law, of religion, of philosophy. By acquiring this one passport to European thought, the mediæval youth had attained what years of study and an accumulation of linguistic lore will not now provide. For, ever since the Renaissance, or certainly the Reformation, the *Aufklärung* in other directions has been the growth of confusion in this. A struggle seems to have arisen among the modern Romance languages, which of them should be the successor to Latin. After a sudden and early growth of Italian, which must at one time have seemed to men the natural heir—Provençal was only the common language of artificial Love—French succeeded in occupying the civilised courts and the polite society of Europe. If the old French monarchy and aristocracy had not been swept away by the terrible Revolution; if France had not ruined her primacy in courtliness, and had not for a time become the dread and the horror of all Europe, it is quite possible that French might have become the exclusive international medium. But the mercantile preponderance of England and the national antagonism of Germany raised up rivals to her supremacy. And since the assertion of nationality was identified with the speaking of a special language, all hope of any agreement has disappeared. When I was young, it was fairly assumed that a working knowledge of English, French, and German would open to the student all the stores of European learning. Nothing can now be further from the truth. Not only are there scientific and literary works of international importance—I exclude mere poetry and small talk—in Italian and Greek, and far more in Dutch, but there are mines of knowledge only to be reached by acquiring Russian and Hungarian. I am told that the geological and zoological observations over the huge area of Asiatic Russia are now published in Russian Transactions; I know that the most interesting Reports on Hungarian social and political questions are now in Hungarian yellow books. Some years ago all these things were printed in French or German. Now we must spend half our youth in acquiring a series of foreign tongues, and the remainder in lamenting that what we have acquired is insufficient.

Is there to be no limit to this absurdity? It is only recently that I was sent a pronouncement regarding the Irish (Celtic) language, signed, I grieve to say, by a Protestant bishop and canon, among other names which represent either hostility to England or mere gratuitous folly, recommending that an agitation should be commenced to prevent the appointment of any officials in the south and west counties who could not speak Irish, and suggesting other means of galvanising into life a most difficult and useless tongue—not only useless, but a mischievous obstacle to civilisation.

We can see in the signal example of Wales how a country

adjoining the most civilised population in Europe, and under its laws, can be kept barbarous by upholding its own obsolete language. The sentimentality of confining Welsh appointments to those who speak Welsh is lowering the standard of Welsh officials to a most melancholy extent. The further the Welsh-speaking remnant falls behind in the march of civilisation, the worse the evil will become. One shudders to think of such principles applied in Ireland.[1] But the sense of humour in our people is our great safeguard. The only advice I can offer to the signatories of the monstrous document I lately received is to urge them to agitate for the resuscitation of Cornish and of Manx. They might also turn their attention to the dying languages of the Maories and the natives of Australia.

The general result is that not only is no advance being made towards a better mutual understanding among civilised nations, but that every miserable remnant of barbarism, every vanquished and half-extinct language which has lost its literary worth, and has become a hindrance to the commercial and political progress of the world, is now coddled and pampered as if it were the most precious product of the human mind.

But let me not be misunderstood. I am very far from imagining that it would be either possible or useful to supplant the language of any nation by an artificial or foreign growth. The extraordinary diversity of tongues in the world—Terrien de la Couperie had counted at least 800—not only points to the great fact that the invention of language is natural to man in every clime and circumstance; it marks and perpetuates psychological differences of great moment in national character; it has supplied us with all the splendour and the variety of many great masterpieces, none of which is capable of showing its perfection in any other dress than its own. But I am now considering language merely as a means of easy and wide communication among them. It is indeed no damage to France that Breton, Walloon, Provençal, Basque are spoken in its provinces, but only so long as French is the imperial language of the courts, of Parliament, of science. The languages of special corners of the world are like their national costumes, interesting and picturesque; but to wear national costume out in the great world is only found practical with one profession—that of wet-nurse.[2] Elsewhere we must seek it either in the artist's studio or at the fancy ball. Provided, then, there be an imperial language in use, not only jargons or dialectical varieties, but even distinct languages, are to be regarded with indulgence and consideration. The test point is this: which is made compulsory, the imperial or the local tongue? If the former, we are advancing,

---

[1] There is no country in which sham excuses, political and religious, for appointing incompetent men to responsible posts flourish more signally than in Ireland. Are we now to add a new sham, the linguistic excuse?

[2] Probably because it suggests rural innocence and health.

if the latter, we are receding, in civilisation. To give examples. Since Hungary was so ill advised as to discard German as its State language, and has introduced its Tartar language into the schools and public offices as the national and necessary language, it is losing touch with the rest of Europe, and drifting away into the herd of semi-Oriental nationalities which are seeking to establish doubtful claims to be included in the peerage of European culture.[3] So long as Wales, or the sentimental English government of Wales, will appoint no bishop or curate that cannot preach in Welsh, it is certain that the majority even of really civilised Welshmen will be excluded from serving their country in this department, and so Wales will in future contribute even less than she has done to British greatness. If, on the other hand, Berkeley and Swift, Goldsmith and Sheridan, Grattan and Burke had been compelled to speak and write in Irish, for the sake of official promotion, or to soothe national sensibilities, not only would the English-speaking world, but Ireland herself, have suffered immeasurable damage. So far as purely national sentiment requires it, let us have poetry and prose in every tongue : let the Scotch heart beat faster to the jargon of Burns, or the Dorsetshire to that of Barnes ; let us have the flavour of each nationality, and the perfume of its finest bloom, expressed in myriad tongues ; but when we come to international questions, imperial policy, discoveries in science, history, economic and social problems, we should surely insist upon some limitation in the vehicle employed. As a matter of fact, we do censure the modern vagaries on this subject. We neglect even valuable dissertations written in out-of-the-way tongues. The author loses most of the recognition which he would receive if he addressed the civilised world ; he too often consoles himself, however, with that most silly and yet engrossing of modern illusions, a patriotic pride in his own jargon as the finest language of the world.

Having now stated the mischief, I should proceed to consider the means, actual or possible, by which we might remedy, partially at least, this great obstacle to our progress in civilisation. But hitherto I have only considered the trouble entailed on those who really master several languages ; I ought to say a word before passing on concerning the stone of Tantalus which occupies the time and labour of the average school boy or girl. The tyrannical shams of modern life have imposed it on all systems of secondary or higher education, that they shall at least pretend to teach modern languages. Some of these languages, especially French, are made compulsory in almost all competitive examinations. Every officer in the British army, for example, is now supposed to have qualified in French. How many

[3] I see it reported by the special correspondent of the *Morning Post* at the Millenary celebration in Hungary (7th of May 1896) that German is rapidly losing ground there, and that the Hungarians are quite proud at their success in recovering the preponderance of the Magyar language. Nothing proves more clearly the fact that they have not yet appreciated European culture.

of them have any working knowledge of that language? Shall I say not one in every 500? At all events in Egypt a few years ago, when there was a considerable British army there, and many British officers in the Egyptian service, it was a matter of common knowledge that the only officer who could speak French with any correctness to the distinguished visitors who used that tongue was the general commanding, a man brought up in days long anterior to the competitive system. At the same time there was but one officer who had any command of German, and he had been a German dragoon officer for ten years. At that time, at all events, it was manifest that the whole of the hours spent in the attempt to learn French by many hundreds of young men had been absolutely wasted. Many of them told me that they had forgotten every word of the smattering acquired for their examination. And this is so all over the country. In the Irish intermediate examinations, many hundreds of school boys and girls compete in French. I have good reason to know that it is most difficult to find one of them who could translate at sight any average French prose, or even read it out, so that any Frenchman could by any chance understand it. To understand spoken French, or to reply to a question in that language, is not even part of the training, as they are examined on paper only, and do not learn even the rudiments of French pronunciation! *Risum teneatis amici!* Was there ever so complete an instance of teaching a dead language? But indeed it is no laughing matter, seeing that millions of hours of labour are absolutely wasted by the absurdities of modern education. Those who succeed in mastering a language have at least laid up one valuable deposit, upon which they can draw hereafter, though under a more perfect civilisation this labour need not have been required of them; those who attempt and fail, or who merely strive to qualify in a book examination with the intention of throwing the subject aside forthwith, are a far larger class, and the amount of force wasted in this manner is one of the most disgraceful extravagances of our modern life.[4]

Let me not be told that all this applies equally to the study of the dead classical languages. The Latin learned by a candidate for the army does not profess to be intended for conversation; it is therefore

---

[4] Here is an instructive anecdote in point. It happened that an examiner, when controlling an examination in French, set one of Daudet's books of short essays as a specimen of the modern language. When candidates complained that they could not find in their dictionaries the words used, it 'transpired,' as the papers say, that they had nothing but the vocabularies at the end of their elementary lesson books to consult. He thereupon published a recommendation to use Littré's abridged Dictionary, an excellent book, which costs 11s. 8d. net. Since that time the majority of the candidates dropped French. They had no idea of investing 11s. 8d. in a book perfectly useless to them when the examination was over. Besides, modern education must not cost anything; it is a mere engine for winning prizes without any outlay beyond time.

no sham; the Latin grammar is and must remain of use to him, not only whenever he desires to learn a foreign language, but whenever he aspires to a literary use of his own. But the objection is too stale and oft refuted to require another word. I only desired, before passing on to the discussion of the remedies for our Babel, to impress upon the reader that the increase in the number of current European languages has been accompanied with an increased pressure upon our youth to learn them; and that this pressure produces a waste of millions of valuable hours every year among those who fail in the task, whether from natural stupidity, or from incompetent and antiquated teaching, or from a rotten and ridiculous system of examinations. The evil is therefore more aggravated than it ever was, and requires more urgent consideration.

No remedy can be proposed with any chance of a hearing if the author shows himself ignorant of previous solutions. The most obvious condition of success in so difficult a problem is to know what others have essayed; and if they have failed, to understand the causes of such failure.

The system adopted by the Chinese and surrounding peoples may be called thoroughly successful in its way, but is nevertheless out of the question for our purpose. By the use of a system of writing which does not represent sounds (words), but the things themselves (images or ideas), they have attained to a mode of representing their thoughts which can be expressed in many different languages. The Japanese, Corean, or Mandschu educated man can read and write the same signs, while each of them pronounces these signs according to his own tongue. Thus, any one of them, if educated in this system of writing, can converse *in writing* with any other, though the languages spoken by each are wholly distinct. Of course, a graphic system not of sounds but of ideas must be very cumbrous; a mandarin requires to know at least 2,000 signs for his literary idiom; but what is the labour of learning these in comparison with the labour of learning even one of the languages required? This is therefore a very reasonable solution, though it falls short of establishing a common system for conversation. Nor is there any possibility that we should ever again set up an ideographic system of writing in the world. The advantages of our phonetic alphabet are too obvious.[5]

I have spoken above of the far more satisfactory mediæval solution of speaking and writing Latin in addition to one's mother tongue.

---

[5] Nevertheless one man at least has been so impressed by the Chinese solution that he has proposed one for European consideration. Here is the title of his book on ideography, quoted, with a short account of his system, by Professor Max Müller in the second series of his *Lectures on the Science of Language*: *Mémoire sur la possibilité et la facilité de former une écriture générale au moyen de laquelle tous les peuples puissent s'entendre mutuellement sans que les uns connaissent la langue des autres:* par Don Sinibaldo de Mas, Envoyé Extr. et Ministre Plén. de S.M.C. en Chine. Paris, 1863.

We can hardly call it a solution, since it grew up in Europe through the force of circumstances. Latin, having been the official language of the Roman Empire, became the language of the Church and of the Law, and so survived among the diverging nationalities of the early middle ages. The only difficulty to answer is: why did it ever fail? Why did so sensible a system ever make place to our modern confusion? The reply which occurs to me is this: Latin was not confined to be the mere instrument of international communication: as such it even still has considerable vogue in the learned world; but in the early middle ages Latin was not only the vehicle of Law and of Religion, it even aspired to express the private feelings of men and to supplant local poetry and familiar prose; thus it became identified with the tyranny of Church, of State, of Scholasticism, which the Reformation overthrew. While the Church intoned in Latin, the Reformers made it a principle to preach in 'the language understanded of the people.' While the wits of the Renaissance published their polished conceits and artificial loves in Latin verse, sterner men sang the ruder words of deeper passions, of honest convictions, in their own tongues. Thus the reaction against mediæval systems brought with it the reaction against their language, and with the domination, perhaps even the tyranny, of Latin, there was swept away the great and useful function which it was performing as an international language.

Since the monarchy of Latin has given way to the oligarchy of five or six leading languages—an oligarchy now threatening to degenerate into a democracy of numerous outlandish tongues—several attempts have been made to construct a common vehicle of communication. I shall mention but two. These are the philosophical attempt of Bishop Wilkins (1688) and the recent scheme called Volapük. The bold and thorough-going plan of Bishop Wilkins may most easily be comprehended by the sketch of Professor Max Müller in the book above cited. It is there shown that Leibnitz was imbued with the same notions, probably borrowed from the Bishop's work. Wilkins aimed at a complete rehandling both of language and writing. He proposed to classify all the objects in nature afresh, classify the sounds which should represent them, classify the signs correspondingly, and so to construct a perfectly logical and complete system of sounds and signs, absolutely independent of all existing languages and graphic systems. The Professor's initial objection to this remarkable proposal is that any classification of nature must be defective, that it must require modifications with the increase of knowledge, and so imply disturbances of the system of sounds and signs. It is not worth making this objection, which, by the way, applies to many living tongues, when there remains a far larger and deeper difficulty. Language is a growth, and not an invention. All the resources of science cannot construct a piece of tissue, which will live and grow, though all the animal and vegetable

If it is a most difficult feat to invent and impose upon human use even one new word, how chimerical is it to impose upon mankind a new and wholly artificial language! Leibnitz, who had taken cognisance of this system, was full of it shortly before his death, but we need not for one moment imagine that even his genius could have imposed upon the world an invented language, however philosophically and scientifically perfect.

The recent attempt—I mean the system calling itself Volapük—was devised by a man [6] who apparently had heard of this difficulty, and who felt that known words or roots for ordinary objects, however wanting in logical order or relation, would be far more acceptable than syllables of wholly arbitrary value. The inventor was probably struck by the existence of Pigeon or Trade English, which is in actual use, not only in China, but among savages on almost all trade routes in America and Africa, modified, of course, in each case by the native language. The general features of this valuable medium of communication are a very small and practical vocabulary, consisting partly of native words for objects, partly of common English words; a disregard of grammatical forms, beyond the absolute necessity of being intelligible; and a great deal of gesture, to help out the deficiencies of so scanty a system of speech. Thus the savages of the world, dealing with English or English-speaking traders, seem to have removed the obstacle which still divides and estranges civilised nations.[7] This the inventors of Volapük proposed to do, not by inventing a wholly new and arbitrary language, but by compounding a new jargon, made up of a selection of roots and forms from the living languages of Europe. The history of this bold attempt is curious and instructive. Taken up by many people with great expectations, taught for a year or two even in counting-houses in North Germany, and in their corresponding houses abroad, accepted for a moment with great hopes, and showing many symptoms of success, it has disappeared so suddenly, and yet so noiselessly, that I suppose the very name is unknown to the younger portion of my readers. Yet eight years ago it was a matter of general talk, not only among students of language, but in commercial houses. Its sudden death seems to have taken place about 1890, for I cannot find any new editions of the grammar or lexicon in English after that date, and it was undoubtedly the passive resistance of English which killed it. The original inventor seems to have had the idea of opposing and displacing English consciously before him. Neither the vocabulary nor the simple processes of English was admitted in his language. Both vowel and

<hr>

[6] Father J. M. Schleyer of Litzelstetten, in Baden, who first published his system in 1880.

[7] Even in the Bismarck Archipelago (let him that readeth understand!) this trade English is current, and not German, which seems quite inadaptable to such uses.

consonant sounds foreign to English were employed, and there is
not a single sentence in any Volapük book of which any Englishman
could even guess the general sense, any more than he could guess at
a sentence in Hungarian. The very name of the language has a
sound *ü*, which English ears with difficulty distinguish, and English
tongues fail to pronounce. It is very amusing to see how the handbooks published in America or England endeavour to gloze over or
to deny this original hostility to English. One of them says that
English is the natural guide to Volapük, and that English people
have a great advantage in learning it. Moreover that forty per cent.
of the roots are derived from English. More impudent falsehoods
could hardly be imagined.[8] The whole principle of the new grammar
was *inflectional*, working by suffixes and affixes, a process wellnigh
strange to us. The odious paradigms of verbs emerge again with
additional complications from the limbo to which they were consigned with our Latin grammars. Will the reader desire a specimen
of this odious jargon?

I loved	älöfob
Thou lovest	älöfol
He loved	älöfom
She loved	älöfof
It loved	älöfos
We loved	älöfon
Thou lovest thyself . . .	älöfolok
You loved	älöfons

Which of the two systems is the easier to learn? Obviously,
that in which the persons are made distinct and are conscious subjects,
not hidden in senseless terminations only to be distinguished by dead
memory. What shall we say of the invention of new roots (appearing in the above suffixes) for the ordinary pronouns, when so many
and such ancient languages had already come into accord upon these
perpetually recurring ideas?

In the face of these grotesque absurdities, only saved from the
charge of lunacy by the orderly and systematic arrangement of
nonsense words and forms, the wonder is, not why such a system
should have promptly died, but why it ever has shown active signs
of life and progress. Its advocates tell us that there have been forty
attempts at various times to invent a non-national language. No
wonder they are all dead and buried, when this, the latest and
probably the most ingenious, offends so egregiously against common-
sense, against the present conditions of the world, against that fundamental law of progress—to make the best of what we have. In the

---

[8] In the case of roots common to English with French or German it is quite
manifest that the author borrowed them from the latter languages, and they are so
disguised that no English reader can recognise them.

cemetery of buried projects which this century has to show, it occupies the newest grave, and on the fresh tombstone we may write its epitaph : *Fad of fads*.

It remains for us to try the only other solution. As the savages of the world have modified English to suit their purposes, adopting this one foreign language for international communication in addition to their own, so we must endeavour to persuade civilised men to be content to adopt one common language for the same purpose, while they cherish their own for national and for literary use. In the last century French held this place as the language of diplomacy in the courts of Europe, and even now, though French influence is manifestly decaying throughout the world, though French commerce is waning,[9] we often hear claims of the old supremacy, and at Athens or even at Alexandria (to our shame be it spoken), French is a more frequent medium of communication than English. But in spite of the stupid indifference of our rulers, who will not see that language is one of the great sources of a nation's influence, English enterprise and English trade make it perfectly impossible for any other nation to impose its language on the world. From this aspect we may include under English the great Republic of the West, which not only speaks English all over North America, but which leavens the cargoes of foreigners that arrive almost daily at her ports, and insists that, whatever may be their nationality or speech, they shall accommodate themselves to the condition of understanding and speaking English. If we add to the influence of the United States that of the English colonies all over the world, the preponderance of English is so great that we only wonder why our language has not long since become not only the trading language (Handelsprache), but the language of common intercourse throughout the nations of the world. That it will become so in time is very probable, if English commerce and English wealth continue to expand at their present rate. If the number of persons who expect to receive money from the English, and to whom therefore a knowledge of our language is profitable, keeps continually increasing, the growth of English influence and English speech is a matter of certainty.

The great obstacle at present lies in that international jealousy of which I have recently spoken in this Review. That 'jealous female' France is furious at the wane of her old supremacy in language. The French are, moreover, very bad linguists, worse even than the English, and very naturally strive against the necessity of a new burden upon their education. The Germans, who learn languages easily (though not well), feel bound to assert the nationality of their new empire against all foreign influences, fortunately against

---

[9] This is freely admitted by French observers; cf. the instructive article of the Vicomte G. d'Avenel in the *Revue des deux Mondes* for the 1st of March 1896.

French above all, thus putting obstacles far more than we do in the way of the diffusion of that language. The Hungarians and Czechs, however, are limiting, on their side, the spread of German, and Italian officers are no longer required to know French for their competitive examinations. All these mutual jealousies are important factors in the problem; they give unwilling aid to the final predominance of English.

Probably the main obstacles in the way of this most desirable end come from ourselves. Two classes are specially to blame : our diplomats and our pedants. The former allow every opportunity to pass where the use of English might fairly be asserted—sometimes from mere stupidity in not estimating its importance, or from pride in the assertion of mere military or naval preponderance; sometimes (though rarely) from the vanity of airing their own proficiency in a foreign language; sometimes out of that insane folly which consists in humouring the sensibilities of jealous neighbours; from these causes, or from sheer indifference, there is no steady assertion of the English tongue in our colonial or foreign diplomacy. Of these reasons the policy of consideration for foreign sensibilities is not only the most utterly foolish, but the most ridiculous, for it makes concessions without the smallest chance of their motive being appreciated. To postulate delicate tact and tender sympathy for the feelings of others as the mainspring of any English surrender must seem perfectly grotesque to any foreign observer even when the facts are so. If, for example, Lord Cromer concedes that French (beside Arabic) shall be the official language of Egypt, is it likely that any Frenchman will attribute this most damaging concession to his suavity and sympathetic tact, and not to a fear of French threats? And yet, owing to this want of proper self-assertion in England, the noble American schools in Egypt, and all the other influences in the country that had wellnigh Anglicised it a few years ago, have been allowed to make way for the teaching of French, and the consequent spread of the influence of a local French press bitterly hostile to England, and spreading every sort of calumny against us among the natives. This blunder even reacts upon neighbouring nations. Is it likely that the Greeks, a most intelligent nation, would now be teaching their children French as their European language, if they had seen that English was becoming the leading speech of Alexandria, and thus of the Levant? They are indeed shortsighted in not perceiving the steady and inevitable decay of French influence in Europe; in fifty years they will see it plainly enough. What I here complain of is that our politicians, who could by steady pressure accelerate the progress of English speaking in the world, only interfere to delay it. Have they ever conciliated one solitary foreigner by these ignorances or negligences?

The other great impediment to the rapid and certain spread of

English speaking and writing comes from the pedants, who find bad arguments to support the conservative spirit of the vulgar, and protest against any step which may remove the great difficulty in the way of foreigners learning English. Our grammar is very easy, our grammatical forms very few and simple; our spelling is the great obstacle. For a long time it has not represented our pronunciation with any approach to consistency or accuracy. Yet the pedants, as well as the public, insist upon maintaining our often irrational spelling as not only an essential of the language, but as the main test whether an Englishman is educated or not. It is, of course, the easiest test for slave-driven examiners to use in making artificial differences among their myriad candidates. Three or four mistakes in our absurd spelling will exclude from the army a young man who has every natural quality to be a good soldier. Even the few little timid changes made by American use, in the direction of omitting useless letters, are regarded with dislike, and accounted vulgarisms, by our purists. Truly, if they set before their minds, not the convenience of Civil Service examiners, not the stupid adherence to an irrational and artificial orthography, not the isolation of England, but the great future which her language might have in traversing the whole world, they could see that some concessions at all events might be made to the wants of all the foreign world, some release from the enormous tax of time upon our own children in having to spell contrary to their utterance.

Am I then a disciple of Mr. Pitman, and do I actually advocate the horrors of phonetic spelling? As a new system, no. A page of the *Fonetic Nuz* is to me as disgusting as to any purist in spelling. The advocates of that system have gone too fast and too far. They were, like the advocates of Volapük, too rash in offending popular prejudices, and they have met with their punishment. They did not realise that as language is not an invention but a growth, so spelling is a growth, and will not be reformed by a revolution, but by a quiet and rational pressure in a proper direction. If every literary man would do but a little in that way, even our generation would see a great change. But we must emancipate ourselves from the tyranny of printers as well as pedants. I found that it required some little persuasion to make the former print *rime, rythm, sovran,* and a few other such reforms, and I should certainly have reverted to the eighteenth-century *tho',* were it not that I could not face *do'* (dough). But these faint and insignificant beginnings should be followed up by many others, especially warning the reformers that they need not expect, or even aim at, uniformity in the earlier stages of the campaign. The real and only object for the present generation is to accustom the vulgar English public to a certain indulgence or laxity in spelling, so that gradually we may approach—I will not say a phonetic, but—a reasonably consistent orthography. For then every foreigner will find his task lightened; he will have some chance of learning English from books; any violations of use he commits by over-phonetic spelling will· not be counted to him as a deadly crime against our language. And then in a short time, in spite of the jealousies that will arise, the British tongue, like British gold, will probably pervade the world.

The reader will give me credit, I hope, for opposing all wild and sudden expedients. The examples of Volapük and of phonetic spelling are sufficient warnings that any such policy only retards the great object which every promoter of Imperial British interests should have in view. But adopting as our motto *Festina lente,* I have yet one suggestion to offer which may probably, like all such suggestions, however moderate, be regarded at first with scorn, ultimately with interest and approval. It is based upon the historic parallel of what was done by the Greeks when they stood in face of a problem analogous to ours. There came a period, about the time that Rome absorbed and unified the kingdoms about the eastern Mediterranean, when Greek became the language of commerce, and even of polite intercourse, from the Tigris to the Atlantic Ocean, from the Red Sea to the British Channel. It was the interest of both Greeks and barbarians that many should learn to use Greek. How did the Greeks, a clever people, meet this demand? for their language was one of exceeding richness and complexity of forms, of literary dialects, of constructions. In the first place the varieties of spelling produced by writing the dialects were abolished. All the Greek intended for common intercourse was written in a *common dialect*, though, of course, great varieties of pronunciation must have remained. So far modern English is agreed with them. Though we may speak, we do not write, dialects in the books intended for business, for science, or for international use. The Greeks had this advantage over us, that their spelling of this common dialect was, if not phonetic, at least rational and consistent, except in one particular. But in this lay a great difficulty for foreigners. The Greek accent was not at all determined by the quantity of the vowels, and so a foreigner reading out a manuscript of the second century B.C. would make such mistakes as to render him unintelligible to Greek natives who heard him. That is not a matter of conjecture or probability; it may be tested by any one to-day in Greece. If an Oxford or Cambridge scholar carries his ' quantities ' with him to the Peloponnesus, he will find himself hopelessly unintelligible, and he will hardly understand one word of what the people say, even when the words are good classical Greek.[10]

---

[10] In the simplest words this curious difficulty occurs. For example Ἡ παρθένος βιβλίον ἔχει, pronounced as our classical people barbarously pronounce it, has no meaning whatever to a Greek. To the correct Η παρθένος βιβλίον ἔχει, he might answer Μάλιστα, but would not recognise our Μαλίστα. For with him, as with us, quantity and accent are nearly identical.

English people do not, I believe, realise how completely useless it is to speak any language with wrong accent. Let us read out the following example quickly to ordinary hearers, and how many will understand it? 'He was misled up to his démise by mendacious evidence and illusóry promises. The interpréter intérpŏsĕd so that the juror éscăpĕd uninjúred.'

How, then, did the Greeks meet this difficulty, and help the Romans and Orientals who desired to learn their language? They put accents on their words, a perfect novelty, and very probably one which the purists of the day beheld with disgust.[11] But by this means, and without altering their spelling, they gave a practical guide to foreigners and greatly facilitated the spread of Greek throughout the world. Why not adopt the same device as regards English? I have known many a British traveller puzzled in Ireland because he was ignorant of the accents on our proper names. Why not therefore write Drógheda, Athenrý, Achónry, Athý, &c., and save trouble? And then why not gradually and tentatively distinguish by accents thóugh and tough, plágue and ágúe, according to any systèm which may be found most simple and convenient? A paragraph at the opening of the Grammar would be sufficient to explain it. Whether we should ever require the elaborate distinctions of the Greeks, whether a rude unscientific attempt might not be more effective than the systems of grammarians, these are questions which need not be discussed till some trial has been made.

Here, then, is the sum of the whole matter. The civilised world is undergoing a terrible waste of time and labour in the now compulsory acquiring of many languages, and in the main even this labour is thrown away, because most people do not advance far enough to use any foreign language. Moreover the great proportion of such students want foreign languages not to study their literature—a high and refined pursuit—but for practical purposes, in order to communicate with various natives, and in order to learn what they have to say on scientific or practical subjects. It is obvious that the use of one common language in addition to the mother tongue of each people would produce an enormous saving of time, and tend to the nearer and better knowledge of the world's progress among them all. This position of the common language was once attained by Greek, then in a wider sense by Latin, both of which commanded not only the business transactions, but even the literature of the world for some centuries. Since the abandonment of Latin in favour of the tongue of each European nation within its own area, confusion has prevailed, until the political predominance of France for a time imposed French as the language of diplomacy upon Europe, and more recently until the mercantile predominance of England and

[11] There is, moreover, clear evidence that this novelty was gradually introduced, and took some time to prevail.

America has imposed English as the language of commerce upon the trading routes of the world. Nevertheless the other civilised nations of Europe hold fast to their respective tongues as a matter of jealous patriotism, and have even broken down the primacy of French in the field of diplomacy. Moreover France is waning in population and in power, while the English-speaking races are waxing. The attempt to settle the problem by inventing an arbitrary tongue has been ineffectual, and will never succeed in the face of practical languages, which are the natural growth of the human mind, spoken and understood already by many millions of men. Nor will a common system of signs like the Chinese be of much avail in trade, where speaking is far more important even among the educated minority than writing, an art which the majority of the world has never yet acquired. In spite, therefore, of many serious obstacles, English will gain the victory and become the world-language. Some of these obstacles, such as the jealousy of neighbouring nations, we cannot obviate; others, which consist in certain anomalies affecting our orthography and hindering the quick acquisition of English by foreigners, we should endeavour to diminish by practical common sense, by disregarding the pedant and the purist, and by encouraging such gradual and moderate licenses as may make English easier, without violating the traditions or the spirit of our great heritage.

J. P. MAHAFFY.

AT a recent bye-election in the West of England an English politician was reported to have said as follows :—

> Land is the property of the people. You must never forget this one main
> principle of difference in property as between land and articles of manufacture.
> We can make boots and coats, build cathedrals, railways, canals, bridges, tunnels,
> all the other articles which we associate with the necessities of modern life, but
> no man ever made land. No man ever made an acre one foot longer or one foot
> broader. The land is the property of the nation, given to the people by the Great
> Creator for the purpose of toiling upon it and obtaining from it food and susten-
> ance.

This is fine logic to preach to agricultural labourers, but it will
hardly hold water. It would perhaps surprise the speaker of the
above words if he were told that land, as we understand it in
civilised countries, is almost as much an article of manufacture as
any of the articles above enumerated ; yet such is the case.

It is the capitalist who has gradually given to the soil, on which
dwell populous communities, its greatest fertility and productiveness,
and has also given the means of housing its cultivators, its stock, and
its produce.

Agriculture is an industry that requires, perhaps, more capital
than any other : the owner finds four-fifths of this capital, in the
shape of houses, buildings, drainage, fences, roads, gates, soil
improvements, &c. &c.; the occupier finds the remaining fifth, in
stock and implements.

There are also labourers' houses to be built, let as a rule at rents
hardly sufficient to keep them in repair, or actually merged in the
farm rental in the majority of cases.

At the present time rent is little more than a fair interest asked
by the capitalist for the amount of money he has tied up on the land
he owns ; nothing is more untrue than that it is the land as land
only (*i.e.* raw land) in respect of which the owner receives rent ; the
fact is that very little rent, if any, is paid in respect of land as land
only.

The estimated expenditure by owners on the agricultural land of

Great Britain since the beginning of the century is about 700,000,000*l.*, while the net income receivable, after paying all outgoings and expenses, is little more than 35,000,000*l.* ; it is, therefore, not too much to say that the owners get little more than a moderate interest on the capital invested by themselves and their predecessors even during the present century. How many landowners are there in England at the present time who would not gladly accept as the price of their estates the amount expended upon them during the last thirty or forty years ?

When the colonial farmer settles upon a tract of land which Government may have granted to him for nothing, or for a small sum of money, he has to borrow, at high rates of interest, sufficient money to build his house, drain, clear, irrigate, plant, fence, and otherwise develop the land, and construct a farm out of a wilderness ; he, in fact, in many instances eventually pays a higher rent than the European farmer in the interest on these loans; and in addition there is this difference : in the older countries bad times are met by a reduction of rent, and consequently a diminution in the rate of interest paid on the capital invested in the land ; in the newer countries, when times go against the farmer, and he makes no profit, the capitalists, fearing their money is in danger, will no longer lend without higher interest. This is shown especially in America by the numbers of heavily mortgaged and derelict farms. Thus it often happens that while European farmers, and especially English farmers, are in many instances paying 2*l.* or 3*l.* per cent. per annum in respect of the capital invested in their farms, colonial farmers are not infrequently paying 2*l.* or 3*l.* per cent. per month.

During the last two hundred years land has been changed in Europe from comparative waste into flourishing fertility, almost entirely at the owners' expense and with undoubted advantage to the community at large.

In no part of Europe has the effect of capital been so strongly marked as in that delightful and practical country which occupies the central portion of the north-west corner of the European continent. Little Holland, as she has been aptly called, has been to a large extent reclaimed from the sea, marsh and lake, at an enormous cost, and a large sum has to be annually spent in keeping up her protective works.

Anyone who will take the trouble to visit this small but flourishing State cannot fail to be struck with the immense amount of capital and labour which has been, and is being, expended in order to make her what she is. She is inhabited by an enterprising and pertinacious race, closely allied to ourselves, whose industry and good sense have stamped their features on the land ; go where you will, all is order, neatness, and punctuality.

The means of locomotion are excellent and varied, both by land

and water. In addition to the main lines of railway the country is intersected by canals, on which steamers and trekschuits constantly ply; it has excellent roads, and is further covered by a network of light railways, by which one can go anywhere in ease and comfort at a very moderate cost.

The advantages of these latter institutions to the agricultural population cannot be overestimated, affording, as they do, a cheap and easy method of conveying agriculturists and their produce to the nearest market towns. Anybody who is sceptical as to the advantages of light railways has only to visit Holland for a few days to be convinced of their usefulness and excellence. No doubt from its flatness this country is peculiarly adapted to their construction, but we believe that there are many large districts in England which would offer almost equal facilities, and which would be very greatly helped and improved by their construction, if only the Board of Trade could relax its restrictions.

The system of dairy farming in Holland differs in many respects from our own, and in many respects it is superior. The temptation of sending milk to large cities, which is doing so much to deteriorate many of the English dairy districts, does not exist to the same extent for the Dutch farmers.

They have to turn their milk into dairy products, such as cheese and butter, and they have looked about to see what is the most economical and best way of accomplishing this end; in consequence they have adopted what in England is still practically in its infancy, viz. co-operative farming.

All over Holland and Friesland are to be found numerous cheese and butter factories, conducted on the very best principles, and turning out goods which compare very favourably with what we can ourselves produce. The Friesland butter, though it has been severely competed with by Denmark, has on the whole held its own, being of uniform make and possessing good keeping qualities.

The mode usually adopted in starting a factory is as follows: A certain district of, say, fifteen to twenty farms, of from fifty to 120 acres, is mapped out, and a factory is erected on the most central and convenient spot for all, usually in close proximity to a canal or light railway (often both); the money for building the factory is either borrowed or subscribed for by the farmers. Each person delivers daily to the factory the amount of milk yielded by his dairy cows, and takes back his proportion of whey, skim and butter milk, on which he feeds his calves and pigs.

A manager is appointed, whose fixed salary includes the wages of his subordinates, and he and his assistants make the cheese or butter, as the case may be, and he markets the same. At the end of every three months the accounts are balanced, the expenses are deducted from the gross receipts, and the balance of profit is divided amongst the various farmers, in proportion to the amount of milk each has delivered during the period in question.

This is true co-operation, and it is in this practical and simple manner that most of the dairy farms are worked.

There are, however, some factories that are owned by private companies, the shareholders being generally farmers. In this case the milk is bought and paid for at an agreed rate from the neighbouring farmers, and the company takes the risk of manufacture and fluctuation of markets.

There are some districts where the factory system is not adopted, and the farmers make their goods at their own farmhouse and take them to market themselves; but the factory system is most prevalent.

The price of milk in the best districts of North Holland, where the milk is of first quality, has ruled this summer about 4½ cents per litre (and lower), equal to 4·04*d*. per English gallon, and in Friesland the average price for twelve months works out about 3·6 cents per litre, or 3·29*d*. per English gallon.

The price for the summer months of this year in the western counties of England has been a little over 4·73*d*. per gallon. But in the winter months the English farmer, who sells his milk in towns, would get a considerably better price than the Dutch farmer, who has to make goods all the year round at home or in factories. It will be seen, therefore, that the English farmer is now getting a better price for his milk than his Dutch neighbours.[1]

The great bulk of the dairy waste products, such as whey and skim milk, is given to calves and young stock, while many pigs are fatted for pork; but there are practically no bacon factories, as in Denmark and Sweden.

Although in numerous instances—in fact, 57·5 per cent.—the owner of land in Holland cultivates it himself, the balance of some two million acres is let, and let at rents which, considering the low price of produce, appear to be surprisingly good ones.

In the district round Beemster, which comprises some of the

---

[1] The prices issued by a large condensed milk factory in the West of England in March 1896 for the following twelve months are as follows:

	d.			
1896, April, May, June	4½	per imperial gallon.		
1896, July, August, September . . .	5	,,	,,	,,
October 1896 and March 1897 . . .	5¾	,,	,,	,,
November 1896 and February 1897 . .	6¾	,,	,,	,,
December 1896 and January 1897 . .	8	,,	,,	,,

This gives an average for the twelve months of 5·80*d*. or 5⅘*d*. per imperial gallon, the six summer months being 4·73*d*. and the six winter months 6·86*d*.

These prices are about equal to those given by London milk contractors in the same district for the same period, the distance from London being between ninety and a hundred miles.

richest land in North Holland, there are many farms whose rental runs from 3*l.* to 4*l.* per acre, besides rates amounting to 7*s.* 6*d.* per acre and more payable by the tenant for drainage, roads, schools, and canals ; the owner, however, in these cases paying the taxes in connection with the farm and supplying material for repair of house and buildings, &c., the tenant doing the labour. In other districts where land is not so good a rent equal to 2*l.* 10*s.* or 3*l.* per. acre is paid.

The quality of land in Holland in most districts is no doubt excellent, but there are many dairy districts in England and Ireland where it is naturally no better, and in some instances superior, the rents, however, of which are much lower.

The Beemster Polder has been reclaimed during comparatively modern times, and the dykes which keep it from inundation are some of the finest in Holland.

The expense of its original construction was very large, and a heavy annual rate per acre is required to keep it in repair and pay the expense of the pumping station.

The old method of pumping out the water from these reclaimed and enclosed districts, by means of windmills, is now rapidly giving way to steam power, and it is probable that in a few years' time the old picturesque windmills, which were at one time such a feature in a Dutch landscape, will be no more seen.

There was a spot in the neighbourhood of Zandam where not long ago 400 windmills could be seen at one time, supplying power to oil-mills, flourmills, sawmills, &c., besides pumping ; this number has decreased by half during the last few years, and probably will get less every year.

Dutch farm houses and buildings are models of excellence and cleanliness ; fresh paint, shining glass, and burnished brasswork are conspicuous everywhere.

They are constructed in a sound and economical manner, the farm buildings and house being all under one roof. First comes the house, oftener than not facing the north or east, the advantage of the southern and western aspect being given to the cattle. The dwelling is slightly raised above the level of the ground, so as to give windows and ventilation to the dairy, which is usually underneath it ; it is roomy and comfortable, without, however, any great show or display. A narrow passage separates the house from the farm buildings, but is covered at the top by the continuous roof, which extends from the house to the buildings; the farmer can thus go from his own house to see his cattle without exposure to the elements. The buildings consist of cow byres, bull, cow, and calf pens, hay barn, corn and cake lofts, &c. &c.

Although, perhaps, not as picturesque as the straggling farm buildings we see in England, with the house standing by itself in its own grounds and gardens, it is practically more efficient, and admirably suited to the size of the farms, which not often exceed 100 English acres.

The amount of stock kept is largely in excess of even the best dairy districts in our country, forty or fifty milking cows being frequently carried by a hundred-acre farm.

The buildings are kept scrupulously clean; though it can hardly be believed, it is not an uncommon event to see a farmer slip his wooden sabots off before going into his own cow byre, in order that the floor, the bricks of which are polished like a mirror, should not be soiled. This may, perhaps, be considered a hypersensitiveness in favour of cleanliness, but it is typical of the race.

The same excellence of upkeep may be observed in the management of the land; it is kept in the highest possible state of flourishing fertility; the most is made of everything. Compost and manure heaps (pictures of neatness) appear everywhere, supplemented in many cases by the mud dredged out from the dykes and canals, the latter forming a valuable adjunct to the manure derived from the cattle; nothing is wasted.

The passion for cleanliness and good order appears equally among the labouring class. The villages are models, planted with trees and laid out with walks. Down the centre in many of the principal villages runs a light railway, giving access to the adjoining neighbourhoods, towns, and villages. There is usually a hall, or *stadhuis*, of some sort, an excellent school, and in many instances a kiosk or stand for a band, used on occasions of village holidays and festivities.

On the outskirts of the village, and sometimes inside it, is the butter and cheese factory. Some persons have an idea that these factories in foreign countries are roughly constructed buildings, run up with no regard to permanancy or appearance. Such, however, is not the case in Holland; the factories are usually excellent buildings, and in many cases ornamentally constructed of brick and stone, fitted up with all modern improvements, and lighted by electricity.

The cattle in Holland are almost universally the old black and white Dutch or Friesland breed; they are large and hardy animals, carry a good amount of flesh, and are good milkers. The quality of their milk is of somewhat a low standard, but they yield immense quantities, some cows giving as much as thirty-two litres (seven English gallons) per diem, a result of years of patient breeding for dairy purposes mainly, and unsurpassed, we imagine, by an English breed of cattle.

The farmers are at great pains to keep up the standard of their stock and to improve the breed, keeping careful registers and entering their stock in the national herd books; for this purpose they are helped by the State, the latter keeping stud animals for the use of certain neighbourhoods. In other districts the farmers themselves combine and purchase high-class bulls for the use of certain areas.

The bulls are kept at some central point, and are looked after and fed at the expense of the society they belong to.

This is an admirable plan; it could be wished that English dairy farmers would adopt this system, as it would much help to maintain and improve their stock. Many of the bulls used in the British dairy districts are inferior beasts, often being a calf saved from the herd on the farm, and in-breeding is thus perpetuated, with unsatisfactory results; or else, what is, if anything, worse, 'pedigree' bull calves, purchased and descended from herds bred for generations to specially produce beef instead of milk.

The Dutch breed of cattle is much sought after by Americans and South Africans, who buy a great many prize and pedigree beasts. Some farmers especially lay themselves out for breeding high-class cattle, and do a large trade in pedigree beasts.

The marketing of dairy produce is carried on in Holland much the same as it is in England; three profits are taken before the goods reach the consumer.

There is first the cheese and butter factor, who attends the markets and buys direct from the producer; secondly, the provision merchant, who buys in turn from the factor; and thirdly, the retailer, who buys from the provision merchant.

It is an unsatisfactory method, but it seems an inevitable one: the middleman appears to be indispensable, and, whatever prices are, he always takes care to get a profit. In some cases factories sell direct to the provision merchant, and thus escape the factor; but generally the latter individual is called in to assist in the sales, and often a better price is obtained through him than by dealing direct with the merchant in the towns.

In one respect the Dutch marketing arrangements are superior to ours. In most of the large market towns there is an official weighing house. The officials attached to this establishment unload the cheese arriving by rail and boat, and after its sale weigh it and affix the Government stamp certifying the weight; they then again load it, in ship or waggon, to its new destination. All this is done at a trifling cost, and has many advantages, the principal one being that both vendor and purchaser are bound by the Government figures, thus avoiding all disputes as to weight, which so often arise at home, especially with regard to an article like cheese, which loses rapidly if kept for any time and not passed into immediate consumption.

In England it often happens that the factor keeps the cheese he buys for a rising market, and then wants to put the loss of weight on to the farmer from whom it is purchased. This is unfair, as the farmer is supposed to have the weight of the cheese at the time of selling. Many kinds of cheese improve by keeping and become more valuable; the factor gets the advantage of this, but wants the farmer to pay for it and thus derive an extra profit.

Farm labourers in Holland are well paid ; in many districts they receive 7 to 9 guilders, or from 12*s*. to 15*s*., per week, besides a meal of bread and milk or coffee in the morning. Although wages are good, the men are well worth the money, and their labour is really cheap. It is no exaggeration to say that they do nearly twice the work of our West-country labourers, though it must be borne in mind that the best of the latter go off into the towns, leaving only the inferior hands.

The cows in Holland are milked at daybreak ; it is general in the summer months for the milking to be done at 4 A.M. and 4 P.M., a thing almost unknown in England. The day from sunrise till sunset is devoted to unremitting labour, though it must be admitted that the number of holidays and days devoted to festivities are more numerous than our own.

Dutch labourers are cheerful, honest, and contented, and take an interest in the farm on which they work and in their master's welfare ; moreover they have not yet lost the charm of courtesy, which is dying out so rapidly in our own country districts ; nine out of ten persons will salute those whom they meet, even if strangers. It is said that one of the kings of France was saluted by a beggar in the street, and returned the salutation ; on being remonstrated with by his companions for acknowledging the courtesy of so mean an individual, his Majesty replied that 'they could hardly desire that the beggar they had passed should be a better gentleman than himself.' The rural Dutchman has taken this principle for his own, and prides himself on acting up to it.

Dutch farmers complain of low prices and of the difficulty of making profits at all commensurate with those received years ago ; yet it appears that in the case of rented farms there have been no reductions at all to be compared with those given by English landlords to their tenants, notwithstanding that the rents are undoubtedly higher than those paid in this country and the prices received for produce are lower. We have already quoted the price paid for milk. Dutch cheese has been quoted this summer in the English market at 40*s*. per cwt. for the best Endams and a less price for Goudas, though it is fair to say that, with our usual craze for cheapness, only inferior Dutch cheese is bought by England.

The highest price, however, that has been realised during the past summer at any of the markets for the best cheese made is 26 guilders per cwt., about 44*s*. in English money. The wholesale price of Friesland butter, the greater part of which comes to England, has been this summer 84*s*. per cwt., or 9*d*. per lb.

The best English cheese, such as Cheshire and Cheddar, has been selling during the summer months at from 50*s*. to 70*s*., according to quality, while English butter was selling for the summer months at an average of 1*s*. per lb.

How is it, then, that our English dairy farmers complain that they make no profits and are beaten by foreign competition, when a country like Holland, with higher rents and lower prices, paying much the same wages to their labourers, and having to contend with a more rigorous climate, can succeed?

There is, we are afraid, no doubt that from want of combination, and slowness of action, English dairy farmers in many districts are being beaten. Many run in the old grooves and grow more slipshod and inattentive to their business than ever. Their idea seems to be how they are to make a profit with the least possible trouble to themselves. Milk-selling is their *beau idéal* of happiness. If they can only get a good contract for their milk they rest content and are happy, quite oblivious as to whether the fertility of their farms is maintained or not. If markets go against them, their first impulse is to run to their landlord for a further reduction of rent, or cry to Government to give them a dole of some kind or other. They affect to despise factories or other methods of cheap production; technical and secondary education they regard with apathy; while light railways they laugh at. Their only idea of combination is one to bring pressure upon Parliament to help them in some pecuniary form or other, though they will attend any number of meetings to hear speeches on protection or bimetallism.

Our farmers by their own indolence often make markets for foreigners. In the great cheese-producing grounds of Wiltshire, Dorsetshire, and Somersetshire the feeding and fattening of pigs from dairy refuse, combined with barley meal, has formed in the past, and still forms, a great source of profit to the dairy farmer. Wiltshire bacon is proverbial for its excellence, and there are factories there, containing every modern appliance and most elaborate machinery, capable of killing and curing several thousand pigs weekly.

The companies who own these factories, which have the effect of giving immediate market to the farmers for their fat pigs at good prices, have impressed upon them the necessity of producing a pig which in shape, size, and quality shall defy competition. Yet our farmers have done very little to improve their breeds, and have allowed Denmark and Canada, two large dairy countries, to produce a breed of pigs which in shape, size, and profitableness, though not in quality, is superior to their own, and from which an article is produced which has certainly affected this branch of industry.

In Denmark fifteen years ago the bacon industry was practically unknown; the pigs there were gaunt creatures of prehistoric type, quite unsuited to the English market; yet in a few years these enterprising Danes have, by careful attention to breeding and feeding, produced a pig which, from a bacon-curer's point of view, is perfect in shape and most profitable to deal with. Though for various reasons they can never hope to produce such a fine quality of meat as our

English-fed swine furnish, they have produced in an incredibly short space of time a formidable competitor; moreover the percentage of soft or inferior pigs, arising from careless and improper feeding, is in Denmark not more than 4 or 5 per cent., while in England it is often 10 to 15. If the West-country English farmer had paid more attention to the breeding and feeding of his swine, he might have prevented Denmark from obtaining the strong hold on the English market which she has at the present time.

It is the same with butter. Our farmers do not seem to realise that what the large centres of England want is an article of good uniform quality which they can rely on getting all the year round. The big provision merchants in London and elsewhere have given up English butter in despair, and now get their supply almost entirely from abroad.

There is a large agricultural district in England where the price of butter is ruled by the price quoted from a market in which not fifty pounds of butter are sold weekly; and it is a fact that the farmers of this district, merely because they will not combine to produce uniformity of quality and steadiness of price, are receiving twopence per pound less than two factories not ten miles away.

We do not mean to say that all British farmers are such as are above described; we should be very sorry to think such was the case. There are many excellent farmers still existent in England—men of energy, thought, enterprise, and intelligence; but unfortunately they are in a minority, and have not yet been able to carry their feebler brethren with them.

It must also be admitted that some individual dairies are capable of turning out an article of such superlative excellence that it cannot be matched by any factory make; for instance, it is possible for very skilled dairy hands on some farms to make a Cheshire or Cheddar cheese of that silky, flaky quality so much prized by experts. Of such quality as this there is very little made, and it is doubtful whether a factory which has to mix its milk will ever be able to turn it out, though factories can produce a uniform article of first-rate quality which can be depended on, and which is better than the usual product of farmhouses.

If any skilled dairyman possesses or rents a farm on which he can produce goods as above mentioned, he does well to stay at home and devote his labours to his own ground; but the majority of English farmers would do well to brush the cobwebs from their eyes, and, while observing what is done in other countries, look forward to an intelligent adaptation of our great industry to its new surroundings.

After what we have heard and seen in other countries, it seems that to argue that agriculture is a ruined industry and can never recover is misleading.

In comparing Dutch and English dairy farming, one of the most striking lessons is that while the Dutch farmer endeavours to increase the fertility of the soil which he cultivates by using all his waste products of dairy manufacturing, such as separated milk, skim milk, buttermilk, and whey, in rearing and feeding additional stock, the Englishman in similar circumstances attaches, alas! little importance to the serious loss entailed by the depreciation of his farm in sending all products away.

This latter constantly treats it as a hardship, should he deal with a cheese or butter factory, to be asked to take back separated milk, whey, or any other dairy waste, so sought after and reckoned valuable in Holland. In consequence his calves are sold within the first week or two of their birth—to be, perhaps, purchased back in an adult stage. Few or no pigs are fed, or, if so, often on artificial feeding stuffs of an inferior quality. An insufficient amount of manure is made, and that only from his milch cows, and as a natural result his pastures become impoverished.

It is then that the tenant comes to his landlord to complain that the farm is not what it used to be, and will not carry the same amount of stock. This complaint is the basis for a further demand for assistance from the landlord; and so year by year we see in certain districts the English dairy farmer drifting into a dependent system, which means ruin to himself and loss of interest to his landlord on his original outlay, instead of, after the manner of the Hollander and the Dane, laying himself out with all his energies to produce economically a larger and better supply of those commodities for which there is a demand actually at his own door.

The system of milk-selling has largely contributed to the present state of affairs. The dairy farmers have not been in the past forced to prevent the intrusion of foreign competition, which has practically taken their entire trade in milk products. It is now acknowledged that milk-selling under its present conditions and organisation is largely overdone, in consequence of so many arable farmers having taken to this industry, and is subject to many hindrances and vexations. On the other hand $3\frac{1}{2}d.$ to $4d.$ appears to be the ruling price for milk in Continental countries which compete with us in butter and cheese. English factories cannot, therefore, afford to pay much more and succeed. If, therefore, the English farmer is dissatisfied with $6d.$ a gallon, which he gets by selling his milk in towns, how can he be expected to be satisfied with the prices offered by factories?

We do not say that it is impossible for pasture farmers to sell off all their milk and yet keep their land in good heart, for this can be done by heavy expenditure in purchased feeding stuffs and, what is now sadly uncommon, thorough and conscientious manuring; nor would our strictures apply to this type of farmer.[2] The energetic,

[2] An instance has come before the notice of the writers of a dairy farm taken in hand seven years ago by a wealthy and energetic landowner. The farm was in an

liberal-minded business man is, however, still handicapped by the want of a more complete and scientific knowledge in the art of production and combination, such as we see outside this country, and which during the last few years has enabled the Dutchman, Dane, and Swede to openly take our trade away from us, though the cost of production has been much the same.

It is now, however, a matter of necessity for the pasture farmers to endeavour to make up lost ground. In the fierce competition of the present day they have got behindhand and are lagging in the race. Indiscriminate reductions of rent by large and rich landlords have rather tended to pauperise them than help them. They must have patience, and endeavour to educate themselves and their children into better business habits and methods, and take lessons from some of our foreign neighbours, many of which are afforded by the practical inhabitants of the little country which has mainly been the subject of this paper.

H. Herbert Smith.
Ernest C. Trepplin.

impoverished condition, and carried a herd of thirty-five cows. It has been highly manured and subjected to the very best treatment. It now carries seventy cows and cuts large crops of hay. It claims to show that during the seven years it has paid the old rent fixed in 1870, interest at 5 per cent. on capital, and has made in addition a very considerable profit. The whole of the milk has been sold off the farm since it was taken in hand.

THE late Lord Leighton's work has been for more than forty years before the world. Since his first great picture of Cimabue's Madonna was exhibited in the Royal Academy he was almost every year a contributor to the great show at Burlington House. His position as an artist has been so freely discussed, admirers and detractors have so long been ranged in opposite camps, that one might suppose that there was nothing new to be said about him; yet, strange as it may seem, except for a few reproductions in Mr. Ernest Rhys's book and elsewhere, the most characteristic part of his work, and, as many will think, the best, remains quite unknown to the general public.

He left behind him a vast number of drawings of exquisite beauty, which will be exhibited in the course of the coming winter, and which will, one may venture to think, attract considerable attention and admiration. They amount to a record of his life and a statement of his artistic creed.

Painters may be divided into two classes, viz. those who seek pre-eminently for pictorial effect of light or colour and those who look first for beauty of form and composition—in other words, those who seek to make a beautiful representation of an object and those who seek to make a representation of a beautiful object. The divergence of the two may not appear great at first sight, but it leads to astonishingly different results. Correggio, the Venetians, and Rembrandt are typical representatives of the first (Sir Joshua was contented with any sitter so long as he had 'a high light on his nose'), the Florentines, the Romans, and Mantegna of the second. Leighton's sympathies were with the latter. That he could see effect and loved colour is made sufficiently clear in his pictures and still more in his sketches, but his real affections were given to form.

One saw it in his method of designing. He began not, as most painters do nowadays, with a sketch of an effect of light or colour, but with an outline. Of late years he used generally to talk to, or, as he was pleased to say, consult, a friend before beginning a picture, and what he would show was a small outline, two or three inches high at the utmost, enclosed in bounding lines as a frame. Whole pages of small designs such as these, in which the germs of his best known

pictures are to be recognised, will be found. The sketch had
to be considered according to the salient and retreating parts, as
one might consider a relief. Raphael's pictures, which are always
planned like coloured bas-reliefs, were probably begun in the same
way.

The first sketch being settled, he proceeded to make drawings
from the model. First he drew from the nude. In many cases
there are evidences of his having tried several models before satisfying
himself. Then, when this was accomplished, the study from the
nude was transferred in outline to another paper. The same model,
draped, was carefully brought into the same pose, and the draperies
having been, after repeated failures, cast in a form which pleased
him, were drawn in over the outlined figure. These drawings of
drapery are most elaborate and beautiful, done generally in black
and white chalk on blue or brown paper, to save time, as no model
can sit for ever.

The next stage was to square off the first small design on to the
full-sized canvas, to draw in the figure from the studies in monochrome, and put the draperies on to it.

You had now an entire picture in monochrome, and the designs
in this state were generally most beautiful and complete. A friend
of his, himself an artist as well as an art patron, once besought him
to sell him a picture, 'The Idyll,' in this condition. Unhappily
Leighton took it as a reflection upon his powers of colouring and
refused.

This businesslike method of working flowed directly from the
nature of the man. His mind was extraordinarily, even disconcertingly
clear. It stripped everything it approached of all fog of prepposses-
sion or mistiness of thought. He detested the indefinite either
in speech or in Art. A singular light towards the understanding of
his mind is that he never painted a haze in his life. Mist is the
differentiating characteristic of our climate, and he delighted in
English landscape, as is proved by the following incident. When
George Mason first returned to England from Italy, where he had
painted his first pictures, and looked at the English landscape in his
own beautiful county of Derbyshire, he said there was nothing in it
to paint. It was Leighton who showed him what to do. He went
down to Derbyshire, and in his presence and that of Signor Costa,
who was with Mason, he drew in a book, which is now in the possession of Lord Carlisle, numerous small sketches for pictures. The
visit decided Mason's career. The best pictures of one of the most
delightful artists England has yet brought forth would never have
been painted but for Leighton's appreciation of his native scenery.
Yet he himself, intensely English and aggressively patriotic as he
was, never cared to paint that cardinal fact of our climate in virtue
of which English landscape is the loveliest in the world. In his

mind and in his eye everything is clear, defined, and as it were in three dimensions. He looks all round it. His landscape backgrounds are so modelled that you may pick your way from point to point to the extremest distance. The minds of most of us are a more or less clear space fading off into a misty region peopled with vague longings, unfinished thoughts, and indefinite shapes. Not so Leighton's. He could sympathise with others who grope to their thoughts through a poetic haze, but he never allowed his own work to be infected by it. His astonishingly active intelligence followed the thought to the horizon, and so far as that horizon extended he saw with a startling clearness. In his drawings a character so marked could not fail to assert itself.

His hand had been exercised from an early age upon all manner of subjects—horses, cows, cats, and poultry, architecture, caricature, and, above all, on the human figure. His industry was almost incredible. Already before his departure for Italy he had acquired in German artistic circles a wide reputation as being able to draw anything. The earlier studies from the nude show a conscientious adherence to clumsy German models, and are interesting chiefly for their faithfulness. But he grew rapidly more and more distinguished in his style.

As for draperies in that school, they were but little considered. A student was expected to be able to invent them, and Leighton with his perfectly clear head was a great adept at it. There are several elaborate drawings of that time with complicated draperies, done entirely *de chic*, as he told me himself, which if rather stiff look astonishingly well. The most remarkable one is the water colour of the 'Plague of Florence,' in which he assured me that all the draperies again were done out of his head.

When he left Germany to continue his studies in Rome he learnt the error of evolving draperies out of his moral consciousness, and never again trusted himself to put in anything without warrant from nature. It is true that the folds were not such as would naturally fall about the figure. They were carefully and even elaborately arranged. He would spend hours in arranging folds which he would copy in half an hour; but he never drew again out of his head. Experience had taught him the danger of trusting to intuition, as leading surely to mannerism, and it took shape in a remark of his late in life on being shown a student's drawing with the recommendation that the student had done it all out of his head. 'How lucky,' he said, 'to be able to get it out!'

Careful lead-pencil drawing, so much practised by Ingres, Delaroche, and the French school generally in the first half of this century, was still the fashion when Leighton was a student. It is a material which lends itself to, and indeed demands, a perfectly definite outline; and in all the Academy studies done in pencil and the exercises in composition done for his master, Steinle, one always notices a remorseless contour. The finer of his performances in this method begin in the years 1853 and 1854, during his stay in Rome, before his success with the Cimabue. The studies of hands, of which there are a number, are wonderful in their perfect delicacy and firmness of outline. Many heads also belong to this period—heads of his friends, male and female, and of models—and a most extra- ordinary piece of landscape representing the Albano hills, all modelled with astounding precision.

But the finest of all, except the famous 'Lemon Tree,' which is in silver point and was done in 1859, are the product of a visit to Algeria in 1857. I do not believe that more perfect drawings, better defined or more entirely realised, than these studies of heads of Moors, of camels, &c., were ever executed by the hand of man. They are not of the nature fashionable in this year of grace. They are not particularly summary, nor do they look as if they had been done in a moment or without any trouble. The drawings in question are as complete as if they came from the hand of Lionardo or Holbein.

Of the 'Lemon Tree' and of the 'Byzantine Well,' another draw- ing in silver point, Mr. Ruskin says, 'These two perfect early draw- ings determine for you without appeal the question respecting necessity of delineation as the first skill of a painter. Of all our present masters Sir Frederic Leighton delights most in softly blended colours, and his ideal of beauty is more nearly that of Correggio than any since Correggio's time. But you see by what precision of terminal outline he at first restrained and exalted his beautiful gift of "Vaghezza." '

After this period for working drawings, not for show but for use in his pictures, he took to using chalks and tinted paper. It is far the readiest method. His industry in this material is staggering. For the Daphnephoria, besides finished clay models of a group of three figures, and of one single figure, there remain over thirty-six drawings; for 'Cimon and Iphigenia,' two models and fifty-six drawings; for the captive Andromache, fifty-nine; for 'Solitude,' a single figure, nine; for the 'Return of Proserpine,' nineteen, and so on. Few of these are mere sketches. Most of them are careful and for their purpose finished drawings. At times, one must admit, his delight in handling the pencil ran away with him, and he would repeat a whole study for no apparent purpose, but as a rule he kept rigidly to a severe course of progressive definition.

Besides working drawings there are numberless designs and projects for pictures in various materials. Some are done without models, as exercises in composition; others are elaborated sketches. Enchanting groups will be found amongst them, full of tenderness and graceful fancy. During the intervals of work when the model was resting he made innumerable little sketches as he or she moved about the studio, and it was from notes made at these moments that several of his most natural and graceful figures were derived. These charming little suggestions, often several on one sheet, will recall to many the best of those bewitching terra-cottas which have been recovered of late years at Tanagra. They are slightly but sufficiently indicated, and generally with a certain insistence on the silhouette.

This is a point worth pausing upon for a moment. The insistence on the silhouette is even more marked in what I have called the exercises in composition. He considered it of the first importance and made it the subject of his most anxious study. 'The outline,' he said once to me, 'should be always changing in its subordinate parts, but it should be simple in its general contour.' Careful observation of the studies for the Daphnephoria and the South Kensington frescoes will reveal how he acted on this maxim. Not only single figures but whole groups are contained in one carefully considered bounding line. It is, perhaps, most obvious of all in the 'Arts of War,' which is, therefore, well worth the close attention of any student who has sufficient power of analysis to sift the wheat from the chaff in it.

To assist his outline Leighton made a most scientific study of draperies. In the heavy materials of the clothing used in the period in which he placed the 'Arts of War' he found opportunities for breadth and enrichment of the contour, of which he made liberal use. For the 'Arts of Peace' and for the Daphnephoria, which are placed in the classical period, he employed softer tissues, which fill out the figure less opulently, but the same care is discernible to conceal such parts of the figure as would look poor in that particular pose, and to fill up gaps that would give a meagre effect.

It was this quality of silhouette which gave his figures their charm and grace. In the present moment, when impressionism and painting as distinct from designing holds, and is likely to hold, the field in England, it is well to remind the rising generation that their predecessors had some merits of their own, though of a different kind. Good outline-designing may not be one of those virtues which tell most in a gallery, but it is not to be despised.

He frequently admitted that he was never so much at home with the brush as with the point. Whatever he may have been with the first, no one, after seeing this collection, will deny that he was a master of the latter. There is no trace of the square blocking which is taught in the modern French schools, the effect of which is to train the eye to a certain dry correctness which is perceptible in all but the very best French drawing. The great Italians never drew in this chip-chop fashion, and their line, if occasionally over-rich, is never poor. Even accomplished artists are apt to overlook the difference between good drawing and fine drawing. I have heard it said by some who should know better that such a drawing as the 'Lemon

Tree,' or any other of those studies of plant life in which Leighton delighted, is a mere exercise of patience. It undoubtedly is an exercise of patience, and a severe one, but it is a great deal more. To appreciate the vitality of the curves and twists of the leaves, and to follow them with such exquisite fineness of undulating line, is not given to all. It needs a hand like that *ineffabile mano sinistra* of Lionardo's to do it.

Our artist's handling of black and white continued to increase in vigour and facility until, in the studies made for ' The Sea giving up her Dead,' ' Perseus and Andromeda,' ' The Phœnicians in Cornwall,' and for other designs of the last few years, we have the most powerful things he ever did. It would not be unfair to say that they surpass any drawings ever made in England.

The great group of ' The Sea giving up her Dead ' is one which no other painter in this country could have attempted with any chance of success. It shows astounding mastery. Unfortunately, in common with some other designs done by Leighton for St. Paul's, it did not find favour with the clerical authorities. It was dubbed irreligious, a criticism which it is not for me to dispute beyond saying that it applies with equal force to the Sistine ceiling. Anyhow it was a grand piece of work, and it would be much to be regretted if no use is ever made in St. Paul's of the cartoon he executed of it.

Such drawings as those I am now speaking of, or reproductions of them, ought to be hung up in the schools of Art all over the country as examples for students. They are invaluable lessons. However eminent a man may be in other departments of the art, in colour, in sentiment, or in decorative effect, he can never be called a master of his craft unless he can draw the human figure with facility. The severe training it requires is the only path to thoroughness such as it is the aim of all academies to teach. The study of the human figure is like that of the dead languages. It is not an end in itself. Though occasional nude figures do find their way into exhibitions, they are year by year less welcomed, except it may be as exercises and proofs of proficiency. But the figure remains the indispensable basis of Art education, and the man who can draw and paint it can express anything he has in his heart.

This is a time when it is necessary to bear this in mind. It is the fashion to paint, and every one does it. We are flooded with clever amateurs. There is a quantity of their work in the Salon and in the Academy. Too good to be rejected, whatever they do is nevertheless always wanting in ' bottom.' Nothing is in reserve. Where they excel is in the cheaper and more effective parts of the art, in the light and shade or the colour. Now these are just the parts which Leighton left to the last. He spoke of them once to me as ' the jam on the bread-and-butter,' the solid foundation being the drawing, which amateurs are always in haste to get over. He rather lingered than hurried over the earlier stages. But then he was superficial in nothing. Besides the thoroughness of his drawing he had done all he could to perfect himself in other respects. He was learned in all that the Greeks or Italians had done, and had scientifically analysed their works. He had read everything of value treating of methods and mediums. He had anatomy at his fingers' ends, and his system of procedure was one carefully thought out for the production of the best work in the best way. In fact, he may be held up to younger generations as the very type of the professional craftsman.

When all the evidence of labour given by his drawings is seen it will, I fear, be a shock to many. The belief that an artist's life is an easy one will never be eradicated from the mind of the majority. They will probably continue to think that Art is a charming accomplishment, which, if somewhat difficult to acquire, is, when once learnt, a pleasant employment in moments of inspiration. But if anything would bring it home to them that it is not so, one would suppose it would be these drawings. For here we see a man not only while young and winning his way in the world, but still when loaded with honours and with business, going through the same mill every time he sits down to paint a picture—indeed, ever toiling harder and growing more fastidious as he feels the years before him grow fewer, until finally by continual exertion is brought on a fatal malady and death, which, if he would but have consented to take his ease, the doctors think he might have averted.

But Leighton's indomitable character would yield to nothing less than death. Turning over the portfolios we see it written more legibly than if it were set down in a journal. Here was a man pursued with ambition to excel, clear-headed, sparingly emotional, a man of intellect and iron will. If he was not exactly a poet in the sense of displaying a warm sympathy with human nature, he was eminently so in the sense that he had a cult and love for beauty. He had an ideal, which he pursued with an unswerving passion. It was his habit and his creed to keep his pictures generally impersonal, but now and again his heart appeared in them, and once at any rate the springs of his innermost life were committed to canvas in a picture which was the type of his general mental attitude, viz. ' The Spirit of the Summits.'

S. P. COCKERELL.

THE CONDITIONS·OF LIFE AFTER DEATH

MEN'S minds in both hemispheres have been drawn with fresh interest to the problems connected with man's persistent life beyond the tomb by the turning of Mr. Gladstone's ever bright and eager intellect in that direction.   But though his treatment of the subject has given fresh point to the perennial inquiry : 'Whither do we go?' the interest aroused by his articles is due to more than the eminence of the writer.   More than ever in this age of doubt and of challenge of all traditions does man yearn for a definite knowledge of his future, nay, for some sure knowledge that he has a future at all.   It is not enough that heavenly visions shall soothe his heart ; his intellect demands satisfaction and refuses to be silenced by authority.   The time seems ripe to offer an answer that includes all that is true in the clashing replies of many creeds, that affirms the verifiability of the facts of the *post-mortem* states, and removes the whole question from the region of doubt into that of investigation and study.   If the statement made be regarded in the light of a possible hypothesis and be applied to the many jostling declarations already before us, it will be found to explain much that seems incredible to some while passionately asserted by others, to reconcile allegations that appear contradictory because they are partial, to illuminate propositions that are obscure because they need analysis and rearrangement.   Each must judge for himself whether the hypothesis be sufficiently credible to be taken on trial as a theory, and time alone can decide whether the theory shall ultimately be accepted as a plain record of the facts in Nature.

Believers in the continuing life of man may be grouped into three great classes :

1. Those who believe on the authority of documents—many of them of great antiquity—documents containing statements either directly written by living persons who claimed to possess first-hand knowledge on the matter in question, or written down by the followers of such persons from their oral teachings.   This class includes all the members of the religions of the world who base their belief in man's survival after death on the testimony of prophets and seers as recorded in their several scriptures.

2. Those who believe on the authority of statements professing to be made by denizens of the invisible world, who know by personal experience the conditions they describe. This class includes all spiritualists and also all religionists who accept as part of their scriptures revelations on this matter made by Gods, angels, or spirits.

3. Those who believe on the authority of what they claim as their own first-hand experience, their own investigations—carried on while they are still in the body—of the states usually reached only through the gateway of death. To this class may be added those who accept from them directly their first-hand testimony on various corroborative grounds satisfactory to themselves.

It is with this last class that this article is chiefly concerned, for their methods and results are less familiar to the public than those of classes 1 and 2. But we need to note a few preliminary points about the two latter.

Religionists of all faiths are at one as regards man's survival after death, but they differ widely as to the conditions which will surround him in the *post-mortem* states, and as to the permanency or transitoriness of their duration. Almost all believe that man after death passes into a transitional state, in which there may be much suffering wherein he shakes off gradually the faults of his lower nature, to enter purified into a condition of bliss. The majority regard this blissful state as of long but limited duration, to be followed by a return of the soul to earth, to pass through another mundane experience, the evolutionary life of the soul being made up of long periods of extra-corporeal existence, separated from each other by relatively brief plunges into corporeal life. The minority allot to each soul, whether it be of high or of low type, but one lesson hour on earth to be followed by endless ages elsewhere, the rapture or the torture of eternity being determined—according to a rapidly decreasing school—by the incidents of the brief earthly span ; as to details there is much variety of opinion, some believing that eternity will be spent in progress, others that the soul will remain crystallised in an immediately perfected beatitude.

However much religionists may quarrel over the nature of the *post-mortem* states, no balanced judgment can deny weight to their complete consensus of opinion that 'Not all of me shall die.' The quarrels are due to the partiality of the different sets of believers, who are apt to claim uniqueness for their several heavens to the exclusion of the heavens of others, as they claim uniqueness for their several scriptures to the exclusion of the scriptures of others—forgetting that all scriptures have their share of inspiration, all heavens their repre-- sentatives in space. But the agreement is due to the deeply rooted conviction in all human hearts, breathed into them by the spirit within them all, that the life of the body is not the life of the man, and that death has no power over all that is noblest in his nature.

All these religionists are further committed to the belief that men in the past have been able to penetrate beyond the veil of death, and to bring back records of life in the world invisible to fleshly eyes.

Spiritualists—to use the name adopted by many of class 2—show similar agreement as to the continuance of life and similar diversity in details. The descriptions given by ‘spirits’ of *post-mortem* existence vary from those of the commonest replicas of earthly conditions to those of highly etherealised and unfettered states of being ; and they generally avoid the error of exclusion, and do not attempt to reduce the invisible world to a sameness which does not characterise the visible. The evidence adduced by spiritualists as to man's continued existence cannot lightly be waved aside as incredible nor be crushed under the imputation of fraud. Frauds indeed there have been, sometimes connived at, sometimes contrived by mediums, sometimes imposed upon them hypnotically by sitters determined to ‘expose’ them, and often caused by the ‘controls’ to whom they blindly yield themselves. But when all frauds are allowed for and sifted out, there remains a residuum of hard facts, testified to by persons of clear judgment, keen intelligence and unimpeachable veracity, that no thoughtful investigator can afford to disregard. The inferences drawn from the facts may be open to challenge, but the facts themselves will bear the closest scrutiny, and it is right to remember as to the inferences that the most thoughtful and careful spiritualists do not now ascribe all the phenomena of the séance room to disembodied human intelligences.

Let us turn to class 3. Mesmeric and hypnotic investigations, carried on by men of science, have amply demonstrated the truth of the contention put forward by occultists in all ages, that the consciousness of man includes far more than is shown in his everyday waking consciousness, and that in the deeper hypnotic states is unveiled a consciousness so completely individualised that it regards itself, and is recognised by others, as separate from and superior to the consciousness working in the physical brain. This higher individualised consciousness is regarded by occultists as the real or inner man, and as existing in everyone, in however latent a condition ; the consciousness working in the brain, closely entangled with the body and with the animal nature of man, is looked upon by them as a merely personal consciousness concerned with the present life, put forth by the true consciousness, the human soul, for the carrying on of the lower nature, but so hampered and blinded by its gross surroundings that it does not recognise its real identity with the soul, and fails to understand the purpose of its putting forth into earthly life—the gathering of experience for the development and evolution of the soul that lives for ever. All agree—religionists, spiritualists and occultists alike—that the human soul leaves the body at ‘ the change that men call death ;’ spiritualists allege that, in the case of mediums at least, it can leave the body during earth life, and allow another entity to take possession of and control the body; occultists declare that it can leave the body at will and return to it at will, bringing back and impressing on the physical brain the experiences it may have undergone during its extra-corporeal travels.

The human soul is not bodiless; it has a body of subtle matter, too fine to be seen by the physical eye—the 'spiritual body' of St. Paul—and is further clothed with two lower but still subtle bodies; in these the soul can exercise all its perceptive faculties far more perfectly than when it is encumbered by the grosser body of flesh. It can withdraw itself from the latter—which then remains asleep or entranced, as the case may be, emptied of intellectual consciousness—and is then, for the time being, a 'disembodied' intelligence, 'like unto the angels,' and is free to range at will and in full self-consciousness the worlds that are usually entered through the gateway of death. It can there observe, compare, and record the phenomena of those regions, and thus gain an experimental knowledge of their inhabitants and conditions. True, it is subject to errors, as it is here, from careless observation, hasty generalisations from partial knowledge, inferences biassed by prejudices and preconceived opinions. But it is on the way to acquire valuable information, and its errors will be corrected by riper study and by the repeated investigations of other observers. The faculties of the soul improve by use in its subtle bodies as much as they do in its physical vehicle, and must be evolved, educated and trained by slow degrees and steady practice. There is no royal road to knowledge for the soul either in the physical or in the subtle bodies, and law rules in other regions as it does here.

The observer, then, of the phenomena of *post-mortem* states is the human soul, using the organs of the subtle bodies instead of those of the gross. When it has developed the power of energising the subtle bodies, it is not, however, necessary that it should absolutely quit the physical body in order to use these greatly extended powers of observation. By practice it can exercise these while remaining 'wide awake' in the physical world, and two or more people may sit together with all their physical faculties active and yet observe the phenomena of the subtle worlds, communicate their observations to each other in the ordinary way, and discuss and compare the objects they are studying.

It is admitted on all hands by religious people that prophets and seers exercised these powers of the soul in the past, but they are not prepared to admit that man can do now what man has done. If the fact be admitted for any period in human history, there is no *a priori* impossibility in its repetition: whether it is being now repeated is a matter of evidence, which each can examine for himself. But it may be asked, Can any one investigate the subtler realms of Nature and reverify individually the observations made by others, thus obtaining first-hand knowledge of the persistence of individual consciousness beyond the grave? The answer is of the same nature as would be made in reply to a similar question in the study of any other science: Any one can do it who has sufficient perseverance and sufficient capacity, and who can devote to the work sufficient time. To be a specialist in the science of the soul is as rare, even rarer, than to be a specialist in any other branch of learning, and while the gaining of first-hand and thorough acquaintance with the invisible world is theoretically open to any one—like the voyage to the North Pole—it is practically open to few at the present stage of development. In time all men will visit and become familiar with the invisible regions—the time when the inner powers will unfold naturally in due course of evolution, but that time is not yet.

Without entering fully into details, it may be well to indicate the general training followed by a student who desires to separate soul and body.

He must begin by practising extreme temperance in all things, cultivating an equable and serene state of mind; his life must be clean and his thoughts pure, his body held in strict subjection to the soul, and his mind trained to occupy itself with noble and lofty themes; he must habitually practise compassion, sympathy, helpfulness to others, with indifference to troubles and pleasures affecting himself, and he must cultivate courage, steadfastness and devotion. In fact he must live the religion and ethics that other people for the most part only talk. Having by persevering practice learned to control his mind to some extent, so that he is able to keep it fixed on one line of thought for some little time, he must begin its more rigid training by a daily practice of concentration on some difficult or abstract subject, or on some lofty object of devotion; this concentration means the firm fixing of the mind on one single point, without wandering, and without yielding to any distractions caused by external objects, by the activity of the senses, or by that of the mind itself. It must be braced up to an unswerving steadiness and fixity, until gradually it will learn so to withdraw its attention from the outer world and from the body that the senses will remain quiet and still while the mind is intensely alive, with all its energies drawn inward to be launched at a single point of thought, the highest to which it can attain. When it is able to hold itself thus with comparative ease, it is ready for a further step, and by a strong but calm effort of the will it can throw itself beyond the highest thought it can reach *while working in the physical brain*, and in that effort will rise to and unite itself with the higher consciousness and find itself free of the body. When this is done there is no sense of sleep or dream nor any loss of consciousness; the man finds himself outside his body, but as though he had merely slipped off a weighty encumbrance, not as though he had lost any part of himself; he is not really 'disembodied,' but has risen out of his gross body 'in a body of light,' which obeys his thought and serves as a beautiful and perfect instrument for carrying out his will. In this he is free of the subtle worlds, but will need to train his faculties long and carefully for reliable work under the new conditions.

Freedom from the body may be obtained in other ways : by the rapt intensity of devotion or by special methods that may be imparted by a great teacher to his disciple. Whatever the way, the end is the same—the setting free of the soul in full consciousness, able to examine its new surroundings in regions beyond the treading of the man of flesh. At will it can return to the body and re-enter it, and under these circumstances it can impress on the brain-mind, and thus retain while in the body, the memory of the experiences it has undergone. As said above, it can also use its subtle senses without leaving the physical body, and this is often a convenient way of carrying on investigations.

To turn to the investigations themselves. When the soul at death leaves the body of flesh it is clothed in a violet-grey body made of ethers, or of matter of different densities, all rarer than the gases of our earth; it is in these kinds of ethers that light, electricity, Röntgen rays &c. find the medium in which they express themselves as 'modes of motion.' The soul remains but for a few hours in this etheric counterpart of its fleshly form, and is generally in a dreamy state while in it; it quickly shakes it off, thus divesting itself of all the matter belonging to the physical world, and enters the region which comprises the hells of various religions, the purgatory of the Roman Catholics, the summerland of the Spiritualists, the intermediate states of the Hindus and Buddhists, the land of desires (Kâmaloka) or astral plane of the Theosophists. The conditions there are extremely various, but may be classified under seven headings or regions, the soul in one region not being conscious of the souls in the other regions but capable of seeing and communicating with those in its own. These regions differ in the densities of the matter that enters into the composition of all forms existing in them, and it is these differences of matter that form the barriers preventing inter-communications ; souls dwelling in one can no more come into touch with souls dwelling in another than a deep-sea fish can hold a conversation with an eagle high-poised in air—the medium necessary to the life of the one would be destructive to the life of the other. A trained occultist can pass into any of these regions at will, having learned how to adapt himself to them, but the untrained soul is not thus unfettered, but must remain within the limitations suited to its moral and mental conditions. The general principle that determines its place is as follows : Into the 'astral' body—in which the soul finds itself when the body of flesh and its etheric counterpart have dropped off—enter the different kinds of matter belonging to the seven regions aforesaid, just as the many chemical elements making up the physical world enter into the physical body of man. During the earth life this astral body interpenetrated the physical, and being worked upon both by the physical body and the mind, its composition was determined by theirs. Gross and unclean living, indulgence in animal passions and appetites, thicken and coarsen the astral body, drawing into it the coarser kinds of astral matter, while a temperate and pure life, control of the lower nature, and high and unselfish thoughts, attract to it the finest and rarest sorts of astral materials. Similar causes, as we know, work similar effects on the physical body, and the effects are more marked on the astral, owing to its more plastic nature. These differences between astral bodies, I may say in passing, are quite perceptible during earth life to the trained vision, so that it is easy to foresee the nature of the intermediate life that the soul will undergo after death. If a soul has led a pure life while on earth, has subjugated completely the animal nature, and is not aroused either by a persistent and keen interest in earth life or by clamorous regrets and longings from its friends, it sleeps through these seven regions, ' enwrapped in rosy dreams,' until, the astral body having in its turn dropped away, it awakens to the bliss of the world beyond. All others, whose astral bodies are impure, dwell for a while in the regions necessary for their purification.

Seventh, or lowest, region. This region must be taken by itself, for it represents all the truth that there is in the descriptions of the hells of all the religions. It is gloomy, dreary, with atmosphere heavy beyond description; to walk through it is like walking through clinging viscous mud. Save for this the souls make their own torment, for here are murderers, profligates, drunkards, criminals of brutal types, suicides, all full of fierce unsatiated passions, seething with revenge, hatred, longings after vicious indulgences which the loss of the physical body incapacitates them from ' enjoying.' Just as they were on earth save for the body, and every passion showing itself unbridled, they rage and raven, and they crowd round all foul resorts on our earth, gloating over crimes and filthy orgies, stimulating those in the body to fresh accesses of debauchery and crime. Earth-bound are they till they wear out their passions, and when these wear out the soul passes on.

Sixth, fifth, and fourth regions. These are still within touch of earth, and resemble earth in their general appearance, each becoming finer as we ascend. Into the lowest of these immense numbers pass at death, and are held there until the trivial and petty side of life exhausts its dwarfing and limiting effects on the soul. Here souls are delayed who set all their interest on trifles, and here also those who let the lower nature largely rule them and who died with its appetites still demanding attention. The souls awake here are mostly dissatisfied, uneasy, restless, with more or less actual suffering according to the vigour of the wishes they cannot gratify; some undergo much positive pain from this cause, and are long delayed ere these earthly longings are exhausted. Many lengthen their stay by seeking to communicate with the earth, in whose interests they are entangled, by means of mediums, who allow them to use their physical bodies for this purpose, thus supplying the loss of their own. As for the most part these earth-bound souls are of small intelligence, their communications are of no more general interest than was their conversation when they were in the body, and—just as on earth—they are positive in proportion to their ignorance, representing the whole astral world as identical with their own very limited area.

Third region. Inhabited by souls of narrow intelligence, but of good life and crude religious beliefs. Literalists of every faith who were filled with selfish longings for their own salvation in the most materialistic of heavens here find an appropriate, and to them enjoyable, home, surrounded by the very conditions they believed in. The religious and philanthropic busybodies who cared more to carry out their own fads and impose their own ways on their neighbours than to unselfishly work for the increase of human virtue and happiness, are here much *en évidence*, carrying on reformatories, refuges, schools, to their own great satisfaction, and much delighted are they to still push an astral finger into an earthly pie with the help of a subservient medium whom they patronise with lofty condescension. They build astral churches and schools and houses, astral cities, reproducing the materialistic heavens they coveted; and though to keener vision their erections are imperfect, even pathetically grotesque, they find them all-sufficing. People of the same religions flock together, but minor subdivisions seem to be largely forgotten.

Second region. Resembles the third in many ways, but is far more refined, and is largely inhabited by souls of more cultured type, but who were much dominated by selfishness in their devotion to artistic and intellectual pursuits, and who prostituted their talents to the gratification of the desire-nature in a refined and delicate way. Religionists, too, of a slightly higher type than those in the third region, are here delayed, working off their cruder ideas. From here again souls will communicate with ordinary mediums of the better sort, mostly pouring out moral platitudes of more or less maudlin sentimentality, occasionally rising into feeble eloquence of a verbose and prosy kind.

First region. A by no means repellent limbo, where men of much intellectual power working on materialistic lines are apt to be long delayed, their keen interest in physical ways of thinking and in earthly methods of gaining knowledge holding them back from freedom. A great mathematician, for instance, was met, fettered by his intense desire to forward his line of discovery on earth, and oblivious or sceptical of the far more effective mental activities that would be his in a higher world.

To all souls sooner or later—save to those who during earth life never felt one touch of unselfish love, of intellectual aspiration, of recognition of something higher than themselves—there comes a time when the bonds of the astral body are shaken off and left behind as an astral corpse, or ' shell,' while the soul sinks into brief unconsciousness, to be awakened by a sense of bliss intense, undreamed of, the bliss of the heaven-world, of the world to which by its own nature it belongs. At first it knows nothing beyond this bliss unspeakable, but soon begin to dawn on it the faces most loved on earth, and it arouses itself to see around it, amid ripples of living light and exquisite melody, the radiant images of all who during earth life were dear. Let us leave it a moment to its joy while we look at the heavenly places.

' Heaven' for the Christian and the Moslem, Devaloka (the land of the Shining Ones, the Gods) for the Hindu, Sukhavatî (the infinitely happy) for the Buddhist, Devachan for the Theosophist. This Devachan is a specially guarded part of the vast world of the mind, protected against the incursion of evil (and therefore of sorrow) by the great spiritual intelligences who guide and overlook the whole of human evolution. The world of which it is a part is the third concerned in the general evolution of man—the physical and astral worlds being the other two. It is the world to which man's higher nature belongs, both by its powers and by the constitution of the ' mental body ; ' that is, the outer organism in which the soul works in all its mental activities. This is a poorly organised and cloudy mass while the soul is little developed, gradually becoming a nobly organised, glorious, and definitely outlined form of divine beauty as the soul evolves. This is the last and the most subtle garment of the soul, immediately clothing the immortal soul-body that lasts throughout the ages of time, the ' spiritual body' of St. Paul.[1] Each of these demands notice, for they function in the *post-mortem* states. The world of the mind (like the astral and the physical) has its seven regions, which fall under two main headings ; the lower four supply the materials of the body through which the soul works as mind by reason, judgment, &c. The higher three yield the materials for the immortal body, through which the soul exercises its highest functions such as intuition and conscience.

[1] I am uneasily conscious that the complexity of the human constitution is apt to puzzle and even irritate people accustomed only to the primitive or savage simplicity of ' soul and body.' But every student must analyse if he is to understand, and a scientist dealing only with the physical body separates it into six distinct systems, according as the life is working in the nervous, muscular, digestive, circulatory, respiratory, or bony system.

All the souls, then, that are dwelling in the four lower of the heavenly regions are clad in this mind-body, and freely exercise all mental powers; but these powers are creative in a way that down here we can hardly realise. On earth a painter, a sculptor, a musician, dreams dreams of exquisite beauty, creating their visions by the powers of the mind, but when they seek to embody them in the coarse materials of earth they fall far short of the mental creation. The marble is too resistant for perfect form, the pigments too muddy for perfect colour. In heaven, all they think is at once reproduced in form, for the rare and subtle matter of the heaven-world is 'mind-stuff,' the medium in which the mind normally works when free from passion, and it takes shape with every mental impulse. Each man, therefore, in a very real sense, makes his own heaven, and the beauty of his surroundings is indefinitely increased, according to the wealth and energy of his mind. As the soul develops its powers, its heaven grows more and more subtle and exquisite; all the limitations in heaven are self-created, and its heaven expands and deepens with the expansion and deepening of the soul. While the soul is weak and selfish, narrow and ill-developed, its heaven shares these pettinesses, but it is always the best that is in the soul, how-ever poor that best may be. Here, as everywhere else, 'God is not mocked; and whatsoever a man soweth that shall he also reap.' In the heaven-world all earth's higher experiences are assimilated, and the thoughts, aspirations, and efforts of the earth-life are worked up into the powers and faculties of the soul; hence the more of these it takes with it the more it grows and develops. Schemes of benefi-cence for which power and skill to accomplish were lacking in the past life are there worked out in thought, and the power and skill are developed as faculties of the soul, to be put into use in a future life on earth; the clever and earnest student develops· to be reborn as a genius, the devotee to be reborn as a saint. Round each soul also throng those it loved in life, and every image of the loved ones that live in the heart becomes a living companion of the soul in the heavenly places. And here again comes in limitation, but now in those who enter into the soul's paradise. Exactly in proportion to the development of the soul in a man's friends is the reality of their presence in his heaven. He, as it were, makes the outward image of his friend, but the soul of his friend vitalises the image in proportion to its own growth and expansion. The illusions of earth, though lessened, are not escaped from in the lower heavens, though contact is more real and more immediate. For it must never be forgotten that these heavens are part of a great evolutionary scheme, and until man has found the real self his own unreality makes him subject to illusions. Let us take the heavens in order.

Seventh or lowest region.—Here are the souls whose noblest part on 'earth was love for family and friends, narrow but sincere, and sometimes unselfish—souls but little developed, little influenced by religious emotion, or the higher aspects of human life. They lead but a very slightly progressive life, but enjoy all the bliss their narrow capacity is able to receive, the highest happiness they are able to imagine.

Sixth region.—Here may be observed souls of every religious faith, steeped in religious ecstasy, worshipping God under the forms their piety sought on earth, losing themselves in the rapture of devotion, in communion with the objects they adore. For the Divine Love they sought meets each under the form that was worshipped, and no soul feels itself amid strangers in its heavenly bliss; the Hindu finds his God under the beloved form of Shri Krishna, the Christian his under that of the Christ. For the roads taken by devotion are many, but the goal of all is one. Very beautiful are some of the family groups in this region gathered round the living and loving image of the God worshipped on earth in the family circle, the Divine veiling Itself as the child Christ or as Bala Krishna, to meet the ideal of the loving and still child-like souls.

Fifth region.—The souls that are found in this region have added to their faith works in abundance, and during their earth-life performed much worship by labour for their fellows. At every step the observer meets those who showed love to God by love to man, and who are reaping the reward of their good deeds by increasing powers of usefulness and increasing wisdom in their direction. These will yield many of the great philanthropists of yet unborn centuries, who will be born on earth with innate dower of unselfish love and of power to achieve.

Fourth region.—Most various perhaps of all the heavens are the inhabitants of this, for here all the powers of more advanced souls find their active exercise. Here we see souls into whose heavenly visions enter great teachers of the race, even those greatest ones who were worshipped as divine as well as learned from as masters. Here they instruct as pupils the souls that on earth sought them as teachers, and swift is the progress made by the eager souls who drink in the heavenly wisdom. As teachers and light-bringers shall they go back to earth, born with the birthmark of the teacher's high office on them. In this heaven also are found the kings of art and literature, so growing in their loftier power that they shall be reborn with genius as a birthright. And others who failed, though greatly aspiring, are here transmuting longings into power, and searchers into Nature are learning her hidden secrets, to return as great ' discoverers ' to earth. But time would fail me to tell of all the wonders and the beauties of these lower heavens, the marvels of their living colours, the ineffable harmony of their melodious sounds.

souls themselves, freed from all garments of illusion, face to face with Truth. To this high dwelling rises the consciousness of every child of man ere he reincarnates on earth ; the vast majority touch its lowest level but for a moment, for the undeveloped soul is but faintly, dreamily self-conscious at that height, almost as the unborn babe in its mother's womb. None the less is that embryonic creature the soul itself, and into it, as into an undying receptacle, passes everything that is pure and valuable gathered by means of its lower bodies or vehicles during its earthly, astral, and devachanic lives. By these experiences alone it grows, develops, becomes mature, and in that third heaven we may study myriads upon myriads of souls, some temporarily connected with physical bodies, but the great majority without them. They are all stages of development, from the embryonic to the comparatively mature. The latter spend part of their heavenly life fully self-conscious in that region, seeing life as it really is, things in their essence, not in their illusory phenomenal aspects.

In the succeeding region are souls highly developed in intellect and in moral character, rapidly maturing towards human perfection. They remember all their past and can see the causes working towards future results ; they are in full and close communion with souls of development similar to their own, helping and being helped ; during the brief periods of incarnation on earth they are able to guide their physical vehicles and manifest a high, noble, and strong character ; self-consciousness has been evolved, never again to be lost, and they are nearly ready for the step which shall unite the higher and lower minds, and make full and free communication possible between the soul and its physical, astral, and mental bodies. This accomplished, the memory of the past can enter the waking physical brain, and the man remembers the long series of his past incarnations.

It skills not to speak of the highest of the heavens, where the souls of masters and initiates have their home. Enough that from that region are poured down upon earth streams of intellectual force and energy of the loftiest kinds. The intellectual life of the world has there its root ; thence genius receives its purest inspirations, and blessed are the embodied souls on whom its radiance falls.

Such, poorly and feebly told, are some of the conditions of the life after death as observed and studied by some amongst us who are training themselves for such investigations. Nothing has here been said which may not at a certain stage of development be seen without leaving the physical body, without losing touch of the waking consciousness. Needless also to add that to all such observers—and indeed to many also who are immediately around them—death becomes a mere incident of small importance, a mere 'change, that men call death.'   Death is but a birth into a wider life, a return from brief exile to the soul's true home, a passing from a prison into the freedom of the outer air.   There are states of consciousness in which, to quote Lord Tennyson, 'Death seems a ludicrous impossibility,' and when these have been experienced, no doubt as to 'life after death' can ever again arise.   For life is then seen to be unbroken, unbreakable, and 'death is swallowed up of life.'

ANNIE BESANT.

LAND PURCHASE IN IRELAND

LAND Purchase in Ireland began its career in the year 1870. Before that time it did not form an article of the creed of either of the political parties of the State. Mr. Bright had advocated the creation of a peasant proprietary in Ireland by means of State aid, just as Mr. John Stuart Mill had advocated the adequate representation of minorities in Parliament. Both suggestions had been listened to somewhat languidly. They were regarded as the hobbies of two distinguished men who ought perhaps to be humoured, if the humouring did not cost too much ; and so Birmingham was formed into a three-cornered constituency, the Bright clauses, as they were called, were tacked on to Mr. Gladstone's Land Bill in 1870, and a million sterling was voted by Parliament to work them. The clauses proved a complete failure. At the end of ten years less than one half of the million voted had been utilised, or, in other words, the capital sum employed in carrying out land purchase in an entire decade was not more than a twentieth or thirtieth part of a single year's rental of agricultural Ireland.

The purchase sections of Mr. Gladstone's Irish Land Act of 1881 were scarcely more successful. In the four years which succeeded the passing of that measure the advances made under it to tenants for the purchase of their holdings amounted to little more than a quarter of a million sterling.

The plan on which land sales to tenants in Ireland are conducted is this. The tenant agrees to buy and the landlord to sell; the purchase money (or part of it, as the case may be) is advanced to the landlord by the State ; the tenant becomes liable to the State for the repayment of it, not in a bulk sum, but by instalments spread over a number of years, which instalments comprise both interest on the sum advanced and a sinking fund in discharge of the principal.

By the Bright clauses of 1870 the State advance was limited to two-thirds, and by the Land Act of 1881 to three-fourths of the purchase money of the holding, and it was repayable by instalments at the rate of 5 per cent. per annum on the amount advanced, which instalments would in thirty-five years pay off both principal and interest.

It may be asked why was it that these provisions were so little

availed of. The Bright clauses of 1870 were doomed from the first.
The landlords in 1870 and for several years afterwards were not
anxious to sell to their tenants. There was a brisk market at that
time for their properties. The outside public were ready and eager
to buy up at high prices whatever land was offered for sale. It
was more troublesome to sell an estate piecemeal to individual
tenants than to sell it *en bloc* to a capitalist, and naturally the
vendors selected the course which gave them less trouble and not
less profit.

By the year 1881 the condition of Ireland had greatly changed.
She had gone through the bad years of 1877, 1878, and the disastrous
year of 1879. All people interested in land had become scared.
Mortgagees had ceased to lend on land, banks were calling in what
they had already lent, rents were falling into arrear, outsiders would
not bid for landed properties. The only possible purchasers were
now the tenants, and to them many landlords were willing to sell on
terms which by comparison with the prices of land in 1870 were
cheap indeed. The tenants did not avail themselves of the landlords'
willingness to sell. The Land Act of 1881 had just given to them
for the first time the right of going into court to get a fair rent fixed
on their holdings, and from this operation they hoped to gain a substantial reduction in their rents. They argued that, the lower their
rent might be, the lower would be the purchase money which the
landlord was likely to accept for his interest in the land, and therefore the tenants were not anxious to buy until they had first got
their rents fixed. But even had both landlords and tenants been
able to agree upon the price, there still remained an almost
insuperable difficulty in carrying out the sales. The Land Commission could not advance more than three-fourths of the purchase money.
Where was the remaining one-fourth to come from? The majority of
the tenants had not the means of making it up. The banks were not
disposed to lend it, and the landlord, who would have been willing to
sell if the transaction was to be a sale out-and-out might be pardoned
for thinking that he would not increase either his wealth or his comfort by ceasing to be a landlord in order that he might become a
puisne mortgagee of his tenant. As such mortgagee, he would have
as much trouble in collecting his interest as he had hitherto experienced in collecting his rent, while his remedies in the event of default
would be less speedy and effectual.

It was plain to practical men in Ireland that no substantial progress could be made towards creating a peasant proprietary until the
Land Commission was empowered to advance the entire of the purchase
money, and until, by some means or other, the annual instalments in
repayment of it were reduced below 5 per cent.

In June 1885 Mr. Gladstone's Government resigned, and a Conservative Government came into office, Lord Ashbourne being their

Lord Chancellor for Ireland and a member of the Cabinet. By 1885 a substantial number of Irish tenants had got their rents reduced and fixed by the Land Commission. Mr. Parnell saw that the time had come when a workable scheme of Land Purchase would probably be of service to the tenants. The landlords were anxious for such a scheme, because there were still no outside purchasers in the land markets. Both Liberals and Conservatives were pledged to the principle of advancing the entire purchase money. The moment was opportune for dealing with the question. Within one month after their acceptance of office, Lord Ashbourne, on behalf of his Government, introduced in the House of Lords his Land Purchase Bill, which has ever since been popularly known as 'Lord Ashbourne's Act.'

Possibly the best fortune which a Bill can meet with is that it should be very fully discussed ; the next best is that it should not be discussed at all. The latter was the fate of Lord Ashbourne's Bill. The discussion in both Houses was perfunctory. In neither House did the Committee stage occupy more than one sitting.

The scheme of purchase provided by the Ashbourne Bill was that the Land Commission, on the part of the State, should advance the entire purchase money of the holding, and that the tenant should repay the amount by instalments at the rate of 4 per cent. on the purchase money, which instalments would in forty-nine years extinguish the principal as well as pay the interest accruing meanwhile. This scheme had one great merit—simplicity. A tenant agreed to buy his holding for 1,000$l.$ He had not to produce any of this sum out of his own stores. It was all advanced for him, and he could see at a glance that in exchange for escaping from his rent, whatever it might be, he became liable for a definite annual sum, 40$l.$—$i.e.$ 4 per cent. on 1,000$l.$ for forty-nine years.

Compared with previous Land Purchase Acts, the Ashbourne Act was a distinct success. In two years more land was sold to tenants by one firm of solicitors alone than had been sold over all Ireland during the whole career of the Bright clauses of 1870 and the Land Act of 1881.

In no year did the advances under the Bright clauses reach 90,000$l.$, while in some years they were well below 20,000$l.$ In only one year did the advances under the Land Act of 1881 reach 100,000$l.$, while in the year immediately preceding the passing of the Ashbourne Act they had shrunk to less than 22,000$l.$ Five years' working of the Ashbourne Act showed that the advances under it had averaged over one million and a quarter sterling per annum.

By 1887 the advances made, together with those applied for, but not actually paid out, had practically exhausted the 5,000,000$l.$ voted by the Ashbourne Act, and Parliament thereupon voted another five millions sterling for land purchase in Ireland. This second sum was applied for as rapidly as the first, and before 1891 it was plain that it would again become necessary to apply to Parliament. What we needed at the time was a little more money, coupled with a little more simplification of procedure in order to avail ourselves of the money. What we got in 1891 was an offer of a large sum of money coupled with a complication of procedure which made it very difficult to avail ourselves of the money at all.

Sales at once began to languish. Instead of utilising, as under the Ashbourne Act, more than one million and a quarter sterling per annum, the Land Commission advanced under the Act of 1891 less than half a million in the same period.

The reader must take on faith the assertion that the failure of the Act of 1891 was due to the complexity of its procedure, and he will do so the more readily when he knows that his only other alternative is to wade through a disquisition on the 'Purchaser's Insurance Money,' 'County per-centage,' 'Annual value,' &c., terms which have now fortunately been relegated to the limbo of history, and the explanation of which would be to the average English reader about as interesting as a dissertation on the law of hypothec or on the incidents of multiple-poinding.

An Irish tenant invited to buy his farm by the payment of annual instalments naturally asked what those instalments would amount to. The information which he regarded as vital before committing himself to signing the agreement to purchase was just what neither the land-lord's solicitor nor his own advisers could supply him with. Under the Ashbourne Act he could see at once that if he agreed to purchase his holding for 1,000*l.* he would have to pay 40*l.* a year, neither more nor less, for forty-nine years. In a similar case, under the Act of 1891, before signing his agreement, he could learn only that for five years he would have to pay certainly not *less* than 40*l.* a year, but that possibly he might for these years have to pay substantially more. He could not be certain of his liability until he had first signed his agreement and then applied to the Land Commission. Even the decision of the Commissioner was not final, it was subject to appeal. Why the com-plications which caused the falling off in sales should have been in-troduced into the Bill, it is not now easy to say. It was currently reported at the time that they were due to the fears of some sup-porters of the Government, especially in the North of Ireland, who had succeeded in persuading themselves and others that if land purchase were allowed to go forward on the lines of Lord Ashbourne's Act there would soon be such a rush of tenants to purchase their holdings as to cause serious trouble and danger to those landlords who wished not to sell but to continue as landlords. Elaborate checks were provided to ward off the danger of this anticipated rush.

Looking back now at what had taken place under the Ashbourne Act, and at what took place under the Act of 1891, it is difficult to believe that the supposed danger had any real existence. The Ashbourne Act had worked steadily, but certainly not with excessive rapidity. A million and a quarter per annum throughout the whole of Ireland was not an alarming sum for the Land Commission to have advanced, and there was no reason to suppose that tenants who had not made a rush to buy before between 1885 and 1890 would make a dangerous rush between 1891 and 1896.

The returns of the Land Commission show that the largest amount advanced for purchase in any one year was a little over a million and a half, and that was in the year 1887. In 1888 the amount advanced was less than that in 1887, and in each of the years 1889 and 1890 it was less than the amount advanced in 1888. Therefore, the tendency apparently was not towards increased rapidity, but rather towards increased slowness.

If the complicated checks introduced by the Act of 1891 had been omitted, it is more than probable that the sales of land in Ireland would not in any year have reached the amount of 2,000,000*l.* sterling, and it will scarcely be contended that sales at this rate could cause a danger to any class in Ireland or to the Treasury.

If the solution of the Irish Land Question is to be looked for in the creation of a peasant proprietary in substantial numbers, it must be conceded that the Act of 1891, by reducing the annual output of State money from a million and a quarter to less than half a million per annum, was a serious misfortune to all persons interested in Irish land.

By Mr. Gerald Balfour's Land Act of this session an effort has been made to cause an expansion in the land market, which the Act of 1891 contracted, and the means adopted to bring about the change are simple.

The Act of 1896 enables the tenant to know what is the *maximum* instalment he must pay on his purchase money in any one year. For the first ten years after the purchase he must pay instalments at the rate of 4*l.* per cent. per annum. Of this, 2*l.* 15*s.* represents interest and 1*l.* 5*s.* represents the sinking fund. At the end of the first decade these instalments will be reduced by reason of the sinking fund having in the meantime paid off portion of the principal. During the next decade the tenant will have to pay 4 per cent. upon the amount of the principal not paid off at the end of the first decade, and, similarly, at the end of thirty years from the date of the purchase, the instalment will again be reduced owing to a further part of the principal having been meanwhile paid off by the sinking fund and its accumulations. But now a remarkable difference will be seen between the relative positions of the tenant purchaser and the Treasury under the Act of 1896, as compared with all previous Purchase Acts. Under the Bright clauses of 1870, and under the Act of 1881, the tenant repaid the purchase money by an unvarying

instalment of 5*l*. per cent. for thirty-five years.   By the Ashbourne
Act he repaid it by an unvarying instalment of 4*l*. per cent. for forty-
nine years.   By the Act of 1891 he repaid it by a varying instalment
payable during forty-nine years.   In other words, there was in all
these Acts a contract by the Treasury with the tenant purchaser that,
if he would pay certain sums, they would, out of such sums, credit
him with the reinvestment of the sinking fund at a definite rate of
interest, which rate was, I think, the same as the rate of interest
charged to the tenant.   Under the Act of 1896 there is no such
contract.   No time is mentioned for the cessation of the instalments.
The tenant is only promised that if he pays instalments of 1*l*. 5*s*.
per cent. per annum as a sinking fund, the Treasury will, at the end
of ten years, tell him at what rate they have been able to employ
the money so paid by him.   His sinking fund will of course produce
more or less according to the rate at which the money may have
been so employed.

A tenant who under the Act of 1896 pays his instalments of 4
per cent. for ten years will probably find that he has not redeemed
as much of the principal as he would have redeemed by similar payments for a similar period under any of the previous Acts, because it
is not likely that the Treasury will reinvest the tenant's money at so
high a rate of interest as 2*l*. 15*s*. per cent.

With the data before us it is impossible to forecast with accuracy
the period during which the tenant's instalments will run under this
last Act, but it seems probable that the period of repayment will be
extended from the forty-nine years to sixty-nine or seventy years.

It will be interesting to see how these changes in his liability
will affect the tenant's mind.   The fact that under no circumstances
can he be called on to pay more than 4 per cent. per annum will
undoubtedly attract him, but the indefinite extension of the period
during which instalments must be paid will have a chilling effect.
Often in arranging sales with a tenant I observed that when told he
would have to pay his instalments for forty-nine years, his answer
was, ' But where shall I be in forty-nine years ? ' but then he almost
invariably added, ' Anyway, my son may see the end of the time.'

But seventy years will probably see two generations go to their
graves.   The tenant purchasing under the Act of 1896 will regard
the purchase not as a purchase at all, but as a transaction by which
a perpetual private landlord is exchanged for a practically perpetual
State landlord.

My own impression is that for some short time to come there will
not be any great extension of purchase in Ireland.   The fifteen-year
term for which the rents were fixed under the Act of 1881 has in a
large number of instances expired or is about to expire.   Rightly or
wrongly, the tenants who got their rents fixed in the early years of
the Act's working are persuaded that they were fixed on a higher

basis than those of the tenants who went into court later on, and, therefore, it seems probable that a substantial number of the early tenants will again go into court. As soon as they have got their rents fixed, they may then devote their attention to purchasing if they can induce the landlords to sell upon what they, the tenants, regard as reasonable terms. The Irish tenant, with the training and experience which he has now had, will not rush. He will deliberately weigh the arguments *pro* and *con* before deciding whether he will try to purchase or not. On the one hand, if he continues a tenant, he knows that he can go into court to get his rent fixed at the end of each judicial term, and if the times grow worse he may count on further reductions of his already reduced rent. On the other hand, if he agrees to purchase, he secures such an immediate reduction as is represented by 4 per cent. on his purchase money compared with the rent to which he is at present liable, and at the end of ten, twenty, and thirty years respectively, he will get such further reductions as are represented by a cessation of interest on the portion of his purchase money which shall have been paid off by his sinking fund.

As he now has security of tenure, it is hard to say whether the prospect of 'outsiders' being found willing to purchase the landlord's interest in the land will appreciably increase the tenant's anxiety to buy ; but it is worthy of remark that in one instance an 'outsider' has, during the present year, purchased a very large estate in Ireland occupied by tenants, an event unheard of for several years past, and in the Landed Estates Court some few outside bidders have lately appeared. The exceptionally low rate of money, with the consequent inflation of nearly all classes of securities, has a tendency to induce capitalists to turn their attention to land as an investment even with the liability of the rents which they purchase being further reduced.

The next question to be considered is, Are the landlords likely to sell ? The low rate of money will from one point of view be a temptation to a landowner to sell, because it has driven to a very high premium the stock in which he will be paid if he does sell to his tenants. A landlord so selling is paid not in cash but in land stock, which now stands at a premium of about 10 per cent., so that if he agrees to a sale to his tenants for, say, 10,000*l.*, he will in reality receive not ten but eleven thousand pounds. On the other hand, the lowness of money has driven all good stocks so high that he may find it difficult to invest his money in any reasonably safe security without submitting to a loss of income greater than he is prepared to face. All of which would go to show that a landlord who has moderate encumbrances on his property is more likely to sell part at least of his estate than will be the landlord who is wholly unencumbered, or who is so heavily encumbered that he is living on the narrow margin between tenants' existing rents and mortgagees' existing interest. In

so far as the purchase money of the land can be utilised to pay off mortgages, it can be more advantageously employed than if the landlord
had to invest it in the purchase of stock securities at their present
price, because the rate of interest which Irish mortgages bear is comparatively high.   If the sum realised by a sale will not produce more
than will pay what is due to the encumbrancers, the impoverished landlord of course will have no inducement to sell.   But it may be that
the interests of the mortgagees might be best served by selling the
estates to the tenants, and now, even if the owner wishes to prevent
the sale, he will be powerless to do so because the Act of 1896 declares
that 'a mortgagee in possession with power of sale shall for all the
purposes of the Land Purchase Acts be deemed to be a landlord.'

This provision tends to place the landlord at the mercy of his
mortgagee, and a few years ago, if it had been passed, the landlord
would have been powerless because it was absolutely impossible to
get capitalists to take up Irish mortgages.   For the last year or two
a marked change in this branch of the money market has taken
place.   The public are again willing to lend money on Irish land.
I do not mean to say that a heavily encumbered Irish landlord could,
as in the ' good old times,' borrow on his estate more than he has
already charged it with, but he can find people willing to step into
the shoes of those in whom existing charges are vested, and in so
far he is more independent of his encumbrancers than he has been
at any time from 1880 to 1894.

Everything considered, it seems likely that there will no more be
a rush on the part of the landlords to sell than there will be on the
part of tenants to purchase, but fair steady progress may be hoped
for in the Land Purchase Department, and this progress will be
materially assisted if the Land Commission will broadly interpret
and courageously use the permission, which Mr. Gerald Balfour's
Act gives them, to 'dispense with the whole or any part of the
guarantee deposit being made or retained if they think the security
for the repayment of the advance is sufficient without it.'

The guarantee deposit was not without its advantages.   It soothed
the nervous taxpayer to know that when public money was advanced
to purchase a holding it was secured not alone by charging the holding itself, but also by impounding part of the purchase money.   But
the taxpayer is not so nervous as he was in relation to land purchase.
The published reports of the Land Commission have reassured him.
The public loss on their sales has been practically nil.   Up to the
31st of March, 1896, the Land Commission had collected in principal
and interest from tenant purchasers over two millions and a quarter
sterling.   The total arrear due on that date was 4,389*l.*, and it was
calculated that most of this would be collected within two or three
months.

In the face of such figures as these the Land Commission need them to trust to the holding alone as security for their money. The very fact that they are trusting to the holding alone will make their valuers all the more cautious when reporting on the value of the land upon which the public money is to be lent, and experience has now proved that if due caution be used in valuing the holding the purchase money will be quite secure without subjecting the landlord to the annoyance of accepting his purchase money piecemeal.

Not the least important provisions in Mr. Gerald Balfour's Act are those dealing with the Landed Estates Court. This is a peculiarly Irish institution; it has no counterpart in England or Scotland. It was established in order to bring to a rapid sale the estates of landlords, especially of encumbered landlords—incidentally it was empowered to collect the rents of the estates pending the proceedings to a sale. For years past it has almost ceased to be a Court of sale—it has become a colossal land agent. In the debate on Lord Ashbourne's Bill in 1885 it was stated that, even then, the sales on the Landed Estates Court had dropped from 1,500,000l. per annum to 150,000l. per annum. The Court is choked with estates brought in nominally in order that they might be sold, but really in order that a sale might be averted, and an official receiver permanently employed to collect the rents.

The Court is now agent over probably a twelfth of the agricultural rental of Ireland, and Parliament has decided that this state of things shall not continue. Where an estate in Court is hopelessly encumbered or is one over which a receiver has been appointed, the Judge is, by section 40, empowered to request the Land Commission to cause it to be inspected and valued; and when the Land Commission shall have complied with this request the Judge of the Landed Estates Court is directed to offer to the tenants on the estate to sell their holdings to them on such terms as may seem to him just.

Before making the offer to the tenants the Judge is directed to hear all parties interested, but he can act quite independently of their consent or refusal. Upon the working out of this section by the Land Judge and the Land Commission, more than upon any other known factor, will, in my opinion, depend for years to come the success or failure of land purchase in Ireland.

GEORGE FOTTRELL.

TURKISH MISGOVERNMENT

I

THE retirement of Lord Rosebery from the Liberal leadership relieves the Radical Opposition of its chief difficulty in regard to Eastern politics, or at least makes it possible to propose a true line of conduct to the party which shall not be met by a jingo *non possumus*. Mr. Gladstone, Sir William Harcourt, Mr. John Morley, are always open to friendly argument where this is based on a true sympathy for liberty; and it is not, perhaps, altogether vain to remind them at times of their own past lapses where a wider interpretation of their admitted principles is pleaded for. I make bold, therefore, to put my view before them of their present Armenian agitation, to point out where I think they are in error, and to suggest what seems to me a more practical plan than any they have yet suggested for gaining the end they have in view. This I take to be the speedy relief of the Armenians from their present persecution, and an early, humane, and perhaps final, settlement of the whole Eastern Question. I believe all to be within their reach; but it can only be through their initial acknowledgment of great errors in the past, and the conversion of England, through their own conversion, to as great a work of reparation in the present.

First, then, as to their past lapses. The Liberal leaders in their pronouncements are astonished and indignant at the crimes they see perpetrated at Constantinople and in Asia Minor, at the Sultan Abdul Hamid's duplicity in the matter of reforms, at his arbitrary misgovernment, and at the Armenian blood that he has shed in torrents. I think, nevertheless, that if they would examine their own consciences a little closely, they would find that the present outrageous condition of things at Constantinople is one very largely, indeed principally, of their own contriving.

To begin at the very beginning—the Cyprus Convention and the Treaty of Berlin. It is true that out of office Mr. Gladstone and his colleagues denounced these arrangements strongly, but in office afterwards they persistently upheld and made use of them, and, indeed, on some points intensified their ill consequences. The full story of the results have been so far-reaching, and are still so vitally affecting the situation, that I will make no apology for relating its chief episode here. The story, as I remember it well at the time—and it cannot in its main facts be gainsaid—is this. When the Congress met at Berlin in the early summer of 1878, one of the first of its acts was to take from each of the Ambassadors present a declaration that he came to it with clean hands—that is to say, free of all secret engagement between his Government and any other Government represented at the Congress. This declaration Lord Beaconsfield and Lord Salisbury gave with the rest. A few days after, however, the text of the Cyprus Convention was published in London by the *Globe* newspaper, which had obtained it from Mr. Marvin, a man employed as translator at the Foreign Office, and who had for money betrayed it to the press. The incident was within a little of breaking up the Congress. The French and Russian Ambassadors declared themselves outraged at the English ill-faith, and M. Waddington went so far as to order his trunks to be packed for leaving Berlin. The situation was only saved by Prince Bismarck's intervention and the great personal ascendency Lord Beaconsfield had acquired at the Congress. It was compromised on the following terms of English surrender. Lord Beaconsfield agreed with M. Waddington:

1. That France, as a set-off for Cyprus, should be allowed on the first convenient pretext and without opposition from England to occupy Tunis ;

2. That, in the appointments then making in Egypt by the Finance Commission, France should march *pari passu* with England ; and

3. That the old French claim of protecting the Latin Church in Syria should be acknowledged.

On these conditions M. Waddington was for the time detached from the Russian influence, and Lord Beaconsfield was able to return to London in triumph, having secured, according to his well-known boast, a ' Peace with Honour.' Nevertheless, the germ of the whole of our subsequent troubles in the East, including the French and Russian alliance, may be distinctly traced to the incident above related, and it is necessary to remember it now if we are to understand the full difficulty in which we are involved. Its first embarrassing result was the establishment in 1879 of the Anglo-French financial control in Egypt ; its second, the violation of the Ottoman territory in Tunis, with our connivance, in 1881 ; the third, the failure of our moral influence with Turkey and all the Powers, leaving us charged with the fate of Asia Minor, and, at the same time, impotent to control it for good. Now, of course the initial blame in this scandalous affair was not the Liberal Party's. Mr Gladstone denounced it as strongly as the rules of official etiquette, which always screen the worst Foreign Office deliquencies, would allow. But what I would beg Liberals to consider is, that neither in 1880, when Mr. Gladstone returned to office, nor at any subsequent period of Liberal ascendency, has the smallest serious attempt been made to undo or repair the wrong. Mr. Gladstone in office became undistinguishable in his treatment of the Eastern Question from Lord Beaconsfield. He neither withdrew from the responsibility in Egypt, nor refused his connivance with France when the time came for redeeming Lord Beaconsfield's bond in Tunis, nor did he abrogate the Cyprus engagement. All that he did to modify his predecessor's policy was to relax the vigilance of English supervision in Asia Minor by withdrawing the perambulating Consuls Lord Salisbury had appointed, and so to leave the Armenians and other Ottoman subjects more completely than ever at the Sultan's mercy. He retained unaltered the obligations of the Convention, while neutralising its purpose—what little there was in it—for good ; and, above all, and to the disappointment of everyone who had followed his noble declarations of disinterestedness out of office, he retained Cyprus, England's unholy 'backshish' in the affair. To the present day it is inexplicable to me how the great Liberal statesman of 1880 should thus have stultified his declarations and swerved from his principles.

A still stronger case for Liberal repentance is that of Mr. Gladstone's action two years later in Egypt, and one that more vitally affects the present unhappy situation among the Sultan's subjects. In 1881 and 1882 there was everywhere in the Ottoman Empire a strong movement in favour of reform. All the intelligence, all the education, all the humanity of the empire was on the side of a liberal interpretation of the Sheria, or Moslem law, of religious tolerance, and, above all, of constitutional government. Rightly or wrongly, all that was best in the empire had turned to this European panacea for a remedy. On the other side stood the reactionist fanaticism of the uneducated, the rabble of the towns, and this same Sultan Abdul Hamid. The moment was a critical one. The constitutional party, weakened by the issue of the Russian war, was being hard pressed by Abdul Hamid at Constantinople ; the liberal Grand Sherif of Mecca had just been assassinated and replaced by a reactionist ; the Sultan was beginning to assert his leadership of the Panislamic movement. Still the issue of the struggle was far from decided against liberty, and in Egypt, at any rate, the constitutional party were carrying all before them. They had wrung a Constitution from the Khedive, and were determined on reform. All the enlightened Moslem world, and in large measure the Christian world, too, of the Ottoman provinces were looking on, their hopes centred on the Egyptian success. It was at this critical juncture that Mr. Gladstone allowed himself to be persuaded—we all remember in what financial interests—to intervene and crush the movement. He pleaded in excuse that he was paying a debt of honour, that he was bound by international engagements and I know not what else. What he seems, however, to have forgotten, but it is very necessary Liberals should remember it, is that in order to effect his purpose he called in the aid of the very forces of inhumanity he is now denouncing, with an effect altogether disastrous to Eastern liberty. It is on historical record that in the month of June 1882, after threatening the Egyptian nationalists in vain, Her Majesty's Government appealed to this very Sultan, Abdul Hamid, for help to crush their movement and dispose of their leader, *by Oriental methods.* The English Liberal press of the day even went so far as to explain that Dervish Pasha, the Sultan's right-hand man, borrowed for the occasion, was specially fitted for his work, inasmuch as he was 'notoriously unscrupulous.' It is also historical that within a few days only of Dervish's arrival in Egypt the Alexandrian riots and massacres occurred. Our ships then bombarded Alexandria; but meeting still with a national resistance, we obtained from Abdul Hamid a decree of rebellion against Arabi, armed with which our English army finally occupied Cairo. It is not too much to say that the overthrow of the Egyptian nationalists at Tel-el-Kebir, *under warrant of the Sultan,* and the non-fulfilment of Mr. Gladstone's promise, made through Lord Dufferin, of restoring some kind of constitutional government at Cairo, sealed the fate of liberty throughout the Ottoman Empire, and with it of all chance of internal reform.

Nor is this quite all. Abdul Hamid, supreme now over the constitutional party in Turkey, was resolved to take vengeance on the defeated Liberal leaders. In 1883, encouraged by the complicity of the Powers, including England, he had Midhat, the constitutional ex-Prime Minister, arrested and tried on a false charge of murder, brought before a packed tribunal at Constantinople, condemned, and sentenced to death. It is within my personal knowledge that English evidence of the highest official kind could have been adduced at the trial, clearing Midhat of the charge. Yet, for reasons of English state, that evidence was withheld. Midhat's sentence, momentarily commuted to perpetual imprisonment, was carried out as soon as the public had ceased to busy itself about him. By the Sultan's order he was beheaded privately in prison at Taïf, in Arabia, and his head was forwarded to Constantinople.

Things having been so in the past, however completely now forgotten (to me they are poignant and ever-living memories), I confess to a little scepticism as to the fundamental right of the Liberal leaders of the present agitation to act as justiciaries on Abdul Hamid, or to 'wield the sword of the Almighty' in a new crusade. I will, however, assume that in their inner consciences they acknowledge they were wrong, and are anxious seriously now to repair the ruin of the Eastern world. It is terribly late to begin. They are no longer in office. Their full opportunity is past. They are discredited in

Europe, doubly discredited in the Turkish Empire. But still they can do something, if only they have the courage to come forward and say fairly to their followers : ' We have misled you all these sixteen years. We have been blind, leaders of the blind. Our eyes are now open ; we will all go back to our principles of 1880.'

Assuming this, let us see how the Armenian question really stands. Down to the year 1893 our responsibility for reforms in Asia Minor was studiously forgotten and left alone by our diplomacy. The Armenian question was considered impossible of solution at the Foreign Office, and all that was done with it was from time to time to trot it out as a possible counter-question to the troublesome one of Egypt. It was a common saying with our diplomatists that there were two ' clichés,' or stock answers, with which Abdul Hamid could always be met and frightened if he showed any inclination to join France on the Egyptian question. The Arabian Caliphate was one of them ; Armenia was the other. It was in this spirit, and no other, that Lord Rosebery, who held a brief for the occupation of Egypt, approached the question in 1893. I was at Constantinople in that year, and I know well that there was nothing more serious in his earlier moves than this : a special inquiry had just been made, in conjunction with the American Embassy, into the condition of affairs in Armenia, but its result had been to show that there was no sufficient element there of resident Armenian population to justify an attempt at encouraging the creation of an autonomous State. The whole Christian population of the provinces was less than one in five compared with the Mohammedan, and in only one small villayet did it stand in a majority. It was therefore admitted by both Embassies that the autonomous movement could not be supported with any chance of success. The Armenians were suffering great oppression, morally justifying them in their resort to a trial of strength with their master ; but it was without chance of success, nor had it become as yet even a ' desperate necessity,' caused by any fixed purpose of their destruction. The Armenian movement was already a political one, having its base in England, and it enjoyed the sympathy and assistance of the Armenians in Russia. Such was the report of 1893, which has not, I think, been published. Nevertheless, Lord Rosebery, little in earnest except diplomatically, encouraged the movement from time to time, toying with it for the sake of Egypt, and to please Armenian sympathisers in the Liberal camp at home. Later, it is quite certain that the stronger action taken by our Embassy at Constantinople was due to his direct orders. The misfortune of the affair is this—that the encouragement of England, official and unofficial, is beyond all doubt the cause of the present Armenian disasters. These poor people, not understanding the needs of our diplomacy, and believing that their hour of political deliverance, under England's protection, was at hand, resolved in 1895 upon a great venture, and organised their movement on the active revolutionary lines which in other countries have proved successful. This hardened the Sultan's heart, and it is clear that he then resolved on their destruction. I was again at Constantinople in September and October 1895, when the first riots there occurred, and I was never in the smallest doubt of the Sultan's personal responsibility. Abdul Hamid is far too powerful a despot for a single blow to have been struck against a single Armenian in his capital without his orders. His motive, however, must not be mistaken. Abdul Hamid, though the head of the reactionary party, is not himself a fanatic. His action has been dictated solely in the interest of a political or, perhaps, to speak more accurately still, a dynastic and personal end. He stood, indeed, according to the phrase, between the devil and the deep sea; and he knew that he must crush the Armenians or himself be crushed. This is his one excuse. I do not give it as a sufficient one, but still as a fact to be noted. His mode of repression is only the old-fashioned Turkish one of massacre, which we ourselves made it possible for him to use in this year of grace, 1896, when we helped him, fourteen years ago, to put down the constitutional party and become the absolute lord he is.

Another matter which it much behoves our Liberal leaders to consider, and which they do not seem as yet to realise, is that in Abdul Hamid's terrible work of repression he has throughout had the countenance and approval of Russia. Of this my visit to Constantinople last year gave me a complete assurance; and its reason is not difficult to seize. Half the Armenian provinces have for the last twenty years been incorporated in the Russian Empire, and from the moment the Armenian movement became one for autonomy it was doomed in Russian opinion. The Russians have a jingoism of their own, which tolerates no other national sentiment within the empire but the Russian; and the Armenians, with their undying tradition of an independent kingdom, one of the most ancient in the world, are, in their eyes, an obstacle and a rock of offence to be removed. As Christians even they do not command full sympathy in Russia, for they belong to a branch of the Orthodox Church which is out of communion with the Russian, and which especially repudiates the religious headship of the Czar. Lastly, their alliance with Russian Nihilists, and their Anarchist methods, have closed the door against official sympathy. As long as M. de Giers was alive something of the old tradition of Russian policy, which championed the Christians in Turkey, survived; but with the advent of Prince Lobanof this finally disappeared, and has given place to a new policy of alliance with the Sultan, as representative there of order. English sympathy has only made matters worse for the Armenians in Russian eyes, and the Russian attitude towards them now is: 'We leave you to England to help you if she can.' Even in the matter of the Sultan's methods I

could not help being reminded at Constantinople of their close similarity to those used by Russia towards the Ruthenian Poles.   These
have been ground under the harrow of the Czar's penal laws, and occasionally of popular violences, now systematically for thirty years, man,
woman, and child, till they have abandoned their Catholic faith and
are to-day fanatic members of the Russian orthodoxy.   The Polish
question has thereby been solved for ever ; and, coming as I did from
Russian Poland, I seemed to see in the forced conversion of the
Armenians of Asia Minor only a page of violence a little overdone,
but taken from the Russian book.   It is the extreme, therefore, of
rashness on the part of the Liberal leaders of the present agitation
to rest their hopes of dethroning Abdul Hamid on Russian intervention.   Abdul Hamid has, I fear, too faithfully been doing Russian
work to be seriously dealt with by Russia as a criminal.

What, then, is it possible for England to do ?   There are here, as
usual, the traditional three courses.   The first is to go blindly into a
war with the Sultan.   With regard to this I am bound to say that
every law of honour—unless, as Mr. Gladstone puts it, the word
'honour' is to be expunged from our dictionaries—prescribes and
necessitates such a war.   We have taken the Armenians solemnly by
treaty under our protection, receiving substantial payment from their
master, for the protective right, in the island of Cyprus.   We have
encouraged them for our own purposes to organise themselves and
rebel, and the Sultan has now got them by the throat, and, backed
by Europe, is defying us to come on and deliver them.   If we do
not go to war we shall be sitting down under the greatest affront we
ever suffered as a nation.   We bombarded Alexandria because a
couple of hundred of the Alexandrian rabble, with Sir Beauchamp
Seymour's valet, had lost their lives.   Here some scores of thousands
of peaceful citizens have perished through our fault, and we have
done nothing but talk.   Nevertheless, I do not suppose we shall fight.
We never do except against a half-armed foe ; and here we should
find all Europe fully armed at the Sultan's back.   The second course,
therefore—to do nothing—will be open to us, and I am inclined to
think we shall choose it.   Lord Rosebery recommends it, and Lord
Rosebery represents trade and finance, our great English gods.   A
third course, however, I will recommend to the consideration of
Liberal England, which I believe to be perfectly sound and feasible,
and, if we have the moral courage to confess our wrong, perfectly
within our reach.   This is to advocate and insist on our Government
arranging without delay with the Powers most interested for a new
European Congress.   I do not see anywhere that this has been suggested in England, yet it is the only true and worthy solution of
the problem for us, the only practical escape we have from our
dishonour.

The conditions on which Lord Salisbury could, if he would, move the great European Powers to meet in a new Congress on the Eastern question are these. First, England must go into the matter absolutely clean handed; not as at Berlin, but with a firm and avowed determination to take nothing whatever of advantage for herself in the arrangements to be made. The clearing of her own honour, now dragged vilely in the mire, must be her sole and all-sufficient reward. Secondly, she must come as a suppliant for her Armenian *protégés*, not as one with rights, for she is not ready to fight for them. Thirdly, she must not expect the question of the Armenians to be settled alone. Europe would not fash herself only for these. England must be ready to see the whole Ottoman case treated without any reserve whatever, her one condition being the rescue of her Christian friends. Fourthly, it follows from this that the Egyptian question must be discussed with the rest of the Ottoman questions. It is mere folly to imagine that France and Russia, having got complete control of the Armenian case, will solve it to our liking, except as part and parcel of a general bargain. It is equally folly to suppose that they would be content with Cyprus. Neither Power cares a straw for Cyprus, nor, I imagine, would take it at a gift. The only proof we can show of our disinterested zeal for the Armenians is to put Egypt with them on the table of the Congress. Fifthly, there must be no subterfuge or mental reservation about the Soudan. I hear people talk about ending the occupation of Egypt some day by an annexation of the Upper Nile. But such talk is useless now. The Powers would not consent to it in any arrangements made, short, perhaps, of a final partition of the Ottoman Empire. Sixthly, we must not expect such a partition to be agreed to. None of the Powers are quite ready for it. It would be too dangerous a scramble. All that could this and next year be reasonably expected would be an intervention at Constantinople to re-establish the authority of the Porte as opposed to the Palace, to disband the Sultan's guard, and to establish some sort of financial control on the Bosphorus, with a throwing open of the Dardanelles. In the Armenian provinces, Russia might at the same time consent to give protection to the Christians, and secure them from further massacre. I believe this to be the extreme outside of what it would be reasonable to expect. But we should have gained our object—the highest one of all. Our honour would have been saved, and we should have regained the right to speak with authority as an honest Government in regard to the final settlement.

Let those, therefore, who really care about honour and duty and humanity, not for the sake of self-laudation on platforms, or for the amusement of denouncing the sins of others, but because they are sincerely ashamed of England's shame, rally to this idea. It is a far more practical one than any of the little half-measures as yet propounded, and, as I have said before, is one easily within our reach.

All we have to do is to persuade our fellow-countrymen to keep their promises about Egypt, and face the truth that we cannot remain there for ever, and arrange the terms of our going. The rest will come easily and pleasantly. Lord Rosebery, with his brief for the occupation, is fortunately gone from the supreme Liberal councils. Let the Liberal Party rise to the full height of the occasion, and it will convert England again, as it did in 1880; while if, on the contrary, we harden our hearts in the face of a pretty well united world, which laughs angrily at our fine moral talk, and points contemptuously at Cyprus and Egypt hanging out of our coat-tail pockets, it may well happen that we shall lose not only these and our honour before many years are out, but the whole of our overgrown Empire besides— God forbid that I should be justified in adding our national independence at home as well as Empire.

WILFRID SCAWEN BLUNT.

II

THE time seems to have come when discussion of the measures that should be taken to settle the Turkish question should be carried beyond the limit to which it has hitherto been confined.

Various proposals have been made, some very drastic. We have been invited to force the Dardanelles—to depose the Sultan—to write a joint Note demanding reforms—to give Russia a free hand—to adopt certain unrevealed, indirect methods of exciting pressure, and so on ; but these are only the first steps, and give no clue to what the succeeding steps should be, still less to the ultimate aim which should be kept in view in order to permanently dispose of this dangerous question.

The accompanying letter, which was written by General Charles Gordon in 1881, is remarkably *à propos* to the present situation. This keen observer and experienced administrator rejects at once two methods which may be suggested, either that the country should be governed and administered by a foreign power, or that the existing government ('The Pachas') should be trusted to reform the administration under foreign pressure. He falls back on the idea that the Turkish peoples themselves should be given the power to control and check those whose misgovernment has turned countries once rich and flourishing into poor and depopulated deserts whose only idea of administration is by robbery, and whose only method of preserving order is by terror and massacre.

This object he would effect, broadly speaking, by extending to the provinces which are still under the Turkish Government constitutions such as have been adopted in those which have been taken away from it, viz. Roumania, Bulgaria, Eastern Roumelia, &c., countries which apparently only require to be let alone in order that they may develop their strength and regain their prosperity.

Difficulties in carrying out this proposal may no doubt be suggested, but it may be that still greater difficulties would attend any other solution of the question ; and it has at least the merit that it evades many of the thorny obstacles which arise from the mutual jealousy of the Powers.

E. F. Du Cane.

8 Victoria Grove, Gloucester Road, Kensington :
January 16, 1881.

My dear Du Cane,

I send you the Blue Book, Condition of Asia Minor &c , but I think you will, on looking over it, see that it merely contains for the most part a description of the deplorable state of the Turkish provinces, and does not in any way— or at any rate only indirectly—show how the misgovernment is to be remedied.

In fact the perusal is wearisome, as there is no decided remedy proposed, though amelioration is suggested by insisting on this and that being forced on the Porte.

I consider that any promise or statement of the Turkish Pachas to improve or remedy any evil are to be deemed utterly insincere, will be carried out with a pure intuition to evade the spirit, and only to comply with the letter while under pressure.

I consider that enforced reform can be only exotic and ephemeral, that it will fall to the ground when it is no longer enforced.

I consider it is quite hopeless for foreigners to attempt to dictate how the administration, collection of taxes, &c. (of which this Blue Book is full) are to be performed.

I consider that unless the people of Turkey will not take up the remedy of the abuses of their government, it is hopeless thinking of any progress being made against the Turkish Pachas by foreigners which will be permanent.

I therefore say that the unique way to deal with misgovernment in Turkey is to call on the Turkish peoples to execute them.

1. The Turkish peoples know exactly the full extent of the corruption and rottenness of their government ; they know how and in what way any remedy they may enact will act on the country. They are in every way interested, for themselves and their children, in obtaining a good government ; whereas to the Turkish Pachas, so long as they can fill their purses it is all they care.

2. To put the power in the hands of the Turkish peoples is a fair, perfectly just effort on the part of foreign governments ; it is merely the supporting of the Sultan's own design when he gave his constitution. Foreign governments who support this liberation of the Turkish people cannot be accused of intrigue or selfishness ; they will gain the sympathy of the peoples, whereas now what have they got ? Have they the sympathy of either the Sultan or Pachas or peoples ? and, judging from the Blue Book, they, or at least our government, are overloading their heads with details of administration, when the whole foundation on which the success of these details rests is thoroughly rotten.

A foreign government is no match for the Sultan and the Pachas : it has not the knowledge necessary to cope with them : it is the Turkish peoples who alone have the power to hold their own, besides which no foreign government has any right to interfere. It may be said that the foreign government interferes in virtue of promises, but these promises were <i>extorted</i> and are not valid.

By the way foreign governments are now working they are inevitably drifting, day by day, into still increasing interference with the internal affairs of Turkey, and are helping to band Sultan, Pachas, and peoples against any improvement. Such interference must end in serious complications, and can in no way further the professed object—improved government.

No individual Pacha, let him be one of the exceptions to the usual rule, can now stand against the influences of the Sultan and the parasite Pachas; the fact of his being backed by this or that foreign government will be (whenever the time comes when that foreign government'becomes urgent in its demands for reform) the cause of his downfall, and will be explained at large that he is dismissed because he is a tool of this or that government; but if this *rara avis*, an upright Pacha, was found, and if he was backed by the peoples of Turkey, it would go hard with the Sultan and his ring ere they flew in the face of their peoples in dismissing him.

It is urged that the Turkish peoples are not fit for representative government. Well, look at Roumania and Bulgaria, and, in some degree, to Roumelia; they succeed very fairly. If the peoples never have a chance, they will never be able to show what they can do. Had we waited till our monarchs or our lords had given us representative assemblies, we would be without them to this day.

What I maintain, therefore, is that our government should unceasingly try, with other governments, *to get the Midhat constitution reconstituted*; that they should leave that very dubiously just (in fact it may be called iniquitous) policy of forcing unwilling peoples under the yoke of other peoples, which is not only unfair to the coerced and ceded peoples, but is a grave mistake, for by it are laid the seeds of future troubles.

To collect all these reports may be useful enough for those who have the time and patience to read them, but what do all these reports tend to elucidate? Simply that the government of Turkey is utterly rotten, that the peoples are miserable and discontented, that the sole object of the Sultan and his Pachas is to drag the entrails of the provinces into their palaces at Constantinople. There may be petty schemes here and there for improvements, but it is like painting up the bulwarks of a vessel which is rotten at the bottom.

I say, too, that at any moment, in the event of the death of the Sultan, most serious events may take place: who is to take his place? who is to nominate his successor? The reconstituted chamber of the Midhat Constitution would at any rate prevent any great catastrophe, and I have no doubt would so coerce the new Sultan as to obtain full promise to benefit the country.

Believe me, my dear Du Cane,

Yours sincerely,

C. E. GORDON.

The Editor of THE NINETEENTH CENTURY *cannot undertake
to return unaccepted MSS.*

THE

NINETEENTH

CENTURY

No. CCXXXVIII—December 1896

THE OLNEY DOCTRINE
AND AMERICA'S NEW FOREIGN POLICY

That the settlement of the Venezuela question, so far as it is in the
power of Great Britain and the United States to settle it, should
be received with general satisfaction in this country, is extremely
natural; that it should be treated as a matter scarcely important
enough to rouse interest, or require other than hasty and perfunctory
comment, is rather curious. Not ten months ago it was viewed with
passionate emotion on one side of the Atlantic, with perturbed and
painful anxiety on the other; now it drifts quietly away in a mist
of half-understood detail, and we scarcely turn our heads to look at
it as it disappears below the political horizon. The experts will
have a good deal to do with it before it is quite disposed of; but
it may now reasonably be hoped that it will be left in the condition in which it will concern the diplomatists and the lawyers
alone, and will not again run any risk of interesting the general
public.

The precise effect and meaning of the settlement not very many
Englishmen have been at the pains to ascertain, nor are they likely
to do so. The common sentiment echoes the prudent and well-
calculated levity with which Lord Salisbury treated the subject in his
Guildhall speech. Most of us are much inclined to agree with the
Prime Minister that after all the whole affair was one of no great
moment to the people of this country. A trumpery dispute, about
some leagues of swamp and forest, with a fifth-rate Republic, on one

of the odd corners of the Empire! Surely the wearied Titan has
other things to think about. Even if there is 'auriferous territory'
involved, there are plenty of gold mines elsewhere.

With all the careful 'coaching' he got from laborious journalists
who had worked up the maps and the blue-books, it is probable that
the man in the street and the man in the club, on either side of the
Atlantic, never quite made out where the Cuyuni River ran or what
the Schomburgk line was. He became excited over the question
when he heard, if he was an American, that the Britisher was trying
to violate the sacred Doctrine of Monroe; if an Englishman, when
he was told that the United States was attempting to bully us out of
something which a British colony 'might justly claim as its own.
Now that his political guides and leaders have informed him that a
compromise has been arranged which is satisfactory to the honour of
both parties, he is quite content to forget the whole affair. In this
country there is assuredly no disposition to look narrowly at the terms
of settlement, or weigh too strictly the gains and losses in the diplomatic bargain. It is assumed—for the exact details are not yet
known, and when they are known they probably will not be generally
understood—that while we have given way to the United States, by
admitting its right to intervene in the dispute, we have secured the
substantial securities for which, as the guardians of British Guiana,
we were mainly contending. An equitable arrangement has been
made by which the long-established prescriptive occupation of the
inhabitants of the older colonial territories is recognised; subject to
this we are to arbitrate on the whole debatable district, as the United
States Government has all along demanded. If there are some who
feel that, supposing this arrangement to be prudent and just, it might
have been most suitably made *before* instead of *after* Mr. Cleveland's
Message: if they find a certain humiliation in the fact that this
solution, so long refused to diplomatic pressure, has been somewhat
precipitately granted when diplomacy was backed by a threat of war,
they are in the minority. There is no denying the fact that in concluding the Arbitration Treaty, Lord Salisbury has satisfied the great body
of his countrymen. The prevalent sentiment is one of impatient relief.
We are glad to be done with a vexatious business; we are only somewhat annoyed to think that, trivial as we are now led to believe it
really was, it should have given us some months of occasional anxiety
and some moments of genuine alarm.

But though the boundary question is in itself of no very great
importance, the same cannot be said of the episode of American intervention, or of the process by which it has been terminated. On the
contrary. It would not be surprising if the future historian of the
nineteenth and twentieth centuries should come to consider this series
of occurrences as the beginning of a new epoch in international relations; and he even may see cause to regard it as the most significant

ahd pregnant event of all this *annus mirabilis* 1896. It is true its'
importance and interest are much more for the people of the United'
States than for Englishmen, though the latter too .are very closely
concerned in it.   For Americans the assertion, and the partial recognition, of the new version of the Monroe Doctrine, laid down by Mr.
Olney last summer, may have consequences that will be felt for generations.   It is strange that this aspect of the matter has received
very little attention in America and next to none in this country.
Both nations are content to welcome the fact—which indeed is gratifying enough in itself—that their rulers, after getting to high words,
and after hesitating as it seemed on the very brink of a serious
quarrel, have contrived to adjust all differences by an arbitration
arrangement, and have even made the incident the occasion of settling
the draft of a General Treaty of Arbitration.   In the exultation or
the relief with which this comfortable escape from a most awkward
embarrassment is hailed, it is forgotten that, before the solution had
been reached, principles had been asserted, and precedents laid down,
which must become part, if not of International Law, at any rate of
public policy.   A novel attempt has been made to define the attitude
of the United States towards the other Governments of the two
Americas.   A fresh article has been added to the code which regu-
lates the relations of the civilised Powers to one another.   How far
the new system extends, and what its precise meaning and validity
may be, are questions which the recent transactions have left in much
uncertainty.   They are at least worth some consideration.

There are, I know, observers who deny that any such striking
results as those suggested have been developed in the course of the
Anglo-American negotiations.   Nothing, they would say, is changed ;
there is only a treaty the more.   There is a tendency among some
American journalists, who have specially supported the action of Mr.
Cleveland and Mr. Olney, to minimise the importance of the State
Secretary's famous Despatch.   They refuse to admit that there has
been any change in the policy of the United States, or that anything
said or done in connection with the Venezuela frontier dispute has
seriously modified international relations.   The *Times* correspondent
at Washington has asserted this opinion with a good deal of emphasis ;
and it seems to have been adopted, after some hesitation, by his
employers in London.   We have been told that the new Monroe
Doctrine does not seem very materially to differ from the old one.[1]
These, however, are the second thoughts of the *Times*.   A day or two
previously that journal had committed itself to a much more serious
and more logical opinion on the meaning of the Washington compact :

From the point of view of the United States the arrangement is a concession
by Great Britain of the most far-reaching kind. It admits a principle that in
respect of South American Republics the United States may not only intervene in

[1] See the *Times*, November 16, 1896.

disputes, but may entirely supersede the original disputant and assume exclusive control of the negotiations. Great Britain cannot, of course, bind any other nation by her action in this matter, but she has set up a precedent which may in future be quoted with 'great effect against herself, and she has greatly strengthened the hands of the United States Government in any dispute that may arise in the future between a South American Republic and a European Power in which the United States may desire to intervene.

If we choose to turn back to a time before this 'far-reaching' concession had been made, and when it was believed that it would not be made, we shall find the same conviction asserted in still more emphatic language. ' It must be observed that the Monroe Doctrine on which Mr. Olney relies has received an entirely new development in his Despatch and in Mr. Cleveland's Message. . . . Lord Salisbury expresses his full concurrence in the view "that any disturbance of the existing territorial distribution in the Western Hemisphere by any fresh acquisition on the part of any European State would be a highly inexpedient change." But the recognition of this expediency does not cover the deductions from the Monroe Doctrine which Mr. Olney's Despatch puts forward, and which President Cleveland makes the basis of the most astounding proposal, perhaps, that has ever been advanced by any Government, in time of peace, since the days of Napoleon. . . . It is impossible to admit that the interests of the United States are affected by every frontier dispute between our colonies and their neighbours, and that therefore the right of imposing arbitration in every case of the kind must be conceded.' I quote from the *Times* of the 18th of December, the day after the publication of President Cleveland's Message ; I might quote from almost any other English newspaper of that date. The universal opinion in this country at the time was that the claims advanced by Mr. Olney were a great innovation. And what Lord Salisbury said last autumn, what nine out of ten intelligent Englishmen said last winter, what a number of the most learned and authoritative of American jurists urged as soon as they were made acquainted with the text of the Secretary of State's Note, competent foreign observers continue to maintain still. The best informed French and German journalists—seldom inclined to view the aspirations and pretensions of Great Britain with indulgence—declared that Lord Salisbury had the better of the argumentative duel ; and, though they acknowledge the equity and prudence of the compromise which has been reached, they think it necessary to point out that it involves possibilities of considerable gravity, not merely to England and the United States, but also to the civilised world in general. The *Cologne Gazette*—echoing what is said to be the view of the German Foreign Office—insists that a precedent has been established by the joint action of the two Anglo-Saxon Powers, the effects of which are likely to be felt long after the British Guiana boundary question has been forgotten. ' We wish to take the first opportunity of declaring,' said the Rhenish newspaper, in an article which was reproduced with approval by the semi-official *Norddeutsche Zeitung*, 'that the precedent in question is at most an English, and in no way a European, precedent.' Nevertheless the German writer admits that the United States has entered upon a line of policy from which it cannot easily withdraw, and that in the future, and in the light of this Venezuela transaction, American public opinion will unhesitatingly demand the intervention of the Federal Government in any dispute between an American State and a European Power, whether territorial questions be involved or not. The *Temps*, which is the best instructed of French newspapers where foreign affairs are involved, writes in a similar strain. What specially concerns Frenchmen, it argues, is the countenance Great Britain has given to a novel and extreme deduction from the Monroe Doctrine :

Ainsi, du consentement exprès du Royaume-Uni, le gouvernement de Washington se verra investi du droit de s'immiscer dans toute querelle territoriale entre une puissance européenne et un Etat du nouveau monde. Il obtiendra le droit de se porter fort, même sans mandat exprès, pour l'un de ses clients. Il pourra, d'accord avec la puissance européenne engagée dans le litige, mais sans l'intervention de l'Etat américain que représente l'autre partie, régler souverainement le mode, les conditions, la forme et le fonds de la solution destinée à mettre fin au conflit.

Ce sont là de bien grosses innovations en matière de droit international. Elles consacrent la suprématie absolue des Etats-Unis dans leur hémisphère.

There can be no doubt that these French and German publicists are right. Great changes in the relations of the European Powers towards the States of the American continent, and in the relations of those States to one another, have been produced by the assertion on one side, and the admission, at least in part, on the other, of that new and enlarged version of the Monroe principle, which may be conveniently known as the Olney Doctrine.

This Doctrine is embodied in the Despatch, so often referred to, of the 20th of July, 1895, emphasised and clinched in Mr. Cleveland's famous Message to Congress. The Despatch is a very verbose, voluminous, and elaborate document, couched in a rhetorical style such as is not commonly employed in formal State Papers. But though its argument is loose and its phraseology singularly wanting in scientific precision, its general meaning is clear enough. To put it briefly Mr. Olney's main propositions are that 'American questions are for American decision;' that no European Power has the right to intervene forcibly in the affairs of the continent, or to seek territorial extension at the expense of any existing American State; that the United States, owing to its superior size and power, is the protector and champion of all other American nations; and that it has the right and duty to intervene in all territorial disputes in the Western Hemisphere, whether such disputes directly affect its interests or not These propositions are deduced from a variety of general statements

of principle, some of which are of a very remarkable and original
character, such for instance as the axiom that ' permanent political
union between a European and an American State is unnatural and
inexpedient.' Lord Salisbury, as the representative of an empire
which includes Canada, thought it necessary to place on record his
' emphatic denial' of this extraordinary proposition, and of many
other statements of fact and theories of politics which Mr. Olney's
Despatch contained; nor did he assent to the State Secretary's view
that ' American questions are for American decision,' or concede that
general right of intervention in the affairs of the continent which the
United States Government claimed. But in that strangely confused
and indefinite system which is called International Law, acts go for
more than words. If the jurist will be able to turn to the cogent
piece of argument in which Lord Salisbury dismissed the new interpretation of the Monroe Doctrine, the statesman will point to the fact
that the Government over which Lord Salisbury presided did eventually comply with the cardinal demand this new interpretation embodied. Whatever we may think of Mr. Olney's historical and juris-
tical generalisations, we cannot deny that Her Majesty's Government
has admitted his two main assertions of practical policy. His long
Despatch ' boils down' to this : the general right of the United States
to intervene in American disputes in order to secure that they shall
be solved by methods which the Government of the Union considers
just and equitable. When the two Secretaries of State come to close
quarters in their Despatches, the argument really turns on this point.
You have only the right to intervene on *any question* which affects
your interests, said Lord Salisbury, whether the question be in
America or elsewhere. You may interfere between Venezuela and
British Guiana it is true, but merely on the same grounds as you
might have interfered, if you had thought proper, between China and
Japan. Not at all, said Mr. Olney; we are not bound to consider
whether we have special interests in the matter. The United States
may intervene because it *is* the United States—' not simply by reason
of its high character as a civilised State, nor because wisdom and
justice and equity are the invariable characteristics of the dealings
of the United States ; ' but also because, 'in addition to all other
grounds, its infinite resources, combined with its isolated position,
render it master of the situation.' In other words, the United States,
being by far the largest and the strongest of American Powers, definitely asserts its right to a paramount control of the States-system of
the continent. And this claim, it must be repeated, Lord Salisbury
has conceded. No one has been able to show that any special interests of the United States have been involved, or that the Republic
is more directly affected by the Guiana boundary question than
Mexico or Peru, or any other American State. If we have recognised
the American claim to determine this dispute, without the invitation

of one disputant, and over the head of the other, it is an admission of
the political hegemony of the United States in the two Americas.
The precedent has been established which it is the chief object of the
Olney Doctrine to set up.

It may be said that this precedent is not binding in the tribunal
of diplomacy. As I have just shown French and German protests
have already been issued, and it will be open to any foreign Governments, if the occasion should arise, to declare that the general system
of International Law cannot be modified by a private arrangement
between two Powers. But if the civilised world is not committed to
the fundamental article of the new Doctrine, the United States is;
and that is the true importance of the matter. We have seen how
President Monroe's Message—which was in fact a purely academic
commentary on events, not followed, or intended to be followed, by
definite action—has become an inseparable part of the public policy
of the United States, and has assumed in the eyes of American
citizens a sanctity almost equal to that of the Constitution itself.
Probably the same weight of authority will not attach to the policy
laid down by President Cleveland and Mr. Olney. But authority
it will have: the authority of an accomplished fact, and the
authority of a successful vindication of a principle which could
not be subsequently abandoned without some appearance of humiliation. America is a democratic country, in which the sovereign is
an electorate keenly alive to the national dignity and impulsively
quick to resent any sacrifice of the national honour. Nothing helps
a party in difficulties more than a show of spirit in foreign affairs, nor
injures it worse than any suspicion of weakness or pusillanimity.
What has been gained by the assertion of the Olney Doctrine cannot
be lost. Successive Secretaries and Presidents must take care that
this high-water mark is not obliterated, if indeed it is not pushed
further outwards. One would not give much for the political fortunes
of an American statesman, who let it be known that he thought the
precedent of 1896 was a mistake, and that he saw no reason why
American questions should be reserved for American decision, or why
a dispute between two Powers, neither of which approached to within
many hundreds of miles of the United States, could not be left to
settle itself without calling for the intervention of Washington. No
politician could now say that; no party could afford to support him
if he did. The United States is practically bound to intervene as
protector, champion, and judge in equity whenever territorial changes
on the American continent are contemplated, or the rights of an
American State are menaced; to intervene by diplomacy if that will
suffice, by fleets and armies if it will not.

It is not the object of these few pages to discuss the wisdom or
justice of this new policy, but merely to point out that new it is and
that it must carry with it new, and weighty, consequences. Many

Englishmen will feel a good deal of sympathy with the spirit that animates it. The violent language of Mr. Olney's Note, its fulsome and excessive laudation of the United States, its contemptuous disregard of the susceptibilities of other great nations, and its glaring misrepresentations of fact and history, caused natural offence in this country. Behind, however, its extravagances and perversities there lies a sentiment for which, even in its audacity, Englishmen must feel a certain respect. 'We are the " biggest " and also the best Power in America, and we mean not merely to " boss the show," but to see that the show is run upon the lines we approve. We are Republicans, and we think everybody else ought to be Republicans, because that is the best form of government, and makes people more virtuous than any other.[2] We don't want European influence or European political methods here. We intend to keep America for the Americans, and make all the peoples of the continent work up to the standard set by ourselves. Therefore no fresh European Powers are to get a hand in, and those that are in already are to be cleared out as soon as convenient.' Mr. Olney does not quite say this, but it is what his arguments really mean. And if the end could be attained, if it were possible to keep the New World free from the strife, the ambitions, the wearing intrigues, the jealous rivalries, the burden of armaments, the constant dread, and sometimes the awful reality, of war, which have saddened the Old—what Englishman would seek to put obstacles in the way of realising the comfortable dream? By all means, he would say, let the Americans try the experiment. Only, from the depth of an Old-World experience that ranges over two thousand years of fierce conflict among the nations, he may be permitted to remind Americans that the experiment is no cheap and easy one. It will need something more than large words and elevated sentiments to carry it to a successful conclusion.

Even in embarking upon the modified form of this enterprise which I take to be implied in the Olney Doctrine, the United States has saddled itself with a vast addition to its burdens and its duties. It has asserted—successfully asserted—for itself a claim to be the general protector and arbiter of the American continent. The responsibility thus assumed is a heavy one. Nothing like it has existed in the world since the downfall of the Roman Empire. Many powerful modern States have exercised a hegemony, or supremacy, over independent, civilised neighbours ; but no other has yet attempted to regulate the affairs of a whole quarter of the habitable globe, or to make itself answerable for a large number of separate States, many of them of enormous extent, and some of them hundreds or even

---

[2] 'The people of the United States have a vital interest in the cause of popular self-government. . . . They believe it to be for the healing of all nations, and that civilisation must either advance or retrograde accordingly as its supremacy is extended or curtailed.'—*Mr. Olney's Despatch.*

thousands of miles distant from its own frontiers. The continent of America is not like Africa. It is not a no-man's land, inhabited by masterless savages. Except the white desolate wastes of the far North, where the continent breaks up among the Polar seas, and a comparatively insignificant tract in the extreme South, all America —North, Central, and South—is, nominally at least, subject to the rule of some organised Government recognised by the family of nations, and administered by men of European blood, professing the Christian religion. Whatever may be the actual facts, in theory, and in the view of International Law, the other Governments of the Americas have as much right to call themselves civilised, and to claim all the immunities and prerogatives of civilisation, as that of Washington itself; and some at least of their States have existed, under settled rule, as dependencies of European Powers, as long as the United States or longer. Nor are these groups of countries, which are henceforth to consider themselves under the tutelage of the Republic, insignificant in resources, or in the possibilities of future wealth and greatness. The Union, it is true, is a mighty Realm, with its seventy millions of people, its vast area of fertile and temperate land, its abounding prosperity, and its magnificent industrial development. Few Englishmen would be inclined to underrate the power and the splendour of the noblest of the daughter States which have sprung from the womb of the Mother of Nations. But the tall shadow of the Republic has perhaps unduly dwarfed the proportions of others who share with it the heritage of the Western world. We need not forget that alongside the United States there lies a country, still under the Imperial Crown of Britain, which may also be called great, in all the elements that make for greatness, except an abundant population ; and even that may come before long. In thirty years' time the Dominion of Canada may have grown into a nation with ten or fifteen millions of people, mostly of British descent : a nation large enough to claim its right to be treated on terms of political equality with any neighbour, however populous and powerful. And if we leave Canada out of account, the Republics of South America and Central America are not so unimportant that their political control can be easy, even for a country so vigorous and powerful as the United States. Mismanaged as it has been by bad government, and retarded in its material development by war, bankruptcy, slavery, and revolution, there is the possibility of a great. future before Spanish and Portuguese America. Great, in certain ways, it is already. Mexico has a population of 10,000,000, and an area equal to all the countries of Western Europe together ; Brazil is larger than Europe, and larger than the United States, excluding Alaska ; the Argentine Republic has fertile land enough to support the combined population of England, France, and Germany ; and even the smaller Republics of the North are larger than

most European monarchies.   These States are not merely huge tracts
of uninhabitable desert, like that immense blank area of 'light soil'
which makes French Africa fill so much space on the map.   Nearly the
whole of South and Central America is well watered, and it is lavishly
endowed by nature with vegetable and mineral wealth; a considerable
portion has a climate which does not forbid settlement by men of the
Caucasian race.   Of this splendid slice of the earth's surface much is
still almost virgin to the foot of man.   The immense dominion which
is called Brazil has only fourteen millions of inhabitants, including
negroes and Indians.   The Argentine is less populous than Belgium.
Ecuador, Colombia, Venezuela, even Peru and Chili, are still only
half-explored lands. · Who can doubt that these vast expanses of
fruitful soil cannot be left for ever to a handful of traders and
political adventurers in a few ports and capitals, and to sparse
agricultural settlements round the rim of the coast and along the
lower course of the great rivers ?   And who can fail to believe that
as South America fills up its haphazard political arrangements, its
accidental and unnatural geographical distribution will be altered ?
The future history of the continent is likely to be more adventurous
than its past.   New states will be created ; the old ones will fall to
pieces ; there must be convulsions and cataclysms, and probably a
struggle for territory, which cannot well be otherwise than violent.
There is another point worth considering, though strangely little
attention has been bestowed on it in this country.[3]   When the reconstruction of South America begins, it will be difficult to exclude
the European nations from a share in the scramble.   Some of them
may be drawn into it by the natural evolution of events and probably
very much against their will.   But then the countries of Europe are
full, and over full ; their surplus population is brimming over into
the other quarters of the world ; cupidity, industrial enterprise, the
desire to gain the necessaries of life on easier terms than they can be
got in comparatively poor countries not fitted to sustain a large
population from their own resources, are driving them to the outer-
most parts of the world, in numbers larger than ever

Rhene or the Danaw from their populous sands

poured upon the fields of Italy.   The problem is really less interesting for us than for some others.   Within the limits of the Empire
there is good land enough to hold the increase of the British Isles
for a hundred years to come.   But the German, the Belgian, the
Austrian, the Italian, the Alsatian, the Sclavonian, the Scandinavian,
pressed abroad by ambition or sheer hunger—where are they to go ?
At present they go mostly to the United States ; but the United
States is not anxious to have them, aud will not take them much
longer.   There is Africa ; but Africa is already a failure, since it

---

[3] See, however, an admirable article in the *Spectator* for November 14, in which
some of the considerations here suggested are presented in a very striking manner.

begins to be plain that the amount of land suited for settlement is strictly limited and a very large part of all that is worth having is in the possession of a Power which cannot be deprived of its dependencies till the strongest navy in the world has been mastered. What every European State wants is a colony capable of sustaining in comfort a few millions of its own people. It is not at all improbable that Germany, for instance, will find such a colony in Southern Brazil, and Italy on the Rio Platá. Let us suppose—not an extravagant supposition—that some time in the early part of the next century a couple of millions of Germans find themselves living in Southern Brazil, and that they also find the government of a gang of half-caste attorneys and political adventurers at Rio Janeiro no longer tolerable. The Uitlanders revolt and are beaten; they appeal to their own Government for protection and annexation. What will the United States do? It might annex South Brazil, or all Brazil, itself; or it might merely signify that the Monroe Doctrine, with its authorised glosses, required it to warn off Germany, and leave the inhabitants of Brazil to fight out the question among themselves. In the former case it would have acquired a Territory or a new State, of enormous extent, inhabited by an alien race, separated from the rest of the Union by hundreds of miles of sea and land, and needing a military force, much larger than the whole of the present United States Army, to police and protect it. In the other case, the civilising mission of the United States, of which Mr. Olney speaks, might be fulfilled by consigning a nobly fertile region and an industrious population to some such welter of anarchy and murderously savage warfare as that which devastated Paraguay and almost exterminated its male inhabitants thirty years ago. There is another alternative. It is conceivable that even the prestige of the United States might not be sufficient to induce a powerful European monarchy to abandon a large population of its own subjects without a struggle; and if the United States declined to annex Brazil, Germany might take some forcible action which would effectually impede that American State from 'shaping for itself its own political fortunes and destinies.' But this would be 'antagonising the interests and inviting the opposition of the United States,' and according to the Olney Doctrine would have to be opposed by the forces of the Union. Whichever alternative is taken the result would involve an addition to the external responsibilities, and an increase of the warlike resources, of the United States.

This last result seems to be inevitable. No nation can expect to take over the political control of an entire continent, to make itself answerable for permanently maintaining the existing geographical divisions of a group of States so large and (in some cases) so distant as those of the two Americas, and to secure the integrity against colonisation, annexation, or other forcible intrusion, of territories at once so tempting, so weak, and in such a condition of economic and industrial infancy, without being in a position to give effect to its wishes. If the scramble for South America once begins, neither the latent resources nor the moral influence of the United States will avail to protect its clients without the display of effective material strength. The Republic will be compelled to provide itself with some of those burdensome appendages to political predomi- nance, under which the peoples of this continent have suffered. Amateur diplomatists may contrive to conduct the external affairs of a nation which is seldom called upon to concern itself with what happens beyond its own borders ; they will require to be replaced by an elaborately (and expensively) trained staff of experts. Both the army and the navy must be brought a good deal closer to the Euro- pean standard. A levy of militiamen and civilian volunteers can no more be relied upon to furnish a completely equipped army corps for service in South America than a fleet of cruisers can be safely left to face a squadron of battleships. President Cleveland has at last provided the United States with a definite and positive foreign policy. It will remain for President Cleveland's successors to supply the country with the means of adequately discharging the responsibilities which this policy necessarily involves. The old Monroe Doctrine was one of self-centred isolation. A country, which aimed as far as possible at having no political relations with foreign States, could almost dispense with the luxury of fleets and armies. But the New Monroe Doctrine (which in some respects is rather the antithesis than the legitimate development of its predecessor) cannot assuredly be maintained unless the citizens of the Republic are prepared to endure burdens and incur obligations from which hitherto they have been enviably free.

SIDNEY LOW.

MANNING THE NAVY IN TIME OF WAR

THE reply given by Mr. Goschen [1] to the question asked by Mr. Webster in the House of Commons on the 23rd of July, seems to indicate that the Government intend to provide for the deficiencies, admitted on all hands to exist in the personnel of the navy, by a further increase in the permanent force. The moment seems specially opportune for the consideration of the grave question of the manning of the navy in war. Shall the permanent force be raised to the strength required in war, or shall we look to an adequate and well-trained reserve for meeting the war requirements of the navy? That the country and the Government should come to a right decision on this question is of supreme national importance.

First let us inquire what number of men are required to man the navy in time of war. In the *Naval Annual* for 1895 and 1896 detailed estimates are given of the numbers required for every ship built or building. The figures are as follows :—

	Men
Ships built or building 1895	97,700
Ships laid down 1895	6,200
Ships laid down 1896	10,450
Total	114,350

This total requirement of 114,000 men could not under ordinary circumstances be reached until the year 1900 ; but before the vessels of the 1895 and 1896 programmes are completed our requirements will probably be diminished by over 7,000 men, owing to the elimination of obsolete ships now on the navy list. It must also be borne in mind that every ship on the list would not be ready for sea at the outbreak of war. There will always be ships in the dockyard reserve requiring extensive and therefore lengthy repairs to make them ready

[1] Mr. Goschen said : ' With regard to reserves of sailors and marines nothing has happened since I submitted the Navy Estimates to induce me to depart in either direction from that steady continuous proportionate increase in the number of men which is rendered necessary by the extension of the fleet. I asked the House for an increase of about 5,000 men when I submitted my last estimate. I must decline to anticipate a statement which I shall have to make next year as to the further increase which will be required.'

for commission. Upon a full consideration of all our possible requirements in relation to manning, it is safe to say that in 1900 we
shall need about 105,000 men. This figure is in close accord with
the estimate given by Lord Charles Beresford at the Liverpool
Chamber of Commerce. What are the numbers at present available?
We have 85,800 men available for sea-service in the navy, and 25,000
men not adequately trained in the naval reserve. Some deduction
being made for sickness, and for the absence of naval reserve men on
distant voyages, it is clear that we shall have barely sufficient men to
man all our available ships. There is certainly no margin to make
good 'the wastage of war,' whether due to losses in action or any
other cause. In dealing with the manning of the navy, we are bound
to keep in view the large demands which would be made in order to
enable the country to employ to the fullest extent, should necessity
arise, its unparalleled resources for the supply of ships and war material. Our private shipbuilding yards are capable of constructing
simultaneously at least twenty battleships and forty cruisers. In a
struggle with a first-class naval power these splendid resources ought
to be employed to their utmost capacity; but they must remain
absolutely valueless to the nation without men to utilise the ships
which could be constructed in a few months.

Past experience shows that the number of men required in time
of peace is no criterion of the number required in war. In the three
great wars in which we were engaged in the latter half of the last
century, we required from four to eight times the number of men
serving in the navy in the intervening years of peace. In the
Crimean War we doubled the force that we had maintained in the
previous period of peace; and this although we were fighting against
an enemy that was not very powerful at sea. The press-gang and
the bounty system were the two principal methods employed in old
days to bring the personnel of the navy up to war strength. Public
opinion would not allow the navy to be recruited again by the brutal
method of impressment. The bounty system is costly and unsatisfactory. Obviously it must prove ineffective if the seamen were not
in existence. The Report of the Committee on the Manning of the
Mercantile Marine contains the latest evidence that British seamen
are diminishing in numbers and probably also in quality.

Our deficiencies being admitted, what steps are we to take to
remedy them? In recent years the additions to strength have been
mainly in the permanent force. In nine years there has been an
increase of over 31,000 in the numbers voted for the navy. During
the last five years nearly 19,000 men have been added to the numbers
available for sea-service. Recent experience has shown that the pay,
the conditions of employment, and the prospects of promotion, are
sufficient to attract as many recruits for the navy as we require. No
one would dispute the contention of naval officers, that it is better to

man our ships with men who have been trained from youth in the ranks of the navy, than with reserve men who have had little if any training in a sea-going man-of-war. To depend almost entirely on a permanent force would place the country under an intolerable burden of expenditure. For the year 1896 no less than 8,000,000l. have been voted for wages, victualling, clothing, half-pay and pensions. In the Naval Works Bill are included 1,145,000l. for Naval Barracks at Chatham, Portsmouth, and Keyham, and 341,000l. for a Naval Hospital at Chatham. It must also be borne in mind that the navy estimates have not yet begun to show the increase in non-effective charges owing to the recent additions to the numbers borne. A large non-effective vote is unsatisfactory in any branch of the public service. The recent additions to the personnel must ultimately raise the non-effective vote in the Navy Estimates to 50 per cent. above its present amount; and even if a change should take place in our policy now, it would be many years before the charge could be again reduced. An addition to the shipbuilding vote is an increase for one or two years only; an addition to the number of men creates a charge on the Exchequer which will be felt for more than half a century.

In the present state of public feeling the Admiralty would have little difficulty in obtaining the sanction of Parliament for a large expenditure. The recent increase in the Navy Estimates has coincided with a revival of commercial prosperity and a budget surplus. The burden has been little felt by the general body of tax-payers. It would not be wisdom on the part of those responsible for the naval defence of the country to take full advantage of the present state of public feeling, and to rely on the maintenance of the prosperous condition of the revenue which we have lately enjoyed. In a period of falling revenue, and when the political atmosphere is less clouded, demands are certain to be made for a reduction in the expenditure of our great spending departments. Any reduction in the Navy Estimates will be made in the future, as in the past, in the shipbuilding vote. Far-seeing statesmen will do well to put some check on the disposition to be lavish in the hour of prosperity. It may be followed by a reaction, and in the end do more to endanger than to establish our naval supremacy. We believe, as we have stated over and over again, that we shall waste our national resources if we attempt to maintain in peace the full numbers required to man the fleet in time of war.

The alternative is to take steps to create a reserve strong both in numbers and efficiency. The existing naval reserve, though undoubtedly valuable, leaves much to be desired. Neither in numbers, nor in completeness of training, is the force as satisfactory as we could wish. It has been proposed that a reserve should be created by passing men rapidly through the fleet, the navy being utilised to some extent as a training ground for the merchant service. Lord

Charles Beresford, in the address already referred to, has given a detailed scheme for carrying this policy into effect. Under this scheme, which may be briefly summarised, 5,000 men are to be enrolled annually for five years' service. On completion of their engagement in the navy, they would be entered in a first-class reserve, and would receive a retaining fee of 12*l*. a year subject to their putting in 28 days' drill. In addition, 5,000 men would be enrolled annually in a second-class reserve, who would get two months' training in the year, one of which must be on board a sea-going man-of-war. These men would receive a retaining fee of 8*l*. a year, instead of the 2*l*. 10*s*. now paid. Entries of second-class reserve men to cease at the end of seven years. At the end of eleven years the reserve would thus be raised to 35,000 men in the first class, and 35,000 in the second class. The total cost of a reserve of 90,000 men is estimated at 840,000*l*. a year, plus 600,000*l*. per annum for training, or a total cost of 1,440,000*l*. This would be roughly 20*l*. a man, excluding officers, the cost of the existing reserve being 10*l*. a man, including officers.

The objections to the institution of a short-service system in the navy are too serious to be disregarded. The following are the most important :—

(1) If two classes of the permanent force engaged for different periods were serving indiscriminately in the same ships, it would lead almost inevitably to a reconsideration and shortening of the longer period of service. This objection was urged with much force by Lord Spencer in the debate which took place some two years ago in the House of Lords.

(2) Men who have served their earlier years at sea in the navy would not take kindly to the merchant service, where the conditions of employment are not so good, and the work is harder. An absolute proof that the navy is the more attractive service is afforded by the fact that there is no difficulty in securing as many boys as we want for the navy, while there is a great and increasing difficulty in keeping up the supply of British-born seamen in the merchant service.

(3) The short-service system is very costly in proportion to the results attained. It has been estimated that every bluejacket entered as a boy costs the country 200*l*. before he becomes efficient. Under the system recently instituted in the 'Northampton,' by which boys are entered at a later age, and are only six months under training, the cost may be materially reduced. The *Times'* report does not tell us at what age or under what system Lord Charles Beresford proposes to enter first-class naval reserve men. In any case a reserve man under his scheme could not be created in less than five years, and of the five years he would probably be two years under training. It is true that during the remainder of the five

years he would be available for service in the fleet; but we have already more men than are necessary in peace. Our object should therefore be to keep naval reserve men as short a period in the fleet as is consistent with securing efficiency. Lord Charles Beresford points out that we must, in order to train reserve men, commission more ships and have shorter commissions. As a result of shortening the length of commissions we should have a large increase in the numbers of men practically unemployed in our home ports, and involving the necessity for additional accommodation in naval barracks and harbour ships. In the view of some of our best naval authorities, our seamen already spend too little time at sea. It would certainly be detrimental to the efficiency of the service to increase the time now spent in harbour.

Under the scheme which is described later, a naval reserve man would be qualified by four years' training in the merchant service, to be followed by serving a year or six months in the navy. As compared with Lord Charles Beresford's plan, it would be obviously less costly. With an equal number of ships in commission, from five to ten times the number of naval reserve men could be turned out in the same period. Every year that a prospective naval reserve man remains in the fleet after he is efficient his services are lost to the reserve. He is costing the country a great deal more, and he does not increase the strength of the personnel for war purposes. A somewhat similar objection applied to the recent entry of 100 naval reserve officers on the lieutenants' list of the Royal Navy.

On the above grounds we must reject the proposal to create a naval reserve through a short-service system, and endeavour to develop a well-trained reserve on other lines. The existing sources of supply for the naval reserve are the mercantile marine and the fishing population of the United Kingdom. We have a further source of supply in the seafaring and fishing population of the colonies, more especially of Canada, which has never yet been touched. Let us briefly examine the possibilities of the various resources on which we might be able to rely.

The mercantile marine has proved itself well able to supply the number of officers that would be required for the navy on the out-break of war. If training in the navy were rigidly insisted on as a condition of promotion from the junior ranks of the Royal Naval Reserve, the reserve of officers would become as valuable from the point of view of efficiency as it already is in respect of numbers. The case is very different if we turn to the mercantile marine for the supply of men. In the Report of the Committee on the Manning of the Mercantile Marine (par. 28) we read: ' It would appear that in 1891 the whole number of seamen employed in the foreign trade of the United Kingdom was 131,375, of whom 22,052 were foreigners and 21,332 were lascars, nearly 23 per cent. in all being non-

British.' The proportion of foreigners and lascars in the different ratings is given in the following table :—

—	Total	Foreigners	Lascars	Per Cent. non-British
A.B.'s	40,625	12,226	6,953	47
Petty Officers . . .	9,309	2,154	1,377	38
Firemen	24,733	3,224	7,475	43
Ordinary Seamen . .	3,431	489	nil	14
Boys	1,207	104	143	20
Apprentices . . .	3,619	Very few foreigners	—	—

The most unsatisfactory feature in the above returns is the fact that 19,179 out of a total of 40,625 A.B.'s, or 47 per cent., are either foreigners or lascars. Bad as the situation is at present, it exhibits no tendency to improve. In a subsequent paragraph the Committee point out that the existing unrestricted admission of foreigners and lascars may eventually result in further diminishing, outside of the Royal Navy, the number of British seamen. The reasons for the change that has already taken place and is still going on are summed up by the Committee in the following sentences :—

(1) The British seaman who has qualified himself for the rating of A.B. by 4 years' service before the mast may sign articles with Scandinavians and men of other nationalties, some of whom possess no proof of qualification and no adequate knowledge of the English language.

(2) Any deterioration of British seamen which may now exist is not owing to the decadence of our countrymen nor to their dislike for the sea, but to the lack of sufficient attraction in the sea service as at present constituted to draw and hold the best class of British workmen, and to the insufficient number of boys in training to supply the necessary waste in the number of A.B.'s.[2]

What are the remedies for the existing unsatisfactory state of things ? How can the mercantile marine become again what it once was, a valuable support for the navy in time of war ? The Manning Committee make the following suggestions :—

(1) Training ships or schools, where boys intended for sea service could obtain technical instruction in seamanship, should be established at the public expense at our seaports. Boys of 17 years of age or over having obtained certificates of competency in such training ships should be entitled at once to the rating of O.S. (ordinary seaman).

(2) A candidate for the rating of A.B. should be 19 years of age or over, and have had *three* years' service at sea as a deck hand. No man should be permitted to be employed as an A.B. who cannot prove his title to that rating.

(3) The candidate for the rating of O.S. should be 17 years of

[2] Similar conclusions are arrived at in the *Naval Annual*, p. 214.

(4) Foreigners who are candidates for the rating of A.B. or O.S. should be required to show the appropriate sea service, and to have an adequate knowledge of the English language.

With the other recommendations of the Committee, such as the fixing of a manning scale, we need not concern ourselves here. Seamen as a body are in favour of compulsory rating, and it is clear that if the recommendations of the Committee were carried into effect, British seamen would be in a great measure protected from that undue foreign competition with which they at present have to contend, and probably the efficiency of the personnel of the British mercantile marine would be materially improved. On these grounds the writer concurs in the recommendation of the Committee to establish a compulsory rating for seamen. The proposal to establish ships at the expense of the State to train boys for the mercantile marine is more difficult of acceptance. The grave national danger to which we are exposed under present conditions could alone justify the State in training men for a particular profession. In any case the proposal could only be entertained upon the condition that the State were to have some claim on the services of these men when trained. As less open to objection, the scheme put forward by Lord Brassey many years ago in his book on *British Seamen*, and reproduced in the *Naval Annual* this year, seems well worthy of consideration. Shipowners are to be encouraged to enter boys, under engagement, at the end of their four years' apprenticeship, to do a year's training in the navy; a subsidy of $20l.$ to be paid to the shipowner and $15l.$ to the boy, $10l.$ of which would only be paid on his joining the navy for his year of service. For reasons given later it is possible that a subsidy of $10l.$ to the shipowner and $10l.$ to the boy would suffice. At the conclusion of his period of training—that is to say, at or about the age of 19 or 20—the State-aided apprentice would, if efficient, become eligible for the first-class naval reserve, and would return to his employment in the mercantile marine as an A.B. The naval reserve man who had once done his training in a man-of-war would be kept efficient by a month's drill annually, provided that once in three years the month's drill was performed in a sea-going man-of-war. Under this scheme the State, instead of undertaking the whole cost and the whole responsibility of training men for the merchant service, would assist the merchant service to train men for itself. Both the navy and the mercantile marine would have a hand in the training of the men, and both would reap the benefit of the supply coming forward. It would be far less costly to assist shipowners to train boys in their own ships at sea, than to establish harbour ships with an expensive staff, as proposed by the Manning

Committee. Boys trained at sea would be more efficient seamen than boys trained in harbour ships.

From some points of view it might be preferable to combine both systems of training, giving a boy one or two years' training in a harbour ship, and two years' training at sea, before he entered the navy for his year of service. It would be more costly than the proposal of Lord Brassey, but it would not be so costly as the proposal of the Manning Committee, because fewer harbour ships would be needed to train the same number of boys.

The Manning Committee complain that they did not receive from masters and officers in active service such information and assistance as their experience would have enabled them to afford. It will therefore be interesting to refer to two conferences held at Government House, Melbourne, one in August and the other in September 1896, to which the masters of all sailing ships of 1,000 tons and over there in the port were invited. There was a ready response to the invitation. The proposals of the Manning Committee and the scheme as sketched were laid before the first conference. These were afterwards printed and circulated to the gentlemen who had attended. At the second conference, to which also the masters of both steam ships and sailing vessels were invited, the proposals were considered in detail. Two shipmasters handed in valuable papers dealing with the whole question of the manning of the mercantile marine. A summary of the conclusions arrived at will not be out of place here.

(1) The experience was general that the supply of British seamen was falling off. One master gave a list of his crew in 1877 and 1896. In both years the officers and the seven apprentices carried were British. Of the crew, including carpenter, sailmaker, steward, and cook, sixteen were British and five were foreigners in 1877; six were British and ten were foreigners in 1896.

(2) Those present confirmed the opinion as to the diminution of the supply of British seamen. The pay and conditions of employment of seamen had not improved in the same proportion as those of skilled workmen ashore. The apprenticeship system had been abolished, and shipowners no longer carried boys, who were coming forward to make good the wastage of able seamen. Only eight 'boys' (as distinguished from apprentices) were carried on the fifteen ships represented at the second conference, and some of these were rated as ordinary seamen. A third cause was the competition of improperly qualified foreigners, whom some shipowners preferred to British seamen.

(3) The recommendation of the Manning Committee that there should be a compulsory rating for A.B.'s was unanimously approved, many of the masters urging that a seaman should have a continuous discharge on which his own service should be recorded. All the captains present approved Lord Brassey's proposal. They preferred

the system of training boys at sea, and thought that the time spent in harbour ships would be wasted. Under present conditions, shipowners could not carry out the system of training boys at sea without the assistance of the State during the first year. A boy after being one year at sea would be of value to the shipowner and should begin to receive wages. Owing to this important expression of opinion, the bonus to the shipowner might be 10l. instead of 20l., and the bonus to the apprentice 10l. instead of 15l. as originally suggested. It was further urged that the period of service in the navy should not be less than twelve months. Having completed his training in the navy, the young seaman would be fully qualified for the rating of A.B. in the merchant service.

To sum up the results of these interesting conferences, it was most satisfactory to find that the general sense of practical men was distinctly in favour of the scheme of State-aided apprenticeship which we have endeavoured in the preceding pages to recommend.

Before establishing any system of training seamen either wholly or partially by the State, it must be evident that both the State and the mercantile marine would be able to command the services of the men when trained. This again must depend upon the inducements offered. Under the present regulations a first-class naval reserve man receives a retaining fee of 6l. per annum and a pension of 12l. a year at the age of sixty, besides his pay during drills. The fact that a young man at the age of twenty would be receiving a retaining fee of 6l. a year, in addition to the wages earned as a merchant seaman, would probably attract sufficient numbers. If the present retaining fee fails to attract, it should be raised to 8l. or 10l., the full amount being payable only so long as a man followed the sea as his profession.

The scheme thus briefly explained for improving the quality and increasing the supply of British seamen in the mercantile marine may be modified in detail without impairing the general principle. The main objection is that it would take five years before we began to feel its effects either in the mercantile marine or in the naval reserve. We can, however, claim that it goes to the root of the present unsatisfactory condition of things. Whatever be the scheme adopted, it must take time before an improvement is manifested. For immediately increasing the strength of the naval reserve we must turn to other sources of supply.

The fishing population of the United Kingdom, from which the second-class reserve is now recruited, is unquestionably the most immediately available recruiting ground. Under the present conditions it would not be difficult to enrol more fishermen in the reserve, but we cannot have full efficiency under the existing regulations. We have two points for consideration. First, we have a distinction

of class which does not rest upon merit.   Many competent
authorities consider that the second-class reserve men are fully as
efficient seamen gunners as the men of the first class.   Next, we
have to overcome the reluctance shown by certain classes of fishermen to embark in sea-going ships for their drills.   On these grounds
it is urged that the present distinction between the first and second
class reserve should be abolished.   Two classes should still be maintained, but the classification should depend not on the sources from
which they are recruited but on efficiency.   No man should be
eligible for the first-class reserve until he had served in the navy for
six months or a year.   All naval reserve men should be embarked
from time to time, say once in three years, in a sea-going man-of-war
for their drills, and if possible during manœuvres.   With the stimulus of promotion from the second to the first class, and the possibility
of earning a largely increased retaining fee, there is every reason for
believing that we could raise an additional 10,000 men for the naval
reserve from the fishing population in the near future, and that in
course of time the figure might be increased to 20,000 men.   The
possession of a large nucleus of naval reserve men in the fishing
population presents many advantages.   Fishermen would be available at short notice ; and the withdrawal of a large number of men
from the fishing trade would be less serious to our national interests
than the withdrawal of men from the mercantile marine.

There is another source of supply for a naval reserve in Canada,
Newfoundland, and Australasia.   According to the census of 1891
there were in the provinces of Canada 27,079 fishermen and 13,928
sailors.[3]   According to the returns of the Department of Marine and
Fisheries there were 70,719 fishermen and seamen, of whom 40,447
were in the Maritime Provinces (East) and 12,650 in British Columbia.
The discrepancy between the returns is accounted for by the fact that
a large number of men on the sea-coasts of Canada follow really two
avocations, being farmers as well as fishermen.   The Department of
Fisheries return really shows the number of persons who are so familiar
with the sea as to be perfectly at home on it.   The above figures do
not include Newfoundland.

No exact estimate can be given of the seafaring population of
Australasia.   The most competent authorities whom the writer has
been able to consult on the subject estimate that about 5,000 men

---

[3] By provinces the figures stand as follows :—

	Fishermen	Sailors
Nova Scotia .	14,478	5,425
New Brunswick .	2,926	1,512
Prince Edward's Island	914	539
Quebec	3,433	2,723
Ontario	1,421	2,989
Manitoba	78	30
British Columbia .	3,798	705
N.W. Territories .	31	5

are employed in the intercolonial trade and in fishing. A large proportion of these are foreigners. Comparatively few are colonial-born. No pains have been spared to ascertain, by means of conferences with shipowners, shipmasters, representatives of the Seamen's Union, as well as with the men themselves, whether it would be possible to raise a reserve for the Imperial Navy in the Australasian colonies. There seems little doubt that the high rates of pay, though they have considerably diminished in the last eight years, attract efficient seamen. The foreigners are principally Scandinavians, Danes, or Hollanders. Nearly all are naturalised Australians; they look upon Australia as their home, and would be ready to serve her in case of emergency. The shipowners of Victoria assured the writer that they would give every facility to the men in their employ to perform their annual drills, and would keep their berths open for them. It is clear that a naval reserve could not be established, except with the cordial co-operation of the shipowners. No objection need be anticipated from the Seamen and Firemen's Union. A representative of the Union formed part of a deputation to the commander-in-chief of the station some seven years ago, urging that opportunities should be given to seamen in the colonies to join the naval reserve. To insist that a period of training in the navy should be a qualification for the first-class reserve would operate as a deterrent, at any rate in the Australasian colonies. Objections would probably be overcome if the retaining fee were raised to 10l. The Colonial Governments might be fairly asked to provide a proportion of the increased fee.

The principal difficulty in the way of establishing an Imperial Naval Reserve in Australia by means of a State-aided apprentice system arises from the fact that no sailing ships are employed in the intercolonial trade, and therefore colonial boys would have no opportunity of going to sea, even if they showed a greater desire to do so than at present. This difficulty might be met by an arrangement with owners of sailing ships trading regularly to Australia (*e.g.* the Loch Line) to carry colonial boys.

A further difficulty might result from the fact that most of the colonies already possess naval forces. In Victoria, for instance, there is a permanent force about 180 strong, and a naval brigade or partially paid force about 150 strong, who are required to man the coast-defence ship *Cerberus* and five torpedo boats. In New South Wales the Naval Brigade, which consists largely of time-expired man-of-war's men, is 330 strong. The pay of A.B.'s is 10l. The Naval Artillery Volunteers (they are now really a militia) are 260 strong, and their pay is 8l. No duty afloat appears to be assigned to the Naval Brigade of New South Wales. The naval volunteers man two torpedo boats. South Australia has a permanent force of seventeen all told, and a small naval reserve to man the cruiser *Protector*. Queensland also possesses a Naval Brigade. By arrangement with the Colonial

Governments it might be possible to absorb the colonial naval brigades into the proposed Imperial Naval Reserve. It would probably result in increased efficiency and also be more economical if the British Admiralty took over the floating defences of the colonies.

As regards Canada and Newfoundland, there is the possibility that our naval reserve men might, after we had trained them, be attracted by the high pay offered in the American Navy. Canadians and Newfoundlanders enlist in the American Navy to a considerable extent at present. They would be less likely to serve under a foreign flag if they were able by joining the Imperial Naval Reserve to earn a retaining fee of 10*l*. The Dominion Government might devote to the encouragement of the naval reserve the bounties now given to fishermen.

A special advantage may be noticed in connection with the establishment of a body of reserve men in Australia. They would not only be on the spot, ready to man the reserve ships of the Australian squadron and any merchant cruisers that might be taken up in war time, but they could also furnish drafts for all stations west of the Horn and east of Suez, thus obviating the necessity of sending crews from England and relieving the strain on the home base. This advantage would not only be felt in time of war. If reserve men were regularly employed as suggested in ships on colonial stations, whether in North America or Australia, the number of continuous service men required would be less and the expenditure on the transport of relief crews smaller.

After the experience gained in Canada and Australia during the past few months, the estimate given in the *Naval Annual* for 1896 that in the near future 5,000, and ultimately 10,000 or even 15,000, men could be raised in the colonies does not seem to be exaggerated. Taking all sources of supply into consideration, in three years we might have 40,000 men, whether seamen or stokers, in the naval reserve, distributed as follows :—

Mercantile Marine	15,000
Fishermen	20,000
Colonies	5,000

In ten years the force might be increased to 75,000 men, thus distributed :—

Mercantile Marine	30,000
Fishermen	30,000
Colonies	15,000
Total	75,000

To give an efficient training to such a force is the great practical difficulty in the way. We have already more men in the permanent force than are sufficient for the peace requirements of the fleet, and the difficulty of providing useful employment for the surplus is already being felt. No further increase in the permanent force should be sanctioned. The tendency should rather be towards a reduction as the naval reserve increases in numbers and efficiency. In the meanwhile we shall be obliged to increase the number of ships in commission for training purposes. The existing reserve is certainly not sufficiently trained. It could not be proposed that we should depend more largely on a reserve than we do now, unless there were to be an alteration in the system of training.

The writer fully recognises that the policy advocated in this article is unpopular with the bulk of the naval service. A naval officer naturally would rather man his ship with bluejackets than with partially trained naval reserve men. ' Few if any naval officers have had practical experience in working with reserve men,' writes an old naval officer who has had that experience. ' In the navy to-day officers work with made and trained ship's companies, every individual having been trained from boyhood. In the old wars, officers had to make and train their own ship's companies, and their worth, and the worth of their ships, depended entirely on their capacity to make raw men efficient.' In a squadron of modern battle ships, which will be the first to come in contact with the enemy, it may be desirable that the proportion of reserve men should be small, but even in a modern battle ship there are many stations where a high degree of training is not required. It would be foolish indeed to under-estimate the value of technical knowledge, but, given a sufficient number of bluejackets for special ratings, it should be easier now to turn comparatively untrained men into an efficient crew than it was in the days of Nelson. To deliver a series of broadsides from a battery of Q.F. guns would require far less general training and far less excellence in each individual man than was necessary in the crews who fought the 18- and 32-pounders of a hundred years ago.

A reserve man [says the officer from whom we have already quoted] could never be as good an all-round man as the seaman-gunner and the torpedo-man, and he would not need to be, but it is surprising how quickly he can be trained to efficiency as to the armament of a ship. The drafting of 25 per cent. of reserve men to a cruiser would not lessen her efficiency. Three months after joining it would be impossible to tell (if the reserve men had been in fairly good hands) that they were not continuous service men. There would be no falling off in smartness, but perhaps the reverse by the importation of new blood. In many respects the reserve man is a point or two ahead of the continuous service man. My experience of merchant seamen is that once he recognises that you have no interest in robbing him, and that it gives you no pleasure to see him ill-treated, he does his work with real good-will. Native Australians are rather more intelligent than the average of seafarers, but bend thoroughly well to discipline.

In conclusion, we may briefly summarise the policy advocated in the preceding pages. There is no question concerning the defence of the Empire of more importance at the present moment than the problem of manning the navy in time of war. Our existing resources are insufficient. The policy of maintaining the personnel of the navy in peace at war strength is too costly and too wasteful of our national resources. Rather we should address ourselves to the task of building up a powerful reserve. As a first step, and before adding to the numbers, the conditions of enrolment must be altered so as to secure greater efficiency. Of the three sources of supply the fishing population alone can be relied upon to yield at once a substantial body of recruits. The colonies, which are not at present in a position to make a serious money contribution to the naval defence of the Empire, could furnish good men for a naval reserve. The mercantile marine, which ought to be a valuable support to the navy in war, has been almost exhausted as a source of supply. The large and continually increasing proportion of foreigners in British merchant ships constitutes a grave national danger, only to be removed by measures dealing more comprehensively and more thoroughly with the present deplorable state of things than those partial remedies proposed by Sir Edward Reed's Committee. Ship-owners, in the acute competition with the often subsidised foreigner, cannot be expected to show a preference for British seamen. No remedy is possible without substantial assistance from the State.

T. A. BRASSEY.

TOTAL ABSTINENCE

AND THE TEMPERANCE MOVEMENT

THERE is a sound of thoroughness and even latent generosity in the term 'total abstinence.' It suggests the complete enjoyment associated with a 'whole holiday.' We think of one who is 'every inch' a man, and has the courage of his convictions. We are encouraged in the admiration of those who act up to their principles, and despise a proposal which is 'neither one thing nor the other.' Whatever it may be to astronomers, we look with imperfect interest at an eclipse which is only 'partial.' It was a happy change in the language of its advocates when they began to talk of 'total abstinence' instead of 'teetotalism,' which has a timid, stammering, and insignificant sound.

Though now suggesting an exclusively alcoholic flavour, it is plain that this term covers a large field.

At certain seasons, indeed, or for a while, every man wholly refrains from something which is allowable. He sits down to his meals instead of nibbling at his food all day. Civilised life is regulated by time-tables which are intended to formulate our actions and to prevent business from encroaching upon relaxation. After a temporary way we are all 'total abstainers' from one thing or another. The Sabbath itself was marked by a law of complete prohibition, though it lasted only for a day.

Every right-minded man, however, recognises the desirability of permanent abstinence from what he believes to be radically wrong. He admits no *via media* in the following of righteousness, corresponding to that of 'temperance' in the use of alcohol. He may pardon a weak offender, but he would not allow that a strong man may disregard the extreme rigour of, say, the Ninth Commandment, since he can be trusted not to indulge himself in perjury ' to excess.'

But though the number of universally accepted moral laws may be few, we witness in these days the wide-spread and growing erection of some which are held by their framers to be as essentially imperative as the Ten Commandments themselves, inasmuch as they are assumed to rest, not upon convenience or expediency, but upon facts, the ignorance or disregard of which is fatal to the development and well-being of our nature.

Such is the attitude of those who believe that the 'use' of alcohol or flesh-meat is radically prejudicial to human life.   There are some, indeed, who admit the employment of 'stimulants' under medical advice, but the genuine 'total abstainer' looks on alcohol as always essentially injurious, and those are unjust to him who resent his assertion that the 'temperate' man does more harm to society than the 'drunkard.'   His contention is perfectly logical.   If he really believes alcohol to be irremediably poisonous when present in beverages, any recognition of their use which fails in displaying its evil effect is a bar to that revelation of its nature which he desires to be made and acknowledged, and in the end does more harm to the good cause than the most obvious intemperance, which is an effective object lesson in support of his teaching.

Much the same line is taken by the thoroughgoing vegetarian who traces disease and premature decay to the eating of flesh-meat. He cannot, indeed, point to revolting spectacles of gluttony as the exclusive result of its consumption, since it is possible for a man to sicken himself by eating too much permissible food—such as jam. Thus he points to the health and strength of those who have adopted his diet without injury to themselves.   He not only ransacks history and the literature of science, but quotes the current testimony of simple-feeding races in support of his faith.   He claims to prove by the analysis of grain, fruit, leaf, kernel, nut, and root that these viands provide all things needed for the building and repair of the human body.   If, by the chemistry of nature, a sheep can be made out of grass, and so much corn and water be changed into a horse, he pleads for such a bloodless construction and preservation of man as raises him above the 'carnivora.'   Indeed, the vegetarian looks on the Lord Mayor, so long as he eats the flesh of animals, as no better than the pedigree-cousin of a cannibal.

Both he and the total abstainer rely chiefly upon the testimony of 'science.'   Without our admitting, however, the soundness of its apprehension or use by them, it is remarkable that, in their anxiety to support their claims, some in both parties appeal also to the Bible. One points to a sentence in the first chapter of Genesis, where 'seed' and 'fruit' are announced to be given to man 'for meat,' and some try to prove that the wines of Scripture were unfermented, and therefore not intoxicating.   They had much better all have the courage of their convictions and boldly affirm that 'teetotalism' or 'vegetarianism' can be proved to be vitally true, and therefore worthy of acceptance, by reason of our present knowledge, and that they decline to place any reliance upon what the Scriptures have to say about human diet.   They are wise in doing this, since their case is weakened in the minds of thoughtful men by forced appeals to a book which refers plainly to the eating of flesh and drinking of wine as not only permissible and customary, but ordained and imperative under circumstances of special solemnity.

It is difficult, by the way, to appreciate the position of those total abstainers who permit the use of wine in the reception of the Holy Communion. If an act is wrong in itself, one would think the doing of it to be most indefensible at a moment of supreme expressed devotion to the will or law of God. A Roman Catholic might say that the element had been changed, and was no longer wine, but the Anglican has no such miraculous escape from the paradoxical reflection that in seeking communion with God he has partaken of that which he denounces as a social poison.

Moreover, the divine use of this at the first Lord's Supper indicates no choice of a special liquor 'permissible' on such an occasion, but recognises it as the most widely accepted drink, as bread was the commonest food. Their legitimate combination, indeed, is (at least by the Church of England) assumed to be still in force, since is so referred to in the catechism, where it is admitted that our bodies are strengthened by 'bread and wine.' The position of those Hindoo Christians who are said to have administered the Holy Communion with rice and water (their usual food) is much more logically in accordance with its original institution than that of those who prohibit the use of wine as pernicious at an ordinary meal, and then accept it as a divine representative of strengthening drink, worthy of consecration at a sacred feast.

An unbiassed reader of the Bible, however, can have no doubt that it recognises the use of alcohol, not as exceptional, but as a factor in the common drink of the 'people of God,' about whom it speaks, and thus moderate drinkers keenly resent the misuse of a book whence they claim to draw much in support of their position. They are well advised, however, not to lay too much stress upon a miraculous changing of water into wine, since the advanced scientific 'prohibitionist' is little affected by that which claims to be supernatural evidence. The witness of the Scriptures to the use of fermented liquor by the 'people of God' is of another sort. Look at that from the Old Testament. When the Hebrews came out of Egypt, they left a nation familiar with the use of wine for a land of vineyards. And while on the way they received a minute code of sanitary and sumptuary laws, many of which concerned their diet. They were forbidden to touch certain meats eaten in the country they had left and in that to which they were going. But nothing whatever was said about what they should 'drink,' save in reference to two exceptionally situated classes of people—namely, priests, when about to officiate, and 'Nazarites,' who took peculiar vows.

In the case of these sectaries we read (Numbers vi. 2, 3, 4): 'When either man or woman shall separate themselves to vow a vow of a Nazarite, to separate themselves unto the Lord: he shall separate himself from wine and strong drink, and shall drink no vinegar of wine, or vinegar of strong drink; neither shall he drink any liquor of grapes, nor eat moist grapes or dried. All the days of his separation shall he eat nothing that is made of the vine tree, from the kernel even to the husk.' Thus it would seem that when these were ended, he was at liberty to return to the use of its fruit, for meat or drink.

The other prohibition applies to the priests while officiating, and runs thus (Leviticus x. 8, 9): 'And the Lord spake unto Aaron, saying, Do not drink wine nor strong drink, thou, nor thy sons with thee, when ye go into the tabernacle of the congregation.'

From this it appears that, except under special circumstances, the priest and the people were at liberty to drink 'the vinegar of wine, and the vinegar of strong drink,' as it suited their convenience or taste.

It is notable, moreover, that when the Hebrews were first about to enter Canaan, those who went to spy the land brought back great bunches of grapes as acceptable specimens of its fertility. It abounded with vineyards, which were not (then or subsequently) planted for the produce of fresh fruit alone, since the building of a 'wine-press' is repeatedly associated with their use. And the assumption that this was employed for the purpose of getting grape-juice, to be drunk unfermented, is disposed of by the well-known august illustration which appealed to a general custom: 'No man putteth new wine into old bottles, else the new wine doth burst the bottles, and the wine is spilled, and the bottles will be marred; but new wine must be put into new bottles.' To this is added, in another record of the saying, 'and both are preserved.'

Arguments for the prohibition of intoxicating liquor, or for total abstinence from it as essentially righteous, should be made to rest on social and sanitary considerations which have arisen in later days. Appeals to the Scriptures really tend to weaken the position of teetotallers. At the same time it is ungracious to murmur at those self-denying men who, in part, follow Scriptural examples, and call themselves modern Rechabites or Nazarites. I say pointedly, 'in part,' since, as I have remarked, it was only during 'the days of his separation' that the ancient Nazarite abstained from the 'liquor of grapes;' and the full obligation of the old Rechabite was neither to 'build houses to dwell in, neither to have vineyard, nor field, nor seed.' It should be remembered, however, that the vows taken by these separatists involved no condemnation of wine as essentially injurious, and, in the case of the Rechabites, pointed to a paternally exceptional test of obedience, rather than to such an example of total abstinence as invited general imitation.

But whatever 'abstainers' choose to call themselves now, the self-denial and devotion of their leaders (who need no special safeguard against intemperance) have come to be recognised as some of the most powerful among distinctly organised efforts in promoting temperance, for it is felt that very few drunkards can be reclaimed except by their being obliged or induced to give up the use of any intoxicating liquor altogether. It is almost hopeless to preach 'temperance' to them. Their sole chance of recovery, with most, lies in 'total abstinence,' and (though dipsomaniacs might well be more subjected to coercion) the modern formulated protests against intemperance certainly owe their chief immediate force to the influence of the 'total abstainer.'

Meanwhile the 'moderate drinker' looks on 'temperance' as man's true aim in the conduct of life, and as more agreeable to his full development than 'total abstinence,' since it involves a greater exercise of elevating self-control. Seeing, too, that the Bible denounces the drunkard while it does not forbid the moderate use of 'strong drink,' he appeals to it not only as directly supporting his attitude, but on Scriptural grounds he resents the drinking of wine being classed with customs which disappear in the fuller light of Christianity. Under the Gospel there was a notably emphatic relaxation for believers in the matter of diet. The eating of certain meats was no longer forbidden to the Christian, and no drink was freshly prohibited. Indeed, not only was the vine (repudiated by the Nazarite and Rechabite) chosen as a symbol of excellence by Christ Himself, but when He was called a 'wine-bibber,' in contrast to the Baptist, He said, 'Wisdom is justified of all her children,' and thus left to the world an emphatic example of temperance rather than of total abstinence as best fitted to the doctrine and practice of the new dispensation.

While, therefore, the temperate Christian deplores excess as much as any one, and urges the weak, who cannot command themselves, to abstain altogether from strong drink, he looks on an 'example' in temperance as, rather than total abstinence, the most Christian that can be set, and relies upon the social and religious growth of self-respect for the mitigation of intemperance rather than upon the introduction of a peremptory law (condemning the use of alcohol) which neither the Church nor the Bible has enjoined, though 'excess' in using it is not new, and is denounced by both.

And he does this the more readily because he sees that one class of society has notably changed its drinking habits without the assistance of fresh prohibitory 'vows,' and because he cannot examine Christianity without perceiving that its drift is to lessen the number of imperative commandments ('all the law and the prophets' being said by Christ to 'hang upon' two), and to place the individual recognition of high principles above the multiplication of restrictive ceremonies and rules.

Moreover, apart from the special influence of religion, the 'temperate' man perceives that the Divine economy, seen in Nature itself, is marked throughout by ' compromise,' and the balance of one law against another.   Without affecting any claim to minute scientific perception he can see that there are powers and influences operating in the conduct of the world, any one of which, if uncontrolled, would be fatal to human life.   And yet this does not prohibit the Creator from employing them in providing for the right condition of man. Thus 'temperance' in using and controlling those factors of mortal existence which are hurtful if unlimited in application, would seem to be a nearer approach to divine procedure than a complete rejection of them lest they should do mischief.

In taking this line the ' temperate' man does not admit that he is anywise less sincere in his abhorrence of drunkenness than the total abstainer, nor that his method and hopes are less radically promising and sound.   He bases them upon the great laws of life which cannot be broken without significant suffering, and he believes that the gradual recognition of these is sure to help and test not only the true progress of science and religion, but the conduct of individual life.

HARRY JONES.

THE WORLD BENEATH THE OCEAN

THE book which Dr. Nansen is writing for Archibald Constable & Co. descriptive of his recent expedition will be eagerly awaited by all who are interested in the study of oceanography. In the somewhat discursive and, to all appearance, hastily written papers which appeared in the *Daily Chronicle* the Norwegian explorer only touched lightly on the observations which he had made in connection with this subject. We learn, however, that he took a large number of soundings, and concluded, from the remarkable absence of organic life in the samples brought up from the bottom, that the existing views as to the nature of ocean-bed deposits will have to be modified. No doubt the majority of these soundings were taken with reliable sounding machinery, and not by a line running over a block and recovered by hand, as represented in the sketch accompanying his paper. A word will be said later in this article with regard to the depths and temperatures which he gives.

All observations that add to our knowledge of ocean depths and deposits are of special interest at the present time, when a conference is being held at the Colonial Office concerning the laying of a Pacific cable in depths which will exceed those of the deepest cable already laid, and in deposits of which no practical experience has been gained. It is only since surveys of the sea bottom were first undertaken for the purposes of submarine telegraphy that any knowledge has been gained of the world beneath the ocean. A certain acquaintance, it is true, with marine animals in shallow waters has long existed, and Aristotle, who mentions 180 species in the Ægean Sea, is familiar to the student of natural history in connection with the masticatory organ of the Echinus, or sea-hedgehog, called after the great philosopher 'Aristotle's Lantern.' Some four hundred years later Pliny the Elder enumerates 176 species, which, although four less than Aristotle's list, seemed to afford the gossipy old naturalist very lively satisfaction. 'One must allow,' he says, 'that it is quite impossible to comprise every species of terrestrial animal in one general view for the information of mankind, and yet, by Hercules! in the sea and

ocean, vast as it is, there exists nothing that is unknown to us ; and
—a truly marvellous fact—it is with those things which nature has
concealed in the deep that we are best acquainted.' Pliny's self-
congratulatory vein would have been brought to a speedy termination
if he had known that the complete list included 500,000 species,
though it is only fair to say that 400,000 of them are organisms very
low down in the scale of nature.

The discovery of America and the extended voyages which followed it stimulated interest in matters connected with the ocean.
Sir John Hawkins, the great Elizabethan admiral, believed that if it
were not for the movement of the sea by tides and winds, it would
corrupt the world. This theory was based on an experience off the
Azores, where he was becalmed six months. He relates that the sea
was filled with serpents, adders, and snakes, three to six feet long,
'some green, some black, some yellow, some white,' and so numerous
'that hardly a man could draw a bucket clear of some corruption.'
Is it possible that this account suggested Coleridge's well-known
lines in the *Ancient Mariner?*—

> The very sea did rot; O Christ!
>   That ever this should be!
> Yea, slimy things did crawl with legs
>   Upon the slimy sea.

No scientific attempts to take deep-sea soundings were made
before the seventeenth century. Then Hooke employed a sphere of
wood, well pitched and varnished, which was sunk by a sphere of
iron attached to it by a spring hook. On reaching the bottom the
sphere of wood became released and rose to the surface, the depth of
the sounding being calculated by a formula from the interval between
the time when it was let go and the time when it appeared again. In
1733 two members of the Royal Society, Dr. Stephen Hales and
Dr. Desaguliers, invented a sounder consisting of a glass vessel in
which stood a gauge-tube, the top of which was hermetically sealed,
while the bottom was immersed in mercury, covered with a thin film
of treacle. The mode of sinking, as in Hooke's sounder, was by a
weight, which became detached on reaching the bottom. The pressure
of the water forced the mercury up the glass gauge-tube, and the
treacle marked the highest point reached. The depth was calculated
by Boyle's law of pressure. A hollow sphere attached to the top of
the glass vessel caused it to rise to the surface when the weight was
released. This contrivance of the two learned doctors acted very well in
shallow water, where there was little current, but would have been
useless in great depths, where the pressure would burst the hollow
sphere, or in currents strong enough to carry it out of sight. The
interest of their invention lies in the fact that it anticipated by some
hundred and fifty years Lord Kelvin's sounding tube, which depends

navigation.

Little advance was made in oceanography during the eighteenth century, but in 1818 Sir John Ross in his famous Arctic expedition brought up living specimens from a depth of 1,050 fathoms,[1] by means of a hemp line and a deep-sea clamm, resembling in appearance a self-acting pair of tongs, with large spoon-shaped ends. This achievement was regarded with suspicion by eminent zoologists, and as late as 1859 Edward Forbes, in his *Natural History of European Seas*, insisted on the theory that animal life could not exist at greater depths than 300 or 400 fathoms. The theory was destined to receive a rude shock the following year in the course of some soundings taken by H.M.S. *Bulldog* over a proposed route for the Atlantic cable. During the first portion of the voyage the specimens recovered from the sea bottom were of little interest. But at length striking results were obtained from a sounding in 1,260 fathoms. One can judge of the scientific enthusiasm which the problem aroused by the tone in which Dr. Wallich, the chief naturalist on board, describes the occasion: 'That single sounding, I may be permitted to say, compensated for every disappointment that weather and accident may have previously engendered. At the eleventh hour, and under circumstances the most unfavourable for searching out its secrets, the deep has sent forth the long-coveted message.'

This message consisted of thirteen starfishes, which had become attached to the end of the line as it rested for a short time on the ocean bed. Its announcement was followed by a storm of controversy amongst the scientific men of the day. The idea of a bathymetric line, or life-zero, below which animal existence could not be supported, was not easily abandoned by the partisans of Edward Forbes. They declared that the starfishes came from a higher layer of water, and had 'convulsively embraced' the line on its way from the bottom. But the question was settled beyond all doubt in the latter part of the same year, when a Mediterranean cable, which Professor Fleeming Jenkin hooked from a depth of over 1,000 fathoms for the purpose of repair, came up with evidences of animal life encrusted on its sheathing.

Meanwhile the science of deep-sea sounding had made considerable advances owing to a contrivance invented in 1854 by Brooke, an officer in the United States Navy. Hitherto no sinking weight had been attached to the sounder, and in great depths the increased friction on the line made the rate of descent so slow, that on reaching the bottom there was no perceptible diminution in the speed of running out, the line continuing to descend by its own weight. On one occasion

---

[1] One fathom being 6 feet, 1,000 fathoms is slightly more than $1\frac{1}{8}$ of a statute mile. Throughout this paper depths and lengths are given in statute, not in nautical, miles.

Captain Denham paid out 7,706 fathoms, or 8¾ miles, without getting bottom, and from another ship over 8,300 fathoms, or 10 miles, of line were lowered with the same result. Brooke's invention depended on the same principle as that employed by Hooke two hundred years previously, namely, that of a heavy weight to sink the sounder, the weight becoming detached automatically on reaching the bottom. The difference in the two methods consists in the fact that, instead of a sphere of wood, Brooke used a metal tube, which was lowered and recovered by means of a hemp line. The weight was a large shot or cannon ball with a hole through the centre, by which it was passed over the sounding tube, and suspended in that position by hanging from two metal arms pivoted to the top of the tube. These arms were attached by a looped cord to the hemp line, and during descent were kept upright by the weight of the sounder. On reaching the bottom the strain was removed, the two arms dropped, and the weight slipped off, leaving the sounder free to return by itself.

But, in spite of the heavy weights employed, hemp lines could not be relied upon in deep water where strong currents were present, and in the case of the Gulf Stream it was found almost impossible to get bottom with them. Accordingly, in 1872, Sir William Thomson, now Lord Kelvin, made some experiments with the view of replacing hemp by wire. As far back as 1838 wire had been used for sounding purposes, but it was of so heavy a type that no indication of reaching the bottom could be observed. The type employed by Lord Kelvin was ordinary pianoforte wire, and proved a complete success. The kind now in general use is only $\frac{1}{33}$ of an inch in diameter, and has a breaking strain of 270 lb., or over 19 stone, which is, bulk for bulk, eighteen times as great as that of hemp. On account of its smooth surface and small area it offers extremely small resistance to the water, and gives accurate results in the strongest currents. But it is in the recovery that, owing to its small weight, which is only 13 lb. per mile, the superiority of this wire is most apparent. A length of 2,000 fathoms, or 2¼ miles, can be wound in—even when the ship has started and is steaming eight or nine knots—in twenty-two minutes, that is, at the rate of 540 feet a minute, which is very little slower than the rate of paying out. A similar length of hemp line would take 2½ hours to recover, and this could only be done when the ship was stationary. In temperature soundings, however, it is unwise to trust to a single wire the weight of a series of thermometers, and for this purpose a wire cable, 2·25 mm. or about $\frac{1}{10}$ of an inch in diameter, such as H.S.H. the Prince of Monaco uses on board the *Princess Alice*, is the best.

There have been many different forms of sounders, but the one now used by the Silvertown Cable Company presents the most important features of the majority, and may be taken as a typical one. It is an adaptation of Sigsbee's sounder, and consists of a central tube $1\frac{1}{2}$ inch in diameter, fitted with valves at the top and bottom, through which the water passes as it descends, but which shut down when it reaches the bottom, and inclose a sample of the bottom water. Beneath this main tube are fixed three smaller ones, 16 inches in length and $\frac{1}{2}$ inch in diameter. These sink into the mud and bring up specimens of it for chemical analysis, to determine if the bottom would be likely to prove injurious to the cable.

The sinkers are usually elliptical in shape, so as to offer the least resistance during descent, and are 30, 40 or 60 lb. in weight according to the depth anticipated. A hole runs through them lengthways, sufficiently large to allow them to slip over the sounder, and to be suspended in that position by a looped wire of soft iron hanging from the hooked lower edge of a joint in the metal top piece of the sounder. The two edges work with a shearing action like a pair of scissors, but are kept apart, during the descent, by a small metal catch. On reaching the bottom this catch is released by the slacking of the wire, but when the line is hauled taut again for heaving up, the soft iron wire suspending the weight is cut, and the weight slips off.

Sounding wire is wound on drums 2 feet in diameter (and consequently about one fathom in circumference) in lengths of 2,000 or 4,000 fathoms as required. When first employed for this purpose the wire was not made in more than 100-fathom lengths, and thus, in a piece of 2,000 fathoms, there were nineteen joints. These joints were found to be the weak spots in a line ; but the difficulty has lately been overcome, and wire can now be drawn in continuous lengths of 7 miles without a single joint. The sounding gear on the Silvertown cable ships is at the stern, and the drum of wire rests on a metal carriage, which, for paying out, runs to the end of a platform overhanging the water, so that the wire is reeled off the drum directly into the sea. For recovery, the carriage is wheeled back inboard, and the wire is led round a pulley before reaching the drum, so as to take the direct strain off the latter. The pulley is driven by a small engine fixed on the sounding platform, and from it a belt passes up to the drum and causes it to revolve.

Attached to the drum carriage is an indicator which gives the number of the revolutions of the drum—that is, the number of fathoms paid out. At the commencement of the sounding the indicator is set at zero, and the time each hundred fathoms take in running out is noted. This interval gradually increases, owing to the increased friction of the lengthening line and the greater density of deeper water. A hand brake augments the brake power to balance the augmented weight of line paid out, so that when the sounder reaches the bottom the fact at once becomes apparent by the sudden slacking of the wire.

In sounding for a cable route it is very useful to get the temperature of the water at the bottom. A high temperature decreases, while a low temperature increases, the conductivity of the copper wire through which the electric current flows, as well as the insulation of its gutta-percha covering. In repairing a cable, the knowledge of the temperature in which it lies enables the electrician to localise the fault with much greater accuracy than if no such data were procurable. Accordingly, when taking a sounding, it is usual to lower a thermometer, attaching it to the line just above the sounder. Several kinds of thermometers are used for the purpose. In the 'capsizing thermometer' a metal frame containing the glass tube is pivoted at the bottom inside a larger frame. During descent it is kept in position by a fan screw, which the movement through the water causes to press down upon the top of it. On the line being hauled upwards, the action of the screw is reversed, and the inner frame is free to turn upside down on its pivot. Owing to a contraction in the neck of the bulb, a column of mercury, short or long according to the temperature, breaks off and falls down into the top of the thermometer, giving the temperature on a graduated scale.

Another form of this thermometer is capsized by a weight being sent down the line and falling on a lever. On one occasion a fish, whose curiosity had prompted it to inspect the strange apparatus on its arrival at the bottom, was jammed between the weight and the lever and brought lifeless to the surface. 'It seemed hard,' was the comment in the logbook of the kind-hearted naturalist who accompanied the expedition, 'that creatures living so far from the resources of civilisation should still be exposed to accidents by machinery.'

In medium depths, owing to the fact that in the sea the coldest water is always at the bottom, an ordinary maximum and minimum thermometer will serve the purpose; but in deep water, where the pressure causes an error of $8°$ to $10°$, and sometimes even bursts the thermometer, a Miller-Casella instrument is the best. The bulb of this instrument is inclosed in an outer bulb filled three-quarters full with alcohol, which is warmed so as to expel some of the air before sealing. A cushion is thus formed between the two bulbs, which takes up the pressure, so that the inner bulb remains unaffected by it.

From the point of view of submarine telegraphy, the most important object in sounding is to discover irregularities of the sea bottom, over which it would be dangerous to lay a cable. The majority of the failures of early cables was due to the fact that the ocean bed on which they were to lie had not been properly surveyed. The sea bottom between Ireland and Newfoundland at the time of the first Atlantic cable was declared by Captain Maury, U.S.N., to be a level plateau, apparently placed there by Providence to facilitate telegraphic communication between the two countries. This statement was made after only fourteen soundings, which was little more than one to every hundred miles. Inequalities of three to four hundred fathoms, sufficient to endanger the safety of a cable, might easily exist between any two such points, and subsequent survey has proved this to be often the case. No systematic soundings were made for the Lisbon-Madeira cable, but from those taken it was inferred that the average depth was 2,000 fathoms. During the laying a bank with only 100 fathoms was crossed, and the cable was suspended in a festoon and broken.

With this experience before them, the Silvertown Company determined to make a careful survey for their Cadiz-Tenerife cable. Mr. J. Y. Buchanan, F.R.S., who had been on the scientific staff of the *Challenger*, was on board the *Dacia*, and 552 soundings were taken by that ship alone. Two important banks were discovered. The first of these was a coral patch about six miles long and three and a half miles broad. Its shallowest part showed a depth of 435 fathoms. At one end there was a precipitous wall, 285 fathoms in height. Whilst sounding on this ledge the sounder struck ground at 550 fathoms, tumbled over, and struck again at 620 fathoms, and, continuing to fall, eventually found a resting-place at 835 fathoms.

The second bank at its most shallow point was only forty-nine fathoms below the surface, and also had a perpendicular wall. As this was discovered at night-time, a buoy was put over in 175 fathoms, and the ship lay by, in order to continue the work by daylight. On attempting the following morning to raise the mushroom anchor, to which the buoy was moored, the wire mooring-rope parted at seventy-five fathoms from the bottom, and was found to have been almost chafed through at that point, thus proving the existence of a rough-edged wall, at least an equal distance from the ground. In spite, however, of these numerous soundings, a fresh bank in the direct path of the cable was discovered, during the laying, by a pioneer ship, a little way ahead. It was at night, and a rocket was fired without delay. The engineer in charge of the laying ship, seeing the signal, and noting, by the dynamometer, the decreasing strain on the cable, although too late to avoid the bank, put the ship's engines full speed astern, and paid out a sufficient amount of slack cable to prevent a repetition of the accident which occurred in the Madeira-Lisbon line.

As this experience proves the impossibility, even with numerous soundings, of discovering every inequality which might prove dangerous to a cable, it becomes a question, in the case of a very long line such as the proposed Pacific, what proportion of the whole cost should be devoted to a preliminary survey. In the neighbourhood of land, careful soundings always repay the time devoted to them ; but in wide stretches of mid-ocean, where the bottom is likely to be more uniform, and where work on such an elaborate scale would be a matter of years rather than months, a much greater distance between the soundings becomes imperative. The total length of the Pacific cable route is about 7,000 nautical miles, or three times the length of an average Atlantic cable. A zigzag course, which would give three direct lines of soundings, with thirty miles between the soundings in each particular line (or, altogether, one sounding for every ten miles), would be quite sufficient for practical purposes.

An expedition which was undertaken by the Silvertown Company, to survey a cable route down the west coast of Africa, revealed some interesting facts with regard to the ocean bed in that quarter. A spot called on the Admiralty charts ' The Bottomless Pit,' lying off Little Bassam on the Ivory Coast, was explored, and a depth of 425 fathoms in close proximity to forty-seven and sixty-seven fathoms on either side of it was found. This formed, perhaps, at one time the mouth of the river Akba. Along the eastward end of the Guinea coast the descent from the hundred-fathom line is well marked, but on nearing the area influenced by the outflow of the Niger and the Congo the slope becomes abnormally gentle. Nine-tenths of the rivers of Africa empty themselves into the Gulf of Guinea, and the sand and mud brought down by them have changed the steep descent to a slowly shelving bank. The water, too, of these rivers, which drain a district remarkable for its heavy rainfall, causes the Gulf to be less salt than any other portion of ocean water in the world. While sounding off the Congo, a submarine cañon or gully two miles broad and 242 feet deep was discovered. This cañon was formed, not like a land cañon by the wearing away of the river bed, but by the heaping up of the mud brought down by the stream into banks on either side. The current was so strong here, that during soundings the ship's engines had to be kept half-speed ahead, and with a hemp line it would have been impossible to get reliable results.

The information gathered from various scientific and telegraphic expeditions goes to prove that the normal depth of the Atlantic Ocean is about 2,500 fathoms, or nearly three miles. In some parts, however, it is almost twice as deep, for off Porto Rico in the West Indies, the *Blake*, belonging to the United States Navy, found a depth of 4,561 fathoms, or nearly five and a quarter miles. One of the deepest cables in the Atlantic is that of the South American Company, which in one part, between Senegal and the Island of Fernando Noronha, lies in 2,830 fathoms, or a little more than three miles. When laying a line in this depth it is calculated that, with the ship steaming at eight knots an hour, the length of cable from the stern of the ship to the spot where it touches the ground is over twenty-five miles, and that it takes a particular point in the cable more than two hours and a half to reach the bottom from the time that it first enters the water. The deepest sounding yet recorded was taken early in the present year by H.M.S. *Penguin* in the South Eastern Pacific, about 550 miles to the north-west of New Zealand. This gave 5,155 fathoms, or a depth of nearly six miles.

As a result of these numerous surveys, much valuable information has been obtained with regard to the configuration of ocean beds. Contrary to the opinion formerly held, the bottom of the sea does not present so many striking irregularities as the surface of the earth. Except for islands of volcanic origin and some coral patches, the bed of the Atlantic is an undulating plain of fairly uniform flatness, and may be better compared to a tray with a sharply ascending rim than to a basin. The slope of the land, as a general rule, is continued out into the sea until it reaches a depth of about 100 fathoms, and then increases rapidly to 1,500 and 2,000 fathoms, reaching finally the normal depth of 2,500 fathoms. The area between the 100-fathom line and the shore—usually known as the continental platform—is really submerged land, and if the sea level were suddenly lowered to that extent, England would be connected by dry land to Denmark, Holland, Belgium, France, Ireland, Orkney, and Shetland. Nearly the whole of the North Sea, with the exception of some of the Norwegian fiords, would be laid bare, while the coast of Ireland would be extended 100 miles to the westward. On the other hand, the raising of the sea level to the extent of 100 fathoms would put a large portion of Europe under water, as, indeed, has been several times the case with that continent. Not only in the Atlantic, but in the Pacific, on the west coast of North America especially, the continental platform rises abruptly from the margins of the real oceanic depressed areas, and this phenomenon is one of the strongest arguments in favour of the theory of the permanence of the great ocean beds.

When the Atlantic first came to be sounded in a scientific manner in the course of the *Challenger* expedition, the result, after the great depths previously reported, was generally felt to be disappointing. Sir C. Wyville Thomson,[2] indeed, who was chief of the scientific staff, subsequently described that ocean, with its average of 2,000 fathoms, as a 'thin shell of water.' When, however, it is remembered that over large areas the depth is at least 2,500 fathoms, or 15,000 feet—the height of Mont Blanc—and that in one place a sounding gave 4,561 fathoms, or 27,366 feet—only 2,000 feet less than Mount Everest, the highest point in the world—his expression appears decidedly misleading. The sea level may, in fact, be taken as the relief equator of the globe, almost equidistant from the highest land elevation and the lowest depths of the sea. But while the average height of the land is only 1,000 feet, the average depth of the water is 13,000 feet. Hence an enormous disproportion exists between the mass of land above sea level and the volume of water beneath it. Taking the area of the sea in comparison to the land as $2\frac{3}{4}$ to 1, and multiplying by thirteen, the number of times by

---

[2] Sir Wyville Thomson, who died in 1882, was succeeded in his work by Dr. John Murray, F.R.S., who is responsible for all the volumes containing the reports of this expedition.

which it exceeds it in depth, we find that the total volume of ocean water is thirty-six times the volume of the land above sea level.

But although the ocean bed has some depths almost equal to the highest mountains, it is, as a whole, much more uniform than the land. In the Atlantic, for instance, as already stated, only a few volcanic islands break the regularity of the level plateau at the bottom. Near to the land the sea bottom, as a rule, reproduces the leading features of the coast, and on these depends the distance of the 100-fathom line from the shore. Thus the low east coast of England is subtended by the shallow sandbanks of the North Sea, while the precipitous mountains of Norway find their counterpart in the great depth of its fiords.

Ocean deposits may be arranged according to the depth at which they are found in the following manner :

(1) Shore deposits.

(2) Pteropod ooze.

(3) Globigerina ooze.

(4) Grey ooze.

(5) Red clay.

(6) Radiolarian and Diatom ooze.

The area of shore deposits is, as Professor Geikie has pointed out, the marginal belt of sea floor skirting the land. The sand and mud brought down by rivers sink to the bottom long before they reach the real ocean depths. The Gulf of Guinea is an exceptional case, and the matter brought down in suspension by its numerous rivers can be traced to a distance of nearly 200 miles out to seaward, and to a depth of 1,600 fathoms. Indeed, off the Congo River shore mud has been found 600 miles from its mouth, and in a depth of 3,000 fathoms. But, as a rule, shore deposits rarely extend beyond the 100-fathom line, and their discovery at greater distances has usually been shown to be due to exceptional agencies. Thus some sand brought up from deep soundings off the north-west coast of Africa was proved to have been carried out to sea by the Harmattan, a powerful and extremely dry wind blowing from the desert of Sahara, and bearing with it a fine dust in such large quantities as to throw a plentiful deposit on the decks of vessels 200 or 300 miles from land.

Pteropod and globigerina oozes are formed from the remains of the shells of the small marine organisms which bear those names. The former is not found at greater depths than 1,500 fathoms, and the latter than 2,500 fathoms, owing to the amount of free carbonic acid gas in the water increasing with the depth, and dissolving their delicate shells of carbonate of lime. These oozes are the best for the purposes of submarine telegraphy. They are so yielding that the cable becomes embedded in them, and their presence is a guarantee against strong under-currents, the scouring effects of which have been traced to a depth of 1,000 fathoms. Shore deposits, on the other hand, are often very injurious to the sheathing wires of a cable, owing to the iodine contained in seaweed and decaying vegetable matter, which is known to corrode iron rapidly.

Grey ooze is intermediary between globigerina ooze and red clay, and is evidently a mixture of the two. Red clay itself is formed by the decomposition of pumice-stone, and from minerals containing felspar. The action of the waves washes pumice-stone off volcanic rocks, and, being lighter than water, it floats for a long time on the surface of the sea. Towing nets invariably inclose large quantities when lowered in mid-ocean. Some may also be derived from submarine volcanic disturbances; but whether this is the case or no, it is certain that the red clay deposit formed by it accumulates very slowly. This is proved by the frequent presence of meteoric iron in this deposit. 'I know of no recent discovery in physical geography,' says Professor Geikie, 'more calculated to impress deeply the imagination than the testimony of this meteoric iron from the most distant abysses of the ocean. To be told that mud gathers on the floor of these abysses at an extremely slow rate conveys but a vague notion of the tardiness of the process. But to be told that it gathers so slowly that the very star dust from outer space forms an appreciable part of it, brings home to us, as nothing else could do, the idea of undisturbed and excessively slow accumulation.'

In the red clay are found nodules of almost pure peroxide of manganese, collected round some hard centre like a shark's tooth or a whale's earbone. Curiously enough, no other parts of the structure of large marine animals are recovered from the bottom; but the two just mentioned occur in great abundance, no fewer than 600 shark's teeth and 100 carbones of whales having been brought up on one occasion in a single haul of the dredge. More striking still is the fact that no fossil remains, no portion of a ship, nor any article of human manufacture, has ever been retrieved from the depths of the ocean. A satisfactory explanation of this problem has yet to be forthcoming.

Red clay is deposited in 2,500 to 3,000 fathoms, and beyond that depth Radiolarian and Diatom ooze is found. This ooze is composed of the skeletons of the Radiolaria, or star-shaped organisms, and of the cases of the vegetable Diatoms. As these are of siliceous formation, they are impervious to the action of carbonic acid gas, which dissolves the shells of the Pteropods and Globigerinæ. Diatoms are classed as vegetables owing to their structure, and their mode of reproduction, which is by self-division of the cell. Although individually so small as to be quite invisible to the naked eye, they often occur in such large masses as to give the sea a deep red hue. Mr. J. Y. Buchanan, in the course of his voyage with the *Buccaneer* on the west coast of Africa, passed through a number of 'Diatom banks, one of which was 200 miles long and forty to fifty fathoms deep.

Although the water at the surface was so strongly tinged with red that wide expanses of it could be seen for several miles from the ship, the tow net at the surface recovered very few specimens of the Diatom. When lowered, however, for only a few minutes to a depth of ten fathoms, it came up glutted with a mass of these highly coloured organisms. If they had been present to the same extent on the surface, the water must have acquired a colour as vivid as that of fresh arterial blood.

But the most widely distributed organisms in the upper stratum of ocean water are the larvæ of crustacea, or certain kinds of shell fish in the earlier stages of their development. These larvæ go through a process of diurnal migration, rising to the surface as daylight disappears, and sinking again as it returns, in order to remain in perpetual gloom. Gatherings with a tow net at the surface are consequently always richer at night than during the day. Large catches, however, can be made in daylight by fishing at a depth of fifteen to thirty fathoms. These few vertical fathoms through which the larvæ pass represent climatic changes of some thousands of miles horizontally at the surface ; for at night on the surface they live in water heated to 80° or 85°, while during the day, at a depth of only twenty fathoms, they have to put up with a temperature of 55° to 65°.

As a result of his scientific investigations on board the *Lightning* and the *Porcupine*, Sir C. Wyville Thomson wrote in 1873 : ' The fauna of the deep sea are more rich and varied, and have organisms in many cases more elaborately and delicately formed, and more exquisitely beautiful in their soft shades of colouring and in the rainbow tints of their wonderful phosphorescence, than the fauna of the well-known belt of shallow water which fringes the land.' But later researches have proved that this description is only true of deep-sea animals on the outskirts of the great ocean basins, for the farther they wander from shallow water, the poorer they become. The conditions under which they have to live in the abysmal areas seem very unfavourable to animal existence. The temperature at the bottom of the ocean is nearly down to freezing point, and sometimes actually below it. There is a total absence of light, as far as sunlight is concerned, and there is an enormous pressure, reckoned at about one ton to the square inch in every 1,000 fathoms, which is 160 times greater than that of the atmosphere we live in. At 2,500 fathoms the pressure is thirty times more powerful than the steam pressure of a locomotive when drawing a train. As late as 1880 a leading zoologist explained the existence of deep-sea animals at such depths by assuming that their bodies were composed of solids and liquids of great density, and contained no air. This, however, is not the case with deep-sea fish, which are provided with air-inflated swimming bladders. If one of these fish, in full chase after its prey, happens to ascend beyond a certain level, its bladder becomes distended with the decreased pressure, and carries it, in spite of all its efforts, still higher in its course. In fact, members of this unfortunate class are liable to become victims to the unusual accident of falling upwards, and no doubt meet with a violent death soon after leaving their accustomed level, and long before their bodies reach the surface in a distorted and unnatural state. Even ground sharks, brought up from a depth of no more than 500 fathoms, expire before they gain the surface.

The fauna of the deep sea—with a few exceptions hitherto only known as fossils—are new and specially modified forms of families and genera inhabiting shallow waters in modern times, and have been driven down to the depths of the ocean by their more powerful rivals in the battle of life, much as the ancient Britons were compelled to withdraw to the barren and inaccessible fastnesses of Wales. Some of their organs have undergone considerable modification in correspondence to the changed conditions of their new habitats. Thus down to 900 fathoms their eyes have generally become enlarged, to make the best of the faint light which may possibly penetrate there. After 1,000 fathoms these organs are either still further enlarged or so greatly reduced that in some species they disappear altogether and are replaced by enormously long feelers. The only light at great depths which would enable large eyes to be of any service is the phosphorescence given out by deep-sea animals. We know that at the surface this light is often very powerful, and Sir Wyville Thomson has recorded one occasion on which the sea at night was ' a perfect blaze of phosphorescence, so strong that lights and shadows were thrown on the sails and it was easy to read the smallest print.' It is thought possible by several naturalists that certain portions of the sea bottom may be as brilliantly illumined by this sort of light as the streets of a European city after sunset. Some deep-sea fish have two parallel rows of small circular phosphorescent ·organs running along the whole length of their bodies, and as they glide through the dark waters of the profound abysses they must look like model mailships with rows of shining portholes.

It was at one time held that the temperature of the ocean never descended lower than 39° Fahr., but this unfounded assumption was disproved by the *Challenger* expedition. As low a temperature as 27° has been obtained in the South Atlantic in the neighbourhood of icebergs. The freezing point of salt water is 25° Fahr., and the fact that it contracts steadily down to freezing point instead of expanding again like fresh water when within 4° of it, causes the coldest water to sink always to the bottom. In a sounding of 2,900 fathoms taken in the South Atlantic, the bottom temperature was 32°, and the last 1,000 fathoms might be described as absolutely glacial. The second 1,000 fathoms consisted of water from 32° to 36½°, and in the course of the next 500 fathoms the temperature rose to 40°. The remaining 400 fathoms constituted the warm upper stratum of water, 40° being the limit at which the sun's rays exert any direct heating influence.

In the North Atlantic no lower temperature than 35° is found, and the warm stratum, instead of being only 400 fathoms, is 800 or 900 fathoms deep. One reason for this comparatively high temperature is that a ridge runs at the bottom of the sea right across the ocean from Greenland to Norway, rising above the surface to form Iceland. This ridge is of such a height that the deeper and colder parts of the Arctic basin are unable to communicate with the North Atlantic. Dr. Nansen states that the soundings taken by the *Fram*, whilst drifting with the ice, gave a depth of between 1,600 and 1,900 fathoms, and he thinks that the whole Polar Basin should be considered as a continuation of the deep channel which runs between Spitzbergen and Greenland from what he calls the North Atlantic Ocean. In Norwegian charts the North Atlantic may reach as far as Spitzbergen, instead of terminating, as in English charts, at the latitude of Iceland. But as the Doctor's words are liable to misinterpretation, it is as well to point out that no deep channel exists connecting the Arctic Ocean with the main portion of the North Atlantic Ocean.

The increased depth of the warm stratum is also due to the fact that the waters of tropical latitudes have been heated by the Gulf Stream or Florida current. The Gulf Stream itself dies out in mid-Atlantic, losing its movement, warmth, and deep colour, and becoming mere surface drift. But the ocean water it has heated, gaining a greater specific gravity under the evaporating action of the dry trade winds, sinks downwards, and, mingling with the cooler water below, extends the depth of the warm stratum to 800 or 900 fathoms. The warm stratum is then carried northward by the vertical circulation of the ocean, the cold bottom water from the poles rising near the equator, and the warm surface water from the equator sinking near the poles. This action is attested by the fact that the plane of 40° of temperature rises at the equator from 700 to only 300 fathoms from the surface.

To the vertical circulation of ocean water North-western Europe owes its climate. Without it, England would be subject to the same low temperature as Labrador, and all the Norwegian harbours would be ice-blocked. The temperature of the atmosphere at the North Cape, in Norway, is 14½° below zero, while the temperature of the sea is several degrees above it. The great thickness of the warm stratum enables it to resist for a long time the cold air of northern latitudes, and below the cold ice-water covering the surface of the Polar Sea Dr. Nansen found a deep layer of warmer and salter water, which still preserved a temperature of one degree above freezing-point. The Pacific Ocean, owing to its wider area and to the absence of any such heating agency as the Gulf Stream, is filled to a very large extent with water of glacial or sub-glacial coldness. Surface temperatures taken on the

(1) The abysmal area, from 1,000 fathoms below the sea level downwards.

(2) The transitional area, from 1,000 fathoms below the sea level upwards to the sea level. .

(3) The continental area, including all dry land.

For practical purposes the sea level may be taken as a constant figure, although, even in the same latitudes of one and the same ocean it is not always the same distance from the centre of the globe. The waters of the ocean are attracted by the proximity of huge land ridges, just as the water in a glass is drawn up at the edges. It is . calculated that the surface of the Pacific Ocean is 2,000 feet nearer the earth's centre at the Sandwich Islands than on the coast of Peru. At the present epoch the sea level stands at such a height in the transitional area that its rise or fall would flood or lay bare the largest surface of land. ·If the level rose only 100 fathoms, fourteen million square miles of land would be submerged. If it sank to the same extent, ten million square miles would be exposed. The enormous disproportion between the mean height of the land and the mean depth of the ocean makes it impossible to believe that the land at present above the sea level has ever formed the bottom of oceans as deep and vast as those now existing, a very moderate upheaval of which would suffice to bring about a universal deluge.

ARCHER P. CROUCH.

SOME PEKING POLITICIANS

It is a matter of common knowledge in China that Li Hungchang, when deprived of his viceroyalty and ordered to Peking, was compelled to distribute among the Court officials and others no less a sum than eight million taels, equivalent to about one million sterling, in order to protect himself against the attacks of his political enemies. With the exception of the vastness of the amount there was nothing unusual in this proceeding, as Li has the best reason for knowing, for as a matter of fact he has at stated intervals been long in the habit of paying a very heavy tax on his many incomings to satisfy the cravings of the voracious distributors of patronage at Peking.

The East is the home of bribery and corruption, and probably in no country have these become so generally recognised a feature of official life as in China.   There they flourish and abound, unchecked by morality and uninterfered with by the chief authorities, except on rare occasions when threatened *exposés* compel the Emperor to assume the appearance of virtuous indignation.   It is true that in other Oriental countries, from Eastern Europe to Korea, they exist as part of the natural order of things : the pashas of Turkey exact all that they safely can from the fellaheen, just as Korean mandarins eke out their scanty pay from the tills of the merchants and shopkeepers within their jurisdiction ; but it has been reserved to China to add a refinement to this universal system of extortion by providing a class which fattens on the illegal gains of their brethren in office.

By the political constitution of the country the Emperor is assisted in the administration of the Empire by a host of Ministers, secretaries, and subordinates.   To these must be added a vast crowd of palace officials, all of whom are poorly paid, and who, like their *confrères* in the provinces, are dependent on what they can exact from others to support the necessary dignity of their offices.   But compared with their provincial colleagues these are at a distinct disadvantage. In a provincial government every member of the hierarchy of officials, from the viceroy down to the lowest district magistrate, exercises sway over a greater or less extent of territory.   The wealthier the people within his jurisdiction the better for him.   A rich man is, for several reasons, more easily amenable to pressure than a less well-to-do one. Apart from the fact that he has more funds at his command, he is naturally less willing to encounter the danger of official wrath, which too often brings in its train imprisonment and torture, than one who is inured to hardship by a needy mode of life. He has also a position to maintain, which would suffer loss by the infliction of any indignity, and, further, it is always within the power of the mandarins so to interfere with the prosecution of his business as considerably to check any future accumulation of wealth.

All this is part of the acknowledged system, for which, though bad in every way, there is undoubtedly some excuse to be made. The official incomes of the mandarins

are not sufficient, even with the exercise of the severest economy, to provide for the necessary expenses pertaining to their offices. So fully recognised is this fact that in addition to his legal salary each mandarin receives an anti-extortion allowance, which in most cases is about thirty times as large as his salary. Even with this addition, however, the incomes are disproportionately low, and are quite inadequate to support the dignity of the service. The viceroy of a province, for example, receives about 6,000*l.* a year, a sum which does not do much more than pay the countless clerks, secretaries, messengers, and hangers-on who crowd his Yamên, and all of whom are entirely dependent on his private purse.

In such conditions it has surpassed the wit of Chinamen to find more than one way out of the difficulty. The mandarins must live and the people must pay. Many centuries have so moulded the views and ideas of both oppressed and oppressors that they have been led to regard the existing system as a natural dispensation of Providence, and it is only when the screw is put on beyond the point of endurance that the people consider themselves entitled to complain.

That the wealth often accumulated by provincial officials is enormous there is abundant evidence to show. The fact that Li was, as mentioned above, able to pay down a million sterling and to remain a man of immense wealth speaks for itself. Li entered on official life with nothing, or less than nothing, for he probably had to borrow money to buy his first appointment. Fifty years in the public service have thus enabled him to accumulate a fortune which in the richest countries would be called colossal. Not every one, however, is either able or willing to turn an official career to so very practical a purpose. Li and his brother, the late viceroy of the two Kwang provinces, have earned for themselves an unenviable notoriety for the acquisition of other people's wealth. Not long ago a censor memorialised the Throne on the subject, and drew a striking comparison between the disinterested honesty of a certain viceroy, Tso Tsungt'ang, and the grasping avarice of the Li brothers. The memorial was published in the official *Peking Gazette*, which serves in China the same useful purpose that the London *Gazette* does among ourselves. Nothing appears in its columns without the sanction of the Government, and its utterances acquire, therefore, a greater significance than would be the case were they to appear in the columns of an ordinary newspaper. Hence the censor's accusations are noteworthy, and he frames his charges in these words :—

> The brothers Li have grown wealthy from the proceeds of several tens of years of viceregal power, and the money spent by them to purchase official rank for their sons and nephews is but as grains from well-filled granaries or as drops from the ocean's expanse. . . . If we bring Li to Tso's side and compare the two, if we notice the immense wealth, the power and influence of the scions of the Li and Ts'ên clans (Ts'ên was another offender), and then look at the honest poverty of the more illustrious Tso, it would not take much shrewdness or farsightedness to judge who has been the more honest to the Throne and the greater patriot to his country.

The vast body of provincial officials are probably neither so grasping as the Lis nor so pure-handed as the redoubtable Tso; but they one and all recognise the advantage which they enjoy of having districts to govern and people on the spot to squeeze. The Peking officials are not so happily situated. They have no local jurisdiction, and consequently have no rich merchants or shopkeepers on whom they can draw to supply their wants. Other victims have, therefore, to be found, and just as in nature the devourers of small animals and insects become in their turn the food of larger creatures, so the provincial magnates are called upon to provide support for the members of the central Government. One, and a most unfortunate, result of this general system is that the superior attractions of the provinces induce all the more able and ambitious mandarins to seek service outside the capital, and the direction of the central Government is thus left mainly in the hands of reactionary and less enterprising officials. In all other countries the ablest men are chosen to advise their sovereigns in council, but in Chinese topsy-turveydom the process is reversed, and while the provincial satraps are as a rule able and energetic men, whatever else they may be, the Ministers at Peking are for the most part men who have no other claim to their positions than that of having brought themselves to the notice of the Emperor by the profession of cheap patriotism and ultra-Confucianist views.

Politically the effect of this result is unfortunate, and as regards foreign relations disastrous. The members of the Tsungli Yamên, whose duty it is to transact all foreign business, are composed, with the exception of Li Hungchang, who has been lately appointed to the office, of men whose circle of knowledge is confined almost entirely to the limits of the Empire. They know nothing of the geography or history of foreign countries, and are utterly ignorant of the relative strength and importance of the European nations. Their geographical knowledge has hardly advanced beyond that primitive stage in which China is represented as occupying the greater part of the earth's surface, while all other nations appear as satellites dancing attendance on the Heavenly Empire. This is bad enough, but the most hopeless feature of the position is that, though their ignorance is stupendous, they have no desire to learn better.

It is no exaggeration to say that the vast majority of those who rule the destinies of China have not advanced one step in the direction of progressive ideas since the establishment of the legations at Peking, nearly forty years ago. If the representatives of the foreign Powers could speak out they would have a dismal tale to tell of the obstructive incompetency and the idle impertinences of the officials of the Tsungli Yamên. To men of high-bred culture visits to the Yamên are hours of torture. The mandarins take a delight in flouting and irritating them by all the countless tricks of which Chinamen are past masters, and the more important the business in hand the more trivial are the subjects which they choose to discuss to the exclusion of it.

It is a well-known fact that in 1874 a war between China and Japan on the subject of Formosa was averted by the wisdom and friendly benevolence of the late Sir Thomas Wade. By a happy chance he became, late one afternoon, aware of the terms which would satisfy Japan, and without a moment's hesitation he determined to call at the house of one of the most enlightened members of the Yamên, to put him in possession of the facts. The official in question received him courteously, and undertook that the Japanese terms should be accepted by the Government if Sir Thomas would induce the Japanese minister, who was in the act of leaving Peking, to reopen negotiations. Pleased at the success of his endeavours, Sir Thomas called at the Yamên on the following morning, naturally expecting to be received with cordiality by the representatives of a nation which he had saved from the consequences of a disastrous war. The ministers present, however, made no reference to his friendly intervention, and talked of the weather, the kind of tea they were drinking, and other equally trivial matters, without giving their visitor a chance of broaching the serious topic of the day. This went on for some half-hour or more, until Sir Thomas, losing patience, asked whether they had not heard of his negotiations of the previous day and the happy result which had been arrived at. They answered 'yes, they had,' and there the matter ended for the moment. They in no way acknowledged the inestimable service which had been rendered them; and nothing further would have been said on the subject had not the official on whom Sir Thomas had called the day before chanced to come in, when he repeated the thanks to which he had already given expression. This same policy of tantalising impertinence is pursued now, as then, and at the present moment the anti-foreign element is more than usually rampant at the capital. The man who has the main direction of affairs is a certain Wêng, the quondam tutor of the Emperor and a Confucianist of the Confucianists. For some years he has exercised considerable influence over the Emperor, and has been a consistent opponent of Li Hungchang and all his works.

Au fond the two men are more nearly allied on foreign politics than might be supposed. On the question of principle they are at one, and it is only a matter of policy which divides them. Li Hungchang is an opportunist, and in order to gain his ends would make concessions from which Wêng would turn away his head in disgust. It is well known that with all Li's glib utterances on the question of reforms he is in accord with Wêng in his ultimate opinion of foreigners, and if it were possible again to close the Empire against the 'outer barbarians' Li would be the first to advocate the measure. He shares also in an eminent degree the settled conviction of his countrymen that as regards wisdom and culture they are the salt of the earth. As he remarked to a friend in speaking of the late disasters which have befallen the Empire, 'it would perhaps be a good thing if we were not so scholarly-minded as we are.' He recognises that in mechanical matters Europeans are superior to his countrymen, but there he considers the advantage ceases, and if in his opinion learning exists at all in Europe, it is of a kind that is beneath contempt. But there are undoubtedly those who regard Li as an enlightened statesman in comparison with Wêng. He at least, such hold, recognises that in one direction his countrymen are the inferiors of the 'outer barbarians,' and he has always been ready to give a practical expression to his belief by making use of foreigners in the services under his control. This is true enough, but it represents the full extent of his liberalism. It is noticeable that in Europe he uttered not a single word about the necessity of administrative reforms in China, which lie at the root of every true reform and of even every real mechanical advance in the Empire. Judging from his words, his main desire, and a very natural one in the circumstances, seems to have been to be brought into closer relations with European financiers, and lest this should appear to be too bald an avowal he took care to express at the same time his approval of the introduction of railways into China. Wêng and his friends, on the other hand, would have none of these things. China, they contend, has got on very well for many thousand years without foreign inventions, and they see no need for their introduction now. Their national conceit covers them as with a garment, and they have no compliments to exchange with foreigners or the friends of foreigners. To such a length does the bitter feeling go in Peking that no mandarin ventures to associate with the European representatives, except in the most formal and frigid manner; and natives in foreign employ are afraid to take any notice of their masters in the street, lest they should draw down upon themselves the wrath of the people. No foreigner has ever been entertained socially in the house of any member of the Tsungli Yamên, and, except on the rare occasions when the Emperor has granted audiences to the foreign representatives, no European has ever been admitted within the walls of the Forbidden City. Until lately the reactionary tendency of the Yamên has been tempered by the presence of Grand Secretary Sun, a comparatively enlightened Minister, who has always been anxious to do what he could to promote the real interests of the Empire. In the questions which have arisen between his Government and the foreign representatives he has ever shown a reasonable and conciliatory spirit, and was consequently brought into frequent collision with the Wêng clique. But, as no real charge could be brought against him, he survived their animosity until the conclusion of the Shimonoseki treaty, when the conflict was brought to an issue. Sun, like a true patriot, associated himself with Li in the support of the treaty and advocated its ratification. Wêng and his friends, on the other hand, in their blind ignorance, were prepared rather to wreck their country than acknowledge their defeat at the hands of the despised Wojên, and fought tooth and nail against the proposal. As is well known, Sun and Li carried their point, and the treaty which saved their country from disasters even greater than those which had already befallen it duly received the Emperor's sanction. But, though defeated as to the main issue, Wêng carried on the war to the knife, and unfortunately with such success that, as the *Peking Gazette* lately announced, Sun has been obliged to retire into private life, a step which it was well known had become necessary to protect himself against the personal attacks of his antagonists.

Such are the men who are now guiding the destinies of the Empire, and these are they who, together with the Dowager Empress, the Imperial Princes, and countless palace officials, are able, by the weight of their authority and influence, to dispose of the characters and fortunes of the provincial magnates, who, accepting the position, are willing to purchase their favours by large and continual bribes. Readers of the *Peking Gazette* are familiar with the edicts in which mandarins who have filled fat posts in the provinces are frequently ordered to present themselves before the Throne. To the uninitiated it might appear as though this were intended to be a compliment, but the recipients of the Imperial rescripts know only too well the real meaning of their master's commands. By the nice adjustment of a sliding scale of 'squeezes' the amount which each individual visitor to the capital should be expected to disgorge is perfectly well ascertained, and in the practised hands of the Pekingese officials care is taken to abstract the amount to the last tael.

The repugnance which Li Hungchang has always shown to enter the gates of Peking has been mainly due to the prospect of such a process as that through which he has lately passed. By a tacit arrangement it was agreed that he should only be called upon to visit the capital once in four years, that interval being considered long enough to enable him to accumulate a sufficient surplus to gratify the desires of his hosts.   No such limit, however, was imposed on the frequency of his contributions to the coffers of the Dowager Empress, and during his viceroyalty he poured countless sums into the exchequer of that masterful lady.   In return, according to common rumour, he has unquestionably received good measure, pressed down and running over; for through good report and evil report she has invariably supported him by her influence, and though she has not been able to save him from disgrace, she has succeeded in breaking his falls and has prevented his being trodden underfoot by his enemies. But not only are the coming guests welcomed, but the parting guests are speeded on their way by similar kind attentions.   It is almost as temporarily ruinous to a man's pocket to receive an appointment as it is to return to Peking after the occupancy of a fat post.   So completely is this system looked upon as a matter of course that it is part of the ordinary business of the native bankers to advance the money required by penniless aspirants to office.   Not long since a well-known official found that he was expected to pay nearly a million sterling for his appointment to a rich charge.   Having no means of his own, he betook himself, after the usual custom, to the bankers, who formed a syndicate to supply the amount.   In due time the money was paid and the official entered upon his duties.   Unfortunately the bankers, possessed with a vaulting ambition to recoup themselves at the earliest possible date, pressed unreasonably for the return of their money.   In vain the mandarin set all the usual machinery at work to gather in the spoils; and so increasingly exacting became his creditors that he was driven to make the fatal mistake of out-heroding Herod in his demands for illegal taxes.   For a time the people possessed their souls in patience, but at length the point of endurance was passed, and a loud outcry against his avarice and cruelty went up to the Throne, with such circumstance and persistency that the Emperor was obliged to remove him from his post.   The dismissal of this man was an unmixed good.   The people were relieved from an intolerable tyranny ; and the man himself was punished for his misdeeds.   As to his bankers, it is unnecessary to waste compassion on them for the loss of their money, more especially as they have since doubtless repaid themselves by later and better conducted enterprises.

In every practice, however bad, it is possible to find some trace of good, and we cannot deny that even this iniquitous system has one small advantage.   It unquestionably exercises, as a rule, a moderating influence upon the conduct of the mandarins.   Men who have given such substantial hostages to fortune are less likely to commit themselves to any act which might interfere with their official careers than those who have no such restraining motive.   Admitting that corruption is inevitable, it is well that this pecuniary obligation should serve as an additional inducement to them so to act as to retain their offices until at least the completion of the three years term. The test of good government which is accepted at Peking is neither stringent nor heart-searching. If no widespread complaints are made, if order is preserved, and if the voice of the turtle is heard in the land, the presiding official is accepted as one who is worthy of further employment. The main object of every mandarin is, therefore, to keep his subjects quiet, and, as the case above quoted shows, this desirable state of things is plainly inconsistent with excessive extortion. Mean though the motive is, the necessity of repaying the debt incurred in the purchase of office superinduces a moderate attitude on the part of the mandarins, and puts a check on any unusual display of avarice. So far the people are gainers.

But it is still more patent that the widespread corruption is an almost insuperable obstacle to the introduction of reforms into the administration of the Empire. In a system by which there are vast potentialities for accumulating wealth, and where no shame attaches to the employment of official pilfering, it is impossible to suppose that the body of men whose sordid interests it so effectually serves would be willing to enact a self-denying ordinance to the detriment of their own pockets. The absence of all public opinion in China makes it hopeless to expect that a movement in the direction of peaceful reform can ever emanate from the people. Any progressive action, therefore, must be initiated by the official classes, and these are the last people in the world who would ever attempt to overthrow a system from which they derive so great and direct advantages. The only means by which reforms can be introduced with any chance of success is by so arranging that they should redound to the pecuniary gain of the central Government. The one enlightened measure which is credited to the Empire within the last forty years has been the establishment of the customs service, which is now doing such excellent work under the guidance of Sir Robert Hart. Having begun in a small way, this service now collects a revenue of over 22,000,000[1] taels, every tael of which is accounted for to the Imperial Exchequer. Blind to principle, and completely ignorant of political morality, it would have been hopeless to have induced the Government to adopt the innovation if it had not been possible to convince them of the very practical advantage which would acrue to the Peking Treasury from its acceptance. Under the old arrangement the custom dues were levied by the provincial authorities, who kept the lion's share for themselves and forwarded the surplus to the capital. The extraction of such substantial illegal gains from the pockets of these hereditary peculators was long and bitterly resented, and the proposal that the Foreign Service should collect the duties payable on cargoes carried in native craft as well as in foreign ships was successfully resisted. If when the success of the system by which foreign duties are collected by foreigners has become so plain and palpable it has been found impossible to extend the arrangement to the collection of native duties, it seems hopeless to expect that any widespread system of reform in the administration of the province can ever be introduced. This becomes the more plain when it is recollected that, while the principal men whose incomes were affected by the custom-house reform might be almost counted on the fingers of two hands, any general reorganisation would affect the incomes of every mandarin serving outside the capital. The opposition to it would be, therefore, overwhelming, and any prospect of its institution must be relegated *ad calendas Græcas.*

The only possible directions in which progress can at the present time be made in China are those which can be brought about by the introduction of railways and the opening of mines, and we have lately been informed by Li Hungchang that his whole weight, whatever that may be, will be thrown in their favour. Such utterances as Li favoured us with are easily made, and when it is expected that they will serve the useful purpose of supplying a *quid pro quo* in the shape of favours to be granted to China, we can readily understand his desire to give them publicity. But to make railways—to take their case first—in China is no easy matter. The same obstacle which makes administrative reforms impossible makes the construction of railways in the ordinary way next to impossible. Money is wanted for their construction, and this, putting aside the idea of a foreign loan, can only be obtained from the wealthy non-official classes. But these sections of the community know as well as others that to hand over money to the officials for the construction of railways is as futile a proceeding, except in so far as the advantage to the mandarins is concerned, as throwing it into the sea.

Two edicts have of late been issued on the subject, and both aptly illustrate the state of affairs described above. The first, which appeared last year, approved in principle of the construction of railways generally, and especially of a trunk line from Hankow, on the Yangtsze Kiang, to Peking. The edict was evidently designed to allay the fears likely to be entertained by possible shareholders that the management of the line would drift into the hands of the mandarins. 'We grant,' wrote the Emperor in condescending terms, 'the privilege of building the line to wealthy men and rich merchants of the various provinces, such as shall be able to show a capital of ten million taels and above, in shares or otherwise;' and he also points out the advantages which were likely to accrue to them from the increased traffic and the easy as well as speedy transmission of goods. At the same time they are assured that, as the line will 'be a purely commercial affair, the Government officials shall not interfere either with the gains or losses of the said company.'

This benevolent pronouncement fell flat. The mercantile communities have had some experience of mandarin-managed mercantile and while considerable sums found their way into the pockets of promoters and official managers, the shareholders were left with only small dividends with which to console themselves. ' Once bit twice shy ' is a saying which has full force in China, and the invitation offered by the Chinese Imperial spider to the non-official fly to walk into his parlour was declined with thanks. This proposal having failed, the Emperor and his advisers are endeavouring to gain their end by other means. A second edict has now been issued, in which it is stated that a loan of 30,000,000 taels has been raised in America for the construction of the line, and that, *mirabile dictu*, Shêng Taotai is to be the manager of the undertaking. It would have been bad enough to have put a mandarin of ordinary good character into the post, but to name Shêng for the office is to insure all the worst traditions of mandarin rule. Shêng is a man who has basked in the sunshine of Li Hung-chang's favour, and who, like his patron, has filled his pockets from the proceeds of every undertaking with which he had been connected. It is notorious that at the outbreak of the war between China and Japan Shêng was commissioned to buy in Europe rifles and ammunition for the campaign. The result is well known. The weapons proved to be next to valueless. But, as it turned out, this was of no great importance, for the ammunition provided was so ill adapted for the purpose that it is difficult to imagine circumstances under which they could have been of any use. At the time he was dismissed from his office with contumely. But he is an able man and is well versed in the art of using his ill-gotten gains to smooth the way to future enterprises. The length of the line from Hankow to Peking is 700 miles. If the amount of the loan which is said to have been contracted in America is correct, it would give an average of between 5,000l. and 6,000l. per mile. This ought to be ample for the purpose, and we shall wait with some curiosity the fate of an undertaking which at least promises such excellent results for Shêng's pocket. Judging from the analogy of the one existing railway in China—that from Tientsin to Shanhai Kwan—the line will be proceeded with so long as the money lasts, or until the funds are wanted for some other purpose. During the preparations for the celebration of the Dowager Empress's sixtieth birthday it was found necessary to stop the laying of the Tientsin line, as the sums allotted for the purpose were wanted for the decorations of the Peking streets. *Ex uno disce omnes*, and with Shêng at the prow and Li at the helm it is possible that it will often be found necessary to divert portions of the funds in several directions.[1]

---

[1] Since the above was in type a further secret edict has, according to a Reuter telegram, been issued, in which the sum required for railways has been raised from 30,000,000 taels to 40,000,000, twenty millions of which are to be ' furnished by the

The future of the mining industry in China shares the unfortunate condition of the railways.   There is probably no other country in the world which conceals beneath its surface such rich mineral deposits as China.   Every mineral from coal to gold exists in profusion, and might be a source of boundless wealth to the Empire.   But here again official interference acts as a blight on all enterprise, and a recent attempt to open mines in the rich province of Szech'uen shows that the mandarins are as determined as ever to keep a tight hold on all such lucrative undertakings.   It was proposed by some more than usually enterprising business men to form a company to develop the mineral resources of the province.   They elaborated their proposal in the form of a memorial to the Throne, and in due course the document was returned to the viceroy of the province for his consideration.   His answer was typical.   He expressed surprise that private individuals should have ventured to have made such a proposition, and forthwith issued a proclamation warning the people to have nothing to do with the project, and ordering an official deputy to inspect the capabilities of the proposed mines.   If the report should prove to be satisfactory he undertook to form a company to carry out the work.   The result is not far to seek.   If the work is undertaken at all, it will be done badly and the bulk of the profits will go to enrich the local officials.

Such being the condition of affairs in China, we may well despair of the future of the Empire.   The whole system of administration is rotten to the core, and there is no sign or symptom of any effort towards progressive reforms.   Ninety-nine out of every hundred mandarins are wedded by long habit and by personal interest to the existing system.   A few men doubtless are conscious of a better way, but it would be a mistake to suppose from their rare enlightened sentiments that there is any disposition to throw off the trammels of corruption and wrong which have enwrapped the country for so many centuries.   The whole weight of the nation is in the opposite scale, and the efforts of the infinitesimally small minority of would-be reformers can no more seriously affect the enduring outline of the national polity 'than the successive forests of beech and fir can determine the shape of the everlasting hills from which they spring.'

ROBERT K. DOUGLAS.

Tsungli Yamên from the last loan, and the northern and southern superintendencies will furnish 3,000,000 and 7,000,000 respectively.'   Whence the remaining 20,000,000 taels are to come is not stated.   This would seem to imply that the negotiations for the reported loan from America have broken down.

THE INFLUENCE OF MACHIAVELLI ON
THE REFORMATION IN ENGLAND

In the widespread and immediate influence which they exercised probably no political writings have ever equalled those of Machiavelli. Not that he was the creator of that unscrupulous statecraft with which his name has been for centuries associated; for Machiavellism (to risk the appearance of paradox) existed before Machiavelli, and he did no more than codify and comment on those principles of policy which he saw applied everywhere about him. But, in doing this, he undoubtedly gave a great impetus to their use, his treatise *The Prince* forming a convenient textbook of practical politics, of which European statesmen were not slow to take advantage. Multiplied in numerous editions, this work, with its companion volume, the *Discourses on Livy*, in spite of the loud and horrified denunciations of old-fashioned moralists, soon found its way into every cabinet and council chamber of Europe, and its cynical maxims have left their impress only too clearly on the policies of the sixteenth and seventeenth centuries.

It may, then, in the light of recent events, be not without interest to inquire how far English statesmen of the Reformation period were brought under the sinister influence of Machiavelli's genius, and, more especially, to attempt some estimate of its effect upon their ecclesiastical policy.

At the outset of such an inquiry we are confronted with one striking and significant characteristic of the English Reformation, differentiating it from contemporary movements in other countries— a certain vagueness of outline, by no means altogether due to the obscuring effect of distance, which makes it difficult to arrive at any universally acceptable definition of its principles and aims. As to what happened in Scotland, in Holland, or in Geneva, there can be no controversy. In all of these the revolution was abrupt and thorough, constituting a more or less complete breach with the past; and even in Lutheran Germany and Scandinavia the retention of a large body of Catholic doctrine and ceremonial was far outweighed by the conscious and deliberate breach of the 'Apostolic Succession.' In

England, on the other hand, the movement was from the first largely conservative, avoiding revolutionary methods, intolerant of extremes, advancing cautiously step by step, and careful of all the ties that bound it to the past, so long as these were consistent with the aim of its political leaders—the subservience of the Church to the State.

This striking characteristic of the Reformation in England may have been due to the exigencies of the case, and to the natural tendency of Englishmen to change the spirit rather than the form of their institutions; but it is nevertheless so entirely in accord with Machiavelli's principle that, in making innovations, the substance rather than the form should be changed, that, in so far as it was the result of deliberate policy, it may well have been to some extent inspired by him, more especially as there is abundant proof of his influence on the methods by which the revolution was effected.

That Henry the Eighth was himself directly influenced by any study of *The Prince* may be doubted, though he was himself a typical prince of the Renaissance—in his culture, his learning, his splendour, and his popular manners, no less than in his ' cruelty well applied.' Yet he was not the ideal ruler of Machiavelli, for he succumbed to that all but universal failing of not knowing how to be wholly either good or bad.   'He was,' to use the words of the late Professor Froude, ' divided against himself.   Nine days in ten he was the clear-headed, energetic, powerful statesman ; on the tenth he was looking wistfully to the superstition which he had left.'   In short, he still nursed his theological conscience, and had not yet learned from Machiavelli to regard religion solely as the handmaid of politics.   In Thomas Cromwell, however, he found a minister to whom his objects were thoroughly congenial, and whose methods were less likely to be affected by inconvenient scruples.

That Cromwell's ecclesiastical policy was dictated by motives of zeal for Evangelical religion, or sympathy with persecuted truth, is a view which may appeal to some minds ; but, in the light of available evidence, it is far more probable that the reforming tendencies of the day were merely used by him, in the true Machiavellian spirit, to further the object which he consistently kept in view—the consolidation of an absolute royal power, under the forms of a constitution, by the aid of a subservient parliament and a terrorised Church.   Nor, in spite of the scarcely impartial opinion of the late Professor Froude,[1] is it improbable that this policy was deliberately based upon Machiavelli's teaching.   It is admitted that Cromwell spent many years in Italy, first as a clerk in a commercial house in Florence, and afterwards as a soldier of fortune or engaged in diplomatic service at various Italian Courts.   It is not surprising that a politician trained in the school of the Medici and the Borgias should have welcomed the

---

[1] He dismisses Pole's accusation of Machiavellism against Cromwell in a short footnote (*Hist.* vol. ii. ch. vi. p. 109).

the architecture of his own fortunes ; and there seems no adequate reason (certainly none is given by Professor Froude) for doubting the substantial truth of the accusation of Machiavellism which is brought against Cromwell by Cardinal Pole.

Pole affirms that the immediate cause of his exile was the rise of Cromwell to power, the results of which he dreaded, because he had had an opportunity of judging of that statesman's principles and maxims of government in a conversation he had once had with him on the office of a prudent councillor. 'In this decision,' he says, 'nothing influenced me more than my having from that one interview and conversation easily perceived what kind of government we should have, if that man ever held the reins of power—namely, a government dangerous and destructive to all honest men.' [2] Of this discussion, which had been raised by some reference to Wolsey, the Cardinal proceeds to give an epitome. 'I told him,' he says, 'that it was the duty of a councillor to consider above all things the interest and honour of his sovereign ; and I enlarged on these subjects, as they are enforced by the law of nature and the writings of pious and learned men.' Cromwell, in reply, poured scorn on the opinions of pious and learned men, as themes good enough for sermons or the discussions of the schools, but of little use in practical politics, and decidedly out of favour at the courts of princes. In his opinion a little experience was worth a great deal of theory, and statesmen who based their policy upon books, rather than upon a knowledge of men and affairs, were apt to suffer shipwreck. For the prudent councillor the first thing to do was to study the prince's inclinations—by no means an easy task, since the external deportment of princes so often belies their inner character. 'For it is of the greatest importance that he should in his conversation consistently display an exalted character for religiousness, piety, and the other virtues ; without, however, there being the slightest necessity for his inclinations to coincide with it.' And in this respect the prudent councillor will know how to imitate the prince, a result to be obtained with a very little trouble. The Cardinal was, very naturally, not a little shocked. At this Cromwell expressed no surprise, but told him that, if he were to turn for a while from his studies to the practical affairs of State, he would soon learn the comparative value of experience and theory in the art of government. 'In these matters,' he exclaims, 'a few sentences from a man of experience are worth whole volumes written by a philosopher who has no such experience.' For him a book founded upon empty speculation had no value. Plato's *Republic* had been written about two thousand years, and its maxims had never yet been practically applied. On the other hand, he knew of a book which he

---

[2] Cf. *Apologia ad Carolum V.* An abstract is given by Professor Brewer in his essay on the Royal Supremacy.

would recommend Pole to read, written by a practical man whose
rules and maxims were confirmed by everyday experience, 'a book,'
adds the horrified Cardinal, 'which, though it displayed the style of
a man, I had nevertheless hardly begun to read, when I saw that it
had been penned by the finger of Satan.' This Satanic work was, of
course, Machiavelli's *Prince.*

Others have, indeed, abundantly pointed out the Machiavellian
nature of Cromwell's methods[3]—his government by terror, his elaborate system of spies, his ruthless sweeping aside of all who stood in
his path. As an illustration of this system of tyranny it may suffice
to take one notable instance, closely connected with the Reformation
both in its political and religious aspects. The execution of Sir
Thomas More and Bishop Fisher has always been regarded as the
master crime of the Cromwellian reign of terror. Even Professor
Froude lamented its necessity, though it was, in his opinion, a
necessity.[4] It was, it is true, unfortunate that the affair of the Anne
Boleyn marriage 'told fatally to destroy the appearance of probity of
motive, so indispensable to the defence of the Government;' and Europe,
no doubt labouring under a misconception of the facts, was filled with
indignation. So great, indeed, was this indignation that Henry ' condescended to an explanation.' He directed the magistrates to enlarge
to the people on the malicious treasons of the Bishop of Rochester
and Sir Thomas More. To the King of France, who had ventured to
send a remonstrance, he replied haughtily that 'the English Government had acted on clear proof of treason ; treason so manifest, and
tending so clearly to the total destruction of the commonwealth of this
realm, that the condemned persons were all well worthy, if they had
a thousand lives, to have suffered a ten times more terrible death and
execution than any of them did suffer.'

And what were these terrible treasons about which Henry was so
righteously indignant, as tending to the total subversion of the realm ?
More had been willing to recognise the right of Parliament to alter
the succession ; he had been prepared to keep silence on the royal
supremacy. What he had not been willing to do was to perjure
himself by denying openly his belief in the spiritual supremacy of
the Pope. If this was treason, of every hundred honest men in the
kingdom ninety-nine were traitors.

The treasons for which More was condemned had not been on the
statute book a year. A few months before his arrest it would have
been heresy to affirm what it was now treason to deny. He was not
allowed to escape by retiring into private life, as he wished, but was
hunted out and, contrary to all precedent and all natural justice,
entrapped into incriminating himself. The true reason for their

---

[3] See Brewer, *Introduction to State Papers.*

[4] *History*, vol. ii. p. 385, &c. Cf. Machiavelli, *Discorsi* : ' . . . nessuna Republica
bene ordinata non mai cancellò i demeriti con gli meriti di suoi cittadini.'

unbiassed mind to see in it any real justification. 'They had,' he says, 'chosen to make themselves conspicuous as confessors of Catholic truth ; though prisoners in the Tower, they were in effect the most effectual champions of the Papal claims, and if their disobedience had been passed over the Act could have been enforced against no one.'[5] They were, in fact, those uncompromising and conscientious opponents of the new order whom Machiavelli classes under the name of ' the sons of Brutus,' and who must, in his view, be slain, if the new order is to be maintained.[6]

If, then, the influence of Machiavelli is so clearly traceable on Cromwell's political methods, it is possible that, in its broader aspects also, his policy was derived from the same source. Especially may he have learned from Machiavelli that astuteness by which he recognised that men are often willing to surrender the substance of their rights if they are allowed to retain the shadow, which led him to exercise a despotic government without the open violation of any constitutional form, and, finally, to make the Church the seemingly willing instrument of her own enslavement. And the justification of this Machiavellian policy is found in the comparatively peaceful course of the Reformation in England. The great bulk of the people, Catholic by education, by instinct, and by the strong conservatism of our race, accepted the new order without realising to what it committed them. Later on, when the hopes of a reaction became weaker, the discontent of a small minority might express itself in abortive plots ; but England was spared the horrors of a Thirty Years' War, or of a struggle such as that between the Huguenots and the League ; and when, in the next century, the Puritan Revolution occurred, its motives were political rather than religious. Even in our day this Machiavellian method of reform still bears fruit, in that it can be seriously argued that the Church of England under Henry the Eighth was the willing instrument of her own reformation.

With the fall of Cromwell the influence of Machiavelli on the course of ecclesiastical affairs in England came, for the time, to an end. For his strong and far-sighted, if ruthless, policy there was little sympathy found among the crowd of miserable sycophants who rose upon his ruin, who surrounded the throne during the last years of Henry the Eighth, and held the reins of power under Edward. With Cromwell, as with Machiavelli, the Dudleys, the Seymours, and the Riches had nothing in common, save their unscrupulousness. All grandeur of aim is gone ; and for the great policy of Cromwell they substituted the most sordid of private motives, striving by the same unscrupulous means which he had used for public ends to gratify their personal ambition or avarice. It would

<hr/>

[5] *History*, vol. ii. p. 369.   [6] *Discorsi*, book iii. cap 4.

be a libel on Machiavelli to apply his name to this government of incompetent and selfish factions. It would have been well had they studied *The Prince,* and taken its lessons to heart ; if Somerset had learned from it to avoid the vacillation and want of decision which characterised him, to abstain from hasty and ill-considered innovations in religion, and to recognise that the true strength of a government lies in the goodwill of the people. But the strong policy of Cromwell, in fact, ceased with his death, and it was not until England had been for eleven years, under Edward and Mary, a prey to the misgovernment of unscrupulous adventurers, and doctrinaires, Catholic and Protestant, that the system which he had initiated was revived again by the accession of Elizabeth.

During the reign of Elizabeth, even more than during that of Henry the Eighth, the statecraft of Machiavelli seems to have been consistently applied. The conditions obtaining in England at the time of the Queen's accession were, indeed, not altogether unlike those which had prompted Machiavelli to write his *Discourses.* There was the same danger to be feared both from within and from without— within, the never-ceasing war of religious factions, wasting in futile and bloody controversy the best strength of the nation ; without ' the French king bestriding the realm, having one foot in Calais and the other in Scotland ; steadfast enemies, but no steadfast friends.' [7] In both the *Discourses on Livy* and *The Prince,* whatever differences of principle and method there might be between them, Machiavelli had the same object in view—the healing of the open wounds of Italy and her liberation from the hated bondage of the ' barbarian.' This, with the necessary differences of circumstance, was also the task that lay before Elizabeth. How well she performed it is matter of history and need not be enlarged upon here.[8] We are more concerned with the policy she pursued, and by means of which she raised England, menaced at her accession by the hostility of France and the scarcely less dangerous friendship of Spain, to an unprecedented height of glory and influence among the nations of Europe. This policy, deliberately selected among several alternatives, was as novel as it was successful. How far was it inspired by the writings of Machiavelli ?

There is evidence, which I will adduce later on, to prove that Machiavelli's works were studied by at least one of Elizabeth's advisers. But the Queen was apt to follow her own courses, and it is certain that no policy could have been forced upon her against her own judgment. The brilliant results of her long and glorious reign were, in fact, due to her own genius. For, though she knew how to select and keep her ministers, her relations with them were always

[7] Address to the Council. Cf. Froude, *Hist.* vol. vii. p. 8.

[8] See Bacon's account of the state of England at the time of the Queen's death in 'Observations on a Libel,' &c. (*Works,* vol. iii. p. 40, ed. 1824, London).

regulated on the principles that Machiavelli had laid down;[9] and, whilst she was ever ready to listen to any advice they had to offer, she never allowed her share of the government to be overshadowed by their influence. Even Lord Burleigh, who for thirty-four years continued to enjoy her confidence, was in the habit of deferring to her opinion, and, as Bacon says, 'there never was a councillor of his Lordship's long continuance that was so applicable to Her Majesty's princely resolutions, endeavouring always, after faithful propositions and remonstrances, and these in the best words and the most grateful manner, to rest upon such conclusions as Her Majesty in her own wisdom determineth, and them to execute to the best.'[10] The guiding spirit of Elizabeth's policy, then, is to be sought in the character of the Queen herself, whose personality exercised so extraordinary an influence in directing the tendency of affairs during her reign.

In some respects Elizabeth approached nearer than her father to Machiavelli's ideal prince. The salient characteristics of Henry the Eighth were, indeed, renewed in her; but whereas he had never quite succeeded in burying the theologian in the statesman, his daughter followed Machiavelli in regarding religion mainly as subsidiary to statecraft, not hesitating, as it seemed, to do violence to her own convictions or predilections if by so doing she could further her policy. That her action was consciously based on a study of *The Prince* there seems, indeed, to be no evidence to prove; but there is much to make us suspect that she was not unacquainted with Machiavelli's writings. There is a certain theatrical aspect about both her private and public life, which seems to show that she was acting a carefully studied part;[11] and all the intricacies of her policy appear to have been based upon some consistent theory of statecraft. From Machiavelli it may have been that she borrowed that art of political lying which she carried to the verge of comedy, and which she seemed to regard as part of the essential equipment of every diplomatist.[12] And, if she was proud of her skill in outwitting others, she was even more so of the penetration which enabled her to see through their deceits. 'You deal not,' she writes to James the Sixth, upbraiding him with breaking his word, 'you deal not with one whose experience can take dross for good payments, nor one that easily may be beguiled. No, no! I mind to set to school your craftiest councillor.'[13] Nor was this high opinion of her own powers without foundation. Bacon comments on 'her penetrating sight in

---

[9] 'Observations on a Libel,' &c. (Bacon, vol. iii. p. 40).

[10] Cf. *The Prince*, cap. xxiii.

[11] Theodor Mundt (*Machiavelli u. der Gang der europäischen Politik*) points out the dramatic aspect of *The Prince* : ' It is more the question of the study of a part than of a consistent doctrine.'

[12] Cf. *Prince*, cap. xviii.

[13] Cf. Ellis, *Original Letters*, vol. i. letter ccxv.

discovering every man's ends and drifts ; her inventing wit in contriving plots and overturns ; her foreseeing events ; her usage of.
occasions.' [14]   And if, in these matters, she appeared in a large measure
to realise Machiavelli's conception of a prudent prince, she did so no
less in the broad outlines of her policy.

The great problem which, at the beginning of her reign, Elizabeth
was called on to solve was the question of religion ; and it is in her
religious policy that the influence of Machiavelli may be most clearly
traced.   The crisis of the religious revolution had, indeed, already
passed when she came to the throne.   A few zealots, on one side or.
the other, might be still anxious to fight out the battle to a decisive
conclusion, but the nation as a whole was heartily weary of a
theological warfare which had reduced the country to the verge of
ruin.   The accession of the new queen had brought back streams of
Protestant refugees, breathing vengeance and destruction against
their persecutors, whilst Elizabeth's cautious proceedings during
the first few months of her reign had, for the time, revived the hopes
of the Catholics.   But she had, in fact, determined to favour neither
of the extreme parties.   She knew that in following this course she
would have the support of the bulk of the nation, and, with the
mass of the nation on her side, she could afford to brave the attacks
of the small number, however zealous they might be, who would be
hostile to her system.   Religion, then, was to be no longer the chief
motive of government.   Henceforward the attention of the people
was to be drawn away from the fatal animosities of theology by the
substitution of a new motive for their aspiration, a motive to which
religion was to be subservient ; and the nation, hitherto shattered by
the conflict of rival sects, was to be welded together in a common
opposition to the power and arrogance of Spain.

At the beginning of the reign, indeed, Philip had still hoped to
retain his hold on England, and had offered Elizabeth his alliance.
For a moment she hesitated, as well she might, for, situated as she
was, the offer was a dazzling one.   But she had had the strength
and foresight to refuse it.   And the policy which she pursued instead
was that which Machiavelli had recommended for distracted Italy—
namely, the policy of ' military reorganisation,' [15] or the consolidation
of the people by uniting them in a national conflict with a rival Power.
And just as in Machiavelli the religious motive is made entirely
subservient to the political, so the national religion became during
Elizabeth's reign gradually associated in the minds of the people
with the national opposition to Spain.   Recusancy, which under
Edward the Sixth would have been punished as heresy rather than

[14] 'A Discourse in Praise of Queen Elizabeth,' Bacon's *Works*, vol. iii. p. 35
(London, 1824).
[15] ' Politik der kriegerischen Reorganisation ' (cf. Theodor Mundt, *Machiavelli
und der Gang der europäischen Politik*).

treason, came to be regarded as an offence against the national cause rather than as a religious crime. Elizabeth, in fact, cared little about abstract propositions of theology. She was quite content to renounce her father's title of 'Supreme Head of the Church,' if by doing so she could persuade people to acquiesce more readily in her practical supremacy. She had no desire to 'pry into men's consciences,' but she required that every man should bow to the laws which she had made in the interests of the national unity. And the success of this policy is apparent in the religious tranquillity of the earlier part of her reign, a tranquillity which might have been permanent, had not the bulls of Pius the Fifth blown the smouldering embers of religious zeal once more into a flame; and, even then, the failure of the Catholic plots proves the general soundness of the Queen's policy.

If Elizabeth did not derive her principles and method of government directly from Machiavelli, it is more than probable that they were suggested to her by the most trusted of her ministers, who, without doubt, had studied him to good purpose.

There is, in the library of the British Museum, a volume containing copies of Machiavelli's *Prince* and the *Discourses on Livy* bound up together. These were ostensibly published at Palermo, in 1584, but are judged, from the evidence of certain initial woodcuts, to have been actually printed clandestinely in London by one John Wolfe. On the title-page of this volume, which is elaborately underlined and annotated throughout, is the signature 'W. Cecil.' To attempt to prove that it was Lord Burleigh who owned and annotated this book is tempting; but unhappily honesty compels me to admit that the handwriting is not his, and that in any case at the date of the publication of the volume his signature would have been 'W. Burleigh.' Yet the name of Cecil, in such a connection, is not without significance, and it would have been possible to argue from it, with some plausibility, that Machiavelli's treatises were known to Lord Burleigh. Fortunately, however, there is other and more conclusive evidence to prove the same point.

Burleigh was in the habit, from time to time, of reducing the outlines of any course of policy he advocated to writing, as memorials for the Queen's use. Of these memorials several have been published among his papers, and serve to throw no little light on the character of his policy; one of them being of peculiar value, because it not only proves that Burleigh himself was a disciple of Machiavelli, but enables us to form some estimate of how far Elizabeth's religious policy was directly influenced by the Florentine writer. This document is published under the title of 'Advice of the Lord Treasurer Burleigh to Queen Elizabeth in Matters of Religion and State,'[16] and the most important part of it deals with the question of the

---

[16] Fourth collection of *Somers Tracts*, vol. i. p. 101.

Catholic malcontents. With regard to these there were two courses
open to the Queen. She might either allow them to grow strong, in
the hope of making them contented, or discontent them by making
them weaker, 'for what the mixture of strength and discontent
engenders needs no syllogism to prove:' But to suffer them to be
strong in the hope of making them contented carried with it, in
his opinion, 'but a fair enamelling of a terrible danger;' 'for men's
natures are apt to strive not only against the present smart, but to
revenging by past injury, though they be never so well contented
thereafter.' [17] For on the very first opportunity for revenge that
presents itself 'they will remember not the after slacking but the
former binding, and so much the more when they shall imagine this
relenting to proceed from fear ; for it is the poison of all government
when the subject thinks the prince doth anything more out of fear
than favour.' [18] But, above all, there should be no half-measures ; [19]
for 'no man loves one the better for giving him the bastinado, though
with never so little a cudgel;' 'the course of the most wise, most
politick, and best grounded estates hath ever been to make an
assuredness of friendship, or to take away all power of enmity.' [20]
'Yet here,' he adds, 'I must distinguish between discontent and
despair ; for it sufficeth to weaken the discontented, but there is no
way to kill desperates, which in such number as they are, were as
hard and difficult as impious and ungodly ; and, therefore, though
they must be discontented, I would not have them desperate ; for
amongst many desperate men it is like that some one will bring
forth some desperate deed.' [21]

A comparison with *The Prince* or the *Discourses on Livy*
will show that not only the spirit of the above advice, but in some
cases almost the language in which it is couched, is borrowed from
Machiavelli. And if the conclusion to which Burleigh is led by the
above argument is a just one—namely, that the consciences of the
Catholics should not be forced by compelling them to take an oath
contrary to their belief in the Papal supremacy—he arrives at this
conclusion not because it is wrong to force men's consciences, but
because, in this case, it would be dangerous to the State to do so ;
and, in dealing out any scant measure of justice to the malcontents,
in his opinion 'the furthest point to be sought was but to avoid

[17] *Discorsi*, book iii. p. 4: 'Mai l' ingiurie vecchie non furono cancellate da
beneficii nuovi.' Also *Principe*, cap. vii. end.
[18] *Ibid.*, vol. ii. p. 14; also *Principe*, end of chap. viii.
[19] *Ibid.*, vol. ii. p. 23: 'Ne usarno mai *la via neutrale* in quelli di momento.'
[20] *Ibid.*: 'Quel Principe, che non castiga chi erra, in modo che non possa più
errare, è tenuto o ignorante o vile.' .
[21] *Ibid.* vol. ii. p. 28: 'Notabile a qualunque governa, che mai non debba
tanto poco stimare un' huomo, che c' creda . . . che colui, che è ingiuriato, non si
pensi di vendicarsi con ogni suo pericolo e particular danno.'

It was the carrying out of this policy that enabled the apologists of Elizabeth's administration, Burleigh himself, Walsingham, and Bacon, to vindicate her conduct towards the Catholics by alleging that they were punished, not for conscience sake, but for treason. Yet, however strenuously they might deny that consciences were forced, however frequently they might reiterate that the Government was merely punishing those cases of conscience which had changed their character by exceeding all bounds, and become matters of faction, the fact remained that the limits of conscientious scruple had been arbitrarily fixed by themselves, and that it was their own policy of making religion an instrument for the attainment of political ends which had rendered persecution a State necessity. And through the thin disguise of all their arguments in justification of their repressive policy appears the fact that they themselves were half conscious that their real motive and true justification was the Machiavellian doctrine that all means are permissible that conduce to the well-being of the State.

Machiavellian in its details, the ecclesiastical policy of Elizabeth was, like that of Cromwell, Machiavellian also in its broader aspects. The ecclesiastical settlement under Elizabeth constituted in effect a complete revolution in the religious character of the nation. At her accession the Queen had found the nation, for the most part, Catholic; when she died it was fiercely and unalterably Protestant. And yet of this tremendous change, so skilfully veiled had been the processes, and so carefully conservative the methods, that it was possible for the Government to assert, and to assert with some plausibility, that in the polity of the Church no fundamentally new principles had been introduced. 'In this part (*i.e.* in the religious innovations),' runs a proclamation of Queen Elizabeth,

we know of no other authority, either given or used by us, as Quene and Governor of this Realm, than hath ben by the Lawe of God and this Realm alwayes due to our Progenitors, Soverayns, and Kinges of the same; although true it is that this Authority hath ben in the Tyme of certen of our Progenitors, some hundred years past, as by Lawes, Records, and Storyes doth appere (and specially in the Reign of our noble Father Henry the Eighth and our deare Brother Edward the Sixth) more clearly recognized by all the Estates of the Realme, as the like hath ben in our Tyme; without that thereby we do either challenge or take to us (as malicious Parsons do untruly surmise) any Superiority to ourself to defyne, decyde, or determyn any Article or Poynt of the Chrestian Fayth and Relligion, or to chang any ancient Ceremony of the Church from the Forme before received and observed by the Catholick and Apostolick Church, or the Use of any Function belongyng to any ecclesiastical Person being a Minister of the Word and Sacraments of the Church: But that Authority which is yelded to us and our Crown consisteth in this; that, considering we are by God's Grace the Soverayn Prince and Quene, next under God, and all the People of our Realm are immediately born Subjects to us and to none ells, and that our Realme hath of long time past receaved the Christian Fayth, we are by this Authorite bound to direct all Estates, being subject to us, to live in the Fayth and Obedience of Christian Relligion, and to see the Lawes of God and Man, which are ordained to that end, to be duly observed, and the Offenders against the same duly punished, and consequently to provide that the Chirch may be governed and taught by Arch-Bishops, Bishops, and Ministers accordyng to the ecclesiastical Auncient Pollycy of the Realme, whom we do assist with our soverayn Power . . .[22]

So the clergy are still, according to Elizabeth, supreme in all spiritual matters ; her own function is confined to bringing, as a dutiful daughter of the Catholic Church, the secular power to the aid of religion ! Can this be the same voice that threatened to ' unfrock ' a certain ' proud prelate ' because he tried to defend the property of his see ?

' Whoever desires to introduce reforms into a State,' Machiavelli had written, ' in such manner as to have them accepted, and maintained to everybody's satisfaction, must retain at least the shadow of old institutions, so as to appear to have altered nothing, while in fact the new arrangements are entirely different from the old.' [23]

W. ALISON PHILLIPS.

[22] ' A Declaration of the Queen's Proceedings since her Reign,' published among the *Burleigh Papers*, Haynes, p. 591. This proclamation was issued early in 1570, after the Northern rising. It was previous to the Pope's Bull of 1570, which threw Elizabeth into the arms of the Protestants.

[23] *Discorsi*, vol. i. p. 25.

WE have at this moment throughout the country 19,800 elementary schools under separate management—5,316 of these schools are controlled by School Boards; 14,484 by Voluntary managers. The number of scholars enrolled is, in the Board schools, 2,310,253; in the Voluntary schools 3,015,605. Both sets of schools receive aid from the Central Exchequer upon the same terms. The Board schools supplement their central aid by assistance from the rates; the Voluntary schools have to rest satisfied for their supplementary local income with what they can secure from voluntary contributions, with the result that they are, generally speaking, run much more cheaply than the Board schools. For instance, on behalf of the two million children attending the Board schools, there were drawn from the rates last year as income supplementary to the central grants, three and three-quarter millions; on behalf of the three million Voluntary schools children, the supplemental income was, roughly, three-quarters of a million. The facts, examined from the point of view of the money spent on each child, show that 10s. 4¾d. *less* was spent last year on each child attending the Voluntary schools than on each child attending the Board schools; and, strangely enough, of this financial disability—'intolerable strain,' Mr. Balfour styles it—of 10s. 4¾d., 8s. 9¼d. per child is accounted for in the difference between the payments made on account of teachers in the schools of the two systems, that difference being to the disadvantage of the Voluntary school teachers.

Having got thus far, let me set down two fundamental propositions which should, I think, commend themselves to most persons. The first is this : *If the country is content to send three of its five millions of elementary school children to Voluntary schools, these schools should be adequately supported.* And the second : *It should be the duty of the State to see that teachers in all classes of elementary schools should receive the same pay for the same work.*

The unfairness of the present system is that neither of these fundamental conditions is fulfilled. The ' State-aiders ' amongst the supporters of Denominational schools—and by ' State-aiders ' I mean those who favour the policy of asking for ' special aid ' grants from the Central Exchequer—think they can settle the matter by an appeal for greater help from the Central Exchequer. The 'rate-aiders' contend that it will never be permanently settled till all schools, Denominational and Undenominational, have an equal pull on 'rate' as well as on 'State' assistance. That is the position in a nutshell. It looks simplicity itself. Only the difficulty comes in, as usual, when politicians begin to discuss the terms of settlement, as the Government will probably learn once more early next year.

But whatever the terms of the settlement may be, I think it essential that still another fundamental consideration should be recognised : *That every person whose name is on the rate-book should, by some means or other, be made to contribute his fair share to the local burdens necessary for the maintenance of elementary education.* At present, roughly, two-thirds only of the rateable value, population, and area of the country (for the fraction is about the same in each case) are taxed locally for education, and taxed in the most grotesque and uneven manner as a result of the extraordinary diversities in the size of the administrative areas, the value of the local property, and the measure of local educational needs. The other third of the country tells us it prefers Denominational schools. This preference enables it to escape a local tax for education. In some cases, no doubt, as much is raised locally by voluntary subscriptions as would reach the average level of the compulsory education rate. And in the large urban centres, it should be gratefully admitted, many people not only pay that tax, but subscribe in addition to Denominational schools.

But in the rural districts especially, *the Denominational school too often exists simply and solely that the locality may entirely, or almost entirely, 'contract itself out' of its proper obligations towards the education of the children of the people.* In such districts the schools are either (1) made to live on the central aid alone (1,061 Voluntary schools have no subscriptions and no endowments); or (2) some benevolent forefather of the village having in time past bestowed a little benefaction on the school, present generations consider themselves absolved of any need to dip their hands into their pockets; or (3) the clergyman or the schoolmaster has to worry around with cap in hand coaxing a few guineas out of the Ladies Bountiful, the big farmers, and the Squire.

The result is that we get villages all over the country, and in a rarer number of cases urban districts side by side, in the one case locally taxed up to one, two, and even three shillings in the pound for education ; in the next raising nothing, or next to nothing, locally for educational purposes.

Now, as I have said, I can thoroughly recognise and deeply respect the case of the people who say they prefer Denominational schools, and raise out of their private purses from twenty to thirty shillings a pupil per year—*often in addition to paying the School Board rate*—that the same may be fully maintained. But I am bound to say that I see at the back of a lot of this talk the consideration that under its guise good, thrifty souls are able to wriggle almost entirely out of their local obligations to the education of the children. And if any one be disposed to challenge this statement, let him spend an hour with a Government Blue Book numbered [C—7529] and purchasable for six shillings and sevenpence. I should await the result with interest.

As I have stated, the amount raised from the localities rated was last year three and three-quarter millions; the amount raised by voluntary subscribers was, roughly, three-quarters of a million. If I divide the country into three equal thirds (spreading the three-quarters of a million voluntary subscriptions evenly over the whole country) I get the following interesting statement of facts respecting the local support of education :—

One-third rateable value, population, or area		One-third rateable value, population, or area		One-third rateable value, population, or area	
	£		£		£
(a) Raised from rates . .	0	(a) Raised from rates .	1,875,000	(a) Raised from rates . .	1,875,000
(b) Raised from voluntary subscriptions, &c..	250,000	(b) Raised from voluntary subscriptions, &c.	250,000	(b) Raised from voluntary subscriptions, &c.	250,000
Total raised . £250,000		Total raised £2,125,000		Total raised £2,125,000	

So that, again to rehearse the conclusions :—of the population, area, and rateable value of the country, only two-thirds contribute anything like their proper share to the local support of education. One-third of the country meets its obligation either with (1) nothing at all raised locally, or (2) ' a threepenny voluntary rate ' (which many do not pay at all), or (3) by yielding the guinea, the half-guinea, and the crown to the parson's unremitting importunity. One-third, in a word, gets off by raising a quarter of a million, roughly speaking. *Each of the other thirds raises over eight times as much !* Now, why, I ask, should not everybody be compelled to bear his fair share of this most important communal obligation ? I press my question because amongst the ' rate-aiders ' there are many who would confine rate-aid to districts already rated—this to allay the fears of those who now enjoy immunity from a local charge for education.

The average local school rate in the area taxed is, roughly, $8\frac{1}{2}d$. (It ranges, by the way, in the various localities from the decimal of a penny up to forty pence in the pound.) This, levied over two-thirds of the country, yields three and three-quarter millions. Levied uniformly and universally it would give us five and a half millions, which, together with the seven millions central aid now granted, would provide for some time to come for that educational expansion which Sir John Gorst tells us is so essential—'if we wish to give to the children an education anything like that which is given by our rivals in France, and Germany, and the States, and elsewhere '—but of provision for which, curiously enough, we saw but very little in the lately deceased measure upon the back of which is inscribed Sir John's name. We could do very well, I say, with this five and a half millions of local aid for education, and in securing it we could easily, by a material extension of the areas of collection, equalise the burden as it at present exists.

And this brings me to a consideration of the grossly unfair incidence of the local rate where now levied. Let me levy an imaginary School Board rate of a penny upon a variety of boroughs and rural School Board areas taken at random. In London a penny rate brings in for School Board purposes, roughly, 140,000*l.*; in Liverpool, 13,200*l.*; Manchester, 11,980*l.*; Birmingham, 9,000*l.*; Leeds, 5,660*l.*; Sheffield, 4,820*l.*; Bristol, 4,000*l.*; Newcastle, 3,930*l.*; Cardiff, 3,560*l.*; Nottingham, 3,240*l.*; Brighton, 2,866*l.*; Portsmouth, 2,680*l.*; and Leicester, 2,650*l.* (It would be an interesting study to compare these varying amounts with the Board School needs of each of these great centres, but that is scarcely my present purpose.) I come at once now to some strikingly different incomes from the self-same penny. At Jacobstow, in Cornwall, a penny rate realises 10*l.*; at North Tamerton (Cornwall), 10*l.*; Lanlivery (Cornwall), 6*l.* 5*s.*; Rhoscolyn (Anglesea), 5*l.* 16*s.*; Maes Mynis (Brecon), 6*l.* 15*s.*; Kirkbride (Cumberland), 8*l.* 11*s.*; Clayhanger (Devon), 7*l.* 14*s.*; Ashen (Essex), 6*l.* 3*s.*; Keinton Mandeville (Somerset), 4*l.* 18*s.*; Barnardiston (Suffolk), 3*l.* 18*s.*; and so on.

Of course it is at once admitted that the educational needs of the great urban centres quoted are not to be compared with those of the small rural districts mentioned. But it *is* suggested that there is a far greater disproportion between the proceeds of a similar rate levied in these various localities than there is between their actual educational requirements.

Naturally, we get the sequel to this absurd restriction of the areas over which the local school rate is levied in the heavy burden cast upon many of the rural districts. The following little table may be left to tell its own tale. It should serve, in its way, as a rebuke to those wealthy Londoners especially who are always bewailing their hard fate in having to pay more than Mr. Forster's 'three pence in the pound.'

PARISH SCHOOL BOARDS IN ENGLAND AND WALES, OUT OF A TOTAL OF 2,271, ISSUING PRECEPTS OF

	England	Wales
1*s.* and above in the £	242	50
Over 9*d.* and below 1*s.* in the £	306	43
Over 6*d.* and below 9*d.* in the £	549	103

'every 1*l*. we in London get from the Central Exchequer we have to spend 1*l*. 9*s*. from the rates. This is noisily objected to just now, especially by the West End section of the community, as casting too severe a burden on the locality.

But what about Great Bentley in Essex, where for every pound 'received from the Central Exchequer they had to raise last year over 14*l*. locally. Look at the following list and strike your own comparisons between the amounts raised locally and centrally respectively, remembering also that, in all probability, contiguous with these parishes are others that raise little or nothing locally for their schools.

Parish	Raised locally			Received from Central Aid		
	£	*s.*	*d.*	£	*s.*	*d.*
Flitwick (Beds)	729	5	0	191	5	6
Eastcotts ,, . . .	110	0	0	68	1	0
Castle Thorpe (Bucks) . . .	225	0	0	171	13	0
Dorney ,, . . .	130	0	0	75	8	6
Little Missenden ,, . . .	170	0	0	81	12	6
Stoke Mandeville ,, . . .	85	0	0	30	11	2
Wyrardisbury ,, . . .	200	0	0	120	6	6

I have taken only two of the first three counties in the alphabetical list, but they will serve. Berkshire, the second of the first three counties, furnishes no example in the above list; I put the whole county in instead. *It received last year* 9,037*l*. 7*s*. 8*d*. *from the Central Exchequer, and had to raise in return from local School Board rates* 18,011*l*. 8*s*.!

Well, now, I can restate my case in the form of three queries. Why should not every ratepayer, urban and rural, take his share in the local support of education? Why should not this local support be equalised in such a way as to render the incidence of the burden fair and equitable throughout the country? And why should not all public elementary schools be adequately and fairly financed, not only out of the central but out of the local purse as well?

The last query, of course, raises questions of vital moment in connection with the management and control of the schools, the powers of managers over the appointment of teachers, and the character of the religious instruction imparted to the children. But if the friends of Denominational schools are prepared to go into the question of the local support of education, prepared indeed to urge the claims of their schools upon the local purse—as so many of them are so strenuously anxious to do—it seems to me that the immediate and ultimate effects of the policy may be contemplated with complacency by those who desire to perfect and popularise elementary education throughout the country.

T. J. MACNAMARA.

P.S.—Since the foregoing was written, supporters of Church schools have decided to ask for ' rate-aid,' *but only in districts already rated.* This I view as a pure piece of opportunism. My figures, curiously enough, will serve as a striking comment on this policy, *which increases the burdens of those who already bear, and perpetuates the repudiation of those who now repudiate.* I cannot think that the Government will make such a plan the basis of legislation.

THE COMMERCIAL WAR BETWEEN
GERMANY AND ENGLAND

SOME few years ago the author was rather roughly handled by a portion of the Midland press because he foreshadowed the growing importance of German competition and what this meant to Staffordshire. Recent statistics have demonstrated beyond a doubt that, supreme as Germany proved herself to be in the battlefield when facing France, her victory in the arts of peace is likely to be more far-reaching and complete, and the vanquished in this second combat will not be France but England.

In the war against France the Teutonic legions gathered under the flag of Prussia were splendidly equipped for the campaign, but not more so than are her soldiers of industry to-day.

The main secret of Germany's great industrial progress may be summed up in the words, polytechnic education and philosophic training. The profundity of Germanic philosophy has for long been accepted as an associate of German character.

But this philosophic attribute has generally been considered to be too academic to become of any substantial value to the practical arts and to science involved in the great industrial operations. This impression has proved to be erroneous, for we find that the mental training associated with philosophic study has helped to bring about the formation of the practical philosopher, which more or less perfectly describes the modern German manufacturer, whilst he owes his high theoretic and technical training to the polytechnic curricula which are the envy and the admiration of educational experts.

The training of our Oxford and Cambridge Universities, up to within say twenty-five years ago, was too academic to be of much practical value for the development of the practical art and science. It is not strange therefore that very few of the great advances made in the technical arts by Englishmen were produced by men who had obtained their degrees at our Universities ; whereas most of the advances in technical science traceable to a German origin have been produced by Polytechnic and University men.

The famous Siemens brothers are a characteristic example of the beneficent advantages that the splendid polytechnic training of Germany gives to students who desire or are compelled to prepare for the arena of industrial or commercial combat, and there is little doubt that the offsprings of ingenuity from the inventive brains of the Siemens family would never have reached the eventually perfect maturity they did but for the scientific and practical training the brothers Siemens had received from their polytechnic Alma Mater.   To Germans the delights from that heavenly art, music, have not been merely sensuous; in the early part of this century their organ construction was unrivalled, and this industry was a profitable one.   So to-day their pianos are for general excellence most remarkable, and their piano manufacturers contribute a massive quota towards the material returns that ever follow the well-directed, competent, and sustained efforts of a rational industry.   A nation or race that can produce the galaxy of musicians beginning with Haydn, Handel, and Beethoven, and ending with glorious Wagner, is one to be both feared and respected, and it is not surprising that in the making of the piano for the mass and for the virtuoso the Berlin piano-makers, measured by actual output, are *facile princeps*.   The ability of the Germans as woodcutters has been recognised for centuries, and this ability, which has become almost a generic trait, has enabled them to produce fancy articles of wood that are conqueringly seductive.   In fine-art pottery-work the German artist workmen have turned out from the Dresden kilns objects of art that are unsurpassable in beauty of design, form, and colour, and as in the industrial arts associated with musical-instrument-making, generations of practical exponents of a craft have produced men of unrivalled talent, so the wood-carving and pottery art is still held in all its highest perfection by the German artist workmen.   In the mechanical arts this hereditary talent is held in the highest degree by the English mechanic, and consequently our English mechanical industries, if properly guided and encouraged, will at least for some time to come be easily able to maintain their position of unrivalled superiority (references in proof of this will be given further on); but, handicapped in the mechanical arts as the Germans undoubtedly are, nevertheless their birthright to a polytechnic training has almost counterbalanced their general disadvantages when compared with English mechanics—a proof of this is found in the inventive creations that are essentially mechanical, and which are of undoubtedly German origin.   Instance the Otto Cycle Gas-Engine of Dr. Otto, an invention that almost deserves to rank alongside Watt and Papin's inventions.

The Mannesmann weldless tube, a comparatively recent mechanical and metallurgical invention, is an astonishing example of highly trained German ingenuity.

The Siemens Recuperative Gas Fired Furnace for melting glass

The renowned Krupp has demonstrated that the metallurgical science of steel has been acquired in its most matured excellence by German workmen.

Herr Grüson has brought highly trained intelligence to bear on the production of hardened cast iron known as Grüson-work, and has overcome technical difficulties that were considered almost insurmountable.

The refined precision and the advanced scientific attainments of the controllers of German metallurgical processes have enabled the day-by-day production of finished metal in sheets, the thinness, pliability, and evenness of structure of which are admittedly impossible of attainment in Staffordshire.

Here in England, we have a technical science in iron-making and rolling-mill practice, and by the environment and the hereditary transmission of the experience of over a century we should be almost unassailable by our rivals, and yet we are compelled to admit an inferiority in the quality of production. Our easy *laissez-faire* policy, and reliance on an assumed superiority—because our fathers succeeded we ought to succeed—will not do, that is unless we are to be satisfied amongst industrial nations with an inferior position of rapidly increasing proportion. Not only does the result of polytechnic and philosophic training command a perhaps unwilling admiration, but we are compelled to admit that it is accompanied with a marvellous, if sometimes *unscrupulous*, energy of enterprise, instances of which will be referred to further on.

The trained mental equipment of the German manufacturer enables him to quickly seize upon a process, an idea, or a formula that will be an advantage to him, and not satisfied with what his contemporaries are doing (and in his survey he includes the whole world of industry), he establishes research laboratories of his own; we see the result of this policy (of ever searching for light and leading) in the magnificent development of the chemical industries of Germany.

What she has done for music, Germany has done for chemical science—she has enriched this portal in the great monument that represents man's intellectual triumph of mind over matter by the inscriptions of the names of Bunsen, Helmholtz, Hoffmann, Liebig, and Nobel. Is it surprising that a race capable of producing such intellectual giants should take an easy first in chemical industrial work? German chemical establishments are so well equipped both in personnel and in apparatus that even if a discovery, such as that by Perkins relating to aniline dyes, is effected by an Englishman, they, the German chemists, are the first to draw the honey of material wealth from it, whilst English manufacturers, uncertain of their own knowledge, are afraid to take the financial plunge necessary to make the newly discovered process a marketable one.

Instance again the discovery by British chemists of the value of dilute solutions of potassium cyanide for the recovery of gold, which called for a large quantity of this chemical agent. Again the demand for the agent found the German chemists ready to take advantage of the outcome of British inventors, and by their ability in reducing the cost of the agent they have amplified the demand, and the material results arising from the demand for this agent in the Transvaal alone have recompensed the German chemist for his enterprise.

Here is another example of the rapidity with which they absorb and utilise an improvement—again an English invention.

The basic steel process initiated by Thomas was accepted at once as chemically correct, and whilst English metallurgists were considering whether they should accept it or not, German metallurgists had applied the principle in many of their works. They further rapidly realised that the basic slag residue from this process was amenable to treatment for conversion into a valuable agricultural fertiliser, and they have brought this process into a high state of perfection.

One of the results accruing from the Franco-Prussian War was the annexation of the wonderful industrial area of Mulhausen and its districts. This war gift gave the Germans a nucleus of the perfected and marvellous mechanical arts by which textiles are produced, and any one who visited the French Exhibition of 1889 would realise the perfection, especially in the dyeing and colour printing, which the manufacturers of Mulhausen had attained. The scientific educational methods kept up even after the termination of the *école polytechnique* period by the technical Société Industrielle of Mulhausen, which has produced in the literature of its Proceedings a display of wealth of research of which we in England can offer no equivalent counterpart. In the mechanical arts they have produced in Hirn a theoretic savant who will rank with Clerk-Maxwell, and in the splendid engines designed by Dr. Proell they proved their capacity in high class steam-engine work.

Even in the shipbuilding—a constructional art in which Englishmen have a just claim to be considered the great masters—our position is threatened ; only the other day there was launched from a German yard a first-class armoured battle-ship, perfect it is said to be in every detail, and the Kaiser's delight was quite justified.

Had anyone prophesied twenty years ago such an event as this launch he would have been laughed at.

In the new and bright child of science, alternative current electricity, the philosophically trained German scholar found a subject for which he was fully prepared. There was ample evidence of this displayed at the Frankfort Exhibition seven years ago. Even if the record of improvements in electrical science were confined to the outcome of the *ateliers* of Messrs. Siemens and Halske, it is promising enough; besides, electrical scientists have a never-to-be-forgotten debt due to Germany for initiating the great test of long-distance electric energy transmission between Lauffen and Frankfort. The results displayed to the astonished and wondering eyes of Europe the vista that electrical science offered to electrical engineers in providing power to our industries from sources miles away from the locale of its utilisation.

In the manufacture of instruments of precision, apparatus for scientific research, and for general everyday laboratory work, the Bohemian glass-blowers are simply *sans rival*, and the workers in our laboratories would be in a curious dilemma if German glass-makers could not be relied upon.

It is perhaps unnecessary to refer to the brilliant record of results that in recent years have emanated from the laboratories devoted to the higher branches of scientific research. The work of Helmholtz and Röntgen may be mentioned *en passant*. In the art of printing Germany has led the way for centuries, and musicians especially are highly indebted to the Leipzig press for cheap and clear examples of musical scores.

In the boundary dividing engineering and chemical science the influence of German work is well defined; instance the important improvements effected in the manufacture of Portland cement, itself another English invention.

For the manufacture of bricks and tiles, German science has given us the Hoffmann kiln, a decided improvement in economy and efficiency over the Old English type of kiln.

It would be quite easy and without much strain on the memory to extend the record, already brilliant and far-reaching, of the work accomplished by our foes in the industrial fight—a struggle which daily becomes keener and keener.

German industry owes a debt of gratitude to the late Prince Albert, who, himself an ardent student of science, realised, after his sojourn here had given him a knowledge of our contemporary superiority in industrial operations, that an open display of those processes that had enabled England to attain her then unchallenged position as the supreme industrial and commercial nation in the world would be an incalculable benefit to his German countrymen. The Exhibition of 1851 was, therefore, initiated. The Germans came, they saw, and the question for us is, Will they be allowed to conquer? An Englishman will never withhold a tribute of unenvied praise to genuine and pure effort that hopes to win by honest intent and honest work; but he certainly has a right to protest against a commercial method such as that which the author exposed in the *Leeds Mercury* some ten years ago,[1] and which eventuated ultimately in the passing of the new Merchandise Marks Act. An Englishman also objects, and quite justly, to the utilisation for commercial advancement of political intrigue, of which we have an example in the history of the Government of the South African Republic—an intrigue which has culminated in the boycotting in Government contracts of English-made goods. Instance the Government specification for the electric lighting of Pretoria. Englishmen can have no objection to German success, if honestly won, by quality or cheapness of product, itself the result of fairly paid labour. They cannot understand why the German manufacturer, trained in his student days to respect the principles of honour, if need be up to the rapier point, should descend to commercial manœuvres that are dishonourable in the extreme.

Perhaps *Cui bono?* may be urged against this fair if generous acknowledgment of the proved qualifications of our great industrial competitor; but is it not more prudent to overvalue rather than undervalue the power of an enemy?

Englishmen have no need to be discouraged; they should, however, examine their position, and, if necessary, concentrate their industrial forces.

In all industrial operations where mechanical skill and genius give an English mechanic a free scope for his ability, we are still easily first in the field. Besides, England (and in this term the whole island is included) has natural advantages that Germany lacks.

If an English patriot is inclined to despair, let him visit Glasgow, without doubt the most enlightened city in the empire, even if it is the dirtiest. A sail down the Clyde will give him food for thought; a visit to Tyneside is also inspiring. Manchester, Oldham, Leeds, Sheffield, are strong links in the chain of England's industrial strength; all these industrial centres rely more or less on mechanical pursuits for their material prosperity. The modern cycle manufacture is the industry of to-day; our capacity for doing justice to this class of work has been magnificently proved, and Coventry, yesterday a decadent textile city of romantic associations, is to-day a flourishing city of mechanical industry. The same may be said of Nottingham: the famous lace industry of this midland town is being neglected, whilst its cycle industry is becoming famous. The Derby potteries industry is no longer the staple trade of this flourishing

---

[1] This letter exposed the practice adopted by German merchants in South America of introducing cutlery having the guise of English-made goods, and carrying the trade marks of English makers, but in reality the cutlery was made in Germany and sent to Sheffield for consignment to South America; the object of this mysterious trade procedure being twofold—first, to *undermine* the sterling character of English cutlery; and second, to make way for the undisguised German-made cutlery, which, although inferior to that of genuine Sheffield origin, was superior to the spurious quality.

B. H. Thwaite, C.E.

THE AUTHORSHIP OF 'RULE BRITANNIA'

IF it be true, as Southey has declared, that 'Rule Britannia' will be 'the political hymn of this country as long as she maintains her political power,' it is surely a matter of some importance that the authorship of the ode should be placed beyond all reasonable doubt. Unfortunately, from the very nature of the case, that now seems almost impossible, although, as we shall endeavour to show, the balance of evidence seems to weigh much more heavily in favour of one claimant than of another.   The initial and indeed the main difficulty arises from the fact that 'Rule Britannia' originally formed part of a work written conjointly by James Thomson and David Mallet, who gave absolutely no indication of their respective shares in the composition.   The work in question was the masque of *Alfred,* which was prepared for an entertainment at Cliefden House, Maidenhead, on the 1st of August, 1740.   Cliefden was then the residence of the Prince of Wales, and the occasion was to commemorate the accession of George the First and the birthday of Princess Augusta.

Thomson died eight years after this, and nothing, so far as we know, had been said in the meantime about the authorship of 'Rule Britannia.'   In 1751 Mallet rewrote *Alfred* for Drury Lane Theatre. In his preface he says, 'According to the present arrangement of the fable I was obliged to reject a great deal of what I had written in the other ; neither could I retain of my friend's part more than three or four single speeches and a *part of one song*.'   The italics are ours.   Now the question at once presents itself, What was this 'one song'?   The original *Alfred* contained six lyrical pieces, four of which are called 'songs,' one is called 'stanzas,' and one (' Rule Britannia') an ode.   None of these pieces are distinguished by the name of the writer.   What, then, was the 'one song' of 1751 which Mallet retained as part of Thomson's work in 1740?   Needless to say, the advocates of Mallet affirm that it was not 'Rule Britannia.' They declare that it must have been the song 'From those eternal regions bright,' and they support the opinion by the fact that this song was in 1751 'enlarged into an ode by the addition of some lines and a chorus.'   But Mallet's words, as quoted above, will hardly bear the interpretation which would lead to this conclusion.   He says definitely *retained* 'a part of one song;' and this cannot possibly mean that the song was 'enlarged,' but, on the contrary, that a portion of it was actually deleted, and probably that other words were substituted for the portion thus deleted. This latter reading of Mallet's announcement applies exactly to 'Rule Britannia.'

In the *Alfred* of 1751 Mallet states in a note that three stanzas of the now famous ode had been written by Lord Bolingbroke. On this point there is no doubt; but the views of critics are somewhat divided on the question as to whether Mallet was more likely to ask Bolingbroke's assistance in furbishing up a composition of his (Mallet's) own than to allow him to mutilate a work from the pen of his dead friend. For our part we dismiss entirely the idea of Mallet permitting even Bolingbroke to make so great changes on the song if it were his own work. Bolingbroke was not likely himself to insult the author by offering to make such changes; and Mallet could have no object in asking Bolingbroke to do what, if the original 'Rule Britannia' were his, he was capable of doing much better for himself. Rather such an action on the part of Mallet would have been equal to a public confession of his own inferiority; for we must remember that Bolingbroke was no poet. Nor should we forget the important circumstance that by this time 'Rule Britannia' had sprung into popularity—the one piece in the mask which had achieved that distinction. Mallet was hardly likely to allow Bolingbroke to tamper with a song of his own which, as it stood in 1740, had taken the public fancy; but from what we know of his character we shall not do him much injury by supposing that he withheld the name of the 'one song' and permitted its mutilation lest his 'friend' should have too much credit. 'Rule Britannia' certainly comes under this description. If Mallet wrote the original song he was likely now—in 1751—to say so plainly, considering the success it had meantime attained; while, on the other hand, by saying nothing he left the question as much in his own favour as in Thomson's.

As a matter of fact Mallet never made any specific claim to the authorship of 'Rule Britannia.' The entire mask of *Alfred*, it is true, was printed in the edition of his works published in 1759; but this does not help us in the least, seeing that, even as so printed, the work, according to Mallet's own admission, contained some things from the pen of Thomson. Moreover, while Mallet was still living —namely, in 1762—the original *Alfred* of 1740, including 'Rule Britannia' as a matter of course, was printed by Murdoch in his edition of Thomson. Thus, if the mere printing of the mask established the claim to the ode, we have the matter equally balanced. Something is sought to be made of the fact that 'Rule Britannia' is not included in the editions of Thomson published under the editorship of Lord Lyttleton in 1757 and 1759. This of course is, at the best, only a negative kind of argument; and in estimating its value we need only take into account the utter worthlessness, as an authority, of the editions referred to. The poet confided to Lyttleton the task of bringing out after his death a revised edition of his works. The choice proved to have been in every way unfortunate. In the exercise of his discretionary power Lord Lyttleton 'submitted the text to the most unwarrantable experiments; and, not satisfied with making numerous verbal changes, clearing up obscurities, and correcting the grammar—the points to which Thomson's anxiety seems to have been chiefly directed—he reconstructed entire lines, transposed whole passages, rejected others, and finally struck out the closing hymn, 'because it appeared to good judges that all the matter and thoughts in that hymn are much better expressed in *The Seasons* themselves.' The work of such an editor as this may be dismissed at once as utterly unreliable. Nor, in the present connection, is there any necessity for giving heed to it, remembering that Murdoch came with his splendid edition of Thomson, in two volumes quarto, very shortly after Lord Lyttleton had thus used his 'discretion.'

Mallet's claim to 'Rule Britannia,' it has thus been seen, is only an implied one. All the same it is tolerably clear that he wished the public to look upon him as the author of the ode; and it therefore comes in as a point of interest that Mallet can be shown to have directly claimed as his own some things to which he had no title whatever. Even the much-lauded ballad of 'William and Margaret,' which is always quoted in connection with his name, has been proved by Mr. Chappell to be a barefaced plagiarism of a ballad that was in existence long before Mallet's day. There is no doubt whatever about this; for the original ballad is now in the library of the British Museum, where it is open to all enquirers. Then there is the question of the poem entitled 'A Winter's Day.' How did Mallet deal with that production? Let Mr. Bell, one of Thomson's biographers, tell us. In 1740, he says, the poem was

communicated to the *Gentleman's Magazine* as having been written by a Scottish clergyman, and 'corrected by an eminent hand.' Mallet, according to the construction put upon certain allusions in his letters, apparently claimed the poem as his own, and it has always been included in his works as a piece 'written in a state of melancholy.' This assumption of a right in the verses may be easily explained by the supposition, which other circumstances justify, that Mallet was the 'eminent hand' of the *Gentleman's Magazine*, and that, not being very scrupulous in such matters, he carried off all the honours of the authorship. That the poem was written by Mr. Riccaultoun, however, admits of no reasonable doubt; but that gentleman having written little in this way, and not being very willing to come before the public as a poet, was probably indifferent to the fate of his verses' if indeed, in the seclusion of Hobkirk, he ever heard of the unauthorised use that was made of them.

Is it necessary to show the bearing of all this on the question of Mallet's claim to 'Rule Britannia'? If Mallet thought it worth his while to claim, on the strength of one or two "corrections," the rough and unskilful lines of an obscure poet, it does not require much argument to prove that he would have no qualms about carrying off the honours of a piece so celebrated as the patriotic ode, especially when the real author was no longer alive to assert his rights.

In this connection the character of Mallet should not be overlooked. For all that his friends may say to the contrary, he was a venal hack scribbler of the time, and one must have great reluctance in accepting his own testimony about himself. Macaulay speaks of him as 'a Scotchman of no literary fame, and of infamous character.' Johnson said he was ready for any dirty job, and that he was 'the only Scot whom Scotchmen did not commend.' Dr. Robertson, who knew him well, says that Mallet was 'not sound at heart,' and that he 'made a cat's paw of Thomson.' This description agrees with the character given of him by Lord Loughborough, who says in one of his letters, 'From the knowledge I have of him I feel an unaccountable propensity to believe the contrary of what he tells me.' In short, we have in Mallet a character sufficiently doubtful to put us on our guard in reference to any unsupported evidence, either direct or implied, which he may have put forward in favour of himself. Dr. Dinsdale, his biographer, has followed the too common plan of biographers by making a hero of his subject, but there is more than a set-off in the contemporary evidence on the other side.

It has often been remarked that the internal evidence of 'Rule Britannia' is all in favour of Thomson's authorship. This, at best, is a dangerous kind of argument ; and, unfortunately, there is too much similarity between Thomson and Mallet to make it of much use in the present case. 'Mallet's blank verse seems to my ear the echo of Thomson,' says Johnson. 'Their minor poems,' remarks one of Thomson's biographers, 'are much of the same order, and have the same common features. Their verses to their Amandas might be exchanged without injustice ; and it is not possible to determine by internal evidence their respective claims to the songs in the mask of *Alfred*, which was a joint production.' At the same time it is worthy of remark that Thomson has frequently dealt with patriotic themes ; witness his 'Liberty' and 'Britannia,' two productions which, in spirit, very much resemble the celebrated ode. He was an enthusiastic advocate of liberty, making constant appeals to freedom and Great Britain, while he was also a warm admirer of heroes and legislators. As Mr. Logie Robertson has pointed out, there is not a single image or idea in 'Rule Britannia' which does not occur, or recur, elsewhere in the general body of his poetry. Nothing like this can be said of Mallet. That Thomson's known songs, for the most part, carry with them no lyrical rhythm is not much to the point in this question. No fact is more fully established than this, that even a writer of very moderate ability, while producing scores of songs, may produce no more than one of undying merit.

The question of the authorship of ' Rule Britannia' will probably, however, never be definitely settled. Thomson left it in doubt ; so did Mallet. Neither directly claimed the ode, and although many of their contemporaries must have known the facts, they found no occasion to speak out on the matter, with the result that one more of our national songs has been added to the list of controverted subjects. If only Murdoch, the friend and biographer of Thomson, had told what he knew ! If only Mallet had been plain and straightforward, and declared either himself or Thomson to be the author ! Happily for our posterity we are more careful about our honours in these later days.

J. CUTHBERT HADDEN.

ON THE SELLING OF BOOKS

FEW questions have given rise to more speculation than those connected with the distributing and selling of books. They are frequently enigmas even to those who are behind the scenes, and are conversant with the methods by which the enormous output of books reaches the reading public.

To authors, publishers, and booksellers the subject is one of vast importance. Could a definite solution of the question be arrived at much heart-burning (especially on the part of young authors) would be obviated.

In discussing this question, all reference to the literary quality of books is purposely omitted. A timely work on a subject of passing importance will frequently sell, be the book good or bad. It is, therefore, of books as articles of commerce, and of the best means of attracting public attention to them, that this paper will treat.

Before entering upon the details of the problem, it will be of interest to glance at the means by which books, when they are issued by the publishers, find their way to the shop of the retail bookseller. It is generally assumed that the booksellers obtain the whole of their supply of books direct from the publisher. Such is not, however, the case ; for by the multiplying of new books and the continued additions made to the list of publishers, it would be almost impossible for a retail bookseller to keep in stock all the books issued even by one publisher.

He has, therefore, to rely upon the wholesale bookseller, who acts as chief distributing agent for the publisher. This arrangement, it may be said, has been found indispensable by the retail bookseller and of great utility by the publisher. It is from the wholesale establishment that the former obtains his daily supplies, and here, also, he directs most of his inquiries for information. The knowledge available at these establishments is encyclopædic, as indeed it must needs be, since it is expected to embrace the titles, prices, &c., of all books that have been published, as well as of those announced for publication.

The extent of the wholesale trade may be judged from the statement, recently made, that the principal distributing house had over a million books always in stock. On a busy day, few sights are more interesting than the counters of these establishments.

Here congregate in noisy haste the messengers from the various retail houses ('collectors' they are called), who are seeking for books which are 'not in stock' with the shopkeepers.

The books required are usually issued by different publishers, and no matter what the size or cost of the book may be, it can generally be obtained at one of these great emporiums of literature.

Many and varied are the enquiries made by the 'collectors,' and when it is stated that, in addition to the trade at the counter, 1,500 letters were received at one of these establishments from country customers in one day, resulting in the despatch of seven hundred or eight hundred parcels, it will be readily understood that the labour involved in grappling with the details of the work must be prodigious.

As to modes of business, each new book when ready for publication is brought to these establishments for 'subscription'—that is, to ascertain how many copies will be bought. The sale of a book is often greatly influenced by the number purchased at this time. During the busy autumn season as many as seventy new books are sometimes submitted for 'subscription' in one day.

In the distribution of books to the public the most important medium is undoubtedly the intelligent bookseller. We use the term 'intelligent bookseller' advisedly, because there are now many calling themselves booksellers who are not rightly so named. To the latter one saleable article stands upon the same footing as another; for in handling a book he looks upon it simply as an article of commerce upon which he can get his share of profit. On the other hand, the intelligent bookseller can always make himself felt as an important factor in the sale of books, if he stocks them carefully, and takes every opportunity of pointing out their various merits to his customers. In this way he can do more to promote sales than any number of advertisements, be the mediums ever so carefully and judiciously selected. Indeed, many instances could be cited in which a bookseller has himself disposed of a large portion of an edition solely by this system of introduction. He may also do much by the careful distribution of prospectuses among his book-buying *clientèle*. Consider also what a useful advertising medium is the counter of the intelligent bookseller's shop. The majority of his customers, belonging as they do to the cultured and well-to-do class, will naturally examine any book which appears unique or striking in its authorship or its appearance. Interest is thus aroused and conversation promoted; the book is mentioned to friends and talked about at the dinner table or in the smoking-room; a demand is by these means created, the result of which it is difficult to estimate.

Many articles have been written and much correspondence has from time to time appeared in literary journals upon the decay of bookselling, but it is in booksellers themselves, rather than in book-selling, that this decay is most noticeable. Probably one reason for this is the want of interest shown by the leaders of the trade, especially in London, to the various organisations which would materially affect the education and improvement of its younger members. The fact of apprenticeship being somewhat out of date has also, without doubt, lessened the business capabilities and literary knowledge of the assistant. Perhaps some day a leader may come forward who will attempt the reorganisation of the trade institutions, and establish an educational or technical guild for the encouragement of knowledge in the bookseller of the future. This might well be undertaken by the Stationers' Company, which was founded as far back as 1403, and in that year completed its organisation as a guild of book dealers. The term *Stationarii* was then applied to the booksellers of the University towns. If some educational scheme could be devised the well-informed bookseller would be the rule, rather than, as is now unfortunately the case, the exception.

There never was a period when so many books were published as the present. The annual return issued by the *Publishers' Circular* shows that, during the year 1895, 5,581 new books and 935 new editions were published. From the same source we learn that an advance of nearly 50 per cent. in poetry was made, by comparison with the previous year. Yet we hear it said that poetry is not read nowadays. What, then, becomes of all the volumes of verse issued, if they are not read? there is no question as to the quantity produced. This activity should make the trade of the bookseller more important, and should lead to a corresponding increase in his business; but, unfortunately, there has sprung up during the last few years many additional channels of distribution, such as the Stores, &c., which, from the bookseller's point of view, are not satisfactory.

Advertising is, next to the bookseller, the most important factor in the sale of books. In England publishers spend larger sums in advertising than in any other country in the world, some indeed spending thousands of pounds annually in trying to make their books sell. Many devices are resorted to, and great ingenuity is displayed in the attempt to find out the best channels for advertising class or technical books, in order that the public for which a particular work is intended may be reached.

Much has yet to be done before the present system of advertising can be said to bring an adequate return. Most publishers have certain fixed mediums, but it is open to question if proper care and thought are always given in making the selection.

A case came under my notice not long since, in which an author spent over 200*l.* in advertising his book, but even this did not result in the sale of a *single copy*. On the other hand, only 10*l.* was expended on a popular 3*s.* 6*d.* book upon publication, and within twelve months nearly 80,000 copies were disposed of. This would seem to show that no amount of advertising will make a bad book popular beyond the author's circle of friends and admirers, while a good book will make its way with little advertising, without friends, and often in the face of adverse criticisms.

Authors themselves frequently show great originality in attracting public attention. Sometimes it is by a speech, sometimes through a clerical friend in the pulpit, a member of Parliament in the House, or by correspondence in the Press. These methods, and others not less ingenious, are resorted to in order to keep their name and that of their book before the public. Of course, where an author already possesses considerable social or political influence, the matter is upon quite a different footing. The ' new author' (to use the cant phrase) appears to have instituted better methods of making himself known. He usually belongs to a clique of men who write of each other in the Press, and talk of each other at their club, in drawing-rooms ; in season or out of season matters not, so that they are talked about. Cases could be mentioned in which an author has ordered copies of his recently published book from several booksellers, stating that he would call for them in a few days. This he failed to do, and the booksellers have been obliged to place the copies in their stock. It is hardly necessary to add that this system of increasing sales can only be practised once during the author's lifetime.

The commercial traveller is an important factor in the publisher's machinery, and is, if an intelligent man, of great importance in promoting the sale of books. By becoming acquainted with the works he is selling, he is enabled to influence a bookseller in stocking a book, and thus initiate what has already been referred to as of great importance to the vitality of a book.

It occasionally happens that publishers themselves are to blame for the inability of the bookseller to dispose of the copies of a work which he has purchased from them, in consequence of the former over-estimating the value or importance of the book. In the majority of instances the publisher relies upon the opinion of his ' reader,' and although in most cases this opinion is a correct one, yet it may be that the ' reader' has no sympathy with the subject under consideration, or an insufficient knowledge of the requirements of the public, and thus his opinion is practically worthless. Many MSS. have been refused on these grounds, which have afterwards been published with marked success. The case of a very popular work on the subject of science and religion occurs to me as I write. It was rejected by one publisher on the ground of its unscientific character (such was his ' reader's' report), but being read by another in sympathy with its subject, it was immediately accepted, and a great success was secured.

The bookseller is frequently heard to complain that so many books are issued without any apparent *raison d'être*. This is, of course, quite a publisher's question, and with the great activity shown by the writers of the day, it must indeed be difficult to discriminate. Take the public expression of opinion of two representative publishers, Mr. F. Macmillan and Mr. A. Chatto. The former, at a recent dinner, stated that his firm only accepted 22 out of 315 MSS. submitted to them in one year, and the latter in a Press interview asserted that his firm retained on an average about 13 out of 500. If the bookseller could, in all cases, rely upon each book being carefully and judiciously selected by the publisher, much of the dead stock which is the bane of bookselling would disappear. Pot-boilers will always be produced, but if they could be dealt with as such, and not as serious literary efforts, it would be better for all concerned.

There is a practice of recent growth (probably imported from America) which must not be overlooked here. A publisher who is on the eve of issuing some book, which he thinks will be of general interest, sends out to the writers of paragraphs in the columns of literary gossip in the various papers scraps of information respecting the work, and details of the author's personality. The appearance of such information, given at intervals, whets the appetite of the public, and is frequently of great value in creating a demand for the book.

' Log-rolling' has sometimes a considerable effect on sales, but the paragraphs employed for this purpose must be very carefully written, and as judiciously distributed. The system is by no means a healthy one.

Reviews of books in the various journals have now less influence than formerly on sales, and are frequently of interest to the author only. A few years ago a favourable review in the *Times* or the *Spectator* was certain to send a book through at least one edition. It has been suggested that, in order to obtain a perfectly independent criticism, every editor or reviewer should purchase the book to be noticed. This arrangement might possibly result in a more healthy and impartial review, but it is doubtful if it would be as satisfactory to the author who is anxious for an opinion upon his work. The present system of sending out so plentifully presentation copies of books is certainly open to abuse, as they are frequently disposed of by the reviewer, and so interfere with legitimate sales.

Two cases might be mentioned, in passing, in which the Press has played an important part in the fortunes of books. During the Franco-German war a little *brochure* was issued, entitled *The Fight at Dame Europa's School*. This was declined by many London publishers, and finally issued in the country, a very small edition only being printed. A notice of it appeared in the *Times*, and such was the demand created thereby, that about 200,000 copies were eventually sold. The other case was that of *Called Back*, by Hugh Conway. This work was brought out in the country as an annual. It was noticed in a society journal, and so flattering was the review that the author's reputation was at once established. Between 300,000 and 400,000 copies were finally disposed of.

Occasionally one of our leading statesmen mentions a book to illustrate a point in a speech.   This is certain. to. cause inquiries to be made for the work.   Unfortunately these instances are less frequent than in former years.   If men like John Bright, .Lord Beaconsfield, or Mr. Gladstone, in the heyday of their popularity, quoted from a particular publication, the result was to influence considerably the fortunes of the book.   Many will remember the latter's masterly criticism of *Robert Elsmere* in this Review, which did so much towards the making of the success of this book.   From the same statesman letters of criticism are frequently received by authors and publishers, proving the interest he still takes in current literature, as well as materially influencing the sale of the book in question.

Fashion and fads are answerable for the sale of much of the fiction of to-day, when so many political and social questions are freely ventilated in the novel.   From the days of Richardson to those of Thackeray the novel was the vehicle through which polite society was discussed, the facts and lessons of history were reviewed or enforced, and social chit-chat of all kinds chronicled.   Now we have novels in which are to be found discussions upon philosophy, religion, Home Rule, the eternal ' Woman' problem, and every other question that agitates the public mind.   Be it society, moral or immoral, or the latest theories or discoveries in science, medicine, or surgery, each is manipulated with a freedom that would have made our forefathers blush for shame.

Though no rule can be laid down that will entirely regulate the sale of books, yet I have no hesitation in stating that a certain sale can always be relied on for a book that really has value in it.   To obtain this let it be one into which the author has put his best thoughts from a realistic or ideal standpoint, let it be carefully written and rewritten, so that its merit may come up to the standard of literary culture. Then let it be well printed and attractively bound, and issued by a publisher who has a reputation to maintain.   The publisher will see that the distributing agencies before mentioned work it well with the booksellers, and will advertise it judiciously, and if possible get it talked about.   By these means if a large sale is not secured there will, at least, be one satisfactory alike to author, publisher, and bookseller.

The trade of bookselling is at the present time in a most unenviable condition, and is, I think, suffering more acutely from competition than any other.   For years past discounts have been steadily increasing, and it is now a question if the bottom has not been reached.   If this be the case, it is reasonable to suppose that the trade may yet be placed upon a more satisfactory basis, although, for the moment, the Publishers' Association and the Association of Booksellers do not appear to be working in harmony to this end. If a better understanding is arrived. at between these two bodies, a satisfactory (and remunerative) condition.

One word upon the future of bookselling. There are in our midst a large number of pessimists, who, because in many instances they do not adapt themselves to the altered conditions of the trade, or feel themselves capable of grappling with the present enormous output of books, think that the end of our modern bookseller is within measurable distance. But I maintain that the existence of the bookseller is a necessity, and it will always be so. By the spread of education the bookseller becomes part of the nation's educational machinery. Further, by his trade, in connection with that of the publisher, who by the issue and sale of books, more especially those dealing with technical and educational subjects, makes all professions and most trades possible, and as it has been in the past so in the future, the bookseller's shop should be a centre of influence and intelligence.

I am fully convinced that the bookseller who has a well-informed mind and one always capable of development, who takes an interest in his trade because he loves books, and who has business capabilities worthy of his trade, is bound to make more than a bare living. He will not now, probably, leave a fortune behind him, but he will have the satisfaction of being associated with the greatest minds of his age, as well as with that distinguishing characteristic of a nation's intelligence, its literature. Booksellers may console themselves by being classed with those who follow literature as a profession, and of whom Froude has said, ' It happens to be the only occupation in which wages are not given in proportion to the goodness of the work done.'

J. Shaylor
(of Simpkin, Marshall, & Co., Limited.)

A SEVENTEENTH CENTURY

CHESTERFIELD

IN the year 1656 Dorothy Osborne wrote the last of her love letters to Sir William Temple; the same year saw the publication by her uncle Francis Osborne of his once famous treatise, *Advice to a Son.* Though the writings of both are contemporaneous, though they were both members of the same family, it would be impossible to find two people more totally opposed, both in their views of life and in their modes of thought. Both alike possessed the art of vividly expressing their own personality in their writings, both alike are typical of their time, both give us a real insight into the feelings and interests of their day. Yet they are as wide as the poles asunder. Different in literary style, in politics, in temperament, and in their situation in life, as well as in their ages, they have given us two pictures of the society of the time, which, though both bearing the stamp of truth, resemble each other in hardly a single detail. Thanks to the energy of Mr. Parry, Dorothy Osborne is now well known, and it is unnecessary to call attention to the romantic charm of her letters and the unaffected grace of her style; once rescued from oblivion, she can never again be forgotten. Her story and her delightful self are drawn with a freshness and sureness of touch that will always awaken the sympathy of any reader in every age; they are so absolutely human. How astonished she would be if she could know that her letters, written for the eye of one alone, had been made into a book and published. How astonished and how alarmed, for we find her writing of Lady Newcastle:

'Have you seen a book of poems newly come out, made by my Lady Newcastle? For God's sake send it to me. They say 'tis ten times more extravagant than her dress. Sure the poor woman is a little distracted, she could never be so ridiculous else as to venture at writing books.' A sentiment which even that sour old misogynist Francis Osborne would have approved. They would have agreed in little else; and yet had not the difficult course of love at last run

Francis Osborne himself would have been no less surprised at his niece's late-grown reputation, when his own name has been so completely forgotten. But he too has had his own share of fame. The *Advice* was published at Oxford in 1656; it was at once greedily bought up, and was especially admired by young scholars. In two years it passed through six editions. In 1658 certain godly ministers in the University, whom Mr. Osborne did not scruple to describe as high-nosed hypocrites, detected a flavour of Atheism in the book, and brought it under the notice of the Vice-Chancellor, Dr. Conant. He refused to burn it publicly, as they demanded ('such was the stupid enthusiasm of those times'), but caused its sale to be prohibited. Its popularity was at once assured, and the sale spread rapidly. Sir William Petty told Pepys that the three most popular works of the day were Brown's *Religio Medici*, Butler's *Hudibras*, and Osborne's *Advice*. The last and twenty-second edition in a complete collection of his works was published in 1722, but from that time it steadily declined in favour. It was contemptuously noticed by Johnson, and this, with the exception of a reference by Sir W. Scott to Osborne's historical writings, is the last we hear of our author till the present day.

Soon after its publication a part of the *Advice*, from its misogynistic character, aroused great debate, and a violent controversy in print raged for some time. John Heydon, the astrologer, took up the cudgels on behalf of women, and published in 1658, under the pseudonym of Eugenius Theodidactus, his *Advice to a Daughter*. The astrologer does not mince his words in criticism. To him Francis Osborne is 'a diseased Maccabee,' a person 'whose mind, could it be looked into, would prove infinitely more monstrous than his body,' 'a monkey who has gnawed away his tail,' and seeks to persuade his son to do likewise; 'a clumsy, doting old wittal,' author of 'a profane, Atheistical old pamphlet.' He continually apostrophises

Osborne in the intervals of his argument with such exclamations as the following: 'You crampt Compendium,' 'Sir Kirk Dragooner,' 'You Purlew of a Metempsychosis,' 'Spleen of a Blue-stockinged Justice,' 'Pigwiggin Myrmidon,' 'Fleabitten Canonick Weed,' 'Camel,' 'Lybian Proselyte,' 'Neast Gull of a young Apocrypha.'

Osborne died that same year, without replying to this remarkable effusion, but his cause was taken up by one T. P., who rushed into print with a work called *Advice to Balaam's Ass, or Momus catechised.* It is described on the title page as an 'Answer to a certain scurrilous and abusive scribbler, one John Heydon, author of *Advice to a Daughter,*' and certainly T. P. did not neglect to pay back the astrologer in his own coin. He describes him as one 'who, by the interposition of his opacous and ridiculous conceptions, malapertly endeavours to eclipse the splendour of an eminent author.' After rating him soundly as a 'Master of Gotham College, a grand proficient in Bacchus' school, and meriting to be chief professor of Billingsgate,' he addresses him as 'thou embryo of a history, thou cadet of a pamphleteer, thou Geoffrey in swabberslops, thou little negro, mounted on the elephant of thine own folly,' and advises him in 'the next book you choke the Preis with (for all your works are very dry), prostrate yourself in an ingenious recantation at the feet of grave and learned Mr. Osborne.' He concludes, 'I fight this great gyant, whose thundering name would affright many, although nothing is able to terrify me, except non-permission to subscribe myself, Your ready servant, T. P.'

Such were the amenities of literary and educational controversy in the days of the Commonwealth.

The author of this notable work, the object of so much admiration and so much abuse, was born in 1593. He was the youngest of the five sons of Sir John Osborne, of Chicksands Priory. To the neglect of his education, as he tells us, he was kept at home till his sixteenth year, and then met with the usual fate of a younger son in those days—he was sent to London to seek his fortune. Hanging about the Court, he attracted the attention of the Earl of Pembroke, who made him a steward in his household, and finally master of his horse. Later he obtained a post in the office of the Lord Treasurer's Remembrancer, which seems to have been a sort of family perquisite. About 1650 he removed to live at Oxford, partly to superintend the education of his son, to whom the *Advice* is addressed, and for whom he procured a Fellowship at All Souls', and partly, no doubt, because then, as now, Oxford was a pleasant place of residence. Here, through the influence of his brother-in-law, Colonel William Draper, a strong Parliamentarian, he obtained some employment under the Commonwealth.

These are the bare outlines of his life, but they tell us little that can account for the extraordinary cynicism that animates his work, and the gloomy pessimism that is apparent on every page. The 'Advice' is that of a man thoroughly beaten and battered in the tempest of life, prematurely aged and soured by many disappointments and sorrows, a man utterly devoid of any enthusiasm or strong belief, who feels that the world is a bad one, and can only be made tolerable by following the dictates of prudence and avoiding rather than surmounting obstacles. Mingled with all this, he displays much worldly shrewdness and true observation; but though his directions are generally extremely moral in themselves, yet they are often based upon very unworthy motives. Osborne belonged to a type which must have been very common at the time: excellent, quiet men, good citizens, thoroughly commonplace in sentiment, but above all heartily sick of the turmoil and clatter of those 'intoxicated times.' In politics they called themselves Parliamentarians, because they hoped from that side most chance of settled government, but they were far removed from out and out partisanship, and indeed were ready to change over without difficulty to whichever party seemed most likely to succed.

The lines of party cleavage were extremely vaguely defined; Osborne speaks approvingly of Charles the First in spite of his own proclivities. Possibly the position he took up may have estranged him from his family, for the Osbornes were a sturdy race of Cavaliers, and Sir Peter, his brother, lost health and fortune in fighting for the King. But difference in politics could coexist with the closest ties of family intimacy, witness the Verney family—Sir Edmund, the standard-bearer, lost his life at Edgehill in the royal cause, Sir Ralph, his son, was a Parliament man, while another son, Edmund, was an enthusiastic Cavalier and was massacred at Drogheda. The account of himself given by Lilly, the astrologer, in his autobiography, sums up the views of a good many of his contemporaries. 'At first,' he says, ' I was more Cavalier than Roundhead, but afterwards I engaged body and soul in the cause of the Parliament, but still with much affection to his Majesty's person and unto monarchy.' The wide prevalence of such sentiments goes far to account for the ease with which the Restoration was accomplished.

The *Advice* is divided into five sections, on Studies, Love and Marriage, Travel, Government, and Religion. A second part was afterwards published, but this is of little importance compared with the first, and its aphorisms are much more commonplace and obvious. The section on Studies contains much shrewd observation on men and manners, dressed in language sometimes very quaint and epigrammatic. It lays down some directions for study, which sound oddly to modern ears, and its maxims of conduct, if generally sound and prudent, are not based upon very exalted motives.

Some of his general principles of education are worth quoting for their felicity of expression. 'A few books well studied and throughly digested nourish the understanding more than hundreds gargled in the mouth, as ordinary students use,' and ' huge volumes, like the ox roasted whole at Bartholomew Fair, may proclaim plenty of labour and inventions, but afford less of what is delicate, savoury and well concocted, than smaller pieces.'

An observation upon ' collegiate discipline, that all the reverence to superiors learned in the Hall and Chapel is lost in the irreverent discourse you have of them in your chambers,' would seem to us to indicate that Osborne had a true appreciation of undergraduate ways, but the eagle eye of Heydon detected in the simple words a design to restore the Jesuitical doctrine of passive obedience.

Osborne has a wholesome feeling that ' a sole academick education renders men pedantick,' and accordingly urges on his son not to ' take them for a pattern that do make all places to rattle with Latin and Greek.' When he comes to discuss particular studies, he, as an historian himself, has a regard for history, but thinks it all the same full of likely falsehood. The ordinary University course has of course to be the basis, but, if time allows, some inspection should be made into physic, for 'the intricacy of the study is not great,' and ' it will add to your welcome wherever you go, it being usual especially for ladies to yield no less reverence to their physicians than to their confessors.' Surely grave and learned Mr. Osborne must have noted that down in the hot days of youth, when the fair sex was not always so disagreeable to him, and we cannot think that he had much acquaintance with Dr. Harvey and his doctrines.

Languages, again, are strictly condemned, especially for an intending diplomat, because treating with foreign princes in their own tongue is beneath English dignity ; moreover, an interpreter will give time to recall a hasty speech and afford leisure for deliberation. ' It is besides too much an honouring of their tongue and undervaluing your own to profess yourself a master therein, especially since they scorn to learn yours.' The first and wisest Earl of Pembroke thought so too, 'for he did return an answer to the Spanish Ambassador in Welsh, for which I have heard him highly commended,' though probably not by the Spaniard. Poetry proclaims your head like ' ships of war, fuller of trimming than lading, and music is likewise condemned, especially for women, for they 'do not rarely decline in modesty proportionately to the progress they make in Musick, and (if handsome) are traps baited at both ends, and catch strangers as often as their husbands, no less tired with the one than the other.'

If the son Osborne followed the advice of his father, he must have been a very respectable and cautious citizen, but he could not have in the Gospel. But great persons in distress must be avoided; he must never go bail either for friends or relations; only persons who are likely to be useful must be courted, and these at the least expense. In saving another he is to 'beware of drowning himself, for swimming is good, but not out of your depth.' The great receipt for success in life is Impudence. 'It is as useful in a court as armour in a camp, and by it Scotchmen go further with a shilling than an Englishman can ordinarily pass for a crown.' It is a curious commentary on the times that Osborne should have thought it necessary to warn his son that 'it is an office unbecoming a gentleman to be an Intelligencer, which in real truth is no better than a spy.' Unfortunately the reason appears to be that they 'are often tortured and die miserably.' Yet Tom Verney, that incorrigible rogue of the Verney family, in spite of adding this profession to many other low and disreputable practices, managed to reach the ripe age of over ninety years, though possibly he died miserably at last.

Under the same head of Studies come a number of very miscellaneous directions for the conduct of life; this excellent father does not hesitate to descend into very minute details. We will hope that he was moved rather by general considerations than by the particular behaviour of his son, the Fellow of All Souls', when he warned him not to eat at meals 'as long as you are able, especially in England, where meat, aptest to inveagle the stomach, comes last,' to get up as soon as sleep left him, and not to drink, 'being hot, unless Sack,' not a very satisfying drink, we should have thought, to the thirsty soul even of a fellow of a college. 'Such thirst,' he goes on, 'is better quenched by gargles, Liquorish, a cherry or Tobacco, the use of which I neither persuade nor prohibit, having taken it myself since sixteen without any extraordinary marks of good or ill, but cannot approve of nosing or swallowing it down.'

Apparently the youth of sixteen had occasionally indulged in other solaces besides tobacco, if we may judge from the feeling way he writes in his old age about drunkenness. 'If unfortunately overtaken by such a distemper, do not move from the place you received it in, by which some part of the shame may be avoided and more of the danger attending the irregular motions of this giddy spirit.'

A thorough condemnation of the distemper would have been more becoming, especially from so respectable a mentor, but on the question of duelling he is certainly ahead of his time. From a different point of view he might be said to display a thoroughly craven temper.

After so many years spent amid alarms of war, the smell of blood is absolutely hateful to him—wit is a better defence than the sword. Although ' if an injury hath been received of so rank a nature as to extort (in point of honour) an unsavoury word, never suitable to the mouth of a gentleman, swordsmen do advise to second it with a blow by way of prevention ; yet this their decree not being confirmed by Act of Parliament, I cannot find it suitable with Prudence or Religion to make the sword the Umpire.'   Caution descends into timidity when we are told ' not to prosecute a coward too far, lest he turn valiant to your disadvantage,' but it is more in place in the recommendation ' not to speak disgracefully of any at ordinaries or public meetings, lest some friend or kinsmen being there should force you to a base recantation.'

Francis Osborne is no lion-hearted hero ; certainly he will venture no risks for distressed damsels, even in the modern form of ' Ushering them to Plays, Maskes or other such public Spectacles.'   That should be avoided nearly on the same principles that ' dogs are not to be carried to Court for fear of such as may spurn them.'   We cannot praise very highly the morality which condemns making love to a married woman, because it increases ' not only the sin, but also the danger ; neither can you, if questioned by her husband, use with hope of victory any sharper weapon than Repentance sheathed in a modest excuse.'

But these disparaging remarks on woman are merely the preliminary murmurs of the storm that is about to burst on their devoted heads.   In the section on Love and Marriage, Francis Osborne gives his dislike for the sex full play.   Nothing is too bad for them— they are the curse of life.   No doubt the good Francis was not eager to provide his son with an allowance sufficient for maintaining a wife, but such a desire cannot wholly account for the intense passion with which he denounces marriage.   In the conclusion of his work he tells us that it is founded on his own miserable experience, and we cannot help suspecting that in the days before he wooed the excellent Anne Draper he must have met with some cruel disappointment which lasted on through his married life and permanently soured his temper.   Still, however forgiving a wife may be to her husband's past, even the most accommodating spouse must have felt some indignation when she read her husband's remarks on marriage.

If ever marriages were on all sides happy (which is no schism to doubt of), experience never found them amongst such as had no other nealing but what they received from the flames of love.   Those virtues and graces and reciprocal desires bewitched affection expected to meet and enjoy, fruition and experience will find absent, and nothing left but a Painted Box which children and time will empty of delight, leaving diseases behind, and at best incurable antiquity.

Love is a storm in which all must be tossed, but we must not be shipwrecked by trusting to its false glamour, for marriage is a precipice yawning before the unwary like a trap set for flies. Many are led into it by the attractions of beauty, and the dreadful result is graphically painted: 'Make not a celebrated beauty the object of your choice, unless you are ambitious of rendering your house as populous as a confectioner's shop, to which the gaudy wasps no less than the liquorish flies make it their business to resort in hope of obtaining a lick at your Honeypot.' The poor crowded-out husband is forbidden the luxury of rudeness; he must 'attend in patience, till his Worship, or perhaps his Lordship, hath pumped his wit dry, having no more compliments left, but to take his leave.' Even as regards beauty itself, if you consider it alone, 'quite discharged from such debentures as it owes to the arts of Tirewomen, Tailors, Shoemakers, and perhaps Painters, you will find the remains so inconsiderable as scarce to deserve your present thoughts.'

There is no remedy anywhere, for the English Laws (even in the days when there was no thought of Married Women's Property Acts or female franchise) 'are composed so far in favour of wives as if our ancestors had sent women to their Parliaments, whilst their Heads were a-woolgathering at home.'

It may indeed be 'strongly presumed that the hand of policy first hung this Padlock' (of marriage) 'on the liberty of men, and after custom had lost the key, the Church, according to her wonted subtlety, took upon her to protect it.' 'Nevertheless the wily priests are so tender of their own conveniences, as to forbid all marriage to themselves upon as heavy a punishment as they do Polygamy unto others. While to render it more glib to the wider swallow of the much abused Laity they have gilt it with the glorious epithet of a Sacrament, which yet they loath to clog their stomachs withall.' Truly a curious theory of the origin of priestly celibacy. In Dorothy Osborne's letters there is a remarkable parallel to this passage.

What an age we do live in, where 'tis a miracle if in ten couples that are married, two of them live so as not to publish to the world that they cannot agree. I begin to be of your opinion of him that (when the Roman church just propounded whether it were not convenient for priests not to marry) said that it might be convenient enough, but sure it was not our Saviour's intention, for He commanded that all should take up their cross and follow Him, and for his part he was confident that there was no such cross as a wife.

And yet two centuries have rolled away and marriage still flourishes as an institution, and still people are found to announce its supposed failure as a new and startling phenomenon of the present day. Two centuries hence somebody will probably be making the same discovery.

But Francis Osborne is no faddist; he draws rein a little: he recognises that marriage may be a necessity after all, he remembers that he too has a wife (whose virtues, he prudently adds, are inferior to none), and, like the sensible worldly man he is, goes on to show how union with these 'peevish daughters of our beldame Eve' may best be made endurable. The best brought up dowager could not disapprove of his principles. 'Though nothing can wholly disengage marriage from such inconveniences as may obstruct felicity, yet they are best palliated under a great estate, all other arguments receiving commonly refutation from Time and Experience.' 'The yoke of Marriage must be lined with the richest stuff and softest outward conveniences, else it will gall your neck and heart,' and a 'Poor marriage entitles shame and misery upon Posterity, who receive little warmth from the Vertue, much less from the Beauty of their mother.' But when we have once made up our minds to marry an heiress, we must proceed with extreme caution; popular rumour is so apt 'to dilate a portion. or jointure beyond its natural limits.' We must look well to our settlements, lest they lead to litigation, 'by which husbands are tied to a black box more miserable than that of Pandora, there being in the Law hope of nothing but troubles and injustice.'

A widow is worst of all, for she often has her fortune tied up so as to 'make him thrash for a pension, who ought to command all.' Ladies were probably smaller in stature in those days; it would not be always safe to apply the remedy of wife-beating now. These concessions made, Osborne begins to be alarmed lest he has gone too far, and lest his son should construe his words into a general approval of marriage. This cannot be allowed on any terms, and a solemn warning is given that 'to hang a neat wench, like a fair picture, in your heart and turn host to a bare holly bush, is so high a blasphemy against discretion that would exceed pity and forgiveness, especially in relation to you, that have had these rocks marked out for you on all sides by the advice of an indulgent father.' It is to be hoped that the indulgence was shown in practice, for the father goes on to point out that children are mere nuisances, nothing more to us than the paring of our nails, whose loss should be accepted with composure. Even the wish to have a successor to carry on the family name is very silly: 'it is the poorest way of immortalising that can be, and as natural to a cobbler as a prince, and not seldom reached out by a grave stone.'

But above all, again and again, he cries, Do not marry for Love— once make yourself a pupil to him, and 'he shall persuade you to make a league with misery, and embrace Beggary for a friend, and after this you are capable of no higher honour than to be registered in one of his Martyrological Ballads and sung by Dairy Maids to a pitiful tune.'

There is no record of how the son received all this excellent of his father's early life it is certain that he would have smiled a good deal. There is extant a letter of his to a friend in which, in language extraordinarily coarse and vulgar, he persuades him not to marry a rich but very ugly and deformed old maid, for reasons quite different to these sage arguments. And there is also another letter, which might have been written by some gay Cavalier, to two sisters, one black and the other fair, so that ' I might comprize in one letter the total sum of all the perfection in womanhood,' and ending, ' To both I remain an equal captive.' Still more, the enemy of poetry and the stern hater of women once committed himself so far as to write ' Lines to a Looking-glass.'

> Tell me, dear glass, by what strange art
> Thou bearest her image without breaking,
> When the same form doth burst my heart
> Just at the moment I am speaking.

Perhaps, if the original of that image had been less obdurate, the *Advice* might have been very different in tone. At any rate the romance had long since passed, and whether this was the key to his sombre temper or not, Francis would have rated soundly any such outburst from his son. But we see that he had reason for his concluding remark, ' Youth may at present make much of this look like blasphemy, but when so many winters have snowed on your head as on your father's, you will think it canonical and fit to be read to posterity.'

Love and Marriage disposed of, Osborne turns to the discussion of Travel. The Englishman was ever a globe-trotter, but at that time the Continent was particularly crowded with refugees of all kinds, and, if we can trust Osborne's remarks upon the Englishman abroad, it is not difficult to account for their bad reputation. English clergymen abroad are peculiarly distasteful to him, and indeed all Englishmen should be avoided, because they are so quarrelsome and inclined to mock at foreign ways and indulge in odious comparisons, which land them in dangerous disputes. He gives much careful advice about the danger of inns or chance acquaintances, and the folly of bestowing tips at your departure when you have no intention of returning ; one injunction in particular is very quaintly worded— namely, to avoid giving or receiving any favours from women, ' there being none any ways acceptable, to which some Ruffin (in Italy called Braves, who will murder a man for a crown) doth not pretend an interest, either as a husband, kinsman or servant.'

In fact, so many are the dangers of travel, that it is very doubtful whether any should travel at all, but here we must yield to popular opinion ; yet ' those only should travel (and that only in company with Ambassadors or persons of quality) who carry over large and thriving talents, and do not bury them in the Levity of France, the Pride of Spain, and the Treachery of Italy.' If people are not well educated, by travelling they merely add 'Affectation to Folly and Atheism to Curiosity—like the factors of Solomon they bring home Apes and Peacocks as well as Gold.'

The two remaining sections contain Osborne's views on Government and Religion. They are such as might have been expected from the author of a pamphlet persuading to a 'mutual compliance with the present government.' Throughout there runs the same worldly shrewdness, mixed with a cowardice so great as almost to amount to folly, and a tendency to choose the winning side so eager as to be almost imprudent. 'A quick evasion cannot but be deemed better than a buried valour,' that was the mainspring of his policy. 'Submit quickly,' he says, 'to any power Providence shall be pleased to mount into the saddle without inquiring into their rights,' and 'give any acknowledgment required by authority,' and 'be not licorish after change, for he that seeks perfection upon earth, leaves nothing new for the saints to find in heaven.'

How a man of such truly conservative principles can ever have been a Roundhead is difficult to conceive, till we remember that to follow the winning side was a higher principle still: loyalty he could not understand; he could not make his living by the King, so why should he support him? Rather, he says, 'follow the stream of the City of London; it is sure to win.' Yet for all this kind of sordidness one or two redeeming virtues shine out. Osborne is no snob. 'Despise none for meanness of birth, yet do not ordinarily make them your companions, unless you find them clarified by excellent parts or guilded by fortune or powers.'

Osborne's attitude to the politics of the day was that of a spectator, and he can observe and criticise with some acuteness; but we cannot respect a man who stands aside in such momentous times, though there must have been many of like mind with him. The opportunist principles which are at least excusable in politics become repulsive when applied to religion. God and the magistrates are coupled together as nearly equal objects of reverence; the conscience should be kept tender, 'but not so raw as to winch and kick at all you understand not, nor let it baffle your wit out of the bounds of discretion.'

But with all this Osborne has a kind of saving common-sense and philosophic toleration about him, which makes him appear very much ahead of his times, and retrieves our bad opinion of him. That 'Religions do not naturally differ so much in themselves as fiery and uncharitable men pretend,' is one of the cardinal points of his faith.

On the subject of witchcraft he is especially sensible. It is common among us,' and his blame of the 'ignorance of the judges, malice of the witnesses, and stupidity of the poor parties accused.' He goes on :

Be therefore not hasty to register all you understand not in the black calendar of Hell, as some have done by the weapon salve, passing by the cure of the King's evil, altogether as improbable to the sense. Neither rashly condemn all you meet with that contradicts the common received opinion, lest you remain a fool upon record, as the Pope doth that anathematised the Bishop of Salzburg for maintaining Antipodes, since the branding of one truth contains more disrepute than the broaching of ten errors.

The spirit of worldly prudence, the fear of disrepute, is still his motive at bottom, and the same appears in his advice (strange from a son of the owner of Chicksands Priory) 'not to let the cheapness or conveniency of Church lands tempt you to their purchase; for tho' I have not observed vengeance so nimble in this world as divines pretend,' yet the enmity of the clergy, supported as they are by ' prayers or policy,' is not to be lightly encountered, and there is also the 'danger and shame of refunding in case a contrary zeal should possess the people.'

The last paragraph in the section on Religion seems to hint that ' grave and learned Mr. Osborne' once yielded to the Puritan failing of preaching sermons at inopportune moments, and suffered in consequence. He is wiser now, for he writes : ' Do not use funereous discourses before Princes or men in power, who hate nothing so much as the thought of their own mortality, and, therefore, are unlike to be pleased with the messengers of it.'

Though princes and men in power may hate the thought of their own mortality, the prospect of death has no terrors for Francis Osborne. To him it is but a haven of rest, almost ardently desired after long tossing on the waters of affliction. Nothing can be more touching and pathetic than the change which comes over him as he contemplates his approaching end. Standing in the presence of the Veiled Figure, with the shadows fast deepening around him, the crust of cynicism and worldly prudence crumbles away, the mistaken wisdom of experience turns suddenly to nothingness, the scoffing voice is hushed, and out of the depth of his heart he speaks the truth at last. He seems to forget all that he has written in the bitterness of his soul; after all, he, too, has had a wife and children, he knows the feelings of a husband and a father, nature is too strong for him, and his final maxims are of the old-fashioned type, more profitable and more true than the new-fangled systems of a thousand cynical philosophers.

' Bear always,' he says, ' a filial reverence to your dear mother, and let not her old age, if she attain it, seem tedious unto you.'

'Therefore, in case of my death (which weariness of the world will not suffer me to adjourn so much as by a wish), do not proportion your respect by the mode of other sons, but to the greatness of her desert, beyond requital in relation to us both.'   'Continue in love and amity with your sister, and help her when you are able.'

It may be silly to wish for children to immortalise your name, but yet our stern critic is found exclaiming, 'Let no time expunge his memory, that gave you the first tincture of erudition, to which he was more invited by love than profit, no less than his incomparable wife.'

He turns to directions for his funeral.

Bury me simply, for he that lies under the Herse of Heaven is convertible into sweet herbs and flowers, that may rest in such bosoms as would shriek at the Ugly Buggs may possibly be found crawling in the magnificent tomb of Henry the Seventh. That man were better forgotten that hath nothing of greater moment to register his name by than a grave.

Neither can I apprehend such horror in Death as some do that render their lives miserable to avoid it, meeting it oftentimes by the same way they take to shun it. Death, if he may be guesst at by his elder brother Sleep (borne before he was thought of, and fell upon Adam, ere he fell from his Maker), cannot be so terrible a messenger, being not without much ease, if not some voluptuousness. Besides, nothing in this world is worth coming from the house-top to fetch it, much less from the deep Grave, furnished with all things because empty of desires.

Empty of desires, yes, but empty too, as far as Osborne was concerned, of hopes and beliefs, and possibly the feeling that life as well as death was no less empty, was no small factor in the gloom that overshadowed him. How sadly he writes, 'If a stronger propensity to Religion resides in Age than Youth (which I wish I had no cause to doubt of), it relates more to the Temperature of the Body, than any Improvement of the mind;' and his creed, as he sums it up, is but cold and comfortless. 'To conclude, let us serve God with what reverence we are able, and do all the good we can, making as little unnecessary work for repentance as is possible.'

An elastic formula, serving equally for the saint and the sinner, good, perhaps, in practice with some great principle as a motive behind it, but bad as an ideal.

Francis Osborne was not and could not be a preacher of high ideals ; his advice is a true reflex of himself, with all his frailties and failings. No one is more aware of these than himself; conceit was certainly not among his faults, and after travelling so long in his company we cannot but feel some affection and pity for him as he concludes :

Thus I have left you finished, dear son, a Picture of the World; in this at least like it, that it is frail and confused, being an original and not a copy, no more foreign help having been employed in it than what my own miserable experience had imprinted in my memory. And as you have by trial already found the

> Now you are taught to Live ; there's nothing I
> Esteem worth learning, but the way to Die.

There let us leave him ; he has long been resting in the haven he desired, but he ought not to be wholly forgotten, for though his other merits may be disputed, at least he can express himself in good English. Peace be to his ashes; he had but little ease in life.

SIDNEY PEEL.

THE
SUPERFLUOUS VACCINATION COMMISSION

THE Report of the Royal Commission on Vaccination can hardly be
said to have justified its existence. It is, indeed, in more senses
than one, a weighty document, and it embodies the results of a most
painstaking inquiry, in the course of which an enormous mass of
evidence from almost every witness who had a fact, or an opinion
however foolish, to communicate was sifted with the most scrupulous
care.   And what is the outcome of all this labour?   In its
scientific aspect vaccination is left precisely as it was.   The medical
profession, which alone is competent to judge in the matter, is
practically unanimous in looking upon the question as absolutely
settled ; as far as it is concerned, therefore, nothing is changed
by the Report ; it is but one blue-book the more.   The oppo-
neuts of vaccination, who are, for the most part, incapable of
appreciating scientific evidence, will certainly not be converted by
the Report ; it gives them, indeed, arguments of the most convincing
nature, but it cannot give them understanding.   As regards the
political aspect of the question the Report is a compromise, and as
such pleases no one.   The tenderness shown for conscientious
objectors is not enough for the stalwarts who denounce vaccination
as an· unclean thing, and appears mere weakness to the advocates
of a policy of Thorough in its enforcement.   The majority of the
Commissioners evidently thought that it would ·be impolitic to
carry their conclusions on the scientific reference to their logical
issue, and they seem, if I may use a metaphor appropriate to the
subject, to have attenuated their recommendations to a degree which
they considered adapted to the tolerance of their recalcitrant colleagues.   The virus was made as benign as possible, but Dr. Collins
and Mr. Picton showed themselves ' naturally insusceptible.'

   To my mind the appointment of the Commission was a mistake.
It was not needed ; it was badly constituted for the purpose in view ;
and its deliberations were protracted to a degree that deprived the
ultimate findings of much of the value that would have been attached
to them had they been arrived at with less apparent doubt and hesitancy.   In saying that it was badly constituted, I mean that although

were, with one or two exceptions, chosen rather on the ground or general eminence than of any special knowledge of the subject. In particular there was not a single one who could be regarded as a representative of pathology. It has been said that this is the day of old men. However this may be in politics and in other departments of intellectual activity, it is emphatically not the case in medicine. Hence 'general eminence' is an inadequate equipment for the solution of problems of pathology—a science which in its modern form has grown up within the last twenty years. Fortunately in so plain a case as that submitted to the Commission it was impossible for any body of men trained in scientific methods and in the weighing of evidence to come to any but one conclusion. Their outrageously protracted deliberations, however, not unnaturally unsettled people's faith in vaccination, and kept the law in a state of suspended animation; and the evil they have thus done lives after them. It now rests with the Legislature to decide whether the law shall be quickened anew into vigorous life or become practically a dead letter. My own view as to the duty of the Government in the matter is clear, and will be frankly stated later. But something must first be said about the Report and the conclusions to be drawn therefrom.

After so unconscionable a length of incubation, there was reason to fear that the Report might prove to be an addled egg. This, however, is not the case as far as facts and deductions are concerned. The case for vaccination has been reinforced by modern instances; some doubtful points have been elucidated; and, above all, the 'antivacks,' if I may be allowed to use a word which has the sanction of Edward Jenner himself, have been allowed to have their say to an extent which testifies to the almost superhuman power of endurance of the Commissioners. The case for anti-vaccination was, in fact, presented as it never has been before, and the presence upon the Commission of an *advocatus diaboli* of such knowledge and ability as my friend Dr. W. J. Collins ensured that every scrap of evidence against vaccination should be given its full weight. These circumstances make the fact that eleven out of thirteen Commissioners—including men accustomed to sift and weigh evidence, like Lord Herschell, Mr. Dugdale, and Mr. Meadows-White—gave their decision unequivocally in its favour of special significance.

It is important that this point should be set in the clearest possible light. The antivaccinists profess to see in the Report a victory for their cause. One is not surprised to. read this kind of stuff in certain inconsiderable quarters; but one did not expect to find it in respectable newspapers. Yet the chief organ of Radicalism went so far as to say : ' Our own reading of the Report is that the Commissioners have been heartily glad to escape from the intolerable position of spreading by force a faith which has lost its hold on them.' Any one who can read such a meaning into the plain language of the Report must be gifted with the exegetic ingenuity of an Ignatius Donelly, or afflicted with that worst form of mental blindness which will not see.

The Commissioners themselves express the hope that their Report ' will stimulate belief in the efficacy of vaccination.' It is, indeed, well calculated to do so ; and it would have been strange if faith in Jenner's discovery had lost its hold on men who had had before them so irresistible an array of evidence as to the good which it has done to mankind.

Before summarising the evidence, it will be instructive to glance backwards for a moment at small-pox as it was before Jenner drew its fangs. About the middle of the eighteenth century the celebrated mathematician Daniel Bernouilli estimated that it claimed fifteen millions of victims every twenty-five years, giving an annual holocaust of six hundred thousand. Haygarth, a careful writer, computed that only 5 per cent. of mankind escaped the disease. But that which to my mind is more convincing than statistics is the fact that our forefathers looked upon small-pox as a scourge from which there was practically no hope of escape. As early as the ninth century we find a Jewish physician stating that the disease *fere omnibus accidit.* The Arabian physician Rhases, who is mentioned by Dr. Collins as the writer to whom we owe the first description of the disease, says that hardly any one escapes it. At the end of the sixteenth century Kellwaye, the author of the first systematic treatise on the disease in the English language, quoted by Dr. C. Creighton in his *History of Epidemics in Great Britain,* says he ' need not greatly stand upon the description of this disease, because it is a thing well known unto most people.' Buchan, writing towards the end of the last century, in his *Domestic Medicine,* so long the medical oracle of the British household, says that small-pox ' is now become so general that very few escape it at one time or another ;' and adds, 'This disease is so generally known that a minute description of it is unnecessary.' To appreciate the full force of this testimony, it must be borne in mind that Buchan was writing, not for medical readers, but for the general public.

Sir Gilbert Blane stated to a Committee of the House of Commons that in the closing years of the last century an adult person who had not had small-pox was scarcely to be met with or heard of in the United Kingdom. Other countries were not less afflicted. In Russia it was calculated that one out of every seven children born died of small-pox. In France it was computed to cause one-tenth of the deaths from all causes. In Germany, the popular belief in the practical impossibility of escaping small-pox found expression in the proverb ' Von Pocken und Liebe bleiben nur Wenige frei.' Thanks to vaccination, that proverb is now decidedly musty in the land of its birth.

With the passing away of the eighteenth century came the dawn of a new era. In England, in Sweden, in Denmark, and in other countries of Western Europe, and in the United States the first quarter of the present century was marked by a striking decrease in the number of deaths from small-pox. It is needless to quote authorities or to give statistics in proof of this statement, for it is admitted by Dr. Collins and Mr. Picton themselves. The only question is whether the decrease was due to vaccination or to some other cause. On this point the Commissioners speak with no nucertain sound. They find that the cause of the decline was the protective influence of vaccination, which made itself felt more and more as the practice came into more general use ; and they find strong confirmation of this view in the fact that 'such information as is available goes to show that in the countries where vaccination did not become general, small-pox prevailed in the first quarter of the nineteenth century very much as it had prevailed in the eighteenth.'

It is not till 1837 that what may be termed the modern history of the disease begins, as far as England is concerned. In that year the present system of registration of deaths came into existence. As regards Scotland a similar record dates only from 1855, and as regards Ireland from 1864. The legislative enactments relative to vaccination in the several parts of the United Kingdom correspond roughly to these periods. If vaccination is an effective protection against small-pox, one would expect to find that in proportion as it is more strictly enforced, the more marked is the decrease in the prevalence of the disease.

In England Acts 'to extend the practice of vaccination' were passed in 1840 and 1841 ; in 1853 it was made compulsory, but the provisions for carrying out the intention of the Legislature were very imperfect ; in 1867 the laws relating to vaccination were consolidated and amended, and power was given to Unions to appoint paid officers whose duty it should be to vaccinate free of charge all children brought to them for the purpose. In a number of Unions, however, the power was not exercised, and in the early part of 1871 there were still a great many Unions in which vaccination officers had not been appointed. In that year an Act was passed making the appointment of such officers in all Unions compulsory, and providing for the better carrying out of the law.

Taking the period from 1837 to 1894 as a whole the official records show a very marked decline in the death-rate from small-pox.

In 1838 the number of deaths from small-pox (together with those from chicken-pox [1]) to every 100,000 living was 106. In 1842, the year following the passage of the first Vaccination Act, the proportion had fallen to seventeen. From that date down to 1853 it was never above forty. Since 1853, when vaccination was made compulsory, only in six years (1858, 1863, 1864, 1865, 1871 and 1872) has it exceeded twenty. The years 1871–72 represent a period of widespread prevalence and exceptional severity of the disease; yet even in these years the mortality did not reach the proportion in 1838. Since then only in five years (1873, 1876, 1877, 1881 and 1884) has the ratio of deaths from small-pox (and chicken-pox) to every 100,000 living exceeded ten; and in no single year has it exceeded twenty. For the years 1886 to 1894 the corresponding figures are 1, 2, 4, ·4, ·4, ·5, 2, 5, 3.

In Scotland the death-rate from small-pox (and chicken-pox) in 1855 was forty-eight to every 100,000 living. In 1863 vaccination was made compulsory, and in 1865 the proportion had fallen to twelve, in 1866 to six, in 1867 to three, and in 1868 to ·5. In 1871–72 Scotland was visited by the prevailing epidemic, though to a much smaller extent than England; the death-rate from small-pox rose to forty-four in 1871 and to seventy-four in 1872. Since 1877 the proportion of deaths from small-pox alone to every 100,000 living has only once reached three, and in fourteen of these eighteen years it has been a fraction, only twice reaching ·5. In 1890 and 1891 it was 0.

In Ireland vaccination was made compulsory in 1863. From data furnished by the Census returns of 1841, 1851 and 1861 the Commissioners estimate that the average annual death-rate from small-pox in Ireland per 100,000 living was seventy-three in the inter-censal period 1831–1841; forty-nine in the period 1841–51, and twenty-one in the period 1851–61. In 1864 the death-rate from small-pox alone to every 100,000 living was fifteen. In 1865 the proportion had fallen to eight, in 1866 to three, and in the four following years it was never above ·6. Ireland did not escape the tidal wave of small-pox which swept over the United Kingdom in 1871; the proportion of deaths from the disease in 1872 was sixty. Since then it has only once been above sixteen; and from 1881–1894 it has only once reached three.

Broadly speaking, therefore, increase of vaccination has been followed by decrease of small-pox in the three kingdoms during the last fifty to sixty years. There have been considerable fluctuations, but these are accounted for by other factors, such as what Sydenham

---

[1] In the Registrar-General's abstracts for the periods 1838–42 and 1847–54 no distinction is made between the deaths from small-pox and those from chicken-pox. The mortality from the latter disease is, however, too insignificant to be a disturbing factor of any importance. The Commissioners have, however, added it on in their ables in ord er to make the basis of comparison absolutely fair.

called 'epidemic constitution,' which exercise a disturbing influence; these are still very imperfectly known, and under present conditions cannot be controlled. The great epidemic of 1870–73 was an example of such disturbing influence. In the old days before vaccination the disease was wont every now and then to assume a special malignity for which no cause could be assigned. As vaccination has not yet completely destroyed the disease, its diffusion and intensity are still subject to considerable variations, though to a vastly less degree than in the pre-vaccination era. This is evident on comparing the havoc wrought by small-pox in 1871, which, so far, has been by far the worst year under compulsory vaccination, with that of the epidemics of the last century. In 1871, of 514,879 deaths from all causes, 23,062 were from small-pox, or barely 4½ per cent., a proportion which in London in the last century was exceeded no fewer than ninety-three times. Of the 100 years there were only seven in which the London small-pox death-rate (per 1,000 deaths from all causes) was less than that of the year 1871 in England and Wales as a whole.[2]

The experience of other countries—notably of Prussia and Sweden, which are well-vaccinated countries as compared with Austria, Russia and Spain, which are ill vaccinated—teaches the same lesson. It would be easy to give decisive statistical proof of this, but it is impossible to do so within the space at my disposal; moreover, the argument may well rest on our own records, which are more easily verifiable.

Not only has there been an immense reduction in the prevalence and fatality of small-pox, but a remarkable change has taken place in its incidence in respect of age. Before vaccination came into use small-pox was the very Moloch of diseases. The Commissioners find that in all records of epidemics in which the ages are given, the mortality was mainly among infants; and they give some striking examples of its fatality among them.

The 'slaughter of the innocents' caused by small-pox in the pre-vaccination era is easily explained by the want of any protection in the case of young children. Adults suffered less not because the disease is a respecter of age, but because, as a rule, it spares those whom it has once touched. As the greater part of the adult population had had small-pox in early life, grown-up people were protected against the disease as most of us are at the present day against measles and whooping cough. Vaccination changed this, and as its protective power is greatest within a few years of its performance, and tends to die out at a later period, adults who now are only in exceptional cases protected by a previous attack of small-pox are—unless they have been re-vaccinated—much more liable to attack than young children. Of the fact of a change of incidence of small-pox in point of age there is no doubt, and it is admitted by the dissentients them-

[2] J. C. McVail, *Vaccination Vindicated*, p. 44.

selves. No figures could be more eloquent than the fact that whereas Buchan, writing in the last century for the guidance of anxious mothers, thought it needless to describe minutely the symptoms of small-pox because they were known to all, Professor Henoch, of Berlin, one of the greatest authorities on diseases of children at the present day, writing for doctors, in his great work dealing with that special branch of medicine, has ' excluded variola, which is very rarely met with nowadays.' [3]

That the cause of the change of age incidence is to be found in vaccination appears clearly from the statistics given in the Report as to recent epidemics—at Sheffield in 1877–88 ; at Dewsbury in 1891–92 ; at Leicester in 1892–93 ; in London in 1892–93 ; at Warrington in 1892–93 ; and in Gloucester in 1895–96.

While at Leicester, Gloucester, and Dewsbury the deaths under ten years of age were more than one-half, in London they were considerably less than one-half, and at Sheffield and Warrington about one-quarter of the total deaths. Now the vaccination returns prove that at Sheffield and Warrington the unvaccinated element was relatively small, while in London and Dewsbury it was considerable, and at Leicester and Gloucester it was very large. In correspondence with this we find that the death-rate from small-pox among children was relatively small at Sheffield and Warrington, considerable in London and Dewsbury, and high at Leicester and Gloucester. In the two last-named towns the fatality among children approximated to that of the pre-vaccination era, which was just what was to be expected in places where the means of protection had practically ceased to be employed. Similar variations in respect of the age of the victims have been equally conspicuous in other epidemies both in this country and abroad. No such change is observable in measles, whooping cough, or scarlet fever, a fact which strongly suggests that in the case of small-pox some special counteracting influence is at work. What is this if it is not vaccination ? There is no other point of difference in the six towns referred to at all adequate to account for so striking a difference in the incidence of fatal small-pox.

If vaccination is to any appreciable extent a safeguard against small-pox, there should be an appreciable difference in favour of those who have been vaccinated as regards the fatality of the disease. The epidemics specially studied by the Commissioners give statistics which are particularly valuable, as they refer to events so recent that full information about them was procurable, and every conceivable precaution against error was taken in their preparation.

Taking the six towns just mentioned together, the total number of persons attacked was 11,065, of whom 1,283, or 20·9 per cent., died.

[3] *Lectures on Children's Diseases*, Sydenham Society's Translation (London, 1889). Author's Preface to First Edition, 1881.

Of the whole number 2,321 were unvaccinated; of these 822, or 35·4 per cent., were attacked. Of these 2,321 unvaccinated persons attacked, 1,449 were under ten years of age, and of these 523, or 36·0 per cent., died. 870 were over ten; of these 299, or 34·3 per cent., died. It should be noted that the fatality of the disease in two classes under ten and over ten among the unvaccinated was almost identical (36·0 under ten; 34·3 over ten).

Deducting the 2,321 unvaccinated persons from the total number attacked, there remain 8,744 to be counted as vaccinated. Of these 461, or 5·2 per cent., died, as against 35·4 per cent. in the unvaccinated class. Taking children under ten only, the total number attacked in the six towns was 2,038, of whom 539, or 26·4 per cent., died. Deducting the 1,449 recorded as unvaccinated, we have 589 recorded as vaccinated; among these there were 16 deaths, a mortality rate of 2·7 per cent. Of persons over ten years of age 9,001 were attacked, and of these 744, or 8·2 per cent., died. Deducting from these the 870 classed as unvaccinated, we have 8,131 vaccinated persons who were attacked, of whom 445, or 5·4 per cent., died. Therefore the proportion of the death-rate to all attacks was 35·4 in the unvaccinated as compared with 5·2 in the vaccinated class; or, taking children under ten alone, the mortality in the unvaccinated was 36·0 per cent., as compared with 2·7 in the vaccinated class. Excluding all children under one year from both classes, so as to avoid loading the unvaccinated class with infants under three months, we get to the results set forth below :—

Vaccinated	Unvaccinated
Attacks, 570; deaths, 16	Attacks, 1,235; deaths, 375
Fatality, 2·8 per cent.	Fatality, 30·3 per cent.

Thus the proportion of deaths in the unvaccinated was largely in excess of that in the vaccinated class in these epidemics, and the fact is equally plain whether the several towns are considered separately or all the six are reckoned together. Conclusive testimony to the same effect is borne by the records of the Highgate, Homerton, and Fulham small-pox hospitals.

That vaccination protects not only against death but also against attack, is shown by the statistics given in the Report as to the epidemics at Sheffield, Warrington, Dewsbury, and Gloucester, which all show a much higher rate of attack among the unvaccinated than among the vaccinated. The difference is particularly marked in the case of children under ten. Space will not allow of the figures being given in detail, but the essential facts are shown in the table on the next page.

Vaccination also greatly lessens the severity of the disease where it fails to protect against attack. The statistics of the six recent epidemics taken by the Commissioners as test cases show this

	Attack rate under 10		Attack rate over 10	
	Vaccinated	Unvaccinated	Vaccinated	Unvaccinated
Sheffield	7·9	67·6	28·3	53·6
Warrington	4·4	54·5	29·9	57·6
Dewsbury	10·2	50·8	27·7	53·4
Leicester	2·5	35·3	22·2	47·6
Gloucester	8·8	46·3	32·2	50·0

conclusively as regards all ages ; and if children under the age of ten are considered separately, the proportion of severe attacks in the vaccinated class was in all the towns quite insignificant.

Enough has been said to show that, on the figures which have been quoted, the odds are greatly in favour of the vaccinated as against the unvaccinated. What is there that distinguishes the favoured class from the other ? Only vaccination. At any rate, if the protective influence is not vaccination, it is something which stands thereto in a relation like that of Leibnitz's ' pre-established harmony ; ' for practical purposes, therefore, it would be prudent to act as if the connection between vaccination and lessened small-pox mortality were indeed cause and effect.

It may be admitted that some change in opinion has taken place among medical men as to the abiding efficacy of a single vaccination. Yet the change has been neither so sudden nor so great as the opponents of vaccination appear to believe. Jenner himself, in the first flush of the enthusiasm of discovery, not unnaturally enough over-rated the protective power of his vaccine ; but experience brought better knowledge. Vaccination cannot reasonably be ex- pected to do more than small-pox itself, and one attack of that disease is not, it is well known, an infallible preservative against another. But that is surely not a sufficient reason for refusing to profit by such usefulness as vaccination has. How great that is the evidence already given is amply sufficient to show, but the full measure of the efficacy of what the dissentients call the ' protective rite ' will be better appreciated if the results of revaccination are taken into account. At Sheffield and Warrington revaccination was carried out among policemen and postmen, and though these men were, from the nature of their duties, much more exposed to contagion than ordinary people, no case of small-pox was reported among them. Small-pox is the most contagious of all diseases, and attendants in small-pox hospitals might therefore be expected to show a very high rate of attack. In the Sheffield hospitals, during the epidemic of 1887–88, of eighty attendants who had been re-vaccinated not one contracted small-pox. At Leicester, of twenty-eight attendants in the hospital, six declined to be re-vaccinated. Of the whole number, six were attacked and one died. Five of these, including the fatal case, were among the six who refused to be re-vaccinated. At the Highgate Hospital, during the thirty-five years before 1871, not a single nurse or servant was attacked; since then, up to the date of the Report, only one case had occurred, so that there is now a record of sixty years at this hospital with only one case among the attendants. The person attacked was a gardener, and alone of all the staff had not been re-vaccinated. The case of Prussia, where small-pox has been practically extinct since the introduction of compulsory re-vaccination in 1874, is an *instantia crucis.*

In short, what Virchow calls the brute force of statistics is all on the side of vaccination. The irresistible nature of the argument lies not merely in the strength of the separate statistical details, but in their cumulative force. A fact, or a series of figures here or there, may be of doubtful import, but the mass of evidence, taken together, all points one way. The case for vaccination is very strong, that for re-vaccination is overwhelming.

Even from the brief summary here given of the evidence laid before the Commission, it will be seen that the effect as well as the intention of the Report is to stimulate belief in the protective power of vaccination; nor do I see anything in the statement of the dissentient Commissioners calculated to neutralise that effect. From the scientific point of view they object to vaccination on two grounds: that it is useless as a means of protection against small-pox; and that in a not inconsiderable proportion of cases it is injurious to the health of those who undergo it. They do not, it is true, explicitly affirm that vaccination has no protective power. They rather 'hint a doubt and hesitate dislike,' but the drift of their argument is, to show that vaccination is a useless 'rite.' The enormous diminution in the prevalence of small-pox since the 'rite' came into use is attributed to sanitary betterment. The discontinuance of inoculation is adduced as a secondary cause. As to this I may remark that the argument which Dr. Collins and Mr. Allanson Picton found upon it is an example of the inconsistencies into which the opponents of vaccination are betrayed by their eagerness to find weapons against it. Their point is that, inasmuch as the practice of inoculation kept small-pox alive, the mere substitution of a non-contagious process like vaccination must have had a striking effect upon the small-pox death-rate. But, on the other hand, they maintain that the vaccinations in London which made so strong an impression on the medical profession at the beginning of the century, and which formed the source of supply of matter, not only for this country but for the others in which the practice was introduced, were in fact 'mild variolations,' the lymph used in them having been in fact small-pox matter. As vaccination spread over the greater part of the civilised world with marvellous rapidity, it is evident, that if the matter was, as the dissentients contend, really

variolous, there must for some time have been an increase rather
than a discontinuance of inoculation.   On the dissentients' own
showing, therefore, there should have been a corresponding increase
of small-pox.

With regard to the improvement in sanitary conditions, in order
to establish even *prima facie* a relation of cause and effect between
that and the decrease of 'small-pox, it must be shown that the
improvement began before the decrease became manifest.   The decline of small-pox was not only great but sudden in all the countries
where vaccination was adopted; if sanitary betterment was the
cause, this betterment must have begun in Great Britain, Sweden,
Denmark, and throughout Western Europe generally as at sound of
trumpet.   Is there any evidence of such a sudden and widespread
awakening to the need for a sanitary new birth at the beginning of
the century?   The first comprehensive enactment which laid the
foundation of our sanitary progress was the Public Health Act of
1848, and this Act had to be extended by much subsequent legislation.   Dr. Collins and Mr. Picton quote two or three writers who, in
the last century and in the early part of this, preached the gospel of
isolation as a means of controlling contagious diseases, but these men
were in advance of their generation; moreover, they were prophets
crying in the wilderness.   How little their teaching had influenced
practice even in the most enlightened quarters is shown by the
following passage from Miss Eve Blantyre Simpson's recently published *Life* of her father, Sir James Young Simpson, who is himself,
by the way, referred to by the dissentients as the author of ' a proposal to stamp out small-pox and other contagious diseases ' by
isolation :

> About 1868 [the very year the ' proposal ' in question was published] one of
> his resident assistants, Dr. Aitken, took scarlet fever in Queen Street. He was
> relegated to a top flat, and orders given for his isolation ; but Jarvis, who had an
> old-fashioned dislike to nurses, attended the sick doctor himself, and continued his
> work downstairs [the said Jarvis was the Cerberus of the medical oracle's door].
> We from the schoolroom liked the victim who was isolated ; and, against orders,
> paid him visits and learned our lessons in his room. We had taken all the usual
> infectious diseases—measles, chicken-pox, and scarlet fever—in gangs together, for
> once one got it in those days it was the fashion for the others to follow suit at the
> same time by herding together. I suppose nowadays no day school would receive
> a pupil who came from a house where an infectious case was laid up, but such a
> thing then was not dreamed of, though my father, by suggesting that the mode of
> stamping out such complaints should form part of every nursery education, was
> held as Quixotic.

Had Miss Simpson been writing of a period less than three quarters
of a century earlier, she would have certainly included small-pox
among the ' usual infectious diseases.'   The opponents of vaccination
may fairly be asked to explain how it is that small-pox alone among
these had ceased to be a terror to the household.   **The official**

statistics given in the Report show that within the last forty or fifty years there has been no reduction in the mortality from measles and scarlet fever at all comparable to the decline in the mortality from small-pox. The same holds good of whooping cough. The dissentients say that these diseases cannot fairly be compared with small-pox inasmuch as they affect chiefly children. But why do they find their victims mainly among children? Because most adults have already had them. It used to be just the same as regards small-pox; how is it that sanitation which is credited with the victory over the worst scourge has suffered such ignominious defeat at the hands of the milder ones? Again how is it that diphtheria has increased and is increasing in spite of better hygiene? There is much more reason *a priori* for thinking that diphtheria would be influenced by sanitary measures than that small-pox would be so; yet diphtheria is the mere despair of the sanitarian. The dissentients lay great stress on the great diminution in 'fevers' shown in the Registrar-General's Report, which is unquestionably in large measure the result of sanitary betterment. I say 'in large measure,' because part of the diminution is merely apparent, being due to the classification in other groups of several diseases formerly included among 'fevers.' The chief fevers are malarial fever, typhus, and typhoid. Of all these the cause is definitely known and can be removed—in the case of malaria by the drainage of marshes, in that of typhus by the prevention of over-crowding, and in that of typhoid by the removal and destruction of the specific poison. There is, however, no shadow of evidence that small-pox can be repressed by such measures. Sanitation may help recovery from small-pox but it cannot prevent infection. But granting that sanitation may have some influence in reducing the prevalence of small-pox, it may safely be assumed that the advantage gained in that way is more than counterbalanced by the increased facilities of communication, which make the diffusion of infectious disease immensely more easy and more rapid than it was even in the first half of the present century.

As for the injurious effects upon the health attributed to vaccination, even if they were as frequent and as serious as Dr. Collins and Mr. Picton believe, they would not to my mind weigh in the scale against its advantages. The harmful consequences imputed to the vaccine lymph are at the worst infinitely less than those of small-pox. Few at the present day, even among the members of the medical profession, have seen a bad case of small-pox in its untamed ferocity. To our forefathers it was only too familiar, and the almost feverish eagerness with which they accepted vaccination, in spite of solemn warnings of all kinds of possible and impossible mischief may be taken as a measure of the dread with which they regarded the disease from which it was to preserve them.

Dr. Ogle estimates that for the period 1881 to 1889 the proportion of deaths among primary vaccinations was one in 14,159, and the Commissioners think that for the years 1886–91 it was not substantially different. In Scotland, during the years 1883–90, the proportion was one in 38,872, the difference probably being due to the fact that in Scotland vaccination is performed within the first six months instead of the first three of life, and the majority of children are vaccinated in their own homes. Even assuming, therefore, that all the deaths certified as being connected with vaccination are so connected—which is not the case—the risk to life is very slight.

As regards the possible transmission of disease, it is true that deaths from syphilis have increased during the last twenty years among infants under one year of age. But the statistics show that the bulk of the fatality from the disease falls within the first three months of life, a fact which appears to suggest that it is mostly unvaccinated children who die of it. With regard to erysipelas, that is a disease which largely affects children independently of vaccination, and the Commissioners think the evidence conclusive that there has not been in the last forty years a substantial increase in mortality from erysipelas due to vaccination. It is undeniable, however, that erysipelas does sometimes occur after vaccination, as it does after the most trivial scratches or abrasions; but it is equally certain that attacks of erysipelas are often attributed to vaccination when in reality the one event has only accidentally followed the other. The same thing may be said of skin eruptions; I have myself known vaccination to be postponed for some reason, and the child has within a few days developed a skin affection which would nuquestionably have been thought to be the consequence of vaccination had that been performed.

For my own part, having seen much of the effects of vaccination as a general practitioner, and having had exceptional opportunities during nearly twenty years of seeing affections of various kinds supposed to have been caused by it, in the out-patient department of a large London hospital, I can only state my belief that the injurious consequences fairly attributable to vaccination are few in number, and mostly insignificant in nature. Such as they are, they are almost entirely preventible with proper care. On this point the Commissioners make recommendations which if adopted would make the risk of vaccination practically a negligible quantity.

The existing law as to vaccination is based on the hypothesis that it is an efficient means of protection against small-pox. To the medical profession this is not an hypothesis, but a fact established by larger and more decisive evidence than any other in the whole range of therapeutics. It is significant that of the three medical men in this country, whom I may call the scientific heresiarchs in this matter, two are not, and have not for many years, if ever, been general practitioners; while the third is engaged in a special line of practice in which opportunities of observing the effects of vaccination must be extremely rare. Their objections are founded largely on theoretical considerations which can have little or no weight with those who know the facts from personal observation. The belief of the medical profession in the efficacy of vaccination is fully shared by the Commissioners, only a minority of whom are medical men. Their Report, in fact, justifies in the strongest possible manner the truth of the doctrine on which it is based. It is to be regretted, therefore, that they should have made certain recommendations as to the carrying out of the law, which go far to stultify their own conclusions on the evidence before them. They recommend what amounts to a practical abolition of compulsion. Parents who object to vaccination are to be allowed to follow the dictates of their conscience in the matter. This (not to speak it profanely) seems to me mere foolishness. Many parents feel compelled by what they call their conscience to use strict discipline in bringing up their children, but the law shows no regard for their conscience when the discipline exceeds a certain limit. The Peculiar People have a conscientious objection to medical treatment of any kind, but the law does not, therefore, hold them guiltless if their children die for the want of it. Children are not the chattels of their parents; they are also the property of the State, and the parent's liberty of action as regards his child needs to be limited not only in the interest of the child, but in that of the nation. I therefore consider it in the highest undesirable that the Legislature should give effect to this recommendation, even in the modified form proposed by Mr. Jonathan Hutchinson and Sir W. Guyer Hunter. The opposition to vaccination comes, after all, from a minority which is numerically small; and whatever may be the case as regards other matters, where the public health is concerned a minority has no rights. Vaccination, if it is to do its full measure of good to the community, must be not merely 'compulsory' but compelled. The recommendation of the Commissioners that penalties for nonconformity should be abolished, is only a concession to democracy, which regards medical science with suspicion and dislike; and it is to be feared that it will lead to disastrous consequences for the coming generation if Government does not show itself wiser than the Commissioners.

On the evidence submitted to them, and on their own conclusions after careful sifting of that evidence, their only logical course would have been to recommend compulsory re-vaccination of all children at the age of ten or thereabouts. But if it is too much to ask that re-vaccination should be made compulsory, at least we may ask that it shall be encouraged by the State and by society in every posssible way. It should be insisted on as a regular condition of admission to every branch of the public service. It should be made a condition of passing beyond a certain standard in all

Board Schools; of admission to training ships, reformatories and homes and teaching establishments of all kinds under public control, to all public schools, to the local examinations of the universities, and to the preliminary examinations for the professions. The French Government has just ordered that all persons wishing to enter as medical students in Paris must first be re-vaccinated. This precaution might, with the greatest advantage to the public as well as to individuals, be extended to all professions where a regular apprenticeship is required. It would be well also if it were adopted by railway companies, ship-builders, gas and water companies, owners of factories and warehouses, and all large employers of labour, and by authorities of schools. In fact, a system of rewards for re-vaccination might be established, and it is conceivable that in this way public opinion might be educated to such a degree that it would come to be deemed as disgraceful to be unre-vaccinated as it is now thought to be unwashed.

If the State concerns itself with vaccination at all, it is incumbent on it to exercise strict vigilance over its performance. At present, it must be admitted, it is too often imperfectly performed. I am inclined to think that it would be better to entrust the duty altogether to public vaccinators, who should seek out the persons to be vaccinated at their own homes, and whose work should be under Government inspection. I think also it is the clear duty of the State to make itself responsible for the supply as well as for the use of pure lymph. That there is room for reform in the way vaccination is now carried out, at least in England, is clearly shown by the evidence before the Commissioners; and the Report will have done something to compensate for its evil effects in other ways if it leads to a more efficient and a more careful performance of the operation.

Isolation, which is the substitute proposed for vaccination by the dissentients, is most useful as an ally, but it could not stand alone as a means of protection, for the simple reason that when any strain on the machinery came it would inevitably break down, as it did at Leicester in 1893. 'Compulsory isolation' on any large scale would be far more resisted than vaccination, and if enforced, would be sure to lead sooner or later to the revolt of the rate-payer. In fact, the 'conscience' of recalcitrant parents would be at least as much outraged by isolation as by vaccination, and its enforcement would only lead to the development of a new kind of 'martyr.'

To sum up—I would retain the element of compulsion in full force as far as primary vaccination is concerned, but I would make 'martyrdom' less cheap. Instead of repeated penalties, I would impose one fine sufficiently substantial to act as a deterrent. In case of persistent disobedience I would go the length of temporary disfranchisement, a penalty which is not too great for an act of bad citizenship.

After all, the question of vaccination is one that chiefly concerns the people itself. The medical profession, if it looked at the matter from a purely selfish point of view, would certainly take no trouble to promote a practice which is directly injurious to its material interests. Doctors know how to protect themselves and those dear to them, and if only men and women were in question, they might be content to let them enjoy the freedom which, as Dr. Gregory wrote many years ago, every Englishman values so greatly, of ' doing what is foolish and wrong, and going to the devil his own way.'

But the young, young children, O my brothers!

For the sake of these helpless ones I would earnestly plead that there should be no relaxation of the existing law.

MALCOLM MORRIS.

A SHINTO FUNERAL

AMONG the advisers who in this generation have surrounded the throne of Japan there have been none more valued by both Emperor and people, none who, by wise counsels and devoted loyalty, have contributed more to raise the ancient empire to the position which it occupies to-day, than Prince Taruhito Arisugawa, whose death caused universal mourning throughout the land.

A man of high principle, and steadfast, upright, honest character, he joined to the ardent patriotism which is a Japanese characteristic a warm personal affection for the Emperor; and by his caution and wisdom he was a constant influence for good in all state affairs. A prince of the blood, but by birth no nearer than a fourth cousin of the Emperor, the Japanese custom of adoption gave him the position of uncle to the latter, and he was, whether by birth or by reason of this adoption is uncertain, heir presumptive to the throne next in succession to the crown prince.

When, at the beginning of the war with China, Hiroshima was fixed on as the headquarters of the army, he accompanied the Emperor thither, and, as chief of the general staff, was ever in his place at the counsels of war, and working indefatigably for the success of the plans which his wisdom did so much to formulate.

If we reckon, as we surely must do, among the brave men who have given their lives for their country those whom disease has stricken down while they were leading armies to victory, Prince Arisugawa's name must be included in the number. The staff at Hiroshima, following in that the example set them by the Emperor, have kept constantly before their minds the hardships and privations endured by the troops, and have regulated their own lives by a standard which they have striven to approximate to that which is possible for their soldiers.

Prince Arisugawa was sixty-one; not an old man, but still past the age when such exertions and privations can be undergone with impunity, and there appears to be no doubt that when, in December, he was attacked by typhoid fever, the strain to which his constitution from Hiroshima to his summer palace at Maiko, near Kobi, and there he was tenderly nursed by his wife and by his daughter-in-law, the wife of his adopted son (and younger brother) Prince Takihito Arisugawa, until the end came.

Prince Takihito, who is hardly more than half the age of the late prince, young enough to be in reality his son, holds the rank of commander in the navy, and was at his post on board the *Matsushima Kan*, Admiral Ito's flagship, off Port Arthur. Though he had been ordered home by the Emperor, he arrived too late. The body had been embalmed in order that he might look once more on his father's face, the funeral ceremonies delayed that he might conduct them, and so he, with the princesses and their suite, brought their dead home to his palace in Tokyo.

The long, smooth, easy journey by the well-worked railway forces our thoughts back by contrast, though it is but a short way back as to time, and suggests to us what, thirty or forty years ago, would have been the magnificent progress of this dead prince, borne to his burial up the Hokaido.

The special train was timed to reach Tokyo at one o'clock in the morning, so as to avoid any publicity; and not till the next day, when the body lay in the Arisugawa palace, was the official announcement of the death made. The coffin was placed in an inner chamber, and there came the grand master of ceremonies, bearing gifts for the dead, and a last message from the Emperor. This is a touching and very ancient custom. The body of the dead prince lay robed in the old traditional court dress of richest white, with his mourning family round him. First the gifts, rolls of red and white silk, were presented; then, standing in front of the coffin, the messenger read, or rather intoned, the last greetings of his master:

We wish to express to you, Taruhito, our sense of our many and great obligations to you for your many and great services to us and to our country during your whole life. At the time of the great restoration you took an active part, and by your wise counsel, assisted us greatly. During the present war you have again done us great and good service by your assistance in our deliberations. You have been a pillar of support to us. To our infinite sorrow you have not lived to see the end of the war. Unfortunately it has pleased God to remove you from us, from your country and from your family.

MUTSUHITO.

The scene was profoundly touching and impressive, never to be forgotten by those who witnessed it. The prince was of the Shinto religion, the recognised state religion of Japan, one characteristic of which is a dignified simplicity of form, colour, and ceremonial. There was no public lying in state.　The Emperor's gifts were placed in the coffin of pure white wood, which was then closed, and watched day and night by all the members of the family and by Shinto priests, who, twice a day, said ' masses ' for the repose of the soul of the dead prince.　While this solemn watch was being kept in the inner chamber, crowds came to express their condolences to the living and their respect for the dead, inscribing their names in a volume laid out in the ' genka ' or entrance hall.　The whole city was in mourning.　In the streets, lately so gay with decorations for the new year, no flag or lantern was to be seen.　All music was strictly forbidden.　The accustomed tinkle of the *koto* behind the paper slides of the houses was not heard ; nor the notes of the piano from the schools and homes where young girls labour with patient diligence to add the graces and accomplishments of the West to those which are their birthright ; nor the twang of the *samisen*, played at the street corners by old women with an *air faux* of poverty about them, which is more potent than their strains to charm a *sen* or two from passers-by.　All were silent, and, as is so often the case, their absence seemed more noticeable than their presence had ever been.

The funeral was a national one, twenty thousand dollars having been voted by the diet for the purpose.　The ceremonial to be observed was arranged by a special commission appointed by the Emperor. The imperial burying-ground is more than four miles distant from the Arisugawa palace, and early in the morning the entire route was packed on either side with crowds so quiet and orderly that the gendarmes and police who were there to keep the road did not seem to find any exercise of control necessary.

Tora no mon and *Sakurada mitsuke* are two of the many gates guarding bridges over the moats, which are the great distinctive feature of Tokyo.　In the wide, open space between these two gates the crowd was perhaps greatest, for here the procession may be said to have been formed.　The palace stood at a little distance only, halfway up a steep bill, at the foot of which is the open space just mentioned.　Many carriages and jinrickshas waited below, and, with more than one regiment of soldiers, filled the centre of the space. Crowded round these, save where the road was kept free for the passing of the procession, were those who had come to see the great man borne to his burial.

It was an ideal winter morning, the clear frosty air and the sunshine combining to make all bright things brighter and to light up even the most sombre.　Men, tall on their high wooden *geta*, held up their children on their shoulders.　Girls with brilliant holiday sashes, and with elaborate *kanzashi* in their hair, where whole scenes of naval and military glory are condensed on the top of a hairpin, flitted about hand in hand, too shy to push, looking in vain for a peephole or a coign of vantage. Here, a small boy in a *képi*, bearing in one hand the flag of his country in miniature, and in the other a huge tin trumpet, is hastily checked by his guardians at the moment when he is beginning an inappropriate and unlawful blast on his instrument. There, a very small girl, smiling patiently among the skirts and legs which threaten to smother her and the smaller and equally patient baby bound on her back, is rescued and pulled into a position of some advantage by a very raw recruit who seems to have hardly settled into his unaccustomed uniform. The jinricksha men are there in crowds, standing up in their vehicles, which are drawn up close under the brick wall which surrounds the buildings of the diet. They are mostly elderly and broken-down men, for their stronger fellows are with the armies. Some more daring spirits among the crowd have climbed to the top of the wall; but they are young and something more than thoughtless, for any such overlooking is contrary to good manners, and has been known, when practised quite innocently by foreigners, to give serious offence.

For the most part a solemn silence prevailed, and sadness and awe marked all faces as the enormous procession passed on with all the pomp and circumstance of a military funeral. At a little distance in front of the procession were carried a number of stands of flowers, about twelve hundred in all. The flowers were of many colours, arranged in cones eight or ten feet high, with stands or stems of bamboo, by means of which they were afterwards planted round the grave. Each of these twelve hundred cones was carried by a man in the ancient mourner's dress, namely, a long *kimono* of white linen and a tall black cap with a backward curve in its long peak. Following these came a company of mounted police, with dress and appointments as modern as those of the others were archaic : fine men, with the resolute patience of the drilled policeman very visibly expressed in face and bearing. The *sakaki* came next—the *Cleyera japonica*, the sacred tree of the Shinto religion. These were in great numbers, with roots intact and of considerable size, the gifts of the Emperor and of members of the royal family—a moving forest, whose dark green boughs were relieved by streamers of paper, red and white, bearing on them sacred inscriptions and prayers for the soul's repose.

Then followed many tall standards, red and white—last, towering above the rest twenty feet or more, gleaming and glancing in the sunshine, the standard of the princes of the blood, displaying its rich brocade of white and gold uninscribed, where the name and fame of a meaner man would have been set forth. Next followed a band of spearmen bearing *hoko*, an ancient weapon with a white silk banneret depending from it. Behind these was borne a large coffer of white wood containing the offerings of food to be made to the dead at the grave ; its stand and silken coverings followed. Then came the orders and decorations of the prince : first, the star, ribbon and collar of the Chrysanthemum; then the foreign orders, fifteen in all, each carried on a cushion of black velvet by an officer of high military rank.

A solitary white-robed mourner, bearing a pair of *geta*, high wooden shoes, preceded the coffin. These shoes are for the weary feet of the dead on the last, long journey. On the coffin were laid the uniform hat and coat of the prince, his sword being carried by officers.

A roof or tabernacle of beautifully wrought wood, with closely shut bamboo blinds, concealed the coffin from view during the procession. The bier on which the coffin rested was carried by twenty-four men in the white robes of mourners, under the escort of numerous officers in full uniform.

Behind came the chief mourners, Prince Takihito on foot, in the old mourning garb of Japan—wide *hakama* trousers of black linen, with an overdress of white, and ceremonial black hat. With rough straw sandals on his feet, and a tall staff of bamboo to guide his pilgrim steps, he was a striking and pathetic figure, this mourner brother-son ; at once so representative of all that is oldest and all that is newest in this land of sharp contrasts.

Both preceding and following the bier were many mounted Shinto priests in their white robes, not very unlike those of the mourners, but with certain distinctive features. The master of the ceremonies and gentlemen in waiting followed, in grey linen *hakama*, and the horses of the prince, their trappings veiled in crape, were led by the grooms. The widowed princess and other ladies of the family came after, in close carriages. They wore yellow dresses partly veiled in black. More distant relations wore red and white. High officials in full court dress covered with decorations made this part of the procession most brilliant. Hundreds of carriages and jinrickshas followed. The troops were the Imperial Body Guards preceding the procession, and the Tokyo garrison following—ten thousand men in all.

To the north-west of the city, at the top of a steep, richly wooded hill, is the cemetery of the imperial family. Set apart for the purpose on the removal of the court from Kyoto, twenty-five years ago, no emperor has as yet been laid in it; but several members of the imperial family are buried there, surrounded by ever-increasing groves of the sacred *sakaki*.

The great and once famous Buddhist temple of Gokokuji adjoins the cemetery and crowns the hill. But Buddhism, once almost amalgamated with the indigenous Shintoism, has been pushed farther and farther from it since the restoration to supreme authority of the heaven-descended Emperor, and with a much accelerated impulse

At the foot of the hill, and just inside the gates of the cemetery, the procession paused. Here large tents had been erected, in which food was served to the whole of the vast assembly in little square boxes, each furnished with chopsticks. Crowds of poor people outside afterwards shared in the feast. Beyond these tents a temporary temple had been erected, still at the foot of the ascent, judged too steep to be surmounted by a crowd so immense. This temple, in accordance with the canons of pure Shintoism, was of fair white wood, relieved on the steep roof by gleams of gold. In front of it stretched a broad, square platform, with chairs six deep ranged round it under the shelter of an overhanging roof. Here were seated the guests, all the members of the *corps diplomatique*, a few other foreigners, and all that was most distinguished and representative of Japan.

On an altar in front of the temple stood the coffin, the decorations and orders of the prince being arranged on a table beside it. All around rose, as in a moment, the ring of sacred *sakaki* trees. Up the platform came the chain of Shinto singers in their rich white silk garb, followed by the pathetic figure of the pilgrim mourner; representatives of the Emperor and Empress, scions of the imperial family, great nobles and foreign ministers, ranged themselves in order in their appointed places. The whole formed a scene not to be forgotten. Against the dark background of the pine-clad hill, under the clear pale sky and in the sunshine of the perfect winter's day, rose the artistic white temple. Around it were the tall bright banners and the innumerable cones of brighter flowers. The quaint old-world garments of mourners, priests, and choristers formed a startling contrast to the brilliant uniforms, many of them blazing with decorations, which suited well with the martial bearing and keen, set faces of the men who wore them—the makers of the new Japan, who yet are the very conscious inheritors of the unforgotten traditions of the old.

Around all these swayed the huge crowd, hushed in the extremest solemnity. The weird notes of the ancient Shinto music sounded, swelling and falling in inflections strange to Western ears, and inexpressibly doleful. Then the chief priest advanced to the coffin and presented the offerings—fish, birds, vegetables, fruit, cakes, rice, and wines. A prayer was intoned, after which the priest read from a scroll the eulogium of the prince, setting forth his services to the State, and enumerating his honours and rewards. It concluded thus: 'The deep grief of their imperial majesties and of every member of the imperial family is great. They have sent each one his messenger to present prayers and offerings. Deign graciously, O soul, to accept these offerings, and sleep, O body, unmolested in the depths of this sacred ground.' The reading was followed by the offering of the *gohei*, folded streamers of paper fastened to small branches of the *sakaki*. What inward and spiritual grace is signified and conveyed by these outward symbols is a matter not to be lightly expounded; but they are sacramental tokens never far absent from the lives of the people, and their presentation is the supreme act of worship at each crisis of life wherever the Shinto rites prevail. In measured order—imperial representatives first, their *gohei* bound round with crimson silk, then mourners and friends—each received from the hands of the priest the branch with its waving zigzags of paper, laid it, deeply bowing, upon the altar, and turned away, conducted by the chamberlains.

An endless ceremony it seemed; but nothing tires the patience of a Japanese assembly, least of all a function so solemn as this. At last it was over; the crowd dispersed slowly, and, as the short day closed in, the mourners bore the coffin up the steep ascent to where, deep and granite-lined, the open grave awaited it, under the shelter of yet another newly erected temple. Slowly, and with many prayers, it was lowered, the pilgrim's shoes and the warrior's sword resting together on the top, along with a handful of coins, and a plate of copper bearing a long inscription, in which expressions of grief, eulogy, and reverential worship of the departed all found place. The widow stood by the head of the grave while the mound was heaped high, ten feet or more, above it. The darkness fell before the last prayers were said and the last mourners moved away, save those who took the first turn in the unceasing watch to be kept for fifty days beside the dead.

For this watching, begun in the death chamber, is continued for so long. Priests occupy the temporary houses erected near the grave, and offer up unceasing prayers, not to the dead, although his deification has been recognised in those writings and speeches. We must not be too logical, or we may miss after all the meaning which we and they feel after *O Kami San*. The great God is over all these minor myriads of gods, and *O Kami San's* judgment follows the deeds done in the body. At the end of these fifty days it will be delivered, and the prayers and alms of the survivors will help to weigh down the scale of his virtues; and thus it is that day by day, the men unshaven, and the women with their long black hair floating unbound, those who love him, come and worship at his grave. After the fifty days are over the mourning is relaxed, but there is a monthly celebration at the grave during the first year, and an annual commemoration during seven years or longer.

ALETHEA YAYENO SANNOMIYA

*(English wife of the Vice Grand Master of the Ceremonies
to His Imperial Majesty the Emperor of Japan).*

THE FINANCIAL GRIEVANCE

OF IRELAND

IT need not be a matter of surprise if a good deal is heard next Session of Parliament of the financial grievance of Ireland. At any rate, the Irish public of all sections and all political parties are just now giving fair and ample warning on the subject. It is unfortunately true that there are not many matters on which Nationalists and Unionists, landlords and tenants, peers and peasants, Catholics, Protestants, and Presbyterians are united; but there are some, and one of them is the robbery of Ireland which has been conclusively exposed by the report of the Financial Relations Commission and by the evidence on which it is founded. For the present it would appear as if the political campaign on the one side and on the other in Ireland were about to be suspended in favour of an agitation, participated in by all parties, in support of the demand that the robbery referred to should cease. In Cork, a requisition signed by Unionists, Parnellites, and anti-Parnellites has been presented to the Earl of Bandon, as Lord Lieutenant of the county, to call a general meeting of the county and city to consider the question and pass resolutions in reference to it; Irish public bodies of all kinds are almost every day expressing their minds upon it in emphatic terms; and there can be little doubt that, before Parliament meets, a body of opinion will have been obtained in favour of the popular view, the national character of which cannot possibly be questioned. Even Englishmen will probably admit that it would be strange if all this were not the case. If England were a part, say, of France, as at one time it seemed not impossible that it would become, and if, after several generations of common government and 'indiscriminate' taxation, it were declared by a tribunal mostly composed of Frenchmen that England had been despoiled at the rate of some millions sterling a year by 'the predominant partner,' Englishmen would almost to a certainty take advantage of such a declaration to declare, in their turn, that they would not submit longer than they were compelled to so great an injustice. Moreover, it is felt that this financial grievance is not recognised or admitted in England as widely as could be desired, and that accordingly a vigorous agitation is necessary if redress is soon to be obtained. But the great fact to be noted is that, for the first time probably since the Union, the whole population of Ireland is, as has been said, united on an Irish question, and that, should England resist the Irish demand, it will have, at least on this occasion, no Irish aiders or abettors.

The conclusions of the Financial Relations Commission, which are sufficiently remarkable in themselves, are rendered more so by remembering the constitution of that body. Putting out of account the Irish members of the Commission, who may by some persons be regarded as prejudiced in favour of the Irish view of the question inquired into, but who, however, include Unionists as well as Nationalists in their number, let us see how the rest of the Commission was constituted. To English and Scotch readers it will be sufficient to mention the names of the late Mr. Childers, Lord Farrer, Lord Welby, the late Sir Robert Hamilton, Sir Thomas Sutherland, M.P., Sir David Barbour, Mr. Bertram Currie, and Mr. W. A. Hunter, ex-M.P., to enable them to know that British interests and the interests of the Treasury in especial were amply represented. Indeed, it may be said, without any disparagement whatever to the Irish Commissioners, that British interests were better represented than the interests of Ireland, for no Irish Commissioner possessed the expert knowledge which comes and can only come of such lengthened official experience as that of Mr. Childers, Lord Farrer, Lord Welby, Sir Robert Hamilton, Sir David Barbour, and Mr. Currie. Yet, of the eight British representatives on the Commission, four have signed the joint report to which all the Irish representatives have attached their names; two others, Mr. Childers and Sir Robert Hamilton, would undoubtedly have done so if they had lived; one other, Sir David Barbour, has presented a report of his own, which shows that he too might have followed suit without outraging his conscience; and even the remaining member can hardly be said to deny the main facts. Never before, it may safely be said, has an inquiry by men of such widely divergent views on political and other subjects into a question so complicated, and involving such antagonistic interests, resulted in so practically unanimous a verdict. But this verdict is unusually remarkable for another reason also. The facts and figures on which it is based were mainly supplied by the officials of an English Government, and made out under the directions of the various departments of that Government. No such objection, therefore, can be taken to the evidence by Englishmen as that it was one-sided or insufficient. It is doubtful, however, if such an objection may not properly be made by Irishmen. In this matter Irishmen have always been at a great disadvantage. Not only have they not had the expert skill which official experience alone brings, but they have not had access to the sources of information necessary to determine the question.   I do not, of course, suggest that any fact of importance has been deliberately kept back from the Commission ; but it is quite possible that if Irishmen, unconnected in any way with the Government departments, had before them all the official information possessed by those departments, they might, by reason of looking at matters from a different point of view, not only put a different meaning on some facts and figures that have been furnished, but might even see importance in other facts and figures that have been passed over as of no significance.

But to come now to the actual findings of the Commission. They are five in number, and are as follows :

I. That Great Britain and Ireland must for the purpose of this inquiry be considered as separate entities.

II. That the Act of Union imposed upon Ireland a burden which, as events showed, she was unable to bear.

III. That the increase of taxation laid upon Ireland between 1853 and 1860 was not justified by the then existing circumstances.

IV. That identity of rates of taxation does not necessarily involve equality of burden.

V. That, whilst the actual tax revenue of Ireland is about one-eleventh of that of Great Britain, the relative taxable capacity of Ireland is very much smaller, and is not estimated by any of us as exceeding one-twentieth.

To an Irishman who has been following the course of this financial controversy, the first observation that suggests itself, on reading this series of conclusions, is that they completely justify all that has ever been said upon the subject from the point of view of Ireland.   From time to time during the last half-century Irishmen of every political party have complained of the over-taxation of their country.   The late Mr. O'Neill Daunt, a Repealer of the old school, of whom it may be said that neither his pre-eminent abilities nor his public services have] ever met with adequate appreciation ; The O'Conor Don, a Liberal Unionist ; the late Colonel Dunne, a Conservative, and sometime member of Parliament for Queen's County ; Sir Joseph McKenna, a Home Ruler, and other representative Irishmen, whose names it is needless to mention, have all at various times laid down the main propositions just quoted ; the exact amount, of course, of the excess of Ireland's contribution to the Imperial revenue beyond her proper share being with them all a matter of doubt. But they have all been, as it were, laughed out of court.   That Ireland was unjustly treated in financial matters, either at the time of the Union or afterwards, was a circumstance which no British statesman would admit.   The contrary, indeed, was asserted—namely, that Ireland was unduly favoured.   The fact that she was exempt from certain taxes to which Great Britain was subject, the ' exceptional ' grants and remissions of loans made to her, and the abnormal expenditure upon the government of Ireland, were all pointed to as conclusively showing that that country was really the petted and pampered member of the United Kingdom, and that it was England which really suffered from the working of the existing financial system. Statesmen of both the great British parties have continuously and consistently committed themselves to this view, but most of all, perhaps, Mr. Lowe (afterwards Lord Sherbrooke) and Mr. Gladstone. Again and again Irish members have laid the Irish case before the House of Commons, and have invariably been met with the same answer from the Treasury bench, no matter who might be its occupants. At last, however, the Irish complainants stand justified and their opponents confounded. At last an authoritative declaration has been made that Ireland has, at all events for the last forty or fifty years, been grossly overtaxed, and that at present the over-taxation amounts to at least a sum approaching three millions sterling a year. It is a 'tremendous admission,' as Mr. Morley has said, and Englishmen may still doubt it or refuse to believe it; but there it is, and it will not be and cannot be got rid of by any special pleading however plausible, or by any protests however vehement. It is scarcely too much to say that since the Commission spoke the cause has been finished.

The findings of the Commission, as set forth in the common or joint Report, take up but a very small space, but they embrace practically the whole case; and it may be added that the Supplementary Reports, to speak broadly, are concerned either with setting forth the grounds for those conclusions, or, as regards two of the reports, with vain attempts to explain some or all of them away. Once it is established or admitted—(1) that Great Britain and Ireland are to be treated in this matter as separate entities; (2) that the Act of Union imposed a burden on Ireland which she was unable to bear, and led to her being taxed on the high British level; (3) that the conspicuous increase of taxation laid upon Ireland between 1853 and 1860 was wholly unjustifiable; (4) that so-called uniform rates of taxation do not necessarily involve equality of burden; and (5) that the actual contribution of Ireland to the Imperial revenue is one-eleventh of that of Great Britain, while her taxable capacity is not higher than one-twentieth—almost every other point involved is comparatively unimportant. The establishment of the last-mentioned point alone would be, to use Mr. Morley's phrase, a 'tremendous' fact. Fancy Ireland contributing in the last thirty-five or forty years to the Imperial revenue a sum equal to the cost of some of the biggest wars of the century! No wonder that she has in that very time declined in every element of wealth. Some persons are for ever diving into the depths of economic science, looking here, there, and everywhere for the secret of Ireland's poverty, inventing specious theories, and twisting and turning endless tables of statistics. Is not one, at least, of the chief causes of that poverty big as a mountain, open, palpable? What nation in Europe could long endure a drain of money similar in proportion to that just mentioned? People talk oftentimes of Ireland's great difficulty being want of capital, and of the great advantage to her, in view of that difficulty, of having the credit of England secured to her by the Legislative Union. Does it not strike one irresistibly that she would have capital enough of her own if only the working of the Legislative Union were such as to allow her to keep what she has after paying her proper share of the Imperial expenses? Fancy what could be done for the poverty-stricken West of Ireland if the Congested Districts Board had at its command, not the beggarly sum of 40,000*l.* a year which is its present income, but a million a year of the excess sum now paid by Ireland to the Imperial Treasury! Fancy what could be done throughout the rest of Ireland in reviving industries, in imparting technical education, in constructing railways, in making piers and harbours, if the balance of that sum, amounting at the lowest estimate to a million and three-quarters sterling, were at the disposal of an Irish representative authority! To the ordinary Irishman it is not so much disgusting as maddening to be obliged to listen to far-fetched and often absurd theories regarding Ireland's decline in material prosperity, to homilies on Irish want of thrift and couse-quent want of capital, to refusals of demands for grants for public purposes, and to lectures on the great virtue of self-reliance as con-trasted with the vice of 'looking to the Treasury for everything,' when he knows all the time that that very Treasury is the receptacle into which have flowed during the last forty years alone at least a hundred millions sterling, and probably much more, of Irish capital which, under any fair financial arrangement, would have either remained in the pockets of the Irish people or would have been used in Ireland on reproductive national undertakings.

One great result of the work of the Financial Relations Com-mission is, as has been said, that the controversy as to the facts of the financial grievance of Ireland may be said to be ended. That controversy has no longer any life in it. It may henceforth be regarded as dead and buried. But it is scarcely possible to imagine how completely it is a thing of the past without reading the Supple-mentary Reports of various members of the Commission, including those of the two Commissioners who dissent from the findings of the main body. The truth is, controversy as to the facts is and has been impossible, if we are to assume the truth of the first of the findings of the Commission—viz. that Great Britain and Ireland are to be treated as separate entities. We shall presently deal with that finding; but, assuming it for the present to be true, that asserting the over-taxation of Ireland must necessarily be admitted. It is only by denying its truth that the over-taxation can be disputed by any one, and it is only in this way that Sir David Barbour and Sir Thomas Sutherland do dispute it, if indeed the former can really be regarded in view of all his admissions as a dissentient at all. To arrive at a conclusion on this point it is only necessary to find out, firstly, the relative taxable capacity of Ireland, and, secondly, the amounts contributed in the shape of Imperial taxation by Great Britain and Ireland respectively. As to the former matter, the materials available, it is said, enable one to arrive only at an approximation to the truth. Granted; but when half a dozen or a dozen different tests are applied, and all are found to point in the same general direction, it is the merest trifling to profess to have any doubts as to what is the truth. The only doubt, indeed, that can reasonably arise in the mind of any one is whether the relative capacity of Ireland to bear taxation is even so high as it is put by the majority of the Commission. When one thinks of the vast industries of England, her enormous foreign and colonial trade, and the millions upon millions of money which she is able to lend to or invest in every country under the sun, and then looks at the wretched remnant of Irish trade and commerce which is now left, the tendency of every man who uses his eyes and ears rather than statistics is to suspect that even the most reliable figures tell a delusive tale, and that the capacity of Ireland for taxation, instead of being a twentieth of that of Great Britain, must be very considerably smaller. Again, some doubt has existed as to the amount of revenue actually contributed by Ireland. But there can be no longer any reasonable doubt on this point. So much is admitted even by Sir Thomas Sutherland. 'So much trouble,' he says, 'has been taken recently by the revenue authorities to estimate the duties derived from Great Britain and Ireland respectively, that a fair assurance of the reliable character of these estimates, as estimates, may be entertained.' But, if we have ascertained the relative taxable capacity and the actual taxation of Ireland, the alleged over-taxation is but a necessary inference of arithmetic. Take the next most important finding of the Commission—viz. that the increase of taxation laid upon Ireland between 1853 and 1860 was not justifiable. Here again, if the primary principle laid down be true, viz. that Great Britain and Ireland are to be treated as separate entities, a verdict of the most sweeping condemnation of the financial policy of Mr. Gladstone in the 1853-60 period cannot possibly be evaded. It is simply a necessary conclusion of arithmetic from premises supplied by the Government departments themselves. 'Ireland was entitled, under the Act of Union,' Sir David Barbour says, 'to such exemptions or abatements as her circumstances might require.' Her circumstances in 1853—when the effects of the great famine were still felt—were similar to those of a man reeling under the results of an illness that brought him to the very verge of death; yet the undisputed figures show that, instead of being indulged with 'exemptions or abatements' at that time, Ireland was loaded with an increase of taxation in that and the few subsequent years amounting to over 50 per cent. Even Sir Thomas Sutherland does not dispute this fact. He is only lost in admiration at the success of Mr. Gladstone's scheme for increasing the revenue both in Ireland and in Great Britain. Of the remaining findings of the Commission, one, the fourth, has been described by the hostile critics of the Report of the majority of the Commission as 'an economic truism,' though it absolutely takes the ground from under their own feet when they allege that no injustice can be done when the same taxes are imposed on every one throughout the three kingdoms; while as to the other, the third, it is universally admitted that Ireland was practically made bankrupt in 1817 by the working of the Union arrangements, the only plea in extenuation being that such a result was not contemplated by the benevolent and honest men who brought about the insurrection of '98, and who bribed the Parliament of Ireland wholesale to pass the Union. But, if Ireland was plundered to the extremity of destruction in the first seventeen years of the Union; if, contrary to the Union Act, her taxation was afterwards raised to the high British level without regard to her circumstances, which would have dictated a reduction in taxation; and if, finally, at the present she is found to be contributing to the Imperial Treasury nearly three millions a year more than she ought to contribute in any fair view of the case, the opponents of her demand for relief now have a pretty hard nut to crack.

But, of course, to all this an answer—whether good or bad we shall see—is forthcoming. It is said (1) that Ireland and Great Britain are *not* to be treated as separate entities, but as one country on which uniform rates of taxation are imposed; (2) that if the expenditure on Ireland, which is proportionately much larger than that on Great Britain, be taken into account, Ireland is favoured rather than injured by existing arrangements; (3) that she has been exceptionally favoured, in especial in respect of grants and loans; and (4) that Ireland is to-day actually exempt from certain taxes to which Great Britain is subject. Let us take these pleas in order, and see whether there is in them anything whatever deserving more than a moment's consideration.

We may dispose of the last-mentioned plea first, as it is capable of being dealt with in almost a sentence. The taxes which Great Britain pays, and which Ireland does not pay, amount to just 4,188,300*l.*; and if Ireland paid her share of those taxes, the total result would scarcely be altered to the extent of a decimal. It is to be hoped that we have heard the last, at least, of this precious answer to the Irish case.

The next point is of much greater importance. Is Ireland to be treated in this matter as a separate country, or as a part of Great Britain? Before answering this question, it may be said, parenthetically, that to agree that it should be treated as a part of Great Britain does actually result from the operation of that system. Here comes in the 'economic truism' that 'identity of rates of taxation does not necessarily involve equality of burden.' Even if the claim of Ireland for separate treatment be abandoned, the fact remains that the specious 'uniform' taxation principle may be so applied that it would work the gravest injustice to the population of Ireland. Obviously, to secure this result all that would be necessary would be to tax highly the commodities most favoured by Ireland, and to tax at a low rate those favoured by England. It would be possible in such a case innocently to say, with Sir Thomas Sutherland, that taxes are imposed not on 'different provinces of the kingdom,' but 'on the individual units of the population,' without regard to locality ; and it would be possible at the very same time effectually to rob the 'individual units' of one locality or province for the benefit of the 'individual units' of all the other localities—the very thing that happens when, for instance, an exceptionally heavy tax is placed on the Irishman's whisky, and an exceptionally light one on the Englishman's beer. But the claim of Ireland for separate treatment cannot be abandoned and cannot be disputed by at least those who stand by the Act of Union. The Act of Union specifically provides for separate treatment for Ireland. The authors of the Act in England and Ireland promised that it would so provide, and explained that it did so provide. On this point the following passage from the Supplementary Report of the Chairman and other members of the Commission is conclusive :—

A legislative union might have been brought about without any particular arrangement as to financial matters, and if it were contemplated that after that union Great Britain and Ireland were to be regarded as one country, this is the course that would manifestly have been taken. But this was not the principle adopted. Mr. Pitt and Lord Castlereagh clearly recognised that, even after the union of the legislatures, Ireland would have separate rights, and that one of these rights was that, in the matter of taxation, she should contribute only in proportion to her ability or resources. Were it not for the acknowledgment of this principle, the seventh article of the Act of Union would have been wholly unnecessary. Notwithstanding the fact that Great Britain had a very large debt, and Ireland a comparatively small one, no notice would have been taken of this disparity unless the principle of contribution according to resources was first admitted. This principle being admitted, an adjustment of taxation so as to provide for the requirements of the separate debts became necessary, and the seventh article of the Act of Union was passed.

What answer there can be to this argument by any one who believes that there is any validity in the Act of Union, it is impossible to imagine. It is impossible to have the Act of Union for some of its purposes and not for the rest. One cannot, as the lawyers say, approbate and reprobate. The reply given by Sir David Barbour seems to be rather an explanation of the Irish case than anything else. 'The provision in the Act of Union,' he says, 'as to such particular *exemptions and abatements* as circumstances might appear to demand in the case of Ireland applies equally to Scotland, and was merely intended as a safeguard, in the interests of the poorer countries, on the working of the system of identical taxation throughout the United Kingdom.' The fact that Scotland may be entitled to separate treatment as well as Ireland is hardly a reason for depriving Ireland of *its* rights; and it is perfectly idle to pretend for a moment that such exemptions from and abatement of taxation as would rectify the injustice of imposing the same taxes on both countries are not wholly inconsistent with the maintenance of a system of indiscriminate taxation. But it may be said, perhaps, that, although every section of the seventh or financial article of the Act of Union clearly contemplates separate treatment of Ireland and taxation of Ireland according to certain standards of relative ability actually laid down in the Act, yet that in certain events the same seventh article provides for the indiscriminate taxation which now exists, and that one of those events, namely, the increase of the Irish debt in a prescribed ratio to that of England, has happened. Even this argument will not avail, for the very section of the seventh article which provides for that eventuality provides also that, before equal taxes shall in that eventuality be imposed, Parliament must be satisfied that 'the respective circumstances of the two countries will thenceforth admit of their contributing indiscriminately.' It is needless to say that Parliament never has been and never could have been satisfied of anything of the kind. But the whole idea of Ireland not being entitled to separate treatment is a mere latter-day afterthought. When, a few years ago, Mr. Goschen, as Chancellor of the Exchequer, assented to the first of the series of Financial Returns showing the income derived from and the expenditure on England, Scotland, and Ireland respectively, the notion never struck that able, acute, and certainly not pro-Irish financier. It is entirely too late to resort to it now.

We now come to the argument that the excessive expenditure on Ireland counterbalances the excessive taxation which is wrung from it. Here we come upon another latter-day afterthought. The idea of drawing a distinction between British local charges, Irish local charges, and Imperial charges finds no expression in the Act of Union by virtue of which the present financial system of the United Kingdom exists. It might, therefore, be sufficient for Ireland to say that she stands in this matter upon the Act of Union, which provides most distinctly that 'the Imperial expenditure to which,' as The O'Conor Don's Report puts it, 'Ireland was to contribute in proportion to her resources included all civil government expenditure, no matter in what part of the United Kingdom it took place.' The Act of Union is to stand, or it is not. If it is not to stand, the Irish

Parliament ought to be summoned to meet on an early date in College Green, and provide, as it may please, for the financial needs of Ireland. If it is to stand, then Ireland must get the benefit of such of its provisions as are in her favour, and, if she does, the argument based on excessive expenditure for Irish local purposes disappears. But there are other answers. If expenditure is to be taken into account in arriving at a solution of the question whether Ireland is or is not overtaxed, then we must go back and see how the account stood at various periods since the Union. Suppose we take the decade 1850–60. In the last year of that decade the true revenue derived from Ireland was 7,750,000*l.* ; the estimated local expenditure on Ireland was less than two and a half millions; there was thus a balance for Imperial purposes of nearly five millions and a half. What about the millions that, according to the 'excessive expenditure' theory of to-day, would then at least be due to Ireland ? If expenditure is to be taken into account against Ireland when it is large, it must also be taken into account in its favour when it is small, and if this principle be applied to the past, then scores of millions are due to Ireland now on a balance. Again, why should the charges for the main-tenance of order, the enforcement of the laws, and the collection of the Imperial revenue in Ireland, be considered less Imperial in their character than those for the army and the navy ? Great Britain is, perhaps, more interested in Ireland being peaceful and orderly than Ireland itself; and if this view of the matter be not admitted, then some unexpected consequences must ensue. 'If,' as The O'Conor Don's Report puts it, 'the Imperial expenditure for the maintenance of civil government in Ireland is to be regarded as local because Ireland is mainly or wholly benefited by it, questions may be asked, and must be asked, why the Imperial expenditure on the army and navy should not be charged to Great Britain, because she is mainly interested in and benefited by that expenditure.' The result, it need hardly be added, would be decidedly disadvantageous to Great Britain. But there is one further answer. It is that the excessive expenditure in Ireland is the direct result of British policy. Why, for instance, does the Irish Constabulary cost a million and a half annually instead of half a million, which would be the cost if that force were organised on the same scale as the police in England and Scotland ? Because Great Britain is governing Ireland against her will. Great Britain has been making that experiment for nearly a century with a full knowledge of its financial consequences, and Great Britain alone, accordingly, ought to pay the cost. It would be unjust beyond all precedent to govern Ireland against its will, and then make Ireland pay for the continual failure. Moreover, such expenditure is not re-productive. It is one thing to spend a million on police ; it is another and a very different thing to spend the same sum on harbour works and railways.

Lastly, there is the argument derived from the supposed liberality of Great Britain towards Ireland in the matter of loans and grants. If there is any part of the history of the financial relations of the two countries of which England ought to desire to avoid an investigation, it is that regarding the loans made to Ireland. It is said that out of the loans advanced for British and Irish purposes respectively, ten millions, or one-fifth, have been written off or remitted or treated as a free grant in the case of Ireland, while only one fifty-eighth part has been so treated in the case of Great Britain. What is the fact? 'An examination of the return [regarding loans] shows,' says The O'Conor Don's Report, 'that about' nine millions out of the ten for which Ireland was alleged to be in default were not, in the true sense, loans for local purposes, and that they did not correspond with the advances made to Great Britain.' The truth is that the greater part of the Irish loans consisted of advances by a State department in relief of distress, and were more than repaid by other devices; or on public works, regarding which it may be said that there was no Irish borrower at all, and no independent Irish authority with the least control either in the selection or the execution of the works; and that many or most of the works have been non-reproductive. Of the ten millions remitted more than four millions represented money advanced for the relief of the poor in the time of the great famine, and it was actually on the ground of the remission of that money that the income tax was extended to Ireland. In other words, four millions and something over were remitted, and twenty millions have been collected to recoup the Treasury! This is, indeed, a curious sort of 'liberality to Ireland.' To all this it may be added that, by the arrangements made regarding the interest to be paid on Irish loans, there is the gravest reason to believe that the Treasury is making actually a profit out of lending to Ireland, just as if it were an ordinary money-lender, and that at this very moment a lunatic asylum cannot be built or extended in Ireland without money borrowed from the Government at $3\frac{1}{2}$ per cent., while, if the local authorities were allowed by law to go into the open market for the advances they require for those institutions, they could, in view of the excellent security they can offer, borrow at nearly 1 per cent. less. As for the grants directly made to Ireland, they are scarcely worth talking about, and, as The O'Conor Don's Report shows, those which have been made under the Tramways Act of 1883 have actually proved, from the manner in which they were made available, a distinct injury, and not a benefit, to the Irish ratepayers. It would thus appear that there is really no answer whatever to the Irish case.

It remains to say a word or two as to the manner in which redress may be afforded to Ireland for the injustice which is thus proved to be inflicted upon her and which she has undoubtedly endured for many years. Four principal suggestions have been made on this head. The first is that the control of her own financial concerns

—the power of raising her own revenue and spending her own money —should be restored to Ireland, with or without the obligation of making a fixed annual contribution to Imperial expenses; the second, that the fiscal system of the Empire should be altered either by making the incidence of taxation fall more lightly on Ireland and more heavily on Great Britain, or by returning to the system which prevailed in the earlier part of the century and making certain abatements in the Excise and Customs duties raised in Ireland so as to differentiate them in favour of Ireland from those raised in Great Britain; the third is to allocate a certain large sum annually from the general revenue for the purpose of promoting the material prosperity of Ireland; and the fourth is that reductions should be effected in the existing expenditure in Ireland, and that the sum of those reductions should be applied to more useful public purposes in that country than those to which they are now devoted. Obviously these various suggestions are so important and cover so much new ground that it would be impossible adequately to discuss them at the close of this paper. A few general observations, however, may be made upon them, and the last is specially worthy of note when we consider the quarter from which it comes, and the reasons urged in its support. The first plan would practically mean the concession of a measure of Home Rule; it is highly significant that it is specially favoured by Lord Farrer and Mr. Currie, and in a less degree by Lord Welby, as the only mode of meeting the difficulty. The second would mean a change which many perhaps, even in Ireland, would not prefer to the third plan, which, if properly carried out, would seem likely to confer much greater and more direct benefit on the country, inasmuch as what, after Home Rule, is most wanted is a liberal expenditure of money in reviving and fostering Irish industries of all kinds. The last is the suggestion of Sir David Barbour. It is obviously intended as a means of saving the British taxpayer from the just consequences of his own misdeeds in the past, and there is no doubt that if adopted it would have that effect. But that very fact shows that it would be no redress of the grievance complained of, for Ireland would be still paying the same excessive contribution to Imperial expenditure, although of course it may at the same time be admitted that it would be better for Ireland to have half the sum, say, now paid to the constabulary devoted to technical schools or the improvement of the means of internal communication. But I do not discuss this plan now; I draw attention to it specially to mention that Sir David Barbour advocates it on the following grounds : (I) That the Union arrangements were unfair to Ireland; (2) that the process by which the present system of taxation has been brought about has in practice proved more advantageous to Great Britain than to Ireland; (3) that the circumstances of Ireland were not fairly considered when the great increase of taxation occurred in the 1850–60 period; (4)

that the economic condition of Ireland has been very unsatisfactory for a very long time—in other words, that it has been about as bad as it could be; (5) that Ireland is entitled under the Act of Union to have her circumstances specially considered; and (6) that being the weaker partner the Irish representatives are necessarily a minority in Parliament. All this is pretty strong for a dissentient. After having read it, we wonder why Sir David Barbour was a dissentient at all.

Much, very much, more remains to be said upon this question. But what has been said shows, I hope, why there is an agitation in Ireland at present such, in one respect, as has been rarely witnessed, and it will probably also explain why next Session of Parliament Irish representatives of all political parties will almost certainly be found earnestly demanding that some plan or other shall be adopted to put an end to an injustice as gross of its kind as is to be discovered in history since the days when Sicily was plundered by Verres.

J. J. CLANCY.

P.S.—Since the foregoing pages were written, another Parliamentary return has been issued on the motion of Mr. Joseph A. Pease, M.P., an examination of which will show that the over-taxation of Ireland, which the Royal Commission found to exist, has been considerably aggravated by that great effort of Liberal statesmanship, the Finance Act of 1894. On the lowest estimate the over-taxation of Ireland now amounts to more than three millions sterling a year.

It having been observed that there was little hospitality in London, Johnson : 'Nay, sir, any man who has a name, or who has the power of pleasing, will be very generally invited in London. The man Sterne, I have been told, has had engagements for three months.' Goldsmith : 'And a very dull fellow.' Johnson : 'Why, no, sir.'

ONE of my earliest recollections is a warning which I received from a country gentleman not to read too many books. 'For my part,' he said, ' I only read two books; but I read them over and over again. One is the Bible. The other is *Tristram Shandy.*' Apart from the absurdity of calling the Bible a book, and the indecorum of comparing sacred literature with profane, there is in the writings of Sterne no obvious inspiration from on high. But there are other qualities with which a mundane critic is naturally more competent to deal. Dr. Johnson, who knew better than to call Sterne dull, declared that *Tristram Shandy* would perish because it was odd, and nothing odd could live. *Tristram Shandy*, like Charles the Second, has been an unconscionably long time in dying. It would be an exaggeration to say that Mr. Disraeli was the last man who read *Rasselas*, or that no man living had read *Irene*. But references to these classical compositions would in the best educated company fall exceedingly flat, whereas Uncle Toby's sayings are as well known as Falstaff's, and the 'sub-acid humour' of Mr. Shandy plays, like the wit of Horace, round the cockles of the heart. It is now a pure curiosity of literature that men have lived who imputed dulness to *Tristram Shandy*. Goldsmith, who was not altogether incapable of jealousy, denounced it in the *Citizen of the World* with a bitterness unsuitable to his character, and censured its violations of propriety in language of extraordinary grossness. Horace Walpole informed Sir David Dalrymple that he could not help calling it 'a very insipid and tedious performance,' in which 'the humour was for ever attempted and missed.' That is a description which might be applied by an unfavourable critic to Walpole's own letters, except that it is not easy to understand how, if humour is always missed, there can be any humour at all. ' The great humour,' adds this great critic, ' consists in the whole narrative always going backwards.' That is like the definition propounded by a budding naturalist to Cuvier, in which a crab was called

a red fish that walks backwards. ' Your definition,' said Cuvier, ' would
be perfect but for three facts : a crab is not red, it is not a fish, and it
does not walk backwards.'   Wordsworth thought that *Candide* was
dull, and it is possible that Voltaire might have pronounced with
more reason a similar judgment upon the *Ecclesiastical Sonnets*.   As
a straightforward and consecutive narrative of actual facts, duly set
forth with appropriate comments, *Tristram Shandy* must be
acknowledged, as Mr. Shandy said of the science of fortification, to
have its weak points.   Those who find it dull will probably find *The
Caxtons* amusing, and I recommend them to try.

Mr. Percy Fitzgerald has rewritten his *Life of Sterne*, and has
published some of Sterne's letters not previously printed.   He has
also reproduced the famous autograph contained in the fifth, seventh,
and ninth volumes of the second edition of *Tristram Shandy*.
When Sterne wrote for the public he was a purist in style, if not in
morals.   When he wrote to ladies he was rhapsodical and in every
sense of the word romantic.   He corresponded with his male friends
in a colloquial and rather slipshod fashion, which has nothing very
characteristic about it except indomitable cheerfulness.   Mr. Fitzgerald has disposed of Byron's charge that Sterne ' preferred
whining over a dead ass to relieving a living mother.'   The mother
was an insatiable harpy, and Sterne did relieve her on many occasions.
He was a good-natured if at bottom a selfish man.   He behaved
much better to his wife than Byron, which is not saying much, and
was as fond of his daughter as Wilkes, which is saying a great deal.
It is a strange notion that a man's private life becomes more interesting if he writes good prose or verse.   The late Professor Freeman
protested against setting up a Chair of English Literature at Oxford
if it was only to mean ' chatter about Harriet '—that is, the first
Mrs. Shelley.   Chatter about Jenny—that is, Miss Fourmantel—
is equally devoid of edification.   It was rather a mean sort of economy
on Mr. Sterne's part to use up his old love letters to Mrs. Sterne in
addressing Mrs. Draper.   Nor can the tone of his epistle to Lady
Percy be held up for the imitation of the married and beneficed
clergy.   But, as Captain Shandy exclaimed, ' what is all this to a
man who fears God ? '

Sterne was forty-five when he began *Tristram Shandy*.   He had
lived since his youth chiefly in York and the immediate neighbourhood.   The book was begun as a sort of local satire, in which the
characters were well known and speedily recognised.   What is the
secret of its unfailing charm ?   There is no plot.   There is no
story.   There is no method.   There is no order, not even an alphabetical order, of which an eminent judge said that, though inferior to
chronological order, it was better than no order at all.   There are
only a few characters, some eccentric, others so broadly and typically
human that one is startled by the familiarity and obviousness of

their comments upon novel and unexpected events. Take. for
instance, the scene in the kitchen at Shandy Hall when the news
arrived of Bobby Shandy's death.

'My young master in London is dead,' said Obadiah. A green satin nightgown
of my mother's, which had been twice scoured, was the first idea which Obadiah's
exclamation brought into Susannah's head. Well might Locke write a chapter
upon the imperfections of words. 'Then,' quoth Susannah, 'we must all go into
mourning.' But note a second time: the word *mourning*, notwithstanding
Susannah made use of it herself, failed also of doing its office; it excited not one
single idea, tinged either with grey or black—all was green. The green satin
nightgown hung there still. 'Oh! 'twill be the death of my poor mistress,' cried
Susannah. My mother's whole wardrobe followed. What a procession! Her
red damask, her orange-tawny, her white and yellow hat-strings, her brown taffeta,
her bone-laced caps, her bedgowns and comfortable under-petticoats—not a rag
was left behind. '*No, she will never look up again,*' said Susannah. We had a
fat foolish scullion—my father, I think, kept her for her simplicity. She had
been all autumn struggling with a dropsy. 'He is dead,' said Obadiah; 'he is
certainly dead.' 'So am not I,' said the foolish scullion. 'Here is sad news,
Trim!' cried Susannah, wiping her eyes as Trim stepped into the kitchen.
'Master Bobby is dead and buried.' The funeral was an interpolation of Susannah's.
'We shall have all to go into mourning,' said Susannah. 'I hope not,' said Trim.
'You hope not!' cried Susannah earnestly. The mourning ran not in Trim's
head, whatever it did in Susannah's. 'I hope,' said Trim, explaining himself, 'I
hope in God the news is not true.' 'I heard the letter read with my own ears,'
answered Obadiah, 'and we shall have a terrible piece of work of it in stubbing
the Oxmoor.' [Obadiah knew that Mr. Shandy had proposed to send Bobby
abroad with the money originally intended for the moor.] 'Oh! he's dead,' said
Susannah. 'As sure,' said the scullion, 'as I'm alive.'

Then follows the famous digression upon the dropping of Trim's
hat. ' "Are we not here now," continued the corporal, "and are we
not " (dropping his hat plump upon the ground. and pausing before
he pronounced the word) " gone! in a moment ? " The descent of the
hat was as if a heavy lump of clay had been kneaded into the crown
of it. " Had he flung it, or thrown it, or cast it, or skimmed it, or
squirted it, or let it slip or fall in any possible direction under
heaven, or in the best direction that could be given to it . . . it had
failed, and the effect upon the heart had been lost." ' Sterne goes on
in a style rather more fantastic than usual to treat Trim's hat as the
symbol of all declamatory eloquence and histrionic effect. Nearly
a hundred years after the publication of *Tristram Shandy* Richard
Cobden and John Bright walked home together from the House of
Commons. Mr. Bright had just made the great speech against the
Crimean war, in which he exclaimed, 'The angel of death is abroad
in the land. You can almost hear the beat of his wings.' It is one
of the most justly celebrated passages in modern oratory. 'There was
one moment,' remarked Cobden, 'when I trembled for you. If you
had said "flap" you would have been lost.' Whether Cobden had
read *Tristram Shandy* or not he understood the moral of Trim's hat.

A great French critic, the late M. Taine, in his spirited and

ingenious history of English literature dismisses Sterne with a few
contemptuous pages. He could see nothing in him but the eccentric
and grotesque. But that is to miss the whole reason of Sterne's popularity and the whole source of his power. Dr. Johnson was right in
his general principle, though wrong in his particular instance.
Nothing merely odd does last. *Tristram Shandy* is not merely odd.
Its oddity is on the surface. The author has ways and tricks which
perplex some readers, and annoy others. But they are not of the essence of his work. They are superficial. What lies below is a profound
knowledge of men and women, a subtle sympathy with human weakness, a consummate art of putting the great commonplaces of life in a
form which makes them seem original. ' Difficile est proprie communia
dicere.' It is difficult, but it is worth doing, for the prize is literary
immortality. M. Taine, who so thoroughly appreciated and so nobly
expressed the genius of Swift, could see in Sterne only a writer who
ended where he ought to have begun, who prosed upon the conjugal
endearments of an elderly merchant and his wife, who had strange
theories of trivial things, who dragged in legal pedantry and theological disputes and the jargon of the schools without reason or excuse.
No such book could have lived a hundred and thirty-six years, or
thirty-six without the hundred. It may be that, as Mr. Fitzgerald
says, *Tristram Shandy* is more talked about than read. All the
masterpieces of literature are. If every copy of *Tristram Shandy*
were destroyed to-morrow its influence upon style and thought would
remain. Sterne had one great quality besides humour in common
with Swift. He wrote his own English. I sometimes doubt whether
justice has ever yet been done to the simplicity and beauty of it.
The *Sentimental Journey* and the fragment of autobiography are
almost perfect. The familiar description of the accusing spirit and the
recording angel and Uncle Toby's oath would by the slightest blunder
of taste have been made ridiculous, and the intrusion or even the
misplacement of a word would have spoiled it. As it stands it is
the admiration of every one who reads and the despair of every one
who writes. The brief sketch of Uncle Toby's funeral, characteristically introduced in the middle of a book which leaves him perfectly
well at the end of it, is a flawless and exquisite vignette in words.
Sterne, like Swift, eschewed the mannerisms of his own age. There
is hardly a phrase in *Tristram Shandy* or in *Gulliver's Travels*
which would fix the date of either. They wrote for posterity, and,
unlike the too famous ode, they have reached their address.

It is, perhaps, less strange that M. Taine should underrate Sterne
than that Sterne should have become the rage in the Paris of Louis
Quinze. Whatever may be said of the *Sentimental Journey* there is
no more thoroughly English book than *Tristram Shandy*. But the
Anglomania of 1760 was equal to anything, and the fine French
ladies who thought Hume handsome found that Shandyism was just

the thing to suit them. Sterne's own French seems to have been as bad as Lord Brougham's. But *Tristram Shandy* was translated as it came out, and the Parisians bought it, if they did not read it. Long afterwards Madame de Beaumont, whose humour was not her strong point, carried *Tristram Shandy* about with her among her favourite volumes in the strange company of Voltaire's *Letters* and the Platonic Dialogue which describes the death of Socrates. It was not all Anglomania or affectation. It was also a conclusive tribute to the universality of the book. We know the sources from which Sterne's characters were drawn. Uncle Toby was a compound of his own father, concerning whom he says in the autobiography that ' you might have cheated him ten times a day if nine had not been sufficient for your purpose,' and Captain Hinde, of Preston Castle, in Hertfordshire. Yorick is, of course, himself, or one side of himself, for there is a great deal of Sterne in Mr. Shandy. Mrs. Shandy is said, alas! to have been his wife. Eugenius was John Hall Stevenson, owner of Crazy Castle, which was unfortunately destroyed, and author of *Crazy Tales*, which have been unfortunately preserved. Ernulphus is Bishop Warburton, Dr. Slop is Dr. Burton, and so forth. These facts are not without their interest, and it is still disputed, I believe, whether Dr. Burton was really a Roman Catholic and whether he was actually upset in the mud. The industrious inquirer who set himself to discover whether the husband of the nurse in *Romeo and Juliet* was really a merry man, or whether she was deceived into thinking him so by affectionate partiality for his memory, belonged to a class more numerous than less energetic people might suppose. ' The best in this kind are but shadows, and the worst are no worse, if imagination amend them.' But the shadows outlast the substance. They are too immaterial to feel the hand of death. They are like the songs of the old Greek, αἷσιν ὁ πάντων ἁρπακτὴρ 'Αίδης οὐκ ἐπὶ χεῖρα βαλεῖ. There is not much superficial resemblance between Laurence Sterne and Jane Austen ; but both drew their characters from their own immediate and not remarkable surroundings. Both drew them in such a fashion that all classes of readers can equally enjoy them. The early editions of *Tristram Shandy* bore on the title page a motto from Aristotle which gives the key to the whole work. Men are troubled, said the philosopher, not by facts, but by opinions about facts. Charles Lamb used to call himself a matter of fiction man. Walter Shandy is the type and presentment of the speculative mind. Nothing strikes him as it strikes other people. He judges everything by reference to a theory, and his theories have no necessary connection the one with the other. Yet his unfailing humour shines through his pedantry and, except when he lies on the bed, saves him from appearing ridiculous.

Sterne laughed at his critics, and their successors have not forgiven him. Bishop Warburton, after extolling him, oddly enough, as the English Rabelais, excommunicated · him with bell, book, and candle, as Bishop Monk long afterwards did to Sydney Smith. ·The result in both cases was a. deplorably easy triumph for the inferior clergy. Warburton lives as Ernulphus, and the *Divine Legation* is dead. Monk's *Euripides* reposes in the libraries of the curious. But everybody remembers him in connection with those 'cephalic animalculæ' protesting against the use of small-tooth combs. It is a dangerous thing to run across a man of genius before he is dead. When Boswell depreciated the *Dunciad* Johnson told him that he had missed his chance of immortality by coming too late into the world.· · Thackeray, who devoted half· a lecture to abuse of Sterne, and many volumes to the sincerest form of flattering him, took him, if one may say so with all respect, by the wrong side. The laughter of fools, said the wise man in one of his wisest sayings, is like the crackling of thorns under a pot. To Mr. Thackeray, with his sensitive and beautiful reverence for the serious side of life, Sterne's laughter was hollow and his mockery hideous. Sterne's sentiment, which is no more exclusively Sterne's than it is Shakespeare's or Nature's, may be found in *Esmond* and *The Newcomes* as much as in the *Sentimental Journey* itself. The fascinating spirit of the eighteenth century, as perilous and attractive as the Hill of Venus in mediæval romance, is summed up in Sterne as in no other man. It was the century of Wesley as well as of Voltaire, and of Johnson as well as of Rousseau. Sterne and Wesley hardly seem to belong to the same species. We are not all made to understand each other. Voltaire, with his noble hatred of persecution and love of intellectual freedom, did undoubtedly sometimes direct the terrible engine of his ridicule against 'the last restraint of the powerful and the last hope of the wretched.' Sterne did not. 'There never,' said Trim of his master, ' was a better officer in the king's army, or a better man in God's world,' and the character of Uncle Toby is a faithful portrait lovingly drawn. With the most substantial charge against Sterne's writings I must deal before I conclude. It cannot without affectation be ignored. But I claim for him, in spite of Mr. Thackeray, that the effect of his humour as of his eloquence, of his slightest sketches as of his most finished rhetoric, is to promote a large tolerance, a kindly sympathy, a broad humanity, and a rational justice.

The eighteenth century boasted itself to be the age of reason rather than the age of faith. Sterne poured contempt upon hypocrisy, upon pomposity, upon pretence, upon that peculiar carriage of the body which is adopted to conceal defects of the mind. He took, perhaps, rather too much interest in the relations of the sexes, and undervalued the conventional respectability which at one time earned for English society the applause of an admiring universe. But he hated cruelty, and meanness, and dishonesty, and malice. He knew that it was sentiment which separates man from beast. We cannot 'call up him who left half told the story of Cambuscan bold.' We cannot, alas! finish *Weir of Hermiston*, though it is not improbable that somebody will make the attempt. For my part I feel it even more difficult to bear the loss of that book which was never written, but which would have described Tristram's grand tour through Europe, 'in which, after all, my father (not caring to trust me with any one) attended me himself, with my uncle Toby, and Trim, and Obadiah, and, indeed, most of the family, except my mother, who being taken up with a project of knitting my father a pair of large worsted breeches (the thing is common sense), and she not caring to be put out of her way, she stayed at home, at Shandy Hall, to keep things straight during the expedition.' One fragment only of this precious work survives to excite curiosity for ever, and leave it always unappeased. The scene is Auxerre.

'We'll go, Brother Toby,' said my father, 'whilst dinner is coddling, to the Abbey of St. Germain, if it be only to see those bodies of which Monsieur Sequier has given such a recommendation.' 'I'll go see anybody,' quoth my uncle Toby, for he was all compliance every step of the journey. 'Defend me!' said my father, 'they are all mummies.' 'Then one need not shave,' quoth my uncle Toby. 'Shave! no,' cried my father; ''twill be more like relations to go with our beards on.' So out we sallied, the corporal lending his master his arm and bringing up the rear, to the Abbey of St. Germain. 'Everything is very fine, and very rich, and very superb, and very magnificent,' said my father, addressing himself to the sacristan, who was a younger brother of the order of Benedictines: 'but our curiosity has led us to see the bodies, of which Monsieur Sequier has given the world so exact a description.' The sacristan made a bow, and lighting a torch first, which he had always in the vestry ready for the purpose, he led us into the tomb of St. Heribald. 'This,' said the sacristan, laying his hand upon the tomb, 'was a renowned prince of the house of Bavaria, who, under the successive reigns of Charlemagne, Louis le Débonnaire, and Charles the Bald, bore a great sway in the government, and had a principal hand in bringing everything into order and discipline.' 'Then he has been as great,' said my uncle, 'in the field as in the cabinet. I dare say he has been a gallant soldier.' 'He was a monk,' said the sacristan. My uncle Toby and Trim sought comfort in each other's faces, but found it not. My father clapped both his hands upon his waistcoat, which was a way he had when anything hugely tickled him; for though he hated a monk and the very smell of a monk worse than all the devils in hell, yet the shot hitting my uncle Toby and Trim so much harder than him, 'twas a relative triumph and put him into the gayest humour in the world. 'And pray what do you call this gentleman?' quoth my father rather sportingly. 'This tomb,' said the young Benedictine, looking downwards, 'contains the bones of St. Maxima, who came from Ravenna on purpose to touch the body——' 'Of St. Maximus,' said my father, popping in with his saints before him. 'They were two of the greatest saints in the whole martyrology,' added my father. 'Excuse me,' said the sacristan, ''twas to touch the bones of St. Germain, the builder of the abbey.' 'And what did she get by it?' said my uncle Toby. 'What does any woman get by it?' said my father. '*Martyrdom*,' replied the young Benedictine, making a bow down to the ground, and uttering the word with so humble but decisive a cadence it disarmed my father for a moment. ''Tis supposed,' continued the Benedictine, 'that St. Maxima has lain in this tomb four hundred years before her canonisation.' 'Tis but a slow rise, Brother Toby,' quoth my father, 'in this self-same army of martyrs.' 'A desperate slow one, an' please your Honour,' said Trim, 'unless one could purchase.'. 'I should rather sell out entirely,' quoth my uncle Toby. 'I am pretty much of your opinion, Brother Toby,' said my father.

If *Tristram Shandy* were merely odd, this is just the sort of episode in it which would long ago have ceased to be read or to be readable. It is a digression upon a digression, if indeed terms of arrangement can be applied to a book which has none. It is a more flagrant violation of the unities than can be found even in Shakespeare, and to Shakespeare a man must go if he wants a purer piece of imperishable nature. Uncle Toby, 'all compliance through every step of the journey,' Mr. Shandy, whose 'remarks and reasonings upon the characters, the manners and customs of the countries we passed over were so opposite to those of all other mortal men, particularly those of my uncle Toby and Trim,' and Tristram silently observing for the future, make an even more delightful medley than that strange company which roamed through the best of all possible words under the guidance of M. Pangloss. This is the kind of passage which comment only spoils. But the 'relative triumph' of Mr. Shandy is the touch of a master. It supplies in two words the whole philosophy of popular preaching, in which the most hardened sinners will rejoice, because there is always some one else whom the shot hits so much harder than them. Sterne was not very respectful in his treatment of the Church of Rome. He played sometimes to the Protestant gallery, which still hated 'Papishes and wooden shoes.' But it is to be observed that on this visit to the Abbey of St. Germain the victory rests with the young Benedictine, who is not a humourist, nor a controversialist, but only a Christian gentleman. Sterne, like Swift, held very loosely to the dogmatic theology of his Church. But both of them were too great to make a cheap reputation for wit out of sneers at religion. Swift turned all the tremendous powers of his savage irony against the shallow free-thinkers of his day, and 'that quality of their voluminous writings which the poverty of the English language compels me to call their style.' The one character in *Tristram Shandy* whom Sterne never allows to be made ridiculous is Uncle Toby, and Uncle Toby's rule of life is the Sermon on the Mount. His quaint simplicity, his native shrewdness, his instinctive preference of good and rejection of evil are more than a match for all the learning and all the subtlety of his brother. When Mr. Shandy, in an unusually tedious mood, had begun a discourse upon learned men's solutions of noses, and had been driven wild by the Captain's artless question, 'Can noses be dissolved?' he replied—

'Why, by the solutions of noses, of which I was telling you, I meant, as you might have known, had you favoured me with one grain of attention, the various accounts which learned men of different kinds of knowledge have given the world of the causes of long and short noses.' 'There is no cause but one,' replied my uncle Toby, ' why one man's nose is longer than another, but because that God pleases to have it so.' 'That is Grangousier's solution,' said my father. ' It is he,' continued my uncle Toby, looking up and not regarding my father's interruption, ' who makes us all, and forms and puts us together in such forms and proportions and for such ends as is agreeable to his infinite wisdom.'

'Now, whether we observe it or no,' continued my father (upon another occasion), ' in every sound man's head there is a regular succession of ideas, of one sort or other, which follow each other in train just like——' ' A train of artillery ? ' said my uncle Toby. ' A train of a fiddlestick ! ' quoth my father—' which follow and succeed one another in our minds at certain distances, just like the images in the inside of a lantern turned round by the heat of a candle.' ' I declare,' quoth my uncle Toby, ' mine are more like a smoke-jack.' ' Then, Brother Toby, I have nothing more to say to you upon the subject,' said my father.

Mr. Fitzgerald has a strange theory that *Tristram Shandy* was written with great carelessness, and at headlong speed, resulting in a farrago of nonsense. illuminated by rare gleams of fancy and humour. This reminds me of the Buckinghamshire farmer who, after listening to a speech from his distinguished member at a market dinner, expressed the opinion that Mr. Disraeli was a very good man, but not at all clever. With all respect for Mr. Fitzgerald I venture to affirm that *Tristram Shandy* is one of the most elaborate of human compositions, that there is not a sentence in it but Sterne well knew how it came there, and that its simplicity is the designed consequence of the highest art. Every one must have enjoyed or suffered the experience of forgetting a single line or even a single word in a great poem. The hopeless impossibility of supplying it by any other means than memory impresses upon the mind, like nothing else, what real poetry is.

> Oh, the little more, and how much it is,
> And the little less, and what worlds away !

There is much in *Tristram Shandy* which approaches the pedantic and borders on the dull. Take the Curse of Ernulphus ; cut out of it the running comments of Uncle Toby and Mr. Shandy's famous shake of the head ; forget that Dr. Slop had to read it through himself as a penalty for cursing Obadiah because he had cut his own thumb. The Curse of Ernulphus becomes about as interesting as an essay on Humour with the humour, as it is usually, left out.

It is said that when the Rev. Laurence Sterne preached as prebendary in York Minster many good people left the sacred edifice rather than sit under him. His sermons, including the one which Corporal Trim read, and broke down in reading because it reminded him of his brother Tom and the Inquisition, are not fervidly spiritual. Sometimes, as when he warns wives against pretending to moral or physical advantages, the absence of which may be discovered in the first domestic scuffle, they may be reasonably suspected of a tendency to raise a laugh. It was, however, we are told, his life and not his sermons which scandalised his congregation He kept bad company, such as his cousin Hall Stevenson and the Rev. Robert Lascelles, known as 'Panty,' from his supposed and unclerical resemblance to Pantagruel. Sterne would have done better to adopt a secular career. His cassock never fitted him, and it is incongruous to make love in bands, especially for one who held that talking about love was not making it. But poor Sterne, with all his personal frailties, has been dead nearly a hundred and thirty years. Miss Fourmantel and Mrs. Draper were not difficult conquests. Sterne was, perhaps, not above enjoying *la fanfaronnade des vices qu'il n'avait pas.* We are concerned rather with his works than with him. Soundness of mind and goodness of heart are enshrined in the central figure of Sterne's masterpiece. At this time of day it is more important that one of the great writers of the world should have employed his genius upon the creation of Uncle Toby than that a clergyman of the Church of England should have written to a countess a letter which she had better have destroyed.

There is no episode in Sterne's writings, not even the description of the dead ass, more hackneyed than the story of Le Fevre. It has been much exposed to penny readings, and the professional writer has done his worst with it. But it remains unscathed, and it is worth all the pathetic scenes in Dickens put together. There is one touch in it peculiar to Sterne, and no more to be imitated than the thunderbolt of Jove. Trim is the narrator.

He did not offer to speak to me till I had walked up close to his bedside. 'If you are Captain Shandy's servant,' said he, 'you must present my thanks to your master, with my little Loy's thanks along with them, for his courtesy to me. If he was of Levens's——' said the lieutenant. 'I told him your honour was.' 'Then,' said he, 'I served three campaigns with him in Flanders, and remember him; but 'tis most likely, as I had not the honour of any acquaintance with him, that he knows nothing of me. You will tell him, however, that the person his good nature has laid under obligations to him is one Le Fevre, a lieutenant in Angus's; but he knows me not,' said he a second time, musing. 'Possibly he may my story,' added he. 'Pray tell the Captain I was the ensign at Breda whose wife was most unfortunately killed with a musket shot as she lay in my arms in my tent.' 'I remember the story, an't please your honour,' said I, 'very well.' 'Do you so?' said he, wiping his eyes with his handkerchief; 'then well may I.' In saying this he drew a little ring out of his bosom, which seemed tied with a black riband about his neck, and kissed it twice. 'Here, Billy,' said he. The boy flew across the room to the bedside, and falling down upon his knee took the ring in his hand and kissed it too, then kissed his father, and sat down upon the bed and wept. 'I wish,' said my uncle Toby with a deep sigh, 'I wish, Trim, I was asleep.'

Sterne often appears to be, though perhaps he never really is, diffuse. Certainly no one could say more, and not many could say so much, in a few words. Into *Tristram Shandy* he put himself, as Montaigne, who was sublimely diffuse, put himself into his essays. The sermons are perfunctory, and Dr. Johnson, no bad judge of the article, could not away with them. The *Sentimental Journey* is a perfect work of art.

But, or rather and, it is all of a piece ; it is a single record of fresh impressions. In *Tristram Shandy* are accumulated the experience, the meditations, the observant knowledge of many years. The eccentricity is in the treatment. The substance is elemental, and belongs to the broadest aspects of human nature. Sterne had an intense hatred of cruelty, of injustice, of hypocrisy, and of Puritanism. His religion was the sentimental Deism of the eighteenth century, and he had no abhorrence of the 'lighter vices.' In politics, though he affected, and perhaps felt, indifference to party, he was a mild Whig. Brought up among soldiers and loving them, as the characters of Uncle Toby and Trim show that he did, he hated war, and especially wars of ambition.

My father would often say to Yorick that if any mortal in the whole universe had done such a thing except his brother Toby, it would have been looked upon by the world as one of the most refined satires upon the parade and prancing manner in which Louis the Fourteenth from the beginning of the war, but particularly that very year, had taken the field. 'But 'tis not my brother Toby's nature, kind soul !' my father would add, ' to insult any one.'

Although Sterne was throughout his life the victim of weak health and fled from death, as he himself said, through France and Italy, dying at last in the fifty-sixth year of his age, his spirits were indomitable and his pluck dauntless. No man could be more nobly serious upon themes that moved his admiration, his reverence, or his pity. But he saw many things in odd lights, and his sense of humour never slumbered, not even when it would have been better asleep. The secret of his style, which must, I cannot help thinking, have had some influence upon Newman's, is expressed in his own aphorism that writing is like conversation. Mr. Shandy was fanciful and fantastic, a devourer of musty rubbish which he mistook for literature, and, it must be added, of some good books along with the rest. But Mr. Shandy is a master of racy vernacular, and his most celebrated repartees are in monosyllables. Unlike Swift, Sterne was a student of Shakespeare, and once found himself under the necessity of explaining to a bishop that there were two Yoricks. This prelate— perhaps the same who declared that he did not believe a word of *Gulliver's Travels*—protested that he could not read sermons by the King of Denmark's jester. Mr. Thackeray's criticism is less crude.

Learned men, who find out everything in time, have made the discovery that Sterne was not original. Their ingenuity and industry are not less laudable because they were anticipated by the candour of Sterne himself. He does not, indeed, mention Shakespeare. I suppose that in a treatise on photography one might assume the existence of the sun. But he speaks of his ' dear Rabelais, and still dearer Cervantes.' He quotes a whole heap of philosophers from Aristotle to Locke. ' Read, read, read,' he says, and of his own reading, if Captain Shandy will forgive such a use of the word, he makes a parade. And then we are gravely told by critics whose anti-Shandian beards we can spy under their mufflers, that he did not spin the whole of *Tristram Shandy* out of his own inside. The worthy and laborious Dr. Ferriar is actually at the pains to point out that when Mr. Shandy heard of the death of Bobby he quoted Bacon. He did indeed. He repeated nearly the whole of the Essay on Death, and he enriched it with an exquisite stroke. ' " Cæsar Augustus died in a compliment.". " I hope it was a sincere one," said my uncle Toby. " It was to his wife," replied my father.' Mr. Shandy upon the same mournful occasion, while Susannah's mind wandered towards green satin, quoted also Plato, Cicero, and Sulpicius. Quotation was the breath of his nostrils. He was always quoting. Excellent Dr. Ferriar. But then Sterne did not get all his quotations at first hand. He made a reprehensible use of Burton's *Anatomy of Melancholy*. Sterne was not melancholy, and stood in no need of Burton's anatomical assistance. But he found a good deal of miscellaneous feeding in the famous collections of Democritus Junior, and Sterne was a miscellaneous feeder. Dr. Arnold thought it was wrong to appropriate another man's quotations, even if you verified them first. Dr. Arnold was a Puritan. Sterne was not, and it is likely enough that he sometimes omitted even the process of verification. ' What is that to any body ? ' as Uncle Toby asked when his brother tried to tell him how he came by his ideas. Molière, so Mr. Fraser Rae tells us, did not say, ' Je prends mon bien où je le trouve.' He said, ' Je reprends mon bien,' which is so flat as to be almost legal. But if Molière had said it he would have said a very good thing, and one which an original genius can afford to say. Sterne is not in the least like any of the writers he has been accused of pillaging. Some say that *Tristram Shandy* was suggested by the *Tale of a Tub*. It requires a more powerful imagination than I possess to understand the meaning of the statement. Both works might be included in a treatise on the coarseness of clergymen. But little could come of such a treatise, and it is to be hoped that none will ever be written. When Warburton called Sterne the English Rabelais, his episcopal colleagues, says Horace Walpole, did not know what he meant. The work of the Abbé of Meudon had not come their way. Sterne could speak out. George the Third would not suffer him to be promoted in the Church, and who can say that his Majesty was wrong ? Queen Caroline would have enjoyed *Tristram Shandy*. One cannot imagine her grandson reading it aloud to Queen Charlotte. Sterne, however, risked nothing worse than the loss of a bishopric or a deanery. Rabelais might have been burnt. He wrote furtively and cryptically, wrapping his message to mankind in parables, in anecdotes, and in jokes. He was a passionate humanist, a lover of the classics, and a hater of monks. So much is clear enough to the most superficial reader. There is not much subtlety in *Tristram Shandy*, and no very definite purpose. Pedantry was ridiculous and cruelty odious before the time of Sterne, or of Rabelais. Goethe said of his own writings that a man who had read and digested them would feel a stronger sense of freedom than before, and would be conscious of a wider range of permissible action. Sterne and Rabelais both harp on the hindrance of prudery and superstition, or, as some might say, religion and respectability, to the thorough enjoyment of life. Sterne was not a man of profound learning. He was a desultory, indiscriminate reader, and there are those who consider these adjectives to be epithets of abuse. He could hardly have been acquainted with the romance of Sir Thomas Malory, or he would not have made Mr. Shandy say that no one named Tristram had ever achieved any exploit in the world. The eighteenth century despised the Middle Ages, as may be seen in that detestable poem *La Pucelle*.

There is, I believe, an expurgated edition of *Tristram Shandy*, which begins with the sixth, or it may be with the seventh chapter. I do not know where it ends, nor what the same ingenious editor has done with the *Sentimental Journey*. The occasional impropriety of both works must be regretted, and cannot be denied. Every one knows the story of the lady whom Sterne asked whether she had read *Tristram Shandy*. 'No, Mr. Sterne,' said she, 'and, to be plain with you, I am told that it is not very fit for feminine perusal.' 'Pooh, pooh, ma'am, look at your child there, lolling on the carpet. He shows much that we conceal, but in perfect innocence, my dear ma'am, in perfect innocence.' Mr. Sterne's innocence was not perfect. It is always easy to condemn. It is often difficult to distinguish. There are passages in Sterne of which one can only say that while it would be coarse to print them now it was not coarse to print them then. That, however, is not an exhaustive account of the matter, and does not meet the gravest part of the charge. Sterne treated delicate subjects, and a delicate subject may be defined, for want of a better definition, as one which lends itself to indelicate treatment. By what standard and by what rules is a book like *Tristram Shandy* to be judged? Mr. Ruskin once complained that he was hampered in his moral and religious teaching (though no one would have suspected it) because he could not address the British public as frankly believing or frankly disbelieving in a future life. It does not seem easy to ascertain what the accepted view of indelicacy in literature is. When M. Zola did us the honour of visiting London, a brilliant assemblage, largely composed of fashionable ladies, gathered in the hall of a learned society to hear the gospel of the author of *Nana*. The English translator of M. Zola's works was, if I remember rightly, at the same time languishing in a dungeon for the offence of too faithfully translating them. If *Tristram Shandy* were veiled in the obscurity of the French language, no apology might be necessary for it. But there is between Sterne and Zola a difference deeper and wider than nationality.   M. Zola has no humour.   He deals with vice in deadly earnest, and without any reserve.   When Sterne departs from conventional propriety it is always to raise a laugh, and never for any less avowable purpose.   There is nothing so serious as passion, and laughter is quite incompatible with prurience. Thackeray contrasts the impurity of Sterne with the purity of Goldsmith.   Goldsmith wrote two stanzas which are quite as indecent as anything in Sterne, and not in the least amusing.   ' It cannot be said,' wrote Sir Walter Scott, who had surely, among all great men of letters, the soundest and healthiest mind, ' it cannot be said that the licentious humour of *Tristram Shandy* is of the kind which applies itself to the passions, or is calculated to corrupt society.   But it is a sin against taste, if allowed to be harmless as to morals.   A handful of mud is neither a firebrand nor a stone ; but to fling it about in sport argues coarseness of mind and want of common manners.'   For his sin against taste Sterne has paid the penalty.   He has alienated and repelled many of the readers who would best appreciate his humanity, his pathos, and his eloquence.   If any man cares to see what Shandean license can be without the great qualities which in Sterne's case redeem it, let him dip—he need do no more—into Hall Stevenson's *Crazy Tales*, which were once thought vastly witty and entertaining. A man and his work must be tried by contemporary comparison.   But I do not know that a generation which reads *La Terre* can afford to hold up the hands of horror at the intricacies of Diego and Julia.

There are some things in *Tristram Shandy* which would be better away.   ' The knowledge of evil is not wisdom.'   The tale of Slawkenbergius is tedious, and has happily ceased to be intelligible. Rhinology may not have been more absurd than phrenology, but it is more completely forgotten.   The tale of the Abbess of Andouillets is low, gross, and stupid.   But with these two exceptions there is hardly a dull page in *Tristram Shandy*.   There is, moreover, this to be said for it, that the more innocent the reader the more innocent the book.   M. Zola, who has, as Dr. Pusey said of Lord Westbury and eternal punishment, a personal interest in the question, argues that a book can no more be immoral than a mathematical demonstration or a musical composition.   Morality is a quality of human beings and not of books.   It may be suspected that a fallacy lurks in this generalisation.   It is only as the work of man that books can be regarded as immoral.   The essence of *Tristram Shandy*, as distinguished from its separable and inseparable accidents, is the triumph of moral simplicity and mother wit over metaphysical subtlety and undigested learning.   But the fight is well sustained.   Mr. Shandy is a man of great natural capacity and well able to hold his own in various companies against all comers.   He is always, in his own favourite word, ' argute,' and it is no easy task to dispose of his polemics.   Sterne was too genuine an artist to make Mr. Shandy a

HERBERT PAUL.

A MISTAKEN IMPERIAL CELEBRATION

On the saga-haunted Kyffhäuser mountain, famed by the Barbarossa folk-tale, the German Emperor recently unveiled a colossal equestrian statue of the late Kaiser Wilhelm the First. Combined with it was a sculptured representation of the heroic and immortal ruler and his knights who, in popular belief, were held to sleep in the underground cave or castle until the day came when the ravens would no longer circle round the hill, and he would sally forth with his armed men to restore the country's power and glory. All German children have been taught to learn by heart Rückert's impressive poem, the first three verses of which run thus :—

> Der alte Barbarossa,
> Der Kaiser Friederich,
> Im unterird'schen Schlosse
> Hält er verzaubert sich.
>
> Er ist niemals gestorben,
> Er lebt darin noch jetzt;
> Er hat im Schloss verborgen
> Zum Schlaf sich hingesetzt.
>
> Er hat hinab genommen
> Des Reiches Herrlichkeit,
> Und wird einst wiederkommen
> Mit ihr zu seiner Zeit.

In accordance with this poem, the artist has figured Frederick the Redbeard sitting, under a richly ornamented arch, on his throne, in the act of awaking, clad in the coronation mantle, holding the imperial sword in his hand, with the crown on his long-haired and bearded head. About him, his retinue and his castle-wardens, as well as the dwarfs of the tale, and the horses and hounds, are still sunk in sleep. The whole is said to be a most stately piece of art. As to the dimensions of the equestrian statue, near which two figures stand typifying ancient Germany in the shape of a stalwart warrior, and History as a female, offering a laurel wreath to William the First— they are truly gigantic. The weight of the monument (396 cwt.) is correspondingly enormous. So are the costs, which reach the pretty sum of 1,300,000 mark.

It would, no doubt, be an unduly strict criticism were it pointed out that, historically speaking, Barbarossa wore his hair, as we happen to know from very minute descriptions of his person, rather short. Certainly it might be supposed to have grown, during fully seven centuries, in his subterranean abode, where, in Rückert's words, 'his beard that is not flaxen, but aye of fiery glow, has grown through the marble table on which his chin doth rest.' But a far more serious question is this : Did the folk-tale about the hill-hidden hero who was to bring back golden days of Germany's power and glory, originally refer at all to Frederick the First, called the Redbeard ?

This question must be decidedly answered with a 'No !' In so far, the recent celebration may be said to be founded on a mistake. Close researches in our older literature and popular legends, begun about twenty-five years ago, after the war with France, have proved this in the clearest manner possible. It was not to Barbarossa—as the Italians called the terrible Kaiser, who first fought against the Lombard League of Free Cities—but to his not less celebrated grandson, Frederick the Second, who in his third marriage had an English princess as his wife, that the popular legend originally applied.

This is important because Frederick the Second of Germany, in the early part of the thirteenth century, held in religious matters very advanced views—as much, if not even more so, than his Prussian namesake of the eighteenth century, Frederick the Second, called the Great. The early Hohenstaufen 'King of the Germans and Emperor of the Romans' anticipated, in fact, the views of modern science. And it was upon him—and not upon Barbarossa who had handed over Arnold of Brescia to the Pope, to be burnt as a 'heretic and rebel'—that the dreamy popular fancy set its expectant eyes as the future mythic hope of the German nation.

Frederick the Second had died somewhat suddenly. In the year before he had been thrown on a sick-bed in consequence of the shock given him by an attempt at poisoning. This murderous attempt was made by the medical adviser of his hitherto trusty Chancellor, Petrus de Vinea, who was suspected of being in collusion with Pope Innocent the Fourth. So, at least, it is stated by Matthew Paris. When the report of the Kaiser's death, in 1250, came over the Alps, few would believe it. The world had been so full of his fame that his disappearance was generally discredited among the people. Even the mendicant friars of the Franciscan Order, one of whose members had wrathfully preached against the corruption of the Church and predicted an awful fate for it, helped in spreading the belief in Frederick's continued existence. They looked upon him as the Antichrist, but as the inevitable avenger of clerical wickedness. An old Sibylline saw, 'He lives and yet he lives not,' was therefore applied to him. 'The common folk declared that nobody knew where he abideth,' says a contemporary German chronicle.

The long absence of the Emperor in Italy was favourable to the upholding of this superstitious belief. In our own days we have seen a strange counterpart of such a belief in the case of Napoleon the First and his Austrian consort. In the first years of the Second Empire, Louis Bonaparte and Eugénie—as he himself laughingly told Queen Victoria—were greeted in the South of France by the masses with cries of ' *Enfin voilà le vieux revenu !* ' and ' *Vive Marie-Louise !* ' [1] These personages had never died in popular fancy.

So general was the opinion among the German popular classes in the second part of the thirteenth century, as to the continued existence of Kaiser Frederick the Second, that a number of pseudo-Fredericks arose and were believed in, by many, as genuine. One of them, a certain Tile Kolup, had been able to surround himself with a kind of court for about two years, until he was captured and burnt at Wetzlar as an impostor. ' Only a little bone ' having been found in his ashes, a fresh tale was spread that the Emperor was still not dead, but that he remained alive by divine strength, and would make an end of the priesthood.

The long national struggle against the Papal claim of universal dominion had in those times— many centuries before Luther—gone deep into the minds of the German people. The bloodthirsty cruelties of the Roman Church were loathed by high and low. During the absence of the Emperor Frederick the Second in Italy, a fanatic Grand Inquisitor had consigned, year after year, numberless victims to the flames; among them, even not a few monks suspected of heresy. But at last some noble knights went for him and his associate, and killed them like mad dogs; whereupon the Courts of Inquisition were done away with by the alarmed priestly authorities.

Long before that decisive event, the anti-Papal and anti-priestly spirit had found vent, not only in the Minnesinger poetry, but also in the satires contained in fables about Reynard the Fox, Isegrim, and the whole animal kingdom. And a characteristic sign it was, that members of the clergy itself, men of somewhat more enlightened minds, imbued with sympathy for popular rights, helped in working out these allusive satires against princely, aristocratic, and theocratic arrogance.

We shall, therefore, not be astonished when we find that one of the popular poets of that epoch, Barthel Regenbogen, describes the hoped-for return of Kaiser Frederick, and the beginning of a golden age of peace, in language foreshadowing a great Church Reformation —language which could not possibly apply to the first Hohenstaufen emperor of that name. Regenbogen is usually reckoned among the Minnesinger; and these are often, though erroneously, held to be

---

[1] See *The Life of his Royal Highness the Prince Consort*, by Sir Theodore Martin.

almost exclusively of noble origin. There were, however, a number of handicraftsmen and other commoners among them. Regenbogen himself was a smith. In one of his songs about his love of the poetic art he says that he 'won his bread most wretchedly on the hard anvil, Poverty having besieged him.' In a lay in which he pleads for a friendly feeling between the three classes—the priests, the knights, and the peasants—he maintains that 'the plough does fully its duty.'

Now, in his *Prophecy of the Future*, Regenbogen foretells a great struggle about the two heads of Christendom, which will bring tears to many a mother's child. Robbery and arson will be rampant in the land. But then 'Kaiser Frederick, the sublime and yet mild,' will come and hang his shield on the famed withered tree, when it will bloom and bear fruit again, and peace will be restored, and all heathen kingdoms become subject to him. As to the Jews, Regenbogen shows himself steeped in the prejudices of his time. We can scarcely wonder at it, considering the disgraceful occurrences at this end of the nineteenth century.

But then he predicts that Kaiser Frederick will 'lay low the masterful rule of all the priests. Scarcely the seventh part of them will remain. *The cloisters he will destroy, this highborn Prince. The nuns he will give into marriage;* that I tell you true. They must grow wine and corn for us. When that happens, there will be good years.'

Such a prophecy could not have been made about Barbarossa. It fully fits in with the character of his grandson Frederick the Second, the friend of heathen thinkers, who corresponded with the Sultan of Egypt about philosophical and mathematical questions, and who was accused by the Pope of having written a book, *De Tribus Impostoribus.* Nobody, it is true, has seen that book. Nor can it be proved that Frederick the Second, or anybody else, wrote a work of such a kind. But it is pretty certain that Frederick rejected all supernatural beliefs. In his dealings with the Papacy he did not mince words. 'A dirty priest,' 'a dragon,' 'a roaring lion,' 'a hellish beast:' these were some of his little refined expressions. Truth to say, they were but the echoes of similar insulting deliverances from the Chair of St. Peter against him.

This Hohenstaufen Emperor, rather unlike his forebear, was a man of great intellectual cultivation, a lover of art, and a poet too. Witness his Italian lay, 'Di dolor mi conviene cantare,' an excellent English translation of which, under the title of 'My Lady in Bondage,' is contained in the '*Early Italian Poets*, from Ciullo d'Alcamo to Dante Alighieri,' published years ago in London by Rossetti. Frederick the Second was a wit, moreover, of whom ingenious sayings are recorded. His priestly enemies sometimes accused him of having declared that 'the Jews had been deceived by Moses, the Christians by Christ, the Mahommedans by Mahommed.' At other times they changed the venue by asserting that he was a secret adherent of the doctrines of Mohammed. 'How can I be that?' was his answer, 'seeing that you accuse me of valuing that Prophet as little as the others?'

His clerical antagonists charged him with all kinds of heresy. To a Saracen grandee who asked him about the meaning of the holy wafer, he is said to have replied: 'Our priests would fraudulently make us believe that this is God!' When seeing a priest going with the Holy Host to a dying man, he is alleged to have exclaimed: 'How long is this imposture to go on?' On passing a cornfield, he remarked: 'Here a great many Gods are grown anew!' At various times, it is true, Frederick took occasion to deny the correctness of these reports. Whether he did so from policy in his difficult contest with the Papacy, or because the reports had been over-coloured, it is impossible to make out.

Gregory the Ninth, who spoke about him as 'that King of Pestilence,' was at any rate not far wrong when asserting that Frederick the Second had declared 'men should not believe anything else than what can be proved by the force of reason, as drawn from the laws of Nature' ('homo debet nihil aliud credere nisi quod potest vi et ratione naturæ probari'). Natural history was, in fact, a special study of the gifted German ruler, who combined with a martial disposition and a love for all chivalrous exercises a marked inclination to scientific studies. He had mastered also the languages of all the populations that were under his sceptre: besides German, Italian, French, Arabic, as well as Latin and Greek.

This was the Prince of whom the folk-tale, current for centuries, fabled that some day he would come forth, from his mythic palace in the enchanted mountain, as a Saviour of the distressed Fatherland. The head of the Roman Church and his partisans had treated him as a King of Pestilence, as an Antichrist, and so forth. His own nation remembered him differently.

Certainly he, too, like Barbarossa, had indulged in high-flying Cæsarean aspirations, out of all harmony with his constitutional position. For was he not, after all, simply the elected and deposable head of a nation whose Constitution he was bound to observe, under penalty of being unseated, when proved guilty of a breach of the ground-law before a High Court of Justice? Like Barbarossa also, Frederick the Second was much engaged in useless war for the sake of aggrandisement in Italy, as well as in crusading against the Saracens. Again, even as in the case of his ancestor, his ambitious enterprises abroad were calculated to damage national unity at home. The dukes and princes of the Empire, who, constitutionally speaking, were merely its officials, always tried to use such troublous difficulties abroad for obtaining semi-sovereignty as *domini terræ.*

people at large only remembered his persistent struggle against the arrogance of the Bishop of Rome, who twice raised Imperial Pretenders against Frederick the Second with the aid of spiritual princes in Germany, and placed him under his theocratic anathema. In an access of contemptuous wrath the Kaiser exclaimed on such an occasion: 'How? The Pope has such outrageous boldness? Where comes this boldness from? Where are my crowns? Let them be brought hither!' And they were fetched from his treasury: the Imperial Roman crown; the German kingly crown; the crown of the Two Sicilies; the crown of Burgundy; the crown of Arelat; and eke the crown of Jerusalem!

Enough has been said to show that the dazzling figure of this ruler easily struck the popular imagination, whilst his struggle against the theocratic Pretender to universal dominion enlisted the sympathy of all patriots on his side. In the years of confusion which followed, the tale about his coming return was gradually evolved. At first, his whereabouts was held to be uncertain, his very death being doubted. Then the ever active fancy of the popular mind mythically located him in a splendid palace under the earth.

The Gods, the heroes, and the illustrious rulers of a bygone creed and history had been similarly disposed of in folk-lore. Wodan and his divine associates, though no longer known by their old names; Siegfried, Theodorich, Karl the Great, Henry the Fowler, Otto the Great, and others, were said to have never died, or to sleep in underground palaces in a hill. Many mountains, in northern and southern Germany, were indicated as enchanted abodes of these supposed Immortals. Thus local tales placed the famed Frankish Kaiser Karl in the Desenberg near Warburg; again, near the river Weser; also in the Spessart, in the Donnersberg (so called after Donar, Thunar, or Thor), in the Untersberg, and so forth; and of him, too, it was said that one day he would come forth with a great army.

In the early part of the fourteenth century, the Kyffhäuser mountain, in Thuringia, is first mentioned as the retreat of the 'Emperor Frederick.' Nothing is said yet about the Redbeard. His name was only introduced towards the end of the seventeenth century.

Since the decay of the heathen German religion, 'an Old Man with a flowing beard' had been fabled to dwell in the Kyffhäuser. Perchance, the All-father of the disestablished Teutonic creed, or his son, the red-bearded God of Thunder, had originally been thus enmountained by secret adherents of theirs, who unwillingly yielded to the New Faith which had been forced upon the Saxons by fire and sword.

The ravens which fly around the Kyffhäuser seem indeed to point to the sacred birds of Odin or Wodan. The knights and the whole retinue of the hill-entombed Emperor would represent the blessed heroes of Walhalla.

As the remembrance of that old creed gradually vanished, the heroic figure of a Kaiser and his warriors would be placed in the stead of the earlier divine circle. In the case of the Kyffhäuser, such substitution is the more comprehensible because the Emperors of the Suabian House had possessed a palace in the neighbourhood and often resided there.

Finally, the remembrance of Frederick the Second as an expected Reformer of the Church also became blurred and extinct. It was, however, still strong enough in the beginning of the sixteenth century. In 1521 Luther said that this prophecy about Kaiser Frederick had been practically fulfilled through Frederick the Wise of Saxony, who had supported Holy Scripture, who had been Vicar of the Empire, and who might have been Kaiser himself, had he wished to accept the offer of the crown made to him. A quarter of a century afterwards, when a strange man, who pretended to be the Emperor Frederick, was discovered in the ruins of the Kyffhäuser Castle, there were still superstitious people enough to believe in the truth of such immortality. This belated Pretender was, however, found to be merely a tailor out of his mind.

It appears that the folk-tale—perhaps by way of mixing up the Teutonic All-father with the God of Thunder—had attributed to the mythic hero in the Kyffhäuser a red beard. This detail made the transition from the person of Frederick the Second to that of his grimmer, less cultivated ancestor and namesake, an easy one. So the two figures became gradually blended. The transition was all the easier because the death of Frederick Barbarossa, who was said to have been drowned in the Far East, during a crusade, in the river Seleph, had occurred under somewhat uncertain circumstances, and was therefore also long disbelieved by the masses.

However, it is only as late as 1680 that the name of Barbarossa is given by Prätorius, from folk-lore, as that of the spell-bound dweller in the magic underground castle of the Thuringian hill. Soon afterwards another collector of popular legends reports, in the first years of the eighteenth century, that the enchanted Emperor's beard is red. It was alleged that many a shepherd had seen him come out of the mountain, attracted by the pastoral flute, and that some had been allowed even to take a glance at the sunken imperial splendour in the subterranean vault. In these tales, Barbarossa generally figured as a benevolent friend of the poor—a trait not exactly recorded of him in history; whilst Regenbogen, who evidently meant Frederick the Second, described the latter as both 'the sublime and the mild.'

it has generally been believed that the mythic Man in the Kyffhäuser Mountain had always been identified, in the legend, with Barbarossa. But this is now shown to be an error.

If we wanted to dig deeper in fabulous lore, some curious additional points might be given. One of the German folk-tales had it that some day a great battle would be fought on the Walser Field, where the famed withered tree—a pear tree—stands. On that tree the Kaiser was to hang his shield, and this battle was to herald in the World's End. A Twilight of the Gods, so to say, in heathen Teutonic prophecy. The bad are to be annihilated by the good; Truth and Right will be victorious. The political meaning of the tale here quite disappears. The great massacre, which is to take place, has only a religious significance. Though clothed in Christian garb, the original pagan kernel of the legend is, however, fully discernible— even as in the christianised *Nibelungenlied* the Germanic heathens are recognisable, who in the corresponding Nibelung lays of the Norse Edda have no alloy yet at all from the later religion.

An Asiatic tradition has been quoted from the fourteenth century, to this effect, that the Dominion of the World would some day fall to a prince who would succeed in hanging his shield on a certain withered tree. The Tatars related that this tree stood in Tauris. that is, the Crimea. Other Oriental races spoke of it as standing in the grove of Mamre. It has been pointed out that this myth has some contact with the Hellenic one of the golden fleece which hangs in a sacred grove on a tree, and the acquisition of which was to confer glory, riches, and power.

However, it must not be forgotten that the tale about the withered tree, on which the coming Emperor's shield is to be hung, is an earlier one in Germany itself. Moreover, in the Crimea, which until the eighteenth century was still called Gothia in the official documents of the Greek Church, a population of Gothic descent had remained from olden times. Specimens of its Teutonic speech are traceable down to 1750. The ransomed prisoner from the Turkish galleys, a native of the Crimea, who in the middle of last century furnished these samples of Teutonic language to a learned Jesuit, declared that he knew nothing about Christianity, his countrymen worshipping an ancient tree.[2] Can this have been a long-forgotten symbol of the World Ash, the Teutonic Tree of Existence? And have we here, perhaps, the origin of the tale about the withered

[2] See *The Goths*, by Henry Bradley (London, 1888).

tree 'which is to grow green and to bear fruit once more,' when the Restorer of German power hangs his shield on it?

As Regenbogen has it, who mixes up this myth with the peaceful recovery of the Holy Sepulchre:

> Sô wirt daz urliug alsô groz, niemant kan es gestillen;
> Sô kumt sich keiser Vriderich, der hêr und ouch der milt . . .
> Er vert dort hin zem dürren boum ân allez widerhap,
> Dar an sô henkt er sinen schilt; *er gruonet unde birt.*
> Sô wirt gewunnen daz heilic grap,
> Daz nimmer swert dar umb gezogen wirt.

Actually, on the famous Walserfeld where the great battle was to take place, there stood, until quite recent days, a withered pear tree which in the folk-tale was connected with the old prophecy. After the re-establishment of the German Empire under William the First of Prussia, the tree was felled overnight—owing, it is said, to a suggestion made to the peasant proprietor by Ultramontanes. The cutting down of the old tree was considered almost a sacrilegious act at the time by those who cherish folk-lore traditions. But some observed that the withered trunk might well have gone, seeing that the prophecy had been fulfilled. There are, however, others who do not see such fulfilment in the foundation of an Empire shorn of its Austrian provinces, which had been an integral part of Germany from olden times down to 1866.

Taking all in all, it is manifest that the 'Barbarossa' myth is quite a late graft upon the stem of the original tale about Kaiser Friedrich the Second, the enlightened adversary of priestcraft, the antagonist of the Papacy, the expected Reformer of the Church, and Disestablisher of Monkhood. Many of the sayings attributed to him, which show him in the light of a man who would readily have assented, had he lived in our days, to the doctrines of Darwin, Huxley, and Häckel, would find little countenance, at present, in high quarters at Berlin. It remains a fact, nevertheless, that 600 years ago an elected ruler stood at the head of the German Empire, who held such advanced views, and that his cherished memory had for centuries sunk deep into the people's mind. Considering this earlier and long-sustained conception of the folk-tale, the recent Imperial celebration on the Kyffhäuser may be said to rest on an historical error.

KARL BLIND.

INDEX TO VOL. XL

The titles of articles are printed in italics

Lightning Source UK Ltd.
Milton Keynes UK
UKHW010744011218
333024UK00013B/2083/P